SAP PRESS e-books

Print or e-book, Kindle or iPad, workplace or airplane: Choose where and how to read your SAP PRESS books! You can now get all our titles as e-books, too:

- By download and online access
- For all popular devices
- And, of course, DRM-free

Convinced? Then go to www.sap-press.com and get your e-book today.

SAP® Master Data Governance

PRESS

SAP PRESS is a joint initiative of SAP and Rheinwerk Publishing. The know-how offered by SAP specialists combined with the expertise of Rheinwerk Publishing offers the reader expert books in the field. SAP PRESS features first-hand information and expert advice, and provides useful skills for professional decision-making.

SAP PRESS offers a variety of books on technical and business-related topics for the SAP user. For further information, please visit our website: *www.sap-press.com*.

Teja Atluri, Bardhan, Ghosh, Ghosh, Saha
SAP Data Intelligence: The Comprehensive Guide
2022, 783 pages, hardcover and e-book
www.sap-press.com/5369

Jawad Akhtar
Business Partners in SAP S/4HANA:
The Comprehensive Guide to Customer-Vendor Integration
2022, 353 pages, hardcover and e-book
www.sap-press.com/5468

Saueressig, Stein, Boeder, Kleis
SAP S/4HANA Architecture
2021, 520 pages, hardcover and e-book
www.sap-press.com/5189

Mark Mergaerts, Bert Vanstechelman
SAP S/4HANA System Conversion Guide
2020, 537 pages, hardcover and e-book
www.sap-press.com/5035

Anil Bavaraju
Data Modeling for SAP HANA 2.0
2019, 432 pages, hardcover and e-book
www.sap-press.com/4722

Bikram Dogra, Antony Isacc, Homiar Kalwachwala, Dilip Radhakrishnan, Syama Srinivasan, Sandeep Chahal, Santhosh Cheekoti, Rajani Khambhampati, Vikas Lodha, David Quirk

SAP® Master Data Governance

The Comprehensive Guide

Rheinwerk
Publishing

Editor Hareem Shafi
Copyeditor Julie McNamee
Cover Design Graham Geary
Photo Credit iStockphoto: 174696550/© malerapaso
Layout Design Vera Brauner
Production Kelly O'Callaghan
Typesetting III-satz (Germany)
Printed and bound in Canada, on paper from sustainable sources

ISBN 978-1-4932-2315-2
© 2023 by Rheinwerk Publishing, Inc., Boston (MA)
3rd edition 2023

Library of Congress Cataloging-in-Publication Data
Names: Kalwachwala, Homiar, author.
Title: SAP master data governance : the comprehensive guide to SAP MDG /
   Bikram Dogra, Antony Isacc, Homiar Kalwachwala, Syama Srinivasan, and
   Dilip Radhakrishnan.
Description: 3rd edition. | Bonn ; Boston : Rheinwerk Publishing, 2022. |
   Includes index.
Identifiers: LCCN 2022033756 | ISBN 9781493223152 (hardcover) | ISBN
   9781493223169 (ebook)
Subjects: LCSH: Database management--Computer programs. | SAP HANA
   (Electronic resource)
Classification: LCC QA76.9.D3 K35555 2022 | DDC 005.74--dc23/eng/20220816
LC record available at https://lccn.loc.gov/2022033756

Contents at a Glance

Dear Reader,

Here's something folks don't tell you about your parents moving in with you: suddenly, your house is going to have too many responsible people in it.

You never need to worry that a toddler might go to the corner store to grab some milk. But with adults? If three people poke their heads into the fridge in the morning and notice there are no eggs, by that evening you're going to have three times the eggs you need. In my family, our solution to this problem was a shared shopping list app that tells everyone what we're out of—and when something's been purchased.

No wonder creating a single source of truth is one of the core tenets of SAP Master Data Governance. If people making decisions based on different data can wreak havoc on a family fridge, imagine what it can do to a business!

Of course, there's a lot more to SAP Master Data Governance than providing a single source of truth. The book you hold in your hands is your comprehensive guide to working with SAP Master Data Governance in SAP S/4HANA and SAP ERP.

What did you think about *SAP Master Data Governance: The Comprehensive Guide*? Your comments and suggestions are the most useful tools to help us make our books the best they can be. Please feel free to contact me and share any praise or criticism you may have.

Thank you for purchasing a book from SAP PRESS!

Hareem Shafi
Editor, SAP PRESS

hareems@rheinwerk-publishing.com
www.sap-press.com
Rheinwerk Publishing · Boston, MA

Contents

2   Introduction to SAP Master Data Governance   63

3   SAP Master Data Governance, Cloud Edition   95

4 Deployment Options 123

5 Central Governance: Data Modeling 147

8 Data Quality, Search, and Remediations   291

13 Central Governance: Integration Scenarios

17   Overview of SAP Master Data Governance Complementary Solutions

Preface

Welcome to the third edition of *SAP Master Data Governance* by SAP PRESS.

In this edition, we've added several new chapters, rearranged the flow of chapters, and made changes to the previous content, including new images, screenshots, diagrams, and so on. We added a lot of content that is cloud relevant too. We've improved the quality of the content, and a huge credit for that goes to our SAP Product Management team under Markus Kuppe.

We were overwhelmed by the positive feedback from our first and second editions. Along with all the positive and encouraging feedback, we also received constructive feedback regarding how we could improve this edition. We've taken into consideration all the requests for additional topics and, in certain cases, have further elaborated on technical aspects. We're confident that this edition will meet your raised expectations.

In 2017, Jim Barbaresso said, "Data is the currency of the digital age." For data to be meaningful and valuable for analytics, it's imperative to have flawless master data. This is the premise of master data management. Our book is intended to be a comprehensive guide to implementing master data management scenarios using SAP Master Data Governance on SAP S/4HANA (as well as for SAP ERP). This book is written from business and technical perspectives, and it complements the standard SAP product documentation available online and through Implementation Guide (IMG) help as well as the blogs on the SAP Community website. It also explains the inner workings of the solution with reference to real-life examples from SAP Master Data Governance projects. This book addresses some of the common questions raised by customers and consultants while implementing the solution.

The book serves as a reference to understand how the SAP Master Data Governance solution works. Although not intended to replace the official SAP documentation, the detailed content in this book is balanced for both functional and technical readers. This book has been written based on our personal project experiences. We've provided links to the available SAP product documentations to provide you with additional details. The chapters discuss various configuration options for each functionality as well as their corresponding enhancement options.

In this edition, the book contains information on the recent innovations delivered as part of SAP Master Data Governance on SAP S/4HANA 2021. We've added new topics such as SAP Master Data Governance, cloud edition; deployment options, complementary solution extensions from our partners; and more. The scope of this book covers SAP's standard offerings for governing material master, business partner, customer, supplier, and financial master data domains. This book also uses the framework provided by SAP for extending the previously mentioned models or configuring a completely custom master data object. Also included in this edition is an overview of some of our partner solution extensions. We also have a section on how to stand up your SAP Master Data Governance application in short amount of time using quick-start for SAP Master Data Governance.

Who This Book Is For

This book is structured to interest a broad audience, including business analysts, techno-functional analysts, business process experts, master data experts, solution architects, technical developers, and data scientists. It's targeted for anyone who plans to implement or work on the SAP Master Data Governance solution. The book provides both an overview of the SAP Master Data Governance solution and an in-depth discussion of the various enhancement options, with emphasis on central governance scenarios to help you understand the end-to-end capabilities of the solution.

How This Book Is Organized

This book is based on SAP Master Data Governance on SAP S/4HANA 2021. As this book is meant to provide an overview of SAP Master Data Governance configuration options, it's organized based on the standard Customizing configuration path.

If you're interested in learning more about the central governance scenario and its configuration options, we recommend reading this book sequentially from Chapter 4 through Chapter 15. Be sure to read Chapter 3 to get information on the capabilities of the SAP Master Data Governance, cloud edition. Chapter 8 discusses the data quality management capability available with the SAP Master Data Governance solution. Chapter 9 provides functional and technical insights into consolidation and mass processing scenarios. Chapter 16 provides additional information on the specific solution capabilities of SAP Fiori apps in SAP Master Data Governance, and Chapter 17 provides an overview of SAP Master Data Governance complementary solutions.

The following is a summary of how this book is structured with a brief introduction to each chapter:

- **Chapter 1**
  This chapter starts with an introduction into the various maturity levels in enterprise data management we see across organizations and explains the key organizational drivers for enterprise information management (EIM). Further, the main business drivers for organizations to invest in EIM are also explained. This chapter elucidates various capabilities expected out of EIM solutions and how each of the capabilities come together in helping enterprises govern and manage their enterprise data. Various SAP solutions are introduced that can support an organization in their data management journey, including the newer solutions, which support a

federated data management architecture. The cloud-based data management solutions and the SAP Master Data Governance solution are also introduced in detail.

- **Chapter 2**
  This chapter discusses various components of the SAP Master Data Governance solution. It provides an overview of the key master data domains that are delivered with the SAP Master Data Governance solution and introduces the concept of customer-vendor integration (CVI) in business partner domain. It also provides an overview of master data architecture in cloud-based scenarios.

- **Chapter 3**
  This chapter discusses the latest addition to the SAP Master Data Governance product profile, namely SAP Master Data Governance, cloud edition. The chapter explains how this complementary solution to SAP Master Data Governance on SAP S/4HANA is provided as a service in SAP Business Technology Platform (SAP BTP). It explains the role that SAP One Domain Model and SAP Master Data Integration play in this cloud solution.

- **Chapter 4**
  SAP Master Data Governance comes with various deployment options to cater to the changing business and architectural needs of customers. In this chapter, we'll go deeper into the various deployment options available for SAP Master Data Governance. We'll compare the hub deployment against co-deployment, including the steps involved and the architectural considerations for each of these deployment choices. This chapter explains why quick-start for SAP Master Data Governance is a recommended way to jump-start your SAP Master Data Governance projects and the key business and project benefits of using this approach. We'll also go into detail regarding customizing synchronization, as well as the various tools that can be used and the steps involved in setting them up. Finally, this chapter jumps into on-premise and cloud deployment options of SAP Master Data Governance and what versions of SAP Master Data Governance support each of these deployment choices.

- **Chapter 5**
  This chapter introduces various data modeling aspects of SAP Master Data Governance such as entity types, attributes, relationships, and hierarchies. It describes how these data model building blocks work together using SAP-delivered data models as examples. This chapter provides step-by-step instructions on configurations related to data modeling.

- **Chapter 6**
  In this chapter, we go through the user interface (UI) configurations available as part of the standard central governance solution and the various options available for extending the standard SAP Master Data Governance UI configurations. The chapter starts by providing an overview of the Floorplan Manager framework and discusses the application configurations associated with the standard domains.

- **Chapter 7**

  Process modeling is an important aspect of SAP Master Data Governance. This chapter introduces the essential building blocks of process modeling and then explains how these building blocks are used to design an end-to-end process using various SAP-delivered processes as examples. It then explains how SAP Master Data Governance addresses the handling of single-record and multiple-record processing scenarios. After providing a high-level overview of process modeling for each SAP-delivered master data domain, we discuss workflow modeling and SAP-delivered workflow templates. This chapter also provides an overview of the rule-based workflow and explains its design aspects with a simple example. This chapter ends with an overview of the various Business Add-Ins (BAdIs) provided by SAP to enable additional enhancements to support workflow processes.

- **Chapter 8**

  Improving the quality of the existing master data and preventing bad data from entering the systems are top priorities in most data governance projects. This chapter discusses various techniques and options, including data quality remediation and data quality management for product master data, that can be leveraged in improving the master data quality during the governance process. This chapter also provides some details regarding data quality rules and discusses options for integrating with SAP and non-SAP applications for data standardization and enrichment.

- **Chapter 9**

  In this chapter, we'll explore why data consolidation and mass processing are key capabilities for any data governance solution. We'll also look at the key business use cases supported by consolidation and mass processing capabilities within SAP Master Data Governance. Further in this chapter, we'll go step by step into activating, configuring, and setting up consolidation capabilities within SAP Master Data Governance. We'll take a detailed look at the various standard data models delivered by SAP and their key attributes and capabilities. We'll also discuss process models within the consolidation and mass processing solution, including the steps to configure them, their benefits, and their usage in a data consolidation process. This chapter covers the configuration capabilities available within each step of a consolidation process in detail. After this, we go into step-by-step details of operating and running the consolidation and mass processing solutions. For customers who want to go beyond the standard and extend the consolidation solution for their own special needs, this chapter also discusses in detail the steps involved in extending the standard solution.

- **Chapter 10**

  The ability to analyze master data and the associated data management process is an important part of keeping it clean. This chapter discusses SAP Master Data Governance analytics functionalities. We focus on process reporting, which is available as part of SAP S/4HANA 2021.

- **Chapter 11**

  This chapter explains how to build custom objects for the central governance scenario. It explains the various steps involved in building custom objects using SAP Work Breakdown Structures (WBS) as an example. The chapter provides details on how to build a custom data model, custom UIs, and custom business logic. This is an end-to-end guide and helps you understand how to build an SAP Master Data Governance custom domain to be used in the central governance scenario.

- **Chapter 12**

  One of the key capabilities of SAP Master Data Governance is its ability to distribute and share the governed master data into various other receiving applications within the enterprise landscape, including both SAP and non-SAP systems. In this chapter, we'll look into the key building blocks and configuration steps of the data replication framework within SAP Master Data Governance. We'll detail topics such as filtering, key mapping, value mapping, and distribution models. Because key mapping is a very important concept in data distribution, we'll dig deeper into that topic and do a step-by-step review of the activities involved in setting it up in SAP Master Data Governance. We'll also discuss in detail the data distribution for all standard data domains supported by SAP Master Data Governance, that is, material, business partner, and finance. This chapter also goes into the details of operating data distribution using the data replication framework, including logging, monitoring, and error handling.

- **Chapter 13**

  This chapter focuses on various SAP Master Data Governance integration options and how they can be integrated with other SAP and non-SAP solutions. An overview of SAP Master Data Governance application programming interfaces (APIs) is provided. Some of the common integration requirements are also discussed, such as integration with SAP cloud solutions, SAP Product Lifecycle Management (SAP PLM), SAP Ariba, SAP Cloud for Customer, Central Finance, and so on.

- **Chapter 14**

  Accurate and efficient initial data loads are key to the success of any SAP Master Data Governance project. Various recommendations and factors that influence and help in choosing the right data migration strategy in central governance are explained as part of this chapter. Options for extraction, conversion, and loading techniques are also explained for various master data objects. In addition, step-by-step instructions and recommendations using the data import/export framework and file upload/download options are explained in detail.

- **Chapter 15**

  From reading this chapter, you'll understand how to operate SAP Master Data Governance after go-live and effectively manage SAP Master Data Governance content.

The editions concept is explained in detail, along with recommendations for effective usage of editions after an SAP Master Data Governance go-live. This chapter provides a best practice approach for ongoing data loads and mass processing. It also provides performance optimization and troubleshooting tips for workflow issues and data replication issues, along with a list of commonly used transactions and application programming interfaces (APIs).

- **Chapter 16**
  This chapter focuses on various SAP Fiori apps available as part of the SAP Master Data Governance on SAP S/4HANA 2021 standard delivery. The chapter details the landscape requirements, key capabilities, and extensibility options involving OData service extensions, UI extensions, and so on for these SAP Fiori apps.

- **Chapter 17**
  SAP Master Data Governance is not only a powerful data governance solution but also a powerful data governance platform on which partners and customers can build their own data domains for data governance. In this chapter, we'll look at various complementary solutions available in the market today, which are built using the SAP Master Data Governance framework. We'll cover SAP Master Data Governance, enterprise asset management by Utopia; SAP Asset Information Workbench by Utopia for managing enterprise assets; SAP Master Data Governance, retail and fashion management extension by Utopia; and finally PiLog's Material Master Taxonomy solution. We'll provide a detailed explanation of the quick-start for SAP Master Data Governance offering, including the business and IT benefits and the deliverables. We'll also do a deep dive into the coverage of the quick-start for SAP Master Data Governance solution and the various deployment options supported with this approach.

Acknowledgments

We'd like to dedicate this edition to the frontline workers risking their lives to keep us safe from the COVID pandemic.

The first edition of our SAP Master Data Governance book was a runaway success, and the phenomenal reception to our second edition is owed to the feedback we recieved from our readers. It's challenging to follow up on the heels of a bestselling book. The advantage, of course, is that we've received some great feedback that we have incorporated into this third edition. Our gratitude goes to our customers, partners, and consultants for their feedback and requests that helped us finalize the topics you'll find in this edition. We hope this edition continues to meet your high expectations.

Special appreciation and gratitude go to Markus Kuppe for his unwavering support, enthusiasm, and guidance. We're very obliged to Markus and his team of SAP Master Data Governance product management colleagues at SAP for taking the time to review and provide priceless feedback at such short notice. To Markus Ganser, Christian Geiseler, Elke Menninger, Andreas Seifried, Michael Veth, and Kefang Wang, you are phenomenal colleagues! Our product management colleagues not only invested their personal time in reviewing, but they also made many good suggestions so that the final version is of the best quality and easy to digest.

Our wholehearted thanks also go out to Riccardo Broggi from the SAP Value Prototyping team, and to our SAP BTP consulting team members, Santhosh Cheekoti, Krish Mudaliar, Subbu Chivukula, and Sandeep Chahal, for proofreading our drafts as the first level of reviewers. Rajani Khambhampati from Nike, thank you for taking the time to review during your flights between India and the US and while on vacation.

The selfless acts on the part of our reviewers just mentioned ensured that the content in the book you have in your hands is of the utmost quality. We owe them our warm thanks for their passion for and dedication to the product.

We'd like to express our gratitude to SAP PRESS and Rheinwerk Publishing for their trust and providing us with this incredible opportunity. To Meagan White, Hareem Shafi, and Sean Fesko—this journey would not have been possible without you. We appreciate your guidance, recommendations, and, most of all, your patience as we ventured on this journey together. Thank you so much! Thanks to Graham Geary for designing the book cover and to Julie McNamee for copyediting. We also offer a huge thank you to the entire editorial, production, and marketing teams at Rheinwerk Publishing.

We'd also like to thank David La Plant, and Asim Munshi for their help in standing up the internal SAP Master Data Governance landscape so we could configure and develop the scenarios for screenshots.

Finally, with love, we give heartfelt credit to our family members for their sacrifices. Without their patience and tolerance of our grumpiness, this journey would have just remained an unfulfilled dream.

Cheers!

Conclusion

The intent of this book is to provide you with a comprehensive view of the SAP Master Data Governance solution and its capabilities. This foundation-level knowledge will enable you to research and learn to deal with complex requirements. This book is designed to empower you to configure an SAP Master Data Governance solution to accommodate the requirements of varying complexities across enterprises and industries. You should use this book in conjunction with the official SAP help documentation and the extensibility how-to guides at the SAP Community website. We're confident that this book will lay the groundwork for you to tackle even the most complex SAP Master Data Governance implementations.

For additional SAP Master Data Governance resources, we encourage you to visit the following links:

- Help Portal: *http://help.sap.com/mdg*
- Product landing page: *www.sap.com/mdg*
- SAP Community page: *http://s-prs.co/v558000*
- SAP Notes/SAP Knowledge Base Articles (KBAs): *http://s-prs.co/v558001*
- Product Availability Matrix (PAM): *http://s-prs.co/v558002*

Education is the most powerful weapon which you can use to change the world.
– Nelson Mandela

Education is what remains after one has forgotten what one has learned in school.
– Albert Einstein

Chapter 1

Introduction to Enterprise Information Management

Enterprise information management (EIM) capabilities are a required foundation for all businesses in this digital age. SAP offers an integrated set of solutions that provide key EIM capabilities.

The essential organizational benefit from implementing an enterprise information management (EIM) foundation within a company is the assurance that trusted information is ready at the point of impact to run and innovate the business. This statement cuts to the heart of what customers need and what SAP is trying to achieve through its EIM portfolio.

Let's break this statement down a little further by considering the expression "point of impact," which will vary greatly between different organizations and in the various departments within an organization. For an asset-intensive company, for example, running the maintenance processes efficiently and implementing aspects of predictive maintenance may be the key pain points that need to be addressed. For a telecommunications company, maybe it's getting a 360-degree view into its customers to understand fully what different services their customers are using and what offers might be relevant to a possible cross-sell marketing campaign.

Even within a company, the point of impact will vary greatly. For someone working on the factory floor who needs to order materials to keep production lines moving, the point of impact will be having accurate and reliable supplier information available so that the manufacturing process can continue uninterrupted. The CEO might be interested in getting the latest revenue numbers by product line to use when contemplating a new strategic direction for the company.

A successful EIM platform needs to support activities ranging from tactical requirements for the day-to-day running of the business through to strategic benefits that will help drive the overall corporate strategy of the enterprise. Fully realizing these capabilities will result in significant organizational benefits.

How does SAP Master Data Governance fit into the EIM picture? Throughout this chapter, the entire EIM story will be explained by highlighting where the various solutions offered by SAP provide value and clearly showing the place occupied by SAP Master Data Governance. The master data management and governance capabilities provided by SAP Master Data Governance are critical to any company's EIM strategy.

1.1 Stages of Enterprise Information Management Engagement

Different companies are at different stages of their EIM journey. Some have quite mature, established EIM programs; others recognize the need and are working toward improving the programs in place; and then, of course, there are companies that are just starting down this path or don't even recognize the problem! The good news is that no matter where you currently exist within the world of EIM, there are methodologies and tools to help you move through any existing challenges to a more sophisticated EIM organization. When assessing the current level of EIM sophistication within an enterprise, companies often fall into one of the following categories:

- **Level 1: Recognition**
  The good news is the number of organizations that don't perceive the need for an EIM program is rapidly diminishing. The market is certainly shifting from a perspective where companies need to be educated regarding the need for EIM capabilities to one where companies are looking for solutions to help them address this enterprise need. Organizations at this level of sophistication are at ground zero for their EIM program. They've likely recognized the organizational need in this space but have taken very few meaningful steps to address it. Companies in this space typically are looking for help to get started.

- **Level 2: Reactive**
  At this level, companies understand the challenges they face and are reacting to issues with their enterprise information as they occur. Some data quality initiatives may have been started, and often there is a heavy reliance on IT groups to help support any activities here. Even if some benefits of an EIM program can be realized, these benefits lack true business self-service capabilities and aren't scalable across an enterprise, perhaps requiring a new "mini-project" every time a problem or need in the EIM space is identified.

  This level involves tasks such as data profiling to help the data stewards and other stakeholders understand the data in the enterprise and to recognize where issues exist. After they understand the data issues, the first steps toward a cleansing/data transformation strategy can be made.

- **Level 3: Monitoring**
  Companies here are well on their way. Data quality and process improvement initiatives related to enterprise information have been made with key data issues both identified and remediated. Organizations understand what data problems exist, and they are able to monitor the enterprise and fix issues as they arise. At this level, self-service is starting to become more prominent, and the need for constant IT involvement is diminished.

  Organizationally, people are empowered to focus on enterprise information and are responsible for data quality across the enterprise. Roles such as data stewards exist across key data domains and within key business units to ensure that defined information management standards are followed.

- **Level 4: Proactive**
Organizations at this level have established a high level of information quality and are actively taking steps to prevent future issues from occurring. Clear standards exist so that enterprise information is appropriately governed and controlled. In addition, key tools are in place to enforce these data and process standards, going beyond simply monitoring and correcting any detected problems to preventing such issues from even occurring. High-quality information is distributed across all relevant systems in the enterprise, ensuring timely and trusted information for all transactional, analytical and reporting needs.

  Data stewards and master data specialists will proactively manage and monitor data quality metrics, ensuring that organizational Service Level Agreements (SLAs) related to the maintenance of enterprise information are followed.

  Typically, dedicated data organizations are in place across these companies. This reflects the need to actively address these challenges rather than simply have information management exist as an offshoot of other departments within the enterprise.

- **Level 5: Strategic**
At this level of sophistication, organizations are actively addressing all aspects of information management. Continuous improvement programs are in place looking for new opportunities to drive further value. These organizations are well positioned to ensure that the current high level of information quality will be maintained regardless of any organizational change imposed due to internal or external factors. Information is viewed as a key corporate asset, and opportunities to monetize this asset are exploited.

  Organizations at this level have a very mature and well-defined information management organization, led by a chief data officer who ensures visibility of the EIM program at the highest levels of the company.

A clear goal of any successful EIM program is to drive the organization to increasing levels of sophistication across this scale.

1.2   Organizational Drivers for Enterprise Information Management

To implement an EIM program at your company, key business benefits and drivers must be analyzed and specifically tailored to your organization. Such an analysis will provide a foundation for building a business case to justify this investment.

1.2.1   Enterprise Information Management Benefits and Drivers

As noted earlier, different organizations will be at different points along their EIM journey and will need to determine an approach to expand their program to realize the significant benefits from increasing their level of EIM sophistication. In addition, companies will have different key drivers, pain points, and types of benefits they aim to achieve from an EIM program. Even with all these differences, many of the common organizational drivers can be grouped into the following categories:

- **Improved operational efficiency**

  Well-managed enterprise information drives internal as well as external process excellence within the enterprise. The definition and enforcement of enterprise information standards will ensure high-quality information exists across the enterprise. For example, better customer master data improves the efficiency of sales order processing, allowing a quick turnaround in margin realization, and better material master data enables improved inventory management and production planning.

  Cost savings will be realized across many areas of the business. For example, a reduction in duplicate customer master records will lead to fewer incorrect shipments being made, reducing the need for reshipments while also increasing customer satisfaction. A clear vision and understanding of suppliers and supplier hierarchies will allow for the negotiation of more favorable payment terms and opportunities for significant cost savings by maximizing all possible volume discounts.

  IT costs will be reduced across multiple dimensions as well. Empowering the business to retrieve any required information in a timely fashion will lower IT spend by reducing the need for IT involvement in these day-to-day processes. In addition, IT landscapes can be made simpler by consolidating various enterprise resource planning (ERP) systems and retiring and archiving redundant databases appropriately.

  A well-defined EIM process can actually lead to a reduction in cycle times for master data creation. For example, significant gains in process efficiency can result from ensuring the following:

  - The record is routed to the correct role within an organization at the correct time throughout the master data creation process.
  - Data rules are automatically enforced, reducing the need for rework.
  - Duplicate checks are automatically performed.
  - Completed records are quickly replicated throughout the landscape.

- **Increased regulatory compliance**

  Ensuring that an organization remains compliant with all necessary legal and regulatory requirements is an essential benefit derived from an EIM program. Regulations surrounding data privacy standards—mandating the rules for retention of information as well as ensuring appropriate and timely destruction—are only increasing. Penalties for noncompliance can be quite significant.

For companies with heavy equipment and manufacturing plants, ensuring that all equipment maintenance is performed on the appropriate schedules will help maintain a safe working environment, reducing liability and lost productivity. Having auditable governance processes in heavily regulated industries (e.g., pharmaceutical companies) is required to demonstrate compliance with local and international regulations.

Better accuracy and reliability of financial reporting can also be achieved. The implications of inaccuracies in this space can be a loss of credibility with customers and stockholders, often along with significant penalties and fines. Financial restatements can be quite lengthy and expensive processes with a huge impact on the company's image.

- **More effective decision-making**
  This is likely to be the most lucrative driver for an EIM program within a company. Allowing all key enterprise information to be in the hands of those driving critical strategic decisions will reap significant benefits for an organization.

  Business transformation initiatives, identification of a potential new market for an existing product, or creating a new product to address a compelling customer need all rely on accurate enterprise information. For example, obtaining a deep understanding of how existing customers are using your company's products will allow for appropriate targeting of offers and cross-sell or up-sell campaigns. Analyzing feedback through social media channels and rapidly adjusting to address any issues or to capitalize on a positive trend will result in a significant competitive edge in the market.

  Handling corporate restructuring and merger and acquisition activities with a minimal amount of disruption to day-to-day operations is a key driver. The addition of new systems to a landscape and the seamless onboarding of enterprise information from a merging entity while ensuring that this information will meet any existing standards is a challenging process without a solid EIM foundation in place. The management of strategic divestitures is another significant challenge in this space.

As mentioned, these EIM benefits and drivers are many and varied. Some of the more appropriate drivers will bring different levels of benefit for different industries, and all should be looked at against an organization's specific priorities, current pain points, and strategic goals.

Considering this, a one-size-fits-all approach isn't going to work. A phased and iterative approach is often adopted to help focus on these key organizational drivers in a structured fashion instead of trying to simply solve every problem at the same time. Identifying and targeting the biggest current pain point might be the right approach. Alternatively, it may be more prudent to address some short-term benefits that might be easier to achieve, building some momentum and showing some clear gains and business benefits with an EIM program that can be used to drive an expanded and more widespread program.

1.2.2   Building the Business Case

Whether an organization is just starting out or looking to expand an existing program, building a solid business case for an EIM program is a critical element for success. The most important factors to consider through this process are the following:

- **Specific, defined value drivers**
  Generic benefits typically aren't sufficient to justify organizational spend in the EIM space. Most certainly, these generic benefits will build an interest in digging more deeply into this topic, but simply stating that you're "looking to reduce duplication across your customer master data" isn't specific enough. You must look at all the potential benefits of an EIM program, determine which of these apply to the organization in question, and then determine a defined, measurable, and quantified organizational benefit.

  These benefits can then be measured over time and show clearly that the promised successes have been realized. This will then often be used to build and expand an EIM program, driving additional business benefits across all levels of an organization and further targeting the key pain points that exist in an enterprise.

- **Strategic benefits vs. tactical benefits**
  There is significant value to be obtained from more tactical benefits of an EIM program; aspects such as increasing operational efficiency or achieving cost savings on the manufacturing line are great and should be a part of an overall business case.

  However, if a business case is to attract the interest of the C-Suite, whose buy-in is needed to get the necessary funding for such a program, strategic benefits will need to be assessed and defined. Showing how an EIM program will move the needle via organizational innovation, placing high-quality information at the fingertips of key executives throughout an enterprise, and helping to set and define new markets or new products to bring to market will drive investment into these programs and ensure success.

To provide a specific example of a business case for the need for EIM, let's look at the need for privacy and compliance support. With the increased use of big data/social media data, privacy concerns have been growing regarding individuals' data use.

To protect the privacy and use of individual data, various governments across the globe have started enacting laws in this area. One such law is the General Data Protection Regulation (GDPR), which is an EU regulation on data protection and privacy for all individuals within the European Union. Noncompliant organizations may face heavy fines.

Additionally, other government acts—such as the California Consumer Privacy Act (CCPA)—have been introduced to support privacy concerns. This legislation is California's version of the GDPR and requires that companies provide the following for their customers:

- The right to know what personal information is being collected about them
- The right to know whether their personal information is being sold or disclosed and to whom
- The right to say no to the sale of personal information
- The right to access their personal information
- The right to equal service and price, even if they exercise rights outlined in the bill

These aren't the only two laws introduced; many more include similar requirements.

At the heart of these laws is personal data, which refers to any information relating to an identified or identifiable natural person, also known as the data subject. As you can imagine, personal data is an expansive category in this context. It can include information such as full name, date of birth, Social Security number, driver's license, email addresses, pictures of the person, education records, income and employment history, financial history, vehicle identifiers, fingerprints, DNA information, and much more. Each law often has its own expanded perspective about what qualifies as personal data. Therefore, organizations face a daunting task to first identify all related personal data across the landscape, including their movements and usage, and then to protect the data for further use—both while remaining compliant with regulations. For example, although an individual may request to be forgotten, his transactions can't be removed until the legal limit (e.g., seven years), requiring the lifecycle of all the data to be managed. Figure 1.1 shows the lifecycle of personal data. Data that is no longer needed for the primary processing purpose must be deleted, unless there are other retention periods defined by law or contract; in that case, the data has to be blocked.

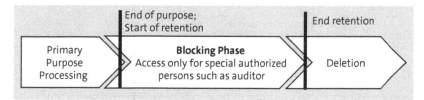

Figure 1.1 Lifecycle of Personal Data

In the EIM space, tools such as SAP Information Steward and SAP Data Intelligence assist in identifying the metadata, tagging the personal metadata across the landscape, and then profiling that data. These tools then allow you to define business rules regarding whether the data is valid and exists, while also identifying the lineage of the data flow across the enterprise. These tools provide a lens into data availability within the enterprise landscape.

Tools such as SAP Master Data Governance provide the support required to govern personal data. For example, SAP Master Data Governance can mark data as end of purpose via the **EOP** flag. This isn't a deletion flag; instead, this flag ensures that the personal data won't be shared with most users who have read access. However, a super user would still have access to transaction data validations for that user.

SAP Master Data Governance also allows you to keep track of the workflow when the **EOP** flag has been set or the mark for delete process has been initiated. It can track information such as who set the flag/initiated the process, the context in which this request was made, and who has approval authority. This provides the full context and traceability for the "right to be forgotten" of the individual's personal data.

SAP Master Data Governance can also be part of SAP S/4HANA: if the deployment is a part of a co-deployment scenario with the transactional system, SAP Master Data Governance will also check whether there are any open transactions before the block is allowed. Blocking personal data isn't allowed until the active transactions are closed.

Essentially, the purpose of SAP Master Data Governance is to provide a single version of truth across the enterprise. That insight into the enterprise data is important to the governance and compliance of the master data during creation and change through integrated staging, approval, and central auditing.

After the **EOP** flag is set or the mark for deletion process is initiated, SAP Information Lifecycle Management (SAP ILM) allows you to archive the data based on the set business rules. SAP ILM manages all archiving, retention, and deletion policies across the enterprise. It provides automatic deletion of data based on policies, enforces the policies required by the regulations, and finally executes e-discovery and legal holds.

Figure 1.2 shows a sample scenario using the **EOP** flag.

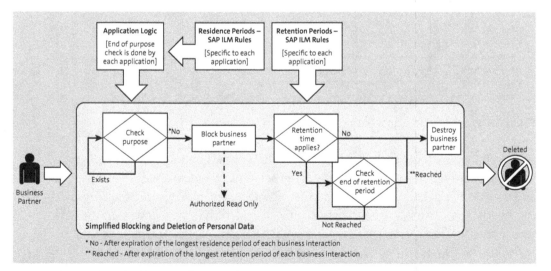

Figure 1.2 End of Purpose (Blocking) Process Flow

1.3 Enterprise Information Management Capabilities

Having addressed and reviewed the organizational challenges and the benefits of an EIM program, next up is an exploration of the core capabilities needed in the EIM world and how SAP offers solutions to deliver these capabilities to the market.

A great model for displaying the delivered EIM capabilities is shown in Figure 1.3. The illustration should be read as a progression, beginning with the architecture and metadata management wedge and progressing around to information lifecycle management. Different companies—depending on their maturity in the EIM space, the complexity of their system landscape, and how much of a priority they have placed on EIM solutions in the past—will be at different stages of this journey or have different compelling needs. However, all companies can derive benefit from all phases of this journey. Let's look at each phase in a little more detail.

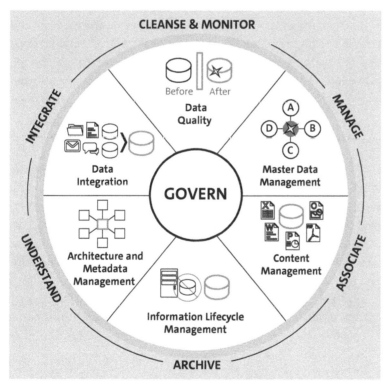

Figure 1.3 EIM Capabilities

1.3.1 Architecture and Metadata Management

During the architecture and metadata management phase, we're looking at companies who could be starting on the EIM path and are looking to understand their organization's data, what issues exist, and where improvements can be made. Such an analysis is always quite revealing. Many companies understand that they have data issues but don't understand the scope of these issues and the key discrepancies that are affecting their productivity. Examining this will involve a data profiling exercise that empirically shows what issues exist, where they exist and how extensive they are. For some companies, this is the first step in a long journey.

One deliverable that will come out of this process is the building of a clearly defined business case for justifying continued investment in this space. The trends revealed in this part of an EIM journey will drive all the subsequent steps in the journey.

1.3.2 Data Integration

With data integration, we're talking about capabilities to access, move, and load all data sources that exist in an enterprise landscape. Software landscapes are often quite complex, and customers will have multiple disparate data stores that are necessary to access and derive insight from. These data stores can be both internal and external and will probably include both SAP and non-SAP sources—for example, transactional systems, data warehouses, external enrichment feeds, and big data sources (e.g., Hadoop). Potentially, this heterogeneous group of system can be a mix of both on-premise and cloud deployments.

1.3.3 Data Quality

In the data quality phase, we're looking at correcting the issues discovered during the architecture and metadata management process by both remediating any existing data issues and by putting solutions in place to monitor the data quality of the enterprise in an ongoing fashion. Tasks addressed here include removing duplicate data, correcting inaccurate data, and enriching incomplete data. Establishing business rules and providing monitoring capabilities to highlight any deviation from these rules are critical to the ongoing data health of an enterprise. Self-service capabilities are important here: business users need to be empowered to build and run these rules to ensure that organizational data standards are being met. Business users own and know the data, so providing them with tools to ensure that it's ready for business use is a critical component in a successful EIM program.

1.3.4 Master Data Management

The capabilities in this part of the wheel are the key focus of this book and they are expanded on significantly in later chapters. The key business need is to manage and govern an organization's master data to ensure data quality across the entire enterprise. By using the previously described capabilities, the data in an organization is now well understood, existing data quality issues have been identified and addressed, and ongoing monitoring rules are in place. However, it's vitally important to ensure that after clean master data has been established, governance processes are in place to keep this data clean. Without this component, an organization will simply return to square one, as the quality of this information will degrade over time unless appropriate governance rules and structures are in place.

Master data management has multiple scenarios that can be implemented based on their use cases, as follows:

- **Consolidation**
  This scenario, shown in Figure 1.4, is where master data has multiple creation points within multiple applications. To identify the uniqueness of the master data and tie the master data transactions together across applications, a golden record needs to be created by matching the master data records from all these applications and merging them in a single entry to create a cluster or group of master data records. This unique record creation is based on a set of defined rules, such as system precedence and the most recent field update. The scenario has been used for analytical purposes, for example, building out spend analytics to consolidate vendor and material master data.

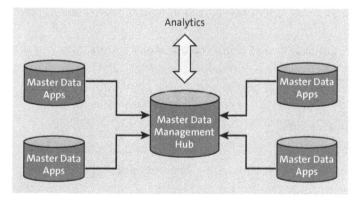

Figure 1.4 Master Data Consolidation

The core capabilities for building the consolidation capabilities are as follows (i.e., data quality, continuous data quality):

- Bring all sources of data together.
- Cleanse, standardize, match, and create the best record.
- Provide data stewardship applications for search/explore and for match/merge/ unmerge.

- **Registry**
  This scenario, shown in Figure 1.5, is used mainly for low latency within the enterprise where applications are found across the geographic landscape with multiple hyperscalers, the public cloud, and the on-premise environment.

The master data records aren't consolidated; however, a token of the records and the key mapping information are tracked across the enterprise application. It's the next step after consolidation and enables data to be linked across the enterprise.

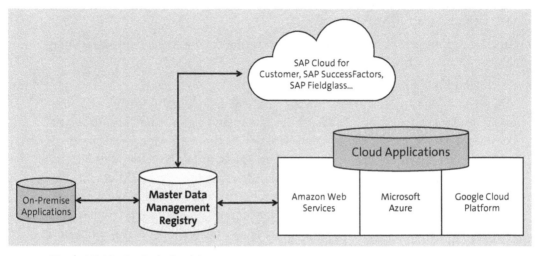

Figure 1.5 Master Data Registry

- **Central management**
  This scenario, shown in Figure 1.6, allows you to create a single version of truth of the master data record with validations and derivations, ensuring that the master data record is created as pristine as possible and then sent across applications. It's the end state—the nirvana. The core capabilities for central master date are as follows:
  - Govern and provide full traceability of the master data record.
  - Provide modeling capabilities with the data stewardship user interface (UI).
  - Provide the business rules framework for data validations and derivation rules.
  - Cleanse and match data.
  - Provide fuzzy search.
  - Provide interfaces to integrate inbound and outbound data.
  - Tie together the core business processes of the application.
- **Hybrid or coexistence**
  This scenario, shown in Figure 1.7, is a mix of all the previous scenarios where master data is authored in various application systems, consolidated into a unique record, and then authored within the central master data scenario. One of the applications can leverage the registry style scenario to ensure that there is always a central repository.

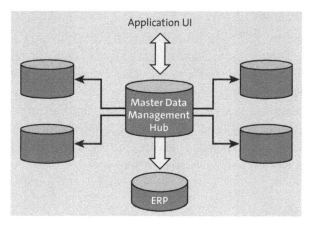

Figure 1.6 Central Master Data Management

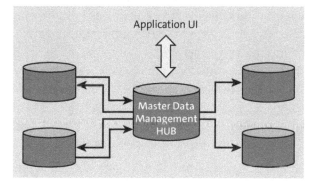

Figure 1.7 Hybrid or Coexistence of Central Master Data Style

1.3.5   Content Management

Although this book's focus is on master data, another important component of an information management strategy is the need to access and manage all the unstructured content that exists within an organization. Think for a second how many Microsoft Word documents, Microsoft Excel files, PDFs, emails, digital media files, manuals, and so on exist in an organization and how much processing is done, both inbound and outbound, that is centered on unstructured content such as invoices, purchase orders, maintenance schedules, delivery notifications, and so on. It's increasingly important to have these documents accessible across the entire enterprise, to have governance and approvals around changes or additions to these documents, and to allow this content to be accessed from within existing business processes. All inbound and outbound documents need to be processed efficiently and accurately. Capabilities here allow organizations to digitize their basement, get away from a mountain of paper, and ensure this content is at the fingertips of those who need it within an enterprise.

1.3.6   Information Lifecycle Management

To comply with regulatory requirements and to continue to run efficiently, organizations need to ensure that retention policies for data and documents are enforced and that archiving procedures are in place. Retention policies will differ depending on the industry involved, on different government regulations, and on the type of information being assessed. Capabilities are needed to apply legal holds to data that should be prevented from being destroyed during any legal proceedings. Archival processes should control that not only the data to be archived is removed but also that none of the associated documents or unstructured content are still in place.

1.3.7   Federated Master Data Landscape

Federated master data management is a concept that is gaining acceptance from master data experts, and it's definitely something you're going to hear more about in the near future. One of the biggest challenges in managing master data has been harmonizing data across a multitude of heterogeneous systems in the enterprise landscape. In many cases, this is a time-consuming and very expensive activity. One of the main reasons is that the same logical object (e.g., customer or supplier) is represented very differently in various systems present in the landscape. These objects are designed as fit for purpose in their respective individual application systems. Trying to align them into a single canonical model is an extremely difficult exercise. With an increasing number of systems in the corporate landscape, this task becomes even more onerous.

Federated master data management and governance tries to overcome this challenge by aligning only on a core set of attributes of the master data and leaving the management of application specific attributes where they are best managed, that is, in their respective application systems. The alignment of the core attributes centrally ensures that you can have a single view of the master data in the landscape. We'll leave governance of application master data to the individual line of business (LoB) systems.

Federated data management lowers total cost of ownership, makes integration seamless, and avoids costly harmonization exercises. In other parts of this chapter, you'll see how SAP is coming up with additional concepts such as SAP One Domain Model to provide such a core data model and how new services such as SAP Master Data Integration and SAP Master Data Orchestration allow access and support in a federated master data landscape architecture.

In a federated master data landscape, the attributes of master data are classified into core master data and application master data attributes

- **Core attributes**
  Common core attributes that are usually identical, for example, name, address, and some global attributes of a supplier or customer. These core attributes can be harmonized and used homogenously across the entire enterprise.

- **Application-specific attributes**
  Application-specific attributes that are defined quite differently in each application or business units, or even geography. Companies often struggle to find a single harmonized approach that meets all stakeholder and business requirements. Often these application-specific master data attributes are important for how the business processes are executed to generate value. It can be quite challenging to harmonize these application-specific attributes on a corporate level.

Figure 1.8 shows an example of core master data attributes and application-specific master data attributes in a heterogeneous landscape.

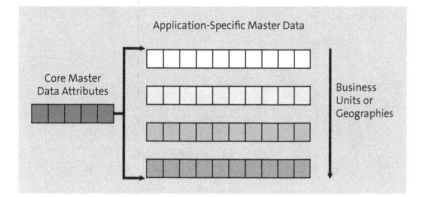

Figure 1.8 Core Master Data and Application Master Data in a Heterogeneous Landscape

This is where the new deployment option of federation of SAP Master Data Governance can help set the right level of centralization and harmonization for effective master data management. In this deployment model, the organization can manage just the core attributes using SAP Master Data Governance, cloud edition, and then syndicate the data across the landscape using SAP Master Data Integration. In the receiving systems, the application-specific master data attributes are then managed. Through this process of federation of SAP Master Data Governance, the organization not only achieves harmonized master data across the entire enterprise but also manages application-specific master data attributes exactly at the place where these are best understood.

SAP Master Data Governance on SAP S/4HANA is supposed to contribute as the first application governing application-specific attributes in a federated SAP Master Data Governance context. This will also allow all existing SAP Master Data Governance customers to expand toward this new federated deployment option, while leveraging all earlier investments made in the SAP Master Data Governance on-premise deployment that they already have.

Federated SAP Master Data Governance deployment is a shared enterprise activity in a network of SAP Master Data Governance systems. Each of the systems in the landscape applies governance and stewardship to a different subset of master data attributes. All of these systems work in coordination and ensure that master data is managed at the exact place in the organization where it's best understood.

Figure 1.9 show a federated master data landscape with core master data management attributes managed at a corporate level with solutions such as SAP Master Data Governance, cloud edition, and application-specific master data attributes managed in their respective application systems in different business units of the corporate landscape.

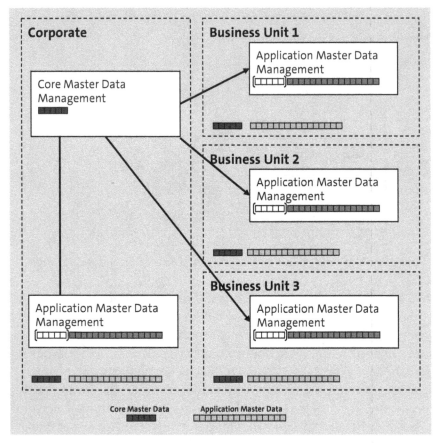

Figure 1.9 Federated Master Data Landscape

1.3.8   SAP One Domain Model

With the emergence of best of breed, LoB cloud applications, the customer landscapes of today are changing rapidly. They are no longer the monolithic ERP-centric landscape of yesteryear's enterprises. But these hybrid landscapes bring complexity of aligning master data across the enterprise. For example, the procurement team uses a solution such as SAP Ariba for qualifying and onboarding new suppliers. At the same time, contract negotiations with the same suppliers are handled on a different contract management system. And when it's time to order from the supplier, the team might use the procurement functions of SAP S/4HANA. Even though the same supplier is available in different systems, their purpose of usage and therefore the information they contain is very specific to the application context in which they are used.

In an intelligent enterprise, when building an integrated end-to-end process such as procure-to-pay or hire-to-retire, it's crucial to have a seamless integration and a single view of the involved master data for the process to work smoothly, especially because different parts of the process will be executed on different solutions within a landscape. SAP One Domain Model is this single representation of the data domain that facilitates an end-to-end seamless integration.

Important to note that SAP One Domain Model isn't a canonical data model, where you try to jam in all the fields of—for example—the supplier master from all the different systems. Rather, SAP One Domain Model is a harmonized single view of a domain that captures only the common and most essential attributes of the master data object, which we've been calling the "core master data." All the other attributes—called the "application master data"—are owned and managed by the applications where they are most relevant. Figure 1.10 shows how various applications can share group of attributes within the context of SAP One Data Model.

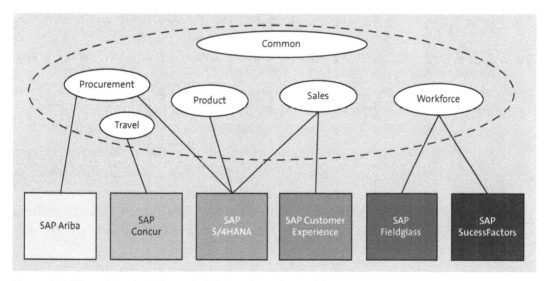

Figure 1.10 Shared Context through SAP One Domain Model

As a developer or integration architect, you can leverage a whole bunch of SAP Master Data Integration service application programming interfaces (APIs) to access both the core master data attributes available in SAP One Domain Model and the application data attributes owned in the respective LoB applications in your landscape—without dealing with specific semantics and protocols for different systems. The SAP Master Data Integration layer provides you with a central access point for the master data in your landscape.

SAP One Domain Model is still a relatively new topic for most SAP customers, but in the coming days, you'll hear more about how it plays a central role in the enterprise landscape.

1.4 Key SAP Solutions for Enterprise Information Management

To address all of these capabilities, SAP has a complete set of products that will take a customer through all stages of an EIM journey. This book will dive into the SAP Master Data Governance offering in detail.

As an overview, the following sections will provide a little more information on the functionality of several of the key offerings in the EIM space.

1.4.1 SAP Data Services

SAP Data Services is a powerful tool that enables organizations to understand and profile their level of data quality, to integrate their data across the enterprise, and to improve and correct issues with this enterprise data.

Extract, transform, and load (ETL) capabilities are important features of the solution, which allow a company to take data from any data source and then ensure a high level of data quality by applying rules, transformations, and filters before loading the data into the required target databases, applications, or business warehouses. These data sources include both big data and cloud sources. Today, SAP Data Services supports many of the most popular big data systems, including Hadoop, SAP HANA, HPE Vertica, NoSQL MongoDB, Google BigQuery, Azure SQL Database, and Amazon Redshift.

All of these data-quality capabilities can be applied to incoming data and can be integrated with your enterprise systems for ensuring high levels of data quality at the point of entry.

Text data processing capabilities are also included, deriving meaning and insight from natural language processing on unstructured text sources, such as Word and PDF documents, as well as other text sources.

A graphic of the most important capabilities of the SAP Data Services solution is shown in Figure 1.11. These capabilities include the following:

- Access and extract structured and unstructured data—SAP and non-SAP—in batches or in real time.
- Transform, cleanse, match, and consolidate data.
- Scale from single to multiple servers for all volumes of data.
- Support a wide variety of SAP and non-SAP targets.

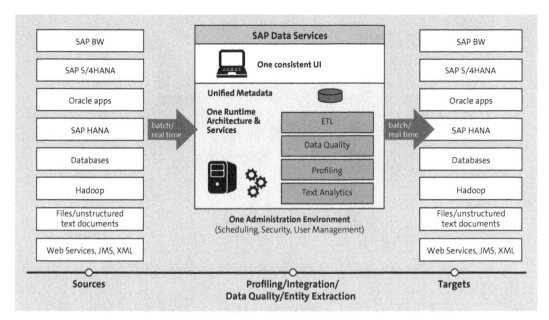

Figure 1.11 SAP Data Services: Key Capabilities

1.4.2 SAP Information Steward

SAP Information Steward takes the power of SAP Data Services and places it in the hands of the business users whose job is to ensure that a high level of data quality is maintained across the enterprise.

The main capabilities of the solution include the ability to profile and monitor data quality across the enterprise; allow key data stakeholders to manage and understand metadata and data lineage across complex landscapes; define business rules, terms, and policies governing data; enhance operational, analytical, and data governance initiatives; and enable collaboration across important roles in a data organization. All of this is achieved through a business-friendly UI incorporating powerful dashboards and scorecards, along with event-driven notifications when thresholds aren't being met.

A graphic of the top capabilities of the SAP Information Steward solution is shown in Figure 1.12. These capabilities include the following:

❶ Discover the business glossary and metadata. Formally develop information policies.

❷ Define business terms, validation rules, and cleansing rules using profiling results.

❸ Enable workflow for data quality task ownership of data assets.

❹ Monitor and resolve data quality issues with preloaded templates.

❺ Analyze data quality using business value analysis to quantify financial impact.

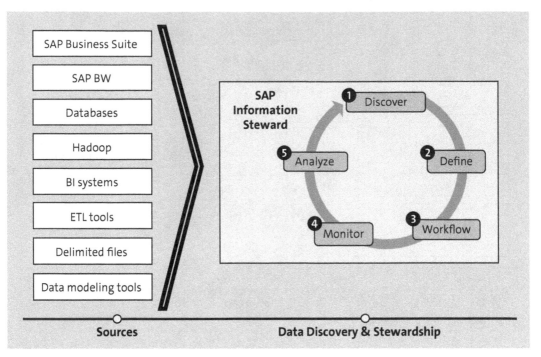

Figure 1.12 SAP Information Steward Key Capabilities

1.4.3   SAP HANA Smart Data Integration and SAP HANA Smart Data Quality

SAP is investing in EIM solutions built natively in the SAP HANA platform. The SAP HANA smart data integration and SAP HANA smart data quality solutions are the foundations of these developments, delivering data integration, data replication, and data quality capabilities to the enterprise.

These solutions allow batch or real-time data replication by applying filters, transformations, and data quality rules as needed across a landscape. Data profiling and data enrichment capabilities are also key use cases.

Along with these benefits comes the ability to develop applications on top of this powerful framework. Some example applications that use these features with the EIM portfolio are SAP Master Data Governance and SAP Agile Data Preparation.

A summary of the main features of SAP HANA smart data quality and SAP HANA smart data integration is provided in Figure 1.13.

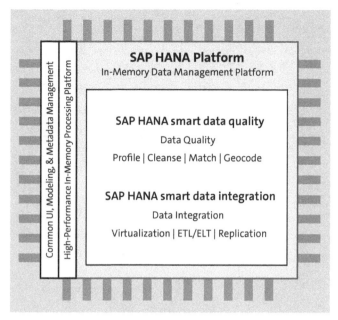

Figure 1.13 SAP HANA Smart Data Quality and SAP HANA Smart Data Integration

1.4.4   SAP Agile Data Preparation

A key market driver in the EIM space is the need for providing tools to allow for self-service data preparation. SAP Agile Data Preparation uses the power of SAP HANA to facilitate self-service data discovery, collaboration, and data preparation, improving both the quality and value of the master data in an enterprise. Organizational benefits will be realized through this trusted data for analytical use cases as well as improving the day-to-day operations of a business.

SAP Agile Data Preparation can be used by different groups within an enterprise, including business users, data stewards, data scientists, and those in the IT department. Business analysts will have the necessary access to a wide variety of data sources across the entire business landscape, allowing for greater visibility into critical enterprise information. IT groups will benefit through the self-service of business users and by allowing for greater control over data standards and security.

The following features and use cases of SAP Agile Data Preparation are noted in Figure 1.14:

- Ingest data from a variety of sources.
- Use for profile data.
- Combine, shape, enrich, or cleanse data.
- Output data for downstream uses.
- Analyze and optimize user processes (IT governance team).

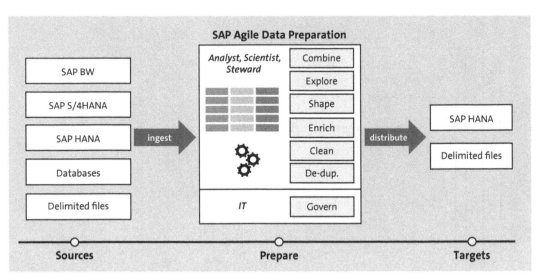

Figure 1.14 SAP Agile Data Preparation: Key Features and Usage

1.4.5   SAP Information Lifecycle Management

When data in an organization reaches the end of its retention period or a system in a landscape is ready to be retired, SAP Information Lifecycle Management (SAP ILM), as depicted in Figure 1.15, will play a critical part in ensuring compliance by following all necessary legal regulations and organizational policies.

Furthermore, data archiving is a key capability of SAP ILM, allowing for data that is no longer needed to support the day-to-day operation of the business to be retired to cheaper, long-term storage.

Retention management is a critical topic that needs to be considered by all organizations to remain compliant in an increasingly complex regulatory environment. Data privacy regulations, such as the EU's GDPR, apply strict standards regarding treatment of personal information. SAP ILM facilitates the definition of policies that will ensure enterprise data is blocked from destruction prior to the appropriate expiration date being reached and will manage the destruction of data after a retention period has been met and the data serves no further business value. SAP ILM is the tool to ensure that personal/sensitive information is blocked when archived. Finally, SAP ILM enables the organization to apply a legal hold on data that would need to be retained throughout a litigation process, for example.

Legacy system decommissioning is another important SAP ILM feature, facilitating the shutting down of any obsolete systems in a landscape and managing the retention rules that need to be applied to any data in those systems. As organizations are moving toward a digital enterprise, the need to shut down legacy systems is only going to increase.

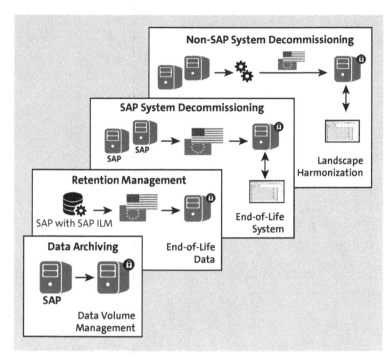

Figure 1.15 SAP ILM Scenarios

1.4.6   SAP Content Management Solutions by OpenText

Another key component of a successful EIM strategy is ensuring that all the unstructured content in an enterprise is managed, governed, and handled in a cost-effective, efficient, and compliant fashion. Consider how many documents, spreadsheets, PDFs, emails, images, videos, and manuals exist in an enterprise. It's vitally important for an organization to ensure that these documents are managed, accessed, and associated with the key enterprise data and processes that relate to them. As organizations move toward a digital core, the need to manage these documents in a controlled fashion is becoming more compelling.

Being able to manage and process all inbound and outbound communication (e.g., invoices, sales orders, purchase orders, delivery notifications, etc.) and internal documents (e.g., policy documents, employee files, technical drawings, maintenance schedules, etc.) as needed is critical to any enterprise. The SAP content management portfolio from OpenText allows organizations to get out from under a mountain of paper and to digitize their enterprise filing cabinet, provides significant process simplification and organizational benefits, and places this digital content at the fingertips of those who need it, where they need it, and when they need it.

Different solution providers are in this market area, but SAP content management solutions are different because they are SAP Solution Extensions, integrating natively with SAP software. This deep content association allows for true enterprise collaboration across both structured master data and unstructured enterprise content. In fact, SAP Extended Enterprise Content Management (SAP Extended ECM) by OpenText can be integrated with SAP Master Data Governance, allowing for the governance and control of both enterprise master data and unstructured content within one governance process.

The following key solutions are part of the SAP content management portfolio:

- SAP Extended ECM (as mentioned previously)
- SAP Archiving and Document Access by OpenText
- SAP Invoice Management by OpenText
- SAP Digital Content Processing by OpenText
- SAP Document Presentment by OpenText

Figure 1.16 demonstrates how content management capabilities can be made a part of and enhance an EIM strategy.

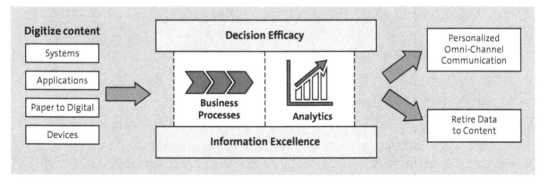

Figure 1.16 SAP Content Management Solutions: Critical Component of an EIM Strategy

1.5   SAP Cloud Solutions for Information Management

As the software industry is moving toward public cloud solutions, SAP has expanded the information management portfolio to support multitenant cloud solutions. SAP Master Data Governance, which is an on-premise solution, can be deployed on any of the hyperscale cloud vendors, such as Amazon Web Services (AWS), Google Cloud Platform (GCP), Microsoft Azure, or on private SAP cloud environment, as a private cloud deployment.

As you'll see in this section, SAP Business Technology Platform (SAP BTP) has gone from strength to strength as a technology foundation on which to build your intelligent enterprise applications, and SAP has made available many EIM solutions on this platform such as SAP Data Intelligence; SAP Master Data Integration, SAP Master Data Orchestration; SAP Data Quality Management, microservices for location data; and so on.

1.5.1 SAP Data Intelligence Cloud

Many of you are likely familiar with the earlier SAP Data Hub solution, which was deployed on-premise and provided data orchestration and management capabilities, as well as dealt with big data handling requirements in the enterprise landscape. Now SAP has evolved this solution further into what is now called SAP Data Intelligence Cloud, by bringing in more intelligent data handling capabilities with machine learning processes and data science capabilities and offering it as a managed service in SAP BTP.

SAP Data Intelligence is a paradigm shift on how integration technologies are leveraged. Previously, when it came to performing application integration, that is, integrating transactional applications among themselves, the integration was performed via middleware and a message bus, which provided very stable integration. Then the technology focus switched toward analytics integration, that is, integrating data from transactional applications toward data warehouses and EIM tools (e.g., SAP Data Services), which provided data quality and transformations before loading the data into the final downstream systems. SAP Data Intelligence is the next generation of integration technology that uses the concept of data fabric to connect, virtualize, integrate, and transform data to build one logical data solution for applications. Figure 1.17 represents the features and functionality embedded within SAP Data Intelligence.

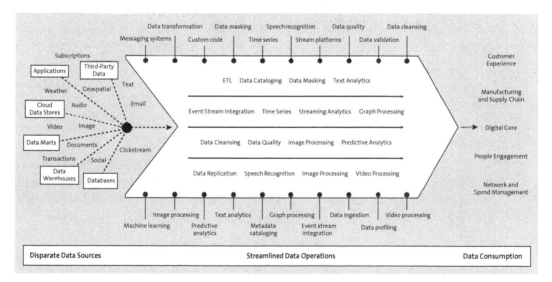

Figure 1.17 SAP Data Intelligence Features and Capabilities

Data orchestration with SAP Data Intelligence is a very new incremental domain, where enterprises are required to deal with disparate kinds of data such as structured and unstructured, cloud and on-premise, and hybrid landscapes. In addition, while integrating with the structured or unstructured data, data science or advanced analytics need to be performed on the data, whose outcomes are then often used back in transactional contexts. SAP Data Intelligence addresses this very new shift in integration technologies—mixing disparate kinds of data and different kinds of advanced processing—because it can't be solved with any of the existing tools. In this domain, SAP Data Intelligence provides strong differentiators and a data orchestration layer that, so far, no other solution offers.

SAP Data Intelligence goes beyond data orchestration by allowing you to manage metadata centrally for all disparate and distributed data sources, providing cataloging, browsing, and profiling capabilities.

You can integrate and orchestrate very diverse data—such as structured, unstructured, and streaming data—with one single tool, solving the data fragmentation issue and overcoming the data integration challenge, which is often a showstopper for many data science and Internet of Things (IoT)-driven innovation initiatives. SAP Data Intelligence provides Lego-like building blocks that allow ingesting, streaming, and subscribing of data. It allows validations, transformations, refinements, and enrichments; leverages machine learning algorithms with Python scripts; and triggers actions or publishes the data. Additionally, SAP Data Intelligence has building blocks for custom coding—including masking of data and image processing—and allowing analytical applications to be built on top of this.

With its extensive machine learning capabilities, SAP Data Intelligence allows you to infuse machine learning capabilities into your data handling and bring them to production very quickly. It provides tools for data modeling, data analysis, and data visualization, all of which can be done with minimal or no programming. If you want to go one step further, it also provides you with a Software Development Kit (SDK) based on Python, which provides you access to all the SAP Data Intelligence functionality via programming.

With SAP Data Intelligence, you can reuse, execute, and orchestrate data processing jobs across several engines—both SAP and open source—and across different locations, minimizing the data movement. SAP Data Intelligence integrates or allows orchestration with existing solutions, including SAP Data Services and SAP Landscape Transformation Replication Server (SAP LT Replication Server). Therefore, for example, SAP Data Services jobs can be integrated with the overall SAP Data Intelligence flowgraphs.

For companies that prefer to run SAP Data Intelligence on-premise rather than on the cloud, an on-premise version of the software is also available from SAP.

1.5.2 SAP Data Quality Management, Microservices for Location Data

SAP Data Quality Management, microservices for location data, is available on SAP BTP and allows you to embed data cleansing and enrichment services within any application system or business process. The solution has prebuilt integrations to SAP solutions such as SAP S/4HANA, SAP Master Data Governance, SAP SuccessFactors, and so on.

The solution enables address cleansing/validation for 240+ countries to correct, validate, format, and standardize address data; it also provides geocoding (return latitude and longitude given an input address) and reverse geocoding (return an address or a list of addresses given a latitude/longitude pair) capabilities. The services can be called from any application via an HTTP POST request containing the address to be processed.

Figure 1.18 gives an overview of the key components involved in the SAP Data Quality Management, microservices for location data. The solution allows you to create correct, consistent, and standardized location information and ensure accurate location analytics.

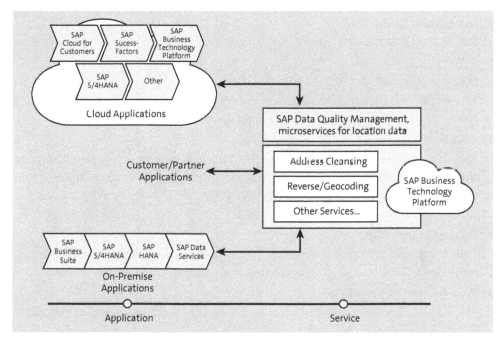

Figure 1.18 SAP Data Quality Management, Microservices for Location Data

1.5.3   Data Attribute Recommendation

The Data Attribute Recommendation service is an offering within the SAP AI Business Services portfolio offered in SAP BTP. The solution allows records to come in as input and provides complex record matching with a nested hierarchy structure. For example, incoming sales data is matched against product data records, including the product hierarchy data. Another example involves tedious manual processes like maintaining complex fields, such as commodity codes, with correct values. This microservice not only predicts the correct values for those fields, including data dependencies, but also trains the model to its needs.

The hierarchy matching microservice has three main functions:

- **Data management**
  This is used to upload training data (data set schema and data set) validate its quality level, preprocess training data, and delete training data.

- **Model manager**
  This is used to train a machine learning model, activate/deactivate a specific trained model, and list and delete all models.

- **Inference**
  This module is used to classify the records using machine learning models and predict the value of missing fields in the incoming data.

Following are the available APIs:

- **Get Authorization API**
  Before accessing any data, this API helps to check if the user has the right authorization to access the data.

- **Data Manager API**
  This API allows uploading new data sets, listing uploaded data sets, and deleting data sets.

- **Data Validation and Data Lifecycle API**
  This API provides validating for data sets uploaded to check if they are compliant with provided schema and to check how many records are available for training purposes. The lifecycle API allows for classifying data records and predicting missing numerical values.

- **Model Manager API**
  This API allows starting machine learning model training, listing all models (currently in training process, already trained, and activated), and deleting models.

- **Training and Deploying Job API**
  This API enables the defining of training and deployment models and working with different model statuses.

- **Inference API**
  This API enables the classifying of records.

1.5.4 SAP Master Data Integration

In the previous section, we touched on two new concepts that are gaining prominence: SAP One Domain Model and federated master data management. One of the key pillars for a federated data concept to work is the ability to access master data easily and be guaranteed that you always get the latest version of the data that you're looking for, irrespective of whether its core master data or application master data.

SAP Master Data Integration is a multitenant public cloud service provided in SAP BTP that allows for simple and consistent access to master data in a heterogenous landscape. The service is based on the SAP One Domain Model concept we mentioned in Section 1.3.8. This means that the data structure used by SAP Master Data Integration for its inbound/outbound processes is aligned with the data schema of SAP One Domain Model. SAP One Domain Model supports many different data domains (the list continues to grow), which can be then accessed using SAP Master Data Integration.

Some features of the service are listed here:

- **Data read and write by multiple systems**
  Multiple client systems can read and write data, provided they have the authorization to do so.

- **Read access logging**
  Access to all sensitive data is logged and recorded; this is a critical feature, especially to support data compliance and privacy requirements such as GDPR.

- **Extensibility**
  The predelivered data models can be extended by customers to support their business needs.

- **Multiversion support**
  The SAP One Domain Model data models are continuously evolving and newer versions are released. However, SAP Master Data Integration supports multiversion read and write, so it's still possible to write data into an older version of SAP One Domain Model and then read it using a schema of a higher version of SAP One Domain Model.

- **Support for REST and OData APIs for data access**
  Data access via REST and OData APIs.

> **Note**
>
> For all the latest information on SAP BTP services, the best place to go is the SAP Discovery Center (*https://discovery-center.cloud.sap/*). Whenever you plan to use SAP Master Data Integration, the SAP Discovery Center will provide the latest information you need to provision, consume, implement, and use the service. The SAP Discovery Center also provides a lot of information on how best to implement different use cases using the service.
>
> For the latest information on the usage and restrictions of SAP Master Data Integration service, refer to SAP Note 2954816.

1.5.5   SAP Master Data Orchestration

In a federated landscape, the abilities to distribute data and to manage ownership of different parts of the master data are important features. These capabilities are provided by the SAP Master Data Orchestration service that works in conjunction with the SAP Master Data Integration service (refer to Section 1.5.4).

The SAP Master Data Orchestration service provides the following apps:

- Manage Distribution Model
- Manage Business Object Type
- Configure Monitoring
- Configure Destination Mapping
- Manage Data Ownership
- Display Distribution Status

Using the SAP Master Data Orchestration layer, it's possible to centrally maintain distribution models, maintain filtering on the models to control which data can be distributed, maintain key mapping information, schedule the distribution, and decide when and to which client systems data should be distributed.

The monitoring capability of SAP Master Data Orchestration works together with the SAP Cloud ALM. The data distribution information is captured by SAP Master Data Orchestration and shared with the SAP Cloud ALM solution, and it can be visualized there.

One of the other important requirements in a federated landscape is the capability to establish ownership of different parts of the master data. For example, address data in a customer master could be owned by a system such as SAP Cloud for Customer because that is the system where the customer data is most likely to be up to date. Whereas organization data such as company code, business partner type, and business area data is typically up to date in the SAP S/4HANA system. Therefore, from an ownership perspective, address data should be owned by SAP Cloud for Customer and the organization level data by SAP S/4HANA.

The owner of the object type typically is the only system that has permission to write and update the master data object type, whereas the other clients can only read that part of the master data. So, we can say the owner of the object type within the landscape is the single source of truth for that data. For the applications accessing customer data, all these data ownership concepts and complexities are fully transparent because the SAP Master Data Integration and SAP Master Data Orchestration services ensure that correct and up-to-date data is passed to every consuming application all the time.

The Data Ownership app, as part of the SAP Master Data Orchestration, allows for listing, modifying, and deleting the ownership of different object types for a given master data object.

If the data object type is changed in one of the client systems that isn't the owner, SAP Master Data Orchestration checks the data ownership and sends the change to the owner of the data object type. The owner system can then either accept or reject this change; if the owner system accepts this change, this change is then distributed to other client systems by the SAP Master Data Orchestration layer.

Going forward, the SAP Master Data Integration and SAP Master Data Orchestration layers will be the key pillars around which master data management in future enterprise landscapes will be built.

1.6   SAP Master Data Governance

Alongside these other EIM offerings sits SAP Master Data Governance. Within the EIM portfolio, SAP Master Data Governance is the key master data management solution from SAP and designed to be complemented by the rest of the portfolio for a complete EIM offering.

Most certainly, understanding your enterprise data is important, and tasks such as cleansing and de-duplicating your records will bring significant value; however, if there isn't a formal mechanism in place to mandate data quality and apply governance standards in an ongoing fashion, the overall quality of the data within the enterprise will degrade quite quickly. As a first step, a company might look to monitor and remediate issues, but, ultimately, preventing data quality issues from even occurring is a major step along the path of advancing the level of EIM sophistication within the enterprise. SAP Master Data Governance is the foremost offering from SAP to provide this business value.

SAP Master Data Governance allows for both the central creation and maintenance of enterprise master data as well as for the consolidation of data from disparate sources into the SAP Master Data Governance application. The SAP Master Data Governance solution allows organizations to use delivered content and leverage a governance framework to build strong governance processes to suit their business requirements.

One of the strengths of SAP Master Data Governance is its alignment with SAP systems, data structures, and architecture. However, it's quite clear that almost no SAP customers have a 100% homogeneous SAP landscape. At a minimum, there are likely custom extensions to SAP data models and likely several non-SAP applications that will benefit from having high-quality master data. SAP Master Data Governance is absolutely designed to cater to such landscapes. SAP Master Data Governance comes with delivered content that gives customers significant out-of-the-box benefits; however, and most importantly, it provides a framework that is completely extensible to allow organizations to benefit from these features across their entire landscape.

Originally, SAP Master Data Governance was developed to address a central governance use case where companies would establish a set of governance processes and rules to control the creation, extension, update, and so on of their enterprise data before distributing this as needed throughout their landscape. This is still seen as a primary use case for the solution. Organizations understand the clear need for addressing this scenario and want this standardization in their enterprise master data. However, a central process with SAP Master Data Governance doesn't necessarily mean having one central group operating globally. The central maintenance of master data can most certainly be distributed throughout an enterprise. Consider, as an example, a global company with different regional subsidiaries setting up a governance process for their material master. SAP Master Data Governance processes could be established to allow, for example, the initial creation of core attributes and then have the process distributed to relevant local centers for the creation of plant or sales organization data. All of these fields would follow global standards—perhaps with regionally approved variations—resulting in one complete, managed, and audited governance process.

It's becoming clearer that there are data management needs beyond this central use case and that organizations are often looking to supplement their central governance processes with the consolidation of data originating from multiple sources. SAP Master Data Governance allows for the consolidation of enterprise data by addressing pure consolidation scenarios. For example, companies might decide to continue to create data in multiple locations and bring these records together into an SAP Master Data Governance system for an analytical use case or for consolidation prior to governance. In addition, companies might want to clean up, standardize, and harmonize their data before centrally governing the data using SAP Master Data Governance. Moreover, some of the more interesting use cases for central governance are around a hybrid approach of both consolidation and central governance. Multiple data sets can be consolidated into a central SAP Master Data Governance instance after some merger or acquisition activities or even in a continuous fashion where there could be a need for periodic external updates to the records stored in SAP Master Data Governance from local or third-party systems or data sources. Figure 1.19 summarizes the different processes for both consolidation and central governance in SAP Master Data Governance.

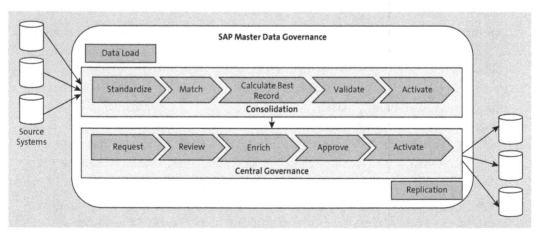

Figure 1.19 SAP Master Data Governance: Consolidation and Central Governance

SAP Master Data Governance is delivered with enterprise content across important domains of master data to allow an organization to govern its critical enterprise attributes:

- **Financials**
  Key financial data is maintained, including general ledger accounts/chart of accounts, cost centers, profit centers, and related hierarchies.

- **Material**
  Material master–relevant data is maintained across all major areas, including material descriptions, units of measure, classification data, quality data, sales data, plant data, and storage and warehouse data.

- **Supplier**
  Common business partner attributes are maintained—for example, name, address, bank details, tax numbers, and the relevant business partner role. In addition, supplier-specific attributes are also stored, such as general data, company code data, and purchasing data. The linkage of business partner data allows for this information to be shared across multiple suppliers with different roles as well as for situations where a supplier might also be a customer.

- **Customer**
  As with supplier, the common business partner attributes are maintained along with the customer-specific attributes, such as general data, company code data, and sales area data.

- **Enterprise asset management (EAM)**
  EAM governance content has been developed as SAP Master Data Governance, enterprise asset management extension by Utopia. This content is relevant to plant maintenance customers and includes such areas as equipment master, functional locations, bills of material (BOMs)—leveraging usage types, functional location BOMs, equipment BOMs, service master, task lists—general, equipment, and functional task lists; measuring points; object links, object networks, and related SAP Linear Asset Management functionality; and industry scenario support for utilities, defense, and fleet management. The solution is further catering to the governance of master data triggered via transactional data creation, such as material serialization for equipment masters.

- **Retail and fashion management**
  Article master governance, which is critically important to all customers in the retail and fashion industries, is provided by SAP Master Data Governance, retail and fashion management extension by Utopia. Areas covered include listings, purchasing and sales views of the article and hierarchies, BOMs, purchase information records, seasons, segmentations, and more.

- **Custom objects**
  SAP Master Data Governance also allows for complete custom domains of master data to be created, for example, for use cases of governing reference data in an enterprise, industry specific-objects, or complete non-SAP objects. The enterprise asset

management extension and the retail and fashion management extension noted earlier were both developed in the SAP Master Data Governance custom objects framework. This allows any objects to be governed and managed on the exact platform as the standard objects delivered with the solution.

Different aspects of content are provided across these domains, such as data models, workflows, UIs (including SAP Fiori content), business roles, and validation rules. With continuous innovations, SAP Master Data Governance now has a data quality management scenario for proactive governance. The solution allows for the creation and implementation of business rules to define data quality checks and then to continuously evaluate, monitor, and fix the failing data via the central governance capabilities of SAP Master Data Governance. The solution provides quality scores, dimensions, and key performance indicators (KPIs).

This architecture and how to extend and customize SAP Master Data Governance to suit the specific needs of an enterprise are explained in detail throughout the rest of the book.

But before wrapping up this section, we'll introduce you to different deployment options available with SAP Master Data Governance today. Initially when SAP Master Data Governance was launched, there was only one deployment option and one type of SAP Master Data Governance solution. But as customers demand more cloud options—both in terms of solution architecture and in terms of operational cost of running their enterprise systems—SAP has come up with a few options on how SAP Master Data Governance could be deployed to avail these cloud benefits.

In the following section, we'll discuss three different options, namely, SAP Master Data Governance, cloud edition; SAP Master Data Governance on SAP S/4HANA Cloud, private edition; and SAP S/4HANA Cloud for master data governance.

1.6.1   SAP Master Data Governance, Cloud Edition

SAP Master Data Governance, cloud edition, is a multitenant, public cloud, software-as-a-service (SaaS) option for SAP Master Data Governance. This solution is built with a modern cloud native architecture and aimed at supporting the federated style of data governance, which we discussed in Section 1.3.7. In line with our federated governance approach, SAP Master Data Governance, cloud edition, is focused on governing the core attributes and leaves the governing of application attributes to the LoB systems and/or SAP Master Data Governance on SAP S/4HANA solution. SAP Master Data Governance, cloud edition, can be considered complementary to SAP Master Data Governance on SAP S/4HANA in a federated, distributed data landscape.

In line with this thinking, SAP Master Data Governance, cloud edition, comes with a data model for business partners covering the core or basic attributes. Other data models will surely be made available in upcoming releases. The data model of SAP

Master Data Governance, cloud edition, is aligned with SAP One Domain Model discussed in Section 1.3.8.

Important to note that SAP Master Data Governance, cloud edition, isn't a replacement for SAP Master Data Governance on SAP S/4HANA; rather, it works hand in hand with it, providing customers with an additional option to bring data governance into part of the business, which could so far not participate in the central data governance that has been set up in the organization.

SAP Master Data Governance, cloud edition, provides data governance, consolidation, and mass processing capabilities. But the capabilities it offers are a subset of the capabilities available in the SAP Master Data Governance on SAP S/4HANA version.

Another important aspect to note is that SAP Master Data Governance, cloud edition, is a multitenant SaaS offering, so you get all the benefits of a native cloud application, including full managed, elastic with faster deployment and roll out. On the other side, this also implies that—like every cloud-native solution—it's something to be consumed and implemented as it is, with minimal extension and changes.

Note

More exciting new capabilities will be introduced in SAP Master Data Governance, cloud edition, so keep track of what is planned by going to *https://roadmaps.sap.com/welcome*.

In Chapter 3 of this book, we'll be delving deeper into SAP Master Data Governance, cloud edition.

1.6.2   SAP Master Data Governance on SAP S/4HANA Cloud, Private Edition

As more and more enterprises start to choose the cloud for their enterprise infrastructure, it becomes very important that SAP Master Data Governance is also available for deployment on private cloud infrastructures. This is where SAP Master Data Governance on SAP S/4HANA Cloud, private cloud edition, comes into the picture. This deployment option has functional parity with SAP Master Data Governance on SAP S/4HANA; in other words, all the functions and features you have on SAP Master Data Governance on SAP S/4HANA are also available on SAP Master Data Governance on SAP S/4HANA Cloud, private edition, with the additional benefits deriving from a full-managed cloud solution.

Like SAP Master Data Governance on SAP S/4HANA, you're also able to build custom objects and extend the predelivered data models and functions. All the details regarding SAP Master Data Governance on SAP S/4HANA described in this book are also supported by SAP Master Data Governance on SAP S/4HANA, private edition.

Unlike SAP Master Data Governance, cloud edition—which is a complementary solution for SAP Master Data Governance on SAP S/4HANA—SAP Master Data Governance on SAP S/4HANA, private edition, is an alternative solution to SAP Master Data Governance on SAP S/4HANA. You don't need both in your landscape, the choice of one deployment model over another should be based on your specific business needs and requirements.

1.6.3   SAP S/4HANA Cloud for Master Data Governance

For customers running the SAP S/4HANA Cloud solution, this option provides them with master data governance capabilities within the cloud system. Nevertheless, the functional scope of SAP Master Data Governance on SAP S/4HANA Cloud is just a subset of the governance functionalities available within SAP Master Data Governance on SAP S/4HANA. This option allows SAP S/4HANA Cloud customers to leverage lightweight governance capabilities locally without being dependent on an external governance system.

SAP S/4HANA Cloud for master data governance supports customer, supplier, and product master data models; it provides consolidation (includes match and merge capabilities), mass processing (includes mass load and maintenance), and data quality management capabilities.

It's important to note that simple mass load and mass maintenance are already part of the SAP S/4HANA Cloud license; if consolidation and mass processing capabilities are also required, then you would need the SAP Master Data Governance on SAP S/4HANA Cloud solution license.

The SAP S/4HANA Cloud solution comes with a whole list of best practice scope items, including the ones for master data governance. You can find all the scope items listed in the SAP Best Practices Explorer at *https://rapid.sap.com/bp/*.

For master data governance, look for the following scope items:

- Master Data Consolidation for Business Partner (1N3)
- Master Data Consolidation for Product (1N1)
- Mass Processing for Business Partner (1N7)

1.7   Summary

The background to EIM we've just gone through is paramount to ensuring that you understand where SAP Master Data Governance fits within this context and the overall organizational benefits of an EIM program. We're now going to dig more deeply into the SAP Master Data Governance topic to explore this solution further in the EIM portfolio offered by SAP.

Chapter 2
Introduction to
SAP Master Data Governance

Master data management is necessary for digital transformation. SAP Master Data Governance enables enterprises to consolidate and govern master data to monitor master data processes and to reduce the total cost of ownership. This chapter discusses the SAP Master Data Governance capabilities and provides information on master data architecture, both for on-premise and in cloud systems.

SAP Master Data Governance enables businesses to consolidate and govern master data. Master data is shared across an enterprise to run business operations, add meaning to transactions, and help manage the unstructured data and associated enterprise metadata. The identification of master data varies from industry to industry and across business process definitions. Master data can also be reference data with less frequent definition changes. SAP Master Data Governance supports key master data objects, such as material master, business partner, customer master, supplier master, contract accounts receivable and payable (FI-CA), internal orders, and finance master data objects such as general ledger accounts, cost center, profit center, and so on. SAP Master Data Governance provides reusable templates and frameworks to extend the standard functionality and to govern custom master data objects. SAP also supports partner-developed solution extensions for master data objects related to enterprise asset management, and to retail article master.

SAP Master Data Governance provides other data management capabilities as well, such as hierarchy processing, mass processing, data integration, data quality evaluation, data quality management, and process analytics, which will be covered in this chapter. Section 2.1 discusses the various SAP Master Data Governance use cases, and Section 2.2 details the core architecture components of SAP Master Data Governance. We'll discuss the SAP Master Data Governance domains in Section 2.3.

2.1 Use Cases

SAP Master Data Governance is the master data management solution for an enterprise. The main SAP Master Data Governance use cases are as follows:

- **Central governance**
  Create and maintain master data in a central system adhering to the data rules and standards. The maintained master data is then replicated to satellite systems, which use the quality master data for the downstream system transactions, as illustrated in Figure 2.1. Up-front governance of master data through a clear and transparent audit trail provides significant business benefits from both process- and business operations perspectives. This eliminates error-prone manual master data maintenance processes in multiple satellite systems. Centralized governance and replication of data to target systems delivers consistent data definition and mapping for master data entities across systems and ensures harmonized master data across enterprises by leveraging the key mapping functionality with SAP Master Data Governance.

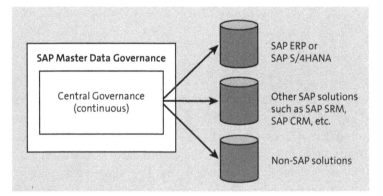

Figure 2.1 Central Governance

- **Consolidation for analytics purpose only**
  Master data is created in separate systems/transactional systems, as needed. The data is then consolidated into a central system by merging and mapping the data to a common data standard, so it can be used for analytics purposes, as illustrated in Figure 2.2.

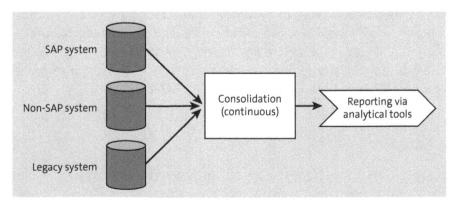

Figure 2.2 Consolidation for Analytics

- **Consolidation for initial load before central governance**
  The consolidation functionalities of merging and best record creation can be used for existing data preparation activities for the central governance scenario. This can be a one-time activity where an enterprise decides to centrally govern the master data and then replicate the data to multiple systems. As part of the initial load, data is extracted, cleansed, and then consolidated using the consolidation scenario, as illustrated in Figure 2.3.

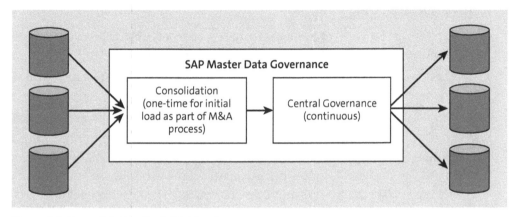

Figure 2.3 Consolidation for Initial Load

- **Consolidation for mergers or acquisitions**
  When new systems are introduced into the landscape, consolidation can be used to harmonize and de-duplicate the new data with the existing data.
- **Continuous hybrid approach**
  Both consolidation and central governance scenarios can be implemented together to refine master data from the source systems and govern the enhanced data through the central governance process, as illustrated in Figure 2.4.

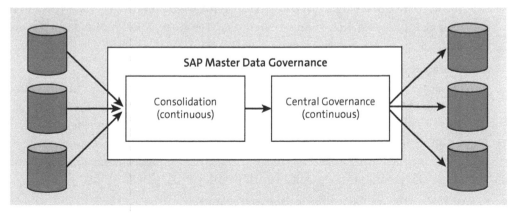

Figure 2.4 Hybrid Approach

To support these use cases, SAP Master Data Governance provides the following functionalities:

- Flexible business-driven/oriented workflow and workflow rules framework are provided to automate master data management processes.

- Tight integration with the SAP data model for key master data domains helps to reduce the total cost of implementation by reusing the data validation and mapping logic. This also helps provide contextual information on the master data record with the linked transactions.

- Frameworks are provided to configure custom master data objects for data management and extension capabilities for standard master data objects.

- Application programming interfaces (APIs) and integration capabilities are provided to enrich the data and provide change logs.

- Built-in master data stewardship tools are provided to monitor data management processes.

- The business rules repository is used to manage data quality rules and analyze data quality for product and business partner master records. Correction of these data quality issues (data quality evaluation) occurs via worklists and embedded analytics.

These functionalities will be discussed in detail in later sections.

2.2   Architecture

This section provides an overview of the SAP Master Data Governance solution architecture and discusses various user interface (UI) options to access this solution.

2.2.1   Overview

SAP Master Data Governance can be used for central and decentralized use cases in a hybrid landscape, based on system requirements. The various SAP Master Data Governance product versions are listed here:

- **SAP Master Data Governance on SAP S/4HANA**
  SAP Master Data Governance on SAP S/4HANA supports consolidation and mass processing for business partner, product master, and custom objects, Central governance of business partner (customer and supplier), product, financial, financial accounting contract account master data and custom objects, data quality management of business partner and product master data, and process analytics. SAP Master Data Governance functionalities are fully integrated with SAP S/4HANA.

- **SAP S/4HANA Cloud for master data governance**
  SAP Master Data Governance functionalities can be used as part of an SAP S/4HANA

Cloud deployment. It provides consolidation, mass processing, and data quality management for business partner and product master data.

- **SAP Master Data Governance, cloud edition**
  This version provides governance of core attributes of business partner master data, leveraging SAP One Domain Model and SAP Master Data Integration. It supports the federated approach of governing the local/application-specific attributes in the decentralized systems. It provides consolidation, central governance, and data quality management functionalities to support the core attributes of business partner data. More details about SAP Master Data Governance, cloud edition, are provided in Chapter 3.

- **SAP Master Data Governance for SAP ERP**
  To use the SAP Master Data Governance functionalities in an SAP ERP system (which isn't in the SAP S/4HANA version), SAP Master Data Governance add-ons needs to be installed to support the central governance, consolidation, and mass processing capabilities. Additional information can be found in SAP Note 2645428.

For the SAP S/4HANA and SAP ERP versions, SAP Master Data Governance leverages the inherent functionalities of the SAP ERP/ABAP application layer, including workflows, Business Rules Framework plus (BRFplus), data replication and distribution, value mapping, key mapping, UI frameworks such as Floorplan Manager, and SAP HANA capabilities such as SAP HANA smart data quality.

Some of the functionalities of SAP Master Data Governance are available only as part of SAP Master Data Governance on SAP S/4HANA:

- Product master and business partner data quality control and evaluation
- Consolidation functionality involving multiple customer and vendor assignments of business partners
- Central governance functionality to use newly added customers and vendors as references for partner functions within the same change request
- Service-oriented architecture (SOA) replication (inbound and outbound) of FI-CA data
- SAP S/4HANA simplifications and enhancements for SAP Master Data Governance
- UI enhancements for material search
- Process and data quality analytics innovations

With SAP HANA smart data quality, postal address validations can be leveraged during the governance process. It's recommended to deploy SAP Master Data Governance on an SAP S/4HANA system.

SAP Master Data Governance provides functionalities to support the following processes:

- Central governance of material master, business partner master, customer master, supplier master, finance master data, contract accounts, internal orders, and custom master data objects
- Consolidation and mass processing scenarios of material master, business partner, and custom objects

SAP Master Data Governance supports these key master data management scenarios via seamless integration with both SAP and non-SAP systems, data quality management, and collaborative business rules management for business partner and product master data.

In addition to these scenarios, additional objects are supported through the SAP Master Data Governance solution extensions by SAP partners.

From a software component installation standpoint, the key software components in SAP Master Data Governance are MDG_APPL and MDG_FND. These components are part of the SAP S/4HANA installation. The functionalities are activated as part of the switch framework, thus providing the freedom to activate the following individually, as needed: SAP Master Data Governance, Customers; SAP Master Data Governance, Supplier; SAP Master Data Governance, Financials; and SAP Master Data Governance, Product. The relationship between classical SAP ERP and SAP Master Data Governance on SAP S/4HANA components can be found in SAP Note 2457268. Each release cycle of SAP Master Data Governance has different revisions of business functions. You can choose to activate the specific business functions, along with their dependencies, as required. The system administrator will activate the switches (Transaction SFW5). The key business functions of SAP Master Data Governance on SAP S/4HANA 2021 are as follows:

- MDG_FOUNDATION_12
- MDG_FINANCIALS_11
- MDG_BUPA_8
- MDG_ERP_SUPPLIER_11
- MDG_ERP_CUSTOMER_10
- MDG_MATERIAL_11

In addition to these business functions, business function MDG_S4_FINANCIALS_8 can be activated for navigation to accounts specific to the general ledger instead of cost elements. This will also enable replication of cost element data to SAP S/4HANA using general ledger account IDocs and SOA. The consolidation, mass processing, and data quality management functions are already part of the SAP S/4HANA installation.

To use SAP Master Data Governance in a system, you need to activate the business functions. MDG_FOUNDATION contains the reusable content used by the central governance functionalities across domains. Thus, this business function is a key dependency for other central governance business functions such as MDG_MATERIAL, MDG_BUPA, MDG_ERP_SUPPLIER, MDG_ERP_CUSTOMER, and so on.

For SAP Master Data Governance 9.2 (used with SAP ERP), the business functions for central governance and consolidation need to be activated. The consolidation business functions are independent of the central governance business functions technically, so companies can install the consolidation functionality in a standalone system if required to support specific use cases.

The generic services offered in SAP Master Data Governance on SAP S/4HANA include the following capabilities:

- **Roles/work centers**
  Template roles are provided to align the standard applications with the enterprise-level roles and responsibilities. These domain- and task-specific roles include data specialist role, read-only role, and so on.

- **UI framework**
  The SAP Master Data Governance UI for central governance is based primarily on Web Dynpro ABAP; consolidation, mass processing, analytics and data quality management UIs are based on SAP Fiori. Additionally, SAP Fiori apps are available for request and approval scenarios for central governance and for analytics applications. SAP Fiori apps are mobile device friendly and provide the same look and feel in both desktop and mobile devices. The various accessibility options for SAP Master Data Governance are discussed in Section 2.2.2.

- **Workflows**
  Out-of-the-box workflow templates are based on SAP Business Workflow. These rules-based workflow templates can be used across domains. The workflow paths can be configured to include serial paths as well as parallel paths. Dynamic workflow paths based on object fields are also possible.

- **Change requests**
  Submission of a change request triggers the workflow. A change request can be used for the creation or maintenance of a single master data record or multiple records. A unique ID, called a change request number, is generated for each change request and used for tracking the request until the workflow process is completed. After the request is approved, master data is created in the underlying master data tables or active area.

- **Staging areas**
  Data in the change request is stored in the staging area until the workflow is successfully completed (discussed in detail in Chapter 3).

- **Search, data quality, and cleansing**
  Master data search is extensive and provides free text and fuzzy search capabilities. SAP Master Data Governance also has embedded data quality solution integrations, such as address cleansing, duplicate check, matching strategy, and so on.

- **Analytics**
  SAP Master Data Governance provides reporting capabilities over the governance processes to track and monitor SAP Master Data Governance change requests and resolve process bottlenecks. Additionally, change logs, Service Level Agreement (SLA), and key performance indicator (KPI) reporting are provided.

- **Data replication import/export**
  The data replication framework helps with replicating data to and from the SAP Master Data Governance system. It leverages SAP application layer components such as IDocs. In addition, replication can be done through web services, remote function call (RFC), and file transfer. It also facilitates mapping objects across the source and target systems. SAP Master Data Governance supports integration with both on-premise and on-demand solutions.

- **Validation/enrichment adapter**
  SAP Master Data Governance supports the validation and enrichment of data based on rules, including checks at various levels. SAP Master Data Governance leverages the rule configurations of the underlying implementation objects. Additional rules/data validation can be configured to be specific to SAP Master Data Governance. Checks can be applied at various levels, including a basic data check, security authorization check, duplicate check, validation rules check, and so on. Enrichment adapters are integrated with the SAP Master Data Governance framework to support data enrichment such as address data, tax information, bank data, and so on.

2.2.2   Available User Interfaces

SAP Master Data Governance applications can be accessed through different UIs and tools. Consolidation, mass processing, and data quality management UIs are based on SAPUI5-based SAP Fiori apps. More information on SAP Fiori apps is provided in Chapter 16. The main UI for central governance scenarios is based on Web Dynpro technology. These Web Dynpro applications are built using the Floorplan Manager framework and are accessible via URL. SAP Master Data Governance groups these applications based on domains and then assigns them to a role. These role menus contain a list of applications corresponding to the domain and can be accessed at runtime through SAP GUI, the SAP Business Client desktop tool, or the SAP Fiori launchpad. SAP Fiori launchpad is the preferred UI option. SAP provides various template roles to model against specific requirements.

SAP Master Data Governance also offers SAP Fiori apps for lean requests and approvals. There are supplementary apps to support SAP Master Data Governance analytics. Consolidation-related apps are based on SAP Fiori apps and can be accessed through SAP Fiori catalog roles as a URL or via an app in a mobile device.

All these apps can also be linked/embedded in other UI solutions such as SAP Enterprise Portal. The following sections provide an overview of these UI technologies and SAP Business Client.

Floorplan Manager

The Floorplan Manager framework allows you to develop Web Dynpro–based applications with a consistent look and feel following SAP's user experience guidelines. Multiple views can be combined to display the required information using predefined floor plans. Standard floor plans are available to display different types of information. Chapter 6, Section 6.1. provides more information on Floorplan Manager and how SAP Master Data Governance leverages this framework. Figure 2.5 shows a UI developed using the Floorplan Manager framework.

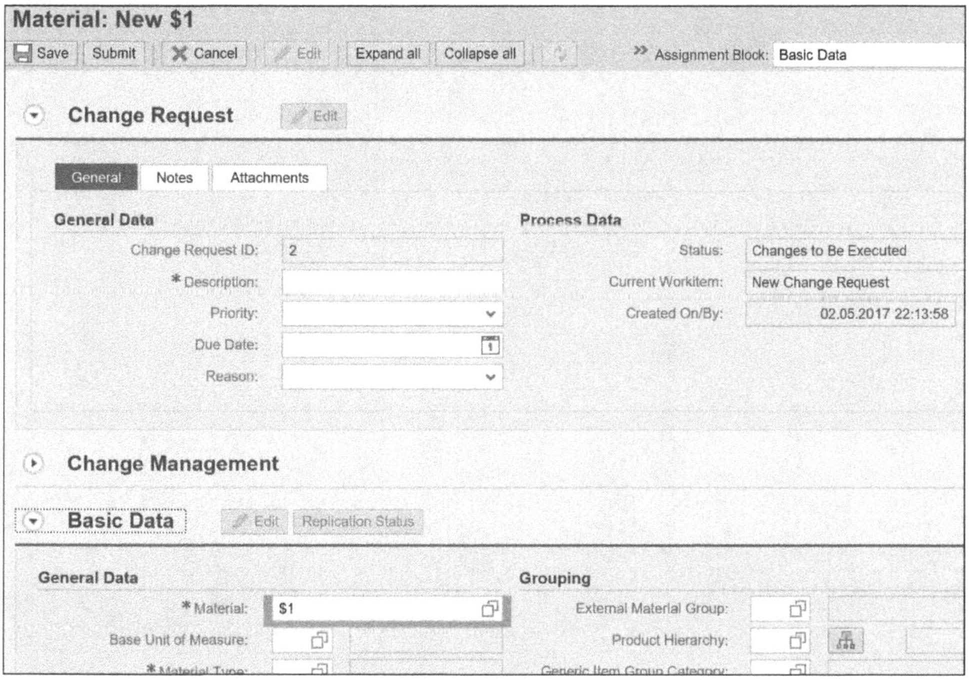

Figure 2.5 Floorplan Manager Look and Feel

SAP Fiori Apps

SAP Fiori provides simple, easy-to-use, role-based apps that can be accessed from mobile and desktop devices. SAP Master Data Governance offers SAP Fiori apps for request and approval scenarios for central governance processing, consolidation functionality, mass processing, data quality management, and process analytics apps. Figure 2.6 shows the look and feel of an SAP Master Data Governance approval screen.

These apps are accessible through the SAP Fiori launchpad. You'll find more information on SAP Fiori apps in SAP Master Data Governance in Chapter 16.

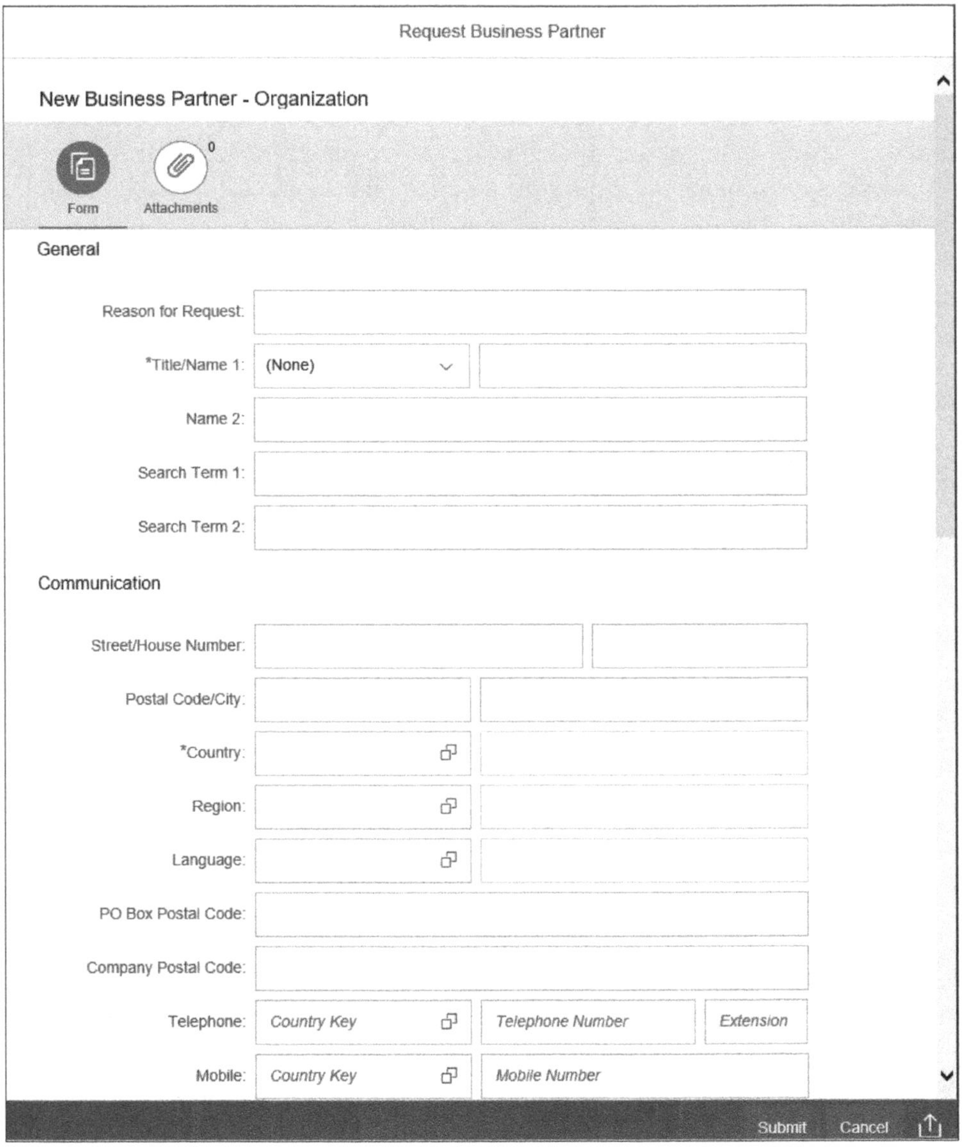

Figure 2.6 SAP Fiori Look and Feel

SAP Business Client

SAP Business Client provides a single point of entry for SAP's business applications. It can host a variety of web-based content, including Web Dynpro applications and SAP GUI applications. Both SAP Business Client and the SAP Fiori launchpad can launch and display SAP Fiori apps and Web Dynpro applications in on-premise SAP S/4HANA systems. Figure 2.7 shows the look and feel of SAP Business Client.

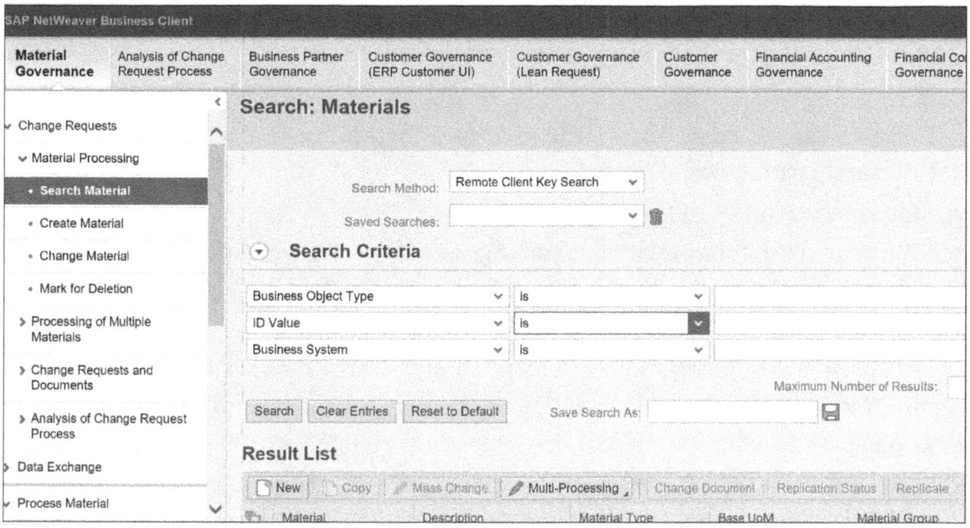

Figure 2.7 SAP Business Client

2.3   Overview of Data Domains

SAP Master Data Governance enables you to govern the following master data objects out of the box as SAP has delivered the required configurations, UIs, data model, and framework to support the governance process. SAP also provides a framework to create custom objects.

- Material/product master
- Business partner
- Supplier
- Customer
- Financial master

The following sections introduce these master data objects from an SAP master data perspective as a foundation to understand the later chapters. We also briefly discuss custom domains.

2.3.1   Material Master

The material master is a central repository of individual material records stored in the system that contains descriptions of all materials an enterprise procures, produces, and keeps in stock. Several functionalities use this single repository of materials, including purchasing, inventory management, material requirements planning (MRP), and invoice verification. Such a central repository of material master records also helps to avoid data redundancy.

A material master record in SAP S/4HANA or SAP ERP can contain the following information, which is organized into various material master views:

- **Accounting**
  Valuation and costing/price calculation information, such as standard price, past price, and future price.

- **Materials planning and control**
  MRP and consumption-based planning/inventory control information, such as safety stock level, planned delivery time, and reorder level for a material.

- **Purchasing**
  Data provided by purchasing for a material, such as the purchasing group responsible for a material, overdelivery and underdelivery tolerances, and the order unit.

- **Storage**
  Storage information for the material along with warehouse data, such as storage conditions and packaging dimensions.

- **Sales and distribution**
  Sales orders and pricing information, such as sales price, delivering plant, and minimum order quantity.

In addition to these views, the material master record also contains information about units of measure, language-specific descriptions, and material classification. Figure 2.8 provides a very high-level overview of the material master, its associated views, and some example fields.

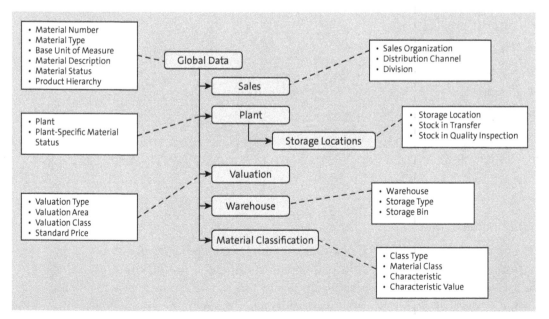

Figure 2.8 Material Master Overview

Chapter 5 provides an overview of how the SAP Master Data Governance data model is structured and how the general master views are structured in SAP Master Data Governance from a data modeling perspective.

Every material record in SAP S/4HANA and SAP ERP requires a material type that is used to define materials with similar attributes. The material type defines what type of material master views and fields are needed for a material record, and it's used for identifying whether the material record can have an externally defined material number or an internally generated number.

Typically, a material master record can go through the following processes, which are supported by SAP Master Data Governance via the change request process:

- Create
- Update
- Extend to additional views/plants
- Flag a material or part of material data, such as a specific plant data or specific sales extension, for deletion
- Mass update

Figure 2.9 shows the **Material Governance Homepage** screen in SAP Master Data Governance.

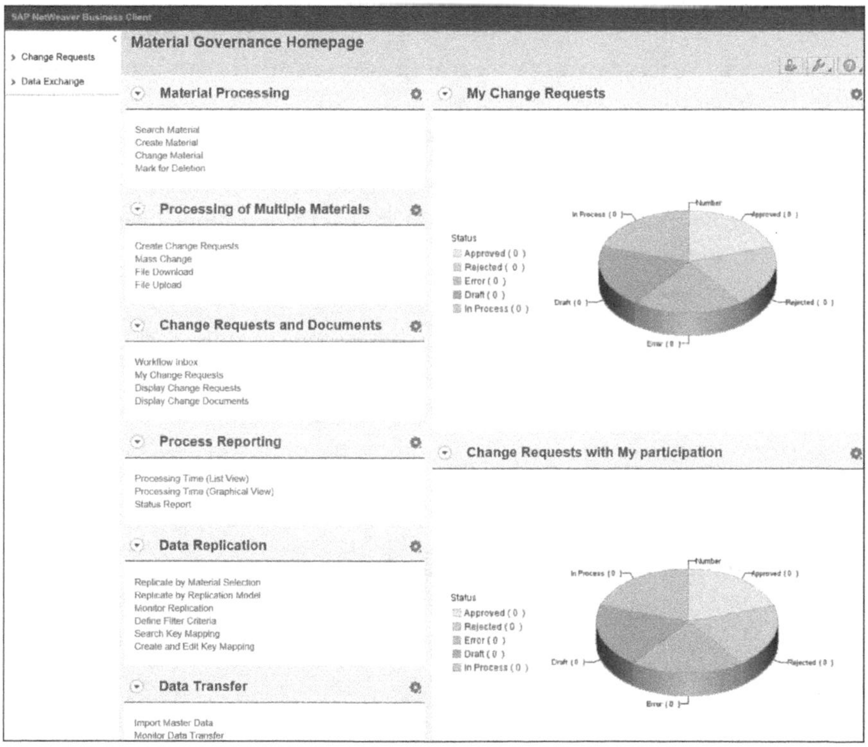

Figure 2.9 Material Governance Homepage Screen

2.3.2   Business Partner, Supplier, and Customer

This section provides an overview of business partner, customer master, and vendor master data objects, which are all connected to each other. This section also provides the functional overview of contract accounts as business partners.

> **Note**
>
> In SAP S/4HANA, the customer master and vendor master are part of the business partner concept. A business partner record can be created with a business partner role of customer and/or vendor to indicate that the business partner acts as customer and/or vendor record.

Business Partner

A *business partner* in SAP terminology is an organization, person, or group of persons or organizations in which the enterprise has a business interest. Business partners can play different roles and can expand to other roles over time. This approach helps in defining the general data of a business partner centrally and avoids creating such data redundantly every time the same business partner assumes a different role. Following are the basic elements that define a business partner:

- **Business partner category**
  Identifies whether a business partner is a natural person (private individual), organization (legal person/entity or part of a legal entity, e.g., a department), or a group.

- **Business partner role**
  Defines various roles played by business partners in an enterprise. The business partner role also drives which views of business partner data need to be maintained. If the business partner is extended to be a vendor, SAP recommends using the vendor (FLVN01) or FI vendor (FLVN00) roles. If the business partner is extended to be a customer, then SAP recommends using customer (FLCU01) or FI customer (FLCU00) roles.

- **Business partner group**
  Like a customer or vendor account group, identifies a group of business partners. A business partner group is also used for assigning number ranges and defining whether numbers are generated internally or assigned externally.

- **Business partner relationship**
  Defines how two business partners are related to each other. A common example in the SAP Master Data Governance context is to assign business partners created with business partner category **Person** as contact persons to the business partner representing an organization.

- **Business partner group hierarchy**
  Defines an organization's structure. SAP Master Data Governance offers governance capabilities for maintaining business partner data.

Figure 2.10 shows the **Business Partner Governance** screen.

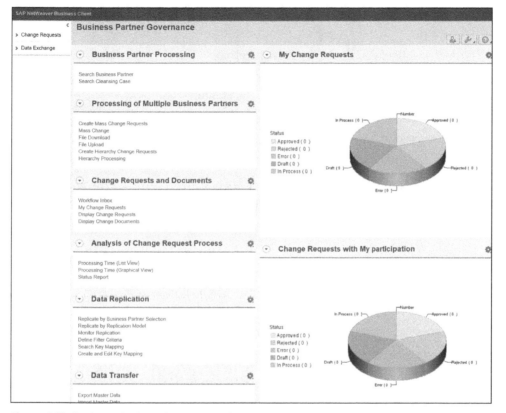

Figure 2.10 Business Partner Governance Screen

Customer Master

The customer master is a central repository of data that an enterprise requires to conduct business with by providing goods and services. A customer master record includes address data and terms of payment, for example. It also controls how business transactions are posted to a customer account and how the posted data is processed. The customer master is stored as individual records, and each record contains the following information:

- Customer's name and address
- Terms of payment
- Contact details
- Customer accounting information
- Customer sales information

All of this data is structured in the customer master in three categories:

- General data
- Company code data
- Sales data

Every customer record must contain a customer account group that determines the role of the customer and other aspects of a customer record. Some examples are as follows:

- Type of number assignment (internal/external)
- Number ranges
- Grouping of customers: sold-to, ship-to, payer, bill-to, and so on
- Screens that are relevant to maintain the customer record that belongs to a specific customer account group
- Partner determination schemas

A customer master record can go through the following processes, which SAP Master Data Governance supports by using a change request process:

- Create
- Update
- Extend to additional company codes/sales organizations
- Flag a customer or part of customer data, such as a specific company code or specific sales extension, for deletion
- Block a customer, specific company code, or sales extension
- Mass update

Figure 2.11 shows the **Customer Governance** screen in SAP Master Data Governance. Note that all processes related to the SAP Master Data Governance, Customer, application are initiated after an appropriate search for the record is made. This ensures that a user is searching for a record before submitting a request for a new customer record.

Vendor Master

The vendor master is a central repository of vendors that supply goods and services to an enterprise. The vendor master is stored as individual vendor records, and each record contains the following information:

- Vendor's name and address
- Currency used for ordering from the vendor
- Terms of payment
- Contact details
- Accounting information required before vendor's invoices are maintained for payment
- Purchasing information required before ordering items from the vendor

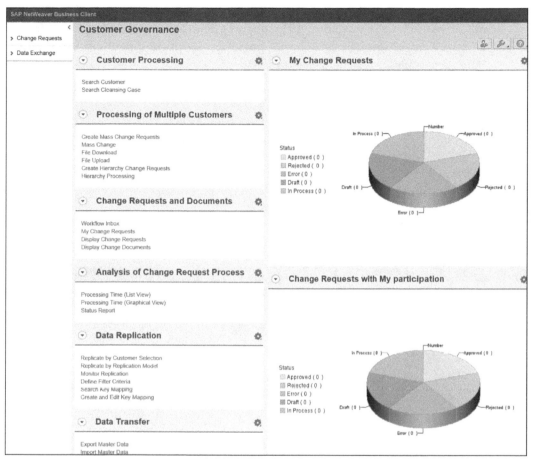

Figure 2.11 Customer Governance Screen

All of this data is structured in the vendor master in three categories:

- General data
- Company code data
- Purchasing data

Every vendor record must contain a vendor account group that determines the role of the vendor and other aspects of a vendor record. Some examples are as follows:

- Type of number assignment (internal/external)
- Number ranges
- Grouping of vendors: one-time vendor, invoicing party, and so on
- Screens that are relevant to maintain the vendor record that belongs to a specific vendor account group
- Partner determination schemas

The SAP Master Data Governance, Supplier, application is used to cover a broader definition than vendor governance and to support the entire business suite. A vendor master record can go through the following processes, which are supported by SAP Master Data Governance using change requests:

- Create
- Update
- Extend to additional company codes/purchasing organizations
- Flag a vendor or part of vendor data, such as a specific company code data or specific purchasing extension, for deletion
- Block a vendor, specific company code, or purchasing extension
- Mass update

Figure 2.12 shows the **Supplier Governance** screen in SAP Master Data Governance.

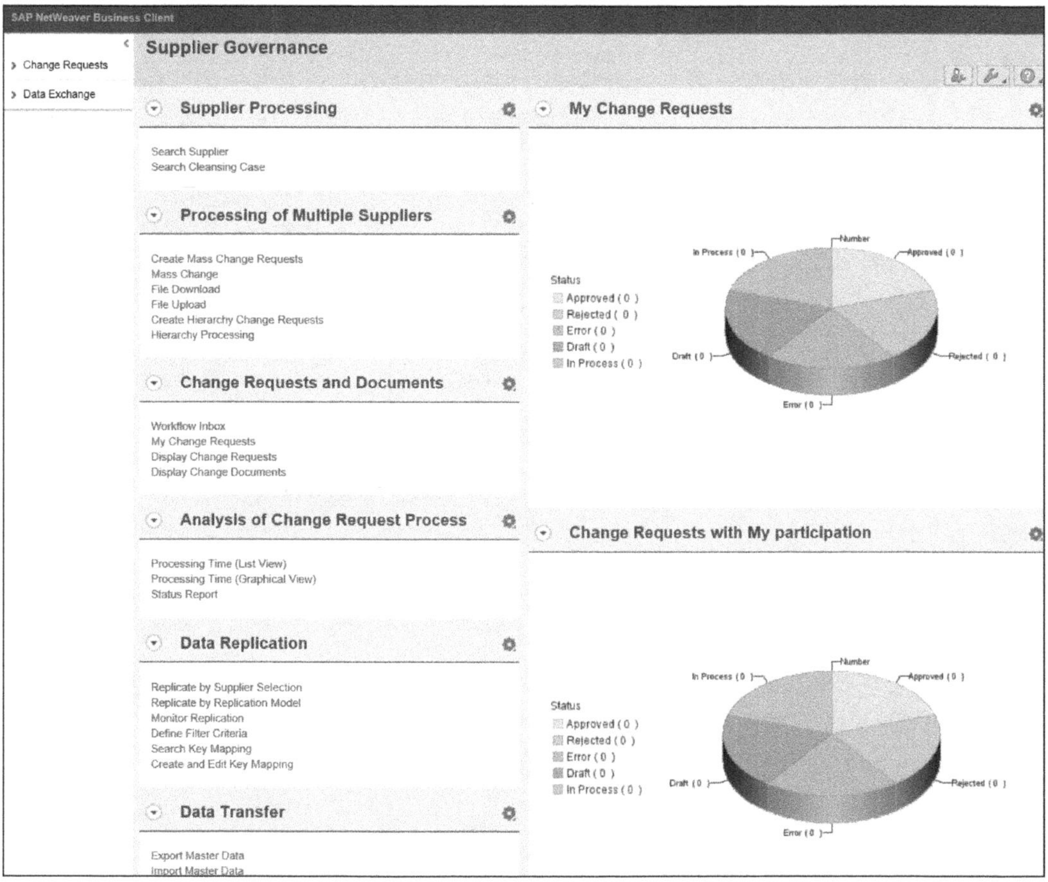

Figure 2.12 Supplier Governance Screen

Note that similar to SAP Master Data Governance, Customer, all processes related to the SAP Master Data Governance, Supplier, application are initiated after an appropriate search for the record is made. This ensures that a user is searching for a record before submitting a request for a new vendor record.

Contract Accounts

Contract accounts (in FI-CA) are typically used in service industries such as utilities, telecom, public sector, and media and require accounts receivables and payables components that can process large volumes. FI-CA doesn't replace the traditional accounts receivable (FI-AR) functionality but represents an alternative subledger for service industries.

Contract accounts are based on business partner records with a restriction that at least one business partner has to be assigned to a contract account. At the same time, a contract account can have more than one business partner assigned to it. Several contract accounts can be assigned to the same business partner. SAP Master Data Governance offers the governance of contract accounts as part of the business partner data model and supports generic core data. Any industry-specific attributes can be accommodated by using extensibility options provided by the SAP Master Data Governance extensibility framework. From the functionality perspective, SAP Master Data Governance supports the create and change contract accounts processes.

2.3.3   Customer-Vendor Integration

Customer-vendor integration (CVI) is a bidirectional setup that enables you to synchronize business partner data with customer/vendor records and vice versa. However, in the context of SAP Master Data Governance, CVI is configured mainly from business partner to customer for SAP Master Data Governance, Customer, and from business partner to vendor for SAP Master Data Governance, Supplier. With the introduction of SAP S/4HANA, SAP has expanded the business partner usage and made the concept of business partner and CVI mandatory for maintaining customer and vendor master data. After the business partner, customer master, and vendor master are configured in the system, CVI configuration can be done by following the IMG path, **SAP Customizing Implementation Guide • Cross-Application Components • Master Data Synchronization • Customer/Vendor Integration**.

Figure 2.13 shows a high-level mapping of relationships among business partner, customer master data, and vendor master data.

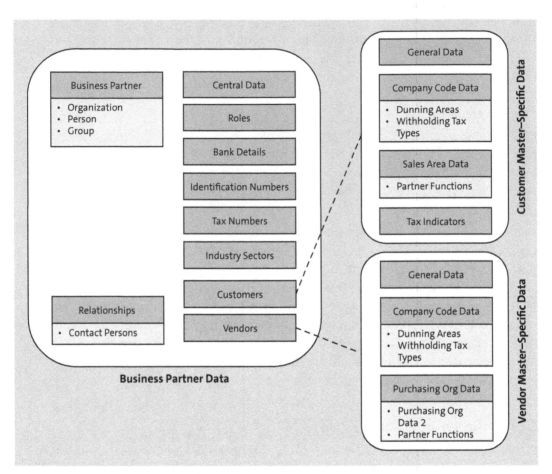

Figure 2.13 Customer-Vendor Integration: Business Partner

The following instructions provide an overview of the minimum setup needed for CVI for business partner synchronization with both the customer master and vendor master:

1. **Activate Postprocessing Office for synchronization.**
   This IMG activity is used to define for which platform objects the Postprocessing Office should be written in case of a synchronization error. For activating CVI, synchronization object (**Syn.Object**) **BP** should be added and activated. The IMG path to perform this activity is **Cross-Application Components · Master Data Synchronization · Synchronization Control · Synchronization Control · Activate PPO Requests for Platform Objects in the Dialog**.
   Figure 2.14 shows the option to activate Postprocessing Office requests.

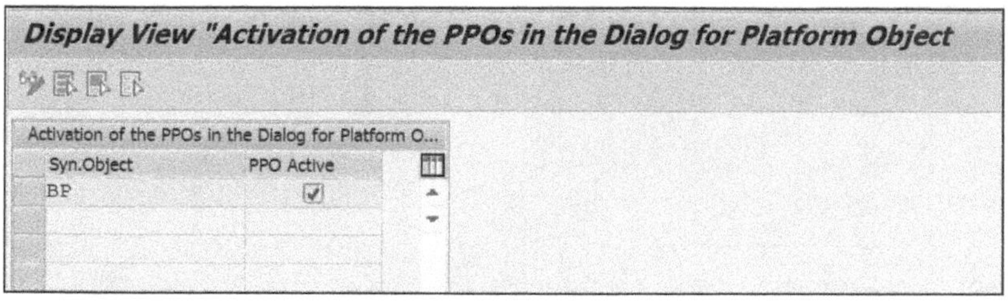

Figure 2.14 Activation of Postprocessing Office Requests

2. **Activate synchronization options.**

This IMG activity is used to define the synchronization option among business partner, customer, and supplier. The IMG path to perform this activity is **Cross-Application Components • Master Data Synchronization • Synchronization Control •
Synchronization Control • Activate Synchronization Options.**

All the options shown in Figure 2.15 must be set as active (**Act.Ind.**) depending on
whether both the SAP Master Data Governance, Customers, application and the SAP
Master Data Governance, Supplier, application are being implemented.

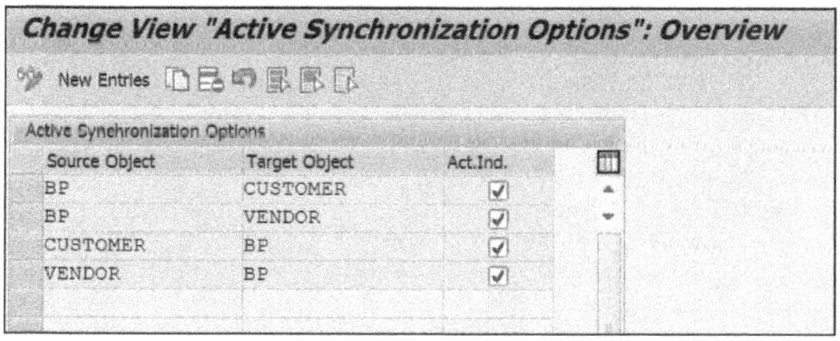

Figure 2.15 Synchronization Options

3. **Activate assignment of contact persons.**

This IMG activity is performed if the processing of contact person data needs to be
synchronized between business partner and customer/vendor master records. The
following attributes for the contact person are synchronized:

- Department numbers
- Functions
- Authority
- **VIP** indicator

You can use the following IMG activities for each contact person attribute: **Cross-
Application Components • Master Data Synchronization • Customer/Vendor Inte-
gration • Business Partner Settings • Settings for Customer Integration • Field
Assignment for Customer Integration • Assign Attributes • Contact Person • Activate
Assignment of Contact Persons.**

Figure 2.16 shows the option to enable contact person assignment.

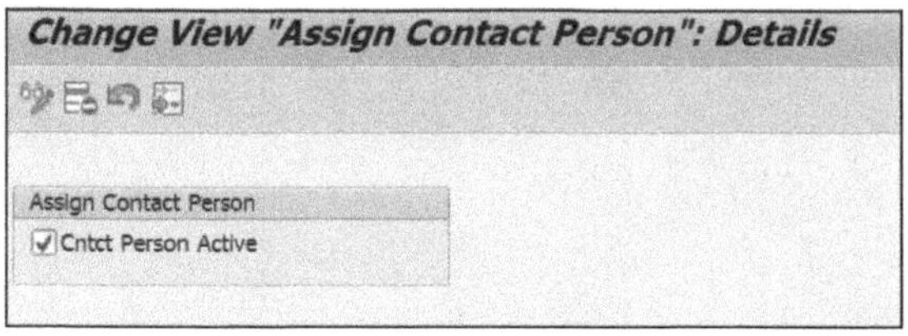

Figure 2.16 Activation of Contact Person Assignment

4. **Assign department numbers for the contact person.**
   In this IMG activity, departments from the business partner are assigned to contact person departments of the customer master. The IMG path to perform this activity is **Cross-Application Components • Master Data Synchronization • Customer/Vendor Integration • Business Partner Settings • Settings for Customer Integration • Field Assignment for Customer Integration • Assign Attributes • Contact Person • Assign Department Numbers for Contact Person.**

   Figure 2.17 shows the assignment of department numbers for a contact person.

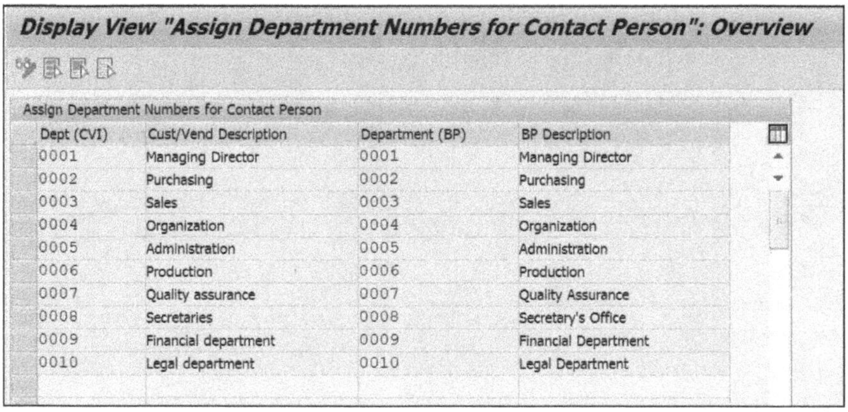

Dept (CVI)	Cust/Vend Description	Department (BP)	BP Description
0001	Managing Director	0001	Managing Director
0002	Purchasing	0002	Purchasing
0003	Sales	0003	Sales
0004	Organization	0004	Organization
0005	Administration	0005	Administration
0006	Production	0006	Production
0007	Quality assurance	0007	Quality Assurance
0008	Secretaries	0008	Secretary's Office
0009	Financial department	0009	Financial Department
0010	Legal department	0010	Legal Department

Figure 2.17 Assigning Department Numbers for Contact Persons

5. **Assign functions of the contact person.**
   In this IMG activity, functions from the business partner are assigned to contact person functions of the customer master. The IMG path to perform this activity is **Cross-Application Components • Master Data Synchronization • Customer/Vendor Integration • Business Partner Settings • Settings for Customer Integration • Field Assignment for Customer Integration • Assign Attributes • Contact Person • Assign Functions of Contact Person.**

   Figure 2.18 shows the assignment of functions of the contact person.

Display View "Assign Functions of Contact Person": Overview

Assign Functions of Contact Person

Function (CVI)	Cust/Vend Description	Function (BP)	BP Description
01	Executive Board	0001	Executive Board
02	Head of Purchasing	0002	Purchasing Manager
03	Head of Sales	0003	Sales Manager
04	Head of Personnel	0004	Head of Personnel
05	Janitor	0005	Quality Officer
06	Head of the Canteen	0006	Production Manager
07	Personal Assistant	0007	Personal Assistant
08	EDP manager	0008	IT Manager
09	Fin.accountg manager	0009	Financial Accounting Manager
10	Marketing Manager	0010	Marketing Manager

Figure 2.18 Assigning Functions of the Contact Person

6. **Assign authority of the contact person.**
   In this IMG activity, authorities from the business partner are assigned to contact
   person authorities of the customer master. The IMG path to perform this activity is
   **Cross-Application Components · Master Data Synchronization · Customer/Vendor
   Integration · Business Partner Settings · Settings for Customer Integration · Field
   Assignment for Customer Integration · Assign Attributes · Contact Person · Assign
   Authority of Contact Person.**

   Figure 2.19 shows the assignment of authority to the contact person.

Display View "Assign Authority of Contact Person": Overview

Assign Authority of Contact Person

PoAtt (CVI)	Cust/Vend Description	Pwr of Att.(BP)	BP Description
1	General authority	1	General Authority
2	No authority	2	No Authority
3	Authorized buyer	3	Authorized Buyer
A	Sole decision maker	4	Sole Decision Maker
H	Main decision maker	5	Main Decision Maker
M	Joint decision maker	6	Joint Decision Maker
W	Decision authority	7	Decision Authority

Figure 2.19 Assigning Authority to the Contact Person

7. **Assign VIP indicator for the contact person.**
   In this IMG activity, the **VIP** indicators from the business partner are assigned to the
   contact person **VIP** indicators of the customer master. The IMG path to perform this
   activity is **Cross-Application Components · Master Data Synchronization · Cus-
   tomer/Vendor Integration · Business Partner Settings · Settings for Customer Integration · Field Assignment for Customer Integration · Assign Attributes · Contact
   Person · Assign VIP Indicator for Contact Person.**

   Figure 2.20 shows the assignment of the **VIP** indicator for the contact person.

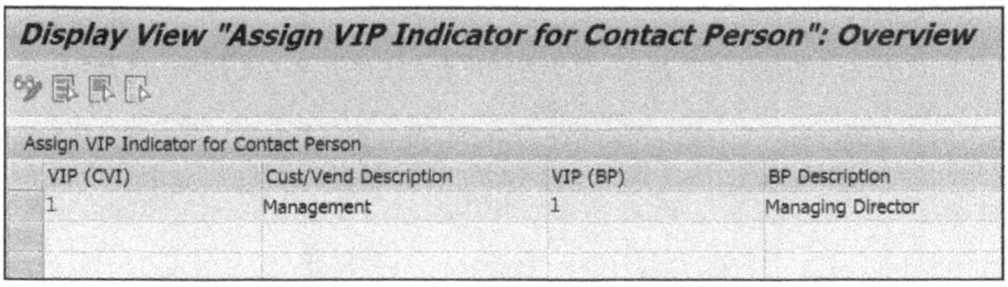

Figure 2.20 Assigning the VIP Indicator for the Contact Person

Some specific CVI settings are needed for customer integration, as follows:

1. **Set the business partner role category in the direction of business partner to customer.**

   This IMG activity is relevant to SAP Master Data Governance, Customers, and is performed to identify the business partner role categories that enable customer integration in the direction of business partner to customer, which is the direction that is relevant for SAP Master Data Governance, Customers, to enable governance on the customer master. Customer (FLCU01) and FI customer (FLCU00) role categories are relevant for SAP Master Data Governance, Customers. The IMG path to perform this activity is **Cross-Application Components** • **Master Data Synchronization** • **Customer/Vendor Integration** • **Business Partner Settings** • **Settings for Customer Integration** • **Set BP Role Category for Direction BP to Customer**.

   Figure 2.21 shows the assignment of business partner role categories in the direction of business partner to customer.

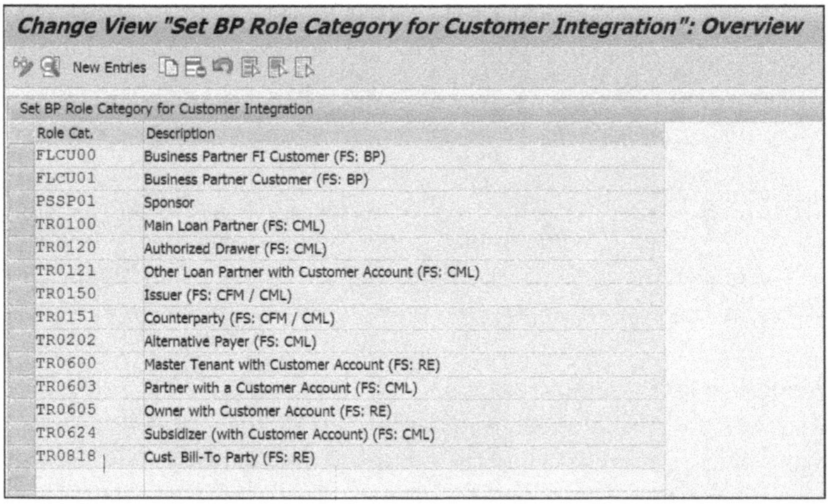

Figure 2.21 Business Partner Role Categories for Customer Integration

Similarly, the IMG activity **Define BP Role for Direction Customer to BP** can be used to define business partner roles in the direction of customer to business partner.

2. **Define the number assignment in the direction of business partner to customer.**
   In this IMG activity, customer account groups are mapped to business partner groups. If the **Same Number** option is chosen, then the number entered or generated at the business partner is copied to the corresponding customer record. The IMG path to perform this activity is **Cross-Application Components · Master Data Synchronization · Customer/Vendor Integration · Business Partner Settings · Settings for Customer Integration · Field Assignment for Customer Integration · Assign Keys · Define Number Assignment for Direction BP to Customer.**

Figure 2.22 shows the assignment of customer account groups to business partner groups along with the **Same Number** checkbox and **Flexible Grouping** checkbox.

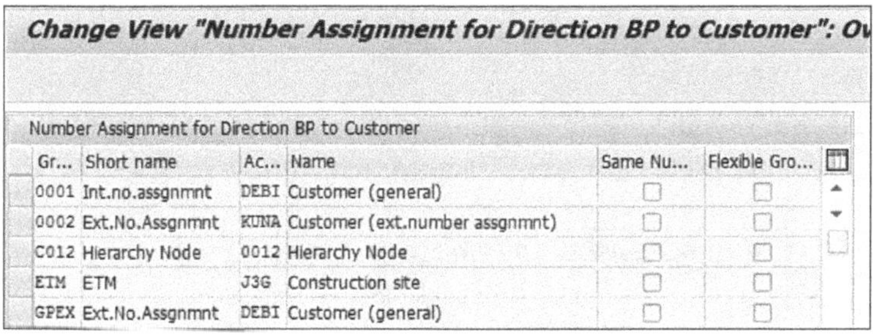

Change View "Number Assignment for Direction BP to Customer": Ov

Number Assignment for Direction BP to Customer

Gr...	Short name	Ac...	Name	Same Nu...	Flexible Gro...
0001	Int.no.assgnmnt	DEBI	Customer (general)	☐	☐
0002	Ext.No.Assgnmnt	KUNA	Customer (ext.number assgnmnt)	☐	☐
C012	Hierarchy Node	0012	Hierarchy Node	☐	☐
ETM	ETM	J3G	Construction site	☐	☐
GPEX	Ext.No.Assgnmnt	DEBI	Customer (general)	☐	☐

Figure 2.22 Business Partner to Customer: Number Assignment

Tip

You should use the same number for the business partner and customer. The following steps need to be considered to enable this in the direction of business partner to customer (the same rules apply to SAP Master Data Governance, Supplier, as well):

1. Set the same number range for the corresponding business partner group and customer account group.
2. Set external numbering for the customer account group, which is mapped to the appropriate business partner group.
3. Select the **Same Numbers** checkbox in the IMG activity as shown earlier.
4. If SAP Master Data Governance is deployed as a hub, and the receiving system is required to have the same number, then set both the corresponding business partner group and customer account group as external. This setup ensures that both the business partner and the customer have the same number across the SAP Master Data Governance hub and receiving SAP S/4HANA or SAP ERP system. If the receiving systems can't be set to external numbering, the key mapping functionality (explained in Chapter 12) can be used.
5. You can use flexible grouping to change the default customer or vendor account group that will be mapped to a business partner group. However, the **Same Numbers** checkbox and the **Flexible Grouping** checkbox can't be selected at the same time.

Some specific CVI settings are also needed for vendor integration, as follows:

1. **Set the business partner role category in the direction of business partner to vendor.**
   This IMG activity is relevant to SAP Master Data Governance, Supplier, and is performed to identify the business partner role categories that enable vendor integration in the direction of business partner to vendor, which is relevant for SAP Master Data Governance, Supplier, to enable governance on the vendor master. Vendor (FLVN01) and FI vendor (FLVN00) role categories are relevant for SAP Master Data Governance, Supplier. The IMG path to perform this activity is **Cross-Application Components • Master Data Synchronization • Customer/Vendor Integration • Business Partner Settings • Settings for Vendor Integration • Set BP Role Category for Direction BP to Vendor**.

   Figure 2.23 shows the assignment of business partner role categories in the direction of the business partner to vendor.

   Similarly, the IMG activity **Define BP Role for Direction Vendor to BP** can be used to define business partner roles in the direction of vendor to business partner.

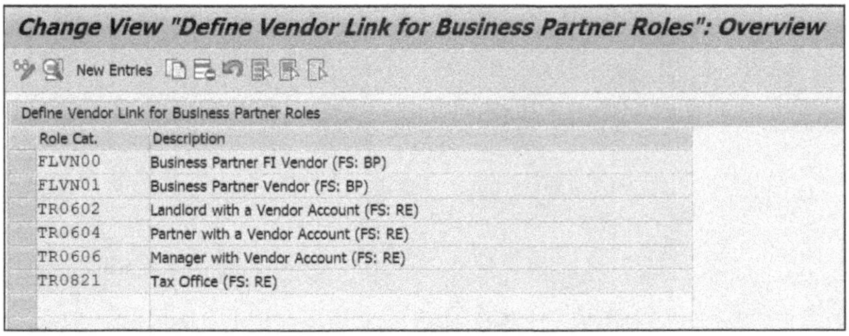

Figure 2.23 Business Partner Role Categories for Vendor Integration

2. **Define the number assignment in the direction of business partner to vendor.**
   In this IMG activity, vendor account groups are mapped to business partner groups. If the **Same Nos.** checkbox is chosen, then the number entered or generated at the business partner is copied to the corresponding vendor record. Figure 2.24 shows the assignment of vendor account groups to business partner groups along with the **Same Nos.** checkbox and **Flex. Grp.** checkbox. The IMG path to perform this activity is **Cross-Application Components • Master Data Synchronization • Customer/Vendor Integration • Business Partner Settings • Settings for Vendor Integration • Field Assignment for Vendor Integration • Assign Keys • Define Number Assignment for Direction BP to Vendor**.

Note

As with the business partner and customer, you should use the same number for the business partner and vendor. The steps to follow are the same.

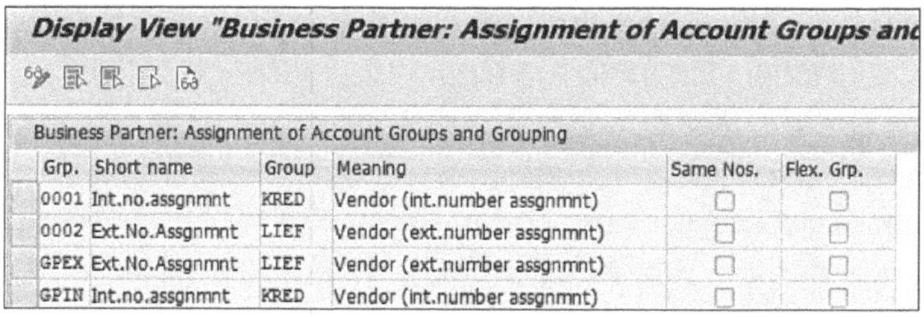

Display View "Business Partner: Assignment of Account Groups and

Business Partner: Assignment of Account Groups and Grouping

Grp.	Short name	Group	Meaning	Same Nos.	Flex. Grp.
0001	Int.no.assgnmnt	KRED	Vendor (int.number assgnmnt)	☐	☐
0002	Ext.No.Assgnmnt	LIEF	Vendor (ext.number assgnmnt)	☐	☐
GPEX	Ext.No.Assgnmnt	LIEF	Vendor (ext.number assgnmnt)	☐	☐
GPIN	Int.no.assgnmnt	KRED	Vendor (int.number assgnmnt)	☐	☐

Figure 2.24 Business Partner to Vendor: Number Assignment

2.3.4 Solution Extension Offerings

SAP Master Data Governance, retail and fashion management extension by Utopia and SAP Master Data Governance, enterprise asset management extension by Utopia are both SAP Solution Extensions offerings from SAP partner Utopia. These solutions are available as add-ins for SAP Master Data Governance on SAP S/4HANA and SAP Master Data Governance for SAP ERP 6.0. In this section, we'll introduce the architecture of these solutions and provide an overview of the data domains, but you'll learn about them in detail in Chapter 17.

Both the solutions are built on the SAP Master Data Governance framework using the SAP Master Data Governance custom data domain and objects in the SAP Solution Extensions partner's namespace. As they are built on the SAP Master Data Governance framework, the look and feel are like other standard out-of-the-box domains of SAP Master Data Governance for business partner and material. They follow a similar release cycle of the standard SAP Master Data Governance offerings. Both the solutions provide out-of-the-box functionality of preconfigured data domains, data structures, workflows, UIs, and so on.

The retail and fashion management extension solution is built using SAP Master Data Governance data model AR (Article Maintenance), whereas the enterprise asset management extension is built using SAP Master Data Governance data model U1 (SAP Master Data Governance, enterprise asset management extension by Utopia). Both data models are built as reuse data models in the partner's namespace.

SAP Master Data Governance data model AR allows you to manage article master data records for the SAP Retail Management and SAP Fashion Management customers. With SAP S/4HANA simplification, the material master model now has an integrated Retail Article master model as well. However, in SAP ERP systems, article master and material master data models are separate and would require the SAP industry solution IS-Retail switch to be turned on as a prerequisite. In addition, SAP ERP doesn't have an SAP Fashion Management–related functionality.

The retail and fashion management extension solution allows you to manage different types of articles, for example, single article, generic articles, variant articles, prepack, sales set, and so on. At the time of writing this book, the retail and fashion management extension solution uses standard IDocs and some specific IDocs developed by the partner for integration and to distribute the article master records.

The enterprise asset management extension solution allows you to manage and govern various enterprise asset master data of SAP Plant Maintenance and service master. Some of the important master data objects are listed here:

- Work center
- Equipment master
- Functional location
- MRO, equipment, and Work Breakdown Structure (WBS) bills of materials (BOMs)
- Service masters
- Task lists
- Maintenance plans
- Maintenance items
- Measuring points

Document links to document management systems for the previously listed master data is also available. Like the retail and fashion management extension, the enterprise asset management extension solution also uses IDocs for integration and to distribute the enterprise asset master data records.

2.3.5   Financials

Following are some of the important financial master data elements and their associated hierarchies that are used in SAP ERP and SAP S/4HANA:

- **SAP General Ledger account**
  SAP General Ledger account data is needed by the SAP General Ledger to determine the account's function. SAP General Ledger account master data is divided into two areas:
  - Chart of accounts: Data that is valid across all company codes.
  - Company code–specific SAP General Ledger accounts: Data that is specific to a company code.

- **Profit center**
  A profit center is a subunit of an organization that is responsible for revenues and costs. Such an organizational unit is created for internal control of the organization.

- **Profit center groups and hierarchy**
  Profit centers with similar characteristics are identified as profit center groups. Similar profit center groups can be combined to form another profit center group, which, in turn, creates a profit center hierarchy.

- **Cost center**
  A cost center is an organizational unit that adds cost to the organization and adds profits indirectly. Unlike profit centers, cost centers add to the organization's profitability indirectly.

- **Cost center groups and hierarchy**
  Cost centers with similar characteristics are identified as cost center groups. Similar cost center groups can be combined to form another cost center group, which, in turn, creates a cost center hierarchy.

- **Cost element**
  A cost element is a cost-relevant item in the chart of accounts and is categorized as either a primary or secondary cost element. Primary cost elements are cost-relevant items in the chart of accounts for which an SAP General Ledger account exists in SAP ERP Financials (SAP ERP FI). A secondary cost element exists in Cost Center Accounting to portray internal value flows. In an SAP system, a secondary cost element can't be created if a primary cost element already exists for the corresponding account.

- **Cost element groups and hierarchy**
  Cost elements with similar characteristics are identified as cost element groups. Similar cost element groups can be combined to form another cost element group, which, in turn, creates a cost element hierarchy.

- **Internal orders**
  An internal order is used to plan, collect, and settle costs of internal jobs and tasks, such as the cost of operations and capital expenditures.

Note

With the introduction of SAP S/4HANA, cost elements are integrated into general ledger accounts and can be distinguished by using the general ledger account type as **Primary** or **Secondary Costs**. From SAP Master Data Governance 9.1 on, SAP delivered the SAP Master Data Governance data model for financials with different codebases depending on the deployment to SAP ERP or SAP S/4HANA (refer to Chapter 5 for additional details).

- If you're using SAP Master Data Governance on SAP S/4HANA, then general ledger accounts are used with account types of **Primary/Secondary Costs** for managing cost elements.
- If SAP Master Data Governance is deployed with SAP ERP, cost elements under financial controlling are used.

Financial master data can keep changing over time, and changes must be kept for reporting and valuation needs. Such data can be maintained with validity periods using valid from and valid to dates.

SAP Master Data Governance, Financials, uses the concept of editions to manage the time dependency of finance master data. By using editions, all planned changes to an existing data or creation of new data are collected and released at a certain date. Objects that use editions inherit the validity dates based on the edition. Chapter 7, Section 7.2.8, describes editions in detail, including how to create and manage them.

SAP Master Data Governance, Financials, contains the following areas:

- **Financial accounting governance**
  Financial accounting governance provides the ability to govern the company, SAP General Ledger accounts, and financial reporting structure hierarchy. Figure 2.25 shows the **Financial Accounting Governance** screen.

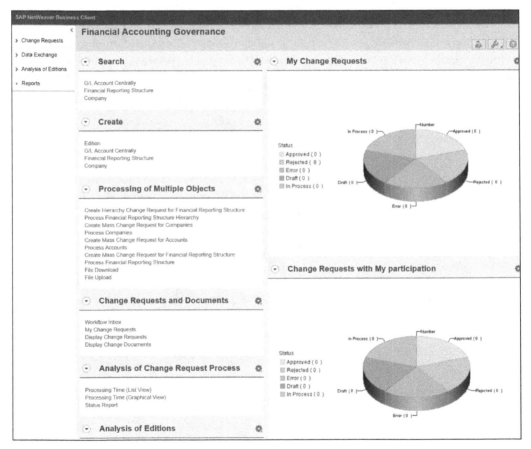

Figure 2.25 Financial Accounting Governance Screen

- **Financial controlling governance**
  Financial controlling governance provides the ability to govern the following controlling-related master data:
  - Profit center
  - Profit center group

- Profit center hierarchy
- Cost center
- Cost center group
- Cost center hierarchy
- Cost element
- Cost element group
- Cost element hierarchy
- Internal order

Figure 2.26 shows the **Financial Controlling Governance** screen.

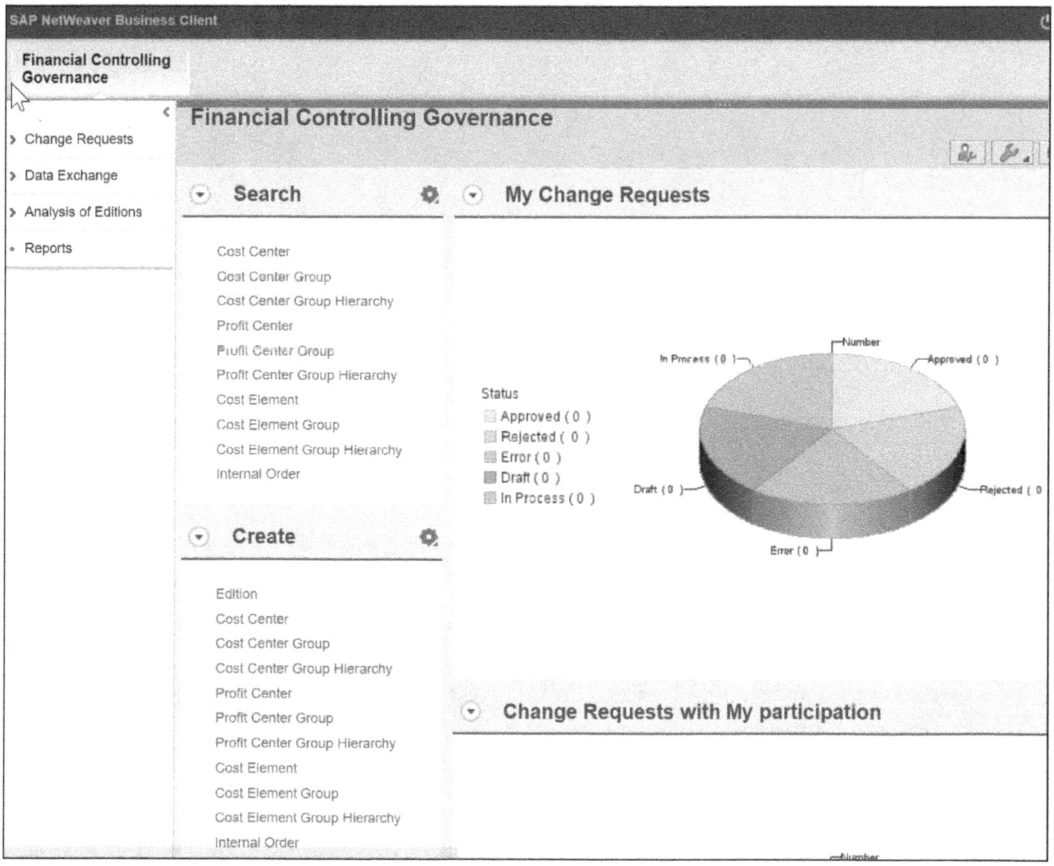

Figure 2.26 Financial Controlling Governance Screen

- **Financial consolidation governance**

  Financial consolidation governance provides the ability to govern financial consolidation–relevant master data such as consolidation unit, item, and associated hierarchies. Figure 2.27 shows the **Financial Consolidation Governance** screen.

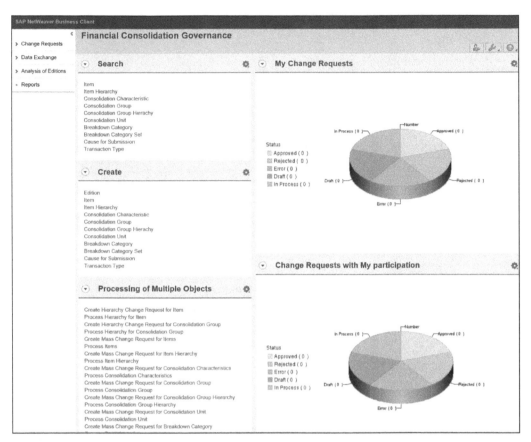

Figure 2.27 Financial Consolidation Governance Screen

Custom Domains

The SAP Master Data Governance framework provides the ability to govern a master data domain that isn't delivered by SAP or by partners as solution extensions. To build a custom domain, end-to-end setup is needed starting with defining the data model. Chapter 11 provides a complete step-by-step process for designing and configuring a custom domain in SAP Master Data Governance.

2.4   Summary

This chapter introduced an overview of the SAP Master Data Governance architecture and available UI options for accessing SAP Master Data Governance. This chapter also explained an overview of master data domains.

In the next chapter, we'll introduce you to SAP Master Data Governance, cloud edition, a complementary solution to SAP Master Data Governance on SAP S/4HANA.

Chapter 3

SAP Master Data Governance, Cloud Edition

SAP Master Data Governance, cloud edition, is a complementary solution to SAP Master Data Governance on SAP S/4HANA and doesn't replace it. It governs core master data attributes that are application-agnostic, and it's based on SAP One Domain Model. It uses SAP Master Data Integration for sharing master data across hybrid landscapes. In addition, it's the cornerstone for federation of SAP Master Data Governance.

In the previous chapter, you learned about SAP Master Data Governance on SAP S/4HANA, a master data management solution that is available as an on-premise and private cloud offering. This solution can be extended with an additional deployment option, called SAP Master Data Governance, cloud edition. SAP Master Data Governance, cloud edition, has been available as a public trial version since February 2021 and became generally available as of May 2021.

In this chapter, we'll see all the features and available process capabilities of SAP Master Data Governance, cloud edition.

3.1 Introduction

SAP Master Data Governance, cloud edition, is a complementary solution to SAP Master Data Governance on SAP S/4HANA. This cloud-native solution allows companies to perform master data governance on core attributes of selected master data. It can be deployed in a public cloud environment on the ABAP environment of SAP Business Technology Platform (SAP BTP), which provides all relevant cloud qualities, for example, scalability, delivered as a service, and so on. As a more affordable and easier-to-implement option, it's available for deployment as a software-as-a-service (SaaS), multitenant system. If companies want to scale up, they can even build this out into a single-tenant, private cloud system just for themselves, providing more resources and flexibility. It can even be consumed as a platform-as-a-service (PaaS) with flexibility to extend data models, user interfaces (UI), and code per the business requirement.

SAP Master Data Governance, cloud edition, shares the same key capabilities with the important processes of SAP Master Data Governance solutions for master data management. The following processes are supported in SAP Master Data Governance, cloud edition.

- **Central governance**
  Centrally govern master data core attributes using staging area, rules, validation, and approval workflows to achieve the desired business outcome and efficiency.

- **Consolidation**
  Consolidate master data into a single view for accurate analytics and operational insights using matching, merging, and best-record calculation.

- **Data quality**
  Manage master data quality by defining and manage rules, as well as enforcing and monitoring quality to ultimately improve data to meet business needs by making corrections using central governance as needed.

We'll examine the preceding processes in depth in Section 3.2.

SAP Master Data Governance, cloud edition, can also provide a nondisruptive additional deployment option for companies that run SAP Master Data Governance on SAP S/4HANA implementations and see a need for a federation of governance. SAP Master Data Governance, cloud edition, is the cornerstone of any federated SAP Master Data Governance deployment. It enables process federation across multiple SAP Master Data Governance systems and leverages SAP Master Data Integration for syndication of master data. (For more information on SAP Master Data Integration and a federated master data landscape, refer to Chapter 1.) Companies that don't see a need for federated governance can continue managing core and application master data in a central hub with SAP Master Data Governance on SAP S/4HANA.

Note

In the SAP S/4HANA product portfolio, there are now three main versions of SAP Master Data Governance:

- **SAP Master Data Governance on SAP S/4HANA**
  This is the on-premise version that is also offered as a private cloud deployment (SAP Master Data Governance on SAP S/4HANA Cloud, private edition). It can be deployed as a standalone hub or can be co-deployed with an existing SAP S/4HANA system.

- **SAP S/4HANA Cloud for master data governance**
  This version isn't meant to be a standalone solution for enterprise-wide master data governance. Instead, it offers capabilities to apply governance to master data within one SAP S/4HANA Cloud system.

- **SAP Master Data Governance, cloud edition**
  This is the latest version in the SAP Master Data Governance product portfolio. It's provided as a service on SAP BTP and is based on core master data attributes of SAP One Domain Model.

A very important thing to note is that SAP Master Data Governance, cloud edition, isn't meant to replace SAP Master Data Governance on SAP S/4HANA. Instead, it extends the solution portfolio of SAP Master Data Governance. The focus is solely on governance of core master data attributes of business partner (customer and supplier) master data domains based on SAP One Domain Model. As such, there are no plans to enhance the data model to any SAP S/4HANA–specific attribute or any other application-specific attributes. There are, however, plans to introduce more domains, such as product, in the future.

Let's look more into this data model now. SAP Master Data Governance, cloud edition, is based on SAP One Domain Model. In the SaaS version, the extensibility of the data model is limited to a predefined maximum scope to provide a true SaaS experience. It can also be consumed as a PaaS version at this point and is limited to a predefined scope. In future PaaS versions of the software, the plan is to provide more flexibility, allowing customers to make simple extensions to the data models and UI. However, by definition, SAP Master Data Governance, cloud edition, is primarily focused on core attributes only. Any extension to the data model should be very carefully thought out and considered, especially when federation to an application platform (e.g., SAP S/4HANA or SAP Ariba) is in scope.

Figure 3.1 shows the initial screen of SAP API Business Hub, which can be reached via *https://api.sap.com/sap-one-domain-model*.

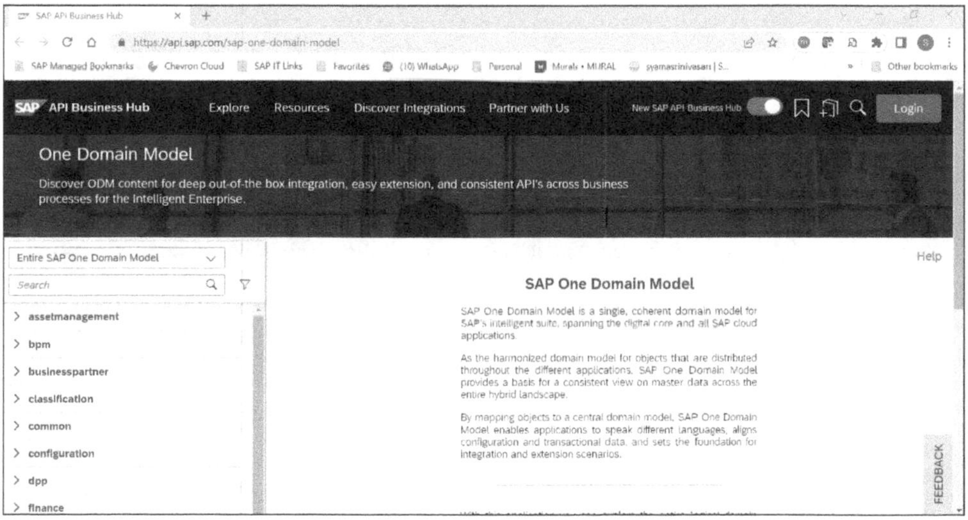

Figure 3.1 Initial Screen of API Business Hub Dedicated to SAP One Domain Model

You can find detailed information of any SAP One Domain Model by filtering and searching for the required model. For example, you can enter "Business Partner" into the search box on the left side of the screen and then select the **BusinessPartner** entity **E** to navigate to the business partner SAP One Domain Model.

Figure 3.2 is a snapshot of some of the business partner entities of SAP One Domain Model. Here, the entity **E Business Partner ❶** is selected. You can also see the title of SAP One Domain Model **❷**, and the version details **❸** of SAP One Domain Model. In this case, the version is **v3.0.0**.

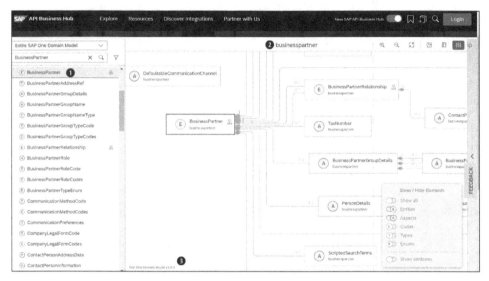

Figure 3.2 Business Partner Entities of SAP One Domain Model

If you want to see all the attributes available in the business partner entity, first select the business partner entity, and then click on the slide button **Show attributes** at bottom of the popup screen next to the selected business partner entity. Then, all the attributes available in the business partner entity are displayed in a separate box, as shown in Figure 3.3.

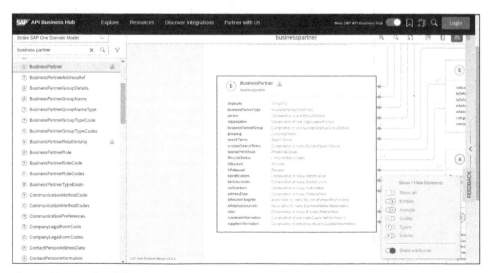

Figure 3.3 Details of the Business Partner Entity

3.2   Overview of Processes in SAP Master Data Governance, Cloud Edition

SAP Master Data Governance, cloud edition, supports all the key capabilities of SAP Master Data Governance. The main difference between the solutions is the scope of master data domains and attributes that each solution addresses. SAP Master Data Governance, cloud edition, provides support to the core attributes of a master data domain, and it's based on SAP One Domain Model. On the other hand, SAP Master Data Governance on SAP S/4HANA covers both core and application-specific attributes of master data, and it's based on SAP S/4HANA's specific data model. At this point in time, only core attributes of the business partner master are in scope for SAP Master Data Governance, cloud edition, and there are plans to introduce other domains, for example, product, in the future; they would also be core attributes aligned with SAP One Domain Model.

3.2.1   Central Governance

Central governance is a core functionality of SAP Master Data Governance. It provides master data management by governing master data records centrally using a dedicated staging area, duplicate checks, workflow approval processes, rules, and validations as required by the business.

A web browser such as Microsoft Edge or Chrome is used to log in to SAP Master Data Governance, cloud edition. Using the URL and logon credentials provided, you log in to SAP Fiori or the SAP BTP launchpad to access various SAP Fiori tiles. The SAP Fiori tiles are typically grouped together in a catalog for each process, and this is based on how the SAP Fiori security roles are set up.

Figure 3.4 shows the SAP Fiori tiles that are available under the **Central Governance for Business Partners** group or catalog to centrally govern the business partner master data.

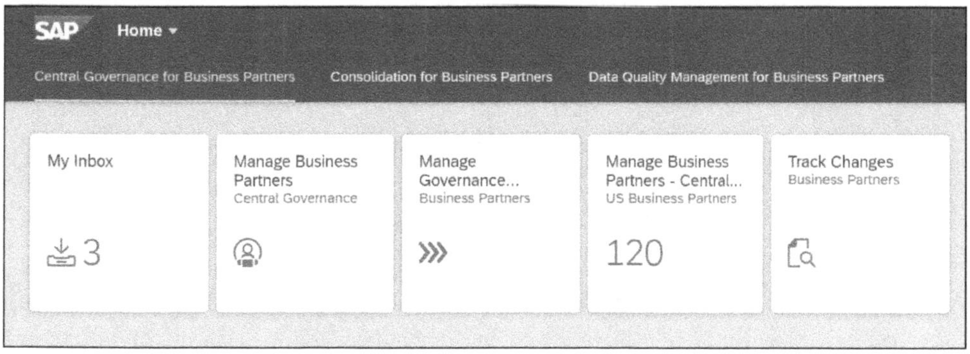

Figure 3.4 Central Governance for Business Partners: SAP Fiori Tiles

Process Overview

Figure 3.5 provides an overview of the Central Governance workflow process steps of business partner single maintenance and mass changes under SAP Master Data Governance, cloud edition. The Manage Business Partners app in SAP Fiori is a single point of entry to display, create, and change business partners. You can use the Manage Governance Processes - Business Partner app to perform mass changes on business partner data. In the next few sections, we'll discuss the processes in detail.

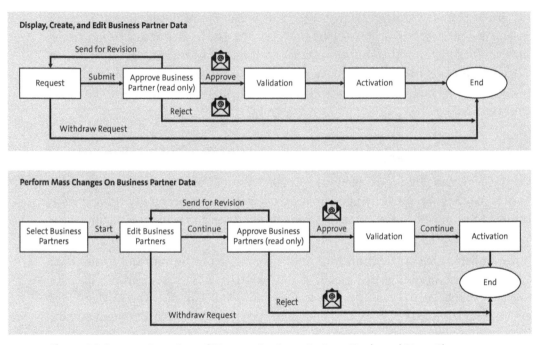

Figure 3.5 Process Overview of Manage Business Partner Single and Mass Changes

Manage Business Partner

The Manage Business Partner - Central Governance app is used to display, create, and edit business partner data. Figure 3.6 shows the app's initial screen in which the top section is the search criteria, and the results are displayed in the bottom section. If your search for business partner isn't successful, you can create a new business partner record using the **Create** button shown in Figure 3.6.

You can also create a mass request for change using the **Process in Mass Request** button shown in Figure 3.6 by selecting multiple business partners from the results of the query.

Alternatively, you can use the Manage Governance Processes - Business Partners app that you saw previously in Figure 3.4 to perform mass changes on business partner data, as discussed in the next section.

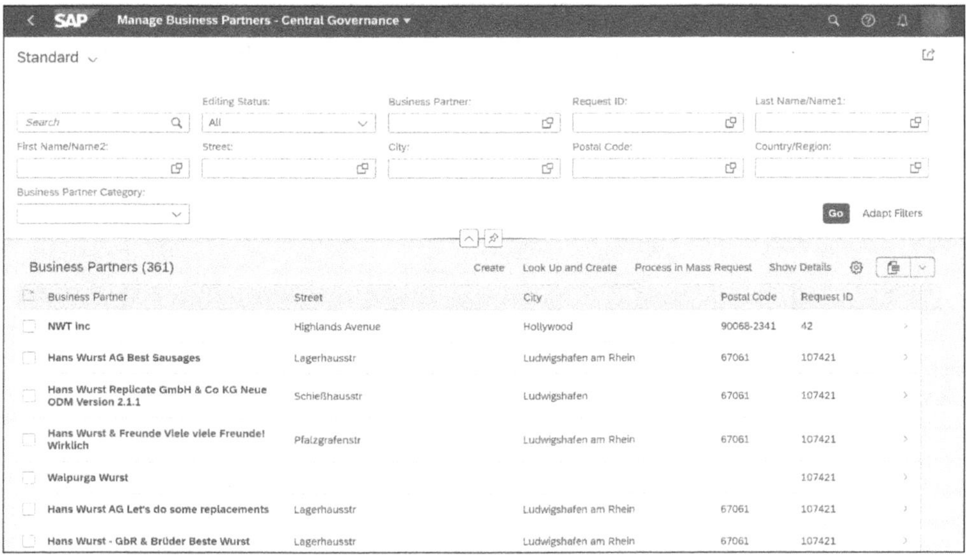

Figure 3.6 Manage Business Partners - Central Governance: Initial Screen

Manage Governance Process and Mass Processing

Figure 3.7 shows the initial screen of the Manage Governance Processes - Business Partners app. By adapting filters and specifying criteria such as date, process requestor, process description, and so on, you can search for any process that has been approved or is pending approval. A new process can also be created from this screen using the **Create** button shown in Figure 3.7. If any old process that isn't required anymore should be deleted, you can select the corresponding row, and then click the **Delete** button.

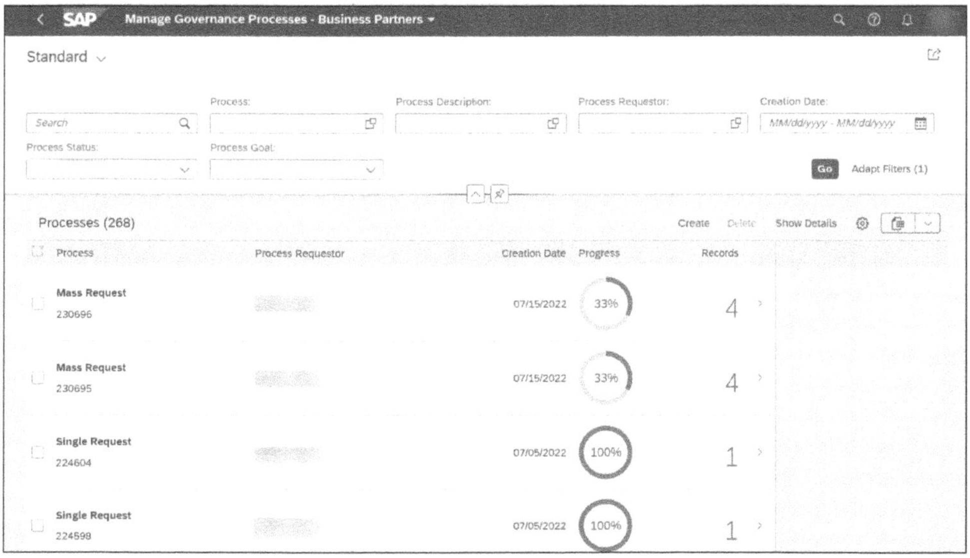

Figure 3.7 Manage Governance Processes - Business Partners: Initial Screen

It's possible to customize the SAP Fiori apps by defaulting certain values in the search query and providing it as a separate SAP Fiori tile as part of the SAP Fiori security role setup. The Manage Business Partners Central Governance - US Business Partners app that you saw previously in Figure 3.4 is a customized version of the Manage Business Partners - Central Governance app with **USA (US)** as a default value in the **Country/Region** field (see Figure 3.8).

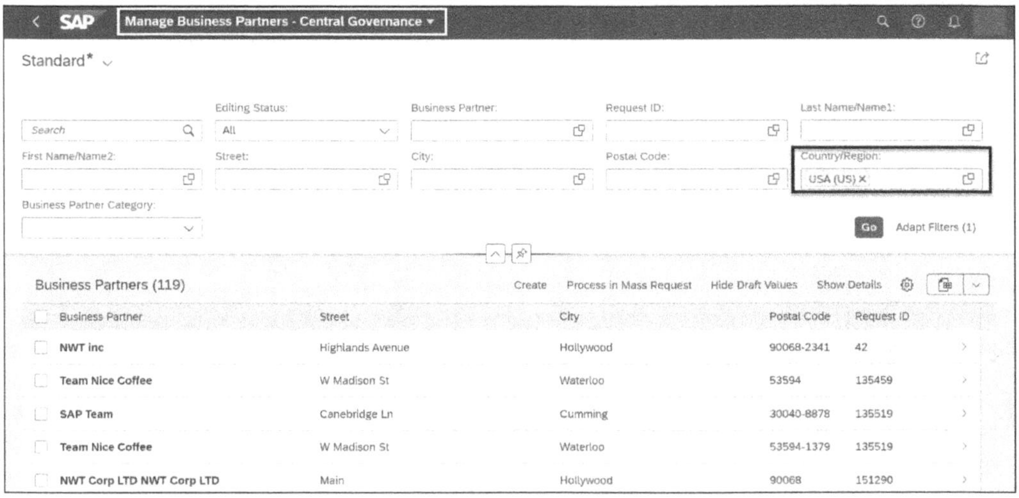

Figure 3.8 Manage Business Partners - Central Governance: US Business Partners

Track Changes

The Track Changes - Business Partners app shown earlier in Figure 3.4 can be used to query and track the changes based on business partner, process ID, and changed dates. Figure 3.9 shows a typical output of this app.

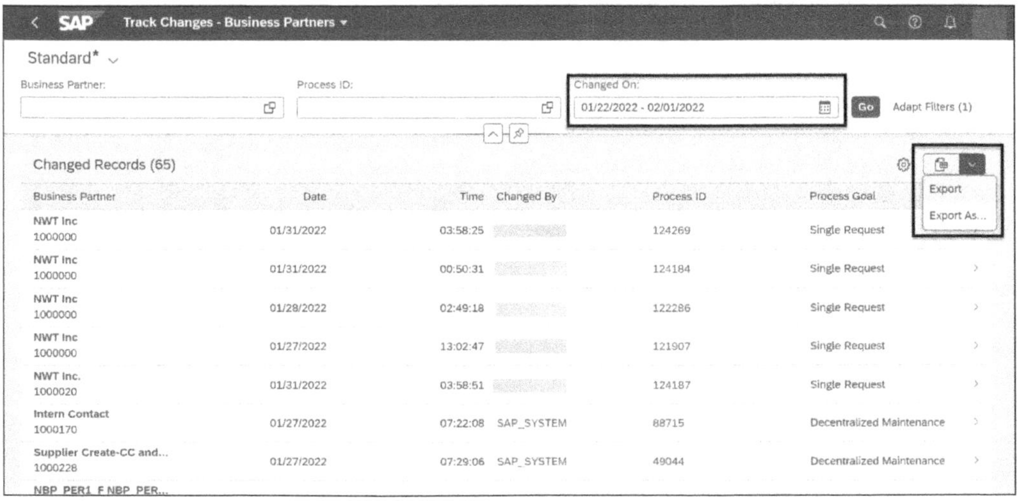

Figure 3.9 Track Changes - Business Partners App

You can further drill down from this screen to business partner and process ID to get more information. There is also an option to export the query results from this screen.

Business Partner Relationships

A business partner relationship represents a commercially relevant connection between two business partners. When creating or editing a business partner record, you can add a relationship to another business partner to reflect this connection. The second business partner can be an existing business partner, or a new business partner, and this relationship can be added in the **Relationships** section during the business partner maintenance.

For any new relationship, you can start by assigning a business partner relationship category. The business partner relationship category describes the features of the business partner relationship.

You can either select an existing business partner for the relationship by selecting an entry in the **Partner ID** field, or you can also create a new business partner by clicking the **Create** button shown earlier in Figure 3.7.

Several **Business Partner Relationship Categories** are available for selection, including **Business Partner Types**, **Cardinality**, and **Time Constraints**.

The assignment options available under business partner relationship cardinality are as follows:

- One-to-one (1:1)
- Many-to-one (n:1)
- Many-to-many (n:m)

The assignment options available under validities and time constraints are as follows:

- **No time constraint**
  Time constraint doesn't apply to the relationship category. This applies to relationship category **Alias (Identity) (Is Identical to)**.

- **Record may have gaps but no overlap**
  Multiple relationships between the same business partners and each relationship can be valid from one point in time to another (x or y) if x and y do not overlap. This applies to relationship category **Marriage (Is Married to)**.

- **Record exists at least once from minimum to maximum**
  You can enter one data record for the validity period. This applies to relationship category **Parent-Child Relationship (Has Child/Is Child of)**.

If you **Create** a new business partner for the relationship, the **Create Business Partner** dropdown list will only offer you the business partner type that is relevant for the chosen relationship category. For example, if the relationship category is **name married to**, you can only select **Person** from the dropdown list, but not **Organization** or **Group**.

Workflow Inbox

The My Inbox app from Figure 3.4 is the workflow inbox that displays all the pending tasks of the user. Figure 3.10 is the typical initial screen of the My Inbox app that displays all the pending tasks of the current logged-on processor. With this app, you can approve or reject the tasks that were submitted by the Manage Business Partners and Manage Governance Processes - Business Partner apps.

The standard **Send for Approval**, **Withdraw Request**, and **Show Log** buttons are available at the bottom-right corner of the screen. The task displayed in Figure 3.10 was generated by System User, which is why you see the **Claim** button at the bottom-right corner. If needed, the processor can claim the task and start working on it.

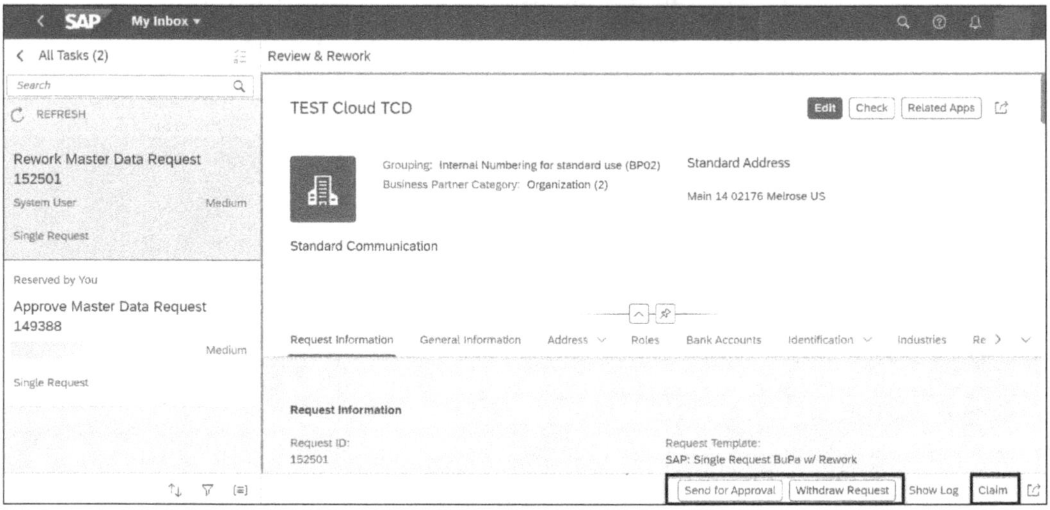

Figure 3.10 My Inbox: Initial Screen

In this section, we discussed various SAP Fiori apps that are available within Central Governance for Business Partners catalog in SAP Master Data Governance, cloud edition. As you can see, these apps are very similar to the ones available in SAP Master Data Governance on SAP S/4HANA.

3.2.2   Consolidation

SAP Master Data Governance, cloud edition, provides the standard consolidation processes for business partners and business partner relationships, and they are quite similar to what is available in the SAP Master Data Governance on SAP S/4HANA system. Figure 3.11 shows the SAP Fiori tiles that lead to the apps available to access the consolidation functionalities in the SAP Master Data Governance, cloud edition, within the **Consolidation for Business Partners** group.

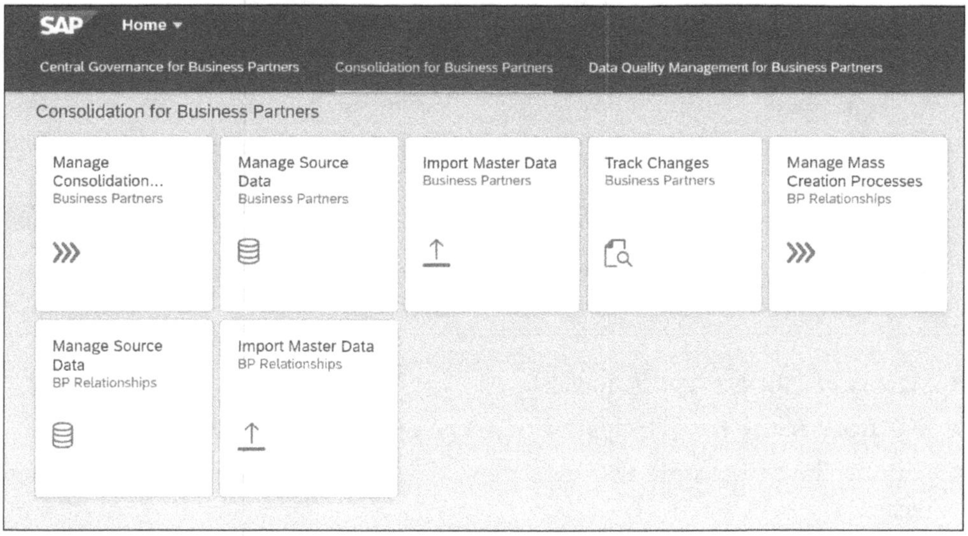

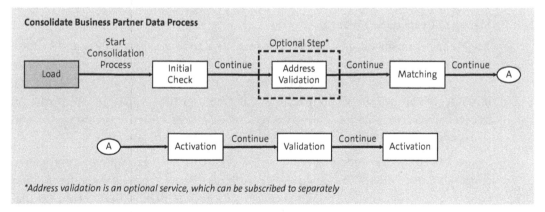

Figure 3.11 Consolidation for Business Partners: SAP Fiori Tiles

Process Overview

Figure 3.12 shows the process to consolidate business partner data from outside into SAP Master Data Governance, cloud edition. This process allows you to collect master data from different data sources and fix inconsistent data to achieve a single representation of master data that comes from multiple sources. After consolidation process, a correlation is established between the master data on source and target systems using key mapping and value mapping.

Figure 3.12 Process Overview of Business Partner Consolidation Process

The process template is predelivered to consolidate business partners only or together with business partner relationships. The following steps are available in the predelivered process template:

- Import master data apps to load data using the spreadsheet format.
- Perform an initial check to validate data consistency after loading the data.
- Address validation using SAP Data Quality Management, microservices for location data.

> **Note**
>
> SAP Data Quality Management, microservices for location data, is an optional subscription service and is discussed in Section 3.4.

- Match capabilities to detect duplicates.
- Match and review the UI to approve/reject potential duplicates.
- Perform the best record calculation step to merge duplicates and create a golden record.
- Use validation and activation to check and activate the loaded data.

> **Address Validation and Enrichment**
>
> Address validation is an optional subscription service that can be subscribed to separately and uses the SAP Data Quality Management, microservices for location data. This service provides an automatic enrichment of address data and an interactive review UI in case of ambiguous or erroneous addresses.
>
> See Section 3.4 for additional information.

Manage Consolidation Process

The **Manage Consolidation - Business Partner** tile shown previously in Figure 3.11 represents the app that allows you to create and manage consolidation processes for business partners in SAP Master Data Governance, cloud edition. Figure 3.13 shows the initial screen of the Manage Consolidation - Business Partners app from which you can search using various attributes, such as process ID, process description, processor, and so on, and then drill down to details from the results of the query.

Figure 3.14 shows the details of one such process. This is an example of a completed consolidation process of the data from SAP Ariba as a data source. As you can see, it has gone through the standard steps (in detail, **Initial Check**, **Matching**, **Best Record Calculation**, **Validation**, and finally **Activation**) of the consolidation process in SAP Master Data Governance. It also displays the details of the process, that is, template, current status, and goal.

To drill down and display the business partners involved in the consolidation process, you can click on the **Show All Changes** hyperlink. Additionally, you can access the audit trail of the process by clicking on the **Show Audit Trail** button.

Figure 3.13 Manage Consolidation Processes - Business Partners: Initial Screen

Figure 3.14 Consolidation Process Details Display Screen

Figure 3.15 shows the aforementioned details screen visualized after clicking the **Show All Changes** visible in Figure 3.14 of the consolidation process screen. From this screen, you can drill down further to check and verify, for every single business partner, which attributes have been changed.

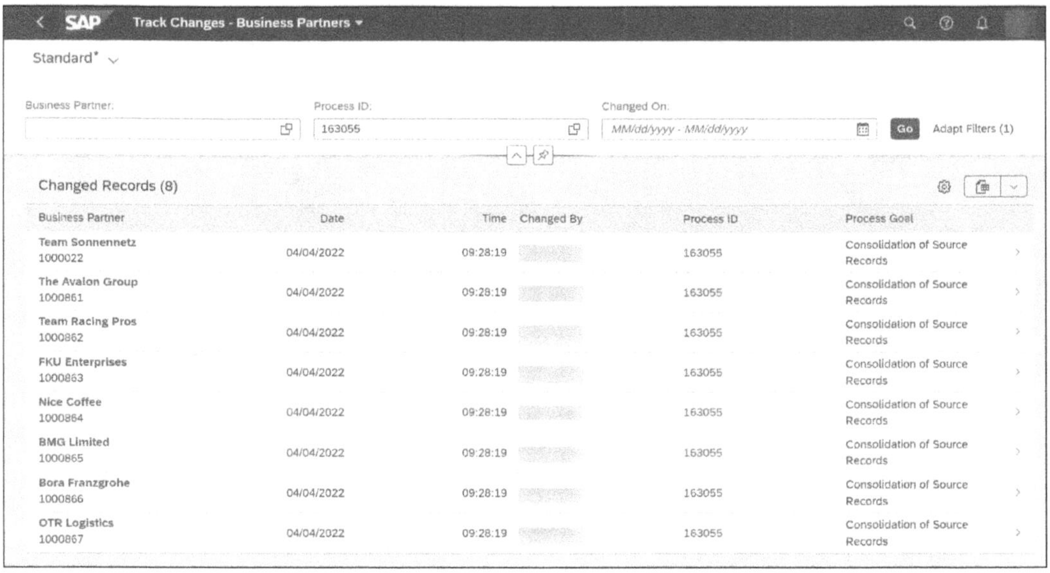

Figure 3.15 Drill Down to Details of Changes Used in the Consolidation Process

Import Master Data

The **Import Master Data - Business Partners** tile shown in Figure 3.11 opens the app that allows you to import the master data to be consolidated. Figure 3.16 shows the initial screen of the Import Master Data - Business Partners app, which provides details about **Source File**, **Source System**, **Data Package**, and **Records** available in each import process.

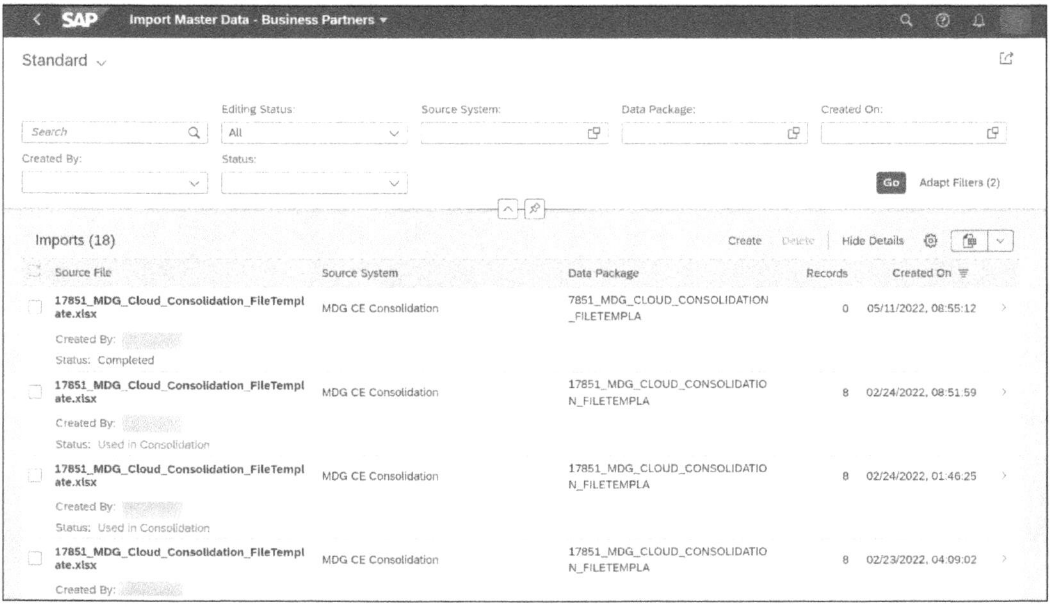

Figure 3.16 Import Master Data - Business Partners App

You can drill down to see details of each import process as needed. You can also choose the **Create** and **Delete** buttons to work with an import process.

Manage Source Data

Figure 3.17 shows the initial screen of the Manage Source Data - Business Partners app. This screen allows you to manage the source data that has been already imported into the system. The **Import Data** hyperlink allows you to start a new import of data. If you want to delete an existing data package, select the row, and click on the **Delete** hyperlink. You can also run a query on data packages and download the results as a file, if needed.

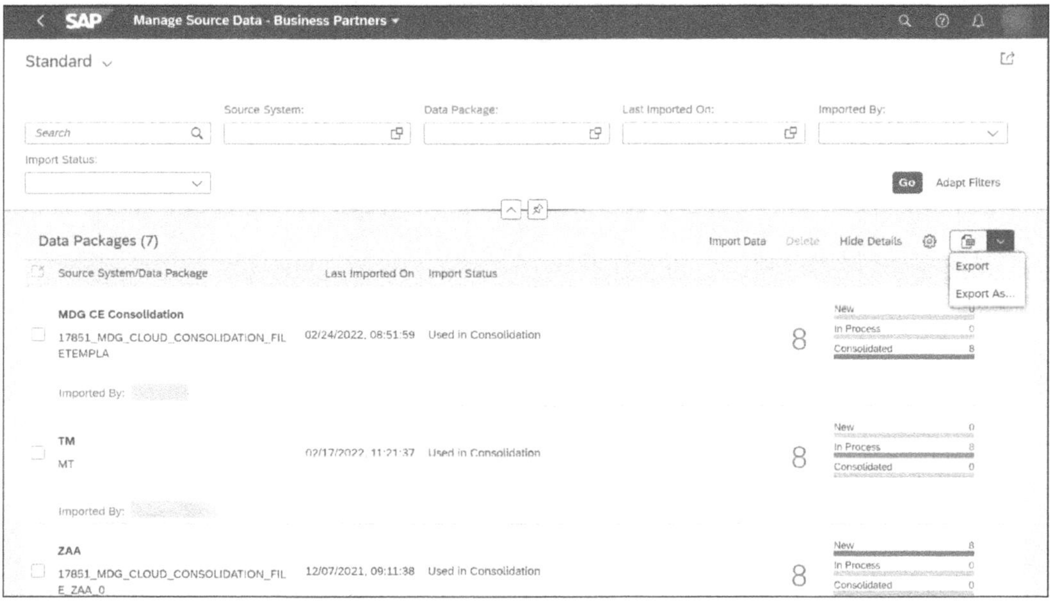

Figure 3.17 Manage Source Data - Business Partners

A similar set of SAP Fiori tiles are available to open the corresponding apps for managing the consolidation process of business partner relationships, as shown earlier in Figure 3.11.

Track Changes

The **Track Changes Business Partners** tile is the same tile that is also present in the **Central Governance for Business Partner** screen shown earlier in Figure 3.4.

In this section, we saw that SAP Master Data Governance, cloud edition, also provides the standard consolidation functionality for business partners and business partner relationships. In the next section, we'll review the data quality management capabilities available for business partners.

3.2.3 Managing Data Quality

The set of data quality management functionalities offered by SAP Master Data Governance, cloud edition, is similar to what is available in SAP Master Data Governance on SAP S/4HANA. The difference is limited only in the scope of attributes available of data quality management.

You can use the **Validation Rules – Business Partners**, **Schedule Data Quality Evaluation**, and **Evaluation Results – Business Partners** apps to manage the quality of your master data. Figure 3.18 shows the corresponding tiles available under the **Data Quality Management for Business Partners** group.

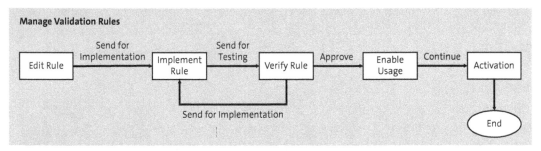

Figure 3.18 Data Quality Management for Business Partners Tiles

Validation Rules for Business Partners

The Validation Rules for Business Partners app allows you to create/edit and manage data quality and validation rules that can be used in the consolidation process and in data quality evaluation jobs. These rules are technically implemented in BRFplus, like the BRFplus validation checks in SAP Master Data Governance on SAP S/4HANA.

Figure 3.19 is the process overview of validation rules used in data quality management.

Manage Validation Rules

Edit Rule → Send for Implementation → Implement Rule → Send for Testing → Verify Rule → Approve → Enable Usage → Continue → Activation

Send for Implementation

End

Figure 3.19 Process Overview of Validation Rules Management

You can use the Validation Rules for Business Partners app to define rules for checking the quality of business partner master data.

Manage Validation Rules

Consider the following important points regarding the usage of the validation rules:

- If the usage **Data Quality Evaluation** is enabled in the definition of the validation rule, the rules are executed during data quality evaluation runs.
- If the usage **Check in Central Governance** is enabled in the definition of the validation rule, the rules can be executed during business partner maintenance.
- If the usage **Check in Consolidation** is enabled in the definition of the validation rule, the rules can be executed during consolidation processes.

Figure 3.20 show the initial overview screen of the Validation Rules for Business Partners app and displays the validation rules that are already available in the system. This screen provides you options to display, review, and manage validation rules, as well as create new ones. Each validation rule contains **Condition Expression (Simplified BRFplus)** and **Scope Expression (Simplified BRFplus)** sections, as shown.

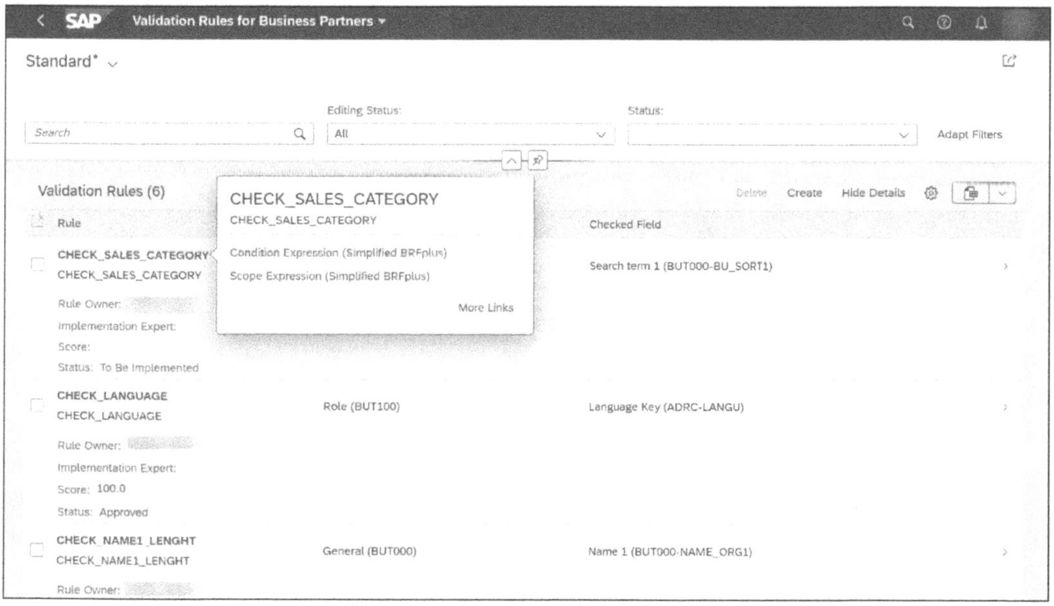

Figure 3.20 Validation Rules for Business Partners: Edit Screen

Figure 3.21 shows the condition expression of the validation rule **CHECK_SALES_CATEGORY**. Note that the system creates the condition expression by appending the suffix **_CON** to the name of the validation rule.

Figure 3.22 shows the scope expression of the validation rule **CHECK_SALES_CATEGORY**. Note that the system creates the scope expression by appending the suffix **_SCP** to the name of the validation rule.

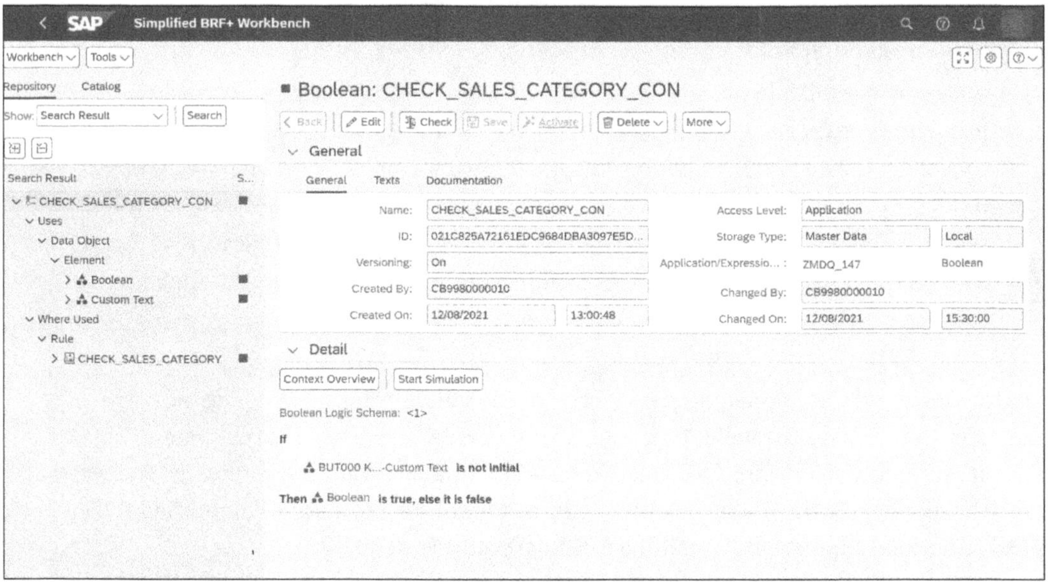

Figure 3.21 Data Quality Validation Rule: Condition Expression

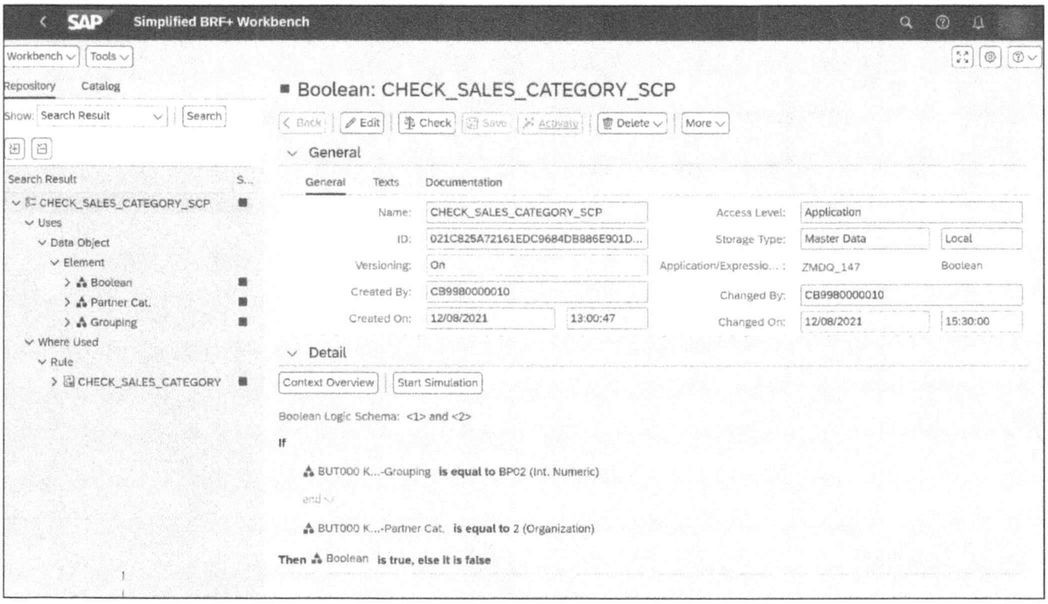

Figure 3.22 Data Quality Validation Rule: Scope Expression

Schedule Data Quality Evaluation

The Schedule Data Quality Evaluation tile shown earlier in Figure 3.18 opens the app that allows you to schedule, create, and manage jobs for evaluating the current quality level of the master data. Figure 3.23 shows the list of data quality jobs based on the selection criteria provided in the top section of the screen. Various options are available here, such as **Create** to create a new data quality job, **Cancel** to cancel the scheduled or running jobs, **Restart** to start a job again, and so on. These jobs are used in the evaluation results that you'll see next.

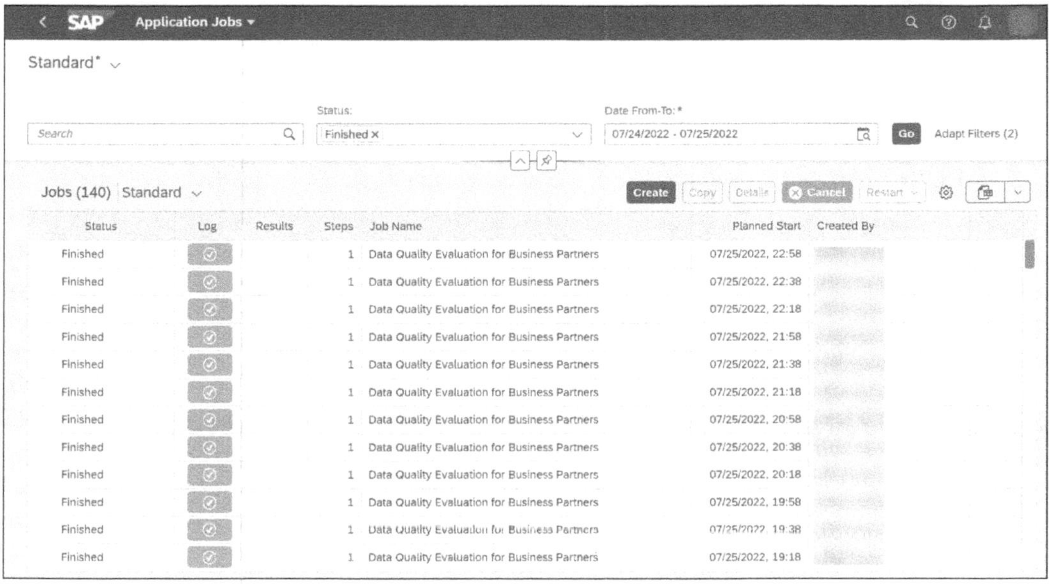

Figure 3.23 Schedule Data Quality Evaluation of Business Partner

Analyzing Data Quality Evaluation Results

Figure 3.24 is the process overview of analyzing and improving the quality of business partner data. The validation rules with the usage **Data Quality Evaluation** enabled in the definition of the validation rule are executed during data quality evaluation runs that are scheduled in the Schedule Data Quality Evaluation app.

The following process can be used to improve the quality of business partner master data:

- Use the Evaluation Results for Business Partners app (tile shown earlier Figure 3.18) to analyze the data quality evaluation results for business partners.
- Select one business partner to change the data in a single request.
- Select multiple business partners to change the data in a mass request.
- The process opens in the Manage Governance Process - Business Partners app shown earlier in Figure 3.7, where you can edit the records and submit the request.
- Approve the process in the Workflow Inbox or My Inbox apps (tiles shown earlier in Figure 3.4).
- With the next evaluation, you can see the improved results in the Evaluation Results for Business Partners app (tile shown earlier in Figure 3.18).

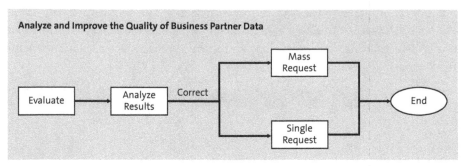

Figure 3.24 Process Overview of Data Quality Evaluation

The Evaluation Results Business Partners app (tile shown earlier in Figure 3.18) provides a very detailed evaluation report, as shown in Figure 3.25, using the validation rules in the data quality evaluation jobs. This is an out-of-the-box analytic report that uses the Analytical List Page (ALP) floorplan from SAP Fiori.

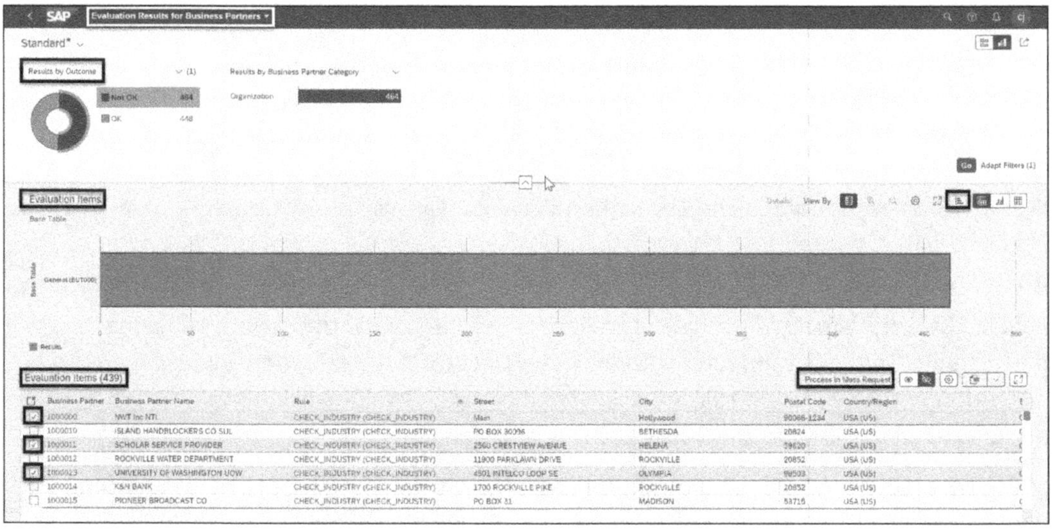

Figure 3.25 Evaluation Results for Business Partners: Initial Screen

Analytical List Page (ALP) Floorplan in SAP Fiori

ALP offers a unique way to analyze data step by step from different perspectives by using different types of charts and drilldown capabilities. Everything can be done seamlessly within one page. The purpose of ALP is to identify interesting areas within data sets, and it provides various tools and options to analyze them further. If required, further processing of the selected subset of data can also be initiated directly from the ALP screen.

Detailed information about ALP can be found at *https://experience.sap.com/fiori-design-web/analytical-list-page/*.

All the important items and options are shown highlighted in boxes in Figure 3.25. The bottom section of the screen provides the list of all business partners used in the analysis of the two sections above. You can drill down directly into any business partner or any validation rule that is applied in the evaluation. If one or more business partners need to be corrected, you can select the corresponding rows in this section and initiate a mass process for business partners directly from this screen by clicking the **Process in Mass Request** button.

Figure 3.26 displays the different types of charts you can select to get a visual analysis of the evaluation items, such as **Bar Chart**, **Column Chart**, **Line Chart**, or **Pie Chart**.

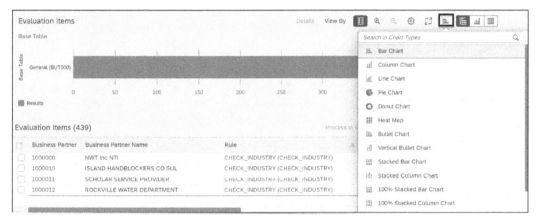

Figure 3.26 Visual Display of Evaluation Items Options of Different Chart Types

Reusing Business Rules Framework Plus Artifacts

The BRFplus artifacts that are in the scope or condition of data quality rules can be reused by other rules. Therefore, consider how activating or changing a BRFplus artifact would affect other rules that use the same artifact. Figure 3.27 shows how reusing BRFplus artifacts can affect other rules.

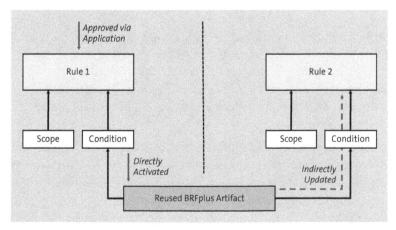

Figure 3.27 Reusing BRFplus Artifacts

The figure shows an example where two different BRFplus validation rules (Rule 1 and Rule 2) share a common BRFplus condition artifact. If you activate or change the reused artifact in Rule 1 directly via the Validation Rules – Business Partner app, it also affects indirectly Rule 2 that uses the same artifact. Therefore, you must take into consideration all the validation rules that reuse a BRFplus artifact and how any changes will impact them.

3.3   Workflow Integration

Workflow capabilities are used in SAP Master Data Governance, cloud edition. The following predefined workflow definitions are provided as default with the processes:

- MDGCloudApprovalWithRework

  This workflow definition is used by the single request and mass request processes. For more information, see the "Display, Create and Edit Your Business Partner Data" and "Perform Mass Changes on Business Partner Data" portions of the process overview shown previously in Figure 3.5.

- MDGCloudBasicApproval

  This workflow definition isn't used in any process template. It's a reduced version of MDGCloudApprovalWithRework without the rework step.

- MDGCloudReworkOnly

  This workflow definition is used for processes triggered by inbound processes in **Data Replication: Initial Load of Business Partner (Core Data) from SAP S/4HANA in Process Overview**. This is an automated process for all valid records coming from SAP Master Data Integration. All valid records are activated automatically. Any erroneous records are automatically split off into a separate process. For these erroneous records, a workflow task is automatically created for a master data specialist to manually correct the data.

> **Note**
>
> In the workflow definitions mentioned here, the task assignments are hard-coded. Depending on your requirements, you can adapt the workflow definitions or create your own workflow definitions. Creating your own workflow definitions is outside the scope of this book. You must refer to the relevant documentation (see *http://s-prs.co/v558007*) on "Developing Applications with Workflow Service in the Cloud Foundry Environment."

This section provided a brief overview of standard workflow capabilities available in SAP Master Data Governance, cloud edition. In the next few sections, we'll discuss the optional components of address validation and attachments that can be used in SAP Master Data Governance, cloud edition. Address validation uses SAP Data Quality Management, microservice for location data; the attachments component uses SAP Document Management Service.

3.4   Address Validation

SAP Data Quality Management, microservices for location data, can be optionally integrated with SAP Master Data Governance, cloud edition, to improve business partner address data. This is an optional feature and requires an additional subscription. The address validation can be used in consolidation and central governance processes of business partners.

Some of the important features available with the integration of this optional service are as follows:

- Verify address per postal authority reference data as correct.
- Standardize the way the address looks and is structured.
- Correct components of an address if incorrect.
- Enhance an address with missing attributes.
- Assign diagnostic codes, which provide insight into the process that assigns the address to reference data.

If you refer to the consolidation process overview shown earlier in Figure 3.12, you can see that the optional address validation step is available in the consolidation process.

In the Central Governance process using the Manage Business Partner app (tile shown earlier in Figure 3.4), you can validate the input address by clicking the **Validate** button shown in Figure 3.28. Before the validation process, the **Validation Status** is **Not Validated**.

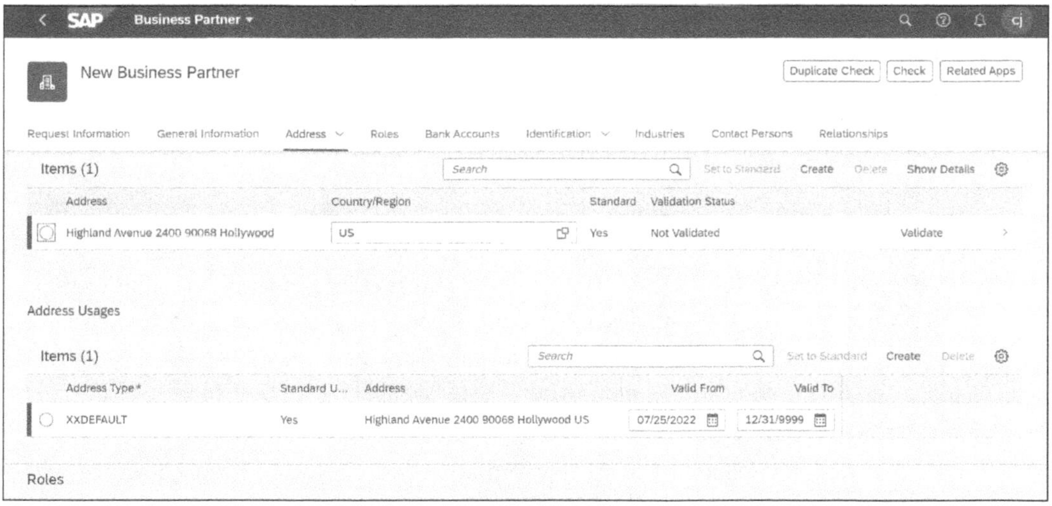

Figure 3.28 New Business Partner Creation: Address Validation

If this optional service is correctly configured, when you click the **Validate** button, the **Validate Address** dialog box opens. Here you can enrich the address in a wizard-like UI. After the enrichment process, you can do one of the following:

- Choose **Accept the Validate Address** to accept the validate address.
- Choose **Use Original Address** if you want to ignore the validation result.

Based on the results of the address validation process, the **Validation Status** will change to one of the following statuses:

- **Accurate**
  Address was already correct when loaded. No improvement was required.
- **Modified**
  Address validation successfully adapted address quality to the required standards.
- **Defective**
  Crucial address information is missing. Address validation could not improve the data; for example, the country isn't defined.
- **Ambiguous**
  User interaction is required as the available data doesn't allow an unambiguous decision.
- **Manually Approved**
  Proposal of address validation is ignored by the user.

Address Validation Using SAP Data Quality Management, Microservices for Location Data

Refer to the configuration guide of the SAP Data Quality Management, microservices for location data to configure this optional service with SAP Master Data Governance, cloud edition. You can find more information in "SAP Data Quality Management, Microservices for Location Data" (*http://s-prs.co/v558003*).

SAP Data Quality Management, microservices for location data, is a service hosted on SAP BTP, and you can access the service via subscription in a subaccount.

To configure and use the SAP Data Quality Management, microservice for location data, in address validation, the configuration steps given here must be performed (find more information in SAP Help Portal by reading "Configure DQM Microservices for SAP Master Data Governance, Cloud Edition" at *http://s-prs.co/v558004*):

1. Enable SAP Data Quality Management, microservices for location data, in the SAP BTP, Neo environment. For more information, see "DQM Microservices in the Neo Environment" at *http://s-prs.co/v558005*.
2. Set up and maintain client certificates.
3. Configure the communication system and communication arrangement.

3.5   Document Management Services

SAP Master Data Governance, cloud edition, can be optionally integrated to SAP Document Management Service to upload and assign attachments to single requests and mass processes in Central Governance. This is an optional service and requires a separate subscription.

SAP Document Management Service is a content management solution on SAP BTP, Cloud Foundry environment. It helps in the management of storing a business's documents. It's based on the Organization for the Advancement of Structured Information Standards (OASIS) industry standard Content Management Interoperability Services (CMIS) and includes features such as versioning, hierarchies, access control, and document management. You can either connect to SAP storage available with SAP Document Management Services or any CMIS-compliant business storage repository.

Documents can be uploaded as file attachments during business partner single requests and mass processes in Central Governance processes using the SAP Document Management service. The process to upload and attach a new file is essentially the same in both single requests and mass processing.

Figure 3.29 shows the Central Governance process during the creation of a new business partner using the Manage Business Partner app discussed previously. To upload and attach a new document, go to the **Request Information** section, and click on the **Files (0)** link.

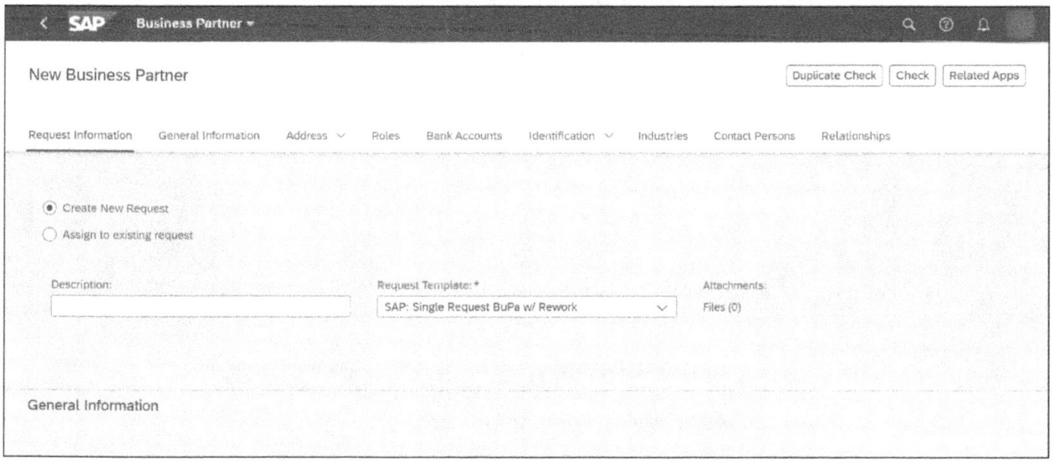

Figure 3.29 Upload New Document: Initial Request Screen

A new screen pops up as shown in Figure 3.30, where you can either drag and drop the document in the box from a local folder or use the **Upload** link to select and upload the document.

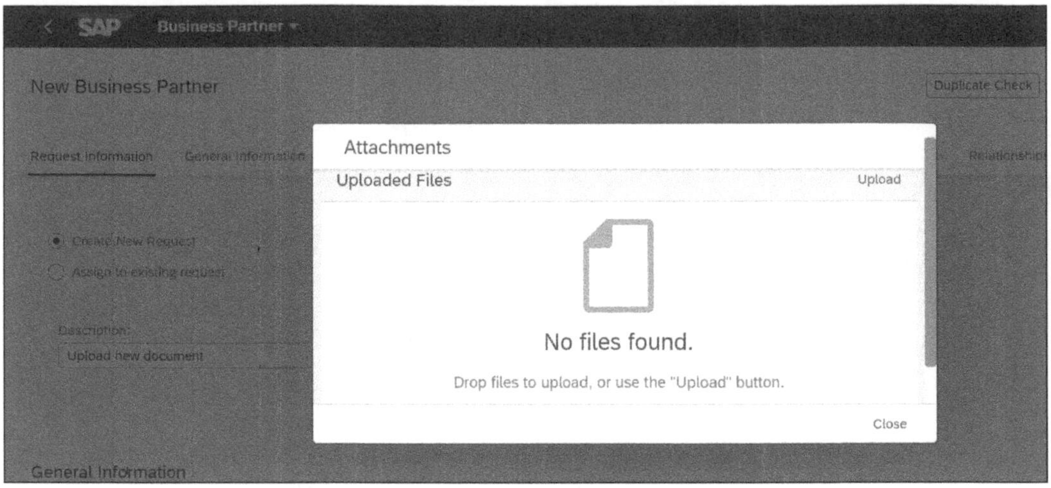

Figure 3.30 Document Attachment: Initial Screen

Figure 3.31 shows the screen after the document is selected and the actual upload process is pending. When you click the **Upload** link, the actual upload and attachment to the request is carried out by the system. This document is uploaded and stored in the SAP Document Management repository, and the link to the document is available as part of the master data request in SAP Master Data Governance, cloud edition.

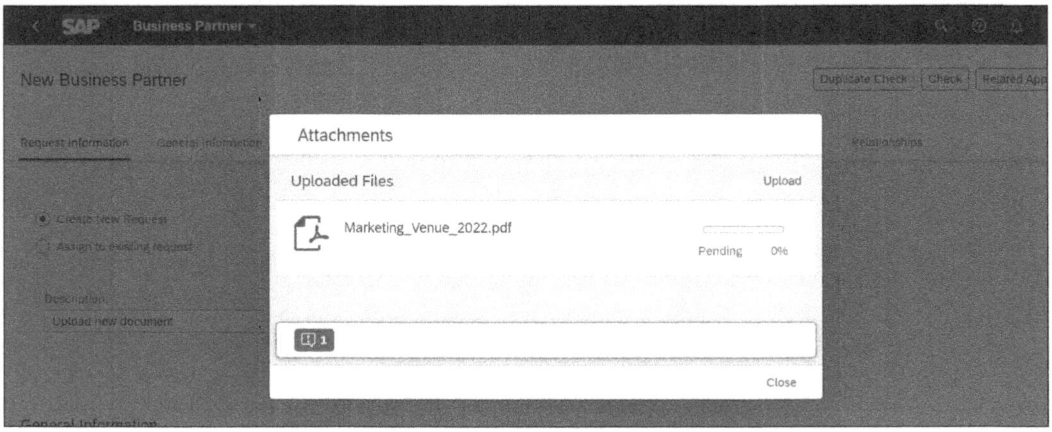

Figure 3.31 Document Attachment: Pending Upload

Figure 3.32 shows the status of the document uploaded and attached in a mass process. Here, you can see the file name and size, along with who uploaded the file and when it was uploaded.

This concludes the overview of all the processes that are available in SAP Master Data Governance, cloud edition.

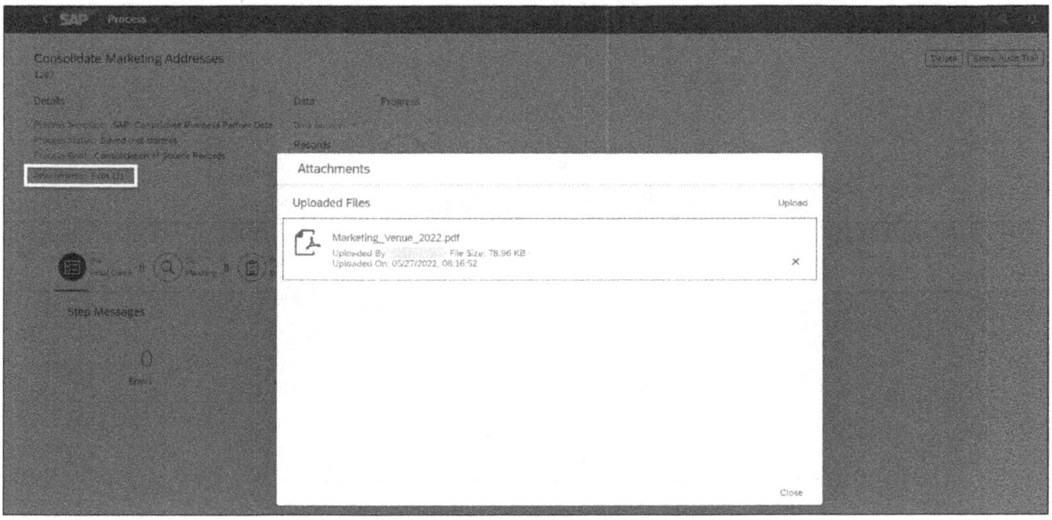

Figure 3.32 Status of Document Uploaded as Attachment

SAP Document Management Service

Refer to the configuration guide of SAP Document Management Service to configure this optional service with SAP Master Data Governance, cloud edition. You can find more information about this optional service in SAP Help Portal at *https://help.sap.com/docs/DOCUMENT_MANAGEMENT*.

3.6 Summary

In this chapter, we reviewed SAP Master Data Governance, cloud edition, in detail. You saw that it's the latest product offering in the product portfolio of SAP for Master Data Governance. It's a complementary solution to SAP Master Data Governance on SAP S/4HANA, and it's *not* meant to replace it. It's implemented as a service on SAP BTP, and it uses SAP Master Data Integration for sharing master data across a hybrid landscape. It's used to manage only the core attributes of the master data and is aligned with SAP One Domain Model. We also analyzed all the available master data governance processes, namely central governance, consolidation of master data, and managing data quality. We also reviewed the optional services available with SAP Master Data Governance, cloud edition, for address validation and document attachments.

In the next chapter, we'll review various deployment options available with SAP Master Data Governance.

Chapter 4
Deployment Options

In today's enterprise landscape, customers want to set up their SAP Master Data Governance systems based on their varied business and IT needs. The setup approach also changes based on the landscape architecture and flow of master data within the landscape. They are looking for options in the business settings, system setup, and deployment of SAP Master Data Governance. In this chapter, we'll look at different deployment options for SAP Master Data Governance to see the benefits of different approaches and compare capabilities. We'll also look at best practice approaches in setting up an SAP Master Data Governance system.

SAP Master Data Governance functionalities are available for configuration after activating the SAP Master Data Governance business functions in the switch framework. There are two different deployment options supported by SAP Master Data Governance:

- **SAP Master Data Governance hub**
  SAP Master Data Governance business functions are activated in a standalone SAP ERP or SAP S/4HANA system.

- **SAP Master Data Governance co-deployed on an operational system**
  The business functions are activated on an operational SAP ERP or SAP S/4HANA system.

There is also another deployment option called *federation of SAP Master Data Governance*. This makes use of the above two deployment options and is covered in detail in Chapter 1, Section 1.3.7. In the federated deployment option, the core master data attributes are typically managed at the corporate level, either using the hub or co-deployed option, and the application-specific master data attributes are managed in a co-deployed SAP Master Data Governance system on an operational SAP ERP or SAP S/4HANA system where they are best understood. This federated approach can also help simplify the Customizing synchronization and even get rid of some very complex and near impossible Customizing synchronization/harmonization scenarios.

4.1   Deployment Options

The SAP Master Data Governance business functions are generally activated on a central hub system, especially if multiple SAP ERP or SAP S/4HANA systems are present in the enterprise landscape, or if some restrictions or business requirements prevent the activation of SAP Master Data Governance functionalities in an existing SAP ERP or SAP S/4HANA system. The SAP Master Data Governance hub and co-deployed options are illustrated in Figure 4.1. The following sections discuss some of the restrictions and limitations that must be considered while determining the deployment approach. We'll also discuss the steps to be considered for the initial build of the SAP Master Data Governance system and for synchronization of Customizing data and reference master data.

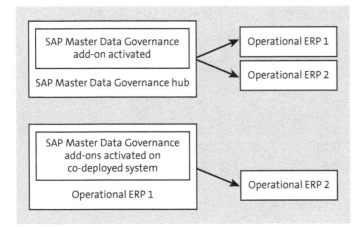

Figure 4.1 Hub Approach versus Co-Deployment Approach

4.1.1   Hub versus Co-Deployment

Numerous industry extensions can be deployed on an operational SAP ERP or SAP S/4HANA system. You must make sure that activation of SAP Master Data Governance business functions is compatible with those industry extensions. For example, SAP Master Data Governance can't be co-deployed if SAP Supplier Relationship Management (SAP SRM) is deployed in the operational SAP ERP system. SAP Master Data Governance also can't be co-deployed when certain industry solutions are activated on an SAP ERP system. Another important aspect to consider is the update strategy of the SAP ERP or SAP S/4HANA system. In a co-deployment situation, an update to SAP Master Data Governance could lead to an upgrade to the underlying SAP ERP system, which might call for end-to-end testing of the SAP ERP business scenarios, in addition to SAP Master Data Governance regression testing. If any new functional changes to the SAP ERP processes were introduced to the system as part of the upgrade, this would require additional effort in change management processes as well. The security aspect needs to be considered when providing access to non-SAP ERP users in SAP ERP to access SAP Master Data Governance.

If the landscape already has a single/central SAP S/4HANA or SAP ERP system, then it's easier to co-deploy SAP Master Data Governance with that system. In a co-deployed system, additional effort to migrate master data and related Customizing configuration is not required. From an end-user perspective, the user interface (UI) navigation will be easier as well. It's recommended that the co-deployment option is considered only on an SAP S/4HANA system to leverage the latest innovations and capabilities that are available exclusively in SAP Master Data Governance on SAP S/4HANA.

> **Activating SAP Master Data Governance Business Functions**
>
> It's recommended that SAP Master Data Governance business functions are activated on the latest version of the SAP S/4HANA system. This will allow customers to make use of any new innovations and capabilities of SAP Master Data Governance that are available uniquely in the SAP S/4HANA version of the solution

If there are multiple systems in the landscape—including SAP and non-SAP systems—but no central system, an ideal approach is to add a new master data hub system for SAP Master Data Governance deployment, although the additional effort required to transport Customizing configuration and migrate master data needs to be considered. The major advantage of this deployment approach is that the upgrade cycle of the SAP Master Data Governance system is independent of the upgrade path of other systems in the landscape. Additionally, more flexibility is available for integrating the hub system with other client systems and additional systems that could be in scope due to mergers and divestments.

The major restrictions to the SAP Master Data Governance co-deploy scenario are as follows:

- Time-dependency for business partners is not enabled.
- SAP SRM can't be co-deployed also with SAP Master Data Governance.
- Industry solutions (other than limited use of Oil and Gas, Retail, Fashion Management, Mining, Discrete Industry and Mill Products [DIMP], and Defense and Security) can't be activated in the system.

> **General Recommendations on Number Range Settings**
>
> When SAP Master Data Governance is deployed in a hub approach, it's highly recommended that the master record numbers—such as the material number, business partner number, and so on—are in sync across the different systems; in this way, the same ID number can be used to search and access a record in the client systems as well in the SAP Master Data Governance hub. However, especially in case of numerous

client systems, it may be difficult to find a common number range; some of the options to consider are as follows:

- **External number assignment in the client system**
  The usage of external numbers in the client system ensures that the ID numbers for newly created records are the same as the hub system records. For already existing records, the SAP Master Data Governance hub system may be loaded with external numbers (same as the existing record numbers). For newly created records, after go-live, you can choose a fixed number range across the systems. If numbers are different across the systems, the key mapping functionality offered by SAP Master Data Governance must be leveraged so that numbers are mapped with the respective system ID.

- **Internal number generation in the client system**
  In this scenario, key mapping is required to map the numbers across the system. The chances that all numbers will be in sync are slim. If replication is done through Application Link Enabling (ALE), the `ALEAUDIT` IDoc may be used to send the internal generated record number back to the hub system.

4.1.2 Limitations and Restrictions

As of this writing, both on-premise and private cloud edition deployment are supported for SAP Master Data Governance. SAP Master Data Governance can be technically deployed on SAP ERP 6.0 or SAP S/4HANA. The general recommendation is to deploy SAP Master Data Governance on an SAP S/4HANA system either in a hub or a co-deployment option.

Note

Some of the key SAP Notes to refer to are as follows (refer to the latest version of the SAP Note listed with respect to the released SAP Master Data Governance version):

- SAP Note 1690202: SAP Master Data Governance and Industry Solutions
- SAP Note 1685823: Release Strategy for SAP Master Data Governance
- SAP Note 2668153: SAP S/4HANA Master Data Governance 2021 Release Information Note
- SAP Note 2656693: Functional Restrictions in MDG for Material in SAP Master Data Governance 9.2 and on SAP S/4HANA 2021
- SAP Note 2656712: Functional Restrictions in MDG for Business Partner/Customer/Supplier in SAP Master Data Governance 9.2 and on SAP S/4HANA 2021
- SAP Note 2700284: SAP Master Data Governance 9.2: Release Information Note
- SAP Note 2645428: Add-On SAP Master Data Governance 9.2 on ERP 6.0 EHP8
- SAP Note 2590829: CMP: Finding and Using the Correct Configuration Guide for "SAP Master Data Governance, Consolidation and Mass Processing"

4.1.3 Initial Build

The initial setup of SAP Master Data Governance in an enterprise varies based on the hub or co-deploy option. If it's a hub deployment, SAP Master Data Governance is installed in a fresh, brand-new system. Customizing configuration data and master data need to be moved from the client systems to the SAP Master Data Governance hub system. When multiple client systems with (potentially) duplicated records are involved, the best practice recommends implementing a data cleansing project to ensure that duplicates aren't loaded into the SAP Master Data Governance hub system. In this case, the consolidation capabilities offered by SAP Master Data Governance can be used to de-duplicate and combine master data coming from multiple systems and finally load an initial set of clean master data into the SAP Master Data Governance hub. (See Chapter 9 for more details on consolidation processes and on the related configuration.) A proper record mapping with respect to the system needs to be configured so that the right data is replicated to the right system from the SAP Master Data Governance hub.

> **Initial Load of Master Data**
>
> In the SAP Master Data Governance hub approach, master data that is under governance must be loaded in the central hub before go-live. It's recommended to load a clean and consolidated set of master data without any duplicates. Because SAP Master Data Governance finance objects—such as accounts, profit centers, cost centers, and so on—are technically implemented as a flex data model, they must be loaded in SAP Master Data Governance staging tables as well.

In a multiple system landscape, based on complexity and type of system, enterprises may go for a new SAP Master Data Governance hub system or—in case a central/leading system already exists—SAP Master Data Governance functionalities may be co-deployed on it. The SAP Master Data Governance co-deployment option is usually chosen if there is only a single operational SAP ERP or SAP S/4HANA system in the landscape, provided there are no restrictions.

The following describes how to set up the systems for these scenarios:

- **Scenario 1: New installation (hub approach)**

  A greenfield implementation (hub approach) of SAP Master Data Governance involves the migration of master data records from the various client/target systems to the hub system, together with the related configuration elements.

  The Customizing configuration data can be moved in several different ways. Customizing transports or Business Configuration Sets (BC Sets) can be leveraged to move specific Customizing configurations from an existing system to SAP Master Data Governance. The automated options include SAP Solution Manager functionalities such as the Customizing Scout and Customizing Distribution tools. If there are multiple systems, the configurations should be harmonized or specific value mapping must be set up in the SAP Master Data Governance/target system before the values are moved.

Another possibility is to use an Application Link Enabling (ALE) Customizing distribution. If there is already a central system that governs the Customizing configurations in the landscape, a system/client copy with Customizing data is also an option, with the major disadvantage that redundant data not related to master records may also be copied.

An option becoming more popular these days is the Cross-Landscape Distribution (XLD) Focused Build for SAP Solution Manager, which leverages the Change Request Management (ChaRM) processes. XLD is a guided procedure that supports the selection of the correct target and automates the distribution of Customizing objects. Although it's not a conflict detection tool, it does allow you to distribute transportable changes from one system to another or across multiple landscapes. Detailed discussion on XLD and the process is outside the scope of this book.

- **Scenario 2: SAP Master Data Governance co-deployed in a central system**
  The major advantage of the co-deployed scenario is that you don't have to move the Customizing nor transfer master data—unless there are other systems in the landscape holding records to be governed. In this case, the delta configuration and data records need to be moved to the co-deployed system.

In cases where SAP Master Data Governance for SAP ERP (less preferred compared to SAP Master Data Governance on SAP S/4HANA) is considered, the choice of the underlying database is also a key factor to be considered for the optimum performance of the solution. SAP HANA is the recommended database for SAP Master Data Governance because it brings several additional functionalities such as improved search, advanced standardization, and matching capabilities (in general, consolidation and mass processing functionalities are limited when SAP Master Data Governance runs on a non-SAP HANA database). SAP Master Data Governance running on SAP HANA provides additional benefits of efficient fuzzy search and duplicate check capabilities, address cleansing, real-time analytics, and so on. SAP HANA as a sidecar scenario for consolidation and mass processing in SAP Master Data Governance isn't supported.

The key configuration options after the system setup are the following:

- Activate business functions using Transaction SFW5.
- Activate BC Sets using Transaction SCPR20. The BC Sets provide preconfigured content for the standard objects. These are domain-specific BC Sets and also common BC Sets for both consolidation and governance use cases.
- Set up the business workflow using Transaction SWU3 (usually done by system administrator). This configuration helps in setting up the basic workflow configuration such as batch user IDs, number ranges for client-specific workflow object

instances, and so on. This configuration enables the SAP system to process SAP business workflows.

- Activate the application services using Transaction SICF. These application services are required to access the predelivered SAP Master Data Governance applications.

- Set up user roles based on predelivered templates.

After completing these initial configuration activities, domain-specific configuration must be executed for the governance and consolidation processes such as setting up search views, assigning agents for change request processing, modeling processes, and so on. These configurations are done using Transaction MDCIMG and Transaction MDGIMG for consolidation and governance scenarios, respectively.

4.1.4   Quick-Start for SAP Master Data Governance

The quick-start for SAP Master Data Governance approach helps to deploy and get started with SAP Master Data Governance very quickly. This is offered from SAP with the aim to enable customers to accelerate their SAP Master Data Governance implementation journey and improve the time to value in an SAP Master Data Governance deployment.

As discussed in the previous section, SAP Master Data Governance can be deployed in various modes— as a hub deployment, a co-deployment, or in a hybrid mode such as the SAP Master Data Governance federated deployment. Irrespective of the deployment option chosen, there are a whole series of steps necessary to configure and get the SAP Master Data Governance system up and running to be able to use the solution for the various master data processes. And these steps have to be repeated for each of your development, quality, and production system, which could consume a lot of time and effort.

The quick-start offering allows you to avoid doing all these repetitive and tedious tasks to enable SAP Master Data Governance in your landscape and provides a prebuilt, pre-configured system that can be readily deployed into your landscape. This shortens the overall timeline from months to weeks in getting your SAP Master Data Governance system up and running. The quick-start can be leveraged in a new SAP Master Data Governance system (greenfield implementation) or can be used to accelerate deployment on an existing SAP Master Data Governance on SAP S/4HANA system (brownfield implementation).

Based on the specific situation, the quick-start function can be leveraged as either of the following:

- **Quick-start template for SAP Master Data Governance**
  This is suitable for greenfield systems and fresh hub deployments.

- **Quick-start service for SAP Master Data Governance**
  This is suitable for brownfield systems and co-deployment options.

The selected option doesn't have any impact in terms of benefits for the SAP Master Data Governance-project team: in both cases, the scope and the delivered content is the same. The primary difference is that, in the "service" approach, timelines are slightly longer—a deployment on a brownfield involves doing additional checks and manual activations on the system before deploying the quick-start package.

These are many benefits of deploying SAP Master Data Governance via such a quick-start approach:

- Deployment of a fully configured SAP Master Data Governance system in a matter of days to weeks
- Availability of a fully configured SAP Master Data Governance system in your design phase for a better fit-gap outcome
- Avoids repetitive configuration of baseline during setup of development, quality, and production tiers
- Template-based approach shortens project implementation and decreases overall project cost and lowers project risk
- Comes fully configured for all standard domains of SAP Master Data Governance, that is, Material, Customer, Supplier, and Financials
- Comes fully configured for all SAP Master Data Governance solutions and functionalities, that is governance, consolidation, mass processing, data quality management, and process analytics
- Comes with lot of dedicated business content, including business rules, validations, workflows, analytical content, and reference configuration content
- Configured based on the SAP recommended best practice approach
- Can be deployed on-premise or as a private cloud deployment, including landscapes hosted by any hyperscalers

More details of quick-start for SAP Master Data Governance are provided in Chapter 17, Section 17.2, of this book.

4.1.5   Customizing Synchronization

When a master data system is deployed as a hub either catering to a single receiving system or as a true central master data governance system, it's important to consider how and where the data that helps maintain master data is managed. In the context of SAP S/4HANA and SAP ERP, such data is known as Customizing data and is defined in a configuration client of a development system and moved to quality and production systems via the transport process. Customizing data is defined as client specific and needs to be copied to other clients if the same data is needed in other clients.

The following subsections provide an overview of the importance of synchronizing Customizing data if SAP Master Data Governance is deployed as a hub, and they describe the options available to synchronize Customizing data. This section also provides a detailed overview and step-by-step instructions on setting up the most recommended and widely used approach to synchronizing Customizing data using SAP Solution Manager.

Overview

It's very common to have SAP Master Data Governance deployed as a hub with one or more SAP S/4HANA or SAP ERP systems in the landscape. In such scenarios, it's important to define which system acts as the "system of record" for the Customizing data. In general, Customizing data is defined and resides in a system where an end-to-end process is defined, typically a system where transactional data is created. It's very uncommon—although possible—to define Customizing data directly in an SAP Master Data Governance hub. Some companies prefer to define process-independent Customizing data in a central hub and distribute the data to other systems. Examples of such data include countries, regions, languages, and units of measure.

Instead of setting up multiple systems as sources of Customizing, other companies prefer to manage this kind of data in a single system where end-to-end processes are maintained (e.g., SAP S/4HANA) and periodically synchronize their Customizing across the system landscape. However, if any of the Customizing data needs to be governed, such data can be modeled as custom objects in SAP Master Data Governance and then distributed to every system that requires such data via replication processes. Chapter 11, provides step-by-step details on how to model and set up a custom object in SAP Master Data Governance.

As discussed earlier, whenever an SAP Master Data Governance hub is set up, it's important to understand that the Customizing data is required and must be synchronized from the system(s) where such data is actually maintained. In case of unharmonized Customizing values, SAP Master Data Governance also provides value mapping capabilities to handle system-specific codes of particular Customizing data. The concept of value mapping is explained in Chapter 12.

Customizing synchronization is a continuous process consisting of two logic phases: a first synchronization performed during the initial setup of the SAP Master Data Governance system and an ongoing resynchronization/delta load to move the "new" values. SAP Transport Management System (TMS) and BC Sets are important aspects in Customizing synchronization. Following is an overview of initial and ongoing synchronization and various options available to perform synchronization of Customizing data:

- **Initial synchronization**
  Depending on how the SAP Master Data Governance hub is installed, the initial synchronization either occurs during the installation process or after installation is complete. Section 4.1 explained various initial build options, and—irrespective of the approach—it's important to synchronize Customizing data from the operational SAP

ERP system and other source systems initially. Building the system and synchronizing the Customizing data based on a set of Customizing object lists is always much cleaner because the initial synchronization is performed based on the objects relevant to the SAP Master Data Governance hub. If the SAP Master Data Governance hub is built as a copy of the operational SAP S/4HANA or SAP ERP system, then a cleansing of the Customizing is required to limit the synchronization only to the relevant Customizing objects.

- **Ongoing synchronization**

  After the initial synchronization, setting up ongoing synchronization is a key aspect of the customization synchronization effort. Various options are available; however, compiling the list of synchronization objects that are relevant to the master data domains maintained in the SAP Master Data Governance hub is essential because all options require such a list. Following are some of the available options:

  - **Semi-automatic synchronization**

    Entries are transported from an operational SAP S/4HANA or SAP ERP system using BC Sets and then imported into the SAP Master Data Governance hub manually. The main disadvantage of this solution is the manual effort involved.

  - **Custom solution**

    It's possible to develop a completely custom solution by pulling only the relevant data into the SAP Master Data Governance hub. The drawback of this approach is the effort involved in building the tool; the advantage is a more controlled extraction of configuration data after the data is available in the relevant operational SAP S/4HANA or SAP ERP systems.

  - **ALE-based Customizing distribution**

    This approach involves setting up ALE between the SAP Master Data Governance hub and operational SAP S/4HANA or SAP ERP systems to capture and synchronize relevant Customizing data.

  - **SAP Solution Manager–based Customizing distribution**

    SAP Solution Manager can be used to simplify the end-to-end Customizing synchronizing process and to monitor it after the initial distribution. The following section discusses this option in more detail as this is used by several companies.

  - **XLD Focused Build for SAP Solution Manager**

    This Focused Build solution for SAP Solution Manager provides an option to set up the distribution of Customizing and to synchronize the Customizing data for identical tables in different system landscapes. It makes use of the ChaRM process to distribute Customizing objects and offers a guided procedure that can be opened from the transport assignment block of the source system. This Focused Build process is a newer approach for distributing Customizing data that is gaining popularity recently.

SAP Solution Manager–Based Customizing Distribution

SAP Solution Manager is widely used for synchronizing Customizing data between multiple SAP systems, including the SAP Master Data Governance hub. This approach helps in automating the Customizing synchronization process and provides the ability to synchronize only the data really required for maintaining master data for the domains implemented in SAP Master Data Governance. SAP Solution Manager has the following tools to support Customizing synchronization:

- **Customizing Scout**
  This tool is used to compare Customizing between two or more systems, and it's capable to analyze the discrepancies in Customizing between the systems based on a predefined list of Customizing objects.

- **Customizing Distribution**
  This tool is used to distribute Customizing from source to target systems based on a predefined list of Customizing objects. This tool can be used to perform initial as well as ongoing distributions of Customizing data:
  - Initial distribution is used to distribute Customizing data from the source to target SAP system, and this process completely overwrites Customizing data in the target system with the data coming from the source system. Therefore, initial distribution is typically used when setting up a new system and customization needs to be replicated from another SAP system.
  - Ongoing distribution picks up only the changes made to Customizing data to any of the objects in the predefined object lists and synchronizes with the target system automatically.

> **Note**
>
> SAP Solution Manager 7.2 offers XLD as part of the Focused Build standalone extension, which also provides the same functionality as Customizing Distribution and has certain advantages compared to Customizing Distribution, especially if ChaRM is being used. Some of the advantages of XLD when compared to Customizing Distribution are as follows:
>
> - Synchronization of workbench objects
> - Integration with ChaRM
>
> XLD provides the ability for synchronizing all Customizing objects or only a defined list of objects. For workbench objects, it's possible to define the synchronization based on the package to which workbench objects are assigned. You can consider XLD in lieu of Customizing Distribution, depending on the implementation requirements, such as tighter integration with ChaRM and distribution of workbench objects.
>
> The rest of the section explains in detail the synchronization of Customizing objects using Customizing Distribution.

Table 4.1 provides a list of authorizations needed for both system administrators and configurators.

Role	SAP Solution Manager	Component Systems
System administrators	■ S_CD_SYSAC ■ S_CS_SYST ■ S_PROJECT ■ S_PROJECTS ■ S_RFCACL	■ S_USER_AUT ■ S_USER_GRP ■ S_USER_PRO ■ S_PROJECT ■ S_PROJECTS ■ S_CTS_ADMI ■ S_TRANSPORT ■ S_RFCACL
Functional configurators	■ S_CD_SYNC ■ S_TABU_RFC ■ S_TABU_DIS ■ S_TABU_CLI	■ S_TABU_CLI ■ S_TABU_DIS ■ S_TABU_LIN ■ S_TABU_RFC ■ S_BCSETS

Table 4.1 Authorization Prerequisites

Sample Processes and Roles

In general, various SAP and non-SAP systems might be involved in managing different types of data (e.g., master data, Customizing/configuration data, transactional data). SAP Master Data Governance is always considered a system of record for master data and any other static data that needs to be governed. Transactional data is always created and maintained in an operational SAP S/4HANA or SAP ERP system. However, configuration data that is defined as part of the end-to-end process setup is also maintained in a system where transactional data is created/maintained. SAP Solution Manager helps in synchronizing such configuration/Customizing data to an SAP Master Data Governance hub.

A three-tier landscape is common in any project implementation. To use SAP Solution Manager for initial and ongoing distribution, it should be part of the implementation project. Figure 4.2 shows a simple process in which SAP Solution Manager–based synchronization is used for ongoing synchronization.

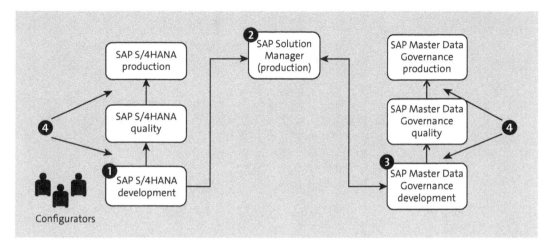

Figure 4.2 SAP Solution Manager-Based Customizing Process for Ongoing Synchronization

The process comprises the following steps:

❶ New configuration is added by configurators in the SAP S/4HANA development system.

❷ Once saved, SAP Solution Manager proposes a transport request in the SAP S/4HANA development system followed by a transport proposed for the SAP Master Data Governance development system.

❸ Entries are recorded in a transport request in the SAP S/4HANA development system. SAP Solution Manager adds the transport entries to a BC Set and activates the BC Set in SAP Master Data Governance.

❹ SAP Master Data Governance and SAP S/4HANA follow their respective transportation paths.

The roles reported in Table 4.2 are for reference purposes only. The best-fitting approach should be identified and followed based on the implementation project setup.

System	Activity	Transaction Code	Role
SAP Solution Manager	Create remote function call (RFC) connections for Customizing Distribution and Customizing Scout	Transaction SM59	System administrators
SAP Solution Manager	Create a project	Transaction SOLAR_PROJECT_ADMIN	System administrators

Table 4.2 High-Level Steps Involved in Customizing Synchronization Setup

System	Activity	Transaction Code	Role
SAP Master Data Governance development	Create synchronization object list	Transaction SCDT_MAPPING	Configurators
SAP Solution Manager	Create synchronization groups with trusted connections to SAP Master Data Governance and SAP ERP systems	Transaction SCDT_GROUPS	Configurators/system administrators
SAP Solution Manager	Create Customizing distribution for the synchronization groups created	Transaction SCDT_SETUP	System administrators

Table 4.2 High-Level Steps Involved in Customizing Synchronization Setup (Cont.)

The various activities introduced in Table 4.2 are explained in the following steps:

1. **Create RFC connections for Customizing Distribution and Customizing Scout.**
   The following RFC connections are needed in SAP Solution Manager for the systems involved in the synchronization process:
   - Customizing Scout:
     - SM_<system ID>CLNT<client>_READ
   - Customizing Distribution:
     - SM_<system ID>CLNT<client>_TRUSTED
     - SM_<system ID>CLNT<client>_BACK

2. **Create a project.**
   This step involves creating an SAP Solution Manager project using Transaction SOLAR_PROJECT_ADMIN and is typically performed by system administrators.

3. **Create a synchronization object list.**
   This step is performed in the SAP Master Data Governance system by functional configurators responsible for maintaining Customizing synchronization using Transaction SCDT_MAPPING. During this step, functional configurators create a synchronization object in the SAP Master Data Governance system and maintain a list of objects that are part of the synchronization objects. These objects are later loaded into SAP Solution Manager during the creation of the synchronization group. When creating the synchronization object, it's important to indicate the relevance of the synchronizing object in the **Relevant for** dropdown, which indicates the main purpose of the synchronization object:

- **Relevant for Comparison and Distribution**
- **Relevant for Comparison Only**
- **Relevant for Initial Distribution Only**
- **Relevant for Distribution by Transport**
- **Relevant for Comparison and Initial Distribution Only**

Figure 4.3 shows an example of creating a synchronization object in the SAP Master Data Governance system along with list of tables added to the synchronization object.

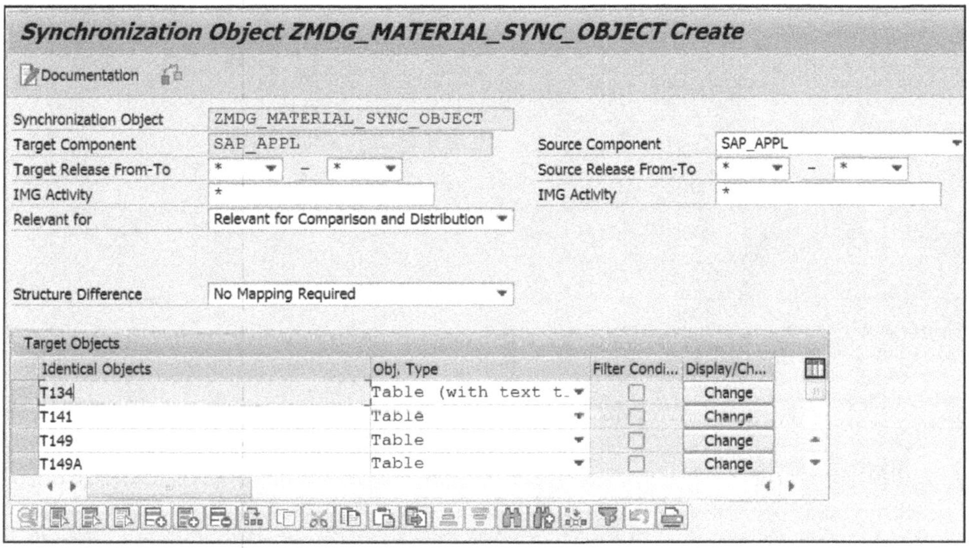

Figure 4.3 Creation of the Synchronization Object

4. **Create synchronization groups.**

   After synchronization objects are created in the SAP Master Data Governance system, the following steps are performed in SAP Solution Manager using Transaction SCDT_GROUPS:

   - **Create the synchronization group and load synchronization objects.**

     This step involves creating a synchronization group by providing the source and target systems and the SAP Solution Manager project. The **Load Object Lists** button provides the ability to load all synchronization object lists maintained in the SAP Master Data Governance system into the SAP Solution Manager system. Figure 4.4 shows an example of synchronization group creation.

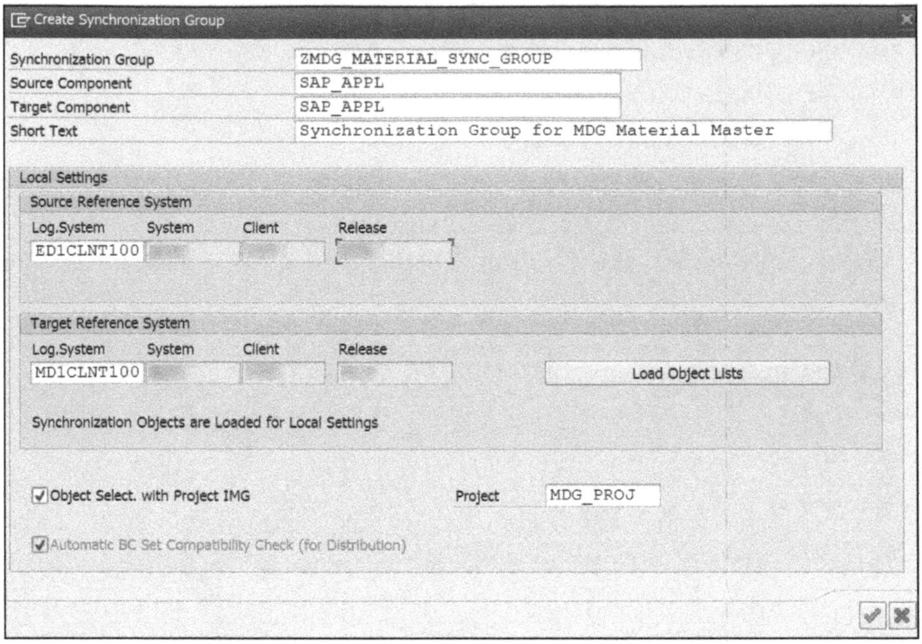

Create Synchronization Group

Synchronization Group	ZMDG_MATERIAL_SYNC_GROUP
Source Component	SAP_APPL
Target Component	SAP_APPL
Short Text	Synchronization Group for MDG Material Master

Local Settings

Source Reference System

Log.System	System	Client	Release
ED1CLNT100			

Target Reference System

Log.System	System	Client	Release	
MD1CLNT100				Load Object Lists

Synchronization Objects are Loaded for Local Settings

☑ Object Select. with Project IMG   Project MDG_PROJ

☑ Automatic BC Set Compatibility Check (for Distribution)

Figure 4.4 Creating a Synchronization Group

> – **Insert synchronization objects under the newly created synchronization group.**
> After the synchronization group is created, and all object lists are loaded from the
> SAP Master Data Governance system, then the next step involves inserting syn-
> chronization objects created in SAP Master Data Governance under the synchro-
> nization group hierarchy. Figure 4.5 and Figure 4.6 provide an overview of this
> step.

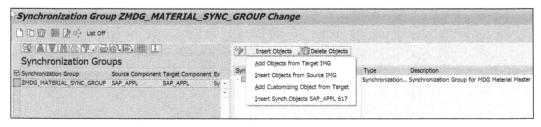

Figure 4.5 Synchronization Group: Insert Objects

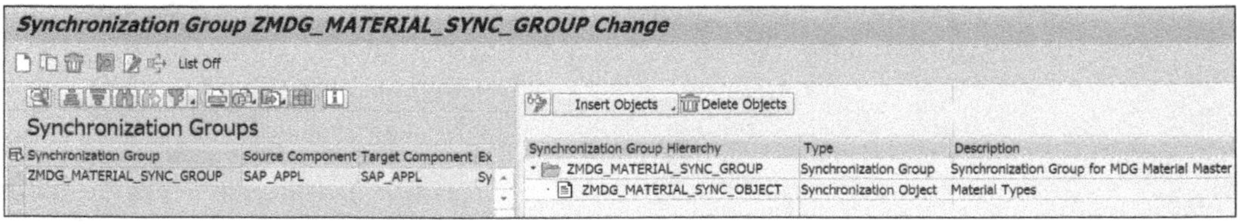

Synchronization Group ZMDG_MATERIAL_SYNC_GROUP Change

List Off

Synchronization Groups

Synchronization Group	Source Component	Target Component	Ex	Synchronization Group Hierarchy	Type	Description
ZMDG_MATERIAL_SYNC_GROUP	SAP_APPL	SAP_APPL	Sy	• ▸ ZMDG_MATERIAL_SYNC_GROUP	Synchronization Group	Synchronization Group for MDG Material Master
				· ▸ ZMDG_MATERIAL_SYNC_OBJECT	Synchronization Object	Material Types

Figure 4.6 Synchronization Group: Hierarchy

5. **Create Customizing Distribution.**

As a next step, Customizing Distribution needs to be created in SAP Solution Manager using Transaction SCDT_SETUP. Creation of Customizing Distribution requires the following:

– Synchronization group created in the previous step

– SAP Solution Manager transport project if that option is chosen

– Source system

– Distribution type:

  • **Timed Distribution**: This option is selected if synchronization needs to occur at predefined times.

  • **At Transport release**: This option is selected if the synchronization needs to be triggered at the time of releasing the transport in the source system.

  • **At Transport recording**: This option is selected if the synchronization needs to be triggered at the time of adding entries to the transport request in the source system.

  • **Initial distribution**: This option is used to indicate that the distribution type is purely for initial distribution.

– Target systems

Figure 4.7 shows an example of creating Customizing Distribution. In this example, **Distribution Type** is set to trigger **Synchronization at Transport Recording**.

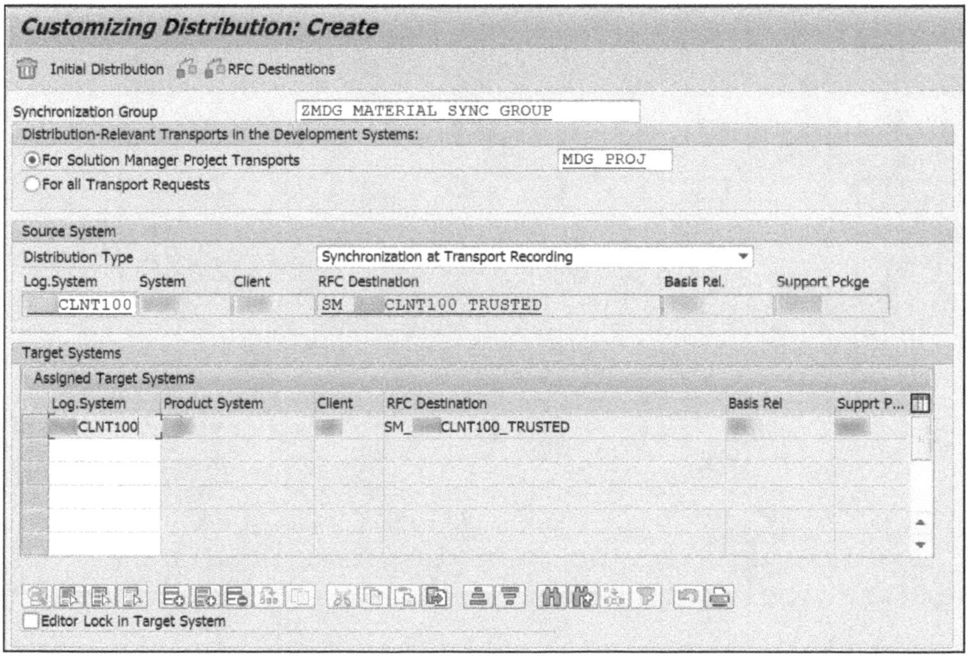

Figure 4.7 Customizing Distribution

Selecting the appropriate distribution type depends on the project requirements. For example, **Synchronization at Transport Recording** immediately triggers as soon as Customizing objects are added to a transport in the source system. In such cases, any customization changes are synchronized immediately to the target SAP Master Data Governance system. This scenario is useful when transports are released after specific test cycles are complete in both the source and target systems.

6. **Display distribution logs.**

   The Customizing Distribution process can be monitored using Transaction SCDT_LOG. This transaction provides the ability to select distribution logs with various selection options, including the following:

   – Distributions based on a source system transport

   – Initial distribution based on a synchronization group

   – SAP Solution Manager project

   – Source and target systems

   – Dates when the distribution occurred

   Figure 4.8 shows Transaction SCDT_LOG and various selection screen options.

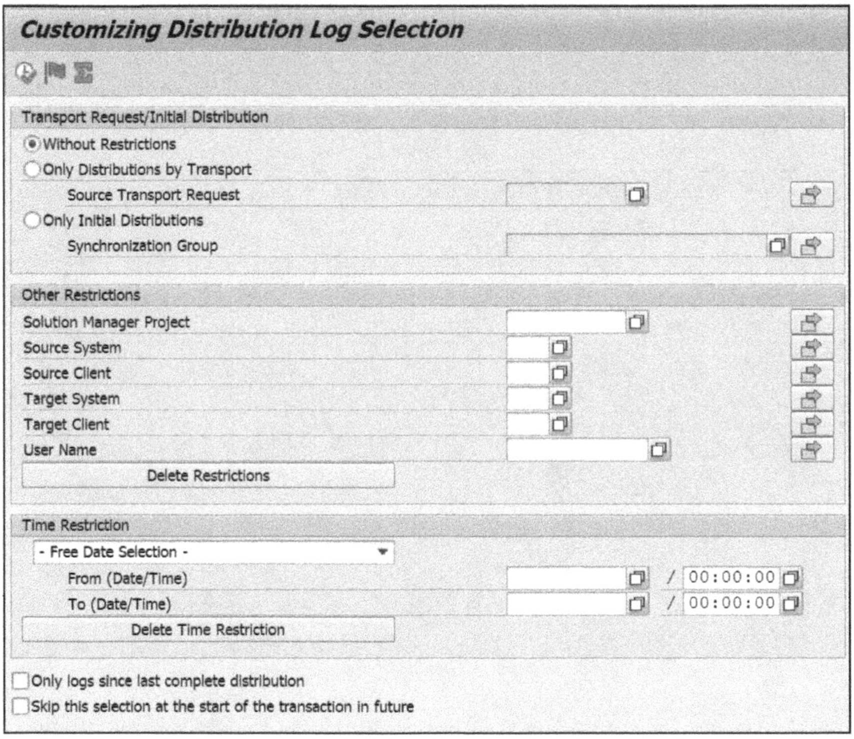

Figure 4.8 Transaction SCDT_LOG: Selection Screen Options

After logs are displayed, you can display details of the generated BC Set. You also can navigate to the BC Set in the target system and to the BC Set activation log directly from the distribution log. Figure 4.9 shows a snapshot of an example distribution log.

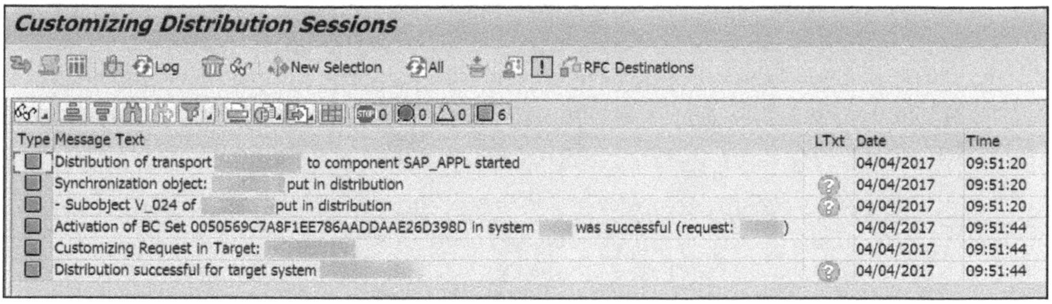

Figure 4.9 Distribution Log Example

You can redistribute any transports from the distribution log itself or trigger distribution of a single transport from a source system to a target system manually via Transaction SCDT_FETCH.

7. **Run Customizing Scout.**

Customizing Scout enables you to compare customization between source and target systems across the entire system landscape based on the predefined list of synchronization objects. Customizing Scout plays an important role in the synchronization process and helps in analyzing the differences in Customizing objects during the initial distribution as well as the ongoing distribution process. Customizing Scout is accessed via Transaction SCOUT in SAP Solution Manager. Figure 4.10 shows the **Customizing Scout - Initial Screen** providing the ability to run comparisons across the system landscape for various system roles between source and target systems.

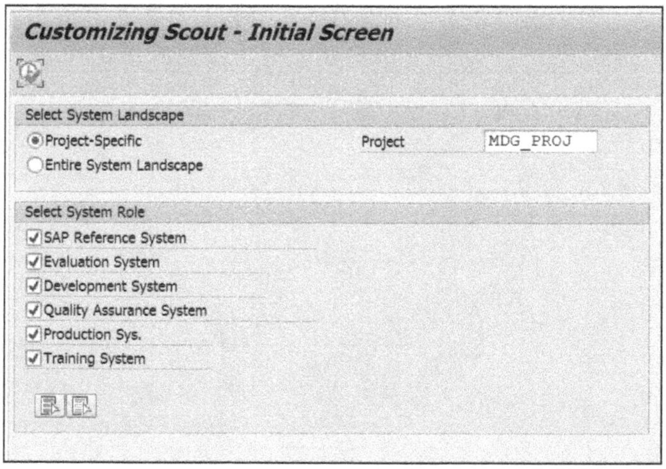

Figure 4.10 Customizing Scout: Comparing Customization across All System Roles in the System Landscape

After a system role is selected and a project is specified, Customizing Scout enables you to select the synchronization group, source system, and target system for comparison. Figure 4.11 provides an example of such a selection.

Customizing Scout comparisons can be run online or in the background. Comparison results provide various options such as an overview of the comparison result and individual Customizing object level comparisons to help further analyze the result. Figure 4.12 shows an example of a Customizing Scout comparison result.

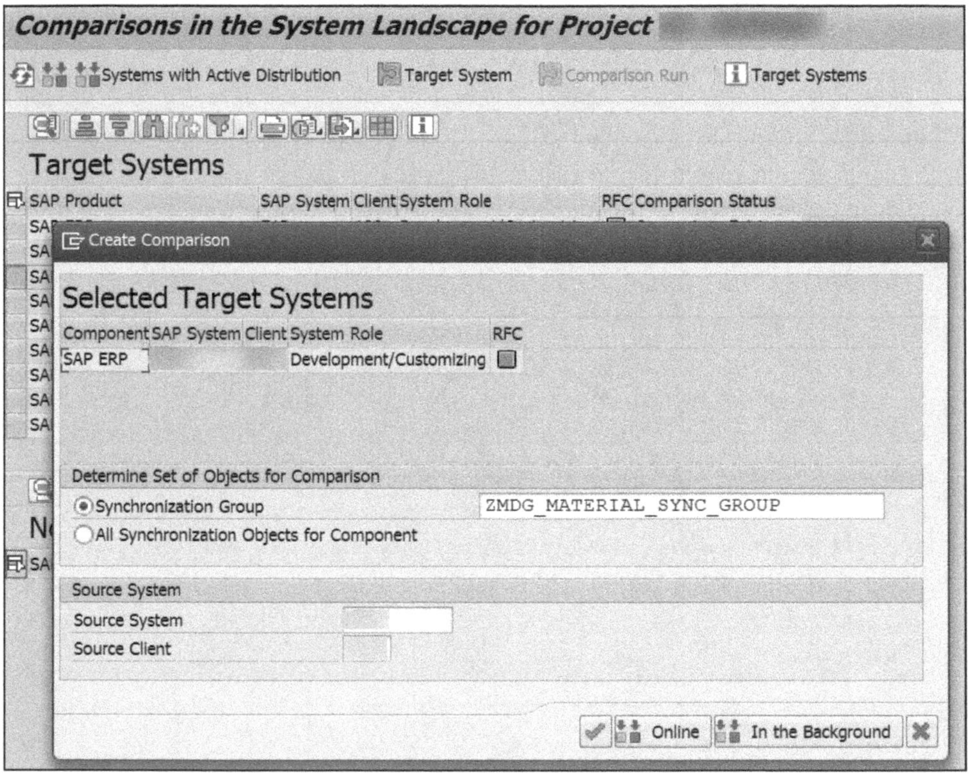

Figure 4.11 Customizing Scout Comparison Based on Synchronization Group

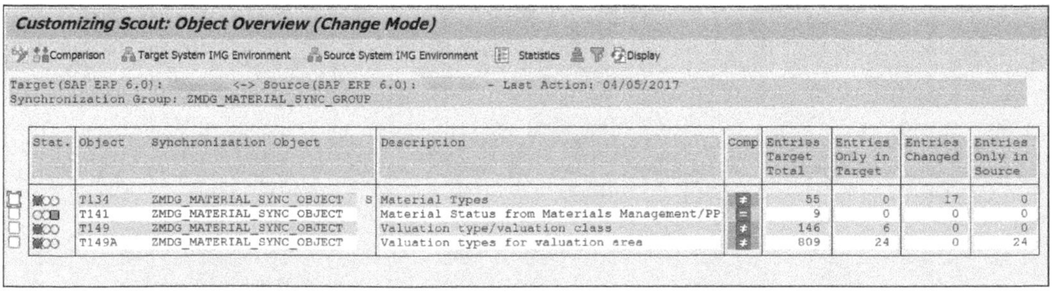

Figure 4.12 Example of a Customizing Scout Comparison Result

4.1.6   Reference Master Data Synchronization

Depending on the master data domains implemented in the SAP Master Data Governance hub, it's not always possible to synchronize all data required to maintain master data using the Customizing Distribution process in SAP Solution Manager. The primary reason for this is that not all such data is maintained as Customizing data. Following are some examples:

- Bank master data
- Material class and characteristics
- Finance master data, such as general ledger accounts and profit centers

> **Note**
>
> If finance master data isn't governed using SAP Master Data Governance, then master data such as general ledger accounts and profit centers needs to be synchronized to the SAP Master Data Governance hub from a system where such data is created to cater to the needs of other domains such as material master or customer master that are governed using SAP Master Data Governance. However, if finance masters are also being managed in the SAP Master Data Governance hub, such information still needs to be replicated to the SAP Master Data Governance hub itself due to the technical nature of the data model for SAP Master Data Governance, Financials (refer to Chapter 5 for additional details).

To synchronize such non-Customizing data, it's very common to set up an ALE-based synchronization process. For example, CLSMAS and CHRMAS IDoc message types can be used for material class and characteristics, and GLMAST and PRCMAS message types can be used for general ledger accounts and profit centers, respectively.

4.1.7   On-Premise versus Cloud Deployment

Traditionally, enterprise systems were deployed on-premise (at the customers own data center), and systems were typically managed by the customer's own IT team or by a system integrator appointed to run and maintain these systems on a customer-owned infrastructure. But with offerings such as infrastructure-as-a-service (IaaS) and software-as-a-service (SaaS) becoming more popular, customers are looking for additional deployment options for their enterprise landscapes. To meet these expectations, SAP Master Data Governance is also available in various deployment options, that is, on-premise deployment or cloud deployment, as described here:

- **On-premise deployment: SAP Master Data Governance on SAP S/4HANA**
  In this approach, SAP Master Data Governance is deployed and managed by the customer in their own infrastructure or in a partner infrastructure. Installation, upgrade, and maintenance of the SAP Master Data Governance system is done by the customer's own IT team or is outsourced to a partner. The customer acquires the

license for SAP Master Data Governance on SAP S/4HANA and then deploys the solution in their environment. Following are some of the characteristics of an on-premise deployment of SAP Master Data Governance:

- Infrastructure: Dedicated landscape on infrastructure operated by the customer (or outsourced to their SI partner).
- License: Classical on-premise license for SAP Master Data Governance on SAP S/4HANA.
- Deployment: Deployed from scratch or by leveraging the quick-start approach.
- Upgrades: Customer IT and project team manage the upgrade and the post-upgrade regression testing.
- Scope Functional scope of SAP Master Data Governance on SAP S/4HANA.
- Extensibility: no restrictions on extensions and enhancements to the SAP Master Data Governance solution.

This has been the traditional way of deploying SAP Master Data Governance and, unless explicitly called out, all the functional and technical capabilities described in this book are available with this version of the SAP Master Data Governance solution.

- **Private cloud deployment: SAP Master Data Governance on SAP S/4HANA Cloud, private edition**

  In this approach, the SAP Master Data Governance solution is deployed on a cloud infrastructure environment operated and managed by SAP; the customer is able to get all the benefits of using SAP Master Data Governance without having to worry about the maintenance of the system. SAP Master Data Governance on SAP S/4HANA Cloud, private edition, comes with the following characteristics:

  - Infrastructure: Dedicated (not shared) landscape on cloud infrastructure operated by SAP (either on an SAP infrastructure or on a hyperscaler infrastructure).
  - License: Subscription for SAP Master Data Governance software.
  - Deployment: Deployment from scratch or by leveraging the quick-start approach.
  - Upgrades: SAP and customer together manage the upgrade process and the regression testing.
  - Scope: Same functional scope as SAP Master Data Governance on SAP S/4HANA.
  - Extensibility: Extension and customer-specific enhancements possible as in SAP Master Data Governance on SAP S/4HANA (in-app extensions).

Note

Irrespective of whether you choose SAP Master Data Governance on SAP S/4HANA or SAP Master Data Governance Cloud on SAP S/4HANA, private edition, the functional scope of the solution is the same.

Besides the previously mentioned options, SAP Master Data Governance is available in public cloud deployment options as listed here.

- **SAP S/4HANA Cloud for master data governance**
  This solution provides data governance capabilities within the SAP S/4HANA public cloud solution. The capabilities of this solution are a subset of the total SAP Master Data Governance capabilities you would have from the SAP Master Data Governance on SAP S/4HANA version. This solution is generally suitable when you want to manage data locally within your SAP S/4HANA Cloud system.

  Important to remember that being a public cloud solution, this solution is hosted in a shared, managed landscape, with minimal capabilities to do in-app extension. SAP Master Data Governance on SAP S/4HANA Cloud supports supplier, customer, and product master data and includes capabilities for consolidation, mass processing, and data quality management.

- **SAP Master Data Governance, cloud edition**
  SAP Master Data Governance, cloud edition, is the latest addition to the SAP Master Data Governance offering portfolio and is a native public cloud version of SAP Master Data Governance. It comes with a subset of capabilities of the SAP Master Data Governance on SAP S/4HANA version and is seen more as a complementary deployment option to SAP Master Data Governance on SAP S/4HANA.

  The main focus of this solution is the governance of the core attributes of the master data object in an enterprise-wide landscape. As a SaaS offering, it provides companies with a quick entry option into master data management, and it's inherently built to support a federated deployment of SAP Master Data Governance.

  Being a public cloud solution, it's to be consumed in a SaaS model and features limited in-app extensions. The solution currently supports the business partner data model and can be used for consolidation, mass processing, governance, and data quality management use cases. The data models are also aligned to the SAP One Domain Model approach explained in Chapter 1, Section 1.3.8.

  Chapter 3 of this book is dedicated to this deployment option and provides a detailed walk through of its capabilities.

Note

These public cloud deployment options for SAP Master Data Governance have a different and limited scope compared to SAP Master Data Governance on SAP S/4HANA. In addition, the scope and purpose of both the public cloud deployment options of SAP Master Data Governance are different from each other.

4.2 Summary

In this chapter, we discussed the various deployment options, namely, such as hub and co-deployment, for SAP Master Data Governance and went into the details on how certain important settings such as number ranges can be configured in an SAP Master Data Governance landscape. We discussed how the deployment approach impacts the flow of Customizing/reference data and various tools and techniques available in synchronizing them in an SAP Master Data Governance landscape. We also compared the on-premise and cloud deployment options available for SAP Master Data Governance. We touched on the quick-Start approach, which is a rapid way of deploying your SAP Master Data Governance system and kick-starting your SAP Master Data Governance implementation journey and its benefits.

The next chapters provide more in-depth details in each of the important areas of SAP Master Data Governance, and we recommend that you refer to both the Table of Contents and the Preface if you're looking for a particular topic.

Chapter 5
Central Governance: Data Modeling

This chapter provides a view into data modeling concepts, including different storage areas and storage types, as well as insights into delivered data models. We'll also discuss entities, attributes, and the relationships between entities. SAP Master Data Governance provides various options to enhance the delivered data models based on business needs.

In previous chapters, we introduced the concept of master data management and SAP's master data management product—SAP Master Data Governance—including how it fits into the overall portfolio of enterprise information management (EIM) products. This chapter introduces the concept of data modeling in SAP Master Data Governance and provides an overview of SAP-delivered data models and their configuration.

The following data models are delivered by SAP as part of SAP Master Data Governance:

- **Material (MM)**
  For governing material master data.
- **Business partner (BP)**
  For governing business partner, customer, supplier, and contract accounts.
- **Financials (0G)**
  For governing financial master data, such as general ledger accounts, cost centers, profit centers, internal orders, and so on.

Note

The following data models are offered as partner solutions developed by Utopia:

- SAP Master Data Governance, retail and fashion management extension by Utopia
- SAP Master Data Governance, enterprise asset management extension by Utopia

---

SAP also provides a framework for extending the data models to create custom data models. Extending SAP delivered data models is explained in Section 5.4 of this chapter, and creating custom data models is explained in Chapter 11, Section 11.2. Let's begin by exploring the data modeling process in SAP Master Data Governance.

5.1   Introduction to Data Modeling in SAP Master Data Governance

A key aspect of governing master data is the ability for all roles involved in the end-to-end governance process to manipulate data collaboratively in a staging environment. Therefore, data currently being used or ready to be used in transactions must be separated from data involved in a governance process. There are two storage areas in the context of SAP Master Data Governance:

- **Staging area**
  Contains data currently in a governance process and has an associated change request.

- **Active area**
  Contains data ready to be consumed by other applications or ready to be distributed to other systems.

In the following sections, we begin with the steps to create or change master data to understand the concept of change requests and staging data versus active data. In the sections that follow, we'll discuss the various elements of data modeling and go through the related configuration steps.

5.1.1   Master Data Create/Change Process

Figure 5.1 illustrates a simple master data create/change process. First, the requester initiates a *change request* for creating or changing a master data record. (We'll discuss the concept of change request in detail in Chapter 7.)

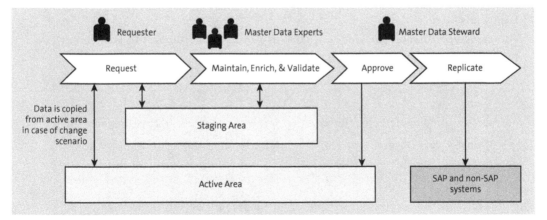

Figure 5.1 Staging and Active Area Concept for Master Data Create Scenario

We'll explore two main scenarios, as follows:

- **Create scenario**
  In a create scenario, request details along with data entered by the requester are stored in the staging area after the requester submits the change request.

- **Change scenario**
  In a change scenario, the master data record is copied from the active area into the staging area, and changes made by the requester, along with change request details, are stored in the staging area.

Master data experts further maintain, enrich, and validate the record to ensure that the master data record submitted by the requester follows data quality rules. During this process, data is read from the staging area and saved back into the staging area if any data changes were made.

The master data steward processes the change request and does the final approval. In this process, the master data record is read from the staging area and is updated into the active area after the final approval step. This process is also known as *activation*. At this point, the master data record is ready to be consumed by any other applications if SAP Master Data Governance is installed in a co-deployment scenario. If SAP Master Data Governance is installed as a hub, once activated, data is ready for replication to other SAP or non-SAP systems.

The active areas in SAP Master Data Governance can be in either flex mode or the reuse active area, as described here:

- **Flex mode**
  In this mode, a new set of database tables is generated when the data model is defined. This mode is used when there are no corresponding SAP S/4HANA or SAP ERP tables or when the activated data in SAP Master Data Governance is intended to be isolated from SAP S/4HANA and SAP ERP tables. If required, data can be replicated to SAP S/4HANA and SAP ERP master data tables. An example of such a scenario is standard SAP Master Data Governance, Financials, objects. All SAP Master Data Governance, Financials, objects are delivered in flex mode to isolate them from financials tables and are only replicated when needed to SAP S/4HANA and SAP ERP master data tables or to transactional SAP S/4HANA and SAP ERP systems if SAP Master Data Governance is deployed as a hub.

- **Reuse active area**
  In this mode, existing SAP S/4HANA and SAP ERP tables are used. As an example, for a material master, these are reuse active area tables MARA, MARC, MARD, and so on. Figure 5.2 shows the difference between the flex and reuse modes of a data model. Data models for material masters and business partners are delivered in the reuse active area mode, which means that after a change request is activated, the corresponding SAP S/4HANA and SAP ERP master data tables are updated.

Data modeling in SAP Master Data Governance involves various elements, such as entity types, attributes, and relationships. Every master data object that needs to be governed using SAP Master Data Governance requires a data model and user interface (UI) to be built on top of it. Every data model in SAP Master Data Governance has several generated database tables that store data during the governance process.

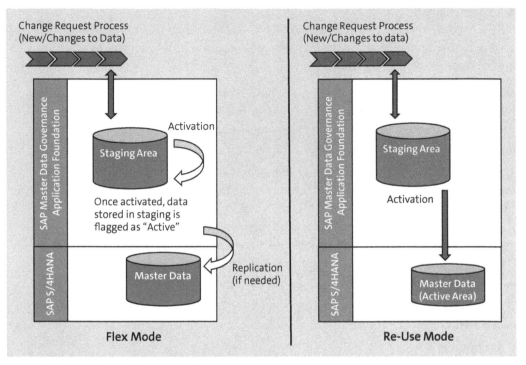

Figure 5.2 Flex and Reuse Modes

> **Note**
>
> In flex mode, the generated database tables use the USMD_ACTIVE field to identify whether the master data record is currently being processed in a change request or is already activated. After the record is activated, data is retained in these tables.
>
> In reuse mode, on the other hand, after a record is activated, data is removed from the generated database tables and moved to reuse active master data tables (e.g., table MARA, table MARC, etc., in the material master).

5.1.2   Entity Types

Different types of master data in a data model are represented by different entity types. SAP Master Data Governance automatically generates the database tables needed for master data processing. Every data model has at least one entity type. An important property of an entity type is **Storage/Usage Type**, which determines the type of information stored, whether entities belonging to an entity type are changeable via a change request or via entities belonging to other entity types, and whether database tables are generated or reused from the active area. The following four storage or usage types are available:

- **1 - Changeable via Change Request; Generated Database Tables**
  This storage and usage type is used for main entities in the data model that are under governance. These entities are linked to change request types (Chapter 7 describes change request types in detail), and data stored in these can be changed via change requests. These entities have persistence, and SAP Master Data Governance automatically generates all necessary database tables, including check tables, text tables, and additional tables needed to store attachments and sets, for example. Key fields of this storage/usage type include the entity type itself, edition (if relevant), and other entity types linked to this entity type via relationships. The `material` entity in the material master data model is an example of a type 1 entity, as shown in Figure 5.3.

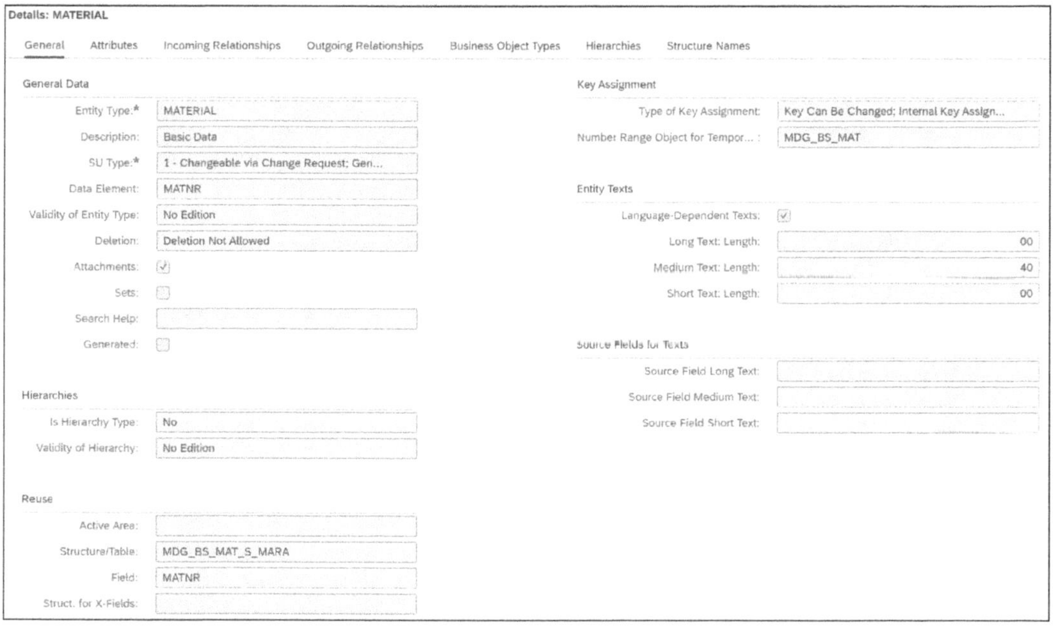

Figure 5.3 Example: Type 1 Entity Type

- **2 - Changeable w/o Change Request; Generated Check/Text Tables**
  This storage and usage type is used for check tables that have persistence in SAP Master Data Governance. Data stored in this storage or usage type can be changed without a change request. SAP Master Data Governance generates only the check tables and text tables with the entity type, as well as with the entity types assigned to the entity type, through leading relationships as fixed key fields. The `DISPO` entity in the business partner data model is an example of a type 2 entity type.

- **3 - Not Changeable via MDG; No Generated Tables**
  This storage and usage type is used for check tables that have no persistence in SAP Master Data Governance. Data stored in this storage or usage type can't be changed

in SAP Master Data Governance. The AKONT entity in the business partner data model is an example of a type 3 entity type.

- **4 - Changeable via Other Entity Type; Generated Database Tables**
  This storage and usage type is used for maintaining dependent data (e.g., plant data for material master and company code, sales data for customer master) and can only be maintained together with an entity of type 1. This entity type needs to be in a relationship with the relationship type leading and assigned as the to-entity type to an entity type with storage and usage type 1. The system generates the check table as described for storage and usage type 1 but also generates the entity types that are assigned through qualifying relationships as key fields. The MARCBASIC entity in the material master data model is an example of a type 4 entity type.

An entity type can have the properties listed in Table 5.1.

Property	Explanation
General Data	
Entity Type	Name of the entity type.
Description	Language-dependent description of the entity type.
SU Type	Determines the generation of database tables for storage of master data.
Data Element	Determines properties such as **Data Type** and **Length** for the entity type to which it's assigned. Data types are restricted to **CHAR**, **NUMC**, or **CUKY**, and length is restricted to 45 characters. Data elements can't be assigned to entity types of storage/usage type 4. Storage/usage types also decide how to represent values if a value table or domain fixed values exist.
Validity of Entity Type	Determines whether the entity type is edition dependent.
Deletion	Determines whether deletion is allowed for the entities of this entity type via the change request process.
Attachments	When selected, attachments can be stored to entities of this entity type, and the system automatically provides a data store for storing these attachments. This can only be selected for entities with storage/usage type 1.
Sets	When selected, sets can be stored to entities of this entity type, and the system automatically provides a data store for this purpose.

Table 5.1 Properties of an Entity Type

Property	Explanation
Search Help	When a search help is assigned to a field, the input help executes the search help instead of reading the data in the check table or the fixed values of the domain of the data element. You should only use search help as an exception.
Generated	Specifies whether entity types were generated or manually created, and those entity types that are generated can't be changed or deleted via the **Edit Data Model** Customizing activity.
Hierarchies	
Is Hierarchy Type	Determines whether an entity type defines a hierarchy, whether hierarchies have versions, and whether they are synchronized.
Validity of Hierarchy	If the Is **Hierarchies Type** option is set to have a version, then this property determines the validity of the hierarchy.
Reuse	
Active Area	When a reuse active area is specified, the system stores active data solely in this reuse active area. The reuse active area can be assigned either at the data model level or at the entity type. When defined at the data model level, all entity types defined in that data model inherit the reuse active area. However, if a separate reuse active area for an entity type is specified at the entity type level, then it overrides the setting inherited from the data model.
Structure/Table	Used to establish the link between an entity type, attribute, or relationship, and a structure or database table defined in the ABAP Dictionary.
Field	Used to establish the link between an attribute or relationship and a field defined in the ABAP Dictionary that is part of a structure or a database table.
Struct. for X-Fields	Used to establish the link between an entity type and an associated structure defined in the ABAP Dictionary that contains a checkbox with type **CHAR** and **Length 1**, with values space and **X** for each resolved attribute.
Key Assignment	
Type of Key Assignment	The following options are available and determine how the key of the entity will be entered during the change request process: ■ **Key Cannot Be Changed; No Internal Key Assignment**: In this case, there is no internal key generation possible, and the user needs to maintain the key manually. After it's maintained, the key can't be changed.

Table 5.1 Properties of an Entity Type (Cont.)

Property	Explanation
Type of Key Assignment (Cont.)	▪ **Internal Key Assignment Only**: SAP Master Data Governance automatically assigns an internal number upon activation of the change request. During the change request process, SAP Master Data Governance assigns a temporary key. ▪ **Key Can Be Changed; No Internal Key Assignment**: The key of the entity needs to be explicitly defined. However, it can be changed as long as the change request isn't activated. ▪ **Key Can Be Changed; Internal Key Assignment Possible**: Either the system can automatically generate a number during the change request activation, or the user can define his own key.
Number Range Object for Temporary Keys	Number range object for specifying temporary keys. For example, the MDG_BS_MAT number range object is specified for the MATERIAL entity type.
Entity Texts	
Language-Dependent Texts	Indicates whether the entity type can have language-dependent texts. Based on this selection, the system automatically includes **Language** as a key field when the database tables are generated for this entity type.
Long Text: Length	Determines the visible length of long text in the UI for this entity type.
Medium Text: Length	Determines the visible length of medium text in the UI for this entity type.
Short Text: Length	Determines the visible length of short text in the UI for this entity type.
Source Fields for Texts	
Source Field Long Text	Applicable to storage/usage type 3 entity types. Determines the check table field that contains long text.
Source Field Medium Text	Applicable to storage/usage type 3 entity types. Determines the check table field that contains medium text.
Source Field Short Text	Applicable to storage/usage type 3 entity types. Determines the check table field that contains short text.

Table 5.1 Properties of an Entity Type (Cont.)

The following is a summary of all storage/usage types:

▪ **Storage type 1:**

  – This storage type is used for entity types that are maintained in SAP Master Data Governance.

- Maintenance is performed via change requests, and these entity types act as entry points for change requests.
- Data storage is generated.
- Additional data modeling is possible and can have attributes and references.
- Data elements such as data type, length, field label, and so on can be assigned.
- Check table and domain fixed values associated with the data element are ignored.
- ⌐F4⌐ is determined based on entries in generated check tables.

- **Storage type 2:**
  - This storage type is used for entity types that can't be maintained in SAP Master Data Governance via change requests but still can be maintained using other means, such as the SAP Master Data Governance file upload mechanism.
  - Data storage is generated.
  - Additional data modeling isn't possible; associated check and text tables are generated.
  - No maintenance occurs via change requests.
  - Mandatory data element assignment occurs for data type, length, field label, and so on.
  - Check tables and domain fixed values associated with the data elements are ignored.
  - ⌐F4⌐ is determined based on entries in the generated check tables.

- **Storage type 3:**
  - This storage type is used for entity types that can't be maintained in SAP Master Data Governance using either the change request process or any other means.
  - No data storage is generated.
  - Additional data modeling isn't possible.
  - No maintenance occurs in SAP Master Data Governance.
  - Mandatory data element assignment occurs for data type, length, field label, and so on.
  - Check table and domain fixed values associated with the data element are used.
  - ⌐F4⌐ is determined based on entries in associated check/text tables and/or domain fixed values associated with the data element. Non-key fields in check tables are ignored.

- **Storage type 4:**
  - This storage type is used for entity types that are maintained in SAP Master Data Governance in the context of another entity type.

- Maintenance is performed via change requests, but these entity types can't act as entry points for the change request. Maintenance is possible via owning the storage type 1 entity type.
- Data storage is generated.
- Additional data modeling is possible and can have attributes and references.

5.1.3   Attributes

An attribute defines a property of an entity type, and an attribute is defined for each property. Alternatively, an attribute can be defined as a storage/usage type 3 entity and linked to the entity type via a relationship (see the next section for details on relationships). An attribute can be defined only for storage/usage type 1 or 4 entity types. Every attribute can have the properties listed in Table 5.2.

Property	Explanation
Attribute	Name of attribute.
Key Field	Indicator to identify attribute as a key field.
Data Element	Determines properties such as data type, length, and field label displayed on the UI and field help for input fields for the attribute to which it's assigned. The domain assigned to the data element determines the allowed values for the value help and the validation of values, either from the domain fixed values or from the assigned check table or text table. If there is no check table or fixed values assigned to the domain, then no input help is available, and no validation is carried out.
Required Entry	Indicator to identify whether the attribute is required for data entry.
Currency/UoM	Currency or unit of measure (UoM) field if the attribute requires a currency or UoM.
Search Help	When a search help is assigned to a field, the input help executes the search help instead of reading the data in the check table or the fixed values of the domain of the data element. Search helps should only be used as an exception.
No Existence Check	Used for deactivating the existence check for attribute values. However, existence checks can't be suppressed for values that are derived from domain fixed values.
Description	Description of attribute.

Table 5.2 Properties of an Attribute

Property	Explanation
Structure/Table	Used to establish the link between an entity type, attribute, or relationship, and a structure or database table defined in the ABAP Dictionary.
Field	Used to establish the link between an attribute or relationship and a field defined in the ABAP Dictionary that is part of a structure or a database table.
Generated	Specifies whether the attribute was generated or manually created, and those attributes that are generated can't be changed or deleted via the **Edit Data Model** Customizing activity.

Table 5.2 Properties of an Attribute (Cont.)

5.1.4 Relationships

If more than one entity type is defined in a data model, a relationship between entity types can be established. A relationship represents a link between entity types. Every relationship has a relationship type and cardinality. Relationship types determine whether one entity type (from-entity type) is at a higher level than another entity type (to-entity type), or whether it should be copied as an attribute of the other entity type in the check table.

The following relationship types are available:

- **Referencing**
  This relationship type is used to specify the from-entity type as an attribute of the to-entity type.

- **Leading**
  If this relationship type is used, then the from-entity type is on a higher level than the to-entity type.

- **Qualifying**
  This relationship type is similar to the leading relationship type with the exception that the qualifying relationship is possible when the to-entity type is of storage/usage type 4.

- **Foreign key relationship**
  This relationship type is used if certain attributes or key fields of the to-entity type use the from-entity type as a foreign key.

Figure 5.4 provides a summary of leading, qualifying, and referencing relationship types.

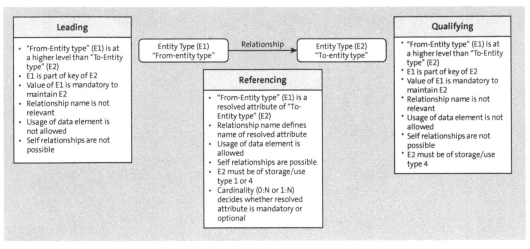

Figure 5.4 Summary of Relationship Types

5.1.5   Hierarchies

SAP Master Data Governance offers modeling hierarchies based on configurations of the entity types. The definition of hierarchies includes setting the hierarchies as edition dependent and synchronous. If a hierarchy is set up for an entity type, the system automatically generates database tables for storing hierarchies. Refer to the hierarchy-related properties explained earlier in Table 5.1. The following sections explain each of these hierarchy-related properties in detail.

Hierarchies Property

The **Is Hierarchy Type** property of an entity type determines whether the entity type defines a hierarchy. If used, it also determines whether the property is version-dependent or synchronized:

- **Version-dependent**
  Version dependency enables a hierarchy to have multiple versions. Hierarchy versions can be defined under Customizing by following the IMG path, **MDGIMG • Process Modeling • Hierarchies • Create Hierarchy Versions**.

- **Synchronized**
  In a synchronized hierarchy, the substructure defined will remain the same throughout. A different structure can't be defined within the same hierarchy or in a different hierarchy for the same entity.

The **Hierarchies** property allows for a combination of version dependent and synchronous hierarchies. Following are the available options:

- **No Hierarchy** (hierarchy can't be set up for the entity type)
- **Yes – Version-Dependent/Synchronized**
- **Yes – Not Version-Dependent/Synchronized**
- **Yes – Not Version-Dependent/Not Synchronized**
- **Yes – Version-Dependent/Not Synchronized**

Validity of Hierarchies

This property is applicable in scenarios where the **Is Hierarchy Type** property is set to have version-dependent hierarchies. Using the property, an entity type can be set to have **Edition** or **No Edition**, and the system uses the edition to delimit the validity of the hierarchy. In such scenarios, an edition needs to be assigned to the hierarchy-defining entity type during hierarchy processing.

Apart from the preceding two properties that are available at the entity type level, there are additional configurations that complete the entire hierarchy setup.

Entity Types for Hierarchies

Using this configuration, you can model the role of additional entity types that are part of a hierarchy setup for a selected entity type. This configuration can be maintained using the IMG path, **MDGIMG • General Settings • Data Modeling • Edit Data Model**, and then selecting the **Entity Types for Hierarchies** view under **Entity Types**.

The following options are available for each entity type in the hierarchy setup:

- **Hierarchy Name**
  If this usage is selected for an entity type, then such entities act as root nodes for a hierarchy and hence define the hierarchy name. For any entity type, to complete a hierarchy setup, an additional entity type needs to be defined with this usage. Such an entity type can't be used as a to-entity type in a leading relationship.

- **No Special Use**
  If entity types are defined with this usage, then they can be used as actual nodes and as lower-level hierarchy nodes in a hierarchy.

- **Ranges Permitted on End Nodes**
  An entity type that is used as a lower node in a hierarchy can have a range of values.

Hierarchy Attribute and Hierarchy Attribute from Reference

Hierarchy attributes can be defined for each relationship between nodes in a hierarchy. These hierarchy attributes are available during hierarchy processing:

- **Hierarchy Attribute**
  Hierarchy attribute for a relationship between nodes is set using data elements.

- **Hierarchy Attribute from Reference**
  Hierarchy attribute for a relationship between nodes is set using a reference to an entity type.

Figure 5.5 shows an example of hierarchy attributes defined for an entity type consolidation group with an **Entity Type** of node consolidation unit (**CONSUNIT**) from **Data Model 0G**.

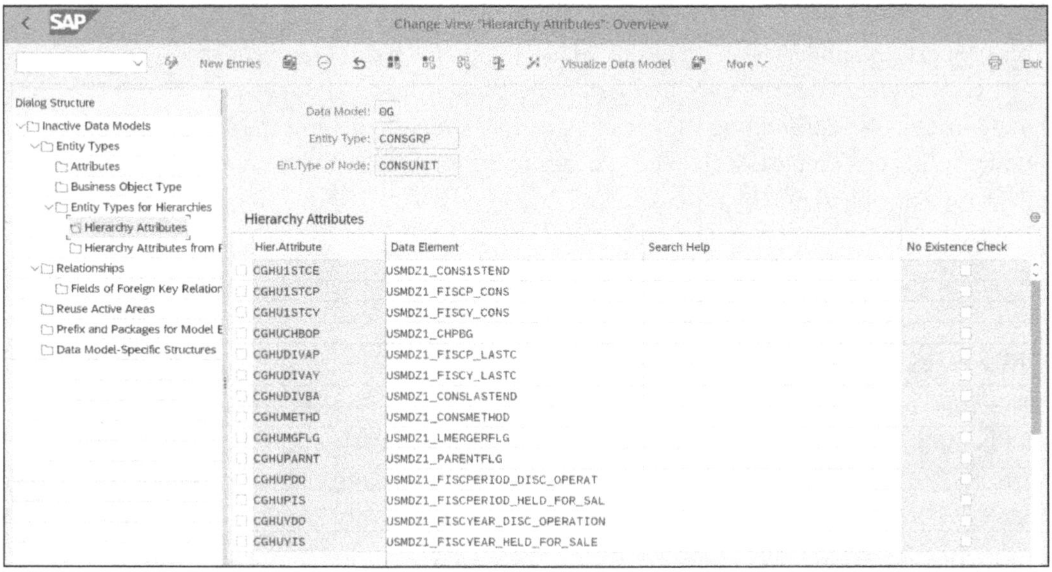

Figure 5.5 Example: Hierarchy Attribute

See Section 5.3.2 to understand how the business partner hierarchy is set up in the business partner data model. Chapter 7, Section 7.4.4, provides details on how to create a hierarchy using an example.

5.1.6   Entity Relationship Model Diagram

As basic data model building blocks were explained in previous sections, this section explains how each of the building blocks comes together to form a data model. This is explained using an entity relationship model (ERM) diagram, as shown in Figure 5.6. The following are some important aspects of a data model and its associated building blocks:

- A data model can have more than one entity type.
- A data model can have many relationships defined.

- An entity type can have one or more attributes.
- Many attributes can have the same data element.
- An entity type can occur in multiple hierarchies.
- Two entity types can have many relationships.

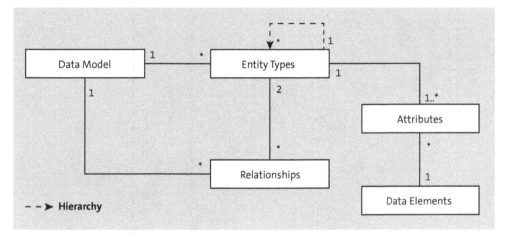

Figure 5.6 ERM Diagram of a Data Model

5.2   Configuring Data Models

SAP Master Data Governance offers all data modeling–related Customizing activities grouped under Transaction MDGIMG. In this section, we'll review all available Customizing nodes under the **Data Modeling** section of Transaction MDGIMG.

5.2.1   Define Business Object Type Codes and Entity Types

In this Customizing activity, new business object type codes can be added for custom data models. For all standard data models, there is no need to add any new business type object codes because SAP has already delivered these. The IMG path for accessing this activity is **MDGIMG • Data Modeling • Define Business Object Type Codes**. Figure 5.7 shows the business object type codes.

If two or more entity types are assigned to the same business object type code, you can specify which entity types should be used by the business object type code. The IMG path for accessing this activity is **MDGIMG • Data Modeling • Define Entity Type to Be Used by Business Object Type**.

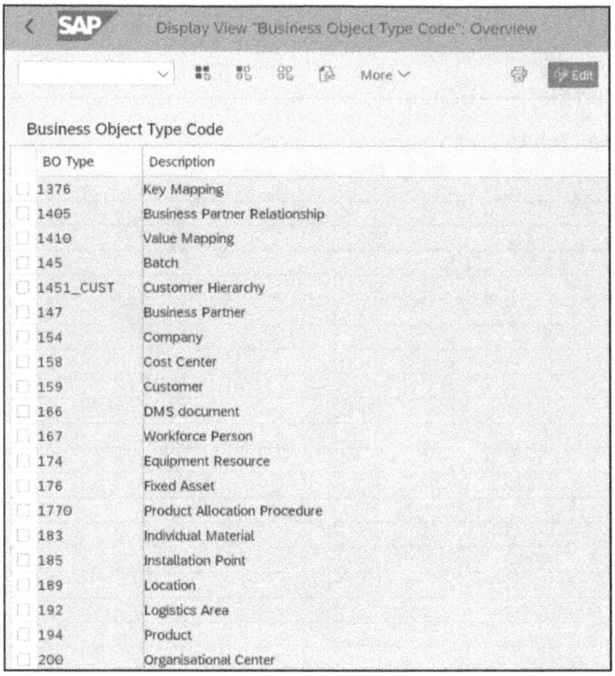

Figure 5.7 Business Object Type Codes

5.2.2 Define Prefixes for Internal Key Assignment

In a data model, when an entity type with internal number assignment is used, a temporary key number range assignment is required (refer to the **Key Assignment** options in Table 5.1). For example, the MATERIAL entity in the material master data model uses the MDG_BS_MAT number range object for temporary keys. Similarly, the BP_HEADER entity type in the business partner data model uses the MDG_BP number range object.

Using this Customizing activity, a prefix can be assigned to the temporary number generated for internal number assignment scenarios to indicate that the generated number is a temporary number (see Figure 5.8). SAP Master Data Governance has **$** as the default **Prefix**, which can be changed if needed. The menu path for accessing this is **MDGIMG • Data Modeling • Define Prefixes for Internal Key Assignment**.

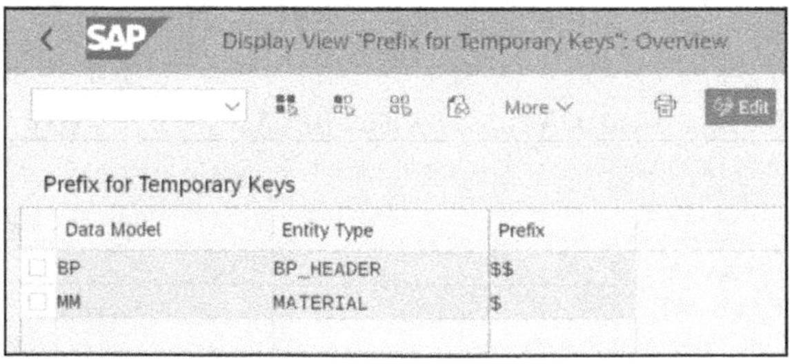

Figure 5.8 Prefix for Temporary Keys

5.2.3   Edit Data Model

This Customizing activity provides an entry point for the entire list of data models available in the system and the list of entities, attributes, and relationships. Various views available in this Customizing activity enable you to extend or create new data models and activate them. The system uses the data model to generate database tables.

This activity can be accessed using two different IMG paths, and each path offers a different way to define or edit data models. Both options, described here, provide a way to access the list of assigned active areas and associated access classes at the data model level:

- **Edit data model functionality using SAP GUI**
  Figure 5.9 shows the business partner data model as an example using this IMG path. This Customizing activity also provides additional functionalities such as **Visualize Data Model** and **Adjust Staging Area of Linked Change Requests**. See the list of reports provided later in this section for additional details.

  The menu path for accessing this is **MDGIMG • Data Modeling • Edit Data Model**.

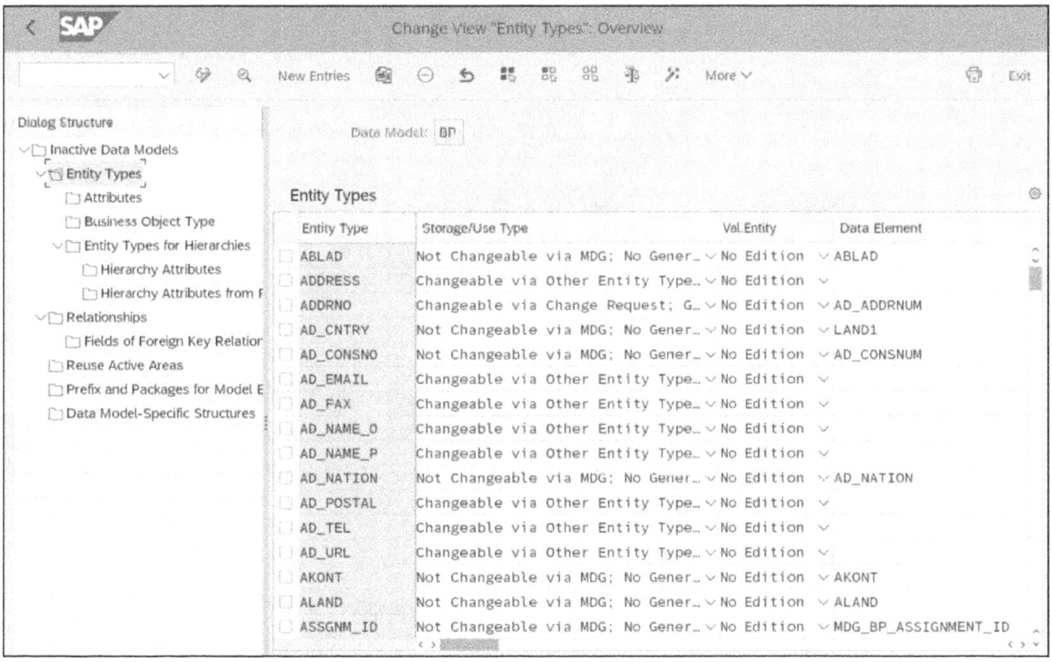

Figure 5.9 Business Partner Data Model: Edit Data Model

- **Configuration Workbench**
  The Configuration Workbench is a Web Dynpro application that acts as an alternative to the **Edit Data Model** Customizing activity. The Configuration Workbench includes all the functions that the **Edit Data Model** Customizing activity provides, presents data model details in a tabular format per entity type, and distinguishes

relationship information into outgoing and incoming relationships for each entity. The Configuration Workbench can also be accessed using Transaction MDGDT.

Figure 5.10 shows the business partner data model using the Configuration Workbench.

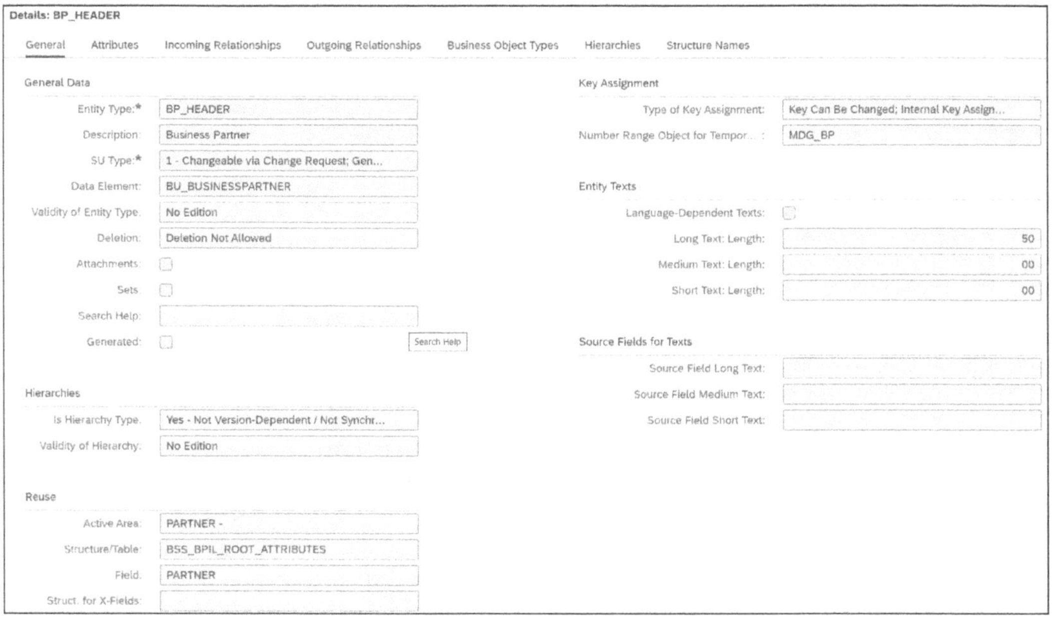

Figure 5.10 Business Partner Data Model: Configuration Workbench

SAP Master Data Governance offers several reports related to data models; the most commonly used are as follows:

- **Visualize Data Model (report USMD_DISPLAY_DATA_MODEL)**
  This report offers a hierarchical view of entity types and attributes in a data model. This report also offers overview, detail view, and graphical display modes as well. Figure 5.11 shows the output of this report for the business partner data model as an example.

- **Data Model Generated Tables (report USMD_DATA_MODEL)**
  This report displays data model entity types and generated database tables. It's also possible to display counts of active and inactive records for each of these tables.

- **Compare Data Model (report USMD_COMPARE_DATA_MODEL)**
  This report compares active and inactive versions of a data model and provides a list of comparison results.

- **Delete Data Model (report USMD_DELETE_DATA_MODEL)**
  This report can be used to delete a data model. This functionality can also be triggered from the **Edit Data Model** IMG node or the Configuration Workbench. However, you should exercise caution because this report deletes the entire data model.

- **Adjust Staging Area of Linked Change Requests (report USMD_ADJUST_STAGING)**
  For the selected data model, this report verifies whether any changes were made to the data model; if yes, it adjusts the change requests that are in process per the changes made in the data model. This report needs to be run in all relevant clients and target systems after data model changes.

Data Model	Name	Field Type	Sto...	Data Element	Referenced Entity Type
∨ BP					
∨ FKKVK	Contract Account				
FKKVK	Contract Account	Entity Type Itself	☑	MDG_FICA_VKONT	
APPLK	Application Area	Attribute	☐	MDG_FICA_APPLK	
FKK_LOEVM	Deletion Flag	Attribute	☐	MDG_FICA_LOEVM	
TXTMI	Description (medium text)	Attribute	☐	USMD_TXTMI	
VKBEZ_UPP	Contract Acct Name	Attribute	☐	MDG_FICA_VKBEZ_UPPERCASE	
VKONA	CtrAcct in LegacySys	Attribute	☐	MDG_FICA_VKONA	
VKTYP	Contract Acct Categ.	Attribute	☐	MDG_FICA_VKTYP	
> FKKVKTD	Contract Account (Time ...				
> FKKTAXEX	Tax Exemptions (Contra...				
∨ BP_SUBHRY	Lower-Level Hierarchy				
BP_SUBHRY	Structure Node	Entity Type Itself	☑	BU_SUBHIERARCHY	
TXTLG	Description (long text)	Attribute	☐	USMD_TXTLG	
∨ BP_REL	DP Relationship				
BP_REL	Relationship Cat.	Entity Type Itself	☑	BU_RELTYP	
PARTNER1	Business partner 1	Key Attribute	☐	BU_PARTNER1	
PARTNER2	Business Partner 2	Key Attribute	☐	BU_PARTNER2	
XDFREL	Standard	Attribute	☐	BU_XDFREL	
> BP_CPGEN	BP relationship contact p...				
∨ BP_HRCHY	Hierarchy				
BP_HRCHY	BPartner Hierarchy	Entity Type Itself	☑	BU_BUSINESSPARTNER_HIER...	
TXTLG	Description (long text)	Attribute	☐	USMD_TXTLG	
∨ BP_HEADER	Business Partner				
BP_HEADER	Business Partner ID	Entity Type Itself	☑	BU_BUSINESSPARTNER	
BP_GUID	BP_GUID	Attribute	☐	CHAR32	
BU_GROUP	Grouping	Attribute	☐	BU_GROUP	
BU_TYPE	BP Category	Attribute	☐	BU_TYPE	
TXTLG	Description (long text)	Attribute	☐	USMD_TXTLG	
> FS_BPTAXC	Tax Compliance				
> FS_BPBANK	Partner is Bank				
> FS_BP1030	Reporting Data				
> FS_BP1012	Ratings				

Figure 5.11 Output of Report USMD_DISPLAY_DATA_MODEL for the Business Partner Data Model

5.2.4   Define Authorization Relevance per Entity Type

This Customizing activity (see Figure 5.12) is used to determine whether the system uses predefined authorizations from the reuse active area or SAP Master Data Governance–specific authorizations using authorization object USMD_MDAT. By default, the system always uses predefined authorizations from the reuse active area. If the option to select SAP Master Data Governance–specific attributes is chosen, then configurations for authorizations at the entity type level and authorization-relevant attributes need to be set up. Note the following:

- If the reuse active area is used, then settings made under **Authorization for Entity Types** and **Authorization-Relevant Attributes** views will be ignored.
- SAP S/4HANA and SAP ERP authorization checks are always performed for the business partner and material master data models; any additional settings performed under this Customizing activity aren't supported.

The menu path for accessing this activity is **MDGIMG · Data Modeling · Define Authorization Relevance per Entity Type**.

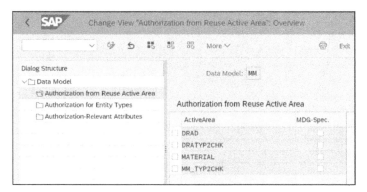

Figure 5.12 Define Authorizations per Entity Type and Attributes

5.2.5 Generate Data Model-Specific Structures

Each data model and entity type can have the following structures in the Data Dictionary:

- PDF-based forms with structures used for the configuration of enterprise services
- Mapping between staging area and reuse active area
- Data replication framework
- Enterprise search
- Field control of attributes
- Field properties of attributes and key fields
- Key fields

This Customizing activity is used to generate the preceding data model–specific structures. These structures need to be regenerated whenever a data model is changed. For all standard data models, these structures are delivered as well. The IMG path for accessing this activity is **MDGIMG · Data Modeling · Generate Data Model-Specific Structures**.

5.2.6   Assign Package and Define Package Groups

When an entity type delivered by SAP is enhanced to include additional attributes, the system automatically writes these attributes to Customizing includes during the generation of data model–specific structures explained in the previous section. In this Customizing activity, a package can be assigned for the Customizing includes used during data model enhancements. The IMG path for accessing this activity is **MDGIMG · Data Modeling · Assign Package for Customizing Include**.

This Customizing activity has views for structures as well as mapping for each data model. Figure 5.13 shows the material master data model structures as an example.

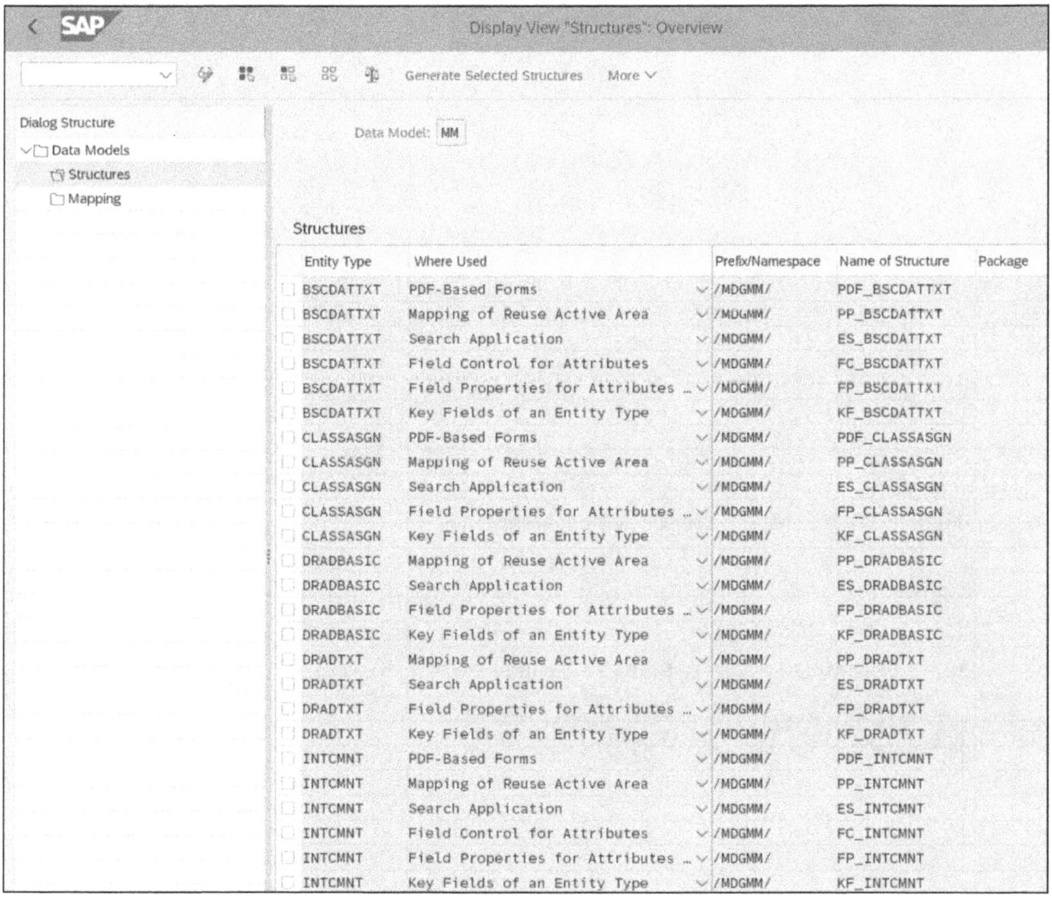

Figure 5.13 Material Master Data Model Structures

Figure 5.14 shows **SMT Mapping from Active Area** and **SMT Mapping to Active Area** for the material master data model as an example.

You can also define package groups that consist of one or more packages. A package group can be assigned to a mapping (see the next section). The F4 help of the transformation tool displays only classes that are contained in one of the specified packages.

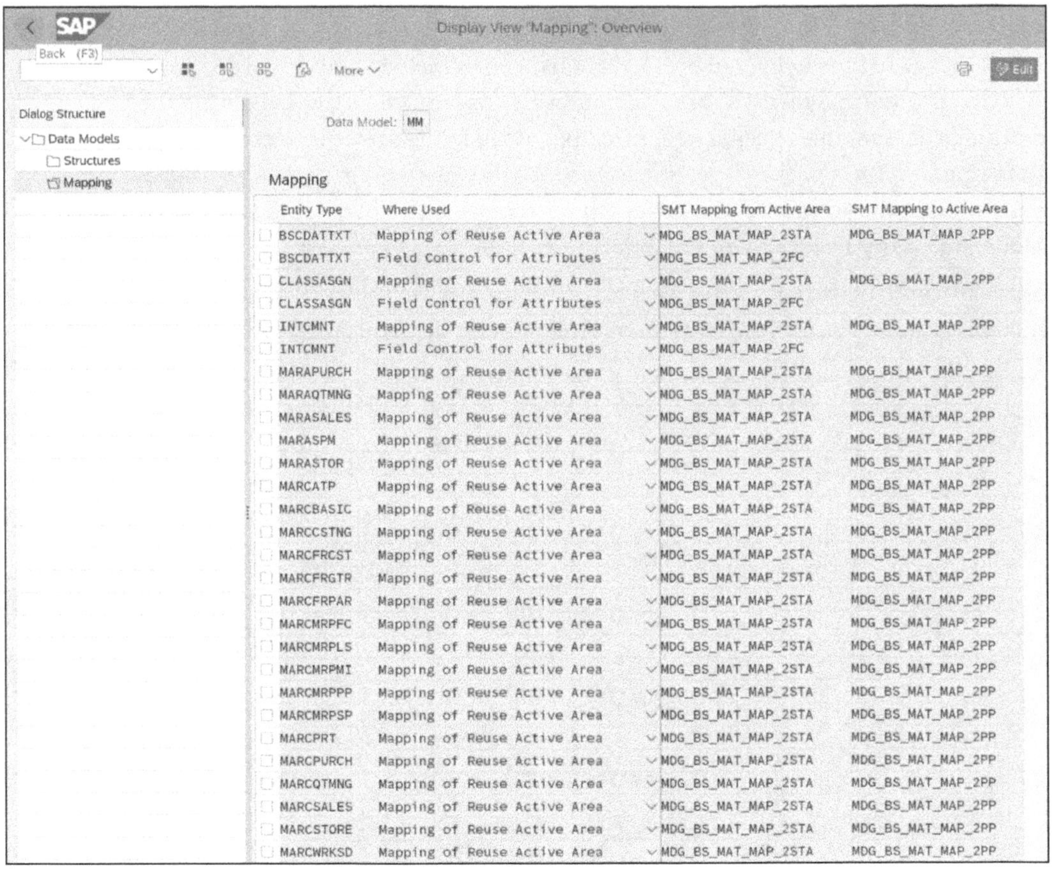

Figure 5.14 Material Master Data Model Mappings

Figure 5.15 shows an example of a package assignment to a material master **Package Group MDG_BS_MM**. The IMG path for accessing this activity is **MDGIMG • Data Modeling • Create and Edit Mappings • Define Package Groups**.

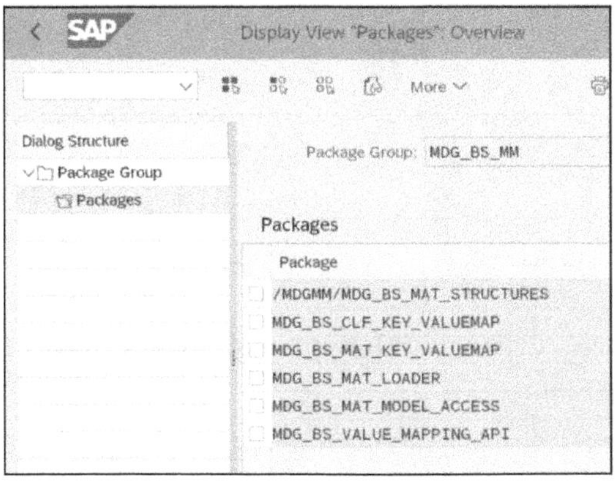

Figure 5.15 An Example of Package Assignment to a Package Group

5.2.7 Service Mapping Tool

You need to understand a bit more about SMT before moving on to the following sections. SMT is a program that enables you to fill target structures using sets of source structures. SMT supports simple and complex mappings, mappings with field transformations, and field checks. The main uses of SMT are to transform SAP internal format to enterprise services format and vice versa.

Figure 5.16 shows an example of mapping for the MDG_BS_MAT_MAP_2STA structure and associated mapping steps. Refer to Section 5.2.5 for details on data model–specific structures and Section 5.2.6 for details on package groups.

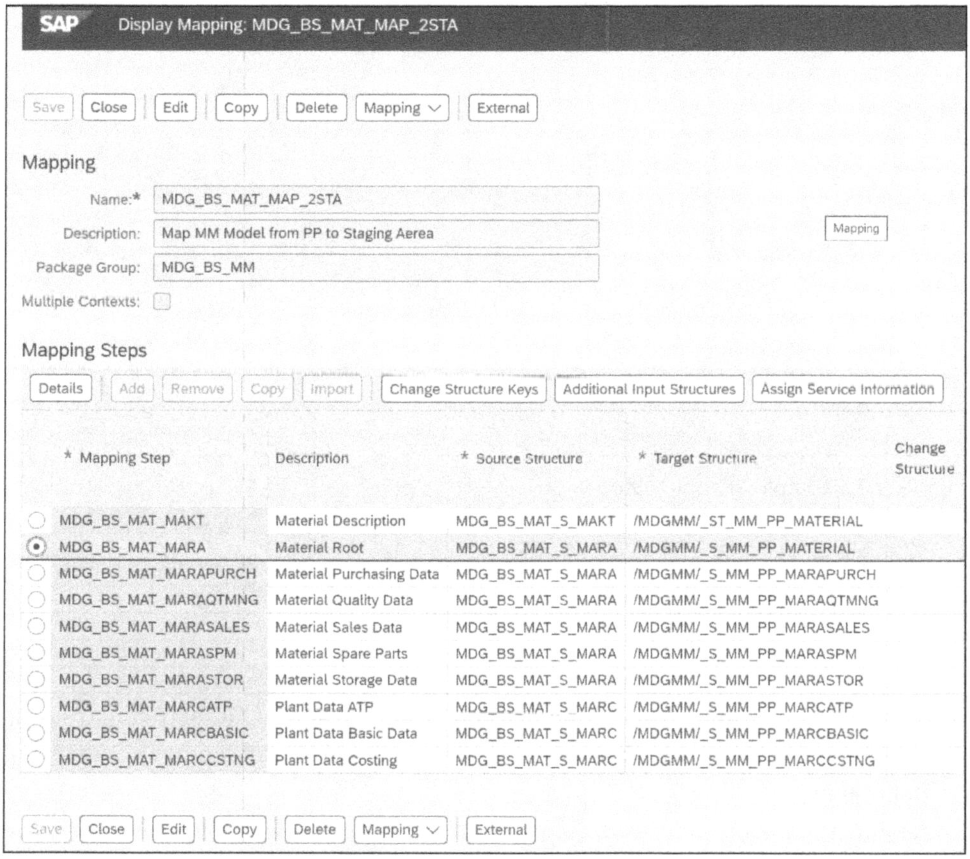

Figure 5.16 Example: SMT Mapping

Figure 5.17 shows mapping step MDG_BS_MAT_MARA as an example along with transformations and field mappings.

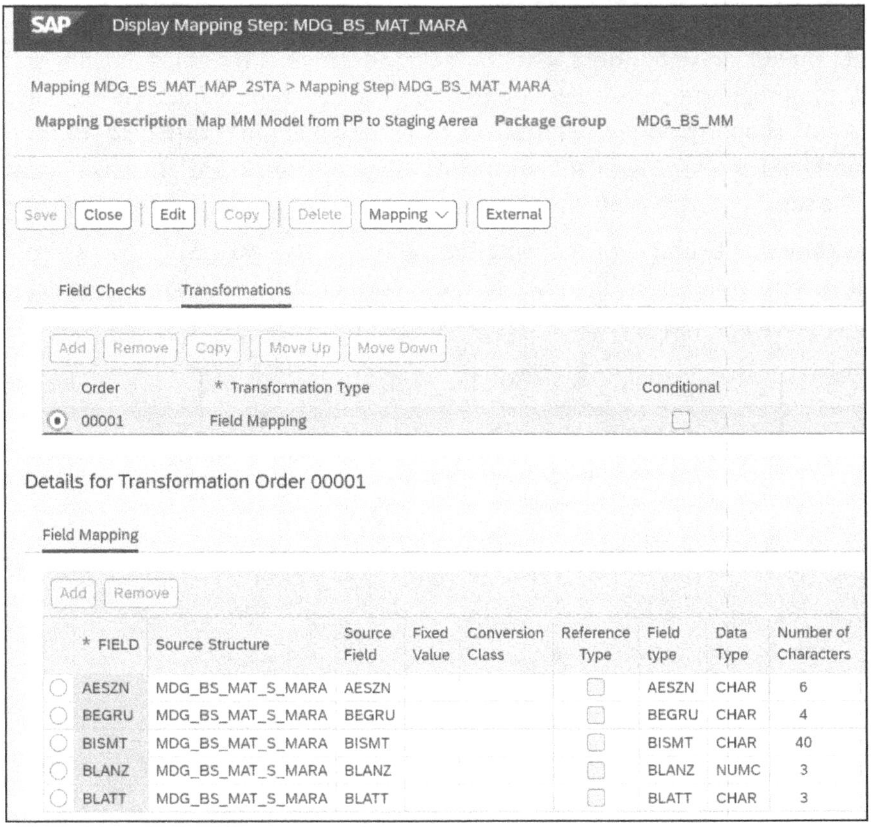

Figure 5.17 Example: Mapping Step

Following are the configurations available for either **Create and Edit Mappings** or **Extend Mappings**:

- **Create and Edit Mappings**
  This Customizing activity is used for creating new mappings and mapping steps, and for creating or editing transformations and field checks. The IMG path for accessing this activity is **MDGIMG • Data Modeling • Create and Edit Mappings • Create and Edit Mappings**.

- **Extend Mappings**
  This Customizing activity is used for extending existing and delivered mappings, but it can't be used to create new mappings or mapping steps. The IMG path for accessing this activity is **MDGIMG • Data Modeling • Extend Mappings • Extend Mappings**.

Now, let's explore the standard data models provided by SAP.

> **Note**
>
> In addition, report RSMT_CHECK can be executed for a specific mapping or for the entire configuration and checks the entire mapping Customizing. The IMG path for accessing this activity is **MDGIMG • Data Modeling • Create and Edit Mappings • Check Customizing**.

5.3   Standard Data Models

In this section, we'll go through the standard data models (material master, business partner, and financial) delivered by SAP at a high level and understand how entities are structured in each data model. This section also covers the scope of each data model.

5.3.1   Material Master Data Model

The material master data model in SAP Master Data Governance covers most of the material master attributes that are commonly used across industries. Figure 5.18 shows an overview of the material master data model.

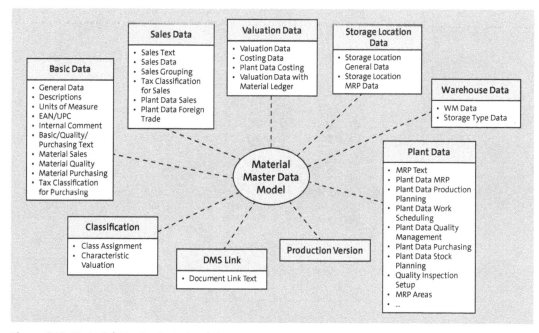

Figure 5.18 Material Master Data Model

Following are some of the highlights of the material master data model:

- Four storage/usage type 1 entity types
- Several type 2 and type 3 entity types acting as check tables
- Several type 4 entity types representing plant data, storage location, valuation, and warehouse data
- No defined hierarchies

Table 5.3 lists **SU Type** 1 and 4 entity types of the material master data model.

Entity Type	SU Type	Description
MATERIAL	1	Basic Data
DRADBASIC	1	Basic Data for Document Link
MATCHGMNG	1	Material Change Management
MKALBASIC	1	Production Version
BSCDATTXT	4	Basic Data Text
CLASSASGN	4	Class Assignment (Classification)
DRADTXT	4	Document Link Text
INTCMNT	4	Internal Comment
MARAPURCH	4	Material Purchasing Data
MARAQTMNG	4	Material Quality Data
MARASALES	4	Material Sales Data
MARASPM	4	Material Service Parts Management
MARASTOR	4	Material Storage Data
MARCATP	4	Plant Data ATP
MARCBASIC	4	Plant Data Basic Data
MARCCSTNG	4	Plant Data Costing
MARCFRCST	4	Plant Data Forecasting
MARCFRGTR	4	Plant Data Foreign Trade
MARCFRPAR	4	Plant Data Forecast Parameters

Table 5.3 Material Master Data Model SU Type 1 and 4 Entity Types

Entity Type	SU Type	Description
MARCMRPFC	4	Plant Data MRP Forecast (View Planning)
MARCMRPLS	4	Plant Data MRP Lot Size (View Lot Size)
MARCMRPMI	4	Plant Data MRP Misc. (View Manufacturing)
MARCMRPPP	4	Plant Data MRP Production Planning (View Material)
MARCMRPSP	4	Plant Data MRP Stock Planning (View Procurement)
MARCPURCH	4	Plant Data Purchasing
MARCQTMNG	4	Plant Data Quality Management
MARCSALES	4	Plant Data Sales
MARCSTORE	4	Plant Data Storage
MARCWRKSD	4	Plant Data Work Scheduling
MARDMRP	4	Storage Location MRP Data for Material
MARDSTOR	4	Storage Location General Data for Material
MBEWACTNG	4	Material Accounting Data
MBEWCSTNG	4	Material Costing Data
MBEWMLAC	4	Material Ledger: Prices
MBEWMLVAL	4	Material Ledger: Period Totals Records Values
MBEWVALUA	4	Material Valuation Data
MDMABASIC	4	MRP Area Basic Data
MEAN_GTIN	4	International Article Numbers (EANs) for Material
MLANPURCH	4	Tax Classification for Purchasing
MLANSALES	4	Tax Classification for Sales
MLGNSTOR	4	Material Warehouse Management Data
MLGTSTOR	4	Material Storage Type Data
MPGDPRODG	4	Material Data for Product Group
MRPTXT	4	Material MRP Text

Table 5.3 Material Master Data Model SU Type 1 and 4 Entity Types (Cont.)

Entity Type	SU Type	Description
MVKEGRPNG	4	Sales Grouping
MVKESALES	4	Sales Data
PURCHTXT	4	Material Purchasing Text
QINSPTXT	4	Material Quality Inspection Text
QMATBASIC	4	Parameters for Inspection Type
SALESTXT	4	Material Sales Text
UNITOFMSR	4	Units of Measure for Material
VALUATION	4	Characteristic Valuation (Classification)

Table 5.3 Material Master Data Model SU Type 1 and 4 Entity Types (Cont.)

Table 5.4 lists the reuse active areas and associated access classes assigned to the material master data model.

Active Area	Description	Access Class
DRAD	Document-object link	CL_MDG_BS_MAT_DRAD_ACCESS
DRATYP2CHK	Type 2 entities (attributes) for document-object link (DRAD)	CL_MDG_BS_MAT_DRAD_TYP2CHK_ACC
MATERIAL	Material master (MM01 – MM03 in active area)	CL_MDG_BS_MAT_ACCESS
MM_TYP2CHK	Type 2 entities (attributes) for material master	CL_MDG_BS_MAT_TYP2CHK_ACCESS

Table 5.4 Material Master Data Model: Reuse Active Areas

Now that you understand all the data model building blocks from Section 5.1, we can focus on the material master data model and understand how some of the entities and relationships are modeled. Figure 5.19 shows the MARCBASIC entity type and its associated relationships as an example. Some of the highlights of this example are as follows:

- The MATERIAL entity has a leading relationship of cardinality 1:N to entity type MARCBASIC.
- The PRCTR entity type has a referencing relationship of cardinality 0:N to entity type MARCBASIC.
- The WERKS entity type has a qualifying relationship of cardinality 1:N to entity type MARCBASIC.

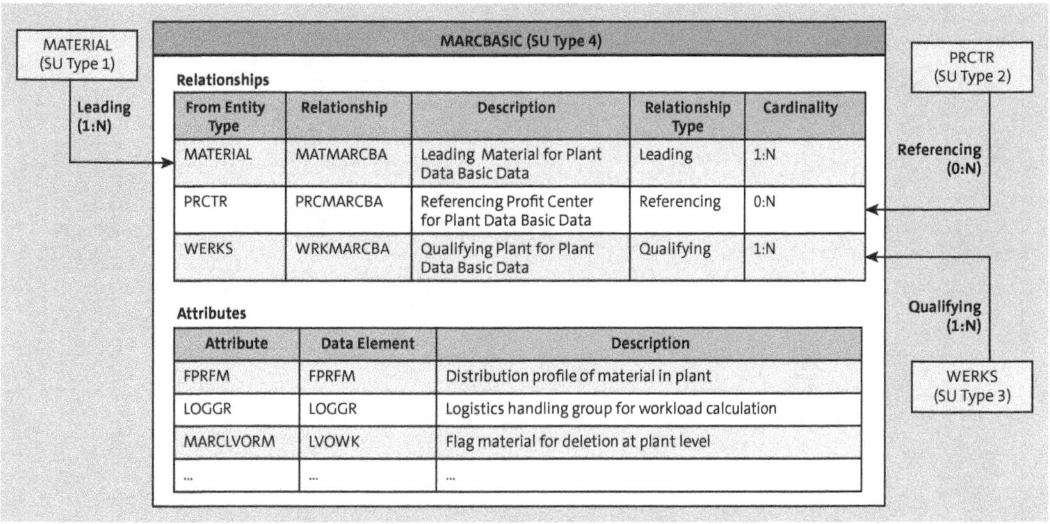

Figure 5.19 Material Master Data Model Example

5.3.2 Business Partner Data Model

The business partner data model caters to business partner, customer master, supplier, and contract account domains in SAP Master Data Governance. This helps in having all common attributes in the appropriate business partner–related entity types. As discussed in Chapter 2, Section 2.3.3, customer-vendor integration (CVI) plays an important role in creating business partner and associated customer/vendor records. Business partner relationships are used for creating customer and supplier contacts in SAP Master Data Governance. Figure 5.20 shows an overview of the business partner data model and how business partner data and corresponding SAP S/4HANA and SAP ERP customer and vendor data are linked.

Some of the highlights of the business partner data model are as follows:

- Multiple storage/usage type 1 entity types are available.
- Multiple type 4 entity types are available.
- Business partner hierarchy is possible.
- Business partner and corresponding SAP S/4HANA and SAP ERP customer and/or vendor data are linked via the multiple assignments entity type.

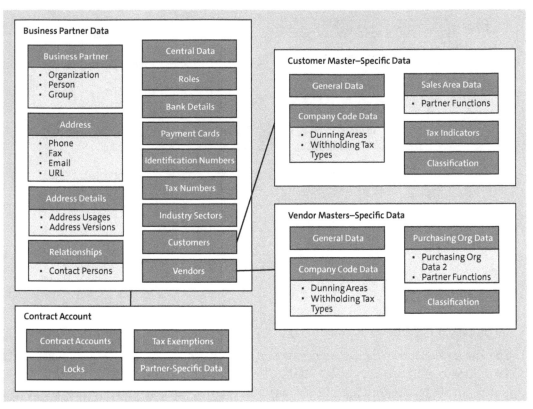

Figure 5.20 Business Partner Data Model

Table 5.5 lists **SU Type** 1 and 4 entity types of the business partner data model.

Entity Type	SU Type	Description
ADDRNO	1	Address Number
BP_HEADER	1	Business Partner
BP_HRCHY	1	Hierarchy
BP_REL	1	Relationships
BP_SUBHRY	1	Lower-Level Hierarchy
FKKVK	1	Contract Account
ADDRESS	4	Address
AD_EMAIL	4	Email Address
AD_FAX	4	Fax Number

Table 5.5 Business Partner

5

Entity Type	SU Type	Description
AD_NAME_O	4	Names of Organizations
AD_NAME_P	4	Names of Persons
AD_POSTAL	4	Physical Address
AD_TEL	4	Telephone Number
AD_URL	4	Internet Address
BP_ADDR	4	Addresses
BP_ADDUSG	4	Address Usage
BP_BKDTL	4	Bank Details
BP_CCDTL	4	Payment Cards
BP_CENTRL	4	Central Data
BP_COMPNY	4	Company Code
BP_CPGEN	4	BP Relationship Contact Person General Data
BP_CUSCLA	4	Customer: Class Assignment (Classification)
BP_CUSDDB	4	Basic Data for Document Link
BP_CUSDUN	4	Dunning Data (Customer)
BP_CUSFCN	4	Customer: Partner Function
BP_CUSGEN	4	General Data (Customer)
BP_CUSTAX	4	Tax Classification for Customer
BP_CUSULP	4	Unloading Points for Customer
BP_CUSVAL	4	Customer: Characteristic Valuation (Classification)
BP_CUSWHT	4	Customer: Extended Withholding Tax
BP_CUS_CC	4	Customer Company Code Data
BP_DUNN	4	Dunning Data
BP_IDNUM	4	Identification Numbers
BP_INDSTR	4	Industry
BP_MLT_AD	4	Multiple Addresses of Customer/Supplier
BP_MLT_AS	4	Multiple Assignment of Customer/Supplier

Table 5.5 Business Partner (Cont.)

Entity Type	SU Type	Description
BP_PORG	4	Purchasing Organization
BP_PORG2	4	Purchasing Data
BP_ROLE	4	Role
BP_SALES	4	Sales Data (Customer)
BP_TAXGRP	4	Tax Groupings (Suppliers)
BP_TAXNUM	4	Tax Numbers
BP_VENCLA	4	Supplier: Class Assignment (Classification)
BP_VENDDB	4	Basic Data for Document Link
BP_VENFCN	4	Supplier: Partner Functions
BP_VENGEN	4	General Data (Supplier)
BP_VENSUB	4	Supplier Subrange
BP_VENVAL	4	Supplier: Characteristic Valuation (Classification)
BP_WHTAX	4	Extended Withholding Tax
BP_WPAD	4	BP Contact Person Workplace Address
CUSCCTXT	4	Texts (Customer Company Code Data)
CUSGENTXT	4	Texts (Customer General Data)
CUSSALTXT	4	Texts (Customer Sales Data)
FKKLOCKS	4	Business Locks (Contract Account)
FKKTAXEX	4	Tax Exemptions (Contract Account)
FKKTXT	4	Texts (Contract Account)
FKKVKCORR	4	Correspondence for Relationship Contract Account<->Partner
FKKVKP	4	Contract Account Partner-Specific (Contract Account)
FKKVKTD	4	Contract Account (Time Dependence)
VENCCTXT	4	Texts (Supplier Company Code Data)
VENGENTXT	4	Texts (Supplier General Data)
VENPOTXT	4	Texts (Supplier Purchasing Organization)
WP_EMAIL	4	Workplace Address: Email Address

Table 5.5 Business Partner (Cont.)

Entity Type	SU Type	Description
WP_FAX	4	Workplace Address: Fax Number
WP_POSTAL	4	Workplace Address: International Versions
WP_TEL	4	Workplace Address: Telephone Number
WP_URL	4	Workplace Address: Internet Address

Table 5.5 Business Partner (Cont.)

Table 5.6 lists the reuse active areas and associated access classes assigned to the business partner data model. Note that the entity types BP_HRCHY and BP_SUBHRY are assigned with SAP Master Data Governance as active areas, which implies that these entity types aren't defined as reuse entity types and don't use the PARTNER reuse active area defined at the business partner data model level.

Active Area	Description	Access Class
CUS_DRAT2C	Type 2 Entities (Attributes) for Document-Object Link (DRAD)	CL_MDG_BS_BP_DRAD_TYP2CHK_ACC
CUS_TYP2CH	Type 2 Entities (e.g., tax classification) for Customer Master	CL_MDG_BS_CUST_TYP2CHK_ACCESS
FKKVK	Contract Account	CL_MDG_FICA_ACCESS_MASTER
PARTNER	N/A	CL_MDG_BS_BP_ACCESS_MASTER
SUP_TYP2CH	Type 2 Entities (e.g., plant) for Vendor Master	CL_MDG_BS_SUPPL_TYP2CHK_ACCESS
VEN_DRAT2C	Type 2 Entities (Attributes) for Document-Object Link (DRAD)	CL_MDG_BS_BP_DRAD_TYP2CHK_ACC

Table 5.6 Business Partner Data Model: Reuse Active Areas

Next let's focus on the business partner data model and understand how some of the entities and relationships are modeled. Figure 5.21 shows how some of the important entity types are related to each other in the business partner data model.

The business partner data model also can model hierarchies for business partners. From the persistence perspective, entity types BP_HRCHY and BP_SUBHRY are modeled to be flex entity types (the active area is defined as "MDG" at the entity type level). It's important to note that the business partner hierarchy isn't related to the SAP S/4HANA and SAP ERP customer or vendor hierarchies.

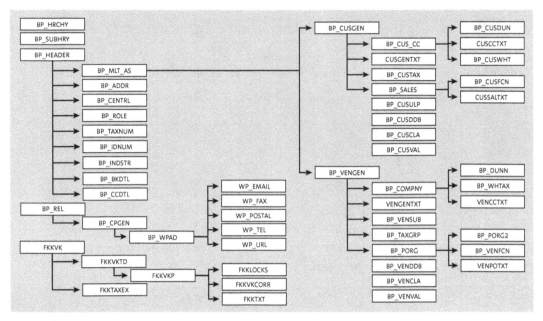

Figure 5.21 Business Partner Data Model: Entity Types

Figure 5.22 shows how entity types BP_HRCHY, BP_SUBHRY, and BP_HEADER are modeled to facilitate hierarchy creation for business partner records.

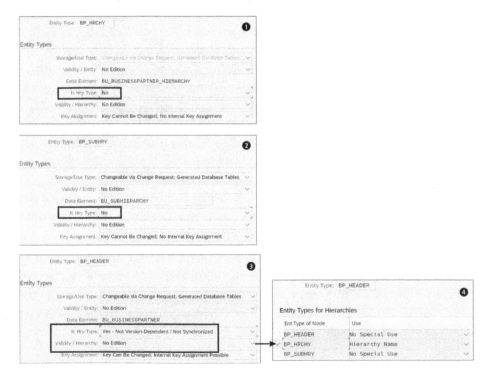

Figure 5.22 Business Partner Data Model: Hierarchy

The following are some important aspects of modeling these three entity types:

- Entity types BP_HRCHY ❶ and BP_SUBHRY ❷ aren't modeled as hierarchies; **Is Hry Type** is set to **No** (as shown Figure 5.22).
- Entity type BP_HEADER ❸ is modeled as a hierarchy; **Is Hry Type** is set to **Yes – Not Version-Dependent/Not Synchronized**.
- For BP_HEADER, the **Entity Types for Hierarchies** customization ❹ is maintained as follows:
  - BP_HRCHY is defined as **Hierarchy Name**.
  - BP_SUBHRY is defined as **No Special Use**.
  - BP_HEADER is defined as **No Special Use**.

Now, let's move on to discuss the financial data model delivered by SAP.

5.3.3   Financial Data Model

The SAP standard financial (0G) data model caters to the data governance of various finance objects such as cost center, profit center, cost element, general ledger account, and so on. Refer to Chapter 2, Section 2.3.5, for a complete list of finance objects in SAP S/4HANA and SAP ERP.

Table 5.7 shows a list of all **SU Type** 1 and 4 entity types of the financial (0G) data model

Entity Type	SU Type	Description
ACCCCDET	1	SAP General Ledger Account (Company Code)
ACCOUNT	1	SAP General Ledger Account (Chart of Accounts)
BDC	1	Breakdown Category
BDCSET	1	Breakdown Category Set
CCTR	1	Cost Center
CCTRG	1	Cost Center Group
CCTRH	1	Cost Center Group Hierarchy
CELEM	1	Cost Element
CELEMG	1	Cost Element Group
CELEMH	1	Cost Element Group Hierarchy
COMPANY	1	Company
CONSCHAR	1	Consolidation Characteristic

Table 5.7 SU Type 1 and 4 Entity Types of the Financial Data Model

Entity Type	SU Type	Description
CONSGRP	1	Consolidation Group
CONSGRPH	1	Consolidation Group Hierarchy
CONSUNIT	1	Consolidation Unit
FRS	1	Financial Reporting Structure
FRSI	1	Financial Reporting Structure Item
FSI	1	Item
FSIH	1	Item Hierarchy
FSIT	1	Text Item
IORDER	1	Internal Order
PCTR	1	Profit Center
PCTRG	1	Profit Center Group
PCTRH	1	Profit Center Group Hierarchy
SUBMPACK	1	Cause for Submission
TRANSTYPE	1	Transaction Type
ACCCCAUDT	4	SAP ERP Audit Information for G/L Account (Company Code)
ACCNTAUDT	4	SAP ERP Audit Information for G/L Account (Chart of Accounts)
BDCSUBSEL	4	Assignments of Subassignments
CCTRAUDIT	4	SAP ERP Audit Information for Cost Center
CELEMAUDT	4	SAP ERP Audit Information for Cost Element
CGGCURR	4	Entity for Currency Assignment
CUVERS	4	Entity Related to Consolidation Unit Entity
FRSITXT	4	Financial Report Texts
FSIAUDIT	4	SAP ERP Audit Information for Item
FSIVERS	4	Entity Related to Item Entity
IORDAUDT	4	ERP Audit Information for Internal Order
PCCCASS	4	Assignments of Profit Centers
PCTRAUDIT	4	SAP ERP Audit Information for Profit Center

Table 5.7 SU Type 1 and 4 Entity Types of the Financial Data Model (Cont.)

Figure 5.23 shows type 1 entity types of the financial data model grouped under three main areas. Note that the financial area also uses profit center, profit center group, and profit center hierarchy.

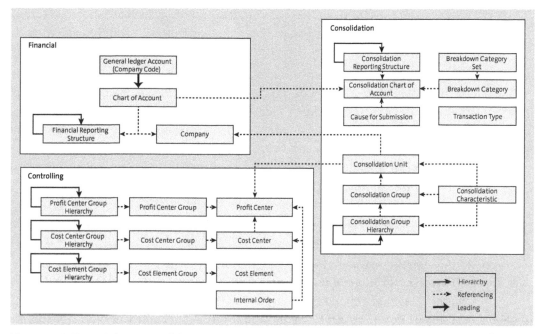

Figure 5.23 Financial Data Model: Type 1 Entity Types

Note

Prior to SAP Master Data Governance 9.1, the 0G data model followed the SAP ERP template; however, now it's split into two different code lines:

- The standalone SAP Master Data Governance 9.2, which can be used with SAP ERP as an add-on
- SAP Master Data Governance on SAP S/4HANA 1809

Refer to SAP Note 202146 for additional details on the list of supported fields in data model 0G and how SAP Master Data Governance on SAP S/4HANA 1809 versus standalone SAP Master Data Governance distinguishes the concept of cost elements.

Note

Internal order governance is delivered only as part of SAP Master Data Governance on SAP S/4HANA 1809 and SAP Master Data Governance 9.2 onward.

5.4   Extending Standard Data Models

The data that needs to be managed and governed via a governance process is determined by the data model definition. The standard content provides the option to configure what data needs to be governed based on the available data entities and attributes of the data model. It also provides the option to add additional entities or attributes that aren't part of the standard data model.

Some common use cases for data model extension are adding industry-specific master data attributes, adding enhanced data fields that already exist in the master data repository tables (extended SAP S/4HANA and SAP ERP tables), adding process-specific attributes, and adding fields that need to exist only in SAP Master Data Governance staging tables and not in SAP S/4HANA and SAP ERP tables (flex option), among others. These requirements can be achieved by adding additional entities or extending the standard entities with new attributes. These new entities can be mapped to the reuse area or can be flex entities. The relationships between the new entities and the existing entities need to be maintained to validate the data. The most common use cases for a data model extension include the following:

- **Adding existing standard fields (reuse option)**
  This involves the requirement to extend the standard SAP Master Data Governance data model with standard fields that aren't part of the SAP Master Data Governance data model. Examples of such fields include those that come with industry-specific solution add-ons, fields related to standard database tables that aren't in the SAP Master Data Governance standard scope, and so on. Based on the number of fields and the type of fields (check tables, text fields, etc.), these fields could be added as attributes to the standard entities or custom entities in the standard data model.

- **Adding custom fields (reuse option)**
  This involves the requirement to extend the standard SAP Master Data Governance data model with custom/enhanced fields that were added to the standard SAP S/4HANA and SAP ERP tables or custom tables that are linked to the standard tables. Based on the number of fields and the type of fields (check tables, text fields, etc.), these fields could be added as attributes to the standard entities or custom entities in the standard data model.

- **Adding custom fields (flex option)**
  This involves the requirement to extend the standard SAP Master Data Governance data model with custom fields that need not be mapped to the active area. Examples of such fields include process-specific fields that are used to determine process flows, fields based on user entry, extending data models with additional flex fields, and so on.

The following sections discuss various steps to implement these data model enhancements, from adding attributes to the standard data model to adding new entities to data models.

5.4.1   Adding Attributes to Standard Data Models

Adding attributes to the standard data model can be accomplished by adding attributes to the existing entities or defining an entity relationship. Attributes can be added only to storage type 1 or type 4 entities. The new entities can be flex entities or reuse entities, based on the entity definition and type of data (master, reference, process-specific, etc.). If the newly added field is part of a check table or has foreign keys, then a storage type 3 entity is defined, and a relationship is configured with the linked entity. If the field already exists in the SAP S/4HANA and SAP ERP tables (reuse option), mappings between the staging and active area need to be maintained through the SMT mapping.

For the business partner data model, if the business partner-related field needs to be part of the customer or vendor UI, CVI mapping needs to be defined to map the field from the business partner model to the corresponding customer or vendor field. Because the finance data model (0G), unlike the material master or business partner data model, is based on the flex option, SMT mapping isn't required.

The customer namespace for adding fields is ZZ or YY. A namespace and custom package need to be provided on configuration; the structures are generated on activation of the data model. They can be visualized in the configuration view to display the graphical model. The generated tables can also be verified by Transaction MDG_DATA_MODEL.

After the data model is extended, the data model is activated and generated so that the extended fields can be used in the governance process. The staging area needs to be adjusted by running report USMD_ADJUST_STAGING, which helps in adjusting the staging area for the linked change requests. The generated structures are used to configure and extend the UIs based on the entity/attribute relationships.

After the attributes to be enhanced or added are identified, the standard data model can be extended. The configuration paths and detailed navigation for each of these extension steps are described in Section 5.2. For the business partner data model enhancements, CVI mapping needs to be updated if the business partner fields need to be mapped to the customer/supplier structure, as discussed in Chapter 2 (Section 2.3.3). You can extend the model by following these steps:

1. Extend the SAP S/4HANA and SAP ERP table (for new reuse fields), if it doesn't already exist (reuse option for business partner and material master data models).

2. Using Transaction MDGIMG, select the data model, and extend it with the new attributes in the corresponding entity definition associated with the SAP S/4HANA and SAP ERP table or with a referencing relationship.

3. Activate the date model.

4. Generate data model–specific structures. Structures for mapping between staging and active areas (for reuse area models) and field properties are mandatory. Other structure usage types (structures for PDF-based forms, for SAP Enterprise Search,

and for field control) may be added as required. Additional metadata structures may need to be extended based on the domain. For example, for the material domain, extend structure `MDG_BS_MAT_S_MAT_DATA`, and check/adjust corresponding table type structures `MDG_BS_MAT_S_<table>*` and `CMD_BS_MAT_S_<table>*`, as needed (for more information, check the help documentation).

5. For the reuse option, enhance the access and respective handler classes (for the business partner model) to read and write in the reuse area. Access classes control the handler class calls. Handler classes need to be enhanced to read and save data for custom entities and attributes. A single handler class is responsible for a single object operation.

6. Define SMT mapping (for reuse fields). This defines the field mapping between the staging area and primary persistence area in both directions so that, upon activation of the change requests, the data is saved to the reuse area (active area).

7. Adjust the staging area for linked change requests.

5.4.2   Adding New Entities to the Data Model

The data model can be extended with additional entities. The data associated with these entities can be stored in SAP Master Data Governance or in SAP S/4HANA and SAP ERP tables upon activation of the change request. The newly defined entities need to be linked to other entities via relationships as defined in Section 5.1.4. The cardinality of the relationship is determined based on the data set.

The steps to extend the standard data model with new entities are the same as those mentioned in Section 5.4.1. For the material data model, the `MDG_BS_MAT_API_SEGMENTS_EXT` Business Add-In (BAdI) is also implemented.

After the data model is extended, the UI needs to be enhanced. For the business partner model, the Generic Interaction Layer (GenIL) model is also extended to connect the data model with the GenIL model, which integrates the model fields to the UI. The mapping of the GenIL model to the data model is done through view cluster `VC_MDG_BS_GENIL_C` (Transaction SM34).

5.5   Summary

This chapter covered the building blocks of SAP Master Data Governance data modeling, including entity types, attributes, and relationships. After introducing the building blocks of data modeling, this chapter covered the customization aspects of data modeling. We covered the standard data models for material master, business partner, and financials, as well as how standard data models are modeled and standard delivered data models can be extended.

In the next chapter, you'll learn about the UI layer of SAP Master Data Governance.

Chapter 6

Central Governance: User Interface Modeling

The main user interface (UI) layer for SAP Master Data Governance is based on Web Dynpro and SAP Fiori technology. The UIs provide a clear and concise user experience. This chapter explains how you can configure the standard UIs for standard domains in central governance scenarios.

A good user experience is a key requirement for any user-centric software application. As SAP Master Data Governance is an enterprise solution involving hundreds of fields per domain, it's very important to display the relevant role-specific information at each governance process step in a user-friendly manner. This will help the data stewards and data analysts make smart decisions with the help of simple and responsive UIs.

The SAP Master Data Governance UI leverages both Web Dynpro technology and SAP Fiori design methodology. The key central governance scenarios leverage mostly Web Dynpro technology; the consolidation and mass processing scenarios leverage the SAP Fiori methodology. SAP Fiori apps available as part of SAP Master Data Governance are discussed in detail in Chapter 16. This chapter describes the SAP Master Data Governance UI configurations, developed using the Floorplan Manager framework, which are available as part of each domain for central governance scenarios. This chapter also provides an overview of the Floorplan Manager toolset.

Section 6.1 provides an overview of Floorplan Manager and standard features provided by the framework. Section 6.2 details the SAP Master Data Governance UI configurations that leverage the Floorplan Manager framework for each domain and the UI configurations that can be done via the SAP Master Data Governance IMG accessed with Transaction MDGIMG. Section 6.3 details the enhancement options available for the UIs.

6.1 Floorplan Manager

Floorplan Manager is based on the Web Dynpro technology paradigm, and it helps developers build UIs on the ABAP application layer with a standardized layout/look and feel. It also provides more flexibility in various configuration options. The Floorplan Manager concept relies on a business object or model for master data object processing. Different types of floorplan templates are available for configuration. These various floorplans display information related to business objects based on the degree of details required and the intended user activity. The Floorplan Manager framework provides the ability to create or adapt the UI configurations in less time. The key components include SAP predefined floorplans, UI building blocks (UIBBs), and the Floorplan Manager configuration editor (flexible user interface designer [FLUID]).

A floorplan can consist of multiple UIBBs. The UIBBs provide a standardized look and feel for form layout, list layout, search, and so on. These UIBBs can be reused across various floorplan applications, which simplifies the development effort of having different variants of the same UI for various roles. The UIBBs can be classified into the following types:

- Generic UIBBs (GUIBBs)
- Reuse UIBBs (RUIBBs)
- Freestyle UIBBs

A Floorplan Manager application configuration is assigned to a floorplan configuration that can contain multiple UIBBs, as shown in Figure 6.1. The UIBBs can be displayed in different layouts with sections/assignment blocks/UIBBs presented in a stacked layout or tabbed layout.

GUIBBs include templates for forms, lists, and so on. RUIBBs include business logic along with UIs. Some examples include notes, attachments, and so on. Freestyle UIBBs are usually generic Web Dynpro components assigned to the Floorplan Manager application using the IF_FPM_UI_BUILDING_BLOCK Web Dynpro interface.

The predefined UIBBs provide a standard look and feel along with a template ABAP class called a feeder class to handle the event processing associated with the UIBB. The GUIBBs come with generic events such as add/delete a row to the table list, and the RUIBBs involve specialized events and error handling specifically for the UIBB functions. For example, they can trigger an error when a note is entered or trigger a specific popup to browse and attach a document to the attachment UIBB. All RUIBBs need to implement the IF_FPM_RUIBB interface.

Standard events trigger the actions in these floorplans. The events are triggered on the initial load of the UIBB and on user action. These events help to perform validations and derivations, as well as to run additional business rules. The feeder classes link the application backend to the generic UIs. Communications between the UIBBs are exchanged using the wiring and SAP Master Data Governance communicator settings. Wiring is used to transfer data between UIBBs. The dependency between UIBBs is also defined in the wiring information during the UI configuration. Floorplan Manager provides various enhancement options to cater to different requirements. These enhancement options are discussed in detail in Section 6.3. For a Web Dynpro component to be recognized as a UIBB by the Floorplan Manager framework, the component should implement the Web Dynpro IF_FPM_UI_BUILDING_BLOCK interface. This interface provides the method definitions required for a component to participate in the Floorplan Manager event loop.

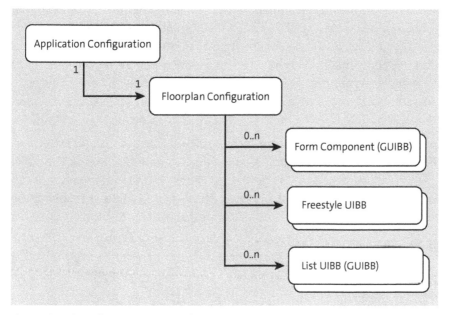

Figure 6.1 Floorplan Manager Application Components

SAP provides the following predefined layouts for Floorplan Manager:

- Overview page floorplan (OVP)
- Guided activities floorplan (GAF)
- Quick activities floorplan (QAF)
- Object instance floorplan (OIF)

Note

For quick reference, the Floorplan Manager application is implemented using one of the following three Web Dynpro components:

- For OVP: FPM_OVP_COMPONENT
- For GAF: FPM_GAF_COMPONENT
- For OIF: FPM_OIF_COMPONENT

The OVP provides an overview of the business object information by listing the attribute/field values of the single business object instance, such as material master data, business partner master data, cost center data, and so on. The layout can be a single-column or multicolumn layout and can also be hierarchical. The OVP is usually used when the user has to review or edit the details of the object instance. A page can contain multiple sections, and each section can contain multiple UIBBs.

In addition to these, toolbars can be configured at various levels. This floorplan is implemented using the FPM_OVP_COMPONENT Web Dynpro component, which has numerous personalization options. The component can be configured using the Floorplan Manager configuration editor, FLUID. Based on the number of fields in the UI, performance impacts to load the UI should be taken into consideration. UIBB rendering configuration can be performed to specify whether a UIBB needs to be collapsed (lazy loading) or expanded at runtime. A workaround for a large number of fields could be to provide a hierarchical layout, where the user drills down based on basic information (e.g., from material basic data → list of plants → plant-specific details).

The example shown in Figure 6.2 has a number of stacked UIBBs. You can see the page title ❶, the page toolbar ❷, and the first section contains tabbed UIBBs ❸. The panel containing UIBBs can be expanded ❹ or collapsed ❺ per your requirements. You can also personalize the display of fields ❻ and the order of stacked UIBBs as required. The personalization and enhancement options of UIs are discussed in Section 6.3.

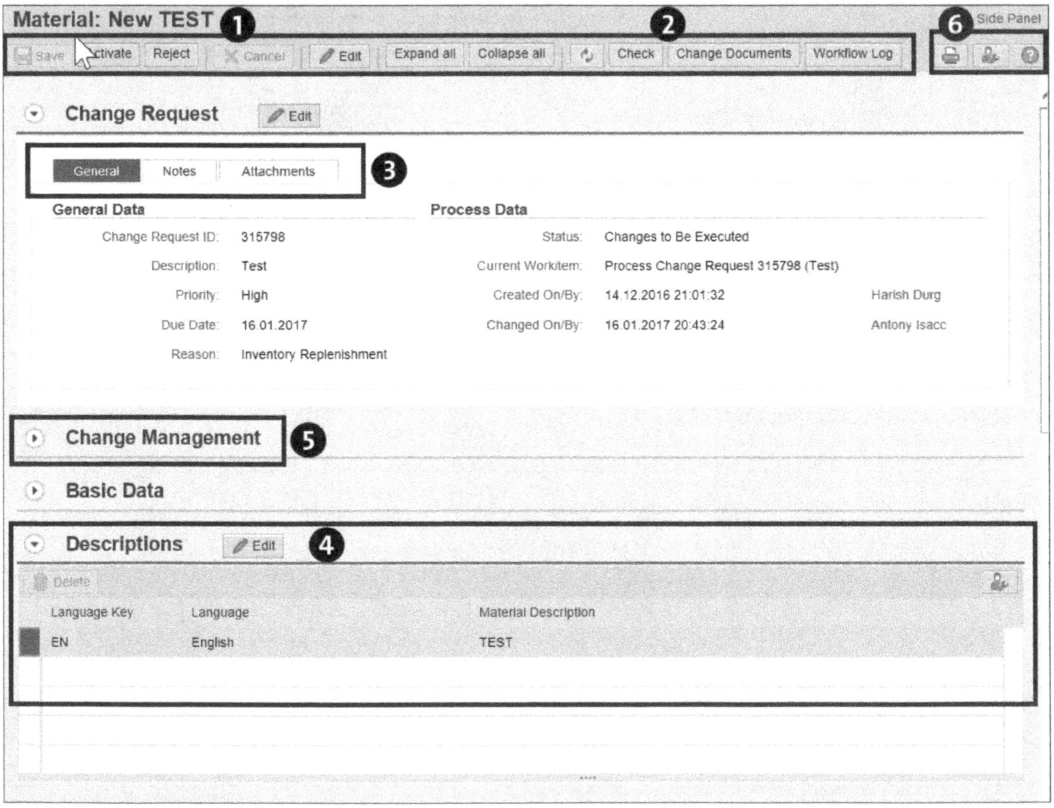

Figure 6.2 Example: OVP Layout

The GAF helps when the user has to take multiple actions based on a sequence of activities/steps. The top section of the GAF provides a road map so you know what step of the process you're in. It's usually used to perform complex activities via a series of logical steps involving tasks and subtasks. This floorplan is implemented using the FPM_ GAF_COMPONENT Web Dynpro component. An example GAF layout is shown in Figure 6.3, as follows:

❶ Page title

❷ Page toolbar

❸ Road maps with sequence of steps (step 3 contains multiple steps, as shown)

❹ UIBB

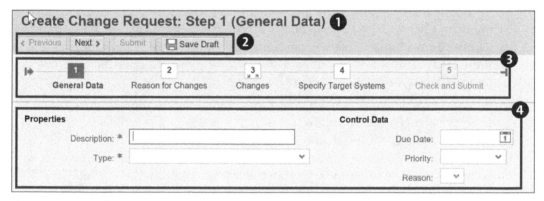

Figure 6.3 Example: GAF Layout

The OIF was used initially to display the object details and for the object maintenance processes. This has been replaced by the OVP floorplan for the new UIs. This floorplan is implemented using the FPM_OIF_COMPONENT Web Dynpro component.

The QAF displays the minimum set of required fields of an object. It's usually realized through the OIF component.

6.2   User Interface Framework

SAP Master Data Governance leverages Floorplan Manager for most central governance scenarios. The consolidation UIs and analytics UIs are based on the SAP Fiori design methodology. Details on all the SAP Fiori UIs available are discussed in Chapter 16.

In the following sections, we'll start with a comprehensive overview of the SAP Master Data Governance UI framework. Then, we'll provide information on the standard Floorplan Manager configurations and applications provided as part of the SAP Master Data Governance content specific to each domain.

6.2.1   Overview

The floorplan applications are linked and grouped under predelivered SAP Master Data Governance roles for each domain. These standard applications cater to each master data activity (e.g., create, change, block, delete, mass processing, etc.). Because they are accessible via URL, you can use a web browser. To access these floorplan applications, you use SAP Business Client or the SAP Fiori launchpad. These URL-based Floorplan Manager applications can also be integrated with the SAP Fiori launchpad/SAP Enterprise Portal or any other web application. The Web Dynpro for ABAP SAP Master Data Governance applications are also delivered in the SAP Fiori theme as part of standard SAP Fiori Catalogues and Roles. SAP Fiori launchpad is the preferred UI for accessing these applications compared to SAP Business Client.

In the standard SAP Master Data Governance content, these applications are tied to template roles (e.g., customer menu role, material steward role, etc.). Based on the access required for each role, you can assign the required application configurations to the users. For each action or activity, additional SAP authorizations need to be provided for table access, field access, action type, and so on.

When accessed via SAP Business Client, the start page of all the domain areas is a homepage. The homepage provides links to each subapplication within the domain area. The menu configured for the SAP role is displayed in the left navigation panel. In the main central area, you see the application view. To view the contextual information with respect to the main application, you can leverage the side panel area, if applicable. Side panels provide additional information regarding the main activity that you're working on via the UI. This is enabled using the Business Context Viewer (BCV) application. The standard BCV content is available using the Business Configuration Set (BC Set) MDGAF_BCV. When accessed via SAP Fiori launchpad, each Web Dynpro for ABAP application is accessed as an SAP Fiori tile based on the role access and associated SAP Fiori catalogs.

For each UI layout, as discussed earlier, you can have separate templates, including an overview page, search page, guided activity page, and so on. OVP is mainly used for SAP Master Data Governance single processing applications, and GAF is mostly used for multistep processing applications. GAF provides a road map view to navigate through multiple steps of a process in a single application. Single processing applications involve the creation or maintenance of a single record at a time, and multiprocessing applications handle multiple records in one process instance.

The following key Web Dynpro applications used to process master data can be grouped into several categories:

- USMD_OVP_GEN, MDGF_OVP_GEN: Single processing of an entity.
- USMD_ENTITY: Collective processing.
- USMD_MASS_CHANGE: Mass change.

Each application configuration is defined for respective domains using application parameters. One key application parameter is USMD_OTC, which refers to the object type code.

The SAP Master Data Governance framework provides the change request UIBB (CRUIBB) and the validity UIBB. CRUIBBs provide the change request header information, such as description, priority, created date, created by, and so on. Validity UIBBs display the time validity details of the edition-based entities. These UIBBS are integrated with the object-specific Web Dynpro applications using the SAP Master Data Governance communicator settings at runtime. Each domain area has the following group of similar applications that cater to specific functions, as the name suggests:

- **Homepage**
  Provides links to other applications and gives an overview of the number of requests submitted/approved from a logon user perspective. This entry page for all the applications associated with a domain area is configured using Transaction LPD_CUST (Launchpad Configuration). Homepage is applicable only when accessing via SAP Business Client. When accessing via SAP Fiori launchpad, all the required apps are displayed as SAP Fiori tiles.

- **Worklist**
  Serves as the workflow inbox for the SAP Master Data Governance work items. This is the main activity center of the governance process, which data stewards and process approvers review the list of change requests to be processed. You can personalize the UI by adding additional predefined attributes as columns. Figure 6.4 shows a sample worklist. Based on the lead selection of a work item, you can see a preview of the change request. The Web Dynpro application related to this functionality is USMD_CREQUEST_POWL with component configuration USMD_WORKCENTER_FMDM.

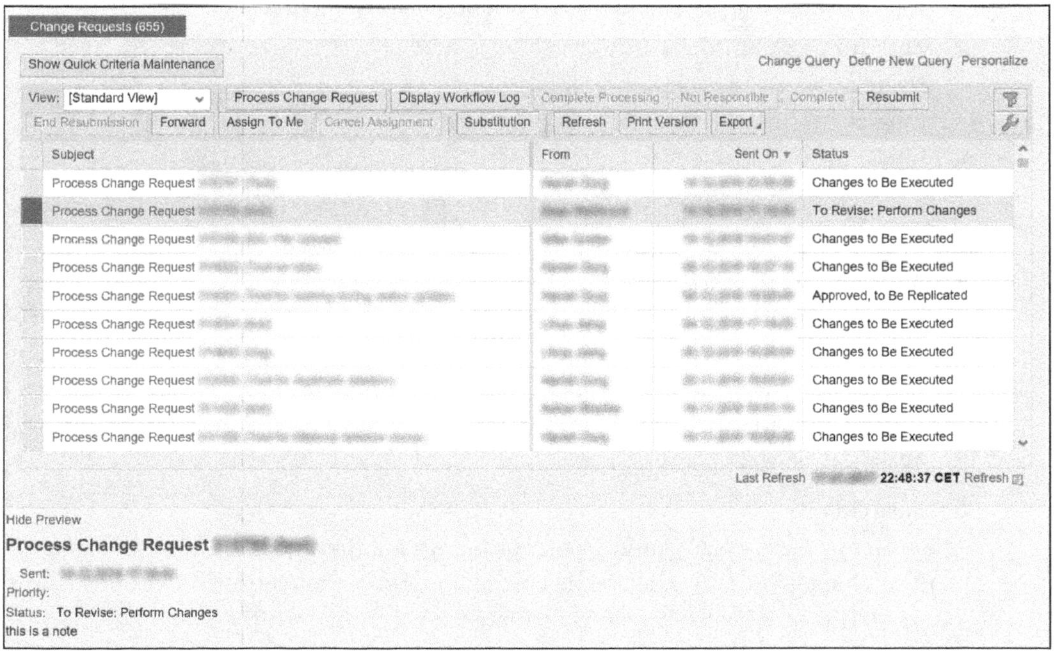

Figure 6.4 Worklist

- **Search**
  Allows you to search records across both the staging area and the active area. The search application (USMD_SEARCH) can leverage different types of search providers such as SAP HANA–based search, database search, SAP NetWeaver Enterprise Search, SAP HANA enterprise search, or an external search provider. The search could be exact search or fuzzy search based on the search provider. The application provides the ability for users to save the search criterion. Multiple search fields can be selected in one single search. The search fields are derived from the respective data model fields of the domain chosen. The toolbar at the search result list provides the key actions to handle existing records or to create new records. Some of the toolbar actions include creating a new record, copying an existing record, performing multiprocessing on a selection of records, checking the status of the records, and more. More details on the search configuration are discussed in Chapter 8.

- **Create**
  Provides the functionality to create a single record request for the governance process. You can create a record from scratch or can copy from an existing record as a template.

- **Change**
  Provides the functionality to change a single record and has a layout similar to the create application. It also provides the functionality to use templates for some domains such as for material objects. Templates can be used to add organizational units such as plants, distribution channels, sales organizations, and so on to a material record based on the values of an existing master data record.

- **Mark for deletion/block/unblock**
  Creates a workflow request to mark/unmark the record as obsolete or to block/unblock master data records.

- **Copy**
  Creates a new record request based on an existing record. It can be used to copy based on an existing change request/master data record or parts of them.

- **Multiple-record processing**
  Changes the field values of multiple records in a single change request. It displays records in a tabular format, enabling users to change select field values. The scope of the associated change request can be limited to specific entities of the data model, so that parallel change requests can be triggered for a record to change the different object-specific views of a record.

- **Mass change**
  Replaces a field value of multiple records with another value. This is similar to the mass change SAP GUI transaction. On submission of the request, a workflow is triggered. The Web Dynpro application related to this functionality is USMD_MASS_CHANGE.

- **Create and edit key mapping**
  Helps data stewards update key mapping information manually. You can add,

update, and delete the mapping information by providing the object type, business system, and object ID for an existing record. The Web Dynpro application related to this functionality is `MDG_BS_WD_ID_MATCH_SERVICE`.

- **Search key mapping**
  Provides the functionality to search the key mapping information by providing the object type, object ID, and business system. The associated Web Dynpro application is `MDG_BS_WD_ANALYSE_IDM`.

- **File upload**
  Performs an entity-dependent file upload request. The request submission triggers a workflow process. The associated Web Dynpro application is `USMD_FILE_UPLOAD`.

- **File download**
  Performs an entity-dependent file download. The request submission triggers a workflow process. The associated Web Dynpro application is `USMD_FILE_DOWNLOAD`.

- **Import master data**
  Imports data and can be accessed through Transaction DTIMPORT. You can select whether the data import/postprocessing should undergo the governance process. For a large number of records, scheduling and parallel processing settings can be maintained before the execution of the data import. The data file could be in an XML or an IDoc format. If the data file is in an external format, you can select the appropriate custom converter settings.

- **Convert master data**
  Converts master data from an external format, such as a Microsoft Excel file into XML format.

- **Export master data**
  Exports the data for other data sources. The data export application can be accessed through Transaction DTEXPORT.

- **Monitor data transfer**
  Helps to monitor the data transfer. You can search for the data transfer status based on a number of search attributes, such as object type, job run number, date, user, and so on.

- **Replicate by object selection**
  Helps to replicate the data by business object. Single or multiple records can be replicated to selected target systems. The application also displays the replication log information. This application is mainly used for manual replication by data stewards as part of issue remediation.

- **Replicate by replication model**
  Replicates records based on the replication model. You can filter the systems based on the replication model and select the records to be replicated.

- **Monitor replication**
  Monitors the replication of data from the hub system to the client system. You can

filter the logs by severity/class, replication mode, and so on. The application provides the functionality to choose the replication mode and business object as well.

- **Define filter criteria**
  Defines the replication filter criterion by replication model, business object, communication channel, and data segments. This configuration helps filter the replication of data from the hub system to the target systems.

- **My change request**
  Provides the list of change requests associated with the user. You can filter this view based on the date and by created requests, processed requests, and to-be-processed requests. The Web Dynpro application related to this functionality is USMD_EDITION_CREQUEST with component configuration USMD_EDITION_CREQUEST_OIF.

- **Display change requests**
  Helps you search for change requests based on change request attributes such as created date, change request type, created on, and so on. This application helps look up the status of a change request as well.

- **Display change documents**
  Displays the list of changes associated with an object and its associated attributes. The report provides information about origin of change documents, type of change, count of changes, change request number if the change originated from SAP Master Data Governance, and so on. There are additional filters for the view such as overview and changed attributes view with descriptions.

- **Processing time (list view)**
  Lists the number of change requests processed during a selected time frame with priority. It provides information regarding change request analytics such as Service Level Agreement (SLA) violations based on priority and defined key performance indicators (KPIs). You can drill down the report to view more information based on data model, change request type, and so on. More information on analytics is provided in Chapter 10.

- **Status report (list view)**
  Provides information on the number of requests created versus approved versus rejected in a time frame. You can drill down this report to view details based on data model and change request type to view the individual change request details. More information on analytics is provided in Chapter 10.

- **Hierarchy processing**
  Creates and maintains hierarchy levels for master data objects. You can create new hierarchies or add more levels to the existing hierarchy and assign master data objects to the level. This application is part of the mass processing functionality to create a mass change request and trigger a governance workflow. This is mainly applicable for the business partner model, finance model, and custom objects. The Web Dynpro application used is USMD_ENTITY.

- **Edition comparison**

  Compares editions to identify objects and changes associated with each edition. The Web Dynpro application related to this is USMD_EDITION_COMPARE. Editions are mainly used for finance data objects as well as custom objects, if needed. Edition history can be viewed using the USMD_EDITION_HISTORY2 Web Dynpro application.

- **Distribution monitor**

  Monitors the replication of data records based on editions in both a hierarchy view and a standard view. The application lists the edition with the respective replication model and provides the status.

- **Workflow log**

  Provides the status of a workflow work item to let you know the step where the request is pending or the history of the request. The Web Dynpro application related to this is USMD_CREQUEST_PROTOCOL2.

- **Application log**

  Provides the error, warning, and information messages related to an application based on the object. The Web Dynpro application related to this is USMD_APPLICATION_LOG.

- **Where-used list**

  Provides the related information of an object in the system and lists objects related to the object specified. The Web Dynpro application related to this is USMD_WHERE_USED.

- **Remote where-used list**

  Provides the where-used information of an object based on a remote system. Mapping information is used to retrieve the required information. The Web Dynpro application related to this is USMD_REMOTE_WHERE_USED.

- **Cleansing case**

  Mainly used for merging duplicate business partner object records. You can search for potential duplicates and create cleansing cases.

The process analytical UIs available as part of SAP Master Data Governance delivery are discussed in Chapter 10. Other domain-specific UI applications are also available for finance, custom domains, hierarchy processing, and so on. These domain-specific application configurations are discussed in Section 6.2.3, Section 6.2.4, and Section 6.2.5.

Each of these applications can be enhanced to meet custom requirements. The enhancement options are made using the Floorplan Manager framework. Floorplan Manager leverages the active SAP Master Data Governance data model to get the field properties for the Floorplan Manager UI field catalog. This is enabled using application-specific abstraction layers such as the Business Object Layer (BOL) and Generic Interaction Layer (GenIL) frameworks. The GenIL framework helps abstract the complex data management logic and provides a structure based on the defined data model and the assigned classes. The standard domains have standard classes for search, dynamic query, hierarchy list, and so on. These are created after the data model is activated and data structures are generated.

You can view the dynamic GenIL objects using Transaction GENIL_MODEL_BROWSER and can test queries using Transaction GENIL_BOL_BROWSER. These transactions are illustrated in Figure 6.5 and Figure 6.6. GenIL objects are linked to UI fields based on data model definition. After the data model is activated, the GenIL structures are generated based on the entity types and entity-relationship types. These are then assigned to the UIBB configuration.

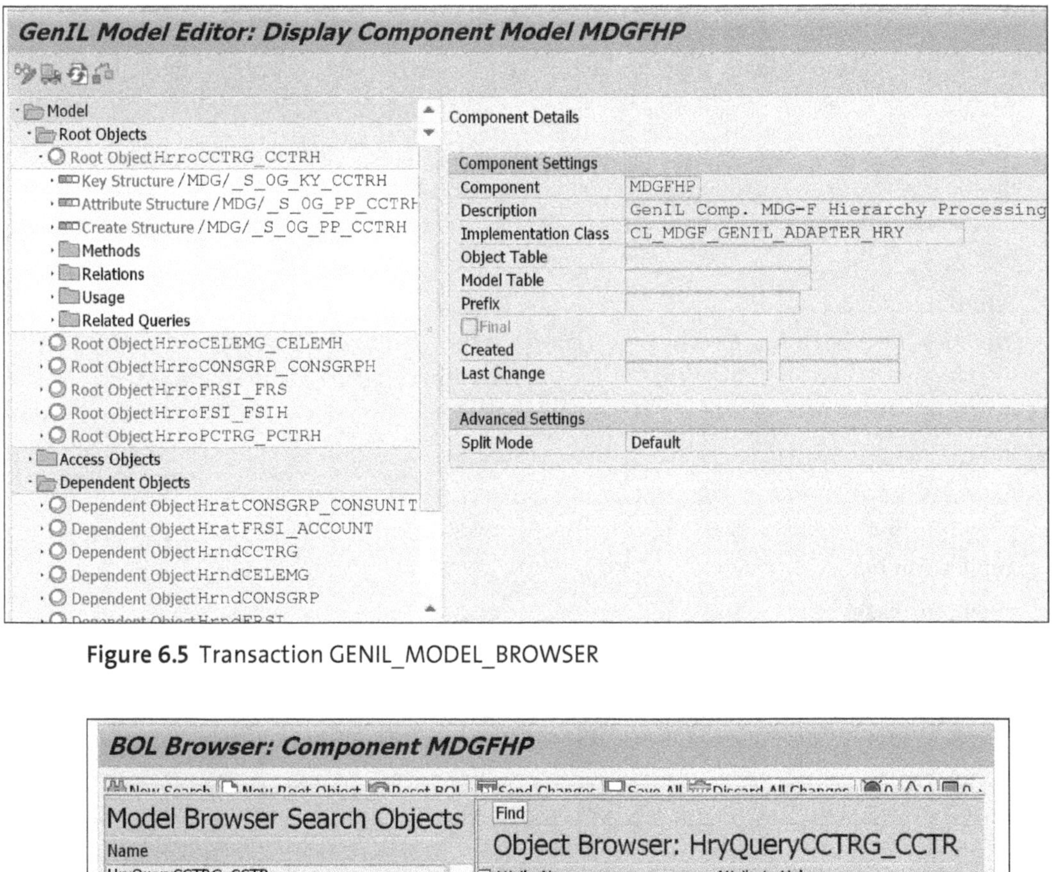

Figure 6.5 Transaction GENIL_MODEL_BROWSER

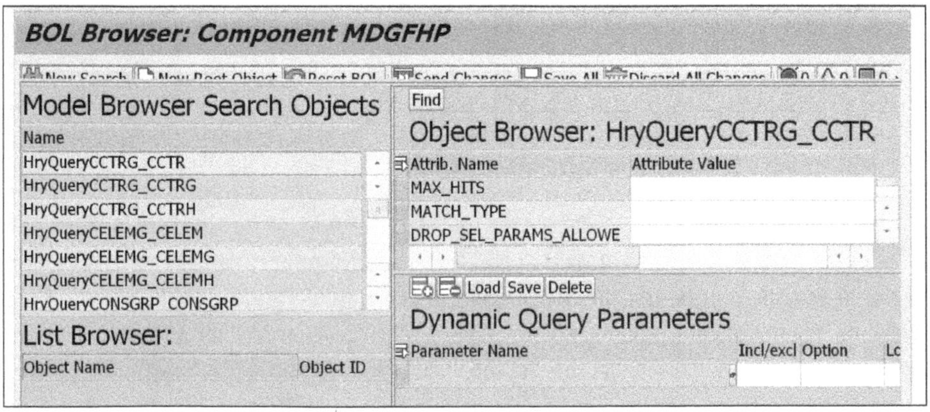

Figure 6.6 Transaction GENIL_BOL_BROWSER

The material UI leverages a different integration framework and is discussed in detail in Section 6.2.3. However, the BOL and GenIL contents are generated nevertheless. The BOL/GenIL contents contain entity names, attributes, and relations mapped to root objects, structures, dependent objects, and associated object classes and methods. These provide a uniform interface for the integration between the application layer and presentation layer. Data objects based on the business partner data model, finance data model (0G), and custom objects leverage the GenIL framework. The GenIL data models are dynamically generated by its implementation class on the activation of the data model. They are mapped to the data model structure as follows:

- Type 1 entity is generated as a root object.
- Type 4 entity is generated as a dependent object.
- Relationships are generated as GenIL relations.
- Additional queries and query result objects are generated to search on the type 1 entity.
- A dependent object is generated to support the text processing capabilities if the type 1 entity supports multilingual descriptions.
- Two dependent objects are generated to support the type 1 attachments: one for attachment processing, and another for handling popups.
- The entity attributes and related structures are transferred to the GenIL key and attribute structures.

Each Floorplan Manager application has the field layout and the associated ABAP class to contain the processing logic. The main ABAP class associated with the UIBB is called the feeder class. The feeder class logic helps in dynamically modifying or enhancing the field layout and field properties. With the help of SAP Master Data Governance application programming interfaces (APIs), you can retrieve the metadata information of the change request as well as the data model to make complex enhancements.

Each UIBB can have its feeder class and the main entity. The feeder class inherits from the main class provided as part of SAP delivery.

After the process modeling section configuration is done, you can provide the action and change request type as application parameters. You can also have a generic OVP Floorplan Manager configuration and provide the application parameters as necessary, thus, reusing the UI. Different UI configurations can also be based on each workflow/ approval step.

6.2.2 Configuration

To help you configure the SAP Master Data Governance applications, SAP provides configuration views based on SAP Master Data Governance data models to enable and disable fields in the SAP Master Data Governance UI. You can perform these configuration activities (see Figure 6.7) via the IMG path in Transaction MGIMG: **Master Data Governance · General Settings · UI Modeling**.

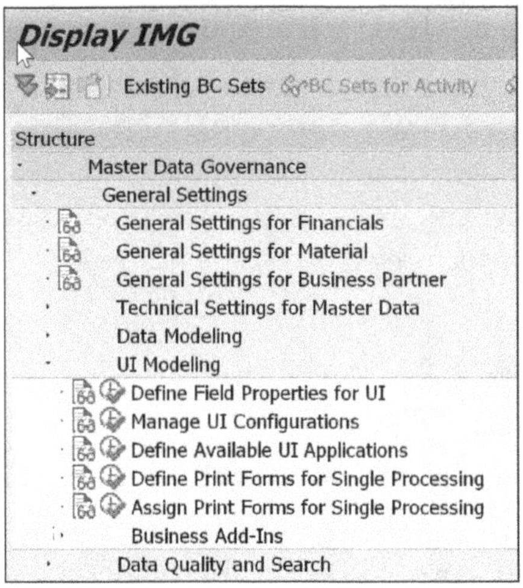

Figure 6.7 UI Modeling for SAP Master Data Governance

These configuration options allow you to change the field properties of the UI, manage UI configurations, modify the field visibility and values using Business Add-Ins (BAdIs), and so on. SAP Master Data Governance also allows you to print the UI pages as printable forms, which is especially helpful when you want to print the details of a specific object such as material master/customer details. Each of the IMG configuration activities are defined as follows:

- **Define Field Properties for UI**
  You can set whether a type 1 entity defined in the data model can be changed via a change request and set the field-level properties. The IMG path for accessing this is **Master Data Governance · General Settings · UI Modeling · Define Field Properties for UI**.

  On execution of this Customizing activity, you can select the data model for which the properties need to be defined. There are two configuration views with this activity. As illustrated in Figure 6.8, the **Hide Entity Types** view is used to select the type 1 entities that need not be associated with a change request and to upload/download applications, such as other related type 1 entities of the material master data model: DRADBASIC and MATCHGMNG. The root object for the material master model is the type 1 entity MATERIAL, which is linked to the change request. As the other type 1 entities are maintained through the MATERIAL entity, they need not be selected and linked to a change request. This configuration also hides these entity fields from applications such as selection screens, mass changes, search results lists, data cleansing, and so on. The configurations of the standard data objects are automatically enabled via activation of standard BC Sets. Custom entities that need not be displayed in these applications need to be listed in this Customizing activity.

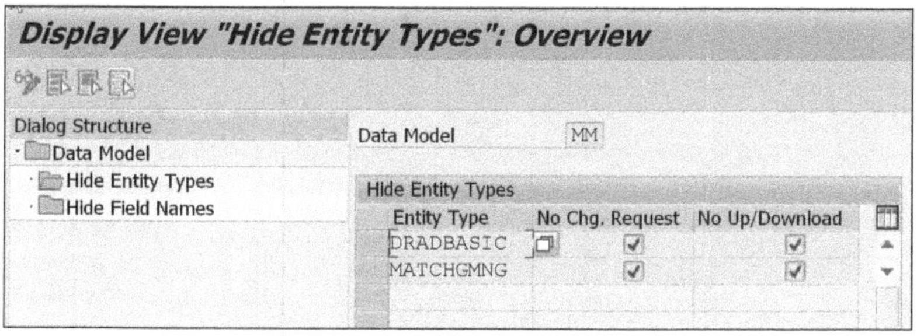

Figure 6.8 Define Field Properties of the UI

In the **Hide Field Names** configuration view, you can disable specific fields from the search criterion, search result list configuration, mass change, and data cleansing (for the business partner data model) UIs (Figure 6.9).

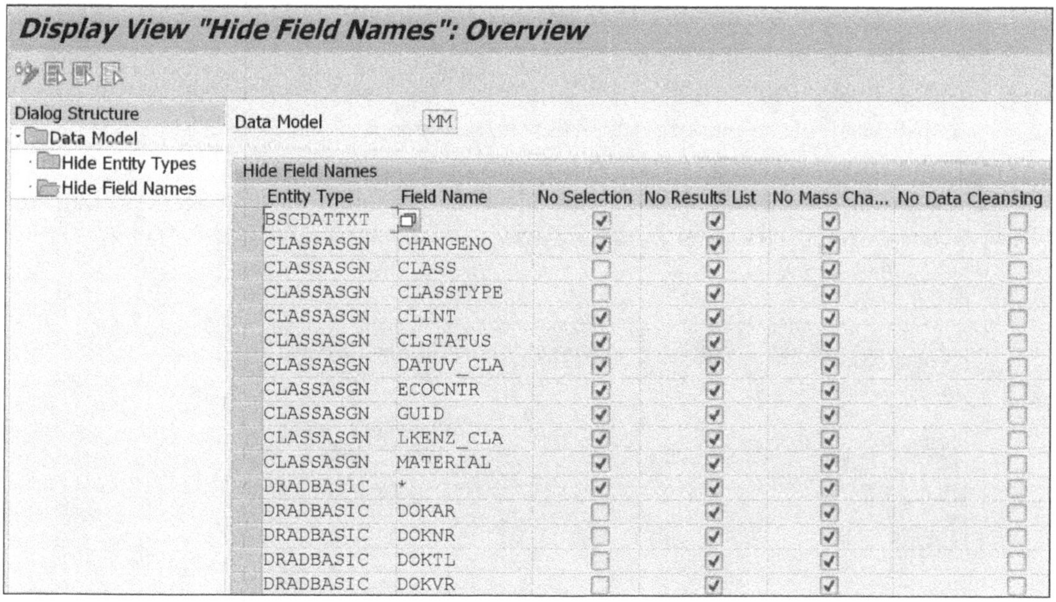

Figure 6.9 Field Level UI Adaptations

- **Manage UI Configurations**
  You can view the standard UI configurations and create configurations based on standard SAP Master Data Governance applications. You can enhance the configurations to meet your needs, as shown in Figure 6.10. Another option is to edit the UI configurations using Transaction SE80. The IMG path for accessing this is **Master Data Governance • General Settings • UI Modeling • Manage UI Configurations**.

Manage UI Configurations

Copy

View: [Standard View] ⌄   Print Version   Export

Data Model	Application	Application Configuration	UI Configuration	Communicator Status	Description
0G	MDGF_OVP_GEN	MDGF_0G_OVP_CCTR	MDGF_0G_CCTR_OVP	▣ Details	Application Configuration f
0G	MDGF_OVP_GEN	MDGF_0G_OVP_CCTRG	MDGF_0G_CCTRG_OVP	▣ Details	Application Configuration f
0G	MDGF_OVP_GEN	MDGF_0G_OVP_CCTRH	MDGF_0G_CCTRH_OVP	▣ Details	Application Configuration f
0G	MDGF_OVP_GEN	MDGF_0G_OVP_CELEM	MDGF_0G_CELEM_OVP	▣ Details	Application Configuration f
0G	MDGF_OVP_GEN	MDGF_0G_OVP_CELEMG	MDGF_0G_CELEMG_OVP	▣ Details	Application Configuration f
0G	MDGF_OVP_GEN	MDGF_0G_OVP_CELEMH	MDGF_0G_CELEMH_OVP	▣ Details	Application Configuration f
0G	MDGF_OVP_GEN	MDGF_0G_OVP_COMPANY	MDGF_0G_COMPANY_OVP	▣ Details	Application Configuration f
0G	MDGF_OVP_GEN	MDGF_0G_OVP_CONSCHAR	MDGF_0G_CONSCHAR_OVP	▣ Details	Application Configuration f
0G	MDGF_OVP_GEN	MDGF_0G_OVP_CONSGRP	MDGF_0G_CONSGRP_OVP	▣ Details	Application Configuration f
0G	MDGF_OVP_GEN	MDGF_0G_OVP_CONSGRPH	MDGF_0G_CONSGRPH_OVP	▣ Details	Application Configuration f
0G	MDGF_OVP_GEN	MDGF_0G_OVP_CONSUNIT	MDGF_0G_CONSUNIT_OVP	▣ Details	Application Configuration f
0G	MDGF_OVP_GEN	MDGF_0G_OVP_CO_ACCOUNT	MDGF_0G_CO_ACCOUNT_OVP	▣ Details	Application Configuration f
0G	MDGF_OVP_GEN	MDGF_0G_OVP_CO_REPORT	MDGF_0G_CO_REPORT_OVP	▣ Details	Application Configuration f

Figure 6.10 Manage UI Configurations

- **Define Available UI Applications**
  This Customizing activity lists the standard UI configurations that are used in the
  SAP Master Data Governance processes, as shown in Figure 6.11. If a custom UI configuration needs to be linked to an SAP Master Data Governance business activity or
  a change request, it must be listed in this configuration view. The IMG path for
  accessing this is **Master Data Governance · General Settings · UI Modeling · Define
  Available UI Applications**.

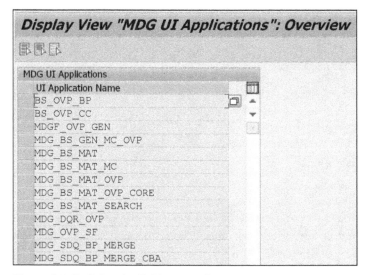

Figure 6.11 Defining Available UI Applications

- **Define Print Forms for Single Processing/Assign Print Forms for Single Processing**
  The **Define Print Forms for Single Processing** and **Assign Print Forms for Single Processing** Customizing activities are used to create and assign accessible PDF forms. The IMG paths for accessing these activities are **Master Data Governance • General Settings • UI Modeling • Define Print Forms for Single Processing** and **Master Data Governance • General Settings • UI Modeling • Assign Print Forms for Single Processing**.

  When you click on the **Print Preview** button in the single processing UI screen, the respective forms are displayed. This Customizing activity allows you to configure the print forms to the respective entity of a data mode. The data from the single processing UI of the entity is mapped to the print form fields. Standard print forms are available for some standard objects. Adding additional forms or enhancements to the custom form can be done using Transaction SFP. Figure 6.12 shows the standard print forms available for the material master data model as an example.

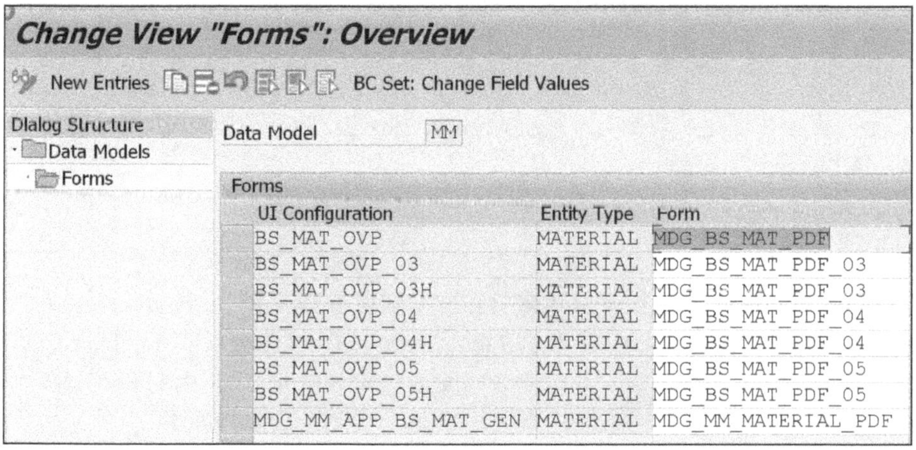

Figure 6.12 Assigning Print Forms

- **BAdI: Adjust User Interfaces for Single Processing**
  This BAdI is used to enhance the single processing UI that uses the Web Dynpro application component USMD_ENTITY_VALUE2. This filter-dependent BAdI can be used to define and adjust the attributes, initialize data fields displayed in the UI, restrict the dropdown/input help values, dynamically control the field visibility, define navigation targets for hyperlinks, check lead selection changes in a table UI element, and so on. Figure 6.13 shows the sample implementations of the BAdI. This BAdI is obsolete with the newer SAP Master Data Governance releases (since SAP Master Data Governance with SAP ERP 6.0 EHP 6 and above). Refer to SAP Note 1606341 for more information.

BAdI Implementations

Implementations for BAdI Definition USMD_UI_EVENT2

Actve(IMG)	Actve(Impl.)	Enhancement Implementation	BAdI Implementation	Description
☑	☑	MDG_UI_EVENT_CUSTOMER	MDG_UI_EVENT_CUSTOMER	UI BAdI Implementati
☑	☑	MDG_UI_EVENT_SUPPLIER	MDG_UI_EVENT_SUPPLIER	UI BAdI implementati
☑	☑	MDG_UI_EVENT_VENDOR	MDG_UI_EVENT_VENDOR	Implementation for v
☑	☑	MDG_FND_SAMPLE_UI_BADI	MDG_FND_SAMPLE_UI_BADI	Example UI BAdI Impl
☑	☑	USMDZ2_IMP_UI_BADI_NEW	USMDZ2_IMP_UI_BADI_NEW	Implementation: Adju
☑	☑	MDG_BS_MAT_GEN	BADI_MDG_BS_MAT	UI BADI Implementati
☑	☑	MDG_FND_SAMPLE_UI_BADI_T1	MDG_FND_SAMPLE_UI_BADI_T1	Implementation: Adju

Figure 6.13 Adjust UIs for Single Processing

- **BAdI: Change Data to be Printed**
  This filter-independent BAdI is used to adjust the field values displayed in the print forms. Data model–specific filter values may be added to separate the implementations. Figure 6.14 shows a sample implementation of this BAdI.

BAdI Implementations

Implementations for BAdI Definition USMD_PRINT_FORM

Actve(IMG)	Actve(Impl.)	Enhancement Implementation	BAdI Implementation	Description
☑	☑	USMDZ2_IMP_PRINT_FORM	USMDZ2_IMP_PRINT_FORM	Implementation: PDF-bas
☑	☑	MDG_MM_PRINT_FORM	MDG_MM_PRINT_FORM	Material Print Form

Figure 6.14 Change Data to Be Printed

6.2.3 Material Master

UIs for material master governance leverage the Service Provider Infrastructure (SPI) framework for integration between the UI (Floorplan Manager) and the database layer. The metadata for the material data model can be viewed through the SPI Metadata Browser (Transaction MDB) with application building block ID (ABBID) MDG_MAT.

The SPI framework is part of the SAP Business Suite foundation (SAP_BS_FND) and connects the application backend with the UI layer. A high-level architecture diagram of Floorplan Manager–SPI integration (FSI) is depicted in Figure 6.15. The SAP Master Data Governance material domain SPI application is identified by the ABBID MDG_MAT. The material data model is exposed via a hierarchical node model. The metadata is defined through the CL_MDG_BS_MAT_MP metadata provider class. The application data flow is handled through the CL_MDG_BS_MAT_SP service provider class. These two ABAP classes encompass the SPI interfaces. These are delivered standard for integrating the data with the Floorplan Manager framework via the feeder classes for each UIBB in the UI layer. The FSI layer enables this in the UI layer.

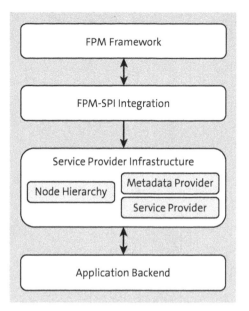

Figure 6.15 SPI Framework Integration

The key SPI entities for SAP Master Data Governance materials are shown in Figure 6.16. The hierarchical SPI node structure is similar to the data model with entities and attributes. Actions are defined to implement the various events to be triggered in the round trip. Any enhancements to the nodes and attributes need to be done using the metadata provider class.

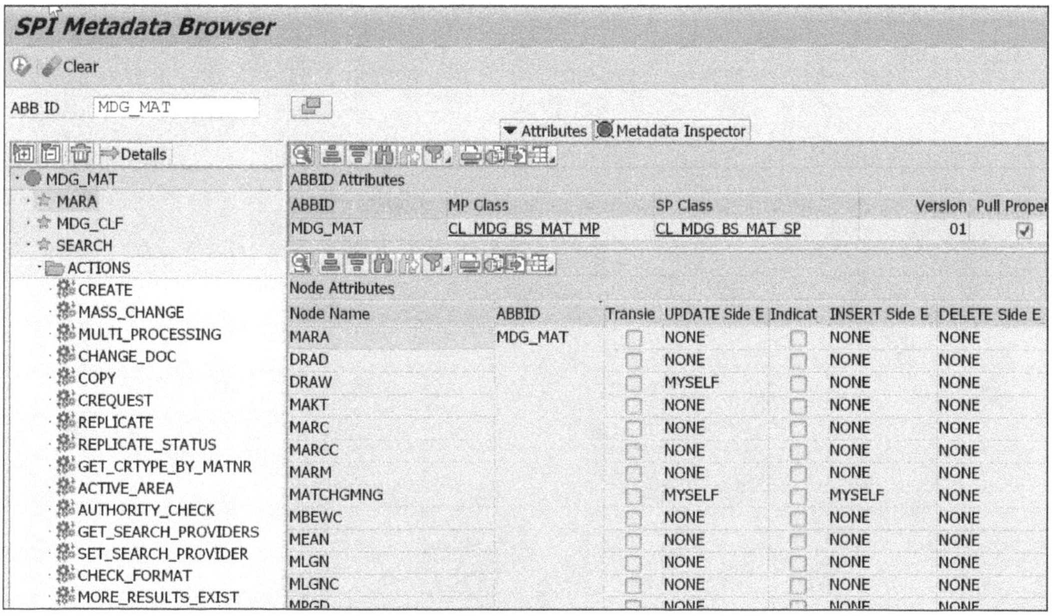

Figure 6.16 SAP Master Data Governance Material SPI Metadata

ABBID, SPI node name, entity, and so on are passed as the feeder class parameters for each UIBB in the floorplan, as shown in Figure 6.17. The communication between UIBBs is implemented through wiring by FSI.

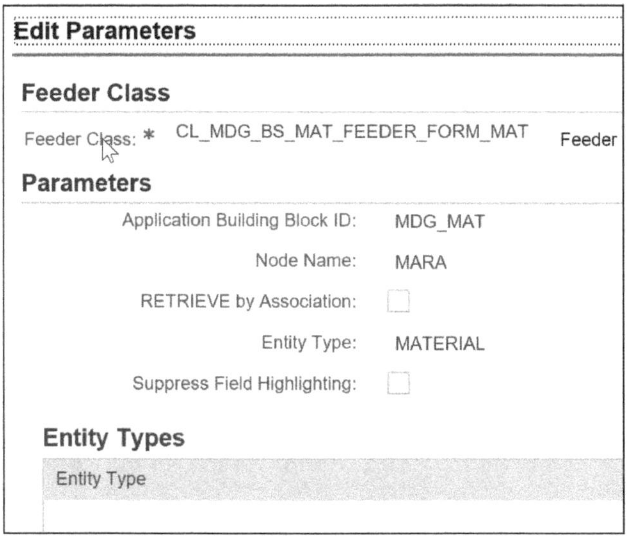

Figure 6.17 SPI Entities as Feeder Class Parameters

The SAP Master Data Governance **Material Governance Homepage** screen, shown in Figure 6.18, is the starting point for the material master governance process when logged in via SAP Business Client.

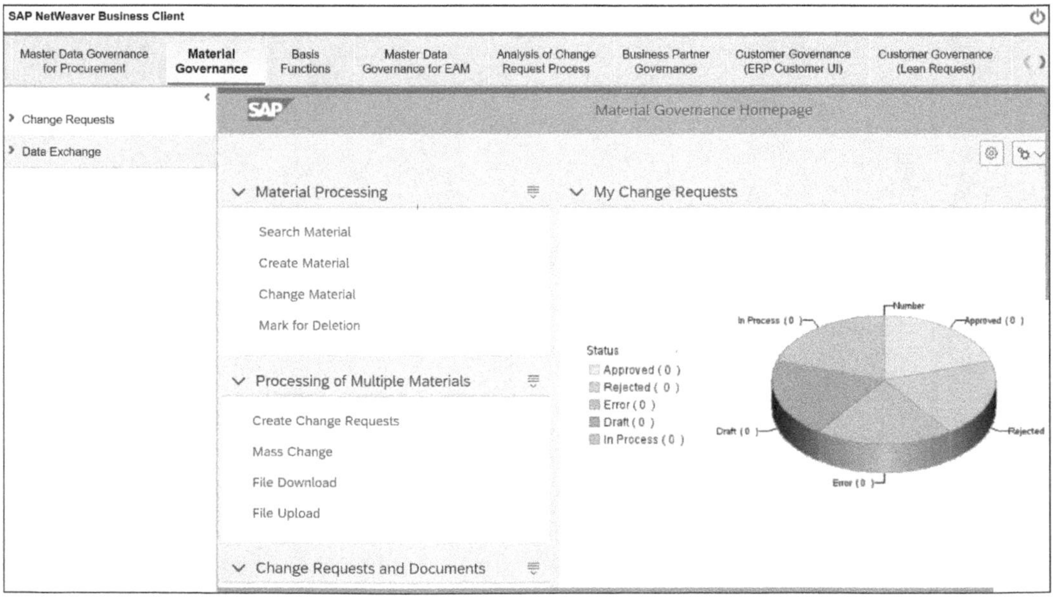

Figure 6.18 Material Governance Homepage Screen

The Material Governance Web Dynpro applications, when accessed through SAP Fiori launchpad, are shown in Figure 6.19. The SAP Fiori apps such as Change Requests Inbox, My Change Requests, Manage Material Governance, and so on corresponds to the respective Web Dynpro–based applications.

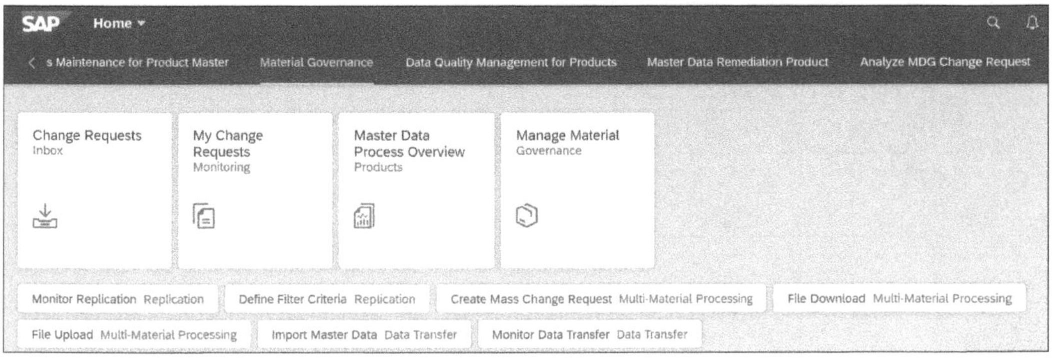

Figure 6.19 Material Governance SAP Fiori Tiles

The Web Dynpro application configurations of key material master governance UI applications (as of SAP Master Data Governance on SAP S/4HANA 2021) are listed in Table 6.1. The SAP Fiori launchpad role, containing these apps, is SAP_BR_PRODMASTER_ SPECIALIST.

Description	Application Configuration	Component Configuration
Search Material	MDG_BS_MAT_SEARCH_09	MDG_BS_MAT_CLS_SEARCH_OVP_09
Create/Change Material	BS_MAT_OVP_09/09H	BS_MAT_OVP_LAYOUT_09/09H

Table 6.1 SAP Master Data Governance Material Master UI Application Configuration

6.2.4   Business Partner, Customer, Supplier, and FI Contract Account Governance

UIs for business partner governance leverage the BOL and GenIL frameworks for data abstraction. The GenIL objects are automatically generated on activation of the data model, and enhancing the generated GenIL objects is forbidden. This abstraction layer provides greater flexibility to link the UI/presentation layer to the business data layer via APIs. The feeder classes for the UIBBs implement the BOL interfaces for data transfers associated with the GenIL root object/data model entity. A high-level architecture of BOL and GenIL integration is depicted in Figure 6.20.

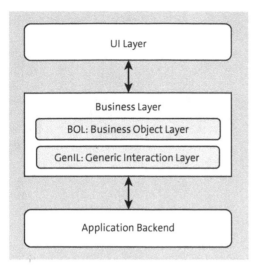

Figure 6.20 BOL/GenIL Layer Integration

The GenIL objects for the business partner data model can be accessed through Transaction GENIL_MODEL_BROWSER for component BUPA and enhancement BUPA_CUSP, as shown in Figure 6.21. These address the needs for the customer and supplier master data governance along with the business partner master data.

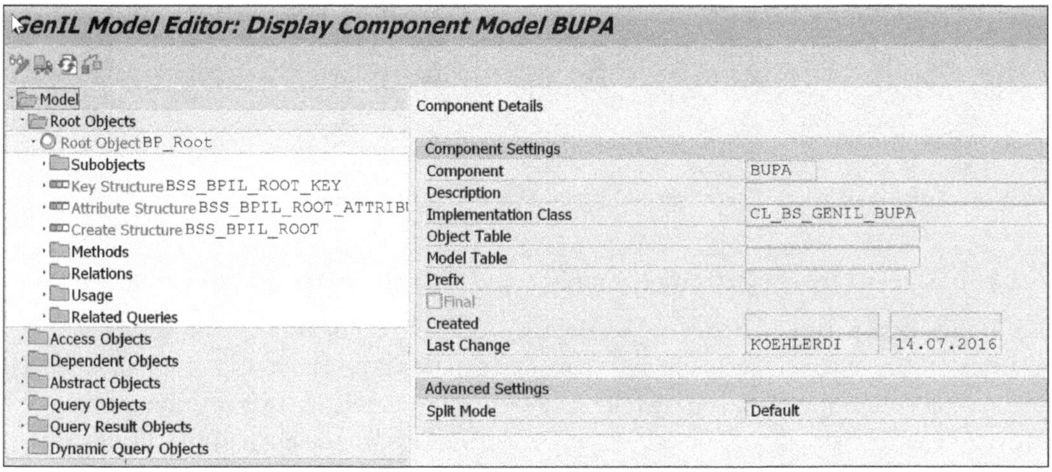

Figure 6.21 GenIL Root Object BUPA for the Business Partner Model

The UI applications related to the business partner data model are grouped into four roles based on the partner types: business partner governance, customer governance, supplier governance, and contract account governance. These roles provide the respective starting pages for accessing the applications. Figure 6.22 shows the **Business Partner Governance** screen when accessed via the SAP Business Client.

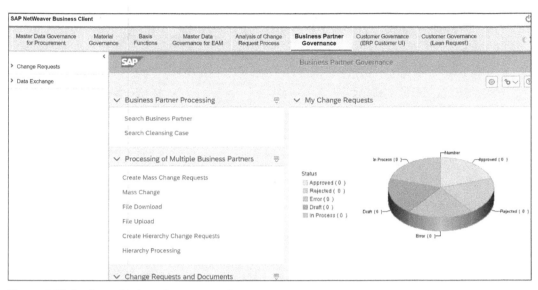

Figure 6.22 Business Partner Governance Screen

Business Partner Governance Web Dynpro applications, when accessed through SAP Fiori launchpad, is shown in Figure 6.23. The SAP Fiori apps, such as Change Requests Inbox, My Change Requests, Manage Business Partner Governance, and so on, correspond to respective Web Dynpro–based applications.

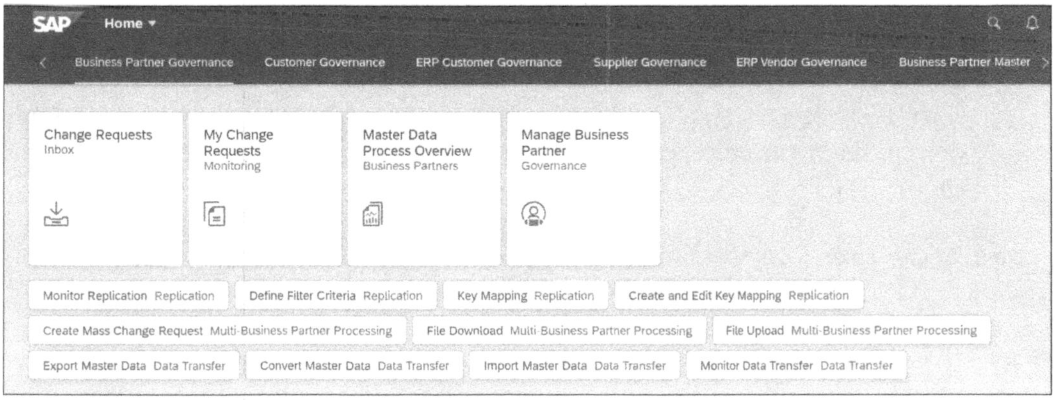

Figure 6.23 Business Partner Governance SAP Fiori Tiles

The Web Dynpro application configurations of key business partner, customer, supplier, and FI Contract Account governance UI applications are listed in Table 6.2. The versions of these applications vary with the SAP Master Data Governance release. The SAP Fiori launchpad role, containing these apps, is SAP_BR_BUPA_MASTER_SPECIALIST.

The Search Business Partner: Drill Down Search application is a SAPUI5 application based on SAP HANA search.

Description	Application Configuration	Component Configuration
Search/Create/Change Business Partner	BS_OVP_BP	BS_BP_OVP
Search/Create Cleansing Case	BS_OVP_CC	BS_CC_OVP
Search/Create/Change Customer	BS_OVP_CU	BS_CU_OVP
Search/Create/Change Supplier	BS_OVP_SP	BS_SP_OVP
Create Hierarchy Change Requests/Change Requests	USMD_CREQUEST_CREATE	USMD_CREQUEST_CREATE_GAF
Hierarchy Processing	USMD_ENTITY	USMD_ENTITY_OIF
Mass Change	USMD_MASS_CHANGE	USMD_MASS_CHANGE_GAF
Search/Create/Change FI Contract Account	MDG_OVP_FICA	MDG_FICA_OVP

Table 6.2 SAP Master Data Governance Business Partner Object UI Application Configurations

6.2.5   Financial Domains

UIs for the finance master data object also leverage the layers in BOL and GenIL. The generated GenIL objects for the finance data model can be accessed through the MDGF and MDGFHP components. The MDGFHP component is used for hierarchy processing functions in the single processing UIs. The GenIL data for SAP Master Data Governance is shown in Figure 6.24.

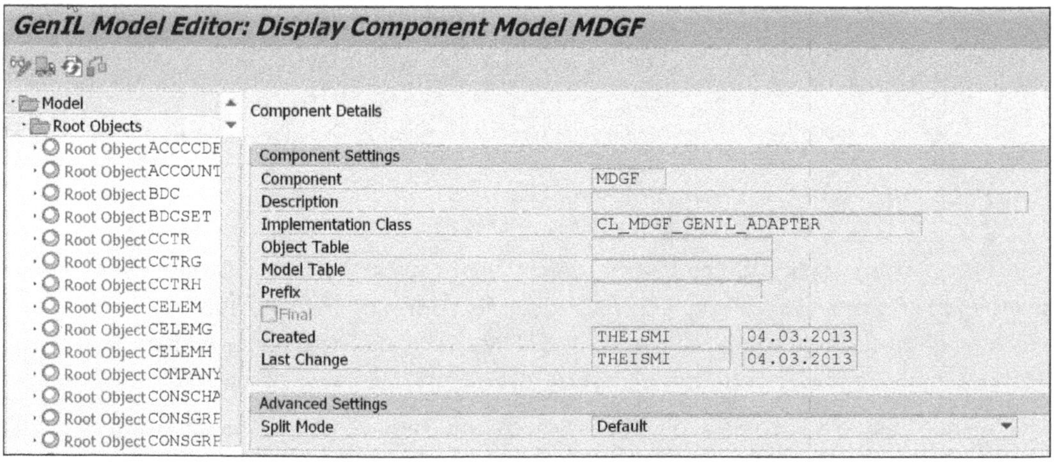

Figure 6.24 GenIL Root Object MDGF for the Finance Master Data Model

The SAP Master Data Governance, Financials, UI applications are grouped under three main groups. Each group corresponds to roles such as display role, requester role, menu role, specialist role, steward role, and so on. The role versions are dependent on SAP Master Data Governance releases. The requester roles for each group are as follows:

- **SAP_MDGF_ACC_REQ_08: Financial accounting governance**
  This constitutes the finance objects, such as SAP General Ledger accounts, financial reporting structure, and company.

- **SAP_MDGF_CO_REQ_07: Financial consolidation governance**
  This constitutes objects such as item, item hierarchy, consolidation characteristic, consolidation group, consolidation group hierarchy, consolidation unit, breakdown category, breakdown category set, cause for submission, and transaction type.

- **SAP_MDGF_CTR_REQ_07: Financial controlling governance**
  This constitutes objects such as cost center, cost center group, cost center group hierarchy, profit center, profit center group hierarchy, cost element, cost element group, and cost element group hierarchy.

The Web Dynpro application configurations of some of the key finance object-related governance UI applications are listed in Table 6.3. The versions of these applications vary with the SAP Master Data Governance release. The SAP Fiori launchpad role, containing these apps, is SAP_BR_MASTER_SPECIALIST_FIN.

Description	Application Configuration	Component Configuration
Search/Create/Change SAP General Ledger Account	MDGF_OG_OVP_FI_ACCOUNT	MDGF_OG_FI_ACCOUNT_OVP
Search/Create/Change Financial Reporting Structure	MDGF_OG_OVP_FI_REPORT	MDGF_OG_FI_REPORT_OVP
Search/Create/Change Company	MDGF_OG_OVP_COMPANY	MDGF_OG_COMPANY_OVP
Create Edition	USMD_EDITION	USMD_EDITION_OIF
Search/Create/Change Item (Consolidation)	MDGF_OG_OVP_CO_ACCOUNT	MDGF_OG_CO_ACCOUNT_OVP
Search/Create/Change Item Hierarchy	MDGF_OG_OVP_CO_REPORT	MDGF_OG_CO_REPORT_OVP
Search/Create/Change Consolidation Characteristic	MDGF_OG_OVP_CONSCHAR	MDGF_OG_CONSCHAR_OVP
Search/Create/Change Consolidation Group	MDGF_OG_OVP_CONSGRP	MDGF_OG_CONSGRP_OVP

Table 6.3 SAP Master Data Governance Finance Objects UI Application Configurations

Description	Application Configuration	Component Configuration
Search/Create/Change Consolidation Group Hierarchy	MDGF_OG_OVP_CONSGRPH	MDGF_OG_CONSGRPH_OVP
Search/Create/Change Consolidation Unit	MDGF_OG_OVP_CONSUNIT	MDGF_OG_CONSUNIT_OVP
Search/Create/Change Breakdown Category	MDGF_OG_OVP_BDC	MDGF_OG_BDC_OVP
Search/Create/Change Breakdown Category Set	MDGF_OG_OVP_BDCSET	MDGF_OG_BDCSET_OVP
Search/Create/Change Cause for Submission	MDGF_OG_OVP_SUBMPACK	MDGF_OG_SUBMPACK_OVP
Search/Create/Change Transaction Type	MDGF_OG_OVP_TRANSTYPE	MDGF_OG_TRANSTYPE_OVP
Search/Create/Change Cost Center	MDGF_OG_OVP_CCTR	MDGF_OG_CCTR_OVP
Search/Create/Change Cost Center Group	MDGF_OG_OVP_CCTRG	MDGF_OG_CCTRG_OVP
Search/Create/Change Cost Center Group Hierarchy	MDGF_OG_OVP_CCTRH	MDGF_OG_CCTRH_OVP
Search/Create/Change Profit Center	MDGF_OG_OVP_PCTR	MDGF_OG_PCTR_OVP
Search/Create/Change Profit Center Group	MDGF_OG_OVP_PCTRG	MDGF_OG_PCTRG_OVP
Search/Create/Change Profit Center Group Hierarchy	MDGF_OG_OVP_PCTRH	MDGF_OG_PCTRH_OVP
Search/Create/Change Cost Element	MDGF_OG_OVP_CELEM	MDGF_OG_CELEM_OVP
Search/Create/Change Cost Element Group	MDGF_OG_OVP_CELEMG	MDGF_OG_CELEMG_OVP
Search/Create/Change Cost Element Group Hierarchy	MDGF_OG_OVP_CELEMH	MDGF_OG_CELEMH_OVP
Internal Order	MDGF_OG_OVP_IORDER	MDGF_OG_OVP_IORDER

Table 6.3 SAP Master Data Governance Finance Objects UI Application Configurations (Cont.)

6.3   Enhancing the SAP-Delivered User Interface

The Floorplan Manager–based UIs provides greater flexibility in enhancements based on requirements. Each component of a Floorplan Manager application can be adapted to custom requirements. These adaptations can be made to all UIs, including single-object processing UIs, multiple-record processing UIs, search UIs, and so on. For more information, refer to SAP Note 1619534.

Multiple adaptation options—both configuration and coding—exist for Floorplan Manager applications. Because Floorplan Manager applications are based on Web Dynpro ABAP, the same enhancement options can be adopted here as well. The various UI adaptation options are as follows:

- Customizing
- Personalizing
- Enhancement
- Context-based adaptations
- Copy application configuration (**Deep-Copy**)
- Modification
- Change request UI BAdIs

These are discussed in detail in the following sections.

6.3.1   Customizing

The changes made to the component Customizing layer are stored as delta to the original component, so it's modification-free. This is client specific. Future upgrades won't affect the Customizing changes made. The component Customizing affects all users of the Web Dynpro application. Customizing can be done both during runtime and design time.

To open an application in the Customizing layer during runtime, as show in Figure 6.25, the `sap-config-mode=x` URL parameter needs to be added to the application URL, or the `FPM_CONFIG_EXPERT` system parameter must be set in the user profile to provide the Customizing options for the user.

Figure 6.25 Customizing at Runtime

A developer can make changes during design time in the Customizing layer through FLUID (the CUSTOMIZE_COMPONENT Web Dynpro application). Figure 6.26 shows the **Create Customizing** option in FLUID. The other options shown, such as **Enhance** and **Deep-Copy**, will be discussed in the following sections. Some of the examples for client-wide Customizing changes include hiding the standard UIBBs/fields, changing the page title, making changes to the application layout (column layout), and so on.

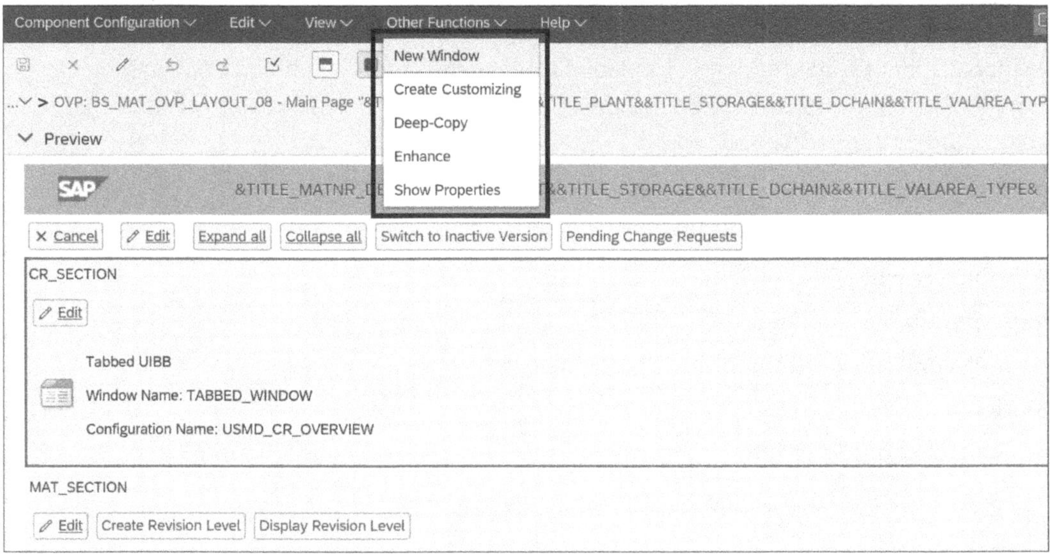

Figure 6.26 Adaptation Options (Design Time): Create Customizing, Deep-Copy, and Enhance

6.3.2   Personalizing

User-specific personalization can be done at the personalization layer only during runtime by the end user through the **User Settings** context menu entry in the application (see Figure 6.27).

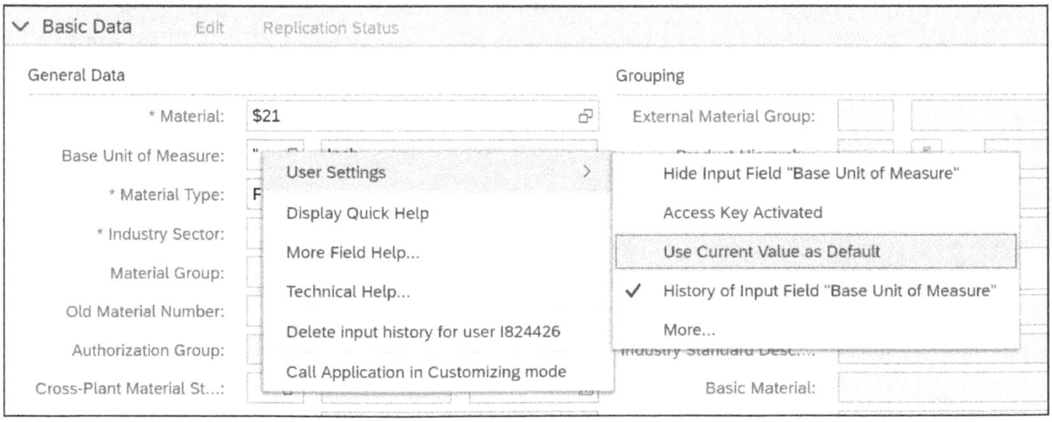

Figure 6.27 Example: User Personalization

It can be used to hide fields/UIBBs, to default field values, to rearrange table layouts, to change application layouts, and so on. The changes made to this layer are stored in the personalization layer and are retrieved each time the user accesses the application. No code changes can be done in the personalization layer by the user.

An end user can enhance the UI via personalization options. These changes are visible only to the specific user who made the changes. Some examples of personalization include rearranging the table columns, reducing the number of rows to be listed in a table layout, defaulting field values, and hiding fields that aren't used frequently. The personalization settings of a component/configuration can be viewed using the WD_ ANALYZE_CONFIG_USER application or using Transaction FPM_WB (Floorplan Manager Workbench). The personalization option can be disabled for specific applications using the application configuration settings.

6.3.3   Enhancement

Floorplan Manager enhancement changes include both code and configuration changes, which can take effect across clients. These enhancements aren't overwritten on upgrades. The changes are effective across the system for all users. Some of the examples of enhancement changes include adding a new button, making changes to/ adding a UIBB, and configuring custom feeder classes.

Search helps for the UI fields can be derived from the domain/data element definition or through the feeder class implementation, as part of the UI configuration. You should implement search helps and filters in the UI configuration. You can also create custom UIBBs, and the corresponding wire configuration need to be assigned with respect to relationships with other UIBBs.

6.3.4   Context-Based Adaptations

Context-based adaptations (CBAs) can be used to change the UI based on the application data chosen during runtime. They can be configured based on conditional logic and field values. The adaptation schema can be enhanced to add additional fields and dimensions to display the UI dynamically based on application runtime parameters. This configuration isn't overwritten on future upgrades. The adaptation schema and related dimensions can be maintained through the Floorplan Manager FPM_VC_ADAPT_ SCHEMA view cluster. The application parameters are mapped to the schema dimensions and evaluated for adaptations at the start of the application load. CBA can be configured for each UIBB in FLUID, as shown in Figure 6.28. Examples of CBA dimensions include business object type code, action, change request type, workflow step, and so on.

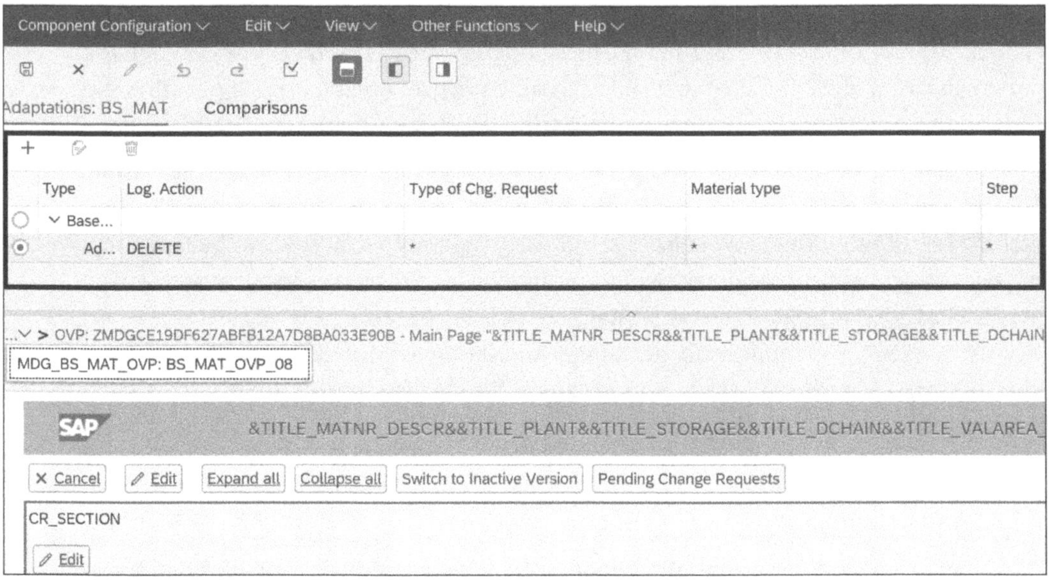

Figure 6.28 CBA Configuration

6.3.5   Copy Application Configuration (Deep-Copy)

Another option to customize the UI application is to copy the standard application configuration and make enhancements on the copied application configuration. This method isn't preferred because future upgrades (corrections/improvements) to the standard application won't be implemented in the copied application. The copied application remains in the custom namespace. Either both the delivered application configuration and dependent UI configuration layout can be copied (deep-copy) or just the application configuration can be copied with the reuse of the standard delivered UI configuration layout. This could also lead to creation of a custom SAP Master Data Governance communicator configuration. SAP Master Data Governance communicator configuration requires the same name as the Web Dynpro application configuration.

The new application configurations need to be linked with the logical action and business activity associated with the change request type. The Customizing paths to do this task are in Transaction MDGIMG: **Master Data Governance, Central Governance • General Settings • Process Modeling • Business Activities • Link Log. Actions with UI Application and Bus. Activity: Custom Definition** and **Master Data Governance, Central Governance • General Settings • Process Modeling • Business Activities • Link Logical Actions with Bus. Activity: Custom Definition**. Figure 6.29 and Figure 6.30 illustrate these custom material master UI configurations.

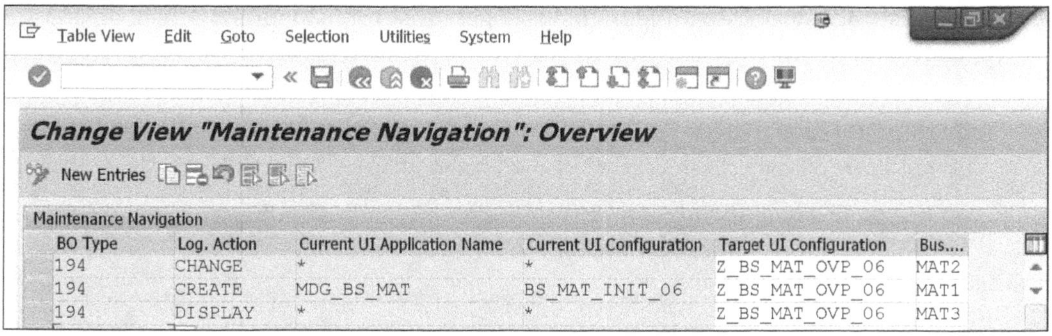

Figure 6.29 Link Logical Actions with UI Application and Business Activity: Custom Definition

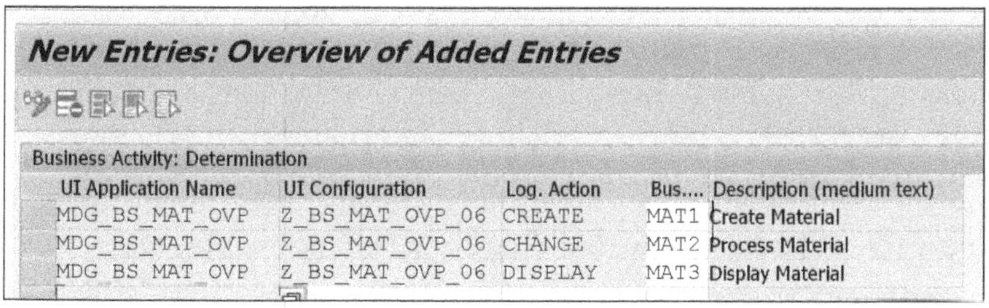

Figure 6.30 Link Logical Actions with Business Activity: Custom Definition

6.3.6   Modification

This option leads to configuration changes to the standard application, but it isn't recommended. Changes through modification will be overwritten on further upgrades.

The Web Dynpro application configurations can be edited by using the WD_ANALYZE_CONFIG_COMP and WD_ANALYZE_CONFIG_APPL application configurations. It's recommended to use a common approach to adapt the UI, instead of mixing the various approaches. This helps in performance as well as management of the application. SAP Screen Personas can also be used to enhance the look and feel of the Web Dynpro application.

Different UI configurations can be configured for each central governance workflow step using the Customizing activity in the path of Transaction MDGIMG: **Master Data Governance, Central Governance** • **General Settings** • **Process Modeling** • **Change Requests** • **Configure Properties of Change Request Step**. The various UI configurations can be adapted using CBA instead of creating separate application configurations for each workflow step.

The homepages can also be customized or configured to rearrange the layout, to hide the sections, and so on. Additional configurations can be done through Transaction LPD_CUST.

In addition to the previously mentioned major UI enhancement approaches, other possible areas include enhancement via code (feeder classes, transient fields, handler classes, BAdIs, etc.) and configuration of application settings (application parameters to control application behaviors such as input field history, defer participation of collapsed UIBBS on initial load, etc.).

In short, the actual UI displayed to the user is determined by the following adaptations or enhancements:

- Personalization (user dependent)
- Enhancements (client-/system-wide for all users)
- CBA (in the start of the application based on dynamic runtime parameters)
- Base configuration

To perform the UI configurations, an active data model with an entity of storage type 1 should exist, and the active data model should be assigned to the R_FMDM_MODEL user personalization object using Transaction SPERS_MAINT. The right approach to enhancing the standard UI configuration is determined based on the number and type of changes, as discussed earlier.

6.3.7   Change Request User Interface Building Block Enhancement BAdIs

BAdI USMD_CREQUEST_INTEGRATION can be used to enhance the change request UIBB. Its implementation can be filtered based on the data model. It uses the IF_EX_USMD_CRE-QUEST_INTEGR interface with methods to filter change request types, auto-fill the change request attributes, and set the change request field properties. This BAdI implementation can be used to auto-populate/derive change request header attributes such as description, notes, reason code, and due date based on data model, entity, edition, change request type, and so on. The implementation also helps set the field properties of these header attributes, such as setting the reason or priority of a change request to a required field. The BAdI definition is shown in Figure 6.31. This is in addition to the possibilities to check and derivations that can be configured using Business Rules Framework plus (BRFplus), based on the data model.

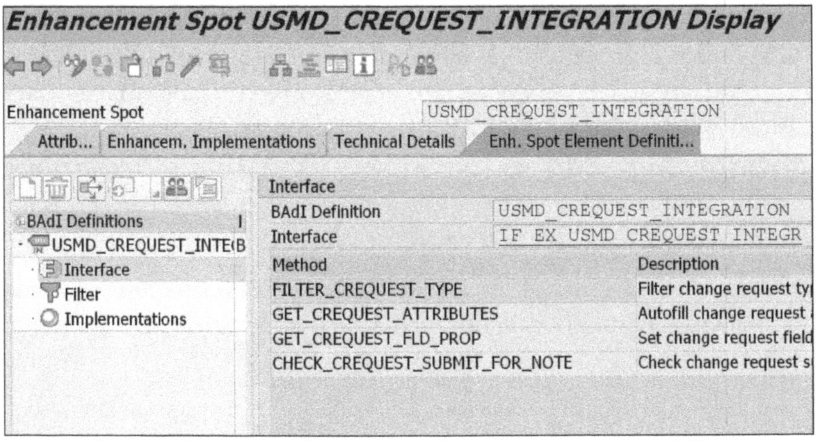

Figure 6.31 BAdI USMD_CREQUEST_INTEGRATION

6.4   Summary

This chapter discussed the UI framework and applications associated with central governance scenarios and provided an overview of the Floorplan Manager framework. The chapter also discussed the various configurations that need to be carried out to set up UIs for each domain and available enhancement options. The next chapters will detail how to integrate these UIs with governance processes.

6

Chapter 7
Central Governance: Process Modeling

This chapter explains how an end-to-end master data maintenance process is set up in SAP Master Data Governance from a central master data governance point of view. We'll cover standard workflow templates, explain how rule-based workflows are defined, and provide an overview of multiple-record processing available in SAP Master Data Governance.

After introducing the high-level architecture in Chapter 2, we discussed two important aspects of SAP Master Data Governance in Chapter 5 and Chapter 6: data modeling and user interface (UI) modeling, respectively. With the knowledge gained in previous chapters, this chapter discusses the most important aspect of SAP Master Data Governance: central master data governance. A key aspect of central master data governance is setting up an end-to-end process to maintain create, read, update, delete (CRUD) operations on master data objects, as well as how to configure workflows to support the end-to-end processes. Various building blocks of process modeling are used to set up the end-to-end process to support central governance.

This chapter begins by introducing the concept of defining governance scope and explaining the concept of the change request and the various building blocks involved in setting up the change request process. Section 7.3 and Section 7.4, respectively, provide an overview of single- and multiple-object processing from a process modeling perspective. Section 7.5 introduces the workflow modeling associated with a change request process and provides an overview of some of the SAP-delivered workflow templates. This section ends with explaining an important aspect of workflow modeling, a generic rule-based workflow template, and the process of designing a rule-based workflow using a simple example.

7.1 Governance Scope

In a master data governance scenario, apart from defining a governance organization, it's also important to define the scope of the governance for each data model. For example, some enterprises may govern only parts of the data that are considered global, whereas other enterprises may bring global as well as local attributes into the scope of the governance process. SAP Master Data Governance offers the capability to define the governance scope for each data model; by default, all entity types and attributes are governed. The governance scope for each data model can be configured via the following IMG path: **MDGIMG · General Settings · Process Modeling · Define Governance Scope**.

When an entity type, attribute, or referencing relationship is set to *not* be governed, such attributes are made read-only by SAP Master Data Governance automatically, and data can't be maintained or derived into those fields via field derivation logic. The following always need to be governed:

- Storage and usage type 1 entity types (attributes and referencing relationships can still be ungoverned)
- Key fields of an entity type
- Mandatory fields

It's highly recommended to remove ungoverned fields from the UI to avoid any confusion for the users of the system. It's also important to verify change request step properties for the ungoverned attributes and fine-tune them as needed. Any changes made to the governance scope will affect how the fields are handled during the change request process and during data loads. Following is a summary of the impact:

- **Single-record processing**
  Attributes removed from governance are automatically changed to read-only in the UI, and all related checks are disabled.

- **Mass change**
  Ungoverned fields can't be updated using the mass change process.

- **File upload**
  All ungoverned fields are ignored.

- **File download**
  Ungoverned fields are included in the download file. However, the comments section in the downloaded file indicates that fields weren't part of the governance scope.

- **Data export**
  Ungoverned fields are included in the exported file.

- **Data import**
  If the data is imported directly into the active area, then the governed fields as well as ungoverned fields are updated. However, if the governance option is selected, and the imported data goes through a change request process, the ungoverned fields are ignored.

> **Note**
>
> The USMD_GOVERNANCE_SCOPE Business Add-In (BAdI) can be used for setting governance rules. The SET_GOV_SCOPE_FORCED method can be used to force governance scope, and the CHECK_GOV_SCOPE method can be used to implement application-specific checks on governance scope.

> **Tip**
>
> Changing the governance scope of fields from **Yes** to **No** doesn't automatically remove ungoverned fields from the interfaces between SAP Master Data Governance and the target systems. Additional steps in the interfaces to suppress ungoverned fields need to be taken to avoid overwriting the values in the receiving system.

Figure 7.1 shows an example of governance scope configuration for the business partner data model.

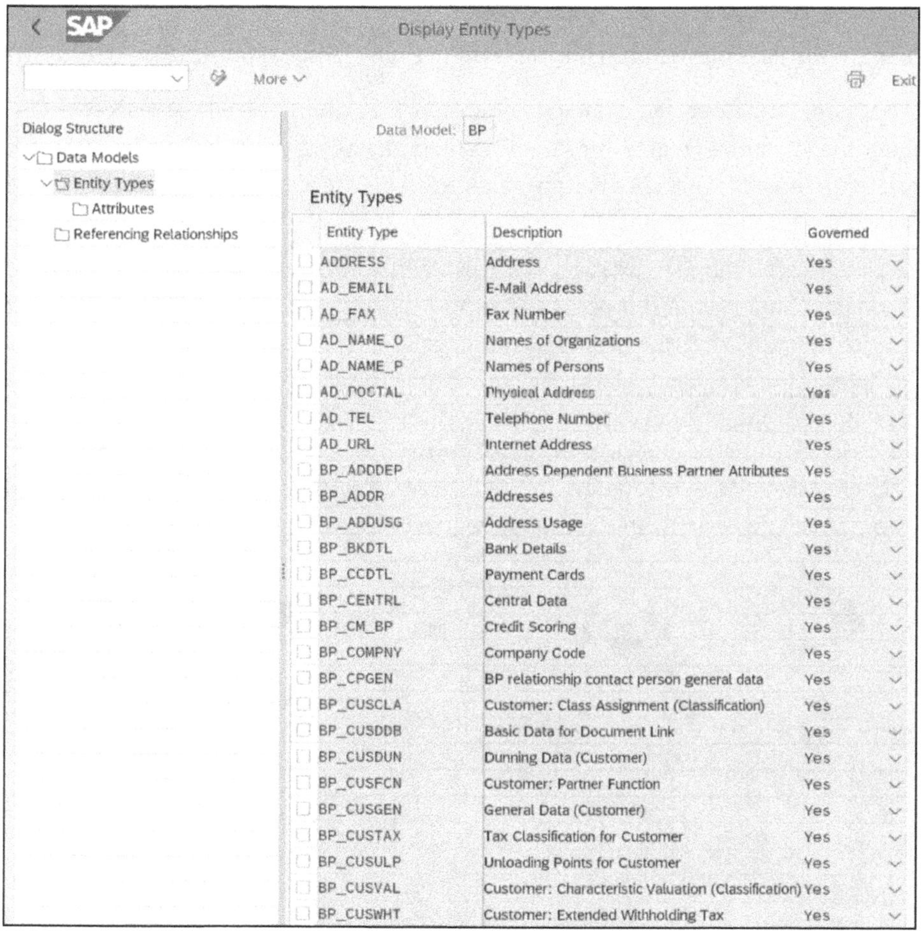

Figure 7.1 Governance Scope for Business Partner Data Model

7.2 Change Requests

In Chapter 5, we briefly discussed change requests in SAP Master Data Governance. A *change request*, in this context, is a container of changes made to a master data object that contains additional details on the relevant process. A change request supports day-to-day CRUD operations by associating a predefined process, data enrichment, and data quality rules. The data enrichment process can be a manual enrichment of data or can be sourced from an external organization via automated enrichment. Data quality rules can be mandatory field checks, conditional mandatory checks, or the derived value of a field based on the value maintained in another field. Following are the common questions that can arise when a typical CRUD process is initiated:

- What are the next steps involved in the process?
- What is the status of the request at each change request step?
- Who can process each change request step?
- What are the possible actions you can take for each change request step?

An SAP Master Data Governance change request process supports all these scenarios. A change request can be created for either a single master data record or for multiple master data records; this distinction is defined at the change request type level (explained later in this section).

Figure 7.2 shows a change request process with two approvals. Existing master data is changed via a change request process and submitted to master data experts for further data enrichment. During the process, data is validated based on preconfigured data quality rules. After the master data experts approve the change request, it's routed to a master data steward for final approval who verifies the data changes and approves the change request. Until the change request is approved, all changes made are stored only in the staging area, which means any transactions that consume the master data record don't contain changes made in the change request process.

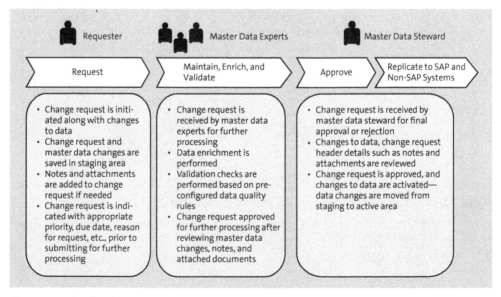

Figure 7.2 Simple Change Request Process

The following sections provide an overview of all the building blocks involved in configuring an end-to-end change request process, starting with an overview of a change request header followed by all the configuration steps.

7.2.1   Change Request Header

Figure 7.3 shows an example of a change request header.

Figure 7.3 Change Request Header: General Details

A change request header can contain the following details:

- **Change Request**
  A unique change request number is auto-generated by SAP Master Data Governance. The number range for change request IDs is controlled via number range object USMD_CREQ.

- **Description**
  This mandatory field is used to identify the change request. All work items in the change request process display the change request description as part of the work item description, so it's important to identify a change request with a meaningful description.

- **Priority**
  Priorities are used to indicate the priority of the change request to the processors of the change request. Priorities can be configured by following the IMG path, **MDGIMG •
  General Settings • Process Modeling • Change Requests • Define Priorities for Change
  Requests**.

- **Due Date**
  Requesters of a change request can indicate a due date for the change request. Adding a due date helps the processors of the change request sort the change requests accordingly.

- **Reason**
  A requester can select a reason for requesting a change request from a preconfigured list of reasons. Configuring a predefined list of reasons helps in terms of maintaining

a uniform set of reasons and in reporting. These are configured per change request type by following the IMG path, **MDGIMG • General Settings • Process Modeling • Change Requests • Define Reasons for Change Requests.**

- **Status**
  A change request can have different statuses, indicated in this field, based on the current process step. A change request status can be set with one of the following permitted processing options:
  - **No Processing**: Objects of a change request can't be changed. With this status, the UI is always set to read-only.
  - **Changing Object List**: Additional objects can be added or deleted from a change request.
  - **Execution of Changes**: Along with the ability to add or delete objects of a change request, changes to the objects are also permitted.

  Figure 7.4 shows a list of SAP-delivered change request statuses and their associated permitted processing. Additional statuses can be configured by following the IMG path, **MDGIMG • General Settings • Process Modeling • Change Requests • Edit Statuses of Change Requests.**

Note

Change request statuses **05 - Final Check Approved** and **06 - Final Check Rejected** mark the completion of a change request and indicate that the change request can't be processed anymore. Any other status indicates that the change request is still open for processing.

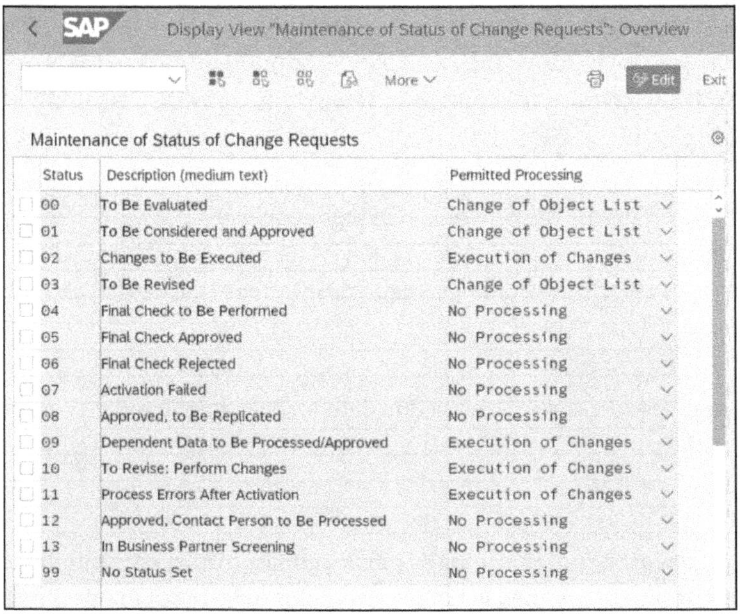

Status	Description (medium text)	Permitted Processing
00	To Be Evaluated	Change of Object List
01	To Be Considered and Approved	Change of Object List
02	Changes to Be Executed	Execution of Changes
03	To Be Revised	Change of Object List
04	Final Check to Be Performed	No Processing
05	Final Check Approved	No Processing
06	Final Check Rejected	No Processing
07	Activation Failed	No Processing
08	Approved, to Be Replicated	No Processing
09	Dependent Data to Be Processed/Approved	Execution of Changes
10	To Revise: Perform Changes	Execution of Changes
11	Process Errors After Activation	Execution of Changes
12	Approved, Contact Person to Be Processed	No Processing
13	In Business Partner Screening	No Processing
99	No Status Set	No Processing

Figure 7.4 Change Request: Statuses

- **Notes**

  The change request header enables you to add notes (Figure 7.5), which can be additional information that will help processors of the change request and also act as a collaboration platform between requesters and processors during the change request process.

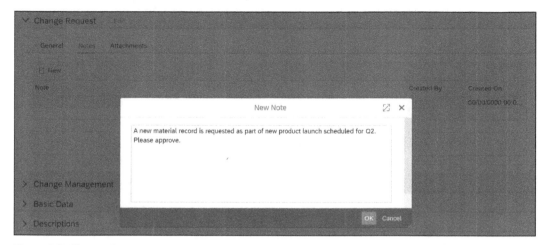

Figure 7.5 Change Request: Notes

- **Attachments**

  Attachments to justify the need for initiating a change request or any document to meet any compliance or regulatory needs can be attached under the **Attachments** tab of a change request (Figure 7.6). Note that the attachments remain specific to the change request itself but aren't attached to the master data object.

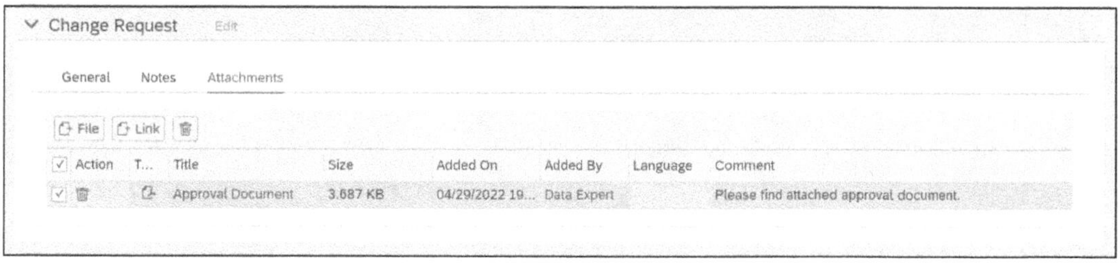

Action	T...	Title	Size	Added On	Added By	Language	Comment
🗑		Approval Document	3.687 KB	04/29/2022 19...	Data Expert		Please find attached approval document.

Figure 7.6 Change Request: Attachments

- **Target Systems**

  If the **Target Systems** checkbox is enabled at the change request type, then the change request header displays the **Target Systems** tab. It provides an option to select target systems that are specific to the change request being created.

- **Rejection Reasons**

  Reasons for rejecting a change request can be configured in the system for each change request type and can be selected while rejecting a change request. Later sections in this chapter explain how to enforce selecting the preconfigured rejection reasons when a change request is rejected. Rejection reasons can be configured by following the IMG path, **MDGIMG • General Settings • Process Modeling • Change Requests • Define Rejection Reasons for Change Requests**.

7.2.2 Logical Action

Logical actions, such as creating, displaying, or changing, are used by the system to choose a UI via linked business activities. We recommend that you use the list of logical actions that SAP provides (see Figure 7.7). If needed, logical actions can be displayed using IMG path, **MDGIMG • General Settings • Process Modeling • Business Activities • Define Logical Actions**.

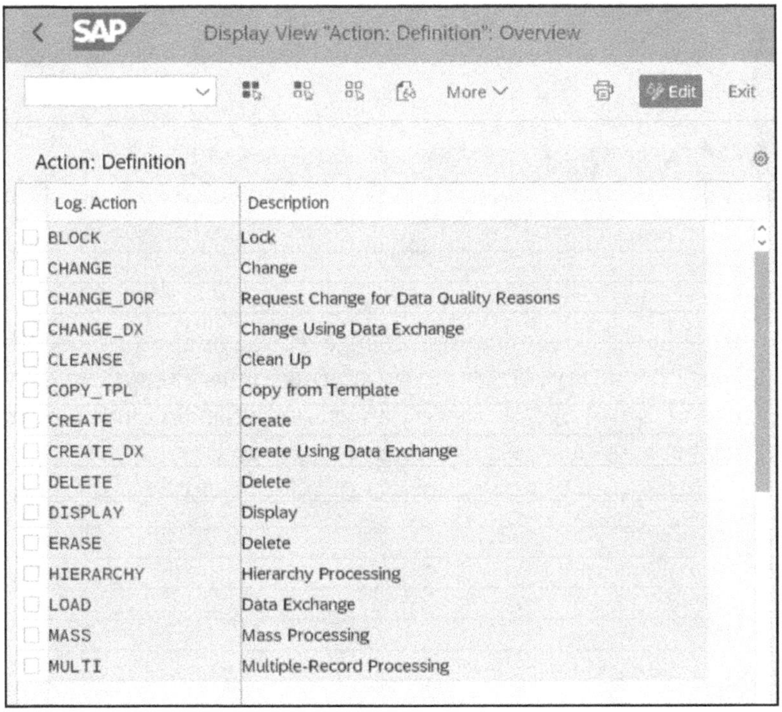
Display View "Action: Definition": Overview
More
Edit
Exit
Action: Definition
Log. Action
Description
BLOCK
Lock
CHANGE
Change
CHANGE_DQR
Request Change for Data Quality Reasons
CHANGE_DX
Change Using Data Exchange
CLEANSE
Clean Up
COPY_TPL
Copy from Template
CREATE
Create
CREATE_DX
Create Using Data Exchange
DELETE
Delete
DISPLAY
Display
ERASE
Delete
HIERARCHY
Hierarchy Processing
LOAD
Data Exchange
MASS
Mass Processing
MULTI
Multiple-Record Processing

Figure 7.7 All the SAP-Delivered Logical Actions

7.2.3 Business Activity

A business activity is created with a link to a logical action, data model, and business object, which means every business activity is unique to a data model and business object. A few examples are as follows:

- For the business partner data model and business object type 159 (customer), CUP1 (create customer) is the business activity for creating customers.

- For the business partner data model and business object type 266 (supplier), SUP1 (create supplier) is the business activity for creating suppliers.
- For business partner data model and business object type 147 (business partner), BPP1 (create business partner) is the business activity for creating business partners.

We recommend using the SAP-delivered business activities for all standard data models unless a custom data model is created or custom type 1 entity types need to be processed. If needed, business activities can be configured using the IMG path, **MDGIMG • General Settings • Process Modeling • Business Activities • Create Business Activity.**

Figure 7.8 shows an example of business activities delivered by SAP for the material master data model.

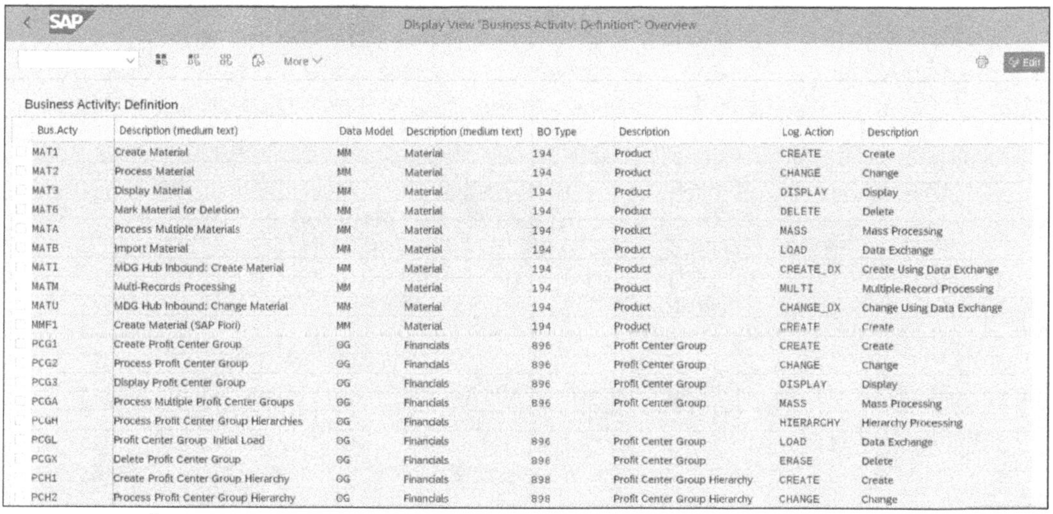
Display View "Business Activity: Definition": Overview

Business Activity: Definition

Bus.Acty	Description (medium text)	Data Model	Description (medium text)	BO Type	Description	Log. Action	Description
MAT1	Create Material	MM	Material	194	Product	CREATE	Create
MAT2	Process Material	MM	Material	194	Product	CHANGE	Change
MAT3	Display Material	MM	Material	194	Product	DISPLAY	Display
MAT6	Mark Material for Deletion	MM	Material	194	Product	DELETE	Delete
MATA	Process Multiple Materials	MM	Material	194	Product	MASS	Mass Processing
MATB	Import Material	MM	Material	194	Product	LOAD	Data Exchange
MATI	MDG Hub Inbound: Create Material	MM	Material	194	Product	CREATE_DX	Create Using Data Exchange
MATM	Multi-Records Processing	MM	Material	194	Product	MULTI	Multiple-Record Processing
MATU	MDG Hub Inbound: Change Material	MM	Material	194	Product	CHANGE_DX	Change Using Data Exchange
MMF1	Create Material (SAP Fiori)	MM	Material	194	Product	CREATE	Create
PCG1	Create Profit Center Group	OG	Financials	896	Profit Center Group	CREATE	Create
PCG2	Process Profit Center Group	OG	Financials	896	Profit Center Group	CHANGE	Change
PCG3	Display Profit Center Group	OG	Financials	896	Profit Center Group	DISPLAY	Display
PCGA	Process Multiple Profit Center Groups	OG	Financials	896	Profit Center Group	MASS	Mass Processing
PCGH	Process Profit Center Group Hierarchies	OG	Financials			HIERARCHY	Hierarchy Processing
PCGL	Profit Center Group Initial Load	OG	Financials	896	Profit Center Group	LOAD	Data Exchange
PCGX	Delete Profit Center Group	OG	Financials	896	Profit Center Group	ERASE	Delete
PCH1	Create Profit Center Group Hierarchy	OG	Financials	898	Profit Center Group Hierarchy	CREATE	Create
PCH2	Process Profit Center Group Hierarchy	OG	Financials	898	Profit Center Group Hierarchy	CHANGE	Change

Figure 7.8 Business Activities for the Material Master Data Model

Chapter 6 explained various aspects of UI modeling and SAP-delivered UI applications. These UI applications are linked to logical actions and business activities. The following configurations explain IMG activities related to logical actions:

- **Link logical actions with a UI application and business activity**
  The target UI application is derived based on the business object type code, logical action, and current UI application. For displaying standard settings, follow the IMG path, **MDGIMG • General Settings • Process Modeling • Business Activities • Link Log. Actions with UI Application and Bus. Act.: Standard Definition**. For defining custom settings for custom applications, follow the IMG path, **MDGIMG • General Settings • Process Modeling • Business Activities • Link Log. Actions with UI Application and Bus. Activity: Custom Definition.**
- **Link logical actions with a business activity**
  For each UI application and logical activity, a business activity is linked. For displaying standard settings, follow the IMG path, **MDGIMG • General Settings • Process**

Modeling • Business Activities • Link Logical Actions with Business Activity: Standard Definition. For defining custom settings for custom applications, follow the IMG path, **MDGIMG • General Settings • Process Modeling • Business Activities • Link Logical Actions with Business Activity: Custom Definition.**

7.2.4   Change Request Type

Every change request is associated with a change request type. Either you select a change request type during creation of a change request, or the system automatically determines the type based on the action initiated if there is only one change request type associated. A change request type can have the properties listed in Table 7.1.

Property	Explanation
Data Model	Identifies with which data model the change request type is associated. When a data model is assigned, then the change requests created are edition independent.
Edition Type	Defines various properties that are valid for all editions of the same type, such as data model, data-specific time period, entity types, and so on (editions and edition types are described later in this section).
Objects Required	Indicates whether an entity needs to be specified during change request creation.
Single Object	Indicates whether the change request can contain more than one entity of the main entity type specified for the change request type.
Parallel	Indicates whether a parallel change request can be enabled for the storage and usage type 4 entities maintained under allowed entity types.
Main Entity Type	Indicates the entity type for which change requests are created.
Workflow	Indicates the SAP Business Workflow template that is followed during the change request process.
Target System	Indicates whether target systems to which data is replicated can be specified.
Default	Indicates the default change request type used by background processes for the combination of logical action and business activity.
UI Application Name and UI Configuration	Specified if a specific UI needs to be determined based on the change request type.
Switch Classification	Allows lean classification to be set for a change request type. This is applicable only to change request types with the material master data model.

Table 7.1 Properties of a Change Request Type

The IMG path for configuring a change request type is **MDGIMG · General Settings · Process Modeling · Change Requests · Create Change Request Type**.

For each change request type, you can configure the scope of the entity level, linking of business activities, and Service Level Agreements (SLAs), which we'll explore in the following sections.

Scope on Entity Level

For a specific change request type, if the parallel change request option is selected, then the entity types that can be changed using this change request type are specified. An example of such a scenario includes various plant-specific entity types included under this configuration to enable plant-level change request types. Figure 7.9 shows the example configuration of the scope on the entity type level with a material parallel change request.

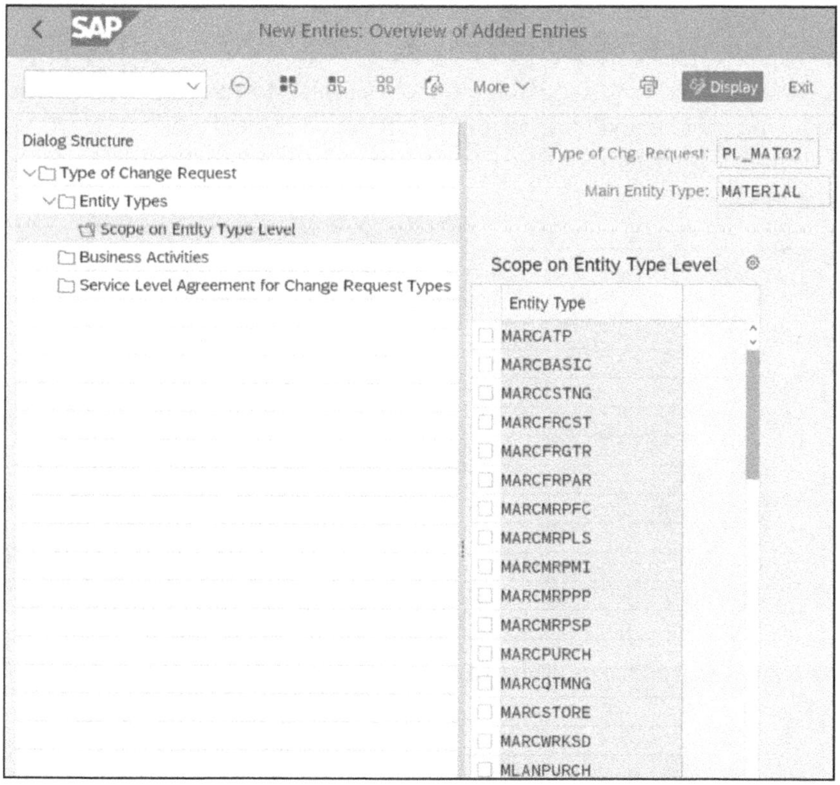

Figure 7.9 Example: Scope on Entity for a Parallel Change Request Type

Linked Business Activities

Business activities are linked to a change request. Because the logical action is already linked to the UI configuration and work center links, linking the business activity to the change request type enables you to automatically initiate a change request of a specific type if only one change request type is linked to a business activity. Figure 7.10 shows an example of a business activity **MAT1** linked to change request type **MATL01**.

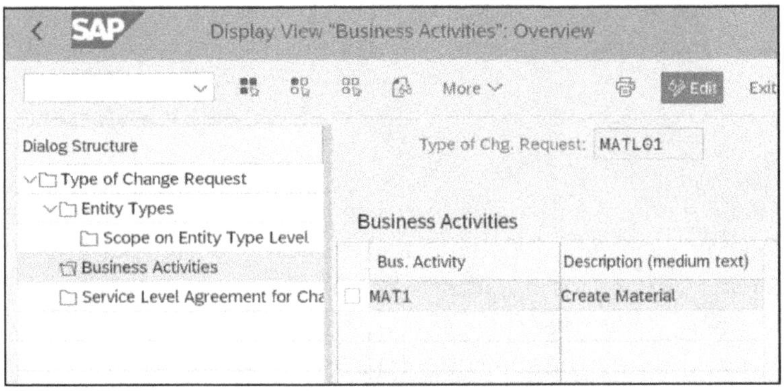

Figure 7.10 Example: Business Activity Linked to a Change Request Type

Service Level Agreement for Change Request Type

SLAs can be defined at the change request type level for each priority, and these defined SLAs are used during process analytics (see Chapter 10 for additional details). Figure 7.11 shows an example of an SLA definition for the **MATL01** change request type for each priority we configured earlier.

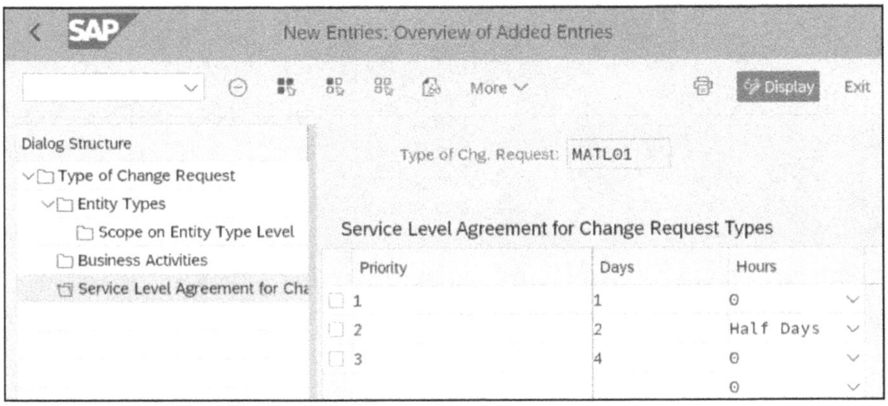

Figure 7.11 Example: SLA for a Change Request Type

Note

Remembering what you now know about logical actions, business activities, and change request types, the following summarizes how they are linked to each other:

- A business activity is linked to a logical action.
- A change request type is linked to a business activity.

Figure 7.12 shows an example of how logical action ❶, business activity ❷, and change request type ❸ are used in a material create process.

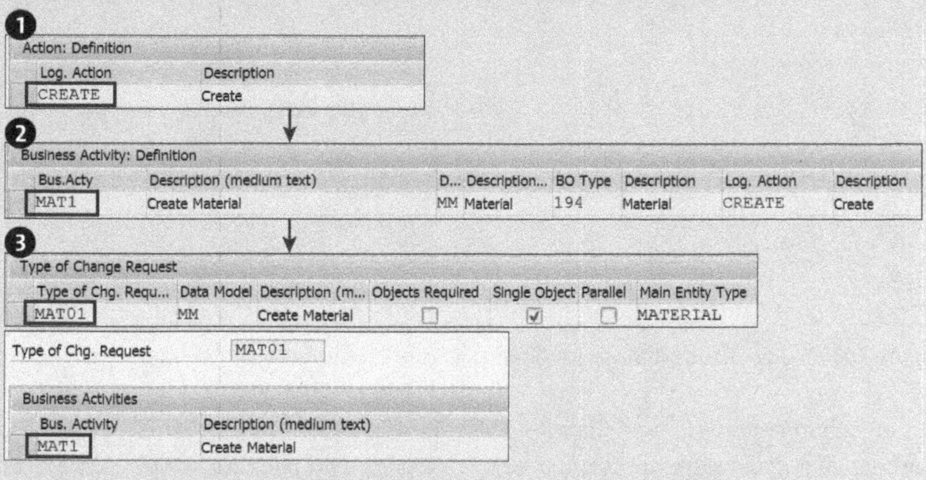

Figure 7.12 Links between Logical Action, Business Activity, and Change Request Type

7.2.5   Change Request Steps

Change request steps are identified as dialog or background steps in a change request process. The process of configuring change request steps differs based on the workflow template used (workflow templates and rule-based workflow are discussed in Section 7.5). The following sections provide details on how to configure change request steps based on workflow template and change request step properties.

Change request processors can use Change Request Tracker to monitor change request progress. They can view the current workflow step, all previously executed dialog workflow steps, and all future steps needed until the change request is successfully approved. This is also referred to as the "golden path" or "happy path." Change Request Tracker can be called up via the **What's Next** link available in the **Change Request UIBB** section.

Configuring Change Request Steps

For any change request type that has a standard rule-based workflow template setup, change request steps are configured using the following IMG path: **MDGIMG · General Settings · Process Modeling · Workflow · Rule-Based Workflow · Define Change Request Steps for Rule-Based Workflow**.

The next step in the configuration defines the ID of the next dialog step following the current step along that golden or happy path of the current change request.

Figure 7.13 shows an example of change request steps configured for change request type **MAT01**, which is configured with a rule-based workflow template.

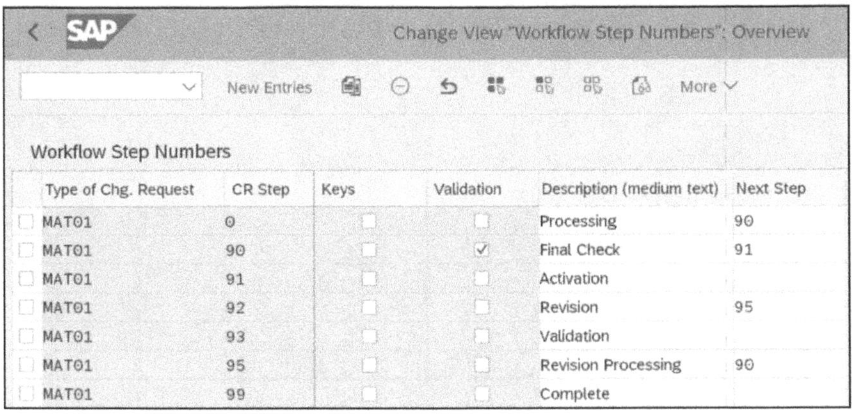

Type of Chg. Request	CR Step	Keys	Validation	Description (medium text)	Next Step
MAT01	0	☐	☐	Processing	90
MAT01	90	☐	☑	Final Check	91
MAT01	91	☐	☐	Activation	
MAT01	92	☐	☐	Revision	95
MAT01	93	☐	☐	Validation	
MAT01	95	☐	☐	Revision Processing	90
MAT01	99	☐	☐	Complete	

Figure 7.13 Change Request Steps for Change Request Types with a Rule-Based Workflow

For any change request type that has a workflow template setup that isn't rule based, the change request steps are configured by following IMG path, **MDGIMG • General Settings • Process Modeling • Workflow • Other MDG Workflows • Define Change Request Step Numbers.**

Figure 7.14 shows the step configuration for workflow template **WS54400001**, which is used for change request type CUST1P2 (create customer, parallel workflow) as an example.

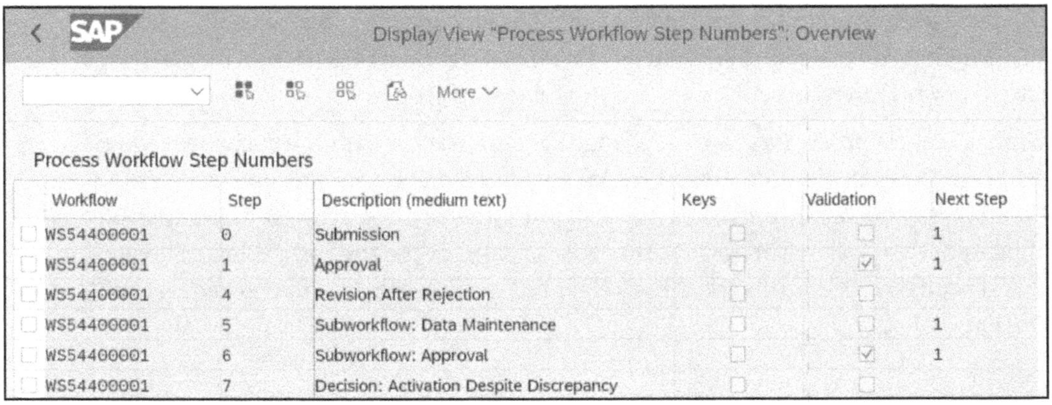

Workflow	Step	Description (medium text)	Keys	Validation	Next Step
WS54400001	0	Submission	☐	☐	1
WS54400001	1	Approval	☐	☑	1
WS54400001	4	Revision After Rejection	☐	☐	
WS54400001	5	Subworkflow: Data Maintenance	☐	☐	1
WS54400001	6	Subworkflow: Approval	☐	☑	1
WS54400001	7	Decision: Activation Despite Discrepancy	☐	☐	

Figure 7.14 Workflow Steps for Workflow Template WS54400001

Configuring a change request step involves the following:

- **Change request type (for rule-based workflow) or workflow template (for other workflow templates)**
  A change request type denotes the object used for managing changes to master data. A change request contains the objects a user wants to create or change, along with information about the changes.

- **Change request step number and description**

  Each change request may have one or more change request steps; each change request step defines the associated processors, checks, entity types, UI, and so on.

- **Keys**

  In a change request process, keys for the entity being changed need to be entered. However, the change request process in SAP Master Data Governance provides the flexibility to delay entering the key of an entity until the final step in the process. The **Keys** checkbox indicates the final step in the process by which the key must be entered.

- **Validation**

  The **Validation** checkbox indicates the final execution of all validations and is a prerequisite for completing all actions for the change request step. Typically, all validation checks must be completed before final activation of the change request occurs.

Properties

In a change request process, configurations at the change request step can be made to control the following:

- How various checks and data enrichment are performed
- Whether entity types and attributes are relevant and required
- The setup of a different UI for each change request step

Figure 7.15 shows change request steps for change request type **MAT01** as an example.

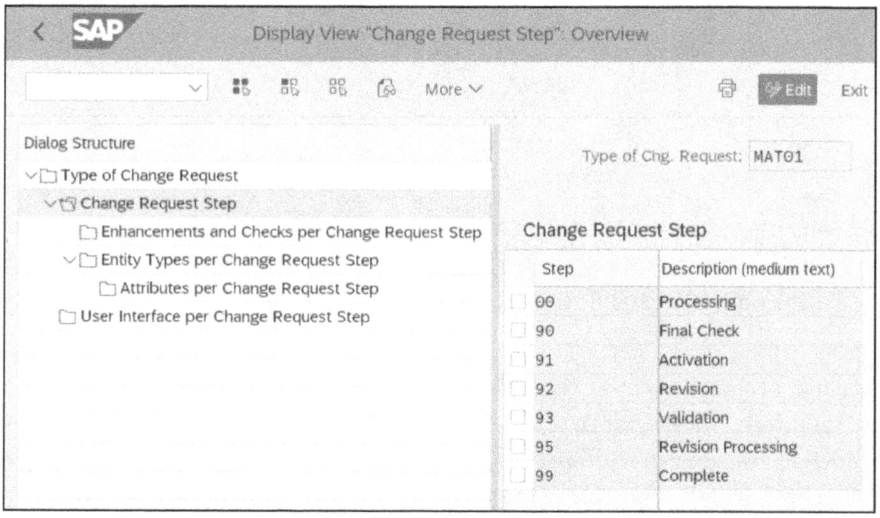

Figure 7.15 Change Request Steps for Change Request Type MAT01

Change request step properties can be configured by following the IMG path, **MDGIMG • General Settings • Process Modeling • Change Requests • Configure Properties of Change Request Step**.

The enhancements and checks triggered for a specific change request step can be controlled. Typically, every change request goes through various checks performed by the system, and for each change request step, you can control the behavior of these checks. Following is a list of checks performed by SAP Master Data Governance:

- Basic check
- Authorization check
- Duplicate check
- Validation rules configured in Business Rules Framework plus (BRFplus)
- Validation rules developed using BAdIs
- Existence check
- Reuse area check
- Validation rules (data quality)

Along with these checks, the system also performs any additional data enrichments (see Chapter 8 for details regarding enrichment spots and how they are configured). Figure 7.16 shows an example of enhancements and checks for change request type **MAT01** (create material) and **00** (submission).

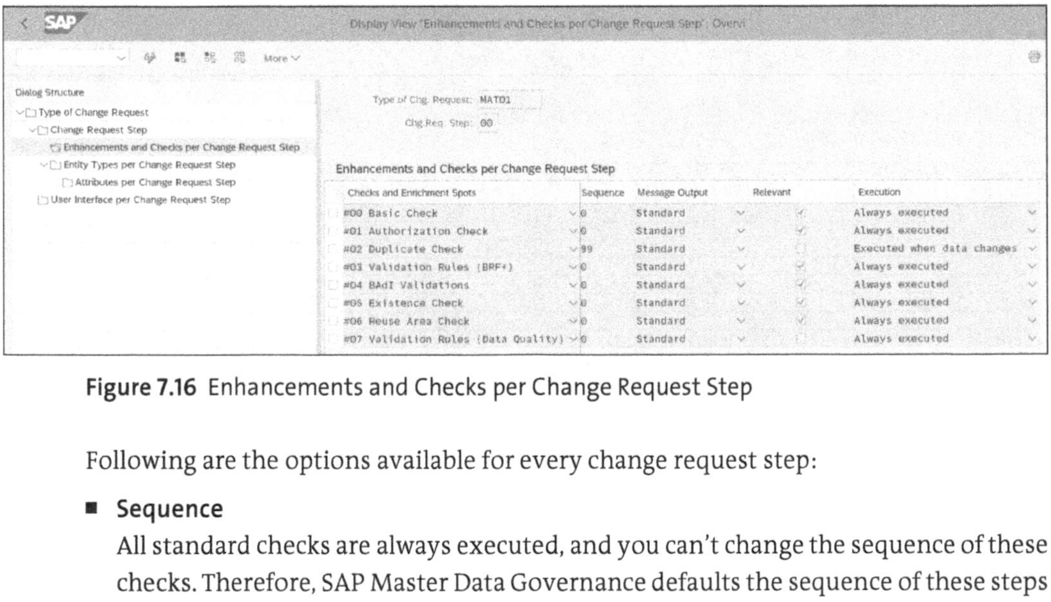

Figure 7.16 Enhancements and Checks per Change Request Step

Following are the options available for every change request step:

- **Sequence**
  All standard checks are always executed, and you can't change the sequence of these checks. Therefore, SAP Master Data Governance defaults the sequence of these steps to 0, which isn't changeable, indicating that they are executed first. Similarly, the duplicate check is always performed at the very end, so the sequence for this check is always defaulted to 99 and isn't changeable. You can change the sequence of execution for all enrichments. It's important to check the dependencies between enrichments and indicate the sequence accordingly. For example, address enrichment needs to be performed before determining tax jurisdiction, which depends on address parameters.

- **Message Output**

  Message output type determines whether a processor of a change request step can process the change request without addressing the outcome of the checks performed. Because the change request process is a collaborative process, sometimes a requester who is creating a new record may not be an expert in completing various parts of the data. In such scenarios, the change request can't be submitted without addressing the errors. SAP Master Data Governance addresses this problem by providing an option to display error messages as warnings for a specific change request step. However, before activation of the change request, all checks are performed. There are two options to choose from:

  - **Standard**: Messages are displayed as standard messages on the UI.

  - **Issue Error Messages as Warnings**: All error messages are displayed as warnings. Authorization and hierarchy checks are the only exceptions.

- **Relevant**

  It's possible to select whether a specific check is relevant for the change request step or not. Except the basic check, all other checks and enrichments can be set as not relevant if needed.

- **Execution**

  Provides an option to trigger checks either as always executed or only when data is changed. For example, duplicate checks don't always have to be triggered and can be triggered only when relevant data is changed.

The following properties can be set for entity types and attributes for each change request step:

- **Field Properties**

  Field properties can be defined for each change request step to determine if the entity types and attributes are relevant. This can be configured both at the entity type level and the individual attribute level. Following is a list of available options for **Field Properties**:

  - **Standard**: System retains the required field settings based on the data model required field setting or based on the check derived from a BAdI or from a reuse active area. If it's set at the entity type, then all the attributes in the entity type inherit the same setting. However, if the property for an attribute is set to be different from the entity type level setting, then the field property takes precedence.

  - **No Required Field Check**: All required fields are set to optional for the change request step. If this is set at an entity type level, all attributes inherit the property and can't be changed.

  - **Not Relevant**: All system checks are ignored, and the field becomes read-only. If this is set at an entity type level, all attributes inherit the property and can't be changed.

- **CheckLogic**
  Check logic can be used to determine if all the enhancements and checks are performed for the change request step or if only basic checks are performed.

  Figure 7.17 shows an example of entity type level properties for change request type **MAT01** and step **00**.

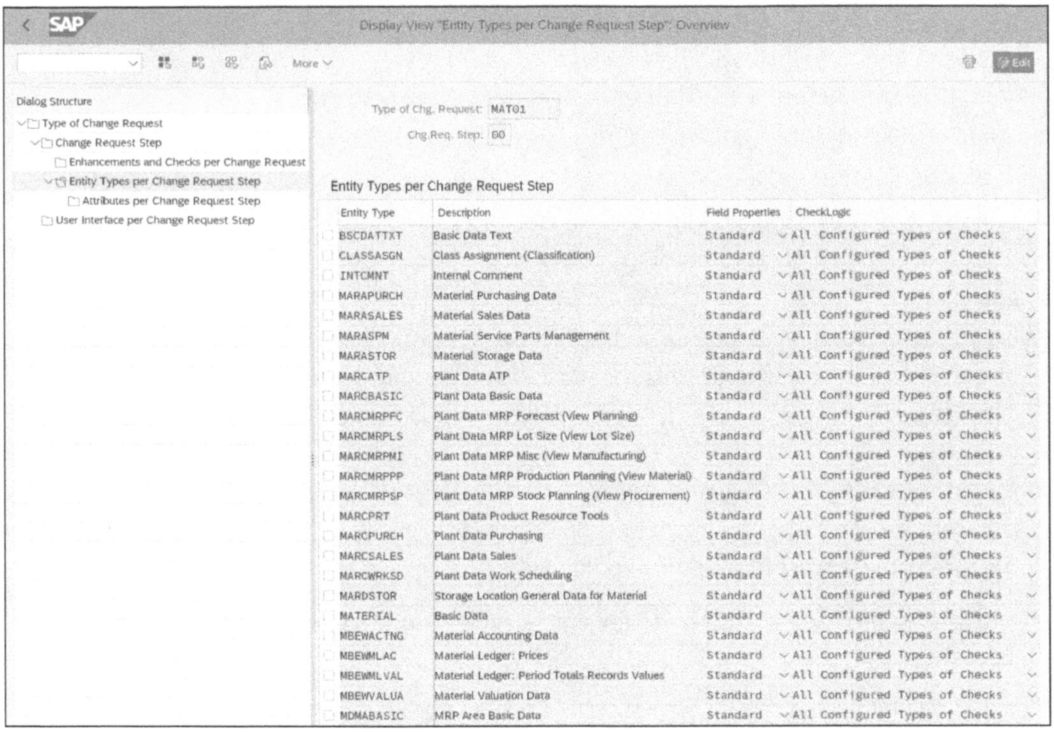

Figure 7.17 Entity Type Properties for a Change Request Step

For each change request step, a separate UI can be configured. When configured, the change request step UI is displayed when the change request process is at that change request step. SAP Master Data Governance also displays all changes highlighted in a different color, which can be disabled at the change request step level.

7.2.6   Change Request Actions and Step Types

In this section, we'll explain the various change request actions delivered by SAP and how a step type is formed using these change request actions.

Change Request Actions

You can take certain change request actions during a change request step, and these actions correspond to UI buttons for processing a change request when defined as part of a step type (explained in the next section). Actions can be defined with the following:

- **Description**
  A text description of the action.
- **Pushbutton Text**
  Text to be displayed on a pushbutton.
- **Quick Info Text**
  Text displayed as a quick info or tooltip for a pushbutton.
- **Check**
  Indicates whether all checks need to be executed without errors for the action to be completed.
- **Note**
  Indicates whether entry of a note is required for completing the action.
- **Reason**
  Indicates whether entry of a rejection reason is required for completing the action.

Figure 7.18 shows some of the actions delivered by SAP. Except for **Disagree**, **Reject**, **Send for Revision**, and **Withdraw**, all checks are implicitly performed for other actions, and the work item can't be completed if the checks return any errors.

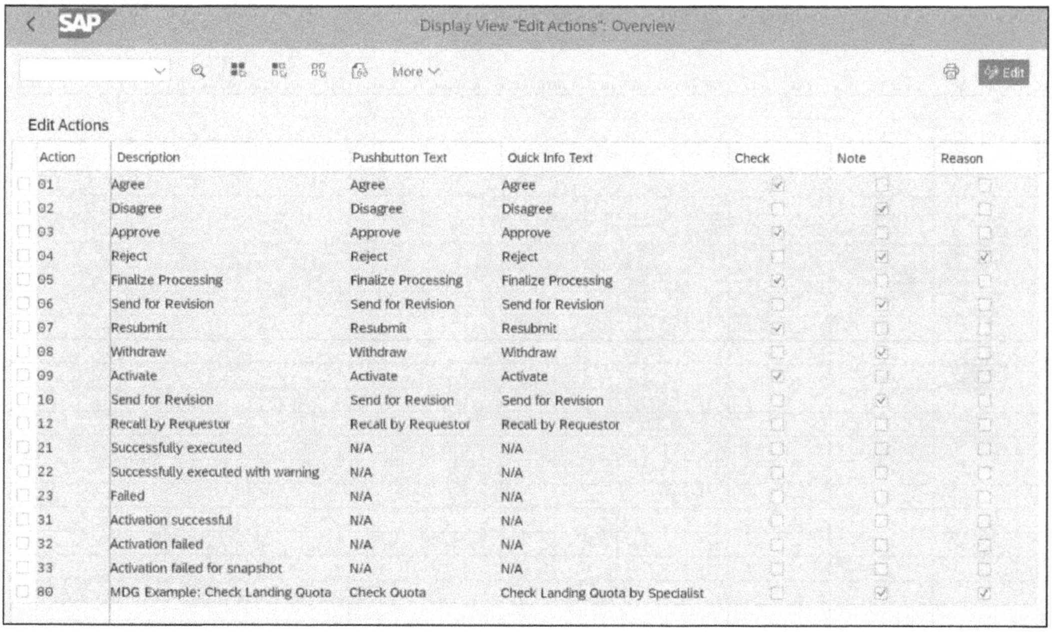
Display View "Edit Actions": Overview

Edit Actions

Action	Description	Pushbutton Text	Quick Info Text	Check	Note	Reason
01	Agree	Agree	Agree	✓		
02	Disagree	Disagree	Disagree		✓	
03	Approve	Approve	Approve	✓		
04	Reject	Reject	Reject		✓	✓
05	Finalize Processing	Finalize Processing	Finalize Processing	✓		
06	Send for Revision	Send for Revision	Send for Revision		✓	
07	Resubmit	Resubmit	Resubmit	✓		
08	Withdraw	Withdraw	Withdraw		✓	
09	Activate	Activate	Activate	✓		
10	Send for Revision	Send for Revision	Send for Revision		✓	
12	Recall by Requestor	Recall by Requestor	Recall by Requestor			
21	Successfully executed	N/A	N/A			
22	Successfully executed with warning	N/A	N/A			
23	Failed	N/A	N/A			
31	Activation successful	N/A	N/A			
32	Activation failed	N/A	N/A			
33	Activation failed for snapshot	N/A	N/A			
80	MDG Example: Check Landing Quota	Check Quota	Check Landing Quota by Specialist		✓	✓

Figure 7.18 Definition of Change Request Actions

Change request actions can be configured by following the IMG path, **MDGIMG • General Settings • Process Modeling • Workflow • Define Change Request Actions.**

Change Request Step Types

Change request step types are used to assign a set of user actions to workflow tasks that aren't in the background. These step types once associated with actions determine the possible user actions on a UI. For a workflow that isn't rule-based, step types are assigned using the Workflow Builder, whereas for a rule-based workflow, step types are assigned using BRFplus. **Save** and **Check** are two actions that are implicitly available in all step types. During the definition of a step type, possible actions are configured, along with the sequence, which determines the order of the corresponding UI buttons. Figure 7.19 shows an example of a standard step type and the associated action assignment. Figure 7.20 shows an example of the same step types and actions from a material approver's UI perspective.

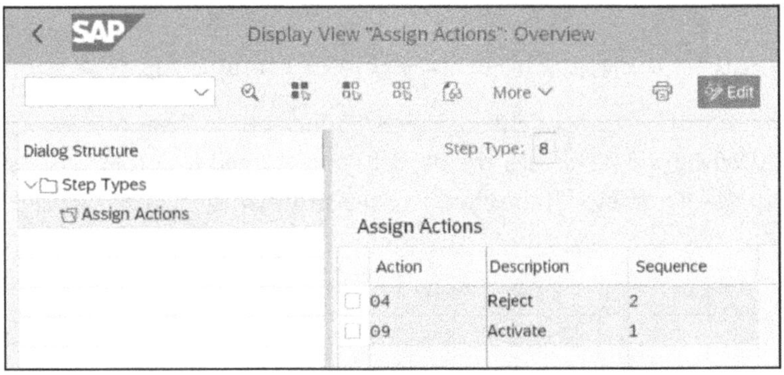

Figure 7.19 Step Type and Action Assignment

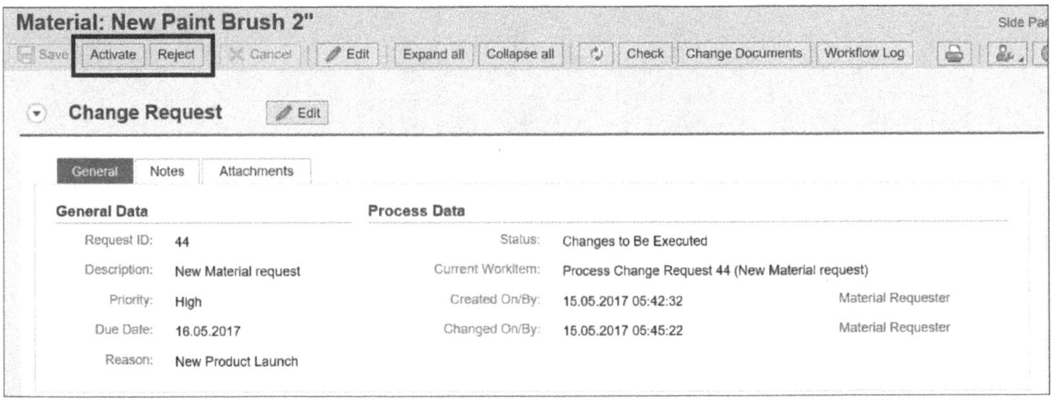

Figure 7.20 Step Types and Actions Represented on a UI

Change request step types can be configured by following the IMG path, **MDGIMG • General Settings • Process Modeling • Workflow • Define Change Request Step Types and Assign Actions.**

Now that we've discussed all the building blocks of a change request, let's consider how these come together. Figure 7.21 shows individual building blocks of a change request process setup and how they are related to each other.

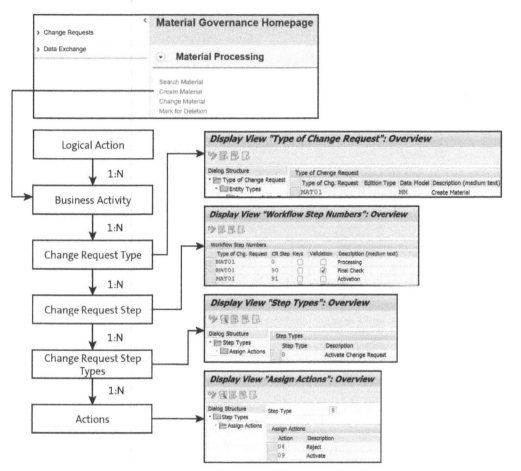

Figure 7.21 Change Request Process Setup

7.2.7   User Interface Determination

Previous sections explained the end-to-end change request process setup. Some of these building blocks of the change request process include assignment of UI configurations. Based on various configurations, SAP Master Data Governance determines the UI. Following is a list of various configurations where UI assignment is configured:

- **Change request step level UI assignment**
  When a change request specific step requires a different UI, it's assigned at the change request step level configuration. Refer to Section 7.2.5 for more details.

- **UI assigned at the logical action and business object type combination**
  Refer to Section 7.2.3 for more details.

- **UI assigned at the change request type**
  Refer to Section 7.2.4 for more details.

- **UI adaptations such as context-based adaptation (CBA), customization, or personalization**
  Refer to Chapter 6 for additional details.

Figure 7.22 shows the sequence of the UI determination process. If the UI is defined at a change request step level, then the specified UI is determined.

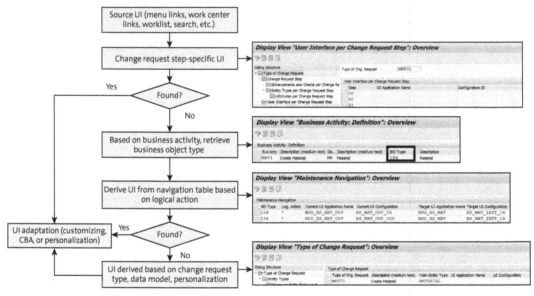

Figure 7.22 Change Request UI Determination

7.2.8   Editions

An *edition* enables time-dependent maintenance of master data. Financial master data objects, such as cost centers and profit centers, require time-dependent master data, so editions are used. Such time-dependent master data objects automatically inherit the valid-from date from the edition's valid-from date. Editions are used to schedule changes to master data and in SAP Master Data Governance. Editions allow you to combine either the changes that are logically related or those that need to be valid from the same date. It's possible to use editions for custom objects modeled in SAP Master Data Governance if the objects are modeled as flex objects. The typical edition-based process follows these steps:

1. Create the edition, and provide validity dates.
2. Initiate the change request process for all changes that are related to each other or that become active from the validity date of the edition.

3. Release the edition after all change requests are approved, rejected, or withdrawn.

4. Replicate the change requests to target systems after approval, via a manual replication, or after release of the edition.

For any master data object being changed, the valid-to date depends on whether there is a next change scheduled or not. If there is no scheduled change, then the validity is until the end of time. However, if there is a next change scheduled, then the valid-to date is changed to the beginning of the next scheduled change. Chapter 15 explains editions in detail, including the strategies to use while creating editions and how to release and monitor editions.

Editions are always created with a reference to an edition type, which identifies the data model and entity types that can be processed in an edition. SAP delivers an edition type 0G_ALL, which is defined with all entity types and can be used in the finance (0G) data model.

An edition type is defined with the following:

- Name of the edition type and description
- Data model to which the edition type is linked
- Whether the edition has period-specific or date-specific validity
- Fiscal year variant
- Indicator to identify if the edition type is retired

> **Note**
>
> An edition type can be retired only if there are no open editions. After an edition type is retired, change requests can't be created referencing that edition type. A retired edition type can't be activated or used in consistency checks.

Figure 7.23 shows the **0G_ALL** edition type, and Figure 7.24 shows a list of all entity types assigned to the **0G_ALL** edition type.

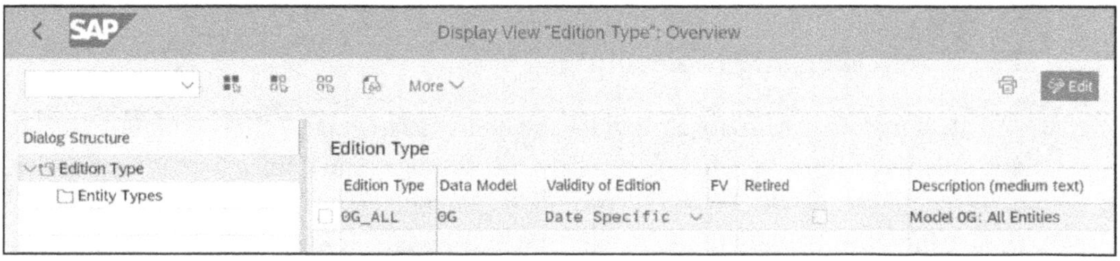

Figure 7.23 0G_ALL Edition Type

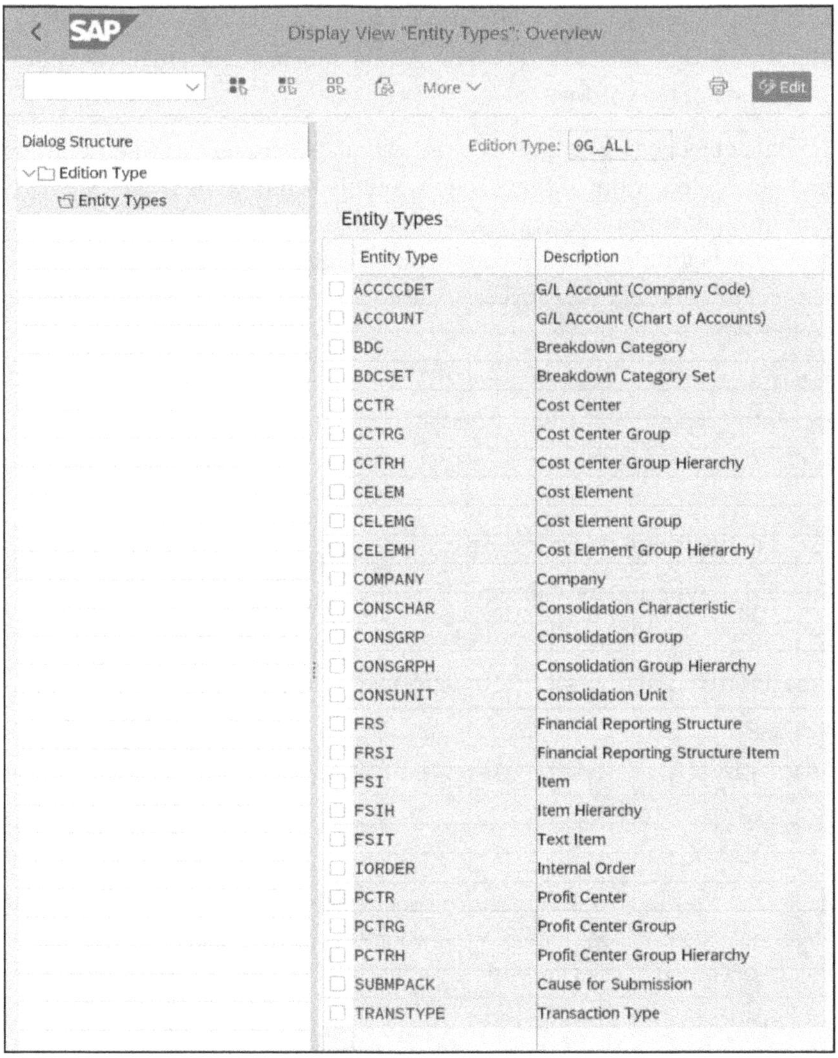

Figure 7.24 Entity Types in the OG_ALL Edition Type

7.3   Single-Record Processing

SAP Master Data Governance provides the ability to manage either a single record or multiple records via the change request process. How many objects a change request can contain is controlled at the corresponding change request type by using the **Single Object** checkbox. Each of the SAP-delivered master data domains offers various single-record processing and multiple-record processing capabilities, as described in the following sections. You'll get an overview of the central governance scenarios for each domain. Processing a customer master using a remote system as a scenario and SAP-delivered Business Context Viewer (BCV) side panel content is also briefly discussed.

7.3.1   Central Master Data Governance Scenarios

In this section, we'll discuss central master data governance scenarios for each of the SAP-delivered domains. Each of the sections provides an overview of scenarios, as well as lists of SAP-delivered change request types and associated workflow templates.

Material Master

The material master provides the ability to search, change, and mark a material for deletion. In SAP Master Data Governance, it's possible to extend the material to multiple plant and sales extensions in a create or change process. SAP Master Data Governance supports the following processes that can be accessed via homepage links or work center links:

- Search
- Create Material
- Change Material
- Mark for Deletion

The search screen provides the ability to navigate to all available processes in the material master, including multiple-record processing. Table 7.2 shows a list of all SAP-delivered change request types, including SAP Fiori–specific change request types.

> **Note**
>
> SAP change request types and associated configurations, including rule-based workflow links for material, are delivered via BC Set MDGM_MDG_MATERIAL_CR_TYPE_8B. This BC Set is valid from SAP Master Data Governance on SAP S/4HANA 2021 and SAP Master Data Governance for SAP ERP 9.2.
>
> The SAP-delivered BC Set for material change request types can be activated using Transaction MDG_BS_MAT_CR_BCST08.

Change Request Type	Description	Workflow
MAT01	Create Material	WS60800086
MAT02	Process Material	WS60800086
MAT06	Mark Material for Deletion	WS60800086
MATL01	Create Material w. Lean Classification	WS60800086
MATL02	Process Material w. Lean Classification	WS60800086
MMF1P1	Create Material (SAP Fiori)	WS60800086

Table 7.2 Material Master Single-Object Change Request Types

Table 7.3 shows a subset of these change request types and how they are linked to corresponding UI links in Figure 7.25, business activities, and logical actions.

Change Request Type	Description	Business Activity	Logical Action
❶ MAT01	Create Material	MAT1	CREATE
❷ MAT02	Process Material	MAT2	CHANGE
❸ MAT06	Mark Material for Deletion	MAT6	DELETE

Table 7.3 Material Master Single-Object Change Request Types

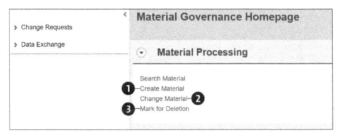

Figure 7.25 Material Processing Links

Business Partner

Business partner governance provides the ability to search for business partner records for various maintenance activities as well as for cleansing cases. SAP Master Data Governance supports a number of maintenance processes that can be accessed directly from a search results view, such as mass change, manual replication, mark for deletion, block/unblock, change, and so on. This ensures that the user is directed to the search screen and will search for an existing business partner record before initiating a new record. SAP Master Data Governance also supports the creation of business partners of type organization, person, and group. The business partner type *person* is used for creating a person (e.g., contact persons). Types *organization* and *group* are used for creating a business partner that is an organization or a group (e.g., customer or supplier records). Table 7.4 shows a list of all SAP-delivered change request types, including an SAP Fiori–specific change request type.

> **Note**
>
> SAP change request types and associated configurations, including rule-based workflow links for business partners, are delivered via BC Set CA-MDG-APP-BP_VC_USMD110_C07. This BC Set is valid from SAP Master Data Governance on SAP S/4HANA 2021 and SAP Master Data Governance for SAP ERP 9.2.
>
> The SAP-delivered BC Set for business partner change request types can be activated using Transaction MDG_BS_BP_CR_BCSET10.

Change Request Type	Description	Workflow
BP1P1	Create Business Partner	WS60800086
BP1P2	Create Bus. Partner w. Hry. Assignment	WS60800086
BP2P1	Process Business Partner	WS60800086
BP2P2	Process Bus. Partner w. Hry. Assignment	WS60800086
BP5P1	Block/Unblock Business Partner	WS60800086
BP6P1	Mark Business Partner for Deletion	WS60800086
BPCC1	Process Business Partner Cleansing Case	WS60800086
BPCC2	Process Business Partner Cleansing Case	WS60800086
BPF1P1	Create Business Partner (SAP Fiori)	WS60800086

Table 7.4 Change Request Types for Business Partners

Along with the business partner search, it's possible to search for business partner cleansing scenarios. See Chapter 8 for additional details on how to create cleansing scenarios. Change request type BPCC1 is used for processing cleansing cases.

Customer Master

Customer master governance provides the ability to govern customer master data via various available processes. Search for an existing customer record, create, update, block, and mark for deletion are the single-object change request processes available under customer master governance. Table 7.5 shows a list of all SAP-delivered change request types, including an SAP Fiori-specific change request type.

Change Request Type	Description	Workflow
CUST1P2	Create Customer (Parallel WF)	WS54400001
CUST1P3	Create Customer w. Hierarchy Assignment	WS54300003
CUST2P1	Process Customer	WS54300003
CUST2P2	Process Customer w. Hierarchy Assignment	WS54300003
CUST5P1	Block/Unblock Customer	WS54300003
CUST6P1	Mark Customer for Deletion	WS54300003
CUF1P1	Create Customer (SAP Fiori)	WS60800086

Table 7.5 Change Request Types for Customer

Change Request Type	Description	Workflow
CUSTHI01	Local Maintenance: Create Customer	WS46000023
CUSTHI02	Local Maintenance: Process Customer	WS46000027
CUSTL1	Create ERP Customer (Lean Request)	WS54300004
CUF2P1	Process Customer (SAP Fiori)	WS60800086

Table 7.5 Change Request Types for Customer (Cont.)

> **Note**
>
> SAP change request types for customer are delivered via BC Set CA-MDG-APP-CUS_VC_USMD110_C09 and can be activated using Transaction MDG_BS_CUS_CR_BCSET13. This BC Set is valid from SAP Master Data Governance on SAP S/4HANA 2021 and SAP Master Data Governance for SAP ERP 9.2.
>
> SAP delivers SAP ERP customer UI-related change request types via BC Set CA-MDG-APP-CL_VC_USMD110_C02, which can be activated using Transaction MDG_BS_CL_CR_BCSET2. This BC Set is valid from SAP Master Data Governance 7.0 onward and, despite the name, is applicable to both SAP ERP and SAP S/4HANA.

Supplier Master

Supplier master governance provides the ability to govern supplier data via various available processes. Search for an existing supplier record, create, update, block, and mark for deletion are the single-object change request processes available under customer master governance. Table 7.6 shows a list of all SAP-delivered change request types, including an SAP Fiori–specific change request type.

> **Note**
>
> SAP change request types for supplier are delivered via BC Set CA-MDG-APP-SUP_VC_USMD110_C10 and can be activated using Transaction MDG_BS_SUP_CRBCSET13. This BC Set is valid from SAP Master Data Governance on SAP S/4HANA 2021 and SAP Master Data Governance for SAP ERP 9.2.
>
> SAP delivers SAP ERP vendor UI-related change request types via BC Set CA- CA-MDG-APP-VL_VC_USMD110_C04, which can be activated using Transaction MDG_BS_VL_CR_BCSET4. This BC Set is valid from SAP Master Data Governance 7.0 onward and, as earlier, is applicable to both SAP ERP and SAP S/4HANA.

Change Request Type	Description	Workflow
SUPPL1P1	Create Supplier	WS54300005
SUPPL1P2	Create Supplier w. Hierarchy Assignment	WS54300003
SUPPL2P1	Process Supplier	WS54300007
SUPPL2P2	Process Supplier w. Hierarchy Assignment	WS54300003
SUPPL5P1	Block/Unblock Supplier	WS60800059
SUPPL6P1	Mark Supplier for Deletion	WS60800068
SUF1P1	Create Supplier (SAP Fiori)	WS60800086

Table 7.6 Change Request Types for Supplier

Contract Account Master Data

Contract accounts provide the ability to govern contract accounts receivable and pay-able (FI-CA) master data. In FI-CA, each business partner posting is assigned to one business partner and one contract account. Contract accounts are part of the business partner data model in SAP Master Data Governance and provide the ability to search and create new contract accounts. Table 7.7 shows a list of change request types delivered for contract accounts.

> **Note**
>
> SAP change request types for contract accounts are delivered as part of BC Set CA-MDG-APP-FKK_VC_USMD110_01. This BC Set is valid from SAP Master Data Governance 9.1 onward.

Change Request Type	Description	Workflow
FKK1P1	Create Contract Account	WS60800086
FKK2P1	Change Contract Account	WS60800086
FKKIP1	Local Maint.: Create Contract Account	WS78500004
FKKUP1	Local Maint.: Change Contract Account	WS78500004

Table 7.7 Change Request Types for Contract Account

Financial Master Data

SAP delivers separate work centers to manage financial governance subareas. Each of these work centers provides the ability to manage the financial objects that fall under the governance area.

Financial governance for accounting provides the ability to search and create company, general ledger accounts, and financial reporting structure hierarchy. Table 7.8 shows a list of all SAP-delivered change request types for financial accounting governance and associated workflow templates.

Change Request Type	Main Entity Type	Description	Workflow
ACC1P1	ACCOUNT	Create Account	WS75700040
ACC1P2	ACCOUNT	Create Account with Hry. Assignments	WS75700040
ACC2P1	ACCOUNT	Process Account	WS75700040
ACC2P2	ACCOUNT	Process Account with Hry. Assignments	WS75700040
ACC5P1	ACCOUNT	Block/Unblock Account	WS75700040
ACC6P1	ACCOUNT	Mark Account for Deletion	WS75700040
ACCXP1	ACCOUNT	Delete Account	WS75700040
CMP1P1	COMPANY	Create Company	WS75700040
CMP2P1	COMPANY	Process Company	WS75700040
CMPXP1	COMPANY	Delete Company	WS75700040
FRS1P1	FRS	Create Financial Reporting Structure	WS75700040
FRS2P1	FRS	Process Financial Reporting Structure	WS75700040
FRSXP1	FRS	Delete Financial Reporting Structure	WS75700040

Table 7.8 Change Request Types for Financial Accounting Governance

Financial governance for controlling provides the ability to search and create the following controlling-related master data:

- Profit center
- Profit center group
- Profit center hierarchy
- Cost center
- Cost center group
- Cost center hierarchy
- Cost element

- Cost element group
- Cost element hierarchy
- Internal orders

> **Note**
>
> Internal order governance is delivered starting with SAP Master Data Governance 9.2 and SAP Master Data Governance on SAP S/4HANA 1809.

Table 7.9 shows a list of all SAP-delivered change request types for financial controlling governance and associated workflow templates. SAP also delivers SAP Fiori–based change request types for creating cost centers and profit centers.

Change Request Type	Main Entity Type	Description	Workflow
CCG1P1	CCTRG	Create Cost Center Group	WS75700040
CCG1P2	CCTRG	Create CCTR Group with Hry. Assignments	WS75700040
CCG2P1	CCTRG	Process Cost Center Group	WS75700040
CCG2P2	CCTRG	Process CCTR Group w. Hry. Assignments	WS75700040
CCGXP1	CCTRG	Delete Cost Center Group	WS75700040
CCH1P1	CCTRH	Create Cost Center Group Hierarchy	WS75700040
CCH2P1	CCTRH	Process Cost Center Group Hierarchy	WS75700040
CCHXP1	CCTRH	Delete Cost Center Group Hierarchy	WS75700040
CCT1P1	CCTR	Create Cost Center	WS75700040
CCT1P2	CCTR	Create Cost Center with Hry. Assignments	WS75700040
CCT2P1	CCTR	Process Cost Center	WS75700040
CCT2P2	CCTR	Process Cost Center w. Hry. Assignments	WS75700040
CCTFP1	CCTR	Create Cost Center (SAP Fiori)	WS60800086
CCTXP1	CCTR	Delete Cost Center	WS75700040

Table 7.9 Change Request Types for Financial Controlling Governance

Change Request Type	Main Entity Type	Description	Workflow
CEG1P1	CELEMG	Create Cost Element Group	WS75700040
CEG1P2	CELEMG	Create CELEM Group w. Hry. Assignments	WS75700040
CEG2P1	CELEMG	Process Cost Element Group	WS75700040
CEG2P2	CELEMG	Process CELEM Group w. Hry. Assignments	WS75700040
CEGXP1	CELEMG	Delete Cost Element Group	WS75700040
CEH1P1	CELEMH	Create Cost Element Group Hierarchy	WS75700040
CEH2P1	CELEMH	Process Cost Element Group Hierarchy	WS75700040
CEHXP1	CELEMH	Delete Cost Element Group Hierarchy	WS75700040
CEL1P1	CELEM	Create Cost Element	WS75700040
CEL1P2	CELEM	Create Cost Element w. Hry. Assignments	WS75700040
CEL2P1	CELEM	Process Cost Element	WS75700040
CEL2P2	CELEM	Process Cost Element w. Hry. Assignments	WS75700040
CELXP1	CELEM	Delete Cost Element	WS75700040
IOR1P1	IORDER	Create Internal Order	WS75700040
IOR2P1	IORDER	Process Internal Order	WS75700040
PCG1P1	PCTRG	Create Profit Center Group	WS75700040
PCG1P2	PCTRG	Create PCTR Group with Hry. Assignments	WS75700040
PCG2P1	PCTRG	Process Profit Center Group	WS75700040
PCG2P2	PCTRG	Process PCTR Group with Hry. Assignments	WS75700040
PCGXP1	PCTRG	Delete Profit Center Group	WS75700040
PCH1P1	PCTRH	Create Profit Center Group Hierarchy	WS75700040

Table 7.9 Change Request Types for Financial Controlling Governance (Cont.)

Change Request Type	Main Entity Type	Description	Workflow
PCH2P1	PCTRH	Process Profit Center Group Hierarchy	WS75700040
PCHXP1	PCTRH	Delete Profit Center Group Hierarchy	WS75700040
PCT1P1	PCTR	Create Profit Center	WS75700040
PCT1P2	PCTR	Create Profit Center w. Hry. Assignments	WS75700040
PCT2P1	PCTR	Process Profit Center	WS75700040
PCT2P2	PCTR	Process Profit Ctr. w. Hry. Assignments	WS75700040
PCTFP1	PCTR	Create Profit Center (SAP Fiori)	WS60800086
PCTXP1	PCTR	Delete Profit Center	WS75700040

Table 7.9 Change Request Types for Financial Controlling Governance (Cont.)

Financial governance for consolidation provides the ability to search and create financial consolidation-relevant master data such as consolidation unit, item, and associated hierarchies. Table 7.10 shows a list of all SAP-delivered change request types for financial governance for consolidation and associated workflow templates.

Change Request Type	Main Entity Type	Description	Workflow
BCG1P1	BDC	Create Breakdown Category	WS75700040
BCG2P1	BDC	Process Breakdown Category	WS75700040
BCGXP1	BDC	Delete Breakdown Category	WS75700040
BCS1P1	BDCSET	Create Breakdown Category Set	WS75700040
BCS2P1	BDCSET	Process Breakdown Category Set	WS75700040
BCSXP1	BDCSET	Delete Breakdown Category Set	WS75700040
CCC1P1	CONSCHAR	Create Consolidation Characteristics	WS75700040
CCC2P1	CONSCHAR	Process Consolidation Characteristics	WS75700040
CCCXP1	CONSCHAR	Delete Consolidation Characteristics	WS75700040

Table 7.10 Change Request Types for Financial Consolidation Governance

Change Request Type	Main Entity Type	Description	Workflow
CGH1P1	CONSGRPH	Create Consolidation Group Hierarchy	WS75700040
CGH2P1	CONSGRPH	Process Consolidation Group Hierarchy	WS75700040
CGHXP1	CONSGRPH	Delete Consolidation Group Hierarchy	WS75700040
CGR1P1	CONSGRP	Create Consolidation Group	WS75700040
CGR2P1	CONSGRP	Process Consolidation Group	WS75700040
CGRXP1	CONSGRP	Delete Consolidation Group	WS75700040
CRS1P1	FSIH	Create Item Hierarchy	WS75700040
CRS2P1	FSIH	Process Item Hierarchy	WS75700040
CRSXP1	FSIH	Delete Item Hierarchy	WS75700040
CUT1P1	CONSUNIT	Create Consolidation Unit	WS75700040
CUT2P1	CONSUNIT	Process Consolidation Unit	WS75700040
CUTXP1	CONSUNIT	Delete Consolidation Unit	WS75700040
FSI1P1	FSI	Create Item	WS75700040
FSI2P1	FSI	Process Item	WS75700040
FSI5P1	FSI	Block/Unblock Item	WS75700040
FSI6P1	FSI	Mark Item for Deletion	WS75700040
FSIXP1	FSI	Delete Item	WS75700040
SMP1P1	SUBMPACK	Create Cause for Submission	WS75700040
SMP2P1	SUBMPACK	Process Cause for Submission	WS75700040
SMPXP1	SUBMPACK	Delete Cause for Submission	WS75700040
TTP1P1	TRANSTYPE	Create Transaction Type	WS75700040
TTP2P1	TRANSTYPE	Process Transaction Type	WS75700040
TTPXP1	TRANSTYPE	Delete Transaction Type	WS75700040

Table 7.10 Change Request Types for Financial Consolidation Governance (Cont.)

Note

SAP change request types for governance of finance master data are delivered via BC Set `CA-MDG-APP-FIN_CR_TYPES_08`. This BC Set is valid from SAP Master Data Governance 9.2 onward.

SAP-delivered BC Set for customer change request types can be activated using Transaction MDG_BS_VL_CR_BCSET4.

7.3.2   Processing Customer on a Client System

In SAP Master Data Governance, if you need to maintain a customer record directly in a client system with a quick turnaround, rather than initiating changes from a hub system, changes are initiated directly in a client system. Figure 7.26 provides an overview as well as the following steps involved in a typical process:

1. Search for a record on the client system as well as the SAP Master Data Governance hub.

2. If the record is found on the hub and isn't available in the client system, the copy process is initiated to copy the record from the hub to the client system.

3. Once copied, any changes to the record are initiated locally in the client system.

4. After all changes in the client system are complete, changes are transferred back to the hub.

5. The governance process is initiated in the hub. Once approved, changes are replicated to all client systems.

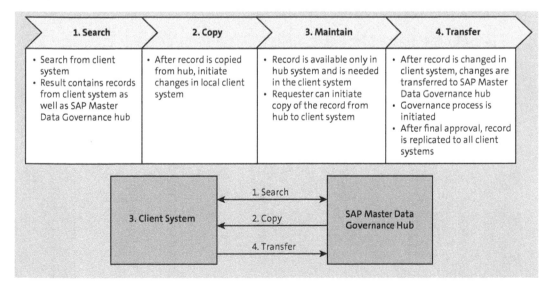

Figure 7.26 SAP Master Data Governance, Customers: On the Client (SAP ERP)

> **Note**
>
> This functionality is activated via business function `MDG_CUST_ERPCLIENT_1`. If the client system is moved to SAP S/4HANA, this functionality isn't applicable anymore because the customer data is maintained via the business partner.

7.3.3   Business Context Viewer Side Panels

SAP provides BCV side panel content to give you a direct overview of changes or of certain transactional data associated with the master data record. In addition to the side panel for **Changes Overview**, which is available across all domains, there are certain domain-specific side panels delivered by SAP as follows:

- **Material master**
  - **Sales Overview**: Sales orders created for the current material master.
  - **Production Overview**: Production orders created for the current material master.
  - **Purchasing Overview**: Purchase orders created for the current material master.
- **Customer master**
  - **Sales Overview**: Sales orders created for the current customer number.
- **Supplier master**
  - **Purchasing Overview**: Purchase orders created for the current vendor number.

Figure 7.27 shows the side panel for the **Changes Overview** on a material master UI. If SAP Master Data Governance is installed as a hub, it's possible to retrieve an overview of transactional data for the selected master data record from the transactional SAP S/4HANA or SAP ERP system.

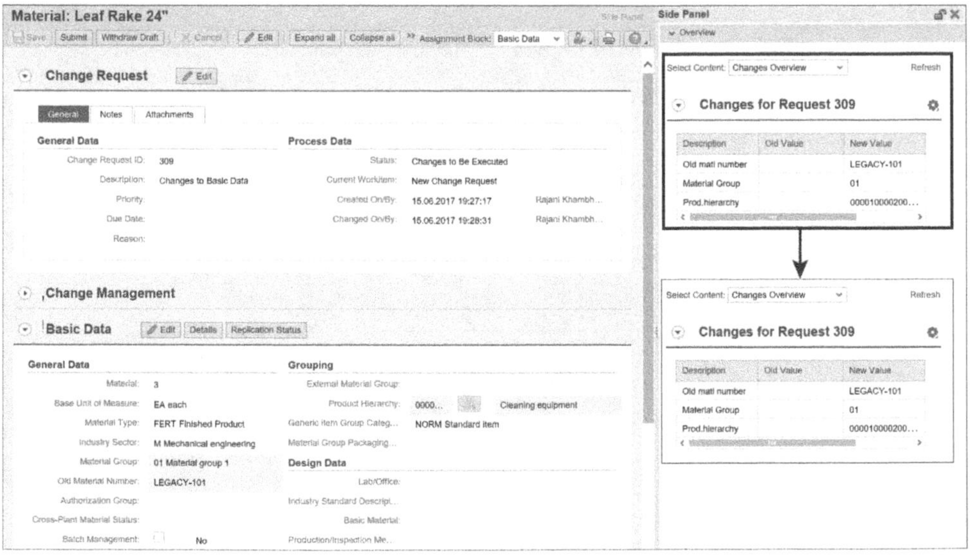

Figure 7.27 BCV Side Panel for "Changes Overview"

7.4 Multiple Object Processing

As explained in Section 7.3, the **Single Object** checkbox in the change request type definition controls whether a change request created for the change request type contains a single object or multiple objects. Following is a list of various processes—some batch processes and some interactive, such as hierarchy processing—where multiple objects are changed within a single change request:

- Mass change
- File upload/file download
- Data import process
- Hierarchy processing
- Multiple-record processing

Figure 7.28 shows the mass change account (**ACCAP1**) change request type as an example. For all SAP-delivered change request types, associated logical actions indicate the type of multiple-record processing. Table 7.11 provides a list of various processes related to multiple records and associated logical actions.

Display View "Type of Change Request": Overview

Dialog Structure	Type of Change Request									
• ▸ Type of Change Request	Type of Chg. Request	Edition Type	Data Model	Description (medium text)	Objects Required	Single Object	Parallel	Main Entity Type	Workflow
• ▸ Entity Types	ACCAP1	0G_ALL		Mass Change Account	☐	☐	☐		WS7570
• ▸ Scope on Entity Type Level									

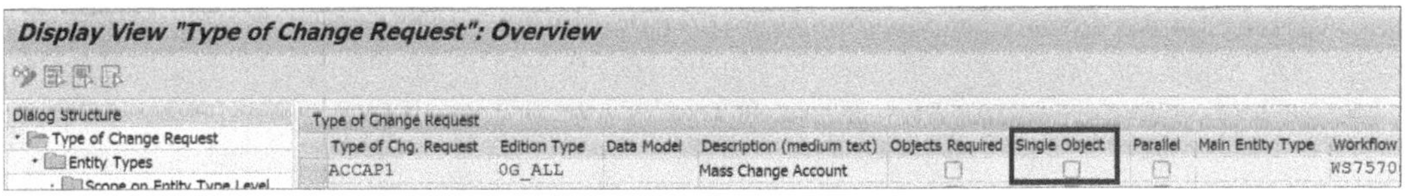

Figure 7.28 Multiple Object Change Request Type

Process	Logical Action	Description
Mass change and file upload	MASS	Mass processing
Data import	LOAD	Data exchange
Hierarchy processing	HIERARCHY	Hierarchy processing
Multiprocessing	MULTI	Multiple object processing

Table 7.11 Logical Actions Associated with Multiple-Record Processing

7.4.1 Mass Change

The mass change process is available for all domains in SAP Master Data Governance and enables you to change multiple records with the following options:

- Update the same value for one field across all selected records.
- Initialize a field across all selected records.

This process is very intuitive and enables you to add the mass change process to an already created mass change request. Unlike single-record processing, the mass change process involves creating a mass change request before initiating the mass change process. Figure 7.29 shows the UI links for the mass change process using a business partner as an example.

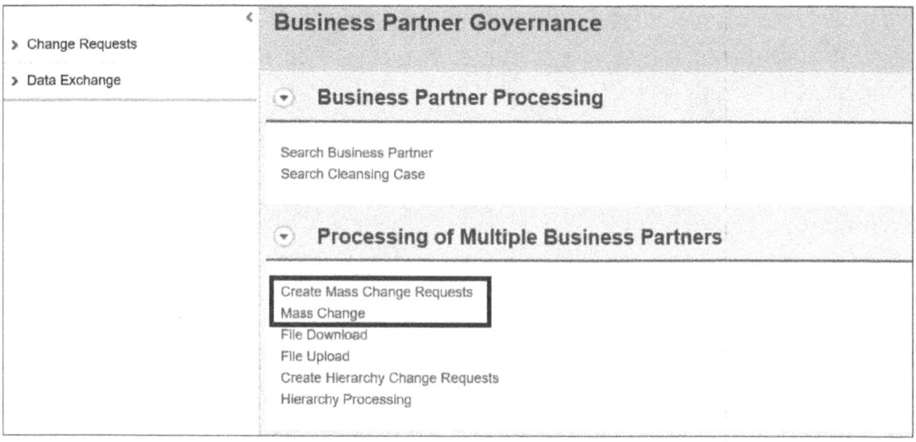

Figure 7.29 UI Links for Creating a Mass Change Request and Mass Change

See Chapter 15, Section 15.2.1, for additional details on the mass change functionality.

7.4.2   File Upload/Download

File upload and file download are entity type-based processes that are used for uploading and downloading file entries, respectively. Both the mass change process and the file upload process use change request types with business activities linked to the MASS logical action. Figure 7.30 shows the links involved in a file upload process using business partner as an example. It's very common to use the file download option as an intermediate step to generate a file template for the upload process.

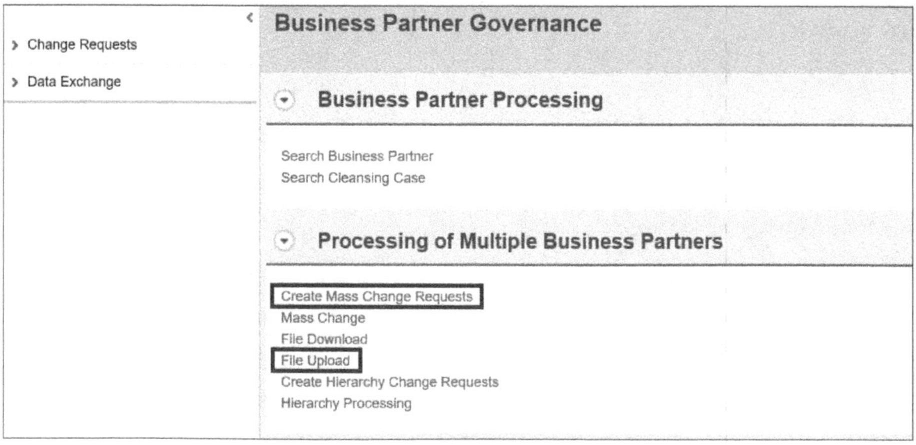

Figure 7.30 UI Links for Creating Mass Change Requests and File Upload

File upload is used for the initial data loads for flex data models, so it's used for financial master data as well as custom objects. Chapter 14, Section 14.2.3, explains the file upload/download functionality in detail. Table 7.12 shows a list of mass change request types that can be used for both mass change and file upload processes.

Change Request Type	Description	Workflow
OG_ALL	OG: All Entities	WS75700027
OG_CO	OG: Controlling Entities	WS75700040
OG_CONS	OG: Consolidation Entities	WS75700040
OG_FIN	OG: Financial Accounting Entities	WS75700040
ACCAP1	Mass Change Account	WS75700040
BCGAP1	Mass Change Breakdown Category	WS75700040
BCSAP1	Mass Change Breakdown Category Set	WS75700040
CCCAP1	Mass Change Consolidation Characteristic	WS75700040
CCGAP1	Mass Change Cost Center Group	WS75700040
CCHAP1	Mass Change Cost Center Group Hierarchy	WS75700040
CCTAP1	Mass Change Cost Center	WS75700040
CEGAP1	Mass Change Cost Element Group	WS75700040
CEHAP1	Mass Change Cost Element Group Hierarchy	WS75700040
CELAP1	Mass Change Cost Element	WS75700040
CGHAP1	Mass Change Consolidation Group Hierarchy	WS75700040
CGRAP1	Mass Change Consolidation Group	WS75700040
CMPAP1	Mass Change Company	WS75700040
CRSAP1	Mass Change Item Hierarchy	WS75700040
CUTAP1	Mass Change Consolidation Unit	WS75700040
FRSAP1	Mass Change Fin. Reporting Structure	WS75700040
FSIAP1	Mass Change Item	WS75700040
PCGAP1	Mass Change Profit Center Group	WS75700040
PCHAP1	Mass Change Profit Center Group Hierarch	WS75700040
PCTAP1	Mass Change Profit Center	WS75700040
SMPAP1	Mass Change Cause for Submission	WS75700040
TTPAP1	Mass Change Transaction Type	WS75700040

Table 7.12 Mass Change Request Types

Change Request Type	Description	Workflow
BPMP2	Business Partner Mass Maintenance	WS60800095
MATOA	Process Multiple Materials	WS60800086
MATLOA	Process Multiple Materials w. Lean Class	WS60800086

Table 7.12 Mass Change Request Types (Cont.)

7.4.3   Data Import Process

Data import, which is part of the data import framework, is used for initial data loads into SAP Master Data Governance. Data import is initiated by using Transaction DTIM-PORT. By default, the data import framework is designed to import data into the active area directly. However, there is an option to initiate governance during the import process. After the **Governance** checkbox is selected, a change request type needs to be selected. The system automatically filters change request types based on the object and those that are linked to logical action LOAD. Figure 7.31 shows an example of the **Import Master Data and Mapping Information** data import screen with the **Governance** checkbox selected. Note that the **Change Request Type** dropdown shows only the **MATOB** change request type, which is linked to logical action LOAD via business activity MATB.

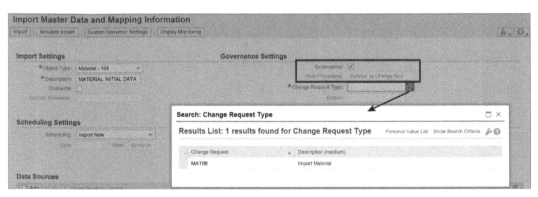

Figure 7.31 Data Import: Governance Checkbox

See Chapter 14, Section 14.2.1, for additional details on the data import framework. Table 7.13 shows a list of change request types that can be used for the data import process, which means all change request types listed are linked to the LOAD logical action.

Change Request Type	Description	Workflow
ACCLP1	Account Initial Load	WS75700040
CCTLP1	Cost Center Initial Load	WS75700040
CELLP1	Cost Element Initial Load	WS75700040

Table 7.13 Change Request Types for Data Import

Change Request Type	Description	Workflow
CMPLP1	Company Initial Load	WS75700040
FKKLP1	Contract Account Initial Load	WS72100006
FSILP1	Item Initial Load	WS75700040
IOR1LP1	Internal Order Initial Load	WS75700040
PCTLP1	Profit Center Initial Load	WS75700040
BPLP2	Business Partner Initial Load	WS72100006
MATOB	Import Material	WS60800086
MATLOB	Import Material w. Lean Classification	WS60800086

Table 7.13 Change Request Types for Data Import (Cont.)

7.4.4   Hierarchy Processing

SAP Master Data Governance allows you to create or edit hierarchies. Entity types need to be defined at the data model level. Chapter 5, Section 5.1.5, explains the configurations that enable an entity type as a hierarchy. Section 5.3.2 in the same chapter provides an example of a business partner hierarchy from a data modeling perspective. With the understanding of the configurations performed at data modeling, we'll now discuss how a hierarchy can be created in SAP Master Data Governance. We'll use the same business partner hierarchy as an example. SAP Master Data Governance enables you to create a change request type for hierarchies up-front, or the change request type can be created during the hierarchy creation process. Figure 7.32 shows the UI links for creating a hierarchy change request first ❶ and then initiating the hierarchy processing ❷.

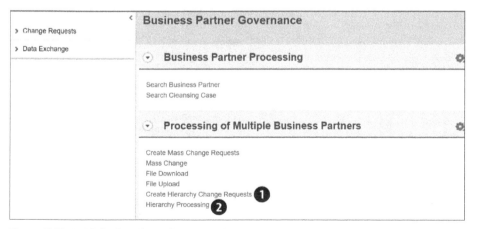

Figure 7.32 UI Links for Hierarchy Processing

Now, let's go through the steps to create a hierarchy using the business partner hierarchy as an example. SAP Master Data Governance enables you to create a new hierarchy or insert nodes into an existing hierarchy. Figure 7.33 shows an example of creating a new hierarchy.

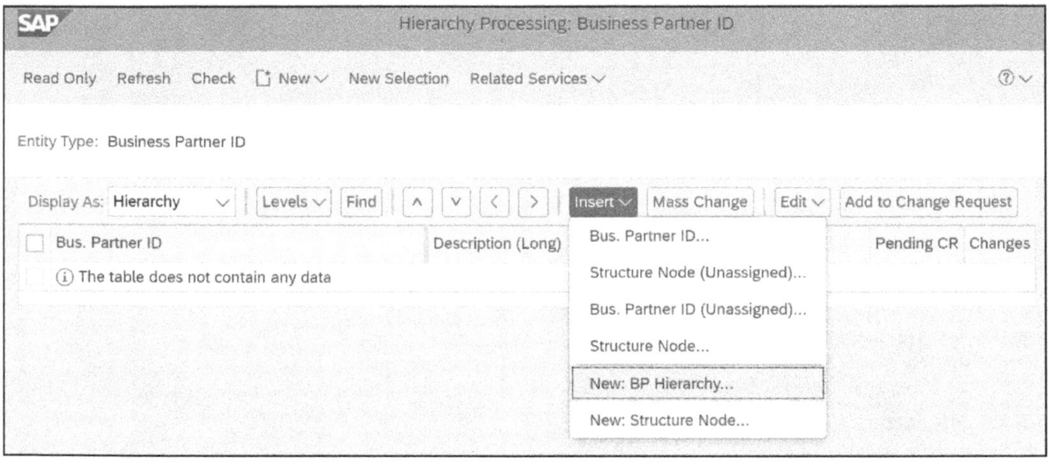

Figure 7.33 Hierarchy Processing: Creating a New Business Partner Hierarchy

New structure nodes can be created for the new hierarchy that is created. If unassigned structure nodes have already been created, they can be assigned as well. Figure 7.34 shows a new structure node being inserted into a hierarchy.

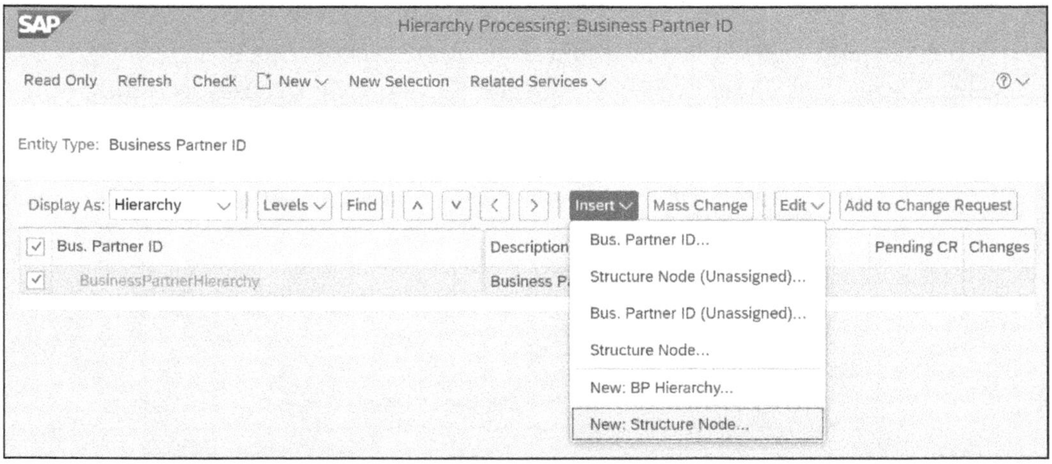

Figure 7.34 Hierarchy Processing: Inserting a Structure Node

You can insert nodes as subnodes, and you can move the nodes after they are created. Nodes can be moved up or down at the same level by selecting up or down arrows. Right and left arrows allow you to rank the selected node higher or lower in the hierarchy. Figure 7.35 shows an example of moving node **USA** as the subnode under **North America** by lowering the rank for the node.

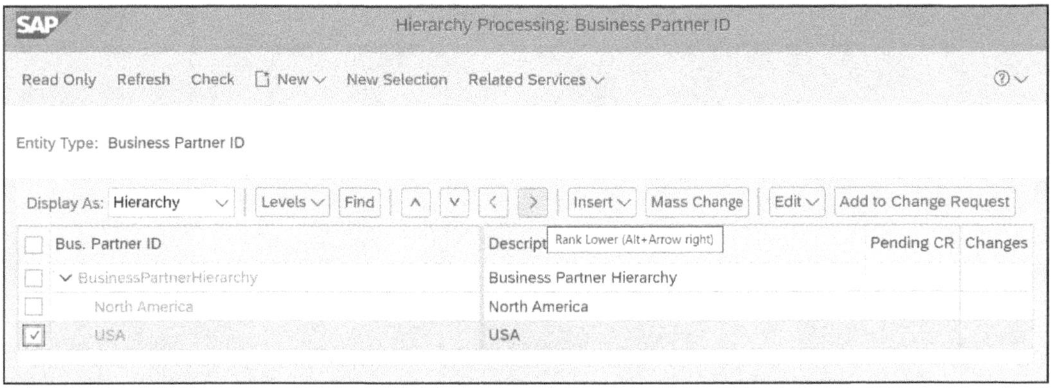

Figure 7.35 Hierarchy Processing: Moving a Node as a Subnode by Lowering the Rank

Figure 7.36 shows a structure node being inserted as a subnode instead of lowering the rank later. In this example, **Austria** is inserted as a subnode of **Europe** during the creation process.

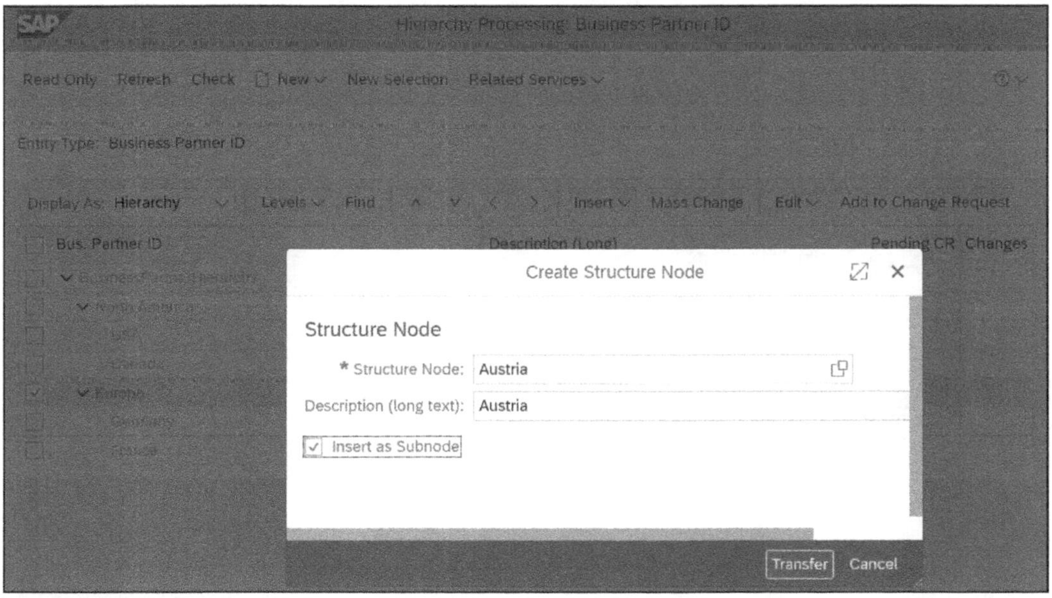

Figure 7.36 Hierarchy Processing: Creating a Structure Node and Inserting as a Subnode

Existing business partner IDs can be inserted into a hierarchy. As an example, the following steps show the process of inserting business partner **1000150** under an existing structure node as a subnode. To insert an existing business partner ID under a specific hierarchy node, follow these two steps:

1. Select the node, click on the **Insert** button, and then click on **Bus. Partner ID**, as shown in Figure 7.37.

2. Enter the **Business Partner ID** in the popup, as shown in Figure 7.38.

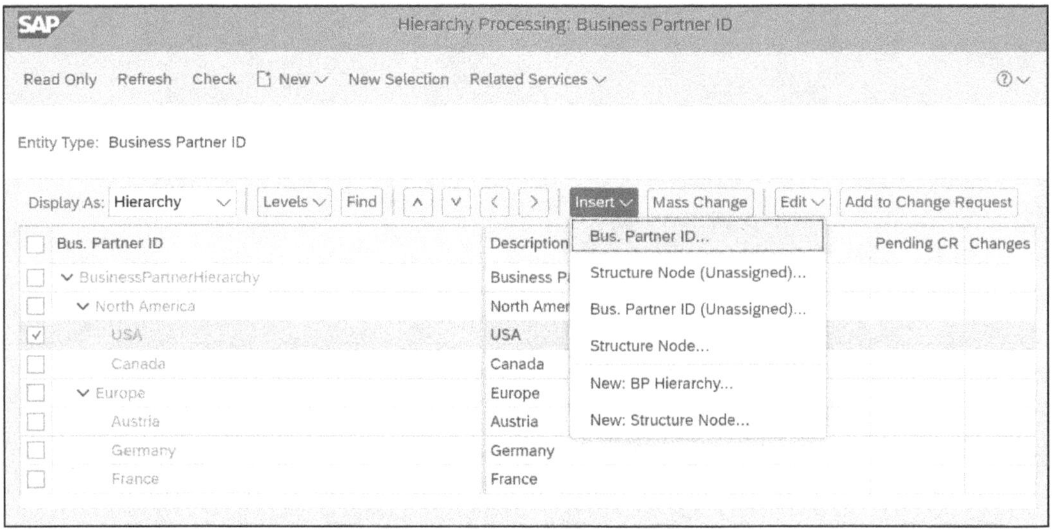

Figure 7.37 Hierarchy Processing: Inserting a Business Partner ID

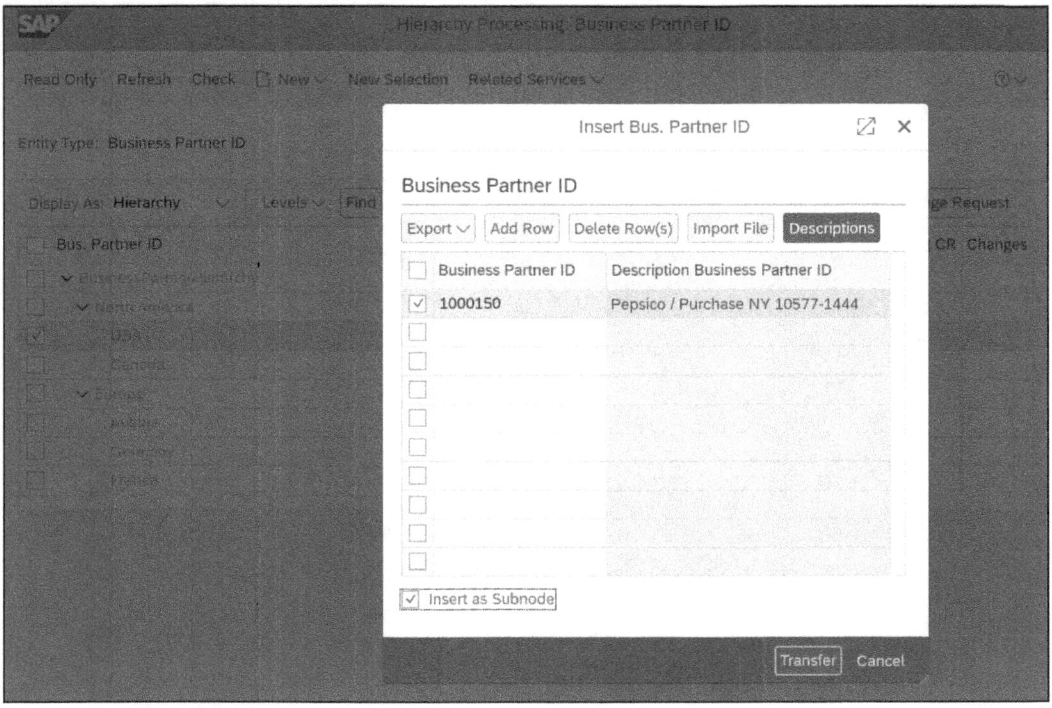

Figure 7.38 Hierarchy Processing: Inserting a Business Partner ID as a Subnode

Figure 7.39 shows the hierarchy after the **Bus. Partner ID** is inserted as a subnode.

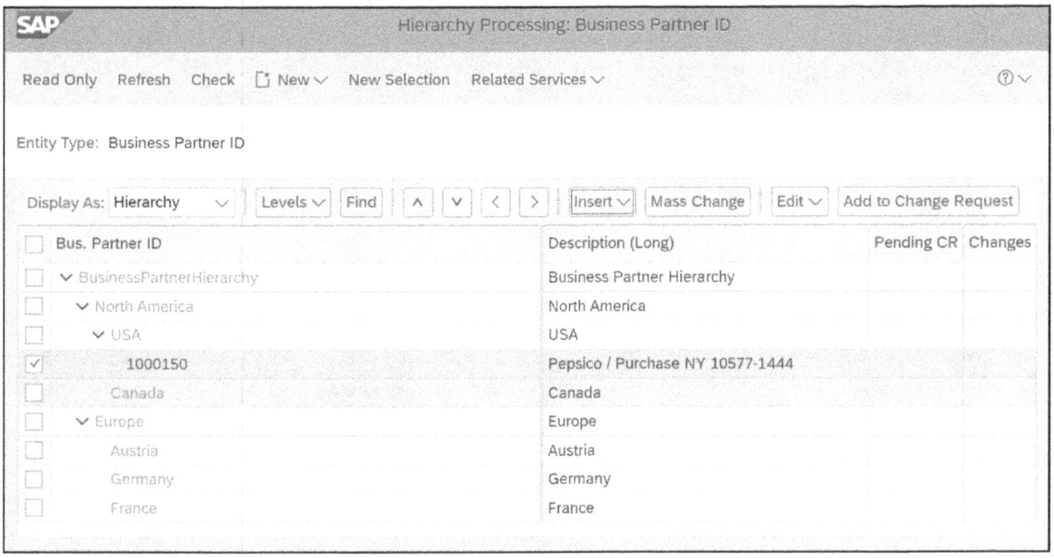

Figure 7.39 Hierarchy Processing: Business Partner Hierarchy with Business Partner ID

You can create a hierarchy processing change request during the save process and add the new hierarchy under the change request, as shown in Figure 7.40.

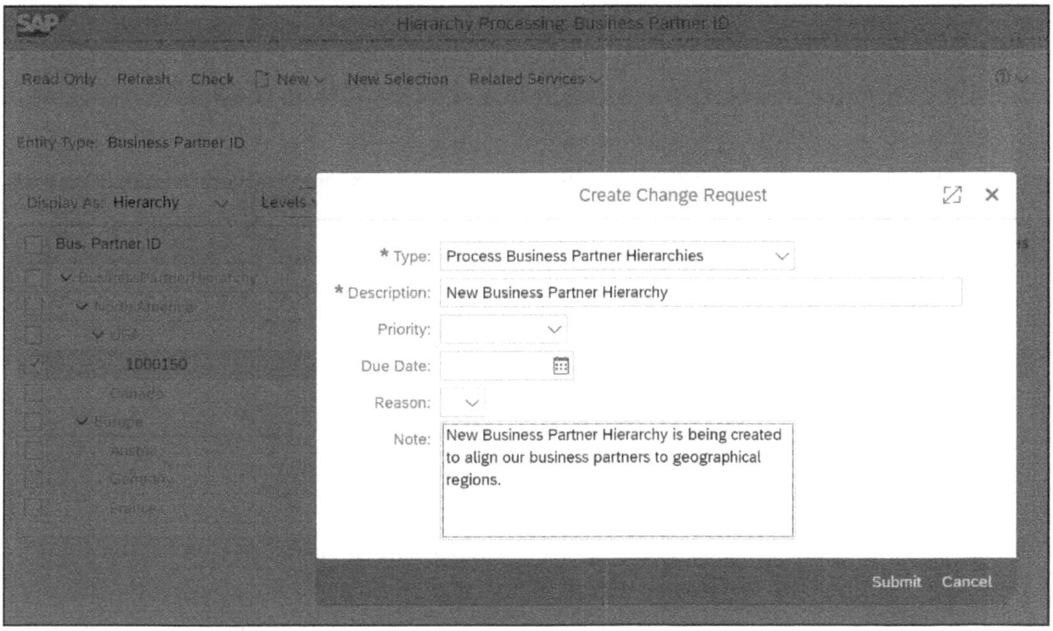

Figure 7.40 Hierarchy Processing: Creating a Change Request upon Save

Once saved in a change request, the links to pending change requests for the nodes and change documents for all parent nodes are displayed. As shown in Figure 7.41, the **Pending CR** column provides a link to pending change requests for each node in the hierarchy, and the **Changes** column provides a link to the change documents.

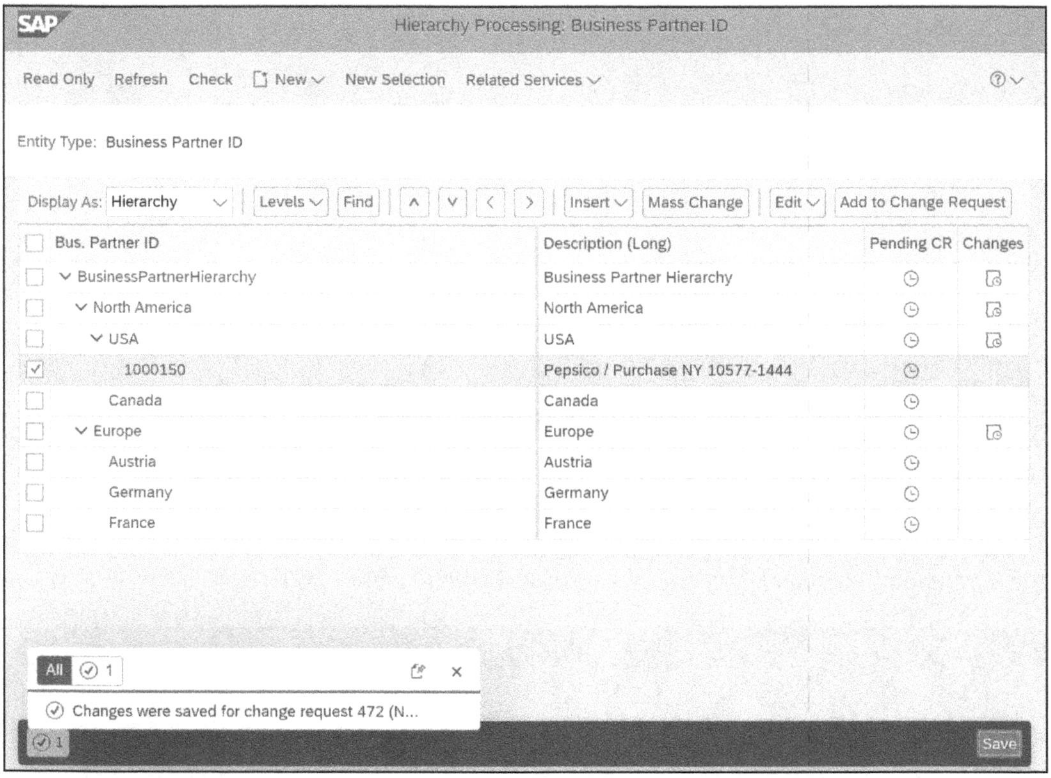

Figure 7.41 Hierarchy Processing: Pending Change Requests and Change Documents for Hierarchy Nodes

Hierarchy processing change request types are linked to business activities, which are linked to the HIERARCHY logical action. Table 7.14 shows a list of change request types that can be used for hierarchy processing for the respective entity types.

Change Request Type	Description	Main Entity Type	Workflow
BPHP2	Process Business Partner Hierarchies	BP_HEADER	WS60800095
CCGHP1	Process Cost Center Group Hierarchies	CCTRG	WS75700040
CEGHP1	Process Cost Element Group Hierarchies	CELEMG	WS75700040

Table 7.14 Hierarchy Change Request Types

Change Request Type	Description	Main Entity Type	Workflow
CGRHP1	Process Consolidation Group Hierarchies	CONSGRP	WS75700040
CRSHP1	Process Item Hierarchies	FSI	WS75700040
FRSHP1	Process Fin. Rep. Structure Hierarchies	FRSI	WS75700040
PCGHP1	Process Profit Center Group Hierarchies	PCTRG	WS75700040

Table 7.14 Hierarchy Change Request Types (Cont.)

SAP Master Data Governance also enables you to define the scope for hierarchy-specific changes, which dictates the ability to create parallel change requests to a hierarchy belonging to a specific hierarchy type. SAP Master Data Governance offers a configurable interlocking feature that can be used to define the level of interlocking of hierarchy nodes when changes are saved to a change request. The IMG path to define interlocking is **MDGIMG • General Settings • Process Modeling • Hierarchies • Define Scope for Changes**.

Figure 7.42 shows an example of the scope for changes set for a business partner hierarchy. When a hierarchy or part of the hierarchy is interlocked, then any changes to the locked node need to be added to the pending change request. All other nodes that aren't locked can be changed under a new change request.

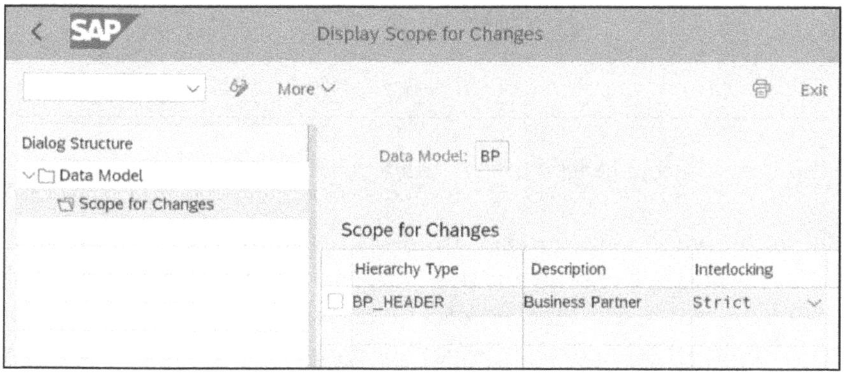

Figure 7.42 Scope for Hierarchy Changes for a Business Partner Hierarchy

The options available for **Interlocking** are as follows:

- **Loose**
  This interlocking option only locks the nodes assigned to the parent node of the node currently being changed.

■ **Strict**

This interlocking option locks all parent nodes up to the root node as well as all child nodes up to the end nodes of the parent node of the node currently being changed.

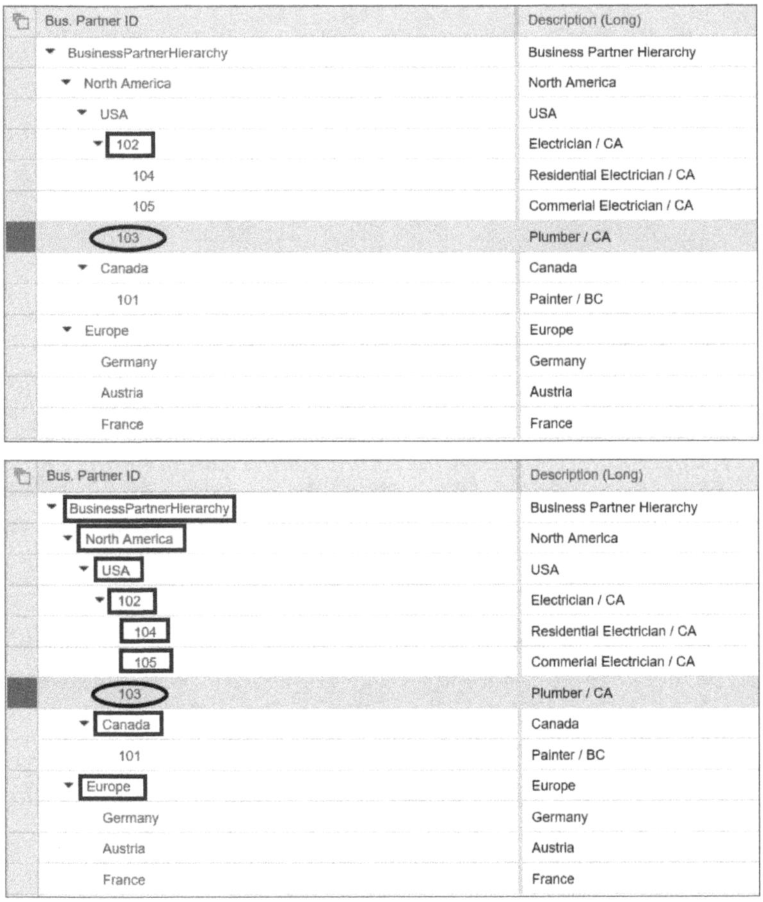

Bus. Partner ID	Description (Long)
▼ BusinessPartnerHierarchy	Business Partner Hierarchy
▼ North America	North America
▼ USA	USA
▼ 102	Electrician / CA
104	Residential Electrician / CA
105	Commerial Electrician / CA
103	Plumber / CA
▼ Canada	Canada
101	Painter / BC
▼ Europe	Europe
Germany	Germany
Austria	Austria
France	France

Bus. Partner ID	Description (Long)
▼ BusinessPartnerHierarchy	Business Partner Hierarchy
▼ North America	North America
▼ USA	USA
▼ 102	Electrician / CA
104	Residential Electrician / CA
105	Commerial Electrician / CA
103	Plumber / CA
▼ Canada	Canada
101	Painter / BC
▼ Europe	Europe
Germany	Germany
Austria	Austria
France	France

Figure 7.43 Scope for Hierarchy Changes: Concept of Interlocking

Figure 7.43 shows the interlocking concept with an example. In this example, business partner **103** was added to the hierarchy, and **USA** is its parent node. The ovals represent the node(s) being changed/add and the rectangles represent the interlocked nodes. In this example, loose and strict interlocking impact the entire hierarchy as follows:

■ **Loose**

Because **USA** is the parent node of **103**, all immediate child nodes of **USA** are locked. In this example, **102** is locked.

■ **Strict**

Because **USA** is a parent node of **103**, all nodes above parent node **USA** are locked, and all child nodes below **USA** are locked.

7.4.5   Multiple-Record Processing

SAP Master Data Governance enables you to process multiple records via the **Multi-Processing** option available on the search results view for material, customer, and supplier domains. SAP delivers several change request types to support this process. Figure 7.44 shows the **Multi-Processing** options to initiate multiprocessing from the search results screen for the material master. After one of the available options is selected, SAP Master Data Governance provides you with a list of available change request types, as shown in Figure 7.45.

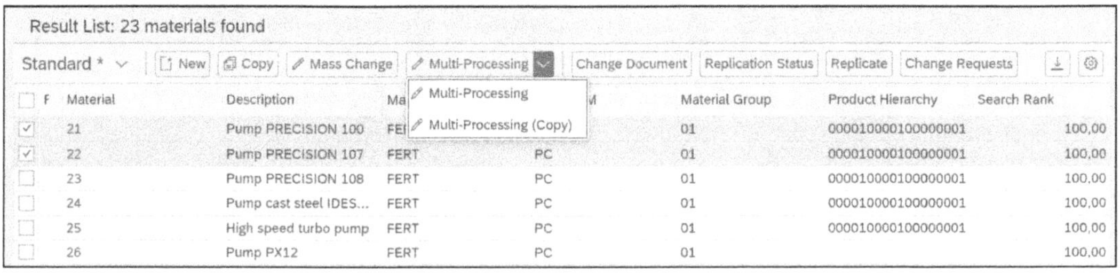

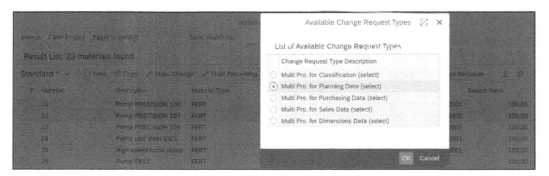

Figure 7.44 Material Master Multi-Processing Options from the Search Results List

Figure 7.45 Material Multi-Processing Change Request Type Selection

Multiprocessing change request types are linked to business activities that are linked to the MULTI logical action. Table 7.15 shows a list of change request types that can be used for multiprocessing; this list is also presented while initiating multiprocessing.

Change Request Type	Description	Workflow
MATLMRP	Multi Pro. for Planning Data (select)	WS60800086
MATLPUR	Multi Pro. for Purchasing Data (select)	WS60800086
MATLSAL	Multi Pro. for Sales Data (select)	WS60800086
MATLUOM	Multi Pro. for Dimensions Data (select)	WS60800086

Table 7.15 Multiprocessing Change Request Types

Change Request Type	Description	Workflow
MATMRP	Multi Pro. for Planning Data (full)	WS60800086
MATPUR	Multi Pro. for Purchasing Data (full)	WS60800086
MATSAL	Multi Pro. for Sales Data (full)	WS60800086
MATUOM	Multi Pro. for Dimensions Data (full)	WS60800086
MATLCLF	Multi Pro. for Classification (select)	WS60800086
CUSTMRP1	Multi Processing for Customer Financials	WS54300003
CUSTMRP2	Multi Processing for Customer Sales	WS54300003
SUPPMRP1	Multi Processing for Supplier Financials	WS54300003
SUPPMRP2	Multi Processing for Supplier Purchasing	WS54300003

Table 7.15 Multiprocessing Change Request Types (Cont.)

7.5 Workflow Process Modeling

Workflow definition is an integral part of SAP Master Data Governance change request processing. SAP Master Data Governance uses workflows to manage central governance scenarios; as such, a workflow template is specified as part of the change request type configuration. SAP delivers the BUS2250 object type (SAP Master Data Governance Change Request) for workflows associated with change requests. Event type linkage for BUS2250 must be activated for the CREATED event with the settings shown in Figure 7.46 by following the IMG path, **MDGIMG · General Settings · Process Modeling · Workflow · Activate Event Type Linkage**.

To ensure that processors of a change request step are selected as current agents at runtime and that they receive the work item, a dialog task needs to be categorized as a general task. If the task isn't enabled as a general task, and if a processor is assigned to a change request step that isn't assigned as a possible agent, then the workflow will end in an error. To complete the configuration, follow IMG path, **MDGIMG · General Settings · Process Modeling · Workflow · Configure Workflow Tasks**, and then perform the following steps:

1. For application component **CA-MDG-AF**, choose **Assign Agents**.
2. Set all activities (denoted by **TS***) that aren't set as **Background Task** to be **General Task** (see Figure 7.47).

Follow the same procedure for all nonbackground activities within the components of the SAP Master Data Governance application that will be used.

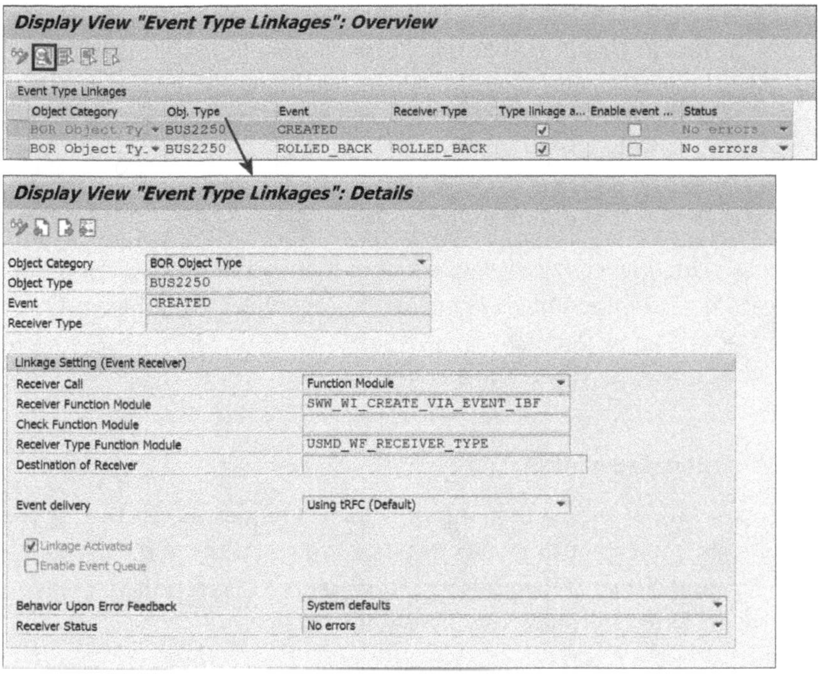

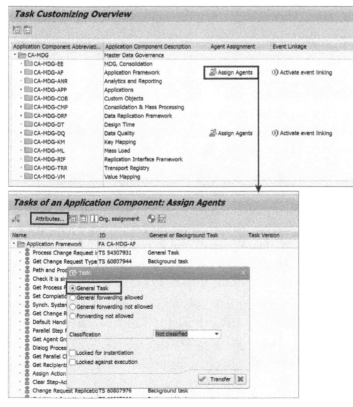

Figure 7.46 Event Type Linkage Activation

Figure 7.47 Configuring Workflow Items

> **Note**
>
> SAP Master Data Governance uses the workflow system batch user (WF-BATCH) to process background tasks. Therefore, it's important to provide required authorizations to the WF-BATCH user. Refer to SAP Note 1650993 for appropriate authorization requirements.

Section 7.5.1 provides a high-level overview of some of the workflow templates delivered by SAP for each domain. Section 7.5.2 provides an overview and an example of designing a rule-based workflow template. Finally, Section 7.5.3 provides a list of available BAdIs that can be used as part of workflow modeling.

7.5.1 Standard Workflow Templates

SAP delivers several workflow templates along with change request types. During the initial project phase, it's important to review the standard workflow templates delivered by SAP to understand if they fit the project requirements. This section provides an overview of some of the workflow templates delivered by SAP.

Material Master

All change request types delivered for the material master use workflow template WS60800086, which is a rule-based workflow. We'll go through rule-based workflows in detail in Section 7.5.2.

Business Partner

All single-object change request types delivered for the business partner use workflow template WS60800086, which is a rule-based workflow. Business partner hierarchy and mass maintenance change request types use workflow template WS60800095. Workflow template WS72100006 is used by the business partner initial load change request type.

Supplier

SAP provides various workflow templates to manage supplier CRUD processes in SAP Master Data Governance. As explained in Chapter 2, Section 2.3.2, vendor master data in SAP S/4HANA and SAP ERP consists of three parts: central data, purchasing organization data, and company code data. SAP-delivered workflow templates for supplier governance are designed to work on these three individual blocks of data.

The supplier create process uses workflow template WS54300005, which is explained at a high level in Figure 7.48. Following is a summary of how this workflow is designed:

- The master data requester initiates a change request using SAP Master Data Governance, Supplier, and then submits it after maintaining central data, company code, and purchasing organization data.

- The master data specialist reviews and approves the central data.

- Purchasing specialists responsible for maintaining purchasing data for each purchasing organization enrich the data and submit the change request for purchasing specialist approval.

- Financial specialists responsible for maintaining company code data for each company code enrich the data and submit the change request for financial specialist approval.

- After central data, purchasing organization data, and company code data is approved, the change request is activated and, if needed, replicated to the receiving systems.

- The workflow also provides the flexibility to send back individual blocks of data to the requesters if the approvers need clarification or rework.

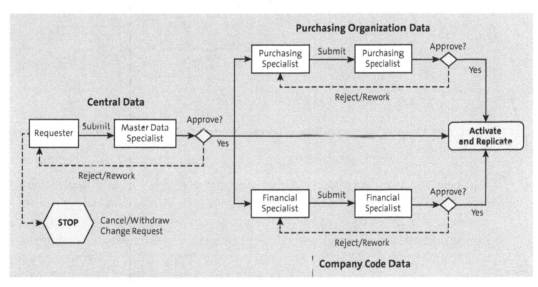

Figure 7.48 Workflow Template for the Supplier Create Process

Like the create process workflow illustrated in Figure 7.48, workflow templates related to the remaining processes, such as change, block/unblock, and mark for deletion, also follow the principle of three major blocks of data: central, purchasing organization, and company code data. Figure 7.49 provides an overview of these workflows, and the following is a summary of how these workflows are designed:

- The master data requester initiates a change request using SAP Master Data Governance, Supplier, and then submits it after making the required changes to central data, purchasing organization data, or company code data.

- Depending on the data that is changed, the workflow is routed to the appropriate master data specialists for approval.

- Once approved, the change request is activated and, if needed, replicated to the receiving systems.

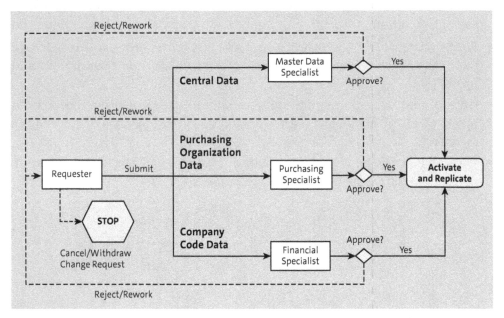

Figure 7.49 Workflow Template for the Supplier Change, Block/Unblock, and Mark for Deletion Processes

The agent determination process for these supplier workflow templates is determined using a BRFplus table. Agents are determined for each change request type, change request step, purchasing organization, company code, and central data combination. For the purposes of the supplier workflow template, SAP delivers the BRFplus application MDG_BS_ECC_SUPPLIER_WORKFLOW, along with the AGENT_DETERMINATION function. To assign a processor, follow the IMG path, **MDGIMG • Master Data Governance for Supplier • Workflow • Assign Processor to Change Request Step Number in BRFplus for Supplier**.

In the GET_AGENT decision table, you'll perform the following tasks:

- Specify the type of change request and the change request step number.
- If the change request step requires agent determination based on purchasing organization, company code, or central flag, maintain those values.
- Assign a processor by entering the object type and the processor ID.

Figure 7.50 shows an example of how the GET_AGENT entries look, as well as an overview of all the links. As shown, the workflow is determined based on the change request type, and change request steps are assigned based on the workflow in the change request step configuration. In terms of available object types, it's possible to enter a **Job**, **Organizational Unit**, **Position**, or **User** ID.

Change Req. Type	Change Req. Step	Comp. Code	Purch. Org	Central Data Chng	Obj Type	ID
SUPPL1P1	01				US	User1
SUPPL1P1	04				US	User2
SUPPL1P1	05	CC01			US	User3
SUPPL1P1	05		PO01		US	User4
SUPPL1P1	06	CC01			US	User5
SUPPL1P1	06		PO01		US	User6
SUPPL1P1	07				US	User7

Display View "Process Workflow Step Numbers": Ov

Process Workflow Step Numbers

Workflow	Step	Description (medium text)
WS54300005	0	Submission
WS54300005	1	Approval
WS54300005	4	Revision After Rejection
WS54300005	5	Subworkflow: Data Maintenance
WS54300005	6	Subworkflow: Approval
WS54300005	7	Decision: Activation Despite Discrepancy

Value	Text
C	Job
O	Organizational Unit
S	Position
US	User

Maintenance of Type of Change Request

Type of Chg. Request	Data Model	Description (medium text)	Objects Required	Single Object	Parallel	Main Entity Type	Workflow
SUPPL1P1	BP	Create Supplier	☐	☑	☐	BP_HEADER	WS54300005

Figure 7.50 Example: Agent Assignment for the Supplier Workflow

Customer

The customer master create workflow process is designed like the supplier create workflow. Customer master data in SAP S/4HANA and SAP ERP consists of three parts: central data, sales area data, and company code data. SAP-delivered workflow templates for customer governance are designed to work on these three individual blocks of data. The customer create process workflow template is shown at a high level in Figure 7.51.

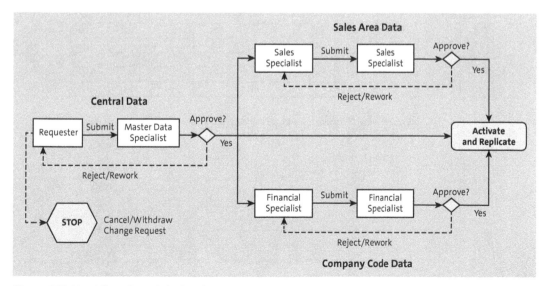

Figure 7.51 Workflow Template for the Customer Create Process

Following is a summary of how this workflow is designed:

1. The master data requester initiates a change request using SAP Master Data Governance, Customers, and then submits it after maintaining central data, company code, and sales area data.

2. The master data specialist reviews and approves the central data.

3. Sales specialists responsible for maintaining sales data for each sales area enrich the data and submit the change request for sales specialist approval.

4. Financial specialists responsible for maintaining company code data for each company code enrich the data and submit the change request for financial specialist approval.

5. After the central data, sales area data, and company code data is approved, the change request is activated and, if needed, replicated to the receiving systems.

The workflow also provides the flexibility to send back individual blocks of data to the requesters if the approvers need clarification or rework.

Like the supplier workflow templates, the agent determination process for these customer workflow templates is determined using a BRFplus table. Agents are determined for each change request type, change request step, sales area, company code, and central data combination. For the purposes of the customer workflow template, SAP delivers the BRFplus application MDG_BS_ECC_CUSTOMER_WORKFLOW along with the AGENT_DETERMINATION function. To assign a processor, follow the IMG path, **MDGIMG • Master Data Governance for Customer • Workflow • Assign Processor to Change Request Step Number in BRFplus for Customer.**

Change Req. Type	Change Req. Step	Comp. Code	Sales Org	Distr. Channel	Division	Central Data Chng	Obj Type	ID
CUST1P2	01						US	User1
CUST1P2	04						US	User2
CUST1P2	05	CC01					US	User3
CUST1P2	05		SO01	01	01		US	User4
CUST1P2	06	CC01					US	User5
CUST1P2	06		SO01	01	01		US	User6
CUST1P2	07						US	User7

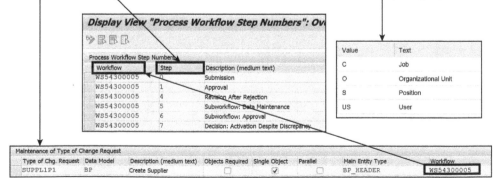

Figure 7.52 Example: Agent Assignment for the Customer Workflow

In the GET_AGENT decision table, you'll perform the following actions:

- Specify the type of change request and the change request step number.
- If the change request step requires agent determination based on sales area, company code, or central flag, maintain those values.
- Assign a processor by entering the object type and the processor ID.

Figure 7.52 provides an example of the GET_AGENT decision table entries and how the change request type, workflow, and step number are linked.

Financials

SAP Master Data Governance, Financials, provides a simple workflow template (WS75700040), advanced workflow template (WS75700027), and an extended workflow template (WS75700043). Following is an overview of these templates:

- **Simple workflow template**
  The change request is created, and required changes are maintained. Simple workflow allows execution and approval of changes at the change request level.

- **Advanced workflow template**
  The change request is created, objects (entity types to be changed) are maintained, and required changes are made. Advanced workflow allows execution and approval of changes on an individual object level.

- **Extended workflow template**
  This template allows execution and approval of changes on an individual object level and allows control of steps by entity types.

Figure 7.53 provides an overview of the simple workflow process.

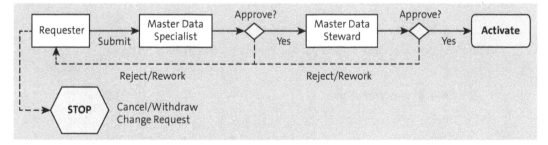

Figure 7.53 SAP Master Data Governance, Financials: Simple Workflow

The high-level steps involved in the simple workflow process are as follows:

1. The requester submits a request to the master data specialist.
2. The master data specialist reviews the request and, if approved, the master data steward receives the workflow task for further approval. The master data steward

can then approve the request for final activation or send it back to the requester for rework.

3. The master data specialist or master data steward can send the request back to the requester for rework.

4. The requester can either resubmit after rework is complete or withdraw.

Figure 7.54 provides an overview of the extended workflow, and following are the high-level steps involved:

1. The requester submits a request to the master data specialist.

2. Multiple master data specialists receive workflow tasks. After all specialists review and approve the request, the master data manager receives the workflow task for further approval.

3. The master data manager reviews and approves the request.

4. The master data manager receives the request for final approval, and, once approved, the change request is activated.

5. During the end-to-end process, any single master data steward, master data manager, or processor can send the request back to the requester for rework.

6. The requester can either resubmit after the rework is complete or withdraw.

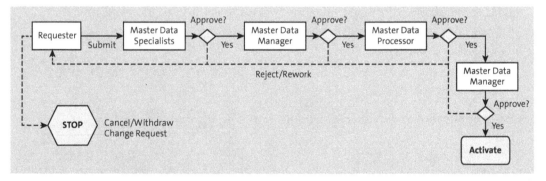

Figure 7.54 SAP Master Data Governance, Financials: Advanced Workflow

7.5.2 Rule-Based Workflows

SAP delivers a rule-based workflow template (WS60800086), which is configurable using a BRFplus decision table and can be used for any change request process where SAP-delivered workflow templates don't suit the project-specific requirements. Using a rule-based workflow also helps avoid the effort involved in copying SAP-delivered workflow templates and adapting them to suit the project requirements. If the process deviation is only minor, SAP-delivered templates can be copied and adapted. However, if the process deviates significantly from the SAP-delivered workflow templates, then using a rule-based workflow template is more flexible. The following sections provide an overview of the rule-based workflow template, associated decision tables, and an example of designing a simple workflow process.

Introduction to Rule-Based Workflows

In a rule-based workflow, the change request process is configured using decision tables for each change request type. Based on the current workflow step and action performed, decision tables determine the next change request step, status, and agents in the workflow process. For each change request type for which a rule-based workflow is configured, a separate BRFplus application is generated by the system with an application name that contains the change request type.

The generated BRFplus application contains the required functions, rulesets, and decision tables. The rule-based workflow itself is generic and isn't specific to a domain, data model, or change request type. The logic built in the template caters to determining the change request process based on the configuration entries maintained in the decision tables of the system-generated BRFplus application. Each decision table has generated input and result columns. For each input column entry maintained in the decision table, result columns determine the output for the process. Each generated BRFplus application contains the following three decision tables:

- **Single-value decision table**
  This decision table is generated by the system with the name DT_SINGLE_VAL_<Change Request Type>. Based on the current change request step, the UI action performed, and a few other parameters maintained as part of the input columns, the results will be returned with values for the next change request step, status, and so on. Table 7.16 provides an overview of the single-value decision table columns.

Column	Column Type	Details
CR Previous Step	Condition	Previously processed change request step.
Previous Action	Condition	Previously processed change request action.
Chng. Req. Priority	Condition	Current change request priority.
Chng. Req. Reason	Condition	Current change request reason.
CR Rejection Reason	Condition	Rejection reason for the change request.
CR Parent Step	Condition	Used for defining parallel workflow processes and indicates the step from which parallel processing is initiated.
Parallel Agt Grp No.	Condition	Used for defining parallel workflow processes and indicates the agent group number of subprocesses.

Table 7.16 Single-Value Decision Columns

Column	Column Type	Details
Condition Alias	Result	Identifies a unique condition defined in a single-value table. Each condition alias must have at least one corresponding entry either in the user agent decision table or the nonuser agent decision table.
New Chng. Req. Step	Result	Next step in the process.
New CR Status	Result	New change request status.
Hours to Completion	Result	Expected number of hours for completion of the work item. If not completed, an email notification is sent.
Merge Type	Result	Used for merging the results after parallel processing into the higher-level process. Merge type is **B** to indicate BAdI implementation.
Merge Parameter	Result	Used along with **Merge Type** with a value of the service name used for the BAdI implementation.
Dyn Agt Sel Service	Result	Service name used for implementation of BAdI: Dynamic Selection of Agent in Rule-Based Workflow.

Table 7.16 Single-Value Decision Columns (Cont.)

- **User agent decision table**

  This decision table is generated by the system with the name `DT_USER_AGT_GRP_<Change Request Type>` and is used to determine processors and UI actions for a change request step. Table 7.17 provides an overview of the user agent decision table columns.

Column	Column Type	Details
Condition Alias	Condition	Condition alias maintained in a single-value decision table to identify a condition that requires user action.
User Agt Grp No.	Result	Value maintained to identify the user agent maintained in **User Agent Value**. For parallel processing, different user agent group numbers are entered to identify each subprocess with the same condition alias.
Step Type	Result	Step type for the condition alias, which defines the UI actions for the change request step.
User Agent Type	Result	Identifies the type of user agent: user, role, job, organization unit, position, or special user.

Table 7.17 User Agent Decision Columns

Column	Column Type	Details
User Agent Value	Result	Depending on the user agent type, either a user or a group value is maintained. Special values such as **INIT** (initiator of the change request step) and **LAST** (last processor) can also be maintained.

Table 7.17 User Agent Decision Columns (Cont.)

- **Nonuser agent decision table**

  This decision table is generated by the system with the name DT_NON_USER_AGT_GRP_ <Change Request Type> and is used to determine background steps involved for a change request step. Table 7.18 provides an overview of the nonuser agent decision table columns.

Column	Column Type	Details
Condition Alias	Condition	Condition alias maintained in a single-value decision table to identify a condition that requires a background action.
Agent Group	Result	Works along with the **Process Pattern** column to identify if there are multiple process patterns for a parallel process.
Process Pattern	Result	Identifies process patterns. (See Table 7.19 for more details.)
Service Name	Result	Service name depending on the process pattern.

Table 7.18 Nonuser Agent Decision Columns

Figure 7.55 provides an overview of a BRFplus application and associated decision tables, as follows:

❶ BRFplus application

❷ Nonuser agent decision table

❸ User agent decision table

❹ Single value decision table

❺ Decision table entries

As you can see, when the corresponding configuration activity is initiated, the first step requires entry of a change request type, which is used by the system to generate the BRFplus application.

The system generates the following:

- USMD_SSW_CATA_MAT01: BRFplus application
- DT_SINGLE_VAL_MAT01: Single-value decision table

281

- DT_USER_AGT_GRP_MAT01: User agent decision table
- DT_NON_USER_AGT_GRP_MAT01: Nonuser agent decision table

Process Definition of Rule-Based Workflow

✓ Continue

＊Type of Change Request: MAT01   ⬚ Create Material

↓

Business Rule Framework plus

Workbench ⌄ | Tools ⌄

Repository **Catalog**   ⬚   ● Decision Table: DT_SINGLE_VAL_MAT01

Switch to Other Catalog ▶↓ ▶↑   ‹ Back | ✎ Edit | ⬚ Check | ⬚ Save | ⬚ Activate | 🗑 Delete ⌄ | More ⌄

Catalog Structure   ⊦ S..   **General**

▾ USMD_SSW_CATA_MAT01 ❶   **Detail**
  ▸ ⬚ BRFp_Appl
  ▸ ⬚ TRIGGER_FUNCTION   Export To Excel | Context Overview | Start Simulation
  ▸ ⬚ RULE_SET
  ▸ ⬚ DT_SERVICE_NAME   **Table Contents**
  ▾ ⬚ DECISION_TABLE   Find: Next | Previous

CR Previous Step	Previous Action	Chng. Req. Priority
=00 (Processing) ❺		
=90 (Final Check)	=09 (Activate)	
=90 (Final Check)	=04 (Reject)	
=91 (Activation)	=31 (Activation successful)	
=91 (Activation)	<>31 (Activation successful)	

DT_NON_USER_AGT_GRP_MAT01 ❷ · ▪
DT_USER_AGT_GRP_MAT01 ❸ · ▪
DT_SINGLE_VAL_MAT01 ❹ · ▪

Figure 7.55 BRFplus Application for MAT01 Change Request Type

Figure 7.56 shows how these decision tables are linked to each other. As shown, the condition alias defined for each row in a single-value decision table becomes a link between the single value decision table ❶ and the user agent decision table ❷ or nonuser agent decision table ❸.

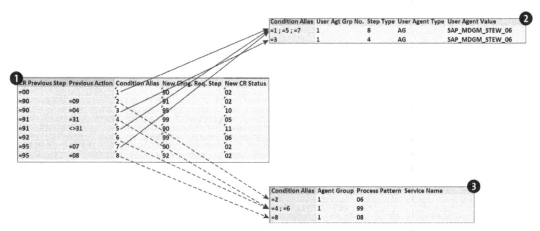

Figure 7.56 Decision Tables and Condition Alias

As discussed in Table 7.18, the nonuser agent decision table uses process patterns to identify background steps involved in a rule-based workflow. We'll now take a look at these process patterns.

Several workflow basic steps are grouped together to form a process pattern used to control the flow of the change request process. Rule-based workflows continue to run in a loop until the process pattern to complete the workflow is found. Table 7.19 provides a list of process patterns.

Code	Process Pattern Name	Comments
01	UI Dialog	Used when user interaction is needed on a change request step, and hence used in user agent decision tables.
02	Call Synchronous Method	Used to include any operations that aren't provided by SAP.
03	Call Sub-Workflow	Used to initiate a subworkflow with the workflow name maintained in the **Service Name** column of the nonuser agent decision table.
04	Call Data Replication	Used for initiating the data replication process after the change request is activated.
05	Activation (Do Not Bypass Snapshot)	Used for activation of the change request. Any changes made to master data tables while the change request was in process trigger a failure of activation process, and the result is set for the **Previous Action** column.
06	Activation (Bypass Snapshot)	Used for activation of the change request. Unlike process pattern 05, this process pattern activates and overwrites any master data changes made while the change request was in process.
07	Validate Change Request	Used for validating change request data.
08	Roll Back Change Request	Used for initiating roll back of changes made using a change request process.
98	Error	Used for error handling.
99	Complete (Sub-)Workflow	Use for indicating the completion of the rule-based workflow.

Table 7.19 Rule-Based Workflow: Process Patterns

Figure 7.57 provides an overview of the rule-based workflow template defined with various process patterns and loops through until the 99-complete process pattern is found.

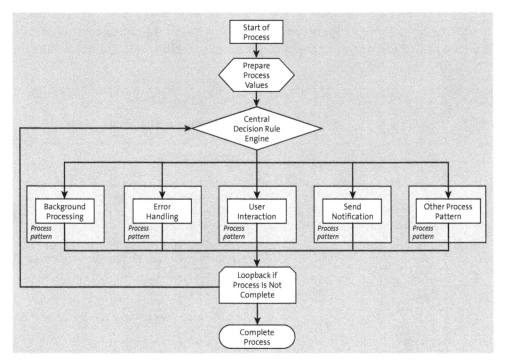

Figure 7.57 Rule-Based Workflow: High-Level Design

Designing a Simple Rule-Based Workflow

In this section, we'll design a simple process using a rule-based workflow template offered by SAP. Some of the change request types delivered by SAP via BC Sets contain required configuration and decision table entries if the change request type delivered is configured with a rule-based workflow. The main goal of this section is to explain the design aspects involved in a rule-based workflow by using the following simple process (also shown in Figure 7.58):

1. A requester initiates the change request process and submits the change request after entering all required data.

2. The master data reviewer receives the work item, reviews the data, and, if agrees, approves the change request.

3. The master data approver receives the work item, reviews the data, and, if agrees, approves the change request.

4. The system initiates the activation process and activates the change request.

5. If either the master data reviewer or the approver disagrees during the process, they can send the change request back to the requester.

6. The requester receives the work item and submits it back after the rework is done or withdraws the change request.

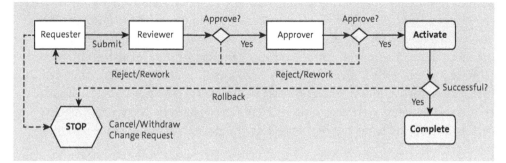

Figure 7.58 Sample Process Considered for Rule-Based Workflow Design

To design this process, you need to consider the following configuration items:

- What change request steps are involved?
- What are the UI actions each person in the end-to-end process can have for a specific change request step? For example, what possible UI actions can the master data reviewer take?
- What is the change request status for each change request step?
- What change request steps are acted upon by the system or the user?

As a first step, identify all possible steps involved in the process, identify each condition involved in the process, and then name it with a condition alias. Then start identifying the UI actions, step types, and change request status that are applicable to a specific change request step. Figure 7.59 provides an overview of the step types and UI actions we chose based on the standard SAP-delivered step type and action configurations.

	Activity performed		Change Request Actions		Step Type	
Requester	Submit	Initial change request submission	--	Not applicable for initial submission		
	Resubmit	Change request submission/withdraw as part of rework	07	Resubmit	4	Revise change request
	Withdraw		08	Withdraw		
Reviewer	Approve	Approve change request and send to approver	03	Approve	2	Approve change request
	Reject	Reject change request and send back to requester for rework	04	Reject		
Approver	Activate	Approve change request and initiate activation	09	Activate	5	Activate change request
	Send for Revision	Send change request back to requester for rework	10	Send for revision		

Figure 7.59 Defining Actions and Step Types for Each User Interaction

If needed, you can create additional step types and actions. For additional details, refer to Section 7.2.6 for change request actions and change request step types.

Similarly, start identifying the change request steps and statuses for each change request step. It's helpful if the process is drawn by identifying all the design elements discussed earlier. This process makes it easy to translate the design into appropriate decision tables. Figure 7.60 shows how our sample process translates into a change request process with individual design elements, including steps that involve user interaction, such as approve and reject, as well as background activities, such as activation. As a next step, start designing decision tables based on the change request process. Following are some important aspects you need to consider while designing the process:

- All identified change request steps and conditions need to be part of single value decision table.
- The first step, which is a change request submission, is always considered step 00.
- All conditions that involve user interaction will be maintained in the user agent decision table with the appropriate agent type and agent value.
- All conditions that involve background processing will be maintained in the non-user agent decision table.

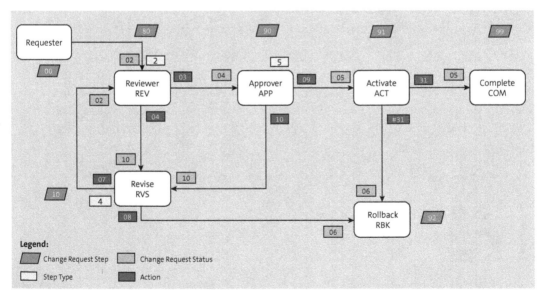

Figure 7.60 Change Request Process Design for a Sample Process

Based on the change request process designed, Figure 7.61 shows all three decision tables populated with all conditions.

Single-Value Decision Table

CR Previous Step	Previous Action	Condition Alias	New Chng. Req. Step	New CR Status
00		REV	80	02
80	03	APP	90	04
80	04	RVS	10	10
90	09	ACT	91	05
90	10	RVS	10	10
91	31	COM	99	05
91	#31	RBK	92	06
10	07	REV	80	02
10	08	RBK	92	06

Non-User Agent Decision Table

Condition Alias	User Agt Grp No.	Process Pattern	Service Name
ACT	001	06	
COM	001	99	
RLB	001	08	

User Agent Decision Table

Condition Alias	User Agt Grp No.	Step Type	User Agent Type	User Agent Value
REV	001	2	O/C/S/AG/US/SU	<Agent>
APP	001	5	90	<Agent>
RVS	001	4	10	<Agent>

Figure 7.61 Decision Tables for a Sample Process

Tip

BRFplus provides functionality to export into and import from Microsoft Excel for decision tables, as shown in Figure 7.62. This provides the advantage of manipulating the decision table entries in Microsoft Excel and importing back into the decision tables.

SAP provides simple rule-based workflow entries for all change request types that are delivered with the rule-based workflow template. Decision tables associated with such change request types can be used as a starting point for designing the required process.

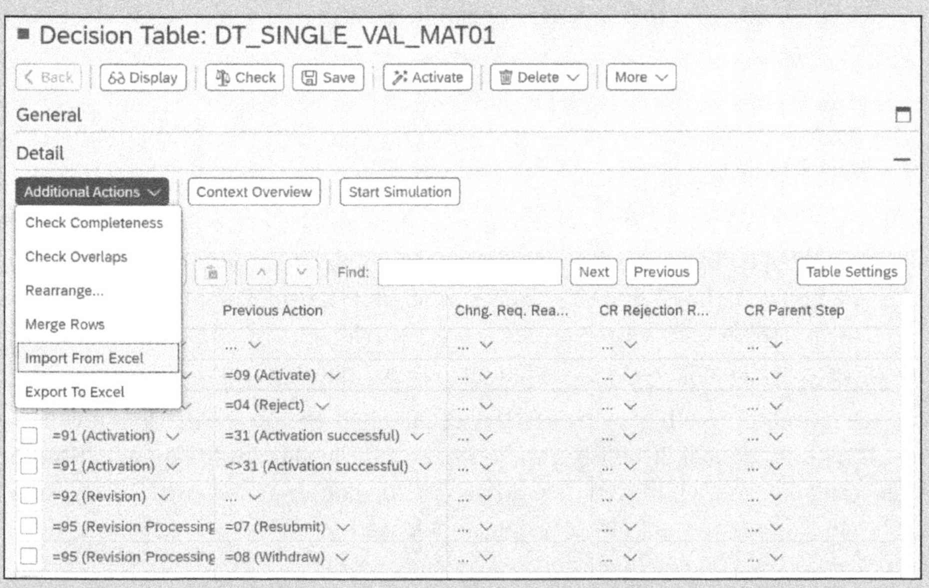

Figure 7.62 Decision Table Export to and Import from Microsoft Excel Functionalities

7.5.3   Available Business Add-Ins

SAP offers various BAdIs for enhancement of workflow-related functionalities. The following BAdIs are available for rule-based workflows:

- **Rule Context Preparation for Rule-Based Workflow** (USMD_SSW_RULE_CONTEXT_PRE-PARE)

  This BAdI is implemented to prepare a BRFplus rule context in a rule-based workflow. When you need to enhance decision tables with additional columns, data for such columns needs to be passed to the BRFplus rule context. For example, you might need to enhance a single-value decision table with the material type as a condition column. To pass the material type selected in the change request data, method PREPARE_RULE_CONTEXT of this BAdI needs to be implemented.

- **Calling of System Method for Rule-Based Workflow** (USMD_SSW_SYSTEM_METHOD_CALLER)

  This BAdI is used to implement the calling of a system method in a rule-based workflow.

- **Dynamic Selection of Agent in Rule-Based Workflow** (USMD_SSW_DYNAMIC_AGENT_SELECT)

  Using this BAdI, agents can be dynamically determined.

- **Handling of Parallel Results in Rule-Based Workflow** (USMD_SSW_PARA_RESULT_HAN-DLER)

  The HANDLE_PARALLEL_RESULT method in this BAdI is used to implement the results of a parallel workflow merge in a rule-based workflow.

- **Check User Agent/Nonuser Agent Table for Rule-Based Workflow** (USMD_SSW_CHECK_AGENT_TABLE)

- This BAdI can be used to implement dynamic checks on user agent or nonuser agent decision tables.

7.6   Summary

In this chapter, we covered the end-to-end modeling aspects of the change request process. We started by introducing the individual building blocks involved in the process and explained how they connect with each other and translate into an end-to-end process. This chapter also provided various processes available for single records and multiple records in a change request, including design aspects of hierarchies.

With the foundation gained in the first half of this chapter, you learned about workflow process modeling capabilities from an overview of some of the standard workflow templates available for each master data domain. This chapter ended with a discussion of rule-based workflows and how to design a rule-based workflow using a simple process as an example. We also included a list of available BAdIs.

In the next chapter, we'll discuss the data quality and search capabilities available in SAP Master Data Governance. We'll also discuss the SAP Master Data Governance framework available for integrating with SAP and non-SAP applications. Chapter 8 also provides an overview of data quality management and data quality remediation.

7

Chapter 8

Data Quality, Search, and Remediations

SAP Master Data Governance offers data quality and search options, as well as validation techniques, duplicate check capabilities, and data enrichment functionalities. Data quality management and data quality remediation functionalities further strengthen the solution by helping to better manage business rules and providing options for data cleaning.

Poor master data quality creates many challenges for any organization irrespective of its size, business line, or geographic location. Many of these challenges are visible and measurable, whereas some challenges affect the growth and profitability indirectly. Quantifying the losses and impact of duplicate, inaccurate, and untrusted data may not be an easy task. No department or process remains insulated from the harm caused by poor master data quality. A common challenge includes reduced sales effectiveness due to a missing single version of truth in which business transactions are compromised due to hidden facts. The lack of transparency and data duplication in the systems may lessen the procurement made by procurement executives, which removes any advantageous edge while negotiating contracts with suppliers. Lack of real time collaboration with the front office can have a visible impact on realizing the go-to-market strategies of the company. In addition, critical business decisions can be wrong if data isn't reliable and consistent.

Some of the common challenges that can arise due to poor master data quality are listed here:

- Risk of noncompliance with the Sarbanes-Oxley Act (SOX), International Financial Reporting Standards (IFRS), General Data Protection Regulation (GDPR), Sunshine Act, and so on
- Lack of consistent consolidated information in real time
- Increased maintenance of master data in the form of rework in identification and correction
- Reduced transparency due to missing consolidated views across the company landscape
- Lost opportunity for potential benefits through better available facts that can be leveraged during negotiations with business partners

- Wrong deliveries to/from business partners due to incorrect master data
- Inaccurate reporting resulting in business decisions made on inconsistent data
- Increased inventory due to inconsistent or duplicate master data
- Production disruptions out of confusion and lack of transparency
- Wrong or missed payments to business partners

With SAP Master Data Governance, companies can take proactive actions by avoiding any inappropriate, invalid, or inconsistent data before that data becomes part of the active database and available operationally for business users, thereby improving the overall accuracy and reliability of the master data. However, remember that good quality master data isn't a one-time endeavor, but it's an ongoing journey where every opportunity should be leveraged to improve and sustain the quality of master data.

Although the SAP Master Data Governance staging-active concept plays a crucial role in the ability to be proactive during master data governance, the robust capabilities around search and data quality functionalities are the real backbone of the SAP Master Data Governance solution.

In this chapter, after discussing various search helps, match profiles, and search setups, the data quality functionalities in SAP Master Data Governance are explained for the key areas of duplicate check, business rules, and data enrichment needs. Data quality management and data quality remediation for product master data are also discussed in detail in the second half of this chapter.

8.1   Search Functionality

Search capabilities in the SAP Master Data Governance user interface (UI) are designed so that users can directly navigate to various business activities from the same screen.

After an overview of the search functionality, this section discusses the various search help options and match profile configurations available. In addition, we'll cover the extensibility of searches in the context of SAP Master Data Governance.

8.1.1   Overview

As a master data governance best practice, you can initiate most of the business activities by first performing a search in SAP Master Data Governance and navigating directly to other business activities from the search screen itself. The business activities that can be performed from the same search screen are as follows:

- Copy
- Create
- Display

- Change/extend
- Open details
- Mark/unmark for deletion
- Mass change
- Block/unblock
- Replicate using service-oriented architecture (SOA)
- Replicate using Application Link Enabling (ALE)
- Replication logs

To access the SAP Master Data Governance search screen, navigate through Transaction **NWBC** or a suitable app in the SAP Fiori launchpad provided for each data domain, for example, manage supplier, manage customer, and so on. Transaction **NWBC** may prompt you to select an assigned security role. After selecting a suitable assigned security role, go to the homepage, and click **Search**. Figure 8.1 shows a typical search screen for a governed master data object in SAP Master Data Governance.

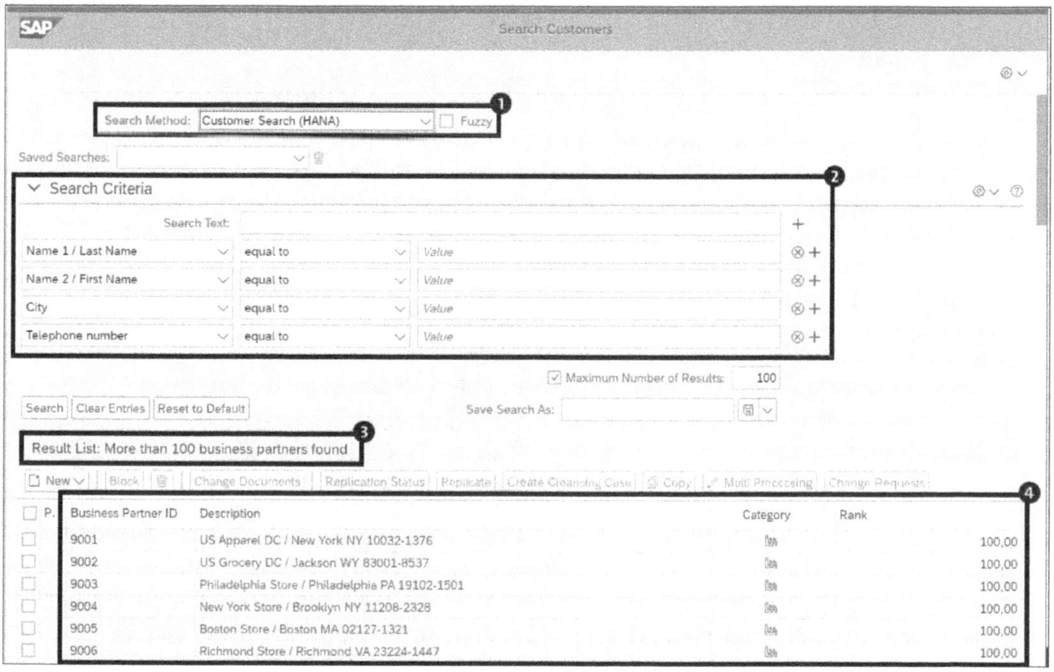

Figure 8.1 Search Screen in the SAP Master Data Governance UI

Here, follow these steps:

❶ **Select search methods.**

In the **Search Method** dropdown, select an appropriate search method to choose the search technology being used. Accuracy and response time may vary based on the search method. Address search, database search, SAP NetWeaver Enterprise Search and SAP HANA enterprise search, remote key search, and SAP HANA search are various search applications available for SAP Master Data Governance.

❷ **Provide search criteria.**
In the **Search Criteria** area, select and input the parameters for the search.

❸ **Check result count.**
A value for this attribute signifies the number of successful hits returned by the search method based on the search parameter provided.

❹ **Review results.**
Records that result from the successful search hits based on search criteria are displayed in this section, and you can further check the details by clicking the link for each result record.

8.1.2   Search Applications

In SAP Master Data Governance, search applications are based on different search applications, which can be deployed in many ways. Some commonly used search applications for SAP Master Data Governance include the following:

- **Exact search**
  This search works based on a database query. No additional SAP or non-SAP software components are required for using exact search. Exact search is configured in SAP Master Data Governance search applications as "DB." Database search searches the SAP Master Data Governance and active area tables to retrieve the data based on the search criteria. This exact search method is recommended if there are fewer records to avoid search performance impacts. With the extension to the database tables and generated tables and structures, the database search UI needs to be enhanced to display additional columns in the search result list.

- **SAP NetWeaver Enterprise Search and SAP HANA enterprise search**
  Enterprise search capabilities can be based on SAP HANA database and use fuzzy search capabilities. SAP NetWeaver Enterprise Search and SAP HANA enterprise search support free-text and attribute-based search as well as the capability to search in other databases in the landscape. Both are configured with the name "ES" in SAP Master Data Governance search applications. Standard search connectors are provided to extract data, schedule the indexing, and run the search logic based on the search criterion. Both the reuse area connector and the SAP Master Data Governance connector for the specific domain should be configured to search on the active area as well as the staging data.

  In addition to free-text and attribute-based search, SAP NetWeaver Enterprise Search and SAP HANA enterprise search also support fuzzy search. The search connectors need to be extended with the extended attributes in the data model. To search for custom objects, the custom search object connector template needs to be created using the Customizing path (Transaction **MDGIMG**), **Master Data Governance, Central Governance** · **General Settings** · **Data Quality and Search** · **Create Search Object Con-**

nector Templates. A search object connector is then created based on the template, which helps with indexing, scheduling, and searching the data. The data is retrieved using the access class for the search application.

To implement custom search providers, an access class and search application must be defined. The access class should use the standard search interface IF_USMD_ SEARCH_DATA. The search application is defined via the Customizing path (Transaction **MDGIMG**), **Master Data Governance, Central Governance · General Settings · Data Quality and Search · Define Search Applications**.

To display the newly added fields in the search application, the Customizing settings for the UI field properties need to be set via the Customizing path (Transaction **MDGIMG**), **Master Data Governance, Central Governance · General Settings · UI Modeling · Define Field Properties for UI**. The **No Selection** and **No Results List** checkboxes need to be unchecked accordingly.

- **Fuzzy search for address data**
  Fuzzy search provides error-tolerant searches on address fields. Using this technique, the search will find matches even when users misspell words or enter only partial words for the search.

  This search is based on Business Address Services (BAS) and requires additional software components, for example, SAP Data Quality Management. In SAP Master Data Governance, this search is configured with the search application name "AD." Refer to SAP Note 176559 for more information on using and implementing BAS. Figure 8.2 shows how a fuzzy search for address data works.

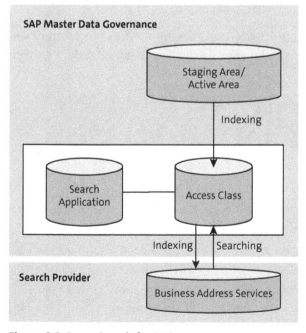

Figure 8.2 Fuzzy Search for BAS

- **Remote client key search**

  In a remote client key search, you can search remotely in other SAP S/4HANA or SAP ERP systems in the landscape by referring to the keys maintained in SAP Master Data Governance key mapping. In search applications, this is configured as "RK." SAP HANA search supports remote client key search.

- **SAP HANA search**

  SAP HANA search is the latest and most powerful search. SAP HANA search views are delivered that can be generated based on requirements. You can also easily extend SAP HANA search. SAP HANA search results are presented with a ranking inside search results using fuzzy search. In SAP Master Data Governance search applications, SAP HANA search is configured as "HA." Check SAP Notes 2281401 and 2302716 for implementing SAP HANA search. More details about setting up SAP HANA search are given in Section 8.1.4.

The IMG activities and configurations related to SAP Master Data Governance **Search and Duplicate Check** are shown in Figure 8.3.

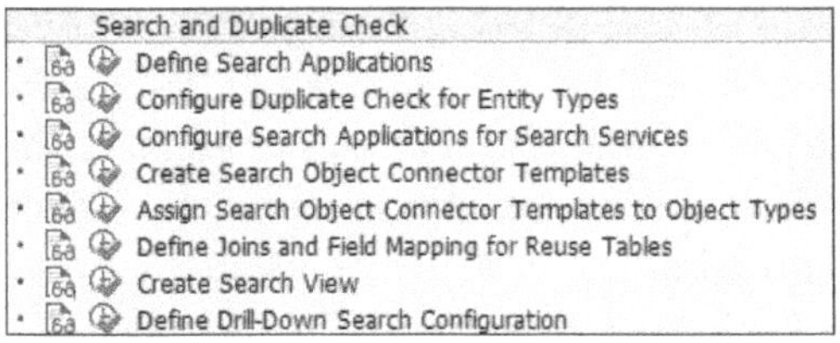

	Search and Duplicate Check
·	Define Search Applications
·	Configure Duplicate Check for Entity Types
·	Configure Search Applications for Search Services
·	Create Search Object Connector Templates
·	Assign Search Object Connector Templates to Object Types
·	Define Joins and Field Mapping for Reuse Tables
·	Create Search View
·	Define Drill-Down Search Configuration

Figure 8.3 Search and Duplicate Check IMG Activities in SAP Master Data Governance

Figure 8.4 shows the standard search applications that are used in SAP Master Data Governance. Based on their own requirements, companies may also define custom search applications.

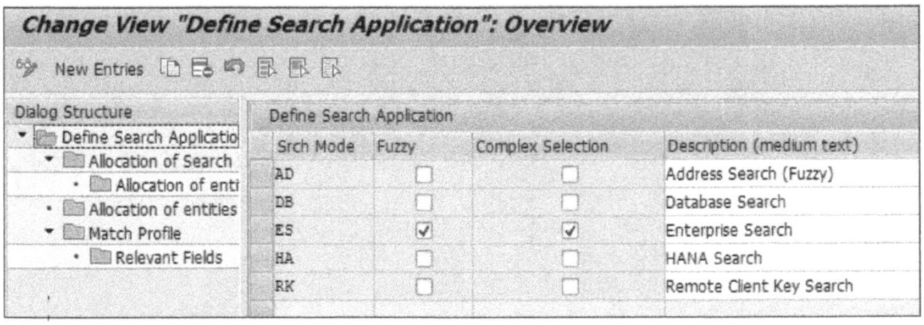

Change View "Define Search Application": Overview

New Entries

Dialog Structure	Define Search Application			
▼ Define Search Applicatio	Srch Mode	Fuzzy	Complex Selection	Description (medium text)
▼ Allocation of Search	AD	☐	☐	Address Search (Fuzzy)
· Allocation of enti	DB	☐	☐	Database Search
· Allocation of entities	ES	☑	☑	Enterprise Search
▼ Match Profile	HA	☐	☐	HANA Search
· Relevant Fields	RK	☐	☐	Remote Client Key Search

Figure 8.4 Define Search Applications

Some of the search providers require the allocation of one or more search helps; for example, SAP HANA search requires the allocation of search views. Database search requires the allocation of search help through the Data Dictionary. Figure 8.5 shows the allocation of search help to search application **HA**.

You can configure data models and entity types that need to be considered by each search help as shown in Figure 8.6.

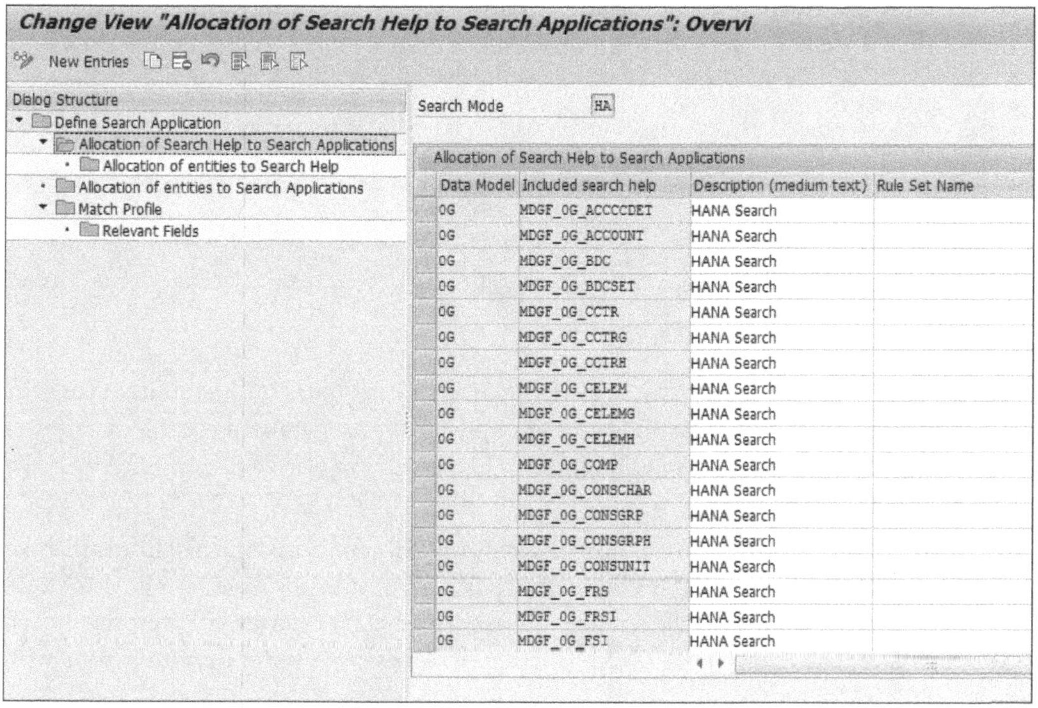

Figure 8.5 Allocation of Search Help to Search Applications

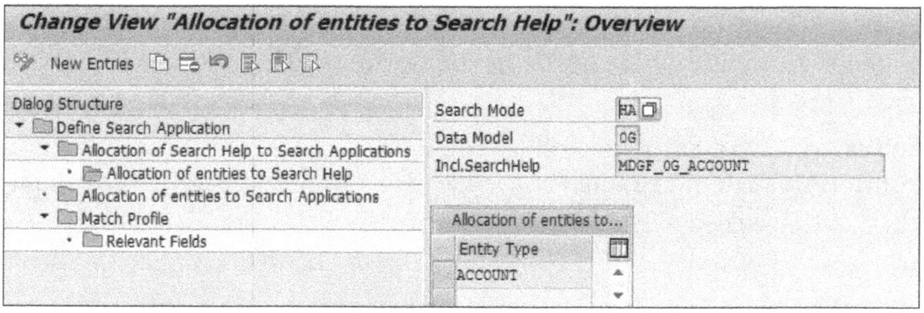

Figure 8.6 Allocation of Entities to Search Help

8.1.3   Match Profiles

Match profiles are used for duplicate checks in SAP Master Data Governance. In match profile configuration, you can specify attributes that should be taken into consideration while the system does a comparison with other database records. Although largely it's the same attributes that define a duplicate master data record, different companies may want to have personalized matching strategies and the flexibility to add or remove attributes that contribute to identifying a duplicate. Figure 8.7 shows some examples of match profiles.

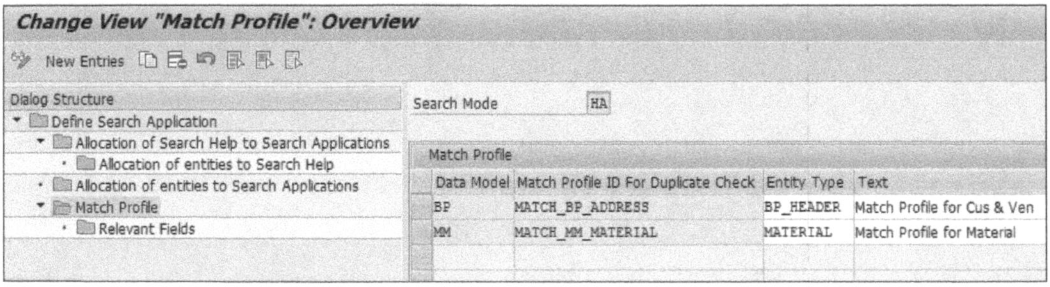

Figure 8.7 Match Profiles

In each match profile, many relevant fields are taken into consideration during the duplicate check. Figure 8.8 shows an example of various parameters set for attributes assigned to a match profile, as follows:

- **Weight**
  This is assigned to an attribute to determine the importance attached to an attribute during the duplicate check and to prioritize the results displayed to the user. Note that the weight isn't relevant for database search (SAP NetWeaver Enterprise Search or SAP HANA enterprise search) and remote key search, but it's typically used with SAP HANA search.

- **Fuzziness**
  The threshold number may have a value ranging anywhere from 0 to 1, in which the higher the fuzziness threshold, the more the attribute values need to match the reference value to be found during search or duplicate check. This setting can't be used with database search.

- **Mandatory**
  This controls whether there should be a value existing for that field before a duplicate check is triggered.

- **Ex. Attr**
  The exclude attribute means the respective attribute would not be taken into consideration while performing a duplicate check, but the field values are displayed to the users for their information.

Parameters are also used to refine the matching strategy to give accurate results. In addition, a sequence can be associated with each of the relevant attributes that signifies the order in which fields should be displayed to the user when the duplicate check pops up on the UI.

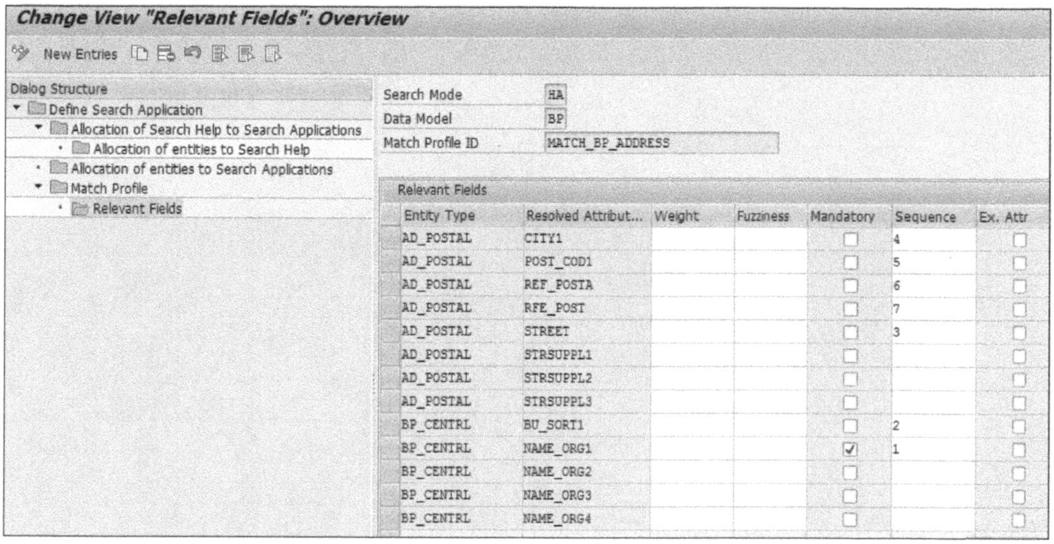

Figure 8.8 Match Profile Relevant Fields

8.1.4   SAP HANA–Based Search Setup

SAP HANA–based search, in addition to SAP NetWeaver Enterprise Search and SAP HANA enterprise search, is one of the most powerful search technologies available today in SAP S/4HANA. It's known for its accuracy and high efficiency. If you have SAP Master Data Governance running on your SAP S/4HANA platform, you get out-of-the-box SAP HANA search capabilities, which are easily configurable without significant effort. SAP HANA search views are delivered for all governed objects in SAP Master Data Governance, and views can be generated based on the exact scope of the project. If SAP Master Data Governance isn't running on an SAP HANA platform, but you have SAP HANA licenses, you can optionally integrate SAP HANA on the side with SAP Master Data Governance and leverage its strong search capabilities during the governance process.

To trigger the Web Dynpro application through which the SAP HANA search views can be generated in SAP Master Data Governance, use menu path (Transaction **MDGIMG**), **Master Data Governance, Central Governance** • **General Settings** • **Data Quality Search** • **Search and Duplicate Check** • **Create Search View**.

Following are the steps for generating the SAP HANA search views:

1. Click on **Create Search View**, and the **MDG Search View** window appears, as shown in Figure 8.9. Through this screen, you can perform various activities needed for generating SAP HANA search views.

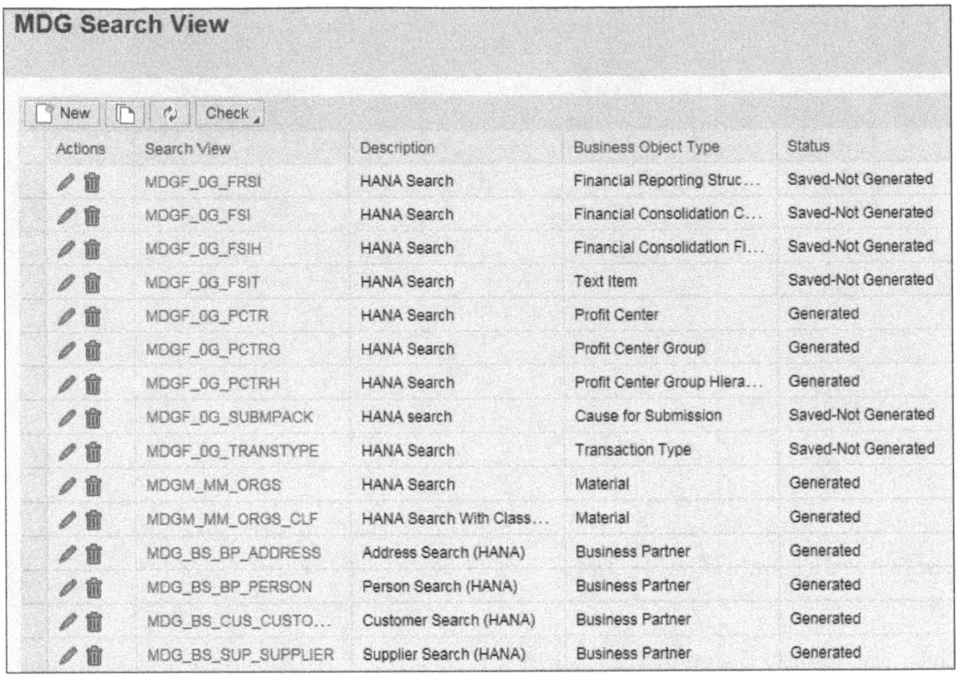

Figure 8.9 SAP HANA Search View in SAP Master Data Governance

2. Select the respective **Search View** for an entity, and click on **Edit** (pencil icon), as shown in Figure 8.10.

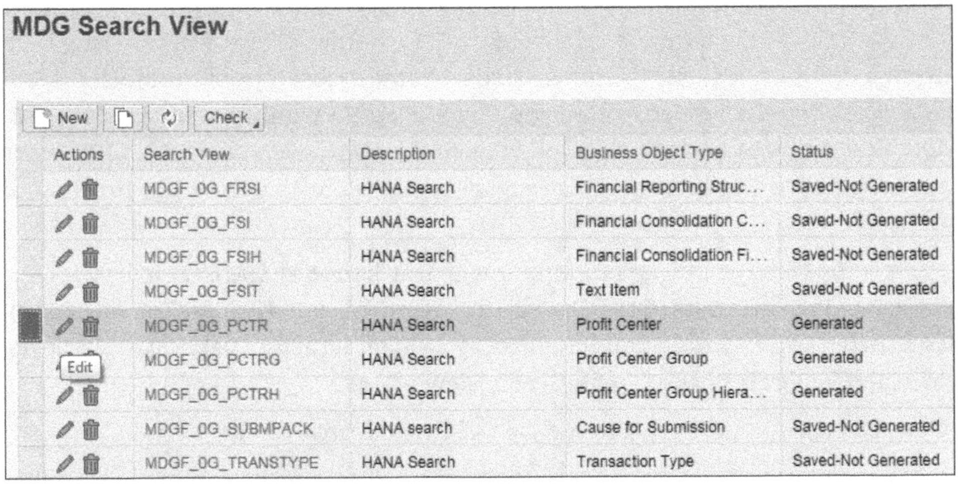

Figure 8.10 Editing an SAP HANA Search View

3. Provide an SAP HANA package name in the **Hana Package** field. Select the **Rule Set** checkbox only if a ruleset should be generated. Click **Next**, as shown in Figure 8.11, to go to the next step for selection of entities and attributes.

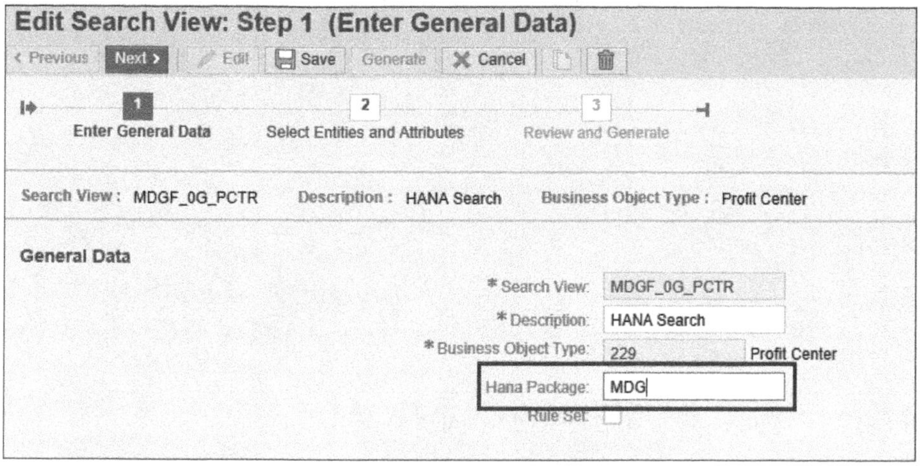

Figure 8.11 Maintaining the SAP HANA Package in General Data

4. Select the entities and attributes that should be part of the search view being generated, and then click **Next**, as shown in Figure 8.12.

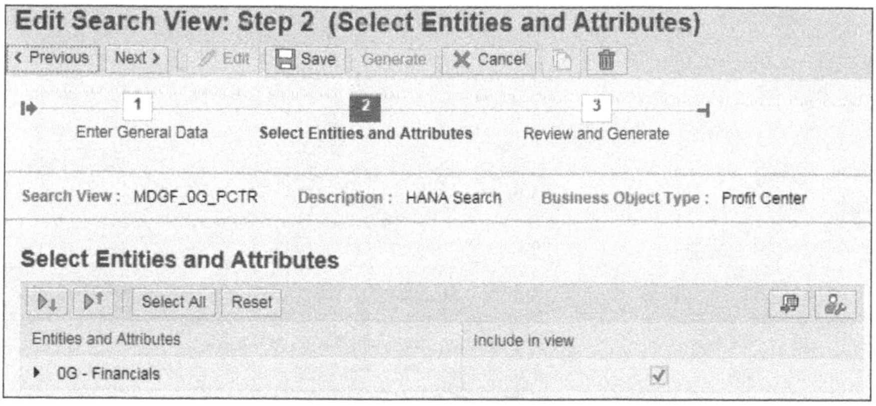

Figure 8.12 Selecting the Entities and Attributes in SAP HANA Search View

5. Click **Save** to save the search view changes in a workbench request. Select an existing workbench transport request using search help, or create a new transport request using Transaction SE10. If required, you can create a search view in the development system and transport it to the test and production systems. The search view must be generated or regenerated in the target (test and production) systems.

6. Click the **Generate** button, as shown in Figure 8.13. After the search view is generated successfully, you can search the properties of an attribute.

7. Go to Transaction **SE80** in SAP Master Data Governance, and select the respective Web Dynpro components. Click on the **Start Configurator** button, as shown in Figure 8.14.

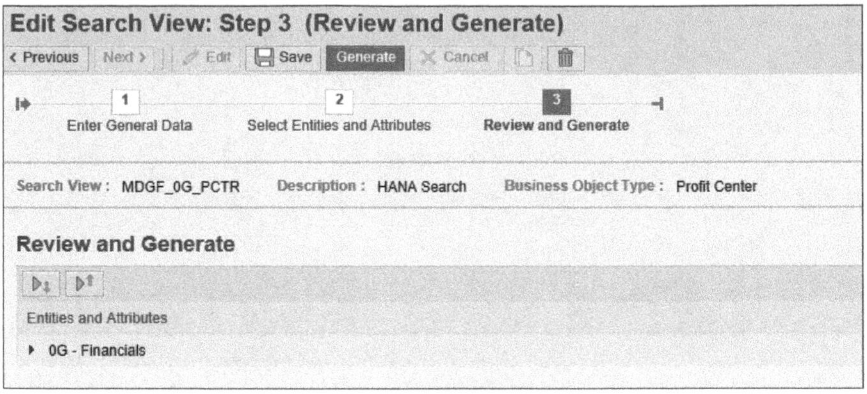

Figure 8.13 Reviewing and Generating the SAP HANA Search View

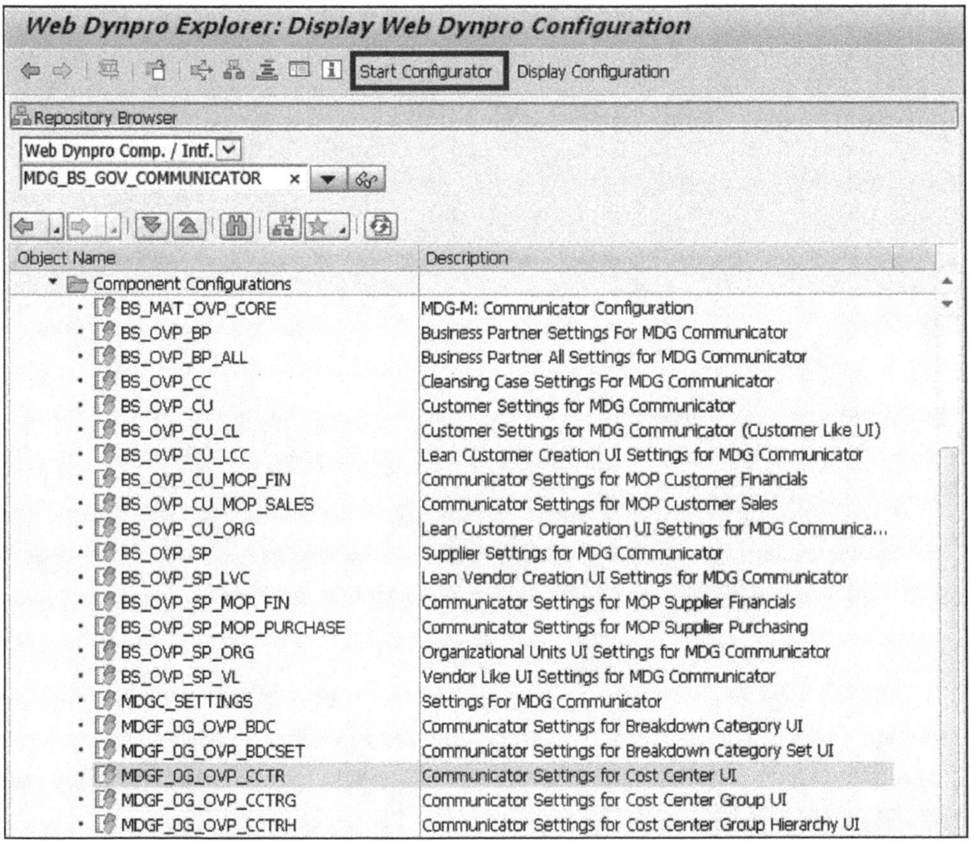

Figure 8.14 Configuration for the Web Dynpro Component through Transaction SE80

8. A new Web Dynpro screen opens in a new window. Click the **Continue in Change Mode** button shown in Figure 8.15.

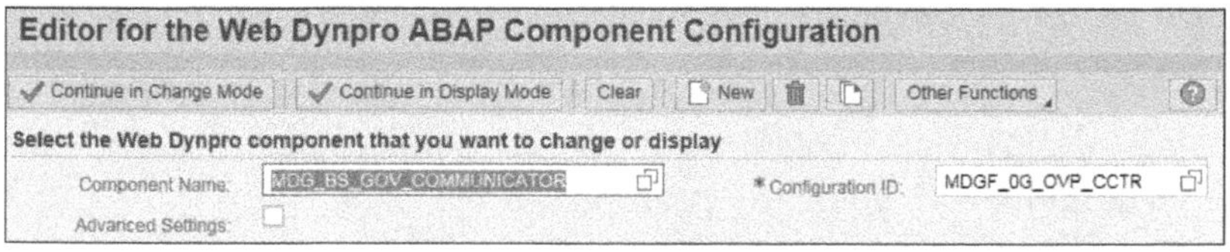

Figure 8.15 Editor for the Web Dynpro ABAP Component Configuration

9. In the new window, select **searchUibbs**, and populate the respective attributes of the element search UI building block (UIBB), that is, **Search Mode**, **Incl.SearchHelp**, **Component**, and **Config ID**. An example configuration for cost center groups is shown in Figure 8.16.

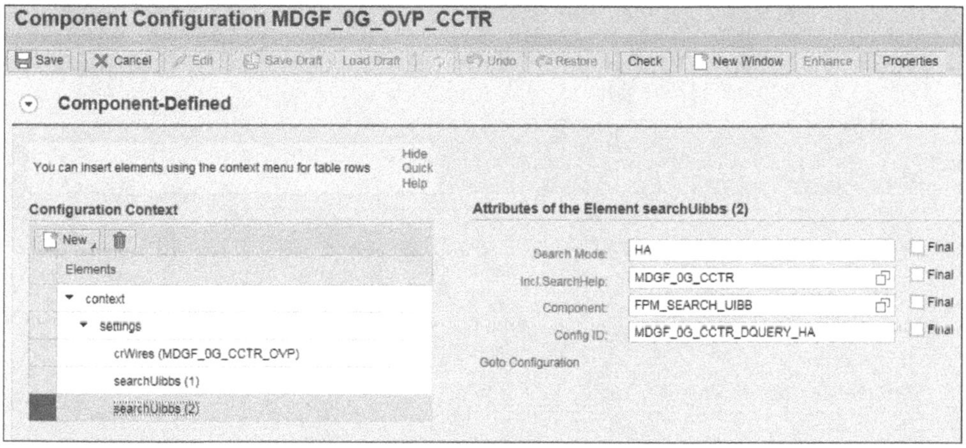

Figure 8.16 Maintaining Attributes of the Element Search UIBBs

10. After completing all these configurations, the search method will be visible in the search screen UI in SAP Master Data Governance. You can select the appropriate search method based on your preferences, as shown in Figure 8.17.

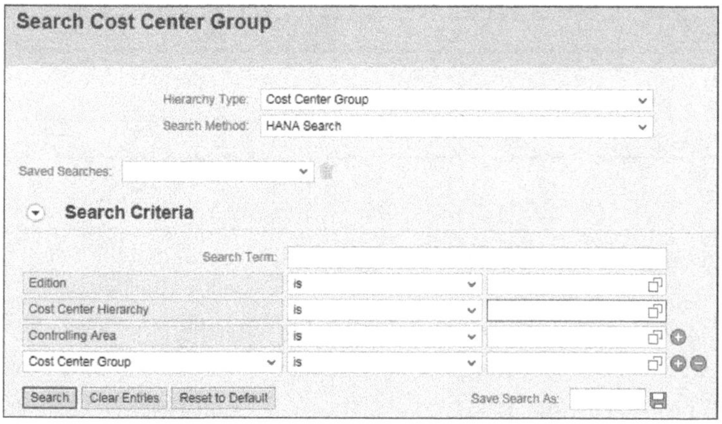

Figure 8.17 Search Using SAP HANA Search in SAP Master Data Governance

8.1.5   SAP HANA Search Extensibility

Due to various business requirements, SAP HANA search may have to be extended to meet your business needs. Let's explore some scenarios where search extensions might become a requirement for your project, as follows:

- **Extending the data model with existing attributes from reuse tables**
  In this case, the extended attributes are available by default for selection in step **2 Select Entities and Attributes** of the SAP HANA search view generation, as shown in the example in Figure 8.18. If these attributes need to be included in the search view, then the flag can be set for the respective attribute. The remaining steps for the configurations remain unchanged as already explained for the SAP HANA search setup.

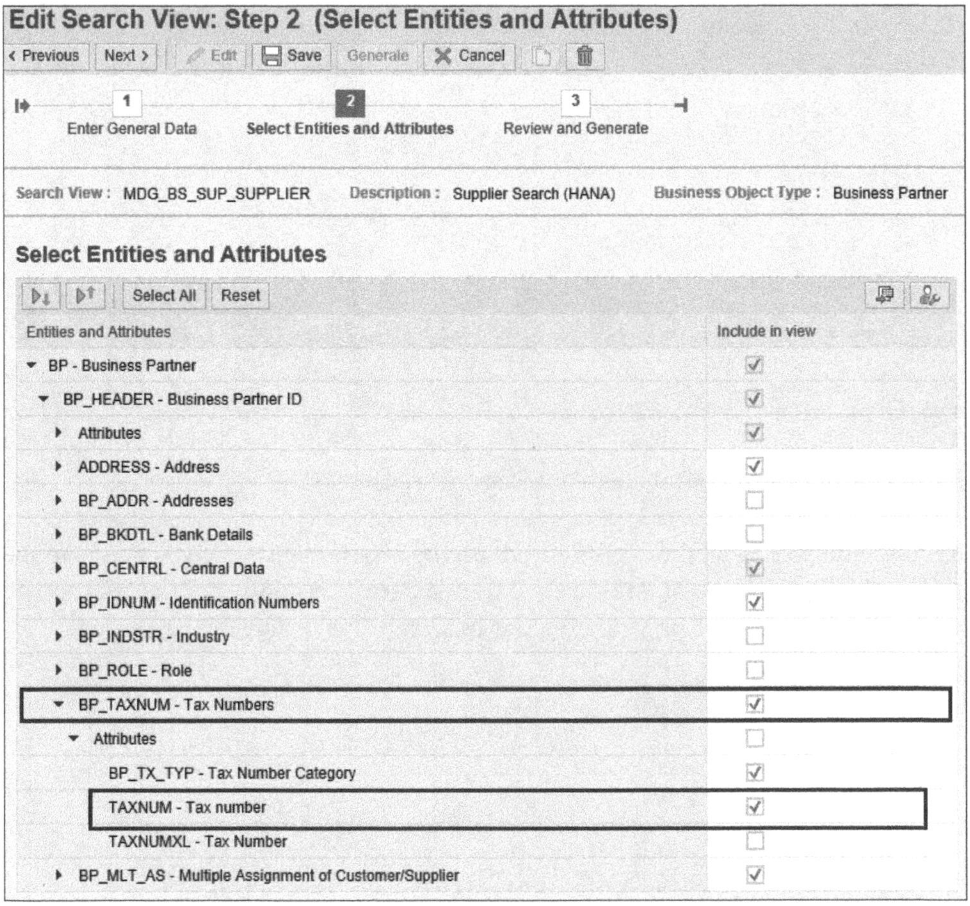

Figure 8.18 Selecting Attributes during the SAP HANA Search View Generation

- **Extending the data model with custom attributes available in backend reuse tables**
  In this scenario as well, without any complex developments, custom fields are by default automatically available for selection, as shown in Figure 8.18. If these

attributes need to be included in the search view, then the flag can be set for the respective attribute. The remaining steps for SAP HANA search configurations are the same.

- **Extending the data model with a custom entity in reuse mode**
  To make the new entity fields available for search view, the joins and field mappings configuration needs to be defined for reuse tables. Figure 8.19 shows the configuration screen for defining joins and field mappings for reuse tables. Accordingly, the new entity and its attributes are visible for selection in step **2** of the SAP HANA search view generation. The rest of the steps remain unchanged for this use case.

Change View "Join Attributes": Overview

New Entries

Dialog Structure	Join Attributes					
▼ 📁 Join Attributes	BO Type	Table Name	Table Name	Cardinalit	Join Opera...	Join Type
· 📄 Join Fields	147	T000	ADRP	1:1 Cardinality ▼	Equal	leftOuter
· 📁 Field Mapping	147	BUT000	BUT020	1:N Cardinality ▼	Equal	leftOuter
· 📁 Group Entities	147	BUT000	BUT0BK	1:N Cardinality ▼	Equal	leftOuter
	147	BUT000	BUT0ID	1:N Cardinality ▼	Equal	leftOuter
	147	BUT000	BUT0IS	1:N Cardinality ▼	Equal	leftOuter
	147	BUT000	BUT100	1:N Cardinality ▼	Equal	leftOuter
	147	BUT000	CVI_CUST_LINK	1:N Cardinality ▼	Equal	leftOuter
	147	BUT000	CVI_VEND_LINK	1:N Cardinality ▼	Equal	leftOuter
	147	BUT000	DFKKBPTAXNUM	1:N Cardinality ▼	Equal	leftOuter
	147	BUT000	MDG_MLT_ASSGMNT	1:N Cardinality ▼	Equal	leftOuter
	147	BUT020	ADR12	1:N Cardinality ▼	Equal	leftOuter
	147	BUT020	ADR2	1:N Cardinality ▼	Equal	leftOuter
	147	BUT020	ADR3	1:N Cardinality ▼	Equal	leftOuter
	147	BUT020	ADR6	1:N Cardinality ▼	Equal	leftOuter

Figure 8.19 Defining Joins and Field Mappings for Reuse Tables

Following is the IMG path for defining the joins and fields mappings for reuse tables (Transaction **MDGIMG**): **Master Data Governance, Central Governance · General Settings · Data Quality and Search · Search and Duplicate Check · Define Joins and Field Mapping for Reuse Tables**.

- **Extending the data model with a custom entity in flex mode**
  SAP HANA search supports flex entities at the main entity level only. Configuration as explained for the previous scenario needs to be performed for this scenario, and after selection of the flex entity and its attributes, the SAP HANA search view can be saved and generated.

These fields can also be customized in the search attributes dropdown for which it should be ensured that the new fields aren't disabled for search in IMG activities and UI field properties. The **No Selection** property should not have a flag set. To meet any requirements to add new fields in the search results, a new enhancement implementation for the UIBB must be created in Floorplan Manager.

8.2   Duplicate Check

Every organization, irrespective of its size, location, business line, or industry sector, must deal with the challenges of duplicate records in its IT landscape. These duplicates might be in the system knowingly or unknowingly. With focus on and awareness about the importance of good data quality, companies have done a lot of work in this area in recent years, and with the help of technology innovations, they are in a better position to deal with duplicates in their IT landscape. There can be several reasons that duplicate records end up in any company's landscape:

- **Merger and acquisitions**
  A merger or acquisition between companies can often be the reason behind most of the duplicate master data in the landscape. The new systems in the landscape potentially have similar master data records (e.g., vendors, customers, or business partner entities with whom both companies have been doing business). Normally, consolidation or data quality projects during or after the merger help to overcome such duplicates. However, due to various business and strategic reasons, companies do defer the projects needed for consolidating master data.

- **Search methods and technology**
  An inaccurate, slow, or difficult-to-use search may also contribute to the reasons a business user may not be able to complete the due diligence before submitting a new request and, hence, end up creating a duplicate in the system.

- **Manual errors**
  Human error, lack of proper training, and ignorance or lack of awareness on the part of the business users working with master data are also common contributors to duplicate master data.

- **Deliberate due to business reasons**
  Some business partners use different addresses for their sister companies for performing some business functions (e.g., delivery, collection, etc.), so separate vendors and suppliers are created in the system based on different addresses.

- **Different entities with some matching attributes**
  In some cases, master data records have many matching attributes but are genuinely separate, independent entities with no relation that fall under the category of potential duplicates due to the defined matching strategies. A system's matching strategies should be intelligent enough to ignore such cases in the list of potential duplicates.

While two or more records existing in the database representing the same entity are considered duplicates, in daily life, it could be a complex job to differentiate between real duplicates and look-alike, unrelated records. It isn't practical and justified to rely completely on human decisions for 100% accuracy without any human error involved. In addition, for various reasons, it's impossible to lay down a set of business rules and logic that a system can use to determine duplicates with accuracy in all possible scenarios.

Considering the challenges explained earlier, it makes sense to use a hybrid approach with multiple human interventions while leveraging the system search and duplicate check capabilities. The SAP Master Data Governance search and data quality process is very robust and minimizes the probability of duplicates entering the system to almost a negligible amount. Following are the multiple-step approaches used in central governance to handle duplicates more effectively and proactively.

> **Note**
>
> As a best practice before creating a new master data record, the requester should always perform a search in the database to determine whether the entity already exists in the database. Intuitive, accurate, and robust search capabilities in SAP Master Data Governance will help to ensure that the requester doesn't overlook existing records and end up submitting change requests for potential duplicates.

By using search and duplicate check capabilities, the system identifies and presents the list of potential duplicates with respective scores based on defined attributes and threshold limits. While submitting the change request in SAP Master Data Governance, a requester may again get an opportunity to decide if the change request carries a potential duplicate. Figure 8.20 shows the SAP Master Data Governance UI when a potential duplicate is presented.

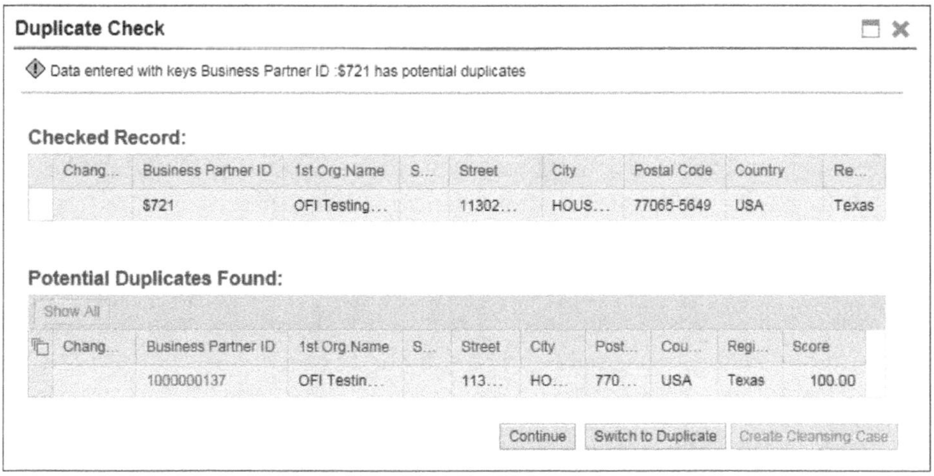

Figure 8.20 A Potential Duplicate Identified and Presented by SAP Master Data Governance

At this time, you have the option to trigger a cleansing case but only between the potential duplicates found and presented in the lower section of the **Duplicate Check** screen where a new governance path will help resolve the existing duplicates. For the new record being submitted, results of the cleansing case may end up merging the records, or the experts may reject the proposal of merging the duplicates if the look-alike records are later identified as different entities.

> **Note**
>
> Cleansing cases in SAP Master Data Governance are supported only for business partner data; no other data domains are supported for this functionality.

Figure 8.21 shows the screen you would see after deciding to continue and ignoring the potential duplicate presented by the system.

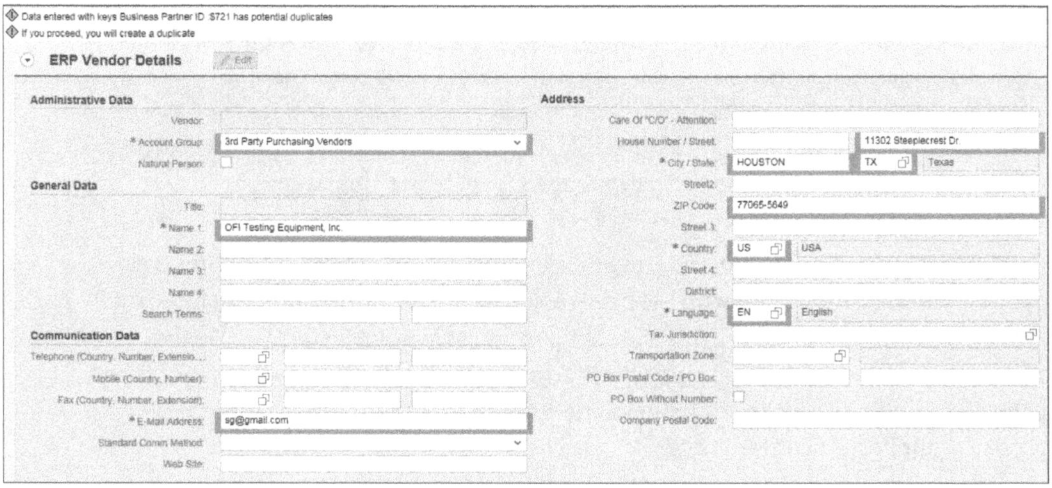

Figure 8.21 SAP Master Data Governance Screen Shown after Deciding to Continue Ignoring Possible Duplicates

Additionally, after the SAP Master Data Governance change request is submitted in the subsequent approval steps, approvers may also receive a list of potential duplicates from the system and can decide to continue, send the change request back, or trigger a cleansing case.

Note that for duplicate check purposes, the SAP Master Data Governance system uses the same search providers as were used for performing the search. Figure 8.22 shows some common search options used during the duplicate check.

As shown in Figure 8.23, in the **Configure Duplicate Check for Entity Types** Customizing activity based on the respective data models, a **Search Mode** is configured as well as the lower threshold (**Low Thres**) and upper threshold (**High Thres**) that should be applied. Low threshold signifies that those records with a matching score less than the low threshold values won't be considered as duplicates, whereas records that have a matching score greater than the low threshold value will be considered as potential duplicates. Records with matching scores greater than or equal to the high thresholds are considered as identical and are still presented to you for subsequent follow-up actions shown in Figure 8.23. Low threshold values are relevant for SAP HANA search, whereas it isn't applicable for database search, remote key search, or SAP NetWeaver Enterprise Search/SAP HANA enterprise search.

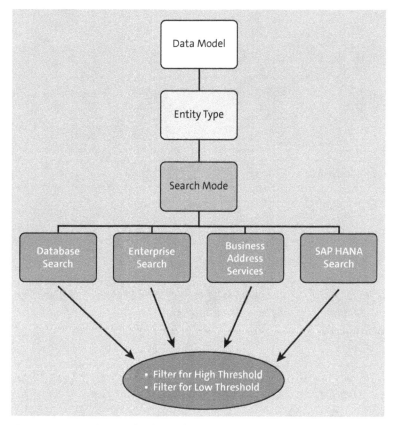

Figure 8.22 Duplicate Check Configurations

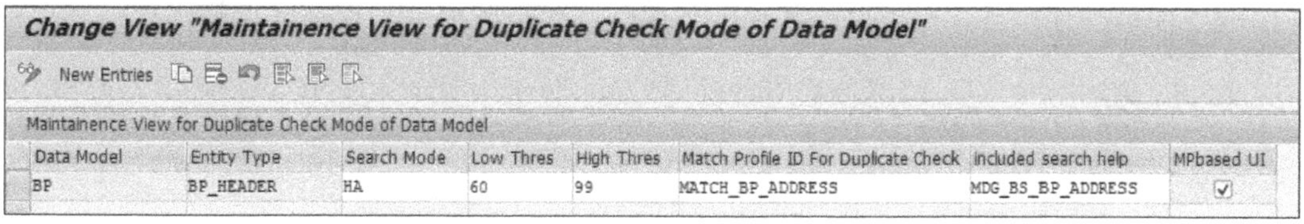

Change View "Maintainence View for Duplicate Check Mode of Data Model"								
New Entries								
Maintainence View for Duplicate Check Mode of Data Model								
Data Model	Entity Type	Search Mode	Low Thres	High Thres	Match Profile ID For Duplicate Check	Included search help	MPbased UI
BP	BP_HEADER	HA	60	99	MATCH_BP_ADDRESS	MDG_BS_BP_ADDRESS	✓

Figure 8.23 Maintenance View for Duplicate Check Mode of Data Model Screen

Additional match profile–related configurations in search applications as required for duplicate check functionality in SAP Master Data Governance were explained in Section 8.1.3.

Figure 8.24 displays a mandatory process modeling configuration required at each change request type step level. This is a prerequisite for triggering duplicate checks for a workflow step.

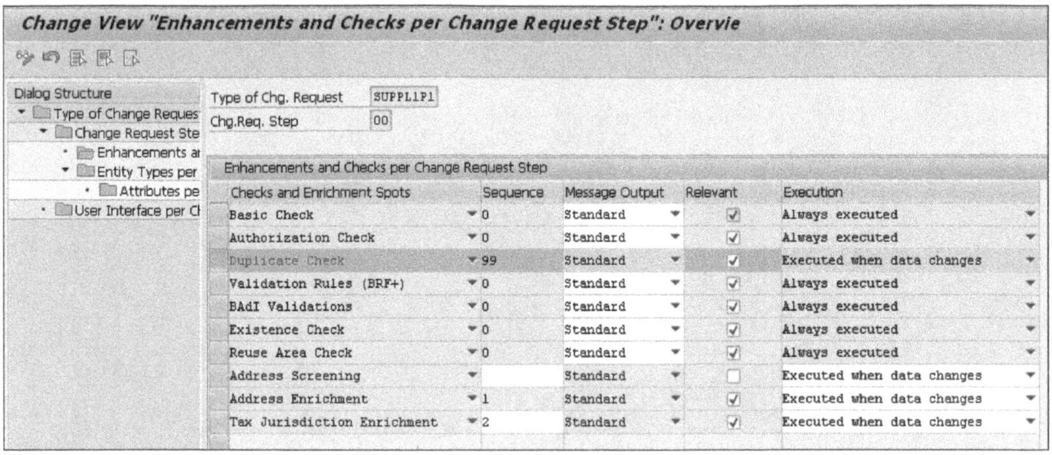

Change View "Enhancements and Checks per Change Request Step": Overvie

Checks and Enrichment Spots	Sequence	Message Output	Relevant	Execution
Basic Check	0	Standard	☑	Always executed
Authorization Check	0	Standard	☑	Always executed
Duplicate Check	99	Standard	☑	Executed when data changes
Validation Rules (BRF+)	0	Standard	☑	Always executed
BAdI Validations	0	Standard	☑	Always executed
Existence Check	0	Standard	☑	Always executed
Reuse Area Check	0	Standard	☑	Always executed
Address Screening		Standard	☐	Executed when data changes
Address Enrichment	1	Standard	☑	Executed when data changes
Tax Jurisdiction Enrichment	2	Standard	☑	Executed when data changes

Type of Chg. Request: SUPPL1P1
Chg.Req. Step: 00

Dialog Structure
- Type of Change Reques
  - Change Request Ste
    - Enhancements a
    - Entity Types per
      - Attributes pe
      - User Interface per Cl

Enhancements and Checks per Change Request Step

Figure 8.24 Duplicate Check Configuration for a Change Request Step

> **Note**
>
> As an SAP Master Data Governance user, if you want to see all column headings and content completely when the duplicate check is carried out, SAP Note 2667744 helps to change the layout of the popup by making the column headings and content readable and auto-resizing dynamically.

8.3   Business Rules in Central Governance

SAP Master Data Governance offers robust capabilities to deal with data quality challenges. It's important to prevent any bad data from entering the system, and this can be achieved in SAP Master Data Governance in a number of ways, as depicted in Figure 8.25.

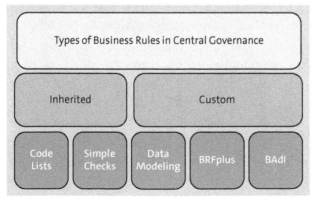

Figure 8.25 Validations in SAP Master Data Governance

Business rules in SAP Master Data Governance are broadly categorized as inherited rules and custom rules. SAP Master Data Governance can reuse some of the SAP ERP and SAP S/4HANA validations, which are termed as inherited validations, for example, code lists, simple checks, and so on. There are also frameworks and Business Add-Ins (BAdIs), called custom rules, delivered by SAP that can be very handy in meeting the data quality requirements of your business. Various types of rules under these categories are explained in the following sections.

8.3.1   Code Lists

SAP Master Data Governance has the built-in intelligence to check the value range tables and fixed sets of values that are assigned against the domain of the respective data element used by an attribute in SAP Master Data Governance. The existence check is performed on the values being maintained by the users in the SAP Master Data Governance UI. Regions, company codes, and payment terms are examples of code list validations in SAP Master Data Governance.

8.3.2   Simple Checks

SAP Master Data Governance does reuse some of the core SAP ERP and SAP S/4HANA configurations, for example, country-based configurations for address checks. SAP Master Data Governance may enforce error, warning, or information messages when users don't adhere to the country-specific address configurations.

Additionally, based on the data element properties format, checks are performed automatically in the SAP Master Data Governance UI when you populate master data in the change request. These checks are inherited from the existing standard data elements. Data elements used by an attribute can be checked in data modeling. You can navigate to the properties of the data element via Transaction **SE11**.

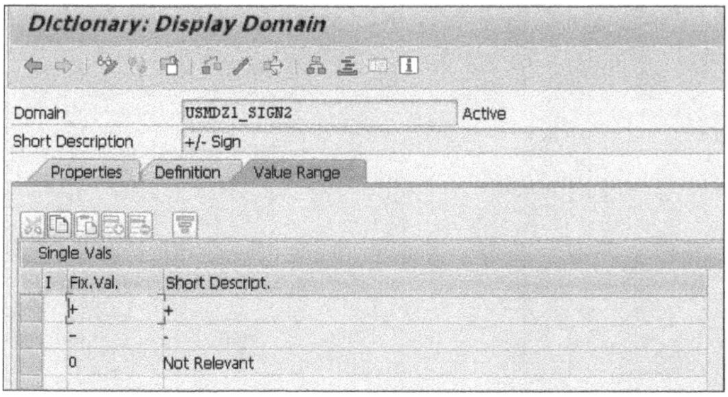

Figure 8.26 Simple Check for Allowed Values Driven by the Data Element

In Figure 8.26, data element USMDZ1_SIGN2 used in the financial statement item (FSI) object allows only "+", "-", and "*" values. In addition, this data type has a length of 1 character as defined in the Data Dictionary. This means during the governance process on the SAP Master Data Governance UI, users can't populate a value larger than the defined length and a value other than "+", "-", and "*", which automatically enforces adherence to data standards and formats without the need for any custom rules.

8.3.3   Checks Based on Data Modeling

Making certain fields mandatory during master data maintenance is a common requirement in any landscape, and SAP Master Data Governance provides many options to meet that requirement. Required attributes in SAP Master Data Governance can be configured easily through data modeling, where, without any coding, certain attributes can be configured as mandatory whenever a specific entity level check is triggered.

Figure 8.27 depicts how you can make an attribute in SAP Master Data Governance mandatory. After the attribute is configured as mandatory, it's highlighted with an "*" next to it, indicating to users the fields that are mandatory to provide a value. Note that any attribute configured as mandatory through data modeling will always be applicable for all workflow steps.

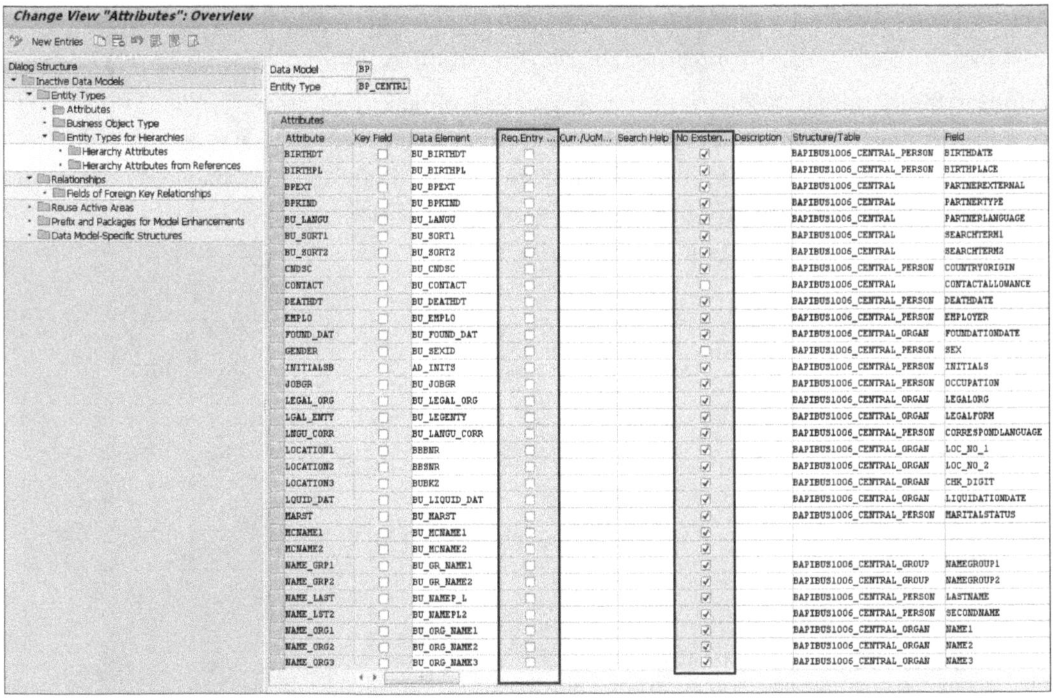

Figure 8.27 Existence Checks in SAP Master Data Governance

The existence checks shown in Figure 8.27 are editable, and based on the specific requirements, they can be checked or unchecked for respective attributes being governed in SAP Master Data Governance. Following is the IMG path where the settings can be checked in SAP Master Data Governance (Transaction **MDGIMG**): **Master Data Governance, Central Governance • General Settings • Data Modeling • Edit Data Model.**

8.3.4 Checks and Validations Based on Business Rules Framework Plus

SAP has provided Business Rules Framework plus (BRFplus) to build business rules easily with simple configurations and no coding. It's easy to use and simple to understand even for consultants and business users who have limited technical knowledge.

Following are some salient features of the BRFplus rule engine:

- BRFplus is part of the ABAP stack with a seamless integration with ABAP-based applications.

- BRFplus enables you to build flexible and customizable business applications with significantly less coding.

- No additional hardware is involved to leverage the BRFplus rule engine.

- No setup costs are involved.

- A separate license isn't required for using BRFplus because it comes complimentary with general SAP licenses.

- BRFplus can be extended easily by additional custom expressions or action types.

- All modeled expressions, conditions, and decision tables can be tested in BRFplus using an integrated simulator.

- Calling BRFplus from the other ABAP applications is easy with just a few lines of code or a remote function call (RFC) web service.

To configure business rules in SAP Master Data Governance using BRFplus, follow menu path (Transaction **MDGIMG**), **Master Data Governance, Central Governance • General Settings • Data Quality and Search • Define Validation and Derivation Rules.** Alternatively, Transaction **USMD_RULE** can also be executed to trigger the Web Dynpro application for defining validation and derivation rules in BRFplus.

After triggering the Web Dynpro–based BRFplus application, an appropriate data model (e.g., financial, material master, business partner, etc.) must be selected for which the rules have to be configured. Rules built in to BRFplus are specific to a data model. Each data model contains its own BRFplus validation rules. Each application contains a **CHECK_ENTITY** folder under which all the check-related functions can be built.

Figure 8.28 shows the navigation options through the **Catalog** view in BRFplus. Figure 8.29 shows the navigation options through the **Repository** view in BRFplus.

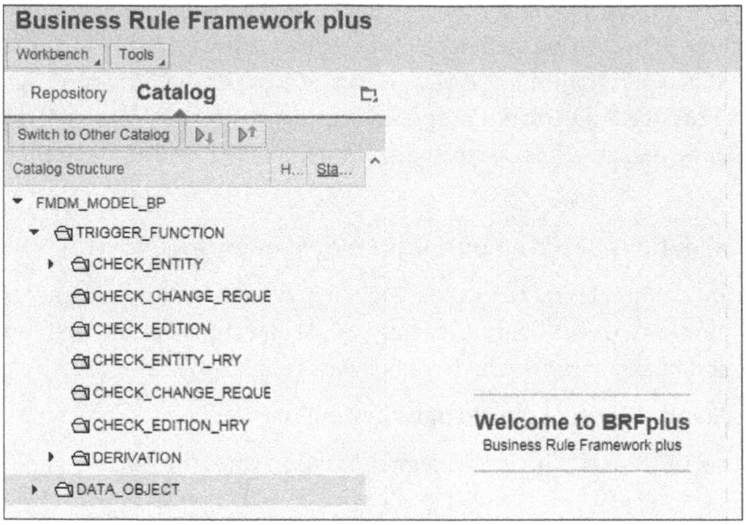

Figure 8.28 BRFplus Landing Page: Catalog View

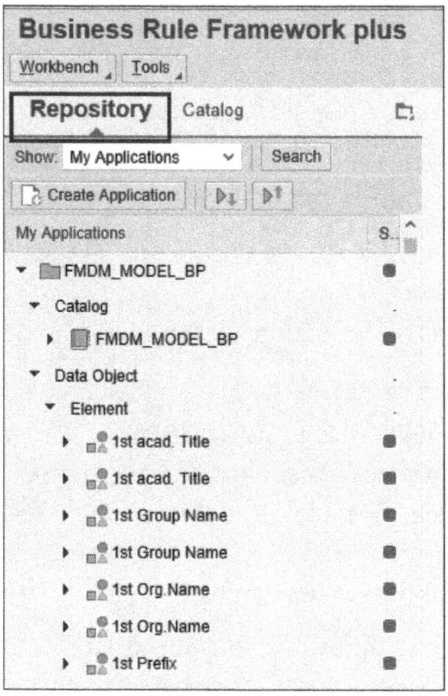

Figure 8.29 BRFplus: Repository View

Figure 8.30 shows various navigational options in BRFplus through the **Workbench**. You can navigate to search a BRFplus object or display objects in a repository. You can also create new applications through this navigational page.

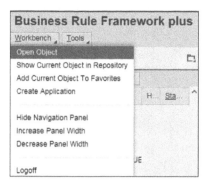

Figure 8.30 BRFplus Workbench Options in SAP Master Data Governance

Figure 8.31 displays various tools available in BRFplus. Some of the commonly used tools are **Application Administration**, **Trace**, **Simulation**, and **Web Service Generation**.

Figure 8.31 BRFplus Tools in SAP Master Data Governance

Figure 8.32 shows the BRFplus view when a new object needs to be searched for.

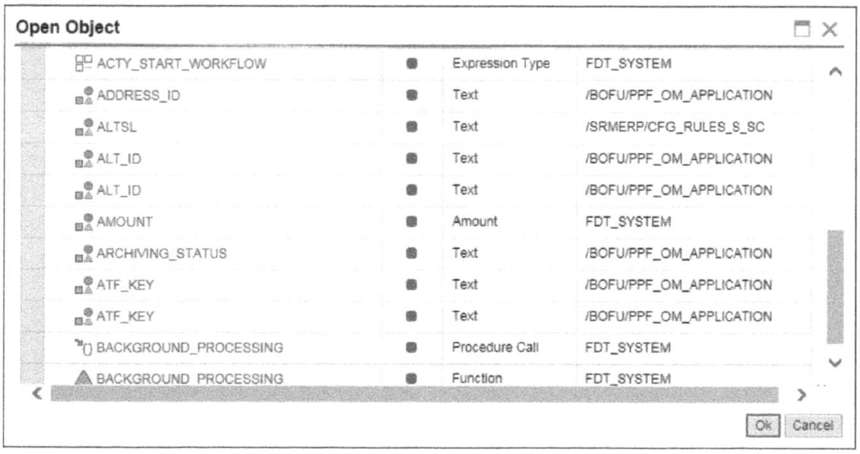

Open Object			
ACTY_START_WORKFLOW	●	Expression Type	FDT_SYSTEM
ADDRESS_ID	●	Text	/BOFU/PPF_OM_APPLICATION
ALTSL	●	Text	/SRMERP/CFG_RULES_S_SC
ALT_ID	●	Text	/BOFU/PPF_OM_APPLICATION
ALT_ID	●	Text	/BOFU/PPF_OM_APPLICATION
AMOUNT	●	Amount	FDT_SYSTEM
ARCHIVING_STATUS	●	Text	/BOFU/PPF_OM_APPLICATION
ATF_KEY	●	Text	/BOFU/PPF_OM_APPLICATION
ATF_KEY	●	Text	/BOFU/PPF_OM_APPLICATION
BACKGROUND_PROCESSING	●	Procedure Call	FDT_SYSTEM
BACKGROUND_PROCESSING	●	Function	FDT_SYSTEM

Ok   Cancel

Figure 8.32 Searching for an Object in BRFplus

Figure 8.33 shows various functions created in the `FMDM_MODEL_BP` application. You can create any number of functions to meet your business requirements. Each of the functions may have one or more rulesets assigned, which you can see by clicking on a function. Views are adjustable, so you can minimize or maximize them. Each object in BRFplus has a unique object ID.

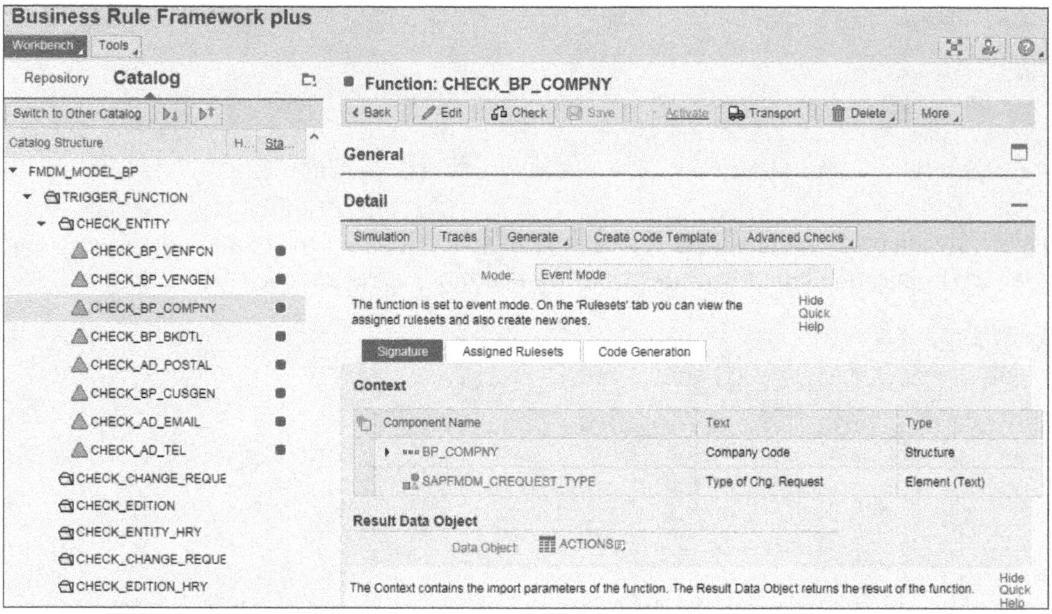

Figure 8.33 Example of a Function: CHECK_BP_COMPNY (Signature Tab)

As shown in Figure 8.34, all rulesets should be in a green **Status** to be operationally usable during the SAP Master Data Governance process.

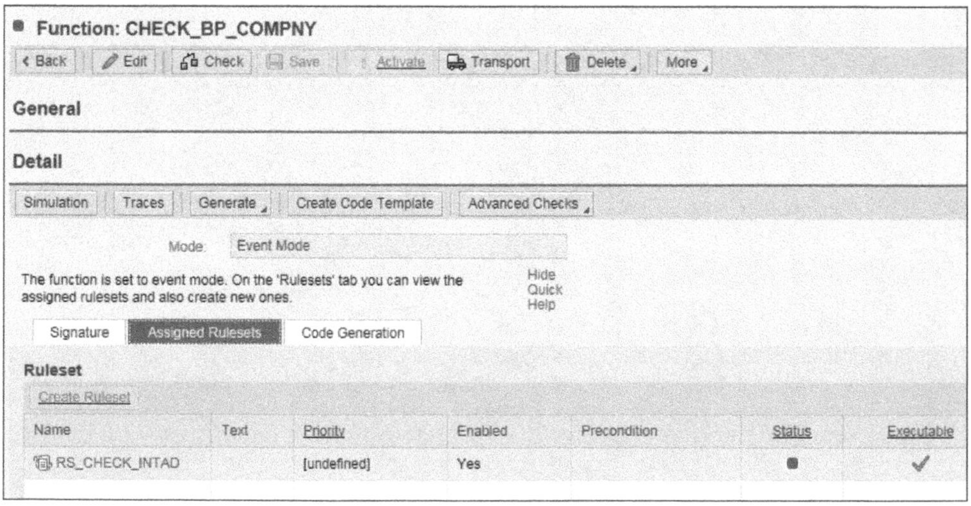

Figure 8.34 Ruleset Assignment to a Function in BRFplus

Note

For the check trigger function, the nodes of a catalog structure must always use the naming convention as CHECK_<Entity Type Name>.

BRFplus applications consist of rulesets containing rules. Rules can be created using different components, such as decision tables, formulas, conditions, expressions, and so on.

These components are reusable in nature. In the example shown in Figure 8.35, there are two rulesets assigned to the CHECK_AD_POSTAL function. You can click on the respective ruleset hyperlinks to drill down and navigate to the details of the rulesets created.

The example implementation shown in Figure 8.36 displays a warning message to SAP Master Data Governance users whenever a postal code value isn't populated for change request types CUSTL1P2 and CUSTL2P1 to processors of workflow steps 00, DP, and CD. The message texts and type can be customized based on the business requirement.

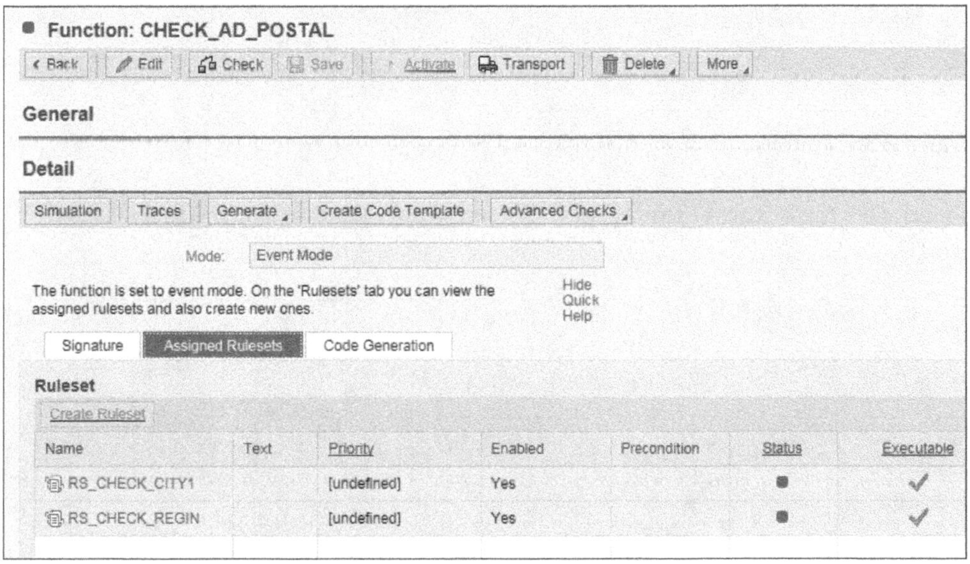

Figure 8.35 Assigned Rulesets to the Function in BRFplus

Note

For the derivation trigger function, nodes of a catalog structure should always use the naming convention DERIVE_<Entity Type Name>. These functions only derive single entities, and cross-entity derivations aren't supported in BRFplus. Cross-entity BAdIs may have to be implemented to achieve complex business requirements.

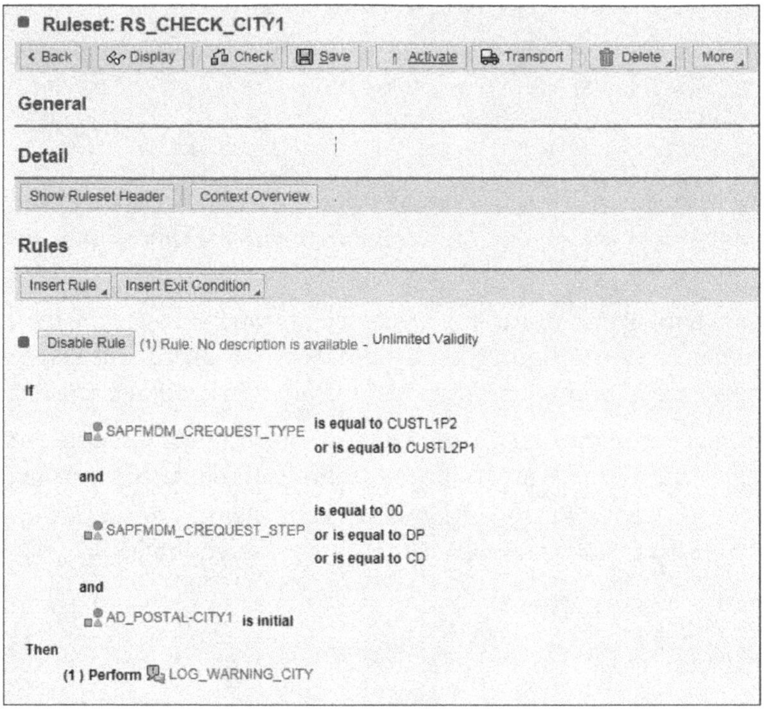

Figure 8.36 Example of a Built-In BRFplus Rule

Figure 8.37 provides an example of the **Signature** view as part of the derivation function.

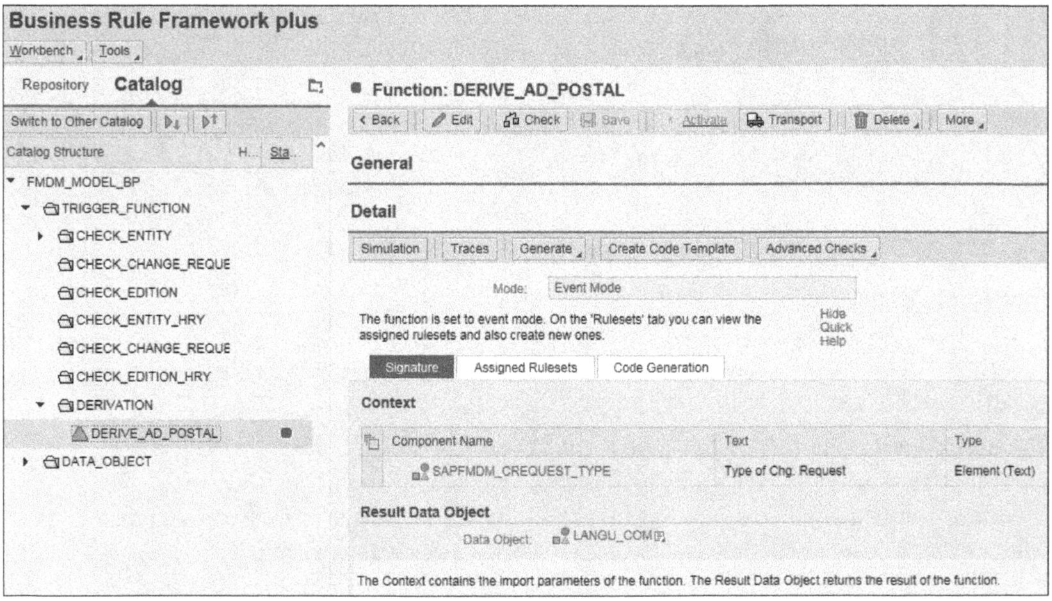

Figure 8.37 Derivation Function Example in BRFplus

The example implementation in Figure 8.38 shows a derivation using a BRFplus rule. In this example based on the change request type ZVENDR01 in SAP Master Data Governance, the language code will be automatically derived to value E.

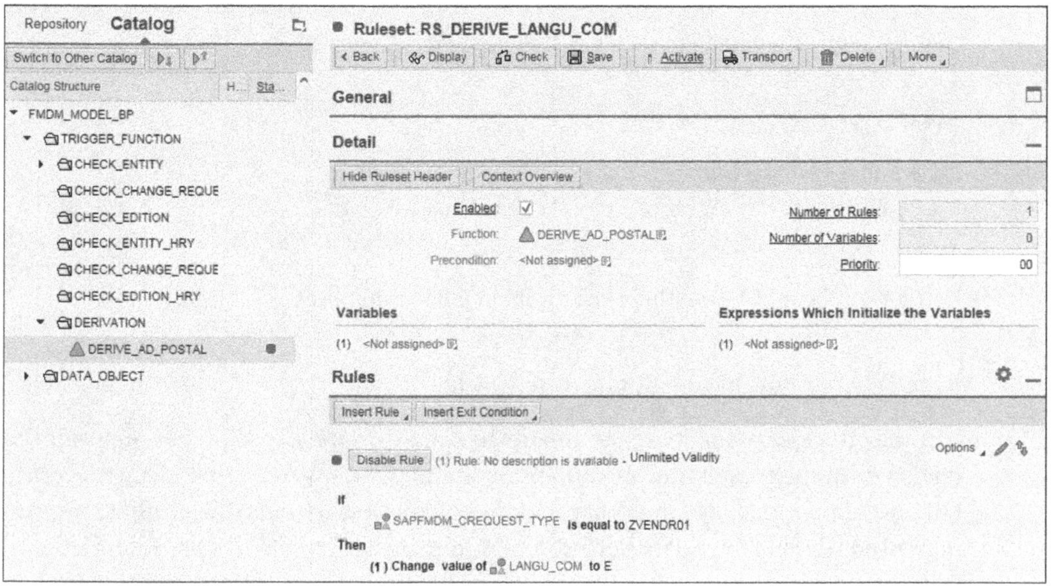

Figure 8.38 Example of a Derivation Rule in BRFplus

Figure 8.39 shows an example of data objects available in the SAP Master Data Governance BRFplus rule engine.

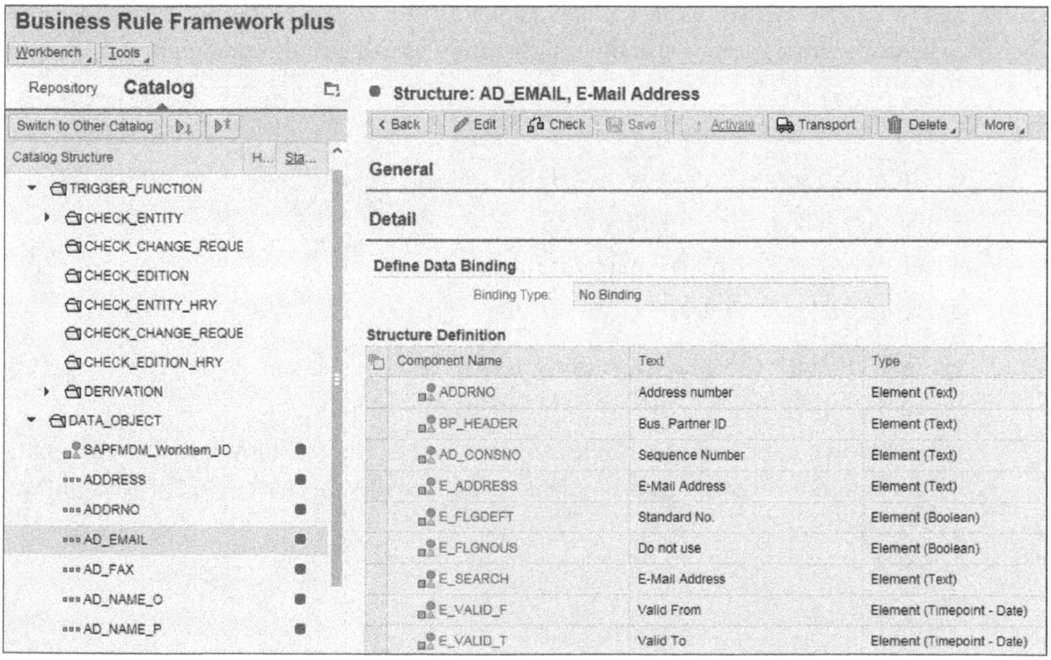

Figure 8.39 Data Objects in BRFplus

Every object in BRFplus has a unique object ID that can be navigated to via the **General** tab, as shown in Figure 8.40.

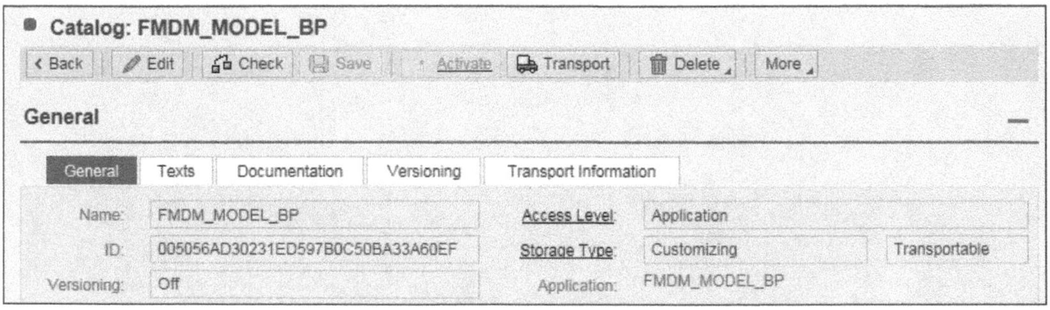

Catalog: FMDM_MODEL_BP						
‹ Back	✎ Edit	⚙ Check	🖫 Save	↑ Activate	🚚 Transport	🗑 Delete ⌄	More ⌄

General   —

General	Texts	Documentation	Versioning	Transport Information

Name:	FMDM_MODEL_BP		Access Level:	Application	
ID:	005056AD30231ED597B0C50BA33A60EF		Storage Type:	Customizing	Transportable
Versioning:	Off		Application:	FMDM_MODEL_BP	

Figure 8.40 General Header Information about BRFplus Application Objects

8.3.5   Validations Based on Business Add-Ins

You may have data quality requirements that are company-specific, yet important to realize from the master data governance point of view. It's recommended to leverage BRFplus, data modeling, and other options to build validations. In certain cases, you may need options to enhance the solution to make it suitable to your requirements. However, there are certain limitations using BRFplus where certain complex data quality requirements are hard to achieve. An example could be the cross-entity validations and derivations. This can't be implemented using BRFplus. This is where you can implement cross-entity BAdIs to achieve the business requirements.

SAP has delivered several BAdIs within the SAP Master Data Governance framework, and these can be used to meet your data quality requirements during governance processes. The process steps to define validation rules using BAdI implementations are as follows:

1. Define the data quality rules.
2. Choose an appropriate data model.
3. Identify an appropriate entity type.
4. Implement a BAdI for the business rule.
5. Define validation rules.

Figure 8.41 shows the IMG screens for various BAdIs that can be leveraged for meeting business requirements related to **Data Quality and Search**.

In the following sections, we'll look into some of the important BAdIs delivered as standard by SAP for various purposes related to data quality and search in SAP Master Data Governance.

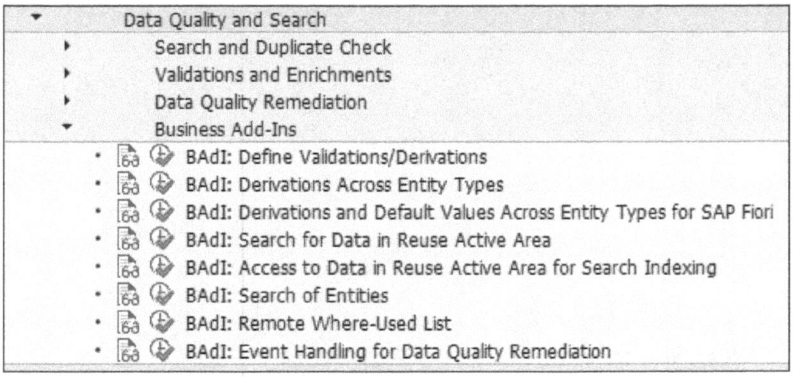

Figure 8.41 SAP Master Data Governance Data Quality and Search BAdIs

USMD_RULE_SERVICE: Define Validations/Derivations

This BAdI can be applied to entities, change requests, and editions, and it's mainly used for implementing customer-specific checks. Following are the methods used in this BAdI while performing various checks and derivations:

- CHECK_ENTITY
- DERIVE_ENTITY
- CHECK_CREQUEST_START
- CHECK_CREQUEST
- CHECK_CREQUEST_FINAL
- CHECK_EDITION_START
- CHECK_EDITION

USMD_RULE_SERVICE_CROSS_ET: Derivations across Entity Types

This BAdI is used for cross-entity derivation scenarios. Data can be changed if the key isn't modified for the associated leading entity with storage and usage type 1. For entity type 4, creation and deletion of data records is possible.

MDG_GW_FIORI_DERIVATIONS: Derivations and Default Values across Entity Types for SAP Fiori

Default values and derivations can be performed for the entity types, which are part of the data model. These values are used in SAP Fiori apps and OData services. Following are the methods used by this BAdI:

- LOAD_DATA
  Loads data for entity types.
- DERIVE_DATA_ON_SUBMIT
  Derives data from submitted entity types.

BAdI MDG_GW_FIORI_DERIVATIONS can be used in various OData services, as follows:

- MDG_PROFITCENTER_SRV
- MDG_COSTCENTER_SRV
- MDG_CUSTOMER_SRV
- MDG_MATERIAL_SRV
- MDG_SUPPLIER_SRV
- MDG_BP_SRV

BADI_SDQ_PP_SEARCH: Search for Data in Reuse Active Area

This BAdI is used primarily in the data quality component and helps in searching for business object types that use a search object connector template for the reuse active area that is different from the SAP Master Data Governance search object connector template. When a search is executed from SAP Master Data Governance, the results are collected by default from the SAP Master Data Governance search object connector.

The following methods are used in this BAdI:

- IF_USMD_SEARCH_DATA~EXECUTE
  This method allows the search for object instances to be executed using a separate search object connector template for the reuse active area.
- SEARCH_PP
  This method can be used to search reuse active areas.
- BADI_SDQ_PP_INITIAL_LOAD_ES
  This can be used for initial extraction of data from a reuse active area. It provides access to data in the reuse active area for search indexing.

This BAdI is used in the data quality component of SAP Master Data Governance when SAP Master Data Governance templates are used instead of creating a new search object connector template for the reuse active area. The template is called during the initial extraction of data for the SAP NetWeaver Enterprise Search or SAP HANA enterprise search indexing so that the data from the reuse active area can also be loaded for indexing, along with the data from the staging area.

This BAdI has two filter parameters:

- IV_DATA_MODEL
- IV_ROOT_ENTITY

USMD_SEARCH: Search for Entities

This BAdI belongs to the application framework component of SAP Master Data Governance and can be used in modifying the Web Dynpro Search for Entities application (USMD_SEARCH).

The following methods are used in this BAdI:

- `INITIALIZE`
  During the initialization, you can change the attributes that are available for the search criteria. You can also add or remove search attributes based on the requirements.

- `PROCESS_EVENT`
  In SAP Master Data Governance, actions can be defined for starting a navigation that is based on logical actions of the framework. These actions can be triggered using this method when registered pushbuttons of the search results table are used.

USMD_REMOTE_WHERE_USED: Remote Where-Used List

This BAdI can be used for displaying a list of values from a remote system. Data model and entity type are the applicable filters for this BAdI.

The `GET_REMOTE_WHERE_USED_LIST` method is used by this BAdI with the following import parameters:

- `IV_ENTITY_TYPE`
  Specifies the entity type that needs to be searched.

- `IT_ENTITY_SEL`
  Contains the key values.

- `IS_REMOTE_SYSTEM`
  Sets the remote destination (only one remote system at a time).

- `IV_MAX_HIT`
  Sets the maximum number of allowed search results.

The following export parameters are also used:

- `ET_RESULT`
  Displays the search results, including business system name, key columns, and so on.

- `ET_MESSAGE`
  Reports error messages.

8.4   Data Enrichment

Data enrichment processes are used to enhance, refine, or otherwise improve the quality of raw data. This idea and similar concepts contribute to making master data a valuable asset for almost any business or enterprise. Although data enrichment can work in many different ways, data enrichment process tools are used with the goal of refining data regarding completeness, accuracy, standardization, verification, and so on. Some examples of data enrichment include spelling correction, auto-population of missing attribute values, and address standardization with reference to postal services. Some of the commonly used data enrichment integration options are SAP Data Quality Management for address standardization, third-party integrations for data enrichment, business partner screening using SAP Business Partner Screening for SAP S/4HANA, and SAP S/4HANA Cloud for data enrichment. These integration options are discussed in the following sections.

8.4.1   Integration with SAP Data Quality Management for Address Standardization

Updated, accurate, and complete addresses of business partners, suppliers, and customers are crucial for the smooth operation of any organization. The efficiency of procurement and sales functions may be affected negatively if addresses for master data records in the system aren't reliable or are incorrect. Manual errors during master data maintenance or incomplete information received from the partners can also cause problems. Address formats in which the master data is maintained can also lead to some data quality issues. Sometimes the same word is found stored in different ways; for example, a street name in an address could be populated as "Avenue", "Ave.", "Av", or "Ave", which all mean the same thing. Therefore, it's important to follow some common standards to avoid data inconsistencies.

These addresses and data formats are important criteria during matching, identification, and standardization processes. If addresses aren't correctly maintained or are maintained in nonstandardized formats, then it may directly affect the de-duplication efforts and data quality.

Considering these challenges, SAP has delivered a specialized tool that helps business users during governance to standardize addresses and identify duplicates in real time. SAP Data Quality Management is installed as a component on SAP Data Services. You can easily activate and integrate SAP Data Quality Management with SAP Master Data Governance via some configuration and without any significant coding.

Following are the SAP Master Data Governance steps involved during address standardization in central governance:

1. Maintain the address.
2. Check the address.
3. Validate the result list.
4. Perform user selection.
5. Correct the address.

SAP Data Quality Management has address directories and rules in its repositories that can be leveraged in real time to compare, standardize, and identify duplicates with reference to the address data populated in the UI by SAP Master Data Governance users. Based on this comparison, SAP Data Quality Management offers a valid list of addresses to SAP Master Data Governance users who can easily and quickly decide if they want to pick any of the standardized address records presented to them.

The following activities are involved in leveraging SAP Data Quality Management for address standardization and duplicate check during the governance process in SAP Master Data Governance.

> **Note**
>
> Some of these steps are performed outside SAP Master Data Governance, so you can refer to the SAP Data Quality Management operational guide for additional information.

1. Install the ABAP add-on in the system.
2. Set up the access server in SAP Data Services.
3. Install SAP Data Quality Management data services components. It's important that all the SAP Data Quality Management components are at the same service pack level.
4. Install the SAP Data Quality Management RFC server.
5. Define the RFC destinations in SAP Master Data Governance.
6. Define **FL_GDQC_SERVER** in Transaction **SM59** in the target client, as shown in Figure 8.42.

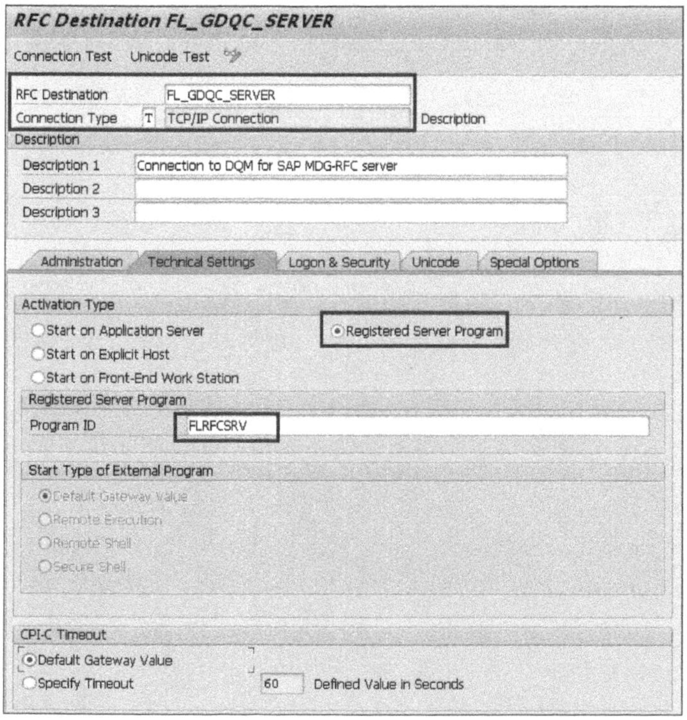

Figure 8.42 Maintaining RFC Destination FL_GDQC_SERVER for SAP Data Quality Management Integration

7. Define **FL_GDQC_BATCH** in Transaction **SM59** of the target client, as shown in Figure 8.43.

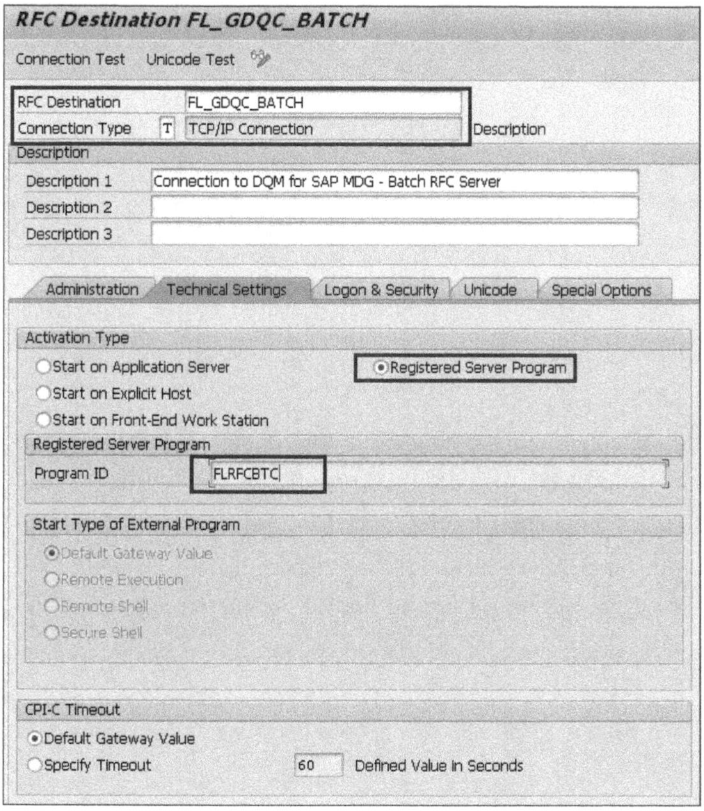

Figure 8.43 Maintain the RFC Destination FL_GDQC_BATCH for SAP Data Quality Management Integration

8. Set up real-time and batch jobs.

9. Configure web services.

10. Follow these configuration steps to use duplicate check with SAP Master Data Governance:

   – Set /FLDQ/namespace to modifiable.

   – Maintain services for the SAP Master Data Governance generic duplicate check by following these steps:

   • Select the business partner data model.

   • Create a service agreement.

   • Configure fields for the duplicate check.

   • Define the match code fields.

- Configure SAP Master Data Governance to use SAP Data Quality Management for duplicate checking by following these steps:
  - Define the search applications.
  - Configure the duplicate check for entity type.
  - Configure the standardization and duplicate check for the change request step.

It's a prerequisite to define the search applications and match profiles to make the duplicate check work for SAP Master Data Governance users. Following is the IMG path for defining the search applications and duplicate checks for the entity type (Transaction **MDGIMG**): **Master Data Governance, Central Governance · General Settings · Data Quality Search · Search and Duplicate Check**.

A change request type being used during the governance process won't trigger a duplicate check unless it's made relevant for duplicate check and address standardization. Following is the IMG path for defining the search applications and duplicate checks for steps of the change request type (Transaction **MDGIMG**): **Master Data Governance, Central Governance · General Settings · Process Modeling · Change Requests · Configure Properties of Change Request Step**.

In addition, Figure 8.44 depicts the configurations needed at the change request step level in process modeling.

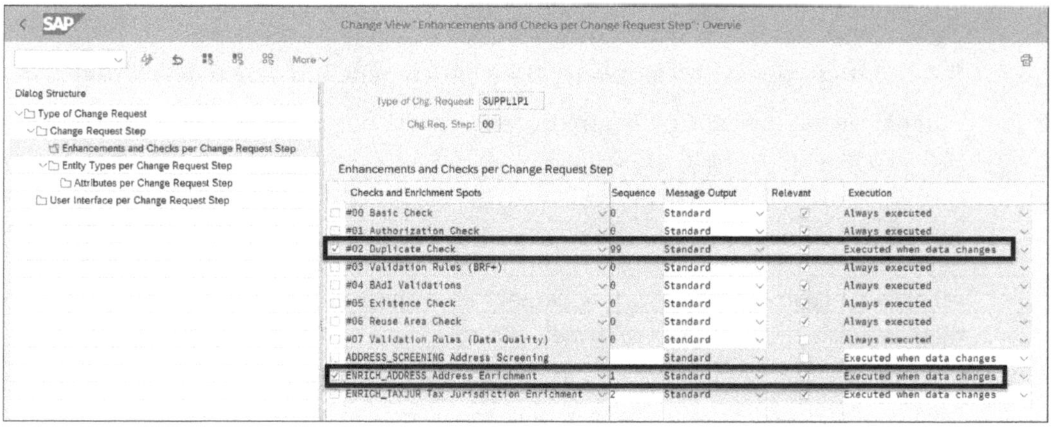

Figure 8.44 Address Enrichment and Duplicate Check Configuration for the Change Request Step

A cloud version of the SAP Data Quality Management, microservice for location data service running on SAP Cloud Platform has been available for the past few years and is becoming increasingly popular. This microservice is a natural evolution of the SAP Data Quality Management to cloud. It can also perform the data quality features of address cleansing and validation, geocoding, and reverse geocoding. This cloud-based microservices solution is available as a subscription that SAP customers can use to integrate with SAP Master Data Governance. This RESTful API cloud-based microservice offers several advantages over the SAP Data Quality Management for address validation. The most important one being that the customer no longer is required to store and manage address directories locally in the repositories. The integration and configuration on the SAP Master Data Governance change request step remains the same. Instead of the address validation call being made to the local address directories in the repositories, the system now makes an external call to the cloud-based microservice. This microservice provides support for 240+ countries. Following are some of the key features:

1. **Address Cleansing**
   - Verify address per postal authority reference data as correct.
   - Standardize the way the address looks and is structured.
   - Correct components of an address if incorrect.
   - Enhance an address with missing attributes.
   - Assign diagnostic codes that describe why the information is incorrect or what was corrected.

2. **Geocoding**
   - Append latitude and longitude when given an address.

3. **Reverse Geocoding**
   - Provide address(es) whe given a latitude and longitude.

8.4.2   Integration with Third-Party Data Enrichment Tools

Companies are increasingly becoming more aware of the advantages and disadvantages of managing master data quality. As discussed in Chapter 5, the master data record consists of several entities and attributes that hold information from various aspects of the business, such as address, tax, organization, characteristics, and so on. Because all this information is stored in the form of various attribute values in the master data, it becomes very important to make sure values stored in the database are complete, accurate, unique, and validated.

For this purpose, to leverage the specialized tools and applications in improving the quality of master data, central governance can be integrated with any number of SAP or non-SAP applications synchronously or asynchronously, such as SAP Global Trade Services (SAP GTS), postal services, Dun & Bradstreet (D&B), and so on. Such service calls can be made by users manually or can be triggered automatically. In addition, background jobs can be used to fetch any such information from external applications.

SAP Master Data Governance provides an enrichment framework that is used for enriching master data during the maintenance and governance process. This framework in SAP Master Data Governance is based on ABAP object-oriented programming and Web Dynpro. Depending on the exact requirements, additional development efforts and skills might be required to use the enrichment framework efficiently for improving data quality.

Figure 8.45 shows the data enrichment framework in SAP Master Data Governance. A number of objects are part of the SAP Master Data Governance enrichment framework: enrichment spots, enrichment adapters, enrichment feeders, and enrichment UI, as described here:

- **Enrichment feeders**
  An enrichment feeder is an implementation of the `IF_USMD_ENRICHMENT_FEEDER` interface for a given enrichment. This is primarily used for data transformation from SAP Master Data Governance format to the format of the enrichment adapter and vice versa. Data transformation refers to data mapping and structure mapping.

- **Enrichment UIs**
  During the enrichment process, the enrichment can have its own UIs, which are displayed when a user interaction is required. The UI should only be a Web Dynpro ABAP component and should implement the `MDG_ENRICHMENT_INTF` Web Dynpro interface.

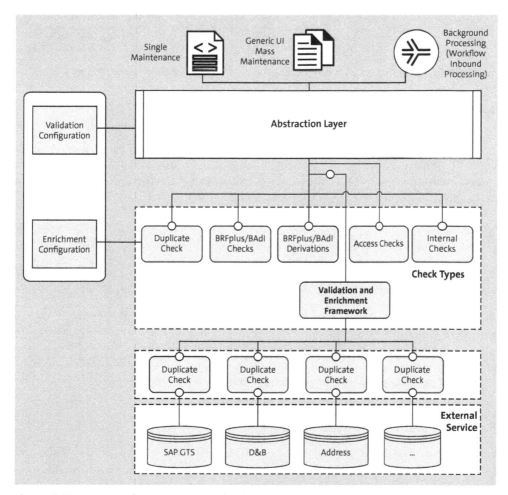

Figure 8.45 Data Enrichment Framework in SAP Master Data Governance

- **Enrichment adapters**

  Enrichment adapters are an implementation of the IF_USMD_ENRICHMENT_ADAPTER interface for a particular enrichment. This enrichment adapter makes a call to the external tools/applications/services to get the necessary data needed for enrichment. A good example of an enrichment adapter is the address enrichment adapter call made to SAP Data Services where it sends the address entered by the SAP Master Data Governance requester on the UI and gets the address data enriched. Some commonly used enrichment adapters are delivered by SAP, but you can always create your own based on specific requirements. Figure 8.46 shows some of the SAP-delivered enrichment adapters in SAP Master Data Governance.

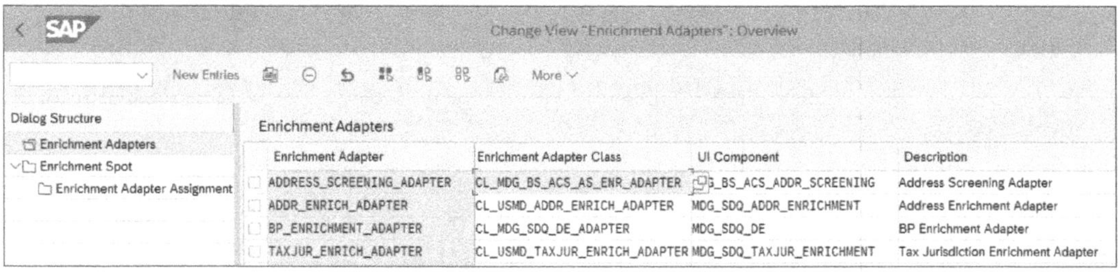

Figure 8.46 SAP-Delivered Enrichment Adapters in SAP Master Data Governance

- **Enrichment spots**

  Enrichment spots are used for defining the placeholder where enrichment of certain data in SAP Master Data Governance is possible. For example, the address enrichment spot supports the enrichment of addresses for business partners, suppliers, and customers. Figure 8.47 shows some of the SAP-delivered enrichment spots in SAP Master Data Governance.

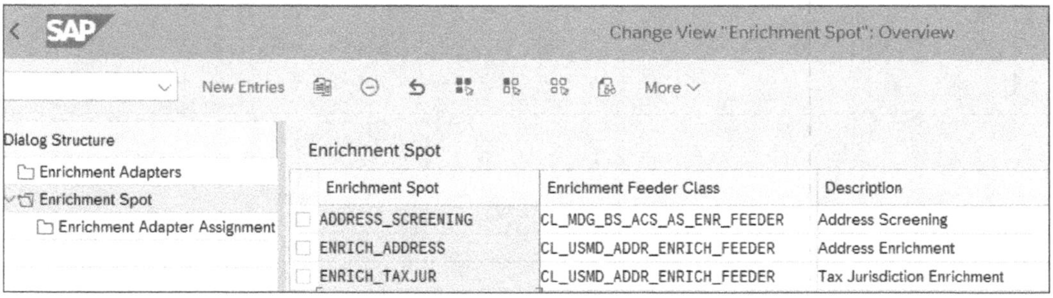

Figure 8.47 SAP-Delivered Enrichment Spots in SAP Master Data Governance

8.4.3 SAP Business Partner Screening for SAP S/4HANA

SAP Business Partner Screening for SAP S/4HANA is part of the SAP Assurance and Compliance software portfolio. SAP Master Data Governance can be optionally integrated with SAP Business Partner Screening for SAP S/4HANA for the purpose of business partner screening. SAP Business Partner Screening for SAP S/4HANA enables enterprises across all industries to check that their business partners are compliant with guidelines, regulations, and legislation by screening them against lists of persons and organizations published by governments and global institutions. SAP Business Partner Screening 1.3 SP00 or higher is required to be installed to enable the integration between SAP Business Partner Screening and SAP Master Data Governance on SAP S/4HANA. SAP Business Partner Screening and central governance can be hosted separately or can be co-deployed on the same SAP S/4HANA system.

SAP Master Data Governance can use the address screening and investigation capabilities of SAP Business Partner Screening. You can perform the address screening of the business partners in the SAP Master Data Governance change requests process. The following two integration options are available in SAP Master Data Governance to integrate with SAP Business Partner Screening:

- **Business partner screening with decision-making in SAP Master Data Governance**
  This integration option allows you to centralize the address screening work in SAP Master Data Governance.

  In this integration scenario, SAP Master Data Governance calls SAP Business Partner Screening to do address screening of the business partner or partners in a change request. The address screening takes place in real time while the change request is being worked on. The master data specialist is responsible for reviewing address screening hits and deciding whether these are confirmed hits or false positives.

- **Business partner screening with decision-making in SAP Business Partner Screening**
  This integration option allows you to have specialists in SAP Business Partner Screening make at least the initial decisions on address screening hits, while the master data specialists in SAP Master Data Governance can concentrate on their work with master data and change requests.

  This integration process is executed as a change request workflow that is started in the SAP Master Data Governance system. The workflow triggers address screening in the business partner screening system. The decision on whether an address screening hit is a confirmed hit is made by the compliance expert in the SAP Business Partner Screening system. As soon as all screening alerts have been completed, the workflow can continue.

  The Customizing in the SAP Master Data Governance system allows the master data specialist to decide how to proceed with the change request. This integration scenario has the following two implementation options in the event of confirmed screening hit:

  - Return the change request to the master data specialist for a manual decision on how to proceed with the change request.
  - Automatically cancel the change request, thus preventing any approval of the change request that has critical compliance problems with business partners.

- These two implementation options share the same technical implementation. You can configure the change request type in Customizing to set the response in the event of a confirmed address screening hit. The response can be a workflow-based manual action or automatic cancellation.

> **Note**
>
> You must choose between the first and second scenario. If you use the second integration scenario, you would be able to use both options based on how you configure the workflows in the change request process.

The business partner screening system uses information in the screening request to determine the detection strategy and the screening list to use. Based on the detection strategy results, the screening system returns the alert and hit information to SAP Master Data Governance. After the alert and hit information is received, the respective SAP Master Data Governance processor decides whether any of the hits are accepted and valid. Based on this decision by the SAP Master Data Governance processor, the alerts are closed in the business partner screening system with either the **Confirmed** or **False Alarm** status. Note that business partner screening can't be successfully performed if only names are provided without addresses.

SAP Business Partner Screening may apply more than one detection strategy to a particular screening request. In addition, more than one alert may be created and presented to the master data specialist. The address screening features of SAP Business Partner Screening ensure that false positives are kept to a minimum and that all address screening hits, whether confirmed or false positive, can be quickly and efficiently cleared. SAP Master Data Governance automatically notifies SAP Business Partner Screening that a change request has been approved or canceled.

> **Note**
>
> When a person or organization is deleted in SAP Master Data Governance with a change request, it isn't automatically replicated in SAP Business Partner Screening. If it's necessary to delete the master data help in SAP Business Partner Screening, you can use Transaction **BPCM_DELETE_ORG** for organization master data and Transaction **BPCM_DELETE_PERSON** for person master data.

SAP Business Partner Screening offers an API for performing business partner screening. This API can be implemented using RFC function modules or enterprise web services. The RFC API is used in the implementation of business partner screening for SAP Master Data Governance.

To use SAP Business Partner Screening in SAP Master Data Governance, make sure the ADDRESS_SCREENING enrichment spot is configured using the following IMG path

(Transaction **MDGIMG**): **Master Data Governance, Central Governance · General Settings · Data Quality and Search · Validations and Enrichment · Define Enrichment Spots**. Figure 8.48 shows the enrichment spot configuration needed for business partner screening in SAP Master Data Governance.

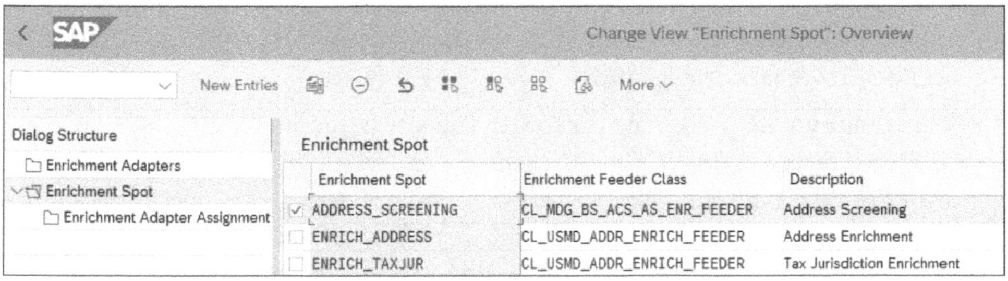

Figure 8.48 Enrichment Spot for Business Partner Screening in SAP Master Data Governance

Following is the IMG path for activating the business partner screening in SAP Master Data Governance process modeling (Transaction **MDGIMG**): **Master Data Governance, Central Governance · General Settings · Process Modeling · Change Requests · Configure Properties of Change Request Step**.

Figure 8.49 shows the business partner screening configuration of the SAP Master Data Governance process modeling.

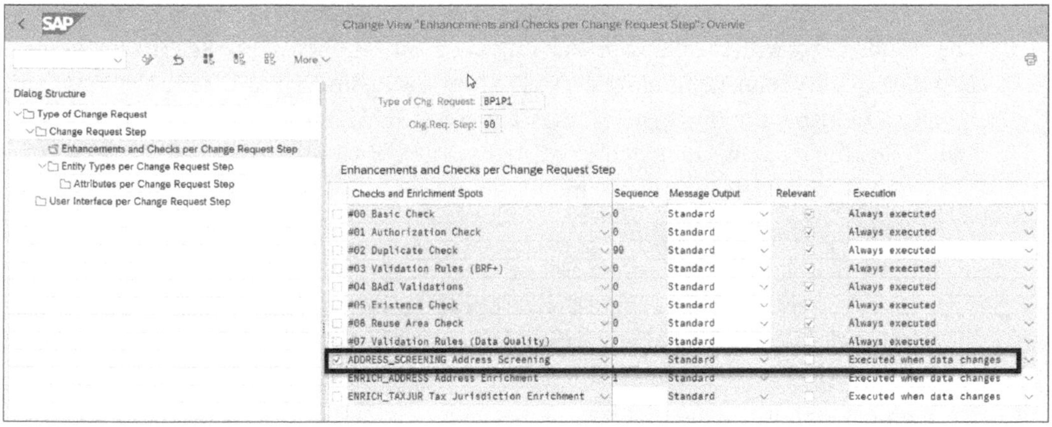

Figure 8.49 Configuring Address Screening in Central Governance

8.5 Managing Data Quality

Starting with the release of SAP S/4HANA 1809 and with every new release of SAP S/4HANA, continuous innovation in data quality management has provided a framework to create consistent quality in master data and helps in continuous data-quality evaluation and monitoring of master data in the system. SAP Data Quality Management for product master was first introduced in SAP Master Data Governance on SAP

S/4HANA 1809, and SAP Data Quality Management for business partner master data was introduced with SAP Master Data Governance on SAP S/4HANA 1909.

In SAP Master Data Governance on SAP S/4HANA 2021, the term "data quality rule" has been replaced by "validation rule." Data quality rule is the new superordinate term for both validation rules and derivation rules. Figure 8.55 in a later section shows the new app titles for the validation rules for business partners and products starting with SAP Master Data Governance on S/4HANA 2021.

SAP Data Quality Management can ensure the quality of product and business partner master data. You can define derivation scenarios to deduce master data based on derivations rules. You can also define validation rules and data quality key performance indicators (KPIs). You can then evaluate the quality of product and business partner master data according to these rules and monitor the current state of the data quality as well as its trend. By analyzing the evaluation results, you can identify areas of data with errors, find potential reasons for error, and initiate corrective actions. You can also use machine learning to mine your master data for new rule suggestions. These rules can be assessed, and, if found valid and useful, they can be added to the set of validation rules. These topics are discussed in the following sections.

8.5.1   Process Overview

One of the primary objectives of master data quality management is to ensure that the data is *fit for purpose*. At the same time, master data quality management must keep pace and evolve with the real-world changes in business operations. Ensuring that master data quality management evolves with how the business processes evolve can be a huge challenge for many organizations. For efficient master data quality management, the following steps are available with SAP Data Quality Management, and they should be carefully considered, planned, and implemented:

1. **Define derivation scenarios.**
   In this first step, you must consider the requirements as defined by business processes. You must use the Define Derivation Scenario app to deduce master data based on rules and a defined scope to ensure data quality. A derivation scenario consists of one or more derivation rules. This allows you to begin small and evolve over time.

2. **Define validation rules.**
   Use the Validation Rules app to define validation rules and to implement these rules in BRFplus for evaluation by the system.

   You can export and import validation rules using the Export Validation Rules and Import Validation Rules apps.

3. **Perform rule mining.**
   Use the Manage Rule Mining and Process Rules from Rule Mining apps to discover new validation rules based on your selected criteria. This process uses machine learning to propose potential rules for data quality evaluation. These proposals can be validated and easily converted to data quality validation rules.

4. **Define data quality KPIs for data quality scores.**
   You can use Configure Data Quality Scores apps to define data quality dimensions and dimension categories with assigned validation rules and specify how data quality scores are calculated to describe KPIs for monitoring data quality.

5. **Evaluate data quality.**
   Using **Evaluate Data Quality** apps, you can create and run an evaluation of your master data according to the validation rules. You can also schedule evaluation jobs, for example, in weekly or biweekly intervals.

6. **Monitor data quality.**
   You can use the **Data Quality Evaluation Overview** apps to display up-to-date status information about current data quality and drill down into the details for further data analysis. If you've configured your own data quality dimensions and scores, you can also display the current scores, trends, and the comparison to the defined thresholds.

7. **Analyze and correct data.**
   You can use the Evaluation Results apps to analyze data quality evaluation results for products and business partners with the goal to find incorrect data, and to investigate potential reasons for incorrect data. After that, you can also start the correction of master data.

Data quality management isn't a one-time static process that you implement and forget. You must keep refining your data quality definition, monitor the data quality, and continually improve it in a constantly evolving process. Figure 8.50 shows the overall objective of data quality management.

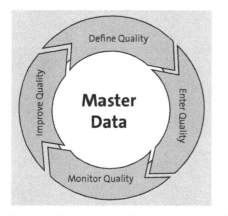

Figure 8.50 Data Quality Management Objectives

With the release of SAP Master Data Governance on SAP S/4HANA 1809, data quality management steps were provided for product master data. SAP Data Quality Management for business partner is available as standard with SAP Master Data Governance on SAP S/4HANA 1909. In SAP Master Data Governance on SAP S/4HANA 2021, the term "data quality rule" has been replaced by "validation rule." As you'll see in later sections, you can define and implement data quality rules, and monitor, evaluate, and analyze data quality by means of data quality scores as KPIs for master data management. By means of this continuous data quality evaluation and monitoring, you can constantly evolve and efficiently manage the challenges of current and future data quality needs.

The SAP Fiori apps available with SAP Master Data Governance on SAP S/4HANA 2021 as standard with the installation are shown in Figure 8.51 for product master data, and Figure 8.52 shows the SAP Fiori apps that are available for business partners.

Note

It's worth noting that the data quality management for business partners and product master data is available *only* with SAP Master Data Governance on SAP S/4HANA. There are no plans to introduce this with SAP Master Data Governance with SAP ERP.

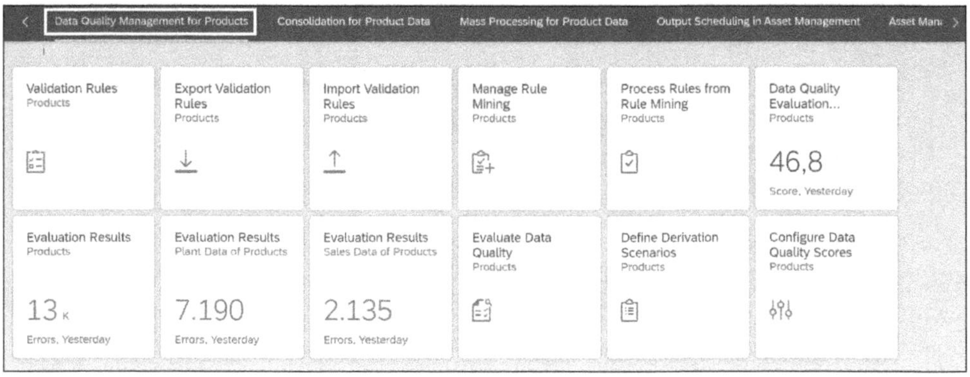

Figure 8.51 SAP Fiori Apps: Master Data Quality Evaluation for Products

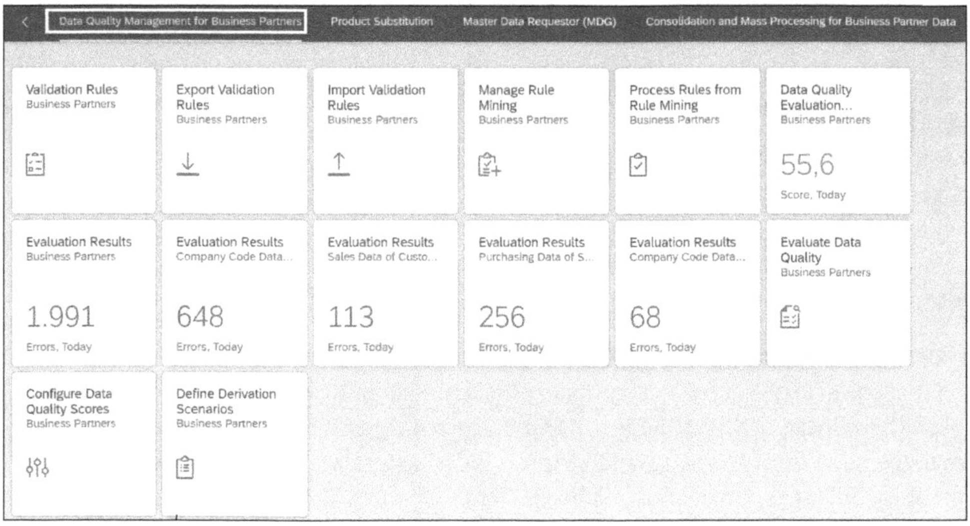

Figure 8.52 SAP Fiori Apps: Master Data Quality Evaluation for Business Partner

In the following sections, we'll discuss each of the preceding SAP Fiori apps in more detail.

8.5.2   Managing Derivation Scenarios

Derivation scenarios are used to deduce master data based on rules and a defined scope. Derivation scenarios are used during master data processes, such as mass processing and consolidation, to ensure data quality.

With the Define Derivation Scenarios app, you can create and edit derivation scenarios. A derivation scenario consists of one or more derivation rules, which control how target values are determined from source values. Figure 8.53 shows the Define Derivation Scenarios apps for Products and Business Partner.

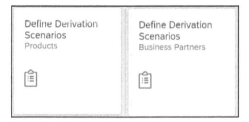

Figure 8.53 SAP Fiori Apps: Define Derivation Scenarios

After launching Define Derivation Scenarios – Business Partners app, initially a list of derivation scenarios available is displayed. To create a new scenario, from this screen, click **Create.** If you want to see the details of an existing scenario, click **Show Details.**

A similar screen for Product is displayed when you click the **Define Derivation Scenarios – Products** tile.

The Define Derivation Scenario app is used to do the following:

- Define and edit derivation scenario, including their details.
- Define and edit one or more derivation rules for each derivation scenario, including their details. Condition and scope expressions must be defined for each derivation rule within a derivation scenario, and it's built for either fields or for tables.
- Decide which rules are executed in consolidation and mass processes.
- Navigate to the BRFplus Workbench to define scope expressions and decision tables.

Figure 8.54 shows the **Define Derivation Scenarios for Business Partners** initial screen that displays the available derivation scenarios and details of one of the derivations. In the derivation details screen, you can define and manage one or more derivations rules for fields and tables.

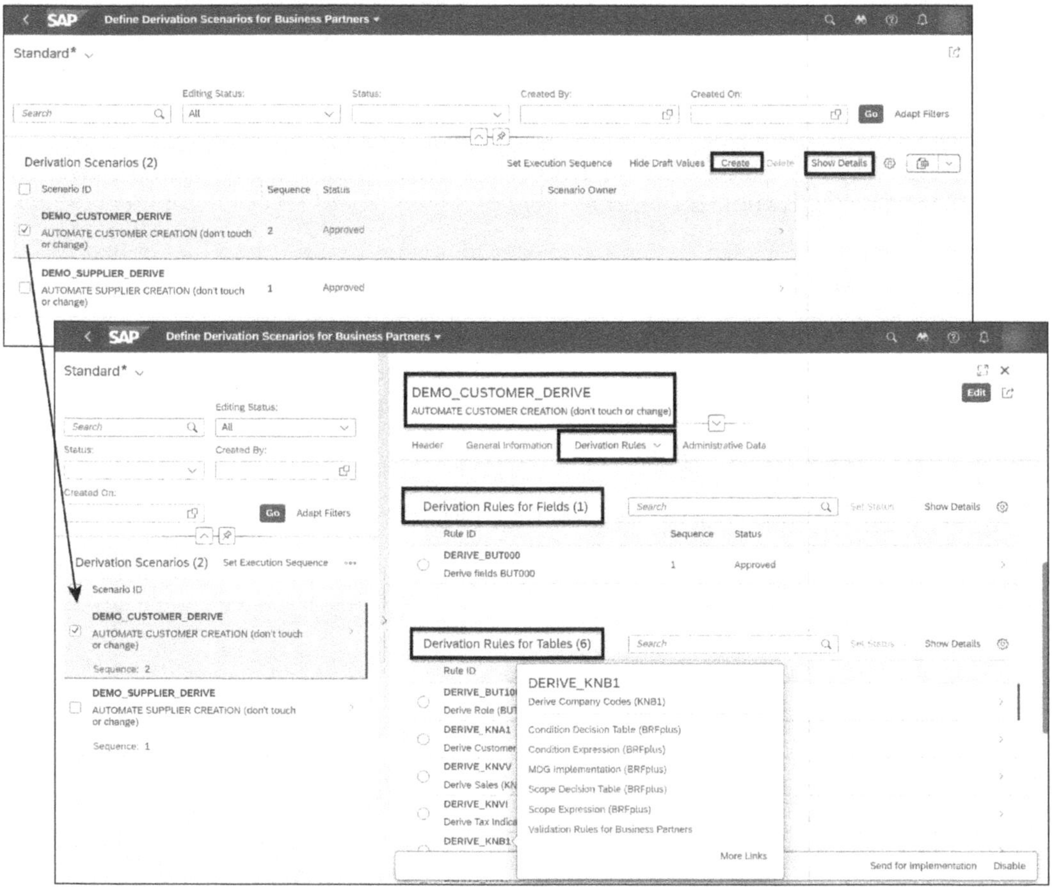

Figure 8.54 List of Derivation Scenarios and Details of a Derivation Scenario

> **Note**
>
> SAP Help Portal provides detailed steps on how to create and implement derivation scenarios.

8.5.3   Manage Validation Rules

For Product and Business Partner, three different sets of SAP Fiori apps are available to manage validation rules. In this section, we'll discuss them in detail.

You can collaboratively define and catalog validation rules in a repository with the rule management process of SAP Master Data Governance. The rules can be implemented with BRFplus to be used for data quality evaluations and for checking data in consolidation and in mass processing. You can also use them for checking data in change requests in Scentral governance. In addition, you can group and import and export rules from one system to another, for example, from a test to a production system.

Figure 8.55 shows the Validation Rules, Export Validation Rules, and Import Validation Rules apps to manage rules management of Business Partners and Products.

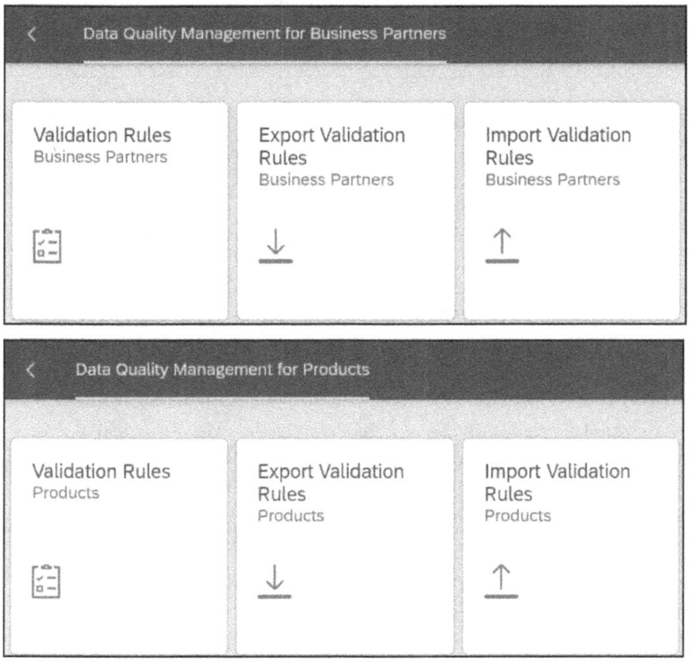

Figure 8.55 SAP Fiori Apps to Manage Validation Rules of Business Partners and Products

As mentioned at the beginning of this section, these apps were introduced with SAP Master Data Governance on SAP S/4HANA 2021. The data quality rules management apps have been replaced by these validation rules management apps.

The apps related to the data quality rules management are as follows:

- **Validation Rules**
  With the Validation Rules app you can collaboratively describe, catalog, and implement rules for data quality using a central rule repository. These validation rules can be used for data quality evaluations and for checking data in change requests, in consolidation, and in mass processing for products and business partners.

- **Export Validation Rules**
  With the Export Validation Rules app, you can export validation rules and the corresponding BRFplus data from one system (e.g., a test system), to later import them into another system (e.g., a production system). The exported rules are prevalidated, and you can view a detailed log per export and per validation rule. You start the

export process in the Validation Rules app by selecting the validation rules for the export and triggering the export process.

- **Import Validation Rules**
  With the Import Validation Rules app, you can create and work with imports. These imports are uploaded files containing validation rules, the corresponding BRFplus data, and administrative data, such as the source system. You can trigger the validation process for selected rules in an import. The imported rules can then be enabled for usage in your master data processes.

The Validation Rules apps allow you to collaboratively describe, catalog, and implement rules for data quality using the central rule repository. These validation rules can be used for data quality evaluations and for checking data in change requests, in consolidation, and in mass processing for products and business partners.

A master data steward can use this app to get structured and comprehensive access to rules as well as to link rules from the rule mining process to validation rules in the central rule repository. You can also trigger the rule export process from this app.

Validation Rules apps use BRFplus to define and implement the **Condition Expression** and **Scope Expression**. The Validation Rules apps can be used to do the following:

- Define rules (e.g., business aspects and responsibilities) and assign one or several usages (e.g., checking data in change request, in consolidation, and in mass processing).
- Define status handling and lifecycle of validation rules.
- Define the technical implementation and execution of rules with BRFplus.
- Assign one or several rule usages to be able to proceed with the rule implementation.
- Configure a message and message severity that will appear in the master data processes where the rule is applied.
- Link rules from the rule mining process to validation rules in the central rule repository. If automatic implementation is supported, the BRFplus implementation is automatically added.
- Start the export of rules, including BRFplus implementation, and download them in OpenOffice XML format.
- Enable or disable the usage for each master data process.
- Display the history of a validation rule by selecting **Show Audit Trail** in the **Administrative Data** section.

When you click the Validation Rules app, it displays a list of available validation rules. You can choose **Create** to create a new validation rule from this screen or click **Show Details** to display additional information about validation rules. If you click on a validation rule, a popup is displayed with hyperlinks for **Condition Expression (BRFplus)** and

Scope Expression (BRFplus). You can navigate to BRFplus to display or manage these expressions.

Figure 8.56 shows a **Validation Rules** list displayed and screenshots of condition expression and scope expression of the validation rule in BRFplus. Note that the **Condition Expression (BRFplus) ❶** name has a suffix **_CON**, whereas the **Scope Expression (BRFplus) ❷** name has a suffix **_SCP**. These suffixes are added by the system during the initial creation of the expressions.

Figure 8.56 Validation Rules and Details of Condition Expression and Scope Expression

We'll discuss the rules mining process after this, and it will be followed by the data quality evaluation process.

8.5.4   Rule Mining Process Overview

This rule mining process was first available with SAP Master Data Governance on SAP S/4HANA 1909. The purpose of the rule mining process is to discover new validation rules based on selected criteria in existing master data. The rule mining process uses machine learning to choose potential rules for the evaluation.

The rule mining process allows the master data steward to collaboratively decide on the business relevancy of the proposed rules and then create and link data quality rules from accepted rules. The complete process involves creating a mining run, executing that run, evaluating the mined rules created by the run, and then linking the mined rules you want to keep with validation rules in the rule repository either by linking to existing validation rules or creating new ones.

The rule mining process can be broken down into two main steps:

- Creating a rule mining run
- Reviewing the rules mined from the run

Figure 8.57 shows the Manage Rules Mining apps for business partners and products, as described in the following list.

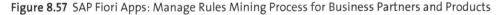

Manage Rule Mining Business Partners	Process Rules from Rule Mining Business Partners
Manage Rule Mining Products	Process Rules from Rule Mining Products

Figure 8.57 SAP Fiori Apps: Manage Rules Mining Process for Business Partners and Products

- Manage Rule Mining
  The Manage Rules Mining app allows you to create and start a rule mining run to discover business rules in your master data records. In a mining run, you can define the focus for a mining run and specify the fields that could be potential condition fields and checked fields for your new rules. When you start the mining run, the system

uses a machine learning algorithm to propose a list of potential rules based on your input. This app assists the master data steward in uncovering potential rules for their master data and so shortens the preparation time of rule definition.

- **Process Rules from Rules Mining**
  The Process Rules from Rules Mining app allows you to review and manage rules generated from rule-mining runs. You can decide to accept the rules or set them for review by others from this app. You can either create a new validation rule directly from the accepted mined rules or link the mined rules to existing validation rules. This app offers many filters and ways of sorting and grouping the rules to help you find and compare interesting rules. For each rule, the app shows you the number of records complying or violating the rule to help you make decisions.

8.5.5 Data Quality Evaluation Process Overview

For evaluating data quality several apps are provided. These data quality evaluation apps collectively enable you to configure how you want your data quality scores to be calculated; create, monitor, and manage data quality evaluation runs; show the quality scores for your data; and analyze, drill down, and correct errors in your data based on evaluation results.

> **Prerequisites to Using These Apps**
>
> Before you can use the data quality evaluation apps, you should have already created and approved validation rules in your system. These validation rules can be created either manually or using the Rules Mining apps.

The data quality evaluation apps can be grouped as follows:

Configure Data Quality Scores Apps

These apps enable you to determine how the system calculates the data quality scores for your data to be used in data quality evaluation runs. You can choose thresholds for your validation rules to apply and the weighted impact of these validation rules.

Figure 8.58 shows the apps that are available to the Configure Data Quality Scores apps for business partners and products.

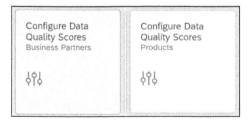

Figure 8.58 SAP Fiori Apps: Configure Data Quality Scores for Business Partners and Products

Evaluate Data Quality

This app allows you to create, execute, and schedule data quality evaluations runs for your chosen domain. You can also delete entire existing runs or choose to delete the results of evaluations and keep their aggregated data to use in score calculation.

Figure 8.59 shows the Evaluate Data Quality apps available for business partners and products.

Figure 8.59 SAP Fiori Apps: Evaluate Data Quality for Business Partners and Products

Figure 8.60 shows an example of the **Evaluation Data Quality for Business Partners** initial screen. From here, you can schedule and create a new process by clicking on **Schedule** and **Create Process**, respectively. If you want to delete results or delete a process, you can select individual or multiple process IDs and then click **Delete Results** or **Delete** a process as needed.

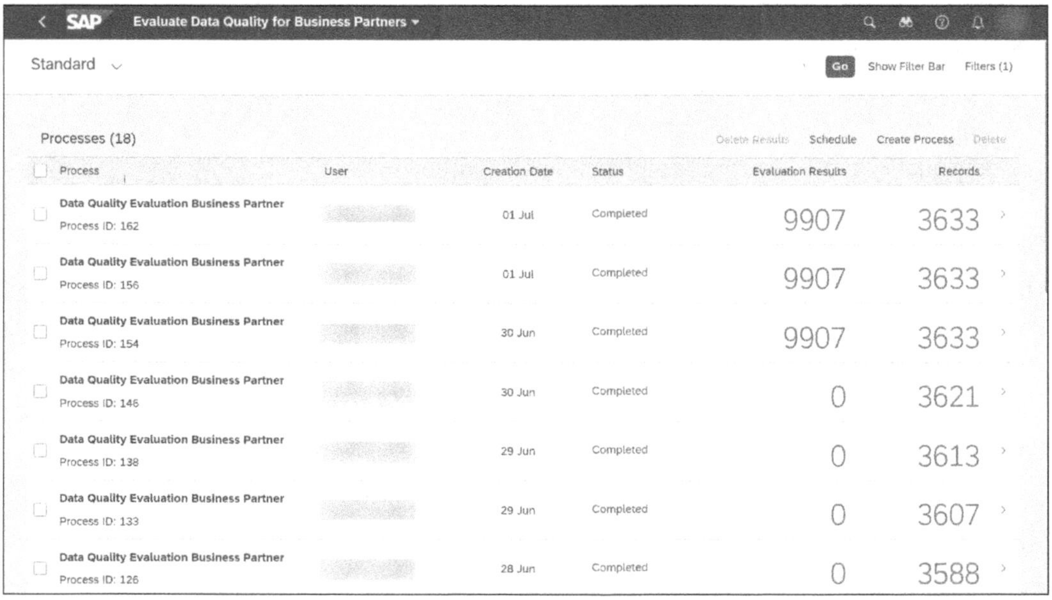

Process	User	Creation Date	Status	Evaluation Results	Records
Data Quality Evaluation Business Partner Process ID: 162		01 Jul	Completed	9907	3633
Data Quality Evaluation Business Partner Process ID: 156		01 Jul	Completed	9907	3633
Data Quality Evaluation Business Partner Process ID: 154		30 Jun	Completed	9907	3633
Data Quality Evaluation Business Partner Process ID: 146		30 Jun	Completed	0	3621
Data Quality Evaluation Business Partner Process ID: 138		29 Jun	Completed	0	3613
Data Quality Evaluation Business Partner Process ID: 133		29 Jun	Completed	0	3607
Data Quality Evaluation Business Partner Process ID: 126		28 Jun	Completed	0	3588

Figure 8.60 Evaluate Data Quality for Business Partners: Initial Screen

Figure 8.61 shows an example of the **Evaluation Data Quality for Products** initial screen. Similar to what we mentioned about business partners, you can schedule and create a new process by clicking on **Schedule** and **Create Process**, respectively. If you want to delete results or delete a process, you can select individual or multiple process IDs and then click **Delete Results** or **Delete** for a process as needed.

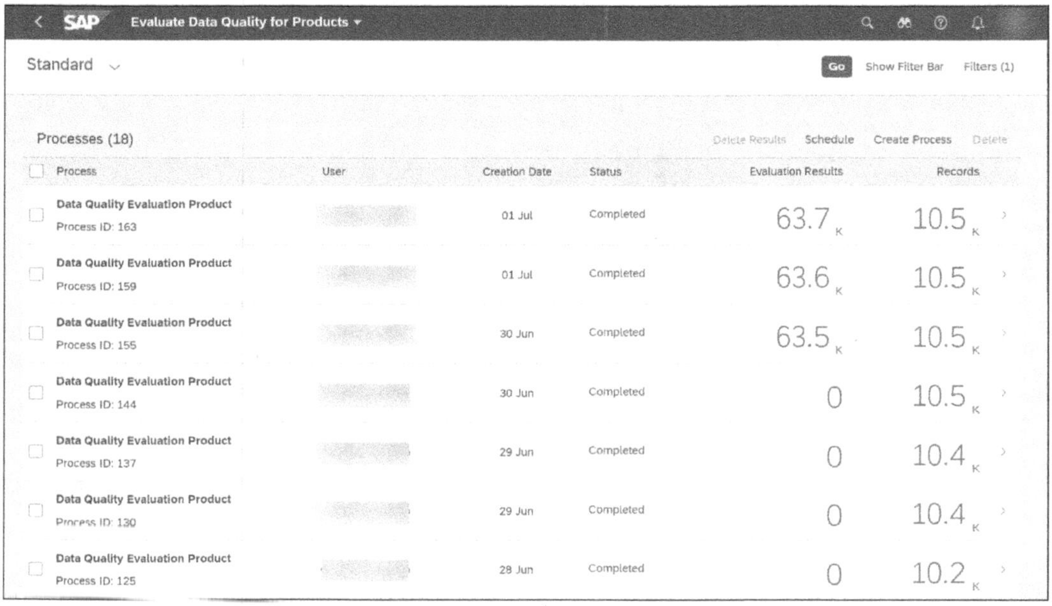

Process	User	Creation Date	Status	Evaluation Results	Records	
Data Quality Evaluation Product Process ID: 163		01 Jul	Completed	63.7 K	10.5 K	>
Data Quality Evaluation Product Process ID: 159		01 Jul	Completed	63.6 K	10.5 K	>
Data Quality Evaluation Product Process ID: 155		30 Jun	Completed	63.5 K	10.5 K	>
Data Quality Evaluation Product Process ID: 144		30 Jun	Completed	0	10.5 K	>
Data Quality Evaluation Product Process ID: 137		29 Jun	Completed	0	10.4 K	>
Data Quality Evaluation Product Process ID: 130		29 Jun	Completed	0	10.4 K	>
Data Quality Evaluation Product Process ID: 125		28 Jun	Completed	0	10.2 K	>

Figure 8.61 Evaluate Data Quality for Products: Initial Screen

Data Quality Evaluation Overview Apps

Evaluating data quality run results can be more complex than they appear initially. The system evaluates each rule and returns the result **OK** or **Not OK** for each rule and data set combination. The simple result has more complex interpretations, and you may use additional apps discussed in the following sections to analyze the evaluation results. Figure 8.62 shows the Data Quality Evaluation Overview apps available for business partners and products.

Figure 8.62 SAP Fiori Apps: Data Quality Evaluation Overview for Business Partners and Products

Figure 8.63 show an example of the **Data Quality Evaluation Overview for Business Partners** initial screen.

Figure 8.63 Data Quality Evaluation Overview for Business Partners: Initial Screen

Figure 8.64 show an example of the **Data Quality Evaluation Overview for Products** initial screen.

Figure 8.64 Data Quality Evaluation Overview for Products: Initial Screen

If you don't see any evaluation results for a validation rule, it may be due to any of the following:

- The rule isn't active, and/or it isn't yet considered in any evaluation.
- The rule was evaluated, but according to the rule's scope, there was no data that produced an outcome.
- The rule was evaluated, and evaluation results were available, but these results were deleted.

If you don't see any evaluation results for an entire evaluation run, it may be due to any of the following:

- The results were deleted using the **Delete Results** action.
- The system automatically deleted the results due to the housekeeping settings of a subsequent evaluation.
- There are no active rules, or no data selected based on the rule scope.

Evaluating the results can be quite complex. If you experience any of the above issues, you can use the Evaluation Results apps discussed in the following sections to analyze the evaluation results.

Business Partner Evaluation Results Apps

The following standard SAP Fiori apps are available for business partner evaluation results:

- Evaluation Results for Business Partners
- Evaluation Results for Sales Data of Customers
- Evaluation Results for Purchasing Data of Suppliers
- Evaluation Results for Company Code Data of Customers
- Evaluation Results for Company Code Data of Suppliers

Figure 8.65 shows the Evaluation Results apps for business partners data quality evaluation.

Figure 8.65 Business Partners Evaluation Results: SAP Fiori Apps

These apps help you analyze data quality evaluation results. They display the evaluation outcome for validation rules applied to your business partner records. You can
determine which business partners have errors and which don't. You can find areas of
bad data or reasons for incorrect data. You can start the correction of data directly from
these apps by selecting the business partners in the display results in these apps.

Figure 8.66 Evaluation Results for Products

You can process a single record, or, by selecting multiple records, you can even start
mass processing to correct the master data in SAP Master Data Central Governance.
You can also export the results to a Microsoft Excel spreadsheet for offline analysis. Figure 8.66 shows an example of the **Evaluation Results for Products** screen.

Product Evaluation Results Apps

The following standard SAP Fiori apps are available for product evaluation results:

- Evaluation Results for Products
- Evaluation Results for Plant Data of Products
- Evaluation Results for Sales Data of Products

Figure 8.67 shows the apps that are available for evaluating results of products data
quality evaluation.

These apps help analyze data quality evaluation results. They display the evaluation
outcome for validation rules applied to your products records. You can determine
which products have errors and which don't. You can find areas of bad data or reasons

for incorrect data. You can start the correction of data directly from these apps by selecting the products in display results in these apps.

Evaluation Results Products	Evaluation Results Plant Data of Products	Evaluation Results Sales Data of Products
13 K	7.190	2.135
Errors, Today	Errors, Today	Errors, Today

Figure 8.67 Products Evaluation Results: SAP Fiori Apps

You can process a single record, or, by selecting multiple records, you can even start mass processing to correct the master data in SAP Master Data Central Governance. You can also export the results to a Microsoft Excel spreadsheet for offline analysis. Figure 8.68 shows an example of the **Evaluation Results for Products** screen.

> **Note: Evaluation Results Apps Implementation**
>
> All the Evaluation Results apps implement the SAP Fiori elements Analytical List Page (ALP) floorplan, and they all share the same behavior. You can find more information about the ALP by navigating to *https://experience.sap.com/fiori-design-web/analytical-list-page/*.
>
> In the following section, we'll use the Evaluation Results for Products app to explain how the ALP works.

With these SAP Fiori apps, you can analyze the data quality evaluation results. The apps display the evaluation outcome for all the validation rules applied in the evaluation. You can analyze products data, plant data of products, and sales data of products based on which app you launch. You can analyze which products have errors and which don't to find areas of bad data or reasons for incorrect data. After you identify the attributes that need to be changed, you can start the correction process directly from the app using the central governance change request process or using the **Change Material** link. You can also initiate a mass change of products. If required, you can download the results to a spreadsheet or send an email and share the results with a colleague directly from the app. Following are some of the key features of these apps:

- Analyze data with errors using filters, diagrams, and sorting based on various product attributes.
- Start the correction of the data with errors using central governance.
- Create prefiltered lists of data to be corrected, and then download or send an email to collaborate with the data owners.

As all three Evaluation Results apps have similar behavior and for the explanation of the functionality, we'll just focus on the Evaluation Results for Products app.

When you launch the Evaluation Results for Products app, you'll see a screen like that shown in Figure 8.68:

❶ **Header with the filter bar**
Here you see displayed **Results by Outcome**, **Results by Product Type**, and **Results by Cross-Plant Product Status**.

❷ **Evaluation item chart**
This is a smart chart for visualization, drilldown, and filtering.

❸ **Evaluation items table**
This is an analytical table for detailed information, action, and export.

Figure 8.68 shows an example of the SAP Fiori element ALP floorplan and provides an overview of the most recent evaluation results in three different sections. The top section ❶ contains the overall results broken down first with the outcome of how many records are **Not OK** and **OK**. The results are further broken down and grouped as **Results by Product Type** and **Results by Cross-Plant Product Status**. By clicking on the **Value Help** icon next to each group of results, you can change the way you see the results grouped by some other attribute.

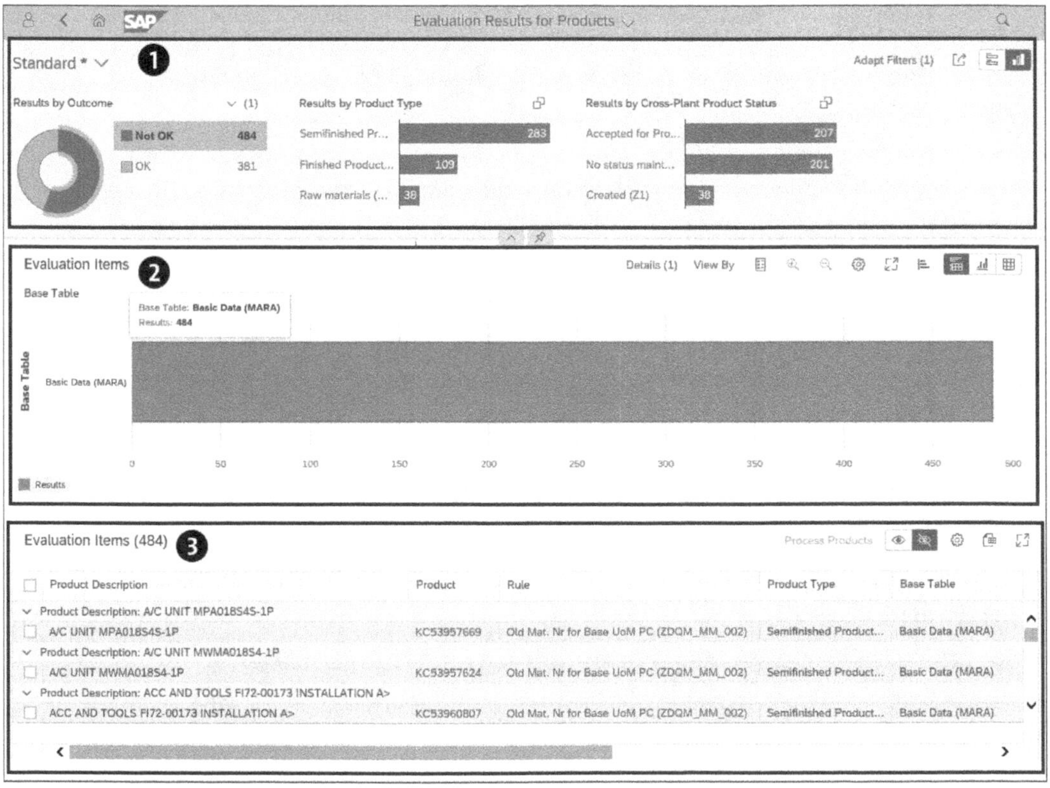

Figure 8.68 Evaluation Results for Products

Whatever you define in the filter bar will influence the data displayed in the chart ❷ and the table ❸. In the top-right corner of this first section, buttons are available to switch between **Compact Filters** and **Adapt Filters** to add more filters.

The middle section ❷ provides a graphical depiction of the evaluation results. This is a smart chart for visualization. The many buttons available in the top-right corner of the section allow you to define your own chart type, choose dimensions from the product master data, select the display attribute, and use filter and drilldown options. You can drill down to see the result by values of almost any field of the product basic data.

The bottom section ❸ gives a list of **Evaluation Items**. This is an analytical table for detailed information, actions, and exports, and it also allows you to add fields from the product basic data section as columns. These and other functions are available in the **Settings** dialog. In Figure 8.68, the list contains **484 Not OK** products. The **Product** number and the **Rule** applied for the record are shown with hyperlinks. By clicking on the hyperlinks, you can drill down to either the active record or the rule applied, respectively.

Figure 8.69 shows the popup screen displaying details of the **Rule** applied in the evaluation. You can drill down further to **Condition Expression (BRFplus)** or **Scope Expression (BRFplus)**. In addition, you can drill down to **Manage Data Quality Rules for Product** to review the rules.

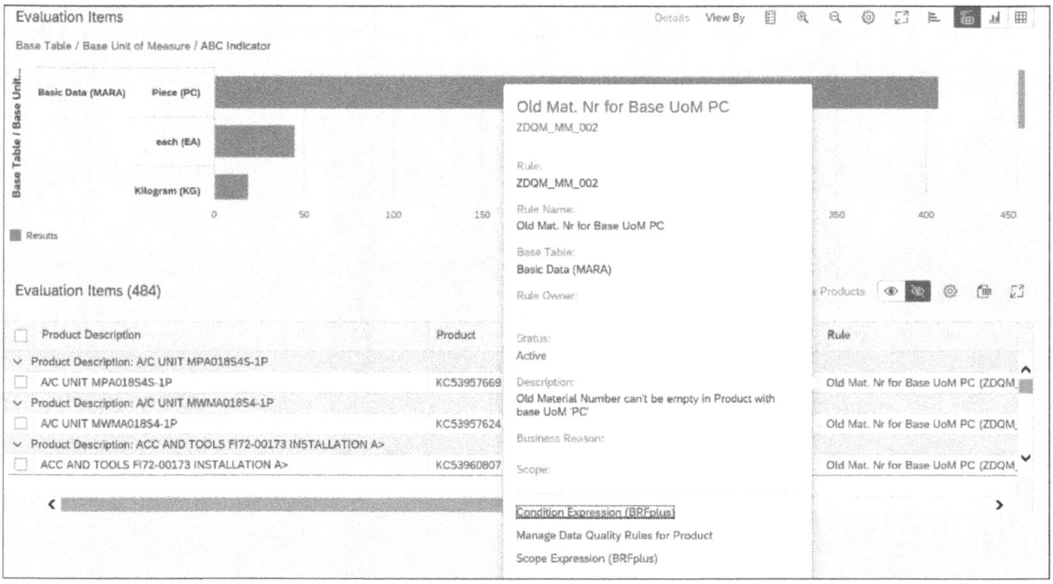

Figure 8.69 Evaluation Items: Rule

If you click on the product hyperlink (**KC53957669**, in our example) instead, you'll see high-level information about the product, as shown in Figure 8.70.

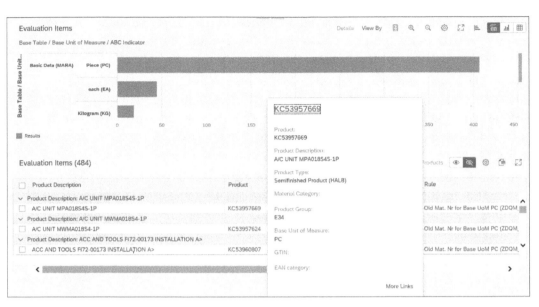

Figure 8.70 Evaluation Items: Product

By clicking on **More Links** in the product information screen, you can drill down further to several other options, as shown in Figure 8.71. Some of the options are to use central governance to change, create, and mark for deletion. Several other options are also available, such as **Display Material, Analyze ALE Appl. Log for MatMaster**, and **Data Replication - Replication**.

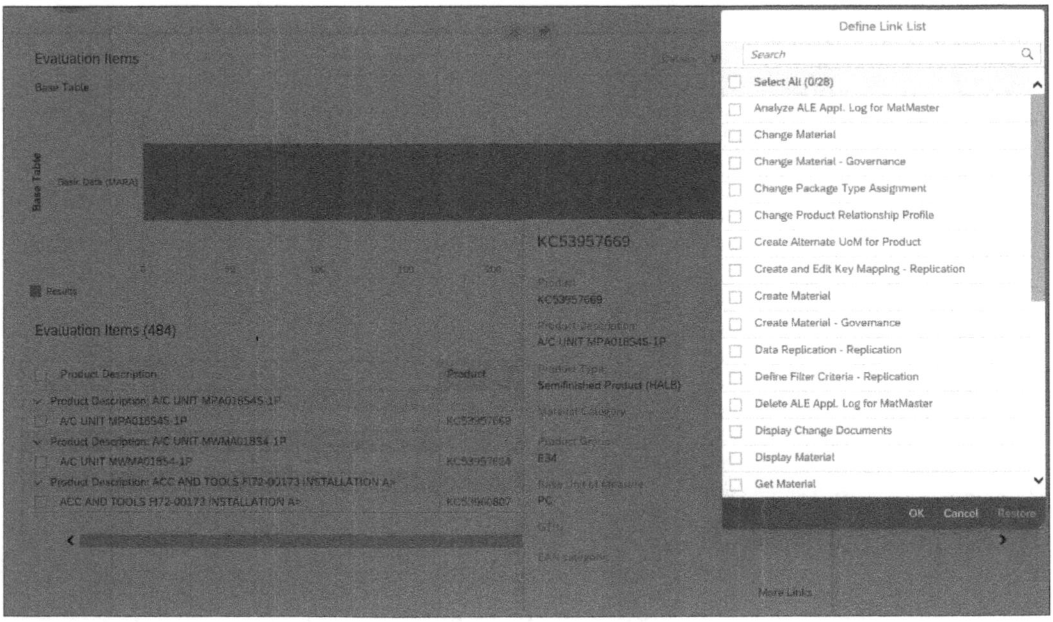

Figure 8.71 More Links for Evaluate Results: Product

If you select the **Change Material - Governance** link, you can navigate to the central governance screen shown in Figure 8.72.

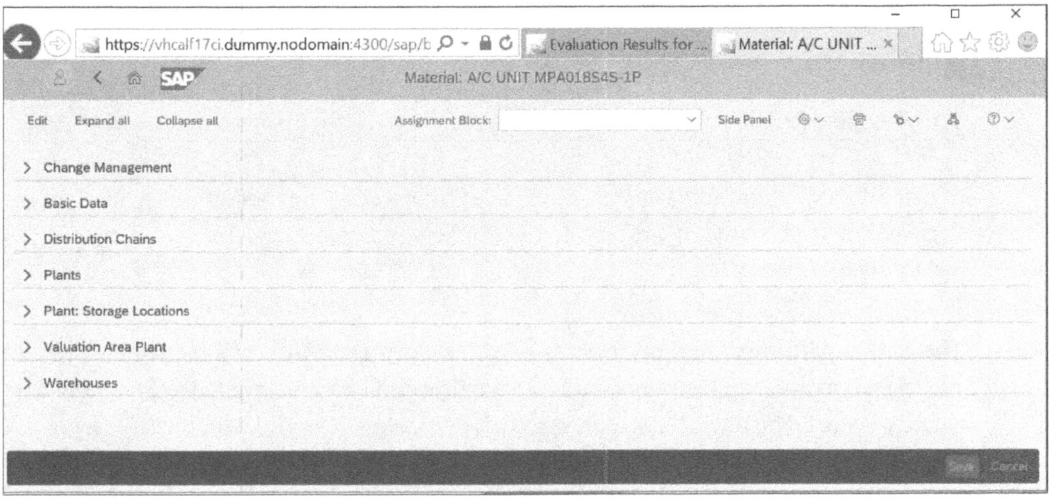

Figure 8.72 Central Governance: Material

The features discussed in this section illustrate the power of these SAP Fiori apps. Many of the icons are arranged to make it more user friendly and intuitive. As soon as you complete the investigation by drilling down to find the bad record that is active in the system, you can initiate the corrective action either by collaborating with the data owner or by using central governance processes to correct the product master data.

8.6   Data Quality Remediation

Earlier versions of SAP Master Data Governance had provided data quality remediation capabilities such as running checks against master data already profiled by external tools (e.g., SAP Information Steward). The remediation process was generally performed via an external tool outside of SAP Master Data Governance, and only the erroneous records were stored in data quality remediation tables in SAP Master Data Governance. Later, the remediation actions to correct the errors were initiated in SAP Master Data Governance.

With the release of SAP Master Data Governance on SAP S/4HANA 1709, the remediation functionality for product master data was enhanced to provide more functions and features to manage this process entirely within SAP Master Data Governance. The following sections give an overview of how the remediation process works in SAP Master Data Governance and how to configure this in the system.

8.6.1   Overview

> **Note**
>
> Starting with SAP S/4HANA 1709, the data quality remediation process was available for product master data. It's also worth noting that the remediation capability is only offered in SAP Master Data Governance on SAP S/4HANA; it's not available with SAP ERP.
>
> As of SAP S/4HANA 1909, it's recommended to use the Managing Data Quality apps covered in previously in Section 8.5. The following section is provided for earlier versions of SAP S/4HANA.

The data quality remediation process in SAP Master Data Governance enables you to control data quality for product data by selecting and validating data to reveal any data quality issues. The remediation process can be started after the data quality issues are identified.

It's recommended that the data quality remediation process is done on a regular basis to ensure that data quality and data governance processes are properly implemented. There is a constant need to keep the quality of master data very high as the business keeps growing and evolving, and as the business processes keep changing. As every master data expert is aware, despite the best of efforts in defining business rules, there is always a chance of data slipping through the crack. Therefore, it's a good idea to revisit data quality on a regular basis to ensure that the quality of master data remains high. If you see an issue with data quality, then erroneous records must be corrected, and some additional rules may have to be put in place to bulletproof your data governance process.

SAP Master Data Governance has provided data quality remediation capabilities in previous versions such as the data quality remediation screen, where you could run checks against your data using SAP Information Steward and other tools. The records with errors can be displayed in the data quality remediation table, and actions can be initiated to correct the errors. In previous versions, evaluation was done with an external tool, and worklists were used for the remediation. Afterward, only the erroneous records or records with errors were loaded into SAP Master Data Governance for further checking and correction. Starting with SAP Master Data Governance on SAP S/4HANA 1709, this functionality has been further enhanced to provide more functions and features to manage the entire process within SAP Master Data Governance itself.

The data quality remediation in SAP Master Data Governance on SAP S/4HANA not only allows you to load error data from external sources but also allows you to select and execute validation on data managed by the SAP Master Data Governance or the SAP S/4HANA system. It also provides an overview screen to get the big picture of the data quality trends in your validation runs and allows you to get more insights into the causes for error. Data quality remediation reuses the consolidation framework for data validation and correction.

The data quality remediation process can be broken down into the steps shown in Figure 8.73.

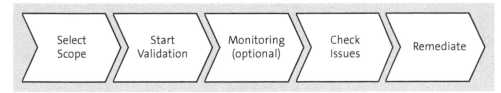

Figure 8.73 Data Quality Remediation for Product Data

These steps are explained in detail in Section 8.6.2. In this section, we'll just explain the terms and try to understand the purpose of each step.

- **Select scope**
  In this initial step, the data is selected for validation. Using the Start Remediation Process for Products app from the SAP Fiori launchpad, select the process template for data quality remediation, and enter a description. Then, select the data to be validated.

- **Start validation**
  Validation of the selected data is started in this step, and the master data quality issues are written into the master data quality worklist.

- **Monitoring**
  This is an optional step that allows you to track the status of the processes.

- **Check issues**
  Review and check issues with the data set that has been validated. The Master Data Quality Worklist app allows you to monitor master data quality issues. In the displayed list, it's possible to filter on object attributes, rulesets, groups, and IDs.

- **Remediate**
  As the last step in the data remediation process, the correction process can be triggered from the app with navigation to single and mass maintenance applications within central governance. Remediation is also possible without using central governance, if needed.

The previous version of SAP Master Data Governance already provided SAP Fiori tiles, as shown in Figure 8.74. These SAP Fiori tiles lead to apps that allow you to import erroneous data records from an external tool and rules descriptions for remediation.

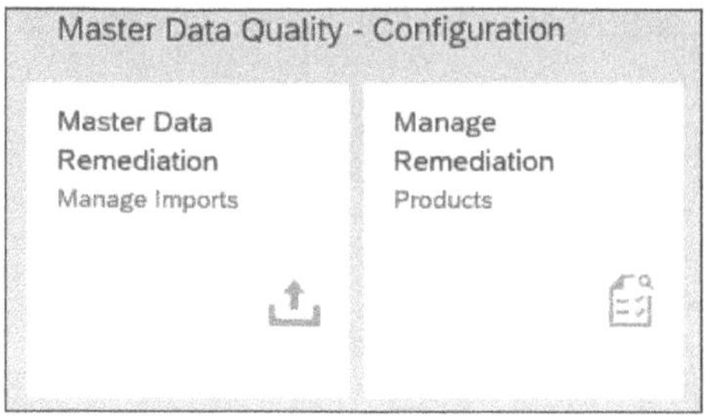

Figure 8.74 Data Quality SAP Fiori Tiles for Import

Starting with SAP Master Data Governance on SAP S/4HANA 1709, this has been further enhanced with more tiles, as shown in Figure 8.75. SAP Fiori apps are provided to get an overview of erroneous data records, to manage remediation processes, and to access a worklist where records with errors appear, including the reason for failure.

Within the SAP Fiori app itself, you can work on the records to correct them and, if needed, to trigger the governance process directly from those screens. It's also possible to trigger either a single maintenance governance process or a mass change process using the mass processing framework for one or more records from the master data quality worklist. Note that you can perform the correction process without using the central governance process.

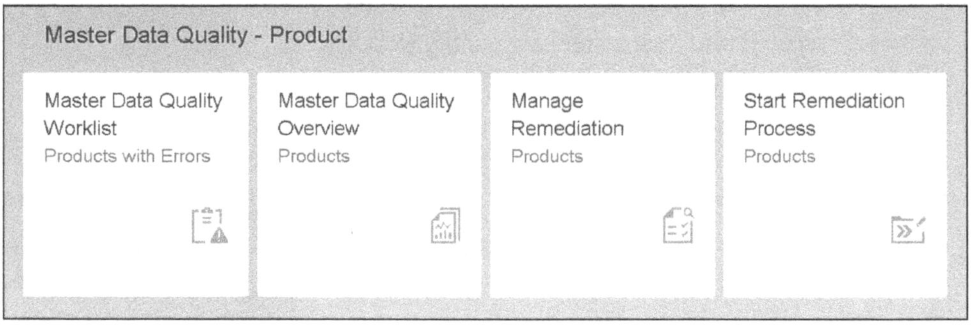

Figure 8.75 Data Quality SAP Fiori Tiles for the Product Master

> **Note**
>
> Use Transaction **MDQIMG** to access the configuration screens for master data remedi-ation. Remember, however, that not all the settings are available in this transaction. For some of the settings (e.g., **Specify Process Template**), you'll have to use Transaction **MDCIMG** where the consolidation settings are located. This is because remediation reuses some of the settings of consolidation.

8.6.2   Remediation Process

The earlier section introduced various terms used in master data remediation and provided an overview of the remediation process steps. In this section, you'll see how these steps are implemented in SAP Master Data Governance for product master data.

Start and Manage Remediation Process

The purpose of the remediation functionality in SAP Master Data Governance is to provide capabilities to run validations on the underlying master data from within SAP Master Data Governance without the need for an additional tool. The remediation process can be started from the Start Remediation Process app. In this app, you can start a remediation process by choosing a preconfigured remediation **Process Template** and providing a **Description** for the process to be configured (see Figure 8.76). After you save this process, you'll be taken to a screen where you can select the subset of data that you want to validate and then run the data through a validation step.

The properties of the process are configured in the Customizing settings for remediation.

For those who are familiar with the consolidation process in SAP Master Data Governance, the layout of the screen will look very similar. All the process steps are visible, and you can stop the process flow after every step to examine the results. The progress bar on top of the screen also shows you how much of the process is completed. You can also use **Rollback** or **Delete** on the process flow and see the audit trail by clicking on **Show Audit Trail** to track what is happening with the process flow you've started.

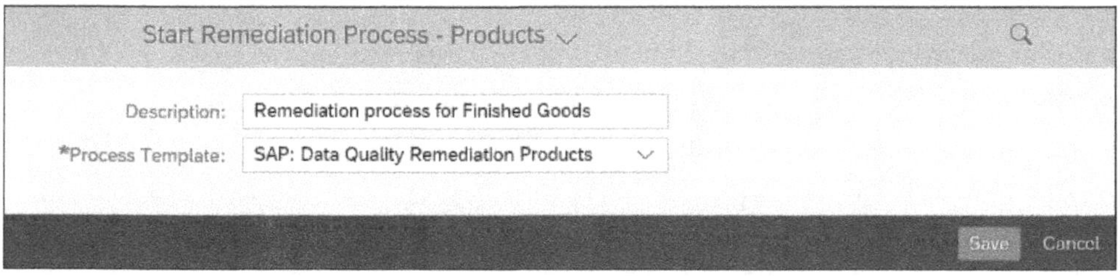

Figure 8.76 Start Remediation Process for Products

The main part of the screen, as shown in Figure 8.77, is used for selecting the records you want to put through the remediation process. Using the set of filters available, you can include records in and exclude records from the remediation flow. Remember that SAP Master Data Governance data remediation capabilities are targeted at records currently within the SAP S/4HANA system from the SAP Master Data Governance tables (for a hub installation), from the SAP S/4HANA product master data tables (for a co-deployed installation), or when you don't have a governance solution in place. So, when you use the (F4) help to select the records for remediation, you're looking at the data in the underlying product master tables.

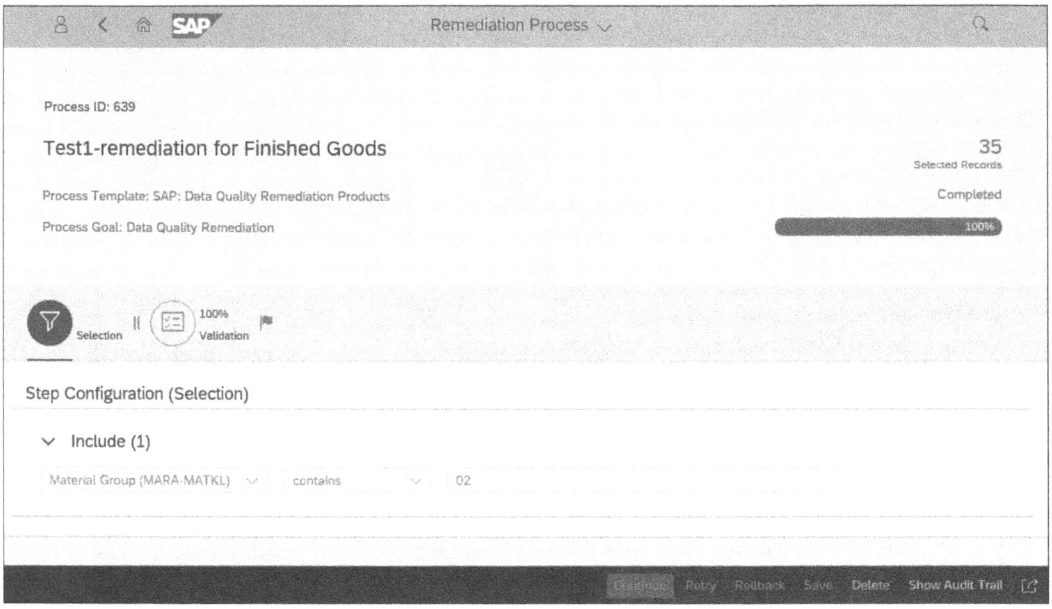

Figure 8.77 Data Selection Screen for Remediation

After the data is selected, the records are sent to the validation step, as shown in Figure 8.78, where they will be checked against a set of rules. Following are the options for these rules:

- Rules enforced by the underlying SAP S/4HANA business logic
- The checks that you've put in place in the central governance process
- BRFplus rules you've specifically configured for validation
- A combination of all the above

These are controlled by the configuration settings you choose and can be further customized using the **Adjust** button. It's possible to choose which of these checks should be executed during the validation step. The results of the validation step can then be optionally written into a worklist, so that a master data expert can review the results and send them for further governance to correct the errors.

> **Tip**
>
> Templates are predelivered in the system. If you follow all the configuration steps in your SAP Master Data Governance guide, you'll be able to use the templates and configuration that are predelivered out of the box. With minimal configuration, you should be able to run your first remediation process for product data.

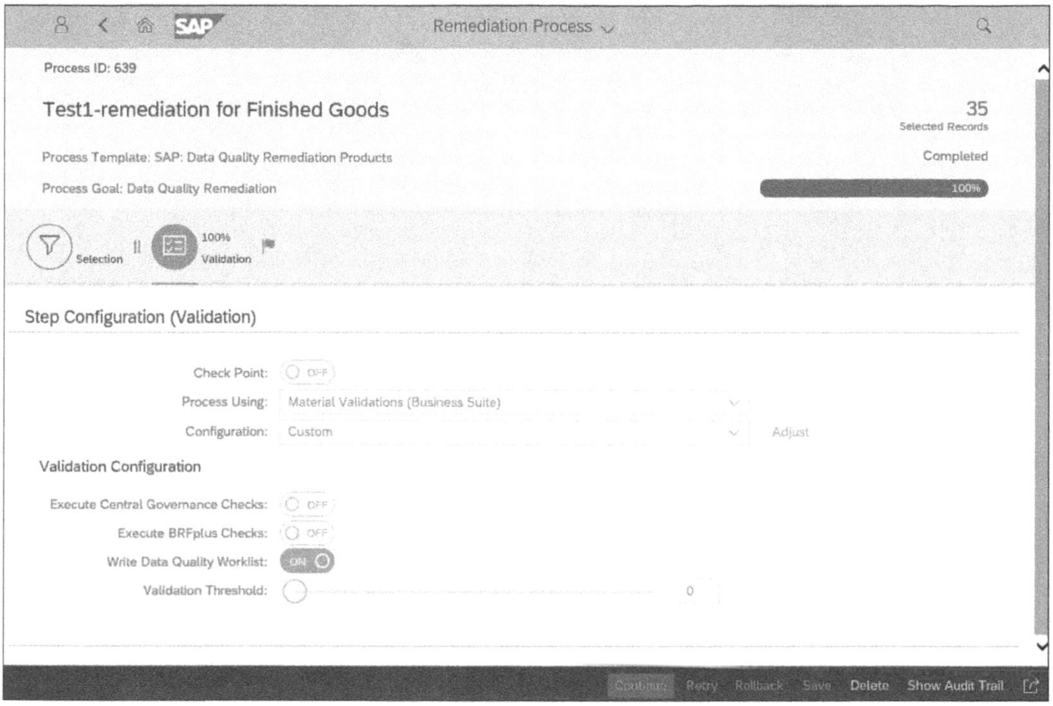

Figure 8.78 Data Remediation Validation Step

Master Data Quality Worklist and Actions

As a master data administrator, for example, you may have to have run the remediation process on your entire set of product data. The process will run in the background, and you can come back later to see if the process has finished and what the results are. Because you've configured the process to write erroneous records into a worklist, you can launch the Master Data Quality Worklist app to look at what errors were identified for the specific run.

Using various sets of filter criteria, you can pull up the list of erroneous records for your selected validation run and investigate details of the errors. Figure 8.79 shows an example of a **Master Data Remediation Worklist for Product** screen showing erroneous products and their attributes.

You can see the products that were caught by the validation step, including product IDs, rules that were violated, product types, and various other attributes for each of the erroneous records. This screen also allows you to filter and sort errors based on various product and process attributes.

After you've filtered the erroneous records into a subset of errors you want to work with, you can set the status for each record and add a note to each record.

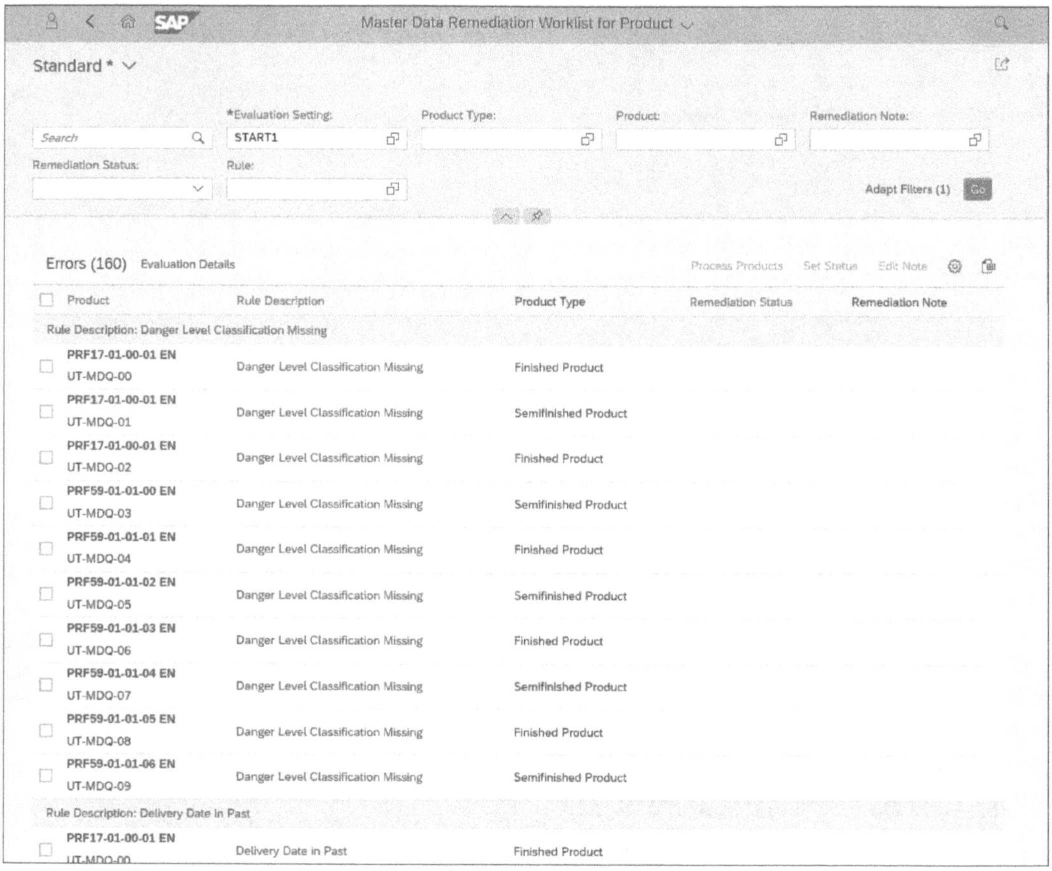

Figure 8.79 Worklist Showing Erroneous Products and Their Attributes

For some of the records, you might also decide to trigger a governance process in SAP Master Data Governance so that appropriate business users will review and correct the erroneous records. From this worklist, you can either trigger single change requests, or choose multiple records to do mass processing using the **Process Products** button.

You can also export the data into a Microsoft Excel spreadsheet and review the worklist offline. If your SAP Fiori apps are integrated to SAP Jam, you can also collaborate with your team via SAP Jam.

> **Tip**
> If you don't have SAP Master Data Governance configured for governance, clicking on the **Process Request** button will take you to the **Product** SAP Fiori tile and then app where you can correct the data errors.

Master Data Quality Overview Dashboard

You can launch the Master Data Quality Overview app to get overview results, as shown in Figure 8.80, of your last run and to get a comparative view of how your last run fared compared to previous runs from, for example, half a year ago.

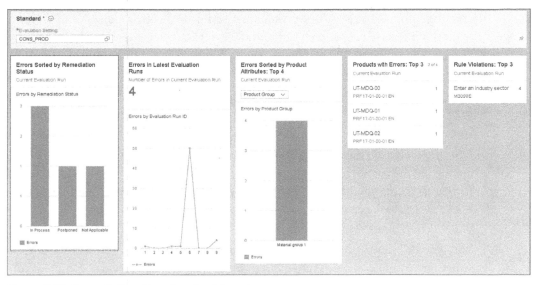

Figure 8.80 Remediation Overview Dashboard

The overview dashboard shows you errors from your last run split into various dimensions:

- **Errors Sorted by Remediation Status**
  As you work through the list of erroneous data, you can set statuses for the data. For example, for false positives, you can set the status to **Not Applicable,** and for those you've already worked on and corrected the errors for, you can set the status to **Finalized.**

  Drilling down on the appropriate status also takes you to a filtered set of records with that status. The master data administrator or steward can quickly get an idea of how much more work is to be done on the error list.

- **Errors in Latest Evaluation Runs**
  This graph shows you how your current run fared in terms of number of errors compared to your last several runs. From here, you can drill down further and click on one of the previous runs to go directly to the list of erroneous records from that run.

  This trend graph also allows you to keep track of how your data quality is progressing and to assess how your data quality is either improving or going down over a period. If you see your data quality going down, it's a clear indicator that you must revisit your business rules for validation to make sure you catch errors even before they are saved on the database.

> **Tip**
>
> The **Evaluation Setting** attribute allows you to group various remediation attributes, such as import type, rule repository, business object type, and so on. This group is then assigned to a process template, which makes it easy for you to assign certain characteristics to your remediation run. The **Evaluation Setting** attribute is a prerequisite entry on most of the remediation screens to get to the right data records and errors.

- **Errors Sorted by Product Attributes**

  This graph shows you the classification of errors based on attributes of the product that caused this error. From the dropdown list, you can change the attribute you want to use and see the appropriate errors.

  This graph also provides the master data steward a good feeling of which attributes are having maximum impact on quality to investigate why the business users creating the data are unable to provide correct values in these fields. For example, providing appropriate onscreen help or using validation features may improve the quality of data entered in these fields.

  You can drill down from here to break the results down based on further dimensions. For example, you can see whether the earlier runs also resulted in more errors due to the product type field or determine which products were the most difficult for end users to classify properly during data entry.

  The drilldown screens also enable you to slice and dice the erroneous records based on various product attributes and across remediation runs. For example, you can add more dimensions to your analysis to see how many errors were caused on a combination of attributes. An example is shown in Figure 8.81. This allows the master data administrator to identify patterns and help plug weak spots in the data create process.

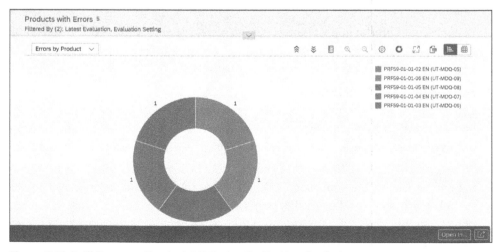

Figure 8.81 Drill Down on Product Attributes for Further Analysis

This screen allows you to further visualize the results in various graphical formats to improve comparison and provide better analysis, as shown in Figure 8.82.

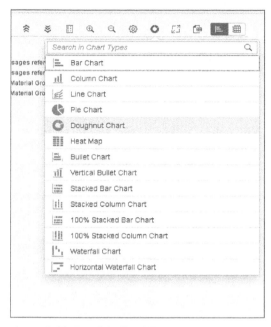

Figure 8.82 Possible Chart Types

You can also toggle between a **List View** and a **Chart View** on this screen. After you've sliced and diced the data and reached the level of classification or grouping that you're looking for, you can jump straight into the records by clicking on the **Open In** button on the bottom of your screen. You can then dive straight into the worklist and start processing the errors.

- **Products with Errors**

  This graph lists the top products that have caused the maximum violations in the current evaluation run. It breaks up the total numbers of errors, groups them by **Product ID**, and gives you a count per product. Again, from here, you can drill down and go to the **List** overview and start processing the errors. For example, if you have product owners in your business dealing with various groups of products, this list will help you identify the product owners with whom you should sit down to analyze this further and see what measures you can take to avoid errors from happening. You can also collaborate with them directly by sending them the list via an email directly from the screen.

- **Rule Violations**

  This graph breaks down the total errors and gives you a count per rule that was violated. It lists the top rules that were violated by maximum number of records. You can drill down to go to the record level and work on the records.

As a master data administrator in your organization, you can also assign different graphs with different attribute level breakdowns to different product owners in your organization. Each product owner gets to see how his products are faring in terms of master data quality. In general, the tiles help you understand the results of the remediation run and act on the results by giving you insights into various attributes and reasons that are leading to data quality violations in your underlying SAP S/4HANA system.

8.6.3   Configuration

As shown in Figure 8.83, a good starting point for master data remediation configuration is Transaction **MDQIMG**. Most of your settings for remediation can be configured from this transaction. However, because remediation reuses some capabilities from consolidation, some of the settings must be done in Transaction **MDCIMG**.

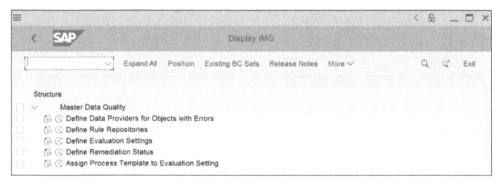

Figure 8.83 Master Data Quality: Remediation Customizing Settings

The **Data Providers of Objects with Errors** Customizing setting allows you to define a logical data source from where you can import data errors, as shown in Figure 8.84. The IMG path is (Transaction **MDQIMG**) **Master Data Quality** • **Define Data Providers for Objects with Errors**.

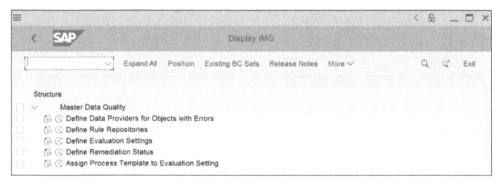

Figure 8.84 Define Data Providers of Objects with Errors

The rule repository is a logical repository for rules from which you can link one logical repository per object type, as shown in Figure 8.85. The IMG path is (Transaction **MDQIMG**): **Master Data Quality • Define Rule Repository**.

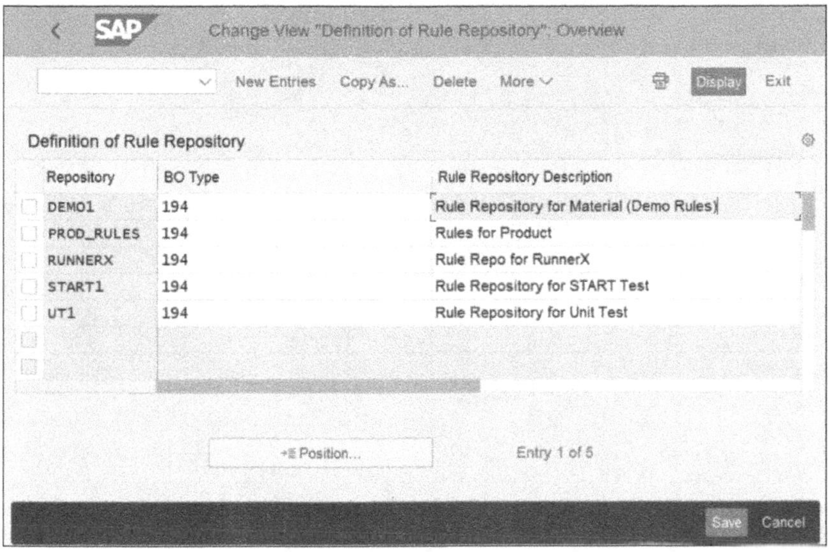

Figure 8.85 Define Rule Repositories

As discussed earlier, **Evaluation Settings** is the Customizing setting that brings together different attributes for your remediation run. As shown in Figure 8.86, you can create an evaluation setting name and then link this with a rule repository, which in turn is bound to a business object type (as of SAP S/4HANA 1709, it was only for product master, BO Type 194). You can also give a description for the **Evaluation Settings** and specify how you plan to bring in the error data.

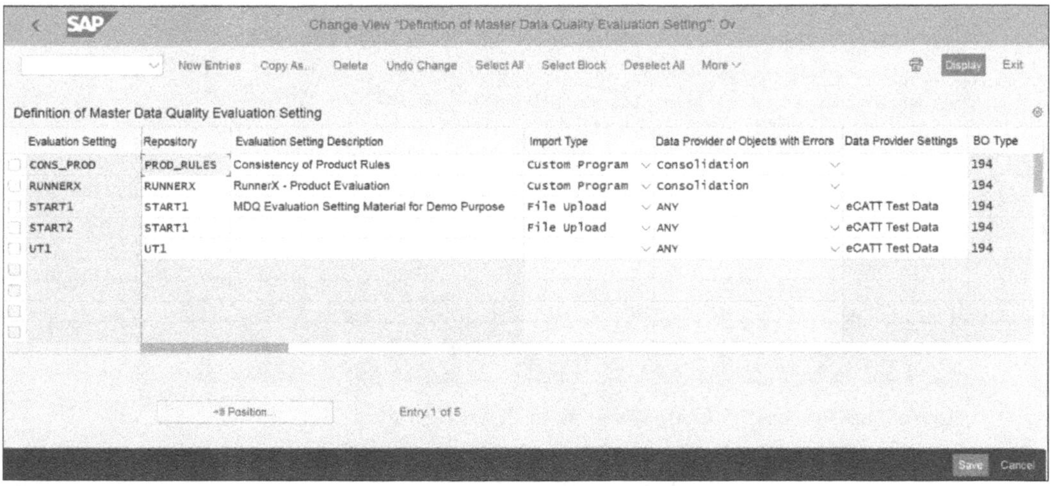

Figure 8.86 Customizing for Evaluation Setting

You can also maintain the description for error status with the **Definition of Status of Error Resolution** Customizing setting, as shown in Figure 8.87. This status is what you'll use in the worklist when setting the status for error records. The IMG path is (Transaction **MDQIMG**): **Master Data Quality · Define Remediation Status**.

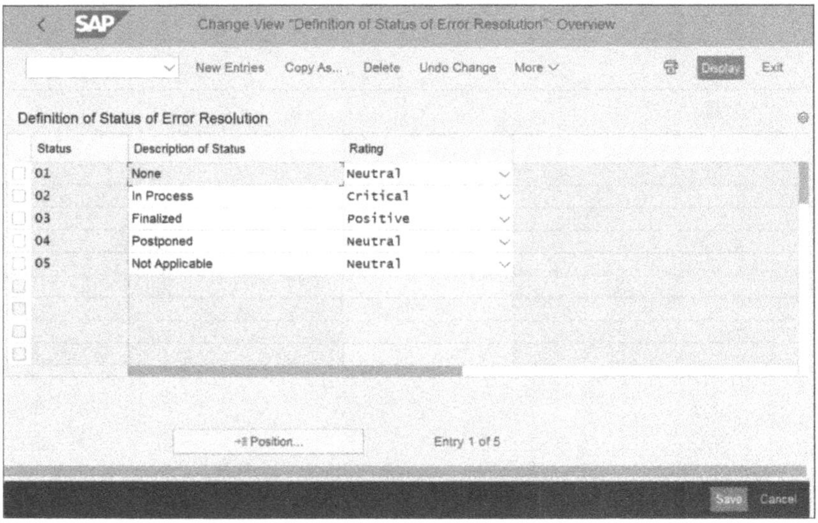

Figure 8.87 Remediation Status Customizing

And, finally, you assign the **Evaluation Settings** to a process template that you'll use for your remediation run, as shown in Figure 8.88. The IMG path is (Transaction MDQIMG): **Master Data Quality · Assign Process Template to Evaluation Setting**.

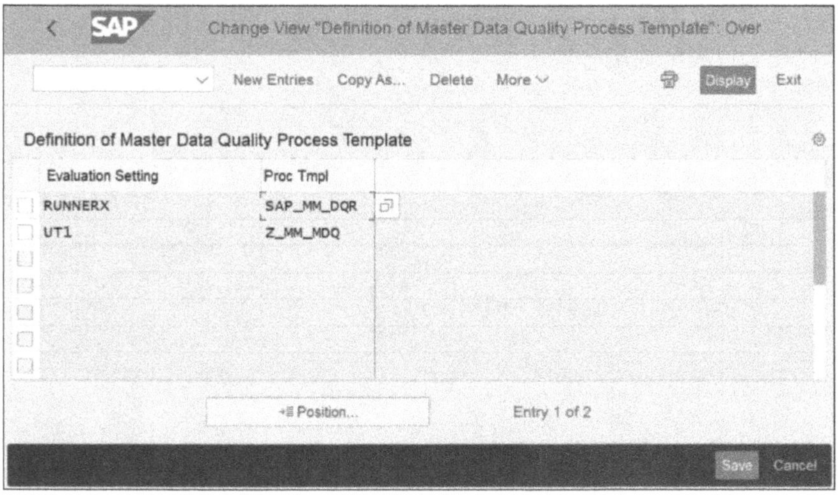

Figure 8.88 Process Template Assignment Customizing

The process template itself, as mentioned earlier, will be configured in the same Customizing setting as your **Consolidation** screen. The IMG path as shown in Figure 8.89 is

(Transaction **MDCIMG**): **Master Data Governance, Consolidation and Mass Processing •
Configure Process Template • Specify Process Template.**

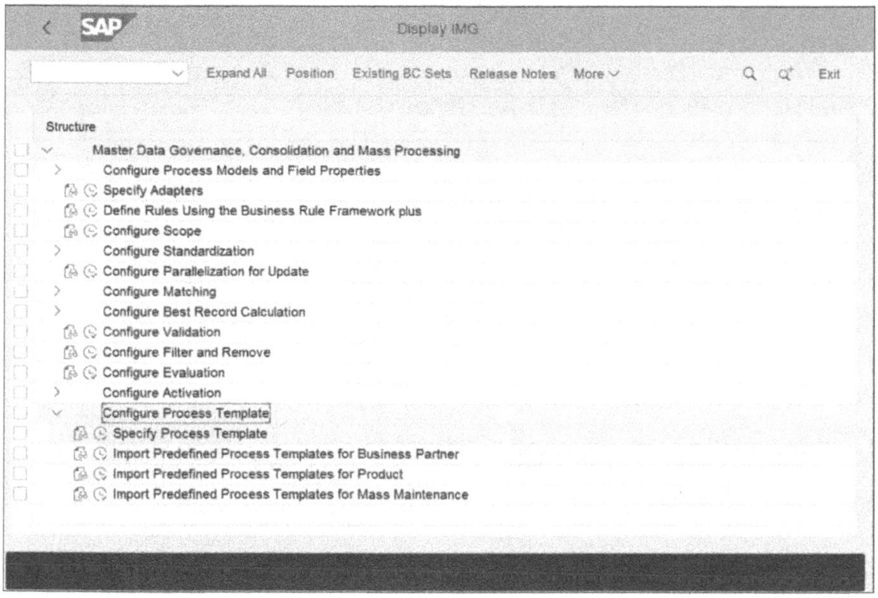

Figure 8.89 Specify Process Template in Transaction MDCIMG

By executing this node, you can drill down to create a **Process Template** (see Figure
8.90).

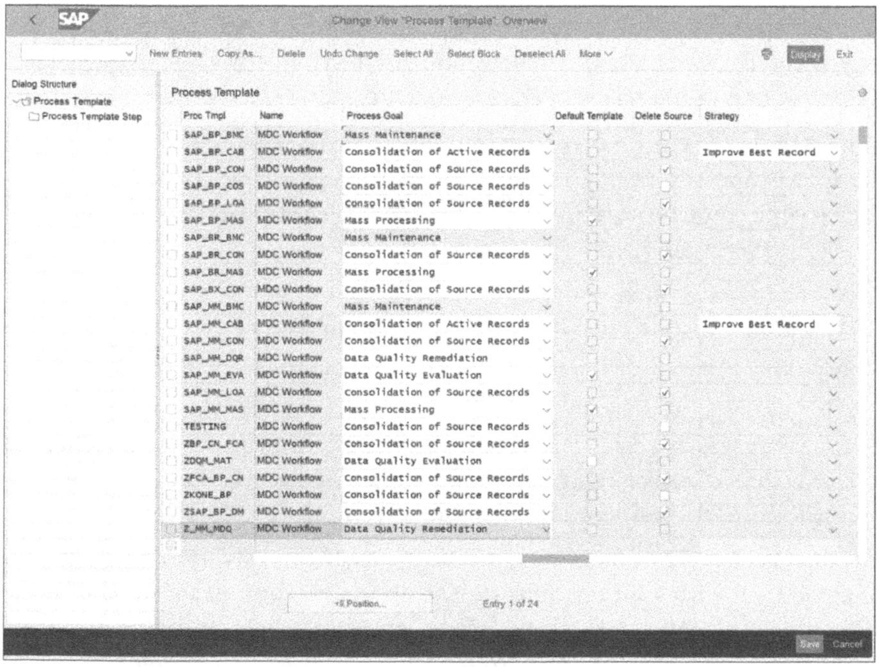

Figure 8.90 Change View "Process Template" Overview Screen

Figure 8.91 shows the details of **Process Template Step**.

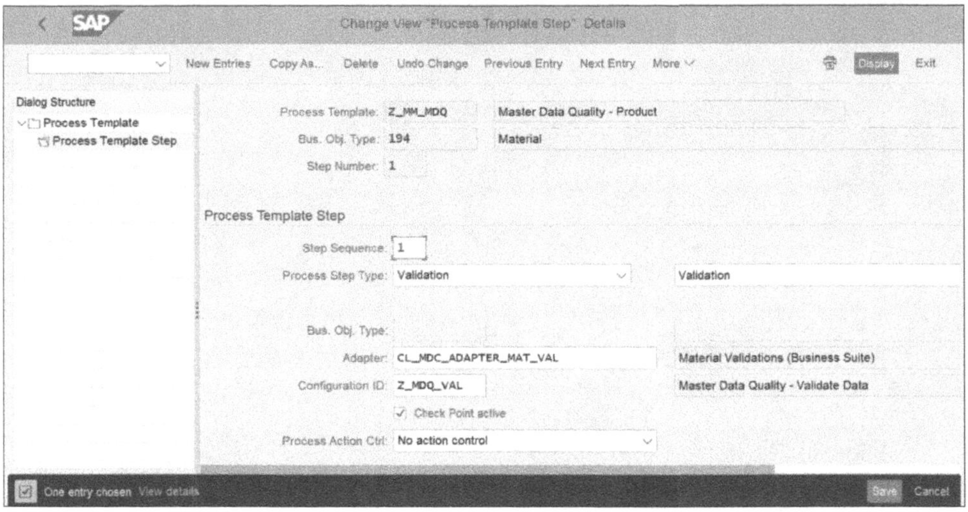

Figure 8.91 Process Template Details

Tip

You'll notice that most of the Customizing settings are already prefilled with entries when you install and activate SAP Master Data Governance. This should be enough for you to start using the system and trying out your first remediation process flow.

Putting all the capabilities together, you can run an end-to-end data remediation process. Now you should have a fair idea of how remediation works. As a review, the logical flow of steps for the end-to-end process are as follows:

1. You start with loading errors coming from an external validation tool using the Manage Import app or selecting a set of records to validate using the Start Remediation Process app. After you've done that, you run the records through validation and write the errors into a worklist.

2. When you have many such remediation processes running, you use the Manage Remediation Process app to keep an eye on different processes to check their status and to get an overview of their dates of creation and completion, number of errors, and so on.

3. After validation, you use the Data Quality Worklist app to look at the details of errors, sort error records based on various attributes, and act on them, for example, by sending them to a governance process for correction.

4. You can then use the Data Quality Overview app to get an overview of your last run and to compare it with your previous runs. It also allows you to slice and dice the error list based on different product criteria to get better insight into what is causing quality issues. You can also drill down to see the root cause of the problem.

> **Note**
>
> Remember that the data quality remediation capabilities of SAP Master Data Governance are only supported in SAP Master Data Governance on SAP S/4HANA starting from 1709 onward and isn't available on SAP Master Data Governance with SAP ERP.

8.7   SAP Master Data Governance: Data Quality Management Content for SAP Analytics Cloud

In addition to the Process and Change Analytics Core Data Services (CDS) views, additional SAP Master Data Governance content can be enabled in SAP Analytics Cloud. Standard SAP Analytics Cloud business content for data quality analysis are available out of the box. The standard business content can be imported into SAP Analytics Cloud to view the SAP Analytics Cloud stories for **SAP Master Data Governance Data Quality Analysis for Business Partners** and **SAP Master Data Governance Data Quality Analysis for Products**. This illustrated in Figure 8.92 and Figure 8.93.

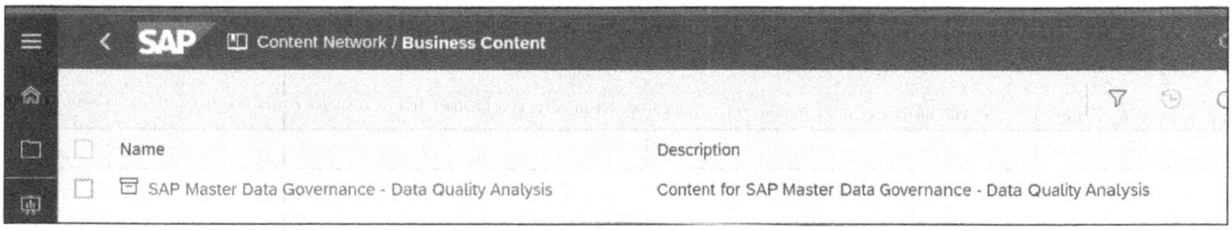

Figure 8.92 SAP Analytics Cloud Business Content for SAP Master Data Governance - Data Quality Analysis

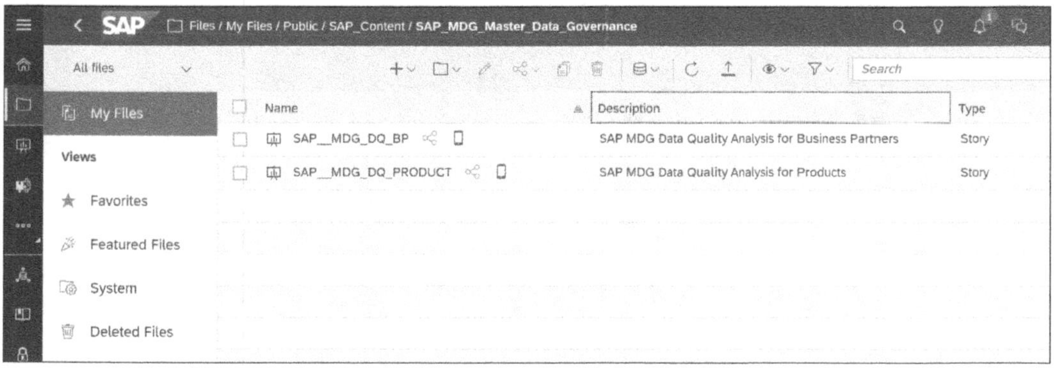

Figure 8.93 SAP Analytics Cloud Dashboards for SAP Master Data Governance Data Quality Analysis

With a live data connection from SAP Master Data Governance system to SAP Analytics Cloud, users can view the master data quality dashboard in SAP Analytics Cloud. Figure

8.94 illustrates the **Data Quality Overview for Business Partners** dashboard, and Figure 8.95 illustrates the **Data Quality Overview for Products** dashboard.

Figure 8.94 SAP Analytics Content - Data Quality Overview for Business Partners

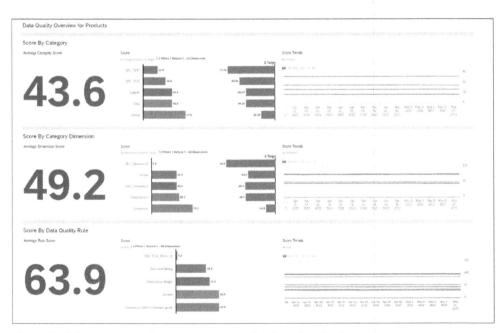

Figure 8.95 SAP Analytics Content - Data Quality Overview for Products

8.8   Summary

This chapter provided an overview of data quality and search functionalities in an SAP Master Data Governance project. It explained various options available in the framework that can be used for improving and maintaining the quality of master data in SAP Master Data Governance. Detailed instructions were also provided to help you when making design decisions and configuring data quality rules using various techniques for different scenarios. Integration components and options between SAP Master Data Governance and other SAP/non-SAP applications and data enrichment tools were also discussed. Duplicate checks and data quality remediation functionalities were explained in detail. Additionally, SAP Data Quality Management for business partners and products functionality in SAP Master Data Governance was discussed in detail. We covered the data quality remediation functionality for getting the master data clean in SAP Master Data Governance with its relevant configurations. A brief introduction to SAP Master Data Governance Data Quality Management standard content for SAP Analytics Cloud was provided.

In the next chapter, you'll learn about the consolidation and mass processing functionality of SAP Master Data Governance available for product and business partner master data.

Chapter 9
Consolidation and Mass Processing

Consolidation and mass processing are key capabilities that help us manage data in large volumes, especially in a distributed master data landscape. In this chapter, consolidation and mass processing scenarios, use cases, and process flows are covered via a walk-through of prerequisite settings and configuration activities. Technical architecture and initial data load options are also discussed. Additionally, the consolidation and mass processing framework for custom objects will be explained in detail along with its various steps.

When master data maintenance is spread across multiple systems, companies have no single view of master data. With different systems or regions having ownership of different segments of the master data, it becomes difficult to coordinate the maintenance and processes, resulting in overall poor data quality. Multiple connections across the multiple source systems complicate the integration environment and hence affect the data quality aspects as well.

There are several business processes in an organization that each interact with one or more master data domains. A cohesive master data management strategy helps elevate the conversation from data quality and governance issues with master data to efficient business processes and practices. Businesses can start to monitor the key performance indicators (KPIs)/business metrics and focus on the success of the business goals. Consolidating the master data into a central master data management hub, is the first step in the process of getting a handle on the problems plaguing the master data in an enterprise. After the master data is centralized, master data teams can focus on introducing governance processes to improve the master data quality.

The SAP Master Data Governance system has been architected as two separate functionalities: consolidation and central governance. These two scenarios are delivered to work as independent solutions addressing various business challenges in the master data management journey, but they can also be optionally integrated with each other to leverage functionalities from both scenarios.

Figure 9.1 shows possible combinations of the consolidation and central governance functionalities that can be used to achieve quality master data while centrally governing ongoing master data maintenance.

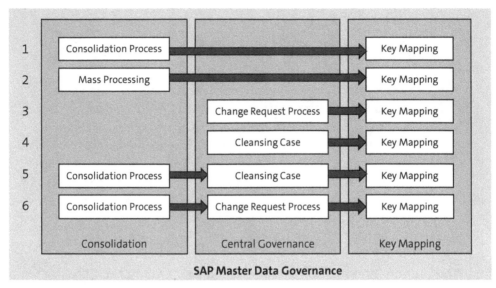

Figure 9.1 Integrated Consolidation and Central Governance Functionalities

The consolidation scenario in SAP Master Data Governance is a pipeline process where the data is staged, standardized, enriched, and, optionally, matched with the existing master data with the view of eliminating duplication. Automated rules then combine the identified duplicate master data to create the best record representation of the master data.

In addition to consolidation capabilities, SAP has also introduced mass processing features. Although it may turn out to be a risky, time-consuming, and costly exercise, master data teams often feel the need to update multiple records in their systems en masse for various business reasons. Even if IT comes out with some quick solutions, they may not be compliant from an auditing perspective and hence expose the company to unnecessary and bigger risks. Not to mention, that without the right set of tools, working with large volumes of data could be slow and error prone.

SAP realized the need to address this common pain point for most companies and delivered the mass processing capability in SAP Master Data Governance. This mass processing functionality uses SAP Fiori as the user interface (UI), allowing master data specialists to perform their mass updates intuitively. The statistics and profiling capabilities provide confidence and transparency while dealing with large volumes of master data.

For recurring loads, variant configurations can be created to make the execution fast by reducing or eliminating unnecessary steps.

Erroneous records in mass processing can be removed from the process during review, and all activities at the process level are tracked with an audit trail available in the SAP Fiori UI.

Mass processing reuses the same technical foundation and framework used by consolidation. Thanks to queuing and parallelization options, even large volumes can be executed without any performance challenges. In addition, you can schedule the updates in background processing. Currently, the mass processing functionality is offered out of the box for business partner, customer, supplier, and material objects. Custom objects are also supported as long as the necessary configurations are complete.

Interestingly, you can use the mass processing capability in different combinations:

- With or without central governance
- Activation with or without a change request
- Integration of mass processing with central governance and reuse of business rules and validations

Currently, objects implemented in SAP Master Data Governance flex mode aren't supported out of the box. The mass processing functionality has multiple steps with different sets of activities performed in each step. These activities will be discussed in more detail later in this chapter.

9.1   Use Cases

Several common use cases motivate companies to use master data consolidation and mass processing capabilities to achieve their organizational goals and clean their master data.

As consolidation and mass processing are relatively new in the master data space, we'll first look at how and where they may fit into your overall enterprise information management (EIM) and governance strategy. We'll also discuss what problems and pain areas can be addressed using consolidation and mass processing.

Following are some common use cases for consolidation

- **New mergers or acquisitions**
  In this very common use case, a company is getting merged with or acquired by another company and thus needs to integrate with systems and reporting applications. For a singular view of what the merged entities look like, it's important to bring together the master data of both organizations, harmonize the data, and arrive at a golden set of records

- **Preparing for central governance**
  For various reasons, most companies have more than one SAP ERP system in their landscape with disparate master data. Now, while trying to align with the corporate goals for their master data, central governance often takes center stage. To realize these goals and make the initiative around central governance successful, it's imperative that existing master data is properly cleansed, enriched, and de-duplicated.

Consolidation helps you prepare your master data before you start governing it centrally.

- **Implementing consolidation with central governance**
Cleansing and consolidating master data isn't an easy and quick job that any tool can perform. It's a lengthy process where thousands of decisions must be made by data owners and data stewards located in different locations. This is a collective process where regional master data experts and stewards across business lines play a significant role when they make decisions about potential duplicates or incomplete data. The consolidation process facilitates user-friendly and accurate decision-making about master data. As a native component, consolidation makes it easy to integrate with central governance and reuse some of the functionalities, including validation and activation processes. Thus, the consolidation scenario complements the implementation of central governance in preparing golden records and avoiding any duplicates being pushed into the central governance repositories during the initial load.

- **Implementing consolidation without central governance**
Not all organizations are able to move to a central governance model right away. This could be due to various reasons, including the nature of your business, the way the organization is structured, or the fact that your master data processes aren't mature enough to enforce a central governance model. So, for the time being, the organization would continue working with master data in a decentralized manner. Nevertheless, they would need a golden set of data from time to time, for various organizations purposes, for example, enterprise-wide reporting such as unified financial reporting or procurement reports, and so on.

> **Note**
>
> It's important to note that, not all functionalities of consolidation and mass processing that are available in SAP Master Data Governance versions on SAP S/4HANA will be available on SAP Master Data Governance with SAP ERP.

Many times, there is a business requirement to change large volumes of records. For example, when a vendor changes the description of many of their materials., some organization change forces you to change the person responsible for a certain type of material group, or some country-level legal changes are put in force, your organization decides to change the way they classify their business partners.

The mass processing solution of SAP Master Data Governance provides you an easy and convenient solution that allows you to select, filter, and change the values of multiple master data records at the same time while ensuring that all changes are audited and transparent.

9.2   Setting Up the Environment for Consolidation and Mass Processing

Consolidation requires configurations to make it operational and running. These configurations control various features and functionalities of consolidation and mass processing. The following subsections cover some prerequisite steps that are generally applicable in a typical consolidation system setup.

9.2.1   Activate Business Functions

Typically, it's necessary for the implementation team to activate relevant business functions for an SAP application as a prerequisite. These SAP business functions in SAP S/4HANA or SAP ERP systems can be activated using Transaction SFW5. Manual activation is required when running SAP Master Data Governance with SAP ERP, whereas these business functions are activated by default if you're using SAP Master Data Governance on SAP S/4HANA. Figure 9.2 shows the initial navigational screen in Transaction SFW5 for a user where consolidation and mass processing business functions can be found.

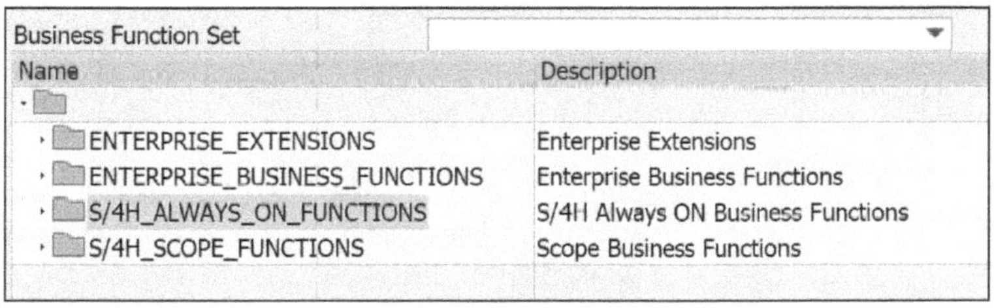

Figure 9.2 Activation of Business Functions

Figure 9.3 shows the business functions relevant for consolidation and mass processing functionalities.

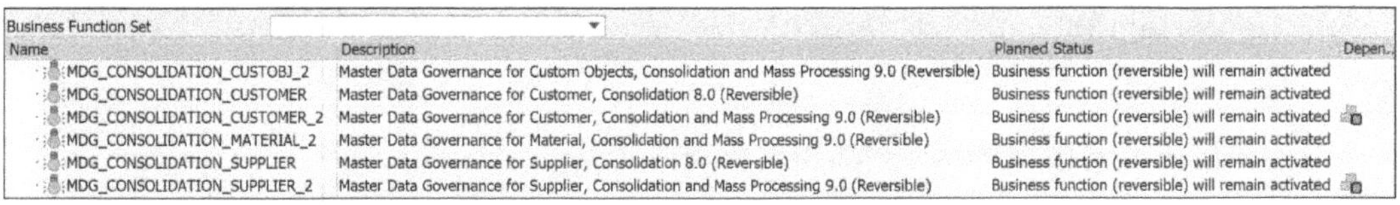

Figure 9.3 Consolidation and Mass Processing Business Functions

9.2.2   Activate Transaction SICF Services

Some of the Transaction SICF services commonly used for consolidation and mass processing are listed in Table 9.1.

Services	Service Name	System	Use
MD_CMPCONFCOS1	MD CMP Configure Custom Objects	SAP Fiori frontend system	SAP Gateway
MD_CMPEXPFILES1	MD CMP Export Master Data into File	SAP Fiori frontend system	SAP Gateway
MD_CMPIMPFILES1	MD CMP Import Master Data from File	SAP Fiori frontend system	SAP Gateway
MD_CMPMANSDATS1	MD CMP Manage Source Data	SAP Fiori frontend system	SAP Gateway
MD_CMPMONPROCS1	MD CMP Monitor Process	SAP Fiori frontend system	SAP Gateway
MD_CMPTRACKCHS1	MD CMP Track Changes	SAP Fiori frontend system	SAP Gateway
MD_CUSTMIZINGS1	MDC Customizing	SAP Fiori frontend system	SAP Gateway
MDC_HDB_MATCH	Match Configurations Overview	Backend system	Web Dynpro
MDC_HDB_MATCH_CONF	Create Match Configuration	Backend system	Web Dynpro
MDG_HDB_SV_GENERATION	Search View Generation	Backend system	Web Dynpro
MDG_HDB_SV_INITIAL	Search View Initial UI	Backend system	Web Dynpro

Table 9.1 Required Consolidation

These services can be activated via the following path in the consolidation system: **Transaction SICF • Provide Service Name • Execute • Activate**.

9.2.3   Authorization Objects and Roles

Table 9.2 lists the authorization objects related to consolidation and mass processing.

Authorization Object	Name
B_BUPA_GRP	Business Partner: Authorization Groups
B_BUPA_RLT	Business Partner: Business Partner Roles
B_BUPR_BZT	Business Partner Relationships: Relationship Categories

Table 9.2 Authorization Objects for Consolidation and Mass Processing

Authorization Object	Name
C_KLAH_BKL	Authorization for Classification
C_TCLA_BKA	Authorization for Class Types
C_TCLS_BER	Authorization for Org. Areas in Classification System
C_TCLS_MNT	Authorization for Characteristics of Org. Area
F_KNA1_BED	Customer: Account Authorization
F_KNA1_GEN	Customer: Central Data
F_LFA1_BEK	Vendor: Account Authorization
F_LFA1_GEN	Vendor: Central Data
M_MATE_MAR	Material Master: Material Types
M_MATE_MAT	Material Master: Materials
M_MATE_WGR	Material Master: Material Groups
MDC_ADMIN	Administrative Permissions
MDC_LOAD	Load Permissions
MDC_MASS	Mass Update Permissions
MDC_MASSBS	Mass Maintenance Permissions
MDC_PFILT	Consolidation Cluster Permissions
MDC_PROOT	Consolidation Root Permissions
S_BGRFC	Authorization Object for NW bgRFC

Table 9.2 Authorization Objects for Consolidation and Mass Processing (Cont.)

The required frontend authorization roles are listed in Table 9.3.

Authorization Role	Name
SAP_BR_BUPA_MASTER_SPECIALIST	Master Data Specialist - Business Partner Data
SAP_BR_BPC_EXPERT: Configuration Expert	Business Process Configuration
SAP_BR_PRODMASTER_SPECIALIST	Master Data Specialist - Product Data

Table 9.3 Standard Frontend Authorization Roles for Consolidation and Mass Processing

The required backend authorization roles are listed in Table 9.4.

Authorization Role	Name
AP_MD_MDC_ADMIN_APP_05	MDG, Consolidation and Mass Processing: Administrator
SAP_MD_MDC_DISP_BP_APP_05	MDG, Consolidation and Mass Processing: Business Partner Display
SAP_MD_MDC_SPEC_BP_APP_05	MDG, Consolidation and Mass Processing: Business Partner Specialist
SAP_MD_MDC_DISP_BP_NOBS_APP_05	MDG, Consolidation and Mass Processing: Business Partner Non-SAP
SAP_MD_MDC_SPEC_BP_NOBS_APP_05	MDG, Consolidation and Mass Processing: Business Partner Non-SAP
SAP_MD_MDC_DISP_MM_APP_05	MDG, Consolidation and Mass Processing: Material Display
SAP_MD_MDC_SPEC_MM_APP_05	MDG, Consolidation and Mass Processing: Material Specialist
SAP_MD_MDC_ADM_CUSTOBJ_APP_05	MDG, Consolidation and Mass Processing: Custom Objects Administrator
SAP_MD_MDC_DISP_CUSTOBJ_APP_05	MDG, Consolidation and Mass Processing: Custom Objects Display Customer
SAP_MD_MDC_SPEC_CUSTOBJ_APP_05	MDG, Consolidation and Mass Processing: Custom Objects Specialist

Table 9.4 Standard Backend Authorization Roles for Consolidation and Mass Processing

9.2.4   Grant Permissions and Privileges for SAP HANA-Based Fuzzy Matching

Following are the permissions to work with views and rulesets in SAP S/4HANA:

- Create packages and write objects into packages
- Create, change, and drop attribute views
- Create, change, and drop SQL views
- Create, execute, and drop rulesets

Following are the privileges to work with views and rulesets in SAP S/4HANA:

- Execute for the EXECUTE_SEARCH_RULE_SET(SYS) object of the SYS schema
- Execute for the GET_PROCEDURE_OBJECTS object of the SYS schema
- Execute for the TRUNCATE_PROCEDURE_OBJECTS object of the SYS schema

9.2.5   Basic Configuration for Background Remote Function Calls

Executing asynchronous web services requires settings to ensure trouble-free processing. For this task, you must configure such system components as AUTOABAP, remote function call (RFC), background RFC (bgRFC), and Internet Communication Framework (ICF) that were set by the web service runtime. Remote-enabled function modules (SRT_TECHNICAL_SETUP, SRT_TECHNICAL_SETUP_RESET) are provided to operate a central configuration. For automated setup of bgRFC, follow SAP Note 1043195, which includes the configuration of a web service runtime.

9.2.6   Determination of Business System

Business systems play a significant role in consolidation and mass processing. It's necessary to differentiate in records/loads from various source systems, maintaining the key mappings automatically based on best record calculation and while replicating to the connected target systems after completion of the consolidation process. To identify the business system, there are two options:

- Connect the SAP Master Data Governance hub system and the source systems to the System Landscape Directory (SLD). To verify the correctness of the SLD content, run Transaction SLDCHECK in the SAP Master Data Governance hub and client systems.
- Implement Business Add-In (BAdI) MDG_IDM_GET_LCL_SYSTEM to determine the local system ID. To implement the BAdI, follow the path, **Master Data Governance · Central governance · General Settings · Data Replication · Define Custom Settings for Data Replication · Define Technical Settings · BAdI: Determination of Local System Name**.

9.2.7   Set Up the Workflow

SAP delivers the standard workflow template WS54500001 for consolidation and mass processing. Linkage type activation settings are needed to make the workflows work for consolidation and mass processing. Transaction SWE2 can be run to verify and configure the necessary settings. The **Linkage Activated** checkbox must be unchecked for other receiver types of the BUS2240 object type and the STARTED event. The receiver type is defined by entering the **Receiver Type Function Module** "MDC_RECEIVER_TYPE_GET". You must ensure that **Receiver Function Module** "SWW_WI_CREATE_VIA_EVENT_IBF" is entered.

Note

Don't enter the workflow template as the **Receiver Type** in type linkage.

The Customizing for the BUS2240 object type is delivered in client 000 in Transaction SWE2.

For more details on setup activities of workflows, refer to Chapter 7.

9.3   SAP-Delivered Data Models

SAP delivers master data objects out of the box as part of the consolidation and mass processing framework. However, the framework also supports creating your own custom objects as needed. Custom objects will be explained in detail later in this chapter.

> **Note**
>
> Not all the objects delivered by SAP and partner solution extensions are delivered with the consolidation and mass processing framework. For nondelivered objects, we'll describe the use of the custom object framework in Section 9.9.

Material and business partner are the only delivered master data objects covered as part of the following SAP-delivered process models:

- Business partner (BO type 147)
- Business partner relationships (BO type 1405)
- Business partner for consolidation (BO type MDC_147)
- Material (BO type 194)

Figure 9.4 shows an example of various sets of business partner, customer, and supplier tables that support the process steps in the consolidation and mass processing framework. Data is imported by loading data in corresponding *_SRC tables and creating data sets that can be used for creating consolidation processes. After a consolidation process is created, the data snapshot is copied to corresponding *_PRC tables with every step.

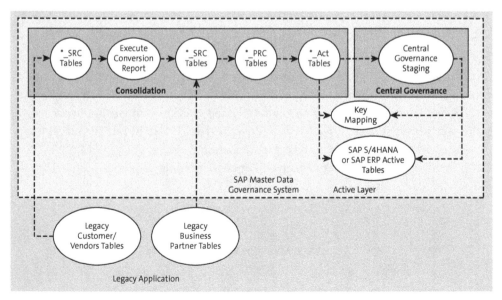

Figure 9.4 Table Types Hosting Data for Consolidation and Mass Processing with Business Partners, Vendors, and Customers: Example Load and Process

For example, in a process template with three process steps, if you're in the second step, then there will be two entries visible against a single record. Similarly, in step 3, there will be three entries for the same corresponding record. However, after activation, all the process step entries for the activated records will be removed from the same *_PRC tables.

> **Note**
>
> Consolidation and mass processing leverage various sets of tables to support their processes. These tables can be accessed by searching for *_SRC, *_PRC, and *_ACT in Transaction SE16N.

9.3.1 Overview of Process Models

Each of the business objects in the consolidation and mass processing process models consists of one or more tables with each table containing one of more fields.

If any data models are extended, it's necessary to generate Business Rules Framework plus (BRFplus) artifacts for any data quality rules. To generate all BRFplus structures and functions for a specific business object, you click on the **Resultant Artifacts** button, choose a package name, and then click on **Apply BRF+ Artifacts**. The IMG path for this configuration is as follows: **Cross-Application Components** • **Processes and Tools for Enterprise Applications** • **Master Data Governance** • **Master Data Governance, Consolidation and Mass Processing** • **Configure Process Models and Field Properties** • **Configure Process Models**.

For each business object, various properties can be configured at the table level or at the field level to control features and behaviors of the application. The table-level properties are listed in Table 9.5 with explanations.

Property	Explanation
Root	Identifies whether the table is a root table
Process	Identifies whether the table is relevant for process data
Omit Rule	Indicates whether the table omits rules for the best records calculation step
BRF+	Indicates whether BRFplus-based business rules are allowed for the table
Hidden	Indicates whether the table will remain hidden from the standard SAP Fiori–based UI
Switch	Indicates the switch ID in the switch framework

Table 9.5 Table-Level Properties

Property	Explanation
Reaction	Indicates whether an object attached to a switch of the switch framework should be displayed or hidden in switch position "On" (possible values: **Display** and **Hide**)
Delete Instance	Signifies a model object's stance regarding its record deletion during the best record calculation step when the UI offers the possibility to delete duplicate data (possible values: **No restriction**, **Prohibit**, and **Allow after Key Mapping**)

Table 9.5 Table-Level Properties (Cont.)

The field-level properties are listed in Table 9.6 with explanations.

Property	Explanation
Technical	Identifies whether a field should be allowed for processing in the material design components framework
Read only	Identifies whether a field should be read-only on the SAP Fiori UI
Selective	Indicates whether a field can be included in the selection criteria on the SAP Fiori UI
Hidden	Identifies whether a field should remain hidden on the SAP Fiori UI

Table 9.6 Field-Level Properties

Note

After changing any configurations in this IMG activity, it's important to clear the cache. To do so for the corresponding business object, click on **Reset Cache**.

9.3.2   Business Partner and Relationships

Similar to central governance, in the consolidation and mass processing framework, business partner is the leading and foundational master data object not only for the business partner data model but also for customer and vendor master data. For any consolidation, mass processing, or central governance operations in SAP Master Data Governance, each of the customer and vendor records must be assigned to a corresponding parent business partner.

Consolidation and mass processing is delivered with three process models related to the business partner object itself. Each of these delivered process models have varying scope coverage as well as some overlaps in terms of the tables that are part of these process models. Appropriate process models should be selected and leveraged based on specific business requirements. A comparison summary of the tables in each of the delivered process models for business partners is shown in Table 9.7.

Business Object Type	Objects Included	Validation	Handover to Central Governance
Business Partner (147)	Business partner, customer, and supplier	The validation uses SAP ERP checks.	Records can be activated with central governance using change requests and cleansing cases or can be activated directly.
Business Partner Relationship (1405)	Business partner relationship	The validation uses SAP ERP checks.	Records can be activated with SAP Master Data Governance using a change request or can be activated directly.
Business Partner for Consolidation (MDC_147)	Business partner, customer, and supplier	SAP doesn't deliver a validation step, so no SAP ERP checks are used.	Records will be stored in their own tables independent of the usual business partner tables. This can be used for analytical use cases; for example, BUT000 data will be stored in table BUT000_ACT.

Table 9.7 Various Delivered Business Partner Object Types and Properties

Table 9.8 provides a comparison summary of business object types delivered for various business partner–related business object types and their respective table coverages as delivered with consolidation and mass processing.

Table Name	Table Description	1405: Business Partner Relationship	147: Business Partner	MDC_147: Business Partner for Consolidation
ADCP	Workplace Data	Yes	No	No
ADR12	Workplace URL	Yes	Yes	Yes
ADR2	Workplace Phone	Yes	Yes	Yes
ADR3	Workplace Fax	Yes	Yes	Yes
ADR6	Workplace Email	Yes	Yes	Yes
ADRC	Address	No	Yes	Yes
ADRP	Person Data	No	Yes	Yes
BUT000	General	No	Yes	Yes

Table 9.8 Tables Supported by Various Business Partner Object Types in the Consolidation and Mass Processing Framework

Table Name	Table Description	1405: Business Partner Relationship	147: Business Partner	MDC_147: Business Partner for Consolidation
BUT020	Technical Link Table for Addresses	No	Yes	Yes
BUT021_FS	Address Usage	No	Yes	Yes
BUT050	General	Yes	No	No
BUT050_TD	Time Dependency	Yes	No	No
BUT051	Contact Person Data	Yes	No	No
BUT052	Workplace Address	Yes	No	No
BUT053	Company Interest	Yes	No	No
BUTOBK	Bank Account	No	Yes	Yes
BUTOID	Identifier	No	Yes	Yes
BUTOIS	Industry	No	Yes	Yes
BUT100	Role	No	Yes	Yes
CVI_CUST_LINK	Technical Link Business Partner to Customer	No	Yes	No
CVI_VEND_LINK	Technical Link Business Partner to Supplier	No	Yes	No
DFKKBPTAXNUM	Tax Number	No	Yes	Yes
KNA1	Customer General	No	Yes	Yes
KNA1_ASSGMNT	Additional SAP ERP Customers	No	Yes	No
KNA1_AUSP	Characteristics (Customer)	No	Yes	No

Table 9.8 Tables Supported by Various Business Partner Object Types in the Consolidation and Mass Processing Framework (Cont.)

Table Name	Table Description	1405: Business Partner Relationship	147: Business Partner	MDC_147: Business Partner for Consolidation
KNA1_INOB_AUSP	Transient Technical Link to Customer Valuations	No	Yes	No
KNA1_INOB_KSSK	Transient Technical Link to Customer Class Assignments	No	Yes	No
KNA1_KSSK	Class Assignment (Customer)	No	Yes	No
KNB1	Company Code (Customer)	No	Yes	Yes
KNB5	Dunning (Customer)	No	Yes	Yes
KNBW	Withholding Tax (Customer)	No	Yes	Yes
KNVI	Tax Indicator	No	Yes	Yes
KNVP	Partner Function (Customer)	No	Yes	Yes
KNVV	Sales Data	No	Yes	Yes
LFA1	Supplier General	No	Yes	Yes
LFA1_ASSGMNT	Additional SAP ERP Vendors	No	Yes	No
LFA1_AUSP	Characteristics (Supplier)	No	Yes	No
LFA1_INOB_KSSK	Transient Technical Link to Supplier Class Assignments	No	Yes	No
LFA1_KSSK	Class Assignment (Supplier)	No	Yes	No
LFB1	Company Code (Supplier)	No	Yes	Yes

Table 9.8 Tables Supported by Various Business Partner Object Types in the Consolidation and Mass Processing Framework (Cont.)

Table Name	Table Description	1405: Business Partner Relationship	147: Business Partner	MDC_147: Business Partner for Consolidation
LFB5	Dunning (Supplier)	No	Yes	Yes
LFBW	Withholding Tax (Supplier)	No	Yes	Yes
LFM1	Purchasing Organization Data	No	Yes	Yes
LFM2	Purchasing Data	No	Yes	Yes
WYT1	Vendor Subrange	No	Yes	Yes
WYT1T	Text Table Vendor Subranges	No	Yes	Yes
WYT3	Partner Function (Supplier)	No	Yes	Yes

Table 9.8 Tables Supported by Various Business Partner Object Types in the Consolidation and Mass Processing Framework (Cont.)

9.3.3   Material

SAP delivers a process model for material with the consolidation and mass processing framework. Its business object type ID is 194. This process model uses SAP ERP checks. For this process model, records can be activated with central governance using change requests, or they can be activated directly after the consolidation process is complete.

Table 9.9 shows a comparison summary of the tables used for materials.

Table Name	Table Description	194: Material
CKMLCR	Material Ledger Prices	Yes
CKMLHD	Material Ledger General	Yes
CKMLPR	Material Ledger Future Prices	Yes
MAKT	Description	Yes
MAPR	Forecasting	Yes
MARA	Basic Data	Yes
MARA_AEOI	Change Management	Yes

Table 9.9 Tables Supported by Material Object Types in the Consolidation and Mass Processing Framework

Table Name	Table Description	194: Material
MARA_AUSP	Characteristics	Yes
MARA_DRAD	Document Assignment	Yes
MARA_DRAD_STXH	Document Assignment: Text General	Yes
MARA_DRAD_STXL	Document Assignment: Text	Yes
MARA_INOB_AUSP	Transient Technical Link to Valuations	Yes
MARA_INOB_KSSK	Transient Technical Link to Class Assignments	Yes
MARA_KSSK	Class Assignment	Yes
MARA_STXH	Basic Data: Text General	Yes
MARA_STXL	Basic Data: Text	Yes
MARC	Plant Data	Yes
MARC_STXH	Plant: Text General	Yes
MARC_STXL	Plant: Text	Yes
MARD	Storage Location	Yes
MARM	Dimensions	Yes
MATERIALID	Material Identification	Yes
MBEW	Accounting	Yes
MDMA	MRPArea	Yes
MEAN	GTIN	Yes
MKAL	Production Version	Yes
MLAN	Tax	Yes
MLGN	Warehouse	Yes
MLGT	Warehouse Storage Type	Yes
MVKE	Sales Data	Yes
MVKE_STXH	Sales: Text General	Yes

Table 9.9 Tables Supported by Material Object Types in the Consolidation and Mass Processing Framework (Cont.)

Table Name	Table Description	194: Material
MVKE_STXL	Sales: Text	Yes
PGMI	Product Group/Member Allocation	Yes
PGZU	Planning Material	Yes
PROP	Forecast Parameters	Yes
QMAT	Inspection Lot	Yes

Table 9.9 Tables Supported by Material Object Types in the Consolidation and Mass Processing Framework (Cont.)

9.4   Process Steps Overview and Configuration

SAP Master Data Governance is meant to facilitate data consistency across multiple applications for streamlined business processes as well as enterprise reporting. Combining and maintaining the master data formerly located in multiple systems in a single hub and linking the records in different systems are the key goals. The consolidation process contributes to achieving these goals with certain process steps and various activities performed at each step.

A typical consolidation and mass processing process is designed with the help of a set of process steps in an appropriate sequence that makes sense from a business requirement perspective. Each of these process steps is required to be assigned to appropriate adapters to run features and functionalities within the application.

SAP delivers several adapters out of the box that can be leveraged for the right combination of business object type and applicable process step.

> **Note**
> - Not all adapters are necessarily applicable on all business object types, but some adapters can be leveraged across different business object types.
> - Not all adapters can necessarily be leveraged for more than one process steps in a given process template.
> - New custom adapters can be created as needed.

Table 9.10 provides a summary of various adapters delivered by SAP for consolidation and mass processing process steps, including for what object types they can be leveraged.

Process Step	Process Step Adapter	Adapter Description	Business Partner Relationship (1405)	Business Partner (147)	Business Partner Consolidation (MDC_147)	Material (194)
Activation	CL_MDC_ADAPT-ER_BP_ACT	Activation for Business Partner		✓	✓	
Activation	CL_MDC_ADAPT-ER_BPREL_ACT	Activation of Business Partner Relationships	✓			
Activation	CL_MDC_ADAPT-ER_MAT_ACT	Activation for Material				✓
Best Record Calculation	CL_MDC_ADAPT-ER_BP_BRC	Business Partner Best Record Calculation		✓	✓	
Best Record Calculation	CL_MDC_ADAPT-ER_BPREL_BRC	BRC for Business Partner Relationships	✓			
Best Record Calculation	CL_MDC_ADAPT-ER_MAT_BRC	Material Best Record Calculation				✓
Edit	CL_MDC_ADAPT-ER_EDI	Interactive Mass Processing	✓	✓		✓
Evaluation	CL_MDQ_RULE_EVALUATION_ADAPTER	Master Data Quality Rule Evaluation				✓
Filter and Remove	CL_MDC_ADAPT-ER_BP_FAR	Delete Business Partners with Incomplete Address Data		✓		
Filter and Remove	CL_MDC_ADAPT-ER_FAR	Filter and Remove	✓	✓		✓
Matching	CL_MDC_ADAPT-ER_986_MTC	New SAP HANA Fuzzy Search				
Matching	CL_MDC_ADAPT-ER_BP_IM_MTC	SAP HANA Smart Data Quality		✓	✓	

Table 9.10 Summary of Delivered Adapters for Various Process Steps and Object Types

Process Step	Process Step Adapter	Adapter Description	Business Partner Relationship (1405)	Business Partner (147)	Business Partner Consolidation (MDC_147)	Material (194)
Matching	CL_MDC_ADAPT-ER_BPREL_METC	Matching of Business Partner Relationships	✓			
Matching	CL_MDC_ADAPT-ER_FUZZY_MTC	SAP HANA Fuzzy Search		✓		✓
Matching	CL_MDC_ADAPT-ER_MAT_MTC	Material Matching (Old Material Number)				✓
Matching	CL_MDC_ADAPT-ER_MTC	New SAP HANA Fuzzy Search		✓		✓
Replication	CL_MDC_ADAPT-ER_BP_REP	Business Partner Replication with DRF		✓		
Replication	CL_MDC_ADAPT-ER_MAT_REP	MDC Material Replication via DRK				✓
Standardization	CL_MDC_ADAPT-ER_BP_IM_STD	SAP HANA Smart Data Quality		✓	✓	
Standardization	CL_MDC_ADAPT-ER_BP_KEY_MAP_STD	Evaluate Key Mapping for Business Partners and SAP ERP Customers/Suppliers		✓		
Standardization	CL_MDC_ADAPT-ER_BP_VALUME-MAP_STD	Evaluate Value Mapping for Business Partners and SAP ERP Customers/Suppliers		✓		
Standardization	CL_MDC_ADAPT-ER_BPREL_STD_VALM	Value Mapping for Business Partner Relationships	✓			
Standardization	CL_MDC_ADAPT-ER_BRF_STD	BRFplus	✓	✓	✓	✓

Table 9.10 Summary of Delivered Adapters for Various Process Steps and Object Types (Cont.)

Process Step	Process Step Adapter	Adapter Description	Business Partner Relationship (1405)	Business Partner (147)	Business Partner Consolidation (MDC_147)	Material (194)
Standardization	CL_MDC_ADAPTER_MAT_KEY_MAP_STD	Evaluate Key Mapping for Material				✓
Standardization	CL_MDC_ADAPTER_MAT_VALMAP_STD	Evaluate Value Mapping for Material				✓
Update	CL_MDC_ADAPTER_BRF_UPD	BRFplus	✓	✓	✓	✓
Validation	CL_MDC_ADAPTER_BP_VAL	Business Partner Validations (SAP Business Suite)		✓		
Validation	CL_MDC_ADAPTER_BPREL_VAL	Validation of Business Partner Relationships	✓			
Validation	CL_MDC_ADAPTER_MAT_VAL	Material Validations (SAP Business Suite)				✓

Table 9.10 Summary of Delivered Adapters for Various Process Steps and Object Types (Cont.)

Now let's look at some details about some commonly used process steps in consolidation and mass processing.

9.4.1   Standardization

Standardization is typically one of the first steps in the consolidation process that normalizes and enriches master data. An example is address validation, which ensures that specific address-related data, such as streets or cities, truly exists.

There are two parts in address validation in consolidation:

- **Enrichment**
  In this process, fields required for performing a business process are missing in the master data; for example, a postal code value is missing for an address with street

name Crescent Plaza Dr. in city Houston, TX. The enrichment process fills in the missing field value to postal code "77077" based on the provided address.

- **Normalization**
  In this process, all occurrences of the same string are delineated in the same way. In such cases, the standard comes from some authority, such as the postal services. An example of normalization is converting a value of a street name from "Crescent Plaza Dr." to "Crescent Plaza Drive".

Following are the adapters used for standardization purposes in the consolidation process:

- `CL_MDC_ADAPTER_BPREL_STD_VALM` (Value Mapping for Business Partner Relationships)
- `CL_MDC_ADAPTER_BP_IM_STD` (SAP HANA Smart Data Quality)
- `CL_MDC_ADAPTER_BP_KEY_MAP_STD` (Evaluate Key Mapping for Business Partners and SAP ERP Customers/Vendors)
- `CL_MDC_ADAPTER_BP_VALUEMAP_STD` (Evaluate Value Mapping for Business Partners and SAP ERP Customers/Vendors)
- `CL_MDC_ADAPTER_BRF_STD` (Business Partner Standardization with BRFplus)
- `CL_MDC_ADAPTER_MAT_KEY_MAP_STD` (Evaluate Key Mapping for Material)
- `CL_MDC_ADAPTER_MAT_VALUEMAP_STD` (Evaluate Value Mapping for Material)

The IMG path for performing standardization activities in consolidation is as follows: **Cross-Application Components • Processes and Tools for Enterprise Applications • Master Data Governance • Consolidation and Mass Processing • Configure Standardization.**

In standardization Customizing activities, parallelization of the standardization adapters for BRFplus, Business Address Services (BAS), key mapping, and value mapping is maintained.

The Customizing activity **Specify Process Template** specifies whether and in what configurations the standardization adapter is used as part of the consolidation process. Note that standardization runs without further configuration, but with parallelization of processes, it can be used for improving the performance during standardization.

Follow these steps in the Customizing activity for parallelization of standardization:

1. Select new entries.
2. Enter a **Config. ID** and **Description.**
3. In the **Number of Processes** field, enter the number of processes you want to be processed in parallel.
4. Enter the **Prefix for Queue Name.**

In addition, through the Customizing activity, Business Configuration Set (BC Set) `CA-MDG-EE-BP_IMHANA_C01` (MDG-BP Consolidation: IM in SAP HANA) can be activated. This

BC Set contains predefined sets of table entries that are required to run the process steps standardization and matching with the adapters for SAP HANA smart data quality.

Setting up the bgRFC inbound destination is a prerequisite for using parallelization during consolidation. You can run Transaction SBGRFCCONF to set up the RFC destination. Click on **Create** to maintain a new **Define Inbound Destination** entry. Enter "MDC_QUEUE_" in the **Prefixes** field.

If the bgRFC destination isn't created manually, users should have authorization object SBGRFC assigned with activity 02 and type 07. In such a case, automatic creation of the inbound destination will occur as soon as a user triggers execution of the consolidation process for the first time.

Figure 9.5 shows the screen visible to consolidation users before executing the standardization step. Click **Continue** to see the standardization results during the consolidation process. Figure 9.6 depicts the result screen after executing the standardization results during the consolidation process.

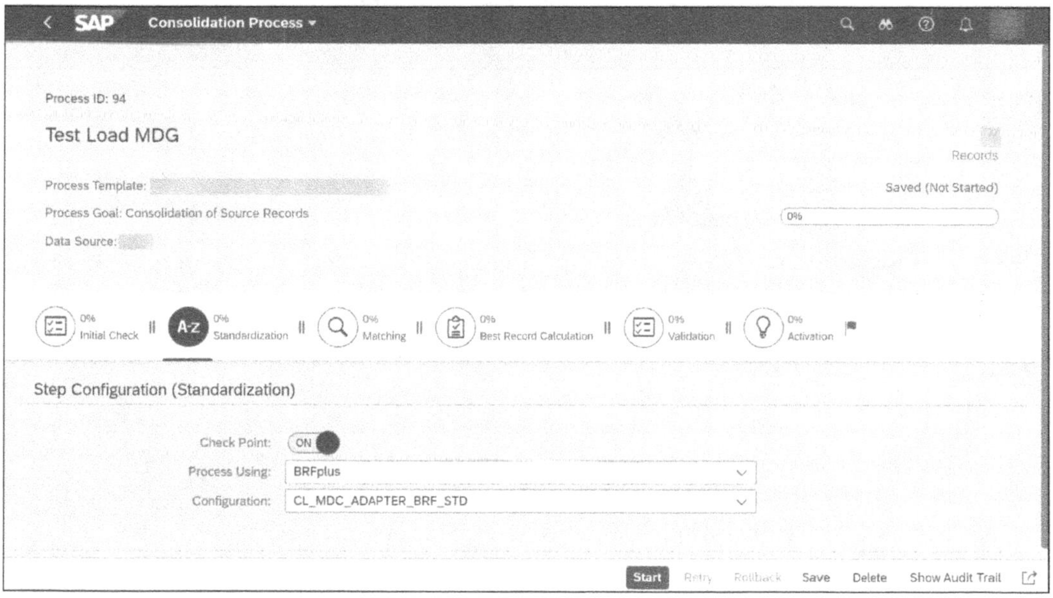

Figure 9.5 Standardization Screen in Consolidation

Further details of the master data can be accessed via the **Results** screen in the standardization step. This screen shows the content of all affected tables in each process step and allows you to navigate between tables using tabs. For example, for a business partner, you can check **Overview**, **General**, **Address**, **Phone**, **Fax**, **Bank Account**, and **Tax Number** information, as shown in Figure 9.7.

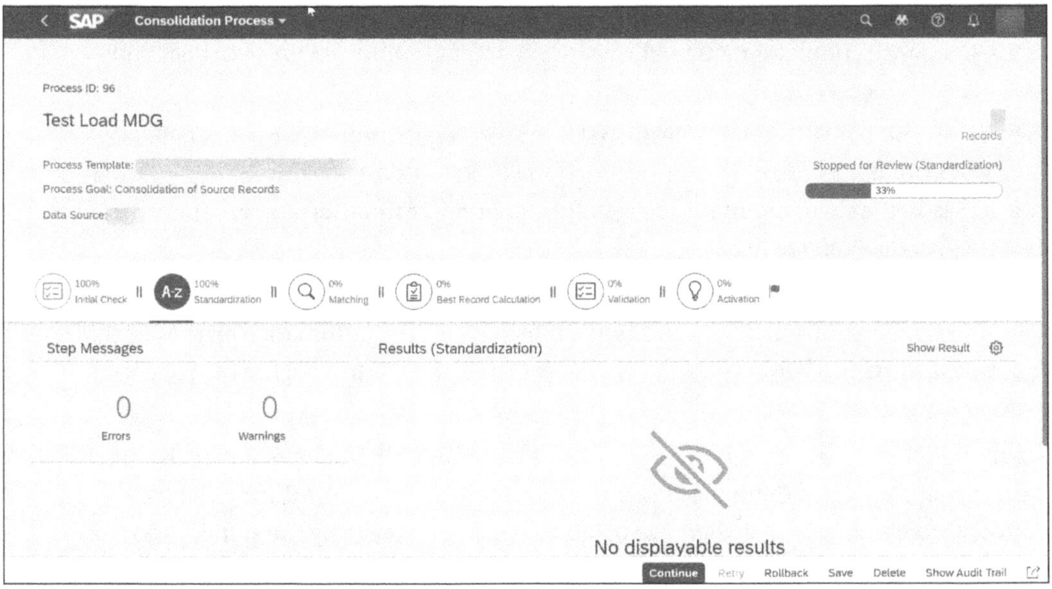

Figure 9.6 Standardization Results during the Consolidation Process

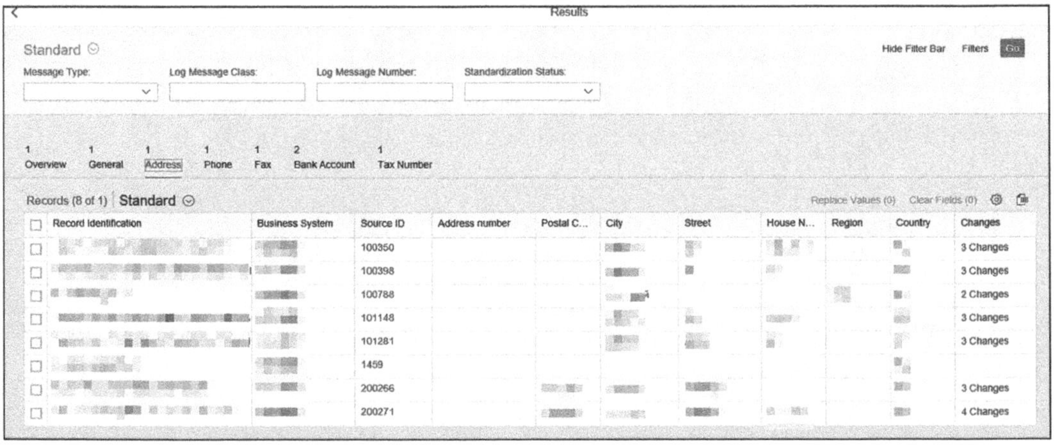

Figure 9.7 Results Screen of the Standardization Step of the Consolidation Process

9.4.2   Update and Edit

You can also perform BRFplus-based checks and data enrichments in consolidation and mass processing to improve the data quality. Adapter CL_MDC_ADAPTER_BRF_UPD (BRF-plus) can be used for this purpose. For more information on how a BRFplus rule can be created, refer to Chapter 8 or check *http://help.sap.com*.

The mass processing functionality also involves editing the master data as part of the process. Adapter CL_MDC_ADAPTER_EDI (Interactive Mass Processing) is delivered for this process step and can be leveraged accordingly.

Figure 9.8 depicts the **Edit** step during a mass processing scenario.

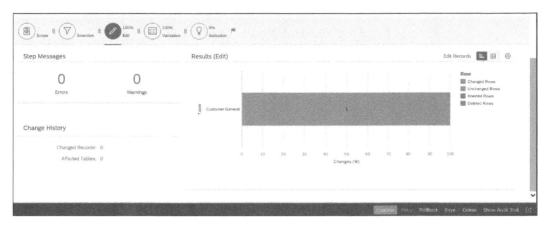

Figure 9.8 User's Screen for Editing in a Mass Processing Process

The **Configure Scope** Customizing activity can be used to configure the default scope for mass process. This default scope is displayed on the **Scope** screen in the SAP Fiori UI. This scope determines the fields that are available in the **Edit** step of the SAP Fiori UI.

To configure the scope, run the Customizing activity under the following IMG path: **Cross-Application Components • Master Data Governance • Consolidation and Mass Processing • Configure Scope**.

Following are the activities to be performed:

1. Select **New Entries**.
2. Enter a **Scope ID** and a **Scope Description**.
3. Enter a **BO Type** using the entry help.
4. Mark the scope you created, and select **Scope Fields**.
5. Select **New Entries**.
6. Enter a **Table** using the entry help.
7. Enter a **Field Name** using the entry help.
8. Choose **Next Entry** to enter more fields.

9.4.3   Matching

Matching in consolidation is performed to check and compare data from various source applications and the active area with the purpose of identifying potential duplicates. Records that are identified as potential duplicates are presented in match groups, and then these match groups are reviewed for potential duplicates. For this purpose, the following adapters are used in the consolidation process:

- `CL_MDC_ADAPTER_BPREL_MTC` (Matching of Business Partner Relationships)
- `CL_MDC_ADAPTER_BP_IM_MTC` (SAP HANA Smart Data Quality)
- `CL_MDC_ADAPTER_FUZZY_MTC` (SAP HANA Fuzzy Search)
- `CL_MDC_ADAPTER_MAT_MTC` (Material Matching – Old Number)
- `CL_MDC_ADAPTER_MTC` (New SAP HANA Fuzzy Search)
- `CL_MDC_ADAPTER_986_MTC` (New SAP HANA Fuzzy Search)

The IMG path for performing matching-related activities in consolidation is **Cross-Application Components · Processes and Tools for Enterprise Applications · Master Data Governance · Consolidation and Mass Processing · Configure Matching.**

Match Configurations for Fuzzy Matching

In this Customizing activity, a match configuration is defined and generated that can be used by SAP HANA for matching master data records while using fuzzy match. These configuration entries are used during the configuration of process templates for assigning step type matching and adapter SAP HANA fuzzy search. After this configuration is maintained, rulesets can be created in SAP HANA Studio to meet the specific requirements, which eventually can be found in the packages created for match configuration.

The SAP HANA fuzzy search is a fast and fault-tolerant search feature that can return records even if the search term has typos or missing letters. While comparing two terms or two strings, scores are created using a fuzzy search algorithm. A higher score means the strings are similar and vice versa. The scores may vary between 0.0 (lowest) and 1.0 (highest).

Note that a prerequisite for performing this activity is that the client must allow cross-client changes. In addition, the ruleset naming convention should be used while performing the configuration in consolidation (i.e., `<Matchconfigurationname>_RULE-SET.searchruleset`).

SAP provides standard match configurations that can be used as a template to define and generate its own matching configurations:

- `BPMATCH1`
- `MAT_MATCH1`

Figure 9.9 depicts the consolidation screens while generating the match configuration. It also shows the standard match configuration delivered out of the box.

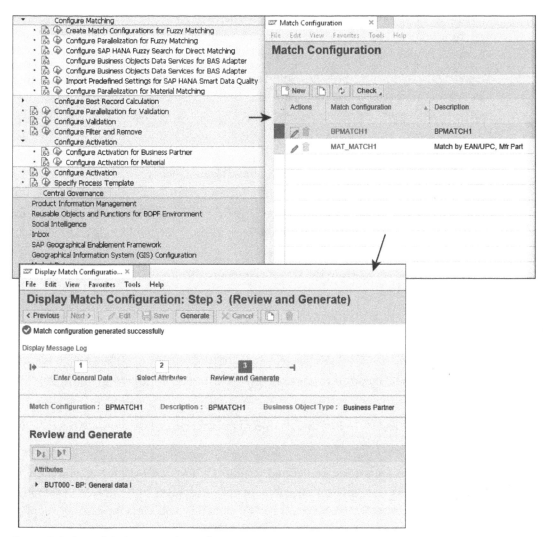

Figure 9.9 Consolidation: Match Configurations

Parallelization for Fuzzy Matching

This Customizing activity determines the number of processes that should be allowed to run in parallel for a given match configuration. In addition, an upper threshold for matches is also defined in this IMG activity for automatically rating two records in the match review process.

> **Note**
>
> In the absence of a choice configured for this IMG activity, the number of processes is considered single processing.

Starting from version SAP Master Data Governance 9.1 and SAP S/4HANA 1709, a new matching adapter for SAP HANA fuzzy search has been provided (CL_MDC_ADAPTER_MTC). This adapter allows a more flexible and easier configuration for the matching rules.

To configure these rules, SAP Fiori app Configure Matching for Consolidation is provided. You can access this app by using the SAP_MDC_BCR_MASTERDATA_ADMIN_T business role (for SAP Master Data Governance with SAP ERP) or SAP_BR_BPC_EXPERT (for SAP Master Data Governance on SAP S/4HANA).

Import Predefined Settings for SAP HANA Smart Data Quality

In this Customizing activity, SAP-delivered BC Set CA-MDG-EE-BP_IMHANA_C01 (MDG-BP Consolidation: IM in SAP HANA) contains predefined sets of table entries that are required to run the matching process steps with the adapters for SAP HANA smart data quality.

From a matching perspective, the BC Set delivered by SAP contains settings for the following matching-related tables:

- Table SIMDQ_CMPRSRC (IM in SAP HANA) for comparing source settings for the match policy
- Table SIMDQ_MTCADDRSTG (IM in SAP HANA) for address settings for the match policy
- Table SIMDQ_MTCFIRMSTG (IM in SAP HANA) for firm settings for the match policy
- Table SIMDQ_MTCPERSTG (IM in SAP HANA) for person settings for the match policy
- Table SIMDQ_MTCCSTMSTG (IM in SAP HANA) for custom component settings for the custom match policy

The IMG path for importing predefined settings for SAP HANA smart data quality in consolidation is **Cross-Application Components • Processes and Tools for Enterprise Applications • Master Data Governance • Consolidation and Mass Processing • Configure Matching • Import Predefined Settings for SAP HANA Smart Data Quality**.

Configure Parallelization for Material Matching

This Customizing activity performs parallelization for adapter CL_MDC_ADAPTER_MAT_MTC for material matching. The matching step checks data from various source systems, loads, and active areas for duplicates. To use parallelization for material matching in consolidation, an RFC destination using bgRFC configuration should already exist.

Figure 9.10 shows a consolidation screen where, after execution of a matching step, results are visible and can be reviewed by users during part of the matching step.

Figure 9.10 Matching Results Summary for Users in the Consolidation Process Step

9.4.4 Best Record Calculation

Best record calculation results in a best record containing the cumulated, most valuable data for each match group identified by the matching process. In other words, in this step for each match group, a best record is calculated. This calculation follows a well-defined process based on a set of rules.

The following adapters support the best record calculation step in consolidation:

- CL_MDC_ADAPTER_BP_BRC (Business Partner Best Record Calculation)
- CL_MDC_ADAPTER_MAT_BRC (Material Best Record Calculation)

The IMG path for performing best record calculation activities in consolidation is **Cross-Application Components • Processes and Tools for Enterprise Applications • Master Data Governance • Consolidation and Mass Processing • Configure Best Record Calculation**.

This Customizing activity provides an overview of the rules for the best record calculation that are part of the standard delivery. You can create new rules based on your business requirements. As stated earlier, in the best record calculation step, the consolidation process calculates a record containing the cumulated, most valuable data for each match group identified by the matching process step. Note that this calculation follows a well-defined process based on certain rules. Figure 9.11 shows the SAP-delivered rules in the IMG, that is, **BRFPLUS**, **COMPLETENESS**, **RECENCY**, and **SOURCE_SYSTEM** settings in consolidation.

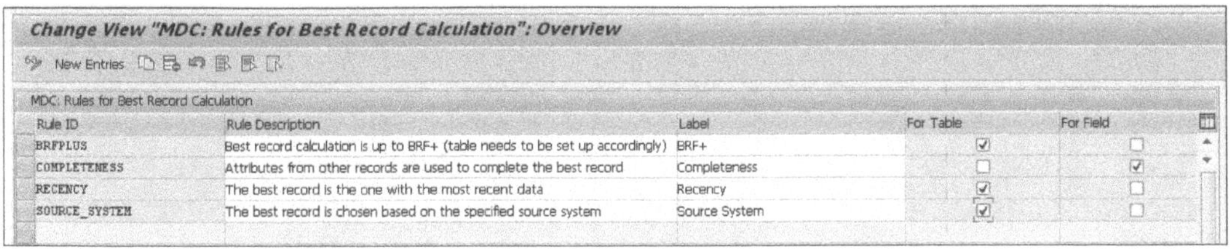

Figure 9.11 IMG Activities: Specifying Rules for Best Record Calculation

Following are some properties of the delivered rules for best record calculation in consolidation:

- When attributes from other records are used to complete the best record, it's called COMPLETENESS. This rule is applied at the field level.
- The best record is the one with the most recent data, which is called RECENCY. This rule is applied at the table level.
- In SOURCE_SYSTEM, the best record is chosen based on the specified source system. This delivered rule is used at the table level.
- Best record calculation can also be based on BRFplus rules, which need to be set up. This rule is applicable at the table level.

After the process matching step has bundled records identified as duplicates into a match group, the system moves these approved records through two steps as described next.

In the first step, the records of a match group are compared at the table level. For a specific table, the source system or the recency can be considered to have higher priority. Depending on this setting, the corresponding data is taken into account for the best record. The information, that is, which source system has a certain priority for a specific table, is maintained in the order of source systems view.

In a second step, the preliminary best record is processed on the field level. If a field doesn't contain data, but completeness is assigned to this field as the highest priority, then the data is completed with data derived from the record with the next higher order. Figure 9.12 shows how an order of rules can be specified using configuration in the best record calculation process step.

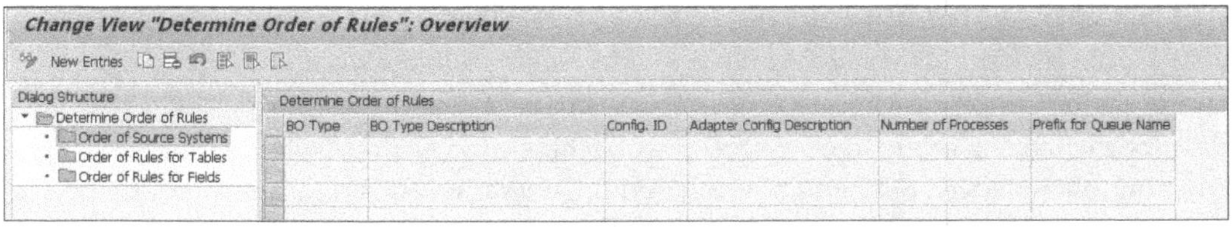

Figure 9.12 Consolidation: Specifying the Order of Rules for Best Record Calculation

With each step, the application indicates the percentage of process completed. Figure 9.13 depicts the best record calculation during consolidation.

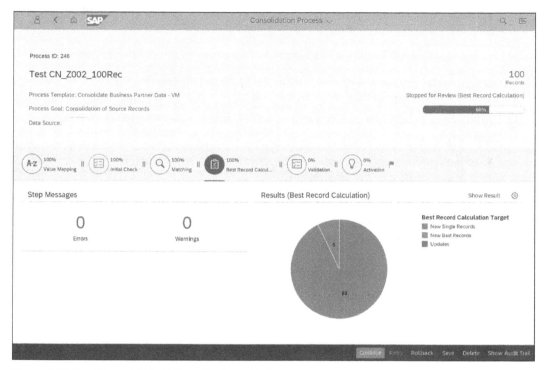

Figure 9.13 Best Record Calculation: Business Partners

You can drill down into the results through this screen. With the help of the **Rollback** button at the bottom, you can roll back to any previous step in the process. In addition, you can rerun the process steps to change settings for the following steps.

9.4.5   Validation

In the validations step, the consolidation process checks the quality of the record to determine if the master data is good enough to meet requirements in the target connected system. The data may be saved if the quality is under the acceptance levels; otherwise, data enrichment can be performed to improve the quality of the data. For this purpose, you can configure parallel processing for the validation step to ensure performance doesn't become a challenge. Following are the adapters that are used during the validation step in the consolidation process for business partner and material business object types:

- CL_MDC_ADAPTER_BP_VAL (Business Partner Validations [SAP Business Suite])
- CL_MDC_ADAPTER_MAT_VAL (Material Validations)
- CL_MDC_ADAPTER_BPREL_VAL (Validation of Business Partner Relationships)

Configurations can be performed to ensure BRFplus and central governance checks are applied on records while they go through the validation step of the consolidation process. Based on the settings, the consolidation process can inherit the following data quality checks:

- Existence checks for reference fields of master data records, such as currency, plants, regions, and so on
- Simple checks, such as address formats, postal code lengths, and so on
- BRFplus modeled business rules and checks
- BAdI-based business rules and checks

The IMG path for performing validation activities in consolidation is **Cross-Application Components · Processes and Tools for Enterprise Applications · Master Data Governance · Consolidation and Mass Processing · Validation.**

> **Note**
> - With the consolidation and mass processing functionalities in the same process template in SAP Master Data Governance, multiple revalidation steps are possible.
> - The rollback functionality allows you to roll back to a specific validation step.
> - For more details on how to create business rules using BRFplus, refer to Chapter 6.

Follow these steps to perform the necessary configuration in the validations step of consolidation and mass processing:

1. Click on **New Entries.**
2. Provide a **Config. ID** and **Description**.
3. In the **Number of Processes** field, enter the number of processes that can be processed in parallel.
4. Enter the **Prefix of the Queue Name.**
5. If you want to execute BRFplus checks, select the **Execute BRFplus Checks** indicator.
6. To execute central governance validation rules, select the **Execute Central Governance Checks (Validation Rules (BRFplus) & BAdI Validations)** indicator.
7. In addition, for filtering the quality of records to the acceptance level, provide a value in the **Threshold** field.

Validation is the fourth step of the consolidation process. Figure 9.14 shows the **Step Configuration (Validation)** screen during the consolidation process. Settings from process templates are adjustable.

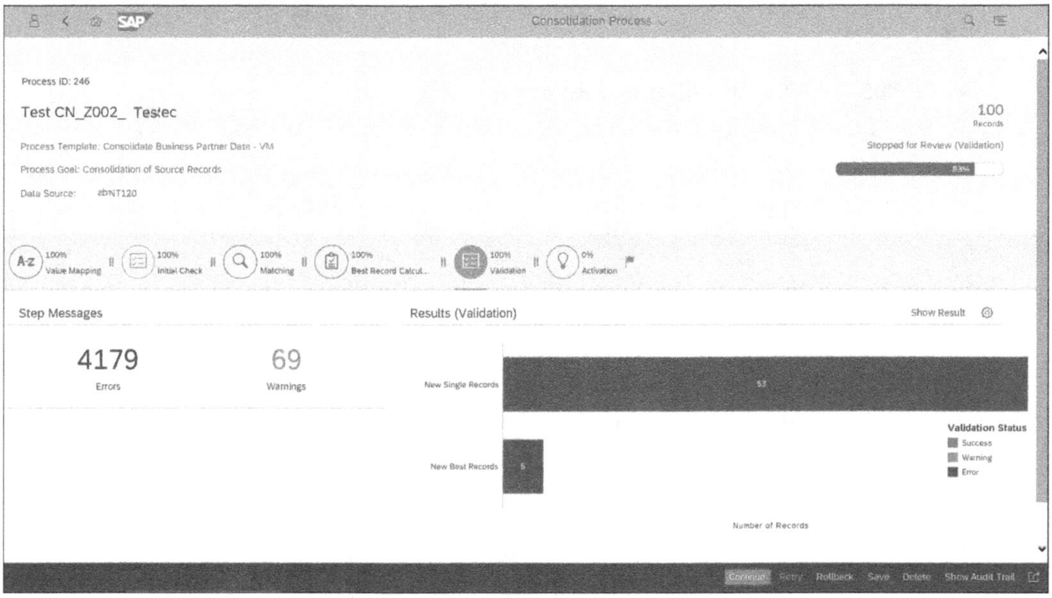

Figure 9.14 Validation Screen during the Consolidation Process

> **Note**
>
> Starting from SAP Master Data Governance on S/4HANA 2020, rules and validations configured in Data Quality Management can be reused in your consolidation and mass processing process flows. You'll learn more about Data Quality Management and how to configure rules in Chapter 8

9.4.6   Filter and Remove

In consolidation, users mainly work on the data quality aspect of multiple records at a time. Hence, it becomes imperative to provide options to filter and remove the unnecessary data during various process steps in consolidation. The filter and remove configuration in consolidation can help to overcome this optional requirement, and you can configure this as a process step. Note that the filter and remove step can be configured only as a successor of matching, best record calculation, or validation. The filter and remove function automatically removes records or moves records into a new duplicate process: after matching, it moves open match groups; after best record calculation, it moves specific groups of records; and after validation, it moves records with warnings or errors.

There are two adapters delivered for this step type:

- **CL_MDC_ADAPTER_BP_FAR (Delete Business Partners with Incomplete Address Data)**
  This adapter helps in removing and deleting all the business partners for which no address data can be found based on the best record calculations. This can be used for object type business partner (147) only.

- **CL_MDC_ADAPTER_FAR (Filter and Remove)**
  Based on the results of the predecessor step, a selection of records is either moved to a parallel consolidation process or removed and deleted. This can be used for object type business partner (147), business partner relationships (1405), and material (194).

9.4.7   Activation

Activation is the final step in the consolidation process where master data will be added in the active area. It's possible to control what should be done with the activated data by maintaining configurations in IMG activities as explained next. Optionally, you can also set up parallelization for the activation process. Normally, there are three possible variations of records for which activation can be applied:

- Records already existing in the active area and hence being updated

- Records that neither exist in the active area nor have any duplicates

- Records that don't exist in the active area but do have potential duplicates

In cases where records could not pass the validations, subsequent specific actions can be configured for each of the systems in scope, including central governance if being used. If central governance is implemented, errored records can also be sent to its staging layer with the help of change request types configured for the scenario to ensure a smooth handshake between the central governance and consolidation functionalities. Following are the adapters used in the activation step of the consolidation process:

- CL_MDC_ADAPTER_BP_ACT (Business Partner Activation in Consolidation)

- CL_MDC_ADAPTER_MAT_ACT (Activation for Material)

- CL_MDC_ADAPTER_BPREL_ACT (Activation of Business Partner Relationships)

The IMG path for performing activation activities in consolidation is **Cross-Application Components • Processes and Tools for Enterprise Applications • Master Data Governance • Consolidation and Mass Processing • Configure Activation for Business Partner**.

Figure 9.15 shows the **Step Configuration (Activation)** execution screen on UI depicting various activation configurations in place.

The following describes the activation-related configuration tasks in consolidation:

1. Click on **New**.
2. Enter a **Configuration ID/Description**.

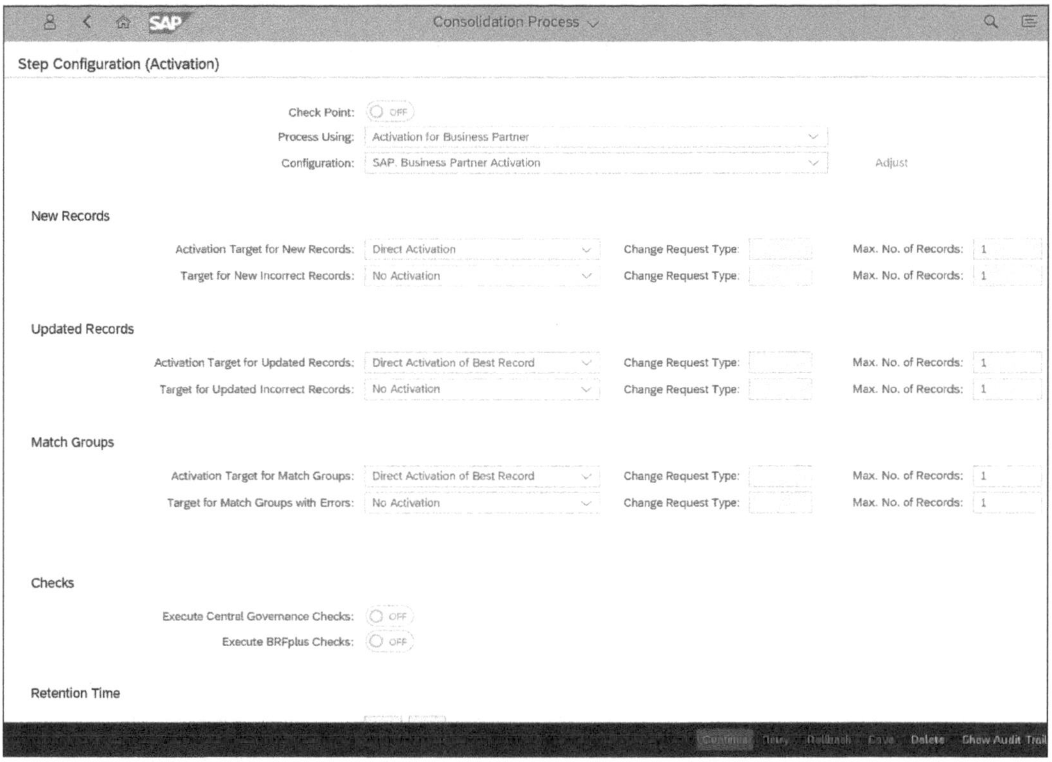

Figure 9.15 Activation Process Step and Configurations during a Consolidation Process

3. In the **Number of Processes** field, enter the number of processes that can be executed in parallel.

4. Enter a prefix in the **Queue Prefix** field.

5. Configure the system settings for **New Records**.

6. In the **New Records** field, select an entry using the input help, and assign a corresponding change request type.

7. In the **New Records with Errors** field, select an entry using the input help, and assign a corresponding change request type.

8. Configure the system settings for **Updated Records**.

9. In the **Updated Records** field, select a value from the list, and assign a corresponding change request type.

10. In the **Updated Records with Errors** field, select a value from the list, and assign a corresponding change request type.

11. Configure the system behavior for **Match Groups**.

12. Select a value from the list and assign a corresponding change request type for this activity.

13. Select a value for the **Match Groups with Errors** field and assign a corresponding change request type.

14. For replicating the records to connected downstream systems, set the **Call DRF after Activation** checkbox. This checkbox is normally set if activation using change requests is used. This flag can't be set in SAP Master Data Governance on SAP S/4HANA. In this environment, the replication will be managed by SAP S/4HANA automatically.

15. If central governance business rules have to be used during the validation process, set the **Execute Central Governance Checks (Validation Rules (BRFplus) & BAdI validation** indicator. If the **BRF+ check** indicator is set, then BRFplus rules will be used during validations.

Activation step configurations for materials can be similar to business partners, or they can be different based on material-specific business requirements. The IMG path for activation configurations of materials is **Cross-Application Components • Processes and Tools for Enterprise Applications • Master Data Governance • Consolidation and Mass Processing • Configure Activation for Material**.

Figure 9.16 shows the IMG configuration screen for activation-specific settings for materials in consolidation.

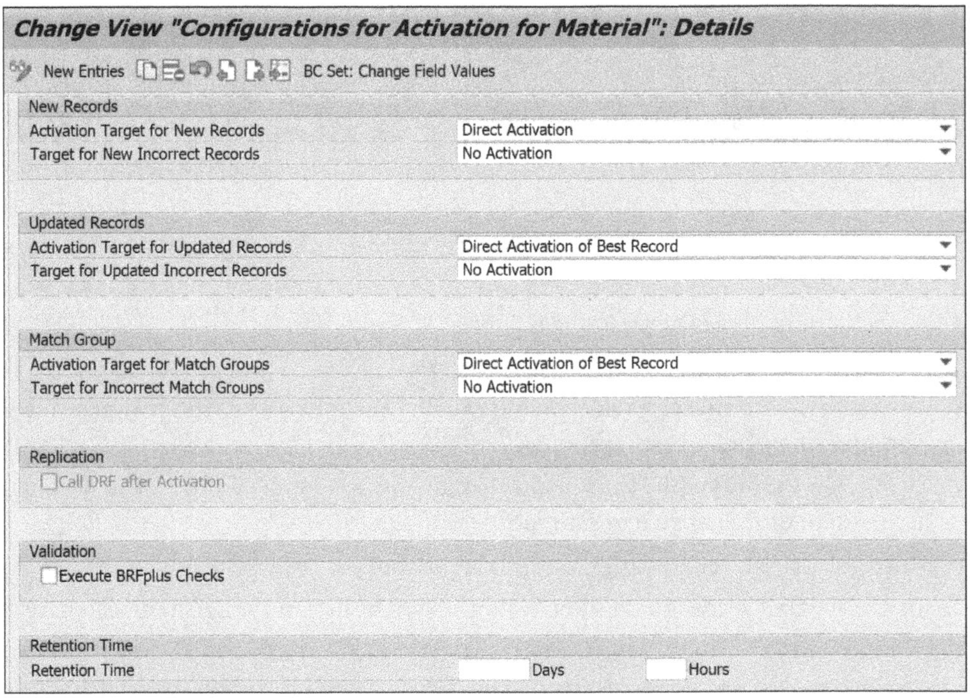

Figure 9.16 Consolidation: Configure Activation for Material

9.4.8   Scheduling Process Steps

Because mass processing and consolidation process steps typically involve very large volumes of data, system administrators are usually worried about the impact of these jobs on the system performance. Most of the time, jobs that are performance intensive are scheduled during off peak business hours or weekends to minimize the impact on other process running in the same system.

With the latest version of SAP Master Data Governance, now we have the capability to schedule the process steps at a predefined date and time (see Figure 9.17).

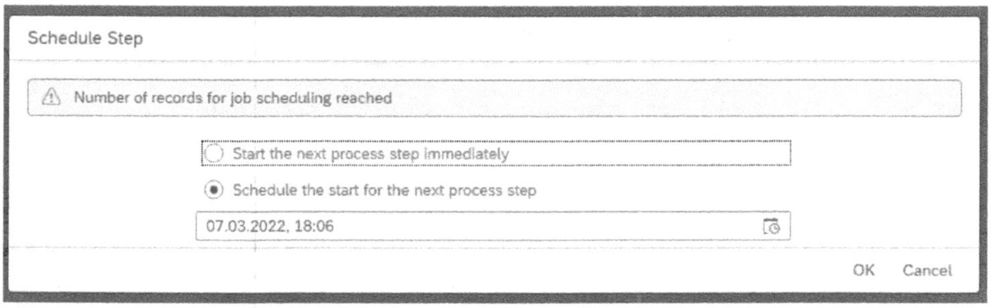

Figure 9.17 Scheduling Process Steps in SAP Master Data Governance Consolidation

In addition, sometimes business requirements dictate that a new golden record is activated or released for productive usage only at preset date and time. For example, you might decide that starting January 1, 2023, you want to start using a new merged business data and not use the old business partner data any more. The scheduling capability could also be useful for these purposes. Scheduling can be configured for the **Validation**, **Activation**, and **Matching** process steps.

Figure 9.18 shows how the configuration of the scheduling can be done. The scheduling function will be triggered based on the number of records in a step. This threshold can be configured.

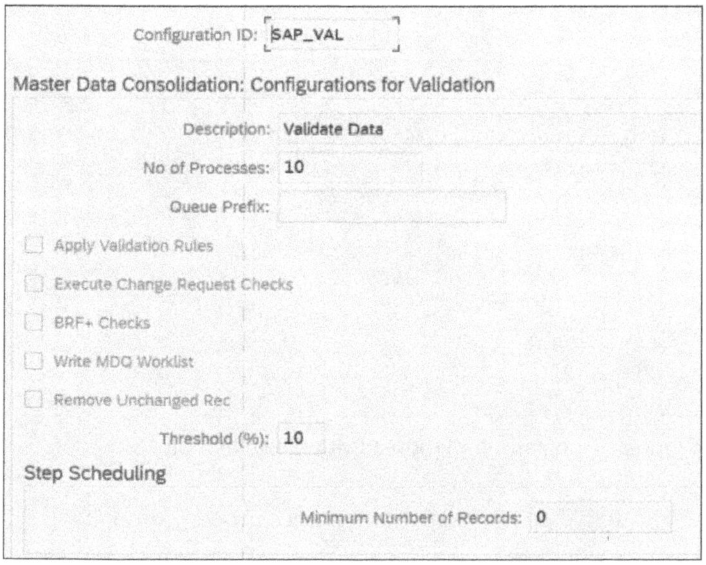

Figure 9.18 Process Step Scheduling: Configuration

9.5   Designing and Configuring Process Templates

The process template used for creating a consolidation or mass process specifies whether and in what sequence the process steps will be executed. The setup of process templates is tied to certain rules concerning the order and recurrence of the individual process steps.

SAP delivers several process templates out of the box in the form of BC Sets. These BC Sets can be activated as needed based on business requirements. Figure 9.19 depicts the BC Sets delivered for consolidation business partner process templates.

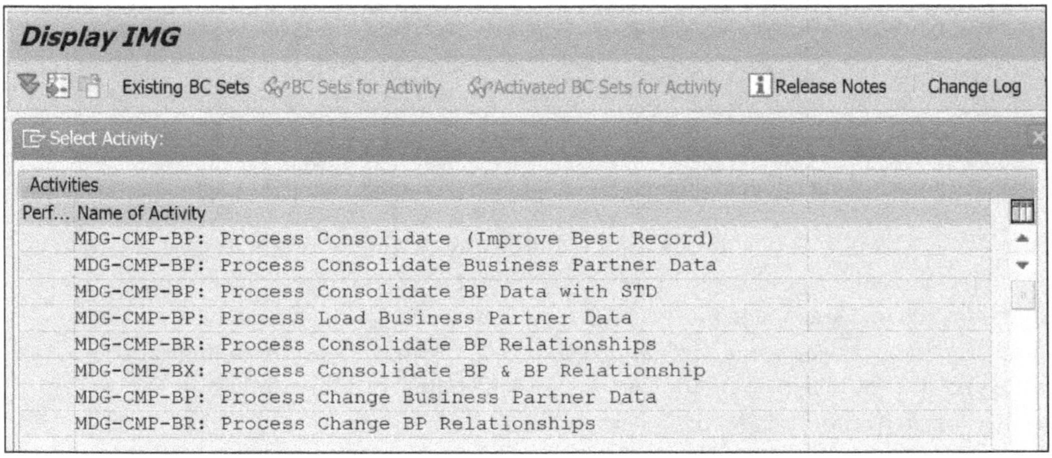

Figure 9.19 SAP-Delivered Process Templates for Business Partner Consolidation

Figure 9.20 depicts the BC Sets delivered for consolidation material master process templates.

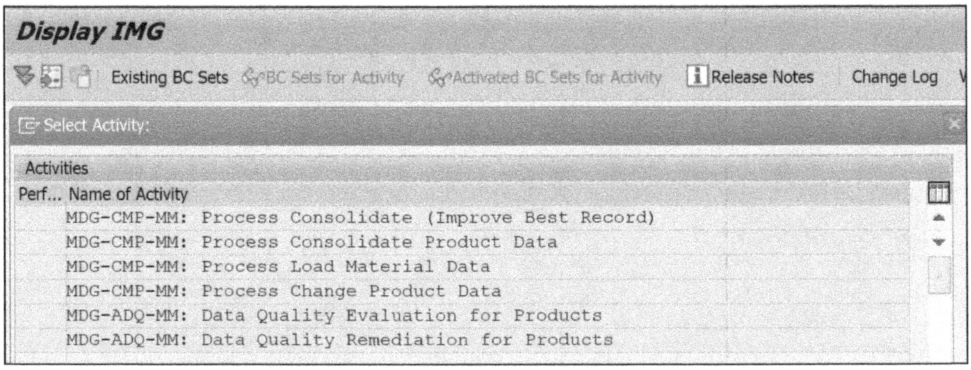

Figure 9.20 SAP-Delivered Process Templates for Product Data Consolidation

Figure 9.21 depicts the BC Sets delivered for mass maintenance process templates.

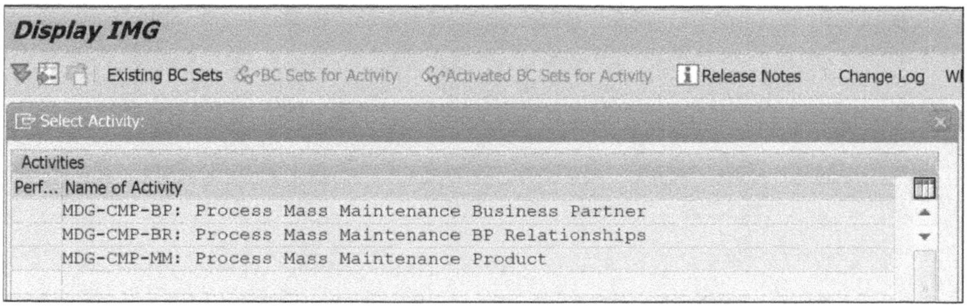

Display IMG

🔻🔁📋 Existing BC Sets ⚙️BC Sets for Activity ⚙️Activated BC Sets for Activity ℹ️ Release Notes Change Log Wl

📋 Select Activity: ✕

Activities

Perf... Name of Activity

 MDG-CMP-BP: Process Mass Maintenance Business Partner
 MDG-CMP-BR: Process Mass Maintenance BP Relationships
 MDG-CMP-MM: Process Mass Maintenance Product

Figure 9.21 SAP-Delivered Process Templates for Mass Maintenance Scenarios

Figure 9.22 depicts the SAP-delivered out-of-the-box process templates with the consolidation and mass processing functionalities.

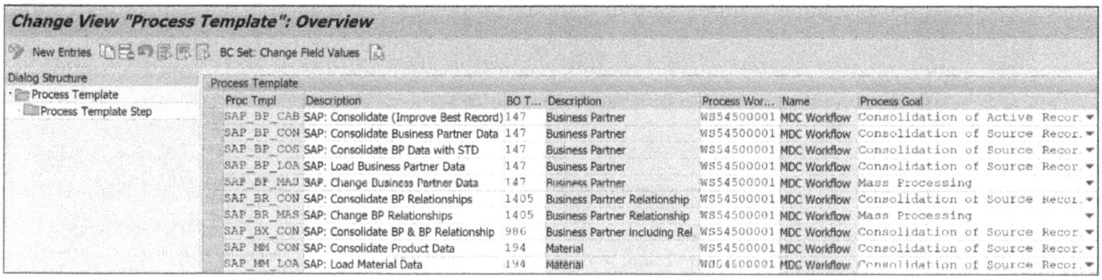

Change View "Process Template": Overview

🔹 New Entries 🗋🗎🗐🗏🗃 BC Set: Change Field Values 🗃

Dialog Structure	Process Template						
• 🗂 Process Template	Proc Tmpl	Description	BO T...	Description	Process Wor...	Name	Process Goal
🗂 Process Template Step	SAP_BP_CAB	SAP: Consolidate (Improve Best Record)	147	Business Partner	WS54500001	MDC Workflow	Consolidation of Active Recor. ▾
	SAP_BP_CON	SAP: Consolidate Business Partner Data	147	Business Partner	WS54500001	MDC Workflow	Consolidation of Source Recor. ▾
	SAP_BP_COS	SAP: Consolidate BP Data with STD	147	Business Partner	WS54500001	MDC Workflow	Consolidation of Source Recor. ▾
	SAP_BP_LOA	SAP: Load Business Partner Data	147	Business Partner	WS54500001	MDC Workflow	Consolidation of Source Recor. ▾
	SAP_BP_MAJ	SAP: Change Business Partner Data	147	Business Partner	WS54500001	MDC Workflow	Mass Processing ▾
	SAP_BR_CON	SAP: Consolidate BP Relationships	1405	Business Partner Relationship	WS54500001	MDC Workflow	Consolidation of Source Recor. ▾
	SAP_BR_MRS	SAP: Change BP Relationships	1405	Business Partner Relationship	WS54500001	MDC Workflow	Mass Processing ▾
	SAP_BX_CON	SAP: Consolidate BP & BP Relationship	986	Business Partner including Rel.	WS54500001	MDC Workflow	Consolidation of Source Recor. ▾
	SAP_MM_CON	SAP: Consolidate Product Data	194	Material	WS54500001	MDC Workflow	Consolidation of Source Recor. ▾
	SAP_MM_LOA	SAP: Load Material Data	194	Material	WS54500001	MDC Workflow	Consolidation of Source Recor. ▾

Figure 9.22 Configuring Process Templates

Additionally, process templates can be created from scratch or by copying any of the delivered process templates based on specific business requirements. Figure 9.23 depicts some of the rules of thumb and principles to be considered while modifying or creating a process template.

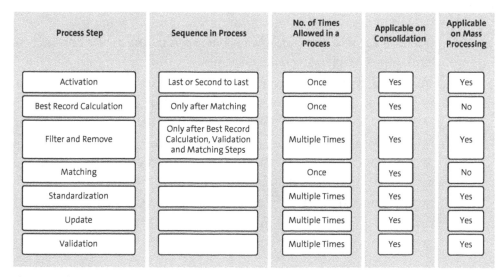

Process Step	Sequence in Process	No. of Times Allowed in a Process	Applicable on Consolidation	Applicable on Mass Processing
Activation	Last or Second to Last	Once	Yes	Yes
Best Record Calculation	Only after Matching	Once	Yes	No
Filter and Remove	Only after Best Record Calculation, Validation and Matching Steps	Multiple Times	Yes	Yes
Matching		Once	Yes	No
Standardization		Multiple Times	Yes	Yes
Update		Multiple Times	Yes	Yes
Validation		Multiple Times	Yes	Yes

Figure 9.23 Process Template Design Principles

Following are some properties that need to be defined while configuring a process template:

1. Go to the following IMG path for performing standardization activities in consolidation: **Cross-Application Components · Processes and Tools for Enterprise Applications · Master Data Governance · Consolidation and Mass Processing · Configure Process Template · Specify Process Template**.

2. Choose **New Entries**.

3. Enter a **Process Template ID**, enter a corresponding **Description**, and select a **Business Object Type** and the **Workflow Template WS54500001**.

4. Use the **Delete Source** indicator if you to configure a default value for the UI.

5. In the **Process Goal** field, use the input help to select the goal of the process out of the following delivered process goals:

   – **Consolidation of Source Records**: As part of this process, goal records can be loaded repeatedly to be consolidated without replication to the source systems after the consolidation process is complete.

   – **Consolidation for Central Maintenance**: In this process, goal records are loaded only once in the hub system; after consolidation, they are replicated back to the source systems. Central governance can also be leveraged to perform the central maintenance.

   – **Consolidation of Active Records**: Active master data records are checked for duplicates, and best records are defined accordingly based on the Customizing. A process strategy is selected for duplicate records to be applied:

     • **Remove Duplicates**: The duplicates are marked for deletion. The key mapping is directed to the best record.

     • **Improve Best Record**: The duplicates are kept unchanged. The key mapping remains unchanged.

     • **Improve All Records**: The duplicates are kept but become copies of the best record. The key mapping remains unchanged.

   – **Mass Processing**: With this process goal, a selection of active records is updated. Process steps matching and best record calculation aren't applicable for this process goal.

   – **Mass Maintenance**: This process goal is applicable for mass maintenance of records. A selection of active records is updated. The process steps matching and best record calculation aren't applicable as part of this process goal.

   – **Data Quality Remediation**: This process goal is selected automatically if you select the **Start Remediation Process** SAP Fiori tile.

Each of the process templates consists of various process template steps. An example configuration for the process template steps delivered for business object type **147 Business Partner** is shown in Figure 9.24.

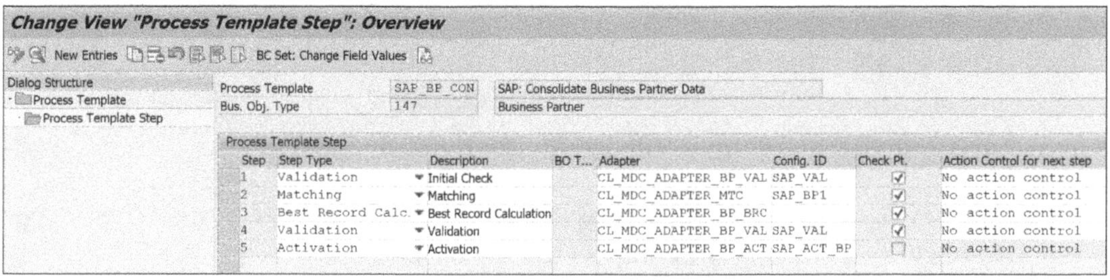

Figure 9.24 Process Template Steps for Consolidating Business Partner Data

This checkpoint checkbox (**Check Pt.**) is an important attribute of a process template that controls the behavior of specific steps during the process. By checking this indicator, the system stops the process for reviewing the data after the process step is finalized. If not checked, the consolidation process will move to the next process step. When **Checkpoint Indicator** is checked using an input help, any of the following options can be applied through another attribute **Action Control for next step**:

- **No action control**
  With this selection, the process can be continued by a user provided the required authorization has been assigned.

- **Apply the four-eyes principle**
  With this selection, the process can be continued for any user except the requestor provided they have necessary authorization. This helps in ensuring segregation of duty for a specific process step.

- **Action is only allowed for requestor**
  With this selection, no one but the requestor of the consolidation process is allowed to execute a process step.

> **Note**
> - Users need to have roles assigned with authorization object MDC_PROOT.
> - **Activity 31 Confirm** has to be assigned to continue the process.
> - **Activity 37 Accept** has to be assigned to continue the process despite unfinished match reviews.

An example configuration for process template steps delivered for business object type **194 Material** is shown in Figure 9.25.

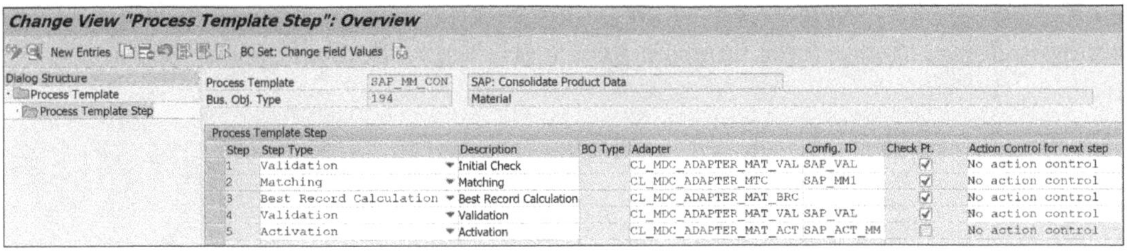

Figure 9.25 Process Template Steps for Consolidating Product Data

An example configuration for process template steps delivered for business object type **1405 Business Partner Relationship** is shown in Figure 9.26.

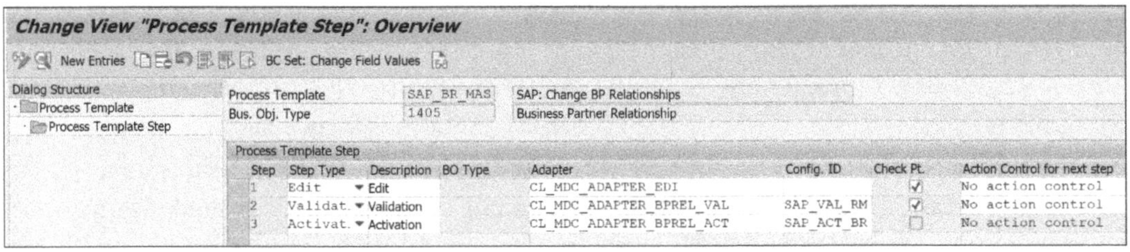

Figure 9.26 Process Template Steps for Business Partner Mass Processing

9.6   Loading Data into Source Tables

To use consolidation functionalities, master data from the source must be loaded in the consolidation application. It's important to note that data must be prepared and transformed into the SAP data structures for the successful processing of the initial load.

SAP has provided several options that can be leveraged for performing initial master data loads in consolidation: SAP Landscape Transformation Replication Server (SAP LT Replication Server), SAP HANA Studio, and comma-separated values (CSV) files-based imports. However, customers can also leverage other extract, transform, and load (ETL) tools with sufficient capabilities to support data loads in consolidation source tables.

For accessing all consolidation-specific source tables, a search can be executed for "*_SRC" in Transaction SE16N to get a list of all relevant tables.

For the upload of data related to organizations, it's also possible to use the customer or vendor data model. In that case report MDC_BP_TRANSFORM_SOURCE_DATA has to be executed to transform the data into the business partner data model after the source tables are filled.

> **Note**
> This report only supports the transformation of data related to business partners of type organizations. It doesn't support the transformation of person-related data.

It's important to consider that while loading data in consolidation, the source ID should be a unique identifier for a specific source system. If data is uploaded using customer or vendor data models, ensure that the IDs remain unique. If there are vendor and customer IDs within the same number range, the IDs can be made unique by adding a prefix.

9.6.1   Import Data for Consolidation

Consolidation supports uploading data from a file without ETL tools. The consolidation framework supports data loads from file types such as CSV, XLS, and XLSX.

As shown in Figure 9.27, multiple SAP Fiori apps are delivered by SAP for importing as well as managing data in the consolidation framework.

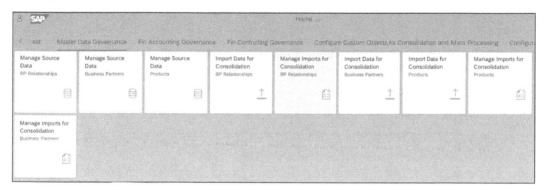

Figure 9.27 Provided SAP Fiori Apps to Perform and Manage Data Imports in Consolidation

Sample and full templates are available for business partners, business partner relationships, and materials for easy downloads and data preparation. As shown in Figure 9.28, through the SAP Fiori app Import Data for Consolidation, users may download these templates and prepare their data accordingly.

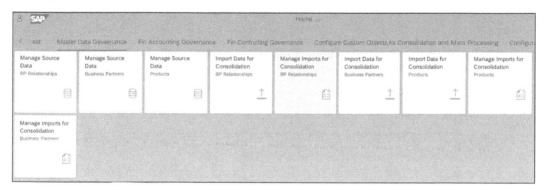

Figure 9.28 Downloading Templates from Consolidation and Mass Processing

Through the **Example Files** and **Full Templates** hyperlinks, a number of templates can be downloaded for the respective object types, as shown in Figure 9.29.

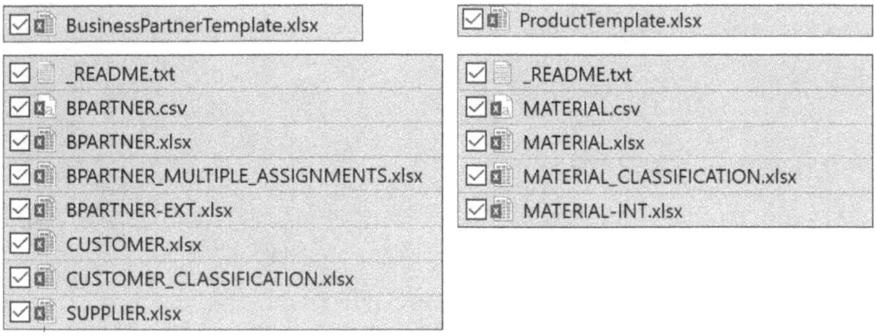

☑ 🔲 BusinessPartnerTemplate.xlsx   ☑ 🔲 ProductTemplate.xlsx

☑ _README.txt   ☑ _README.txt
☑ 🔲 BPARTNER.csv   ☑ 🔲 MATERIAL.csv
☑ 🔲 BPARTNER.xlsx   ☑ 🔲 MATERIAL.xlsx
☑ 🔲 BPARTNER_MULTIPLE_ASSIGNMENTS.xlsx   ☑ 🔲 MATERIAL_CLASSIFICATION.xlsx
☑ 🔲 BPARTNER-EXT.xlsx   ☑ 🔲 MATERIAL-INT.xlsx
☑ 🔲 CUSTOMER.xlsx
☑ 🔲 CUSTOMER_CLASSIFICATION.xlsx
☑ 🔲 SUPPLIER.xlsx

Figure 9.29 Consolidation Import Templates Delivered for Material and Business Partner Object Types

After the data is prepared in the templates, the templates can be used for loading through the Import Data for Consolidation apps, as shown in Figure 9.30. The load will be executed in consolidation source tables by clicking the **Proceed Import** button on the SAP Fiori UI.

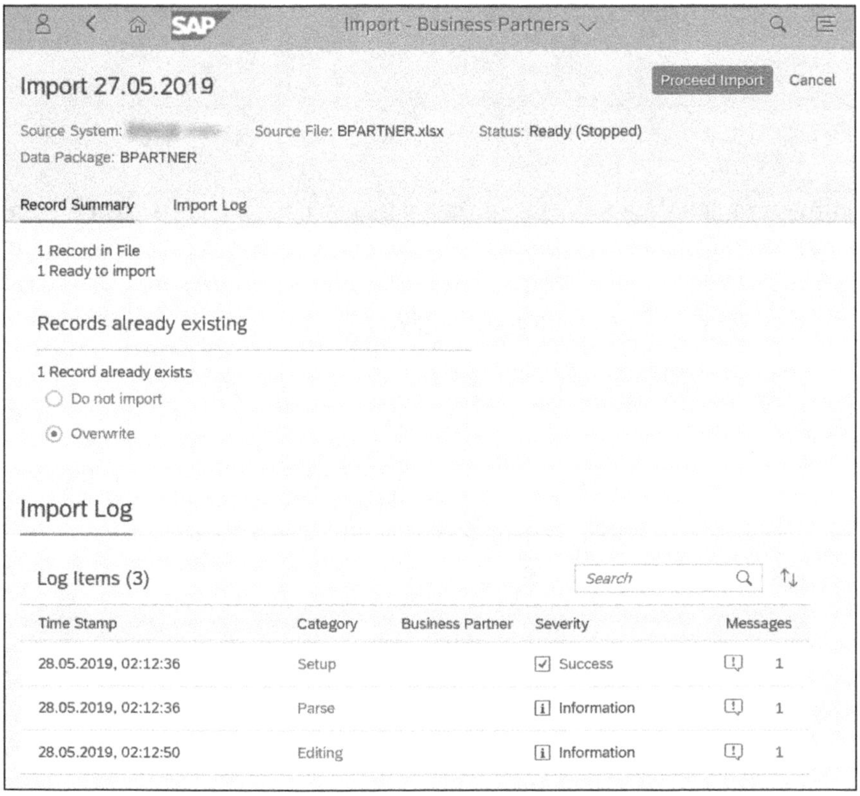

Figure 9.30 Summary and Import Logs after Executing the Files in Consolidation

In the latest version of the consolidation and mass processing functionalities, Export Master Data apps are also delivered for business partners, business partner relationships, and products. These SAP Fiori apps can be leveraged to easily download master data into spreadsheet formats. It's possible to define the field scope to be exported. In addition, the records to be exported can be specifically selected before executing the export. This exported file can be imported again by making necessary changes, hence saving a lot of time in data preparation activities in appropriate formats.

For the business partner, business partner relationships, and materials object types, dedicated SAP Fiori apps are delivered for managing the data imports. Figure 9.31 shows an example for the business partners object where all the data packages imported in source tables can be accessed. In addition, consolidation processes can be directly created from the respective imports.

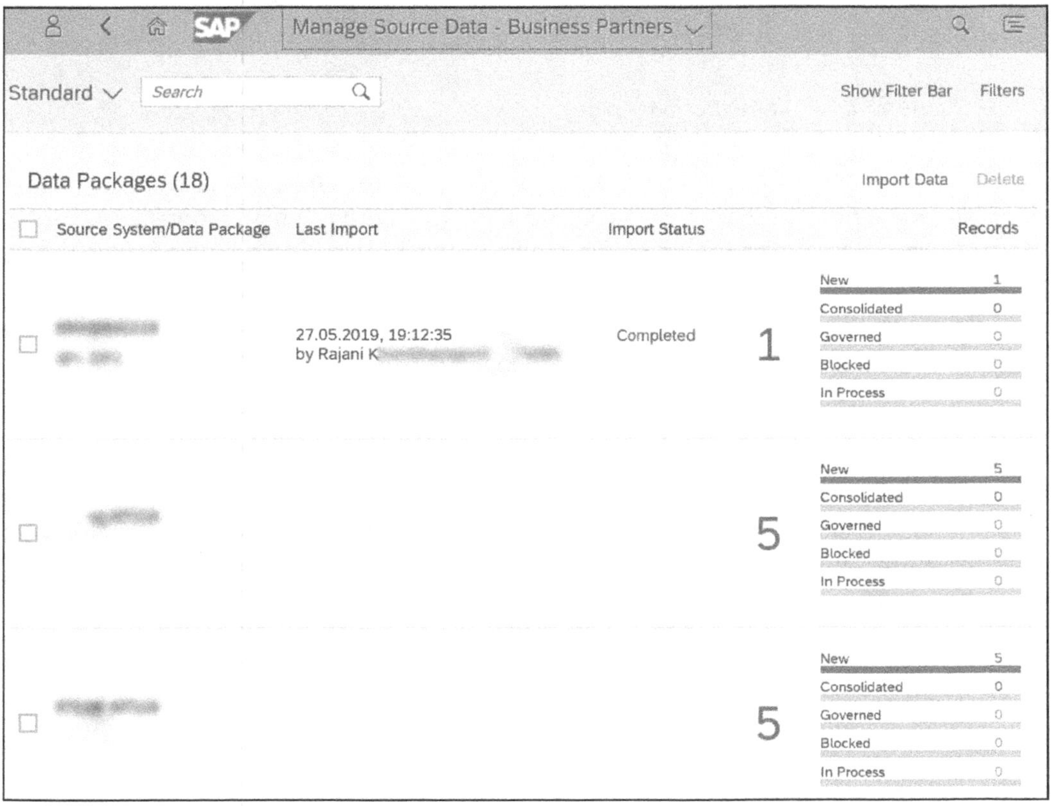

Figure 9.31 Manage Import for Consolidation

9.6.2   SAP Landscape Transformation Replication Server

SAP LT Replication Server is a widely used option by many customers for the purpose of initial loads in consolidation, especially for existing SAP Business Suite models because identical data models are being used. SAP LT Replication Server uses a trigger-based replication approach to pass data from source systems to target SAP HANA–based systems. As shown in Figure 9.32, with SAP LT Replication Server, it's possible to load as well as replicate data in real time or schedule data to be loaded into an SAP HANA database at a later time.

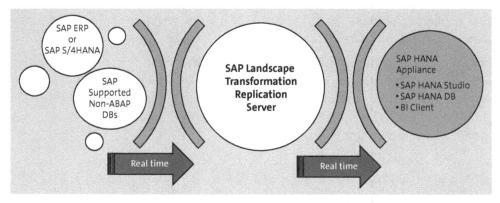

Figure 9.32 SAP LT Replication Server

SAP LT Replication Server has the built-in capability to handle and support conversion between non-Unicode and Unicode data formats. With full integration to SAP HANA Studio, SAP LT Replication Server also has table settings and some simple transformation capabilities. For any complex transformation, specialized ETL tools should be considered. With the help of SAP Solution Manager for SAP HANA, SAP LT Replication Server also has data monitoring functionalities. To access SAP LT Replication Server, use Transaction LTR.

SAP LT Replication Server–based table data provisions provide the following options:

- **Load (Full)**
  This is normally a one-time event used mainly for initial load purposes from a source application.

- **Replicate (Full and Delta Load)**
  With this option, the initial load is triggered along with any delta changes.

- **Stop Replication**
  This option removes the database trigger and logging table completely while ensuring the replication process is stopped for a given table.

- **Suspend**
  This option doesn't remove the database trigger and logging information but just pauses the replication process.

- **Resume**
  This option resumes the suspended replication process.

Following are some salient features while establishing a connection between an SAP application and an SAP HANA–based system:

- A read engine is created in the SAP source system.

- The connection between SAP LT Replication Server and SAP HANA–based systems is established as a database connection.

- The connection between the SAP source applications and SAP LT Replication Server is established as an RFC connection.

- While replicating a table, SAP LT Replication Server creates logging tables in the source system.

- SAP LT Replication Server transforms all metadata table definitions from the ABAP source applications to SAP HANA.

Following are some salient features while performing a data load connection between a non-SAP system and an SAP HANA–based system:

- A read engine is created in SAP LT Replication Server.

- The connection between SAP LT Replication Server and the non-SAP legacy system is established as a database connection.

- The connection between SAP LT Replication Server and SAP HANA–based systems is established as a database connection.

- While replicating a table, SAP LT Replication Server creates logging tables in the source system.

- SAP LT Replication Server transforms all metadata table definitions from the legacy source system to SAP HANA.

9.6.3   SAP HANA Studio

With SAP HANA Studio, it's recommended that data be imported in an interim table first, and then this content from the interim tables can be loaded to source tables using custom ABAP reports or SQL.

9.6.4   Usage of Consolidation Processes for Service-Oriented Architecture Inbound Processing

If service-oriented architecture (SOA) setup has been configured between the source system and the SAP Master Data Governance system, it's possible to automatically create and start consolidation mass processes using the payload data for each SOA message during the SOA inbound processing. However, to make it run, the process templates should be configured accordingly.

9.7   Operating and Running Consolidation and Mass Processing Applications

Consolidation and mass processing are SAP Fiori–based applications. All out-of-the-box operations related to consolidation and mass processing activities can be performed through a set of SAP Fiori apps delivered by SAP.

The consolidation and mass processing SAP Fiori–based UI can be launched through Transaction /UI2/FLP. Alternatively, it can be accessed directly through the application URL.

If SAP Single Sign-On (SAP SSO) is enabled, then by clicking on the SAP Fiori launchpad or the SAP Master Data Governance hyperlink, users will be taken directly to the SAP Fiori homepage. If SAP SSO isn't enabled in a company, Figure 9.33 shows the SAP Fiori logon screen for consolidation and mass processing where users can provide the credentials to log in to the application.

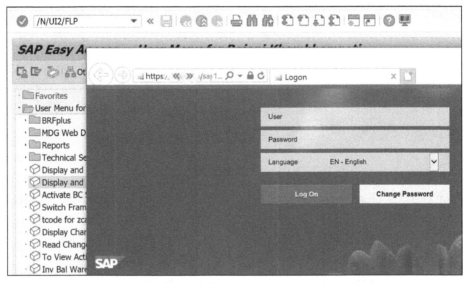

Figure 9.33 SAP Fiori Launchpad Logon for Consolidation and Mass Processing

> **Note**
>
> Unlike central governance, where operational activities can also be performed via the SAP Business Client–based UI, consolidation and mass processing operations can only be performed through SAP Fiori apps.

After you're logged in the application, various SAP Fiori apps can be accessed for starting and managing the consolidation processes and mass processes for business partners, business partner relationships, and materials.

9.7.1   Starting a Consolidation Process

You can use the SAP Fiori–based UI for performing various process steps and activities in consolidation. Figure 9.34 shows the SAP Fiori apps highlighted that are used for supporting various business activities involved in a consolidation process.

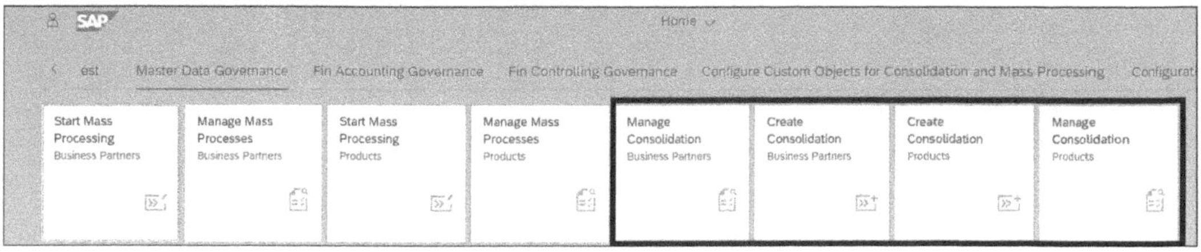

Figure 9.34 SAP-Delivered Consolidation SAP Fiori Apps

For any usage based on the business requirements, a consolidation process has to be created first, as shown in Figure 9.35. Accordingly, an appropriate **Description** with free text should be populated to indicate some information about the consolidation process being executed. Based on the business requirements, **Process Goal** and **Process Template** field values will be populated from a set of preconfigured dropdown values. In addition, a data source must be selected on which the consolidation process can be executed.

Lastly, before creating the consolidation process, a decision must be made regarding whether the source data should be deleted or retained after the consolidation process is complete by checking the appropriate radio button (see Figure 9.35).

As soon as a user clicks on the **Save** button, the system will assign a unique process ID number to the consolidation process. Throughout the consolidation process, its process ID, description, process template, process goal, and selected data source are displayed in the upper section of the UI. The **Start** button in the bottom section of the UI will remain highlighted in blue by default to initiate and execute the consolidation process. Respective process steps will remain highlighted during a consolidation process to give an indication to operators about the progress made and the current status.

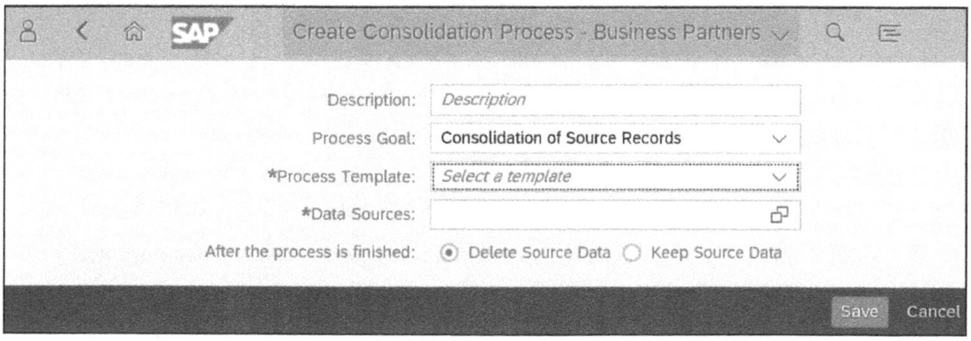

Figure 9.35 Create Consolidation Process: Business Partners Screen

In addition, as shown in Figure 9.36 on the top-right section, you may see the number of records involved in the consolidation process along with the percentage of progress made by the process so far.

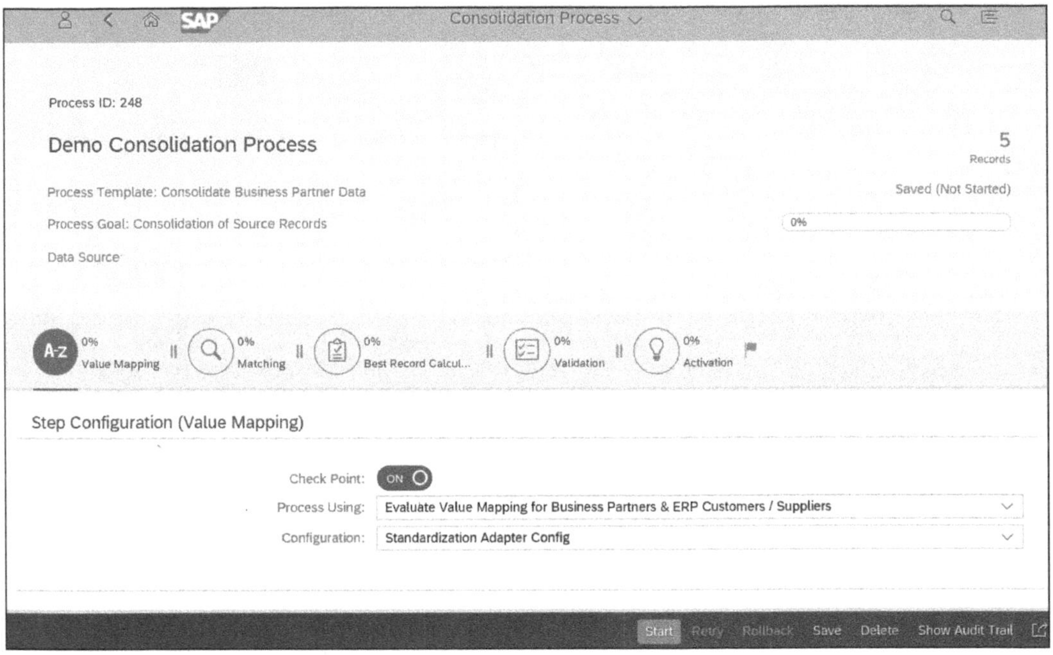

Figure 9.36 Running a Consolidation Process

Remember, either a desktop or a tablet device can be used for creating consolidation scenarios.

9.7.2   Starting Mass Processing

The mass processing functionality helps users update multiple master data records at a time while saving time and improving efficiency. This function is available for business partner, business partner relationships, material master, and custom object domains, if any. To update records, fields and records to be change should be selected first. The application then displays list of fields to change based on the selection made. After the changes are made, the system provides statistics on the changed fields and validates the data. After checking the validations, the application can then be activated during which the data is finally copied from the staging area to the active memory of the application, and replication occurs to various connected downstream systems.

Mass processing can be started for business partners and materials through the highlighted Start Mass Processing apps shown in Figure 9.37.

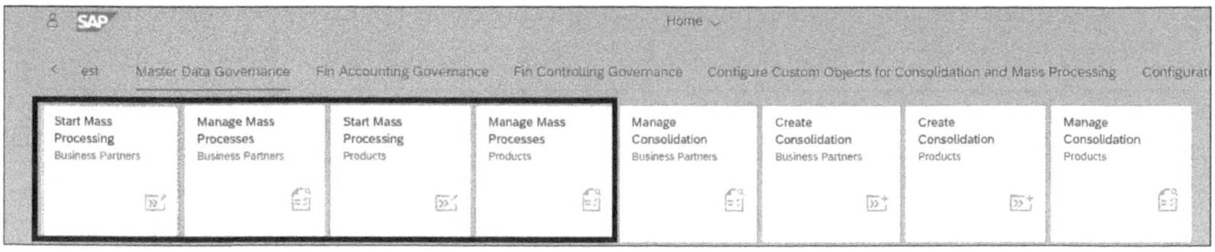

Figure 9.37 SAP-Delivered Mass Processing SAP Fiori Apps

Mass processing can be used with or without central governance. Technically, mass processing uses the same framework as the consolidation capabilities, which provides the flexibility to combine the features in a flexible process configuration. Packaging, queuing, and parallelization contribute to enhanced performance while dealing with large volumes.

Mass processing typically consists of several process steps, including **Start Mass Processing**, **Scope Selection**, **Record Selection**, **Edit**, **Validation**, and **Activation**. Additionally, **Update**, **Filter**, and **Remove** steps can also be added.

9.7.3   Manage Consolidation and Mass Processing Processes

These consolidation and mass processing processes created in SAP Master Data Governance can be effectively managed through SAP Fiori apps. Figure 9.38 shows how a consolidation process can be managed. It's possible to create, delete, and mark processes for deletion. This screen acts as a process monitor for consolidation by providing an overview of all processes in various states and by providing navigation to process details (e.g., process ID, process description, data source, user, creation date, status, process goal, number of records in a specific process, etc.).

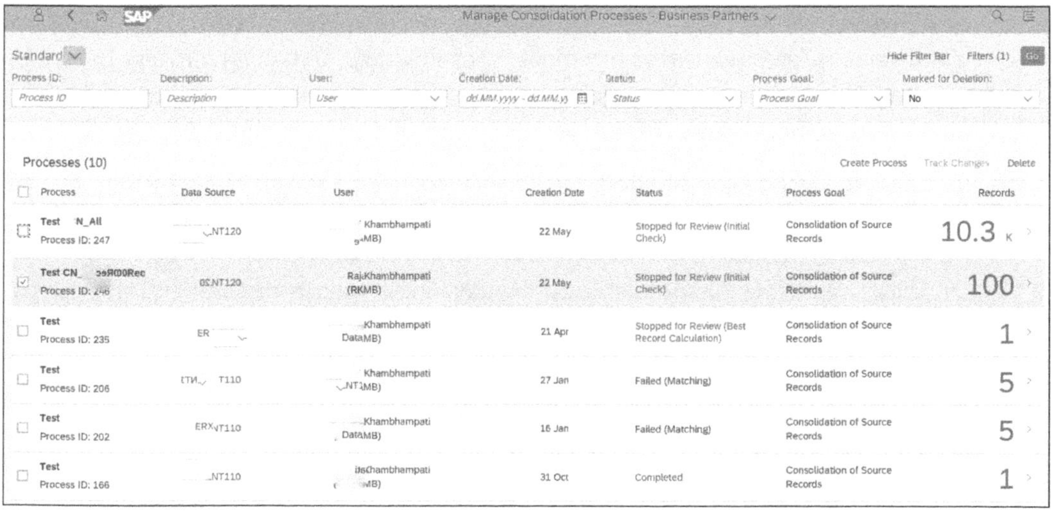

Figure 9.38 Manage Consolidation Processes

As explained earlier in this chapter, during a consolidation process, various steps come into play. From a user's perspective, these steps are sequential, and each step needs various configurations as prerequisites. Figure 9.39 depicts the screen after an initial check step has been executed. The horizontal red, yellow, or green bar will represent initial check results for the respective number of errors, warnings, and successes. A summary of the number errors and warnings in the initial step is provided for information. In addition, for detailed analysis, users may select the appropriate horizontal bar and click on **Show Details**.

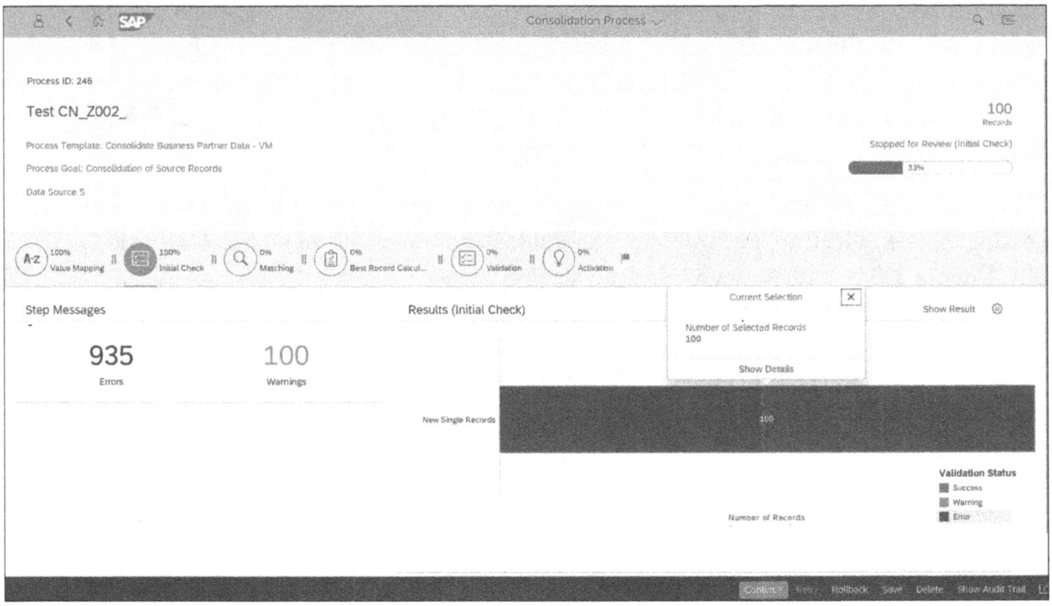

Figure 9.39 Manage Consolidation Process: Initial Check

In **Show Details**, a new screen will open to give record-level information of the actual data being processed through various consolidation and mass processing tables. Through the **Details** column on this screen, the system summarizes the number and the type of error or warning messages per record, as shown in Figure 9.40.

In this step, it's possible to select specific records and to "remove" them from the process being executed. This record removal functionality helps in expediting the processes as it allows users to remove the records with high complexity errors from the process. Sometimes a handful of records may have higher complexity errors with the potential to delay the whole process as they may take comparatively longer to fix. Therefore, from a business priorities perspective, it allows the consolidation process to keep moving.

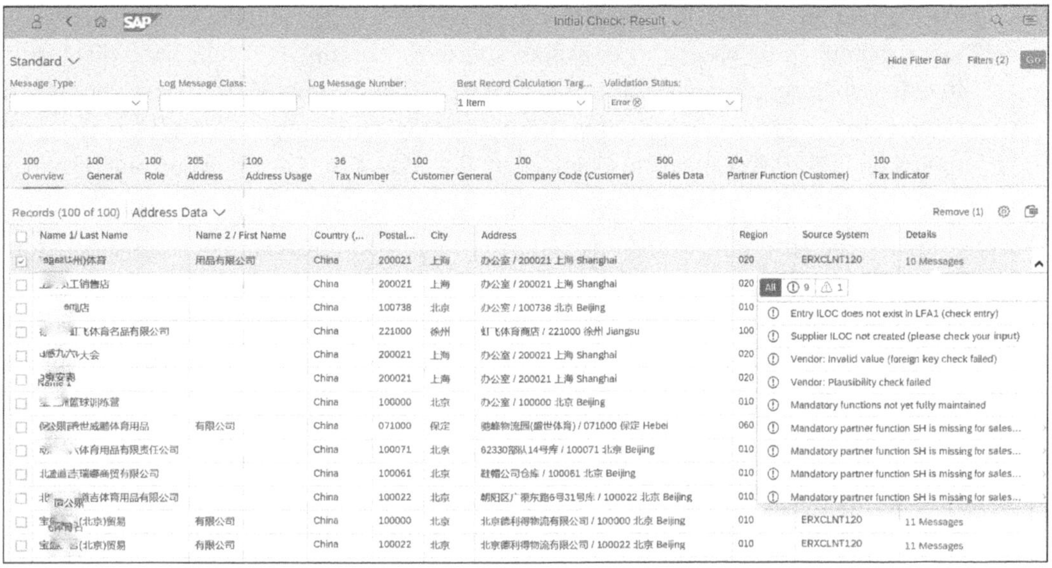

Figure 9.40 Manage Consolidation Processes: Initial Check Result of Business Partners

The matching step is one of the most important steps in a consolidation process and is like the heart of the whole consolidation process when dealing with potential duplicates in data sets. Typically, after a matching step is executed, the SAP Fiori–based UI depicts the summary of the match group information and provides a graphical representation of the matching step summary. This comprises open match groups, approved match groups, and rejected match groups, if any, as shown in Figure 9.41.

Figure 9.41 Manage Consolidation Processes: Matching Step for Business Partners

The horizontal data bar on the matching screen result is typically highlighted in orange when the matching was executed against source records only; the data bars will be blue in color when matching was executed against active records. Match result details can be accessed and reviewed by clicking on the **Match Review** button. After the review, the next step in the process can be executed by clicking on the **Continue** button.

After the match groups are created, the next step in the consolidation process requires users to create the golden records and mark identified duplicate records for deletion. This way, there will always be a clean and de-duplicated view of master data records in the SAP Master Data Governance repository. After the successful execution of this best record calculation step, as shown in Figure 9.42, there are three possible consequences and categorization of records:

- **New Single Records** are highlighted in blue on the pie chart representation.
- **New Best Records** are highlighted in orange on the pie chart representation.
- **Updates** are highlighted in green on the pie chart representation.

A best record calculation step can only be executed in a consolidation process after a match step is completed. Best record calculation isn't applicable for mass processing.

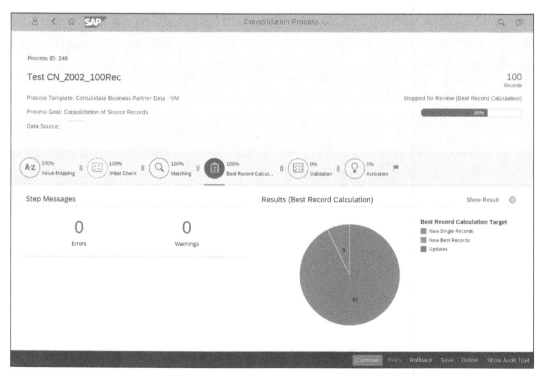

Figure 9.42 Manage Consolidation Processes: Best Record Calculation for Business Partners

Optionally, during any of the process steps, users can view the audit trail of the consolidation process by clicking **Show Audit Trail**. Figure 9.43 shows how audit trails are visible in consolidation. All activities on the process level (continue the process, roll back the process, etc.) are tracked. This audit trail can be displayed in the process UI with the ability to drill down into the details.

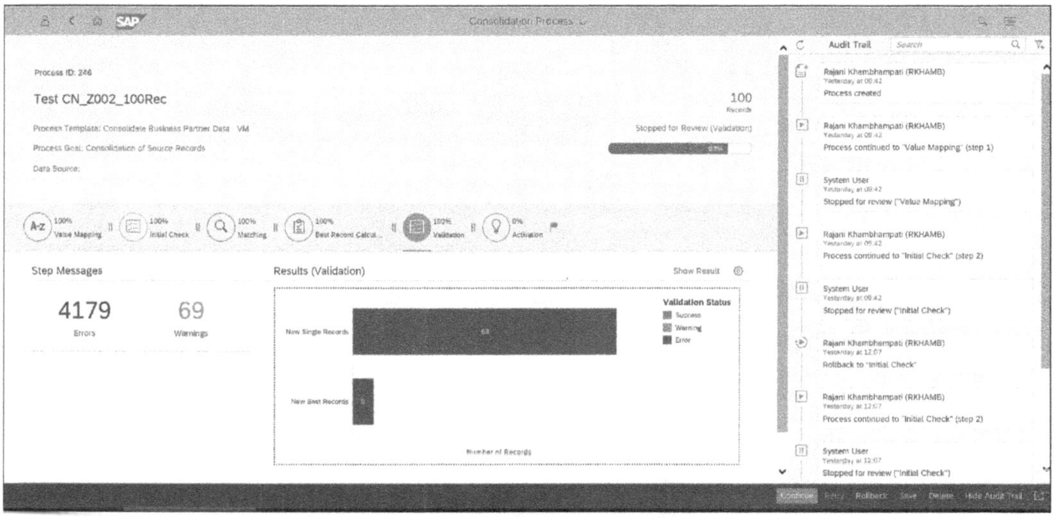

Figure 9.43 Audit Trail View during the Consolidation Process

Note

Starting with version SAP S/4HANA 1809, SAP Master Data Governance supports auditing requirements, including search and display changes of active records (track changes), which is now possible with the consolidation and mass processing function.

Changes can be selected using object ID (material number, business partner number), change date, or process ID.

9.7.4 Troubleshooting Errors in Consolidation and Mass Processing

While dealing with consolidation and mass processing business scenarios, users often have to deal with resolving the data quality issues pertaining to the selected data sets. Multiple validations steps can be added in a consolidation process for effectively managing and catching the data quality issues early and before the activation.

Figure 9.44 shows a user screen after a validation step is executed during a consolidation process.

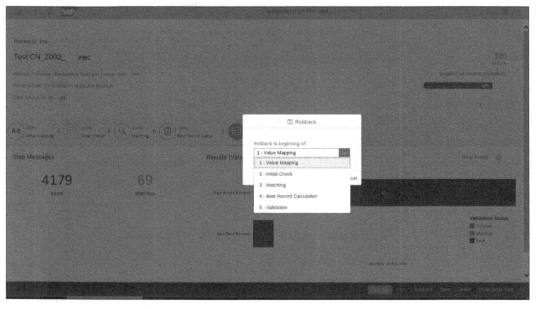

Figure 9.44 Validations Step in a Consolidation Process

If need be, a rollback can be performed to any of the previous steps in the consolidation process, as shown in Figure 9.45.

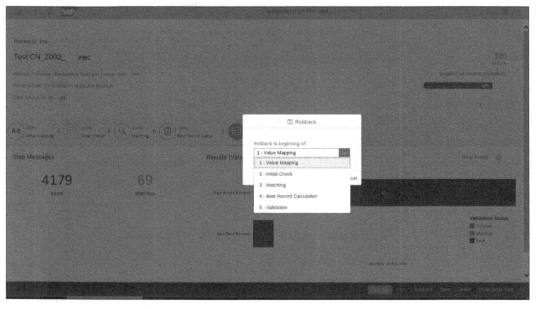

Figure 9.45 Rollback Functionality in a Consolidation Process

While working with consolidation and mass processing, it's important to effectively analyze and manage the errors captured during a process. Although every process step in the SAP Fiori–based UI allows these errors to be accessed and analyzed, for more technical details and deeper analysis, SAP has provided Transaction SWIA, which enables you to process work items as administrator. This comes in handy while zeroing in on a specific error type based on various input parameters, including work item ID, work item properties (i.e., type, status, priority, deadline status, task, task group, top level task, etc.), and selection using time period (i.e., created on). It's possible to create variants for this transaction that can be used for executing quick searches based on the selection parameters. Figure 9.46 depicts the execution screen of Transaction SWIA in SAP.

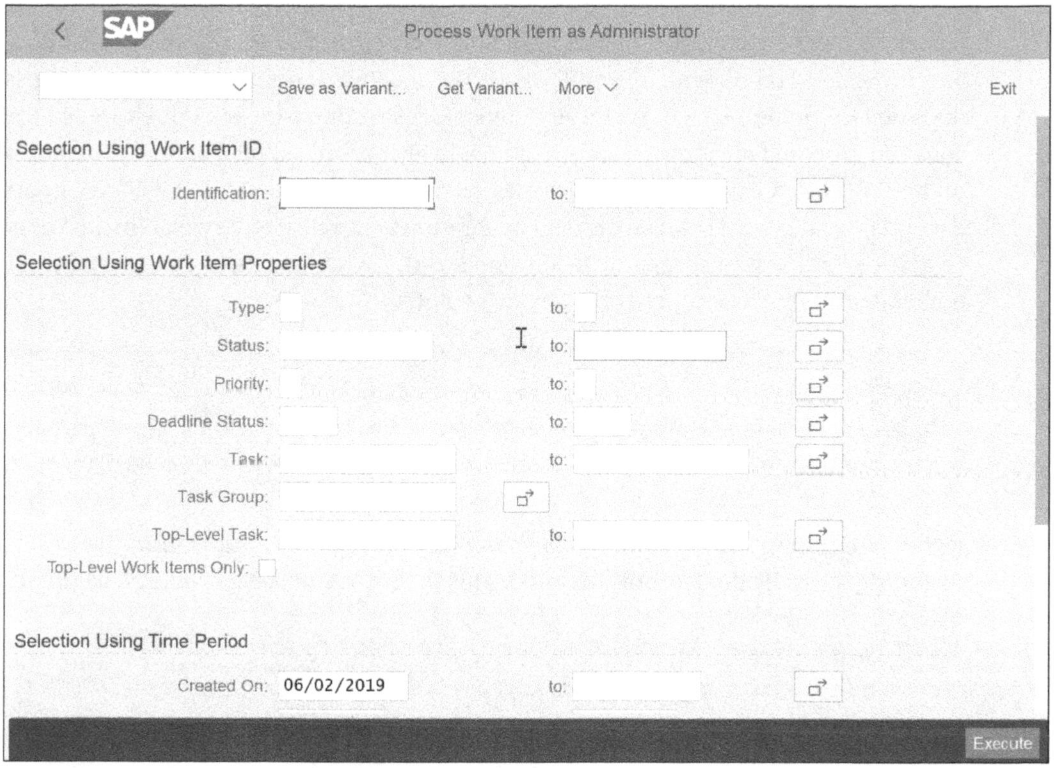

Figure 9.46 Transaction SWIA Input Selection: Process Work Item as Administrator

9.8   Technical Architecture

Consolidation and mass processing is a tool that runs natively on SAP ERP and SAP S/4HANA to provide consolidation and mass processing capabilities along with loosely coupled integrations to central governance.

The following sections will explain the technical architecture of consolidation and mass processing in detail. The sections start with an overview of the consolidation and mass processing architecture, followed by subsections that provide insights about frontend and backend architecture of consolidation and mass processing.

> **Note**
>
> The central governance component and the consolidation and mass processing component are two independent technical components. Either of them can be activated without the other.

9.8.1   Overview

Like central governance, consolidation and mass processing is an add-on to SAP ERP or an embedded component in SAP S/4HANA. Consolidation and mass processing is designed to run on SAP HANA and all other databases supported by SAP. However, the consolidation and mass processing add-on delivers optimized performance when run on an SAP HANA database. Some features, such as fuzzy matching, SAP HANA smart data quality, and SAP HANA smart data integration are exclusively available when consolidation and mass processing is run on an SAP HANA database. Features such as embedded analytics are only available on SAP S/4HANA.

> **Note**
>
> To get further insights into the future direction of consolidation and mass processing, refer to SAP Master Data Governance road maps available at *www.sap.com/roadmaps*.

Figure 9.47 shows the *runtime architecture* of consolidation and mass processing, including the individual technical components in the frontend, backend, and database.

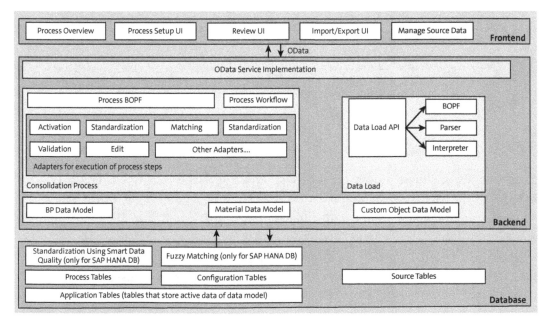

Figure 9.47 Runtime Architecture for Consolidation

> **Note**
>
> Embedded analytics related to consolidation and mass processing will be explained in Chapter 10.

9.8.2   Frontend Architecture

All consolidation and mass processing applications are web applications and run on browsers. No special software (e.g., SAP GUI) is required to run these applications.

> **Note**
>
> Refer to the Product Availability Matrix (PAM) to decide if the browser (and its versions) used by your organization supports consolidation and mass processing applications.

> **Tip**
>
> You can find the version of SAPUI5 supported by your ABAP server by executing the URL *http://[host]:[port]/sap/public/bc/ui5_ui5/*. Replace the [host] and [port] with your server parameters.

Consolidation and mass processing applications are built using the SAPUI5 frontend framework, so they comply fully with SAP Fiori guidelines.

> **Note**
>
> SAPUI5 and SAP Fiori are different. SAP Fiori provides design guidelines and principles for building UIs. SAPUI5 is the underlying technology that is used to build the web applications in compliance with SAP Fiori guidelines.

SAPUI5 is a JavaScript-based frontend framework that imparts the following features natively to consolidation and mass processing applications:

- **Cross platform**
  Consolidation and mass processing applications run across the different browser platforms (Chrome, Internet Explorer, Edge) without the need to install additional add-ons or software. The PAM is the single source of truth to find out the list of browsers (and their versions) supported by consolidation and mass processing. The applications behave consistently across different browser platforms.

- **Responsive**
  Consolidation and mass processing applications are inherently responsive, which means that applications will be rendered well based on the window or screen size

(view port size). The responsiveness of consolidation and mass processing applications ensures usability of applications across screen sizes.

- **Enterprise ready**
  Consolidation and mass processing applications are enterprise-ready applications. SAPUI5 provides internalization support, creates consistent user experience patterns, and supports model-view-controller (MVC) architecture and robust APIs to consume OData services.

- **Extensible**
  The SAPUI5 framework provides a modification-free extensibility framework to enhance SAP-delivered consolidation and mass processing applications to accommodate customer requirements.

SAPUI5 helps a developer concentrate only on business logic; the framework takes care of generating runtime artifacts such as HTML content, Cascading Style Sheets (CSS), and JavaScript libraries.

SAP Fiori launchpad is the central access point for accessing consolidation and mass processing SAP Fiori apps. SAP Fiori launchpad acts as an entry point on desktops, and it provides generic navigation and personalization support.

The entry points for consolidation and mass processing apps are represented as tiles on the launchpad. Tiles are in SAP Fiori groups, and SAP Fiori groups are grouped under catalogs. Users can click on the tile to navigate into the app. Figure 9.48 shows SAP Fiori launchpad and tiles.

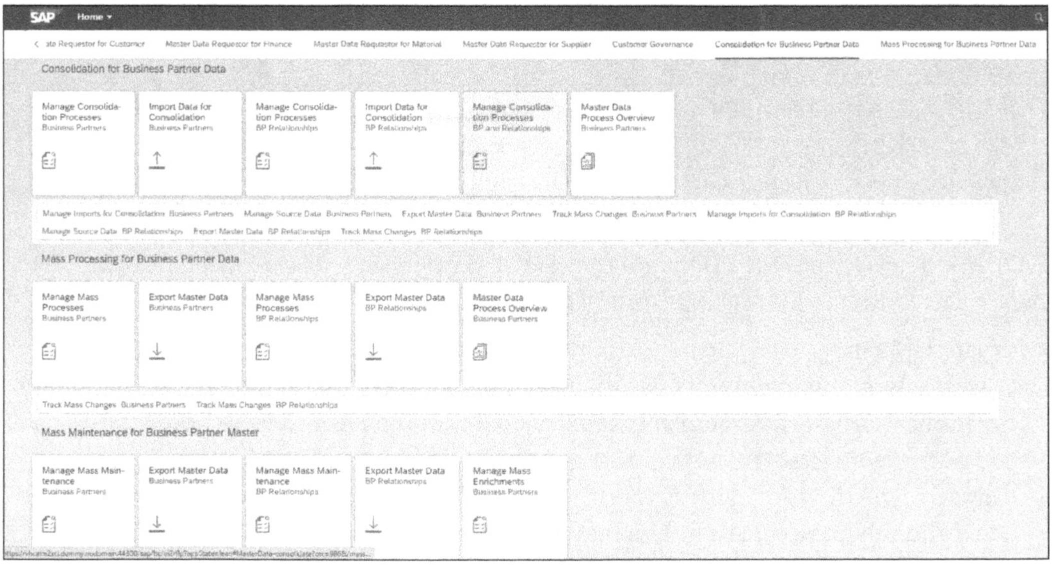

Figure 9.48 SAP Fiori Launchpad: Tiles as App Entry Points

The application can open within the same browser window (or tab) as the launchpad or can open in a new window or tab. When the application is opened within the launchpad, the user can use the navigation services provided by the launchpad to navigate by clicking on the **Back** button. Users can also navigate quickly to another consolidation and mass processing application by entering the name of the application in the search field at the top-right corner. Figure 9.49 shows an example of navigation services ❶ and search services provided by SAP Fiori launchpad, which provide quick access to other applications ❷.

Before we see further details regarding the consolidation and mass processing frontend architecture, it would be a good idea to understand the word "process" in the context of consolidation and mass processing. A *process* is a user-created entity that is used to execute actions such as master data consolidation and master data mass processing using consolidation and mass processing applications.

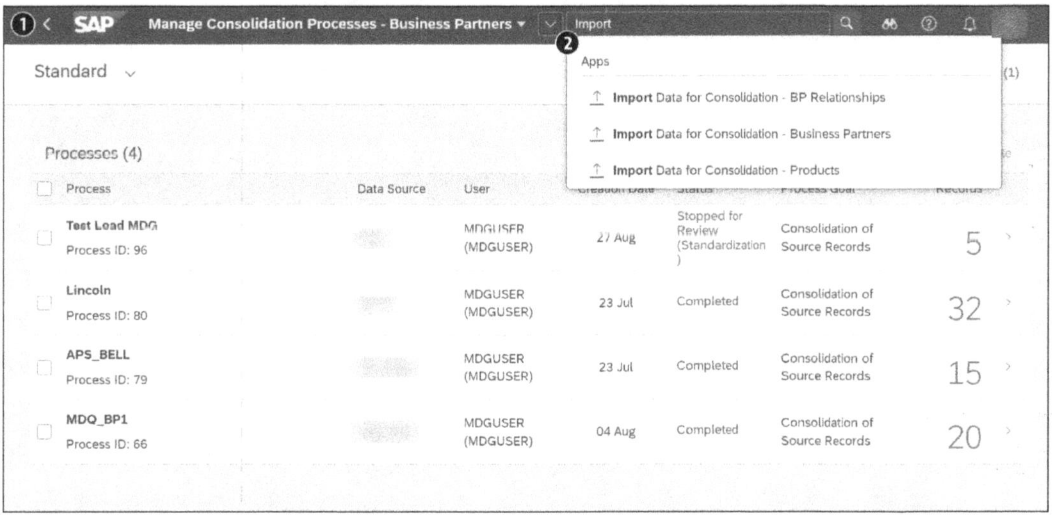

Figure 9.49 Navigation Service and Quick Access to Other Applications Using the Search Field

---

Note

Process can also be used in the context of data quality management and data quality remediation in SAP Master Data Governance; however, these topics aren't in the scope of this chapter. The word *process* in this chapter refers exclusively to the consolidation and mass processing process.

The consolidation and mass processing process is inherently modeled as business object (business partner, material) independent. However, the process is linked to business objects through the process template and URL parameters (otc) during runtime. The process template is specific to a business object, and it's primarily used to model a consolidation process or mass processing process by specifying the following:

- Which steps are executed (e.g., standardization, matching, etc.)
- How steps are executed (EIM adapter or BRFplus adapter)
- In what sequence the steps are executed

Note

Including the activation step is mandatory while configuring a process template for consolidation and mass processing.

Multiple SAP Fiori apps (UIs) are delivered standard as part of consolidation and mass processing. Table 9.11 provides a list of UIs delivered by SAP, along with the SAPUI5 application name in the ABAP repository.

Type of Consolidation and Mass Processing UI	UI Name	Application Name
Process UIs	Process Overview UI	MD_CMPMONPROCS1
	Process Setup UI	
	Process Review UI	
	Mass Edit UI	
Import/export UIs	Import Data for Consolidation	MD_CMPIMPFILES1
	Export Master Data	MD_CMPEXPFILES1
Source data manipulation UIs	Manage Source Data	MD_CMPMANSDATS1
Configuration UIs	Configure Custom Objects for Consolidation and Mass Processing	MD_CMPCONFCOS1

Table 9.11 UIs Delivered by SAP for Consolidation and Mass Processing

Note

The Configure Custom Object for Consolidation and Mass Processing app isn't in the scope of this chapter, but you can refer to *http://s-prs.co/v488302* for more details regarding this SAP Fiori app.

The data source (backend) for all consolidation and mass processing applications is always an ABAP server with consolidation and mass processing components activated. This ABAP server can be SAP S/4HANA, SAP S/4HANA Cloud, or SAP ERP. During runtime, the consolidation and mass processing SAPUI5 applications connect with the ABAP server using OData services for transactional handling of the master data. OData services are often referred to as web SQL. They can be used to perform create, read, update, and delete (CRUD) operations in the ABAP server.

Note

OData services are RESTful services that comply fully with the OData specification. More details about OData can be found at *http://OData.org*.

Another generic frontend architecture principle followed by consolidation and mass processing applications is usage of *hash-based navigation*, which allows the creation of single-page applications. The navigation is done by changing the hash part of the application URL to ensure that the browser doesn't have to reload the page; instead, a call back is triggered that can be handled by SAPUI5 navigation services to navigate to a different SAPUI5 view. The hash part of the URL in SAPUI5 is called the *pattern*. The *route* is a data set that tells the SAPUI5 router which SAPUI5 view is to be loaded based on the pattern in the URL. The SAPUI5 router is initialized with the routes when the application is first loaded. The routes are configured either as metadata in the component definition or as part of *manifest.json*.

Tip

In the MD_CMPMONPROCS1 app, the routes are configured as metadata objects in *component.js*; in the MD_CMPIMPFILES1 app, the routes are configured in *manifest.json*.

The navigation between the launchpad and the consolidation and mass processing application is handled using intent-based navigation. Intent is used to identify the actions that the users want to perform on semantic objects. Intent is used for navigation within the application or to different applications.

Intents include the following parts.

- **Semantic object**
  This represents a business entity, such as a sales order or invoice. Figure 9.50 shows the definition of the MasterData semantic object, which is used for navigation in consolidation and mass processing applications.

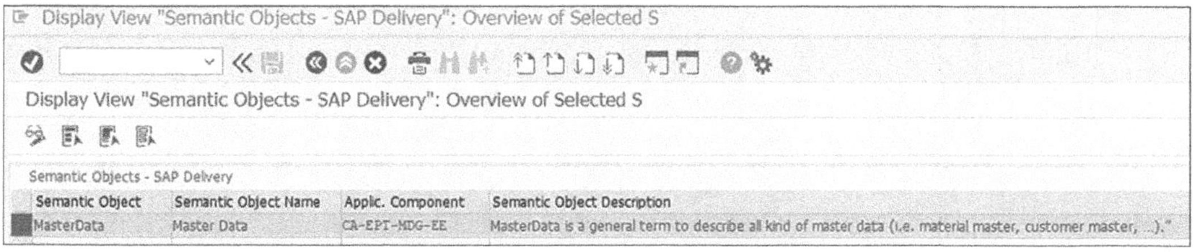

Figure 9.50 Definition of the "MasterData" Semantic Object

- **Action**
  This describes the operation to be performed on the semantic object, for example, `approveSalesOrder`.

- **Semantic object parameters**
  These are the parameters that can be used to define the instance of the semantic object and/or to pass additional data to the application.

Figure 9.51 shows the configuration of the intent-based navigation for consolidation and mass processing applications. Here, the intent (semantic object + action + URL parameters) are configured against the target URL.

Icon	Title	Semantic Object	Action	Parameters	Target URL	Reference	Outdated
	Manage Consolidation Processes	MasterData	consolidate	otc=1405&/massUpdate=	#MasterData-consolidate?otc=1405&/mass Update=		
	Manage Consolidation Processes	MasterData	consolidate	otc=986&/massUpdate=	#MasterData-consolidate?otc=986&/mass Update=		
	Create Consolidation Process	MasterData	consolidate	otc=1405&/viewName=ProcessSetup/standalone=X/massUpdate=/template=/importGuid=	#MasterData-consolidate?otc=1405&/viewName=ProcessSetup/standalone=X/massUpdate=/template=/importGuid=		
	Create Consolidation Process	MasterData	consolidate	otc=986&/viewName=ProcessSetup/standalone=X/massUpdate=/template=/importGuid=	#MasterData-consolidate?otc=986&/viewName=ProcessSetup/standalone=X/massUpdate=/template=/importGuid=		
	Start Mass Processing	MasterData	change	otc=1405&/viewName=ProcessSetup/standalone=X/massUpdate=X/template=/importGuid=	#MasterData-change?otc=1405&/viewName=ProcessSetup/standalone=X/massUpdate=X/template=/importGuid=		
	Manage Mass Processes	MasterData	change	otc=1405&/massUpdate=X	#MasterData-change?otc=1405&/massUpdate=X		
	Import Data for Consolidation	MasterData	import	otc=1405&/viewName=MDCImportCreate/UUID=	#MasterData-import?otc=1405&/viewName=MDCImportCreate/UUID=		
	Manage Imports for Consolidation	MasterData	import	otc=1405&/viewName=MDCImportOverview	#MasterData-import?otc=1405&/viewName=MDCImportOverview		
	Manage Source Data	MasterData	manageSourceData	otc=1405&/viewName=MDCSourcesOverview	#MasterData-manageSourceData?otc=1405&/viewName=MDCSourcesOverview		
	Start Mass Maintenance	MasterData	maintain	otc=1405&/viewName=ProcessSetup/standalone=X/massUpdate=B/template=/importGuid=	#MasterData-maintain?otc=1405&/viewName=ProcessSetup/standalone=X/massUpdate=B/template=/importGuid=		

Figure 9.51 Configuration of Semantic Object, Action, and Parameters against the Target URL

A mandatory requirement of every enterprise web application is Internationalization (i18n). Internationalization is the process of inducing the ability to adapt the application content in various languages.

Internationalization of consolidation and mass processing applications is materialized by storing the UI texts in resource bundle files as key value pairs. The name of each file indicates which language is contained in each bundle file. These files are stored in the *i18n* folder in a SAPUI5 project. However, it's not in the scope of this chapter to explain how these resource bundles are consumed in the SAPUI5 framework.

The current language of the user is determined by the URL parameter `sap-language`. There are other ways to determine the user language, but the language configured in the URL always wins.

Figure 9.52 shows the **Manage Consolidation Process – Business Partner** UI in German based on the URL parameters. The figure also shows the UI rendered in Chinese.

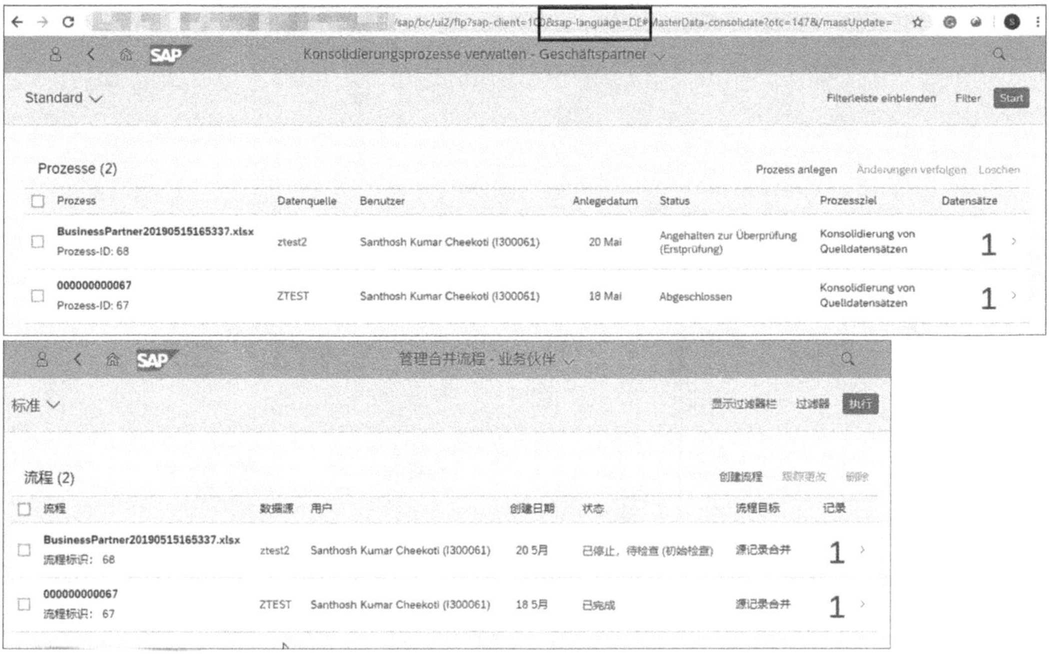

Figure 9.52 Rendering of UI in Different Languages Depending on the URL Parameter Specification of the User Language

Process User Interfaces

The process UIs are used to create, change, delete, and display the consolidation and mass processing process. All the process-related UIs are delivered as SAPUI5 XML views under the application with namespace `mdm.cmd.cmpmonprocs1`. The name of this SAPUI5 application in the ABAP repository is `MD_CMPMONPROCS1`. This single-page application and navigation between different SAPUI5 views is done using hash-based navigation.

View `Main.view.XML` and controller `Main.controller.js` act as the root view and root view controller, respectively, of the component. The root control in the `Main.view.XML` is `sap.m.App`, and the content to aggregation `pages` are added in the runtime by the SAPUI5 router based on the URL parameters during runtime.

> **Note**
>
> The router is initialized with routes and other variables by the component controller.

Figure 9.53 shows how the SAPUI5 control hierarchy is rendered when the Manage Consolidation Process app is opened. The figure shows how view `mdm.cmd.cmpmonprocs1.view.MDCOverview` is added to the pages aggregation of view `mdm.cmd.cmpmonprocs1.Main` during runtime by the SAPUI5 router.

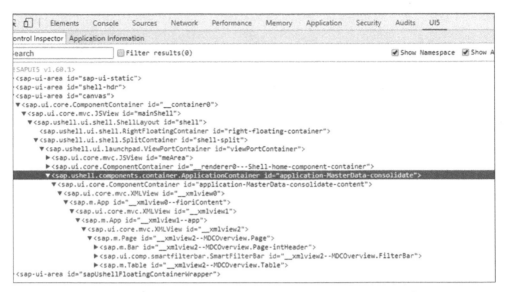

```
R  ⌂  |  Elements   Console   Sources   Network   Performance   Memory   Application   Security   Audits   UI5
ontrol Inspector | Application Information
earch                              Filter results(0)                                    ☑ Show Namespace  ☑ Show A

SAPUI5 v1.60.1>
<sap-ui-area id="sap-ui-static">
<sap-ui-area id="shell-hdr">
<sap-ui-area id="canvas">
▼<sap.ui.core.ComponentContainer id="__container0">
  ▼<sap.ui.core.mvc.JSView id="mainShell">
    ▼<sap.ushell.ui.shell.ShellLayout id="shell">
        <sap.ushell.ui.shell.RightFloatingContainer id="right-floating-container">
      ▼<sap.ushell.ui.shell.SplitContainer id="shell-split">
        ▼<sap.ushell.ui.launchpad.ViewPortContainer id="viewPortContainer">
          ►<sap.ui.core.mvc.JSView id="meArea">
          ►<sap.ui.core.ComponentContainer id="__renderer0---Shell-home-component-container">
          ▼<sap.ushell.components.container.ApplicationContainer id="application-MasterData-consolidate">
            ▼<sap.ui.core.ComponentContainer id="application-MasterData-consolidate-content">
              ▼<sap.ui.core.mvc.XMLView id="__xmlview0">
                ▼<sap.m.App id="__xmlview0--fioriContent">
                  ▼<sap.ui.core.mvc.XMLView id="__xmlview1">
                    ▼<sap.m.App id="__xmlview1--app">
                      ▼<sap.ui.core.mvc.XMLView id="__xmlview2">
                        ▼<sap.m.Page id="__xmlview2--MDCOverview.Page">
                          ►<sap.m.Bar id="__xmlview2--MDCOverview.Page-intHeader">
                          ►<sap.ui.comp.smartfilterbar.SmartFilterBar id="__xmlview2--MDCOverview.FilterBar">
                          ►<sap.m.Table id="__xmlview2--MDCOverview.Table">
<sap-ui-area id="sapUshellFloatingContainerWrapper">
```

Figure 9.53 Control Hierarchy of the Consolidation and Mass Processing Application in Runtime

> **Tip**
>
> Figure 9.53 shows the control hierarchy of the consolidation and mass processing SAPUI5 application using the SAPUI5 Inspector tool. SAPUI5 Inspector is a standard chrome extension for debugging and getting to know SAPUI5 applications. More information about this tool can be found in the GitHub page at *https://github.com/SAP/ui5-inspector*.

Process Overview User Interface

The generic process overview UI displays the list of processes created for a business object (147 for business partner and 194 for material) and a process goal (consolidation or mass processing). Figure 9.54 shows the process overview UI for consolidation processes for business partner.

The name of the SAPUI5 view is MDCOverview for the process overview UI. The view changes its content based on the URL parameters, thus making it flexible and reusable across business objects and process goals. Primarily, this view accepts two URL parameters. Table 9.12 shows the URL parameters required for this SAPUI5 view.

Figure 9.55 shows all the consolidation processes for the business partner because the URL parameter massUpdate is set as null. In this figure, and the next, we can see that it's a hash-based URL ❶ with separate parts for the semantic objects ❷ and the URL parameters ❸.

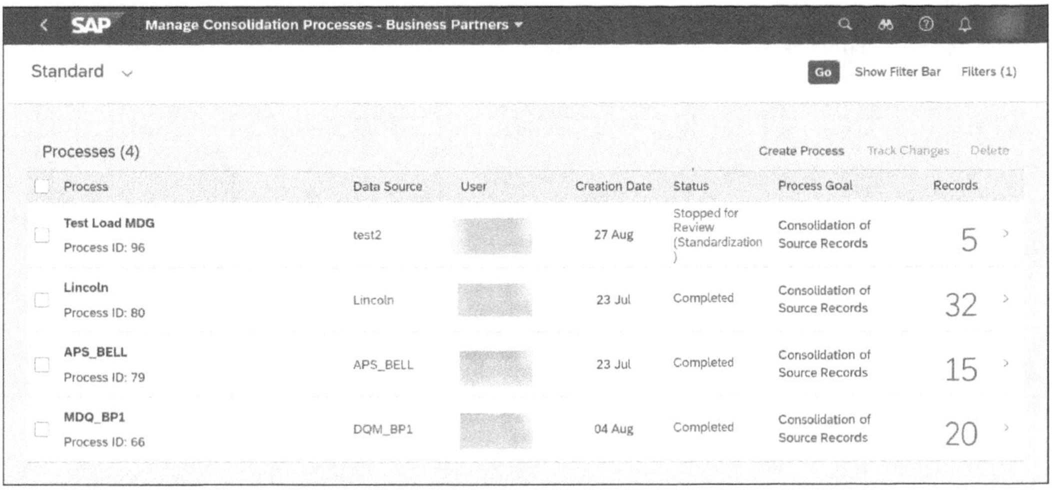

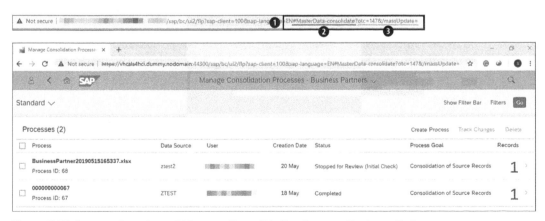

Figure 9.54 Process Overview UI

URL Parameter	Description	Possible Values
otc	Business object This is a mandatory parameter.	■ 147: Business Partner ■ 194: Material ■ 1405: Business Partner Relationships
massUpdate	Indicates whether the application should list only the process with mass update for the business object goal. The value for this URL parameter is optional.	■ X: Mass Update ■ Null: Show only the process with the consolidation for the business object goal ■ B: Basic Mass Update ■ Null: Consolidation

Table 9.12 URL Parameters for the Process Overview UI

Figure 9.55 Process Overview of Manage Consolidation Process: Business Partners

Figure 9.56 shows all the mass processes for business partner because the URL parameter massUpdate is set as X.

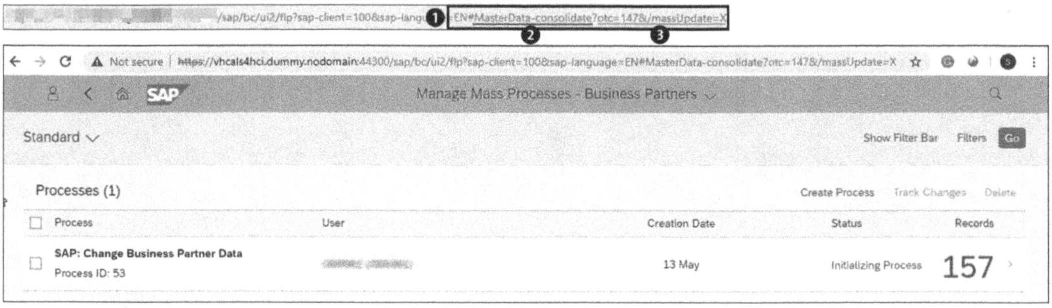

Figure 9.56 Process Overview of Manage Mass Process: Business Partners

The OData service used in the process overview UI changes based on the business object (mentioned as URL parameter otc). Table 9.13 shows business objects and their corresponding OData services that will be invoked by the process overview UI.

Business Object	OData Service
Business Partner (147)	MDC_PROCESS_SRV__147
Material (194)	MDC_PROCESS_SRV__194
Business Partner Relationship (1405)	MDC_PROCESS_SRV__1405

Table 9.13 OData Services for Business Objects Invoked by Consolidation and Mass Processing

XML view MDCOverview is the design-time artifact for the process overview UI. The XML view primarily consists of two UI controls:

- **Smart filter bar**
  This control belongs to the UI library sap.ui.comp.smartfilterbar. During runtime, this control is rendered as a filter bar with input fields to filter the processes based on user-defined filter criteria. By default, this filter bar is hidden, but you can open it by clicking on the **Show Filter Bar** hyperlink. Figure 9.57 shows the smart filter bar in the process overview UI. The filter bar contains the following input fields:
  - **Process ID**
  - **Process Description**
  - **Requestor of the Process**
  - **Process Creation Date**
  - **Process Status**
  - **Process Goal**
  - **Marked for Deletion**

Input fields such as **Process Status**, **Process Goal**, and **Requestor of the Process** will derive the value set from the backend (ABAP server) and from the entity set `DataValueDescriptionSet`. The entity set belongs to the corresponding OData service mentioned in Table 9.13.

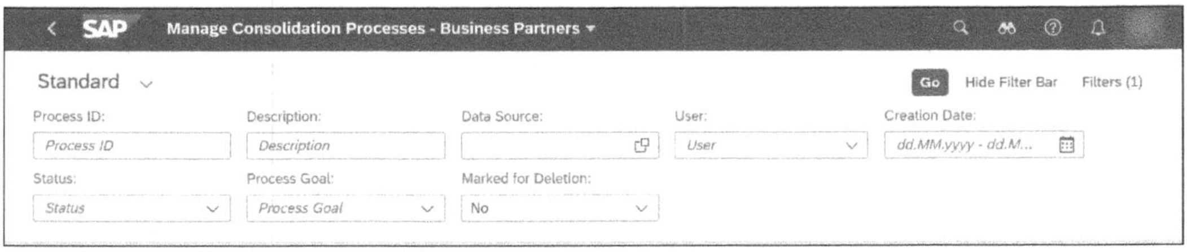

Figure 9.57 Smart Filter Bar, Link to Control Its Visibility, and Input Fields to Enter Filter Criteria

- **Table**

  Table is rendered using the `sap.m.table` library. The table mode property is set as `multiselect`, which means that multiple rows can be selected at the same time. The table has the following events:

  - `toDisplayProc`: This event is triggered when any row on the table is triggered. This event will trigger navigation to SAPUI5 XML view `MDCProcDisplay`.
  - `onSelectionChanged`: This event is triggered whenever selection of a table row is changed. The event handler controls the visibility of buttons in the table toolbar based on the selection.

  The table toolbar has the following buttons:

  - `ProcCreateBtn`: This button is used to create a new process. The handler for the `Press` event of the button is `toCreateProc`. The event handler for this event will trigger navigation to the SAPUI5 XML view `MDCProcSetup`. This button is visible and enabled by default, but only if you have sufficient backend authorization.
  - `ProcDeleteBtn`: This button is used to delete the selected process. The handler for the `Press` event of the button is `deleteProc`. This button isn't enabled by default; the button is enabled only when a table row is selected. Its visibility is controlled by the `onSelectionChanged` event of the table. To delete the process, the view controller will trigger an OData batch request of type `Delete` on the entity set `ROOTSet`.
  - `trackChanges`: This button will trigger navigation to an external UI to display the mass changes done as part of the process. This button is visible only for completed processes.

Figure 9.58 shows the table UI control in the process overview UI. It also shows how the visibility of the buttons in the table toolbar is changed based on the table row selections. The buttons are invisible because the row selection hasn't been made ❶; once one is selected ❷, they become visible.

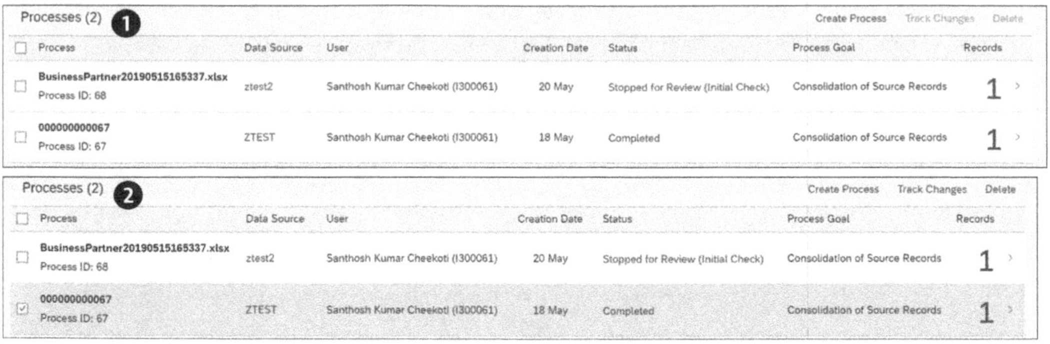

Figure 9.58 Table UI Control in the Process Overview UI

Process Setup User Interface

The process setup UI is used to create processes. Figure 9.59 shows the process setup UI for creating a consolidation process for business partners.

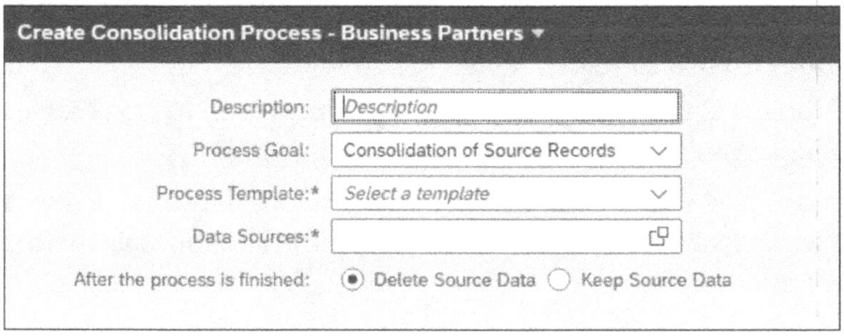

Figure 9.59 Process Setup for Creating a Consolidation Process: Business Partners

This UI can be used to create the following processes:

- **Start Mass Processing**
  The UI starting mass processing is rendered when the URL parameter massUpdate = X.

- **Create Consolidation**
  The UI creating consolidation process is rendered when the URL parameters massUpdate is null.

Note

This process setup UI can also be used to create remediation processes and evaluation processes; however, these processes aren't in the scope of this chapter.

This view has the following fields arranged using layout sap.ui.layout.form.Simple-Form:

- **Description**
  This input field is used to store a meaningful description of the process to be created.

- **Process Goal**
  This field is used to specify the process goal. The value set for this field is derived from domain values of the MDC_PROCESS_GOAL domain. This field is visible only when creating a consolidation process.

- **Process Template**
  This field is used to specify the template for the process. The value set is again fetched using the OData service from entity set DataValueDescriptionSet. The value set during runtime is changed based on the type of process, process goal, and business object.

- **Data Sources**
  This is an input field with value help activated. Using the value help dialog, the user can select multiple data sources. This field visibility is also controlled based on the URL parameters and process goal. If the URL parameter importGuid is mentioned, then this field is hidden, and data from the import GUID will be considered as data sources. This field is only visible for consolidation processes with the consolidation source records goal.

Note

Data source in the context of the process setup UI refers to the source data package belonging to a source system.

Along with the UI control simple form, the SAPUI5 view has a toolbar in the page footer. The toolbar has a ProcDisplayBtn button. The label of this button is **Save**. The press event of the button is handled using event handler toProcDisplay. After this button is clicked, a process will be created by creating an OData entity of type ROOTSet. Although the OData operation is performed asynchronously, the page is set to busy state. If the OData operation is successful, then navigation will be triggered to the SAPUI5 view MDCProcDisplay; if the OData operation fails, then the message handling of the messages from the server will be performed to inform the user about the error and provide the user an option to correct the errors.

Process Display User Interface

The process display UI is where the process execution happens. The UI changes dynamically based on the URL parameters and authorizations. Like other views, the process display UI can be reused for multiple process goals (consolidation, mass processing, evaluation, and remediation). Figure 9.60 shows an example of the process display UI with the consolidation process for business partner. The elements of the UI are as follows:

❶ Process object details

❷ Number of records in the scope of the process

❸ Progress indicator to show the status of the process object

❹ Tab bar where each tab represents one step configured as part of process template

❺ Page footer with all the buttons required to execute the process

❻ KPI UI containing all the key figures of the process step

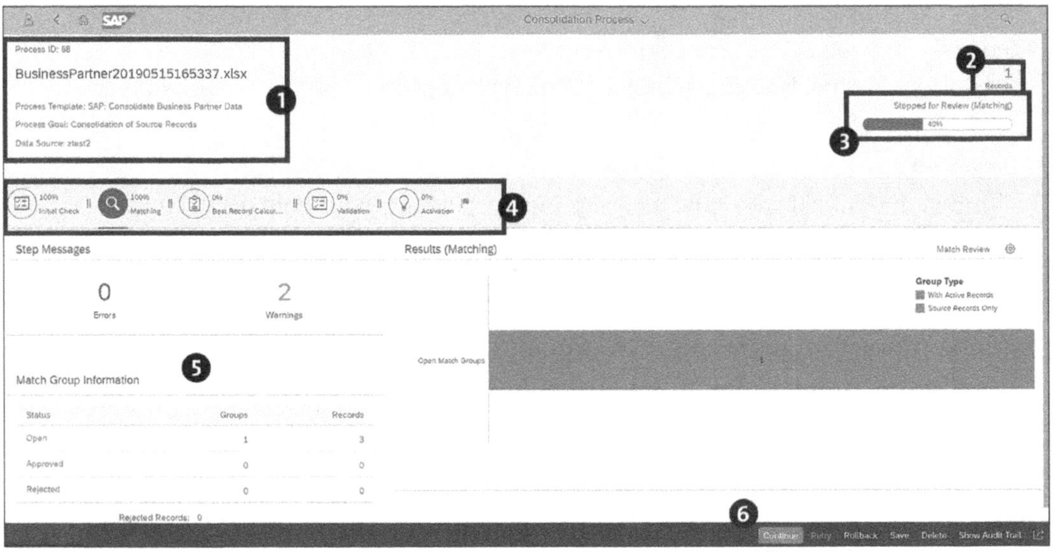

Figure 9.60 Display Process UI for the Business Partner Consolidation Process

The technical name of the SAPUI5 XML view that renders the process display UI is MDCProcDisplay.

All the UI controls in the XML view MDCProcDisplay are wrapped in the layout control sap.ui.layout.DynamicSideContent, which allows additional content to be displayed in a responsive way on the side of existing view controls. The additional content won't overlay the main content; instead, the main content will become narrower and make way for the side content. In the process display UI, the audit trail of the process is displayed as side content. This side content is triggered by clicking on the **Show Audit Trail** button. Figure 9.61 shows different SAPUI5 controls that are rendered when the display process UI is loaded in the browser, as follows:

❶ sap.m.ObjectHeader

❷ MDCStepKPI

❸ Sap.m.IconTabBar

❹ sap.m.Bar

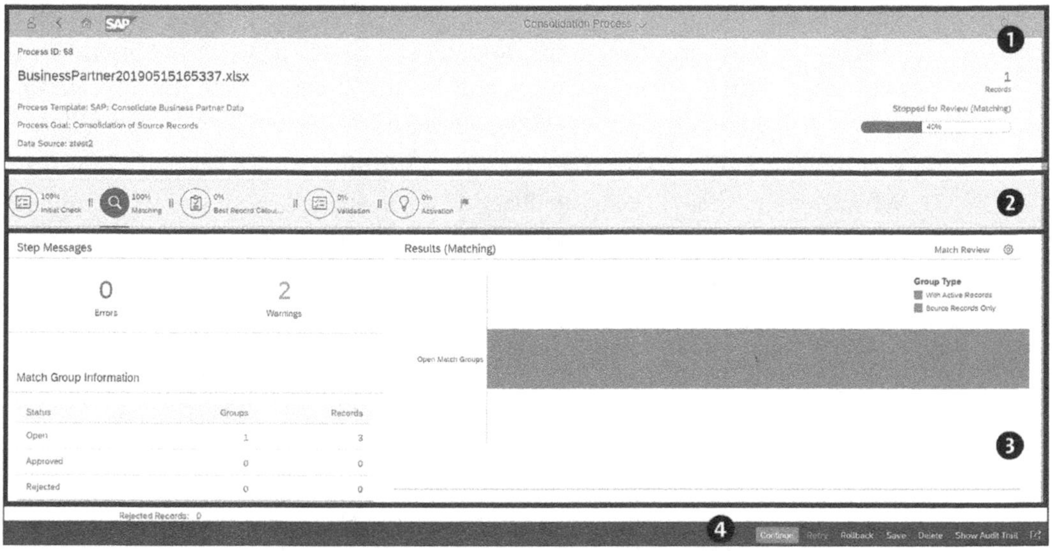

Figure 9.61 Rendering of Different SAPUI5 Controls in the Display Process UI

In Figure 9.61 MDCStepKPI is an XML view that is dynamically added to this page for steps that are completed. For steps that aren't completed, the XML view MDCStepParam will be added.

Following are the different SAPUI5 controls in the process display UI:

- **Object header**
  This display-only control is used to display all the key details of the process, including the **Process ID**. The control is rendered using the SAPUI5 sap.m.ObjectHeader library. The data source for this control is entity set RootSet of the corresponding OData service, as mentioned earlier in Table 9.13.

- **Tab bar**
  This interactive control displays each process step of process template as a tab with icons. During the design time, no tab items are added. During the runtime, a list of steps for the current process is retrieved using an OData service from entity set StepSet. For each step, a tab item of type sap.m.IconTabFilter is added dynamically. The onStepSelect method in the view controller is the handler for the tab bar select event.

  The onStepSelect method takes care of adding the step details view when a tab is selected. If the selected step is in status **Completed**, then this method will add the MDCStepKPI view; if the selected step isn't completed, then the method will render the MDCStepParam view.

- **Page footer**
  The page footer consists of multiple buttons:

- **Retry** button: This button will execute a failed process step again. This button is only visible if the user has authorization to change the process, and the status of the step is **Partially Finished**. When this button is clicked, the function import RETRY_STEP of the corresponding OData service is called by the view controller.
- **Rollback** button: This button will roll back to a previous step selected by the user. When the button is clicked, a **Rollback** dialog is opened, as shown in Figure 9.62. The rollback is executed by calling function import ROLLBACK of the OData service mentioned in Table 9.13.

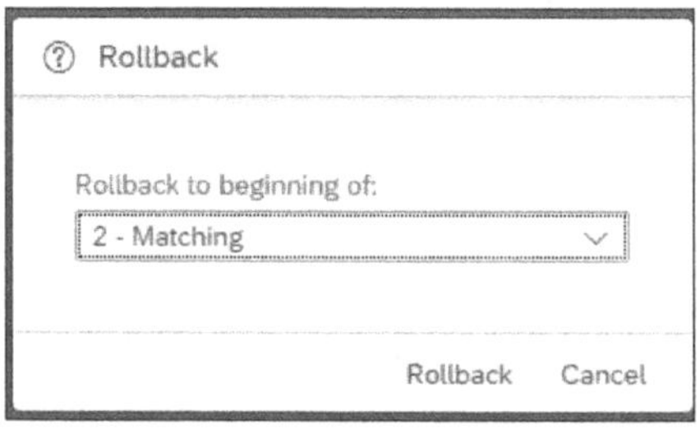

Figure 9.62 Rollback Dialog That Opens When the Rollback Button Is Clicked

- **Save** button: This button is used to save the current state of the process. The Save operation issues an OData put operation on the entity StepSet of the OData service mentioned in Table 9.13.

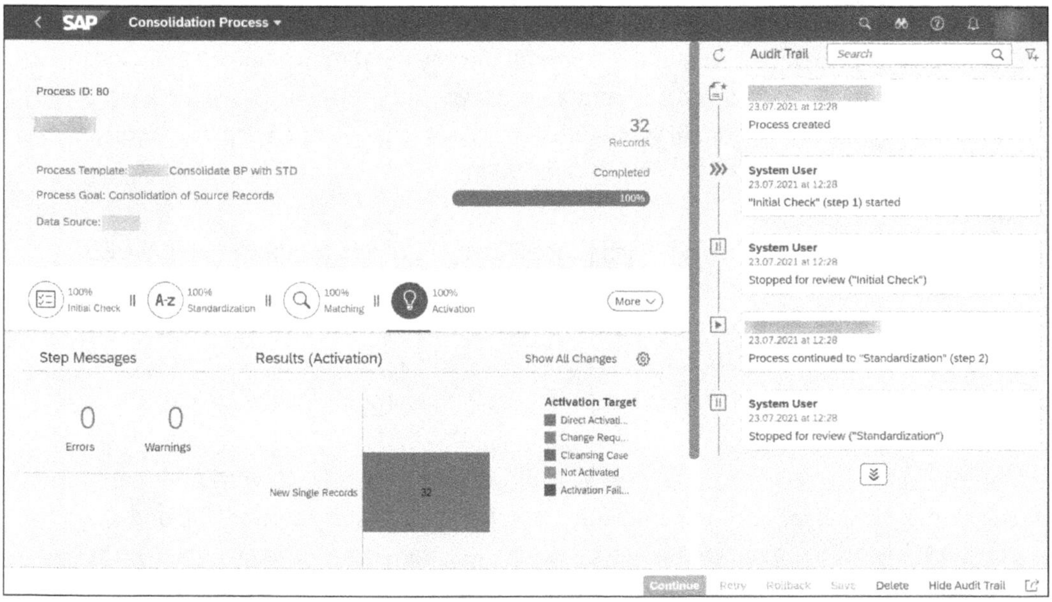

Figure 9.63 Audit Trail Displayed as Side Content in the Process Display UI

- **Delete** button: This button is used to delete the current process, including the process data. This button is only visible if the user has the authorization to delete a process. The delete operation is executed by calling the OData operation `remove` (delete) on the entity `ROOTSet` of the OData service mentioned in Table 9.13.

- **Show/Hide Audit Trail** button: This button opens side content that shows the audit trail of the process. The description of this button toggles between **Show Audit Trail** and **Hide Audit Trail**. When this button is clicked, XML SAPUI5 view `timeline` is rendered as side content of the UI. Figure 9.63 shows the audit trail being rendered as side content in the process display UI.

Match Review User Interface

Matching is a consolidation process step during which the system checks data from various source systems and active areas for duplicates. The duplicates are grouped together in match groups.

Best record calculation is a consolidation process step that contains the cumulated data from the match group.

Both the best record calculation step and the matching step change the meaning or interpretation of source data. It's therefore required to have a review UI for each of these steps, so that the user can see the results. This is where the review UIs come into focus. The match review UI is for reviewing the results of the matching step in a consolidation process, and the best record calculation review UI is for reviewing the results of the best record calculation step. Figure 9.64 shows the match review UI, and Figure 9.65 shows the best record calculation review UI.

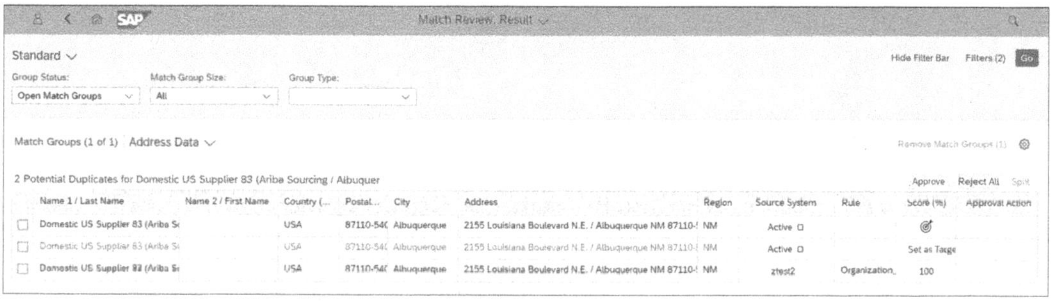

Figure 9.64 Match Review UI

Figure 9.65 Best Record Calculation Review UI

Import Data User Interface

There are two kinds of tables in consolidation and mass processing that are used for staging the data before activation: source tables and process tables. Source tables are used for storing the source data from different source systems, and process tables are used to store the data that is currently being processed in a consolidation and mass processing process.

Loading the data into source tables is an important step before you can start a consolidation process. Data is transferred from source tables to process tables only using a consolidation process. There are many ways to load the data into source tables, and you can even use popular ETL tools. However, if you want to use the native capabilities of consolidation and mass processing, then you must use the import data UI. Like the process UI, the import data UI is also business object independent. This UI loads the data into source tables in data packages. You specify the business object in the URL parameters. Figure 9.66, Figure 9.67, and Figure 9.68 show how the import data UI is rendered for different business objects just by changing the URL parameters.

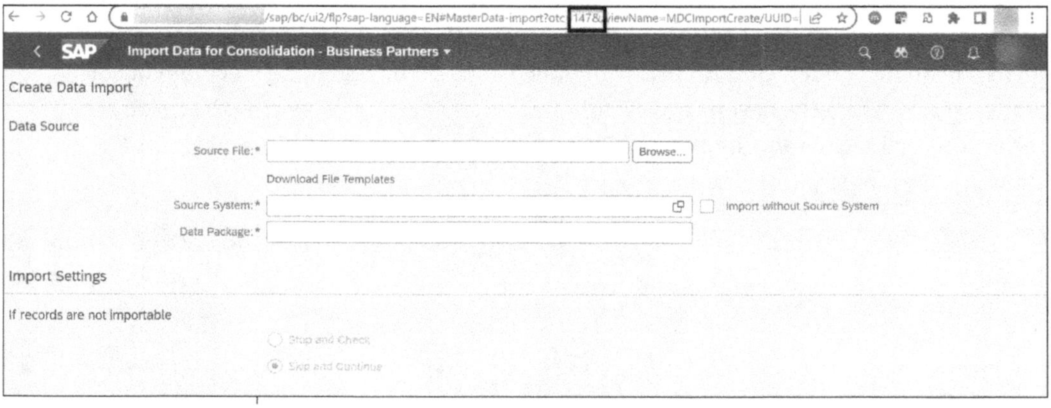

Figure 9.66 Import Data for Consolidation UI for Business Partner

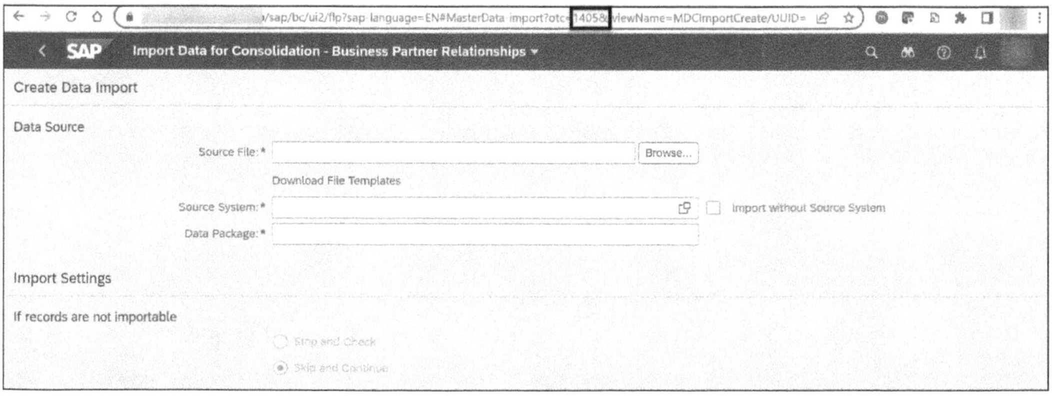

Figure 9.67 Import Data for Consolidation UI for Business Partner Relationships

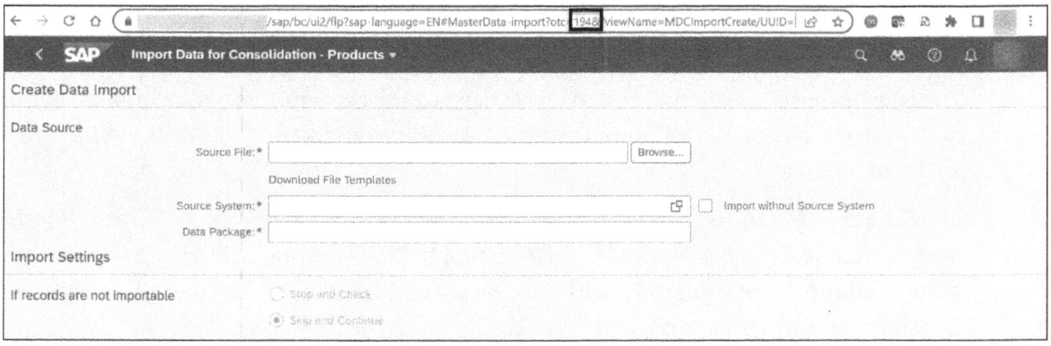

Figure 9.68 Import Data for Consolidation UI for Products

The name of the SAPUI5 application in the ABAP repository is `MD_CMPIMPFILES1`, and the full name space of the application is `mdm.cmd.cmpimportfiles1`. The OData service used by the SAPUI5 application is `MDC_IMPORT_SRV`. The root SAPUI5 XML view for the application is `App.view.XML`, and the controller for the root view is `App.controller.js`. The navigation between the root view and other view of the application is handled by the SAPUI5 router based on the pattern in a hash-based URL. The authorization objects primarily checked in the import data UI are as follows:

- `MDC_PFILT`
- `MDC_LOAD`

Import Overview User Interface

The import overview UI lists all the data imports created. It's a worklist of data imports, except that it's not user specific. The UI will list all the data imports created in the system. Figure 9.69 shows the import overview for business partners. The table is bound to entity set `C_MasterDataImport` of OData service `MDC_IMPORT_SRV`.

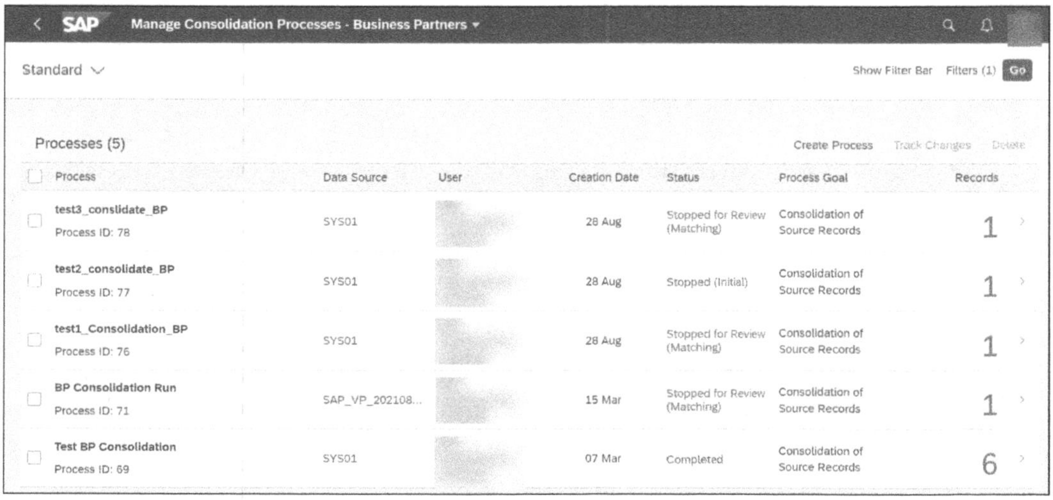

Figure 9.69 Import Overview UI for Business Partners

The smart filter control is rendered using `sap.ui.comp.smartfilterbar`, and the table control is rendered using `sap.m.table`.

The **New Import** button in the overview is used to start creation of a data import. When this button is clicked, the view controller triggers navigation to SAPUI5 XML view `MDCImportCreate`.

The **Delete** button is used to delete a data import. The `press` event of the button is handled by the controller method `onDeleteImport`. This method will trigger an OData request of type `remove` on the entity set `C_MasterDataImport`. When the row is selected, the controller will trigger navigation to the `MDCImportDetails` view.

Import Create User Interface

The import create UI is used to create a data import (see Figure 9.70). This UI is rendered by XML SAPUI5 view `MDCImportCreate`. Navigation to the UI can occur from the import overview UI by clicking on the **New Import** button or by clicking the **Create Import** SAP Fiori tile directly.

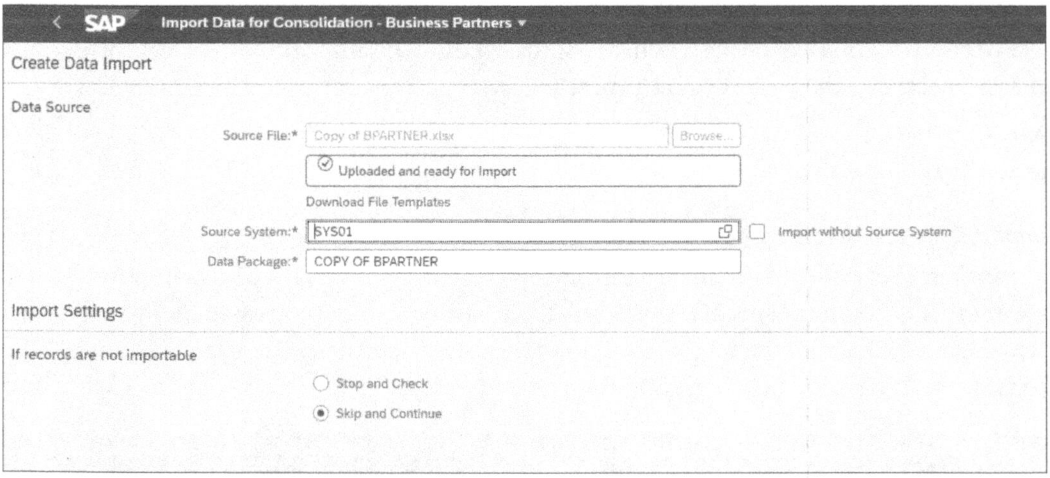

Figure 9.70 Import Create UI

9.8.3   Backend Architecture

The following sections explain the backend architecture of the consolidation and mass processing application.

OData Services

RESTful services conform to the Representational State Transfer (REST) architecture style. HTTP is an example of a RESTful service. OData services are RESTful web services that conform to OData specifications. The payload of an OData service response and request must conform to the OData specifications.

Consolidation and mass processing applications use OData services 2.0 to interact with the backend (SAP NetWeaver Application Server for ABAP).

SAP Gateway is a native framework on SAP NetWeaver AS ABAP. SAP Gateway provides a runtime environment to process an OData client request. SAP Gateway also provides a design-time environment for developing OData services.

OData services are generated based on data models built on entity data model (EDM) concepts. These models are built on SAP Gateway Service Builder using Transaction SEGW.

> **Note**
>
> You can generate core data services (CDS) models and views as OData services via the Service Adaptation Description Language (SADL) and OData annotations. However, this isn't in the scope of this chapter.

All consolidation and mass processing (excluding SAP Data Quality Management and data quality remediation) OData services are primarily based on four SAP Gateway projects:

- `MDC_PROCESS`
  This is the core SAP Gateway project that is responsible for transactional handling of consolidation and mass processing processes. Table 9.14 lists the OData service implementations that are generated based on this SAP Gateway project.

OData Service Name	Description
MDC_PROCESS_SRV	MDC Process Object
MDC_PROCESS_SRV__147	MDC Process Object for Business Partner
MDC_PROCESS_SRV__194	MDC Process Object for Material
MDC_PROCESS_SRV__1405	Service for MDC Business Partner Relationships

Table 9.14 OData Services Generated Based on the MDC_PROCESS SAP Gateway Project

- `MDC_IMPORT`
  This SAP Gateway project is used for generation of OData service `MDC_IMPORT_SRV`, which is primarily used for handling the requests from the import data UI as described in Section 9.8.2. This SAP Gateway project is modeled on the CDS view `C_MasterDataImport`.

- `MDC_EXPORT`
  This SAP Gateway project is used for generation of OData service `MDC_EXPORT_SRV`, which is primarily used to handle OData requests from the export data UI.

Business Object Processing Framework

The Business Object Processing Framework (BOPF) is used to represent a business object as a hierarchal tree of nodes. Each node consists of semantically similar data in the form of elements. BOPF is used for transaction handling of consolidation and mass processing data.

> **Note**
>
> To understand BOPF in detail, refer to the BOPF developer guide at *http://s-prs.co/v488303*.

BOPF Business Object: MDC_PROCESS

This BOPF object represents the process object, which is common for consolidation and mass processing, data quality management, and data quality remediation in SAP Master Data Governance. However, in the current chapter, we refer to the process object only in the context of consolidation and mass processing.

Figure 9.71 shows the BOPF business object model of the MDC_PROCESS object.

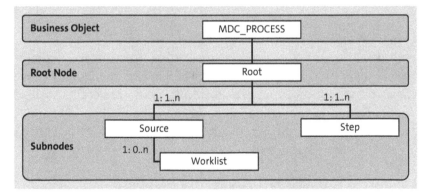

Figure 9.71 Business Object Model for the MDC_PROCESS Object

The structure of the MDC_PROCESS business object can be explained as follows:

- ROOT
  The name of the root node is ROOT. The attributes of the node are represented by Data Dictionary (DDIC) structure MDC_S_PROCESS. Each instance of root node represents one consolidation and mass processing process. Figure 9.72 shows actions, determination, validations, and queries for the ROOT entity.

- SOURCE
  The SOURCE node of the source system record. Each instance of this node represents the source system details, such as number of records and status. You can load data from multiple source systems in one consolidation process, so one ROOT entity can have multiple instances of SOURCE node. The attributes of the SOURCE entity are represented by DDIC structure MDC_S_PROCESS_SOURCE.

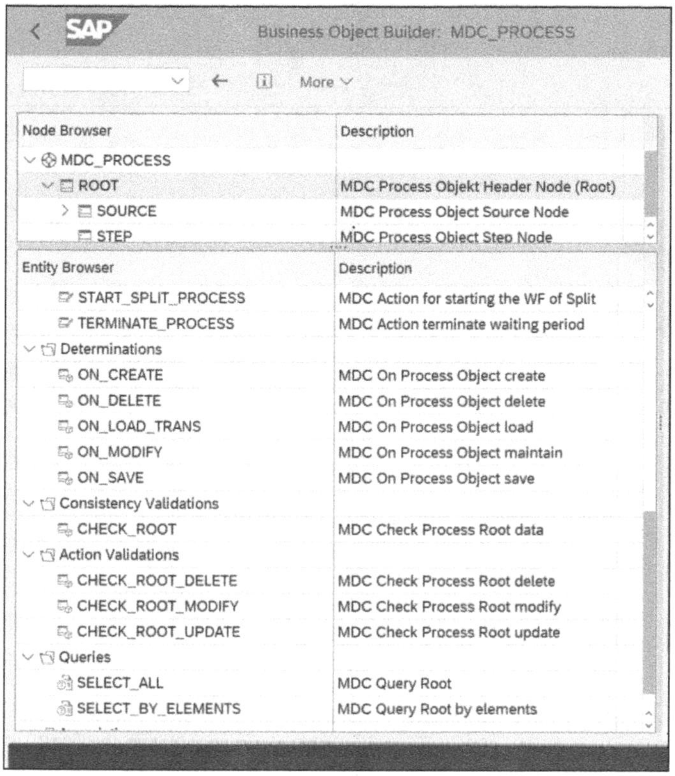

Figure 9.72 Actions, Determinations, Validations, and Queries for the ROOT Entity of BOPF Business Object MDC_PROCESS

- **STEP**

  The STEP node represents each step of a consolidation process. A step can be standardization steps, validation steps, matching steps, and so on. The attributes of the STEP node are represented by DDIC structure MDC_S_PROCESS_STEP.

BOPF Business Object: I_MASTERDATAIMPORTTP

Unlike BOPF business object MDC_PROCESS, this business object is generated from CDS view I_MasterDataImportTP using the @objectModel annotations.

The root node of the business object is I_MASTERDATAIMPORTTP, and the root node has one subnode named I_MASTERDATAIMPORTSTATISTICTP.

Workflows

SAP Business Workflow makes it easy to model business models in the SAP system. Consolidation and mass processing uses SAP Business Workflow to handle the process right from the start (when the user clicks the **Start** button) till the process is complete through activation. SAP Business Workflow is based on Business Object Repository (BOR) objects.

During runtime, the workflow is called by BOPF object MDC_PROCESS, and the workflow that needs to be started is determined based on the process template selected by the user during runtime.

> **Note**
>
> The standard workflow template WS54500001 can't be used to determine agents for different process steps of a process.

SAP delivers workflow template WS54500001 and BOR object BUS2240. This workflow starts on BOR event STARTED ❷. Figure 9.73 shows the start event of workflow template WS54500001 ❶ and the event data that is passed from the event caller to the workflow ❸.

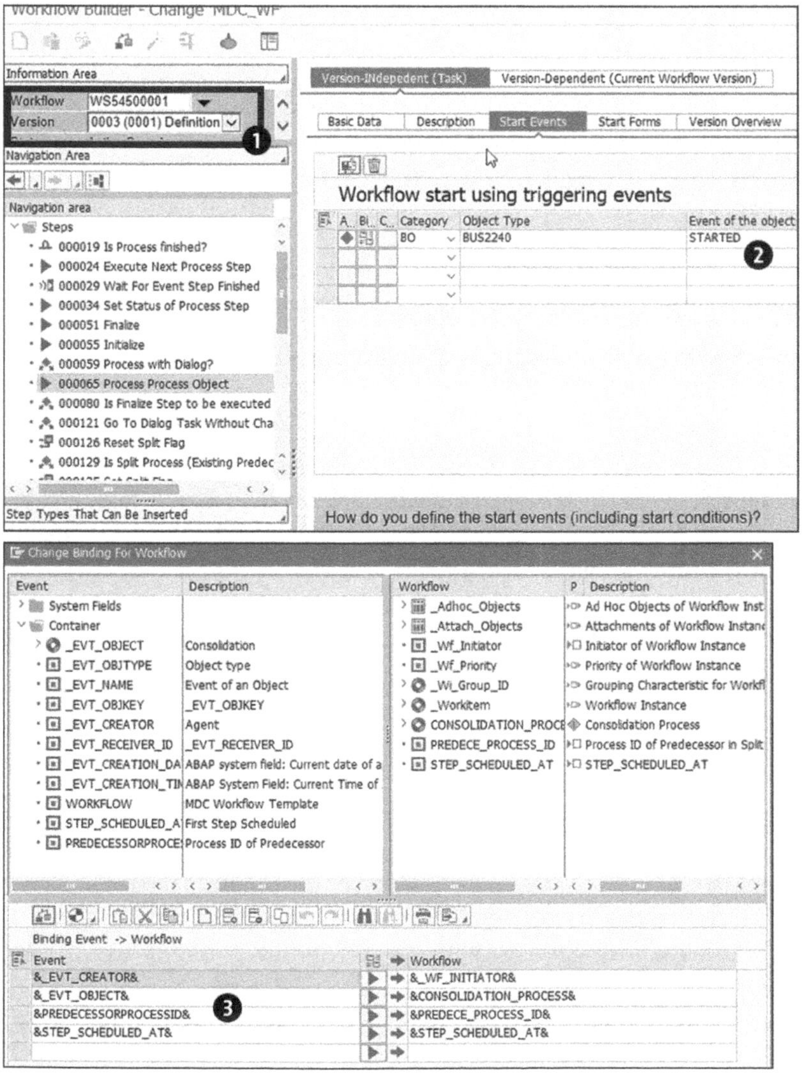

Figure 9.73 Start Events of Workflow Template WS5450001

Adapter Classes

There are two important classes to understand regarding the consolidation and mass processing backend architecture:

- Adapter classes
- Data model classes

Adapter classes are responsible for executing the process step and passing the results of the execution to the consolidation and mass processing framework. Any ABAP class that implements interface IF_MDC_ADAPTER is called an adapter class. Figure 9.74 shows the list of available adapter classes.

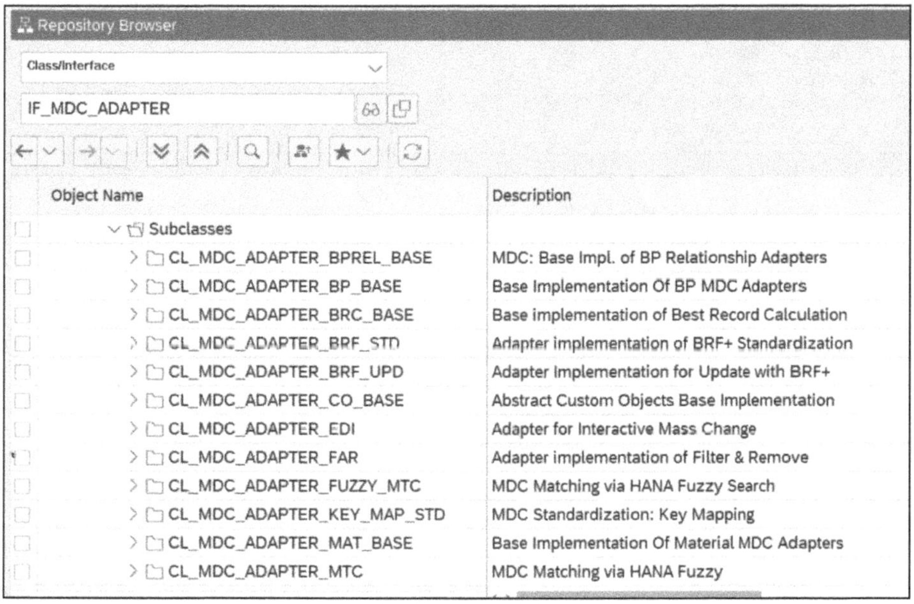

Figure 9.74 List of Available Adapter Classes

Adapter classes are configured against the process step in the process template. For further details on how to set up process templates, Section 9.9.1.

To use an adapter class in the process template, you need to first register the class and assign it to a business object type, as shown in Figure 9.75.

Data model classes are responsible for transaction handling for business object data. They facilitate saving data from consolidation and mass processing process tables to active area tables.

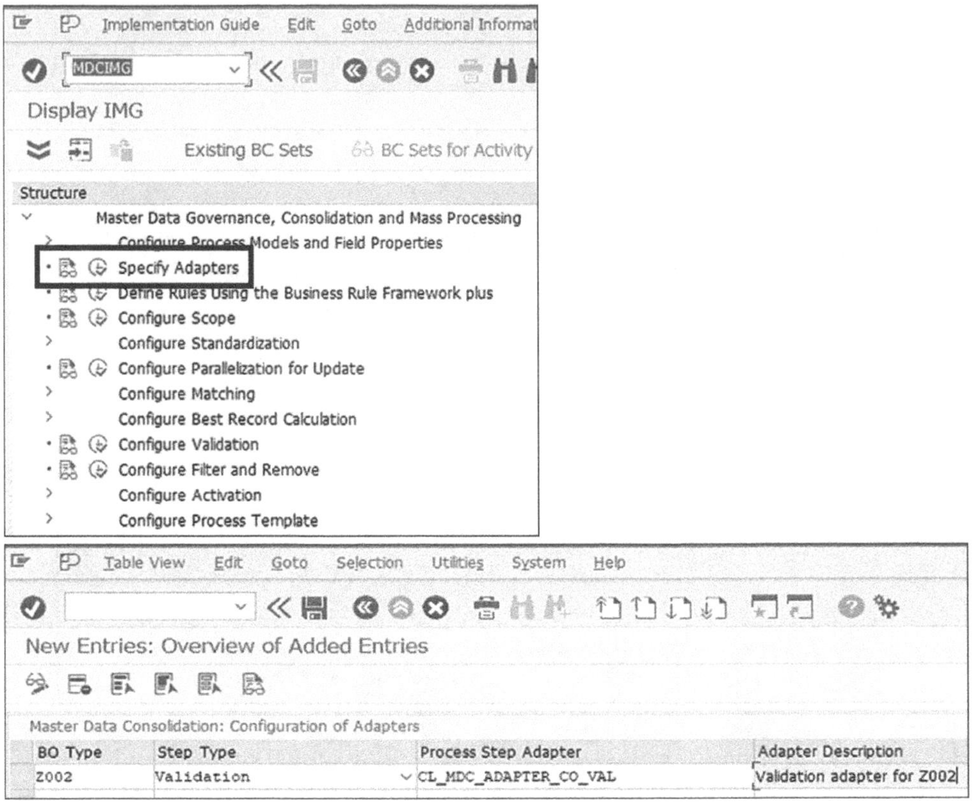

Figure 9.75 Steps to Register and Assign an Adapter Class to a Business Object Type

9.9   Backend Extensibility

The following section describes how to extend consolidation and mass processing by building a custom object for the purchase info record. This example is intended to provide you with a process that will allow you to build any custom object you need for consolidation and mass processing.

9.9.1   Building Custom Objects: Consolidation

In this section, we'll build purchase info records as custom objects in the consolidation and mass processing tool. Before taking a deep dive, however, a little refresher about purchase info records will be helpful.

Sources of supply are data records that store the relationship between materials and vendors. Possible sources of supply are purchase info records and outline purchase agreements (contract and scheduling agreements).

The purchase info record is part of the purchasing department's master data. It contains data concerning the relationship between material and vendor or a material group and vendor. The data stored at the info record level is used as default data in documents such as purchase orders.

Two tables, EINA (Purchasing Info Record: General Data) and EINE (Purchasing Info Record: Purchasing Organization Data), will be used as the foundation for creating a process model for purchase info records in consolidation and mass processing.

> **Caution**
>
> The choice of purchase info record as the custom object use case for consolidation and mass processing is arbitrary. Our intention is to explain the steps needed to create custom objects for consolidation and mass processing. Perform due diligence before making any project decisions based on the content of this chapter.

Create Process Model

Designing the process model is the first step toward building custom objects for consolidation and mass processing. Every process model in consolidation and mass processing is based on active tables. Active tables store the final consolidated, standardized, and processed data.

In simple terms, the process model is the design-time configuration artifact based on which the consolidation and mass processing framework generates source tables, process tables, and status tables. These tables are required to run the consolidation and mass processing process.

The first step toward creating the process model is the creation of a business object.

> **Tip**
>
> SAP provides many business objects out of the box; if your business object already exists, then you can skip this step.

Figure 9.76 shows the creation of business object Z001 for purchase info records. Following are the steps to create the business object:

1. Go to Transaction IDMIMG ❶.
2. Follow the IMG **Enhance Key Mapping Content** · **Define Business Objects** ❷ and ❸.
3. Click on the **New Entries** button ❹.
4. Enter "Z002" in the **BO Type** column ❺.
5. Enter "Purchase Info Record" in the **Description** column ❻.

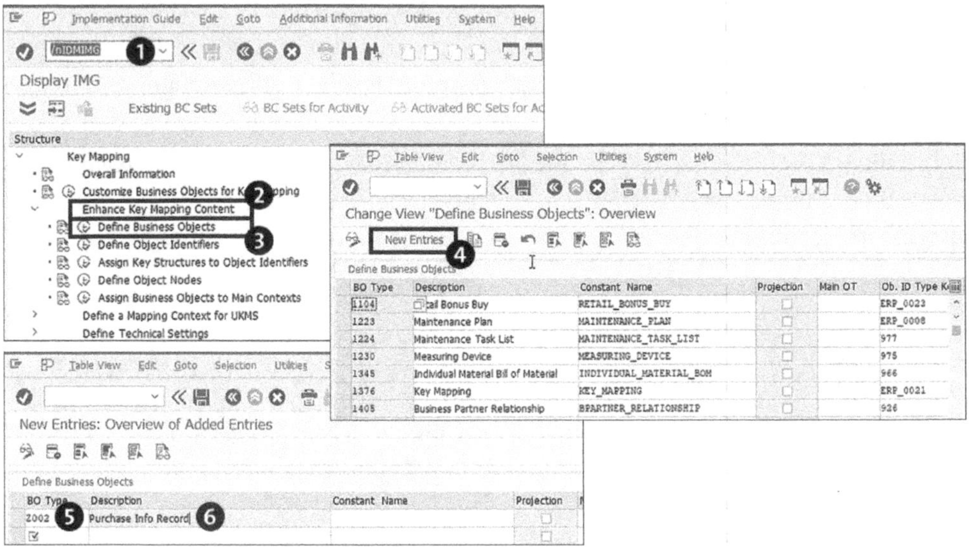

Figure 9.76 Creating Business Object Z001

After the business object is created, you then create the process model. The process model will be created with the business object as the leading entity, which, in this case, is **Z002**.

Following are the steps to create a process model based on a business object (see Figure 9.77):

❶ Go to Transaction MDCMODEL.

❷ Click on the **New Entries** button.

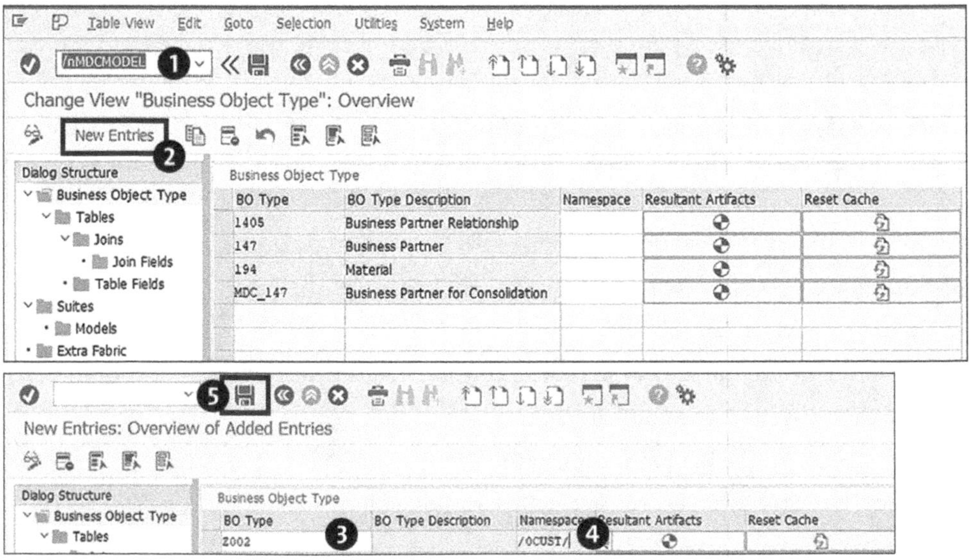

Figure 9.77 Creating Process Model Z002

❸ Enter "Z002" in the **BO Type** column.

❹ Enter "/OCUST/" in the **Namespace** column. (This step is optional; it's only required for partner solutions.)

❺ Click the **Save** button.

After the business object is added to the process model as the leading entity, the next step is to assign the tables to the business object. These tables are the basis for creating the source and process table at a later step. It's mandatory to have one table—and only one table—designated as the root table. When you have multiple tables assigned to the process models, each table should associate to the root table using joins.

Following are the steps to add tables to the process model (see Figure 9.78):

❶ Select **BO Type Z002**.

❷ Click on the **Tables** folder in the **Dialog Structure**.

❸ Click on the **New Entries** button.

❹ Enter "Z1EINA" as the table in the first row. Table Z1EINA will be mapped to active area table EINA in the model classes. We can't enter table EINA due to namespace restrictions.

❺ Designate the table Z1EINA as root table by clicking on the checkbox in the **Root** column. This setting will make active table Z1EINA the root table of BO Type Z002.

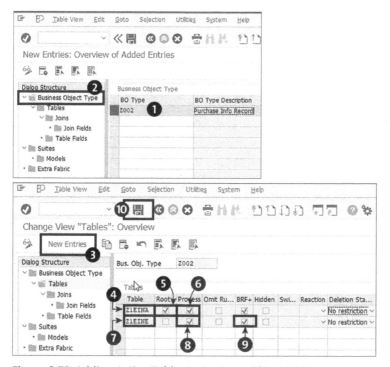

Figure 9.78 Adding Active Tables to Business Object Z002

❻ Designate table Z1EINA as relevant for the process. This setting will ensure that process tables are generated for table Z1EINA.

❼ In the second row, enter active table "Z1EINE".

❽ Designate table Z1EINE as relevant for the process.

❾ Enable generation of BRFplus artifacts for table Z1EINE by selecting the checkbox in the **BRF+** column.

❿ Click on the **Save** button.

Figure 9.78 shows the sequence of steps to add tables to the business object type Z002.

Because multiple tables are added to business object Z002, we need to associate nonroot table Z1EINE to root table Z1EINA using joins and **Join** fields.

Following are the steps to add joins between active tables Z1EINA and Z1EINE using join fields, as shown in Figure 9.79:

❶ Select **Table EINA**.

❷ Double-click on the **Joins** folder in the **Dialog Structure** hierarchy.

❸ Click on **New Entries** to add the join table.

❹ Add "Z1EINE" as the join table.

❺ Select the table as **Process** relevant.

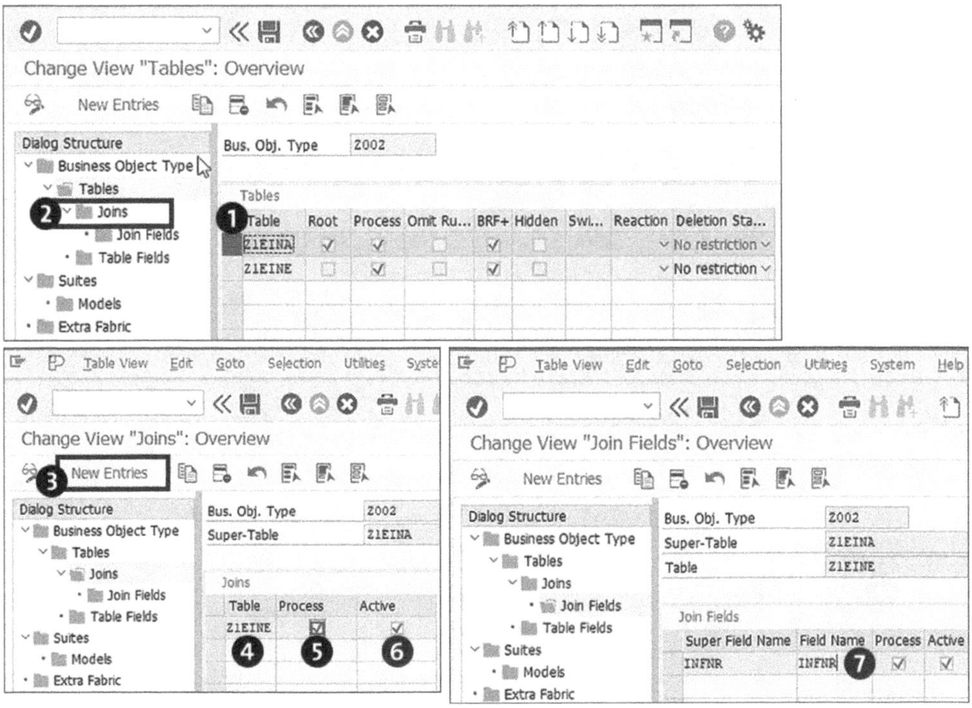

Figure 9.79 Adding Joins between Tables Z1EINA and Z1EINE

❻ Select the table as **Active**.

❼ Select **Z1EINE**, and click on **Join Fields** in the **Dialog Structure** hierarchy. Add field "INFNR" as the join field.

After the tables are added and joins between the tables are established, the basic setup for a process model is complete. It's time now to generate the final artifacts based on the process model configuration. Following are the resultant artifacts that will be generated:

- **Source tables**
  Source tables are used by consolidation and mass processing to stage the data. Before being processed by the consolidation and mass processing process, the data in these tables isn't validated. There is one source table each for table Z1EINE and Z1EINA. The table names end with the _SRC suffix.

- **Process tables**
  Process tables are used by consolidation and mass processing to store the data that is currently being processed. The data in these tables goes through various transformations as the consolidation and mass processing process proceeds from one process step to another. There is one process table each for tables Z1EINE and Z1EINA. The table name ends with the _PRC suffix.

- **Status tables**
  Status tables are used to store the status of each source ID from a source system. These tables end with the _STA suffix.

- **BRFplus application and function for standardization step, update step, and validation step**
  This BRFplus function can be used to add custom logic to transform data at various process steps.

To generate the resultant artifacts, follow these steps:

❶ Click on **Business Object Type** in the **Dialog Structure** hierarchy.

❷ Select the row with **BO Type = Z002**.

❸ Click in the **Resultant Artifacts** column.

❹ In the model maintenance screen, enter package name (here, we've entered "ZMDC1").

❺ In the **Table Keeps** area, there are DDIC objects, and the **Available** column shows if they are currently created. Click on the **Apply Missing** button to generate the missing DDIC artifacts.

❻ The system will generate all the artifacts under package name ZMDC1.

Figure 9.80 shows the list of steps to be performed to generate the DDIC artifacts.

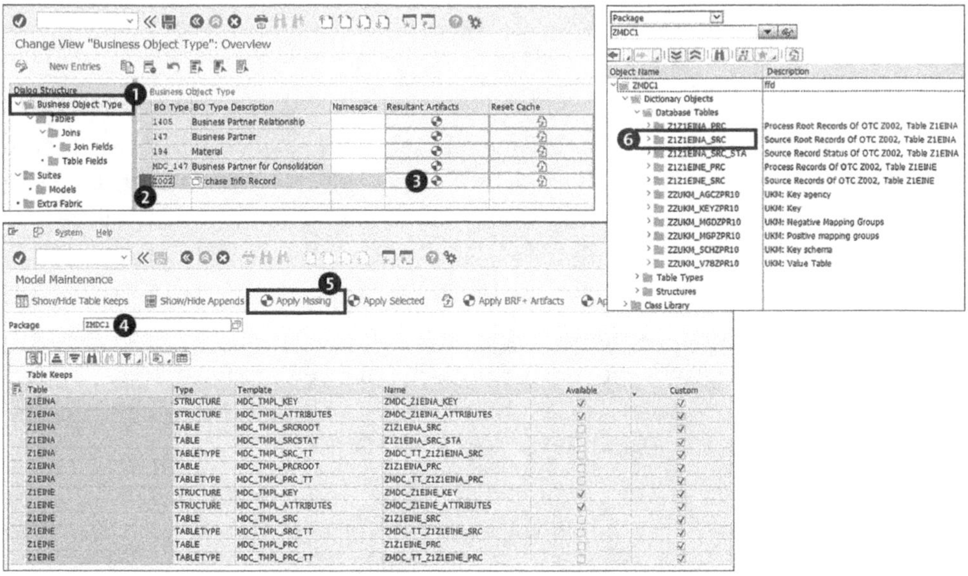

Figure 9.80 Generating Resultant Artifacts for Business Object Z002

After generating all the DDIC objects, you can now generate BRFplus artifacts to use for data standardization later in the chapter. Follow these steps:

❶ In the **Model Maintenance** screen, click on the **Apply BRF+ Artifacts** button.

❷ The log with generated BRFplus artifacts will appear.

Figure 9.81 shows the steps required to generate the BRFplus artifacts.

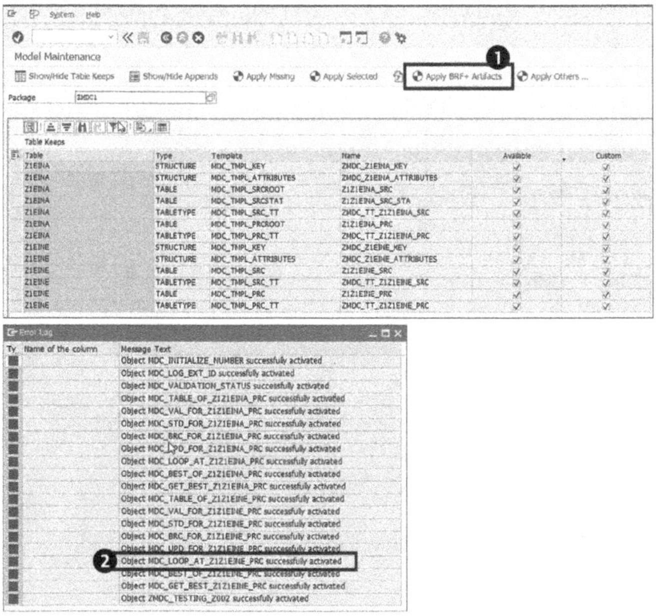

Figure 9.81 Generating the BRFplus artifacts

> **Tip**
>
> Generate BRFplus artifacts only after all the structure and table types relevant for the process model are available in the system.

> **Tip**
>
> It's always a good idea to refresh the cache after making any changes to the process model.

Configure the User Interface

In the previous section, we created a process model and generated all the artifacts required to run a process in the backend. For a human user (dialog user) to start a process for business object type ZOO2, we need to enable a UI. The OData services must also be registered and activated so that the consolidation and mass processing frontend application can access these business object type artifacts.

The first step is to create the service model by following these steps (see Figure 9.82):

❶ Go to Transaction /IWBEP/REG_MODEL.

❷ Enter the **Technical Model Name** as "MDC_PROCESS_MDL__ZOO1".

❸ Enter the **Model Version** as "1".

❹ Click on the **Create** button.

❺ Enter the **Model Provider Class** as "CL_MDC_PROCESS_MPC_EXT".

❻ Enter the **Description**.

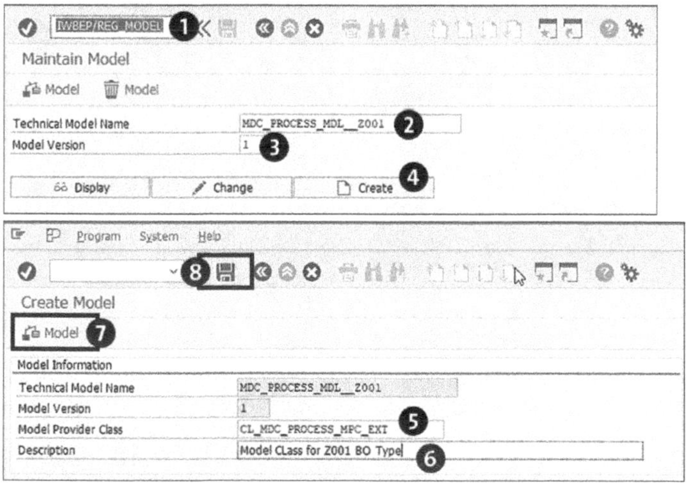

Figure 9.82 Creating the OData Model

❼ Click on the **Check Model** button.

❽ Click on **Save**.

Figure 9.82 depicts the steps to create the OData model.

After the OData model is created, you can create the OData service by following these steps:

❶ Go to Transaction /IWBEP/REG_SERVICE.

❷ Enter the **Technical Service Name** as "MDC_PROCESS_SRV__Z002". The format of the service name should always be MDC_PROCESS_SRV__XX where XX is the business object type. If this format isn't found, then SAPUI5 won't be able to call the OData service.

❸ Enter the **Service Version** as "1".

❹ Click on **Create**.

❺ Enter **Data Provider Class** as "CL_MDC_PROCESS_DPC_EXT".

❻ Enter a **Description**.

❼ Click on **Save**.

❽ Click on the **Assign Model** button to assign the OData model created in the earlier step.

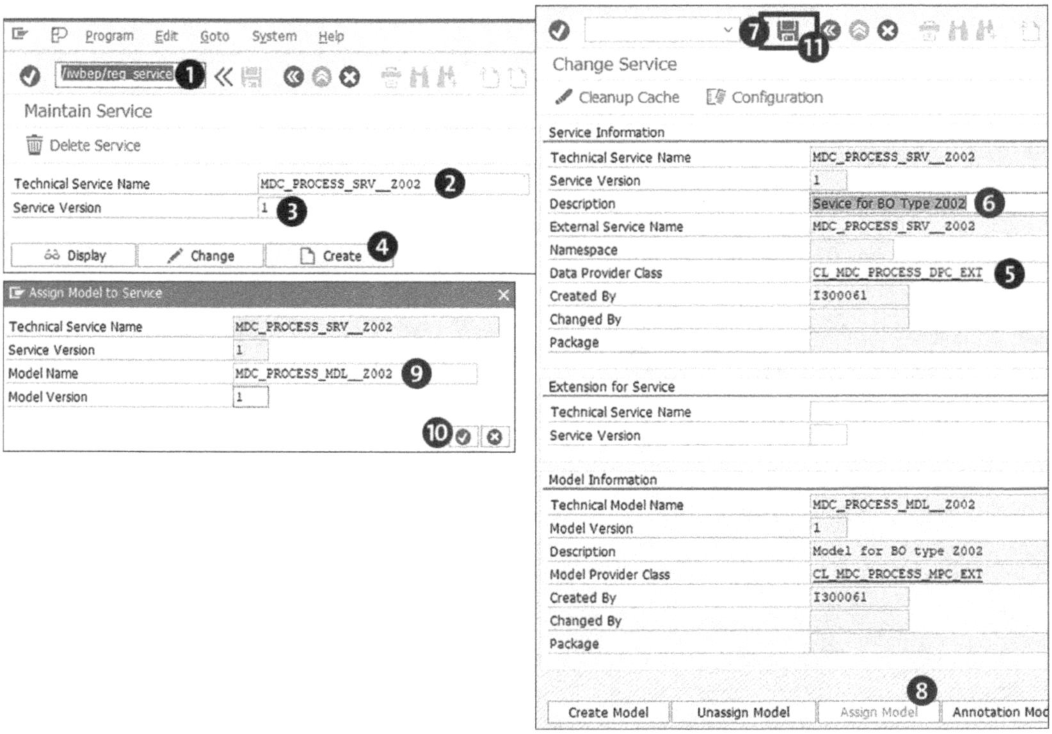

Figure 9.83 Creating the OData Service for Business Object Type Z002

❾ Enter the **Model Name** as "MDC_PROCESS_MDL__Z002".

❿ Click **OK**.

⓫ Click **Save**.

Figure 9.83 shows the steps required to create the OData service.

The next step is to expose OData service MDC_PROCESS_SRV__Z002, so that it can be accessible to consolidation and mass processing SAPUI5 applications from a browser. To expose the service, we need to activate the OData service. Figure 9.84 shows the steps that need to be performed to activate OData service MDC_PROCESS_SRV__Z002. The following steps are carried out in Transaction /IWFND/MAINT_SERVICE (see Figure 9.84):

❶ Click on **Add Service**.

❷ Enter the **System Alias** as "Local". (Local is used here because the demo system has the SAP Gateway server co-deployed.)

❸ Enter the **Technical Service Name** as "MDC_PROCESS_SRV__Z002."

❹ Click on the **Get Services** button.

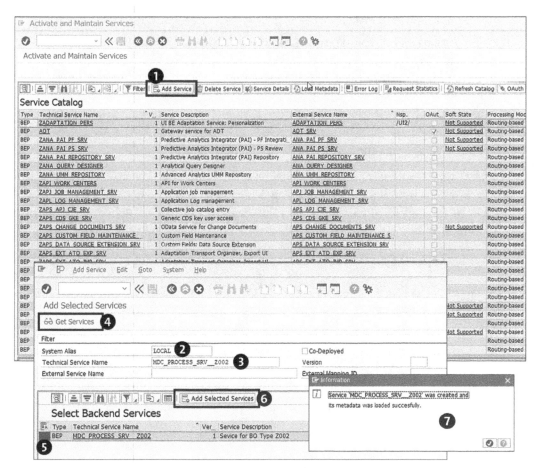

Figure 9.84 Activating the OData Service MDC_PROCESS_SRV__Z002

465

❺ Select the backend service **MDC_PROCESS_SRV__Z002**.

❻ Click on **Add Selected Services**.

❼ The service is activated.

> **Note**
>
> Activation of the OData service should be performed in the frontend server or SAP Gateway server. For the co-deployed mode, the service creation and activation can happen in the same system. The server where this custom object has been built is configured as co-deployed.

SAP Fiori launchpad is the central access point to access consolidation and mass processing applications, so it's imperative that we integrate our new business object into SAP Fiori launchpad. To add tiles for executing consolidation and mass processing for the purchase info record (business object type Z002), follow these steps:

1. Create a new SAP Fiori catalog.
2. Create a new SAP Fiori group.
3. Create a new PFCG role, and add SAP Fiori catalog and SAP Fiori group.
4. Assign users to the PFCG role.

Create an SAP Fiori Catalog

A catalog is a list of SAP Fiori tiles and target mappings. Target mappings map the navigation target (e.g., the namespace of the SAPUI5 application in the ABAP repository) with sematic objects and actions (*Semantic Object + Action = Intent*).

SAP Fiori catalogs are created using the launchpad designer. Launchpad designer can be opened in both the Customizing scope and configuration scope. In the current use case, we're creating a new catalog with tiles to launch the consolidation and mass processing applications, so we'll open the launchpad in the configuration scope.

> **Tip**
>
> Launchpad designer can be opened in the Customizing scope using Transaction /UI2/FLPD_CUST and in the configuration scope using Transaction /UI2/FLPD_CONF.

For the current use case, there are two ways to create catalogs. First, we can copy the standard SAP Fiori catalog for the consolidation and mass processing application and create a new one. We can make the changes in the copied catalog by deleting unnecessary tiles. Second, we can create a completely new catalog. Following are the steps to copy SAP Fiori catalog SAP_CMD_BC_BP_MONPROCS to make a custom SAP Fiori catalog:

❶ Enter Transaction /UI2/FLPD_CUST, to open SAP Fiori launchpad designer.

❷ Enter "SAP_CMD_BC_BP_MON_PROCES" in the search field.

❸ After the search result shows up, select the **SAP_CMD_BC_BP_MON_PROCS** catalog, and drag it to the lower-left corner of the screen to the blue box.

❹ Enter the new **Title** as "CMD-Consolidation and Mass Processing for Purchase Info Records".

❺ Enter the catalog **ID** as "ZMDC1_PIR_CATALOG".

Figure 9.85 depicts the steps to create a new SAP Fiori catalog by copying the standard catalog.

Figure 9.85 Copying Catalog SAP_CMD_BC_BP_MONPROCS to Create Custom Catalog ZMDC1_PIR_CATALOG

After the catalog is created, we need to delete the SAP Fiori tiles that aren't required and change the **OTC** value to **Z002** for each tile. Figure 9.86 shows the list of SAP Fiori tiles in the catalog **ZMDC1_PIR_CATALOG** ❶ and the parameter values for each tile ❷. Notice that the value for parameter **OTC** is **Z002**, which is the business object type based on which we created the process model in the previous Section section.

Icon	Title	Semantic Object	Action	Parameters	Target URL	Refer...	Outd...
⬇	Export Master Data	MasterData	export	otc=Z002&viewName=M DCExportCreate/worklist=	#MasterData-export? otc=Z002&viewName=M DCExportCreate/worklist=		
🗐	Manage Source Data	MasterData	manageSourceData	otc=Z002&viewName=M DCSourcesOverview	#MasterData-manageSourceData? otc=Z002&viewName=M DCSourcesOverview		
🗂	Manage Imports for Consolidation	MasterData	import	otc=Z002&viewName=M DCImportOverview	#MasterData-import? otc=Z002&viewName=M DCImportOverview		
⬆	Import Data for Consolidation	MasterData	import	otc=Z002&viewName=M DCImportCreate/UUID=	#MasterData-import? otc=Z002&viewName=M DCImportCreate/UUID=		
📇	Create Consolidation Process	MasterData	consolidate	otc=Z002&viewName=Pr ocessSetup/standalone=X /massUpdate=/template=/i mportGuid=	#MasterData-consolidate? otc=Z002&viewName=Pr ocessSetup/standalone=X /massUpdate=/template=/i mportGuid=		
🗂	Manage Consolidation Processes	MasterData	consolidate	otc=Z002&massUpdate=	#MasterData-consolidate? otc=Z002&massUpdate=		
📝	Start Mass Processing	MasterData	change	otc=Z002&viewName=Pr ocessSetup/standalone=X /massUpdate=X/template =/importGuid=	#MasterData-change? otc=Z002&viewName=Pr ocessSetup/standalone=X /massUpdate=X/template =/importGuid=		
🗂	Manage Mass Processes	MasterData	change	otc=Z002&massUpdate= X	#MasterData-change? otc=Z002&massUpdate= X		

Figure 9.86 Tiles in the SAP Fiori ZMDC1_PIR_CATALOG Catalog

Create an SAP Fiori Group

For the user to see the tiles readily when he logs into SAP Fiori launchpad, we need to add tiles from the just-created catalog into a new group. The group and catalog are added to the PFCG role in the following sections.

Follow these steps to create SAP Fiori group ZMDC_GRP_PIR:

❶ Click the **Groups** menu.

❷ Click on the **Add** button.

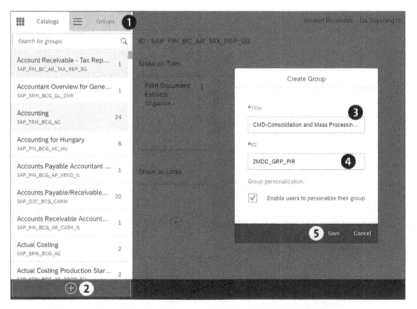

Figure 9.87 Creating SAP Fiori Group ZMDC_GRP_PIR: Part 1

❸ Enter the title "CMD-Consolidation and Mass Process for Purchase Info Rec".

❹ Enter "ZMDC_GRP_PIR" as the group **ID**.

❺ Click on **Save**.

Figure 9.87 depicts the steps to create an SAP Fiori group.

After the SAP Fiori group is created, we need to add the tiles from SAP Fiori catalog ZMDC1_PIR_CATALOG:

❶ Click on the **Add Tiles** button.

❷ Click on the **Value help** button on the **Catalog** field.

❸ In the value help dialog, enter the catalog ID "ZMDC1_PIR_CATALOG".

❹ Double-click on catalog **ZMDC1_PIR_CATALOG** in the result list.

Figure 9.88 depicts the steps required to add tiles from catalog ZMDC1_PIR_CATALOG to group ZMDC_GRP_PIR.

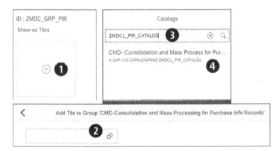

Figure 9.88 Creating SAP Fiori Group ZMDC_GRP_PIR: Part 2

Figure 9.89 shows the arrangement of tiles added from the catalog. If needed, the sequence of the tiles can be changed here.

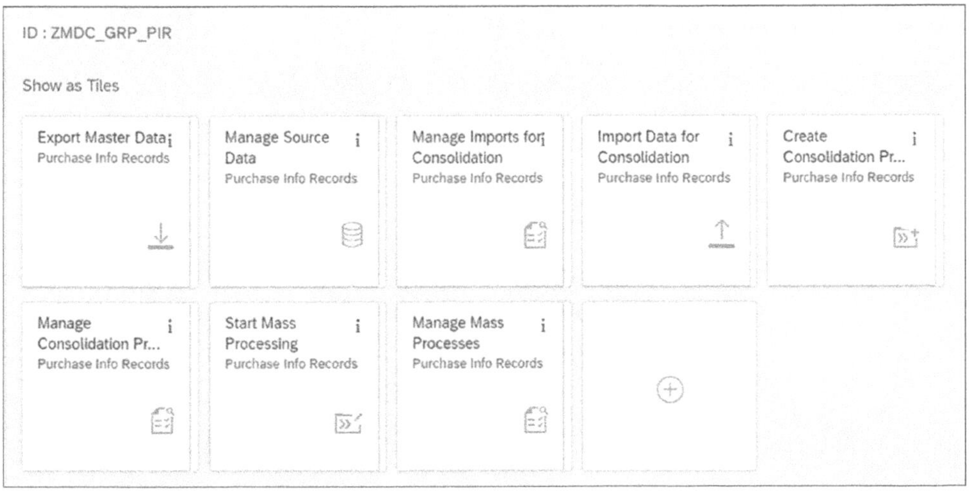

ID : ZMDC_GRP_PIR				
Show as Tiles				
Export Master Data¡ Purchase Info Records	Manage Source i Data Purchase Info Records	Manage Imports for¡ Consolidation Purchase Info Records	Import Data for i Consolidation Purchase Info Records	Create i Consolidation Pr... Purchase Info Records
Manage i Consolidation Pr... Purchase Info Records	Start Mass i Processing Purchase Info Records	Manage Mass i Processes Purchase Info Records		

Figure 9.89 SAP Fiori Group ZMDC_GRP_PIR with Tiles from the ZMDC1_PIR_CATALOG Catalog

Create the PFCG Role

The SAP Fiori catalog and SAP Fiori group that have been created won't yet show up in the user's launchpad. For the group (and thereby the tiles assigned to the group) to show up in the user's launchpad, the user needs to be assigned to the PFCG role. Then, the PFCG role should be assigned the users who need to access the SAP Fiori tiles to execute the consolidation and mass processing process for purchase info records (business object type ZOO2). Figure 9.90 shows the assignment of the SAP Fiori catalog and SAP Fiori role to the PFCG role.

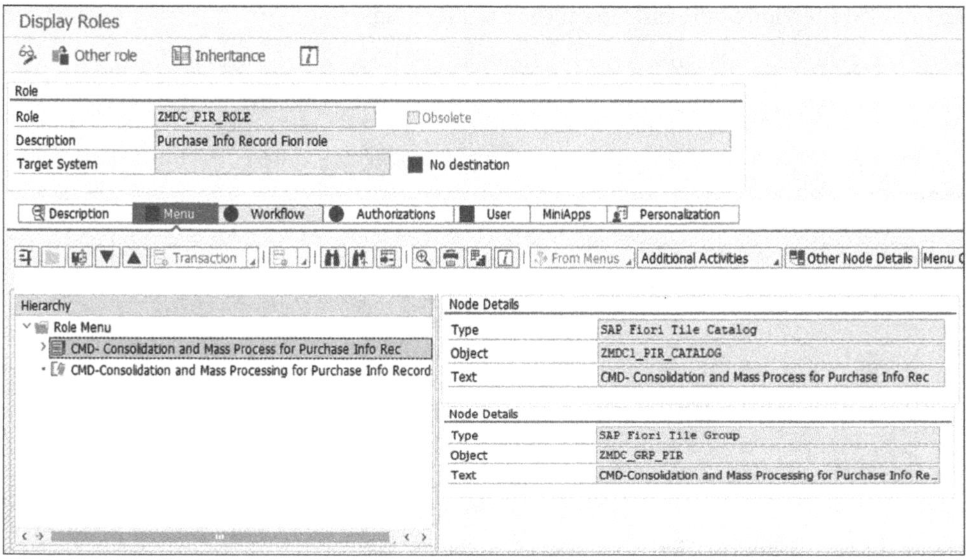

Figure 9.90 Assignment of the SAP Fiori Catalog and SAP Fiori Group to the PFCG Role ZMDC_PIR_ROLE

After the PFCG role is created, users should be assigned to the role so they can see the SAP Fiori tiles in the launchpad (Figure 9.91).

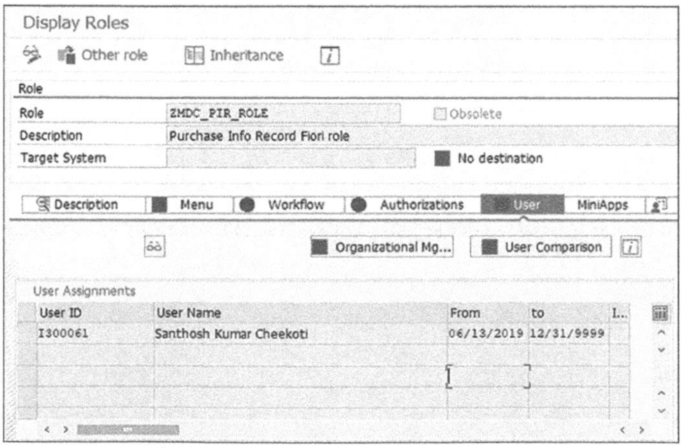

Figure 9.91 Assignment of Users to the PFCG Role

Newly Created SAP Fiori Tiles and Apps

In this section, we'll explore how the tiles have been added to the launchpad and how consolidation and mass processing applications are called with new URL parameters that we configured in the earlier Create an SAP Fiori Catalog section.

SAP Fiori launchpad can be launched from the SAP GUI using Transaction /UI2/FLP or via *https://[host]:[port]/sap/bc/ui2/flp?sap-client=100&sap-language=EN#Shell-home.*

> **Note**
>
> Based on your organization's security strategy, the URL might change if a proxy server is being used. Your system administrator should be able to help you with the right URL.

Figure 9.92 shows the SAP Fiori tiles and SAP Fiori group created for purchase info records (business object type Z002).

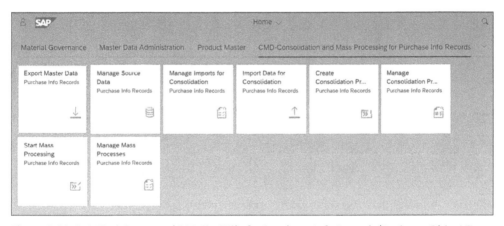

Figure 9.92 SAP Fiori Group and SAP Fiori Tile for Purchase Info Records (Business Object Type Z002)

> **Note**
>
> All the titles of pages in the following sections will show the text "Z002". In the real-time project, this text should show the description maintained in the *i18N.properties* file. Changing the i18N file to reflect the actual description of business object type Z002 isn't in the scope of this chapter.

Figure 9.93 shows the Import Data app for business object type Z002 (purchase info record).

Figure 9.94 shows the Create Consolidation Process app for business object type Z002. The **Process Goal** and **Process Template** fields are empty because we haven't yet completed the process template configuration.

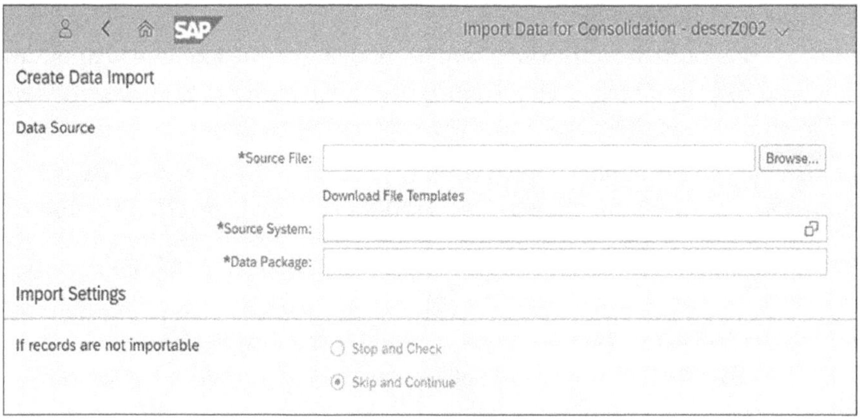

Figure 9.93 Import Data for Consolidation Application for Business Object Type Z002 (Purchase Info Record)

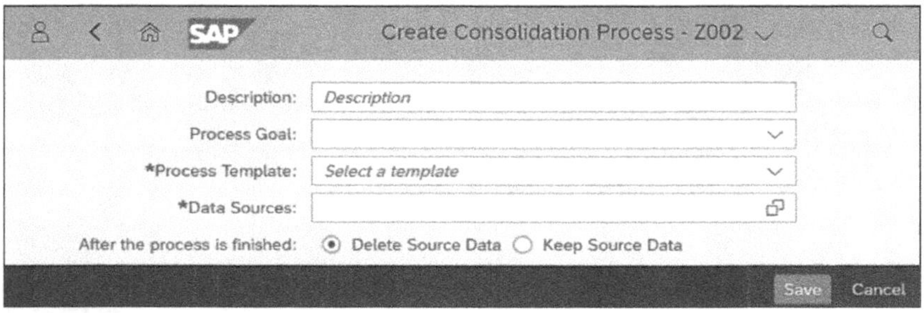

Figure 9.94 Create Consolidation Process UI for Business Object Type Z002

Figure 9.95 shows the Mass Process app for business object type Z002.

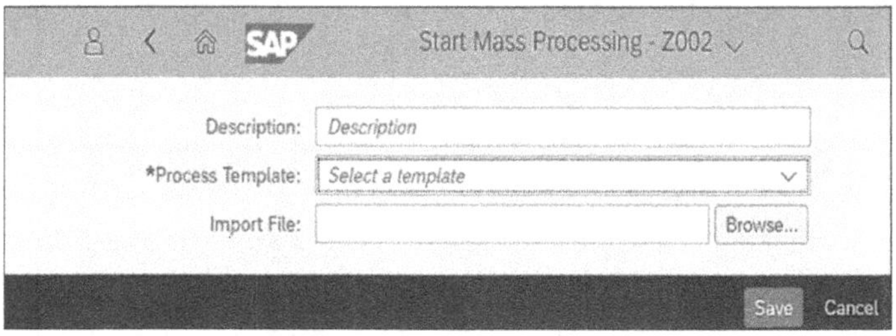

Figure 9.95 Start Mass Processing UI for Business Object Type Z002

Previous sections explained how to adapt SAP-delivered SAP Fiori apps to the custom object Z002. Notably, these UIs are adapted without writing any ABAP code.

Set Up Standardization Rules Using BRFplus

As part of the resultant artifacts generated after the process model is activated, the BRF-plus application and function are also generated. Using consolidation and mass processing standardization, we can perform both.

To explain how to set up standardization steps using BRFplus rules, we'll implement the following business rules:

- Enrich the short text of the purchase info record (EINA-TXZ01) with material number and supplier number.
- Set the default number of days for reminder/expediter (EINA-MAHN1 = 5 days, EINA-MAHN2 = 10 days, EINA-MAHN3 = 15 days).

Before we configure the standardization step for the business object type (ZO02), we need to model the preceding business rules as BRFplus rules, as explained in the following sections. After BRFplus rules are modeled, we can proceed to configure the standardization step.

Following are the steps to open the generated BRFplus application for the business object type (ZO02):

❶ Enter Transaction BRF+.

❷ Click on **Workbench.**

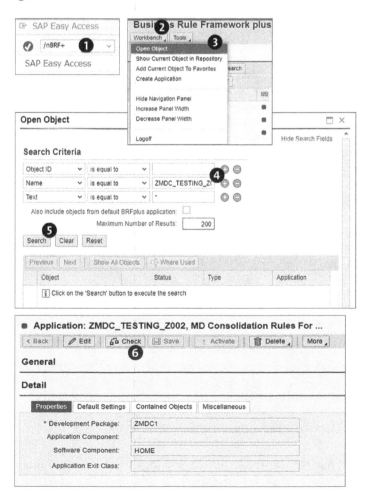

Figure 9.96 Opening the Generated BRFplus Application for Business Object Type ZO02 (Purchase Info Record)

❸ Click **Open Object**.

❹ Enter "ZMDC_TESTING_Z002" in the **Name** field.

❺ Click on **Search**.

❻ The ZMDC_TESTING_Z002 application will open.

Figure 9.96 depicts the steps to open the generated BRFplus application ZMDC_TEST-ING_Z002.

The application includes generated functions. We can add our standardization rules in these generated functions. Our rules primarily focus on table EINA (table Z1EINA in the process model), so we should model our rules in BRFplus function MDC_STD_FOR_Z1Z1EINA_PRC.

Figure 9.97 shows how the BRFplus rules are created to model the business "Default number of days for reminder/expediter" rule.

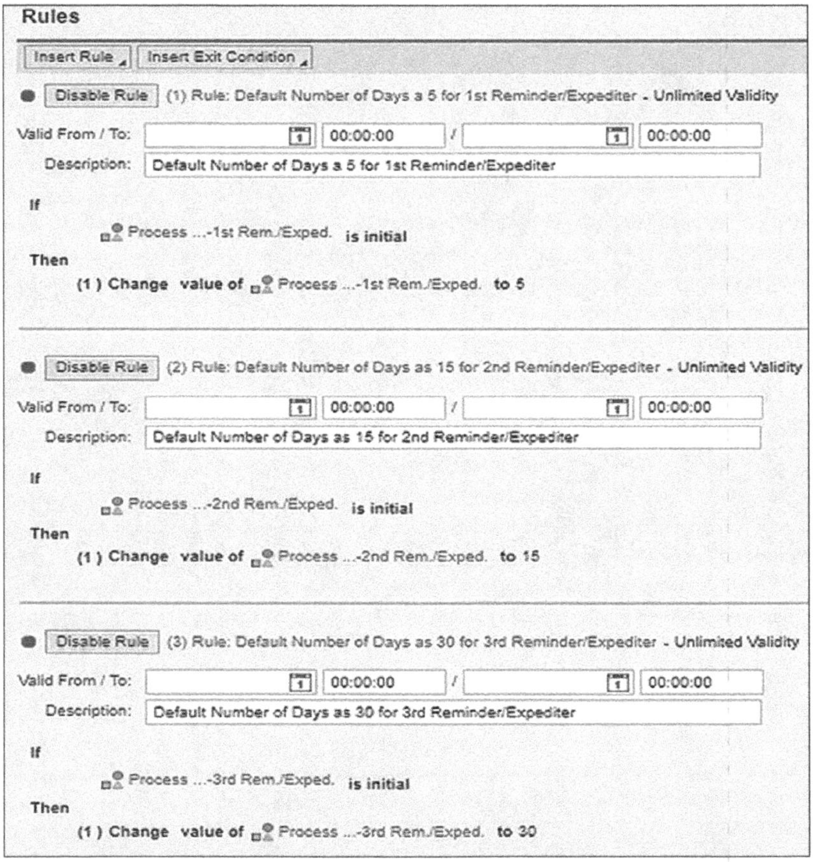

Figure 9.97 BRFplus Rule to Default Number of Days for Reminder/Expedite

Figure 9.98 shows the modeling of the business rule to concatenate the vendor number and material number as purchase info record short text.

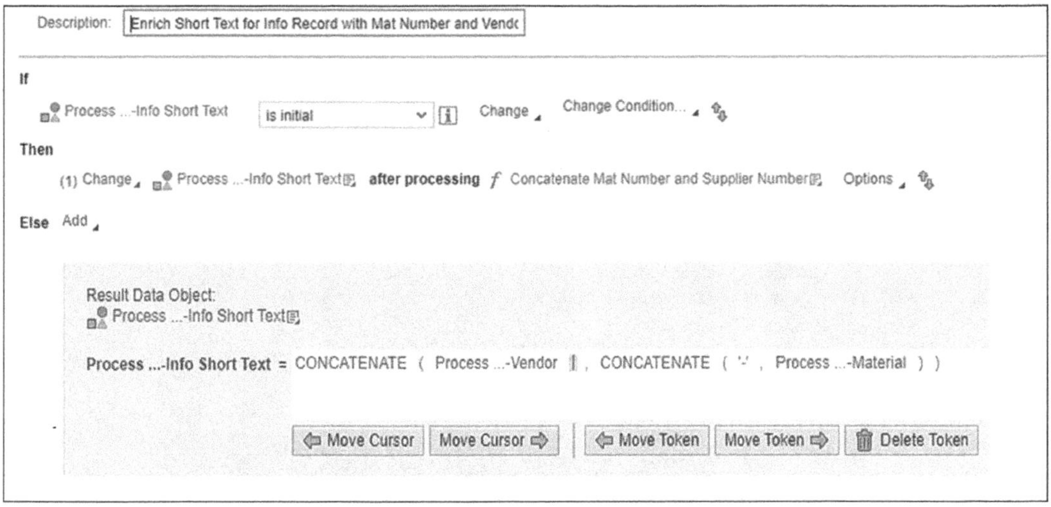

Figure 9.98 Concatenate Vendor and Material as Purchase Info Record Short Text

> **Note**
>
> One of the key value propositions of consolidation and mass processing is parallelization. Parallelization allows the execution of data loads in parallel work processes. Parallelization for standardization can be configured in IMG path **MDCIMG · Configure Standardization · Configure Parallelization for Standardization**. In the current example, we're skipping this step because we don't need parallelization

Set Up Activation

Activation is the process of saving the processed data in the active tables. There are two kinds of activations in consolidation and mass processing:

- **Direct activation**
  Processed data is saved directly in SAP S/4HANA or SAP ERP tables.

- **Activation with change request**
  Processed data is transferred to central governance through change requests.

In our example, purchase info records don't exist as data models in consolidation and mass processing, so we'll use direct activation by default.

If your scenario has a corresponding data model in SAP Master Data Governance, and you want to be able to configure activation differently for different process steps, you must have a custom DDIC object to support the process. However, this isn't in the scope of this book.

Figure 9.99 provides a quick view of how the IMG tree will look when we add a custom IMG activity for configuring activation for business object type Z002.

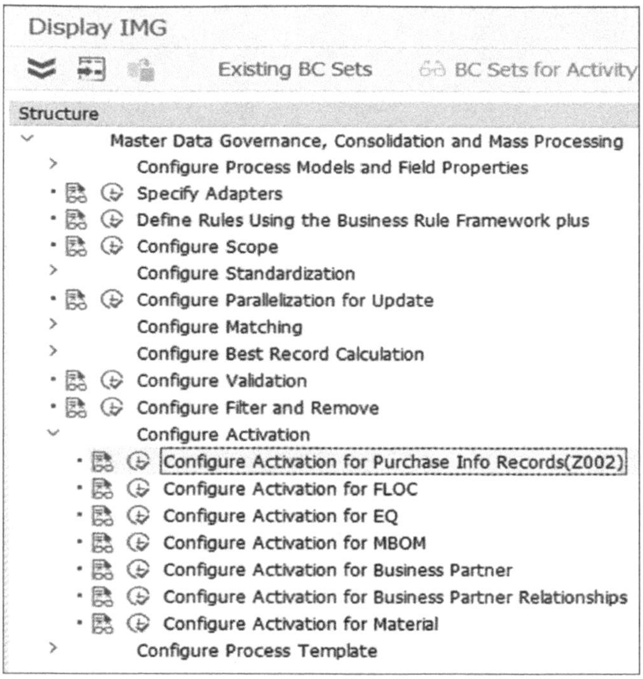

Figure 9.99 Quick Glance at a Custom IMG Activity for Configuring Activation for Purchase Info Records

Set Up the Process Template

The process template is a configuration entity that defines the process steps, step type, and step sequence that are assigned to the business object type.

For the custom object type purchase info record (Z002), we'll design a simple process template as described in Table 9.15.

Step Type	Step Sequence
Standardization	1
Validation	2
Activation	3

Table 9.15 Process Template Design for Business Object Type Z002

Following are the steps to create the process template:

1. Go to Transaction MDCIMG.
2. Go to IMG path **Master Data Governance, Consolidation and Mass PROCESSING** • **Configure Process Template** • **Specify Process Template**.
3. Click on the **New Entries** button.

4. Enter the **Process Template** as "Z002_01".

5. Enter the **Description** as "Consolidate Purchase Info Records".

6. Enter the **Process Workflow** as "WS54500001".

7. Select the **Process Goal** as **Consolidation of Source records**.

8. Click on **Save**.

Figure 9.100 and Figure 9.101 depict the steps to create process templates.

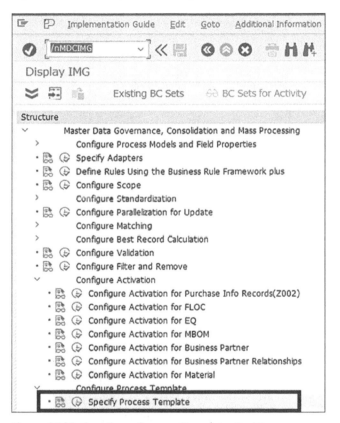

Figure 9.100 Creating a Process Template: Part 1

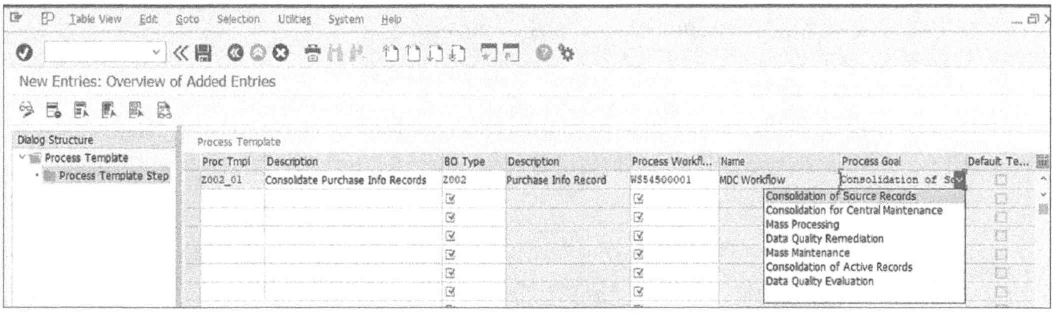

Figure 9.101 Creating a Process Template: Part 2

The configuration of process steps (as described in Table 9.15) is shown in Figure 9.102.

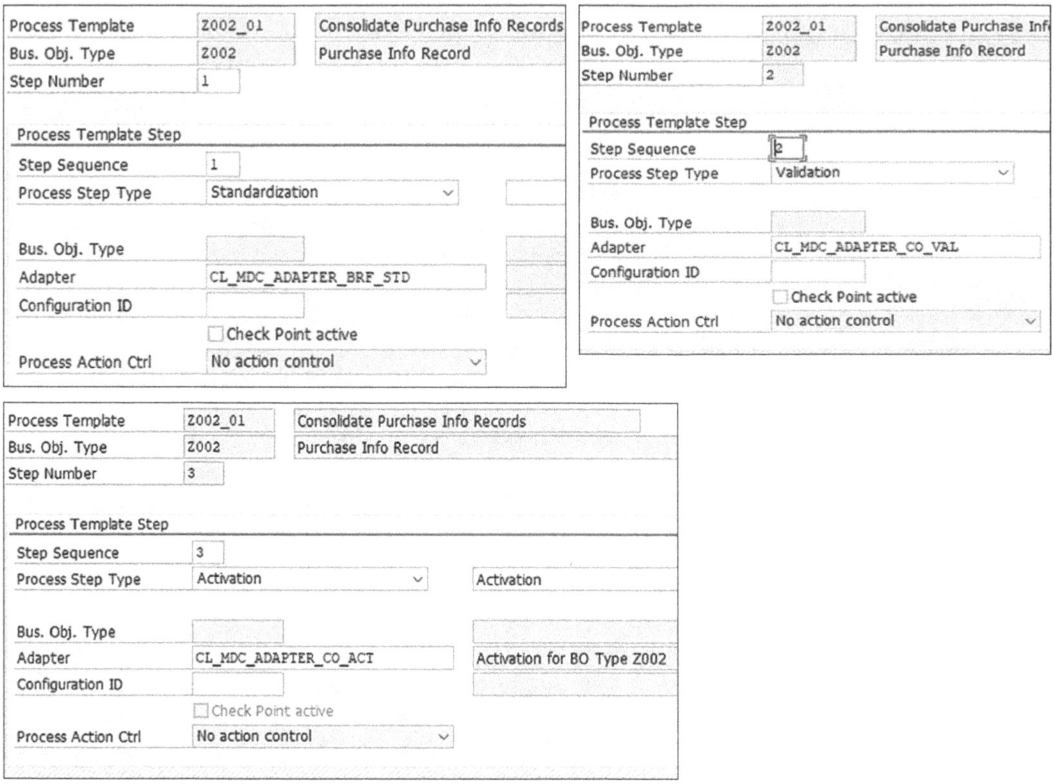

Process Template	Z002_01	Consolidate Purchase Info Records
Bus. Obj. Type	Z002	Purchase Info Record
Step Number	1	

Process Template Step

| Step Sequence | 1 |
| Process Step Type | Standardization ⌄ |

Bus. Obj. Type	
Adapter	CL_MDC_ADAPTER_BRF_STD
Configuration ID	
	☐ Check Point active
Process Action Ctrl	No action control ⌄

Process Template	Z002_01	Consolidate Purchase Inf
Bus. Obj. Type	Z002	Purchase Info Record
Step Number	2	

Process Template Step

| Step Sequence | 2 |
| Process Step Type | Validation ⌄ |

Bus. Obj. Type	
Adapter	CL_MDC_ADAPTER_CO_VAL
Configuration ID	
	☐ Check Point active
Process Action Ctrl	No action control ⌄

Process Template	Z002_01	Consolidate Purchase Info Records
Bus. Obj. Type	Z002	Purchase Info Record
Step Number	3	

Process Template Step

| Step Sequence | 3 |
| Process Step Type | Activation ⌄ | Activation |

Bus. Obj. Type		
Adapter	CL_MDC_ADAPTER_CO_ACT	Activation for BO Type Z002
Configuration ID		
	☐ Check Point active	
Process Action Ctrl	No action control ⌄	

Figure 9.102 Process Step Design

Run the Custom Application

Thus far in this section, we've built all the configurations that are required to establish purchase info records with business object type Z002 as the custom object in the consolidation and mass processing framework. In the following sections, we'll run the consolidation and mass processing application for the custom object. We'll first load the data into source tables, then create a consolidation process to create purchase info records in the backend system, and finally update the key mapping between the source records from files to active records in the backend system.

Source Records Data Set

The source records are the purchase info records from a source system that we're trying to load into the SAP Master Data Governance system. We'll load two records each for table EINA and table EINE.

Figure 9.103 shows the content of the load file for table EINA. It's important to note here that the source **System** ID is **PURCHASING**, and **Source IDs** are **PIR7** and **PIR8**.

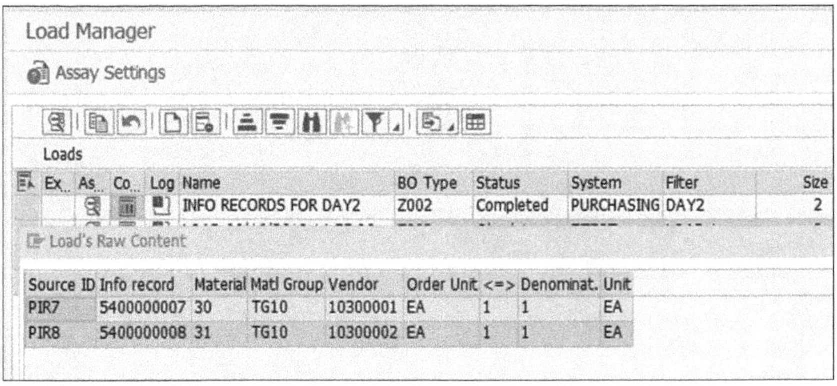

Load Manager

Assay Settings

Loads

Ex..	As..	Co...	Log	Name	BO Type	Status	System	Filter	Size
				INFO RECORDS FOR DAY2	Z002	Completed	PURCHASING	DAY2	2

Load's Raw Content

Source ID	Info record	Material	Matl Group	Vendor	Order Unit	<=>	Denominat.	Unit
PIR7	5400000007	30	TG10	10300001	EA	1	1	EA
PIR8	5400000008	31	TG10	10300002	EA	1	1	EA

Figure 9.103 Content from Load File for Table EINA

Figure 9.104 shows the corresponding entries in table EINE for the entries shown in Figure 9.103.

> **Note**
>
> The load file has been kept simple to focus on showing the consolidation and mass processing custom object framework.

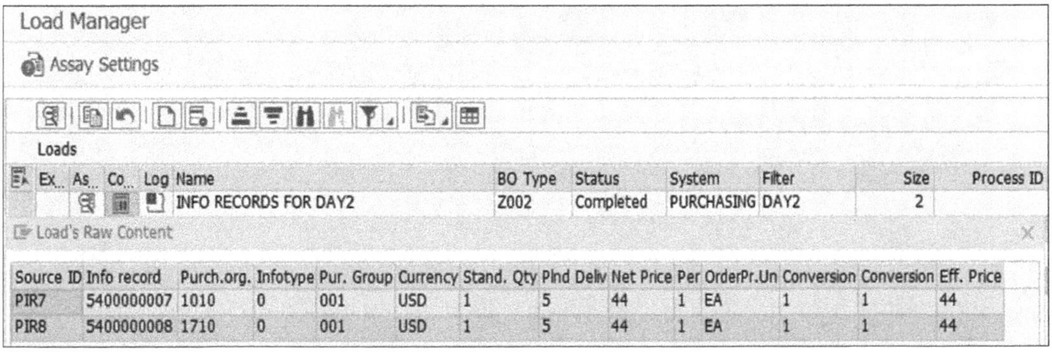

Load Manager

Assay Settings

Loads

Ex..	As..	Co...	Log	Name	BO Type	Status	System	Filter	Size	Process ID
				INFO RECORDS FOR DAY2	Z002	Completed	PURCHASING	DAY2	2	

Load's Raw Content

Source ID	Info record	Purch.org.	Infotype	Pur. Group	Currency	Stand. Qty	Plnd Deliv	Net Price	Per	OrderPr.Un	Conversion	Conversion	Eff. Price
PIR7	5400000007	1010	0	001	USD	1	5	44	1	EA	1	1	44
PIR8	5400000008	1710	0	001	USD	1	5	44	1	EA	1	1	44

Figure 9.104 Content of the Load File for Table EINE

The loaded data can also be seen in the corresponding SAP Fiori apps. Figure 9.105 shows the status of source data in the Manage Source Data – Purchase Info Records app. As shown in the figure, the status of the load shows as **Completed**, which means that source data has been loaded into the source tables of process model Z002.

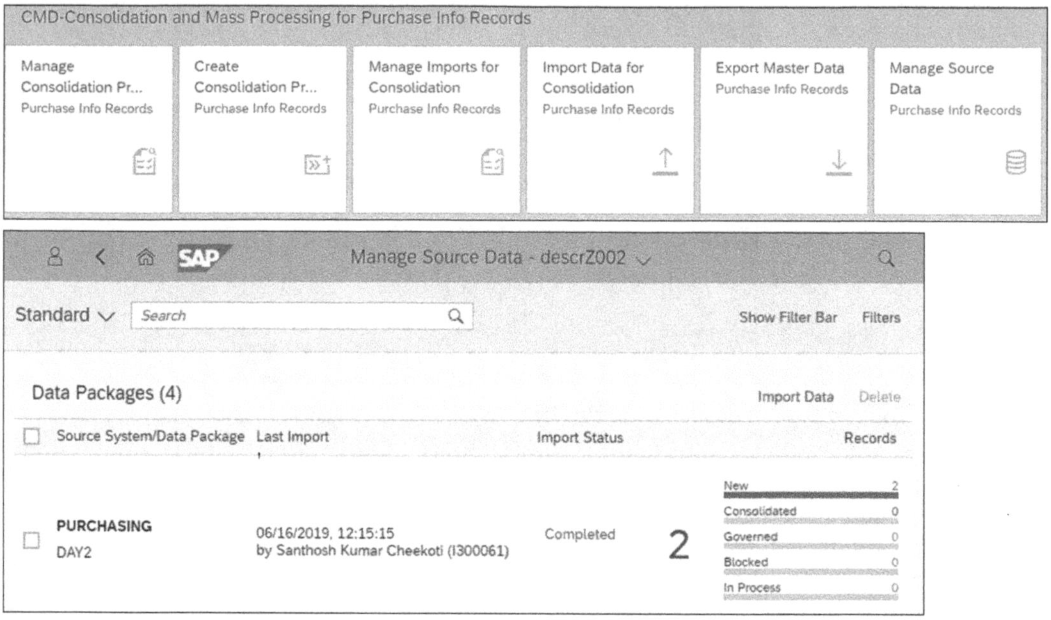

Figure 9.105 Status of Import in the Manage Source Data SAP Fiori App

Figure 9.106 shows the source data in the Manage Imports for Consolidation app.

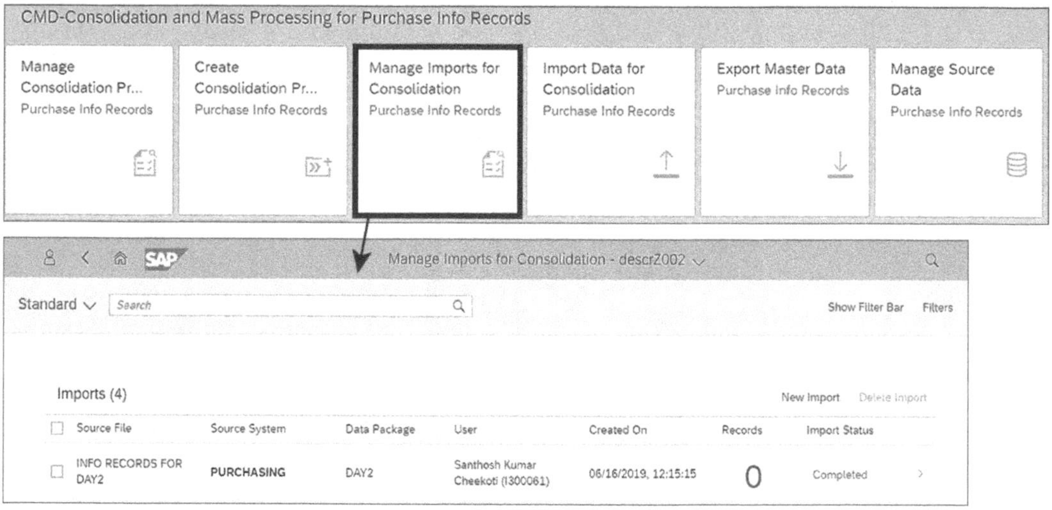

Figure 9.106 Source Data Set Represented in the Manage Imports for Consolidation App

Create a Consolidation Process for Purchase Info Records

In the previous section, you've seen how to import purchase info records data from a source system into source tables of process model Z002. It's important to remember that these source tables have been generated as a result of the configuration we performed in the earlier Section section.

The next logical step is to create a consolidation process for the source records that we just loaded. The consolidation will be created using process template ZOO2_O1, which we configured in the Section section.

The consolidation process can be created by launching the Create Consolidation Process – Purchase Info Records app from SAP Fiori launchpad. Consolidation can also be created using the Manage Consolidation – Process – Purchase Info Records app. Figure 9.107 depicts different ways to navigate to the Create Consolidation screen. The **Create Consolidation Process** screen is described in detail in the Process Setup User Interface section earlier.

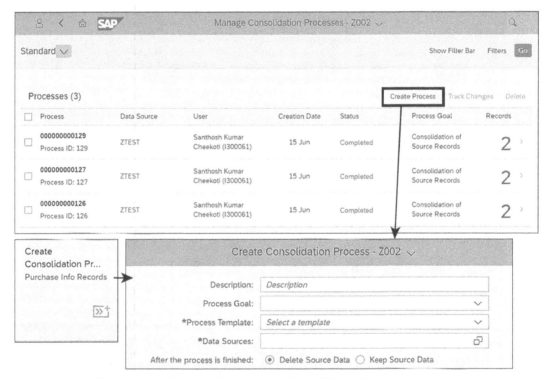

Figure 9.107 Different Ways of Navigating to Create Consolidation Process Screen

In the **Create Consolidation Process** screen, we can create the process. The following steps are required to create the consolidation process for purchase info records for the data set we've loaded in the Source Records Data Set section:

❶ Enter value "Consolidation of PIR" in the **Description** field.

❷ Select **Consolidation of Source Records** in the **Process Goal** field.

❸ Select **Consolidate Purchase Info Records** in **Process Template**. This process template has been configured in the Section section.

❹ Click on the value help button in the **Data Sources** field.

❺ In the value help dialog box, select **Data Package DAY2**.

481

❻ Click on **OK**.

❼ The data package from source system **Purchasing** is added in the **Data Sources** field.

❽ Click on **Save** to create the consolidation process.

The steps in the preceding list are also depicted in Figure 9.108.

Figure 9.108 Creating the Consolidation Process

After the consolidation process has been created, it has to be started explicitly. When the consolidation process is started, the system will execute the first step in the process and transfer the source data from the source tables to the process tables.

Per the process template for business object type ZOO2 (purchase info records) that we configured in the Section section, the process will have the following process steps with a checkpoint at the completion of each step:

- Standardization step (has been configured in the Section section.
- Validation step
- Activation step

Figure 9.109 shows the process display screen for **Process ID 130**. This process was created as part of the preceding section. All the major UI elements on the process display screen are as follows:

❶ Unique process identifier

❷ Process description

❸ Process template

❹ Process goal

❺ Process steps

❻ Number of records (only the number of records from the root table)

❼ Process status

❽ Process progress indicator

❾ Step configuration (contents changes are based on step selection)

❿ Page footer with all the process actions

It also shows steps that will be executed as part of the process lifecycle when the **Start** button is clicked.

Figure 9.109 Process Display Screen

The steps will be executed in sequence as described in the process template. You can't skip execution of any step in the process display steps. Process execution is highly flexible; at each checkpoint, you have the option to roll back to a previous step.

In **Process 130**, when the **Start** button is clicked, the first step that will be executed is standardization. The standardization step will execute all the BRFplus rules that were configured previously.

Figure 9.110 shows the process display UI after the standardization step is completed. Note the informative step analytics that are specific to the standardization step.

Let's take a little bit of a deep dive into what has happened to our source data, in which we configured the following rules as BRFplus rules:

- Enrich the short text of the purchase info record (EINA-TXZ01) with the material number and supplier number.

- Set the default number of days for reminder/expediter (EINA-MAHN1 = 5 days, EINA-MAHN2 = 10 days, EINA-MAHN3 = 15 days).

Figure 9.110 Process Display UI for Process 130 after the Completion of the Standardization Steps

Figure 9.111 Different Options to Navigate to the Results Page

The step analytics shows that two records (which is the total size of our load) have been modified. To determine the records that had been modified and what fields have changed, you have to navigate to the step results page. Figure 9.111 shows the different options to navigate to the results page of a step.

Figure 9.112 shows the results page for the standardization step of process ID 130.

The main content of the page is found in the following three tabs:

- **Overview**
  Contains table UI elements with data from the process tables.

- **Z1EINA**
  Contains table UI elements with data from process root table Z1EINA. This table represents active table EINA.

- **Z1EINE**
  Contains table UI element with data from process table Z1EINE. Process model table Z1EINE is the child element of the root process model table Z1EINA. This table represents active table EINE.

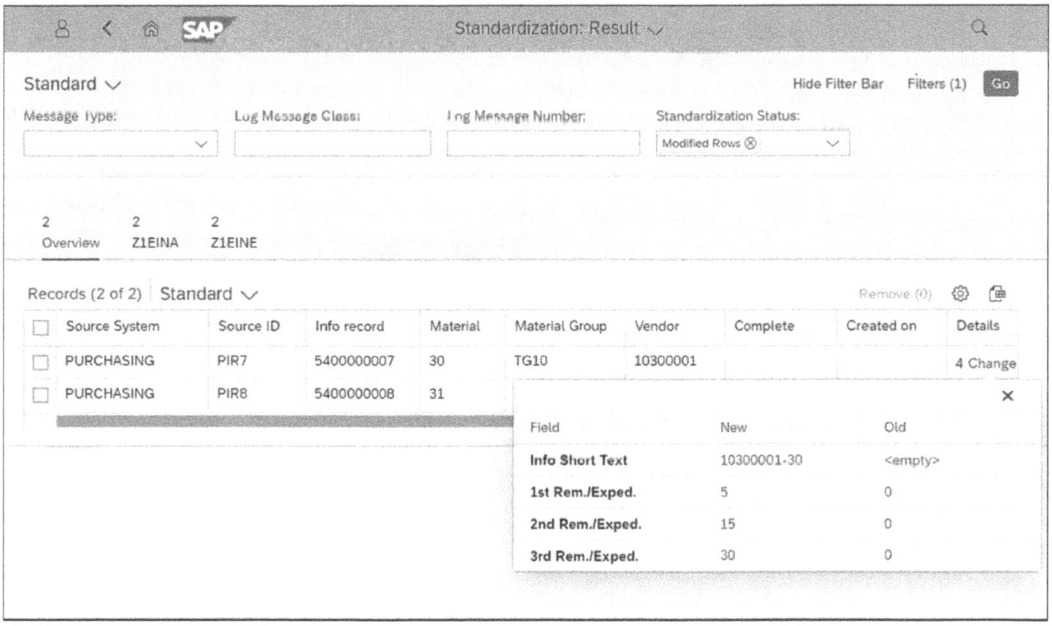

Figure 9.112 Understanding the Result Page for the Standardization Step

As shown in Figure 9.112, the **Details** column is present in every tab. It contains the hyperlink to the popup showing changes performed on the record. The **Change** log popup shown in Figure 9.112 indicates that BRFplus rules configured previously have been performed, and data in process table Z1EINA has changed as expected.

To proceed with the execution of the next process steps for the process with ID 130, click on **Continue**. Consolidation and mass processing then executes the validation step.

Figure 9.113 shows the process display UI with the validation step completed. As with the standardization step, even the validation steps contain step analytics that show the number of records successfully validated and failed records, if applicable. Users can navigate to the results UI to determine which records failed and why. Figure 9.113 also shows that the process has stopped for review because the process template has been configured to trigger a checkpoint after the completion of the validation step.

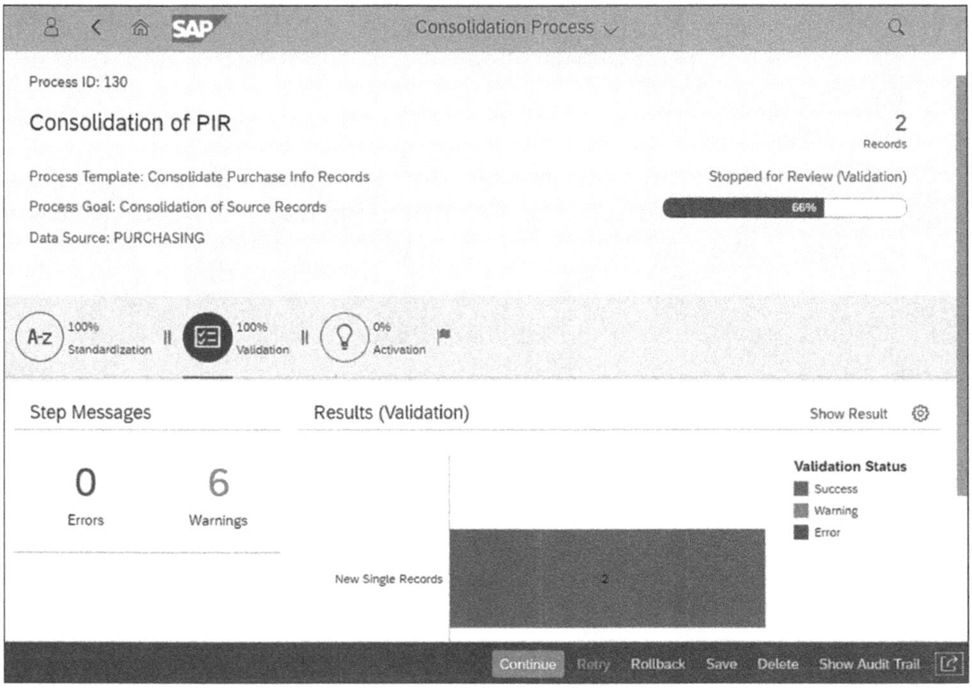

Figure 9.113 Process Display UI with the Completed Validation Step for Process 130

When you click **Continue**, consolidation and mass processing will execute the activation step, which is the next step in the process. Activation is the process of storing the data in the active tables. The active tables in our case are EINA and EINE. The configuration for the activation step can be used to configure the activation target of the activation step. You can use the active area as the activation target or an SAP Master Data Governance change request as the activation target. In the current use case, the purchase info record isn't configured as a custom data model in central governance; therefore, our obvious activation target is the active area.

Figure 9.114 shows the process display UI with status **Completed**, and the activation step also shows **Completed**. The successful completion of activation steps marks the end of Process 130. At the end of the activation steps, the data is transferred to the active area.

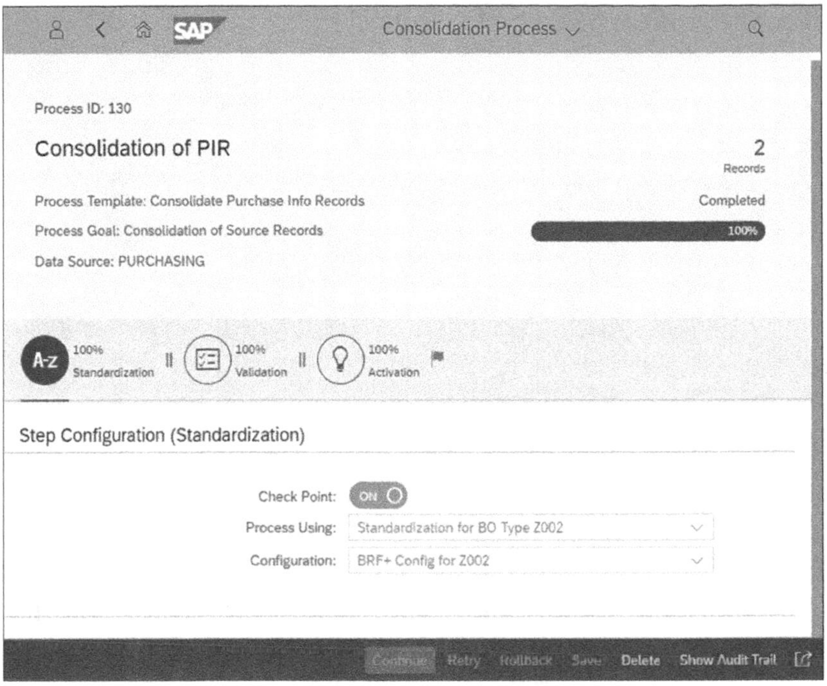

Figure 9.114 Process Display UI with the Activation Step in Completed Status

Side Effects of Process Activation

In the previous section, we created a consolidation process using the data set that we imported into source tables and executed each step of the process. After the process is completed, multiple side effects are triggered. It's important to learn about them to ensure that our consolidation process has achieved the target. The following sections describe the aftermath of process activation.

After the process is completed, first data is transferred to the active area. In our case, tables EINA and EINE are the activation targets. To view the data in the activation area, we need to find the record ID (info record number) in the target area. At this point, all we know is the source ID and source system based on the source file that we loaded in the source tables of model Z002.

Table 9.16 shows the source ID and source system based on the source file. Key mapping help can be used to find the active record ID for source IDs listed in Table 9.16.

Key mapping update is one side effect of process activation. Figure 9.115 and Figure 9.116 show how to search for active records using the search key mapping UI.

Source System	Source ID
Purchasing	PIR7
Purchasing	PIR8

Table 9.16 Source IDs and Source Systems That Were Loaded as Part of the Data Set

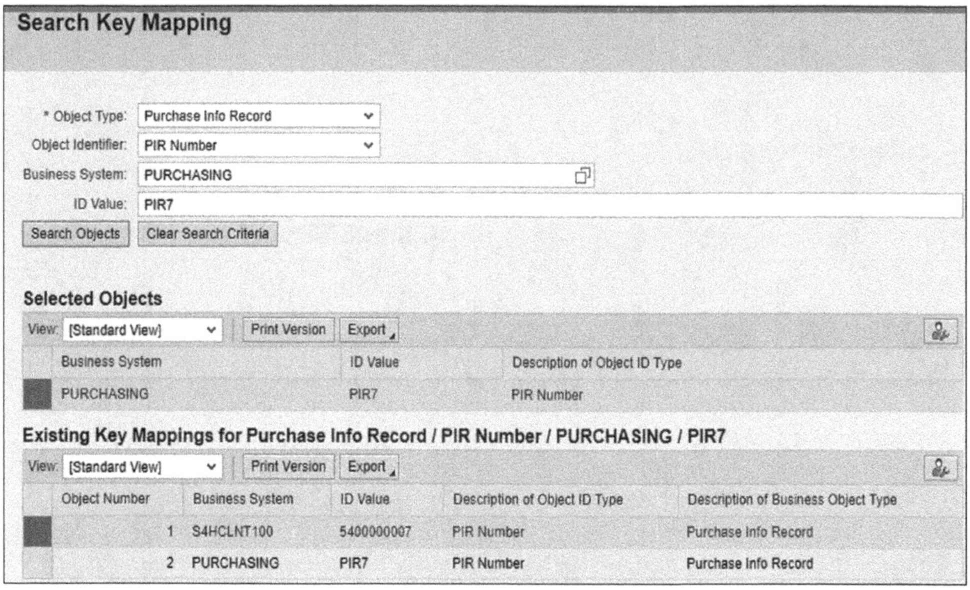

Figure 9.115 Searching for Corresponding Active Record ID for Source System ID PIR7 Using the Search Key Mapping UI

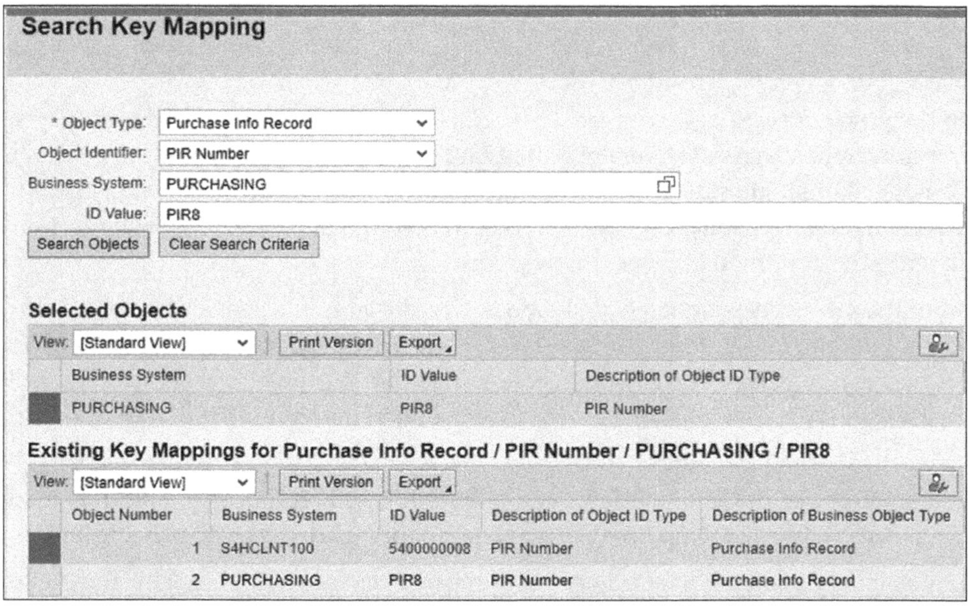

Figure 9.116 Searching for Corresponding Active Record ID for Source System ID PIR8 Using the Search Key Mapping UI

Figure 9.117 shows that data has been successfully created in Transaction ME13.

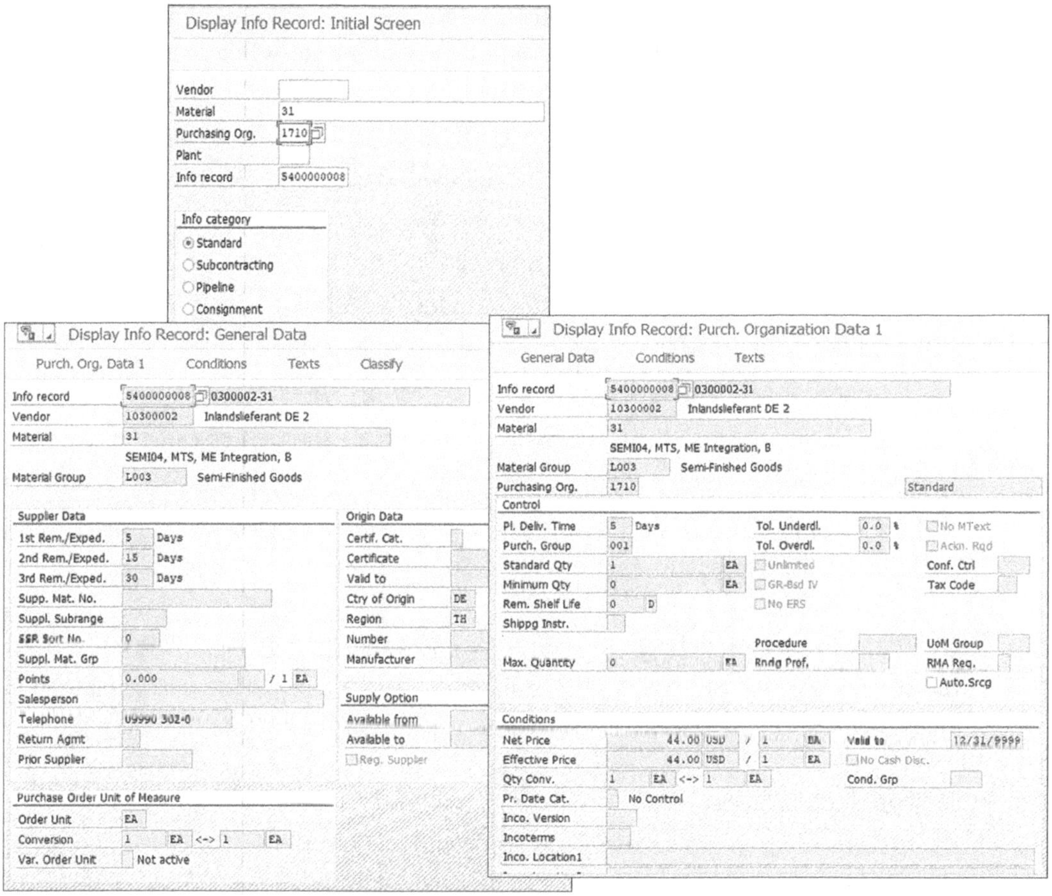

Figure 9.117 Active Data Successfully Created in the Active Area

9.9.2 Building Custom Objects: Mass Processing

In Section 9.9.1, we built and enabled consolidation of purchase info records using the custom object framework of consolidation and mass processing. In the following sections, we'll use the same custom object (purchase info record) to demonstrate the mass processing capabilities of consolidation and mass processing.

As a review, we've created business object type ZOO2 to represent purchase info records. Using this business object type, we've created a process model with process model table Z1EINA (representing active table EINA) and process model table Z1EINE (representing active table Z1EINE). We then set up the standardization step to implement business rules as BRFplus rules followed by the creation of a process template to include BRFplus-based standardization steps, generic activation, and validation steps. Finally, we loaded purchase info records into the system using the newly created configuration.

Now, we'll reuse the same process object (ZOO2) to demonstrate how to configure mass processing capabilities for the custom object and run the consolidation and mass processing application for the custom object.

Following is the use case for this demonstration:

1. The user should be able to select the active purchase info records based on info record number, vendor number, material group, and material number.
2. The user should be able to make changes to these fields:
   - MAHN1: Number of Days for First Reminder/Expediter
   - MAHN2: Number of Days for Second Reminder/Expediter
   - MAHN3: Number of Days for Third Reminder/Expediter
3. After edits are made to the records, the changed data should be validated and then activated.

In the following sections, we'll explain how to implement the preceding use case in consolidation and mass processing.

Create the Process Model

The steps to create a process model for mass processing are the same as explained in the earlier Section section.

Set Up Selection Fields

The first step of mass processing is to select the active records for which mass processing is to be performed. This selection is done using selection fields. Selection fields can be used to define selection criteria to retrieve active records for mass processing.

Following are the steps to set up the selection fields for a process model:

1. Go to Transaction MDCIMG.
2. Go to IMG path, **Master Data Governance, Consolidation and Mass Processing** • **Configure Process Models and Field Properties** • **Configure Process Models**.
3. Execute the IMG activity **Configure Process Models**.
4. Select the **BO Type ZOO2**.
5. Click **Tables** in the **Dialog Structures**.
6. Click on **Table Fields**.
7. Select the fields that you want as **Selective**.

Figure 9.118 shows how to configure table fields of the process table as selective.

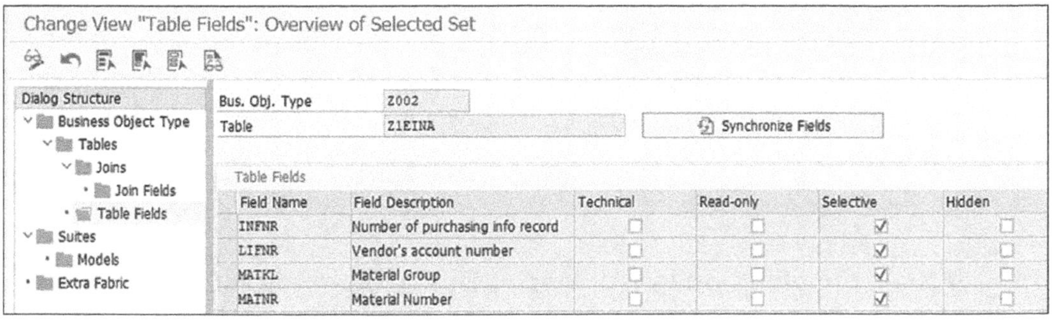

Figure 9.118 Configured Tables Fields as Selective in the Process Model

Set the Editing Scope

Editing scope is a configuration activity to define a group of fields that are available for editing and can be assigned to the process template. When a process of this process template is created, the fields defined in the editing scope are available for editing by default.

Figure 9.119 shows the setup of the edit scope as described in the preceding use case.

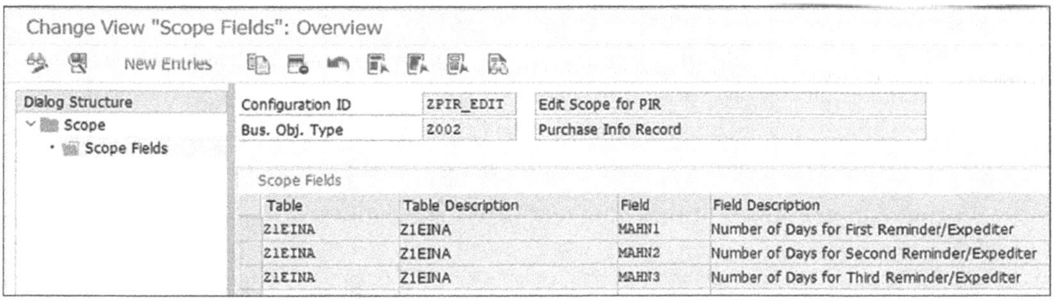

Figure 9.119 Setting the Edit Scope for Business Object Type Z002

Set Up the Process Template

A process template is designated as relevant for mass processing by setting the process goal of the process template as mass processing. Figure 9.120 shows how to set up the process template for mass processing.

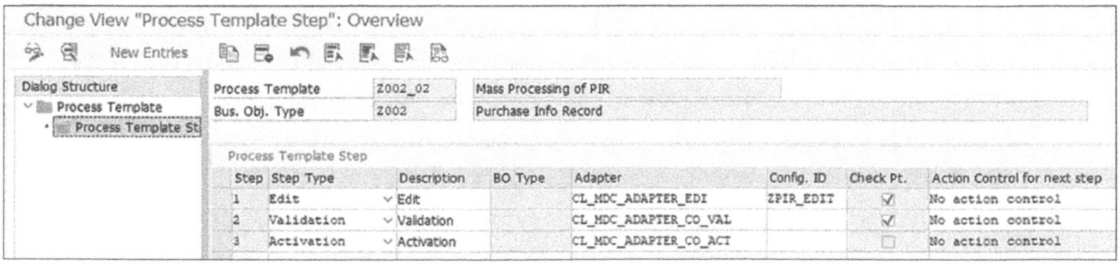

Figure 9.120 Setting Up the Process Template for Mass Processing

> **Note**
>
> In the latest version of SAP Master Data Governance on SAP S/4HANA, mass updating of long text fields is supported. Import and export options are also supported on the long text fields.

9.10   Consolidation in SAP Master Data Governance, Cloud Edition

Before we close this chapter, it's also important to mention that SAP Master Data Governance, cloud edition, the public cloud version of SAP Master Data Governance, also comes with data consolidation capabilities. However, the consolidation capabilities in SAP Master Data Governance, cloud edition, aren't a replacement for the consolidation capabilities in SAP Master Data Governance on SAP S/4HANA, which we've detailed in this chapter. Rather, because SAP Master Data Governance, cloud edition, is focused on governing core attributes of master data, it's more seen as a complementary solution that can be used to consolidate core master data attributes in a federated landscape.

The consolidation capabilities on SAP Master Data Governance, cloud edition, are very similar to SAP Master Data Governance on SAP S/4HANA. However, SAP Master Data Governance, cloud edition, supports only the business partner data object in its current version. It allows you to maintain data sources and import data from various data sources into the consolidation tables. You can then use the consolidation capabilities to consolidate business partner data and create a golden data set.

More data domains will be added to SAP Master Data Governance, cloud edition, in future releases.

We explained SAP Master Data Governance, cloud edition, extensively in Chapter 3, and consolidation capabilities are covered in Section 3.2.2 of that chapter.

9.11   Summary

This chapter provided an overview of the consolidation and mass processing functionalities delivered with SAP Master Data Governance. Various use cases, data loading options, process steps types, and configuration considerations were discussed. We highlighted how consolidation and mass processing functionalities can be leveraged to achieve organizational goals related to master data. Various prerequisite configurations and settings needed for performing several business activities that eventually run the consolidation process were also discussed. We've also provided a set of detailed instructions to help you build custom objects in consolidation as well as mass processing.

In the next chapter, you'll learn about analytical applications for SAP Master Data Governance.

Chapter 10
Data and Process Analytics

The standard content in SAP Master Data Governance provides various analytical applications to monitor both the governance processes as well as the object-specific data for better process efficiency and improved data quality.

10

Organizations need to monitor the governance processes continuously and fine-tune them to reach process maturity. To help with this requirement, you need better analytics functionalities to identify bottlenecks and critical paths in a process. The governance processes should have the flexibility to adjust to varying business needs without compromising on data quality and data standards. After proper empowerment from data governance councils and active data stewards, reduced number of data errors, and automation of the data quality rules, you may identify the need to remove a process task in your workflow or to add an additional check in your workflow process.

You may be concerned that introducing processes and additional checks will increase the time to create and process master data records. However, this doesn't consider the cost savings achieved with the reduction in efforts of data cleansing projects and other parallel projects to create workarounds regarding data quality issues. As the enterprise becomes mature with proven data governance processes, you can reduce the time it takes to create or process master data drastically. To help with the fine-tuning of the process, data stewards need to understand the process bottlenecks. This is where process analytics comes into the picture. SAP Master Data Governance standard content provides various analytical functionalities to report on the process data as well as on the contextual data based on the domain attributes, such as number of requests created by a plant/purchase organization, and so on. These analytical reports will help the process managers allocate the right number of resources and measure the productivity of the human resources required to manage the master data process and improve data quality. The standard out-of-the-box functionality also provides the monitoring of master data changes by specified attribute. This helps in managing critical master data attribute changes and identify areas for process improvements and data governance standards.

This chapter describes the applications available as part of the SAP Master Data Governance analytics functionality. SAP Master Data Governance on SAP S/4HANA process analytics is available to monitor key performance indicators (KPIs) and Service Level Agreements (SLAs) of the processes across various master data scenarios.

Section 10.1 discusses the process analytics content available as part of SAP Master Data Governance on SAP S/4HANA 2021 with SAP Fiori apps and the associated configuration activities that are available for SAP Master Data Governance analytics. Section 10.2 details the configurations required to generate additional views to perform change request analytics using master data attributes, and Section 10.3 details the configurations required to perform change analytics for master data in change requests.

10.1   Process Analytics Overview and Analysis Drilldown

Standard SAP Fiori apps are provided for domain-specific content to analyze and monitor the master data processes and change history of mater data attributes. The technical names and details of these SAP Fiori apps, including the setup, are included in Chapter 16. The key apps provided are as follows:

- Master Data Process Overview for Business Partners
- Master Data Process Overview for Products
- Master Data Process Overview for Financial Data

These apps provide information in the form of actionable cards with drilldown capability to navigate to other SAP Fiori–based analytical apps. The dependent apps for Change Request Analysis, respectively, for each domain are as follows:

- Change Request Analysis for Business Partners
- Change Request Analysis for Products
- Change Request Analysis for Financial Data

Similarly, for Work Item Analysis, the dependent apps include the following:

- Analyze Completed Work Items from Change Requests for Business Partners
- Analyze Completed Work Items from Change Requests for Financial Master Data
- Analyze Completed Work Items from Change Requests for Products
- Monitor Open Work Items from Change Requests for Business Partners
- Monitor Open Work Items from Change Requests for Products
- Monitor Open Work Items from Change Requests for Financial Master Data

The process overview apps provide summary information, in the form of cards, from a user perspective as well as a process perspective. From each card, you can navigate to the respective dependent analysis app. The displayed information includes the following:

- **Total Change Requests**
- **Open Change Requests**
- **Overdue Change Requests**

- Rejected Change Requests
- Change requests with My Participation
- Longest Running Open Change Requests
- Change Requests Older Than 48 hours
- Processing Duration of Finalized Change Requests
- Open Work Items by Responsibility and Status
- Open Work Items
- Average Processing Hours of Completed Work Items
- Total Processing Days of Completed Work Items
- Completed Work Items

For business partner and product master domains, consolidation and mass processing cards are included, as follows:

- Open Consolidation and Mass Processes
- Finished Consolidation and Mass Processes
- Duration of Consolidation and Mass Processes
- Number of Processed Business Partners/Products
- Consolidation Validation Results
- Changed Business Partner/Product Attributes

The Master Data Process Overview for Product app is shown in Figure 10.1.

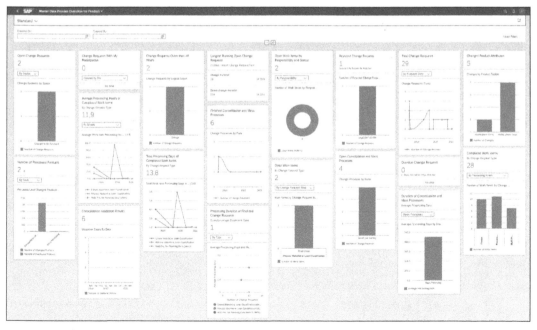

Figure 10.1 Master Data Process Overview for Product App

The cards related to work item analysis are shown in Figure 10.2.

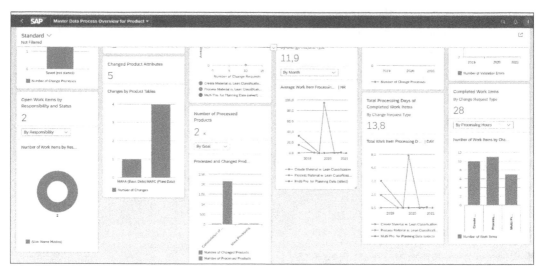

Figure 10.2 Cards for Work Item Analysis

Drilling down on the change request related cards shows the Change Request Analysis of Products app, as shown in Figure 10.3. Similar apps are visible for all domains.

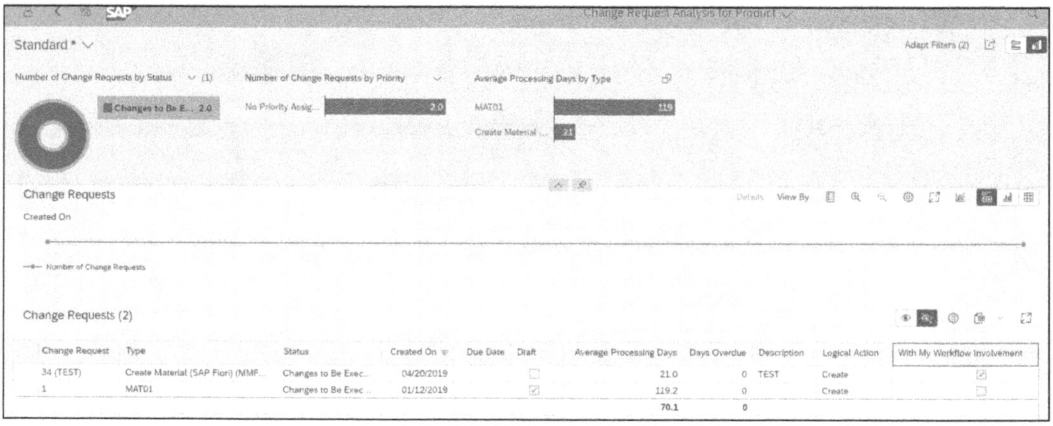

Figure 10.3 Change Request Analysis for Product App

Users can hide/unhide these cards based on personalization preferences, filter the information displayed, and maintain variants for easy access and sharing of user-defined views. The cards can be hidden for the end user using SAP role SAP_UI_FLEX_KEY_USER.

For the Master Data Process Overview for Business Partner and Master Data Process Overview for Products apps, users can filter for the cards based on change requests and for the cards based on consolidation and mass processing for precise selection and analysis of the data, as shown in Figure 10.4.

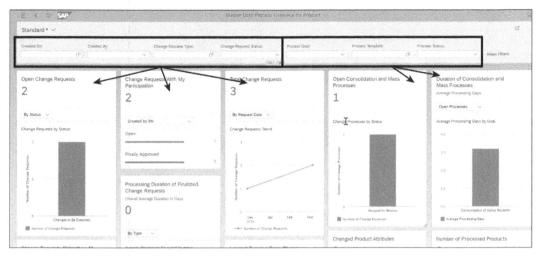

Figure 10.4 Filters for Analysis

In the Master Data Process Overview for Business Partner app, users can filter the results to get customer or supplier master data. By using the filter for **Business Object Type**, you can get the process overview for customer or supplier object–related change request analytics when selecting **Business Partner**, **Customer**, or **Supplier** as the filter. The result can be saved as a variant for customer or supplier for the user, as shown in Figure 10.5.

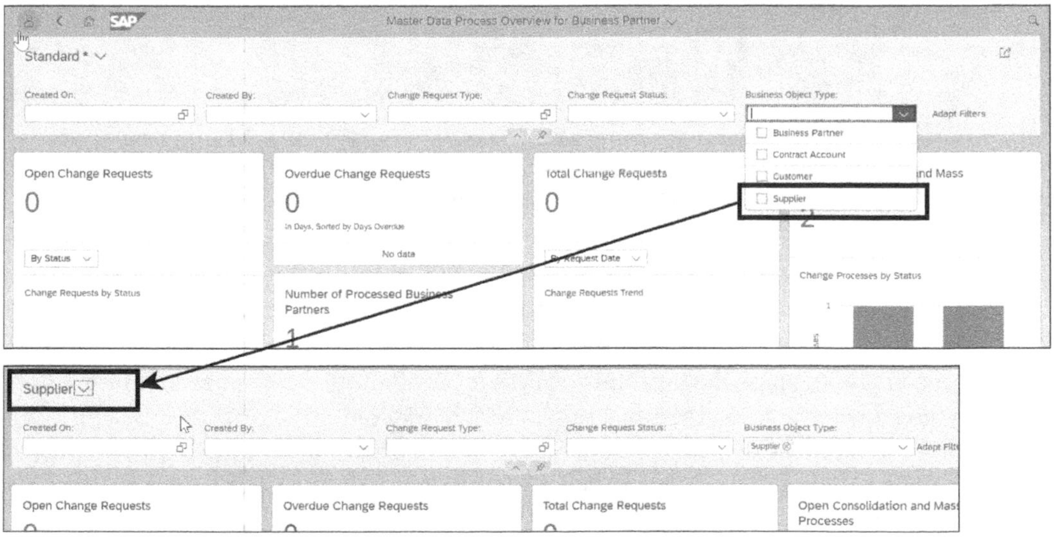

Figure 10.5 Variants for Business Partner Master Data Process Analytics

For financial master data process analytics, users can filter based on edition data. Two predefined application views for **Accounting** and **Controlling** are available, as shown in Figure 10.6.

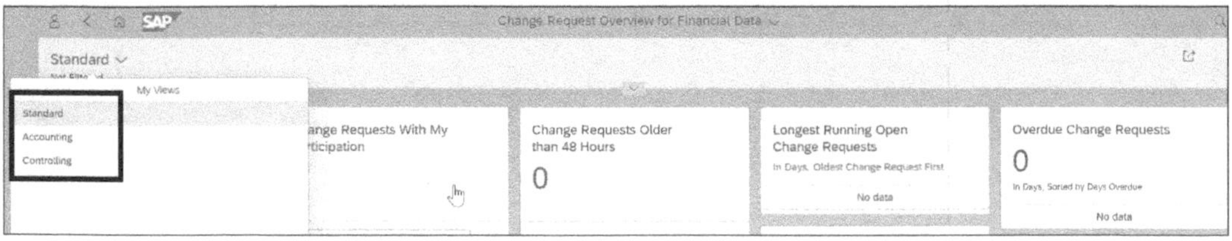

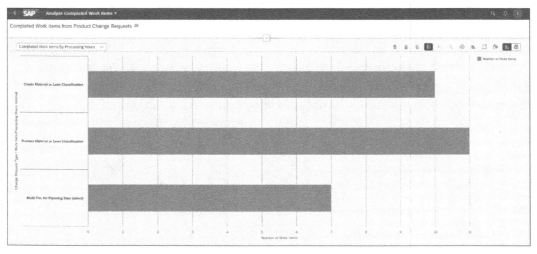

Figure 10.6 Variants for Finance Master Data Process Analytics

The work item analysis app provides information about the process steps such as average time to process a work item. This helps to analyze the work items related to completed as well as open change request processes. These apps are available for custom models as well. Figure 10.7 shows the Analyze Completed Work Items app for Products.

Figure 10.7 Analyze Completed Work Items for Products App

The Customizing activity **Activate Work item Attributes for Process Analytics** (in Transaction MDGIMG: **Master Data Governance, Central Governance • General Settings • Process Analytics**) enables the use of change request attributes and actions for work item analytics apps. The Customizing activity **Configure Time Frames for Process Analytics** allows you to set the time intervals for work item processing and to set the factory calendar, so that the processing times are accordingly evaluated for the work items in the analytical application. Figure 10.8 shows the Customizing view of setting up the factory calendar at the change request type level. This enables you to configure processing time measure in hours/days or workdays in the application.

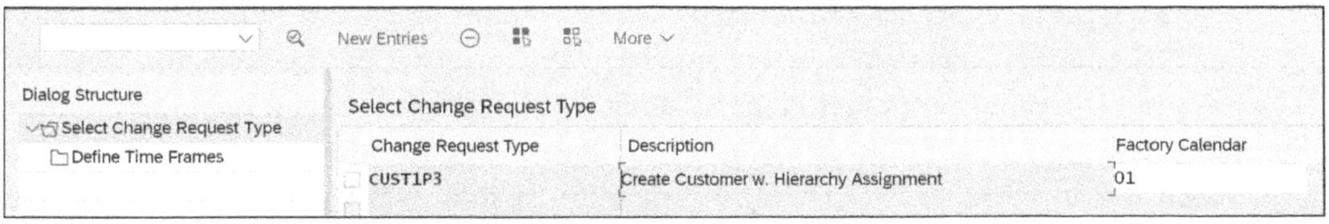

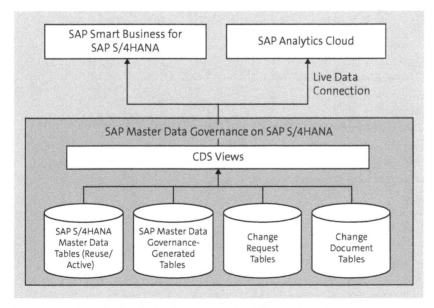

Figure 10.8 Time Frames for Process Analytics

Section 10.2 and Section 10.3 detail the configuration activities required for setting up views for change request analytics using master data attributes and change analytics, respectively.

10.2   Change Request Analytics Using Master Data Attributes

Analysis of SAP Master Data Governance change request processes based on master data attributes help master data stewards/master data specialists monitor the processes, both open and completed, based on different master data dimensions such as plants, company codes, purchasing organizations, sales organizations, material groups, and so on. This data can be configured to support drilldown analytics based on additional attributes. Proper authorization controls can be set up for the display of respective master data attributes based on user role. The standard framework to generate the various analytics views is supported for both standard and custom data models. Therefore, the standard built-in configuration provides the flexibility to create real-time custom reports based on user needs, without compromising the required security controls.

Figure 10.9 SAP Master Data Governance Analytics Architecture

To perform analytics based on master data attributes and to do change analytics on specific master data attributes, there are standard options to generate custom views for further analysis. The standard reports generate analytics core data services (CDS) views that can be exposed to users via SAP Smart Business apps or SAP Analytics Cloud. The solution architecture for CDS view generation is shown in Figure 10.9. Information from the SAP Master Data Governance system tables such as master data tables in the active/reuse area, SAP Master Data Governance staging generated tables, SAP Master Data Governance change request tables, and change document tables are joined per the business requirements and filter criterion to generate the CDS views. These CDS views are consumed via the SAP Smart Business app user interface configuration. These could be consumed via a live data connection to SAP Analytics Cloud as well.

Configuration for process analytics content to enable work item analytics, analytics based on master data attributes, and change analytics can be done using the configuration path via Transaction MDGIMG: **Master Data Governance, Central Governance** · **General Settings** · **Process Analytics**. Figure 10.10 illustrates the configuration path for analytics-related content.

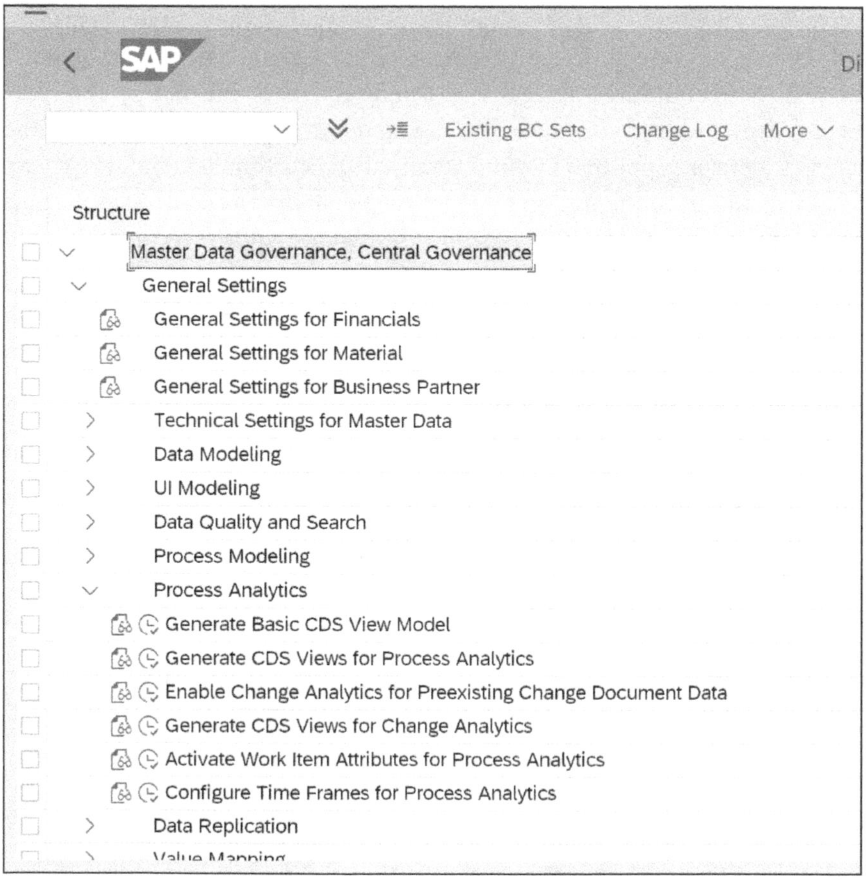

Figure 10.10 Transaction MDGIMG: Process Analytics Configuration Path

The Customizing activity **Generate Basic CDS View Model** is a prerequisite to generate CDS views for process analytics. These CDS views are used to expose the data for analysis. The basic CDS views need to be generated before other CDS views for process and change analytics can be generated in the next steps. Figure 10.11 shows the view to generate the basic CDS view. The CDS views can be generated for an active data model. If any enhancements are made to the data model, such as custom fields, these views need to be regenerated. The view displays the generation status for the data model and the details on the generated CDS views. These views could be combined with other data sources (external to SAP Master Data Governance) with a small effort.

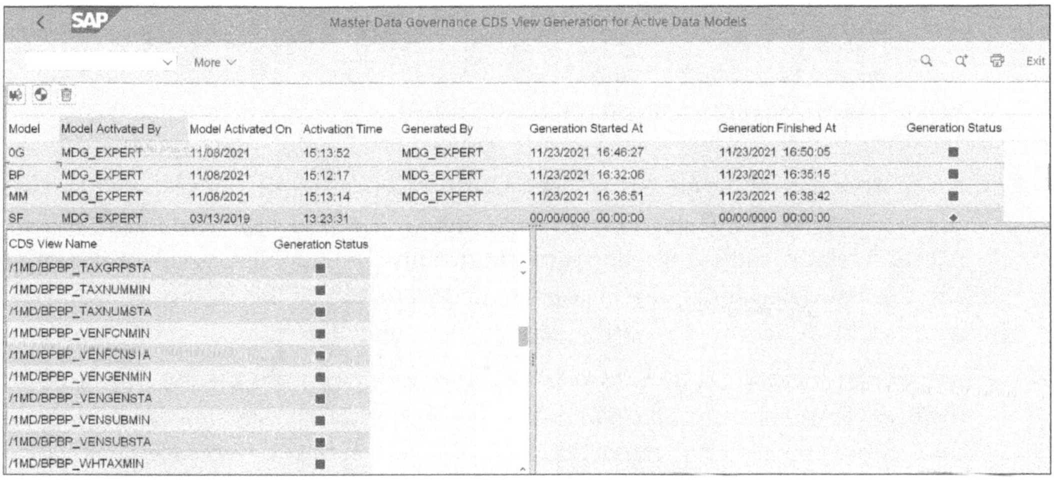

Figure 10.11 Basic CDS View Generation

Once the basic CDS views are generated based on the data model, additional CDS views can be generated with specific fields. The Customizing activity **Generate CDS Views for Process Analytics** can be used to generate the CDS views with various field combinations, as required, for the change request analytics. The data to be included can be filtered, as part of the view generation. The parameter **Analysis target** can be set to define if the analysis should be done on **All Change Requests/Finalized Change Requests/Open Change Requests**. This helps with optimizing the performance of the reports. Figure 10.12 shows the configuration view to select the master data attributes from the data model that need to be displayed in the view for analysis. Master data attributes of type 1 or type 4 entities related to the main entity can be selected. Read access logging for the attributes can be configured at the attribute level.

The included analytical measures are as follows:

- Total number of change requests
- Total change request processing days
- Average change request processing days

- Total change request overdue days
- Average change request overdue days

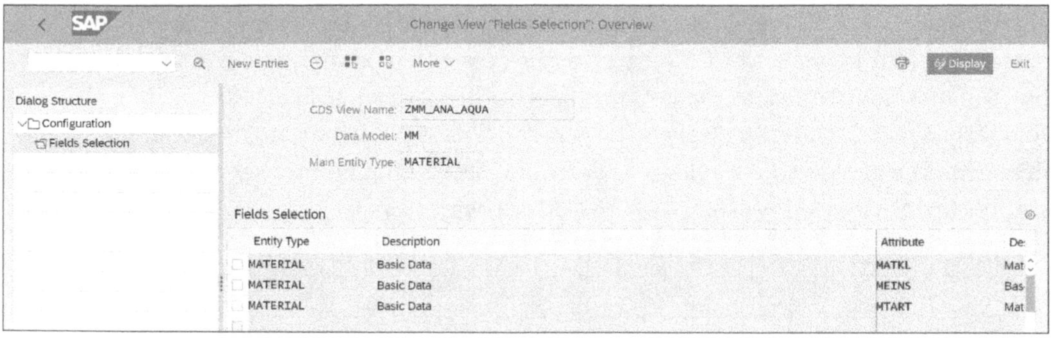

Figure 10.12 Generate CDS Views for Process Analytics

The dimensions for the analytical reports include change request header data, such as change request type, change request description, status, priority, due date, reason, rejection reason, and so on, along with additionally configured master data attributes and the associated entity keys. The generated views can be included in personalized reports with drilldown capabilities based on views and dimensions.

As part of the view generation, associated authorization controls are also generated for the CDS views. For custom fields/entities, the authorization mapping can be done in the Customizing path via Transaction MDGIMG: **Master Data Governance, Central Governance • General Settings • Data Quality and Search • Search and Duplicate Check • Define Joins, Field Mapping, and Authorizations for Reuse Tables**.

The generated CDS views can be consumed via embedded analytical tools such as SAP Smart Business apps or via the SAP Analytics Cloud solution. Figure 10.13 illustrates the SAP Master Data Governance process analytics content in SAP Analytics Cloud.

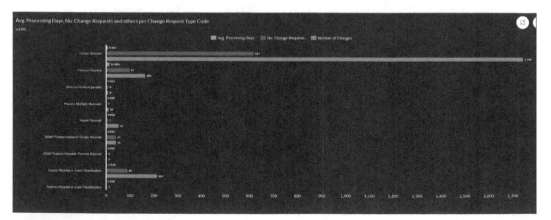

Figure 10.13 SAP Master Data Governance Process Analytics in SAP Analytics Cloud

10.3   Change Analytics for Master Data in Change Requests

Change analytics helps the data stewards/data specialists to get real-time audit reports and insights on specified master data attribute changes. This helps to monitor the business-critical attribute changes.

The included analytical measures are listed here:

- Number of Changes
- Number of Change Requests
- Average/Total Change Request Processing time
- Average/Total Overdue Days

The dimensions for the analytical reports include change request header data, such as change request type, change request description, status, priority, due date, reason, rejection reason, and so on, along with changed attribute details, such as field name, new/old value, action, change by/at, associated field key (based on entity), and the additional attributes configured for drilldown. The generated views can be included in personalized reports with drilldown capabilities based on views and dimensions.

The Customizing activity **Generate CDS Views for Change Analytics** is used to generate the CDS views for change analytics of change requests. It allows you to generate views based on an analysis target of **All Change Requests**, **Final Change Requests**, **Finalized Change Requests with Details**, and **Open Change Requests**, as illustrated in Figure 10.14. Setting the analysis target helps in performance optimization of the report. The generated view contains the number of changes measure in addition to the analytical measures listed for process analytics CDS views. These views are generated based on the change documents shown earlier in Figure 10.9.

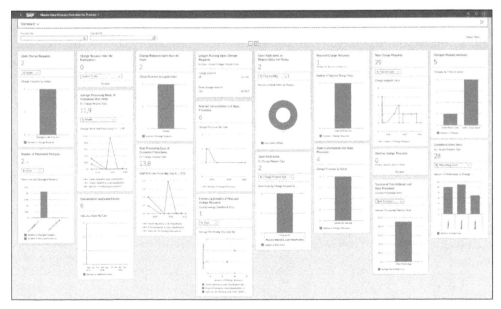

Figure 10.14 Change Analytics CDS View Generation

The attributes required for change analytics can be configured as part of the CDS view generation activity, as shown in Figure 10.15. The attributes should belong to the main entity type of the data model.

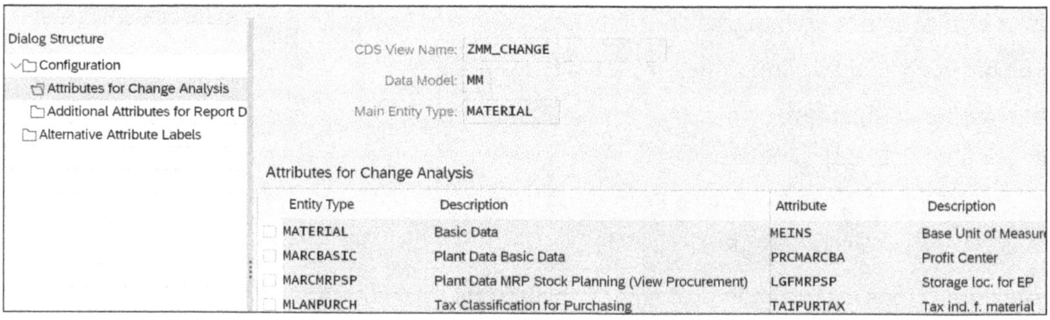

Figure 10.15 Change Analytics CDS View Attributes

Additional attributes (nonnumeric) for report drilldown can be configured as shown in Figure 10.16.

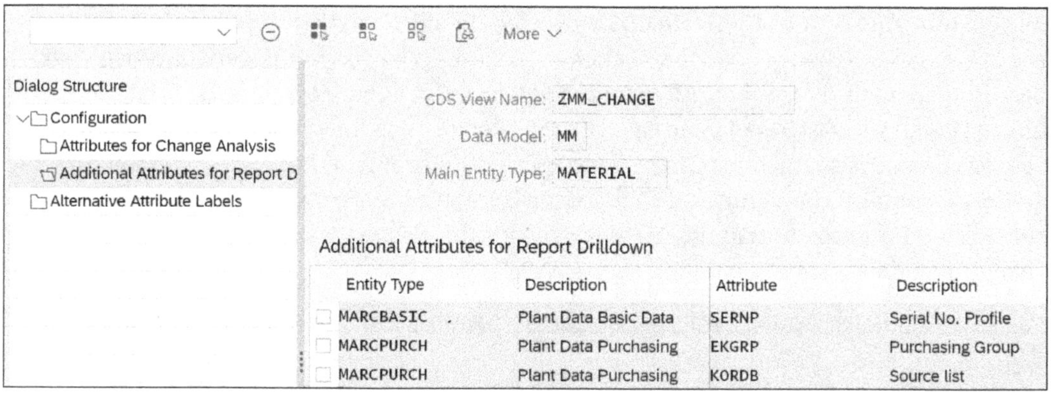

Figure 10.16 Change Analytics CDS View Drilldown Attributes

Alternative attribute labels for the report can be configured per the end user requirement, based on a data element description, as shown in Figure 10.17.

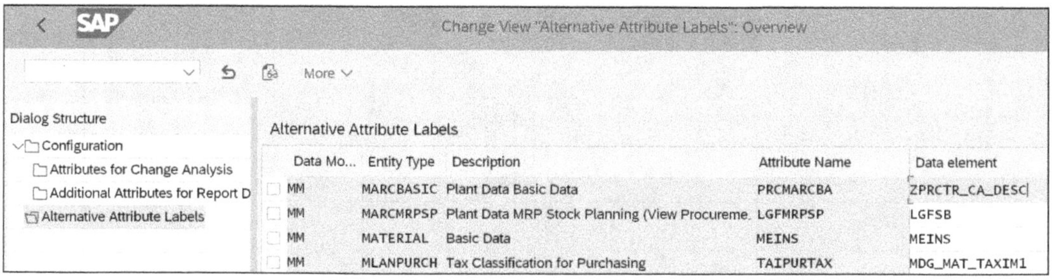

Figure 10.17 Change Analytics CDS View Attribute Alternative Labels

If your chosen attributes in **Attributes for Change Analytics** need read access logging, then choose **Log Domain** on the view level. For **Additional Attributes for Report Drill-Down**, if access logging is needed, choose a **Log Domain** on these attribute levels, as shown in Figure 10.18.

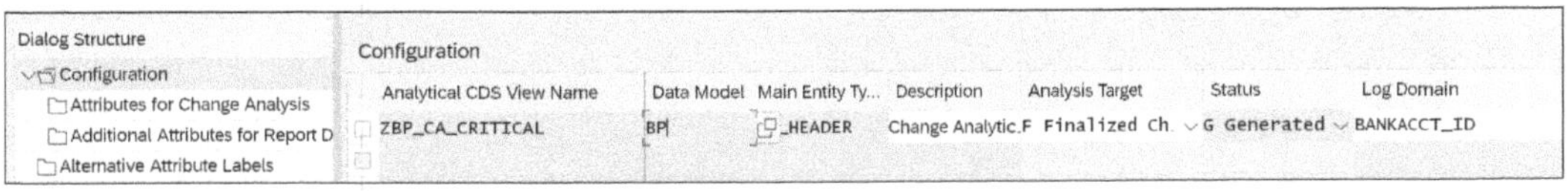

Figure 10.18 CDS View Generation Reading Log Domain

Once the CDS view are generated, the data can be consumed via an SAP Smart Business apps or via other tools such as SAP Analytics Cloud. Figure 10.19 illustrates the **MM Change Analytics** report of the material master attribute. It displays the change history of the unit of measure attribute and also displays additional attributes such as **Plant**, **Purchasing Group**, and so on, in addition to the change request attributes.

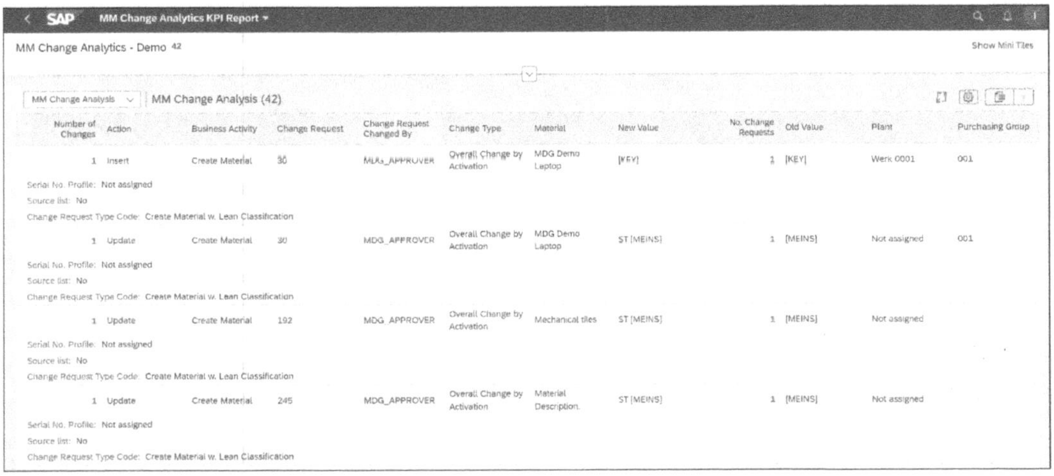

Figure 10.19 Change Analytics Material Master Report

10.4   Summary

This chapter provided information on the key analytical applications available with the SAP S/4HANA 2021 release. The standard analytical content involves analytics for both master data and process information related to the change request information. In addition to the standard generated views, custom views can be generated to expose additional attributes for reporting and further analysis.

The following chapter will give more information on developing central governance custom scenarios in SAP Master Data Governance.

Chapter 11

Central Governance: Building Custom Applications

In this chapter, we'll take an in-depth look into the detailed functionality and usage of the SAP Master Data Governance custom object framework. We'll use the Project System component as an example of building custom SAP Master Data Governance applications using the SAP Master Data Governance custom object framework.

The SAP Master Data Governance custom object framework is provided to help you model and build SAP Master Data Governance applications for the master data objects specific to your business, which aren't provided by standard SAP Master Data Governance models. It can also be used for standard SAP master data objects for which SAP hasn't provided any standard SAP Master Data Governance applications. For example, no out-of-the-box data model and SAP Master Data Governance user interface (UI) applications are delivered for the location master data object, so you can use the custom object framework to build an SAP Master Data Governance application for the location master data object.

The custom object framework ensures that the applications you build are consistent in look and feel with standard applications provided by SAP Master Data Governance. The framework also ensures that custom applications meet SAP guidelines and conform to the SAP Master Data Governance architecture.

The key objective of the custom object framework is to help customers concentrate on modeling the application without worrying about architecture and the technical design under the hood. The custom object framework should also reduce a lot of work by reusing existing SAP Master Data Governance components. For example, you can reuse the existing generic search UI (USMD_SEARCH) to configure any kind of search UI.

In this chapter, we'll explain the SAP Master Data Governance custom object framework using Project System in SAP S/4HANA as an example. This chapter starts by explaining the background and context of Project System and providing a quick overview of custom data models. Next, we describe sequentially the steps to model Work Breakdown Structures (WBSs) in Project System as a custom data model object in SAP Master Data Governance. After the data model is modeled for the custom object WBS, we describe building UI applications based on the data model and configuring process model and data replication for WBS elements. The chapter also covers how to enable security and roles for WBS as custom objects in central governance.

> **Note**
>
> All the instructions in this chapter are equally applicable to SAP ERP Project System (SAP ERP PS) as they are to Project System in SAP S/4HANA. At the time of writing, there are no significant differences between the two systems that impact these instructions.

11.1 Custom Data Models

This section first introduces how Project System business objects are structured and related and then provides an overview of the data models themselves.

11.1.1 Project System in SAP S/4HANA

Project System is a project management solution that provides you with support in all phases of an enterprise project. In SAP S/4HANA, Project System provides structures that can be used to model and organize projects flexibly.

> **Note**
>
> We recommend a little refresher on Project System from publicly available documentation:
>
> - For SAP ERP PS: *http://s-prs.co/v558006*
> - For Project System in SAP S/4HANA: *http://s-prs.co/v488300*

Project system provides two structures for mapping an enterprise project: WBSs and networks. WBSs are used to organize a project in the form of a hierarchy and to map the structure of a project. Networks are used to represent project activities and logical relationships between the project activities. WBSs consist of WBS elements that are arranged in various levels to produce a hierarchical model of the project activities to be carried out.

The following elements are considered master data for the Project System application:

- WBS elements
- Networks
- Activities

Depending on the requirements, you can use WBSs, networks, or both to map your project in the SAP system. However, the scope of this book only includes project definition, WBSs, and WBS elements, not networks and activities.

> **Note**
>
> We're limiting the scope here to concentrate on explaining the SAP Master Data Governance custom object framework. The focus of this chapter isn't to explain the details of Project System, but rather to show how the SAP Master Data Governance custom object framework should be used.

You can have only one WBS assigned to a project. Each WBS can contain multiple WBS elements, as shown in Figure 11.1.

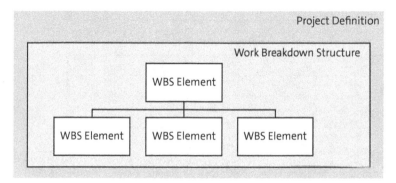

Figure 11.1 Project Definition and the WBS

Following are the different Project System components:

- **Project definition**
  The project definition is used to define the common attributes that are shared across the structures (WBS/network) and structure elements (WBS elements/activities) assigned to the project. Project definition is a mandatory component for creating a project with a network, WBSs, or both. The project definition holds the data that affects the whole project. For example, a controlling area entered in the project is applicable for the whole project. Project definition is also used to define organizational data such as company code, business area, profit center, and plant. This organizational data is defaulted across the WBS elements.

- **WBS**
  The WBS is the model of the project and shows the work packages in a hierarchical structure. Each work package in an enterprise project is represented by WBS elements.

- **WBS elements**
  WBS elements represent a work package in an enterprise project. WBS elements are actual elements that are used as account assignment objects to record costs, and they can also be used as planning elements. WBS elements are arranged in a hierarchical manner, allowing the data to be summarized at any level.

We also need to take a brief look at the data modeling architecture in Project System in SAP S/4HANA. Figure 11.2 shows the various tables that together form the data model for Project System. All data is saved in the tables. This database architecture will be the basis for the SAP Master Data Governance data model. It doesn't make sense to reengineer an already proven and established data model.

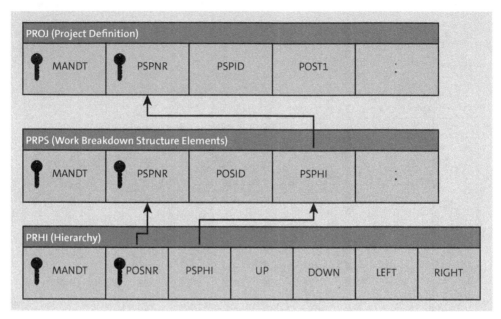

Figure 11.2 Project System Database Architecture in the SAP Business Suite and SAP S/4HANA Core

11.1.2   Data Modeling Tools

The SAP Master Data Governance application framework has its own data modeling tools. SAP Master Data Governance applications are built on top of this data model. An SAP Master Data Governance data model is an abstract model that organizes semantically similar elements of data as entities and attributes, along with relationships between the entities. The SAP Master Data Governance data model acts implicitly as a source of metadata for UI modeling.

The SAP Master Data Governance foundation framework uses the SAP Master Data Governance data model entities, attributes of entities, and relationships between entities to generate the staging area. The *staging area* is an exclusive persistence layer for SAP Master Data Governance, generated from an active SAP Master Data Governance data model. The staging area is used to store both active data and inactive data. Technically, the SAP Master Data Governance staging area is a set of generated database tables, and the SAP Master Data Governance data model is an abstract layer for this staging area. The goal of the data model is to generate these staging area tables correctly and be the single source of information for relationships between various SAP Master Data Governance entities. The SAP Master Data Governance data model is also a source of metadata required for UI modeling.

Following are two storage modes for active data:

- **Reuse mode**

  This mode is used if a data model (tables) already exists in SAP S/4HANA. Usually these are the master data objects that are available as part of the SAP S/4HANA data model but aren't delivered as out-of-the-box SAP Master Data Governance data models.

  To use the reuse active area for the custom data models, you must create an active area and assign the access class to the active area. Figure 11.3 shows how to create the active area and the access class in Transaction MDGIMG.

  The access class acts as a bridge between the SAP Master Data Governance application framework and the reuse area.

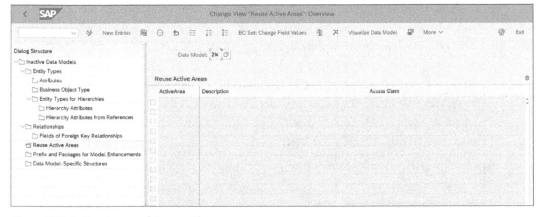

Figure 11.3 Active Area and Access Class

The SAP Master Data Governance access class implements the IF_USMD_PP_ACCESS interface. Table 11.1 provides a brief overview of important access class methods.

Method Name	Method Description
READ_VALUE	This method is used to read the master data from the active area (SAP S/4HANA) tables.
CHECK_DATA	This method is used to perform active area checks. For example, this method can be used to check UI data against the SAP S/4HANA configuration.
SAVE	This method is used to save the data into the SAP S/4HANA table by calling SAP S/4HANA application programming interfaces (APIs).

Table 11.1 List of Important Methods in a Reuse Class

Method Name	Method Description
CHECK_AUTHORITY	This method is used to perform authorization checks using SAP S/4HANA authorization objects.
ENQUEUE	This method is used to set the lock on the objects.
DEQUEUE	This method is used to remove the locks on the objects.

Table 11.1 List of Important Methods in a Reuse Class (Cont.)

- **Flex mode**
  This mode is used if no tables are available in SAP S/4HANA. Usually these are the master data objects that aren't available as part of the standard SAP S/4HANA data model.

  The flex option is also a preferred approach for business objects that require edition management. SAP S/4HANA doesn't have the edition concept; instead, these layers enforce time dependency by using valid-from date, valid-to date, or both as key fields in the table. It would be tedious for the developer to translate these valid-from and valid-to dates to an edition and prepare data slices in terms of editions.

  The flex model comes with only one set of tables. The data model with flex mode saves both the active and inactive data in the SAP Master Data Governance staging area. The SAP Master Data Governance framework fully understands the metadata of these tables. Therefore, a developer needs to develop the access class, which is automatically handled by the framework.

In our current example of WBSs in Project System, we'll choose flex mode because the flex model doesn't require the creation of an active area access class, and our current data model involves a hierarchy.

> **Note**
> A type 1 entity must always be assigned to a business object.

11.2   Create a Custom Data Model

The first step toward building custom SAP Master Data Governance applications is to create a custom data model. The Generic Interaction Layer (GenIL) provides uniform API services to access and manipulate underlying business data. The Business Object Layer (BOL) consumes the GenIL API. The following sections explain how to create the custom data model, entities, and relationships in detail.

11.2.1 Concepts and Prerequisites

The process of creating entities and attributes for custom data model ZW will be described via the following:

- Conceptual data model
- Logical data model
- Physical data model

The conceptual data model is a high-level representation of the data model architecture. The conceptual data model is created with nontechnical names so that project stakeholders such as executives, business users, and business subject matter experts (SMEs) can easily understand the architecture of the data model. The conceptual data model acts as the basis for creating the logical data model.

Figure 11.4 shows the conceptual data model for the WBS in a Project System data model. Note that we didn't include all the fields. The purpose of this diagram is to introduce you to the idea of the conceptual data model, which doesn't require the full details of the data model.

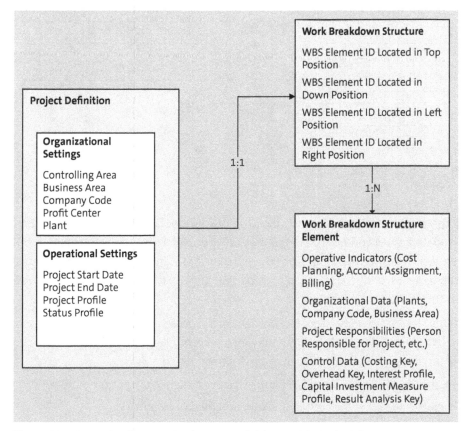

Figure 11.4 Example of Conceptual Data Model for WBS in Project System

Next, the logical data model is a representation of the conceptual data model in terms of entities, attributes, and relationships. The logical data model is normalized by specifying field-level details such as data type and data length.

Figure 11.5 is a logical representation of the WBS in the Project System data model. The figure shows two entities—**Project Definition** and **Work Breakdown Structure Elements**—along with detailed attributes. The figure also shows the cardinality and foreign key relationship between the two entities. The target audience for the logical data model is made up of business SMEs, expert modelers, and application experts (in SAP Master Data Governance in this case).

Project Definition

Field Name	Description	Data Element	Key
PSPID	Project definition (internal)	PS_PSPID	X
POST1	PS: Short description	PS_POST1	
VERNR	Number of the responsible person	PS_VERNR	
ASTNR	Applicant number	PS_ASTNR	
PLFAZ	Project Planned Start Date	PS_PLFAZ	
PLSEZ	Project planned finish date	PS_PLSEZ	
KALID	Factory calendar key	FABKL	
VKOKR	Controlling area for the project	PS_VKOKR	
VBUKR	Company code for the project	PS_VBUKR	
VGSBR	Business area for the project	PS_VGSBR	
WERKS	Plant	WERKS_D	
STORT	Location	PS_STORT	
PRCTR	Profit Center	PRCTR	
PWHIE	Proj Currency	PS_PWHIE	
PROFL	Project Profile	PROFIDPROJ	
BPROF	Budget Profile	BP_BPROFIL	

1:N — Foreign Key Relationship

Work Breakdown Structure Element

Field Name	Description	Data Element	Key
POSID	Work breakdown structure	NUMC08	X
PSPID	Project definition	PS_PSPID	X
PSPNR	WBS Element	PS_POSNR	
POST1	PS: Short description	PS_POST1	
PRART	Project Type	PS_PRART	
PSPRI	Priority	NW_PRIO	
VERNR	Pers.Resp.No.	PS_VERNR	
ASTNR	Applicant no	PS_ASTNR	
FKOKR	Controlling area of	PS_FKOKR	
FKSTL	Responsible cost center	PS_FKSTL	
PLAKZ	Planning Element	PS_PLAKZ	
BELKZ	Account assignment element	PS_BELKZ	
FAKKZ	Billing Element	PS_FAKKZ	
PKOKR	Controlling area for WBS element	PS_PKOKR	
PBUKR	Company code for WBS	PS_PBUKR	
WERKS	Plant	WERKS_D	
PSPID	Current Project Number	PS_PSPID	

Figure 11.5 Representation of WBS in the Project System Logical Data Model in the Form of Entities and Attributes

During this process step, business SMEs describe various attributes (including field length and data type) and how the attributes are grouped. Expert modelers and application experts translate the input from the business SMEs into entities and attributes. After the entities and attributes are designed, the relationships and navigation between the entities are defined.

During this step, the stakeholders also define other data semantics such as the source of value list of the fields. Stakeholders may also determine, if applicable, some of the example attribute dependencies, such as the following:

- The plant value list is the subset of plants that are assigned to the company code.
- The region value list is the subset of values assigned to a country.

Finally, the physical data modeling is the process of creating the actual data model in the system. During this step, you take the outcomes (e.g., design document) from the preceding two steps and implement them in the system. The physical data model is system specific and deeply technical in nature. The actors who perform roles in physical data modeling are usually SAP Master Data Governance data modeling experts and developers.

At this process step, we dig deeper into SAP Master Data Governance and start implementing the logical data model in the system. Figure 11.6 shows that the **Data Model ZW** has been created to represent WBS in Project System. Here the active area is **MDG**, which means that all the active data of this data model will be persisted in the SAP Master Data Governance staging areas. Ensure that the data model name is created in the proper namespace of X*, Y*, and Z*.

Following are the steps to create a data model:

1. Go to IMG path, **Master Data Governance, Central Governance · General Settings · Data Modeling · Edit Data Model**.

2. Click on **New Entries**.

3. Enter the values as shown in Figure 11.6.

4. Click on **Save** and activate the data model.

Inactive Data Models					
Data Model	Description (medium text)		ActiveArea	Prefix/Namespace	Package
✓ ZW	Data Model for SP PS - WBS		MDG	ZMDG	ZMDG

Figure 11.6 Data Model Created for the WBS in the Project System Custom Data Object in SAP Master Data Governance

Following are the steps necessary to create business object code **ZPS**, as shown in Figure 11.7:

1. Go to IMG path, **Master Data Governance, Central Governance · General Settings · Data Modeling · Define Business Object Type Codes**.

2. Click on **New Entries**.

3. Enter "ZPS" as the **BO Type** and "Project Structure" as the **Description**.

4. Click **Save** to save your entries.

> **Note**
>
> This chapter doesn't explain the SAP Master Data Governance data model concepts and definition of data model artifacts. For more information on those topics, refer to Chapter 3.

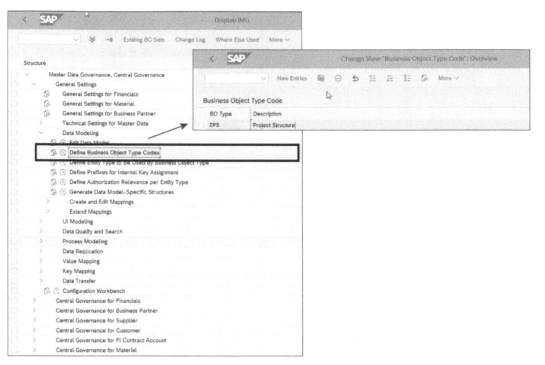

Figure 11.7 Creation of Business Object Type Code "ZPS"

11.2.2   Creating Entities

In the following sections, we'll look at creating entities for your custom data model, starting with type 1 entities before moving on to type 3.

Project Definitions

Every data model should have at least one type 1 entity. In the current example, the project definition is one of the type 1 entities. Figure 11.8 shows the creation of project definition as a type 1 entity with **Entity Type PSPID**.

The relevant features of the entity settings are as follows:

❶ Edition management has been disabled. In the underlying SAP S/4HANA data model, Project System isn't a time-dependent entity.

❷ Every type 1 entity needs a key assigned. We've selected external key for the type 1 entity in accordance with the underlying SAP S/4HANA settings for the project definition.

❸ The project definition can have language-dependent texts.

❹ The **Active Area** field has been left blank; when left blank, the active area of the data model is adopted.

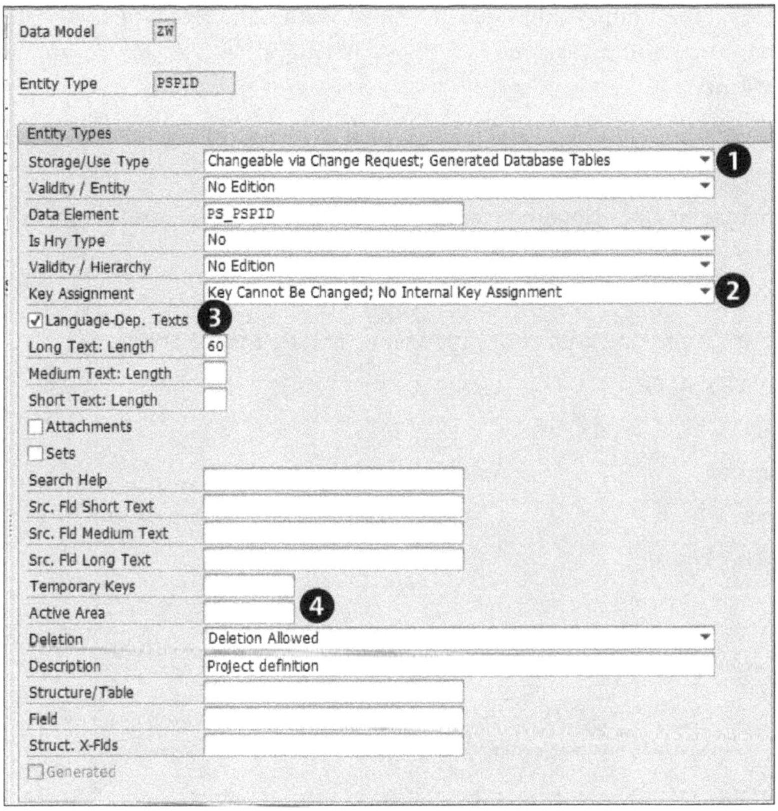

Figure 11.8 Creation of the Project Definition as a Type 1 Entity

Figure 11.9 shows all attributes added to **Entity Type PSPID**.

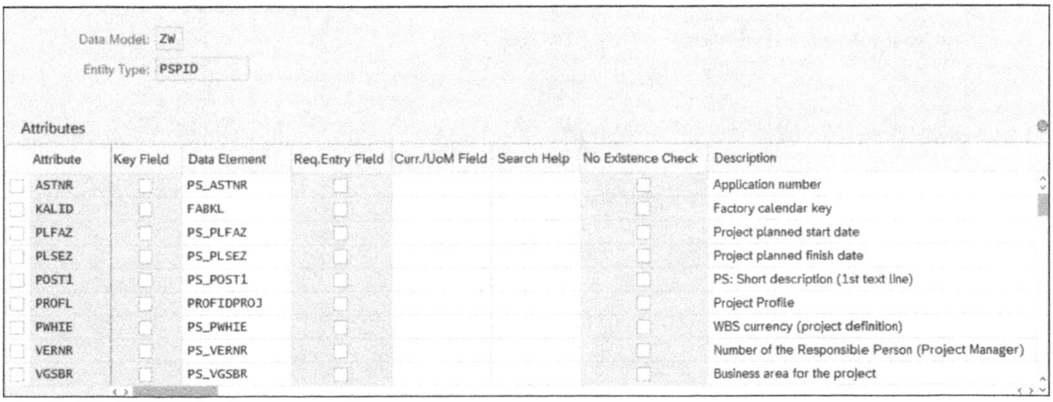

Figure 11.9 Attributes Added to the Type 1 Entity "PSPID"

Entity type PSPID is a type 1 entity and needs to have business object type code ZPS, which you created in Section 11.2.1, assigned to it. This association is used for UI modeling and data replication.

Following are the steps to assign business object type code ZPS to entity type PSPID, as shown in Figure 11.10:

1. Go to IMG path, **Master Data Governance, Central Governance · General Settings · Data Modeling**.

2. Select **Data Model ZW**.

3. Click on **Entity Types**, and open the entity type view for data model **ZW** ❶.

4. Select **Entity Type PSPID** ❷.

5. Open the **Business Object Type** view.

6. Click on **New Entries**.

7. Set the **BO Type** to **ZPS**.

8. Select the **Root** checkbox.

9. Click the **Save** button to save your entries.

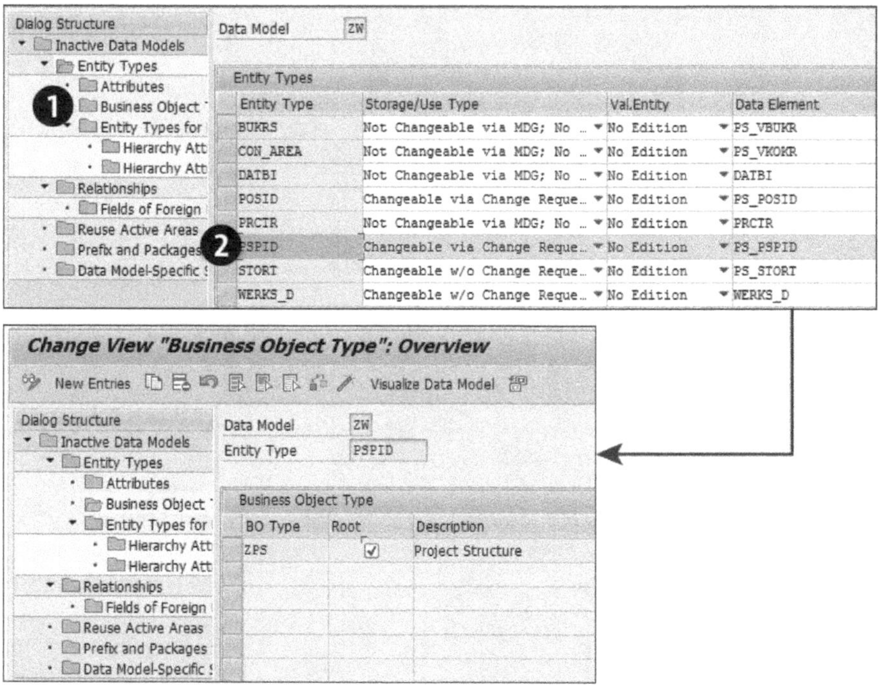

Figure 11.10 Assigning Business Object ZPS to Entity PSPID (Project Definition)

Notice that we've designated entity PSPID as the root object for the business object type ZPS.

Work Breakdown Structure Elements

We'll be creating a WBS element as another type 1 entity, but we'll assign it the same business object as the project definition (PSPID). By assigning it to the same business object as the project definition, we're ensuring that a WBS element can't be replicated alone, and it needs to be replicated through the project definition. Figure 11.11 shows the creation of a type 1 entity for a WBS element.

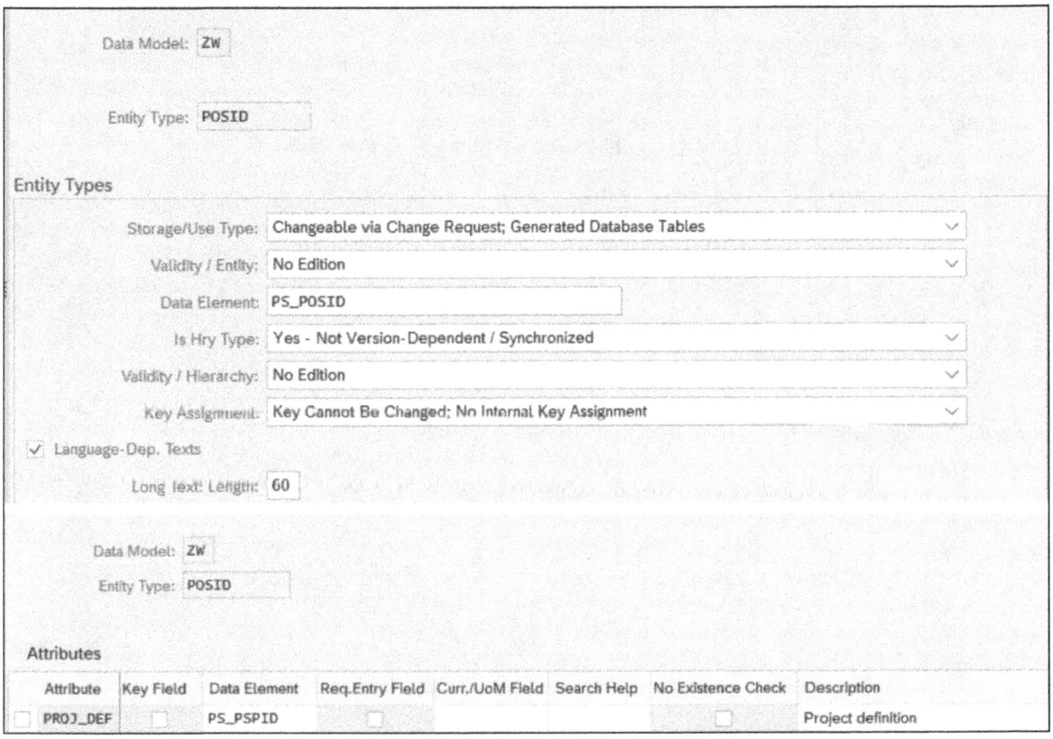

Figure 11.11 Creation of a Type 1 Entity for a WBS Element and Addition of Project Definition as an Attribute

If you look at Figure 11.12, you'll notice that in the underlying reuse active area, there is a foreign key relationship between the tables PROJ and PRPS. We need to replicate a similar kind of relationship in the SAP Master Data Governance data model as well between entities POSID and PSPID. For this purpose, we've added an attribute called PROJ_DEF to entity POSID. This field is used to store the project definition ID of the project to which the WBS element is assigned. This attribute needs to have a foreign key relationship with entity PSPID.

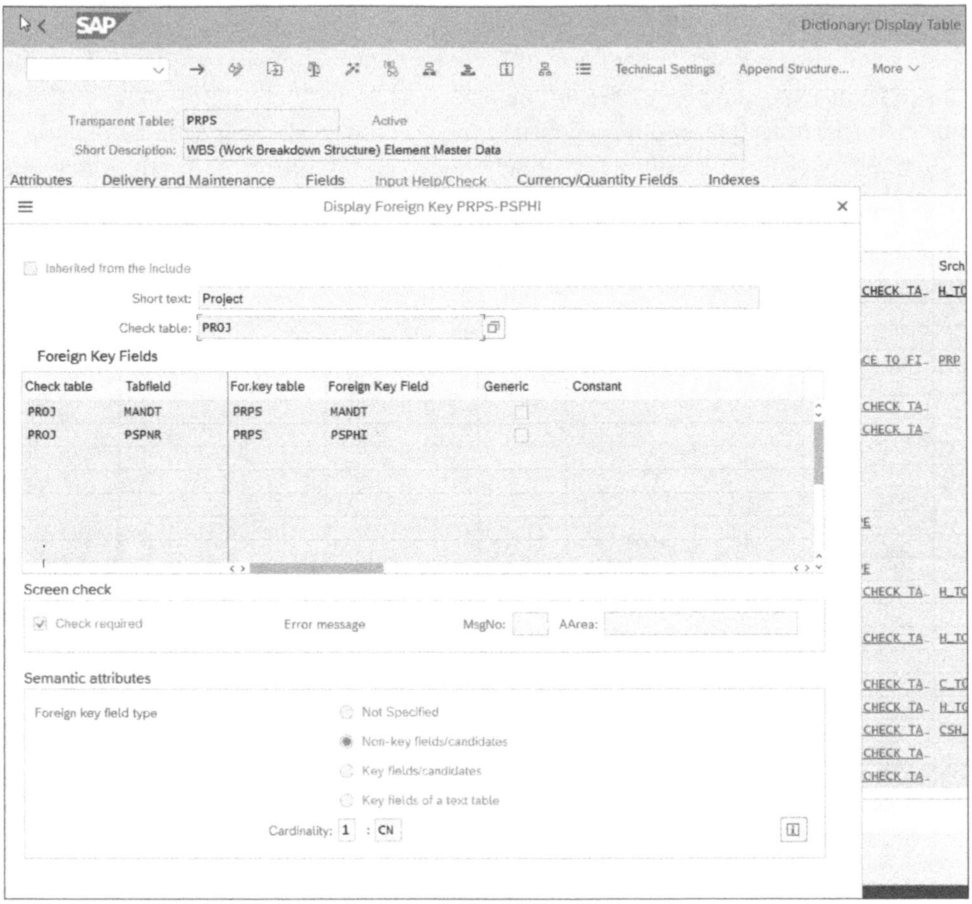

Figure 11.12 Foreign Key Relationship between Tables PROJ and PRPS

The foreign key fields are project definition internal IDs. Because we don't have a project definition internal ID in the data model, we'll establish a similar kind of relationship on the external ID of the project definition. Figure 11.13 shows the modeling steps to implement foreign key relationships between entities PSPID and POSID. Following are the steps that need to be performed to model foreign key relationship between entities PSPID and POSID:

❶ Select a type 1 entity for the WBS element.

❷ Add **Attribute** "PROJ_DEF" under entity POSID.

❸ Create a new foreign key relationship.

❹ Enter "PSPID" as the **"From" Field (Check Table Fld)** and "PROJ_DEF" as the **"To" Field (Foreign Key Field)**.

❺ Once the data model is generated, the project definition will have PSPID as a reference entity.

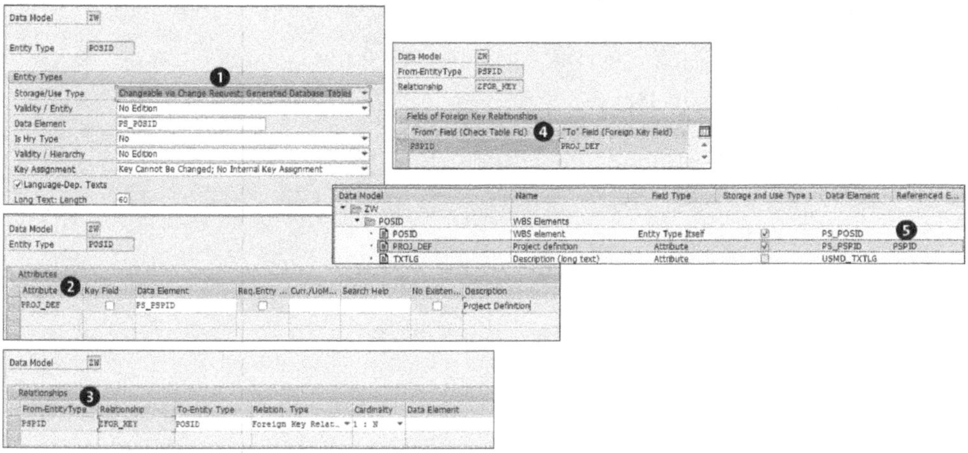

Figure 11.13 SAP Master Data Governance Data Modeling Steps to Implement a Similar Foreign Key Relationship

Entity POSID is also a type 1 entity. You therefore need to assign business object type code ZPS to entity type POSID, as follows (see Figure 11.14):

1. Go to IMG path, **Master Data Governance, Central Governance · General Settings · Data Modeling**.

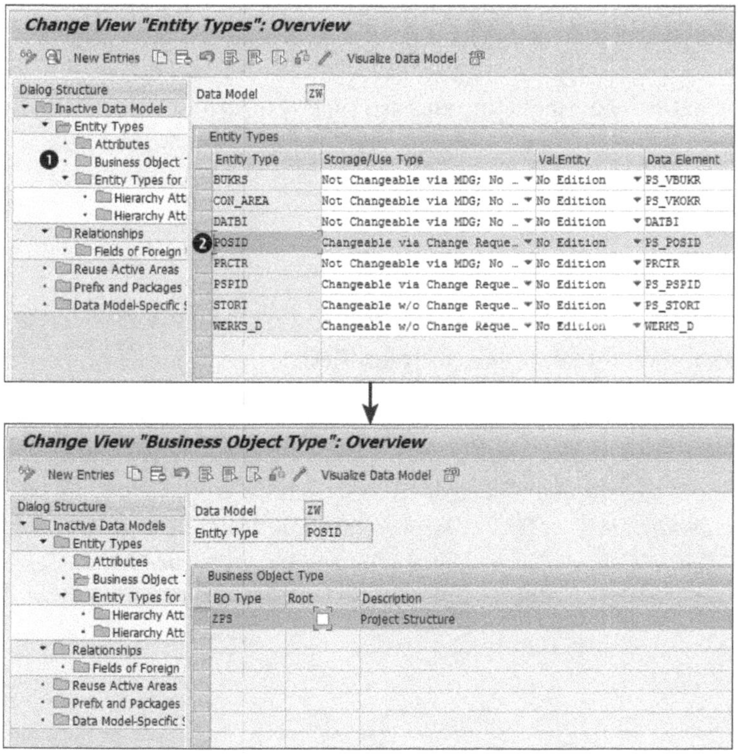

Figure 11.14 Assigning Business Object "ZPS" to Entity "POSID" (WBS Element)

2. Select **Data Model ZW**.

3. Click on **Entity Types**, and open the entity type view for data model **ZW** ❶.

4. Select **Entity Type POSID** ❷.

5. Open **Business Object Type** view.

6. Click on **New Entries**.

7. Set the **BO Type** to **ZPS**.

8. Click the **Save** button to save your entries.

Notice that we haven't enabled POSID as a root object.

Controlling Areas

If you revisit the logical data model, you'll find the following distinct features in the data model:

- The controlling area is present as an attribute both in the project definition and in the WBS element. Therefore, it makes sense to create just one type 3 entity and then assign the same entity as an attribute to the project structure and WBS element entities using referencing relationships.

- The controlling area is one of the key fields in the check tables assigned to other attributes of the data model (e.g., profit center); therefore, it's imperative that you create the controlling area as a type 2 or type 3 entity so that the entity can be used to establish a leading relationship.

Figure 11.15 shows the creation of a controlling area as a type 3 entity and its assignment as an attribute to entity PSPID using a referencing relationship. In this figure, you see the following:

❶ The profit center as a type 2 entity

❷ The valid-to date as a type 2 entity

❸ Adding the profit center as an attribute to PSPID using a referencing relationship

❹ The controlling area and valid-to date as leading entities

Why a Type 3 Entity and Not a Type 2 Entity?

The controlling area is a configuration entity, and the value list of this attribute is maintained in the **Reuse Active Area** (SAP S/4HANA). You do need a separate set of check tables generated in SAP Master Data Governance, and you want the SAP Master Data Governance framework to use the underlying check tables in the **Reuse Active Area**.

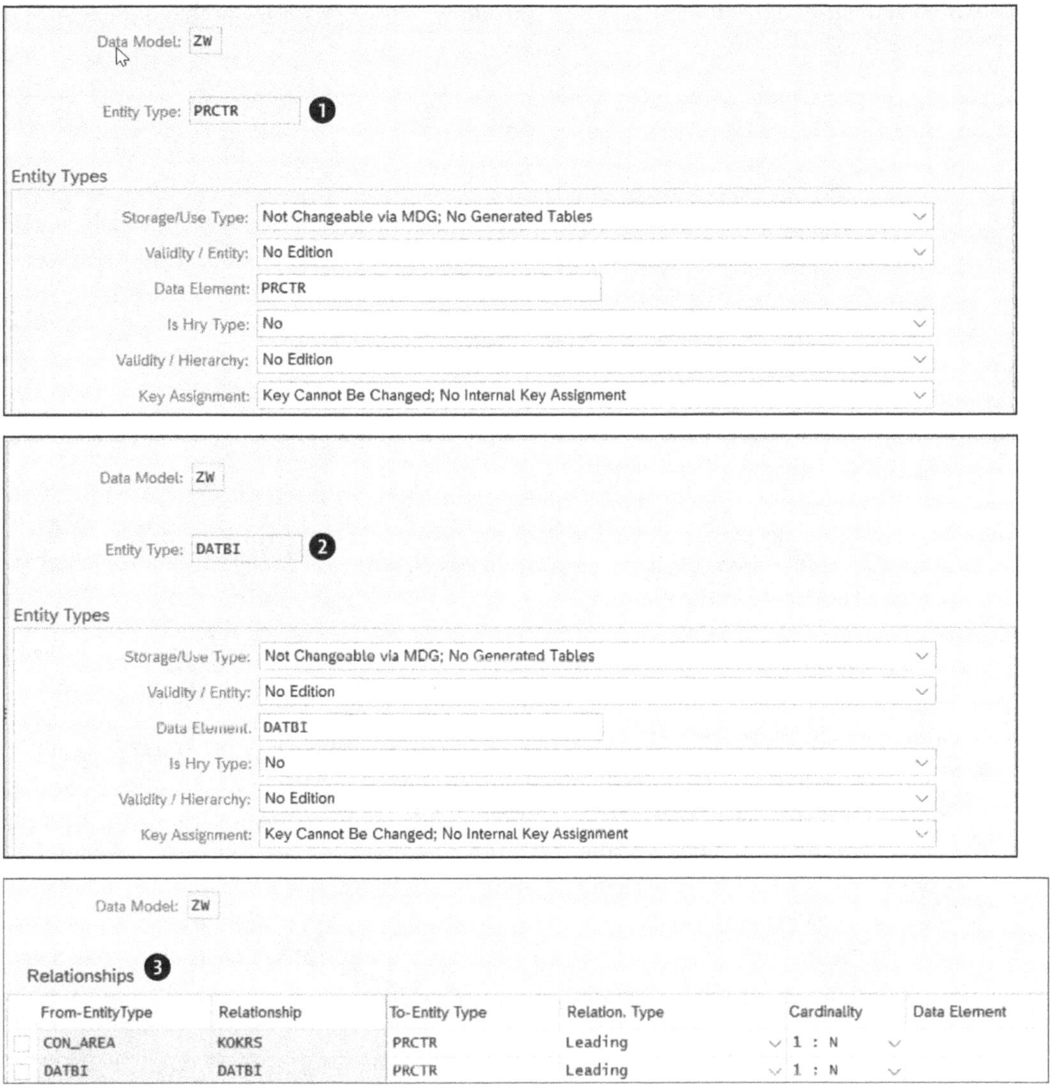

Data Model: **ZW**		
Entity Type: **PRCTR** ❶		
Entity Types		
Storage/Use Type:	Not Changeable via MDG; No Generated Tables	⌄
Validity / Entity:	No Edition	⌄
Data Element:	PRCTR	
Is Hry Type:	No	⌄
Validity / Hierarchy:	No Edition	⌄
Key Assignment:	Key Cannot Be Changed; No Internal Key Assignment	⌄

Data Model: **ZW**		
Entity Type: **DATBI** ❷		
Entity Types		
Storage/Use Type:	Not Changeable via MDG; No Generated Tables	⌄
Validity / Entity:	No Edition	⌄
Data Element:	DATBI	
Is Hry Type:	No	⌄
Validity / Hierarchy:	No Edition	⌄
Key Assignment:	Key Cannot Be Changed; No Internal Key Assignment	⌄

Data Model: **ZW**

Relationships ❸

From-EntityType	Relationship	To-Entity Type	Relation. Type	Cardinality		Data Element
CON_AREA	KOKRS	PRCTR	Leading	⌄ 1 : N	⌄	
DATBI	DATBI	PRCTR	Leading	⌄ 1 : N	⌄	

Figure 11.15 Creation of a Controlling Area as a Type 3 Entity under Data Model ZW

Profit Centers

The project definition (entity PSPID) has profit center as one of the attributes. The profit center has a PRCTR data element, which has table CEPC as a check table. Table CEPC has profit center ID, valid to, and controlling area as key attributes. You can't add profit center as an attribute directly under the type 1 entity PSPID (project definition) because the SAP Master Data Governance data model rules dictate that a check table of an entity's attribute can't have more key fields besides the client (MANDT field) and key field referring to the attribute. Figure 11.16 shows the error message that appears when adding profit center as a direct attribute to type 1 entity PSPID.

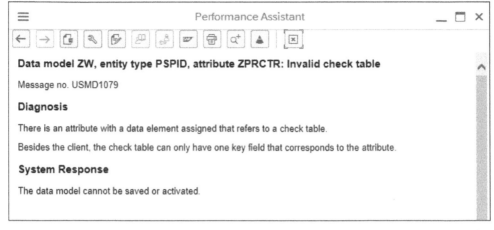

Figure 11.16 Error Message When Trying to Add Profit Center as a Direct Attribute with PRCTR as a Data Element to Entity PSPID

Note

This validation makes sense because the SAP Master Data Governance framework performs a default existence check of the attribute value against the underlying check tables. This check works correctly only if the underlying table has just one key referring to the attribute itself besides the MANDT field. If it has more keys, then the SAP Master Data Governance framework can't perform the check accurately because the SAP Master Data Governance foundation can't populate the full key of the table as it doesn't have sufficient information (metadata) to derive the value of key fields other than the key field referring to the attribute.

To tackle this kind of modeling challenge, perform the following actions, as shown in detail in Figure 11.17:

- Create the attribute (in our example, it's PRCTR) as a type 2 or type 3 entity ❶.
- Create the other key fields of the underlying check table as type 2 or type 3 entities (in our example, the valid-to fields ❷ and controlling area ❸).
- Create a leading relationship between all the type 2/type 3 entities of the key fields and the type 2/type 3 entity of the attribute ❹, ❺.
- Add all the keys and attribute entities as attributes to type 1 or type 4 entities using a referencing relationship ❻.

The figure contains the following panels:

Panel ①

Data Model: ZW
Entity Type: PRCTR ①

Entity Types

Storage/Use Type:	Not Changeable via MDG; No Generated Tables
Validity / Entity:	No Edition
Data Element:	PRCTR
Is Hry Type:	No
Validity / Hierarchy:	No Edition
Key Assignment:	Key Cannot Be Changed; No Internal Key Assignment

Panel ②

Data Model: ZW
Entity Type: DATBI ②

Entity Types

Storage/Use Type:	Not Changeable via MDG; No Generated Tables
Validity / Entity:	No Edition
Data Element:	DATBI
Is Hry Type:	No
Validity / Hierarchy:	No Edition
Key Assignment:	Key Cannot Be Changed; No Internal Key Assignment

Panel ③

Data Model: ZW
Entity Type: CON_AREA ③

Entity Types

Storage/Use Type:	Not Changeable via MDG; No Generated Tables
Validity / Entity:	No Edition
Data Element:	PS_VKOKR
Is Hry Type:	No
Validity / Hierarchy:	No Edition
Key Assignment:	Key Cannot Be Changed; No Internal Key Assignment

Panel ④

Data Model: ZW

Relationships ④

	From-EntityType	Relationship	To-Entity Type	Relation. Type	Cardinality
✓	PRCTR	PRCTR	PSPID	Referencing	0 : N

Panel ⑤

Data Model: ZW

Relationships ⑤

From-EntityType	Relationship	To-Entity Type	Relation. Type	Cardinality	Data Element
CON_AREA	KOKRS	PRCTR	Leading	1 : N	
DATBI	DATBI	PRCTR	Leading	1 : N	

Panel ⑥

Data Model: ZW

Relationships ⑥

From-EntityType	Relationship	To-Entity Type	Relation. Type	Cardinality	Data Element
CON_AREA	VKOKR	PSPID	Referencing	0 : N	
DATBI	DATBI_R	PSPID	Referencing	0 : N	
PRCTR	PRCTR	PSPID	Referencing	0 : N	

Figure 11.17 Modeling of the PRCTR Entity and Check Table Dependencies

Company Codes

Next let's create a company code as a type 3 entity and add the type 3 entity as an attribute to entity PSPID using a referencing relationship. We're adding the company code as a type 3 entity because we must establish a leading relationship later with the plant entity. This relationship is required to ensure that only plants assigned to the project company code are entered.

Figure 11.18 shows the creation of a type 3 entity type for company code. The figure shows how we've added the company code as an attribute to entity PSPID using the referencing relationship from entity type BUKRS to entity type PSPID.

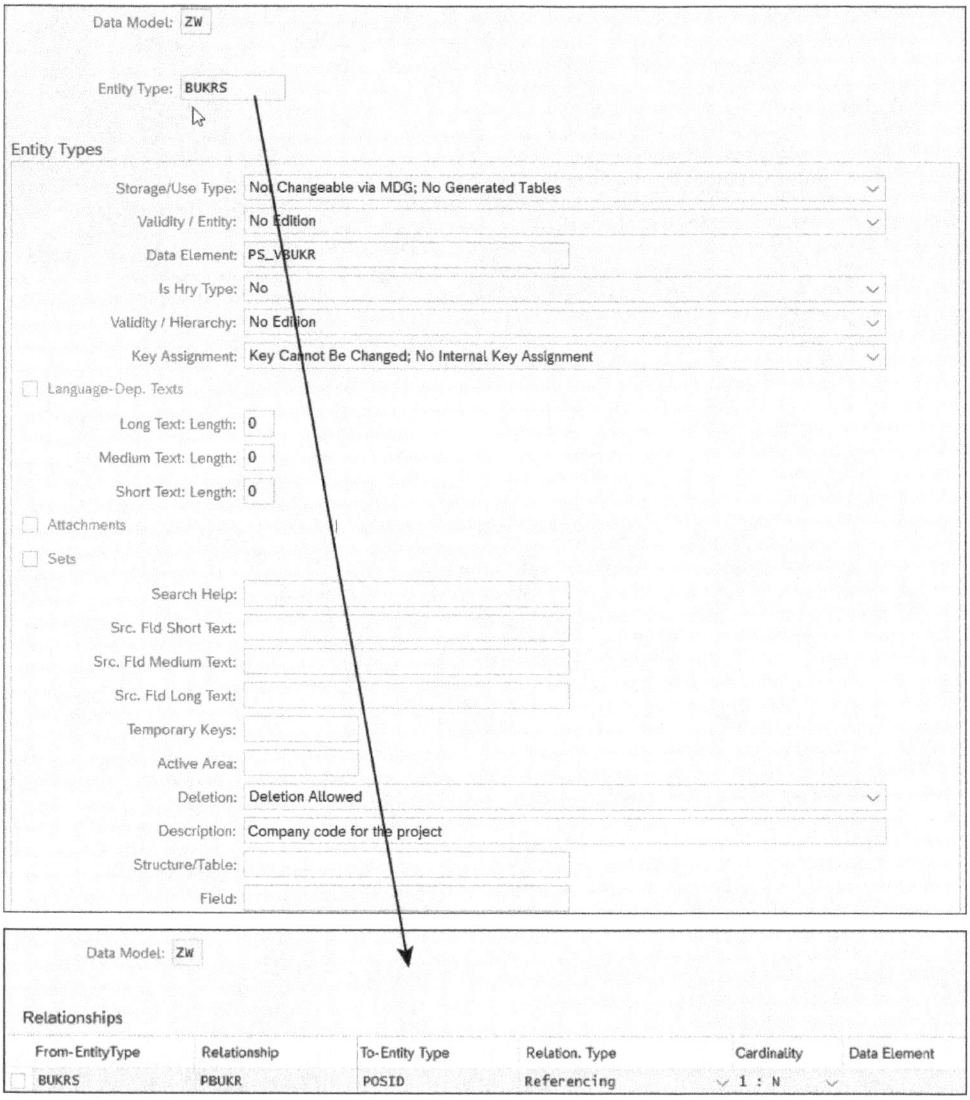

Figure 11.18 Creating Company Code as a Type 3 Entity and Assigning as Attribute to PSPID Using a Referencing Relationship

Plants

Plant is used to define organization data during project definition. In the next section, you'll learn about creation of the location entity type. The underlying check table of the location entity has the plant as a key field. To ensure that the SAP Master Data Governance framework understands this relationship between plant and location, we'll create plant as a type 3 entity because we need it to be part of the leading relationship for the location attribute. Figure 11.19 shows the steps to create plant as a type 3 entity:

❶ Create a type 3 entity for the plant.

❷ Add the plant as an attribute to **PSPID** using a referencing relationship.

Data Model	ZW	
Entity Type	WERKS_D	

Entity Types ❶

Storage/Use Type	Changeable w/o Change Request; Generated Check/Text Tables	▼
Validity / Entity	No Edition	▼
Data Element	WERKS_D	
Is Hry Type	No	▼
Validity / Hierarchy	No Edition	▼
Key Assignment	Key Cannot Be Changed; No Internal Key Assignment	▼
☐Language-Dep. Texts		
Long Text: Length		
Medium Text: Length		
Short Text: Length		
☐Attachments		
☐Sets		
Search Help		
Src. Fld Short Text		
Src. Fld Medium Text		
Src. Fld Long Text		
Temporary Keys		
Active Area		
Deletion	Deletion Allowed	▼
Description	Plant	
Structure/Table		
Field		
Struct. X-Flds		
☐Generated		

Relationships ❷

From-EntityType	Relationship	To-Entity Type	Relation. Type	Cardinality
WERKS_D	WERKS	PSPID	Referencing	▼ 1 : N ▼

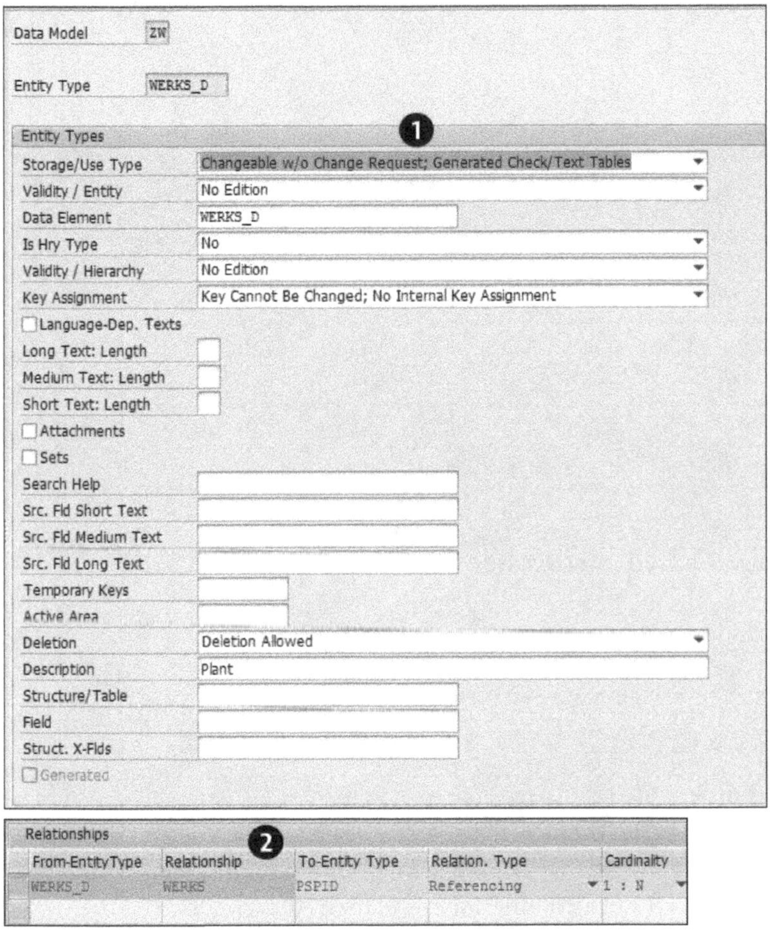

Figure 11.19 Creation of a Plant and Assigning Plant as Attribute Using a Referencing Relationship

Locations

The check table (table T499S) assigned to location has plant and location as key fields. Therefore, as explained before, you need to perform the following activities to be compliant with the SAP Master Data Governance data model rules:

1. Create plant as a type 3 entity. This has already been done in previous steps.

2. Create location as a type 3 entity, as shown in Figure 11.20 ❶.

3. Create a leading relationship between the entity for plant and the entity for location.

4. Create a referencing relationship between the entity for location and entity PSPID ❷.

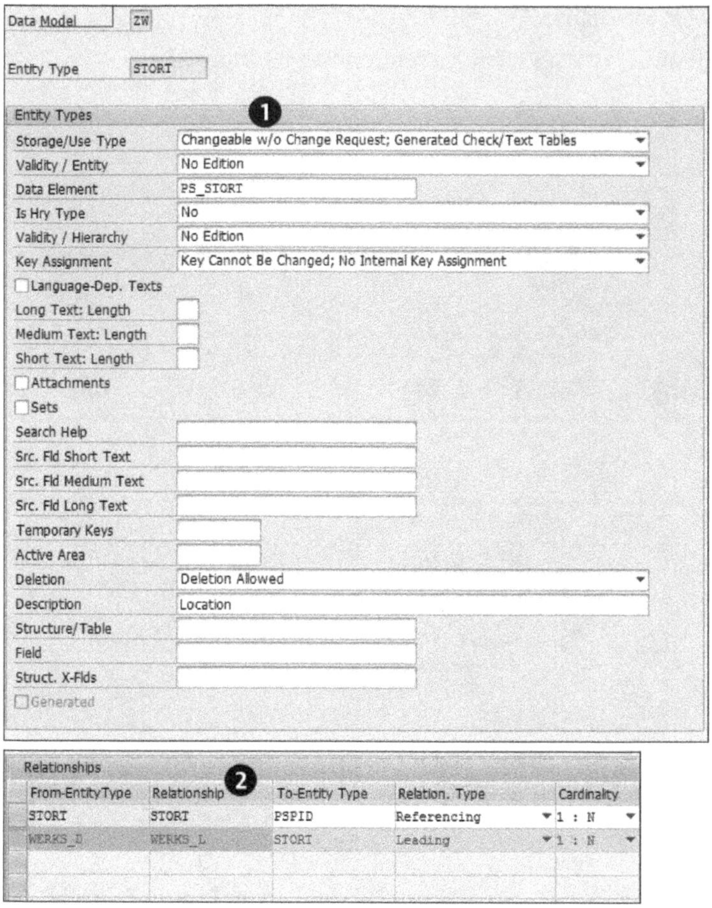

Figure 11.20 Creating an Entity for Location and Its Relationships

Figure 11.21 shows the final list of attributes for entity type POSID.

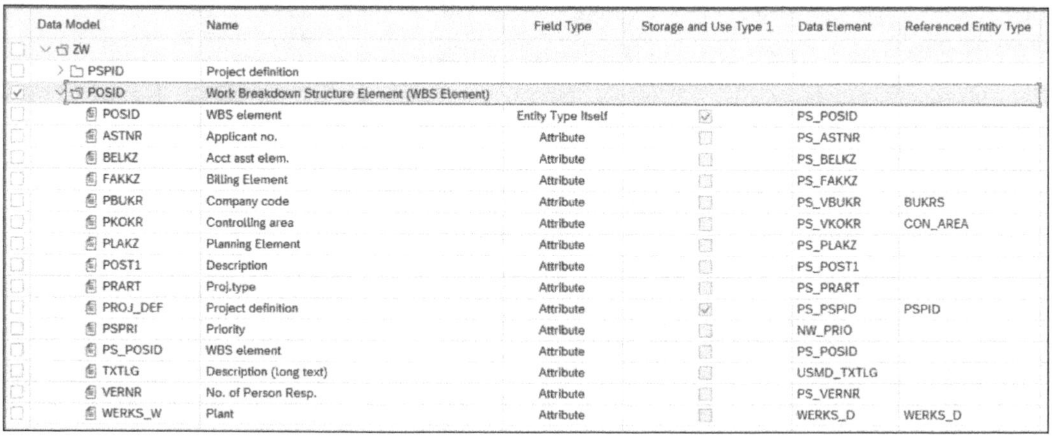

Data Model	Name	Field Type	Storage and Use Type 1	Data Element	Referenced Entity Type
ZW					
PSPID	Project definition				
POSID	Work Breakdown Structure Element (WBS Element)				
POSID	WBS element	Entity Type Itself	☑	PS_POSID	
ASTNR	Applicant no.	Attribute	☐	PS_ASTNR	
BELKZ	Acct asst elem.	Attribute	☐	PS_BELKZ	
FAKKZ	Billing Element	Attribute	☐	PS_FAKKZ	
PBUKR	Company code	Attribute	☐	PS_VBUKR	BUKRS
PKOKR	Controlling area	Attribute	☐	PS_VKOKR	CON_AREA
PLAKZ	Planning Element	Attribute	☐	PS_PLAKZ	
POST1	Description	Attribute	☐	PS_POST1	
PRART	Proj.type	Attribute	☐	PS_PRART	
PROJ_DEF	Project definition	Attribute	☑	PS_PSPID	PSPID
PSPRI	Priority	Attribute	☐	NW_PRIO	
PS_POSID	WBS element	Attribute	☐	PS_POSID	
TXTLG	Description (long text)	Attribute	☐	USMD_TXTLG	
VERNR	No. of Person Resp.	Attribute	☐	PS_VERNR	
WERKS_W	Plant	Attribute	☐	WERKS_D	WERKS_D

Figure 11.21 Final List of Attributes of Entity POSID

11.2.3   Adding Attributes to Entities

Among the list of attributes to be added to entity POSID, there are simple attributes and modeled attributes. Simple attributes can be added directly as attributes to entity POSID. Figure 11.22 shows the list of simple attributes.

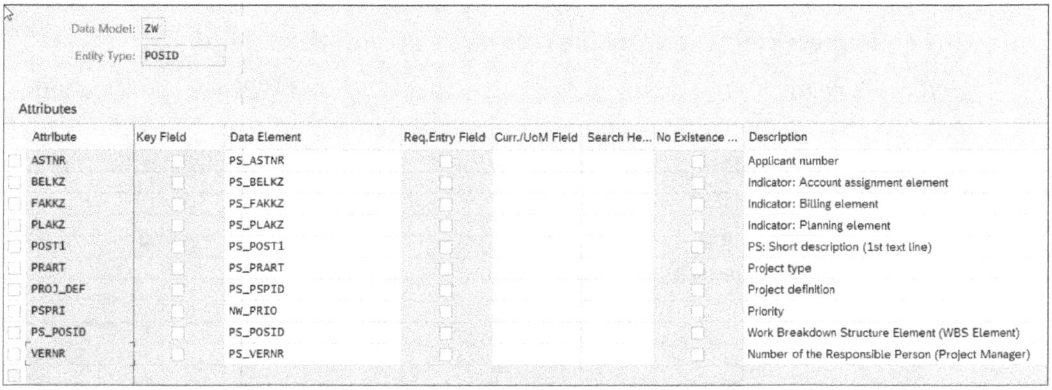

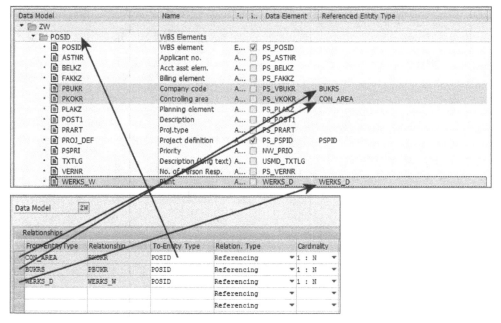

Figure 11.22 Simple Attributes That Can Be Easily Added to Entity Type POSID

The controlling area, company code, and plant of WBS make up the modeled attributes. In previous steps, we already created type 3 entity CON_AREA for the controlling area. We'll now reuse the same entity in a different referencing relationship to entity POSID to add it as an attribute to entity POSID. A similar kind of modeling will be done for company code and plant.

Figure 11.23 Adding Company Code, Controlling Area, and Plant as Attributes to Entity POSID

The process of adding company code, controlling area, and plant as attributes to entity POSID using existing type 3 entities is shown in Figure 11.23. The screen on the top is the final visualization of entity POSID, and the screen on the bottom shows the list of relationships added to data model ZW.

11.2.4   Representing the Work Breakdown Structure Hierarchically

Before we begin, it's important to emphasize that WBSs and WBS elements are different. A WBS is a hierarchical representation of WBS elements, whereas the WBS element represents a work package in a WBS. Entity PSPID represents the project definition, and entity POSID represents the WBS element and not the WBS. In this section, we'll walk through representing the WBS in SAP Master Data Governance using the SAP Master Data Governance hierarchy concept.

Note

Figure 11.24 shows a theoretical hierarchy model, which we're going to build under data model ZW. The purpose of this section is to introduce how to enable and build a hierarchy for a custom data model. You shouldn't attempt to implement the hierarchy model and its design in real-world projects without proper analysis.

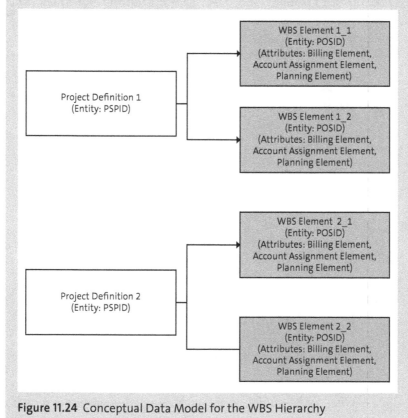

Figure 11.24 Conceptual Data Model for the WBS Hierarchy

The following describes the various hierarchy settings to enable the hierarchy for data model ZW:

- **Hierarchy leading entity**
  The hierarchy leading entity is the type 1 entity in which the hierarchy setting is activated. In our example, we'll configure entity POSID as the leading entity. Figure 11.25 shows the required settings to enable entity type POSID as the hierarchy leading entity.

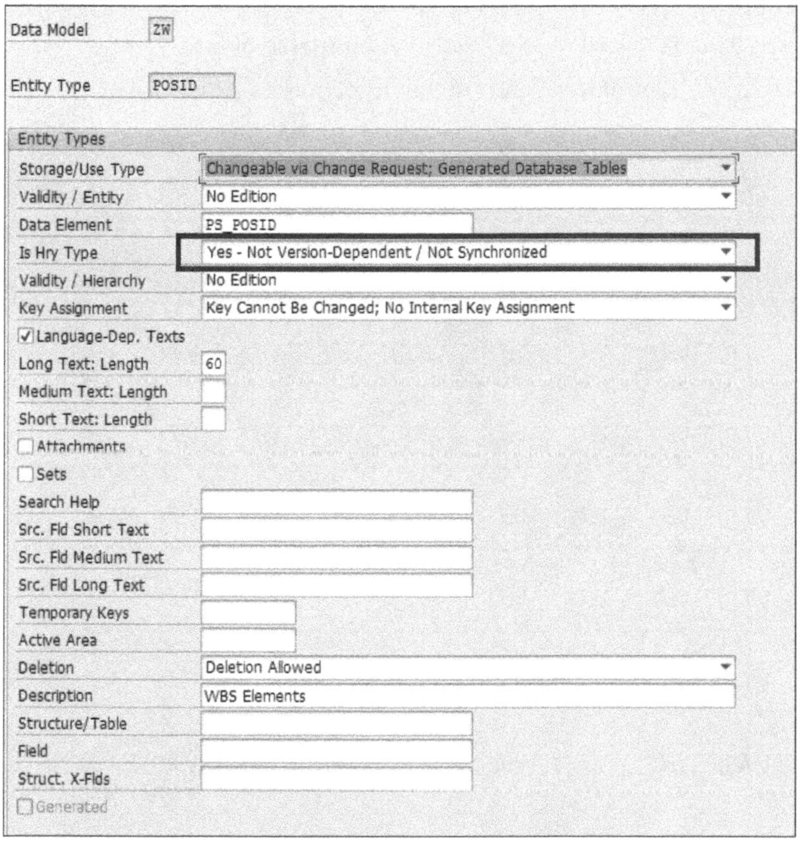

Figure 11.25 Configuring Entity POSID as the Hierarchy Type

- **Hierarchy name**
  Every hierarchy in SAP Master Data Governance must have a single hierarchy name. This hierarchy name is technically a separate type 1 entity. Here, we'll try to replicate the hierarchy model in Project System. The top node in the underlying SAP S/4HANA layer is project definition. The hierarchy name in SAP Master Data Governance is really the top node, so we designate our entity PSPID as the hierarchy name.

- **Additional entity types**
  Entities configured as additional entity types are used for grouping or end nodes

(leaves). You can configure type 1, 2, and 3 entities as additional entity types. Following are two different use types for additional entities:

– No special use: The entity can be used for both grouping and as an end node.

– Ranges permitted on the end node: This entity is an end node with ranges.

Figure 11.26 shows the additional entity type configuration for the leading entity POSID. In our entity, we won't use any additional entity types nor add any attributes to the additional entities. As shown in the figure, we'll add "PSPID" as a **Hierarchy Name**. Following are the steps that need to be performed:

– Select entity **POSID** ❶, and click on **Entity Types for Hierarchies** ❷.

– Add "PSPID" as **Ent. Type of Node** and "Hierarchy Name" as entity **Use** ❸.

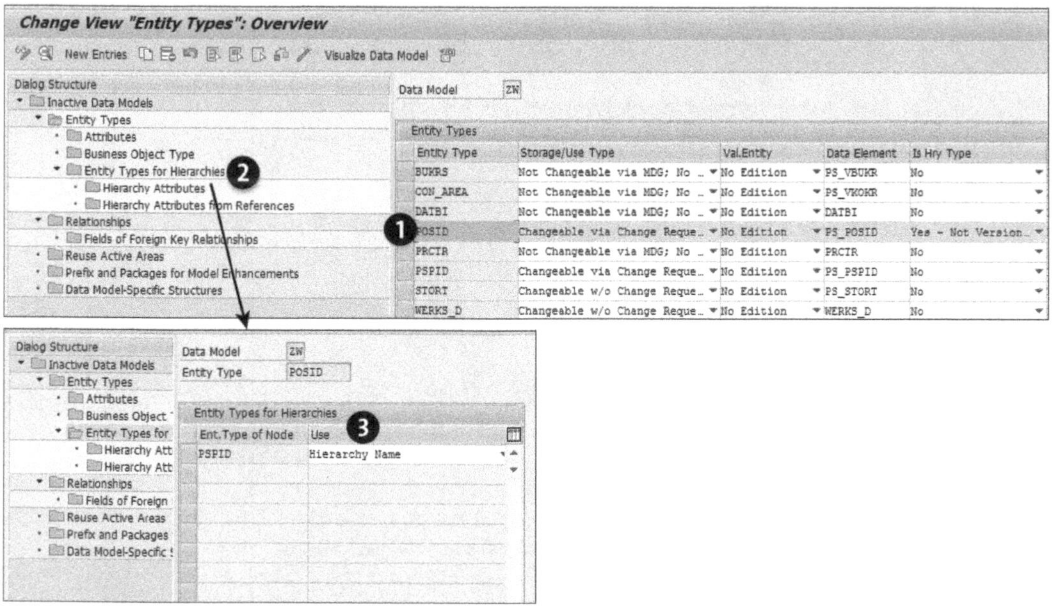

Figure 11.26 Adding Additional Entity Types to the Leading Hierarchy Entity POSID

Note

After creation of every entity and relationship, it's good practice to save your content and activate.

Figure 11.27 shows the entity relationship diagram for data model ZW. It shows a list of entities created so far and relationships (with direction) between the entities.

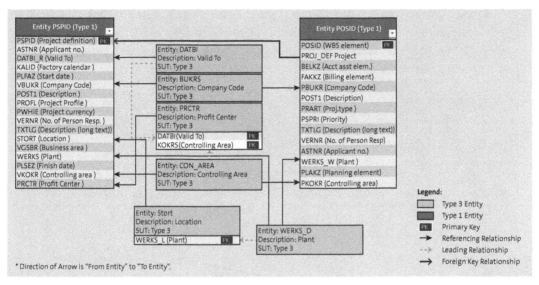

Figure 11.27 Entity Relationship Diagram for Data Model ZW

11.2.5   Generic Interaction Layer Data Model

Every active data model has corresponding GenIL models generated. For custom objects, you'll have at least two GenIL models generated. Following are the GenIL models generated for an active SAP Master Data Governance data model:

- **GenIL model for single processing:** `ZSP_<Data Model>`
  In our current example, the `ZSP_ZW` GenIL model is used in the Single Object Maintenance (SOM) UI.

- **GenIL model for multiple records processing:** `ZMP_<Data Model>`
  In our current example, the `ZMP_ZW` GenIL model is used in the multiple-record processing UI.

- **GenIL model for hierarchy processing:** `ZHP_<Data Model>`
  In our current example, the `ZHP_ZW` GenIL model is used for the hierarchy processing UI.

The GenIL model for hierarchy processing is generated if a hierarchy is activated on a storage use type 1 entity in the SAP Master Data Governance data model.

This GenIL model and its object types (root object, access object, dependent object, query object, and DQuery object) and relationship types (aggregation and associations) are used extensively in SAP Master Data Governance UI modeling.

The GenIL model is generated based on the SAP Master Data Governance data model. Following are some of the generic guidelines followed by SAP Master Data Governance to generate the GenIL model automatically:

- Each storage use type 1 entity is created as a root object in the GenIL data model. Attributes of the entity are created as attribute structures of the root entity. Figure 11.28 shows the corresponding root object generated for type 1 entities POSID and PSPID. In both models, POSID and PSPID are superior objects.

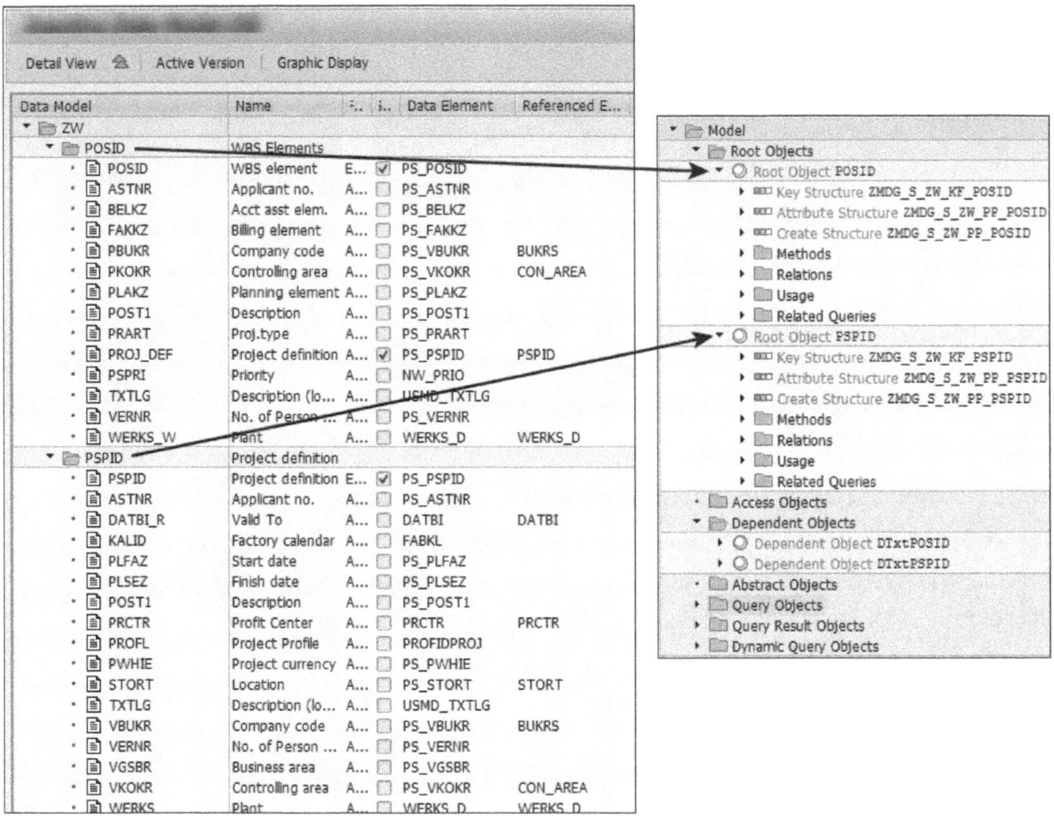

Figure 11.28 Storage Usage Type 1 Entities Project Definition (PSPID) and WBS Elements (POSID)

- Each storage usage type 4 entity in the SAP Master Data Governance data model is created as a dependent object.

- Relations in the SAP Master Data Governance data model are created as relations in the GenIL model.

- Storage usage type 2 and storage usage type 3 entities have no impact on the GenIL model. They can be related to GenIL objects via their superior objects (type 1 or type 4 entities).

- For entities that have language-dependent texts settings activated, dependent objects are generated in a GenIL model. In our data model ZW, both type 1 entities POSID and PSPID have language-dependent texts activated. Therefore, dependent object DtxTPOSID is generated for POSID, and DTxTPSPID is generated for PSPID (see Figure 11.29).

> **Note**
>
> The generation of the GenIL model depends on the SAP Master Data Governance data model, but this book doesn't dive deep into how SAP Master Data Governance entities and relationships are translated into GenIL objects and relationships. This section only provides comparisons specific to the current data model ZW.

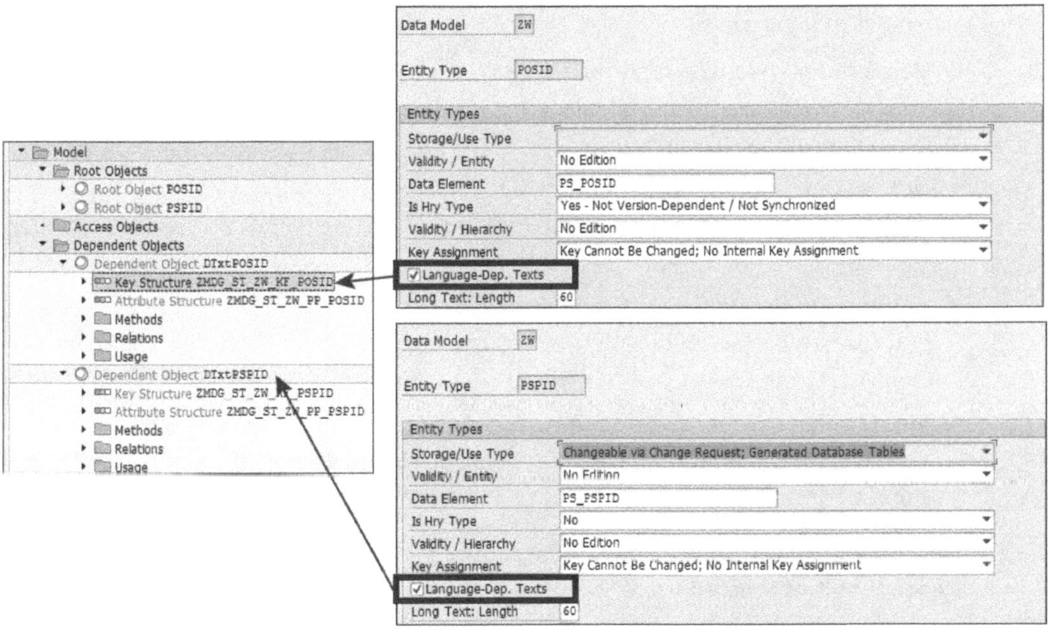

Figure 11.29 Language-Dependent Structures Generated as Dependent Objects

11.2.6 Hierarchy Data Model Types

There are mainly two hierarchy property types that defines what type of hierarchy you would like to develop, and it's one of the properties of the entity. Using a combination of these two properties, you can define four different types of hierarchies in SAP Master Data Governance. The two hierarchy properties—version-dependent and synchronized—are discussed in the following subsections.

Version-Dependent Hierarchy

A version-dependent hierarchy allows for multiple hierarchy versions. These multiple versions of hierarchies enable different views of the hierarchical dependencies. You can define the required hierarchy versions in Customizing under **Process Modeling • Create Hierarchy Versions**.

Synchronized Hierarchy

In a synchronized hierarchy, the structure of the hierarchy's substructures is the same throughout. This means that when an entity of a certain entity type has one or more lower-level entities (in a specific order), this structure is used for all other hierarchies. In this case, you *can't* define a different structure for the entity within the same hierarchy or in another hierarchy.

You can define four different types of hierarchies using a combination of the preceding two types of hierarchies:

- **Version-dependent/synchronized**
  You can define synchronized hierarchies and define different hierarchy versions for the synchronized hierarchy.

- **Not version-dependent/synchronized**
  You can set up synchronized hierarchies only. Defining hierarchy versions isn't permitted.

- **Not version-dependent/not synchronized**
  You can set up hierarchies that aren't synchronized only. Defining hierarchy versions isn't permitted.

- **Version-dependent/not synchronized**
  You can set up hierarchies that are synchronized and define different hierarchy versions.

Note that in Figure 11.29, we've set the property of entity type **POSID** as **Not Version-Dependent/Not Synchronized**.

11.3   Create a Custom User Interface

This section introduces the concept of building the SAP Master Data Governance application UI using the SAP Master Data Governance custom object UI framework.

> **Note**
> The focus of this chapter is on the custom object UI for single-object processing and hierarchy processing. The multiple-object processing UI and cleansing UI aren't in the scope of this chapter.

In the following sections, we first explain the UI architecture of the custom object framework. We then move on to build a search UI and a SOM UI for project definition and WBS (elements and hierarchy).

11.3.1 User Interface Framework

The major building blocks of the custom object UI framework are shown in Figure 11.30.

These building blocks are as follows:

- **User interface**
  The UI technology for the custom object UI is Web Dynpro–based Floorplan Manager. Floorplan Manager enforces consistency in the UI and compliance with UI guidelines by providing generic UI building blocks (GUIBB) and predefined floorplans (e.g., overview page floorplan [OVP] and guided activities floorplan [GAF]). The UI framework supports SAP Business Client, SAP Enterprise Portal, and SAP Fiori launchpad as UI clients. UI clients are the point of entry to web-based applications such as SAP Master Data Governance applications.

> **Note**
>
> More details on the UI application framework are discussed in Chapter 6. In the current chapter, we'll focus on the UI framework for custom objects.

USMD_OVP_GEN is the generic Web Dynpro application delivered by SAP to build the UI for the custom object application. Some of the features of the application are as follows:

- Based on the OVP floorplan
- Implements the FPM_ADAPTABLE_OVP component, which enables context-based adaptations

- **GenIL and Business Object Layer (BOL)**
  The purpose of GenIL is to provide uniform access to the underlying data persistency layer. It encapsulates business object–specific implementation and provides a uniform interface to access data from the persistency layer.

  BOL interfaces with the UI framework to provide the following:

  - Simple, easy-to-use, object-oriented APIs to access GenIL
  - A built-in buffer that automatically decides if data is to be accessed from the buffer or from GenIL (buffering improves the performance of the UI)

The loose coupling of the various building blocks guarantees minimum disruption. For example, if the SAP OData framework has a BOL adapter, then we can easily replace the Floorplan Manager with SAP Fiori without changing the code in the underlying GenIL and BOL framework. This feature is sometimes referred to as "timeless software." We'll never make changes in the BOL because it's just a bridge between the UI and GenIL. We've already discussed in detail the list of GenIL components that are generated for our custom data model ZW.

11

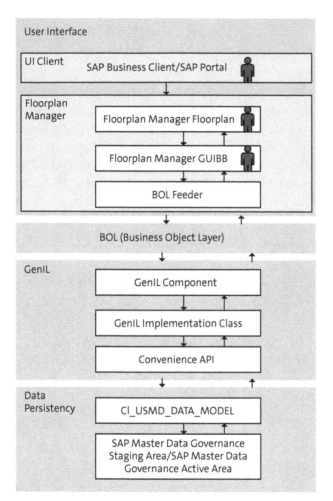

Figure 11.30 Runtime Architecture and Building Blocks of the Custom Object UI Framework

11.3.2   Design and Develop the User Interface

UIs are very important because they are used directly by end users of an enterprise. A great user experience is a must to increase the business value of SAP Master Data Governance custom applications and can provide the following:

- Gains in productivity via reduced number of clicks, maximum information in the least number of screens, and personalizing the UI to end user roles
- Increased user adoption
- Decreased user errors

A bad user experience is the source of user frustrations, low user adoptions, and decreased productivity.

The characteristics of a good UI are as follows:

- **Role based**
  The UI is personalized per job function of the user, and the fields/screens that the user should not see are hidden.

- **Simple UI**
  Clicks are kept to a minimum, and users are only shown what they need to see.

- **Low cost of adoption**
  Training requirements are minimized.

The following sections explain the basic concepts behind the UI design and the development of a search UI.

Design the User Interface

Every custom object UI should respect and follow the data semantics of the underlying SAP Master Data Governance data model. The features of data model ZW are as follows:

- Project definition and WBS elements are the leading objects.
- A WBS element can't exist independently; it always must be created under the project definition.
- Project definition and WBS elements have language-dependent texts.
- Project definition is the top node of the WBS hierarchy.

Taking these features into consideration, we'll design the UI as follows:

- **Search screen as initial page**
  Most SAP-delivered SAP Master Data Governance applications have the search screen as the initial screen that allows users to search for existing business objects. If the object is found, the user opts for changing the business object data or for creating a new business object. We'll adopt a similar design for our custom application as well. The initial screen will be a search screen that provides the option to create a new project. To limit the scope, we won't extend the search screen to search for WBS elements.

- **Main page**
  The main page will have the following components:
  - Project definition: The first UI building block (UIBB) is form based and will be used for maintaining attributes of the project definition.
  - Language-dependent texts for project definition: The second UIBB will be a list UIBB for maintaining language-dependent texts.
  - WBS elements: The third UIBB will be a list UIBB for creating a WBS element under the project definition. The first column in the list UIBB will be an action column that contains buttons to direct the user from the main page to the edit page.

- **Edit page**

  The edit page is used exclusively for maintenance of WBS element data and arranging the WBS elements into the project hierarchy. The edit page will also have buttons to edit the page and to return to the main page. The list of UIBBs in the edit page is as follows:

  - WBS maintenance: The first UIBB is a form UIBB for maintaining WBS element data.

  - Language-dependent texts for WBS elements: The second UIBB in the edit page is a list UIBB used for maintaining language-dependent texts.

  - Hierarchy maintenance UIBB: The last UIBB in the edit page is a hierarchy UIBB used for assigning WBS elements to the project hierarchy.

Note

At the UI design stage, it's a good idea to design your wiring between various Floorplan Manager UIBBs. For example, you can decide which will be the root UIBB and what kind of port will be used to connect a search UIBB and the main page (lead selection or collection).

Develop the Search User Interface

SAP Master Data Governance provides a generic search application called USMD_SEARCH, which can be used to search any data model and type 1 entity using any search provider (database search, SAP HANA, SAP Enterprise Search). There are many scenarios on how to use this generic search UI, and some of them require copying the generic search UI and creating a new one. For some scenarios, you can use it as is just by maintaining the URL parameters.

In our use case, we'll copy the application configuration of the USMD_SEARCH application only to default the application parameter values. To enable the generic search UI, follow these steps:

1. **Step 1: Create search help.**

   The first step toward enabling the generic search UI is to create a search help. The generic UI generates search criteria and a search results area based on the search help. Therefore, assigning search help is mandatory for the generic search UI.

   In the current example, we'll create a search help with SAP HANA as the search mode. Navigate to IMG activity **MDG IMG • Master Data Governance, Central Governance • General Settings • Data Quality and Search • Search and Duplicate Check • Create Search View**.

   This IMG activity is used to create SAP HANA–based search help. Figure 11.31 shows the sequence of actions that needs to take place to create an SAP HANA search view.

After the SAP HANA search view is created, then a search help entry with the same name as the SAP HANA search view will be created in the IMG activity.

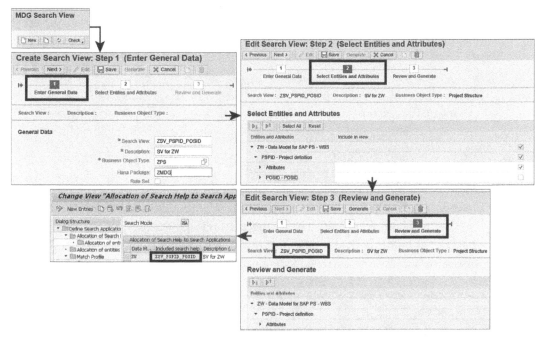

Figure 11.31 Sequence of Steps for Creating Search Help Based on SAP HANA

Note

Remember to create an SAP HANA package in the SAP HANA database before proceeding with the activity to create the SAP HANA search view.

The SAP Master Data Governance search framework creates SAP HANA artifacts such as an attribute view and a ruleset under the SAP HANA package. The framework also creates database procedures to invoke SAP HANA artifacts from the application server.

2. **Step 2: Open the manage UI configurations application from the IMG.**
Go to **MDG IMG • Master Data Governance, Central Governance • General Settings • UI Modeling • Manage UI Configurations.**

This IMG activity is used to manage all the object maintenance-related UIs (e.g., SOM UI, multiple processing UI, search UI). It provides options to copy application configurations and check the status of the SAP Master Data Governance communicator settings. This tool is helpful for users who have no knowledge of navigating the ABAP Workbench for copying and maintaining the SAP Master Data Governance UI applications.

> **Note**
>
> The SAP Master Data Governance communicator technically is an application controller. It plays a key role in integrating the SAP Master Data Governance change request framework with SOM/multiple processing UIs. For example, it's responsible for adding the change request UIBB (CRUIBB) during runtime to the SOM/multiple processing UIs.
>
> Not every SAP Master Data Governance application uses the communicator. SAP Master Data Governance communicator settings aren't relevant for material master applications built using the Service Provider Infrastructure (SPI) framework. However, the communicator is relevant for SAP Master Data Governance applications built using the custom object framework.

3. **Step 3: Create a new generic search application.**
   In the UI, select the application configuration **USMD_SEARCH_TEMPLATE**, and click on the **Copy** button to create a new generic search application configuration. Figure 11.32 shows how to copy the existing template configuration and create a new one. It also shows how we've assigned a data mode, type 1 entity, search help, and search mode as application parameters.

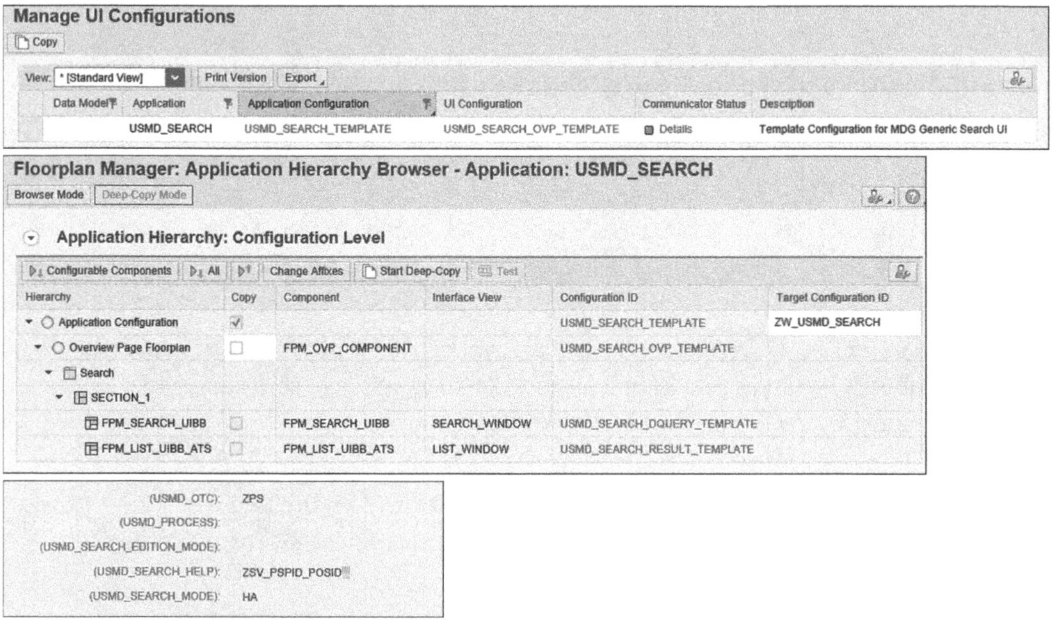

Figure 11.32 Steps to Create a Copy of the Generic Search Template Configuration

The application parameters are used during runtime by the generic search UI to determine the right search help. The application parameters have the following runtime significance:

- When no application parameters are entered, the search control area is rendered in the search UI. The search control area provides an option to select the data model, entity, and search method. These values will be used by the generic search UI to automatically render search criteria and search results.

- The search control area won't be rendered if all the application parameters, such as USMD_MODEL, USMD_ENTITY, and USMD_SEARCH_MODE, are entered.

Figure 11.33 shows the screen of a fully functional search UI application. Note the way the search UI has been rendered, as follows:

❶ The title of the UI appears as **Search: Project definition**. This title has been generated automatically based on the description of the entity assigned in the USMD_ENTITY application parameter.

❷ The **Search Criteria** area is derived automatically from the search help configuration.

❸ The **Result List** area is nothing but keys and attributes of the type 1 entity assigned in the USMD_ENTITY application parameter.

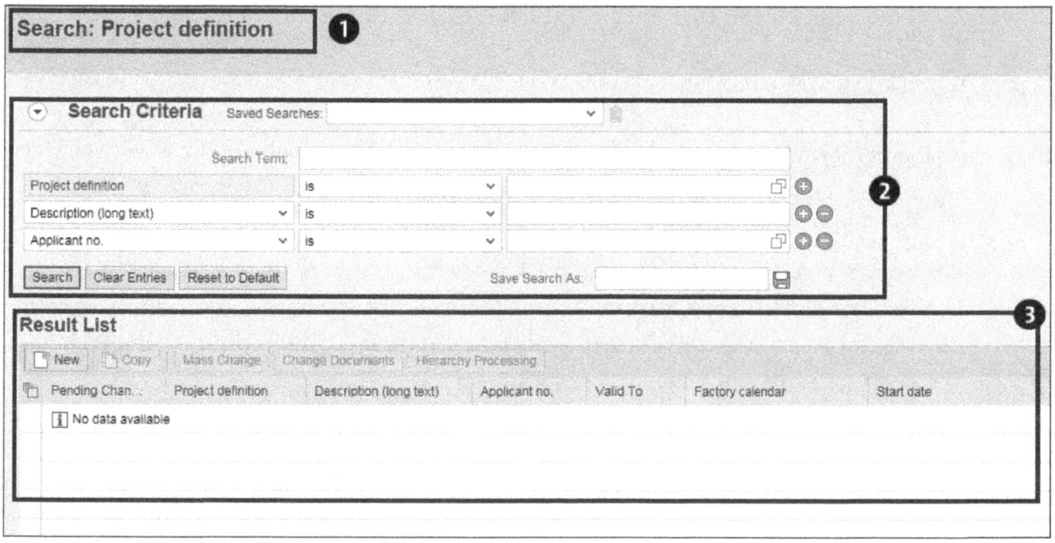

Figure 11.33 A Fully Functional Search UI Application

One very important step that needs to be performed after copying the generic search template configuration is to create the communicator (MDG_BS_GOV_COMMUNICATOR) configuration. The name of the communicator configuration and the search UI application must be the same; if they aren't, then the search UI application won't be rendered correctly. The communicator is responsible for rendering the search criteria and search results areas based on the search help configuration. Therefore, if you find that your search UI doesn't display search criteria and search results correctly, the first thing to check is the communicator settings for the search UI application configuration. Figure 11.34 shows how to configure the communicator.

To begin, click **Details** ❶. On the next screen, change nothing, and click **Save**. The **Details** icon should now be green ❷. In the next section, we'll discuss how to create the actual SOM UI for maintaining the project definition and WBS hierarchy. We'll discuss how the navigation from the search UI to the SOM UI happens in Section 11.4.

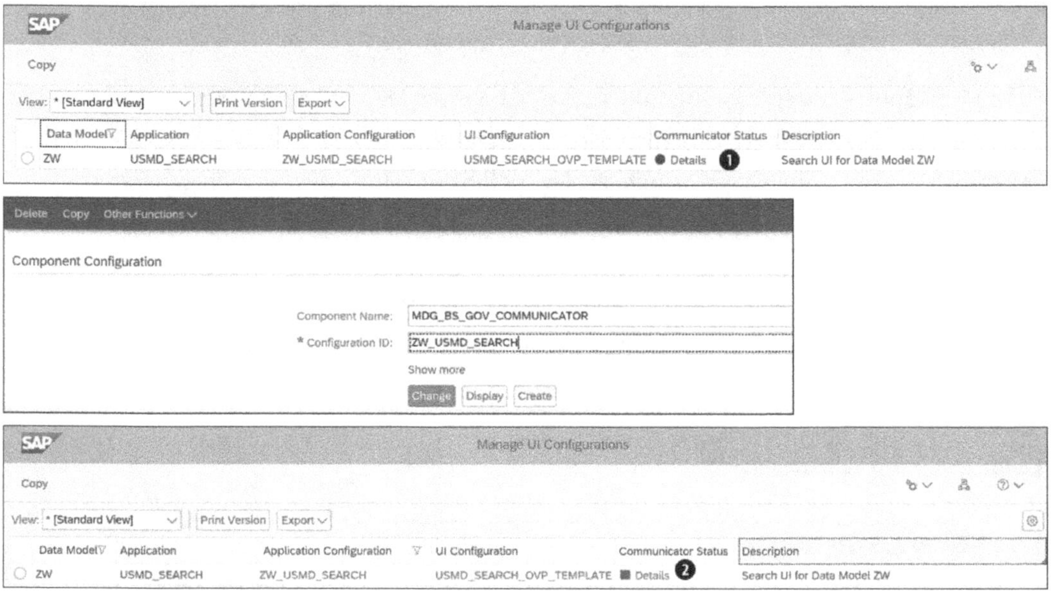

Figure 11.34 Steps to Create the Communicator Configuration

We now have a fully running search UI application. This is the advantage of the SAP Master Data Governance custom object UI framework. We haven't written a single line of code until now, and we've already completed data modeling, configured search help, and copied a template search UI configuration.

11.3.3 Develop a Single Object Maintenance User Interface

In the previous section, we created a search UI; now we'll create a SOM UI for the project definition and WBS hierarchy.

SAP provides template configurations for the USMD_OVP_GEN UI application. The details of the template application configuration and component configuration are as follows:

- Application name: USMD_OVP_GEN
- Application configuration name: USMD_OVP_GEN_TEMPLATE
- Component configuration: USMD_GEN_OVP_TEMPLATE

Figure 11.35 shows how to copy the template SOM UI configuration. On the **Manage UI Configurations** screen, click **Copy**. On the next screen, enter the **Target Configuration ID**, and click **Start Deep-Copy**. Finally, assign your Web Dynpro component. We've also assigned value ZPS to application parameter USMD_OTC. The business object type code ZPS, which is used to derive the data model and main entity during runtime. We've also created an SAP Master Data Governance communicator configuration.

The SAP Master Data Governance communicator is responsible for adding the CRUIBB and corresponding wiring during the runtime to the SOM UI.

> **Note**
>
> Wiring in Floorplan Manager refers to transferring data from the source UIBB to the target UIBB.

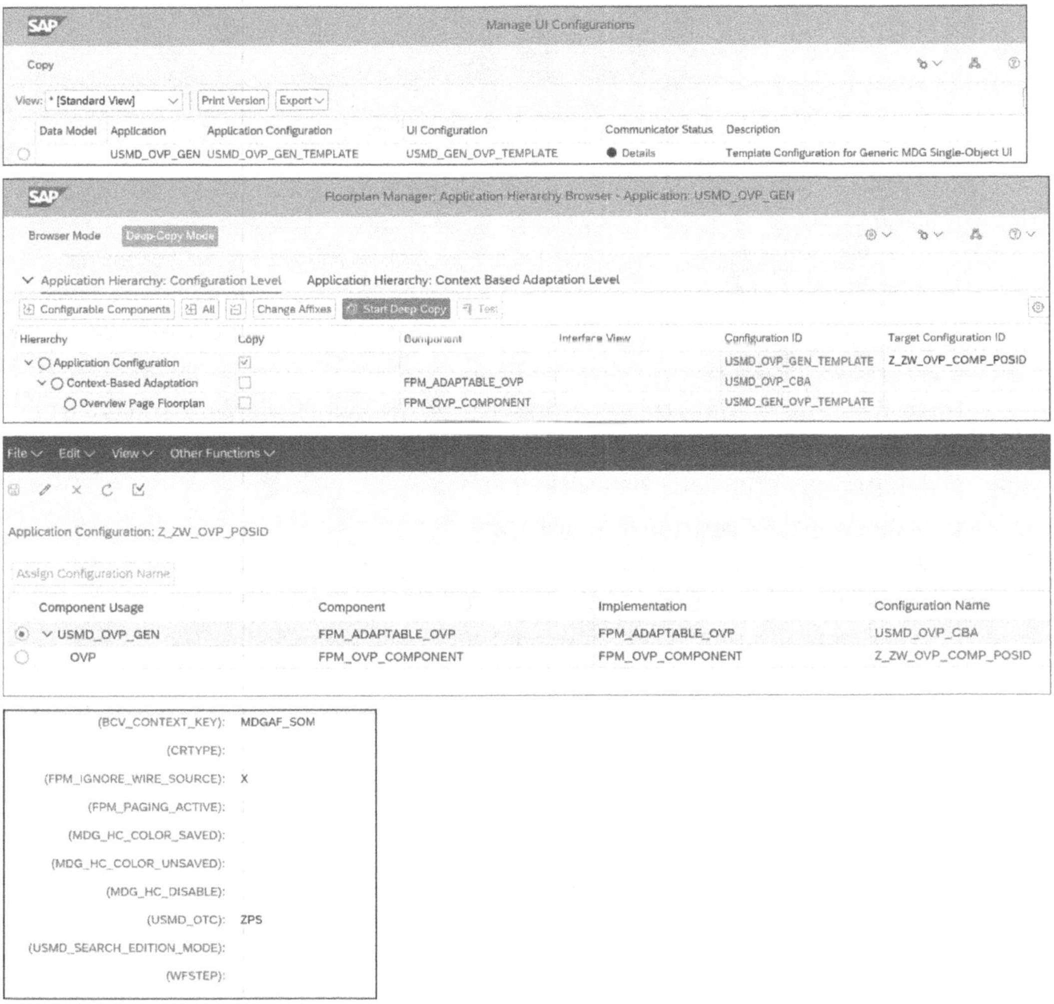

Figure 11.35 Steps Required to Copy the Template Configuration for SOM and Create a New Configuration

When component configuration Z_ZW_OVP_COMP_POSID is opened, by default a main page will be created. You can change the main page ID or retain the default ID, and then you can enter the title of the main page. Ensure that USMD_GEN_OVP is configured as the application controller. Figure 11.36 shows how to create a main page and configure the application controller.

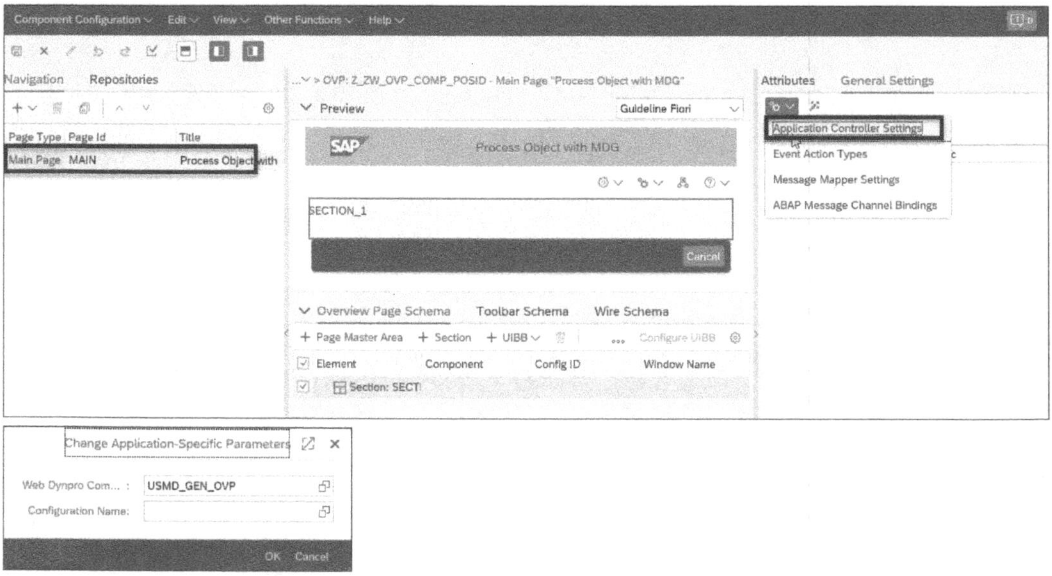

Figure 11.36 Creation of the Main Page and Configuring Application Controller Settings

The steps to perform in this area are as follows:

1. **Main page: Configure the technical UIBB.**
   We start the UI configuration of the main page by creating a technical UIBB. The technical UIBB is never shown in the UI, but it participates in the Floorplan Manager event loop. This UIBB will be the root UIBB in the wire schema. The UIBB will just contain the key fields of entity PSPID.

   Figure 11.37 shows how to add the technical UIBB to the OVP floorplan. Notice that we've enabled the **Hidden Element** attribute ❷ that makes this UIBB hidden but still participates in the event loop. We've added a wire ❶, which has the technical UIBB as the target UIBB but doesn't have a source UIBB. This makes it the root UIBB, which can be instantiated independently.

   Figure 11.38 shows how the technical UIBB is configured in the flexible user interface designer (FLUID), as follows:

   – Class CL_MDG_BS_GUIBB_FORM ❶ is used as a feeder class in the UIBB. This is a generic feeder class provided by SAP Master Data Governance for forms. Every form GUIBB used in the SAP Master Data Governance application should have CL_MDG_BS_GUIBB_FORM or its subclass as the feeder class.

- Click **Display Parameters ②** to add the parameters for the UIBB as **Component** = **ZSP_ZW ③** and **Object Name** = **PSPID ④**. ZSP_ZW is the GenIL component for single-object processing for data model ZW.
- Select the **Editable** checkbox **⑤**.
- This UIBB will only have **Project definition ⑥** as an input field.

Figure 11.37 Adding the Technical UIBB to the OVP Floorplan

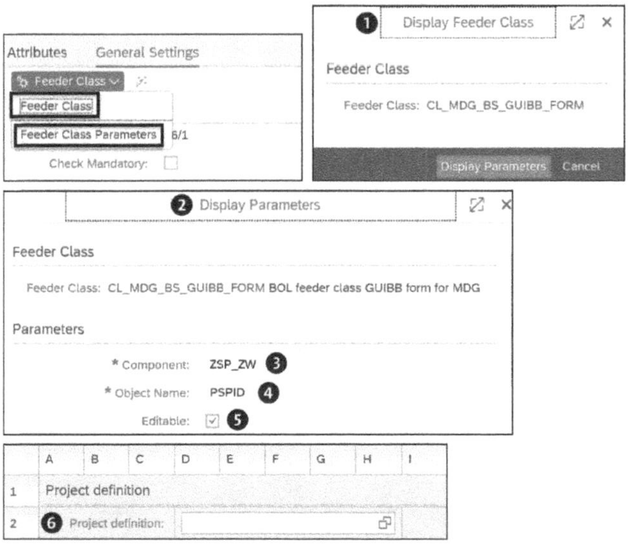

Figure 11.38 Configuring the Technical UIBB in FLUID

2. **Main page: Configure form UIBB for project definition.**

We now add the first visible UIBB of the SOM UI; this UIBB will be a form UIBB and will hold the project definition. We'll also configure a wire with port type as the lead selection from the technical UIBB to form the UIBB of the project definition. Apart from data transfer, this wire will ensure that the technical UIBB is instantiated first.

The feeder class and feeder class parameters will be the same as those of the technical UIBB. Figure 11.39 shows the configured form UIBB with UI elements related to the project definition. Figure 11.40 shows the wiring between the technical UIBB and the form UIBB for the project definition.

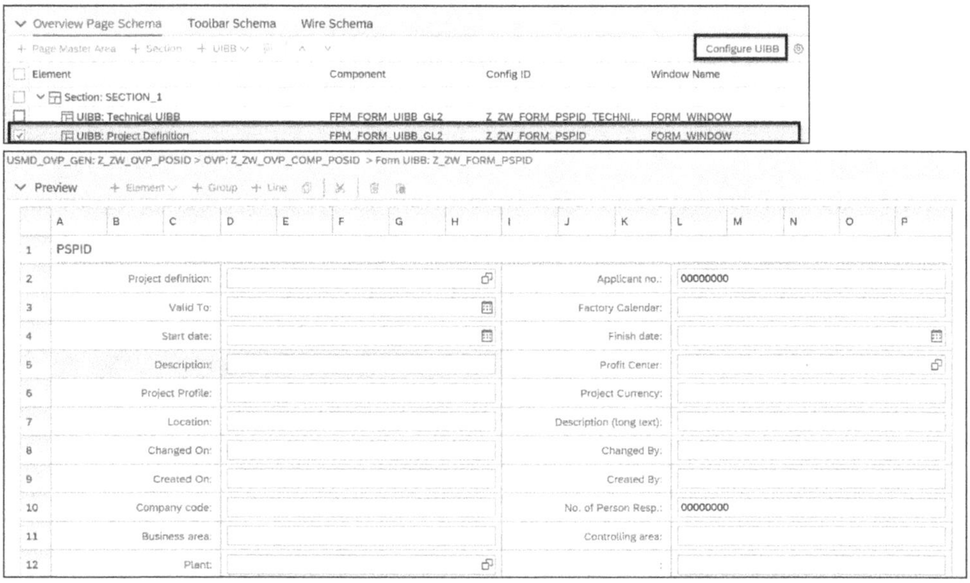

Figure 11.39 Configuring Form UIBB for the Project Definition

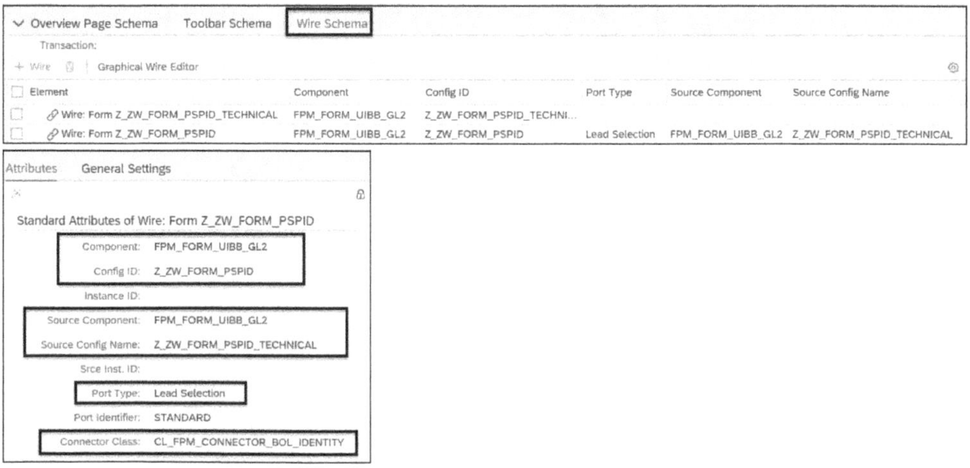

Figure 11.40 Wiring between the Technical UIBB and the Form UIBB for Project Definition

Note

The transaction handler class is used by the UI for handling transaction events such as save, check, and so on. We'll use SAP-delivered transaction handler class CL_MDG_BS_BOL_TRANSACTION. Ideally, the only reason you'll have a custom transaction handler class inheriting a standard class is if you want to influence the transactional events or to influence the messages on transactional events such as save.

When creating a custom transaction handler class, the subclass calls the corresponding superclass methods. If not called, then the delegation from GenIL to MDGAF (application framework) won't happen.

3. **Main page: Configure the list UIBB for language-dependent texts.**

As shown in Figure 11.41 and in Section 11.2.2 previously, the type 1 entity for the project definition (PSPID) has language-dependent texts activated, allowing the description for the project definition to be maintained in multiple languages. To enable this functionality in the UI, you need to add a list UIBB and create a wire between the form UIBB for the project definition and the list UIBB for language-dependent texts. We use CL_MDG_BS_GUIBB_LIST as the feeder class, which is the generic feeder class provided by SAP for list UIBBs in SAP Master Data Governance applications. Figure 11.42 shows the steps to create a list UIBB for language-dependent texts for entity PSPID, as well as the UIBB settings.

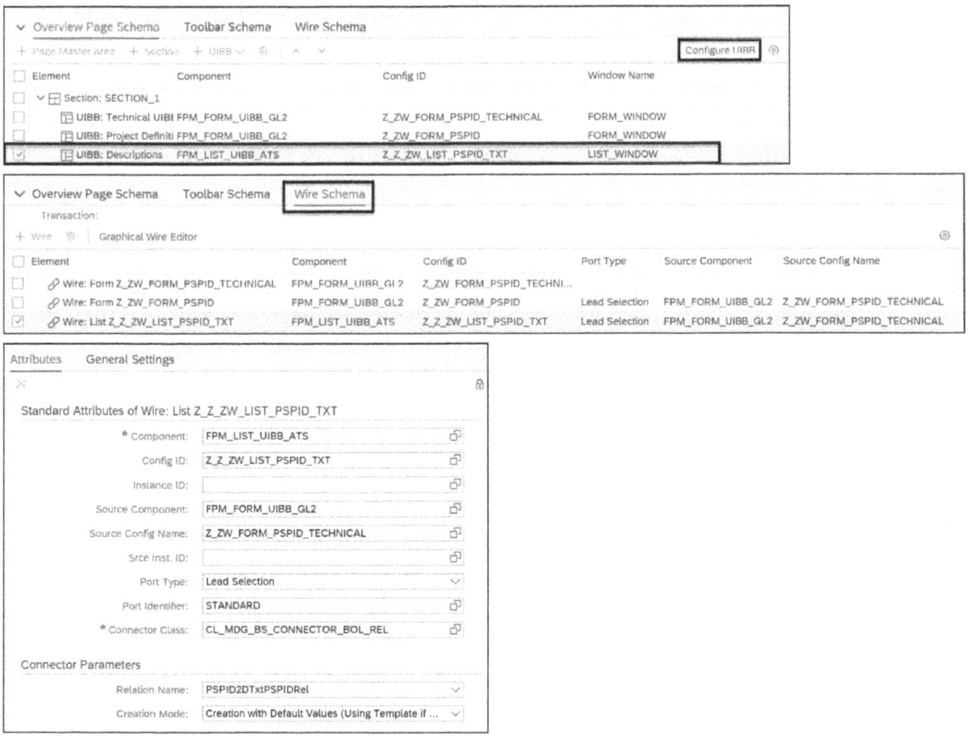

Figure 11.41 Creation of the List UIBB for Language-Dependent Texts and Connection via Wire with Technical UIBB

4. **Main page: Configure the list UIBB for creating and changing WBS elements.**
   A project definition can have multiple WBS elements assigned to it. Each WBS element has its own set of attributes and is assigned to the WBS hierarchy. To meet these requirements, we first create a list UIBB in the main page and then create an edit page; this edit page is tagged as the default edit page for the list UIBB.

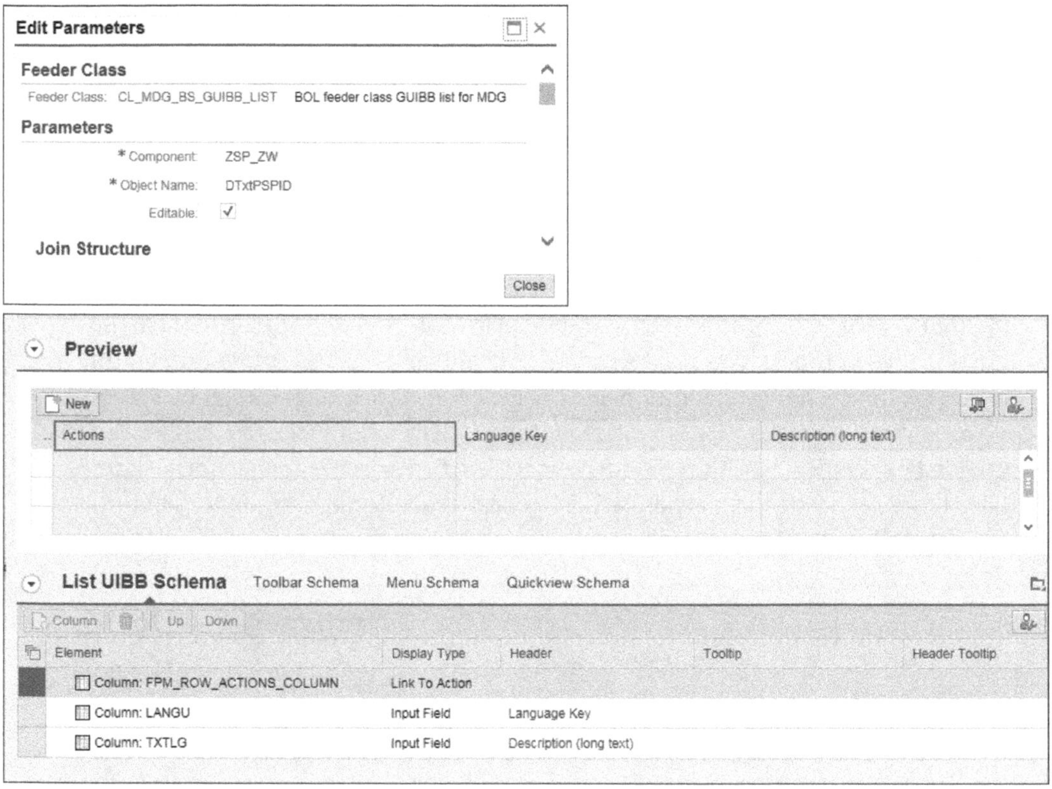

Figure 11.42 List UIBB Configuration for Language-Dependent Texts

The first column in the list UIBB is the **Actions** column. This column holds the button that triggers navigation to the default edit page to maintain the WBS element–specific attributes and assign the WBS element to the hierarchy.

It's very important to note that, per the SAP Master Data Governance data model, both WBS elements and the project definition are type 1 entities. In the GenIL model, these two entities are related via an association relationship. Figure 11.43 shows the steps to create the list UIBB for WBS element maintenance. Figure 11.44 shows the UIBB settings and steps performed to add elements to the list. As mentioned, the first column in the UIBB is the **Actions** column. The standard Floorplan Manager event is configured as one of the actions in this column.

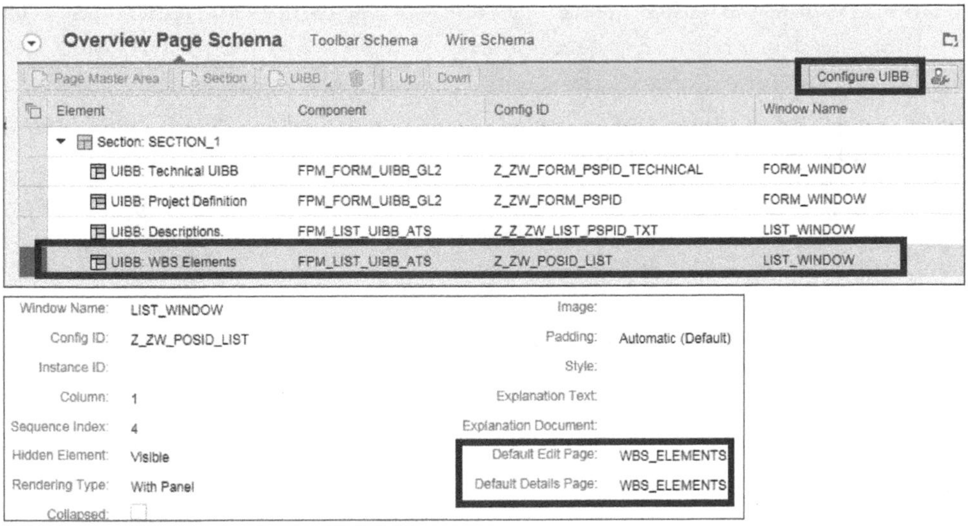

Figure 11.43 Creating the List UIBB for Maintenance of WBS Elements and Assigning the Edit Page as the Default

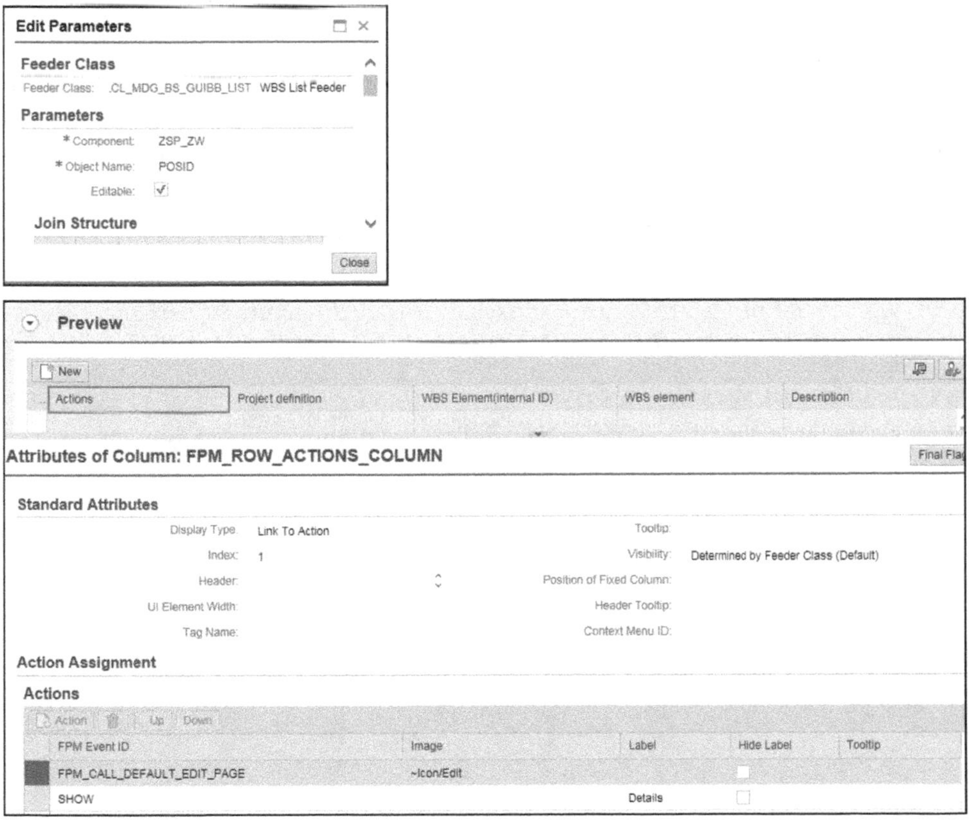

Figure 11.44 Configuring the UI Elements in the List UIBB for WBS Element Maintenance

Figure 11.45 shows the wiring that has been done to transfer the PSPID entity data to the list UIBB. The data is required to default the key of the POSID entity. To do so, we've created a subclass for connector class CL_MDG_BS_CONNECTOR_BOL_ASSOC. We've redefined method CREATE_REL_ENTITY_FROM_TEMPL, which creates an entity based on a relationship and fills up the collection of entities.

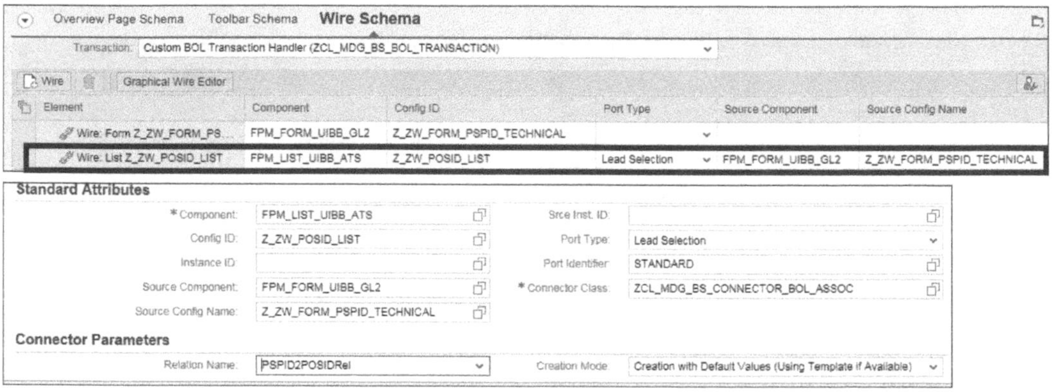

Figure 11.45 Wiring between the Technical UIBB and List UIBB for WBS Maintenance

Figure 11.46 shows the final look of the main page. It's important to note here that we've created a functional UI almost without writing any code. The only code that we've written is in the redefined method of the connector class described earlier. This code could have been easily avoided if we didn't have any relationship in the GenIL model of the association type. This again reemphasizes the reusability of the SAP Master Data Governance custom object framework.

Throughout this chapter, we've only discussed how to create a data model and develop a UI. We haven't needed to concern ourselves with architecture or best practices, as these are provided by the SAP Master Data Governance custom object framework.

Per the UI design discussed in previous sections, navigation to the edit page occurs from the **Action** column of the WBS list UIBB in the main page. This edit page will be used to maintain the WBS attributes and assign WBS elements to the hierarchy. Figure 11.47 shows the edit page for maintaining WBS element attributes.

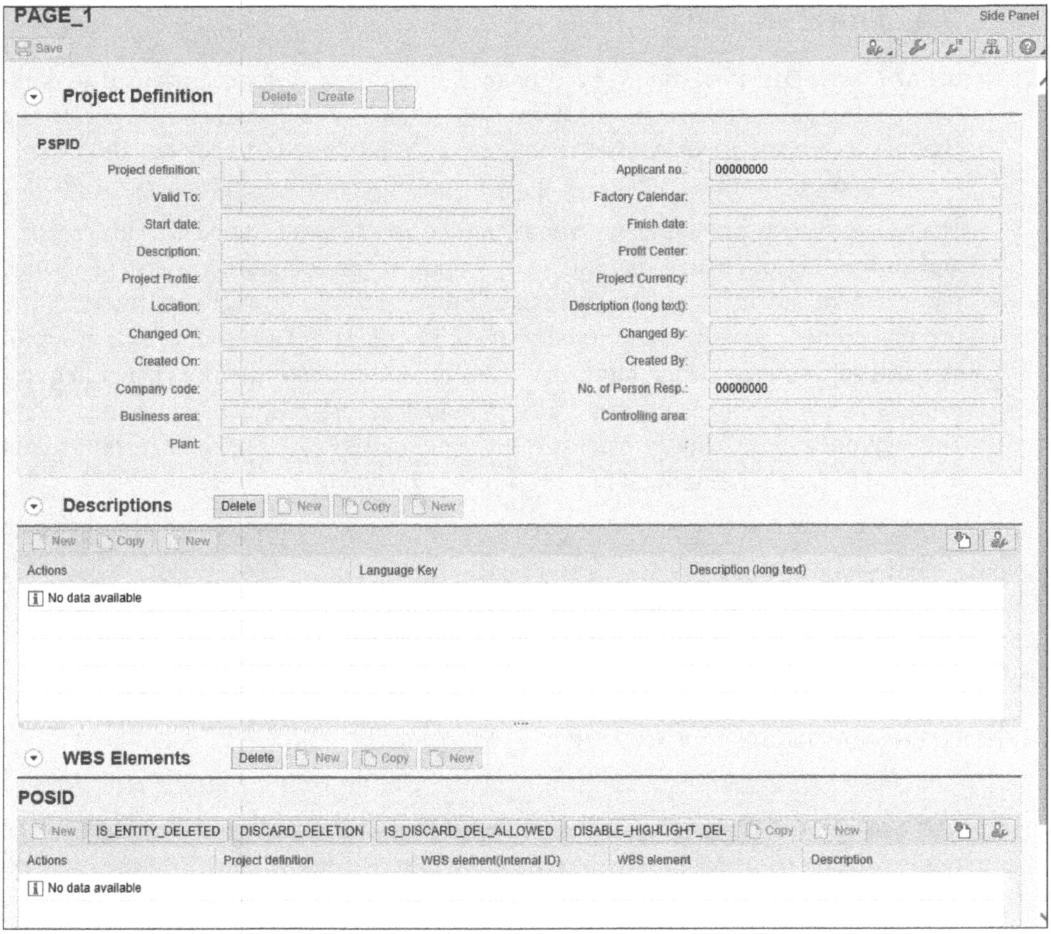

Figure 11.46 Final Look of the Main Page

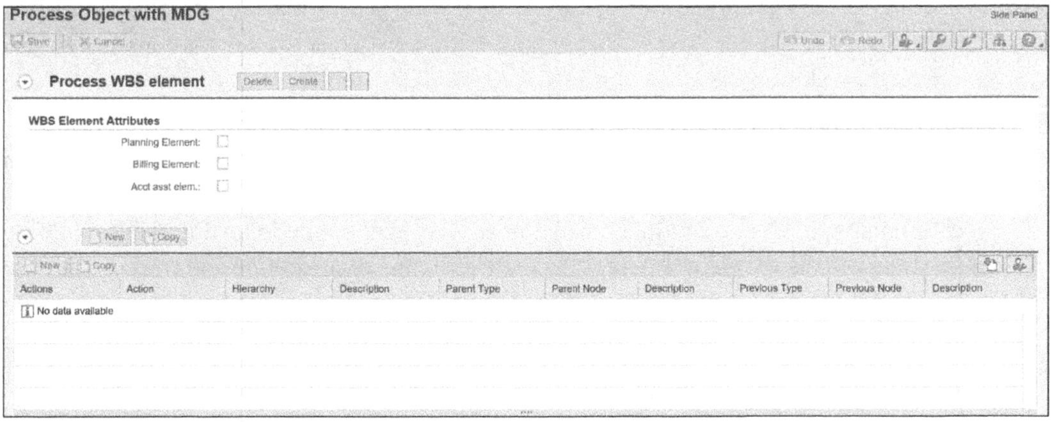

Figure 11.47 Edit Page with WBS Element Attributes and Hierarchy Assignment UIBB

11.4   Process Modeling

In SAP Master Data Governance, every change (including creation) of master data is initiated using a change request, which can be described roughly as a container carrying changes to the master data. After change requests are initiated, they need to be processed before activation/rollback by applying governance rules and collaboration.

The process model provides the required input (metadata) for change request creation and processing of change requests (e.g., workflow for collaboration, list of change request steps, and list of objects that can be processed as part of a change request). The process modeling configuration node in SAP Master Data Governance is a group of semantically similar configuration activities required to execute the change request process. A change request process is a list of sequential or parallel change request steps. The sequence of the change request steps is defined by SAP Business Workflow and assigned to the change request process through the change request type.

> **Note**
>
> Submit and activation/rollback are mandatory change request steps in a change request process. Without the submit step, you can't initiate a change request. It's illogical not to activate/roll back the initiated master data changes through the change request. The SAP Master Data Governance change request framework doesn't explicitly impose this rule.

SAP Master Data Governance reuses the SAP Business Workflow component of the underlying SAP S/4HANA system. Technically, the SAP Master Data Governance workflow is an instance of business object BUS2250.

> **Note**
>
> If a change request has parallel processing, then each parallel step of the change request will have one BUS2250 instance. Therefore, a change request can have multiple BUS2250 instances.

For process modeling, the first step is to create a new business activity to tie an action with the business object and then maintain navigation settings of the custom UI application using business activities and actions, as covered in the following sections. These sections will also explain the steps to create a change request type and the corresponding workflow settings.

11.4.1   Create a New Business Object

The business object is mandatory in SAP Master Data Governance, every type 1 entity, UI application, and outbound implementation in the data replication framework should be assigned to a business object.

The IMG path for creating the business object is **Master Data Governance Central Governance · General Settings · Data Modeling · Define Business Object Type Codes**. Click on **New Entries**, and enter the values as shown in Figure 11.48.

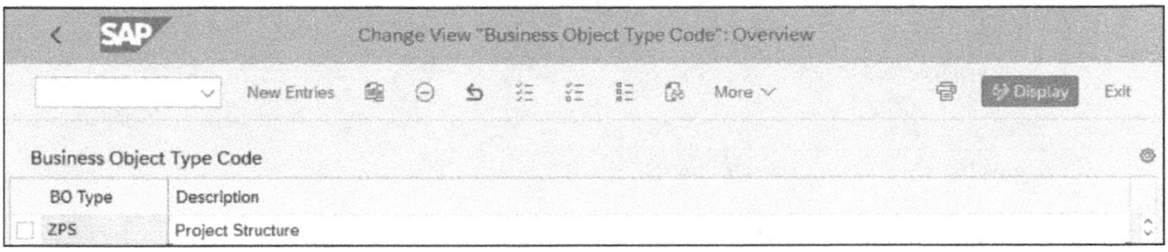

Figure 11.48 Creation of Business Object ZPS to Represent the Custom Data Object for Project System

11.4.2 Create a New Business Activity

To design a business activity, you start by asking the business user what kind of actions (create, change, etc.) he intends to perform and on which business object.

Each combination of logical action and business object becomes one business activity. In our case, we'll create two business activities:

- ZBA1
  Create project definition and WBS elements.

- ZBA2
  Change project definition and assign WBS elements to the project hierarchy.

> **Note**
> In Transaction CJ20N, you can create the project definition and WBS elements and then assign them to the hierarchy. This can't happen in SAP Master Data Governance because the SAP Master Data Governance framework requires the hierarchy's name entity (PSPID) to be active. Therefore, we must create the project definition first, and then we can create WBS elements and assign hierarchies in change mode.

Figure 11.49 shows the list of business activities we've created in the IMG for SAP Master Data Governance. You can follow these steps to create business activities and assign business activities and actions to the business object:

1. Go to IMG path **Master Data Governance, Central Governance · General Settings · Process Modeling · Business Activities · Create Business Activity ❶**.
2. Click on **New Entries ❷**, and enter values for your business activities ❸, ❹.

> **Note**
>
> In Section 11.3.3, we've assigned ZPS as the value for the application configuration parameter USMD_OTC. This value is used during runtime by the SAP Master Data Governance application framework to derive the business activity based on the configuration performed in Section 11.3.3.

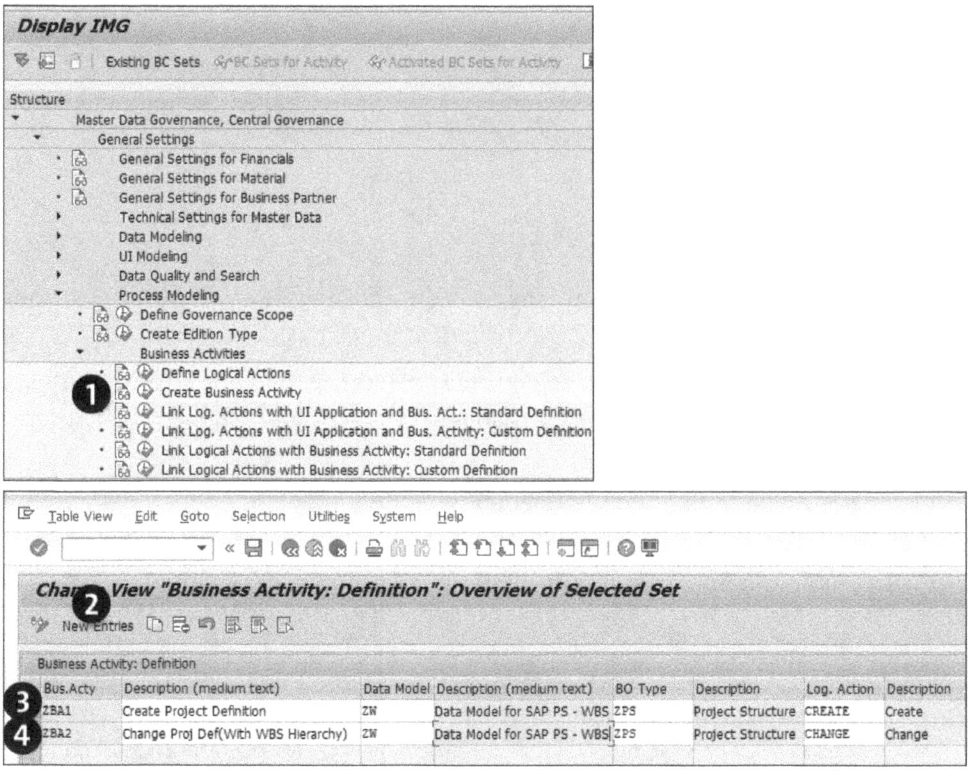

Figure 11.49 Creation of Business Activities for WBS in Project System

11.4.3   Assign Business Activities and Logical Actions to Business Objects

A logical action represents the operation to be performed on the master data by an actor in the process (e.g., create, change, or delete). Business activities add business context to logical actions by linking them with business objects such as create supplier, change material, and delete account. Business activities are defined by assigning an action, data model, and business object.

For our use case, we don't need to create a new action. We'll reuse SAP-delivered actions such as create and change. This is important because we're using the generic search UI, which defaults the create action when the **New** button is clicked.

11.4.4   Maintain Settings for Business Activity Determination

During runtime, the SAP Master Data Governance application framework needs to determine the business activity for various purposes, such as determining the change request type and determining the navigation targets during cross-application UI navigation. Figure 11.50 highlights the list of IMG activities that must be performed to determine the right business activity at runtime.

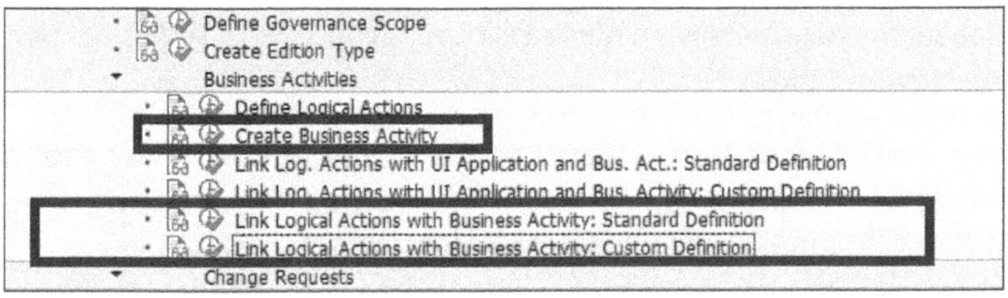

Figure 11.50 IMG Activities Required to Correctly Determine Business Activities at Runtime

Every SAP Master Data Governance application UI—both the SOM UI and the multiple-object processing UI—requires action to be configured as a URL parameter. Action along with business object (parameter USMD_OTC) will be used to determine the business activity. Figure 11.51 shows the settings to determine the business activity for **Data Model ZW**.

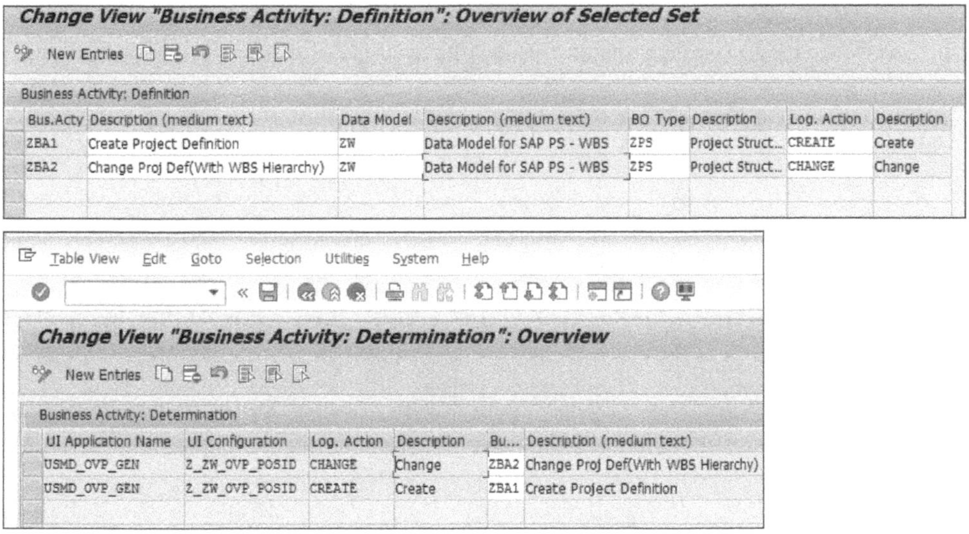

Figure 11.51 Settings for Business Activity Determination for Data Model ZW

SAP Master Data Governance features different kinds of navigation between the UIs:

- **In-place navigation**
  This kind of navigation usually happens within the application and includes navigating from the main page to the edit page, navigating from a dialog box to the main

page, and vice versa. This navigation is handled by the feeder class and UI configuration.

- **Cross-application navigation**
  This kind of navigation happens from one application to another, such as from a generic search UI to the SOM application UI and from the change requests UI to the SOM UI. This kind of navigation is usually handled by configuration, which can be accessed using the path, **Master Data Governance, Central Governance • General Settings • Process Modeling • Business Activities • Link Log. Actions with UI Application and Bus. Activity: Custom Definition.**

Figure 11.52 shows the list of configurations created for cross-application navigation between the generic search UI and the custom object UI for actions create, change, and display. In the figure, the second set of highlighted entries is triggered whenever a **New** button is clicked on the search UI. The first set of highlighted entries is triggered whenever an **Edit** button is clicked on the SOM UI. The last set of entries is triggered whenever a UI is opened to view the active data.

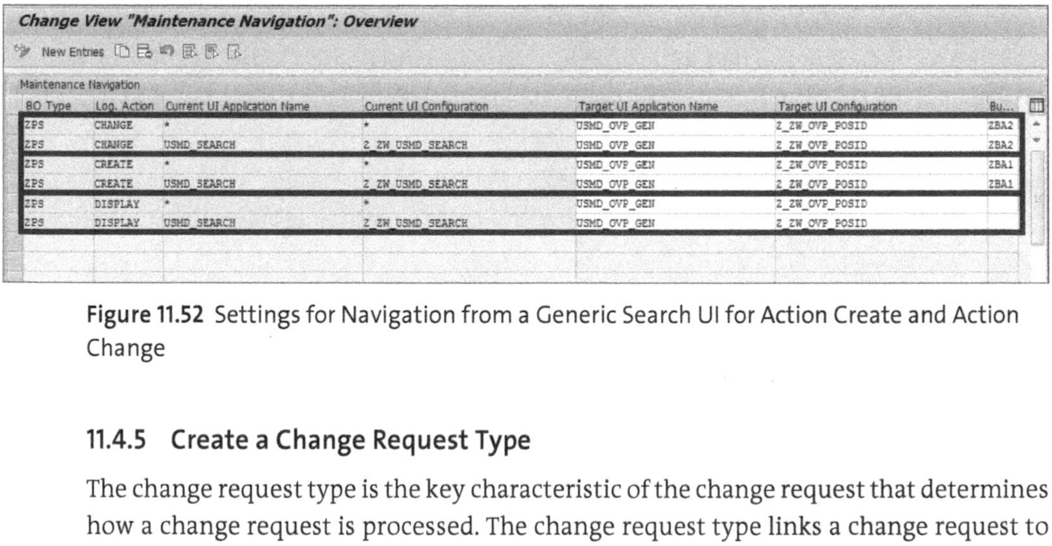
Change View "Maintenance Navigation": Overview

New Entries

Maintenance Navigation

BO Type	Log. Action	Current UI Application Name	Current UI Configuration	Target UI Application Name	Target UI Configuration	Bu...
ZPS	CHANGE	*	*	USMD_OVP_GEN	Z_ZW_OVP_POSID	ZBA2
ZPS	CHANGE	USMD_SEARCH	Z_ZW_USMD_SEARCH	USMD_OVP_GEN	Z_ZW_OVP_POSID	ZBA2
ZPS	CREATE	*	*	USMD_OVP_GEN	Z_ZW_OVP_POSID	ZBA1
ZPS	CREATE	USMD_SEARCH	Z_ZW_USMD_SEARCH	USMD_OVP_GEN	Z_ZW_OVP_POSID	ZBA1
ZPS	DISPLAY	*	*	USMD_OVP_GEN	Z_ZW_OVP_POSID	
ZPS	DISPLAY	USMD_SEARCH	Z_ZW_USMD_SEARCH	USMD_OVP_GEN	Z_ZW_OVP_POSID	

Figure 11.52 Settings for Navigation from a Generic Search UI for Action Create and Action Change

11.4.5 Create a Change Request Type

The change request type is the key characteristic of the change request that determines how a change request is processed. The change request type links a change request to the workflow, data model, and business activities.

In this example, we'll create one change request type for one business activity. Figure 11.53 shows the change request types we've created, as follows:

- **ZPS_01**
  This change request is used for creation of the project definition and WBS elements. We've assigned simple workflow template WS75700040 to the change request. The main entity type for this change request type is PSPID (project definition). The other entity is POSID. Remember that although POSID is a type 1 entity, PSPID is a superior entity to POSID by virtue of the leading relationship from PSPID to POSID. Business activity ZBA1 is assigned to the change request type. This assignment is used at

runtime for change request type determination. Following are the steps to create change request type ZPS_01:

- Go to IMG activity **Master Data Governance, Central Governance · Process Modeling · Change Requests · Create Change Request Type.**
- Click on the **New** button.
- Enter **Type of Chg Request** as "ZPS_01".
- Enter **Data Model** as "ZW".
- Enter **Description** as "Create Projects".
- Select the **Single Object** checkbox.
- Enter **Main Entity Type** as "PSPID".
- Enter the workflow ID "WS75700040" in the **Workflow** field.
- Press ⌊Enter⌋.
- Select the row for change request type **ZPS_01**, and click on **Entity Types**.
- Add entity **POSID** to the list of entity types.
- Select **Business Activity**.
- Add **Business Activity ZBA1** that was created as part of Section 11.4.2.
- Click on **Save**.

- **ZPS_02**

  This change request type is used for changing the project definition, creating new WBS elements, changing WBS elements, and assigning WBS elements to the project definition hierarchy. This change request type, like ZPS_01, also has PSPID as the main entity and POSID as the other entity. Business activity ZBA2 has been assigned to the change request type. Neither change request type has parallel processing enabled. Following are the steps to create change request type ZPS_02:

  - Go to IMG activity **Master Data Governance, Central Governance · Process Modeling · Change Requests · Create Change Request Type.**
  - Click on the **New** button.
  - Enter **Type of Chg Request** as "ZPS_02".
  - Enter **Data Model** as "ZW".
  - Enter **Description** as "Create Projects".
  - Select the **Single Object** checkbox.
  - Enter the **Main Entity Type** as "PSPID".
  - Enter workflow ID "WS75700040" in the **Workflow** field.
  - Press ⌊Enter⌋.
  - Select the row for change request type **ZPS_02**, and click on **Entity Types**.
  - Add entity **POSID** to the list of entity types.
  - Select **Business Activity**.

- Add **Business Activity ZBA2** that was created as part of Section 11.4.2.
- Click on **Save**.

Type of Change Request									
Type of Chg. Requ...	Data Model	Description (medium text)	Single Obj...	Parallel	Main Entity Ty...	Workflow	Target Sys	Default	
ZPS_01	ZW	Create Projects	☑	☐	PSPID	WS75700040	☐	☐	

Type of Chg. Request   ZPS_01

Entity Types					
Entity Type	Scenario	Configuration ID	Optional	Message Output	
POSID			☐	Standard	▼ ▲
PSPID			☐	Standard	▼ ▼

Change View "Business Activities": Overview

New Entries   BC Set: Change Field Values

Dialog Structure	Type of Chg. Request ZPS_01		
▼ Type of Change Reques			
▼ Entity Types	Business Activities		
• Scope on Entity	Bus. Activity	Description (medium text)	
• Business Activities	ZBA1	Create Project Definition	▲
• Service Level Agreer			

- -

Type of Change Request									
Type of Chg. Requ...	Data Model	Description (medium text)	Single Obj...	Parallel	Main Entity Ty...	Workflow	Target Sys	Default	
ZPS_02	ZW	Change proj(With WBSHie...	☑	☐	PSPID	WS75700040	☐	☐	

Type of Chg. Request   ZPS_02

Entity Types					
Entity Type	Scenario	Configuration ID	Optional	Message Output	
POSID			☐	Standard	▼ ▲
PSPID			☐	Standard	▼ ▼

Change View "Business Activities": Overview

New Entries   BC Set: Change Field Values

Dialog Structure	Type of Chg. Request ZPS_02		
▼ Type of Change Reques			
▼ Entity Types	Business Activities		
• Scope on Entity	Bus. Activity	Description (medium text)	
• Business Activities	ZBA2	Change Proj Def(With WBS Hierarchy)	▲
• Service Level Agreer			

Figure 11.53 Change Request Type Configuration

11.4.6   Workflow Settings

We've assigned simple workflow template WS75700040 to both change request type ZPS_01 and ZPS_02. Following are the steps to assign processors to the simple workflow:

1. Go to IMG activity, **Master Data Governance, Central Governance · General Settings · Process Modeling · Workflow · Other MDG Workflows · Assign Processor to Change Request Step Number (Simple Workflow)**.

2. Click on **New Entries**.

3. Enter values in the IMG view, as shown in Figure 11.54. We've used agent type as **US** (user). You also have the option to use roles or organization units.

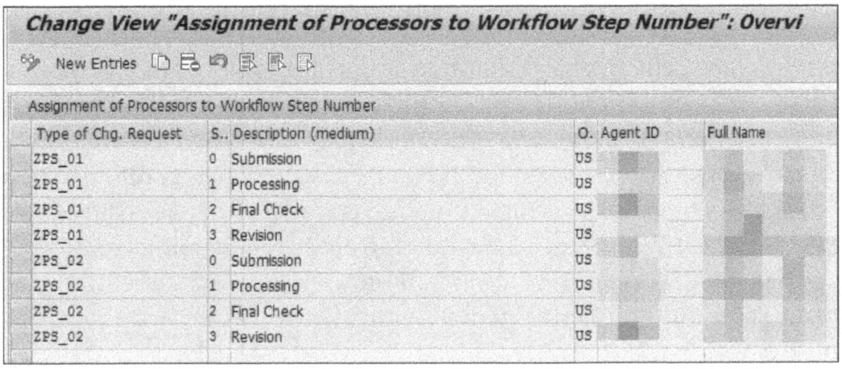

Type of Chg. Request	S..	Description (medium)	O.	Agent ID	Full Name
ZPS_01	0	Submission	US		
ZPS_01	1	Processing	US		
ZPS_01	2	Final Check	US		
ZPS_01	3	Revision	US		
ZPS_02	0	Submission	US		
ZPS_02	1	Processing	US		
ZPS_02	2	Final Check	US		
ZPS_02	3	Revision	US		

Figure 11.54 Assignment of Processors to Workflow Step Number

11.5   Security and Roles

This section explains the concept of security and roles for custom applications. Section 11.5.1 provides an overview of authorization objects delivered by SAP and how to use them to control the security of an SAP Master Data Governance custom application. Section 11.5.2 explains how to create new menu roles and authorization roles. Menu roles are used to configure role-based homepages. Finally, Section 11.5.3 explains how to create a homepage. The homepage that we'll create is based on the Transaction PFCG roles created in Section 11.5.2.

11.5.1   Authorization Objects

Authorization objects provided by SAP are used to restrict access to the SAP Master Data Governance application during runtime and design time. Configuring access to SAP Master Data Governance using authorization objects is highly specific to each company. Therefore, we won't explain this concept in detail in terms of the use case.

The SAP-delivered SAP Master Data Governance application comes with sufficient authorization checks that reuse the underlying SAP S/4HANA authorization objects. This reuse essentially means that if you have supplier master data maintenance roles in an existing SAP S/4HANA system, then this role can be used as-is in the SAP Master Data Governance system as well.

For SAP Master Data Governance custom objects, you can choose to implement authorization checks on existing authorization objects in the access class (if the data model has a reuse active area, and you want to reuse the reuse area authorization objects) or in Business Add-In (BAdI) USMD_RULE_SERVICE (if the data model is in flex mode).

SAP delivers the following generic authorization objects that you can use irrespective of the data model:

- USMD_MDAT

  This authorization object is used to configure restrictions on master data maintenance. The permitted activities for the authorization object are create, change, display, and delete. The authorization fields for this object are USMD_MODEL (data model), ENTITY (entity type), and KEY_FLD1 … KEY_FLD7. The key fields are interpreted depending on the way the configuration is done. If you flag only entities as authorization relevant, then, by default, the key fields of the entities are defined as key fields. Apart from key fields, you can also define attributes of an entity type as authorization relevant. You can only define seven fields as authorization relevant per entity type. These seven fields include the key fields of the entity type. You can configure type 1, 2, and 3 entities as authorization relevant.

- USMD_MDATH

  This authorization object is used to configure restriction on the maintenance of the hierarchy. The permitted activities are create, change, and display. Table 11.2 lists the authorization fields for the object.

Authorization Field	Description	Usage
USMD_MODEL	Data model	Enter the active data model.
ENTITY	Entity type	Specify the entity type for which the hierarchy is defined. The entity type for which the **Is Hry Type** field is configured as **Yes.**
HRYVERS	Hierarchy version	Enter the hierarchy version. This field is relevant only if the hierarchy is version enabled in the hierarchy entity type.
H_KEY_FLD1	Value for key field of ENTITY	Enter the value for the key field of ENTITY.
H_KEY_FLD2	Value for key field of ENTITY	Enter if you have another key field of the entity.
ENTITY_NOD	Entity type of the node	Enter your own ENTITY or entity configured as additional nodes.
N_KEY_FLD1 - N_KEY_FLD1	Value of node key	Enter the value of the node key.

Table 11.2 Authorization Fields for Authorization Object USMD_MDATH

For data models with a reuse active area, you can use authorization objects from the reuse active area; however, you can choose to deactivate the usage and choose to use only the USMD_MDAT authorization object. Figure 11.55 shows the configuration settings to activate SAP Master Data Governance–specific authorization (USMD_MDAT) for the business partner data model.

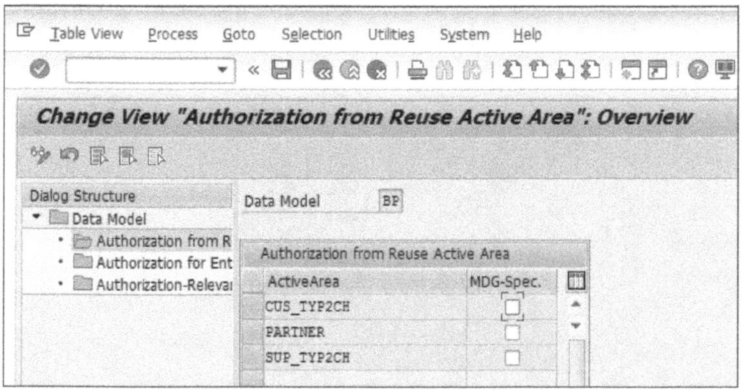

Figure 11.55 Settings to Activate SAP Master Data Governance-Specific Generic Authorization for the Business Partner Data Model

This configuration activity can be accessed via **Master Data Governance, Central Governance • General Settings • Data Modeling • Define Authorization Relevance per Entity Type • Data Model • Authorization from Reuse Active Area**. If you activate this setting, the authorization from the reuse area won't be invoked by default; only USMD_MDAT will be invoked.

Although our data model ZW is configured in flex mode, the USMD_MDAT and USMD_MDATH authorizations aren't invoked by default. You have to mark these entities explicitly as authorization relevant in the configuration path, **Master Data Governance, Central Governance • General Settings • Data Modeling • Define Authorization Relevance per Entity Type • Data Model • Authorization for Entity Types**.

Figure 11.56 shows the settings made in the system to enable entity types PSPID and POSID as authorization relevant.

Following are the steps that need to be performed to enable entity types PSPID and POSID as authorization relevant.

❶ Select **Data Model ZW**.

❷ Click on **Authorization for Entities** in the **Dialog Structure**.

❸ Click on the **Authorization Relevant** checkbox for **Entity Type POSID** and **Key POSID**.

❹ Click on the **Authorization Relevant** checkbox for **Entity Type POSID** and **Key PSPID**.

❺ Click on the **Authorization Relevant** checkbox for **Entity Type PSPID** and **Key PSPID**.

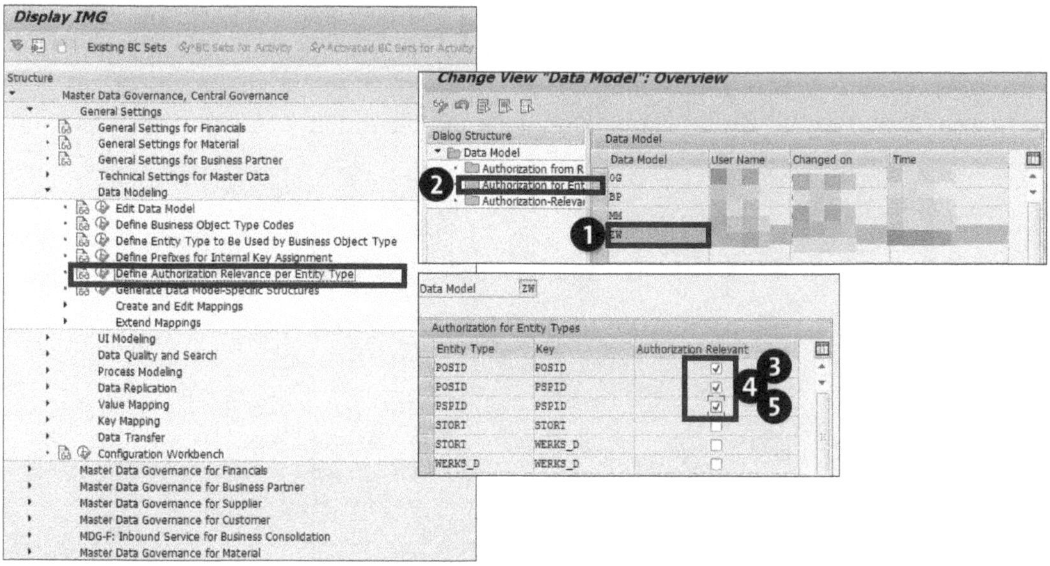

Figure 11.56 Enabling Settings to Make Entities POSID and PSPID Authorization Relevant

11.5.2 Roles

Roles are used for configuring authorization profiles and menus for users. Roles are directly assigned to the user master and can also be used to configure personalization values for users.

The role design guidelines are established differently for every organization. We'll adopt one such approach here. To bring in more flexibility in the role assignment, we'll create separate roles for the menu and authorization profile but group these two roles into a composite role. SAP delivers a template role called SAP_MDGX_MENU_04 for custom objects. We'll copy this role to create two new roles for authorization and menu.

Role for Menu

The role for menu is used exclusively to configure the menu entries in SAP Business Client. This role won't have any authorization maintained.

First, we copy role SAP_MDGX_MENU_04 and create a custom role. Be sure to use your own naming convention here. Figure 11.57 shows the list of steps to create custom menu role ZSAP_MDGZW_MENU_04:

❶ Enter the **Role** as "SAP_MDGX_MENU_04."

❷ Click on the **Copy** button.

❸ In the **to role** field, enter the new menu role name as "ZSAP_MDGZW_MENU_04".

❹ Click on the **Copy all** button in the dialog box.

❺ Add the **Long Text** for the menu role.

❻ Add a **Description** for the menu role.

❼ Click on the **Save** button.

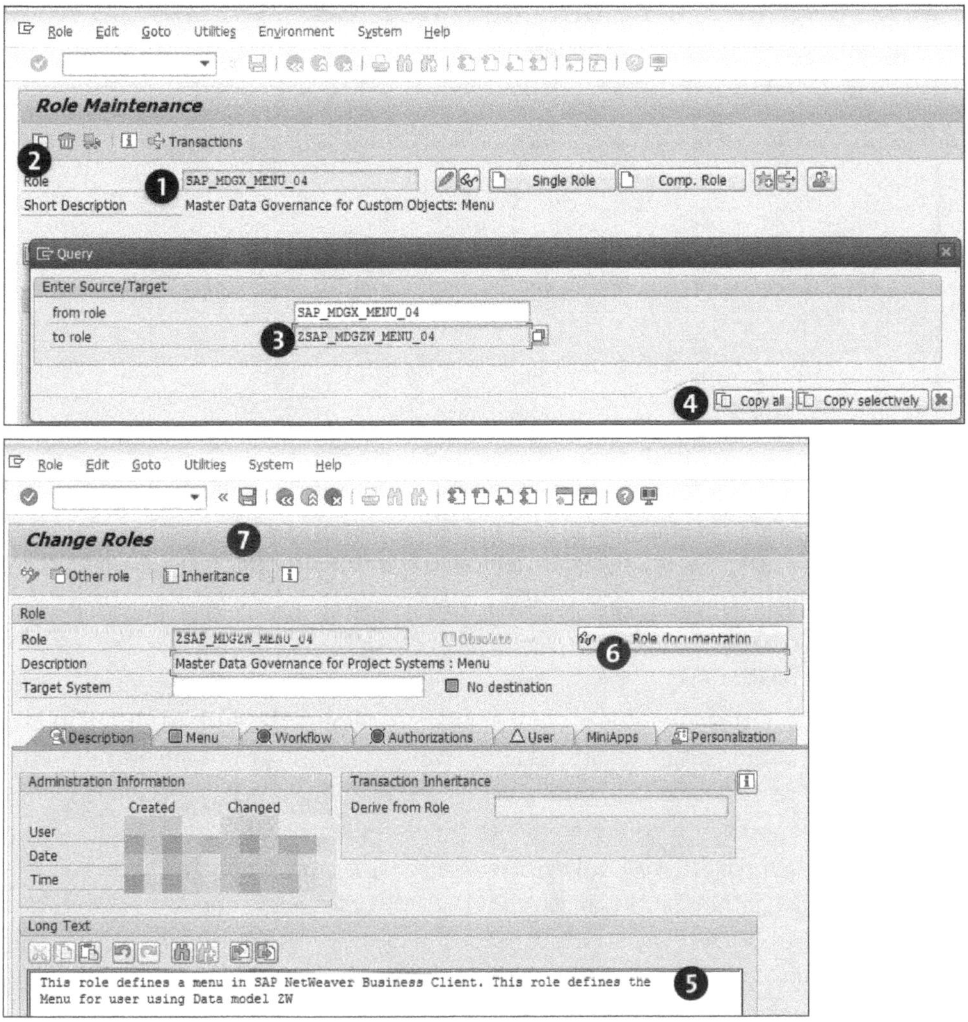

Figure 11.57 Steps to Copy Role SAP_MDGX_MENU_04 into Custom Menu Role ZSAP_MDG-ZW_MENU_04

After the role is created, we adjust the menu entries in the role. We configure the USMD_SEARCH UI we created in Section 11.3.2. Figure 11.58 shows the list of adjustments made to the copied role. Here you can see the following:

❶ Title of the menu role

❷ Personal object worklist

❸ USMD_SEARCH application

❹ Standard menu entries copied from the template role

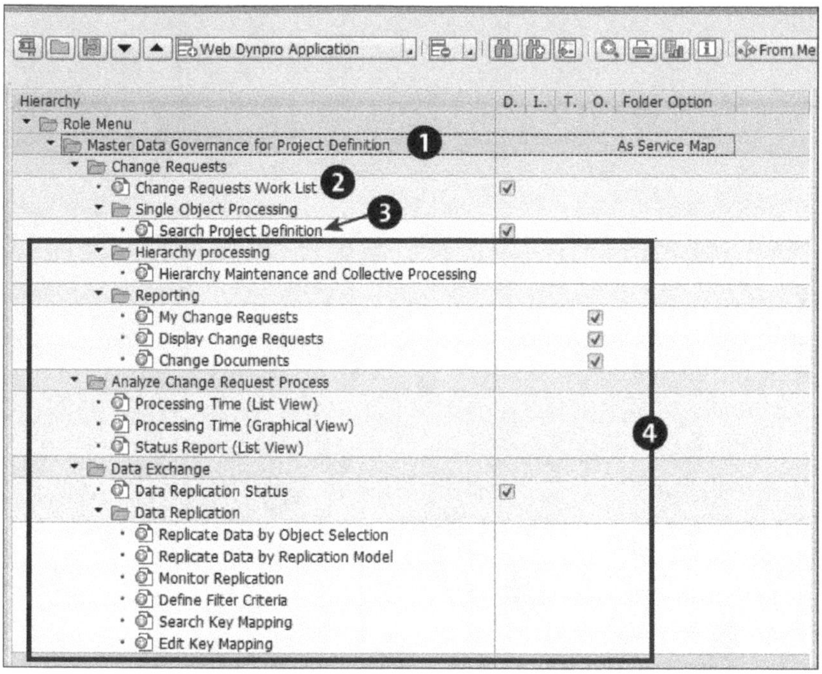

Figure 11.58 Adjusting the Menu Entries of the Copied Role

Role for Authorization

The role for the authorization is used only for maintaining the authorization objects and values for authorization object fields. We won't maintain any menu entries in the role. Here you create one role for one persona. For example, if you have a persona for requester and approver in your governance process, then you'll create two authorization roles. For simplicity, we'll only create one role for admin persona here. You can choose to use an authorization object from the FMDM object class and SAP Master Data Governance. SAP delivers the SAP_MDGX_MENU_04 template role for custom objects; this role should copied and used as a foundation to build custom object-specific roles. Figure 11.59 shows the steps required to copy the template roles:

❶ Enter the **Role** name as "SAP_MDGX_MENU_04".

❷ Click on the **Copy** button.

❸ Enter the new role name as "ZSAP_MDGZW_ADMIN_04" in the **to role** field.

❹ Click on **Copy all**.

Note

We've only used USMD_MDAT and USMD_MDATH authorization objects in the role. Many other authorization objects are delivered by SAP but haven't been used to keep this chapter short and concise. Refer to object class FMDM and SAP Master Data Governance for a list of more authorization objects.

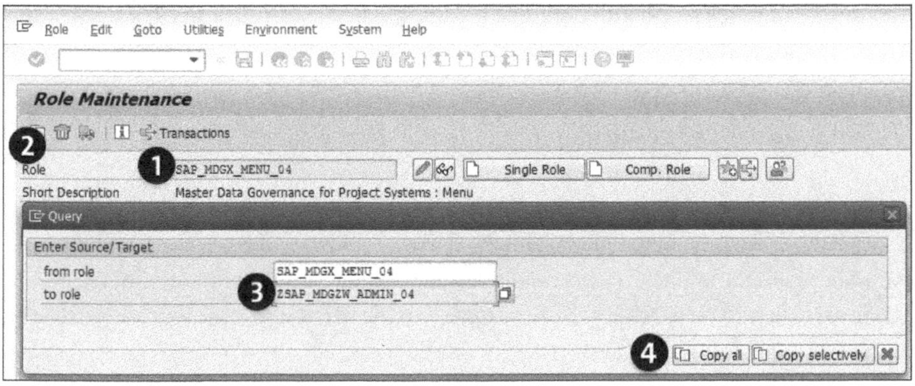

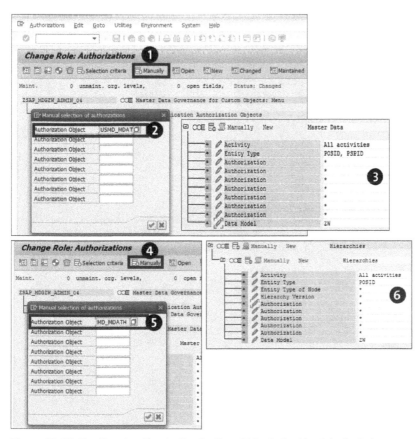

Figure 11.59 Copying the Template Role to the Admin Authorization Role

Figure 11.60 shows how to add the authorization objects to the custom object role for admin, as follows:

❶ Click on the **Manually** button.

❷ Enter "USMD_MDAT" as the **Authorization Object**.

Figure 11.60 Configuring the Authorization Objects for the Admin Role

❸ Select **All activities**, **POSID**, and **PSPID** as entity types for data model **ZW**.

❹ Click on the **Manually** button again.

❺ Enter "USMD_MDATH."

❻ Select **All activities** and **POSID** as entity types for data model **ZW**.

11.5.3   Homepage

A *homepage* is a landing page that is displayed as soon as a user opens the menu role in SAP Business Client. We'll build this homepage using the Page Builder. To create the page configuration, follow these steps:

1. Go to the ABAP Workbench (Transaction SE80).

2. To create an application configuration as shown in Figure 11.61, display Web Dynpro component **WDR_CHIP_PAGE** ❶, select application **WDR_CHIP_PAGE** ❷, and choose **Create/Change Configuration** ❸ from the context menu.

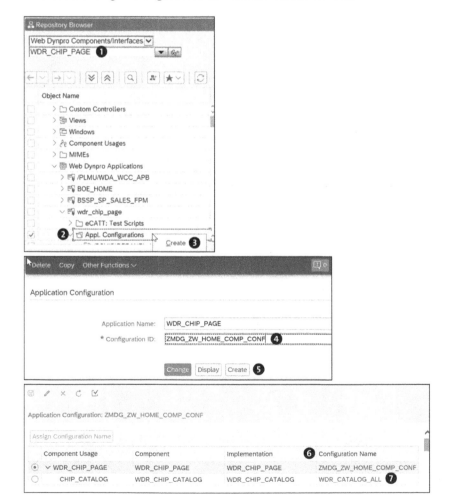

Figure 11.61 Steps to Create Page Configuration for Application WDR_CHIP_PAGE

3. Specify a unique **Configuration ID 4**.

4. Click on the **Change** button **5**, enter the **Configuration Name** as "ZMDG_ZW_ HOME_COMP_CONF" **6**, and enter "WDR_CATALOG_ALL" for **CHIP_CATALOG 7**.

5. Figure 11.62 shows the steps to start the Page Builder in configuration mode. Call the Page Builder by selecting application configuration **ZMDG_ZW_HOME_APPLN_ CONF 1**, and choose **Test 2** from the context menu. The Page Builder is started.

6. Choose the **Adapt Page** button **3** on the top-right corner of the page, and click on **Configuration 4**.

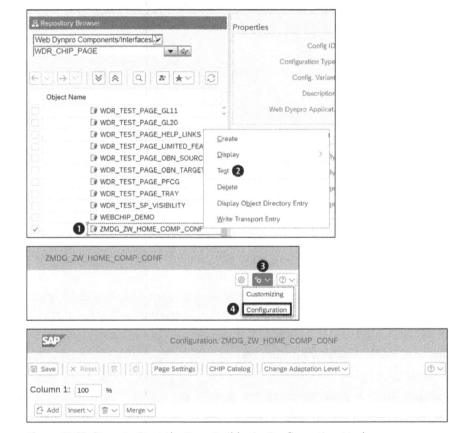

Figure 11.62 Steps to Start the Page Builder in Configuration Mode

7. Figure 11.63 shows the steps to define the page layout. Click on the **Page Settings 1** button on the application toolbar, and enter the title of the page in the **Page Title** field **2**.

8. Click on the **CHIP Catalog 3** button on the application bar, and a side panel for **CHIP Catalog** opens.

9. Search for "PFCG" **4**, and select chip **PFCG Link List 5**. Drag and drop the chip in a row in the Page Builder.

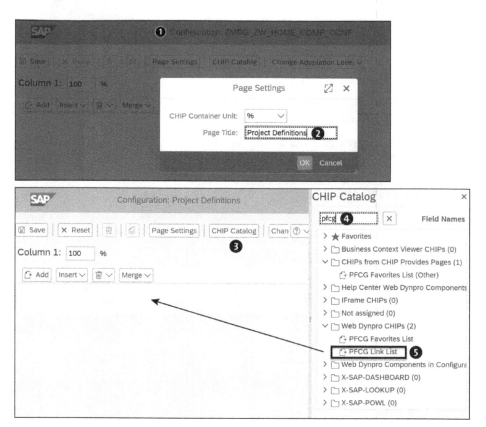

Figure 11.63 Setting Up a Page: Adding the Title and PFCG Link List Chip to the Page Builder

10. After the chip is added, change the title of the chip, and define the link list. Use the application alias configured in the menu role. Figure 11.64 shows the steps. Click on **Settings • Change Tile ❶**.

11. Enter **Title** as "Process Project Definition" ❷.

12. Click on **Define Link List ❸**.

13. Enter the **Application Alias** as "{PBA=ZW_CR_MAIN}" ❹.

14. Repeat this step for all the folders in the role.

15. After the homepage is configured, add the homepage to the PFCG role (see Figure 11.65).

Note

You can add two kinds of chips: PFCG link list and launchpad link list. The second requires configuration of the launchpad in Transaction LPD_CUST. In this chapter, we're using the PFCG link list.

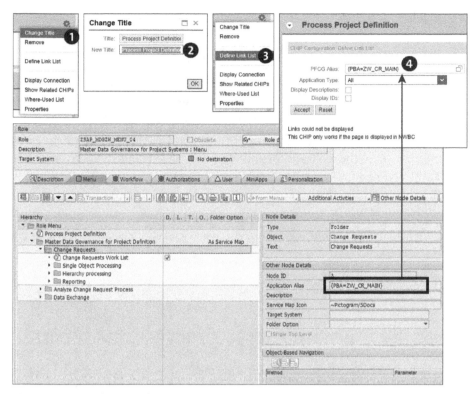

Figure 11.64 Configuring the PFCG Application Alias

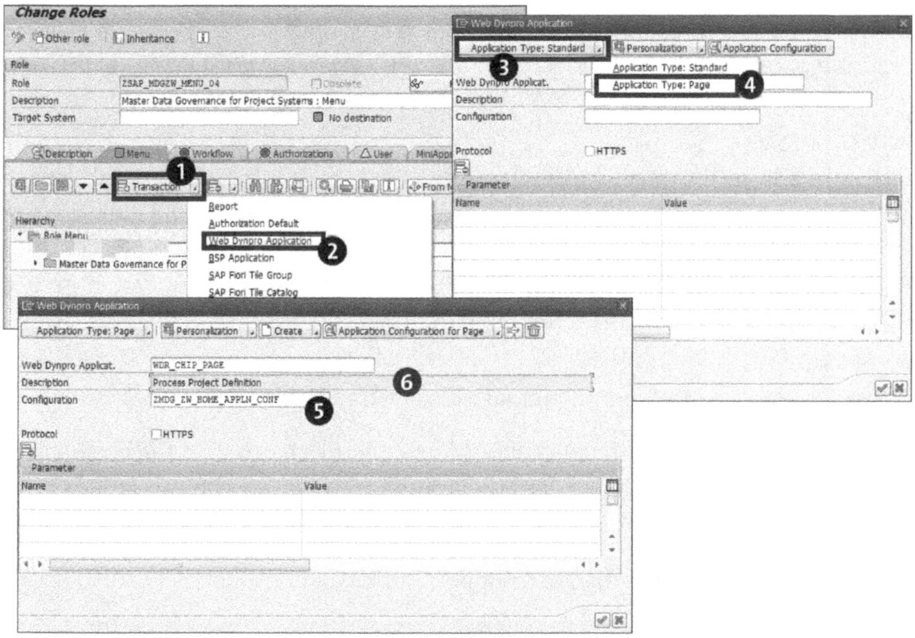

Figure 11.65 Adding the Homepage to the PFCG Role

11.6   Data Replication

Replicating master data to target systems is the final outcome of the central governance process. The change request framework and data replication framework are integrated natively. This integration helps in triggering the data replication soon after a change request is activated, or an edition is released. SAP Master Data Governance custom objects can also use this integration to trigger replication automatically.

Before proceeding with setting up the data replication, we should first choose the communication channel for the replication. In our use case, we're using SAP-delivered IDoc type PROJECT01 and message type PROJECT; therefore, our communication channel is IDoc. The IDoc type PROJECT01 can replicate the project definition, WBS elements, and WBS hierarchy.

The next step is to create the outbound implementation class by implementing interface IF_DRF_OUTBOUND.

In the outbound implementation class, it's mandatory to implement the following four methods:

- **INITIALIZE**
  This method is used to create an instance of the current outbound implementation and send back the instance in the EO_IF_DRF_OUTBOUND exporting field to the data replication framework (outbound controller). This method is also used to pass the table type of the main entity back to the framework; this table type will be filled with keys of objects that are relevant for replication.

- **READ_COMPLETE_DATA**
  This method is used to read the complete data based on the CT_RELEVANT_OBJECTS importing parameter, which contains object keys relevant for replication. It's good to save the data that is read here in the context of the class.

- **MAP_DATA2MESSAGE**
  This method is used to transfer the data from SAP Master Data Governance structures and tables to the message structures and table. It's recommended to use the Service Mapping Tool (SMT) for this purpose. During transformation of data from SAP Master Data Governance structures to message structures, you should invoke the key mapping and value mapping API if required.

- **SEND_MESSAGE**
  This method is used to trigger the actual message transmission process.

In this section, we won't go into detail about how to write the code in the methods of the object implementation class, as this is beyond the scope of the book.

11.6.1   Customizing Settings for Data Replication

This section introduces a list of customized settings that need to be performed to enable replication of custom object data. First, we describe how to define filter objects and assign them to business objects to enable filtering of data based on the target system. Second, we describe how to define object identifiers and outbound implementation.

Define Filter Objects

Filter objects are design-time objects that are used to generate filters. They are used during runtime to filter the data before replication. Refer to Chapter 12 for more information on this topic.

For the current use case, we'll define filter-to-filter projects based on the project definition ID. We'll also reuse the SAP standard CL_USMD_DRF_FILTER filter class. When the data model is activated, the SAP Master Data Governance application framework generates key structures for every type 1 entity; for example, in our use case, the ZMDG_S_ZW_KF_PSPID key structure is generated for entity PSPID. We'll reuse this key structure as a parameter structure. Figure 11.66 shows the definition of **Filter Object ZF_PSPID** and simple explicit **Filter 81**.

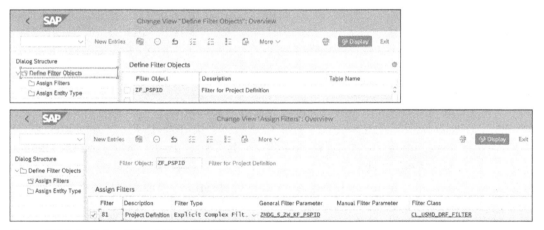

Figure 11.66 Defining Filter Object ZF_PSPID

The IMG activity to define a filter object can be accessed using the following IMG path: **DRF IMG • Data Replication • Enhance Default Settings for Outbound Implementations • Define Filter Objects**.

Assign the Filter Object to the Business Object

We need to assign the filter object to the business object to implicitly assign the filter to the replication model via the business object.

Following are the required steps, as shown in Figure 11.67:

1. Go to IMG activity **DRF IMG • Data Replication • Enhance Default Settings for Outbound Implementations • Define Business Objects and Object Identifiers • Assign Filter Objects To Business Objects**.

2. Click on **New Entries**.

3. In the **Business Object Type** column, enter "ZPS". (This business object was created in Section 11.4.1.)

4. Enter **Filter Object** "ZF_PSPID". (This filter object was created in the previous section.)

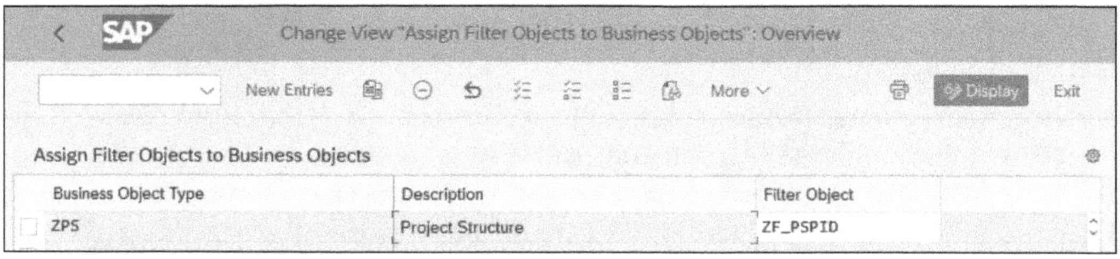

Figure 11.67 Assigning the Filter Object to the Business Object

Define and Assign the Object Identifier

The object identifier defines the structure of the business object key. This information is used by the data replication framework for logging purposes and for updating key mapping during the posting of the ALEAUD inbound IDoc message type. The Customizing activities to define and assign the object identifier are as follows:

1. **Define object identifiers.**

   Define an object identifier code for the object identifier and assign a business object to the object identifier code. Figure 11.68 shows the **Object ID Type ZPROJDEF_CODE** and assignment of **BO Type** code **ZPS** to the identifier. Following are the steps to define the object identifier:

   - Go to IMG menu path, **DRF IMG · Data Replication · Enhance Default Settings for Outbound Implementations · Define Business Objects and Object Identifiers · Define Object Identifiers**.

   - Click on **New Entries**.

   - Enter **Object ID Type** as "ZPROJDEF_CODE".

   - Enter **Description of Object ID Type** as "Object Identifier of ZPS".

   - Enter **BO Type** as "ZPS".

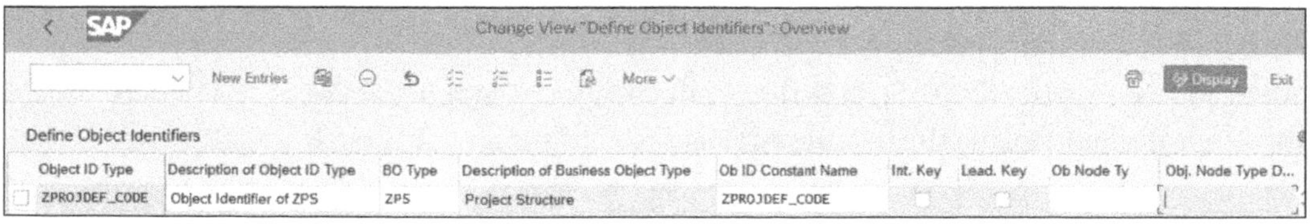

Figure 11.68 Defining the Object Identifier

2. **Assign key structures to object identifiers.**

   After the object identifier is created, assign a structure to the object ID type. Usually, we assign the key structure generated after activation of the data model to the object ID type. It's recommended to always use the structure generated during data model activation because the structure is always updated by the framework based on changes to the data model. Figure 11.69 shows assignment of key structures to the object identifier. Following are the steps to create this assignment:

   - Go to IMG menu path, **DRF IMG · Data Replication · Enhance Default Settings for Outbound Implementations · Define Business Objects and Object Identifiers · Assign Key Structures to Object Identifiers.**
   - Click on **New Entries**, and enter **Object ID Type** as "ZPROJDEF_CODE".
   - Enter **Key Structure** as "ZMDG_S_ZW_DRF_PSPID".
   - Click on **Save.**

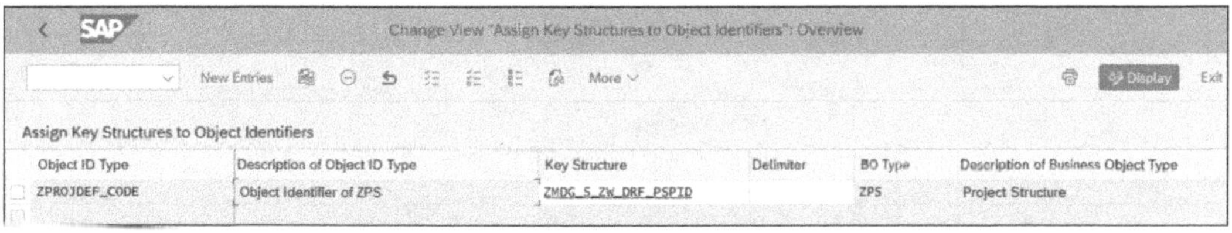

Figure 11.69 Assigning the Object Identifier to the Key Structure

After the object identifier type code is created, and the settings for the code are maintained, assign the object identifier to **BO Type ZPS** (Figure 11.70)

The IMG to assign the object ID type to the business object is **DRF IMG · Data Replication · Enhance Default Settings for Outbound Implementations · Define Business Objects and Object Identifiers · Define Business Objects.**

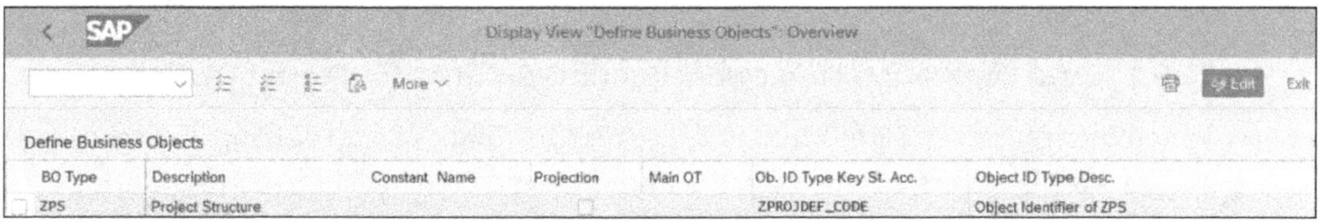

Figure 11.70 Assigning the Object Identifier Type to the Business Object Type

Create Outbound Implementation

The IMG activity for creating the outbound implementation can be accessed using **DRF IMG · Data Replication · Enhance Default Settings for Outbound Implementations · Define Outbound Implementations.**

In this IMG activity, click on the **Create** button, and enter the data given in Table 11.3.

Field Name	Field Value	Explanation
Outbound Implementation	ZPROJ_DEF	Unique ID for outbound implementation
Description	Project Definition IDoc	Meaningful description for project definition
Communication Channel	Replication Via IDoc	Means of data transfer to target system
Outbound Implementation Class	ZCL_ZW_OUTBOUND_IMPL	Name of the outbound implementation class
BO Type	ZPS	Business object type

Table 11.3 Creating Outbound Implementation: Values

Figure 11.71 shows the definition of the outbound implementation.

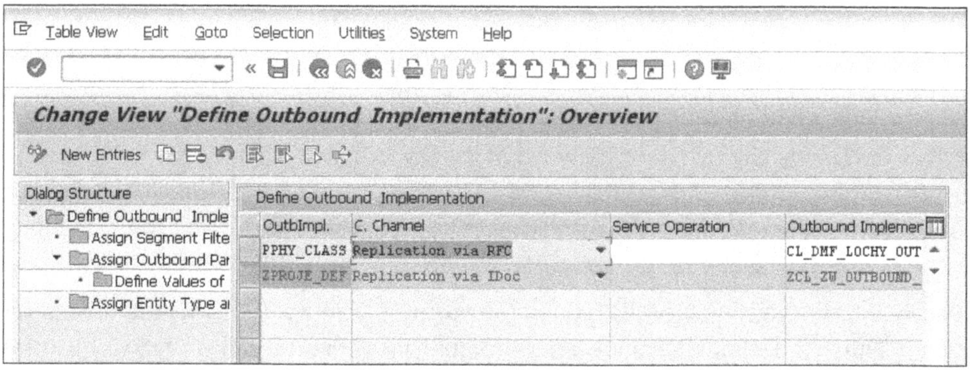

Figure 11.71 Definition of New Outbound Implementation

11.6.2   Data Replication Framework Runtime Settings for Project Definition

When the transfer of data is initiated, the responsibility of transferring is passed on to the data replication framework by the initiator (change request framework during activation, user through ad hoc replication or edition release, or batch program such as DRFOUT). The data replication framework will then consume the Customizing settings to process the data transfer of objects. These settings are called runtime data replication framework settings.

The ultimate aim of the data replication framework is to replicate the right data to the right system in the right channel. The runtime settings are consumed by the data replication framework to achieve this goal.

In this section, we'll perform settings to define the business system and replication model. We'll also link the business system and outbound implementation with the replication model.

Determination of the Local System Name

The data replication framework needs to know the local system name or its own system name. This is used in the runtime by the key mapping framework to populate the source system ID in the outbound message (control record in IDocs and message header in service-oriented architectures [SOAs]).

You can define the local (source) system name in the following ways:

- **System Landscape Directory (SLD)**
  You can define the business system ID for the local system in which SAP Master Data Governance is hosted in SLD. This will be consumed automatically by the data replication framework.

- **BAdI MDG_IDM_GET_LCL_SYSTEM**
  If your system doesn't have an SLD connection, you can use this BAdI to determine the local system name. Refer to the IMG documentation of the BAdI before implementing it.

Define Target Systems

Each target system for replication from SAP Master Data Governance is defined as a business system in the IMG path, **Data Replication • Define Custom Settings for Data Replication • Define Technical Settings • Define Technical Settings for Business Systems**.

Figure 11.72 shows the addition of **Business System ZSYSTEM1**; in our case, it's mandatory to enter the **Logical System** name because our communication channel is IDoc. If an SLD connection exists, then choose the business system from the value help.

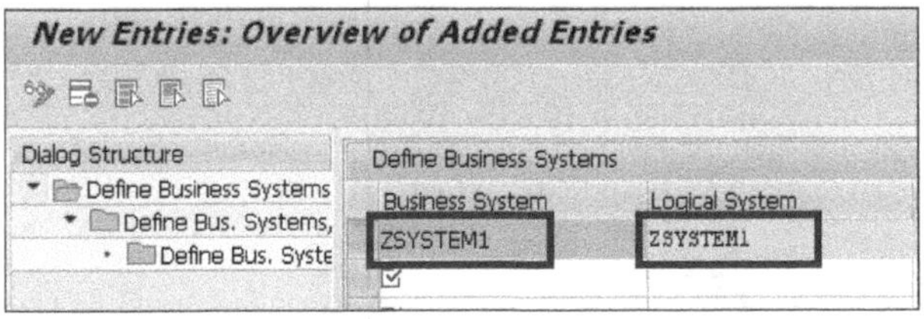

Figure 11.72 Adding ZSYSTEM1 as a Business System

We now must determine what data can be sent to this target system (business system) by assigning business objects to the business system. These settings are used in runtime to validate whether object data can be replicated to a business system. In Figure 11.73, the **BO Type** is assigned to the **Business System**.

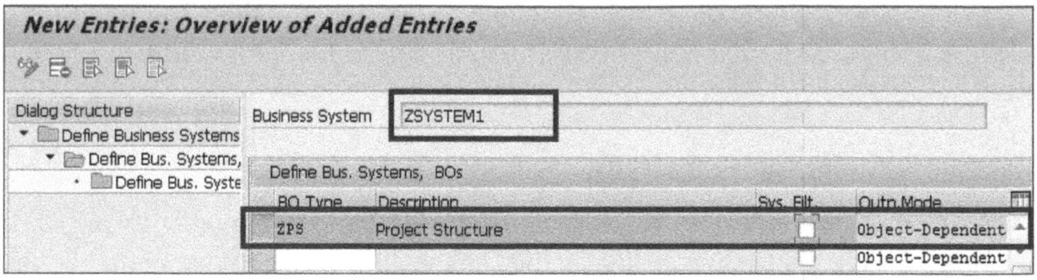

New Entries: Overview of Added Entries

Dialog Structure	Business System	ZSYSTEM1		
▼ ☐ Define Business Systems				
▼ ☐ Define Bus. Systems,	Define Bus. Systems, BOs			
• ☐ Define Bus. Syste	BO Type	Description	Sys. Filt.	Outp.Mode
	ZPS	Project Structure	☐	Object-Dependent
			☐	Object-Dependent

Figure 11.73 Assigning Business Object ZPS (Project Structure) to Business System ZSYSTEM1

Along with the list of valid business objects for the target system, we also need to determine the communication channel between the local system and the target system. In addition to the communication channel, we also need to define more context about key mapping. The data replication framework needs to know if object keys between the local system and the target system are harmonized; if they aren't harmonized, then key mapping should be performed.

> **Note**
>
> The outbound implementation plays a major role in implementing the Customizing settings. For example, if the setting for the **Key Harm.** field is defined as not harmonized, then it's the responsibility of the outbound implementation class to read this setting and decide whether key transformation should be done by invoking the key mapping API. The data replication framework doesn't perform key mapping automatically.

In our example, the project definition has an external number range, so the project definition and WBS will be created with the same ID as the SAP Master Data Governance hub. Figure 11.74 shows the communication channel settings and key harmonization settings for **Business System ZSYSTEM1** and **Bus. Obj. Type ZPS**.

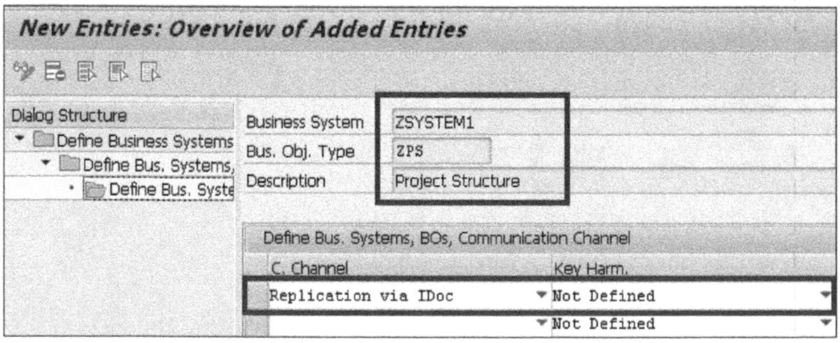

New Entries: Overview of Added Entries

Dialog Structure		
▼ ☐ Define Business Systems	Business System	ZSYSTEM1
▼ ☐ Define Bus. Systems,	Bus. Obj. Type	ZPS
• ☐ Define Bus. Syste	Description	Project Structure
	Define Bus. Systems, BOs, Communication Channel	
	C. Channel	Key Harm.
	Replication via IDoc	▼ Not Defined
		▼ Not Defined

Figure 11.74 Definition of the Communication Channel and Key Harmonization Settings for Business System ZSYSTEM1

Define Replication Model

A replication model is used to group semantically similar outbound implementations and can be defined flexibly depending on the requirements.

You can create a replication model in either of the following ways:

- **Outbound implementation specific**
  You can create one replication model for one outbound implementation, and you can assign multiple business systems to the outbound implementation.

- **Business system specific**
  You can create one replication model for one business system and assign multiple outbound implementations to the replication model. All the outbound implementations will have the same business system assigned.

The best approach will be based on your requirements and landscape; however, many consider a replication model specific to an outbound implementation as highly flexible. Therefore, in our use case, we'll create a replication model specific to an outbound implementation. Figure 11.75 shows the definition of replication model **ZPROJ_DEF**.

The Customizing activity to define the replication model can be accessed using the following path in Transaction DRFIMG: **Data Replication · Define Custom Settings for Data Replication · Define Replication Models**.

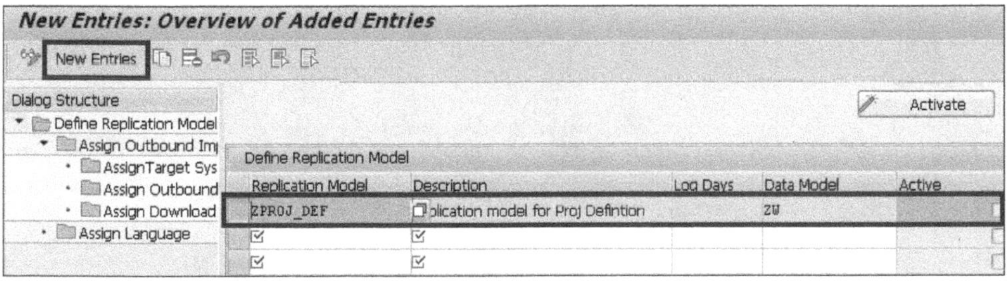

Figure 11.75 Definition of Replication Model ZPROJ_DEF

After creating the project definition, it's mandatory to define at least one outbound implementation to the replication model and assign at least one business system as the target system to the outbound implementation. Figure 11.76 shows the assignment of the outbound implementation to the replication model and the assignment of business system **ZSYSTEM1** as the target system.

After maintaining all the settings, activate the replication model. The system will perform checks to ensure the consistency of the replication model.

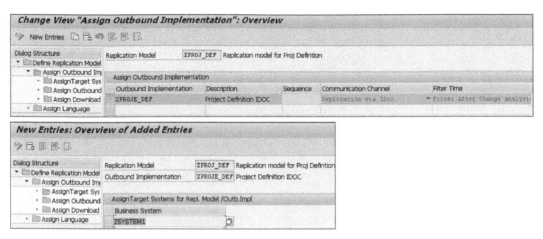

Figure 11.76 Assigning the Outbound Implementation to ZPROJ_DEF and ZSYSTEM1 as the Target System for ZPROJE_DEF

Figure 11.77 shows the activation of replication model ZPROJ_DEF.

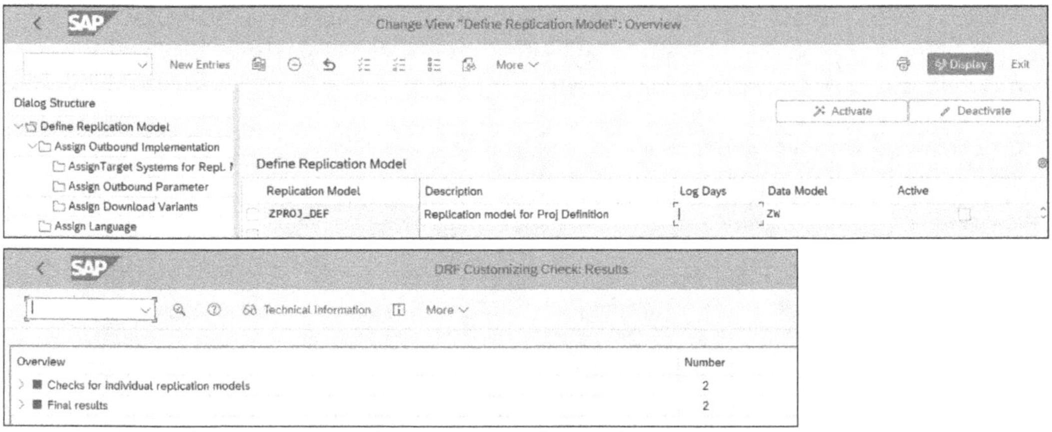

Figure 11.77 Activation of the Replication Model

We've created the ZF_PSPID filter and assigned it to the ZPS business object, which is assigned to the ZPROJE_DEF outbound implementation. The outbound implementation is assigned to the ZPROJ_DEF replication model. Therefore, the ZF_PSPID filter is assigned implicitly to the ZPROJ_DEF replication model. This can be verified in Transaction DRFF. The result of this configuration is shown in Figure 11.78.

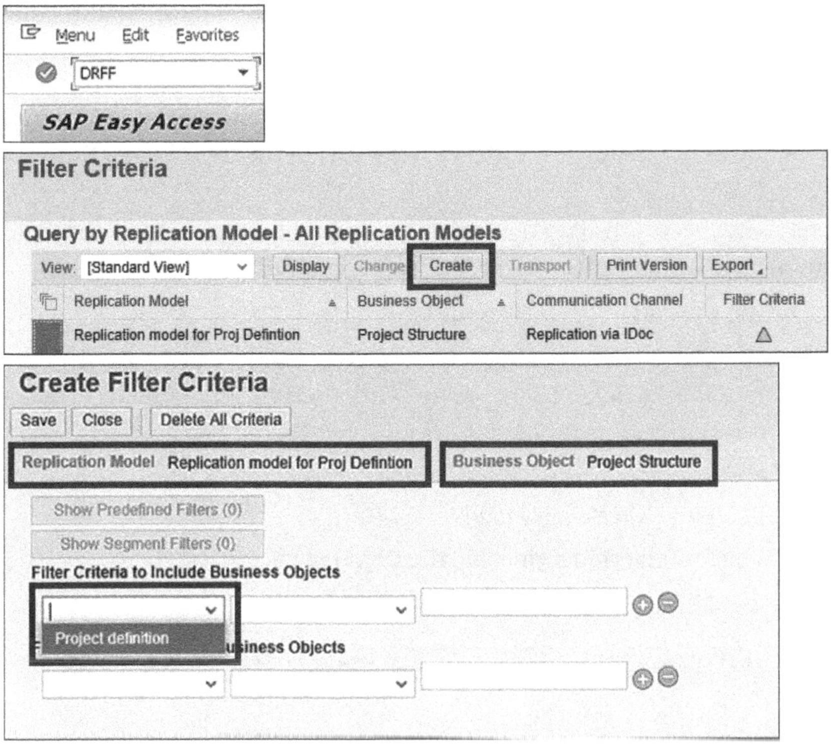

Figure 11.78 Maintaining Filter Criteria for Replication Model ZPROJ_DEF

11.7   Enabling Key Mapping

In an enterprise, the master data coexists in multiple systems, and, in some cases, the same business object is identified by different object keys in different systems. Centrally governing nonharmonized master data from SAP Master Data Governance can be challenging if SAP Master Data Governance doesn't know the identifier of the master data in each target system. The key mapping framework addresses this challenge and provides the ability to map SAP Master Data Governance object identifiers against target system object identifiers.

This key mapping framework provides an API to retrieve this mapping during replication to transform the object identifiers into values that can be understood by the target system.

This section details the steps required to enable key mapping for business object ZPS. All the activities described in Section 11.6.1 must be completed to enable the key mapping for custom business objects.

A business object type code can have multiple object identifier types assigned to it. For example, object ID type 888 (business partner number) and type 889 (business partner UUID) are assigned to the same business object type code 147 (business partner). Object type nodes are used to define whether different object identifiers assigned to the same business object type code can be part of the same mapping group or not. If the keys have to be part of the same mapping group, then assign the same object node to all the object identifier type codes. If the keys have to be stored in different mapping groups, then assign different object nodes to the object identifiers of the same business object type codes.

Our use case has only one key (project definition ID), so we create one object node and assign it to our object identifier that was created in Section 11.6.1.

Following are the steps to create an object node (see Figure 11.79):

1. Go to IMG node **Master Data Governance, Central Governance · General Settings · Data Replication · Enhance Default Settings for Outbound Implementations · Define Object Nodes**.

2. Click on **New Entries**.

3. Enter "ZOBN_ZPS" in the **Obj Node Ty** field.

4. Enter "Object Node for Project Identifier" in the **Obj. Node Type Desc.** field.

5. Click on **Save**.

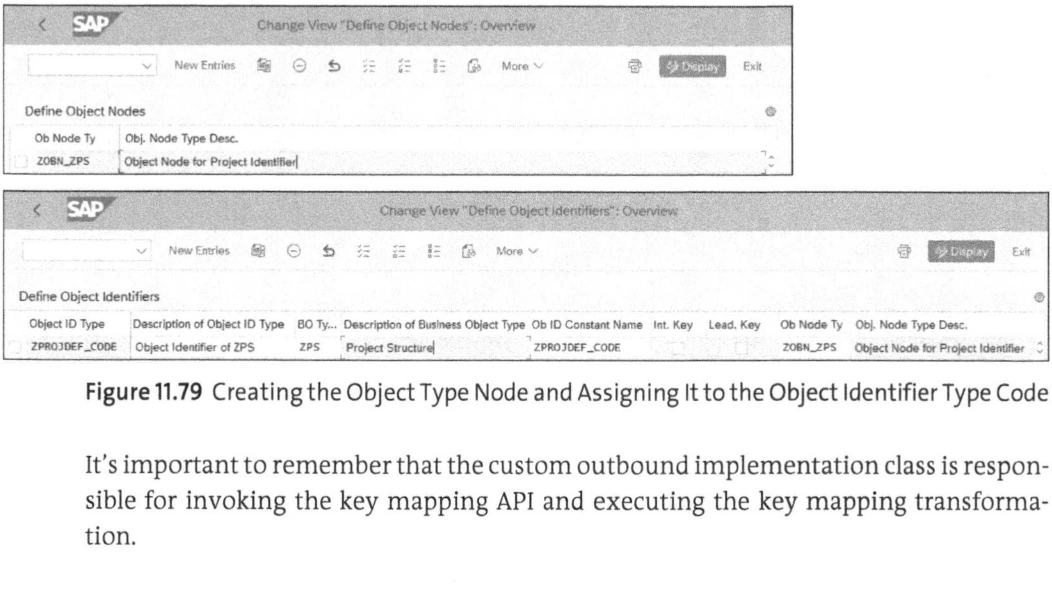

Figure 11.79 Creating the Object Type Node and Assigning It to the Object Identifier Type Code

It's important to remember that the custom outbound implementation class is responsible for invoking the key mapping API and executing the key mapping transformation.

11.8   Enabling Value Mapping

Value mapping is a way of converting source system-specific values to target system-specific values. For example, units of measure of material are maintained using different codes in different target systems. When replicating material data to a target system, the values need to be converted into target system–specific codes. This conversion is achieved using value mapping. Value mapping should be invoked only during the replication.

The first requirement to enable value mapping to the custom data model object is to maintain settings for the data element of the field that needs the value mapping to be triggered. For our example, after the configuration settings are made, value mapping will be performed for every field that refers to the ZBUKRS data element in an outbound message. The following steps are required to maintain these settings (see Figure 11.80):

1. Go to IMG menu path, **VM IMG · Value Mapping · Maintain Value Mapping**.

2. Click on **New Entries**.

3. In the **Object Type** field, select **Data Element** from the dropdown list.

4. In the **Global Data Type** field, enter "ZBUKRS".

5. In the **Input Help** field, enter "CL_MDG_CODE_LIST_PROV_BUKRS".

6. Click on **Save**.

Figure 11.80 Maintaining Value Mapping for the ZBUKRS Data Element

The next step is to maintain the value list for the ZBUKRS date element. The value list is a mapping between the internal code and the external code. The following steps are required to maintain value lists (see Figure 11.81):

1. Go to IMG menu path, **VM IMG · Value Mapping · Maintain Value Mapping**.

2. Select the row with **Global Data Type ZBUKRS**, and click the navigation button in the **Navigation** column.

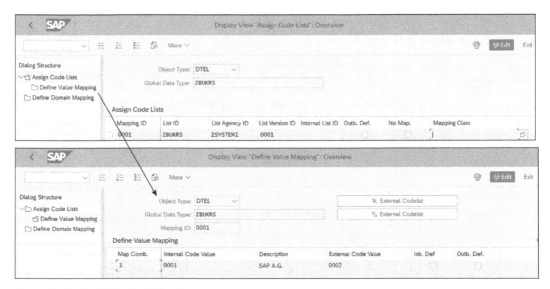

Figure 11.81 Maintaining Value Lists

3. Click on **New Entries**.

4. Enter the **Mapping ID** as "0001".

5. Enter the **List ID** as "ZBUKRS" (this field should always have the same value as the data element name).

6. Enter the **List Agency ID** as "ZSYSTEM1" (this field should always have the same value as the business system ID of the target system).

7. Enter the **List Version ID** as "0001". Increment this value for a new version.

8. Click on **Save**.

9. After the save is completed, select the just-saved row, and click on **Define Value Mapping**.

10. Maintain the **Internal Code Value** and **External Code Value** fields.

11.9   Enabling Notifications

One of the key tasks of a process model design is implementing a real-world business process as a system workflow using SAP Business Workflow. This workflow involves assigning work items to different users during various milestones of the workflow.

Sometimes, these users won't use the SAP Master Data Governance application frequently to execute their day-to-day tasks, so we need a robust notification mechanism to inform them about pending work items in their worklist. These notifications play a very important role in improving the Service Level Agreement (SLA) for SAP Master Data Governance change requests. For these notifications to be effective, they need to be delivered via email.

The extended notification framework informs users of a pending work item in their worklist through an email or SMS. This framework can trigger email with HTML content or email with plain text.

Note

Program SWN_SELSEN is used for selecting the work items for which we need to trigger notifications. The program will also take care of delivering the notifications to the subscribers of the task.

Tip

More information on enabling notifications using the extended notification framework is available at *http://s-prs.co/v488301*.

The extended email notification framework internally uses Business Server Pages (BSPs) to trigger email notifications with HTML content. The BSPs used for workflow-based notifications are configured as message templates via the following menu path (Transaction SWNCONFIG): **Business Scenario** · **Category** · **Assigned Message Templates.**

Figure 11.82 shows the message templates.

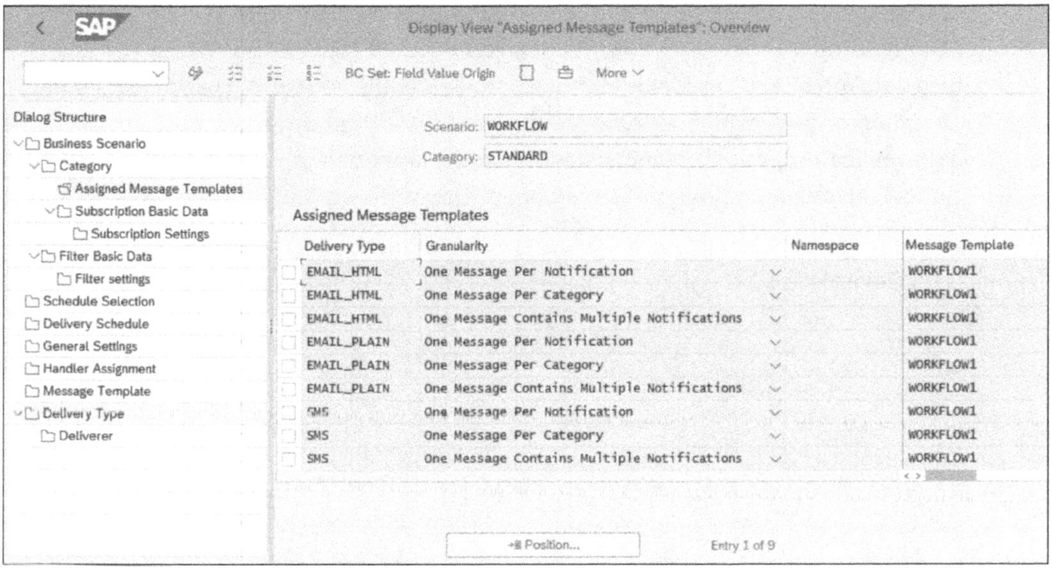

Figure 11.82 List of Message Templates Assigned to Scenario WORKFLOW and Category STANDARD

Each message template is assigned to a BSP application. Figure 11.83 shows the BSP application assigned to **Message Template WORKFLOW1**.

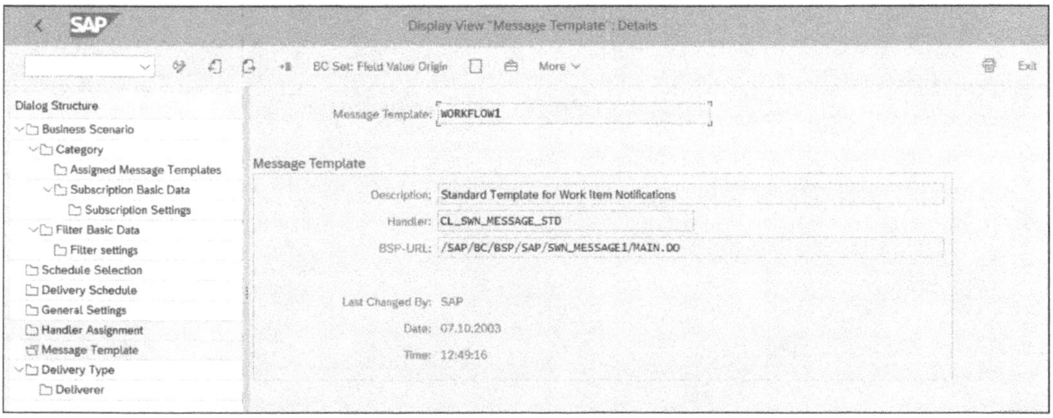

Figure 11.83 BSP Application Assigned to Message Template WORKFLOW1

You can copy this BSP application and create a new BSP application to enhance it and implement customer-specific requirements such as theming and adding URLs to SAP Master Data Governance change requests.

11.10   Summary

This chapter described in detail the custom object framework of central governance. After reading this chapter, you should have a good understanding of how to build custom data models and implement process models and UI on top of custom data models. The chapter also explained how to integrate cross-application components such as date replication, value mapping, key mapping, and enabling email notifications into the SAP Master Data Governance custom object framework.

In the following chapter, we'll discuss the data replication framework for SAP Master Data Governance.

Chapter 12
Data Replication Framework

The data replication framework is used to replicate master data, distribute it to all systems in the enterprise, monitor and trace data replication, and invoke key mapping and value mapping.

In a centralized master data system, it's important to have a robust replication framework to replicate master data to various target systems that consume master data. The data replication framework provides this functionality and solves key challenges such as standardizing master data across the enterprise, distributing data to all systems in the enterprise, easily monitoring and tracing data replication, distributing target system–specific data, and invoking key mapping and value mapping. This framework caters to design time, runtime, and monitoring requirements to replicate master data objects from SAP Master Data Governance to SAP systems and non-SAP systems.

Day-to-day business operations of companies are executed on enterprise system landscapes. SAP ERP and SAP S/4HANA are used by top enterprises of the world to run business processes such as order to cash, procure to pay, record to report, and so on. These enterprise systems consume master data to execute the business processes. For example, order to cash requires customer master data to create sales orders or invoices. Therefore, master data forms a critical component of every business process.

As master data is shared across all the enterprise systems, it makes more sense to maintain, consolidate, and govern master data in a centralized system with an SAP Master Data Governance solution and replicate the master data from SAP Master Data Governance to various target systems in the enterprise. Standardizing master data across the enterprise ensures transactional data integrity.

The data replication framework is a solution framework that enables replication of governed master data across the enterprise. SAP provides most of the design-time objects out of the box. Design-time objects, such as an outbound implementation class, need to be developed and configured only for custom objects using standard templates.

Figure 12.1 shows the various components of the data replication framework. The top part of the diagram shows the different ways you can interact with the data replication framework. You'll primarily interact with the data replication framework to replicate business objects or monitor the replication that has been triggered already. The middle part of the diagram shows various building blocks of the SAP Master Data Governance data replication framework and how they are grouped. Each component in the group interacts with other components of the group to enable replication of active master data from SAP Master Data Governance to its target systems.

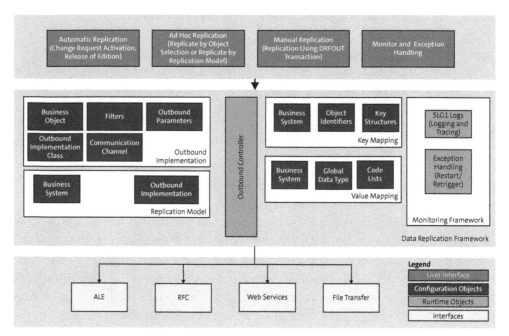

Figure 12.1 Logical Representation of the Data Replication Framework

This chapter is divided into the following sections:

- Section 12.1 describes the basic architecture of the data replication framework by explaining its building blocks and configuration objects.
- Section 12.2 provides an overview of available replication objects for the material master.
- Section 12.3 provides a list of out-of-the-box objects provided by SAP to enable replication of suppliers, customers, and business partners.
- Section 12.4 provides a list of out-of-the-box replication objects for financial master data replication.
- Section 12.5 provides options for replicating master data from SAP Master Data Governance to non-SAP target systems.
- Section 12.6 introduces you to the available options in SAP Master Data Governance to monitor the replication, as well as various other tools that are helpful during day-to-day operations.

12.1   Building Blocks and Configuration Objects

Each of the various building blocks of the data replication framework is an independent component, but all the building blocks interact with each other to enable replication of active master data from SAP Master Data Governance to the target system. Along with the building blocks, we'll discuss various configuration objects of the data replication framework. The configuration objects are used to influence data replication. Finally, we'll look at some steps you can take to enhance the default settings for outbound implementations.

12.1.1 Building Blocks

One of the prerequisites to understanding the data replication framework is to understand the functionality of its various building blocks. This section explains each of the building blocks in detail and describes the configuration settings of each building block, which you can use to characterize the building block or influence its behavior.

Business Objects

Business objects are used to represent real-world business entities in the data replication framework. Business objects can represent a business document (e.g., purchase order), a business partner (e.g., supplier or customer), or a controlling object (e.g., cost center or profit center). SAP Master Data Governance entities assigned to business objects are replicated together.

IMG path **Master Data Governance, Central Governance • Data Modeling • Define Entity Type to Be Used by Business Object Type** is used to define new business object type codes for business objects.

A business object should be assigned to an SAP Master Data Governance entity type. This assignment is used during runtime to decide what entity type data needs to be replicated for a business object. Figure 12.2 shows the configuration activity used for assigning an SAP Master Data Governance entity type to a business object.

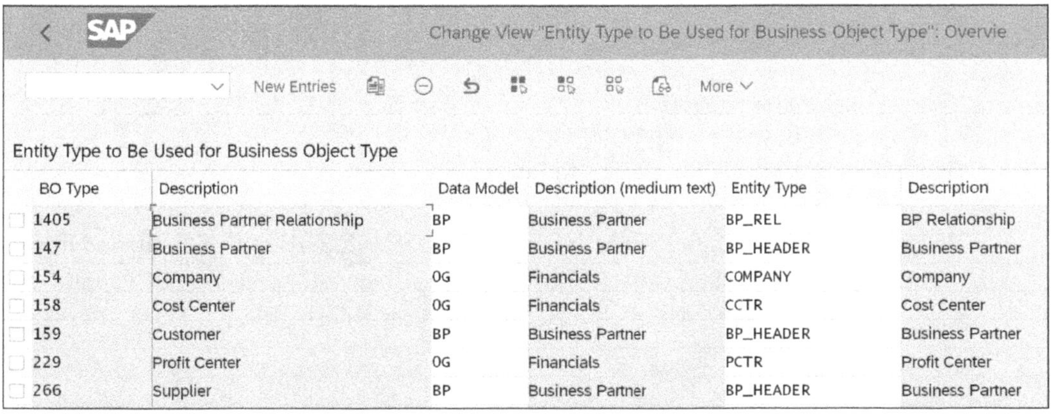

BO Type	Description	Data Model	Description (medium text)	Entity Type	Description
1405	Business Partner Relationship	BP	Business Partner	BP_REL	BP Relationship
147	Business Partner	BP	Business Partner	BP_HEADER	Business Partner
154	Company	OG	Financials	COMPANY	Company
158	Cost Center	OG	Financials	CCTR	Cost Center
159	Customer	BP	Business Partner	BP_HEADER	Business Partner
229	Profit Center	OG	Financials	PCTR	Profit Center
266	Supplier	BP	Business Partner	BP_HEADER	Business Partner

Figure 12.2 IMG Activity Showing an Entity Type Assigned to a Business Object

Common examples of business objects are suppliers, customers, and logical objects, such as cost center and profit center. In the SAP Master Data Governance context, the business object represents either a type 1 or type 4 entity. You can assign the same entity to multiple business objects.

Filter Objects and Filters

In the real world, the SAP Master Data Governance hub needs to replicate master data to multiple target systems. The SAP Master Data Governance hub should be able to apply target system–specific filters to replicate relevant data.

A filter object is used to determine which data can be selected and transferred to the target system. When assigned to a business object, the filter object is used to check the relevance of the data to be replicated to the target system both during initial (or full) replication and during delta replication. In this case, the filter criteria can be configured among any fields of the associated table using simple filters. Filter objects assigned to type 4 entities are called segment filters.

> **Note**
>
> Filter object F_MAT1 represents the plant segment of a material. This filter object directly relates to table MARC. To populate the filter values from table MARC, the table is assigned to the filter object directly. Figure 12.3 shows the F_MAT1 filter object and its association with table MARC ❶. It also shows an example of a filter object that isn't associated with a table ❷.

Figure 12.3 Associating Filter Objects to Tables

IMG path **DRF IMG · Data Replication · Enhance Default Settings for Outbound Implementations · Define Filter Objects** is used to define new filter objects and, if applicable, assign an SAP S/4HANA or SAP ERP table to the filter object.

> **Note**
>
> Another kind of filter object, F_GLACCASS (see Figure 12.3), isn't associated with any SAP S/4HANA or SAP ERP table. For this kind of filter object, either complex filters or implicit filters should be used to determine which business object should be selected for the replication.

Figure 12.4 shows the relationship between a business object and filter objects. Filters are assigned to filter objects. Filters are used to determine the selection criteria for choosing which business object instance is relevant for replication. It's mandatory to assign at least one filter to the filter object, but you can assign multiple filters if you like.

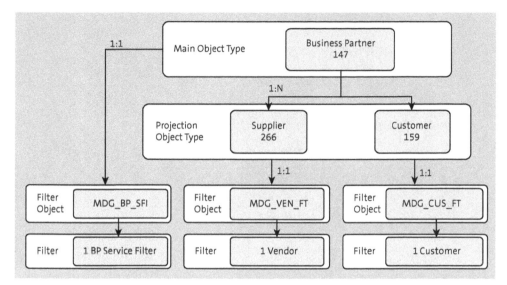

Figure 12.4 Relationship among Business Object, Filter Object, and Filters

Figure 12.5 depicts the hierarchically different kinds of filters.

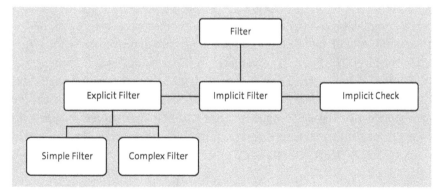

Figure 12.5 Different Kinds of Filters

The different kinds of filters are as follows:

- **Explicit filters**
  With explicit filters, you can specifically mention filter values for the filter parameters. Explicit filters are further divided into the following:
  - Simple explicit filters: This filter directly refers to the table assigned to the filter object. The filter parameters are derived from the structure assigned to the filter.

The fields of the structure must be present in the table assigned to the filter object. The SAP-delivered simple explicit filters can be extended using the append structure concept. The extended fields must be part of the table assigned to the filter object. Figure 12.6 depicts the simple explicit filter. F_MAT1 is the simple explicit filter assigned directly to table MARC in SAP S/4HANA or SAP ERP. The fields of the filter structure look similar to table MARC fields.

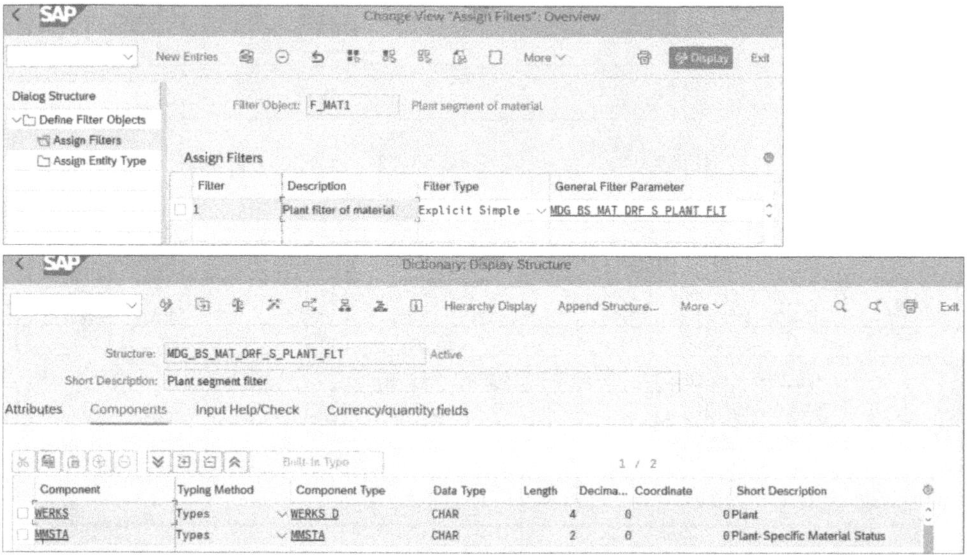

Figure 12.6 Simple Explicit Filter

Complex filters: Complex filters are defined for the filter objects that aren't assigned to the SAP S/4HANA or SAP ERP table. The filter parameters are determined by the structure assigned to the filter. The filter class evaluates the filter values and does the actual filtering. The filter class implements the IF_DRF_FILTER ABAP object interface. Extensions of this kind of filter are complex. The values for the filter parameter can be changed at any time. A filter class is assigned to evaluate the filter values and perform object filtering. The parameter structure determines which filter parameters are available in Transaction DRFF. Figure 12.7 shows an example of a complex filter configured in the system.

Figure 12.7 Explicit Complex Filter

- **Implicit filter and implicit checks**

  Implicit filters and implicit checks are fixed-implemented within each outbound implementation. You can activate such filters and checks in the Customizing for each outbound implementation so that the system executes the relevant filter. Implicit filters are designed to be reused in other outbound implementations, if required; implicit checks, on the other hand, aren't intended for this purpose.

IMG path **DRF IMG • Data Replication • Enhance Default Settings for Outbound Implementations • Define Filter Objects-Assign Filters** is used to assign filters to filter objects.

Outbound Implementations

The outbound implementation defines how the replication of the business object is executed. Outbound implementation defines the communication channel (Application Link Enabling [ALE], remote function call [RFC], web services) of the business object's replication and outbound implementation class. The communication channel denotes the means of transmitting data to target systems of the SAP Master Data Governance system. The available communication channels are as follows:

- Replication via web services
- Replication via IDoc
- Replication via file
- Replication via RFC

The outbound implementation is assigned to the business object directly or indirectly. When the business object is assigned indirectly to an outbound implementation that has web services as the communication channel, the business object is assigned to the service operation, and the service operation is assigned to the outbound implementation. For all other outbound implementations, the business object is assigned directly to the outbound implementation. The outbound implementation class is the IF_DRF_ OUTBOUND ABAP class implementing interface. Outbound parameters are also assigned to outbound implementations.

Following are the functions of an outbound implementation class:

- Read the runtime parameters from the outbound controller and save the parameters in the runtime memory of the outbound implementation class. These parameters are consumed as required during the execution of the outbound implementation class. The outbound implementation class can also decide to excuse itself from further processing by changing the runtime parameters.
- Enrich the filter criteria irrespective of the Customizing settings. Filter criteria defined in the configuration can be enriched based on runtime data values.
- Read the complete data of the relevant objects (after filters are applied, and change analysis is performed) for replication.
- Perform change analysis for direct replication and ad hoc replications.

- Map the replication data from the SAP Master Data Governance format to the replication format.

- Hold the code line to initiate/trigger the replication based on the communication channel of the outbound implementation.

- Perform post-replication steps such as identifying success and error messages, updating the data replication framework log, and so on.

Outbound Parameters

Outbound parameters are assigned to outbound implementations to add more context and conditions to the outbound replication. Following is the list of standard parameters provided out of the box by SAP:

- **Package Size for Bulk Messages**
  This parameter tells the outbound implementation how many messages (one message corresponds to one instance of a business object) are to be packaged into one package. Use this parameter wisely to optimize the performance of the replication. This parameter takes any numeric value.

- **Send Delta Information Only**
  This parameter is used to tell the outbound implementation to replicate only delta changes to the target system. The values for this parameter are **Y** (yes, send delta information only) and **N** (no, don't send the delta information).

- **Size of Parallel Task Delta Analysis**
  This parameter is only applicable when manual data replication is initiated by a user and the user has selected parallel processing. This parameter performs change pointer analysis on the filtered objects in a parallel task.

Business System

A business system in the context of the data replication framework is used to represent the physical system in an enterprise landscape to which master data is replicated. A business system can represent both the local system and target system. Business systems for local systems and target systems are defined in the System Landscape Directory (SLD). If the SLD isn't available, then Business Add-In (BAdI) `MDG_IDM_GET_LCL_SYSTEM` is defined to determine the local system.

Replication Models

Replication models define what data (through outbound implementation) is sent to which system (through the business system) under what conditions (through outbound parameters). Replication models can be activated and deactivated at will.

Key Mapping

Today's enterprise landscapes are highly distributed. The immediate implication of these kinds of landscapes is that a business process is executed across enterprise systems.

Note

The vendor lifecycle is a very good example of executing a business process across systems. The vendor lifecycle involves identifying, onboarding, maintaining, transacting with, and terminating a vendor. In most enterprises, this process is executed across multiple systems. For example, identifying a vendor is done on business network systems such as SAP Ariba. Onboarding and maintenance of vendors is done on a governance system such as SAP Master Data Governance. Transacting with vendors occurs on SAP ERP or SAP S/4HANA systems.

In these kinds of scenarios, due to system limitations or business constraints, it's not possible to maintain the same vendor IDs across all systems. Therefore, you need a repository that keeps track of vendor IDs used by different systems. The solution for this problem is the SAP key mapping framework.

Note

A business object can be identified by different object identifiers in different systems that aren't harmonized. The key mapping framework provides an aid to store the relationship of different object identifiers of the same business object across different systems.

Figure 12.8 shows key mapping using a cost center as an example. The system maps key values of the cost center in different systems against the key value of the cost center in the SAP Master Data Governance hub.

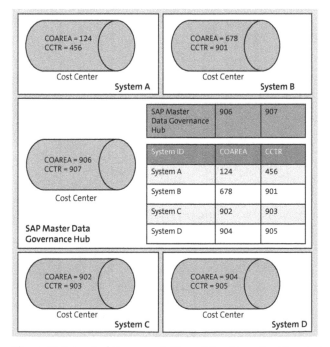

Figure 12.8 Logical Representation of Key Mapping Concept

The key mapping framework is invoked by the outbound implementation using the various key mapping application programming interfaces (APIs). The data replication framework automatically doesn't trigger the key mapping. Key mapping consumers such as the outbound implementation class (for outbound) or proxy class (for inbound) are responsible for invoking the key mapping API to convert the key to a value known to the target system.

The following tools are provided by the key mapping framework:

- **Adjust key mapping after client copy**
  A client copy is performed to copy production data to test systems or to create a new client out of an existing client. When the client copy is done, key mapping tables are copied as they are. The key mapping tables after the client copy need to be adjusted to reflect the new business system ID for the SAP Master Data Governance hub and target systems. Adjusting key mapping to reflect the new business system IDs is done using program RMDG_ADJUST_KEY_MAPPING. This program can also be called using Transaction MDG_ADJUST_IDM. Figure 12.9 shows the selection screen of the program.

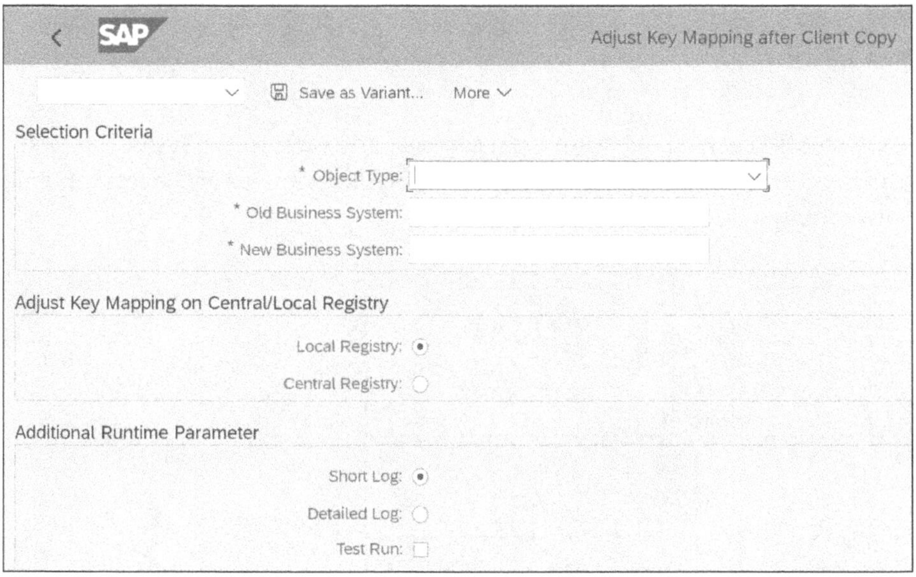

Figure 12.9 Selection Screen of Program RMDG_ADJUST_KEY_MAPPING

Table 12.1 describes some of the options on the program RMDG_ADJUST_MAPPING selection screen.

Selection Element	Description
Object Type	Select the business object type from the dropdown list.

Table 12.1 Selection Screen Elements of Report MDG_ADJUST_KEY_MAPPING

Selection Element	Description
Old Business System	Select the business system ID of the old system, which needs to be replaced for the selected business object.
New Business System	Select the business system ID of the new business system, which replaces the old system business object.
Local Registry	Select this radio button to replace the old business system ID with the new business system ID in the local registry for the selected business object type.
Central Registry	If **Central Registry** is selected, then the same registry might be used by the original client and the new client. Therefore, to cater to both new and old clients, all the selected key mapping entries for the business object are copied first, and then the old business system ID is replaced with the new business system ID in the copied entries.

Table 12.1 Selection Screen Elements of Report MDG_ADJUST_KEY_MAPPING (Cont.)

- **Manual maintenance of key mapping**

  Key mapping is usually updated automatically by the response message from the target system, and the response message will have the keys of the business object in the target system. Sometimes it's required to maintain the key mapping manually for an object using the SAP-delivered MDG_BS_WD_ID_MATCH_SERVIC Web Dynpro user interface (UI). This UI can also be called using Transaction MDG_KM_MAINTAIN. Figure 12.10 depicts the web application to maintain the key mapping manually. Ideally, all SAP-delivered SAP Business Client roles have this UI added to the menu path. To maintain the key mapping UI, you should know the full details.

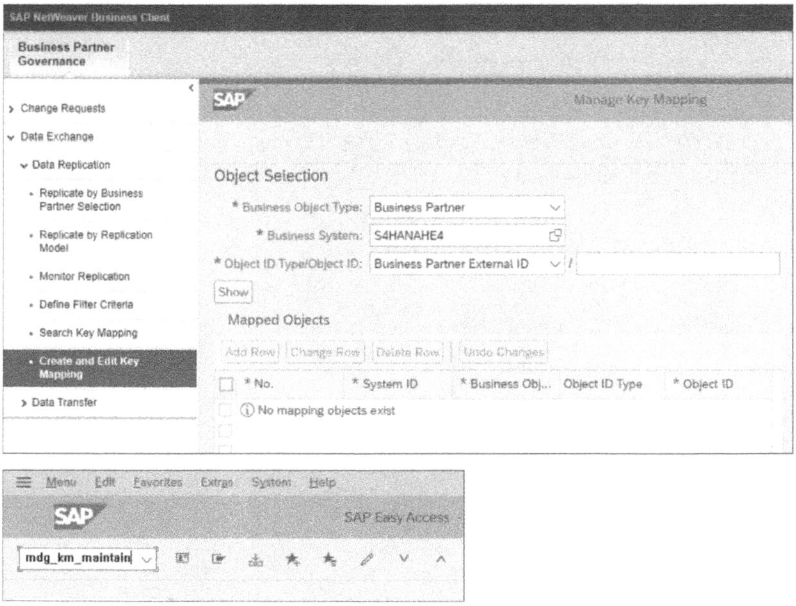

Figure 12.10 Different Ways to Open the Manual Maintenance of the Key Mapping UI

Table 12.2 explains each screen element of the web application.

Screen Element	Description
Business Object Type	The business object value
Business System	The business system ID for which the key mapping entries should be maintained
Object ID Type	The object ID type for the business object
Object ID	The ID value of the object ID type

Table 12.2 Key Mapping Manual Maintenance UI Screen Options

- **Search key mapping**

  By allowing the use of wild cards, this UI is provided to search for the key mapping when you're not sure about the ID value. SAP provides two interfaces for this: a Web Dynpro UI (MDG_BS_WD_ANALYSE_IDM) and an SAP GUI–based UI, which can be accessed via Transaction MDG_ANALYSE_IDM. Figure 12.11 shows the SAP GUI application and web applications used for searching key mapping.

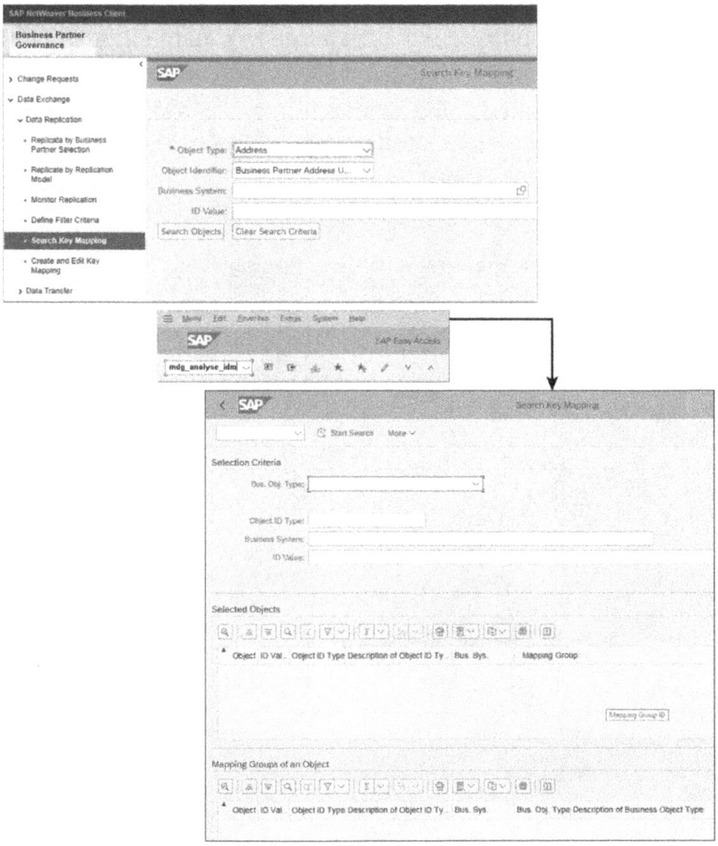

Figure 12.11 Searching Key Mappings

- **SOA services for key mapping**
  SAP Master Data Governance also provides service-oriented architecture (SOA) services that can be used to receive and replicate key mapping information. They also help in checking the status of key mapping information from client systems.

The following lists the SOA services that are published in the SAP API Hub, which can be leveraged for key mapping purposes:

- `KeyMappingBulkReplicateRequest_In`
  This bulk replication services enables you to receive key mapping of supported business object types in the receiver system from the sender system.

- `KeyMappingBulkReplicateRequest_Out`
  This bulk replication service enables you to send key mapping of supported business object types from the receiver system to the sender system.

- `KeyMappingBulkReplicateConfirmation_In`
  This service enables you to get the status of key mapping in the receiver system from the sender system.

- `KeyMappingBulkReplicateConfirmation_Out`
  This service enables you to get the status of key mapping from the receiver system to the sender system.

Value Mapping

Value mapping is a way to handle the conversion of values during replication from a source system–specific value to a target system–specific value. Value mapping is maintained based on a global data type or data element. Value mapping for services-based replication is based on the fact that service-based replication can send the list ID and list agency ID as part of the message.

These details are in turn used by the consuming system to convert the values. ALE doesn't have this ability automatically. In this case, the SAP Master Data Governance system should perform the value mapping in the outbound implementation class before triggering the actual message.

Value mapping can also be maintained as centralized code lists, which can be accessed by every system in the landscape.

Outbound Controller

The outbound controller is responsible for triggering the outbound replication. The outbound controller is technically represented by the `CL_DRF_OUTBOUND` class, which is instantiated during runtime by the calling application (workflow by calling activation step, manual replication, or ad hoc replication).

Replication Modes

The following sections describe the different replication modes available in the SAP Master Data Governance data replication framework.

Direct or Automatic Replication

Direct or automatic replication takes place after a change request is activated, depending on the customization. If a change request isn't edition dependent, replication is triggered after activation by default. For change requests that are edition dependent, automatic replication will depend on the settings of the corresponding edition type. Figure 12.12 shows the logical flow of direct replication until the triggering of the data replication framework outbound controller.

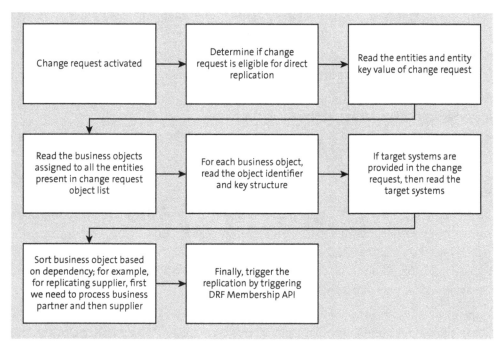

Figure 12.12 Logical Flow of Automatic Replication

Ad Hoc Replication

Ad hoc replication is used when mass replication is required. For example, when a new target system is configured, ad hoc replication is used to replicate all the data to this new system. The process of triggering the replication happens in the background. The ad hoc application for replication is DRF_AD_HOC_REPLICATION. Figure 12.13 shows the technical steps triggered by the ad hoc replication application to determine the relevant objects for replication and the corresponding target systems.

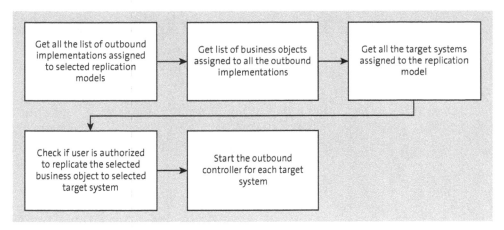

Figure 12.13 Logical Flow of Ad Hoc Replication

Manual Replication

Manual replication is triggered by the user based on object selection. For example, if replication of a business object fails, a master data steward can use this functionality to replicate the objects again. Manual replication can be done in two ways, as follows:

- Using Transaction DRFOUT in SAP GUI
- Using SAP Business Client to replicate business objects based on the object key

Figure 12.14 shows Transaction DRFOUT in SAP GUI. This report is used to create one or multiple outbound messages based on the selection criteria. One major difference between ad hoc replication and Transaction DRFOUT is that when executing Transaction DRFOUT, you can maintain the manual filter criteria, which overwrites the filter criteria maintained in Transaction DRFF.

Table 12.3 describes some of the selection screen fields of Transaction DRFOUT.

Field	Description
Replication Model	Enter the replication model. This field is mandatory.
Outbound Implementation	Enter the outbound implementation.
Replication Mode	- **Initialization**: The system processes all data of the selected outbound implementations that are required for a replication model. - **Changes**: The program analyzes all data that was changed since the last change run or since the last initialization. - **Manual**: The program selects the records based on the filter criteria and replicates the selected data; if no selection criteria is specified, the system replicates all the data for an outbound implementation.

Table 12.3 Transaction DRFOUT Fields in SAP GUI

Field	Description
Parallel Processing	Activate the parallel processing for the outbound data replication.

Table 12.3 Transaction DRFOUT Fields in SAP GUI (Cont.)

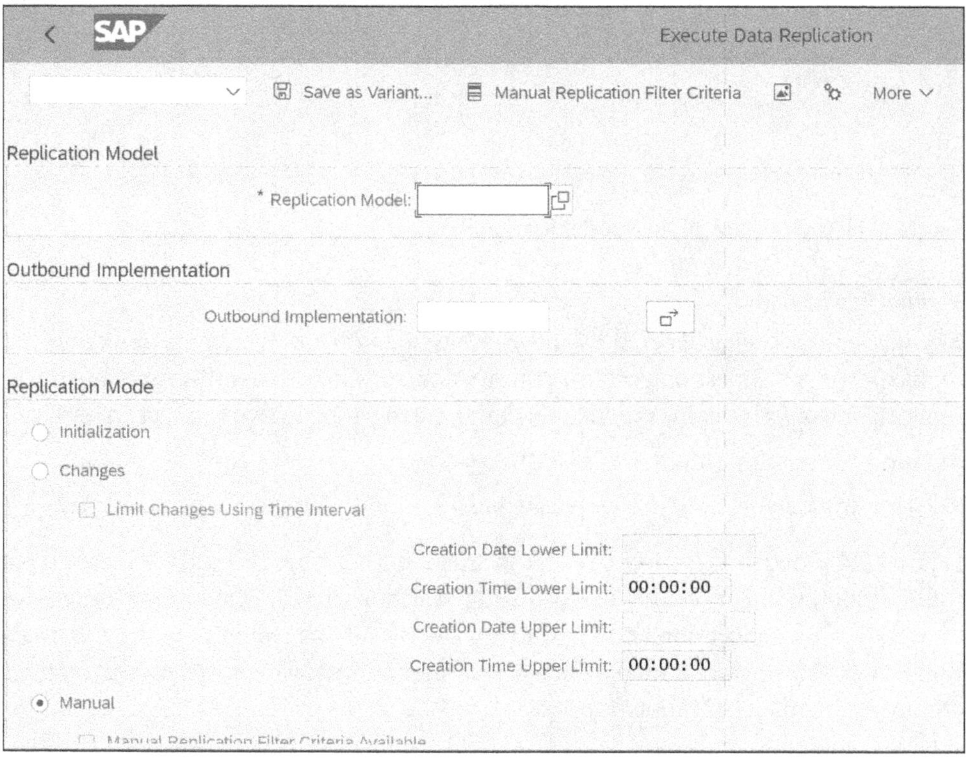

Figure 12.14 SAP GUI Application to Execute the Replication Manually

12.1.2   Configuration Objects

In this section, we'll go into detail about various configuration objects that are available as part of the data replication framework.

Define Custom Settings for Data Replication

This configuration node groups the list of configuration activities that you need to perform to enable data replication of the business object to the target system.

Use IMG path **DRF IMG • Data Replication • Define Custom Settings for Data Replication** to view the configuration activities required for setting up data replication, as shown in Figure 12.15

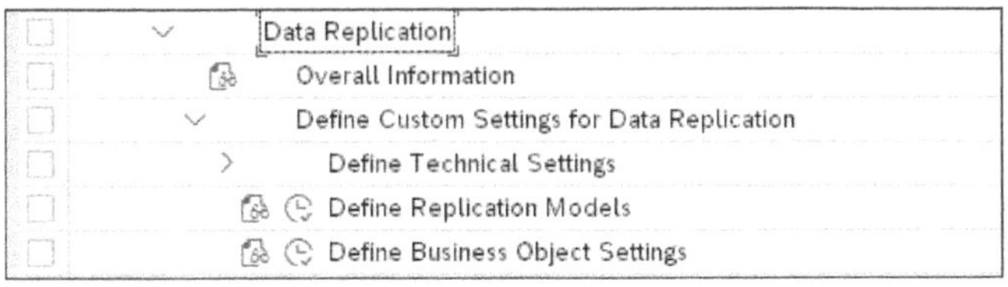

Figure 12.15 IMG Activity to Define Custom Settings for Data Replication

This **Define Technical Settings for Business Systems** IMG activity is used to define the business systems from either the SLD or locally defined logical systems (see Figure 12.16).

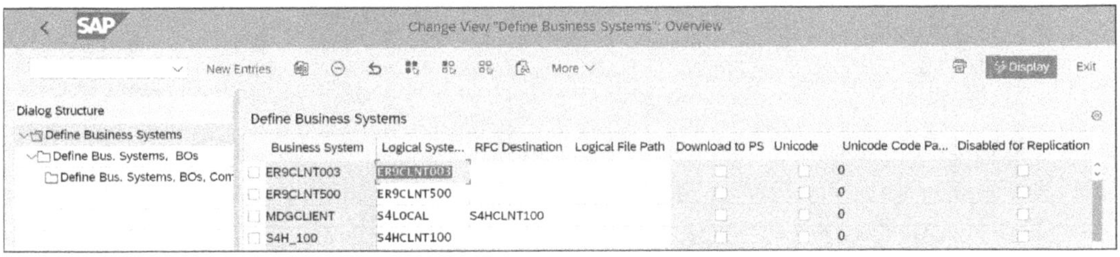

Figure 12.16 Defining Business Systems

IMG path **DRF IMG · Data Replication Define Custom Settings for Data Replication · Define Technical Settings · Define Technical Settings for Business Systems** is used to define the business system and business system settings.

Table 12.4 describes some of the configuration fields of the IMG activity used for defining the business system.

Configuration Field	Description
Business System	Business systems represent a physical or logical enterprise system that needs to be connected to the SAP Master Data Governance system either for inbound or outbound replication. Business systems are added in SLD. If SLD isn't available, business systems can be created locally.
Logical System	Logical system is used when the communication channel is ALE/IDoc. This logical system name is passed on to the IDoc framework to determine the partner profile and generate IDocs for further processing.
RFC Destination	This destination is used when the communication channel between the SAP Master Data Governance system and the target business system is through RFC. This RFC destination must be created in Transaction SM59 before entering in this IMG activity.

Table 12.4 Configuration Fields for Defining a Business System

Configuration Field	Description
Logical File Path	This value is used when the communication channel is replication via file. This value is passed to the outbound implementation during runtime, and the outbound implementation stores the formatted file in this location. The logical file properties must be configured in Transaction FILE in the SAP GUI before entering in this IMG activity.
Unicode	This indicates whether the system accepts Unicode.
Disabled for Replication	This option enables users to disable all kinds of replication to the business system. The replication won't happen even though the corresponding replication model is active.

Table 12.4 Configuration Fields for Defining a Business System (Cont.)

Replication Models

A replication model is a configuration object used for defining required settings for replicating master data to target systems. The replication model is used to define which business object data is replicated to which business system. An active replication model is a prerequisite for successful replication of master data to the target system. Figure 12.17 shows various settings that can be defined for a replication model.

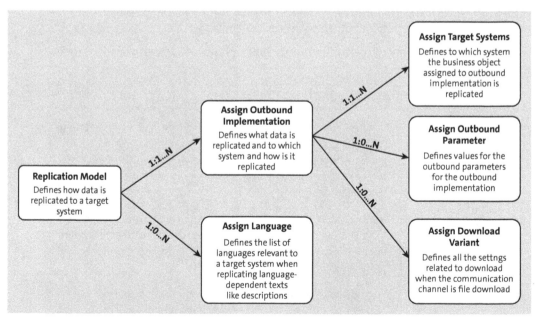

Figure 12.17 Overview of Various IMG Activities to Define a Replication Model

Replication models are used to perform the following actions:

- Define what data should be considered as relevant for a target system.
- Define the target system.
- Define the values for outbound parameters.

Replication models can be activated and deactivated. You can trigger ad hoc replication based on the replication model. The filter values for simple explicit and complex explicit filters are maintained at the replication model level in Transaction DRFF.

The following sections explain in detail various configuration fields used for defining settings for the replication model and assigning the outbound implementation to the replication model.

Define Replication Model

This section introduces configuration fields that can be used to create a new replication model. Figure 12.18 shows configuration for a replication model.

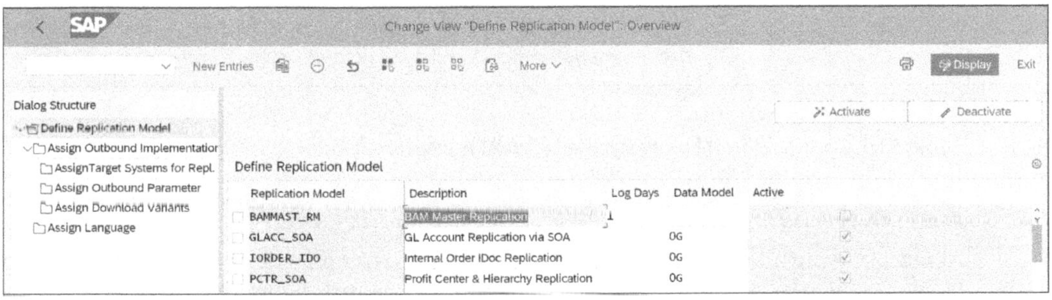

Figure 12.18 IMG Activity to Define a Replication Model

IMG path **DRF IMG · Data Replication · Define Custom Settings for Data Replication · Define Replication Models** is used for defining replication models.

Table 12.5 lists the configuration fields for defining a replication model.

Configuration Field	Description
Replication Model	No standard content for this activity is delivered by SAP. No namespace limitations apply here. A replication model can be created per the target system or per the business object. Configuring the filters per business object limits your ability to maintain the filters per the target system. You're free to create the replication model per your specific requirements.
Description	Provide a description for the replication model. Maintain translations for this description to cater to multilingual users.

Table 12.5 Configuration Fields for the Define Replication Model

Configuration Field	Description
Log Days	The data replication framework stores all the messages issued during replication as an application log (Transaction SLG1) under the FMDM application log object. The value indicates the expiration duration of the application log for the replication log.
Data Model	Assign a replication model to a data model.
Active	This field is disabled for user input. The value for this field can be changed using the **Activate** and **Deactivate** buttons: ■ **Activate**: A consistency check for the replication model is triggered. If the replication model passes the consistency check, then the replication model is activated; otherwise, errors related to the replication model activation are displayed. You can maintain filters only for active data models. ■ **Deactivate**: The replication model is deactivated, and no business objects associated with the outbound implementations assigned to the replication model can be replicated to the corresponding target systems.

Table 12.5 Configuration Fields for the Define Replication Model (Cont.)

Assign Outbound Implementation

At least one outbound implementation should be assigned to a replication model. The sequence of outbound implementation must also be maintained. Figure 12.19 shows the IMG activity for this assignment.

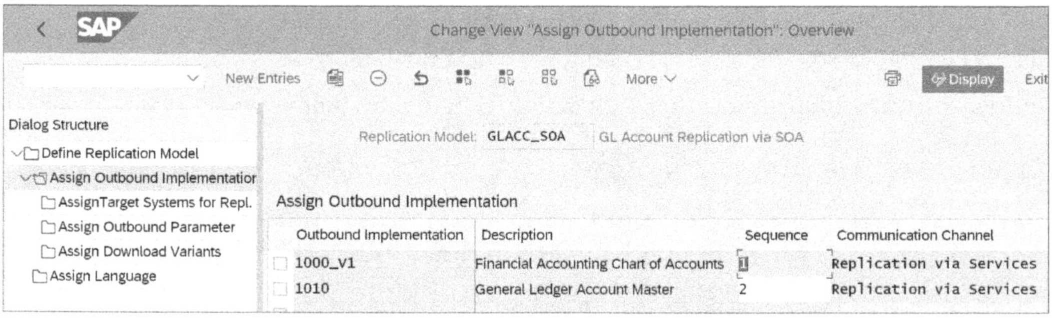

Figure 12.19 IMG Activity to Assign an Outbound Implementation to Replication Models

IMG path **DRF IMG · Data Replication · Define Custom Settings for Data Replication · Define Replication Models · Assign Outbound Implementation** is used to assign an outbound implementation to a replication model.

Table 12.6 explains the configuration fields used for making the assignment.

Configuration Field	Description
Outbound Implementation	Assign the outbound implementation to the replication model. By performing this activity, you implicitly provide the following details to the data replication framework: • What business object is to be replicated? • Which primary filters and segment filters are invoked? • What is the communication channel for the replication of the business object to the target data? • What is the outbound implementation class?
Description	This is a display-only field that stores the description of the outbound implementation defined during its creation.
Sequence	This field accepts absolute numeric values. When more than one outbound implementation is assigned to a replication model, sometimes it's required to sequence the outbound implementations. This is true especially when you have separate business objects (and thereby separate outbound implementations) for the main entity (type 1) and a dependent entity (type 4 entity). In this case, the outbound implementation related to the main entity is triggered first, and then the outbound implementation related to the dependent entity is triggered. For example, general ledger account basic data and general ledger account company code data are represented by two business objects and respective outbound implementations. When replicating these objects to target systems, it makes sense to replicate general ledger account basic data first and company code data next.
Communication Channel	This is a display-only field. The value for this field is derived based on the outbound implementation. This field indicates what mechanism is used to replicate the business object data to the target system. The available communication channels are **Replication via IDoc**, **Replication via services**, **Replication via file**, and **Replication via RFC**.
Filter Time	This field is used to configure whether the filter should be applied after change analysis or before change analysis. This applies only if the current replication is a change message, and delta replication is switched on.

Table 12.6 Configuration Fields for the Assign Outbound Implementation

Your next step is to assign the target system for the replication model/outbound implementation, as shown in Figure 12.20.

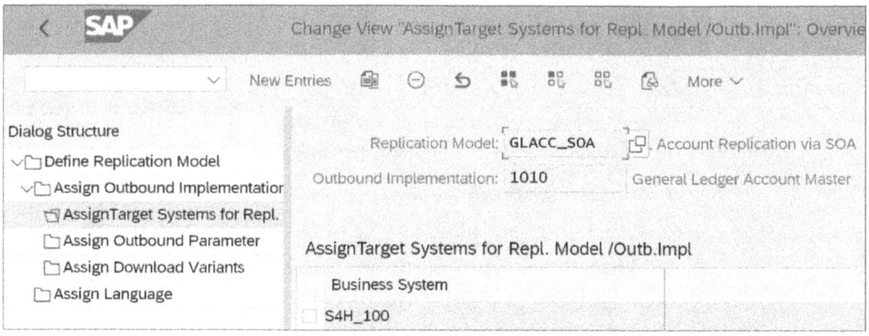

Figure 12.20 IMG Activity Depicting How to Assign a Target System to a Replication Model

IMG path **DRF IMG • Data Replication • Define Custom Settings for Data Replication • Define Replication Models • Assign Outbound Implementation • Assign Target Systems for Repl. Model/Outb.Impl** is used for assigning target systems to outbound implementations. The only new relevant configuration field is **Business System**, the target system that receives the business object data assigned to the outbound implementation. The **Business System** field should be configured as defined in Section 12.1.1.

Finally, you'll need to assign the outbound parameter. The outbound parameter is used to provide more information during runtime to the outbound implementation. Figure 12.21 shows the IMG activity to maintain values for outbound parameters.

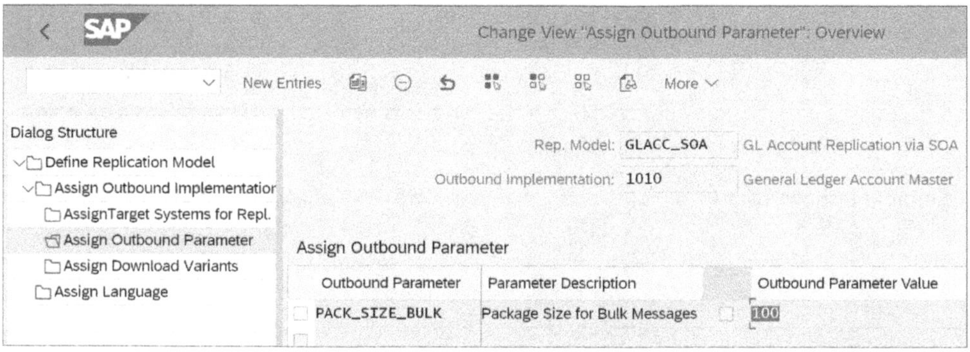

Figure 12.21 IMG Activity Depicting How to Maintain the Values for Outbound Parameters

IMG path **DRFIMG • Data Replication • Define Custom Settings for Data Replication • Define Replication Models • Assign Outbound Implementation • Assign Outbound Parameter** is used to maintain values for outbound implementations.

Table 12.7 describes the configuration fields of the IMG activity.

Configuration Field	Description
Outbound Parameter	This is the outbound parameter name.

Table 12.7 Configuration Fields for the Assign Outbound Parameter to Outbound Implementation Configuration Activity

Configuration Field	Description
Parameter Description	This is the description of the outbound parameter.
Outbound Parameter Value	This field is used to enter the outbound parameter value.
	The characteristics of the parameter should follow the rules specified during the definition of the outbound parameters. For example, the SEND_DELTA_INFO outbound parameter should only have **N** (no) or **Y** (yes) as the outbound parameter value. The PACK_SIZE_BULK outbound parameter should be an integer with a value length as **10**. Failure to follow the specifications will result in an outbound parameter not being evaluated during replications.

Table 12.7 Configuration Fields for the Assign Outbound Parameter to Outbound Implementation Configuration Activity (Cont.)

12.1.3   Enhance Default Settings for Outbound Implementations

The **Enhance Default Settings for Outbound Implementations** IMG node is a grouping of different configuration activities that can be used to either enhance the default settings for outbound implementations or create new settings for outbound implementations (Figure 12.22).

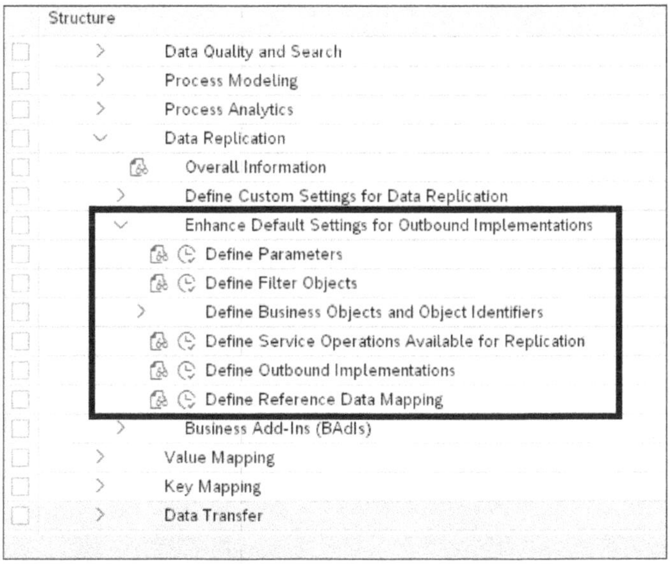

Figure 12.22 IMG Activity Showing Configuration Nodes Available for Outbound Implementations

IMG path **DRF IMG · Data Replication · Enhance Default Settings for Outbound Implementations** is used to view the list of default settings for outbound implementations.

This IMG activity is a grouping of all the configurations related to outbound implementations. The following shows how each is linked to outbound implementations:

- **Parameters (1:N)**
  Used to add more context and replication conditions.

- **Filter objects (1:1)**
  Used by the outbound implementation to evaluate relevant objects for replication.

- **Business object (1:1)**
  Logical representation of a master data object such as supplier.

- **Service operations (1:1)**
  Required only for replication via web services. Defines the enterprise services repository (ESR) name and proxy class.

- **Outbound interface models (1:1)**
  Required only for replication via RFC.

In the following sections, we'll discuss the first three of these in detail. The final two have been omitted because they aren't used very often. The following sections also describe how to define object identifiers for each business object and how to define object nodes to group multiple object identifiers in one mapping group.

Define Parameters

The **Define Parameters** IMG activity is used to define parameters and their technical characteristics. Parameters are assigned to outbound implementations. You can assign multiple parameters to one outbound implementation, and the same parameter can be assigned to multiple outbound implementations. Values for the parameters are assigned while defining the replication model. Refer to Section 12.1.2 for more details.

The parameters, along with parameter values, enrich the runtime environment of the outbound implementation with target system–specific information. Figure 12.23 shows the IMG activity for defining outbound parameters.

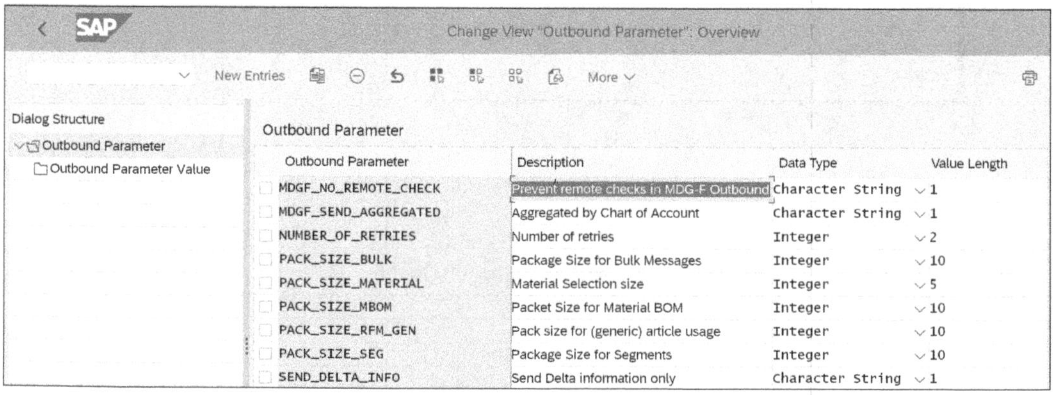

Figure 12.23 IMG Activity to Define Outbound Parameters

IMG path **DRF IMG · Data Replication · Enhance Default Settings for Outbound Implementations · Define Parameters** is used for defining outbound implementation parameters.

Table 12.8 describes the configuration fields of this IMG activity.

Configuration Field	Description
Outbound Parameter	Give a unique identifier to the outbound parameter.
Description	Provide a meaningful description.
Data Type	Select the technical characteristics of the value that can be entered as an outbound parameter value. The list of available values includes **Integer** and **Character String**.
Value Length	Describe the length of the outbound parameter value.

Table 12.8 Configuration Fields for the Define Parameters Configuration Activity

You can define a value list for every outbound parameter to help you configure the correct values when assigning the outbound implementation to the replication model. Figure 12.24 shows the IMG activity for defining parameter values for an outbound parameter.

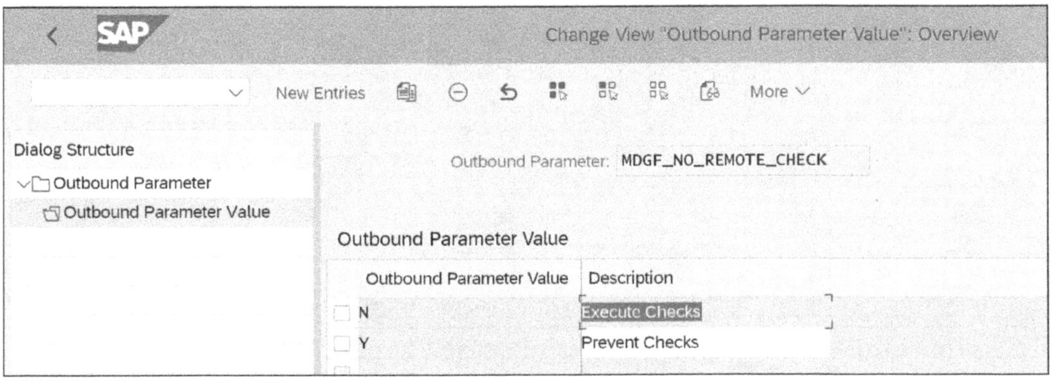

Figure 12.24 IMG Activity Showing How to Configure Outbound Parameter Values for an Outbound Parameter

IMG path **DRF IMG · Data Replication · Enhance Default Settings for Outbound Implementations · Define Parameters · Define Parameter Value** is used for defining outbound parameter values.

Table 12.9 describes the configuration fields of the IMG activity.

Configuration Field	Description
Outbound Parameter Value	This field is used to enter the list of possible values for an outbound parameter. The values must conform to the technical characteristics of the parameter.
Description	This is the logical description of the parameter.

Table 12.9 Configuration Fields for the Define Parameter Values Configuration Activity

Define Filter Objects

This section covers the IMG activity for defining filter objects. For more details on filter objects, refer to Section 12.1.1. Figure 12.25 shows the **Define Filter Objects** IMG activity.

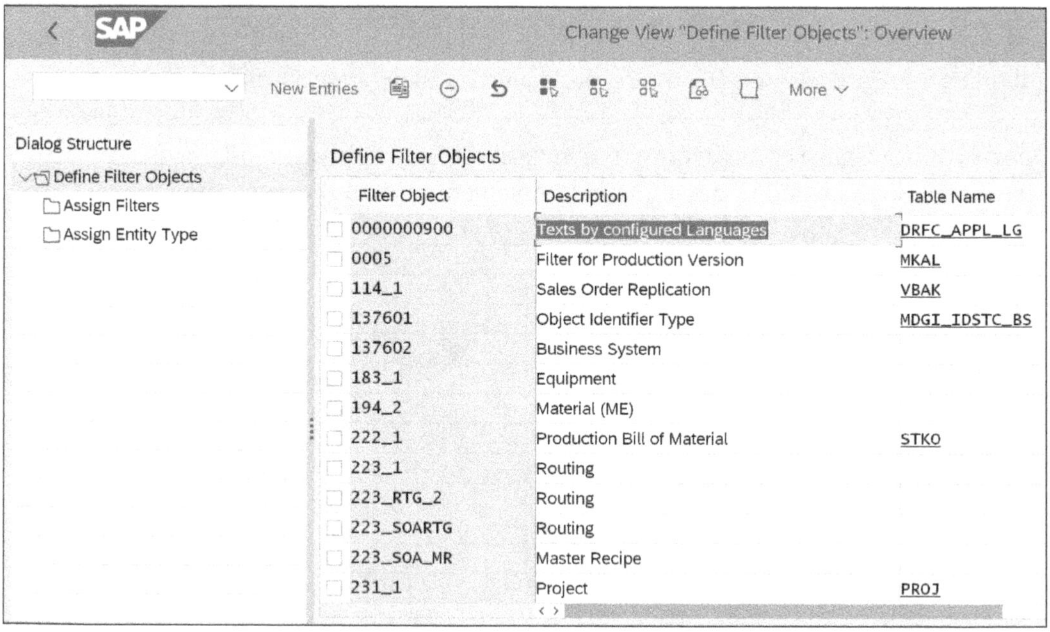

Figure 12.25 IMG Activity Depicting How to Define Filter Objects

IMG path **DRF IMG · Data Replication · Enhance Default Settings for Outbound Implementations · Define Filter Objects** is used for defining new filters or changing the settings for existing filters.

Table 12.10 describes the configuration fields of this IMG activity.

Configuration Field	Description
Filter Object	Enter a unique identifier for the filter object.
Description	Enter a short description of the filter object.

Table 12.10 Configuration Fields for the Define Filters Configuration Activity

Configuration Field	Description
Table Name	Enter the name of the table from which the value list for the filter criteria is selected. This value list is displayed when defining filter criteria in Transaction DRFF. Entry in this field is mandatory if you're defining a simple explicit filter.

Table 12.10 Configuration Fields for the Define Filters Configuration Activity (Cont.)

Filters are assigned to filter objects and are the actual objects that store settings related to the filtering of data. Figure 12.26 shows the IMG activity to **Define Filters Objects**.

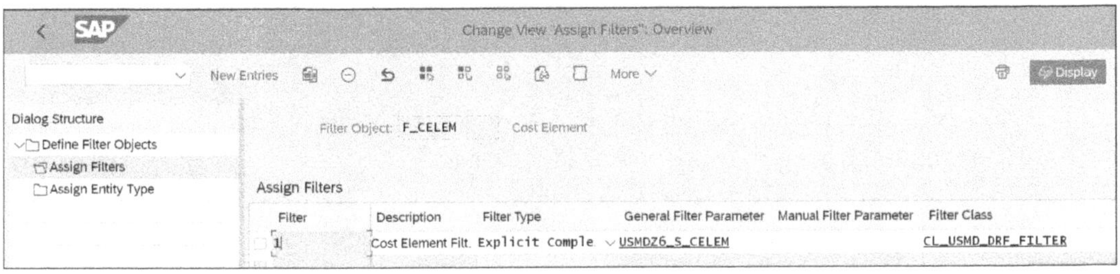

Figure 12.26 IMG Activity Depicting How to Assign Filters to Filter Objects

IMG path **DRF IMG · Data Replication · Enhance Default Settings for Outbound Implementations · Define Filter Objects · Assign Filters** is used for assigning filters to filter objects and defining settings for filters. Table 12.11 describes the configuration fields of this IMG activity.

Configuration Field	Description
Filter	Enter a unique numeric value of length **2** as the filter identifier.
Description	Provide a logical description of the filter.
Filter Type	Specify the type of filter. Refer to Section 12.1.1 for more details.
General Filter Parameter	Enter the name of the structure that holds the filter criteria as fields. For simple explicit filters, this structure should be a subset of the table assigned to the filter object. For other types, this structure is used in the filter class to evaluate the filter criteria. This structure is used during filter criteria configuration in Transaction DRFF. This value is used only for the explicit complex filter.
Manual Filter Parameter	This value is evaluated only for manual replication. It defines the fields for entering the filter criteria during manual replication. This value is used only for the explicit complex filter.
Filter Class	Enter any class that implements the IF_DRF_FILTER interface. This value is only considered for explicit complex filters and implicit filters.

Table 12.11 Configuration Fields for the Assign Filter to Filter Objects Configuration Activity

Finally, you can use the **Assign Entity Type** IMG activity to assign entity types to filter objects. This activity is used mainly in the filter class to read the metadata of the entity to perform data filtering. Figure 12.27 shows an entity being assigned to a filter object.

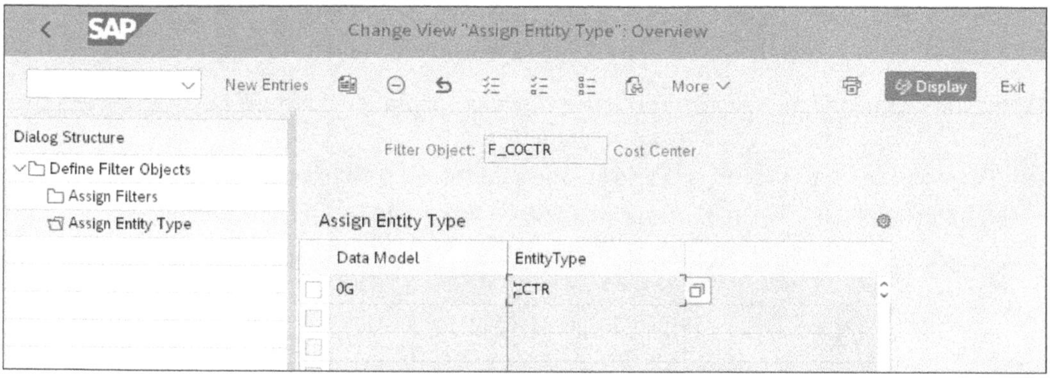

Figure 12.27 Assigning an Entity Type to a Filter Object

IMG path **DRF IMG · Data Replication · Enhance Default Settings for Outbound Implementations · Define Filter Objects · Assign Entity Type** is used for assigning an entity to a filter object.

Table 12.12 describes the configuration fields of this IMG activity.

Configuration Field	Description
Data Model	Enter a valid active data model.
EntityType	Enter a type 1 or type 4 entity.

Table 12.12 Configuration Fields for the Assign Entity Type to Filter Objects Configuration Activity

Define and Assign Business Objects

For more information on business objects, refer to Section 12.1.1. Business object type codes are defined/created in the IMG activity **Master Data Governance, Central Governance · General Settings · Data Modeling · Define Business Object Type Codes**. In the same IMG activity path, you can assign a business object to a data model by assigning the business object to an entity. Figure 12.28 shows the IMG activity used for defining the further attributes of a business object in the context of the data replication framework.

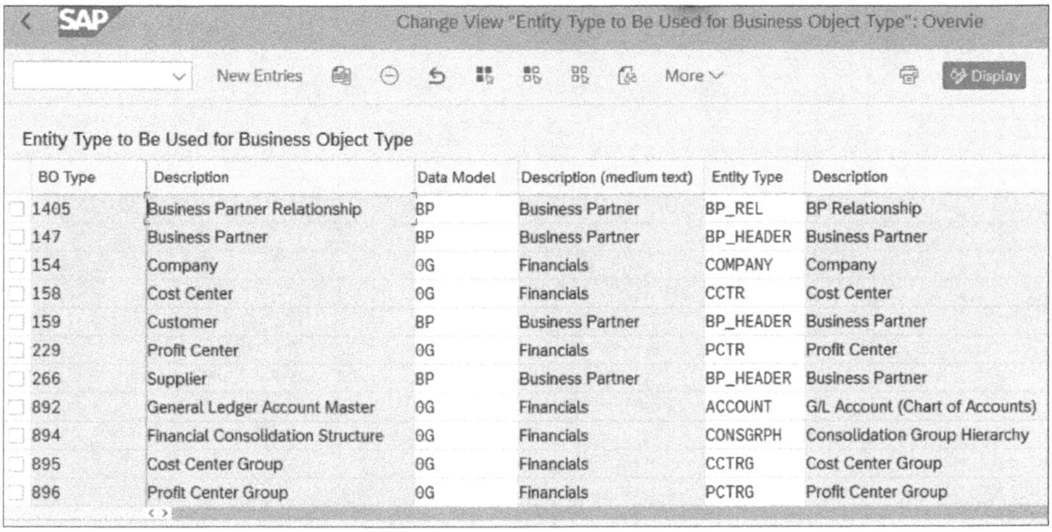

Figure 12.28 Configuration Activity to Define a New Business Object

Table 12.13 describes the configuration fields of the IMG activity.

Configuration Field	Description
BO Type	Unique numeric identifier for the business object.
Description	Text describing the business object in terms of business semantics.
Data model	Data model to which the business object must be assigned.
Entity Type	Type 1 entity of the value entered in the **Data Model** field.

Table 12.13 Configuration Fields for the Definition of a Business Object

After the business objects are defined, they can also have filter objects assigned to them. Filter objects act as aids during the data replication framework runtime to evaluate the relevant instances of business objects based on the filter criteria. This filter criterion is maintained per outbound implementation. Filter objects are assigned to outbound implementations indirectly via business objects. Filter objects are assigned to business objects, and business objects are assigned to outbound implementations. Figure 12.29 shows the IMG activity to **Assign Filter Objects to Business Objects**.

> **Note**
>
> A business object can have only one filter object assigned to it, and an outbound implementation likewise can have only one business object assigned to it. A business object, however, can be assigned to any number of outbound implementations.

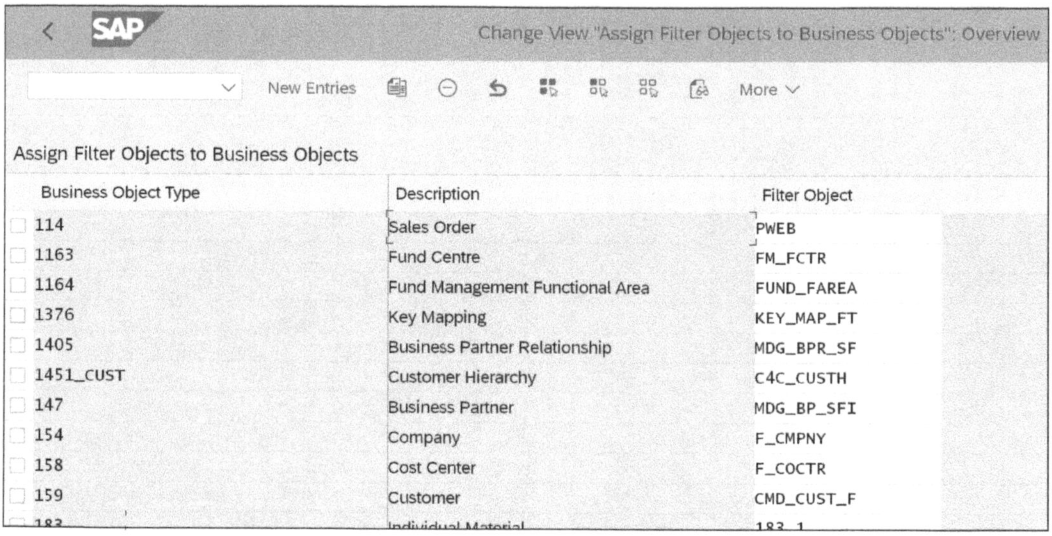

Figure 12.29 Assign Filter Objects to Business Objects

IMG path **DRF IMG · Data Replication · Enhance Default Settings for Outbound Imple-mentations · Define Business Objects and Object Identifiers · Assign Filter Objects to Business Objects** is used for assigning filter objects to business objects.

Table 12.14 describes the configuration fields of this IMG activity.

Configuration Field	Description
Business Object Type	Enter a valid business object.
Description	The text is auto populated from the business object definition.
Filter Object	Enter a valid filter object to be assigned to the filter object.

Table 12.14 Configuration Fields for the Assign Filter Object to Business Object Configuration Activity

Define and Assign Object Identifiers

Object identifiers are Data Dictionary structures that hold the key fields of a business object. In the **DRF IMG · Data Replication · Enhance Default Settings for Outbound Implementations · Define Business Objects and Object Identifiers** IMG activity, object identifiers are assigned to business objects (see Figure 12.30). This IMG activity is mainly consumed by the key mapping framework.

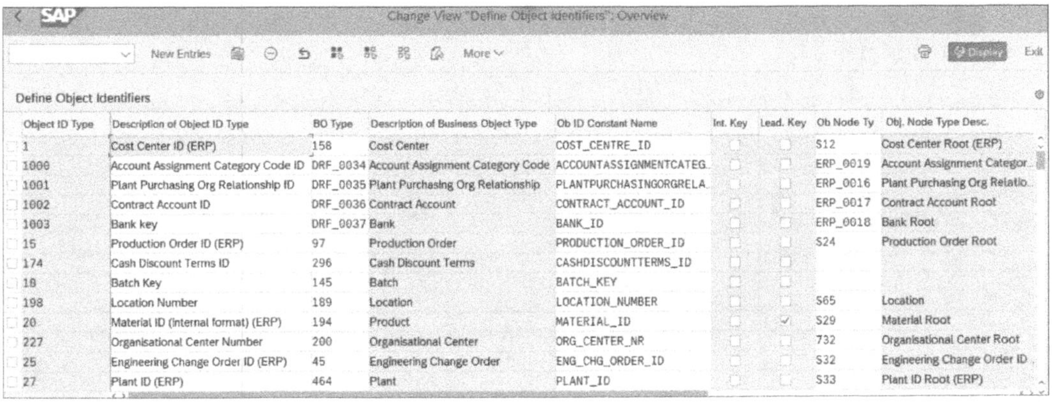

Figure 12.30 Define Object Identifiers

Table 12.15 describes the configuration fields of the IMG activity.

Configuration Field	Description
Object ID Type	This unique identifier of the business object key helps in differentiating between multiple keys of a business object.
Description of Object ID Type	Enter a logical explanation of the business object key that describes it accurately. It helps users understand the object ID type when traversing the key mapping UI.
BO Type	Enter the business object whose key field the object ID type represents. A business object can have multiple keys.
Int. Key	This indicates that the object ID type of the business object uses an internal key.
Lead. Key	For objects that have more than one key, this specifies which key is used for all internal processes, such as data retrieval and maintenance.
No Conv.	This specifies no conversion from internal key to external key.
Obj. Node Type	This acts as an aid for creating the mapping group. If you assign all the object identifiers that belong to one business object to one object type node, they form one mapping group. You can have multiple mapping groups for the same business object.

Table 12.15 Configuration Fields for the Definition Object Identifier for Business Object

After object identifiers have been defined, you can assign key structures to them. In the underlying database tables, all the keys that belong to a mapping group are concatenated and stored. To split the concatenated key into individual key fields, the key structures are used. Figure 12.31 shows the IMG activity to assign structures to object identifiers.

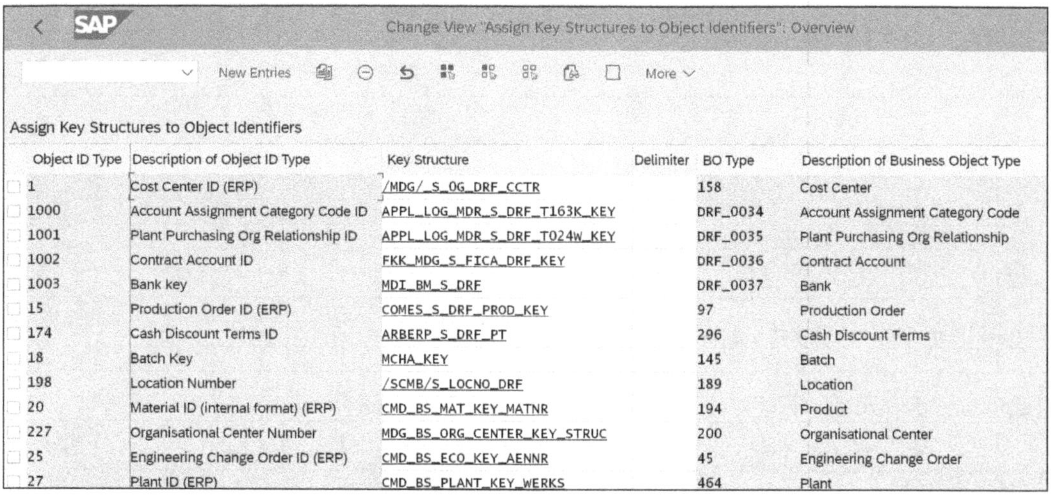

Change View "Assign Key Structures to Object Identifiers": Overview

New Entries More

Assign Key Structures to Object Identifiers

Object ID Type	Description of Object ID Type	Key Structure	Delimiter	BO Type	Description of Business Object Type
1	Cost Center ID (ERP)	/MDG/_S_OG_DRF_CCTR		158	Cost Center
1000	Account Assignment Category Code ID	APPL_LOG_MDR_S_DRF_T163K_KEY		DRF_0034	Account Assignment Category Code
1001	Plant Purchasing Org Relationship ID	APPL_LOG_MDR_S_DRF_T024W_KEY		DRF_0035	Plant Purchasing Org Relationship
1002	Contract Account ID	FKK_MDG_S_FICA_DRF_KEY		DRF_0036	Contract Account
1003	Bank key	MDI_BM_S_DRF		DRF_0037	Bank
15	Production Order ID (ERP)	COMES_S_DRF_PROD_KEY		97	Production Order
174	Cash Discount Terms ID	ARBERP_S_DRF_PT		296	Cash Discount Terms
18	Batch Key	MCHA_KEY		145	Batch
198	Location Number	/SCMB/S_LOCNO_DRF		189	Location
20	Material ID (internal format) (ERP)	CMD_BS_MAT_KEY_MATNR		194	Product
227	Organisational Center Number	MDG_BS_ORG_CENTER_KEY_STRUC		200	Organisational Center
25	Engineering Change Order ID (ERP)	CMD_BS_ECO_KEY_AENNR		45	Engineering Change Order
27	Plant ID (ERP)	CMD_BS_PLANT_KEY_WERKS		464	Plant

Figure 12.31 Assign Key Structures to Object Identifiers

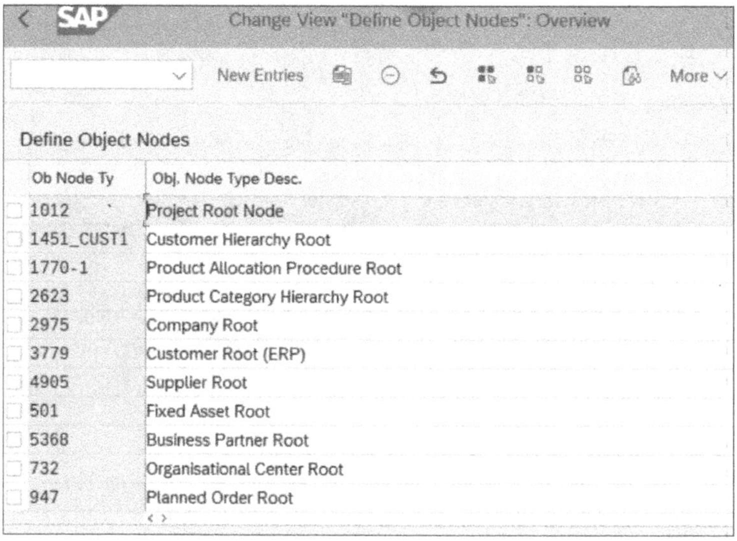

Change View "Define Object Nodes": Overview

New Entries More

Define Object Nodes

Ob Node Ty	Obj. Node Type Desc.
1012	Project Root Node
1451_CUST1	Customer Hierarchy Root
1770-1	Product Allocation Procedure Root
2623	Product Category Hierarchy Root
2975	Company Root
3779	Customer Root (ERP)
4905	Supplier Root
501	Fixed Asset Root
5368	Business Partner Root
732	Organisational Center Root
947	Planned Order Root

Figure 12.32 Define Object Nodes

IMG path **DRF IMG • Data Replication • Enhance Default Settings for Outbound Implementations • Define Business Objects and Object Identifiers • Assign Key Structures to Object Identifiers** is used for assigning key structures to object identifiers.

Table 12.16 describes the configuration fields of the IMG activity.

Configuration Field	Description
Object ID Type	Unique identifier for the object ID type of a business object
Description of Object ID Type	Description of the object ID type of a business object
Key Structure	A Data Dictionary structure containing key fields of the object ID type

Table 12.16 Configuration Fields for the Assign Key Structures to Object Identifiers Configuration Activity

Define Object Nodes

Object nodes are used to group different object ID types belonging to the same business object under one mapping group Figure 12.33 shows an example of different object ID types belonging to business object type **147** being grouped under one object node 5368 (business partner root); by this configuration, all the object ID types are grouped under one mapping group. IMG path **DRF IMG • Data Replication • Enhance Default Settings for Outbound Implementations • Define Business Objects and Object Identifiers • DefineObject Nodes** is used to define object nodes.

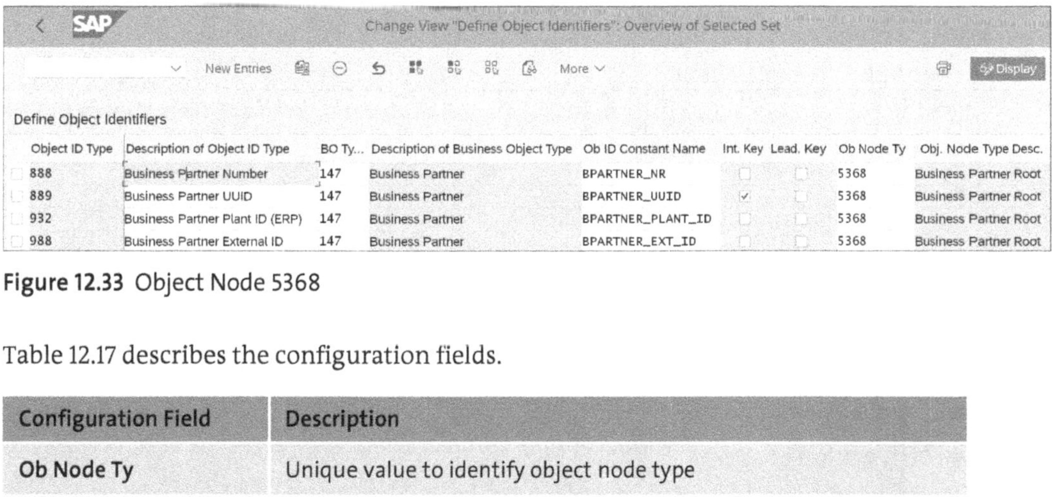

Object ID Type	Description of Object ID Type	BO Ty...	Description of Business Object Type	Ob ID Constant Name	Int. Key	Lead. Key	Ob Node Ty	Obj. Node Type Desc.
888	Business Partner Number	147	Business Partner	BPARTNER_NR	☐	☐	5368	Business Partner Root
889	Business Partner UUID	147	Business Partner	BPARTNER_UUID	☑	☐	5368	Business Partner Root
932	Business Partner Plant ID (ERP)	147	Business Partner	BPARTNER_PLANT_ID	☐	☐	5368	Business Partner Root
988	Business Partner External ID	147	Business Partner	BPARTNER_EXT_ID	☐	☐	5368	Business Partner Root

Figure 12.33 Object Node 5368

Table 12.17 describes the configuration fields.

Configuration Field	Description
Ob Node Ty	Unique value to identify object node type
Obj. Node Type Desc.	Meaningful description of object

Table 12.17 Object Nodes Configuration Fields

12.2   Material Master Replication

SAP provides runtime and design-time artifacts for replicating material from the SAP Master Data Governance hub to any client system. As of version SAP Master Data Governance on SAP S/4HANA 1909 Material/Product master can be replicated using both the ALE- and the SOA-based replication approaches.

Table 12.18 lists the outbound implementation classes delivered by SAP.

Outbound Implementation	Description
I_MAT	This outbound implementation always sends MATMAS (material) CLFMAS (Classification) This doesn't support change analysis.
I_MAT_V2	This new outbound implementation performs change analysis. The following IDoc messages are triggered: ■ MATMAS (material) ■ CLFMAS (classification) ■ DOLMAS (document object links) ■ ECMREV (revision level) ■ QMAT (quality data)
194_3	This is the new SOA-based outbound implementation, which uses the SOA service ProductMDMBulkReplicateRequest_Out

Table 12.18 Outbound Implementations for Material Master Replication

The explicit complex filter object assigned to material is MDG_BS_MAT. It provides the following parameters to filter the material during outbound replication, as shown in Figure 12.34:

■ Plant
■ Material Number
■ Material Group
■ Material Type
■ Industry sector
■ Sales Organization
■ Distribution Channel
■ Storage Location
■ Class Type
■ Class number
■ X-plant matl status
■ X-distr. chain material status

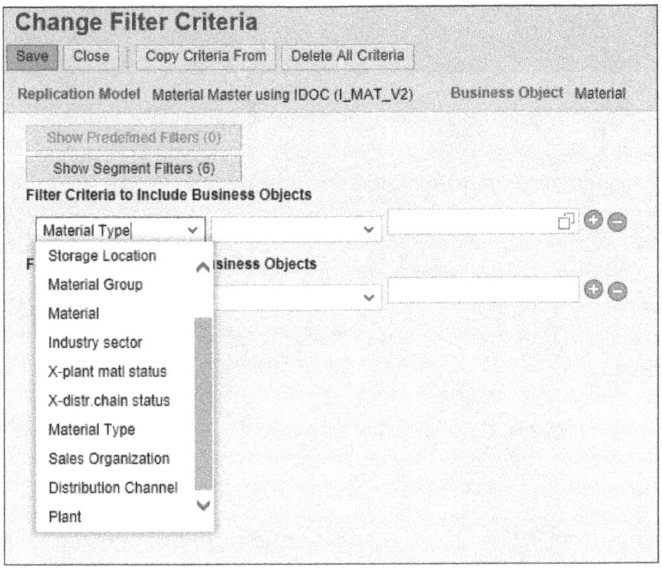

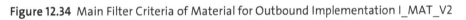

Figure 12.34 Main Filter Criteria of Material for Outbound Implementation I_MAT_V2

Outbound implementations provide the segment filters described in Table 12.19.

Filter Object	Description
F_MAT1	Filter material based on the plant segment filter. This simple explicit filter is based on table MARC. Filter parameters are **Plant**, **Plant-Specific**, and **Material Status**.
F_MAT2	This filter object is used to filter materials based on the sales segment of the material. This is a simple explicit filter based on table MVKE. Filter parameters are **Sales Organization**, **Distribution Channel**, and **Distribution-Chain-Specific Material Status**.
F_MAT3	This filter object is used to filter materials based on the storage segment of a material. This is a simple explicit filter based on table MARD. Filter parameter is **Storage Location**.
F_MAT4	This filter object is used to filter materials based on the tax class segment of a material. This is a simple explicit filter based on table MLAN. Filter parameter is **Departure Country** (country from which the goods are sent).

Table 12.19 Filter Objects Available for the Material Master Domain of SAP Master Data Governance

Filter Object	Description
F_MAT5	This filter object is used to filter materials based on the valuation segment of a material. This is a simple explicit filter based on table MBEW. Filter parameters are **Valuation Area** and **Valuation Type.**
F_MAT6	This filter object is used to filter materials based on the class segment of a material. This is a simple explicit filter based on table KSSK. Filter parameters are **Class Type**, **Change Number**, and **Valid-From Date.**

Table 12.19 Filter Objects Available for the Material Master Domain of SAP Master Data Governance (Cont.)

Figure 12.35 shows the segment filters for the I_MAT_V2 outbound implementation. This filter usually corresponds with type 4 entity types such as plant sales and data. The segment filter is applied only after a filter on a type 1 entity is applied.

To update the key mapping, the ALEAUD IDoc should be configured in the target systems, and AUD2 should be configured as the inbound processing code in the partner profile configuration for ALEAUD in the SAP Master Data Governance hub system.

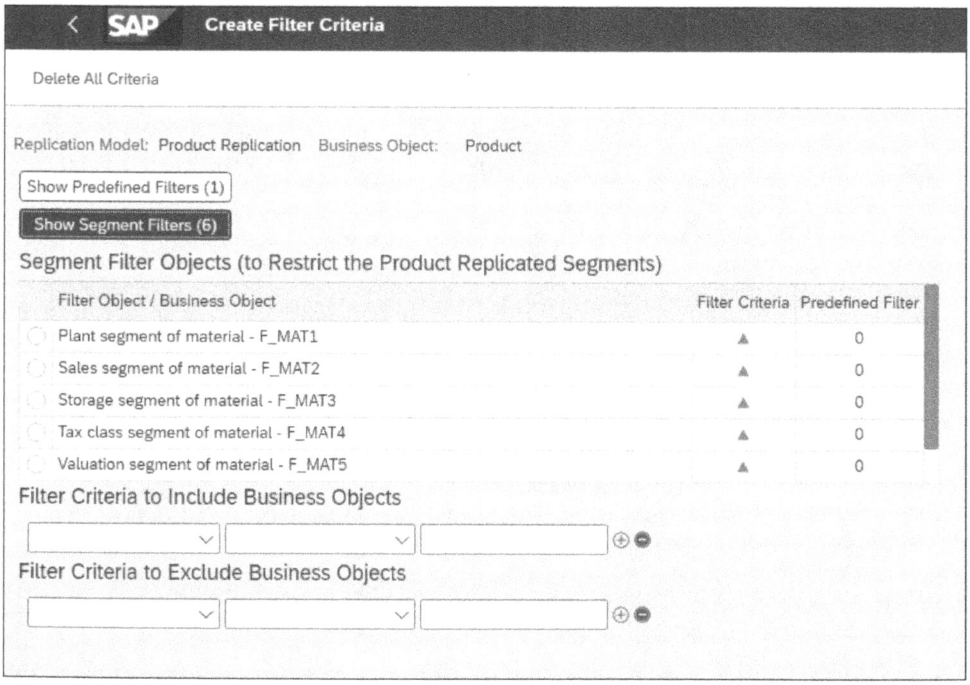

Figure 12.35 Segment Filters Assigned to Outbound Implementation I_MAT_V2

Note

SOA message `ProductMDMBulkReplicateRequest_Out` is used to replicate the product master data from SAP S/4HANA into the client system using the service `CO_MDM_PRD_BULK_REPL_REQ_OUT`. In the SAP S/4HANA system, there is a common data model called Product data model that combines different types of material types such as materials, articles, and so on. This service can be used to replicate not only material data but also article data.

Unlike the older Material SOA service, the Product SOA service supports both the inbound and outbound transfer of data. The Inbound SOA services is used to create a material in the master data governance system hub system from an external system. This service can save data either in the staging area of SAP Master Data Governance or in the active area or create a consolidation process.

During SOA replication of products, you can use Transaction SRT_MONI to monitor the messages.

12.3   Customer, Supplier, and Business Partner Replication

SAP delivers Customizing and runtime objects to enable out-of-the-box replication of business partners and relationships, suppliers, and customers. The replication can take place using SOA or ALE, as described in the following sections.

12.3.1   Service Oriented Architecture-Based Replication

Business partners with their respective vendors and suppliers are replicated using the asynchronous point-to-point enabled SOA services described in Table 12.20.

Name of SOA Service	Description
Businesspartnersuitebulkrep-licaterequest_Out	This SOA service is used to replicate business partners, suppliers, and customers to client systems from the SAP Master Data Governance hub system.
BusinessPartnerSUITEBulkRep-licateRequest_In	This inbound SOA service is used to create a business partner in the SAP Master Data Governance hub system from the external system. This service can save data in the SAP Master Data Governance staging area, directly save in the active area, or create a consolidation process.

Table 12.20 Web Services Available for Replication of Business Partners, Customers, and Suppliers

Name of SOA Service	Description
BusinessPartnerSUITEBulkRep-licateConfirmation_Out	This is the confirmation message triggered by the SAP Master Data Governance hub system to the client system.
BusinessPartnerSUITEBulkRep-licateConfirmation_In	This service is triggered by the client system to the SAP Master Data Governance hub system.

Table 12.20 Web Services Available for Replication of Business Partners, Customers, and Suppliers (Cont.)

These services take care of creating business partners and their respective customers and suppliers. They also take care of updating key mapping and invoking value mapping APIs.

Following are the SOA services used for replicating business partner relationships from SAP Master Data Governance to target systems:

- BusinessPartnerRelationshipSUITEBulkReplicateRequest_Out
- BusinessPartnerRelationshipSUITEBulkReplicateRequest_In
- BusinessPartnerRelationshipSUITEBulkReplicateConfirmation_Out
- BusinessPartnerRelationshipSUITEBulkReplicateConfirmation_In

12.3.2 Application Link Enabling-Based Replication

You can use ALE as a replication mechanism to replicate business partners, suppliers, and customers to client systems from SAP Master Data Governance hub systems. The difference between SOA-based replication and ALE-based replication is that in ALE-based replication, you have separate message types for business partners, suppliers, and customers. ALE messages for business partners won't create suppliers or customers.

The IDoc messages used for replicating customers and suppliers are listed in Table 12.21.

IDoc Message Type	Description
CREMAS, ADRMAS	Customer data, customer address data
DEBMAS, ADRMAS	Supplier data, supplier address data

Table 12.21 IDoc Messages Used for Replication of Customer and Supplier Master Data with Address Data

12.4   Financial Master Data Replication

Financial master data replication can happen through SOA, IDoc, or file protocols. SAP Master Data Governance, Financials, unlike other domains in SAP Master Data Governance, has multiple business objects in one data model. Therefore, this section will discuss the following business object replications: account replication, company replication, cost element replication, profit center replication, cost center replication, and internal order replication.

12.4.1   Account Replication

The entities related to account replication are as follows:

- ACCOUNT
- ACCCCDET

Table 12.22 shows the outbound implementations relevant for account replication.

Outbound Implementation	Communication Channel	Message
1000_V1 (Financial Accounting Chart of Accounts)	SOA	ChartOfAccountsReplication-Request_V1
1002 (Financial Accounting Chart of Accounts File Transfer)	File	N/A
1010 (General Ledger Account Master)	SOA	GeneralLedgerAccountMaster-ReplicationBulkRequest
1011 (General Ledger Account Master File Transfer)	File	N/A
1012 (General Ledger Account Master IDoc)	IDoc	GLMAST

Table 12.22 Outbound Implementations for Replicating General Ledger Accounts via ALE and Web Services

Note

SOA message ChartOfAccountsReplicationRequest_V1 is used for replication ACCOUNT entity attributes and FSI entity attributes; however, this SOA message won't transmit all ACCOUNT attributes. ACCOUNT attributes such as functional area and trading partner are transmitted via SOA message GeneralLedgerAccountMasterReplication-BulkRequest. This is how the SOA messages are designed.

To overcome this design complexity, the outbound implementation class for ACCOUNT will ensure that both SOA messages are triggered whenever an account is replicated. The sequence of these messages is ensured by the data model due to the business object definition. Business object definition 899(ACCOUNT) is defined as prerequisite for 892(ACCCCDET). It's also a good idea to sequence outbound implementation 1000_V1 first and outbound implementation 1010 as second during configuration of the replication model. This kind of restriction doesn't apply for IDocs because both ACCOUNT entities and ACCCCDET entities are part of the GLMAST IDoc.

12.4.2   Company Replication

The entity related to company replication is COMPANY. Table 12.23 shows the list of outbound implementations available for company replication.

Outbound Implementation	Communication Channel	Message
1140	SOA	CompanyReplication-BulkRequest
1141	File	N/A

Table 12.23 Outbound Implementations for Company Replications

12.4.3   Cost Element Replication

In SAP S/4HANA, cost elements don't exist as separate objects. The general ledger account has been extended with account types for primary cost element and secondary cost element; effectively, the cost element in SAP S/4HANA has been merged into general ledger accounts. SAP Master Data Governance on SAP S/4HANA supports replication of cost elements to SAP ERP and SAP S/4HANA, as described in the following sections.

SAP ERP

The SAP Master Data Governance entity for cost element is CELEM. The target tables in SAP ERP client's systems are tables CSKA, CSKB, and CSKU. Cost replication is enabled both via IDoc and SOA.

Table 12.24 contains the list of outbound implementations.

Outbound Implementation	Communication Channel	Message
1180 (Cost Element SOA)	SOA	CostElementReplication-BulkRequest
1181 (Cost Element File Transfer)	File	N/A
1182 (Cost Element IDoc)	IDoc	COELEM

Table 12.24 Cost Element Replication

> **Note**
>
> The target tables in SAP ERP are table CSKA and table CSKB. Table CSKA holds the chart of account data of the cost element. This data isn't time dependent. Table CSKB holds the controlling area–dependent data of the cost element, which is time dependent. The SOA message CostElementReplicationBulkRequest sends data relevant to both table CSKA and table CSKB. For table CSKA–related data, the corresponding outbound implementation will trigger only that latest data. For table CSKB–related data, the outbound implementation will trigger data related to all the time slices when object-based replication or ad hoc replication are used. When the replication is based on change requests or editions, only data corresponding to the edition is sent.

SAP S/4HANA

In SAP S/4HANA, general ledger accounts and their counterpart in the controlling cost element have been merged. In SAP ERP, they remain as separate entities.

To replicate cost elements to SAP S/4HANA, general ledger account SOA services must be used. For more details, refer to Table 12.22. Figure 12.36 shows an overview of how replication is handled from SAP Master Data Governance on SAP S/4HANA to operational SAP S/4HANA and SAP ERP.

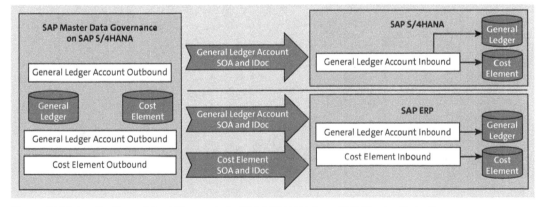

Figure 12.36 Replication of Cost Elements to SAP S/4HANA from SAP Master Data Governance on SAP S/4HANA

12.4.4   Profit Center and Profit Center Hierarchy Replication

The SAP Master Data Governance entity for profit center is PCTR. SAP Master Data Governance supports both ALE-based replication and SOA-based replication. The target tables in the SAP S/4HANA or SAP ERP client are tables CEPC, CEPCT, and CEPC_BUKRS.

Table 12.25 contains the list of outbound implementations for profit centers.

Outbound Implementation	Communication Channel	Message
1120	SOA	ProfitCentreReplication-BulkRequest
1121	File	N/A
1122	IDoc	PRCMAS
1130	SOA	ProfitCentreGroupHierarchy-ReplicationRequest
1131	File	N/A
1132	IDoc	COGRP6

Table 12.25 Outbound Implementations for Profit Center and Profit Center Hierarchy Replication

12.4.5   Cost Center and Cost Center Hierarchy Replication

The SAP Master Data Governance entity for cost center is CCTR. The target SAP S/4HANA (or SAP ERP) tables are tables CSKS and CSKT.

Table 12.26 lists the outbound implementations and their corresponding messages.

Outbound Implementation	Communication Channel	Message
1100 (Cost Center)	SOA	CostCentreReplication-BulkRequest
1101 (Cost Center)	File	N/A
1102 (Cost Center)	IDoc	COSMAS
1110 (Cost Center Hierarchy)	SOA	CostCentreGroupHierarchy-ReplicationRequest_Out
1111 (Cost Center Hierarchy)	File	N/A
1112 (Cost Center Hierarchy)	IDoc	COGRP1

Table 12.26 Outbound Implementations and Corresponding Communication Channels for Cost Center Replication

12.4.6   Internal Order Replication

Internal order is represented in SAP Master Data Governance data OG as type 1 entity IORDER. The target active area table for this entity is table AUFK. Table 12.27 shows the outbound implementations, communication channel, and message for internal order replication

Outbound Implementation	Communication Channel	Message
1201	SOA	InternalOrderBulkReplicate-Request_Out
1200	IDoc	INTERNAL_ORDER

Table 12.27 Outbound Implementations, Communication Channels, and Message IDs for Internal Order Replication

12.5 Replication Options for Non-SAP Systems

This section covers the available options to replicate governed master data to non-SAP systems. Replication options for non-SAP systems are explained in terms of the communication channels supported by SAP Master Data Governance, as follows:

- **Web services**
  Because web services can be consumed by any non-SAP application using open Internet protocols (e.g., HTTP), this is the most appropriate channel for replicating master data to non-SAP systems. Any non-SAP system that can understand Internet protocols can consume a web service provided by the SAP Master Data Governance hub to replicate master data.

  A web service is exposed by an application to other communications. This service can be used by other applications to communicate with applications using HTTP. Web services use simple formats such as Simple Object Access Protocol (SOAP).

- **IDocs**
  IDoc is SAP's proprietary format. Many non-SAP systems don't understand the IDoc format. The proprietary feature of IDoc makes it the least desirable option when replicating to non-SAP systems. However, this shortcoming can be overcome by using middleware such as SAP Process Integration, which can transform the IDoc message to any desirable format that a non-SAP client system can understand. Many non-SAP middleware systems also have IDoc adapters to help them understand the IDoc format.

- **File protocol**
  Replication via file protocol is another best-suited technique to replicate master data to non-SAP client systems. This is suitable when replicating data to systems that desire file-based replication and to systems that don't understand Internet protocols.

> **Note**
>
> RFC is the standard method of communication between SAP systems and isn't a suitable option for replication to non-SAP systems.

12.6   Operations

SAP provides various logging and replication monitoring tools as well as other tools for checking the consistency of the data replication framework, customizing the replication model, deleting the replication log, deleting the replication status, displaying the object-specific replication status, and subscribing objects for data replication.

12.6.1   Logging, Tracing, and Monitoring Tools

The data replication framework triggers replication of business objects to a target system. The actual replication is triggered by the outbound controller, which logs each milestone in the application log. Two of the milestones are filtering and change analysis. Tracing the data replication process is also recorded as part of the application logs. The data replication framework is integrated to the Computing Center Management System (CCMS), so any application log under the Very Important category creates an alert in CCMS. Logs generated by the data replication framework can be accessed using Transaction SLG1 with FMDM as the object.

The out-of-the-box tools provided for monitoring are as follows:

- **Monitoring replication**
  This Web Dynpro UI can be accessed by clicking the hyperlink either on the launchpad or on the navigation pane. This tool is mainly for the master data steward to monitor the replication. Figure 12.37 shows the replication monitoring tools that can be called from the SAP Business Client.

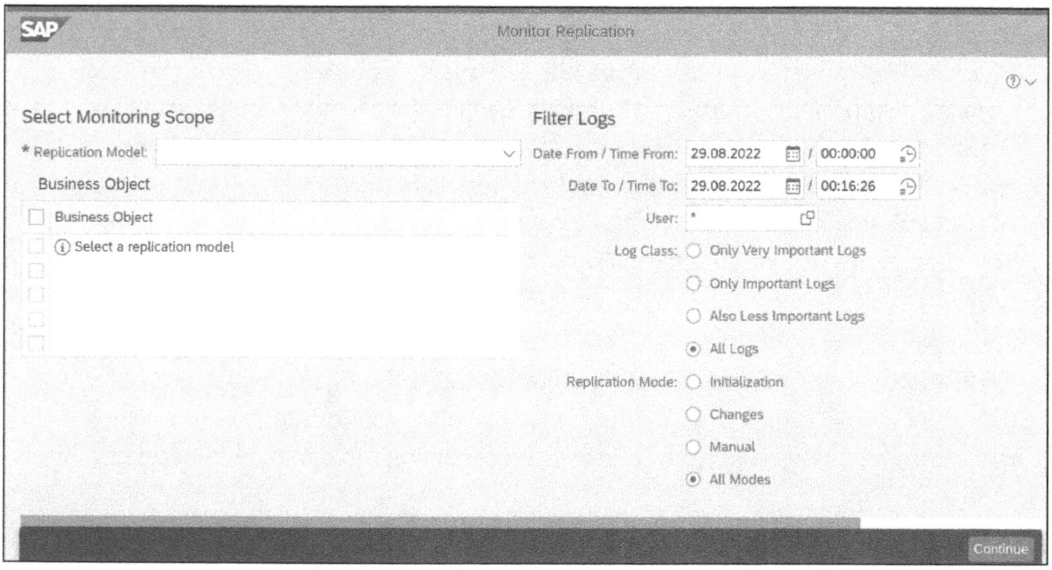

Figure 12.37 Web-Based Replication Monitoring Tool

Table 12.28 describes the fields on the Web UI.

Field	Description
Replication Model	This mandatory field allows you to select only one value.
Business Object	This table displays all the business objects assigned through outbound implementations to the selected replication model. You can select multiple business objects.
Date From/Date To	These fields are used to filter the logs based on the date range.
User	This field is used to filter the logs based on the user who executed the replication.
Log Class	This field is used to filter the logs based on the log class.
Replication Mode	This radio button is used to filter the logs based on the replication mode. The available options are as follows: ■ **Initialization**: Filter the logs that are created when the business object is created through a change request. ■ **Changes**: Display the data replication framework logs that are created when the changes are made to the business object through a change request. ■ **Manual**: Filter the logs that are created when a business object is replicated manually either using Transaction DRFOUT or using the **Replicate by Object Selection** UI. ■ **All Modes**: Displays the data replication framework logs for all the modes mentioned earlier.

Table 12.28 Fields of the Replication Monitoring Tools

■ **Analyze log for outbound implementations (Transaction DRFLOG)**
This tool is accessed in the SAP GUI using Transaction DRFLOG, as shown in Figure 12.38 You can use the various fields to enter the selection criteria. Transaction DRFLOG also enables you to filter the log using the object IDs.

Transaction DRFLOG provides many more capabilities to monitor and analyze the logs. The tool is used by IT experts for troubleshooting and monitoring. Like the monitoring replication web application, this tool displays the application log, but it has more log filtering capabilities. This tool can filter Transaction DRFLOG based on the object IDs of the business object.

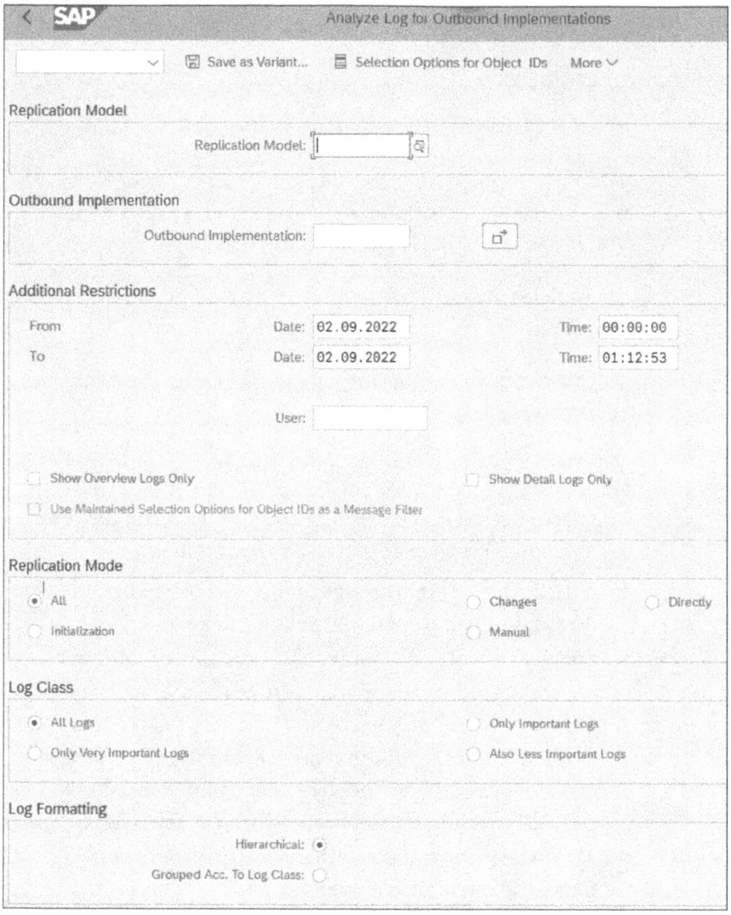

Figure 12.38 Selection Screen of Transaction DRFLOG in the SAP GUI

12.6.2   Change Pointers

SAP Master Data Governance change pointers store the changes (old value and new value) made to business objects along with the change request ID, time stamp, and user who made the changes. These change pointers are used primarily to determine the relevant business object instances during delta replication mode based on the last state of replication to a business system.

SAP Master Data Governance doesn't manage underlying SAP ERP or SAP S/4HANA change pointers. SAP Master Data Governance creates its own change pointers per target system. This kind of storage helps when replicating only delta changes to a target system. Change pointers are created after the save event of the business object. These change pointers shouldn't be confused with the change documents of change requests. Change documents of change requests reuse the existing SAP S/4HANA/SAP ERP change pointer framework.

12.6.3 Check Data Replication Framework Customizing

In the SAP GUI, you can use Transaction DRFCC to access the application to check the correctness of a replication model and business system configuration. Figure 12.39 shows the initial screen of Transaction DRFCC.

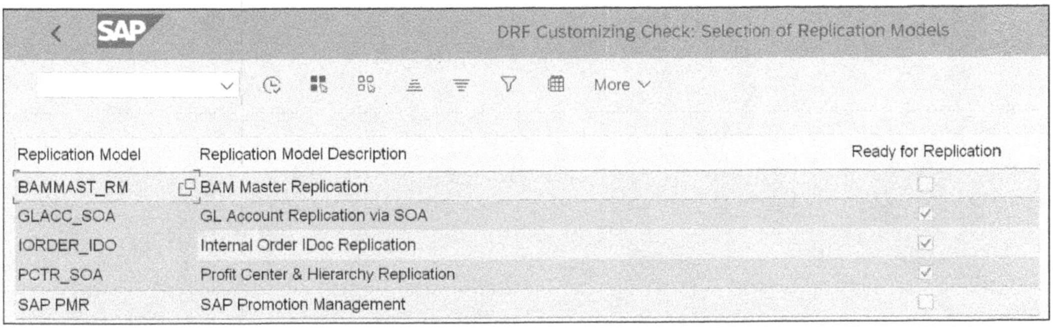

Replication Model	Replication Model Description	Ready for Replication
BAMMAST_RM	BAM Master Replication	☐
GLACC_SOA	GL Account Replication via SOA	☑
IORDER_IDO	Internal Order IDoc Replication	☑
PCTR_SOA	Profit Center & Hierarchy Replication	☑
SAP PMR	SAP Promotion Management	☐

Figure 12.39 Transaction DRFCC in the SAP GUI

This transaction performs the following checks:

- Check if at least one outbound implementation is assigned to a replication model.
- Check whether languages are assigned to a replication model. If languages are assigned, then the system checks if at least one outbound implementation supports the language filter. This setting is defined when creating the outbound implementation. The language filter is used to filter language-dependent texts of a business object based on the languages configured in the replication model.
- Check whether every business object has a filter object configured.
- Check whether all the mandatory outbound parameters are assigned to an outbound implementation in the replication model.
- Check whether a business system is configured for every outbound implementation.
- Check that the business object and target system combination is unique across the replication models.
- Check whether the communication channel configured against the outbound implementation and business system is the same.
- Check whether time dependency and key harmonization settings defined against a business system are consistent with the outbound implementation settings.

12.6.4 Delete Replication Log

The report to delete logs can be accessed in the SAP GUI using Transaction DRFLOGDEL. This report is used to delete the logs based on selection criteria. You should schedule this program in the background to delete expired logs of a replication model. A log's expiration date is controlled by the setting when defining the replication model. Figure 12.40 shows the initial screen of Transaction DRFLOGDEL in the SAP GUI.

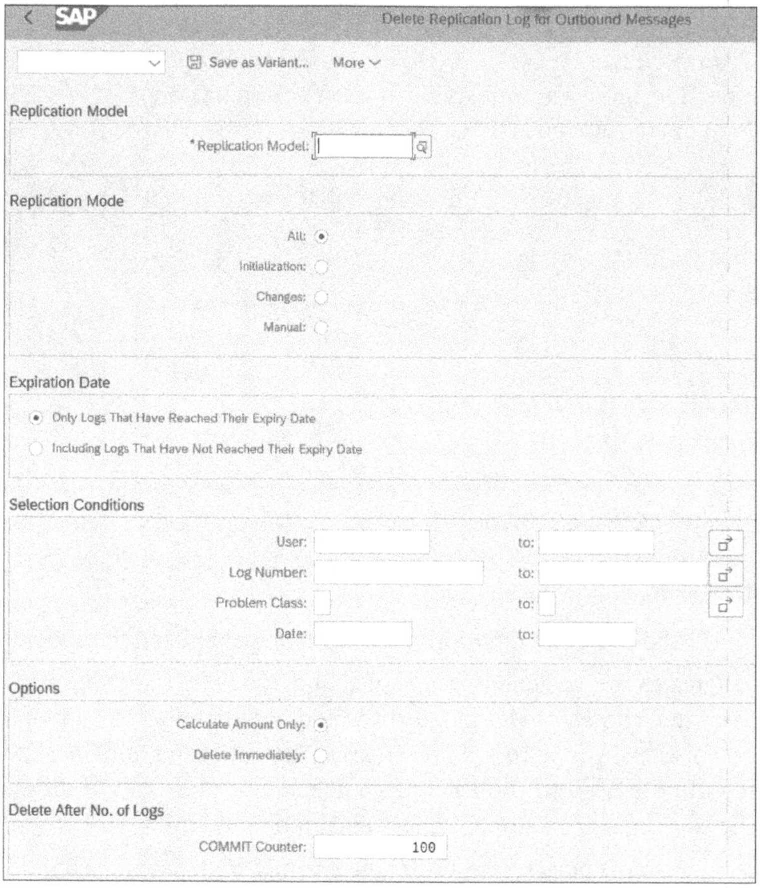

Figure 12.40 Transaction DRFLOGDEL in the SAP GUI

Table 12.29 describes some of the selection screen fields of Transaction DRFLOGDEL.

Field	Description
Replication Model	This selection field is used to enter the replication model whose logs need to be deleted.
Replication Mode	One of the classifying features of data replication framework logs is their replication mode; every data replication framework log clearly shows in the header what the replication mode was when the log was created. Available options are as follows: ■ ALL ■ Initialization ■ Changes ■ Manual

Table 12.29 Fields of Transaction DRFLOGDEL

Field	Description
Expiration Date	This radio button group allows you to choose whether to delete the logs that have expired or delete all the logs irrespective of the expiry date.

Table 12.29 Fields of Transaction DRFLOGDEL (Cont.)

12.6.5   Display Object Replication Status

Transaction DRFRSD is used to display the object replication status in the SAP GUI based on the object ID of the business object (Figure 12.41).

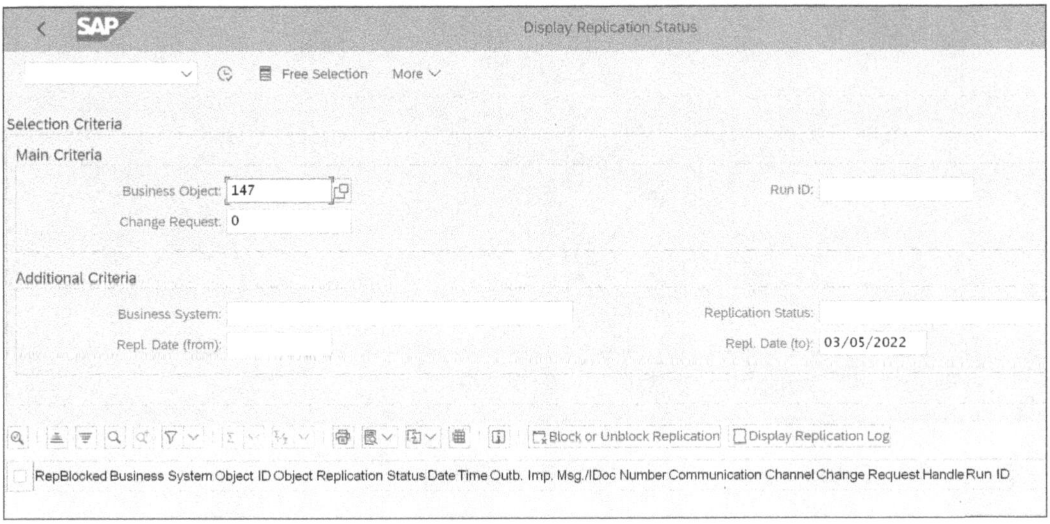

Figure 12.41 Transaction DRFRSD in the SAP GUI

Table 12.30 describes some of the selection screen fields of Transaction DRFRSD.

Field	Description
Business Object	Enter the business object ID of the business object. This field is mandatory if you want to enter the object ID by clicking the free selection icon.
Change Request	Enter the change request ID.
Business System	Enter the target system ID.
Repl. Date From	Enter the date of replication.
Replication Status	Choose the status of the replication.

Table 12.30 Fields for Transaction DRFRS

12.6.6   Delete Replication Status

Transaction DRFRSDEL can be used to delete the replication status of different object IDs per system. This transaction is used when the object status no longer needs to be saved for future reference. Figure 12.42 shows the initial screen of Transaction DRFR-SEDEL.

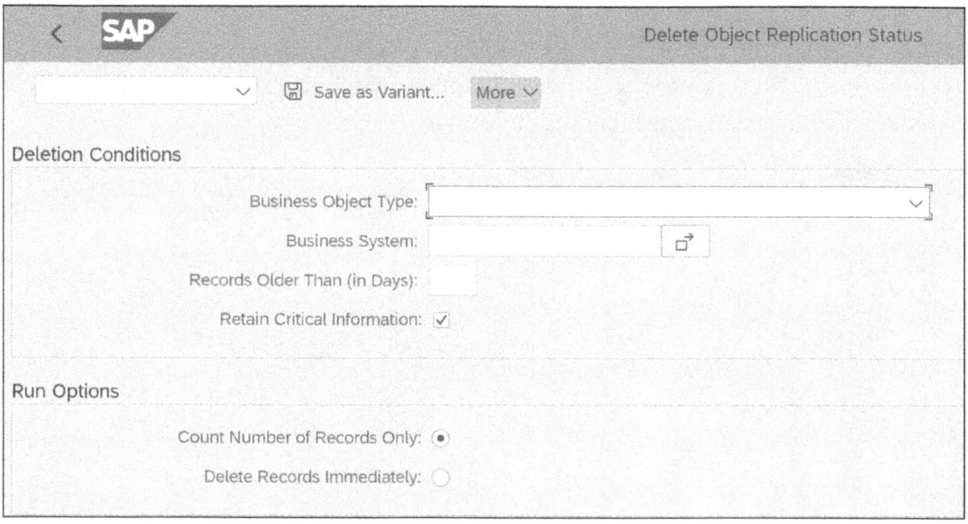

Figure 12.42 Transaction DRFRSDEL in the SAP GUI

12.6.7   Subscribe Objects for Data Replication

This function is used to enable any future data replication of business object instances belonging to a business system. The subscription overrides the filter settings. This function can be accessed using Transaction DRFSUB, as shown in Figure 12.43.

Figure 12.43 Transaction DRFSUB in the SAP GUI

12.7   Summary

After reading this chapter, you should now understand the purpose of the data replication framework, as well as its different components. This chapter explained the basic building blocks of the data replication framework and how they are interconnected. The chapter then provided domain-specific replication details for material, supplier, customer, and business partner. The chapter then concluded with an overview of the different tools that can be used when operating with the data replication framework. In the next chapter, we'll discuss the APIs available in SAP Master Data Governance and the integration scenarios with other SAP solutions.

12

Chapter 13
Central Governance: Integration Scenarios

SAP Master Data Governance integrates with other SAP and non-SAP solutions to support business processes that enhance or require master data. This chapter discusses various application programming interfaces (APIs) of the SAP Master Data Governance application framework and various integration scenarios that are common in SAP Master Data Governance projects.

Master data can be used for the smooth execution of transactions and associated subprocesses. Harmonized master data supports end-to-end business processes involving various business solutions such as SAP Cloud for Customer, SAP Ariba, SAP S/4HANA Cloud, and other associated SAP and non-SAP solutions. This chapter provides an overview of various integration scenarios between SAP Master Data Governance and business applications or third-party solutions. It also introduces the SAP Master Data Governance application programming interfaces (APIs). These APIs enable developers to perform various operations for the SAP Master Data Governance data model and the governance process. In this chapter, Section 13.1 discusses various API methods and operations. Section 13.2 covers the integration scenarios between SAP Master Data Governance and other SAP solutions, and Section 13.3 explores the integration scenarios between SAP Master Data Governance and third-party solutions.

13.1 SAP Master Data Governance Application Programming

You can build multiple SAP Master Data Governance data models that are usually semantically different from each other. Each data model has an active area. Uniform access to the active area of the data model and the SAP Master Data Governance staging area is important for good architecture and increased adoptability.

The SAP Master Data Governance application framework provides a few APIs to enable uniform access to the active area and staging area, as follows:

- Governance API
- Convenience API
- Application Context API

The Governance API and Convenience API can't be used together. Both of these APIs provide buffering capabilities, automatically updating or invalidating the buffer during various events. In the following sections, we'll look at each of these APIs in turn.

13.1.1 Governance Application Programming Interface

The class ID of the Governance API is `CL_USMD_GOV_API`, and the Governance API has a singleton instance. It's typically invoked when the Single Object Maintenance (SOM) user interface (UI) isn't involved. The Governance API is an abstract layer for more complex APIs, such as `CL_USMD_HRY_API_GOV`, `CL_USMD_UI_SERVICES`, `CL_USMD_MODEL`, and `CL_USMD_WF_SERVICE`.

This abstract layer is required to access multiple SAP Master Data Governance APIs, and it has built-in buffering capabilities to improve the performance of SAP Master Data Governance applications. The abstract layer also simplifies developers' jobs because one instance of the Governance API can be used to invoke multiple SAP Master Data Governance APIs, which means developers don't have to create multiple instances of various APIs. The API protects custom application code from becoming incompatible if any of the underlying complex APIs change.

Following are the main functions of the Governance API:

- **Perform hierarchy-related actions**
  Beginning with SAP Master Data Governance 8.0, the Governance API enables you to manipulate hierarchy-related data, such as reading and writing assignments.

- **Perform change request–related actions**
  The Governance API can be used to perform change request actions such as adding an attachment, creating a change request, and getting a change request object list.

- **Perform CRUD actions on an entity locked in a change request**
  The API can be used to perform create, read, update, and delete (CRUD) actions on entity data in change requests. The Governance API can't be used to update data in the active area. Only the activate method of the `BUS2250` business object can update data in the active area. The methods related to this action hide the complexity of underlying API `CL_USMD_MODEL`.

- **Perform action related to a process control**
  The Governance API can also be used by an application to control a process by starting the workflow and validating process data.

- **Perform actions related to a transaction control**
  The SAP Master Data Governance application can execute transaction-wide actions such as **Save** by invoking the Governance API.

13.1.2 Convenience Application Programming Interface

The Convenience API is specifically triggered for all UI-related scenarios (e.g., when the SOM UI or multiple-record processing are called). The framework creates this API instance during runtime. Sitting one level above the Governance API, the Convenience API provides all the functionalities of the Governance API and calls the Governance API internally. The Convenience API offers additional value by bundling multiple features of the Governance API into comprehensive methods (e.g., lock handling) for the various use cases.

The Convenience API can be called only for one change request, which is why SAP forbids the coexistence of Convenience API and Governance API instances. The class ID for the Convenience API is CL_USMD_CONV_SOM_GOV_API.

13.1.3 Application Context Application Programming Interface

The Application Context API is used during application programming to access various pieces of context information. The Application Context API provides methods to save application context information as static variables in the context API class.

This context information is stored temporarily in the application memory. Any component that needs the context information invokes this API and consumes the context information. For example, the SAP Master Data Governance communicator would need the business activity and data mode information to determine the navigation to the target application. The SAP Master Data Governance communicator calls the Application Context API to retrieve the information.

The following context information is available:

- Data model
- Business activity
- Workflow information
- Change request
- Change request type
- Change request step
- Change request index (relevant for parallel processing)
- Workflow item
- Application parameter data

The API can also be used to update application context data in the workflow container. The Application Context API class ID is CL_USMD_APP_CONTEXT.

13.2   Integration with SAP Solutions

SAP Master Data Governance provides various technical integration options via web services, IDocs, remote function calls (RFCs), file transfer, APIs, and so on to interface with other SAP solutions based on their compatibility.

Master data integration scenarios with cloud applications in a hybrid landscape are more common. Business partner and product master data integration across an enterprise enables a single view of the customer, supplier, and product. For cloud-based solutions, SAP Master Data Integration (SAP MDI), based on SAP One Domain Model, can help with federation of data based on events and subscription by consuming systems. Based on OData services, SAP MDI can be used to synchronize core master data attributes across different applications. For partner applications and other non-SAP applications, the integrations could leverage SAP Integration Suite. Information regarding various OData services available for master data can be found in SAP API Business Hub (*https://api.sap.com*).

Integration of SAP Master Data Governance with other solutions varies based on the master data governed and how the governed data fits into the overall enterprise business process/system landscape. Some of the common integration scenarios, with respect to the standard master data objects, such as material master, customer master/supplier master, finance master data objects, and the corresponding data flow, are discussed at a high level in the following sections. Infrastructure considerations, such as on premise or on demand (cloud-based), firewall, service users, and so on, need to be checked with respect to how the technical landscape is set up in the enterprise. It's assumed that the integrated solutions are deployed with the latest or a recent release.

13.2.1   SAP Cloud for Customer

SAP Cloud for Customer helps in managing customer sales and service information. Bidirectional integration of business partner master data is supported with SAP Master Data Governance. Thus, customer data can be maintained in both SAP Master Data Governance as well as the SAP Cloud for Customer system. The standard integration via the business partner SOAP service helps in keeping the data in sync and in preventing duplicate records across the systems.

As the data definitions for a customer differ between SAP Master Data Governance and SAP Cloud for Customer solutions, the standard content takes care of the required transformation logic based on the Customizing system parameter for SAP Cloud for Customer. A merge scenario of business partners in SAP Master Data Governance as part of a consolidation process triggers a merge scenario in SAP Cloud for Customer. The ID mapping distribution from SAP Master Data Governance to SAP Cloud for Customer is supported as well using the key mapping service. SAP Cloud Platform Integration is recommended for integration between SAP cloud solutions and on-premise solutions.

Figure 13.1 illustrates the integration with the SAP Cloud for Customer solution. The integration between SAP Master Data Governance and SAP Cloud for Customer is handled via middleware (e.g., SAP Cloud Platform Integration). Customer data requests from SAP Cloud for Customer (create/change scenario) are triggered using the business partner SOAP service with the SAP Cloud for Customer business partner number as the External ID. The inbound proxy logic in the SAP Master Data Governance hub system runs the matching and consolidation process. If there is a duplicate record already in the SAP Master Data Governance system, a merge scenario is triggered back in SAP Cloud for Customer as part of the replication response back to SAP Cloud for Customer. Additionally, the SAP Master Data Governance system replicates the business partner data to other client systems accordingly.

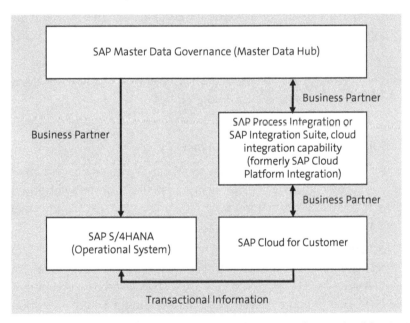

Figure 13.1 SAP Master Data Governance Integration with SAP Cloud for Customer

The following integration scenarios can be considered:

- **New customer from SAP Cloud for Customer**
  When a new customer is created in SAP Cloud for Customer, the data is replicated to the SAP Master Data Governance system. Once the duplicate matching logic is run, the following matching results needs to be considered:
  - No duplicate in SAP Master Data Governance: This is a new record in SAP Master Data Governance.

- Duplicate in SAP Master Data Governance, but not in SAP Cloud for Customer: The record is updated in SAP Master Data Governance, and key mapping is updated.

- Duplicate in SAP Master Data Governance and exists in SAP Cloud for Customer: The record is updated in SAP Master Data Governance and the key mapping is updated which combines the two SAP Cloud for Customer records with the SAP Master Data Governance record ID. The replication response triggers a merge scenario in SAP Cloud for Customer.

- **New customer from SAP Master Data Governance**
  The record is sent to SAP Cloud for Customer and other client systems for creation.

- **Change customer in SAP Cloud for Customer/SAP Master Data Governance**
  The record is updated and replicated to other client systems.

- **Merge two active customer records in SAP Master Data Governance**
  The mappings are updated, and the corresponding records are updated based on the mappings and business decision in the client systems so that the transactions aren't affected.

More information on integration of SAP Cloud for Customer with SAP S/4HANA and SAP Master Data Governance is available in SAP Note 2414514.

13.2.2   SAP Ariba Supplier Lifecycle and Performance

SAP Ariba Supplier Management solutions help in the onboarding and management of suppliers in an enterprise by managing supplier data across all SAP Ariba solutions. It encourages supplier self-registration/maintenance, and, after approval, the information is available for sourcing and contracts.

With SAP Master Data Governance, Supplier, in the landscape, the supplier master data can be transferred between the SAP Master Data Governance system and the SAP Ariba solution using middleware (e.g., SAP Cloud Integration) with web services (service-oriented architecture [SOA]) as the communication mechanism. In the supplier creation process, either SAP Ariba Supplier Management or SAP Master Data Governance can be the leading solution.

With SAP Master Data Governance, Supplier, as the leading system, a duplicate check with the SAP Ariba data needs to be done before creating the supplier. The data is then replicated to the client systems, including SAP ERP or SAP S/4HANA and Ariba Network. Any updates from Ariba Network need to be routed through the SAP Master Data Governance, Supplier, solution for data sync and further replication to other client systems. The SAP Master Data Governance SOA service can be triggered to start the consolidation process for duplicate check and activation of the best record along with the key mapping update. The key mapping needs to be updated for duplicate check process, further updates, and replication. This scenario is illustrated in Figure 13.2. The scenarios for supplier creation and change process, similar to SAP Cloud for Customer scenarios discussed in Section 13.2.1, are applicable in SAP Ariba integration as well.

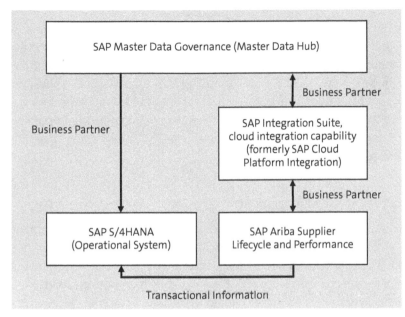

Figure 13.2 SAP Ariba and SAP Master Data Governance Integration

SAP Ariba Cloud Integration add-on software components are required to be installed in SAP S/4HANA. More information on integration of SAP Ariba with SAP S/4HANA and SAP Master Data Governance is available in SAP Note 2926463.

13.2.3 Central Finance

Central Finance is one of the possible deployment approaches when starting the transformation to adopt SAP S/4HANA. It requires replication of finance documents into a Central Finance instance (SAP S/4HANA Finance) to perform consolidated reporting. In a multisystem landscape, Central Finance adds value through a nondisruptive implementation approach to consolidate the systems over time. The Central Finance deployment approach delivers harmonized data for consolidated financial and management reporting.

Data from multiple source systems needs to be mapped to the Central Finance system. SAP Master Data Governance can be leveraged to maintain key master data mappings (e.g., chart of accounts, profit centers, cost centers, business partners, materials, etc.) across various system to have a harmonized data set for reporting. Therefore, when an SAP ERP Financials (SAP ERP FI) posting is pushed from the source system to the Central Finance instance, corresponding master data key values are retrieved with respect to the systems (source system and Central Finance instance mapping in SAP Master

Data Governance). Additionally, functionalities in SAP Master Data Governance, Financials, can be used to govern the SAP ERP FI master data objects, such as SAP General Ledger accounts, hierarchies, and so on.

Thus, SAP Master Data Governance adds value to the Central Finance deployment scenario, along with the management of other master data domains and their respective mappings. (Additional information on Central Finance implementation and configuration is provided in SAP Note 2148893.) SAP Landscape Transformation Replication Server (SAP LT Replication Server) is used to replicate the SAP ERP FI documents from SAP ERP systems to the Central Finance instance. The key mapping information can be pulled from the SAP Master Data Governance tables via SOA services, key mapping APIs, and other interface mechanisms.

13.2.4   SAP Product Lifecycle Management

The SAP Product Lifecycle Management (SAP PLM) solution helps in the management of an organization's product lifecycle processes in product ideation, design, manufacturing, service, and beyond. When a new product or change to an existing product is requested, an engineering change record (ECR) is created to maintain the associated product components (assembly) and make changes to the bill of materials (BOM). This ECR is analyzed and validated by various groups, such as sourcing, manufacturing, marketing, partners, and so on. After this is approved, the change is implemented in the SAP PLM system and replicated to the SAP Business Suite system.

When SAP Master Data Governance, Product, governs the material master in an enterprise, the changed information (from the ECR) needs to be updated in the SAP Master Data Governance system, and then the change needs to be synced with other SAP Master Data Governance client systems, including the core SAP ERP system.

In this scenario, because the need for change is triggered from the SAP PLM system, SAP PLM is the leading system and interfaces with the SAP Master Data Governance system to update the master data fields or to create new material. This avoids the requirement to map the SAP PLM–specific (nonmaster data) fields to the SAP Master Data Governance system. After the SAP Master Data Governance subworkflow is completed, all the records are updated in the client systems.

The SAP PLM system can leverage SAP Master Data Governance APIs to trigger the SAP Master Data Governance change request, and the SAP Master Data Governance system can update the SAP PLM system via the SAP PLM interface to update the information back to complete the ECR workflow process. The material number can be generated in SAP Master Data Governance and sent back to the SAP PLM application before the final SAP Master Data Governance workflow approval, so the SAP PLM process is continued. This scenario is illustrated in Figure 13.3.

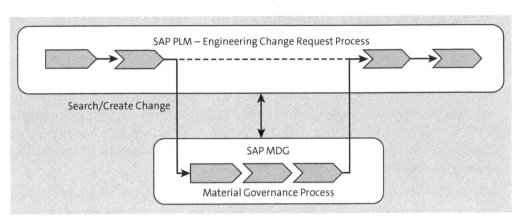

Figure 13.3 SAP PLM to SAP Master Data Governance Integration

13.2.5   SAP Product Content Management

SAP Product Content Management, part of SAP Commerce Cloud, is used for management of product-related content, including catalog products and managed products. It helps to classify and categorize product versions and manage catalog versions, including supplier product catalogs. The product-related content, including unstructured data, is sourced from multiple sources and managed in the SAP Product Content Management solution.

SAP Master Data Governance, Product, and SAP Product Content Management complement each other in managing the product data. The managed product master data can be fed from SAP Master Data Governance, Product, to the SAP Product Content Management solution, and the catalog-only products can be consolidated directly in SAP Product Content Management (see Figure 13.4).

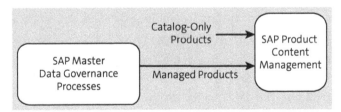

Figure 13.4 SAP Product Content Management and SAP Master Data Governance Integration

Another option is to have all the product content consolidated in the SAP Product Content Management system and the managed product data replicated to the SAP Master Data Governance system for governance; thus, any updates are made in sync between the two systems and other client systems.

13.2.6 SAP Information Lifecycle Management

To conform to data privacy and data protection rules, SAP Master Data Governance can be integrated with SAP Information Lifecycle Management (SAP ILM) for master data lifecycle management. SAP ILM helps to manage the data residence and retention periods with respect to the eventual retirement of data. Data volume management can be handled through data archiving, and data end-of-life can be managed through proper data retention management policies. This reduces system complexity, maintenance costs, and wasteful energy footprint. It also helps to meet audit requirements and ensure legal compliance.

SAP Master Data Governance supports data archiving and integration with SAP ILM for deletion of business partner data. This helps to comply with General Data Protection Regulation (GDPR) for master data. Deletion and blocking of personal data in SAP Master Data Governance can be controlled using SAP ILM. End of purpose (EOP) indicators are used to manage the deletion. The business partners record with EOP indicator is deleted from the central governance, consolidation, and mass processing scenarios. The respective data is masked from the display list, and navigation to masked data is disabled. More information regarding data archiving and read access logging can be found in Chapter 15, Section 15.4 and Section 15.5, respectively. SAP provides additional security authorization objects to control the display, blocking/unblocking, and deletion of data with an EOP indicator. To use the SAP ILM functionalities, the corresponding business functions and dependent components need to be configured. Additional information is available in SAP Note 1825544.

13.2.7 SAP Information Steward

SAP Information Steward mainly helps in analyzing and monitoring the data quality and data integrity across the enterprise. It also helps in metadata management, match review, definition of cleansing packages to parse and standardize the data, and so on.

SAP Information Steward can be used to analyze data for the SAP Master Data Governance data load as well as for continuous monitoring of master data in the SAP Master Data Governance system. SAP Information Steward also complements other data load and consolidation solutions to understand data quality and take remediation steps.

Ongoing data monitoring is a key part of the master data management process cycle. It helps to validate the existing data rules and identify/refine new data rules with respect to changing Customizing, business rules, enterprise structures, and so on. The data errors need to be fixed through a data quality remediation process.

SAP Master Data Governance aids in the data remediation process by leveraging the embedded data quality remediation framework. Data quality scorecards in SAP Information Steward provide insight into the failed data records that didn't meet the predefined data rules. SAP Information Steward also provides match review functionality to check on the data records that match based on configured match rules and derived scores. These records can be reviewed in the SAP Master Data Governance data quality remediation UI, and the data stewards can trigger a change request to correct the data. A new business rule can then be configured in SAP Master Data Governance to make sure that records are corrected as they go through the data management process in SAP Master Data Governance. A sample use case for integration with SAP Information Steward is illustrated in Figure 13.5.

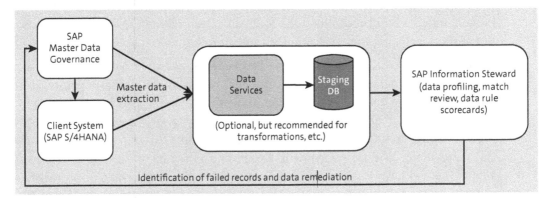

Figure 13.5 Data Remediation Using SAP Information Steward

For integration with a data quality tool, a data quality connector class is implemented with the IF_MDG_DQR_DQ_SERVICE interface. The UI is based on the MDG_DQR_OVP application. The data quality remediation service is configured using Customizing path (Transaction MDGIMG), **Master Data Governance, Central Governance · General Settings · Data Quality and Search · Data Quality Remediation · Define Data Quality Service**. The change request process is defined to remediate the failed records through an SAP Master Data Governance process.

13.3   Integration with Third-Party Solutions

In system landscapes, where the SAP Master Data Governance system should integrate with other solutions, including non-SAP solutions, many options are available. As discussed in previous chapters, master data information can be replicated to or from the SAP Master Data Governance system using enterprise services (both SOAP-based and REST-based services), files, RFCs, business application programming interfaces (BAPIs), or APIs.

If the standard data model will be enhanced with additional entities or attributes, and this information needs to be exchanged with other solutions, the interfaces need to be extended accordingly.

Some of the use cases include integration with address libraries for address check, tax jurisdiction code validation with third-party tax software, integration with non-SAP product lifecycle management solutions, customer relationship management (CRM) solutions, material pricing solutions, and so on. Most of these third-party solutions provide proprietary SAP interfaces to support these scenarios. SAP Master Data Governance can be integrated via open standard interfaces such as web services for real-time communication or via the file mechanism for batch communication. SAP interface mechanisms such as RFCs and IDocs can be used though middleware, preferably SAP Process Integration or SAP Cloud Platform Integration Suite (for cloud-based solutions), for third-party communication and transformations.

Additionally, an enrichment framework can be leveraged to enrich the SAP Master Data Governance data fields. The data can be enriched using an internal or external service. The standard delivery provides the address enrichment logic to integrate with external address libraries and provides the ability to integrate the enrichment UI with the SAP Master Data Governance UI. The key components that need to be defined are the enrichment adapter, enrichment feeder, and enrichment UI. The enrichment adapter should have interface IF_USMD_ENRICHMENT_ADAPTER implemented. It makes a call to the external or internal service to get the data for data enrichment. The enrichment feeder class implements the IF_USMD_ENRICHMENT_FEEDER interface and converts the data from the adapter format to the SAP Master Data Governance format and vice versa. The enrichment UI should be a Web Dynpro ABAP component with the MDG_ENRICHMENT_INTF Web Dynpro interface. A service can have only one adapter implementation and the associated feeder class. The enrichment spots can be leveraged for enrichment of address data, tax jurisdiction data, and so on.

SAP key mapping and value mapping frameworks can be used for mapping the data consumed by both SAP and non-SAP solutions during replication and consolidation processes.

13.4   Summary

This chapter provided an overview of various APIs and a high-level view of common integration scenarios with other solutions. In the next chapter, you'll be introduced to details on how to execute data migration to central governance.

Chapter 14

Master Data Migration

Data migration is an area of vital importance for the success of any master data governance implementation project. This chapter describes the techniques and technology options available in the central governance framework for initial loads with a focus on migrating master data objects from existing SAP ERP systems to the SAP Master Data Governance environment.

Master data by nature is shared centrally and exchanged across business applications, business processes, and different business lines. Master data is vital for executing any business process because it includes data about business partners, customers, suppliers, materials, financials (e.g., cost centers and profit centers), hierarchies, and more. Master data is typically shared by multiple users and groups across an organization, so there is an increased possibility of duplicate, obsolete, and inaccurate master data existing in the current source applications.

Master data extract, transform, and load (ETL) activities can be challenging and time-consuming. In the absence of the right data migration strategy, unexpected hidden data inconsistencies may jeopardize the project timelines and potentially put the whole project at risk. During SAP Master Data Governance implementation projects, the biggest challenge can be the timely and smooth transition of error-free quality master data. Failure to ensure this may potentially affect the current business processes, procedures, and business transactions in the source application.

SAP delivers applications within the central governance framework in addition to some other already available options that help to successfully migrate the master data from the existing SAP ERP to the central governance environment in SAP Master Data Governance.

> **Note**
>
> The data migration approaches based on consolidation and mass processing functionality and on SAP Landscape Transformation Replication Server (SAP LT Replication Server) are covered in Chapter 9, so we won't cover them in this chapter.

14.1   Data Migration Options

In the following sections, we'll first discuss when you may need to perform master data migration. After that, we'll discuss the various technology options available for extraction (from SAP ERP as the source), conversion, and loading into SAP Master Data Governance. In addition, some general recommendations for initial data loads are provided.

14.1.1   Migration Use Cases

Some common use cases where master data migration activities might become a requirement are as follows:

- **New SAP Master Data Governance implementation**
  Master data migration is needed for almost every SAP Master Data Governance implementation. Every organization planning to implement SAP Master Data Governance will have master data in their existing landscape that must be migrated to the SAP Master Data Governance system. However, the scale of the master data migration activities may differ based on the exact scope of the project. Some businesses implement SAP Master Data Governance in a phased manner, so not all master data existing in the current application must be migrated to the SAP Master Data Governance environment.

- **Post go-live maintenance in SAP Master Data Governance**
  For various business reasons, there might be a requirement to create or update multiple records after the SAP Master Data Governance go-live. SAP Master Data Governance data migration options play an important role in meeting such requirements where governance is expected before creating/updating records in bulk. Updating hierarchy information for financial master data in SAP Master Data Governance is a good example in which activities, such as downloading from SAP Master Data Governance and uploading hierarchies back to SAP Master Data Governance after necessary updates, are required.

- **Onboarding new business lines or domains in SAP Master Data Governance**
  If your company goes live with SAP Master Data Governance or adopts a phased rollout approach based on some regions, business units, master data domains, or applications, you may want to expand the SAP Master Data Governance footprint in the landscape for governing master data centrally, and this requires data migration.

- **Merger/acquisition**
  Many organizations acquire new businesses/companies that might be maintaining master data in their own legacy applications. You can adopt a common strategy for all master data maintenance for the organization. To govern all master data centrally using SAP Master Data Governance, such old applications are integrated with SAP Master Data Governance to create the system of record that feeds master data to these applications. Initial data loads are required in such scenarios.

- **Data quality initiatives with specialized data quality tools**
  Very often, businesses take initiatives with a focus on data quality where they plan to run parallel projects using specialized tools/applications during or after the SAP Master Data Governance implementation projects. Such projects need to process data on their end to achieve the specified objectives, which require extraction and loading of master data.

14.1.2   Data Extraction from SAP ERP

Data extraction from existing SAP ERP applications is an important activity in the process of migrating the master data to the SAP Master Data Governance environment. This can be done in several different ways. Some of these options are intuitive, whereas some approaches are proven and more traditional. Your choice for extraction of master data will be based on your project requirements. Some of the data extraction options available in SAP ERP are as follows:

- Remote function call (RFC)
- Table downloads
- SAP Landscape Transformation (SLT)
- Transaction MDMGX–based extraction
- Service-oriented architecture (SOA)
- Other ETL extractors
- Data export framework
- Application Link Enabling (ALE)

Following are some techniques that are widely tried and tested by the organizations in SAP ERP environments. Remember, SAP Master Data Governance runs with SAP ERP when SAP Master Data Governance is an add-on. Therefore, traditional data extraction mechanisms used in SAP ERP systems can also be used in SAP Master Data Governance for extracting master data, if there is a requirement to extract data from SAP Master Data Governance. Some of these traditional extraction options may not be appropriate in some cases when the SAP Master Data Governance flex area is being used as a source for extracting master data. However, in the context of this topic, we'll only discuss in detail the options that are relevant and capable of loading master data directly into the SAP Master Data Governance staging area and not in the backend active area:

- **Application Link Enabling (ALE)**
  ALE is an SAP-supplied technique for transferring data in and out of SAP systems. ALE is considered a traditional and proven way of migrating data within the SAP ecosystem using IDoc formats. This is still seen as an effective and preferred way of migrating master data for objects, including suppliers, customers, and materials data, from any SAP application to SAP Master Data Governance (e.g., objects implemented in reuse mode). However, customer-vendor integration (CVI) setup might

14

be needed to generate corresponding business partners for suppliers and customers in SAP Master Data Governance. In SAP S/4HANA systems, CVI setup is mandatory.

- **Service-oriented architecture (SOA)**
  SOA-based communication is becoming increasingly popular for sending data within and outside SAP environments. SAP provides out-of-the-box web services for various master data objects. SOA is capable of efficiently communicating between two SAP ERP systems and the SAP Master Data Governance system through point-to-point communication as well as mediating through SAP Process Integration. This interface can be used for migrating master data in the SAP Master Data Governance system.

- **SAP Landscape Transformation Replication Server (SAP LT Replication Server)**
  SAP LT Replication Server is a cornerstone in SAP HANA–based landscapes with real-time data replication requirements. With SAP LT Replication Server, you can perform even complex data transformations on the fly in replications from SAP and non-SAP sources. It provides a high-performance technology and methodology that can affectively read, convert, and load the data in the SAP ecosystem.

- **Data export framework**
  The data export framework is provided by SAP for extracting data in XML formats, which are readily acceptable on the SAP Master Data Governance data import framework. Various master data objects can be easily extracted using the data export framework via Transaction DTEXPORT. (This option is explained in more detail in Section 14.2.)

- **Report KBAS_MDGF_SET_DOWNLOAD**
  Extracting hierarchies for SAP Master Data Governance, Financials, objects can be a very complex and tedious task. Therefore, SAP has provided report KBAS_MDGF_SET_DOWNLOAD, which can be executed to easily extract profit center hierarchies, cost center hierarchies, and cost element hierarchies. The extracted data is in *.txt* format, which is compatible with the file upload framework in central governance.

- **Report FBS_MDGF_FRS_DOWNLOAD**
  For extracting SAP Master Data Governance, Financials, reporting structures in central governance for accounting, SAP has delivered report FBS_MDGF_FRS_DOWNLOAD. This report can be executed to extract the file repository server (FRS) from the SAP ERP system. Extracted files are in *.txt* format and can be loaded in central governance through the file upload functionality.

- **Generic SAP NetWeaver Master Data Management (SAP NetWeaver MDM) extractor: Transaction MDMGX**
  Transaction MDMGX-based extraction is provided in the SAP ERP system to extract data in SAP Master Data Governance–supported formats and structures. This extraction is provided by SAP through Transaction MDMGX within an SAP client system. It's available in various SAP systems and can extract master data as well as Customizing data in the XML format. The extracted file can either be downloaded to

the local PC or stored within the application server on which the transaction is running.

- **FTP**
  FTP can also be used to send extracted files to any FTP-based receiver. This method is more successful for extracting financial master data and its hierarchies.

14.1.3   Transaction MDMGX Data Extraction from SAP ERP

As a prerequisite to extracting master data using Transaction MDMGX, you must implement the following SAP Notes on the source SAP systems:

- SAP Note 1783851
- SAP Note 1880169

After implementing the SAP Notes, you can execute Transaction MDMGX in SAP ERP. On the screen shown in Figure 14.1, only **Start Extraction** is relevant. **Generate XSD** isn't required.

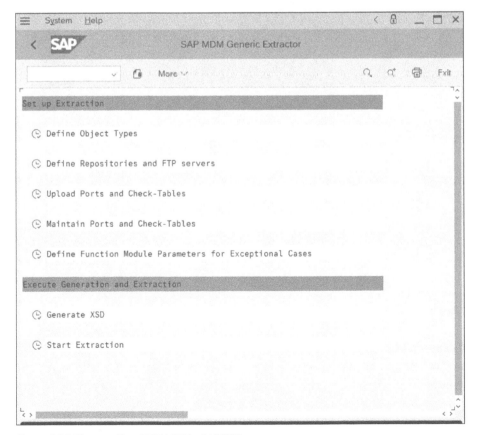

Figure 14.1 Transaction MDMGX in SAP ERP

You can import this extracted data into SAP Master Data Governance using the data import framework. However, to import data into the SAP Master Data Governance staging layer, a valid change request type with a workflow is a prerequisite.

The following steps are performed in Transaction MDMGX of the SAP ERP system from which the data has to be extracted:

1. **Check the object types in Transaction MDMGX.**
   SAP Master Data Governance object types are predefined by SAP. Check that the object types already exist as shown in Figure 14.2.

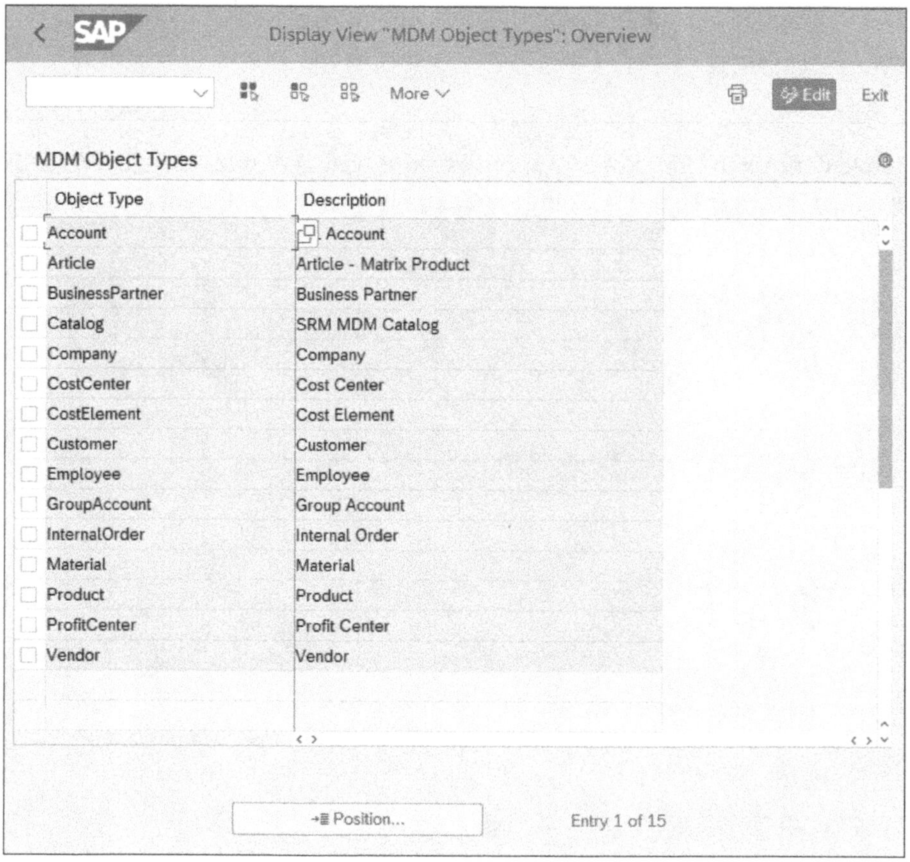

Figure 14.2 Transaction MDMGX: Object Types

2. **Define repositories and FTP servers.**
   Figure 14.3 shows all repositories and FTP servers that must be defined for the extraction of all SAP Master Data Governance, Financials, objects. It's strictly recommended that you create them accordingly using the same names.

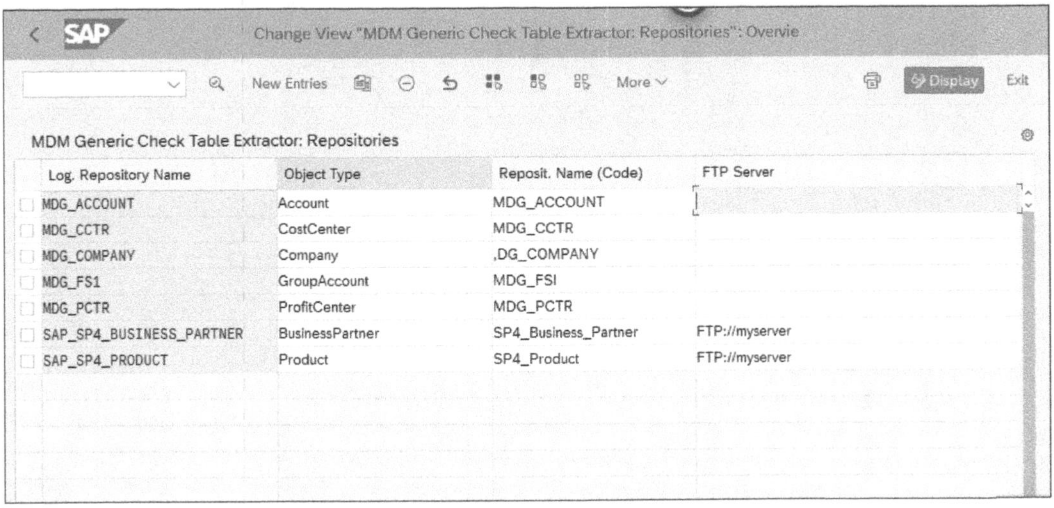

Figure 14.3 Transaction MDMGX: Defining Repositories and FTP Servers

3. **Maintain ports and check tables.**
   Follow these steps to maintain the ports and check tables:
   - Upload the SAP Master Data Governance, Financials, ports and check tables text file into Transaction MDMGX (the text file is attached to SAP Note 1882127). Select **Upload Ports and Check-Tables**.
   - Enter the **Object Type**, and select the locally stored text file. Ensure that the **Remove Header Line** checkbox is set.
   - Execute the upload. After the success message appears, go back to the main menu, and select **Maintain Ports and Check-Tables** to check the ports.
   - Choose system type **R3**, and display the records.

   Figure 14.4 shows where upload ports and check tables are maintained in SAP Master Data Governance.

4. **Define function module parameters for exceptional cases.**
   To overcome the gap between SAP Master Data Governance data models and SAP ERP data models, function modules are required while extracting the data from SAP ERP in the SAP Master Data Governance expected structure and format. There is no general configuration defined for input parameters. It's mandatory to adjust the parameter according to the desired extraction. The parameter must use the common format of an SQL statement. Figure 14.5 shows the system screen for defining function module parameters for exceptional cases.

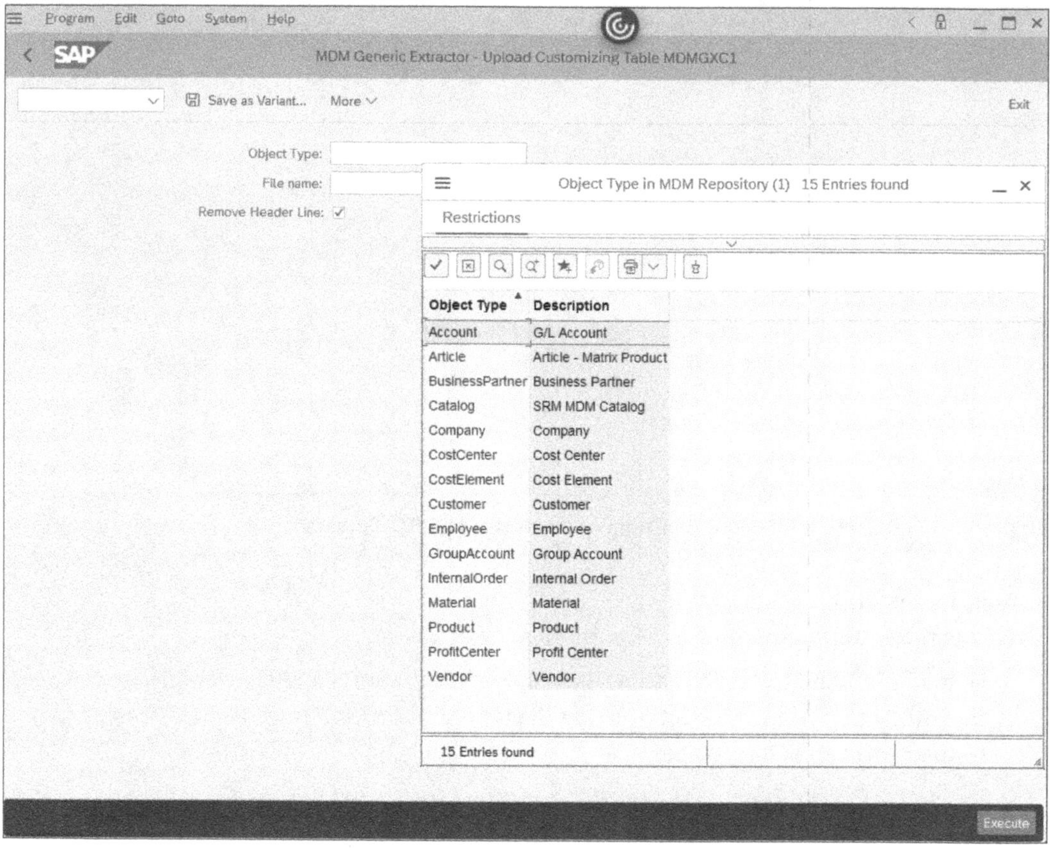

Figure 14.4 Transaction MDMGX: Upload Ports and Check Tables

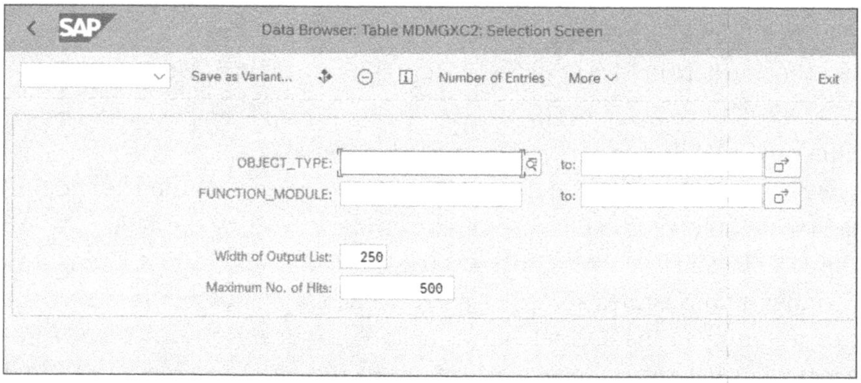

Figure 14.5 Defining Function Module Parameters for Exceptional Cases

5. **Extract the data.**

   Follow these steps to extract the data:

   - In Transaction MDMGX, click **Start Extraction**.

   - Select a repository using the search help.

- If you leave the input fields for **Port Name (Code)** blank, the system tries to extract data for all ports being maintained. If you enter a port, the system will only extract that port's specific data.
- Select the **Local Download** checkbox and use the search help on the **File Directory** field to specify the destination folder for the extracted files.
- Click the execute icon to trigger the extraction.

The Transaction MDMGX extraction process from an SAP ERP system is now complete. This extraction method isn't suitable for hierarchy extractions, but it's normally used for extracting financial master data, such as cost centers, profit centers, and so on.

14.1.4 Data Conversion Option in SAP Master Data Governance

Data conversion is an important part of the data migration process. Normally, for any master data conversion requirements, specialized tools are used for handling any complex transformation requirements, for example, SAP Data Services.

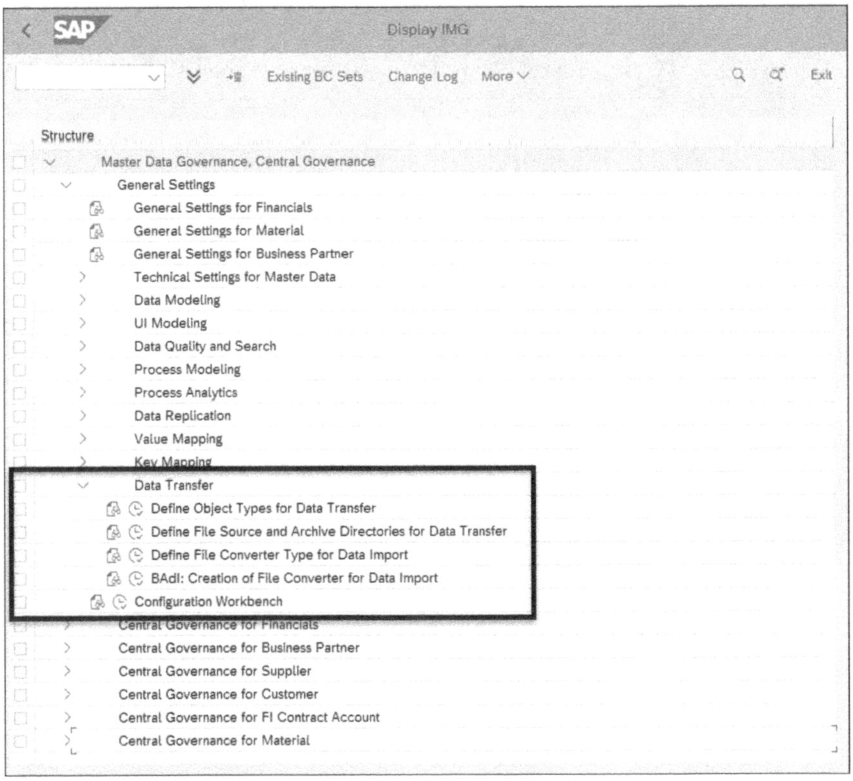

Figure 14.6 Conversion Option in the SAP Master Data Governance Import Framework

The SAP Master Data Governance file import framework supports load files in only certain defined file formats (e.g., XML). However, in some instances, files extracted from source applications may not be available in the expected format for the SAP Master Data Governance data import framework, and specialized conversion tools may not be readily available. Under such scenarios, standard Business Add-In (BAdI) BADI_MDG_FILECONVERTER can be used to perform any conversion activities, including formatting the load files in the desired XML formats. You can navigate to this BAdI using Transaction MDGIMG and by following the path shown in Figure 14.6.

This BAdI provides converter implementations for different file formats, such as *.XLS*. Additionally, the conversion types must be maintained in the Customizing activity via Transaction MDGIMG. This is a filter-dependent BAdI.

While importing the master data in SAP Master Data Governance, you can apply converter settings by selecting the appropriate converter type via **File Import • Custom Converter Settings • Use Search Help • Select Converter Type for the Load • Execute Import after Selecting the Mandatory Parameters**.

You can apply file import converter settings from the screen shown in Figure 14.7.

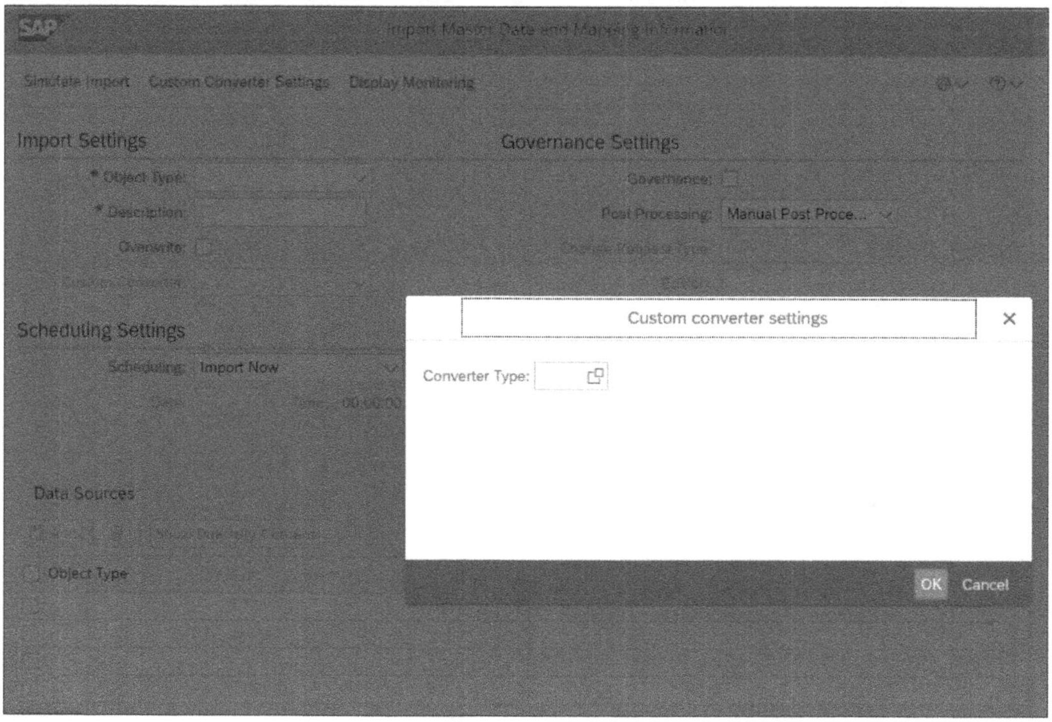

Figure 14.7 Applying Converter Settings during Data Import in SAP Master Data Governance

14.1.5   Data Load Options in SAP Master Data Governance

SAP Master Data Governance works on the concept of *staging* and *active areas* where the governance of the master data will happen in the staging area typically by a workflow process. After the master data is approved at the end of the governance process, the master data is transferred to the active area of SAP Master Data Governance.

Active Area

Several proven options, such as ALE and SOA, can be leveraged for migrating master data from the SAP ERP system to the SAP Master Data Governance system and from one SAP system to another in general. These standard options do have some limitations when it comes to updating the staging area of SAP Master Data Governance for the respective master data objects implemented in flex mode, for example, finance master data objects. SAP Master Data Governance can use these options provided the goal is to migrate data directly to the active area and not to the staging area.

The data import framework provides the option to choose whether the master data load should happen in the staging area or directly to the active area, skipping the staging area completely while loading the master data. However, when using the file upload option, the data is always loaded in the staging area. Some of the options that can be used for loading master data directly into the active area of SAP Master Data Governance include RFC, SAP LT Replication Server, SOA, ALE, data import framework, and the Legacy System Migration Workbench (LSMW).

Staging Area

Objects implemented in flex mode of SAP Master Data Governance use the same SAP Master Data Governance generated tables to store inactive as well as active data. This means for all financial master data objects or other custom objects implemented in flex mode, both active and inactive master data resides in the SAP Master Data Governance area. Therefore, traditional data load options might not be suitable to load the master data. This demands a special framework to load data in the staging area of SAP Master Data Governance. In addition, other objects implemented in reuse mode might need to go through the governance area for various business reasons. Some of the available options capable of loading data in the staging area of SAP Master Data Governance are as follows:

- Data import framework
- File upload framework
- SAP Master Data Governance application programming interfaces (APIs)
- Consolidation and mass processing framework

Consolidation and SAP Master Data Governance APIs are out of scope for this chapter. In this chapter, our focus is primarily to discuss the file import and file upload options in SAP Master Data Governance. Detailed steps about these two options are covered later in Section 14.2.

[»]

> **Note**
>
> For additional details on consolidation and mass processing framework refer to Chapter 9. For more on SAP Master Data Governance APIs, refer to Chapter 13.

14.1.6   General Recommendations for Initial Data Load

Every SAP Master Data Governance project is unique, and a common strategy usually can't be applied to different projects. Numerous decisions and different factors specific to the projects may influence the choice of data migration strategy.

Following are some of the common factors that normally influence the selection of options, and they can be taken into consideration while deciding about the right strategy for migrating data to the SAP Master Data Governance environment:

- **Hub versus co-deployed**

  If you have a single SAP ERP instance in the landscape with SAP Master Data Governance being implemented on top of the operational SAP ERP system, then data migration isn't needed for some of the objects, including customers, suppliers, and materials. CVI setup would be required to generate business partners for customers and suppliers. Because financial master data objects are implemented as flex data model, data migration is still necessary in the SAP Master Data Governance area. In a hub-based SAP Master Data Governance environment, all types of master data must be extracted from the source SAP application and loaded in SAP Master Data Governance.

- **Type of master data object**

  The master data object type is a major influencing factor that plays a role in determining the migration approach. Suppliers, customers, and materials can be loaded using traditional techniques as well as supported by the new data import framework based on XML formats, or consolidation and mass processing framework. However, because the financial (0G) data model in SAP Master Data Governance uses flex mode, the financial master data objects, for example, cost centers, items, general ledger accounts, profit centers, cost elements, and so on, can't use the traditional data load techniques. Even the consolidation and mass processing framework doesn't support objects implemented in flex mode. We must rely on the SAP Master Data Governance data import framework or the SAP Master Data Governance file upload framework. Groups and hierarchy data can't be loaded using the data import framework, so the file upload framework is a suitable option.

- **Volume of master data**

  Like any other data migration project, the volume of master data to be migrated to the new environment can be a compelling factor to choose or not to choose certain available techniques. File upload and data import methods may experience performance issues and challenges beyond certain volumes. The file upload functionality doesn't support queueing or parallelization. Splitting the load files into smaller sizes and parallel processing is recommended to use file import and file upload methods.

- **Number of source applications**
  Landscape complexity and the number of connected systems may determine the overall approach for migrating the data in SAP Master Data Governance. Projects involving multiple source systems may have interdependencies in terms of sequencing and decision-making about the loads. Often such large projects may also involve consolidation requirements in large-scale transformation projects, which might need specialist data quality tools such as enterprise information management (EIM) on SAP HANA, SAP Data Services, and so on. However, in this chapter, we won't be covering consolidation and other data quality requirements. Instead, we'll focus only on extracting and migrating the data into the SAP Master Data Governance environment. Consolidation of master data is covered in Chapter 9, and data quality is discussed in Chapter 8.

- **Validity dates**
  Some of the master data, such as profit center and cost center, is time dependent in nature with validity dates associated with each of the records. Time-dependent master data is governed in SAP Master Data Governance using editions, so it's important to extract and load such data with great sensitivity to avoid any impact on the business processes and transactional data in downstream systems.

- **Data transformation needed**
  Although it's recommended to clean data in the source system before extracting and loading it in SAP Master Data Governance, there may be requirements that specify data transformation needs that require specialized tools to improve the quality of the extracted data. Selection of the ETL tools for such requirements may also influence the data migration strategies. In some cases, data extracted in SAP Data Services can be easily loaded into SAP Master Data Governance using the native capability to integrate the two applications using SOA-based communication.

- **Application technology and version of source system**
  SAP Master Data Governance natively integrates with most of the SAP applications, minimizing the need for any custom developments or mappings. Some of the lower versions of SAP ERP applications doesn't support SOA-based communication, so it may not be viable to use some of the techniques.

- **Data format preferences**
  Due to some existing enterprise strategies in place, you might choose to adhere to a common approach for all data communication within the landscape. Such preferences may also influence the choice of data migration strategy. In addition, some companies try to stick with old and proven techniques (e.g., ALE) because they have the available resource skill sets and are comfortable with these techniques.

- **Governance needed during migration**
  Not all the available data load techniques have the capability to go through the

governance (staging) area of SAP Master Data Governance. If you're planning to use the business rules built into SAP Master Data Governance and/or expect workflow approvals before loading the data in SAP Master Data Governance, you must follow the techniques that can populate the master data first in the staging area before activating it. The file upload and file import options are available for loading master data in the staging area. SAP Master Data Governance, Financials, master data and other custom objects implemented in flex mode must go through the SAP Master Data Governance staging area. However, this is optional for the objects implemented in reuse mode.

- **SAP Master Data Governance implementation approach (big bang vs. phased)**
  Scale, objective, and exact use case of a project may also affect the master data migration strategy. Large-scale big bang implementations tend to involve specialized middleware tools that are responsible for preparing the load files for SAP Master Data Governance.

Tips

Some important considerations during data migration are as follows:

- Hierarchies aren't supported by the file import framework in SAP Master Data Governance, but they can be uploaded using the file upload method.

- File upload may not be the right option for updating objects with multiple entities and complex relationships.

- For custom objects with relatively simple data modeling, file upload can be an easy and reliable option because it involves minimum development.

- For any data model enhancements in SAP Master Data Governance, no enhancements are needed to use the file upload functionalities. However, file import would require some development.

- Data loads can be scheduled while using the file import framework as it supports parallel processing.

- File upload supports text, comma-separated values (CSV), and tab-delimited file formats, whereas file import supports only XML and SOA formats. However, using a BAdI implementation available in SAP Master Data Governance, the file import method can support CSV files.

- Migrate only cleansed data to SAP Master Data Governance. Avoid bringing obsolete master data that is no longer used or required for operational purposes.

- Data cleansing is a complex and time-consuming activity that involves making thousands of decisions. To be successful, start cleaning the master data early and in your existing applications first.

- Leverage the key mapping and value functionality for cross-referencing between legacy and SAP Master Data Governance values.

- Identify key mapping and value mapping requirements early in the project.

- While extracting and loading the time-dependent data, you should use a time slice consisting of the valid-from and valid-to dates as selection criteria. In SAP Master Data Governance, the entity type will be stored within an edition that also has a time slice. At least the valid-from date extracted from the client system should fit into one of the target editions in the SAP Master Data Governance hub.
- For financial master data objects, use the chart of accounts, controlling area, and company codes as selection criteria. This limits the number of records that will be extracted and thus ensures that the change request used for the import in the SAP Master Data Governance hub doesn't get too big.
- SAP recommends the creation of application-specific file directories, which will be bound to unique folders of the application server.

14.2   Data Migration Strategies

With several traditional and new techniques available for migrating the master data into SAP Master Data Governance, it's vital that the right strategy is adopted after considering all important factors related to the master data and specific to your project. In this section, SAP Master Data Governance–specific data loads are described, along with an overview of key mapping and value mapping uploads.

Note

The consolidation and mass processing framework also supports initial load scenarios under its mass processing capabilities. This is a recommended option while loading large volumes of master data. Because this chapter is primarily focused on data migration capabilities available as part of central governance, refer to Chapter 9, Section 9.2, for details on mass processing capabilities.

14.2.1   Data Import/Export Framework

The data import/export framework is a proven technique to export or import master data, key mapping information, and value mapping information. This technique is designed to use XML-based master data load files, which can easily be exported from existing SAP ERP systems. The following sections provide more details about this process and the steps involved in using the data import framework/data export framework.

Data Import Framework

Let's walk through the steps while using the data import framework. First, note that the data import framework requires at least two file directories on the application server to facilitate loads:

- One directory to store the files to be imported
- One directory to store the archived files that have been imported

Physical directories can be created on the application server and mapped to logical directories using Transaction FILE. The IMG path for configuring the directories in Customizing for SAP Master Data Governance is (Transaction MDGIMG) **General Settings · Data Transfer · Define File Source · Archive Directories for Data Transfer**.

The data transfer directories are used for the source files to be imported in SAP Master Data Governance. The archive path directories are needed to place the load files after the successful upload of data in the SAP Master Data Governance staging area. Figure 14.8 shows the screen to define the file source and archive directories for data transfer.

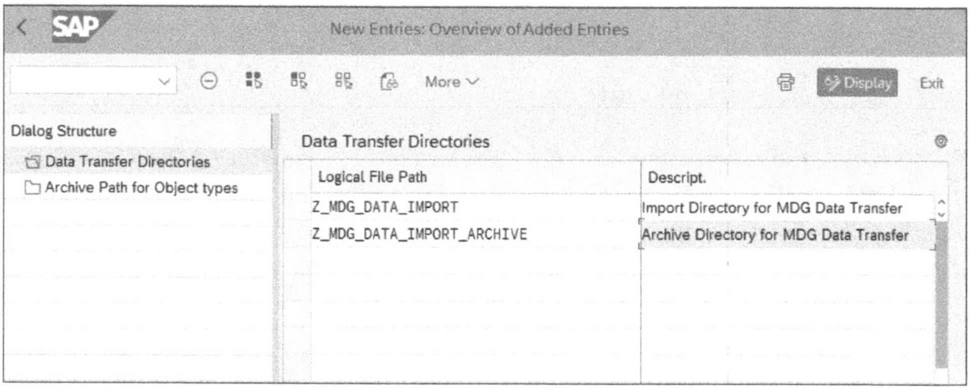

Figure 14.8 Defining the File Source and Archive Directories for Data Transfer

In this step, the master data has already been extracted in XML format and is available on the application server in the designated folder. Extracted files can be uploaded to the application server through Transaction CG3Z. Enter a path on the application server as the storage location in the **Target file on application server** field, and click the **Upload** button to start the upload (see Figure 14.9).

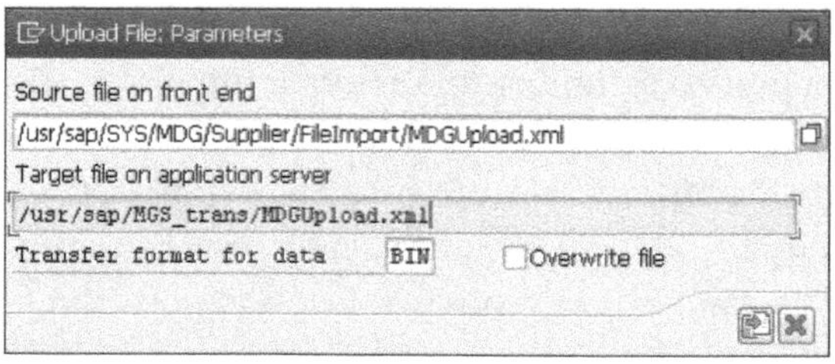

Figure 14.9 Uploading Extracted Files to the Application Server

The four main tasks of the data import process are as follows:

1. **Start the data import framework by following these steps:**
   - Log on to the SAP Master Data Governance hub.

- Run Transaction NWBC.
- Select the appropriate role to navigate to your work center. The example uses role SAP_MDGF_*.
- In the tree menu on the left-hand side, select **Data Exchange**.
- Within **Data Exchange**, navigate to **Data Transfer**.
- Click on **Import Master Data** to go to the main screen for executing the load in SAP Master Data Governance.

Figure 14.10 shows the main screen of the data import framework in SAP Master Data Governance.

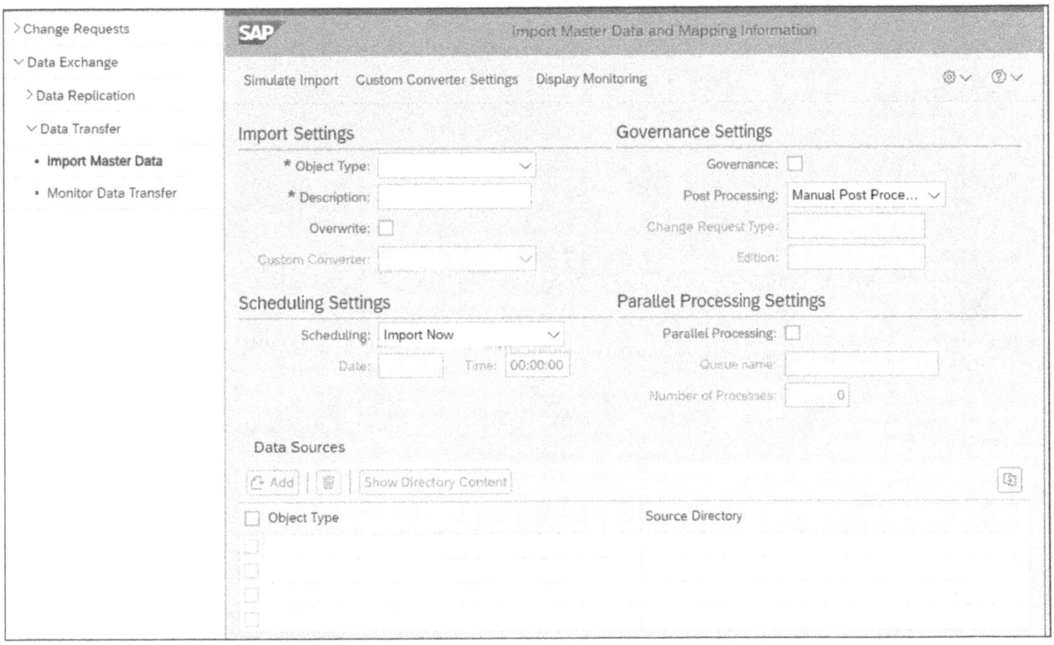

Figure 14.10 The Data Import Framework in SAP Master Data Governance

2. **Prepare for the import of master data.**
The data import framework is a cross-entity type application. It supports importing various entity types for various data models. Entity types are reflected in data import framework object types. Following are the steps required to prepare the upload of master data:

- Choose an object type from the **Object Type** dropdown.
- Enter a **Description** for the import of master data.
- In the **Data Sources** area, click the **Add** button.
- Select the object type, and confirm by clicking **OK**.
- Use the search help for the source directory to select the one option that contains the data to be imported.

- Check the content of the directory by clicking on the **Show Directory Content** button.

- Define a **Change Request Type** and an **Edition** for the import, if applicable.

Import settings can be selected out of the **Object Type** list available in the data import framework, as shown in Figure 14.11.

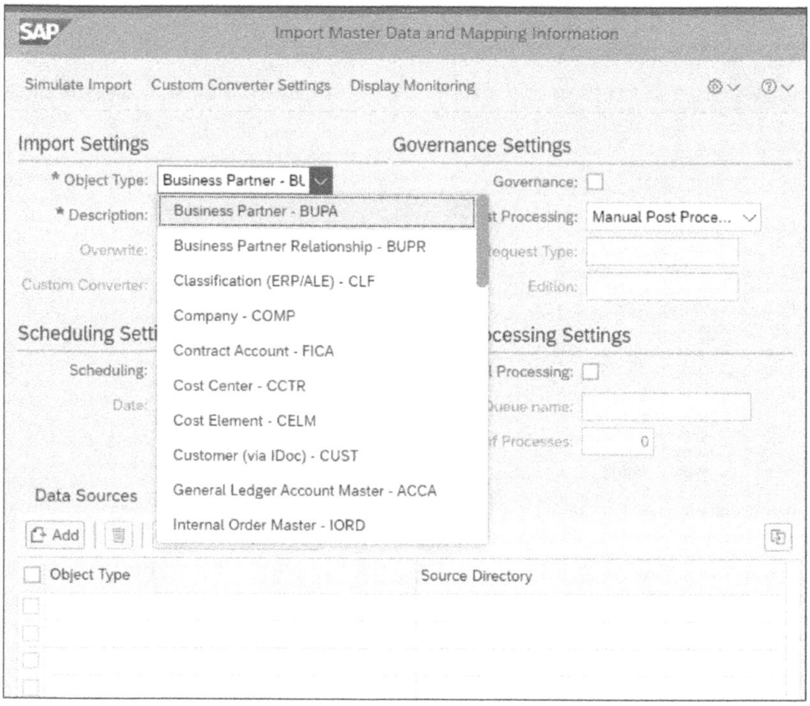

Figure 14.11 Data Import Framework: Import Settings

3. **Simulate the import.**

   Master data import can be simulated in the data import framework before executing the data import. The simulation processes the files ready to be imported and maps them into the target format but without creating a change request. After the simulation has been started, you can select **Display Monitoring** to navigate and analyze the logs during simulation.

4. **Execute the import.**

   The import of master data using the data import framework automatically creates a change request in SAP Master Data Governance. A direct import of the master data into the active area is also possible by skipping the governance process. Following are the detailed steps to be followed:

   - Click on the **Import** button.

   - Note the **Run Number** shown on the user interface.

   - Click the **Display Monitoring** button to navigate to the import logs.

– When the result of the import run status is displayed, expand the data transfer logs. A change request number will be generated in the logs if the load was successful.

– If the import fails, check and rectify the data in the file and then process again. After the load is successful, the load files are automatically transferred to the archive directory.

After a successful load run, the master data is loaded in the staging area in the form of a change request that must be processed according to its workflow definition to ensure the creation of the master data in the active area.

File Export Framework

For operational purposes, after the SAP Master Data Governance go-live, there may be requirements to extract master data from SAP Master Data Governance. File export can be useful for extracting data for SAP Data Services or SAP NetWeaver MDM.

For this purpose, the data export framework can be used for various standard object types. File export can also be performed for key mapping and value mapping information. When SAP Master Data Governance is based on various filtering criteria, the master data can be extracted easily in the SOA-based structures in XML format.

You can provide the object type, export description, variant (if any), communication channel, file prefix, target directory, and target system.

Package sizes, target systems selection, and export scheduling to defined directories are also supported. Mandatory settings that require selecting a parameter value have an asterisk. Master data can be filtered by clicking on **Number of Selected Objects**. After all settings are completed, click on **Export Data** to execute, and generate the exported file in the desired directory. Figure 14.12 shows the screen used to trigger the data export.

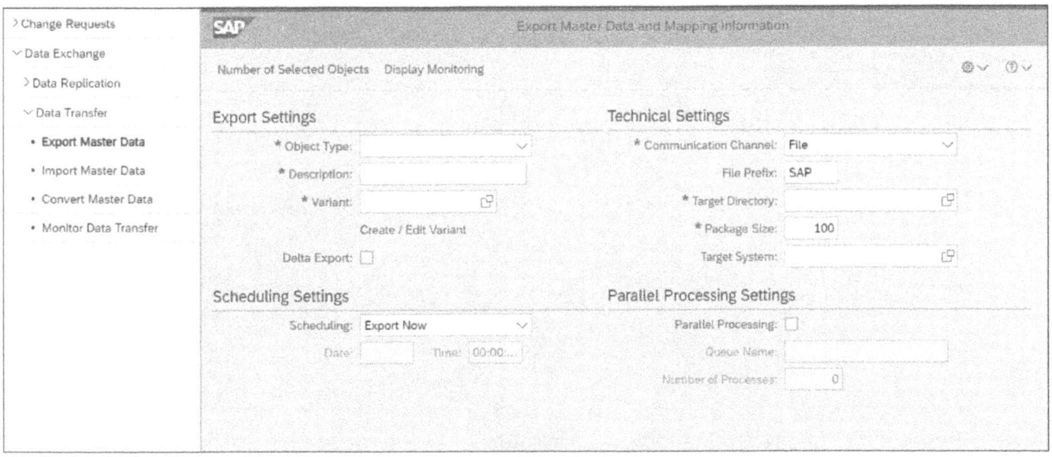

Figure 14.12 Master Data Export Screen in SAP Master Data Governance with Necessary Settings

14.2.2   Key Mapping and Value Mapping

The data import/export framework can also be used for mass creation of key and value mappings. The objects are delivered out of the box and don't need any special settings. For using the data import framework like other master data objects, key mapping and value mapping load files also must be prepared in the right structure for successful loads. In the **Object Types** parameter, **Key Mappings** and **Value Mappings** should be selected for the respective import/export.

Key Mapping Initial Loads

Because SAP Master Data Governance is the central master data governance application responsible for all master data maintenance activities for various downstream systems, it's likely that numbers representing the keys for master data in SAP Master Data Governance aren't the same as the keys maintained in the downstream system for the same record.

Key mapping cross-referencing information can be uploaded in the SAP Master Data Governance framework in bulk uploads. The data import framework in SAP Master Data Governance also facilitates importing key mapping information in SAP Master Data Governance. This cross-referencing information between SAP Master Data Governance and the downstream application can be loaded in SAP Master Data Governance using an XML file for various objects in SAP Master Data Governance.

The SAP Basis structure for each of the objects remains the same while different IDs of the objects get an individual universal unique ID (UUID). Following is the structure in which the IDs are maintained in the key mapping framework:

Group UUID – Object UUID – OTC – OITC – ID value – business system

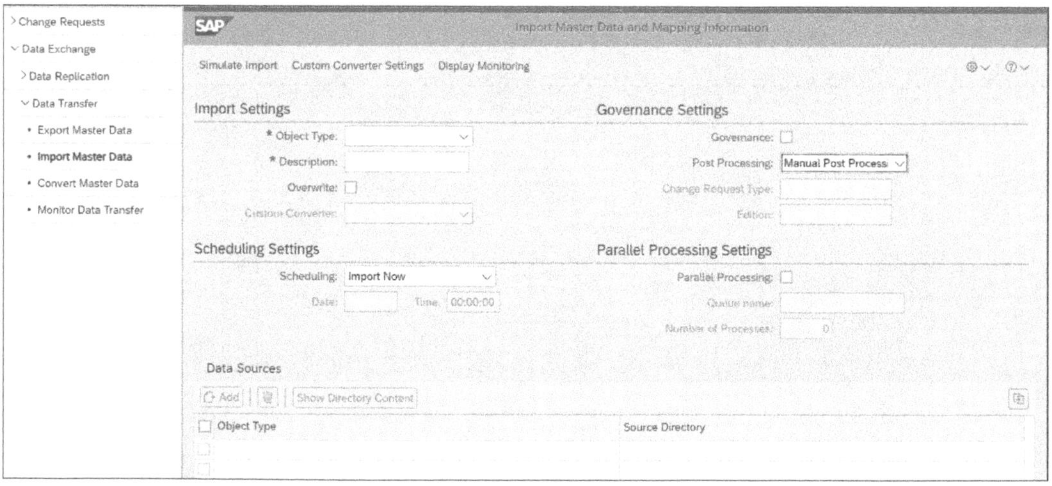

Figure 14.13 Import Key Mapping Information

Transaction MDG_ANALYSE_IDM can be used for analyzing the key mapping information maintained in SAP Master Data Governance, whereas Transaction MDG_KM_MAINTAIN and Transaction MDG_ADJUST_IDM can be used for key mapping maintenance purposes. Figure 14.13 displays the **Import Master Data and Mapping Information** screen in SAP Master Data Governance, which is used for triggering the key mapping import.

After import directories are created and visible through Transaction FILE, you can go to the **Import Master Data** screen and select **Object Type Key Mapping** in the **Select Related Object** area, as shown in Figure 14.14.

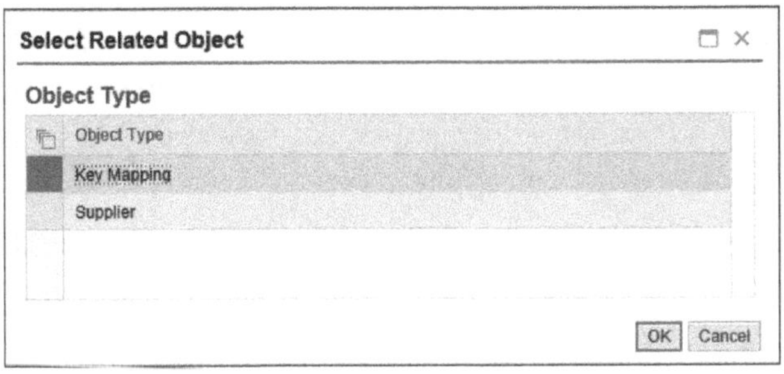

Figure 14.14 Selecting the Object Type during the Key Mapping Load

Select the appropriate source directory where key mapping load files are located by selecting the right source directory defined in SAP Master Data Governance, as shown in Figure 14.15.

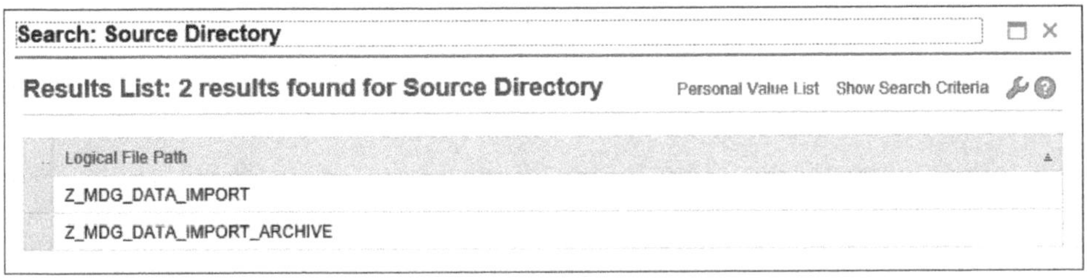

Figure 14.15 Choosing the Source Directory for the Key Mapping Import

Although file import is the recommended option for a key mapping load, there is another option available: program CREATE_MASS_KEY_MAPPING or Transaction CREATE_MASS_ID_MAP. Load files can be in CSV or Microsoft Excel formats and should have values for the following attributes in the same sequence as mentioned here:

- Object Type
- Business System
- Object ID Type
- Object ID

- **External Object Type**
- **External System ID**
- **External Obj. ID Type**
- **External Object ID**

This can be a quick option as files can be prepared easily in Microsoft Excel. However, this method is more suitable for smaller volumes only.

Value Mapping Initial Loads

Nonharmonized master data maintenance in the landscape is a reality in which it isn't unusual that the Customizing values for some reference data are maintained differently between SAP Master Data Governance and SAP ERP applications. However, to support downstream processes and transactions, it might be necessary to send only the old legacy values to the respective downstream applications.

In SAP Master Data Governance projects, very often it's a requirement to maintain a list of legacy codes referencing new values in the SAP Master Data Governance environment. Value mappings can be used to map the code values for Customizing elements that are represented in the system to the code values of a named external list. This external list can be a global code list or a system-specific code list.

Figure 14.16 Example: Load File Prepared for Uploading Value Mapping Using Data Import

Value mappings can be manually maintained in Customizing through the following IMG path: **Master Data Governance, Central Governance · General Settings · Value Mapping**. For the purpose of mass creation of value mappings, the SAP Master Data Governance data import framework can be leveraged for loading value mapping information. Figure 14.16 shows an example of the format in which a load file can be prepared and imported in SAP Master Data Governance.

14.2.3   SAP Master Data Governance File Upload/Download

You can perform an entity-based upload/download in SAP Master Data Governance without any custom developments or enhancements needed using file upload/download. This technique supports CSV-based load files, and it's more suitable for initial loads of custom objects in SAP Master Data Governance, as well as hierarchies and objects with comparatively fewer complex data models. Steps involved in file upload/download are explained in detail in the following sections.

File Upload

File upload is another popular option in the SAP Master Data Governance framework that is used for initial loads by uploading a file in the SAP Master Data Governance staging area. SAP delivers the USMD_FILE_UPLOAD Web Dynpro application, which is used for copying master data from the load file to the SAP Master Data Governance staging area. File upload is always specific to an entity type and should mandatorily belong to an edition if editions are applicable for the entity type.

To avoid reconfiguring the selection parameters each time a file is uploaded using this framework, settings can be saved as a variant. Application logs are updated with each file loaded in the system and can always be accessed via Transaction SLG1 with the FMDM object and the UPLOAD subobject. Figure 14.17 depicts the upload mode options while specifying the impact of the file upload on existing data.

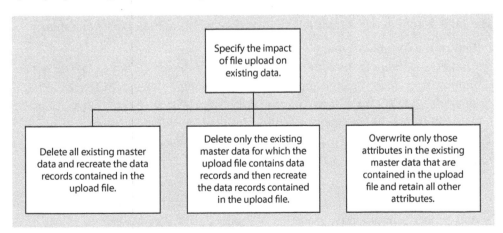

Figure 14.17 Upload Mode Options: Impact of File Upload on Existing Data

File upload can be navigated through the SAP Master Data Governance homepage by clicking on the **File Upload** option under the **Processing of Multiple Objects** section shown in Figure 14.18.

Following are some of the prerequisites required before using the file upload functionality:

- A change request type must exist with a defined workflow in process modeling.
- For uploading data in an already existing change request, the person uploading the file should be the current processor of the respective change request. In addition, the change request status should allow changes in process modeling.
- A data model must have been assigned to you with sufficient security authorizations.
- The file that is to be uploaded is only a text file (e.g., a CSV file).
- Separators applicable on field values can be semicolons, tabs, commas, and any character.
- Files to be uploaded should be available on the application server or presentation server.

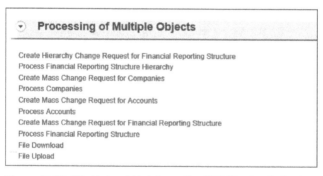

Figure 14.18 File Upload Link from the SAP Master Data Governance Homepage

The SAP Master Data Governance file upload process includes the following steps:

1. **Determine the entity type.**
   Chose the relevant **Entity Type** and **Type of Transfer** to specify which master data of the entity type are to be uploaded (**Attributes, Language-Dependent Texts**, or **Hierarchies**). In addition, if applicable for the entity type, select an appropriate **Edition**. Figure 14.19 shows the **File Upload: Step 1 (Determine Entity Type)** screen.

   The **Language-Dependent Texts** transfer type can be selected only for entity types of 1 that have language-dependent texts.

2. **Define the file structure.**
   Select the available attributes relevant for the file upload by selecting and clicking on **Add** under the appropriate level, that is, **Header** or **Data Row** (see Figure 14.20).

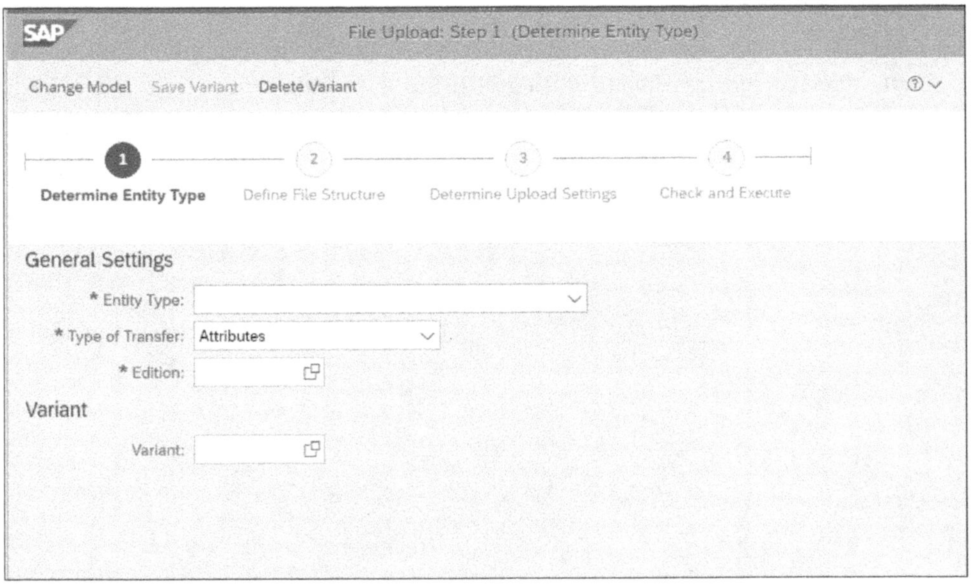

Figure 14.19 File Upload: Determine Entity Type

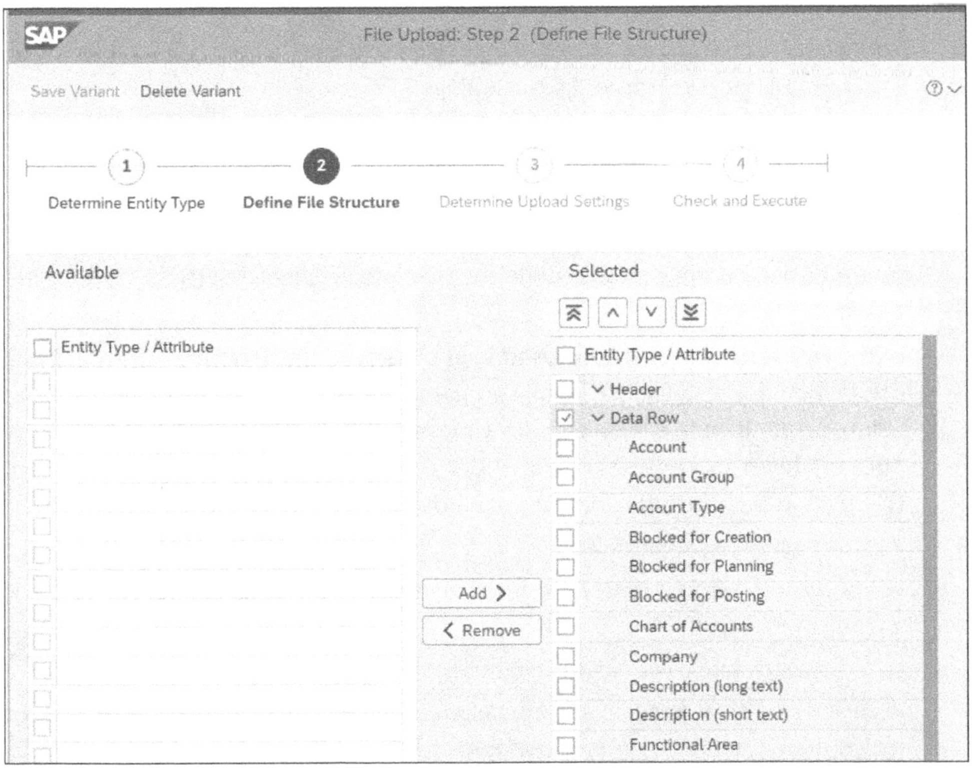

Figure 14.20 File Upload: Define File Structure (Account Entity)

3. **Determine the upload settings.**

In **Step 3** of the file upload process, various settings have to be applied for the load under these categories: **Upload Settings**, **File Store**, and **File Format** (see Figure 14.21).

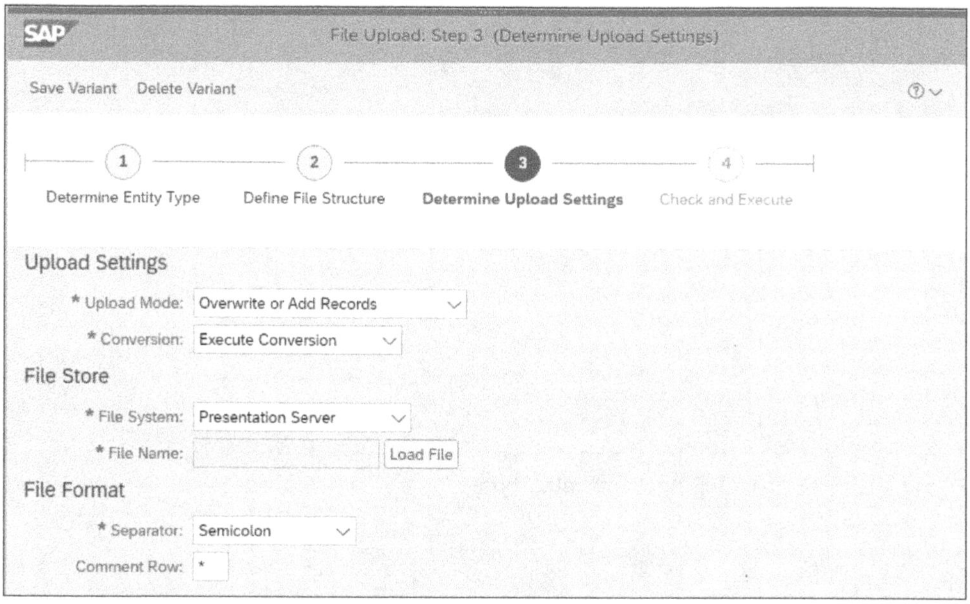

Figure 14.21 File Upload: Determine Upload Settings

These settings are explained in detail, as follows:

- **Upload Mode**

This step should be carefully executed with the right option to make sure only the intended actions are performed via the file upload. **Upload Settings** options are shown in Figure 14.22.

- In the **Delete All and Add Records** upload mode and the **Attributes** transfer type, the system deletes all existing master data. The system then recreates the data records contained in the upload file. Upload mode **Delete All and Add Records** is only offered if the settings of the entity type in data modeling allow deletion. However, this is permitted only if the following are true:

  • The master data to be deleted isn't already used as nodes in a hierarchy.

  • The system automatically deletes master data that is used as leaves in a hierarchy.

  • The master data to be deleted isn't used in any other entity types.

- In the **Overwrite or Add Records** upload mode, the system deletes master data for which there are data records in the upload file. It then recreates the data records contained in the upload file. This upload mode is only offered if the setting of the entity type in data modeling is defined as **Allow for Deletion**. If the upload process doesn't include all the attributes, the system sets the missing attributes to **Initial**.

If attributes that are specified as required entry fields aren't uploaded, the system will issue an error message.

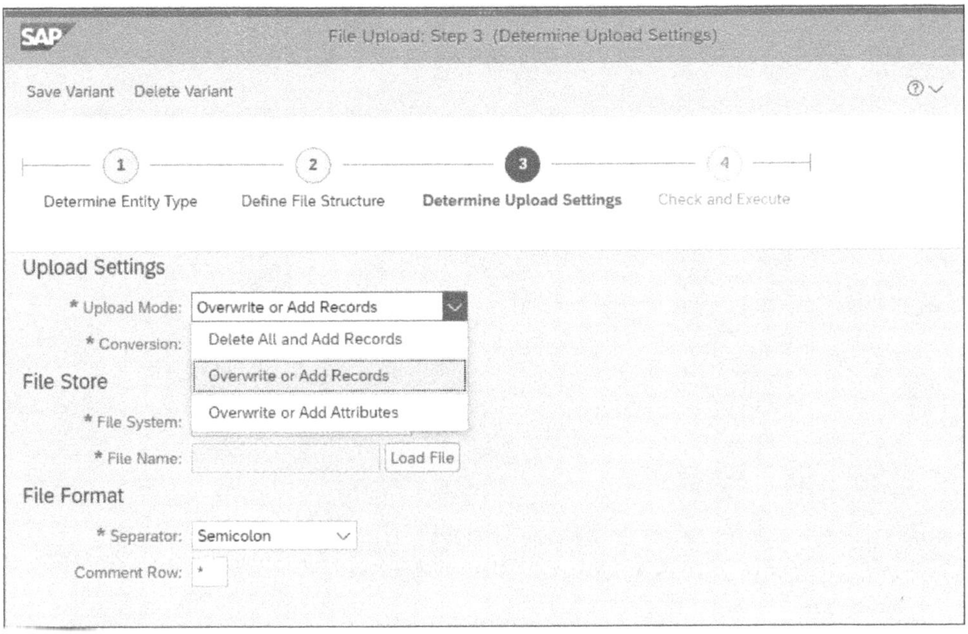

Figure 14.22 Upload Settings: Options for Upload Modes

– In the **Overwrite or Add Attributes** upload mode, the system deletes attributes for which there are attributes available in the upload file. It then recreates the attributes contained in the upload file in the following way:

• If the upload file contains an attribute with an empty value for an existing attribute of the SAP Master Data Governance system, the system overwrites the existing attribute of the SAP Master Data Governance system with the empty value of the upload file.

• If the upload file contains no attribute for an existing attribute of the SAP Master Data Governance system, the system keeps the existing attribute of the SAP Master Data Governance system.

• If the upload file contains an attribute with a filled value for which there was no existing attribute in the SAP Master Data Governance system before, the system adds the attribute from the upload file to the SAP Master Data Governance system.

– **Conversion**

In some file upload scenarios, it may be necessary to convert the format of data records from external to internal format (date values and figures). To specify that the system is to carry out a conversion, you can select the **Execute Conversion** option. **Conversion** options available in **Step 3** of the file upload process are shown in Figure 14.23.

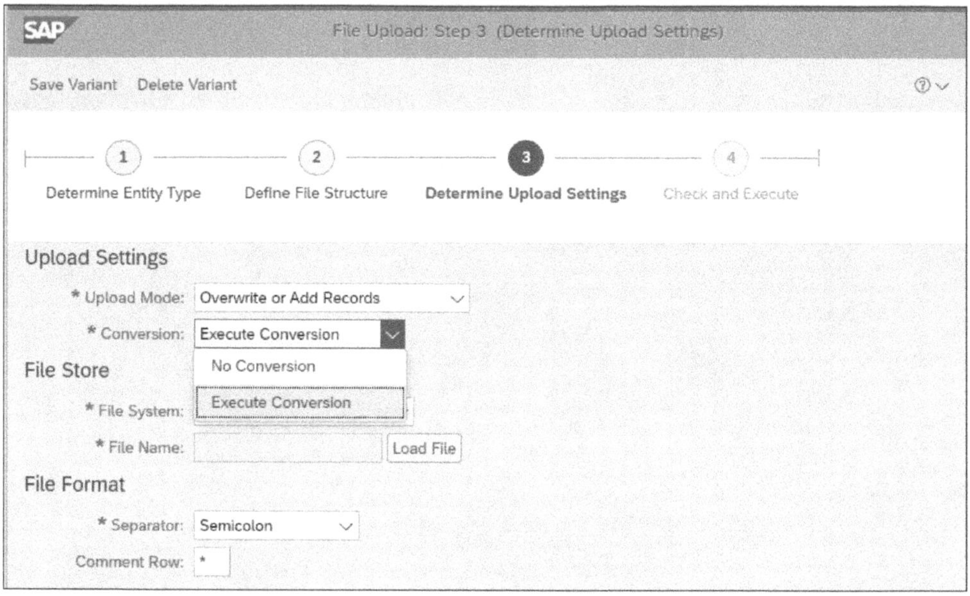

Figure 14.23 File Upload: Select Conversion Settings

- **File Store**

  The file to be uploaded can be stored on either the presentation server (i.e., local PC) or the application server. **File Store** settings selection can be made as shown in Figure 14.24.

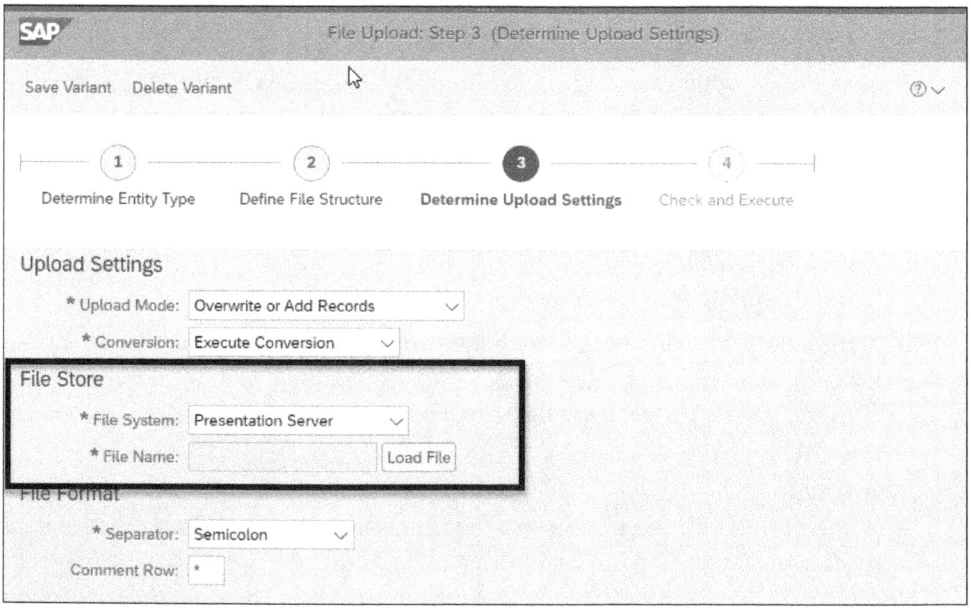

Figure 14.24 File Upload: Select File Store Settings

- **File Format**
  The file upload framework accepts only text files for the file upload. You can specify whether field values are to be separated by a semicolon, tab, comma, or other printable character. It's also possible to select a character that should be used for ignoring a row from the upload file. Figure 14.25 shows the file format separators that can be applied in **Step 3** of the file upload process.

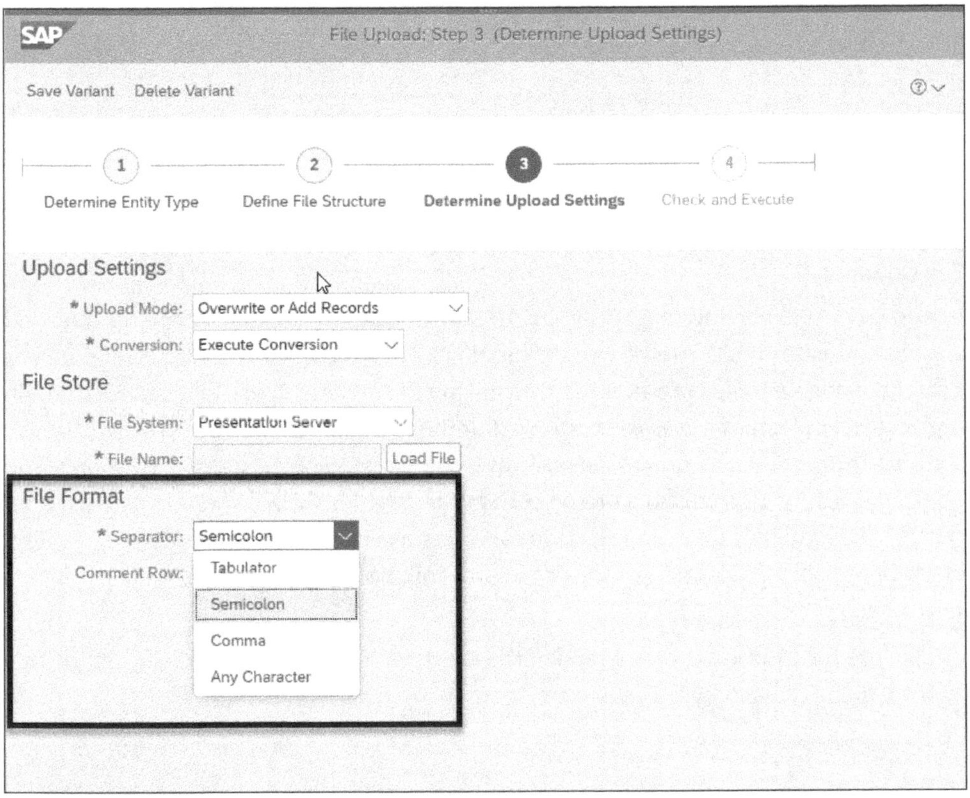

Figure 14.25 File Upload: Selecting the File Format Separator

After the **Upload Settings** are chosen, the system provides an option to select if the load being performed should use an already existing change request type or create a new change request after the load is executed in the final step.

4. **Check and execute.**
   In this step, the system uploads the data in the staging area of SAP Master Data Governance through a change request, provided there are no failed checks in terms of consistency. This is the final review step before executing and loading the data in the change request. Data can be reviewed and analyzed in this step by easily filtering rows with any messages or rows with hard errors. To fix any data inconsistencies, you can go to the previous step to select the updated load file after the data inconsistencies are fixed, avoiding going through the whole process again. Figure 14.26 shows **Step 4** of the file upload process from which the upload is executed.

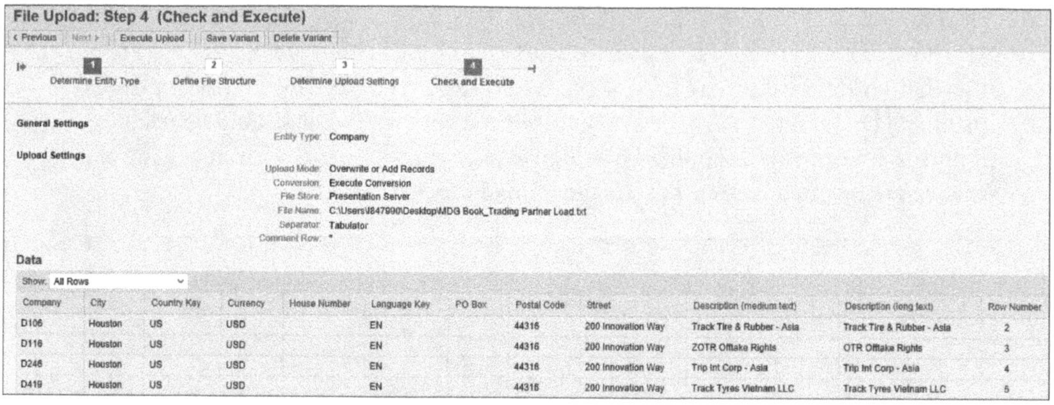

Figure 14.26 File Upload: Check and Execute

File Download

In addition to exporting master data, SAP Master Data Governance provides another simple and easy-to-use method to extract data out of SAP Master Data Governance. You can navigate to this method easily from any SAP Master Data Governance domain homepage, and you can also execute it using the SAP-delivered USMD_FILE_UPLOAD Web Dynpro application. File download is always specific to a selected entity type only and a selected edition (if applicable on the entity type). Variants can be created and used for recurring downloads to avoid selections and settings each time. SAP Master Data Governance file download is a five-step process, as follows:

1. **Determine the entity type.**

   Like the file upload process, **Step 1** of the file download process involves determination of entity types by the user (see Figure 14.27).

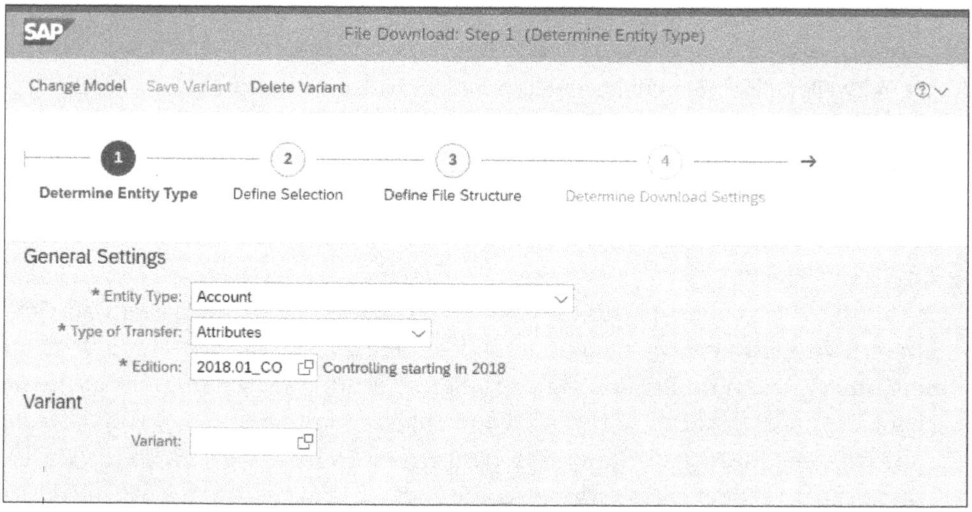

Figure 14.27 File Download: Determine Entity Type

2. **Define selection.**
   In **Step 2** of the file download process, a selection of records must be defined by the user so that only intended records can be extracted out of SAP Master Data Governance (see Figure 14.28).

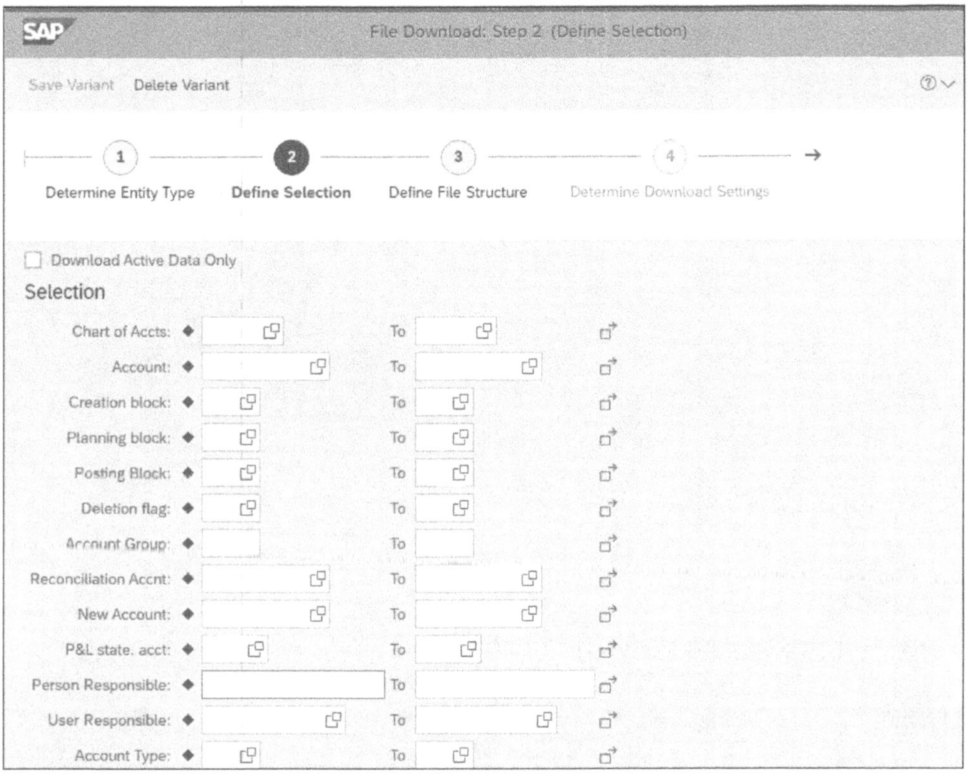

Figure 14.28 File Download: Define Selection

3. **Define the file structure.**
   In **Step 3**, a file structure is defined based on selecting and adding available attributes to the selected attributes (see Figure 14.29). Only the selected attributes will be downloaded accordingly.

4. **Determine the download settings.**
   In **Step 4**, the download settings and file formats are selected, as shown in Figure 14.30.

5. **Check and execute.**
   In **Step 5** of the file upload process, selections parameters can be revised, and the download can be executed by clicking on **Execute Download**, as shown in Figure 14.31.

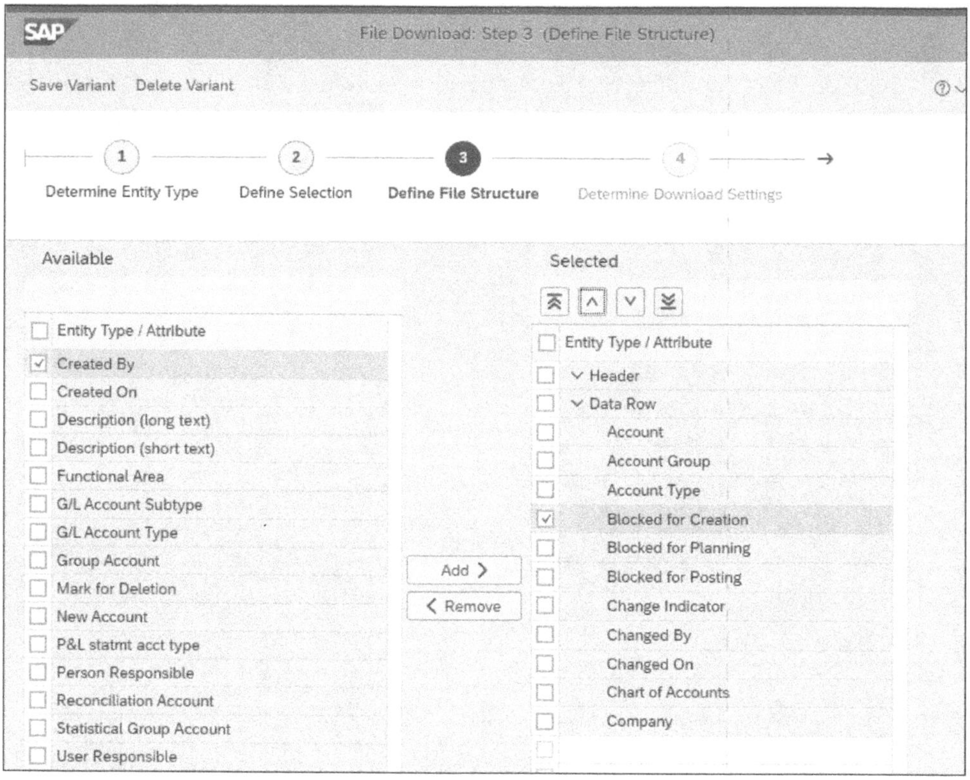

Figure 14.29 File Download: Define File Structure

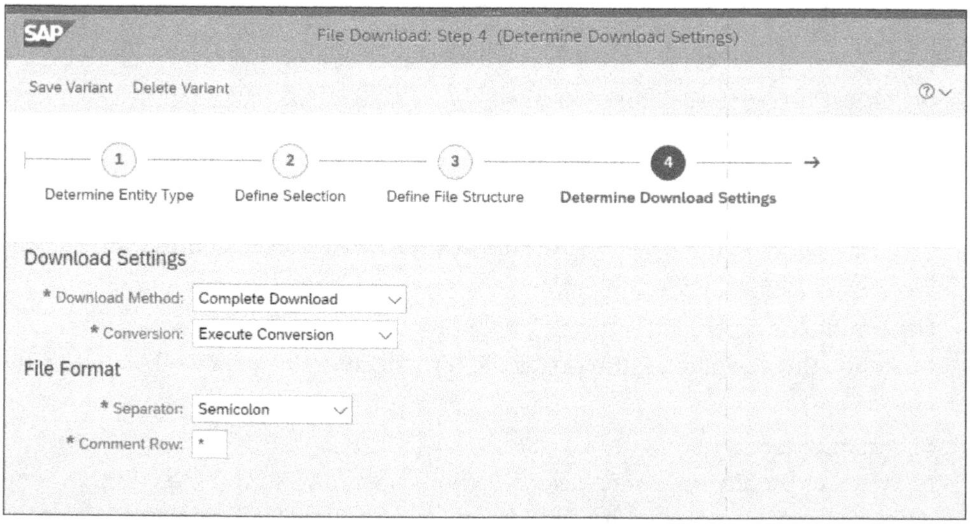

Figure 14.30 File Download: Determine Download Settings

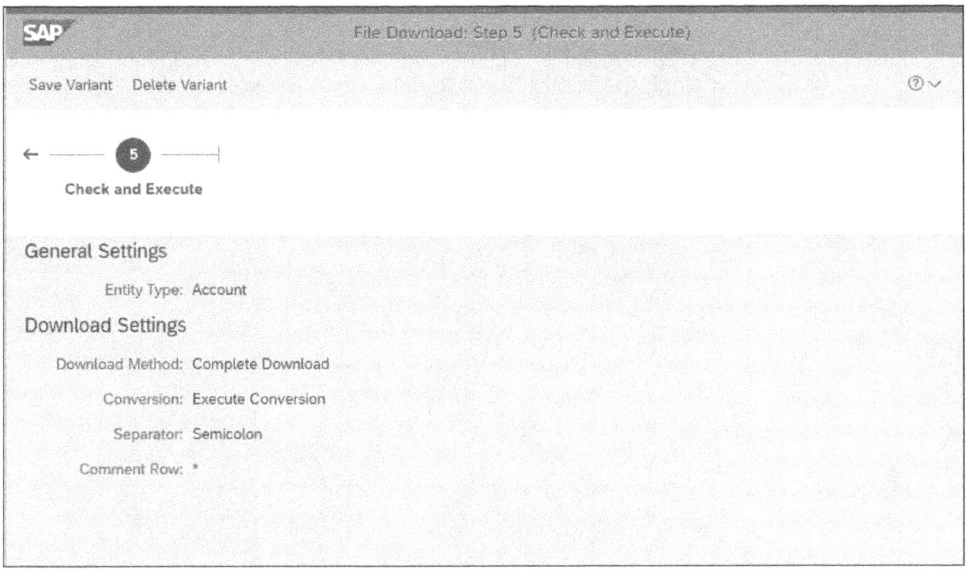

Figure 14.31 File Download: Check and Execute

After executing the download, a screen appears showing the successful download with the number of records. You can now display, save the file, or execute another file upload for this screen, as shown in Figure 14.32.

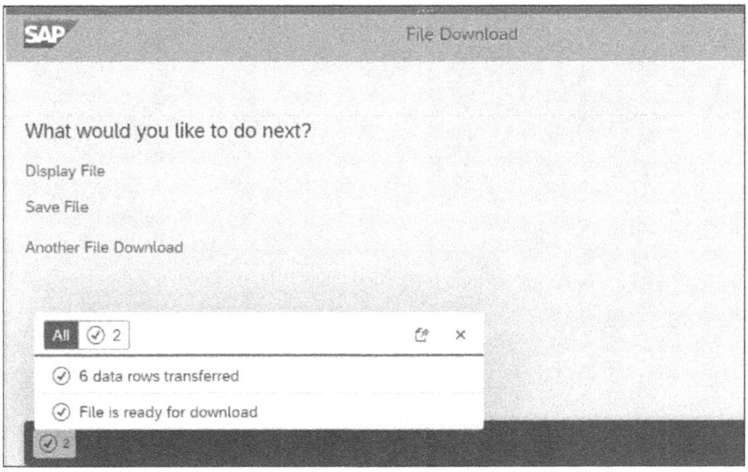

Figure 14.32 System Message after Successful File Download Execution

14.3   Summary

This chapter provided you an overview of data migration in an SAP Master Data Governance project. It explained the various technology options available for master data extraction, conversions capabilities, and master data loads in SAP Master Data Governance. A set of general recommendations were also provided that can help you make the right decisions while adopting a data migration approach for your project. In addition, data migration strategies were discussed in detail with the steps involved with the data export framework, data import framework, file uploads, file downloads, key mapping, and value mapping. In the next chapter, we'll discuss the operational strategies for SAP Master Data Governance, such as ongoing data loads, performance optimization, and data archiving.

Chapter 15

Central Governance: Operational Strategies

This chapter explains some guiding principles on the usage of editions, the data import/export framework, and the file upload/download framework for mass processing in an operational SAP Master Data Governance environment. This chapter also provides some performance optimization tips.

Implementing SAP Master Data Governance is an important step in the master data journey for any company. However, a successful SAP Master Data Governance implementation is only the first step, and it requires continuous monitoring and improvements to mature the master data processes in the organization. Master data teams need to have a proactive strategy in place to prepare, effectively monitor, and make the master data processes more robust while ensuring the system is running smoothly.

In this chapter, we'll cover some of the most important topics that you should pay attention to after SAP Master Data Governance becomes operational. These topics include editions, ongoing data loads, performance optimization, and troubleshooting options.

> **Note**
>
> Editions in SAP Master Data Governance are part of process modeling. For the definition of and concepts about editions, refer to Chapter 7, Section 7.2.8.

15.1 Edition Strategy

Organizations implementing SAP Master Data Governance use editions to manage their master data effectively based on its validity dates. Normally, editions are used mainly for finance organizations; however, editions aren't limited to financial objects, and technically any master data object implemented in flex mode may use editions. With SAP Master Data Governance 7.0 onward, the editions functionality has been improved significantly, and a lot of flexibility has been provided while dealing with editions in SAP Master Data Governance.

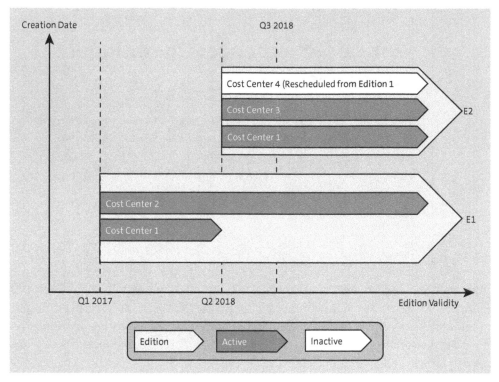

Figure 15.1 Overlapping Flexibility of Editions

Edition management in SAP Master Data Governance was introduced with initial lower releases, but a lot of additional flexibility has been added with the latest SAP Master Data Governance releases (8.0 and 9.0) to enable the master data governance organizations to strategize and use editions more effectively in their master data landscapes. Following are the four new key capabilities with enhanced flexible editions offered with SAP Master Data Governance 8.0, SAP Master Data Governance 9.0, and SAP Master Data Governance on SAP S/4HANA 1809:

- **Flexibility to reschedule changes to new editions**
  Figure 15.1 shows how several open editions can handle the same master data objects. When you create or change a cost center, the valid-from date of the edition defines the valid-from date of the change, as shown with cost center 1 in Figure 15.1. The valid-to date is defined by the *next change* (i.e., in a later edition) of the same cost center. If there is no future planned change, the valid-to date is unlimited, as with cost center 2. You can reschedule open change requests with the related inactive data to another edition, which is useful when you want to release an edition, but some of the change requests are still under the workflow process, as with cost center 4. With the improved concept, you can now use and combine as many editions as needed and reschedule planned changes across editions.

- **More granular control over selection of replication timing**
  You may now decide which replication timing is allowed for each edition. It's possible to replicate all approved change requests together when the edition is released or replicate each change request separately and immediately when approved. In addition, you can determine for each change request whether it will be replicated immediately or held back and replicated together with the edition when it's released.

- **Improved transparency of past and planned changes**
  When displaying any change request in an edition, you now get full transparency about other (planned) changes. The system shows the next already planned and approved change of the same master data object and allows you to jump directly to it. It also provides a link to any pending change that hasn't been approved yet.

- **Intuitive access to the different states of master data valid in certain time frames**
  With a new search parameter (*valid on*), you can intuitively search and display master data and the data's status on a certain date.

The following sections explains the creation, release, and monitoring of editions in SAP Master Data Governance. We also discuss some of the guiding principles to operate editions.

15.1.1 Creating New Editions

Because the edition is a new functionality for many organizations, it's necessary to establish clear responsibilities around creating editions. This provides better control and prevents any confusion about the usage.

The various characteristics needed when creating an edition are as follows:

- Edition technical name
- Edition description
- Edition type
- Validity period
- Replication timing
- Comment

Following are some common guiding principles to consider regarding editions:

- If applied, editions become a prerequisite for creating change requests in SAP Master Data Governance.
- Restrict edition creation authorization only to a defined group/set of users who are responsible for creating the editions. Authorization object USMD_EDTN can be used in SAP Master Data Governance for this purpose.
- Editions have to be created before allowing users to create master data with a particular validity date.

- Because editions control the validity date of the master data, they also influence and control the replication timing for the master data in change requests.
- To provide flexibility to users over the replication of change request data, editions can be created with the **Selected in Each Change Request** option.
- An edition may have any number of change requests assigned to it; however, a change request can be assigned to only a single edition.
- Master data objects using validity dates in SAP Business Suite and SAP S/4HANA applications automatically inherit the valid-from date from the edition's valid-from date, so be sure to select it carefully. Cost center and profit center are classic examples of master data items that inherit the edition validity date into the master data validity date.

The **Create Edition** screen in SAP Master Data Governance is shown in Figure 15.2.

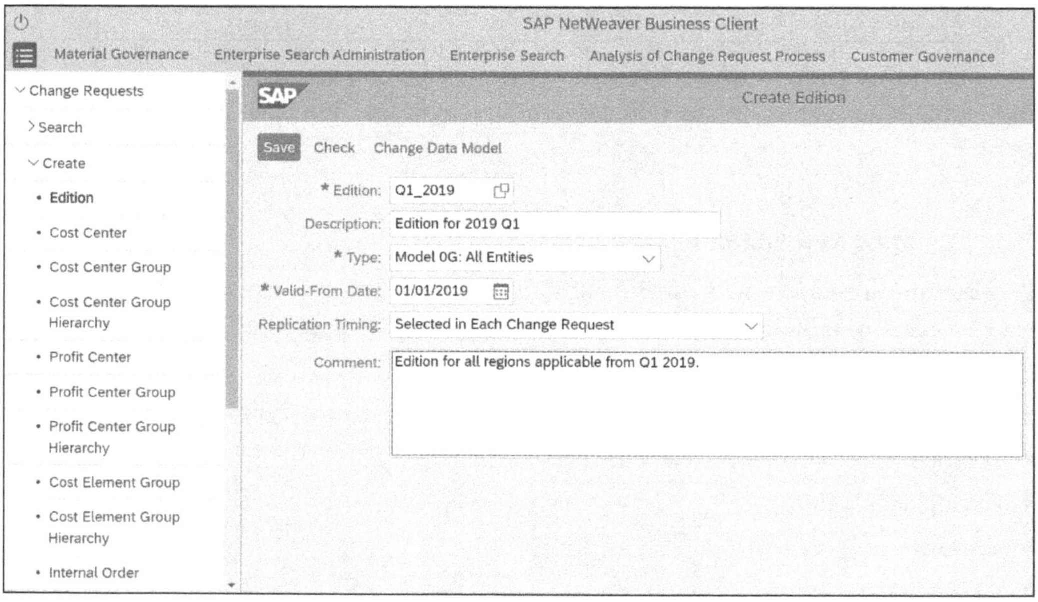

Figure 15.2 Creating an Edition in SAP Master Data Governance

15.1.2   Releasing Editions

Similar to edition creation, it's important to establish a strategy around releasing editions. This process should be centrally controlled with a designated person/group responsible for releasing the edition after it has matured. Following are the methods that are called while checking an edition during the governance process in SAP Master Data Governance:

- CHECK_EDITION_START
- CHECK_EDITION
- CHECK_EDITION_FINAL

Following are some guiding principles that can be used while working on releasing the editions:

- Editions can be marked for release before actual release if no more change requests will be created.
- Always run a validation before releasing the edition.
- The replication to local systems can be triggered by the approval of the single change request or the release of the edition, or it can be done manually.
- An edition can't be released unless the workflow process is completed for all change requests belonging to the same edition.
- Change requests still under the workflow process can be transferred to another edition to clear the way for the release of the existing edition.
- No change request data can be replicated before releasing the editions.
- After an edition is released, no change request can be assigned to it. However, a new edition can be created for updating the master data.
- Use the SAP Master Data Governance distribution monitor for replicating the master data after an edition is released.

Figure 15.3 shows the SAP Master Data Governance screen for releasing the edition, running validations, and navigating to various options from a single screen.

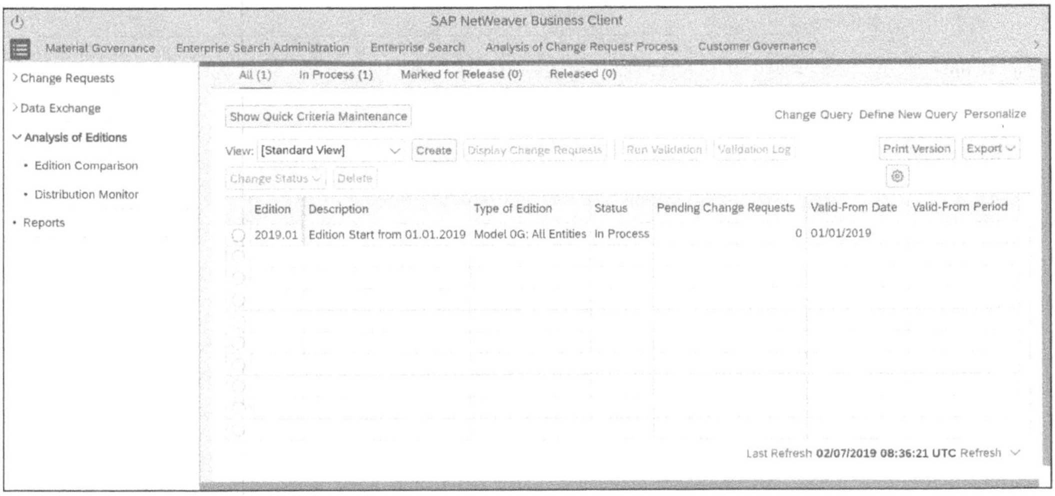

Figure 15.3 Releasing an Edition

15.1.3 Monitoring Editions

The monitoring framework in SAP Master Data Governance provides intuitive access to master data with transparency across time frames. The distribution monitor gives granular control over the timing of data replication to the downstream systems where you can decide the date from which the data should be valid.

Figure 15.4 shows a section from the SAP Master Data Governance **Financial Accounting Governance** screen with various options for analyzing the editions that can be easily navigated with a single click.

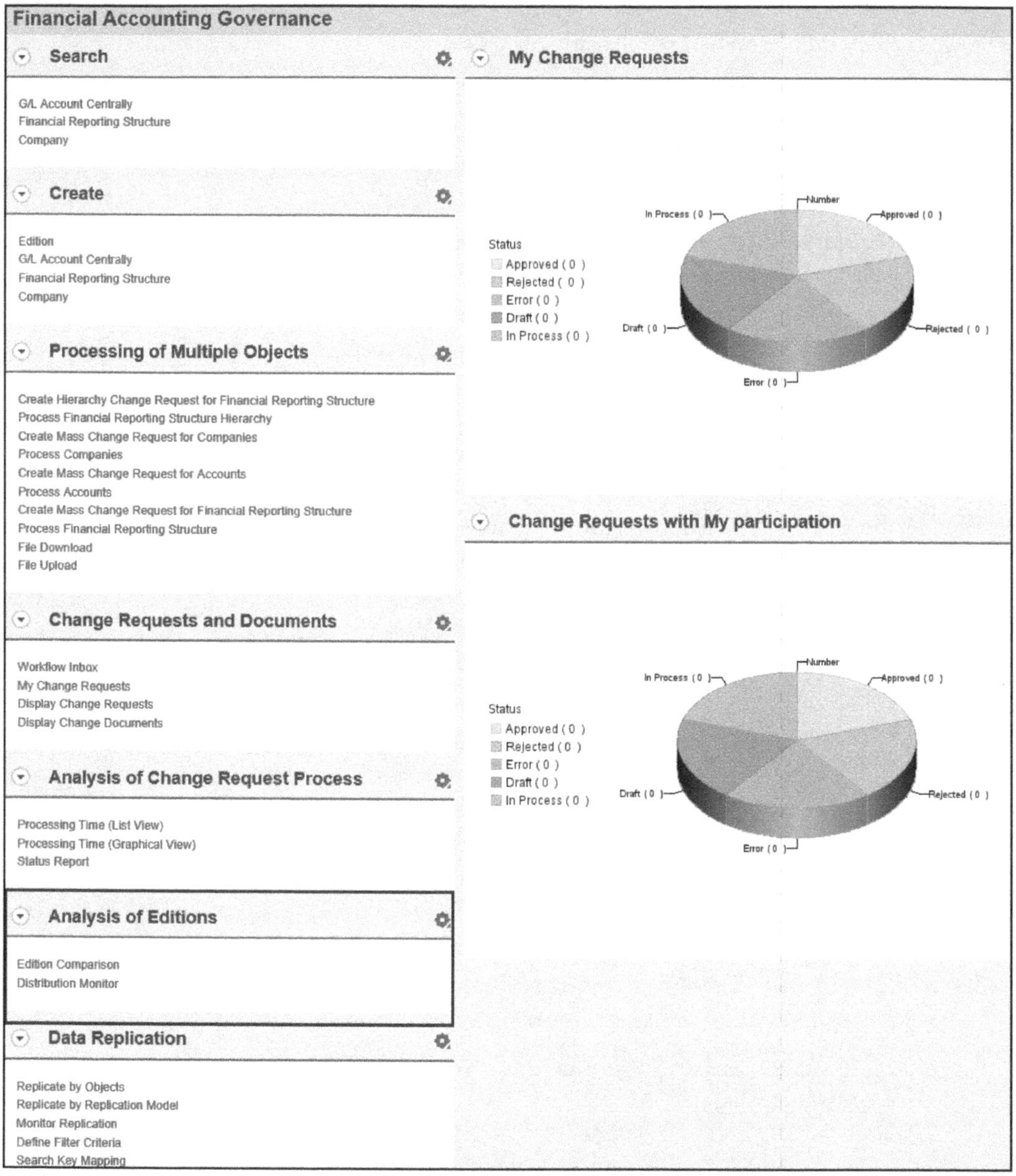

Financial Accounting Governance

- **Search**
  - G/L Account Centrally
  - Financial Reporting Structure
  - Company

- **Create**
  - Edition
  - G/L Account Centrally
  - Financial Reporting Structure
  - Company

- **Processing of Multiple Objects**
  - Create Hierarchy Change Request for Financial Reporting Structure
  - Process Financial Reporting Structure Hierarchy
  - Create Mass Change Request for Companies
  - Process Companies
  - Create Mass Change Request for Accounts
  - Process Accounts
  - Create Mass Change Request for Financial Reporting Structure
  - Process Financial Reporting Structure
  - File Download
  - File Upload

- **Change Requests and Documents**
  - Workflow Inbox
  - My Change Requests
  - Display Change Requests
  - Display Change Documents

- **Analysis of Change Request Process**
  - Processing Time (List View)
  - Processing Time (Graphical View)
  - Status Report

- **Analysis of Editions**
  - Edition Comparison
  - Distribution Monitor

- **Data Replication**
  - Replicate by Objects
  - Replicate by Replication Model
  - Monitor Replication
  - Define Filter Criteria
  - Search Key Mapping

- **My Change Requests**

  Status
  - Approved (0)
  - Rejected (0)
  - Error (0)
  - Draft (0)
  - In Process (0)

- **Change Requests with My participation**

  Status
  - Approved (0)
  - Rejected (0)
  - Error (0)
  - Draft (0)
  - In Process (0)

Figure 15.4 Navigation from the SAP Master Data Governance Screen for Analysis and Monitoring of Editions

Figure 15.5 depicts the SAP Master Data Governance **Analysis of Editions** screen used for analyzing, filtering, and searching editions based on various criteria.

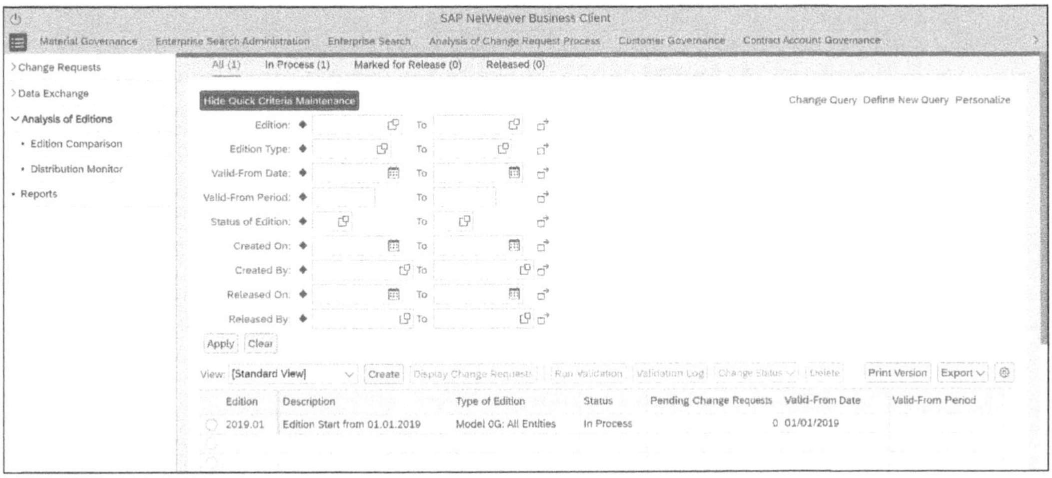

Figure 15.5 Analysis of Editions Screen in SAP Master Data Governance

While working with editions, you'll often need to compare two editions and their master data. SAP Master Data Governance provides an out-of-the-box standard application for comparing two editions for a particular entity type. Further detailed navigation is available after executing the edition comparison. Figure 15.6 depicts how edition comparison can be performed based on entity type.

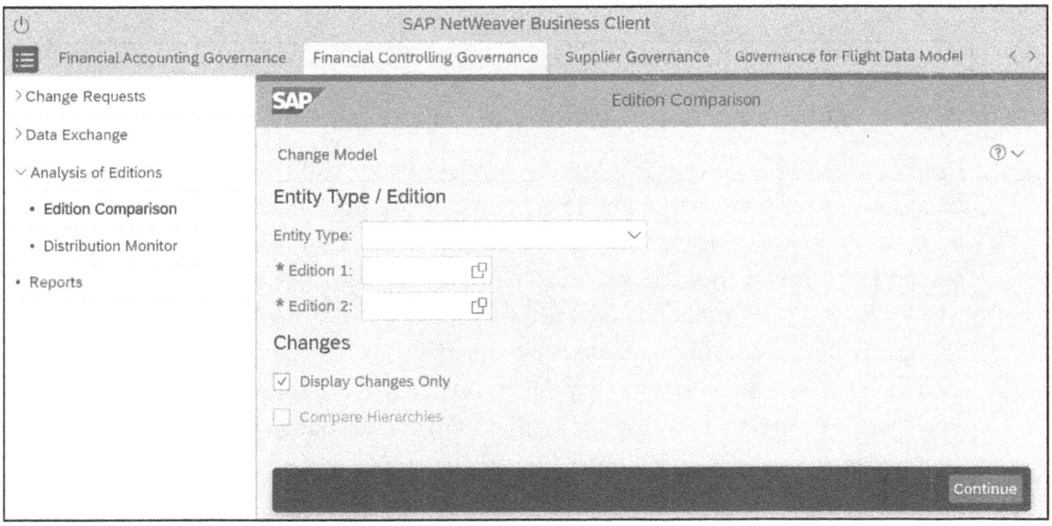

Figure 15.6 Options for Edition Comparison in SAP Master Data Governance

After an edition is released manually, a defined authority in the governance process must select the edition and trigger the replication based on the replication model by clicking on the **Replicate** button. You can monitor replication status and logs on the same screen. For more information on data replication, refer to Chapter 12.

15.2   Ongoing Data Loads

In an operational SAP Master Data Governance environment, businesses often need to perform updates/maintenance on multiple records for various reasons. SAP Master Data Governance offers several options that can be leveraged while dealing with multiple records in SAP Master Data Governance. Multiple object change requests in SAP Master Data Governance support options such as mass change, file data import/export framework, and file upload/download functionality. Note that a change request supported with a workflow process is always needed, even while dealing with multiple records, with the only exception being the file import framework where governance can be skipped.

> **Note**
>
> Initial load and mass processing capabilities in the consolidation and mass processing frameworks are discussed in Chapter 9 and thus not discussed in this chapter. This chapter only covers central governance–specific mass processing capabilities.

In the following sections, some of the commonly used options for post go-live data loads are explained. Depending on exact requirements, suitable options can be used to meet specific business needs. Different options have different capabilities to perform mass loads either first into the SAP Master Data Governance staging area or directly to the SAP Master Data Governance active area.

15.2.1   Creating Mass Change Requests for Mass Loads

Unlike previous versions of SAP Master Data Governance, it's not mandatory to have a mass change request created before actually performing a mass change on records or doing a file upload. Recent SAP Master Data Governance releases (starting with SAP Master Data Governance 8.0) provide an option to create a change request on the fly while performing a mass change or a file upload. However, you still may create a change request in advance and assign it to the mass processing during execution of the load. It's also important to note that the mass change request being assigned should be in a **Change Request** status that allows the changes and change request workflow to be assigned to the current user.

Figure 15.7 depicts various steps in the creation of a mass change request in SAP Master Data Governance:

❶ **General Data**
  In this step, you populate the general attributes of a change request, including a **Description, Edition, Valid From Date, Replication Timing, Due Date, Priority, Reason,** and so on.

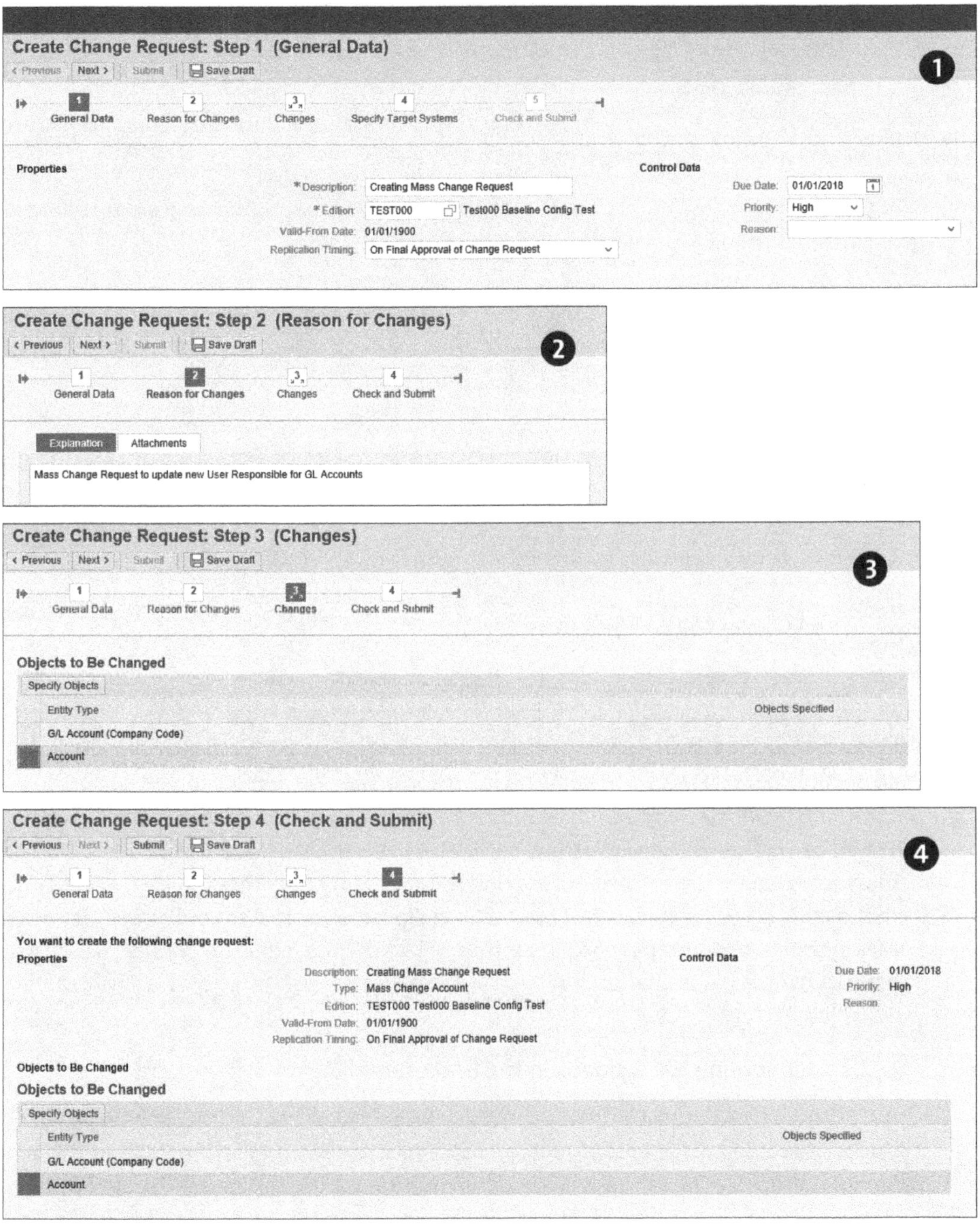

Figure 15.7 Steps to Create a Mass Change Request in SAP Master Data Governance

❷ **Reason for Changes**

In this step, you'll add a detailed explanation of the changes being executed through this mass changes request. This is necessary both for approval as well as for compliance.

❸ **Changes**

In this step, entity types are selected, using which the attributes will be changed.

❹ **Check and Submit**

This step provides a final opportunity to review all the data entered so far before submitting and triggering the workflow.

Figure 15.8 shows the mass change request number. The workflow process is triggered in the background with this message.

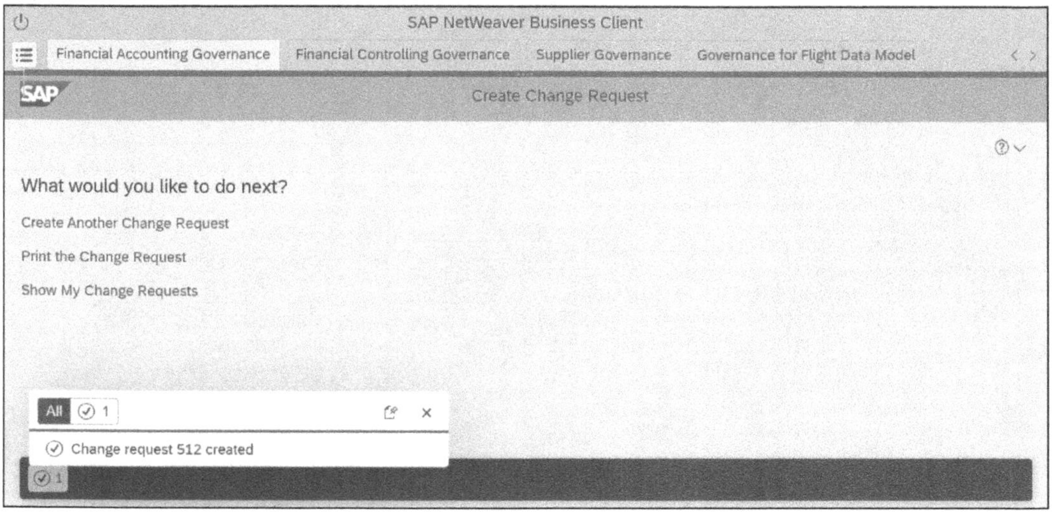

Figure 15.8 System Message after Successful Mass Change Request Creation

The mass maintenance process is no different from the single record process. During mass maintenance, you must ensure that the governance process is duly followed and that data is activated in the SAP Master Data Governance system only after all necessary approvals. For this purpose, a multiple object change request is created, which will have its own workflow path.

15.2.2   Scheduling File Uploads in the Background

Any recurring loads or large files that need to be loaded in SAP Master Data Governance can be scheduled in the background by selecting the files and placing them in the designated directory. You can specify a date and time at which the load should be executed.

Figure 15.9 shows the screen where you can schedule a file upload in SAP Master Data Governance.

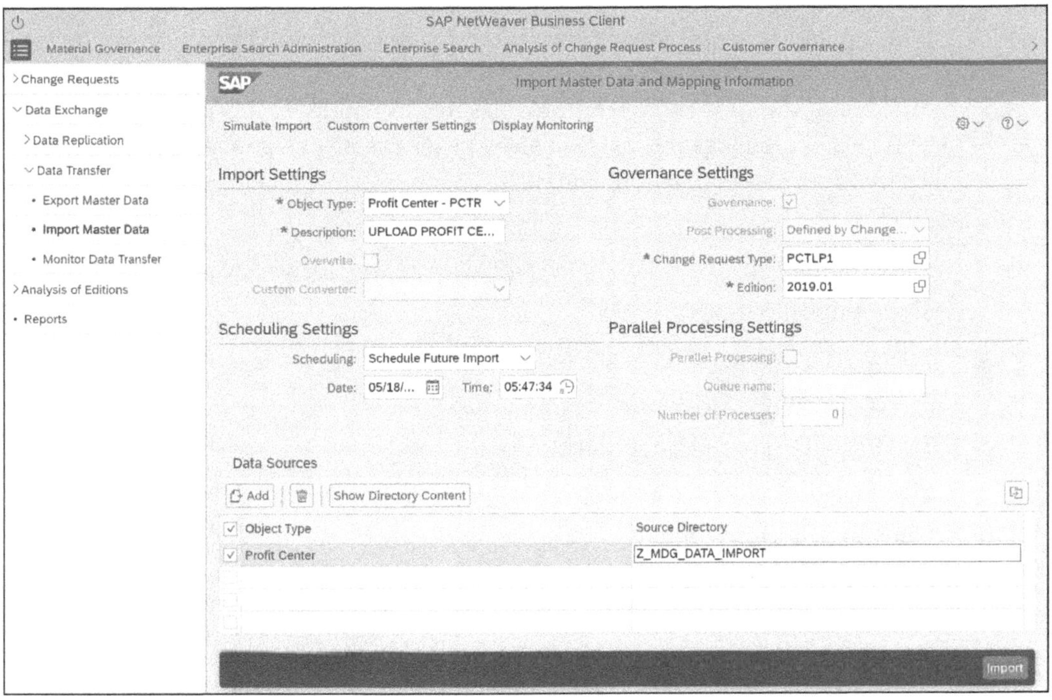

Figure 15.9 Scheduling a File Upload Using the File Import Framework

15.2.3   Operating with the Data Import/Export Framework

The data import/export framework is an XML-based data load application that can be leveraged for loading data in SAP Master Data Governance depending on the use cases. This functionality can be used in data migration for new regions or any new applications coming in the scope of SAP Master Data Governance. Optionally, data can also be exported from SAP Master Data Governance using the export framework and can be loaded back into SAP Master Data Governance using the import framework after necessary updates are made in the XML file.

> **Note**
>
> Detailed steps for using the data import/export framework are explained in Chapter 14.

The following attributes must be selected for exporting a file from SAP Master Data Governance:

- Description
- Variant
- Communication channel
- Target directory

- Package size
- Object type

The data import/export framework provides functionalities to monitor the data transfers and access the logs through the SAP Master Data Governance UI in case of any failed loads. The various actions and their sequence in the data import framework are as follows:

1. Place the load file in the designated SAP Master Data Governance directory.
2. Select import settings.
3. Select the governance setting.
4. Select scheduling settings.
5. Select parallel processing settings.
6. Select custom converter settings.
7. Show the directory content.
8. Simulate the import.
9. Display monitoring.

The data import/export framework also has data monitoring and options for displaying logs. Figure 15.10 shows the options available in SAP Master Data Governance for data monitoring and logs for a particular load.

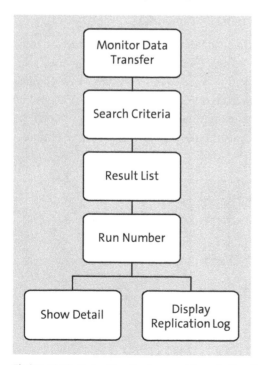

Figure 15.10 Data Monitoring and Logs in the Data Import/Export Framework

15.3 Performance Optimization

You may face some performance challenges after SAP Master Data Governance becomes operational, but you can overcome those challenges by smartly using the functionalities provided and with the help of some tweaks that can improve system performance. Following are some focus areas for system administrators and architects:

- **Parallel processing during data import/export**
  Huge data loads in the SAP Master Data Governance system could cause performance issues. For such scenarios, you can use parallel processing to start multiple processing instances during data export and data import. Settings for parallel processing are defined through Transaction DRFOUT. For more information on data replication, refer to Chapter 12.

- **Periodic deletion of status logs using Transaction DRFRSDEL**
  This task should be executed weekly or on an as-needed basis if a large replication was triggered in the SAP Master Data Governance system. Program RDRF_DELETE_REP_STA deletes the replication status while keeping the last record and the last successful record for each object/target system.

- **File upload performance issue**
  While using the file upload functionality in SAP Master Data Governance, performance might become a concern for large volumes. Depending on the entity and object for which the load is being performed, systems may behave differently. Minimizing the file sizes by keeping the volumes to no more than 10K might help to avoid any performance challenges.

- **Business rules in SAP Master Data Governance**
  Business rules implemented in SAP Master Data Governance might also impact the data import and file uploads in the system. The higher number of rules you have, the more of a load will be placed on the SAP system. Based on your specific requirements, these business rules can be temporarily switched off during data loads in SAP Master Data Governance for the specific change request types via process modeling.

- **Periodic deletion of logs using Transaction DRFLOGDEL**
  Application log data should be written by the data replication framework, and internal log information should be deleted by executing program RDRF_DELETE_LOG at least once a week or more frequently if large-scale replication was triggered in SAP Master Data Governance.

- **Periodic deletion using Transaction MDGCPDEL**
  Execution of this task varies for different objects and depends on the volume of change pointers written. Program MDG_BS_CHANGE_POINTER_TOOLS deletes processed or new change pointers based on the selection.

- **Data replication trigger using Transaction DRFOUT**
  Depending on the business requirements, heavy data loads can be triggered manually or scheduled from SAP Master Data Governance using Transaction DRFOUT and change pointers.

- **Data replication trigger program USMD_EDITION_REPLICATE**
  This program can be executed on or shortly after the valid-from date for changes to the relevant business objects. This can ensure timely replication of data from all approved change requests belonging to an edition after executing the validation.

- **Data virus scan profile in SAP Fiori for SAP Master Data Governance apps**
  Virus scan profile `MDG_BS_FILE_UPLOAD/MDG_VSCAN` can be used when uploading files to the SAP Fiori request apps.

- **Hardware requirements**
  SAP Master Data Governance sizing guides must be strictly followed before tweaking any changes in the system. Sizing guides can be found at *https://www.sap.com/about/benchmark/sizing.html*.

- **Application configuration and user interface building block (UIBBs)**
  In the Floorplan Manager, SAP standard UIBBs can be easily tweaked to optimize performance. Remember, not all the delivered UIBBs are needed by all users and in all scenarios to perform their tasks. Heavy usage of a large number of UIBBs does affect the performance of the system, so keeping the number of UIBBs on the governance UI as small as possible may improve the system's performance.

- **Highlighting changes**
  Highlighting changes in SAP Master Data Governance is an intuitive functionality that helps users focus on the exact updates in the change request at first glance. If needed, deactivation of this functionality may also improve the system's performance.

- **Floorplan Manager**
  Floorplan Manager applications that use context-based adaptation (CBA) may take longer than necessary to start. When starting the SAP application, the Floorplan Manager loads all necessary data for CBA in a prefetch from unbuffered tables. This prefetch can be made faster if these tables are buffered. Therefore, you should consider activating the buffering of table `FPM_ADAPT_SET` using Transaction SE11. For more details, refer to SAP Note 1860705.

15.4 Data Archiving

Due to high maintenance around master data create, read, update, and delete (CRUD) activities in SAP Master Data Governance, it's very likely to have an adverse impact on system performance while also increasing the cost of maintaining the infrastructure and administration activities. In addition, it may become difficult to have cost-efficient system upgrades and migration.

To fix this, you can use Transaction SARA to archive and delete change requests. You then choose the archiving object (`USMD_CR`) where respective tables can be listed that archiving objects can cover. In SAP Master Data Governance, it's possible to archive the growing data related to change requests, including the following:

- USMD120C: Change Request Header
- USMD1210: Change Request: Notes
- USMD1211 and USMD1212: Change Request: Attachments
- USMD1213, USMD1214, and USMD1215: Change Request: Objects
- USMD1216: Change Request: Receiver Systems
- USMD1240: Change Request: Systems
- USMD: Change Documents Created during Change Request Processing
- USMD_ACT: Change Documents after Activation
- USMD2400: Mapping from Top Work Item to Change Request
- USMD_PP_CD: Mapping from Change Documents in Reuse Area to Change Request

Residence time for each change request type plays an important role in the SAP Master Data Governance archiving process. Change requests are archived only if the finalized date falls before the number of days set as a residence time. These dates are stored in the USMD_RELEASED_AT field of table USMD120C.

Following is the IMG path for defining the residence times: **Transaction MDGIMG** · **Master Data Governance, Central Governance** · **Central Governance** · **General Settings** · **Process Modeling** · **Change Requests** · **Change Requests Archiving** · **Define Residence Times**.

> **Note**
>
> The system archives only those change requests that aren't going through a workflow process, that is, change requests that have already attained **CR status** either with the **Final Check Approved** or **Final Check Rejected** status.

15.5   Data Read Access Logging

Read access logging is often required to comply with legal regulations or public standards such as data privacy for respective industry sectors. It's important to protect and restrict access to personal data to ensure data privacy. In some countries, data privacy regulations even require that access to certain personal data be reported to authorities. Companies and public institutions may also want to monitor access to classified or other sensitive data for their own reasons. If no trace or log is kept on who accesses data, it's difficult to track those responsible for any data leaks to the outside world. Read access logging provides this information.

Read access logging is always based on a logging purpose that is freely defined according to the requirements of an organization (e.g., data privacy). This logging purpose is then assigned to each log entry as an attribute, which allows the log data to be classified and organized according to the logging purpose. For example, various archiving rules or reporting can be created based on logging purposes.

SAP Master Data Governance, as an application that manages and governs personal and sensitive data, is required to comply with data privacy regulations. Therefore, the read access logging framework in SAP Master Data Governance can be used to fulfill legal or other regulations, to detect fraud or data theft, for auditing purposes, or for any other internal purpose. SAP Master Data Governance enables read access logging for various functions and interface types, as described in Table 15.1.

Read Access Logging Configuration	Description
MDG_MDC_BANK_DETAILS_OUT_WEB_SERVICES	Bank Details
MDG_MDC_PAYMENTCARD_OUT_WEB_SERVICES	Payment Card Details
MDG_MDC_BANK_DETAILS_IN_WEB_SERVICES	Bank Details
MDG_MDC_PAYMENTCARD_IN_WEB_SERVICES	Payment Card Details
BUPA_INBOUND_MAIN_SAVE_MO9	SAP Master Data Governance Business Partner Bank Details
BUPA_INBOUND_MAIN_SAVE_MO9	SAP Master Data Governance Business Partner Payment Cards
MDG_BP_BANK_ACCOUNT_WEB_DYNPRO	Bank Details for Business Partner
MDG_BUSINESS_PARTNER_CARD_PCA_MASTER_WEB_DYNPRO	Payment Card Details
MDG_BP_PAYMENTCARD_CCARD_WEB_DYNPRO	Payment Card Details
MDG_CUSTOMER_BANK_ACCOUNT_WEB_DYNPRO	Bank Details for Customer
MDG_SUPPLIER_BANKACCOUNT_WEB_DYNPRO	Bank Details for Supplier
MDG_CUSTOMER_PAYMENTCARD_PCA_MASTER_WEB_DYNPRO	Payment Card Details for Customer
MDG_CU_PAYMENTCARD_CCARD_WEB_DYNPRO	Payment Card Details for Customer
MDG_BP_CHNG_DOCS_WEB_DYNPRO	SAP Master Data Governance Business Partner Display Change Documents
MDG/CMP_BANK_SAPGATEWAY	Bank Details
MDC_TRACK_CHANGES_SRV__147	Consolidation and Mass Processing Track Changes Display Business Partner Bank Details SAP Gateway

Table 15.1 Read Access Logging Configurations Available in the SAP Master Data Governance Framework

15.6 Troubleshooting

After SAP Master Data Governance goes live, users may encounter some issues related to workflows and data replication, in addition to other areas. Following are two key recommendations that should be implemented in any SAP Master Data Governance project as part of the operational strategy:

- **Activation failed change requests**
  It's important to define a designated group responsible for receiving all work items in case a change request goes into **Activation Failed** status. This ensures that the change request doesn't remain in **Activation Failed** status and gets due attention even before users are affected. You can build alternative workflow steps in SAP Master Data Governance to reprocess or reroute such change requests for fixing change request activation issues.

- **Computing Center Management System (CCMS)**
  For tracking any issues related to data replication, CCMS-based alert monitoring can be set up.

Additionally, for a quick and accurate root-cause analysis of various post go-live issues, it's important to have a list of commonly used transactions and programs available for reference.

Following are some commonly used transactions and programs in SAP Master Data Governance for any change request failed activations and workflow-related scenarios:

- Transaction SLG1: Analyze Application Log
- Transaction SWIA: Process Work Item as Administrator
- Transaction SWI5: Workload Analysis
- Transaction SWI6: Display Workflows: Select an OBJECT
- Program USMD_DELETE_MODEL
- Program USMD_DELETE_CR
- Transaction SWI1: Selection Report for Work Items
- Transaction USMD_SSW_RULE: Rule-Based Workflow Configuration
- Transaction USMD_RULE: BRFplus Rules
- Transaction SWE2: Change View "Event Type Linkages"

Following are some web UI applications used in data replication:

- MDG_BS_WD_ANALYSE_IDM: Search Key Mapping
- MDG_BS_WD_ID_MATCH_SERVICE: Create and Edit Key Mapping
- MDG_BS_WD_RSI_DISPLAY: Display Replication Status Information
- DRF_FPM_OIF_MONITORING: Application Monitoring
- DRF_ADHOC_REPLICATION: Manual (Ad Hoc) Replication
- DRF_FILTER_POWL_QAF_AC: Define Filter Criteria

15

Following are some common transactions and a report that can be used for troubleshooting and analysis related to data replication:

- Transaction DRFRSD: Replication Status for Business Object/Receiver System
- Transaction DRFLOGDEL: Reorganize DRF Logs
- Report RDSF_MESSAGE_REOUT: Restart Replication for Erroneous Objects
- Transaction DRFOUT: Execute Data Replication
- Transaction MDGCPDEL: Reorganization of SAP Master Data Governance Change Pointer
- Transaction MDG_ANALYZE_IDM: Search Key Mapping
- Transaction DRFSUB: Subscribe Business Objects for Replication
- Transaction MDG_KM_MAINTAIN: Create and Edit Key Mapping
- Transaction DRFLOG: Analyze DRF Logs
- Transaction SRT_TOOLS: SOA Runtime Tools
- Transaction SRT_MONI: Web Service Utilities: Message Monitor
- Transaction SXMB_MONI: Integration Engine: Monitoring
- Transaction DRFIMG: Customizing for Data Replication Framework
- Transaction DRFCC: Check Customizing for Data Replication Framework
- Transaction DRFF: Define Filter Criteria
- Transaction DRFLOG: Analyze Log for Outbound Implementations

Following are some commonly used Governance application programming interfaces (APIs) available in SAP Master Data Governance. These can be handy during troubleshooting of various issues:

- IF_USMD_GOV_API
- IF_USMD_GOV_API_CR_DATA
- IF_USMD_GOV_API_ENTITY
- IF_USMD_GOV_API_PROCESS
- IF_USMD_GOV_API_SERVICES
- IF_USMD_GOV_API_TRANS
- IF_USMD_GOV_API_CR_ACTION

In addition, following are some commonly used Convenience APIs:

- IF_USMD_CONV_SOM_GOV_API
- IF_USMD_CONV_SOM_GOV_CR
- IF_USMD_CONV_SOM_GOV_ENTITY
- IF_USMD_CONV_SOM_GOV_TRANS
- IF_USMD_CONV_SOM_GOV_CR_ACTION

Following are some other commonly used transactions and a program in SAP Master Data Governance for various troubleshooting scenarios:

- Transaction LPD_CUST: Overview of Launch Pads
- Transaction WE21: Ports in IDOC Processing
- Transaction SE80: Object Navigator
- Transaction ST22: ABAP Runtime Errors
- Transaction SU53: Display Authorization Data
- Program USMD_EDITION_REPLICATE: Edition-Based Replication
- Transaction WE19: Test Tool for IDoc Processing
- Transaction AL11: SAP Directories
- Transaction CG3Z: Upload File Parameters
- Transaction BD54: Change View Logical Systems Overview
- Transaction BD82: Generate Partner Profile
- Transaction FILE: Logical File Path Definition Overview
- Transaction CG3Y: Download File Parameters

15

15.7 Summary

This chapter provided an overview of the editions functionality from various aspects, discussed mass changes, and explored file upload options in an operational SAP Master Data Governance environment. The chapter also provided some performance optimizations tips that are often useful in projects. In addition, some commonly used transactions and programs were shared that can help while troubleshooting post go-live issues. From a data management perspective, data archiving and read access logging functionalities in SAP Master Data Governance were also discussed. In the next chapter, you'll learn about SAP Fiori apps for SAP Master Data Governance.

SAP Fiori Applications

With the goal to simplify the user experience (UX) for SAP users, SAP Fiori UX technology provides the same look and feel across all devices and is easy to adopt. This chapter provides an overview of SAP Fiori apps available as part of SAP Master Data Governance on SAP S/4HANA 2021.

The ability to access any application seamlessly via a mobile device is a key need, particularly for casual business application users. To meet the need for accessing SAP Master Data Governance applications via mobile devices, SAP provides SAP Fiori apps. Several SAP Fiori apps are available as part of the standard content. This chapter provides an overview of the SAP Fiori apps available for the SAP Master Data Governance solution. The chapter details the landscape requirements, key capabilities, and extensibility options for the SAP Fiori apps for SAP Master Data Governance.

Section 16.1 provides an overview of SAP Fiori and helps you understand key terminologies used in SAP Fiori development, such as SAP Gateway, OData, and so on. Section 16.2 delves into the details on SAP Fiori apps across all standard domains. Section 16.3 discusses the extensibility options for SAP Fiori apps.

16

16.1 Introduction to SAP Fiori

SAP Fiori is an HTML5-based UX technology using SAPUI5 add-ons. SAP Fiori is the next-generation UX technology allowing users the same look and feel across all kinds of devices—mobile, tablet, and desktop. This provides a consistent UX across all SAP solutions. It adapts to various form factors based on the device. The key criteria for SAP Fiori UX are as follows:

- **Role-based**
  User interfaces (UIs) are task specific to a role.

- **Adaptive**
  The same UX is provided across all types of devices.

- **Coherent**
  The UI is easy to understand.

- **Simple**
  The UX is maintained for a specific user type, specific use case, and minimum screens/navigation.
- **Delightful**
  The UI is easy to use.

SAP Fiori launchpad provides role-based and personalized single point of access to SAP apps. The apps are also role based with a common role definition. The launchpad is context aware and connects related apps, supporting easy bookmarking and collaboration. The SAP Fiori search enables you to search and list recently used/searched apps. You can personalize the homepage based on your preferences. Apps are displayed in the form of a tile in the launchpad, so you can have access to multiple apps, and the corresponding tiles are assigned or grouped in a catalog or group. A central SAP Fiori launchpad could be launched to expose the various SAP Fiori apps from multiple systems in a landscape, instead of using the local SAP Fiori launchpad for each system. In other words, an SAP Master Data Governance business user could navigate to both SAP Master Data Governance hub system–based SAP Fiori apps and local system (e.g.: SAP S/4HANA, SAP Business Suite, or SAP S/4HANA Cloud) or other content provider–specific SAP Fiori apps from a single SAP Fiori launchpad instance. SAP Launchpad service as part of SAP Business Technology Platform (SAP BTP) is an option.

Different SAP Fiori app types include transactional apps, analytical apps, fact sheets, and so on. Transactional apps provide task-based access with guided navigation to perform tasks such as creation or maintenance of objects, and so on. Analytical apps provide insights to processes or key performance indicator (KPI) information. Fact sheets help you search and explore information related to specific objects. SAP Master Data Governance standard content involves transaction apps. The analytical apps associated with SAP Master Data Governance are discussed in detail in Chapter 10.

A high-level architecture diagram of the SAP Fiori system landscape is shown in Figure 16.1. The master/transaction data in the backend system is exposed as Open Data Protocol (OData) services via RESTful application programming interface (API) implementation, and the HTML5/SAPUI5-based SAP Fiori screens consume these services. To expose the data via OData services, the corresponding SAP Fiori UI add-ons are required. With an SAP Master Data Governance system in the landscape, the SAP Master Data Governance data can be exposed via the SAP Fiori frontend server component. Embedded frontend server is the recommended option for an SAP S/4HANA system.

For SAP Master Data Governance on SAP S/4HANA 2021, the SAP Fiori apps are part of the UIS4HOP1 software component. SAP Fiori for SAP S/4HANA can be deployed either in an embedded or hub option. If there are multiple backend systems, a central SAP Fiori launchpad could be considered to navigate the SAP Fiori apps exposed across the various systems. SAP Launchpad service can be used as a UX integrator.

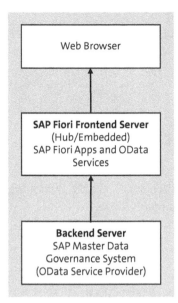

```
                    ┌─────────────────────┐
                    │    Web Browser      │
                    └─────────────────────┘
                              ▲
                              │
                    ┌─────────────────────┐
                    │ SAP Fiori Frontend  │
                    │       Server        │
                    │   (Hub/Embedded)    │
                    │  SAP Fiori Apps and │
                    │    OData Services   │
                    └─────────────────────┘
                              ▲
                              │
                    ┌─────────────────────┐
                    │  Backend Server     │
                    │  SAP Master Data    │
                    │  Governance System  │
                    │ (OData Service      │
                    │    Provider)        │
                    └─────────────────────┘
```

Figure 16.1 SAP Fiori Landscape

16.2   SAP Fiori Applications for SAP Master Data Governance

The key installation components for SAP Fiori apps can be found in the respective installation guide. For example, for SAP Master Data Governance on SAP S/4HANA 2021, the installation information can be found in SAP Note 2590829. The SAP Fiori information for SAP S/4HANA 2021 can be found in SAP Note 3067553.

The SAP Fiori apps reference library provides technical and implementation information on various SAP Fiori apps. The SAP Fiori apps reference library can be accessed via *https://fioriappslibrary.hana.ondemand.com/sap/fix/externalViewer* (e.g., search using application component "CA-MDG" to view the SAP Fiori app information). The standard content also provides SAP Fiori apps for analytics based on core data services (CDS) views. This is explained in detail in Chapter 10.

After the landscape requirements are installed, the key administrative actions to set up the frontend server components and the connection to the backend server/OData service provider need to be executed. These tasks can be performed individually or by executing the predefined task list via the task manager for technical configuration (Transaction STC01). The OData services and Internet Communication Framework (ICF) services corresponding to each SAP Fiori app (SAPUI5 application) can be activated using the task list or Transactions /IWFND/MAINT_SERVICE and SICF, respectively.

The key SAP Fiori apps for central governance functionality are as follows:

Request Business Partner (SAP Master Data Governance)

This app can be used to trigger a request for the creation of a business partner containing basic data. The key implementation objects of the app are as follows:

- OData service: MDG_BP_SRV
- SAPUI5 application: MDG_REQ_BP
- Business role: SAP_MDG_BCR_REQUESTER_T

The Request Business Partner app is shown in Figure 16.2.

- **Request New Cost Center (SAP Master Data Governance)**

  This app can be used to trigger a request for the creation of a cost center containing basic data. The key implementation objects of the app are as follows:

  - OData service: MDG_COSTCENTER_SRV
  - SAPUI5 application: MDG_REQ_CC
  - Business role: SAP_MDG_BCR_REQUESTER_T

  A screenshot of the Request New Cost Center app is shown in Figure 16.3.

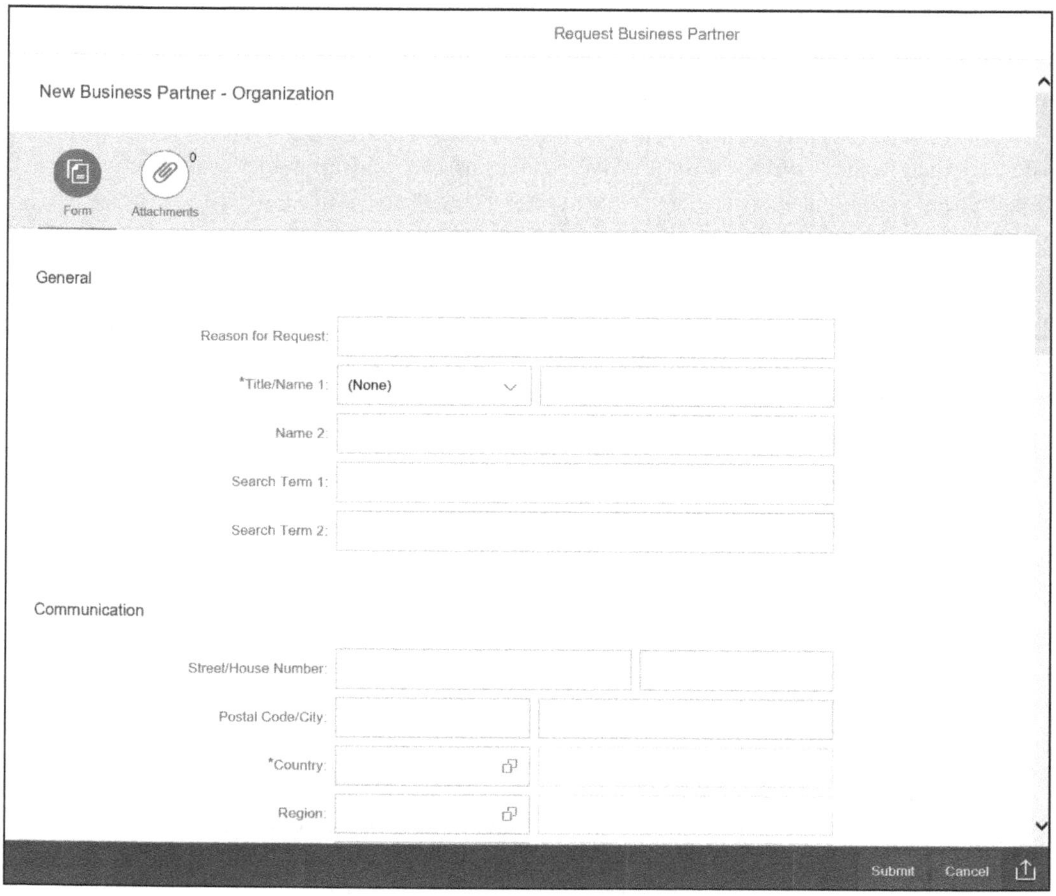

Figure 16.2 Request Business Partner App

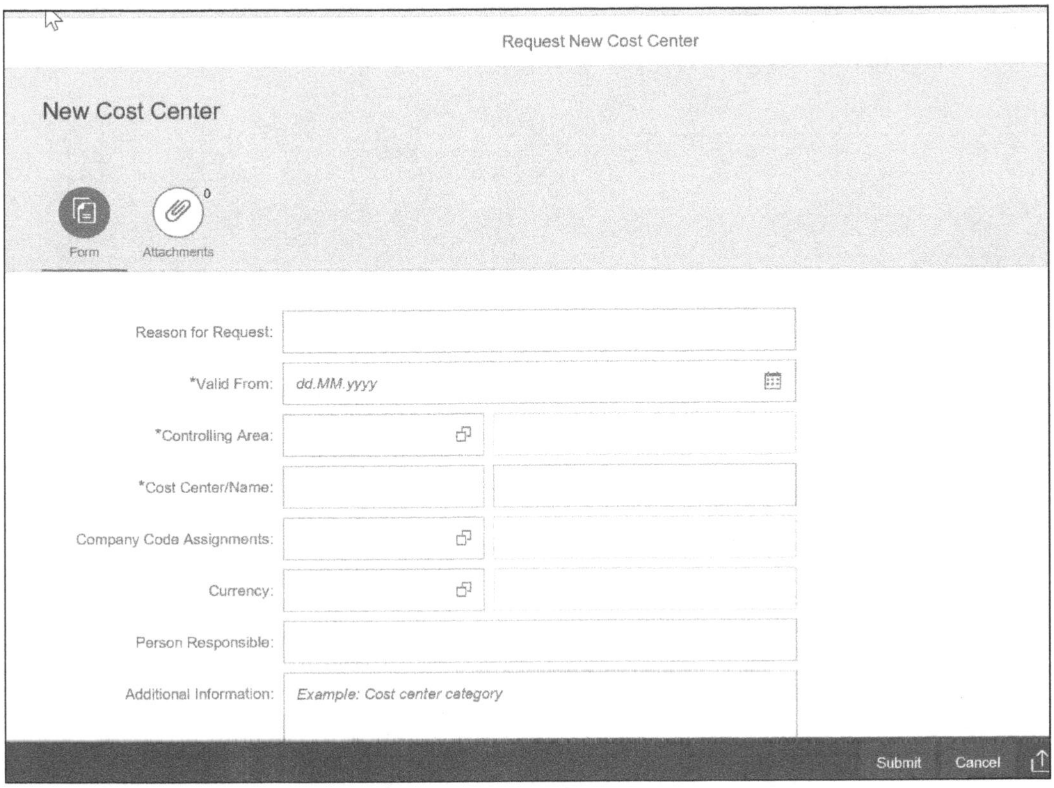

Figure 16.3 Request New Cost Center App

- **Request Customer (SAP Master Data Governance)**
  This app can be used to trigger a request for the creation of a customer master containing basic data. The key implementation objects of the app are as follows:
  - OData service: `MDG_CUSTOMER_SRV`
  - SAPUI5 application: `MDG_REQ_CUST`
  - Business role: `SAP_MDG_BCR_REQUESTER_T`

- **Request Customer Change (SAP Master Data Governance)**
  This app can request changes to customer master data. The key implementation objects of the app are as follows:
  - OData service: `MDG_EDIT_CUSTOMER`
  - SAPUI5 application: `MDG_EDIT_BP`
  - Business role: `SAP_MDG_BCR_REQUESTOR_T`

- **Request Material (SAP Master Data Governance)**
  This app can be used to trigger a request for the creation of a material master containing basic data. The key implementation objects of the app are as follows:
  - OData service: `MDG_MATERIAL_SRV`

    – SAPUI5 application: MDG_REQ_MAT

    – Business role: SAP_MDG_BCR_REQUESTER_T

The Request New Material app is shown in Figure 16.4.

Figure 16.4 Request New Material App

- **Request Profit Center (SAP Master Data Governance)**
  This app can be used to trigger a request for the creation of a profit center containing basic data. The key implementation objects of the app are as follows:
  - OData service: MDG_PROFITCENTER_SRV
  - SAPUI5 application: MDG_REQ_PC
  - Business role: SAP_MDG_BCR_REQUESTER_T
- **Request Supplier (SAP Master Data Governance)**

This app can be used to trigger a request for the creation of a supplier containing basic data. The key implementation objects of the app are as follows:

- OData service: MDG_SUPPLIER_SRV
- SAPUI5 application: MDG_REQ_SUPPL
- Business role: SAP_MDG_BCR_REQUESTER_T

- **Track My Requests (SAP Master Data Governance)**

This app can be used to track the requests submitted. The key implementation objects of the app are as follows:

- OData service: `MDG_MYCR_SRV`
- SAPUI5 application: `MDG_MY_REQ`
- Business role: `SAP_MDG_BCR_REQUESTER_T`

Approve Master Data – Extended
This app is used to approve or reject the change requests submitted. It supports both single-object change requests and multi-object change requests. It also displays information on the data changed as part of the change request. The key implementation objects of the app are as follows:

- OData services: `MDG_APPROVE_CR`, `MDG_CUSTOMER_GENIL_SRV`, `MDG_FINANCIALS`, `MDG_GL_ACCOUNT`, `MDG_MATERIAL_APPROVE_CR_SRV`, `MDG_SUPPLIER_GENIL_SRV`
- SAPUI5 application: `MDG_APPROVE_CR2`
- Business role: `SAP_MDG_BCR_APPROVER_T`

The request and approval apps are linked to the central governance workflows. They have separate change request types. The predefined change request types can be imported by activating the following Business Configuration Sets (BC Sets) for each domain (as of SAP Master Data Governance on SAP S/4HANA 2021):

- `CA-MDG-APP-BP_CR_ODATA_08`: Business partner
- `CA-MDG-APP-CUS_CR_ODATA_09`: Customer
- `CA-MDG-APP-SUP_CR_ODATA_08`: Supplier
- `CA-MDG-APP-FIN_CR_ODATA_06`: Financials
- `MDGM_MDG_MATERIAL_CR_ODATA_08`: Material

The roles `SAP_MDG_BCR_APPROVER_T` and `SAP_MDG_BCR_REQUESTOR_T` are part of software component `UIMDG001` (for more details, see SAP Note 3119307). From an end user perspective, the SAP Fiori apps are accessed via SAP Fiori launchpad (Transaction /UI2/FLP). Additional field-level derivations for SAP Fiori UIs can be defined using the Business Add-In (BAdI) `MDG_GW_FIORI_DERIVATIONS`. The standard BAdI `USMD_RULE_SERVICE`, if already implemented, takes precedence over this BAdI.

The key SAP Fiori apps for change request analysis and process analysis are as follows:

- **Change Request Analysis for Business Partner**
  This app helps to view the analytics related to business partner change request processes. The key implementation objects of the app are as follows:
  - OData service: `MDG_CR_BUPA_ALP_SRV`
  - SAPUI5 application: `MDG_CRBP_ALPS1`
  - Business role: `SAP_BR_BUPA_MASTER_SPECIALIST`

- **Change Request Analysis for Financial Data**
  This app helps to view the analytics related to finance change request processes. The key implementation objects of the app are as follows:
  - OData service: `MDG_CR_FIN_ALP_SRV`
  - SAPUI5 application: `MDG_CRFIN_ALPS1`
  - Business role: `SAP_BR_MASTER_SPECIALIST_FIN`

- **Change Request Analysis for Product**
  This app helps to view the analytics related to product master change request processes. The key implementation objects of the app are as follows:
  - OData service: `MDG_CR_PRODUCT_ALP_SRV`
  - SAPUI5 application: `MD_CRPR_ALPS1`
  - Business role: `SAP_BR_PRODMASTER_SPECIALIST`

- **Master Data Process Overview for Business Partner**
  This app provides a dashboard-like feature to view and drill down to all the master data management processes related to business partners. This includes the central governance, consolidation, and mass processing request and process analytics. It provides both the user-specific information as well as the process-specific information. The information is grouped as cards that can be hidden or unhidden based on user preferences. The key implementation objects of the app are as follows:
  - OData service:OData service: `MDG_MDPROC_BUPA_OVP_SRV`
  - SAPUI5 application: `MDG_PRCBP_OVPS1`
  - Business role: `SAP_BR_BUPA_MASTER_SPECIALIST`

- **Master Data Process Overview for Financial Data**
  This app provides a dashboard-like feature to view and drill down to all the master data management processes related to finance master data objects. This includes the central governance analytics. It provides both the user-specific information as well as the process-specific information. The information is grouped as cards that can be hidden or unhidden based on user preferences. The key implementation objects of the app are as follows:
  - OData service: `MDG_CR_FIN_OVP_SRV`
  - SAPUI5 application: `MDG_CRFIN_OVPS1`
  - Business role: `SAP_BR_MASTER_SPECIALIST_FIN`

- **Master Data Process Overview for Product**
  This app provides a dashboard-like feature to view and drill down to all the master data management processes related to the product master. This includes the central governance, consolidation, and mass processing request and process analytics. It provides both the user-specific information as well as the process-specific information. The information is grouped as cards that can be hidden or unhidden based on user preferences. The key implementation objects of the app are as follows:

- OData service: `MDG_MDPROC_PROD_OVP_SRV`
- SAPUI5 application: `MDG_PRCPR_OVPS1`
- Business role: `SAP_BR_PRODMASTER_SPECIALIST`

- **Analyze Completed Work Items from Change Requests for Business Partners**
  This app provides information about completed change request work items for the business partner domain. Users can drill down to analyze based on a specific time frame. The key implementation objects of the app are as follows:
  - OData service: `C_MDGOVCLSDWRKFLWBPQRY_CDS`
  - SAPUI5 application: `SBRT_APPSS1`
  - Business role: `SAP_BR_BUPA_MASTER_SPECIALIST`

- **Analyze Completed Work Items from Change Requests for Financial Master Data**
  This app provides information about completed change request work items for the finance domain. Users can drill down to analyze based on a specific time frame. The key implementation objects of the app are as follows:
  - OData service: `C_MDGOVOPENWRKFLWFINQRY_CDS`
  - SAPUI5 application: `SBRT_APPSS1`
  - Business role: `SAP_BR_MASTER_SPECIALIST_FIN`

- **Analyze Completed Work Items from Change Requests for Products**
  This app provides information about completed change request work items for the products domain. Users can drill down to analyze based on a specific time frame. The key implementation objects of the app are as follows:
  - OData service: `C_MDGOVCLSDWRKFLWPRODQRY_CDS`
  - SAPUI5 application: `SBRT_APPSS1`
  - Business role: `SAP_BR_PRODMASTER_SPECIALIST`

- **Monitor Open Work Items from Change Requests for Business Partners**
  This app provides information about open change request work items for the business partner domain. Users can drill down to analyze based on a specific time frame. The key implementation objects of the app are as follows:
  - OData service: `C_MDGOVOPENWRKFLWBPQRY_CDS`
  - SAPUI5 application: `SBRT_APPSS1`
  - Business role: `SAP_BR_BUPA_MASTER_SPECIALIST`

- **Monitor Open Work Items from Change Requests for Financial Master Data**
  This app provides information about open change request work items for the finance domain. Users can drill down to view analyze based on a specific time frame. The key implementation objects of the app are as follows:
  - OData service: `C_MDGOVOPENWRKFLWFINQRY_CDS`
  - SAPUI5 application: `SBRT_APPSS1`
  - Business role: `SAP_BR_MASTER_SPECIALIST_FIN`

16

- **Monitor Open Work Items from Change Requests for Products**
  This app provides information about open change request work items for the products domain. Users can drill down to analyze based on a specific time frame. The key implementation objects of the app are as follows:
  - OData service: `C_MDGOVOPENWRKFLWPRODQRY_CDS`
  - SAPUI5 application: `SBRT_APPSS1`
  - Business role: `SAP_BR_PRODMASTER_SPECIALIST`

The key SAP Fiori apps for data quality management are as follows:

- **Manage Rule Mining for Business Partners**
  This app helps to perform data rule mining on business partner master data records per the defined scope and conditions. The key implementation objects of the app are as follows:
  - OData service: `CMD_QLTY_RULE_MINING_SRV`
  - SAPUI5 application: `MD_QRLMNG_A1`, `MD_QRLMNG_S1`
  - Business role: `SAP_BR_BUPA_MASTER_STEWARD`

- **Manage Rule Mining for Products**
  This app helps to perform data rule mining on material master data records per the defined scope and conditions. The key implementation objects of the app are as follows:
  - OData service: `CMD_QLTY_RULE_MINING_SRV`
  - SAPUI5 applications: `MD_QRLMNG_A2`, `MD_QRLMNG_S1`
  - Business role: `SAP_BR_PRODMASTER_STEWARD`

- **Process Rules from Rule Mining for Business Partners**
  This app helps to manage business partner rules proposed as part of rule mining. The key implementation objects of the app are as follows:
  - OData service: `CMD_QLTY_MINED_RULE_SRV`
  - SAPUI5 applications: `MD_QMNDRL_A1`, `MD_QMNDRL_S1`, `MD_QRLMNG_A1`
  - Business role: `SAP_BR_BUPA_MASTER_STEWARD`

- **Process Rules from Rule Mining for Products**
  This app helps to manage material domain rules proposed as part of rule mining. The key implementation objects of the app are as follows:
  - OData service: `CMD_QLTY_MINED_RULE_SRV`
  - SAPUI5 applications: `MD_QMNDRL_A2`, `MD_QMNDRL_S1`, `MD_QRLMNG_A2`
  - Business role: `SAP_BR_PRODMASTER_STEWARD`

- **Configure Data Quality Scores for Business Partners**
  This app helps to configure data quality score calculations based on data quality dimensions and corresponding rules for business partner records. The key implementation objects of the app are as follows:

- OData service: `CMD_QLTY_CONFIGN_SCORE_SRV`
- SAPUI5 applications: `MDQCONFSCORE_A1`, `MD_QCONFSCORES1`
- Business role: `SAP_BR_BUPA_MASTER_STEWARD`

- **Configure Data Quality Scores for Products**
  This app helps to configure data quality score calculations based on data quality dimensions and corresponding rules for product master records. The key implementation objects of the app are as follows:
  - OData service: `CMD_QLTY_CONFIGN_SCORE_SRV`
  - SAPUI5 applications: `MDQCONFSCORE_A2`, `MD_QCONFSCORES1`
  - Business role: `SAP_BR_PRODMASTER_STEWARD`

- **Data Quality Rules for Business Partners/Validation Rules for Business Partners**
  This app helps to define and manage the data quality rules, that are used for business partner data quality evaluations. The key implementation objects of the app are as follows:
  - OData service: `CMD_QLTY_RULES_SRV`
  - SAPUI5 applications: `MD_QRULE_GEN_A1`, `MD_QRULE_GENS1`
  - Business role: `SAP_BR_BUPA_MASTER_STEWARD`

- **Data Quality Rules for Products/Validation Rules for Products**
  This app helps to define and manage the data quality rules that are used for material data quality evaluations. The key implementation objects of the app are as follows:
  - OData service: `CMD_QLTY_RULES_SRV`
  - SAPUI5 applications: `MD_QRULE_GEN_A2`, `MD_QRULE_GENS1`
  - Business role: `SAP_BR_PRODMASTER_STEWARD`

- **Data Quality Score for Business Partners**
  This app provides data quality scores for business partners based on the latest evaluation run. The information can be drilled down to view further details such as score at the dimension level, rule level, and so on. The key implementation objects of the app are as follows:
  - OData services: `/SSB/SMART_BUSINESS_RUNTIME_SRV`, `CMD_QLTY_EVAL_OVP_SRV`
  - SAPUI5 application: `SBRT_APPSS1`
  - Business role: `SAP_BR_BUPA_MASTER_STEWARD`

- **Data Quality Score for Products**
  This app provides data quality scores for business partners based on the latest evaluation run. The information can be drilled down to view further details such as score at the dimension level, rule level, and so on. The key implementation objects of the app are as follows:
  - OData services: `/SSB/SMART_BUSINESS_RUNTIME_SRV`, `CMD_QLTY_EVAL_OVP_SRV`
  - SAPUI5 application: `SBRT_APPSS1`

16

- Business role: `SAP_BR_PRODMASTER_STEWARD`

- **Evaluation Results for Business Partners**
  This app provides the data quality evaluation results for business partner master data. The key implementation objects of the app are as follows:

  - OData service: `CMD_QLTY_BP_GENERAL_ALP_SRV`

  - SAPUI5 application: `MD_QBPGENALPS1`

  - Business role: `SAP_BR_BUPA_MASTER_STEWARD`

- **Evaluation Results for Company Code Data of Customers**
  This app provides the data quality evaluation results for customer company code data. The key implementation objects of the app are as follows:

  - OData service: `CMD_QLTY_BP_CUST_CCODE_ALP_SRV`

  - SAPUI5 application: `MDQCUSTCCALPS1`

  - Business role: `SAP_BR_BUPA_MASTER_STEWARD`

- **Evaluation Results for Company Code Data of Suppliers**
  This app provides the data quality evaluation results for supplier company code data. The key implementation objects of the app are as follows:

  - OData service: `CMD_QLTY_BP_SUPLR_CCODE_ALP_SRV`

  - SAPUI5 application: `MDQSUPLCCALPS1`

  - Business role: `SAP_BR_BUPA_MASTER_STEWARD`

- **Evaluation Results for Purchasing Data of Suppliers**
  This app provides the data quality evaluation results for supplier purchasing data. The key implementation objects of the app are as follows:

  - OData service: `CMD_QLTY_BP_SUPLR_PURG_ALP_SRV`

  - SAPUI5 application: `MDQSUPLPURALPS1`

  - Business role: `SAP_BR_BUPA_MASTER_STEWARD`

- **Evaluation Results for Sales Data of Customers**
  This app provides the data quality evaluation results for customer sales data. The key implementation objects of the app are as follows:

  - OData service: `CMD_QLTY_BP_CUST_SALES_ALP_SRV`

  - SAPUI5 application: `MDQCUSTSLSALPS1`

  - Business role: `SAP_BR_BUPA_MASTER_STEWARD`

- **Export Data Quality Rules for Business Partners/Export Validation Rules for Business Partners**
  This app provides export functionality for business partner data quality rules. The key implementation objects of the app are as follows:

  - OData services: `APL_LOG_MANAGEMENT_SRV`, `CMD_QLTY_RULE_EXPORT_SRV`

  - SAPUI5 applications: `MD_QRULE_EXP_A1`, `MD_QRULE_EXPS1`

  - Business role: `SAP_BR_BUPA_MASTER_STEWARD`

- **Export Data Quality Rules for Products/Export Validation Rules for Products**
  This app provides export functionality for material data quality rules. The key implementation objects of the app are as follows:
  - OData services: `APL_LOG_MANAGEMENT_SRV`, `CMD_QLTY_RULE_EXPORT_SRV`
  - SAPUI5 applications: `MD_QRULE_EXP_A2`, `MD_QRULE_EXPS1`
  - Business role: `SAP_BR_PRODMASTER_STEWARD`

- **Import Data Quality Rules for Business Partners/Import Validation Rules for Business Partners**
  This app provides import functionality for business partner data quality rules. The key implementation objects of the app are as follows:
  - OData services: `APL_LOG_MANAGEMENT_SRV`, `CMD_QLTY_RULE_IMPORT_SRV`
  - SAPUI5 applications: `MD_QRULE_IMP_A1`, `MD_QRULE_IMPS1`

- Business role: `SAP_BR_BUPA_MASTER_STEWARD`

- **Import Data Quality Rules for Products /Import Validation Rules for Products**
  This app provides import functionality for business partner data quality rules. The key implementation objects of the app are as follows:
  - SAPUI5 applications: `MD_QRULE_IMP_A2`, `MD_QRULE_IMPS1`
  - Business role: `SAP_BR_PRODMASTER_STEWARD`

- **Define Derivation Scenarios for Business Partners**
  This app helps to define derivation scenarios for business partner data, as part of data quality management. The key implementation objects of the app are as follows:
  - SAPUI5 application: `MD_Q_DRVSCN_A1`
  - Business roles: `SAP_BR_BUPA_MASTER_STEWARD`

- **Define Derivation Scenarios for Products**
  This app helps to define derivation scenarios for material master data. The key implementation objects of the app are as follows:
  - SAPUI5 application: `MD_Q_DRVSCN_A2`
  - Business role: `SAP_BR_PRODMASTER_STEWARD`

- **Data Quality Evaluation Overview for Business Partners**
  This app provides an overview for business partner master data quality evaluation. The key implementation objects involved in these apps are as follows:
  - OData services: `CMD_QLTY_BP_CUST_CCODE_ALP_SRV`, `CMD_QLTY_BP_CUST_SALES_ALP_SRV`, `CMD_QLTY_BP_GENERAL_ALP_SRV`, `CMD_QLTY_BP_SUPLR_CCODE_ALP_SRV`, `CMD_QLTY_BP_SUPLR_PURG_ALP_SRV`, `CMD_QLTY_EVAL_OVP_SRV`
  - SAPUI5 application: `MD_QEVLBPOVPS1`
  - Business role: `SAP_BR_BUPA_MASTER_STEWARD`

16

- **Data Quality Evaluation Overview for Products**
  This app provides an overview for product master data quality evaluation. The key implementation objects involved in these apps are as follows:
  - OData services: `CMD_QLTY_EVAL_PROD_OVP_SRV`, `CMD_QLTY_PROD_GENERAL_ALP_SRV`, `CMD_QLTY_PROD_PLANT_ALP_SRV`, `CMD_QLTY_PROD_SALES_ALP_SRV`
  - SAPUI5 application: `MD_QEVLPRDOVPS1`
  - Business role: `SAP_BR_PRODMASTER_STEWARD`

- **Data Quality Evaluation Results for Products**
  This app provides the data quality evaluation results for the product master and analyzes data quality issues. The key implementation objects involved in these apps are as follows:
  - OData service: `CMD_QLTY_PROD_GENERAL_ALP_SRV`
  - SAPUI5 application: `MD_QPRDGENALPS1`
  - Business role: `SAP_BR_PRODMASTER_STEWARD`

- **Data Quality Evaluation Results for Plant Data of Products**
  This app provides data quality evaluation results for plant data of the product master and analyzes data quality issues. The key implementation objects involved in these apps are as follows:
  - OData service: `CMD_QLTY_PROD_PLANT_ALP_SRV`
  - SAPUI5 application: `MD_QPRDPLTALPS1`
  - Business role: `SAP_BR_PRODMASTER_STEWARD`

- **Data Quality Evaluation Results for Sales Data of Products**
  This app provides data quality evaluation results for sales data of the product master and analyzes data quality issues. The key implementation objects involved in these apps are as follows:
  - OData service: `CMD_QLTY_PROD_SALES_ALP_SRV`
  - SAPUI5 application: `MD_QPRDSLSALPS1`
  - Business role: `SAP_BR_PRODMASTER_STEWARD`

The SAP Fiori apps for consolidation and mass processing are as follows:

- **SAP Fiori apps for consolidation**
  These apps can be used to consolidate and harmonize business partner/material master data. The key implementation objects of the app are as follows:
  - OData services: `MDC_PROCESS_SRV`, `MDC_PROCESS_SRV_194`, `MDC_PROCESS_SRV_147`, `MDC_PROCESS_SRV_1405`, `MDC_PROCESS_SRV_986`
  - SAPUI5 application: `MD_CMPMONPROCS1`
  - Business roles: `SAP_BR_BUPA_MASTER_SPECIALIST`, `SAP_BR_PRODMASTER_SPECIALIST`

Consolidation and mass processing apps were discussed in depth in Chapter 12. For configuring custom objects consolidation and mass processing, SAPUI5 application MD_CMPCONFCOS1 and OData service MDC_CUSTOM_OBJECT_SRV must be activated. Source data for consolidation can be imported via file through the Import Data for Consolidation app. For the Import Data app to work, the SAPUI5 application MD_CMPIMPFILES1 and OData service MDC_IMPORT_SRV must be activated. The source data for the consolidation process can be managed using the Manage Source Data for Consolidation app. To manage consolidation source data using the SAP Fiori app, SAPUI5 application MD_CMPMANSDATS1 and OData service MDC_MANAGE_SOURCE_DATA_SRV have to be activated.

- **SAP Fiori apps for mass processing**
These apps can be used to mass process master data records for material, business partner (including customer, vendor, and business partner relationships), and custom object domains. The key implementation objects of the app are as follows:
  - OData services: MDC_PROCESS_SRV, MDC_CUSTOM_OBJECT_SRV, MDC_PROCESS_SRV_194, MDC_PROCESS_SRV_147, MDC_PROCESS_SRV_986, MDC_PROCESS_SRV_1405
  - SAPUI5 application: MD_CMPMONPROCS1
  - Business roles: SAP_BR_BUPA_MASTER_SPECIALIST, SAP_BR_PRODMASTER_SPECIALIST

The data to be mass-processed can be exported using the Export Master Data app. For the Export Master Data app to work, SAPUI5 application MD_CMPEXPFILES1 and OData service MDC_EXPORT_SRV have to be activated.

- **Track Mass Changes**
This app helps to track the consolidation and mass process changes. The key implementation objects of the app are as follows:
  - OData services: MDC_TRACK_CHANGES_SRV_1405, MDC_TRACK_CHANGES_SRV_147, MDC_TRACK_CHANGES_SRV_194
  - SAPUI5 application: MD_CMPTRACKCHS1
  - Business roles: SAP_BR_BUPA_MASTER_SPECIALIST, SAP_BR_PRODMASTER_SPECIALIST

16.3 Extensibility Options

The requirement for extending the standard SAP Fiori apps can be triggered through the requirement to personalize the UX of the SAP Fiori apps or to add a new entity or attribute to the data model. The key steps/dependent steps in extending an SAP Fiori app at a high level are as follows:

1. Redefine the OData service (SAP Gateway layer).
2. Extend the UI layer.
3. Extend the launchpad.
4. Use the UI theme designer to enhance the app UX.

Some of these steps can be optional based on the use case. These steps are discussed in the following sections. A technical overview of the various dependencies in an SAP Fiori app is given in Figure 16.5. Some of the standard apps leverage ABAP CDS views.

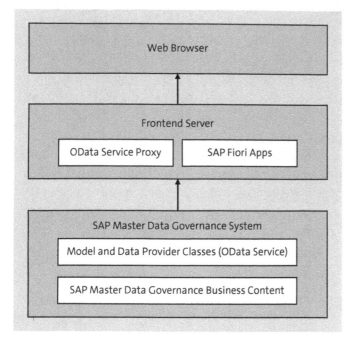

Figure 16.5 Technical Overview of SAP Fiori Components

16.3.1   Redefinition of OData Service

The main use cases for redefinition of the OData service are as follows:

- **Add new fields to an existing entity**
  Additional custom attributes to the data model entity or additional fields for display or calculation could trigger this requirement to add new fields to an existing entity.
- **Add new entities**
  When the SAP Master Data Governance data model is enhanced with a new entity, if those fields are to be used or displayed in the UI, the OData service corresponding to the UI should be extended as well.
- **Add new navigations**
  If two entities need to be linked through relationships, navigation properties are defined, and the respective association sets are configured with the respective cardinality.

The key steps in the redefinition of an OData service are as follows. Some of them are optional based on the requirement. Additional information on the extension of OData service in SAP Gateway Service Builder can be found in SAP Note 1919388.

1. **Create a new extensibility project using Transaction SEGW.**

   The OData service is based on an entity data model (EDM). The create, read, update, and delete (CRUD) methods are used to access and maintain the data. These methods are implemented and defined using two main classes: model provider class and data provider class. A model provider class is used to define the model involving the entity and related properties. A data provider class is used to implement the CRUD methods and function imports.

   The SAP Master Data Governance OData projects in SAP Gateway Service Builder are displayed in Figure 16.6. The leading model provider class and data provider class names associated with each project can be viewed from the property details of the respective data model and service implementation.

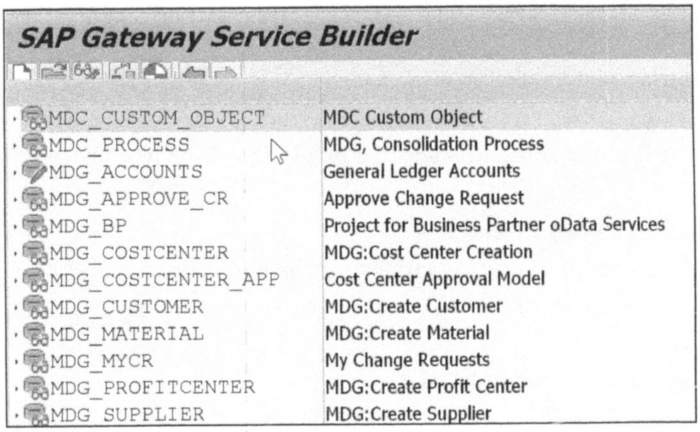

Figure 16.6 SAP Gateway Service Builder Projects for SAP Master Data Governance Scenarios

2. **Redefine the OData service.**

   On redefinition of the service using the SAP Gateway Service Builder (Transaction SEGW) and generation, the provider classes are created that inherit from the base class. Additional logic to pass the data is written in the new provider classes.

3. **Add the custom entity/property.**

   On addition of a new entity, the associated query methods for CRUD operations need to be implemented.

4. **Add the association and navigation property.**

   On addition of an association or a navigation property and referential constraint, the associated query methods need to be updated for the associated entities.

5. **Redefine methods (data provider class).**

   For the extensions, the inherited methods of the data provider class source service needs to be redefined.

6. **Generate the OData project.**

   After the service is redefined, the project is generated so it can be exposed for consumption.

7. **Register and test the new OData project as a new service using Transaction /
   IWFND/MAINT_SERVICE.**
   After the OData service is extended, it's recommended to clear the cache at both the
   SAP Gateway and the SAP Master Data Governance system using Transactions /
   IWFND/CACHE_CLEANUP and /IWBEP/CACHE_CLEANUP, respectively.

16.3.2   Extension of the User Interface Layer

SAP Fiori apps for SAP Master Data Governance, especially the request apps, are lean
apps meant for casual users. It's recommended to limit the UI extensions to be modification free, so that future upgrades don't affect the extensions. The various ways of
enhancing a standard SAP Fiori app are as follows:

- **View modification**
  Hide a UI element in the standard view.

- **View extension**
  Add additional UI elements to the standard view through the extension points available in the view.

- **Controller extension using a hook method**
  Add additional logic at specific places in the controller through the hook methods
  available as part of the standard view.

- **i18n resource extension**
  Change the label texts of the UI elements.

- **View replacement (if required)**
  Replace the standard view.

- **Controller extension (if required)**
  Change the logic of the controller methods.

- **Custom view (if required)**
  Create and add a custom view to the app.

These extension/enhancements can be implemented at the view level and fragment
level through the controller hook methods or through enhancement of the files storing
the metadata information, such as internationalization (i18n) strings, bootstrap *Com-
ponent.js* files, and so on. A SAPUI5 page may include multiple fragment files.

An extension application is created during design time. At runtime, the custom
extended application is merged with the standard app that is referenced in the bootstrap *Component.js* metadata file. It's recommended to adopt a view extension, view
modification, or controller extension via a hook method or i18n resource extension
before considering other extension/UI Customizing options.

The recommended approach for extending the SAP Fiori UI is to use the SAP Business
Application Studio by creating an adaptation project. SAP Business Application Studio
is part of SAP BTP. To create an adaptation project for a standard SAP Fiori app, the app
needs to meet some technical prerequisites such as UI elements compatibility for

adaptation, and so on. As of SAP S/4HANA 2021, some of the central governance SAP Fiori apps (e.g., lean request apps and approver apps), which were built as part of the initial product versions, still need to be extended using SAP Web IDE. SAP Web IDE is the web-based integrated development environment for creating and enhancing HTML5/SAPUI5-based UI applications. SAP Web IDE is shown in Figure 16.7. With SAP BTP, SAP Web IDE has evolved to SAP Business Application Studio. To access an SAP Web IDE tool and connect to an on-premise system, a cloud connector needs to be set up.

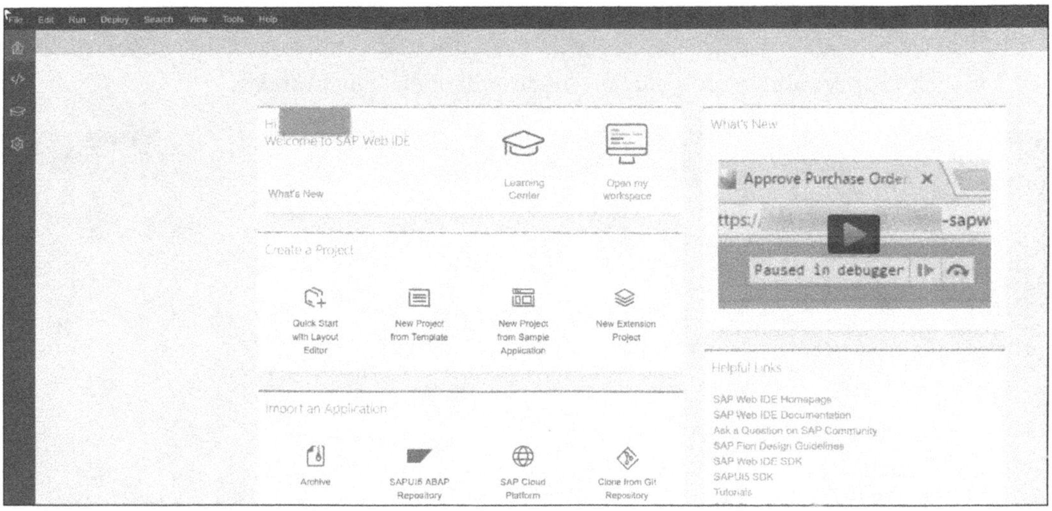

Figure 16.7 SAP Web IDE

The key steps involved in the extension of an SAP Fiori app are as follows:

1. **Create an extension project.**
   You can create an extension project in SAP Web IDE by choosing **File • New • Extension Project**, as shown in Figure 16.8.

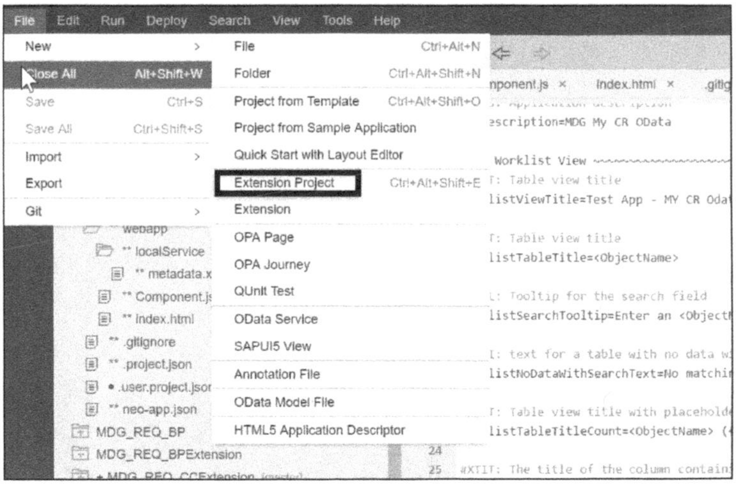

Figure 16.8 Creating a New Extension Project

723

2. **Select the application to extend from the SAP Gateway server.**
Import/select the application from the SAPUI5 ABAP repository, as shown in Figure 16.9. On selection of the system, it lists all the SAPUI5 applications that can be extended. You can filter the required applications from the list. After the base application is selected, SAP Web IDE proposes the extension project name and enables you to import the base application if you choose.

3. **View the project in the extensibility pane.**
After the extension project is created, view the extensibility pane by navigating to **Tools · Extensibility Pane**, as shown in Figure 16.10. This view allows you to preview the application in both preview mode and extensibility mode.

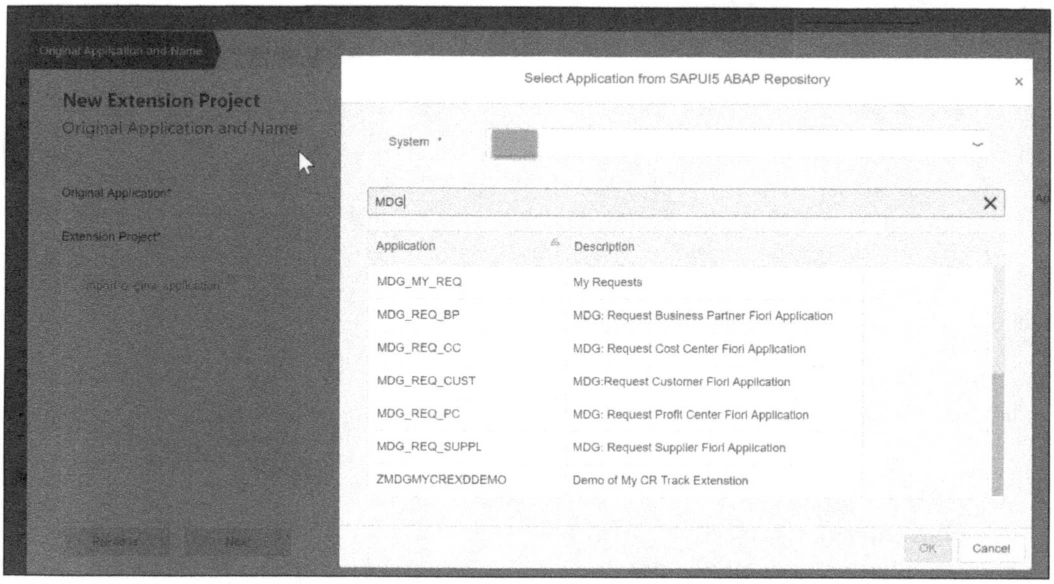

Figure 16.9 Import Project

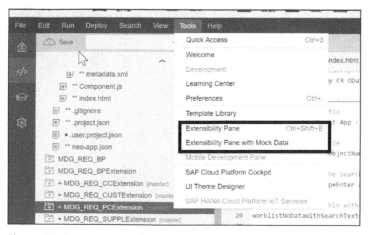

Figure 16.10 Viewing the Extensibility Pane

4. **Select and extend the extension option.**

   The **Outline** section displays the UI elements of the extension project, as shown in Figure 16.11. You can filter this view by extensible elements, extension points, or extended elements. Thus, you can easily identify the extensible options, such as view extensions, controller hook methods, and so on, of an SAP Fiori app through this view. Detailed documentation on each extension option of an SAP Fiori app is available with the associated documentation in the SAP Fiori apps reference library as well as in the SAP Help documentation.

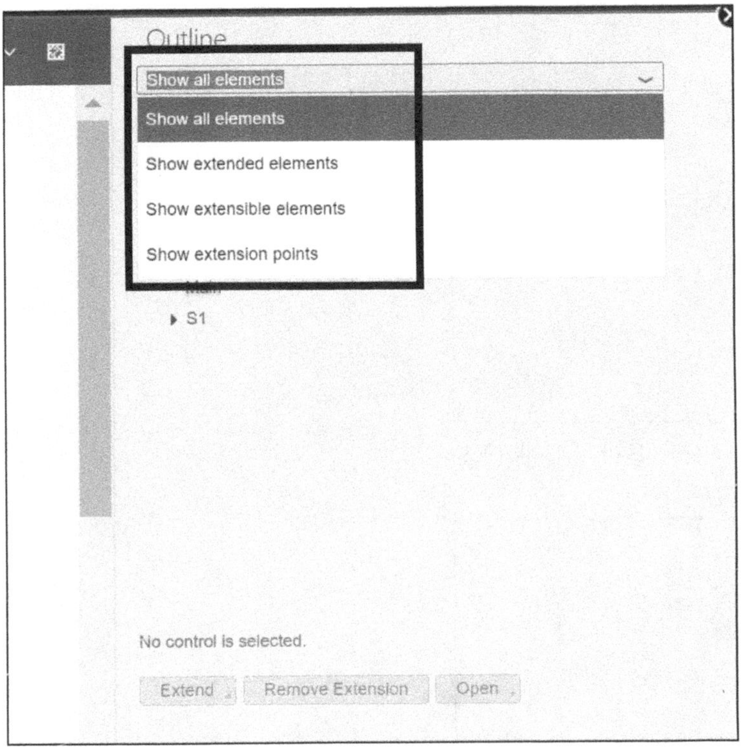

Figure 16.11 Extensibility Pane Outline Options

After an extension point is selected from the **Outline** section, you can extend it by opening the code view to add the additional logic in JavaScript or XML, based on the artifact selected. An example of the MDG_REQ_BP application is shown in Figure 16.12. You can also select the extension option from the UI preview. The respective extension method is auto-selected in the **Outline** section. SAP Web IDE also provides additional extension options, such as hiding a UI element by selection in the context menu, without writing a piece of code because the system automatically generates the required code.

Extension logic can be written in the controller hook methods, as shown in Figure 16.13. After the required elements are extended, you can view the extended elements via filtering in the **Outline** section.

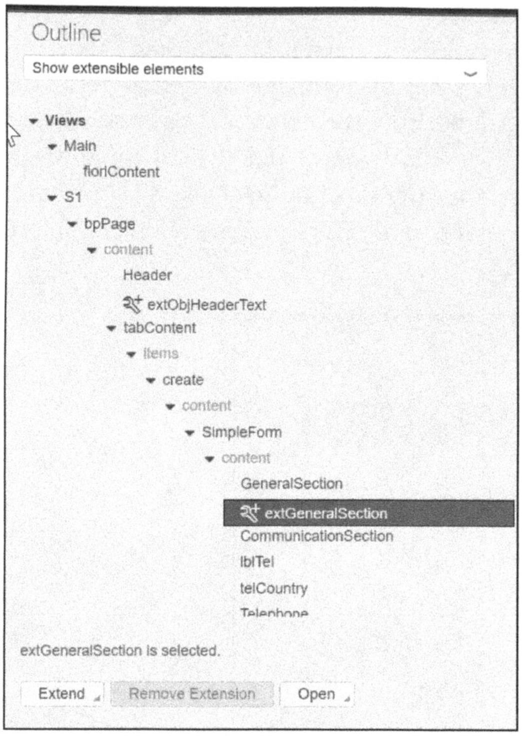

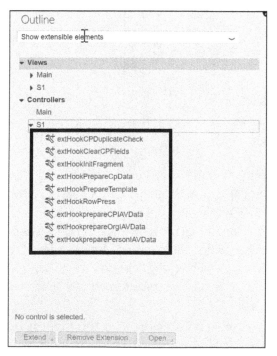

Figure 16.12 Extensible Elements of MDG_REQ_BP

Figure 16.13 Controller Hook Methods

5. **Deploy the extended application to the ABAP repository.**
   After the required enhancements and extensions are performed, you can deploy the application to the SAPUI5 ABAP repository of the SAP Gateway system, as shown in Figure 16.14.

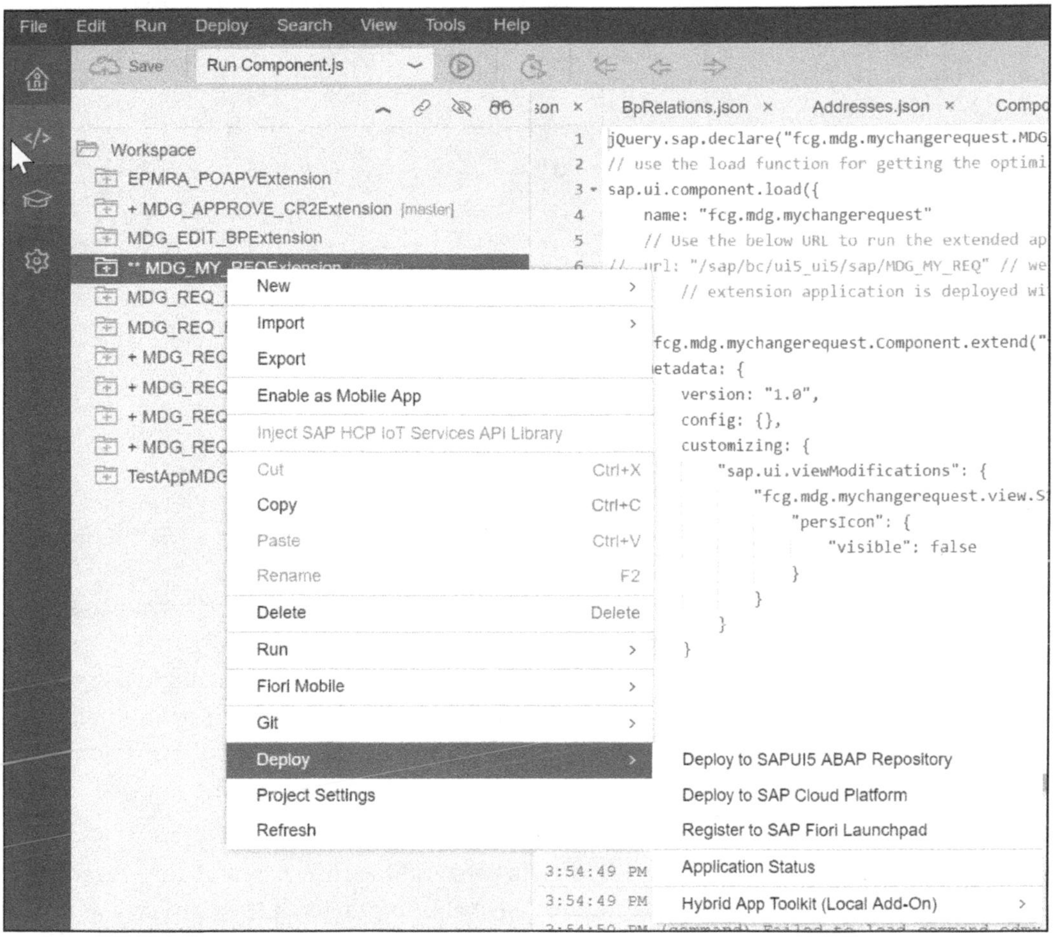

Figure 16.14 Deploying the Extension Application

A similar approach of SAP Fiori app adaptation can be done, for compatible apps, via SAP Business Application Studio, using the adaptation project template as shown in Figure 16.15.

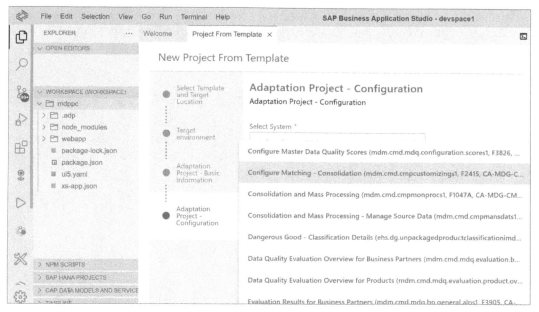

Figure 16.15 Adaptation Project in SAP Business Application Studio

16.3.3   Launchpad Extension

To link the extended app to SAP Fiori launchpad for user access, the launchpad should be extended. An overview of various contents of the launchpad configuration is shown in Figure 16.16. A catalog is a set of apps that a user can add to the homepage, and a group is a set of tiles a user sees on the homepage. A tile corresponds to an application. Target mapping defines the navigation target based on the user authorizations. This intent-based navigation is achieved by specifying the corresponding semantic object, action, and related parameters of an application.

Thus, an application can be configured to behave differently based on the intent specified in the target mapping definition. This helps in providing the right user access as well as providing the right functional/business scope. The definition of catalogs, tiles, and so on is performed using the launchpad designer. The launchpad designer of a configured frontend server can be accessed via *http://<host>:<port>/sap/bc/ui5_ui5/sap/arsrvc_upb_admn/main.html?*.

The steps required to define a catalog as part of the launchpad are as follows:

1. Create the launchpad app using Transaction LPD_CUST.

2. Create a catalog with a new tile and target mapping using the launchpad designer. Provide the intent information of the extended app for navigation.

3. Add the catalog in the **Menu** tab of a new role or to an existing custom role using Transaction PFCG, and assign the role to the user ID.

4. Add the new catalog and tile to the user's homepage using SAP Fiori launchpad (Transaction /UI2/FLP).

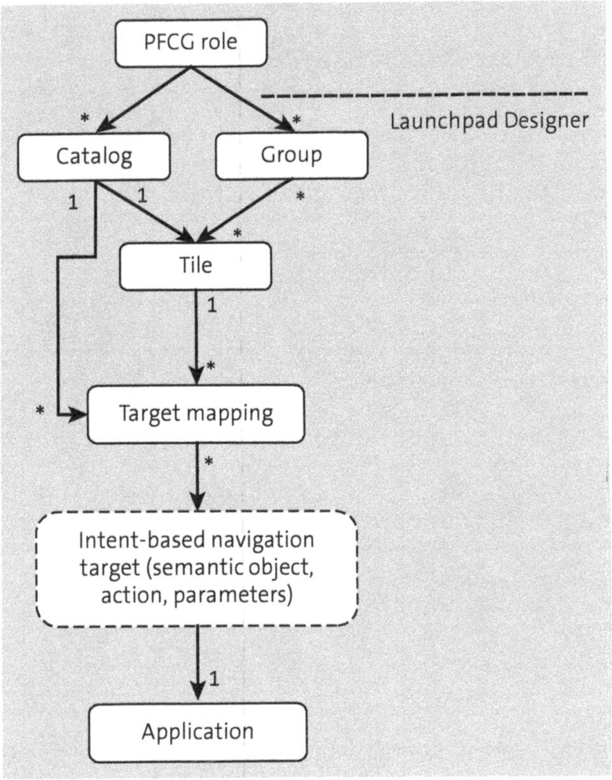

Figure 16.16 Launchpad Content Model

Semantic objects delivered by SAP can be accessed via Transaction /UI2/SEMOBJ_SAP, and custom semantic objects can be accessed via Transaction /UI2/SEMOBJ.

16.3.4   User Interface Theme Designer

The UI theme designer is the browser-based tool used to customize the themes of SAP Fiori launchpad and SAPUI5 applications. You can also create custom themes for SAP UI applications. The UI theme designer can be accessed using Transaction /UI5/THEME_ DESIGNER, as shown in Figure 16.17.

You can access the custom theme using Transaction /UI5/THEME_TOOL, as shown in Figure 16.18. This application is also available as part of SAP BTP. You can export and import the configured custom themes. The launchpad theme can be defined in Transaction /UI2/NWBC_CFG_SAP, and the user-specific theme can be defined in Transaction /UI2/NWBC_CFG_CUST. For more information, refer to SAP Note 1852400.

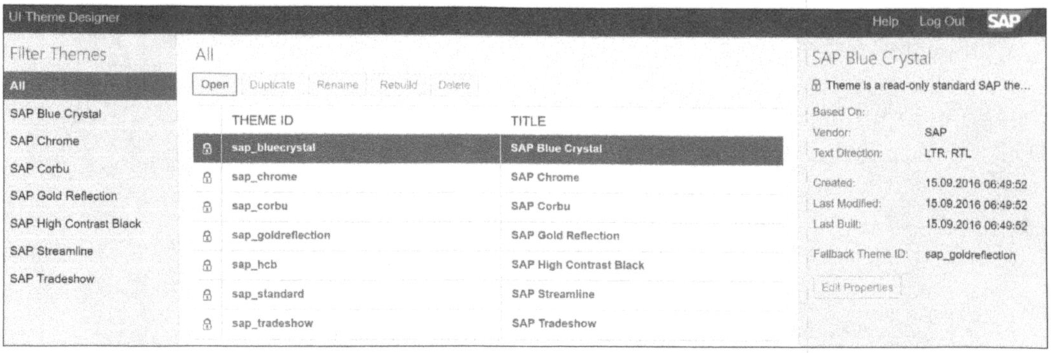

Figure 16.17 UI Theme Designer

Figure 16.18 Custom Themes

16.4   Summary

This chapter gave an overview of SAP Fiori and details about the SAP Fiori apps available as part of SAP Master Data Governance on SAP S/4HANA 2021. The chapter also discussed various extensibility options available for the standard SAP Fiori apps. The consolidation and mass processing functionalities were discussed in more detail in Chapter 9. Data quality management functionality is discussed in more detail in Chapter 8. The next chapter discusses some of the SAP Master Data Governance complementary solutions and SAP Solution Extensions.

Chapter 17

Overview of SAP Master Data Governance Complementary Solutions

There are several SAP Master Data Governance complementary solutions, developed by partners, which bring additional value-added content, including tools, additional master data domains, and support for rapid deployment of SAP Master Data Governance in the customer environment. In this chapter, you'll see some of the important SAP-certified add-on complementary solutions.

SAP Master Data Governance on SAP S/4HANA is a proven leader in the industry in master data management, governance, audit, and data quality areas. So, it's no wonder there are several other SAP partners in the ecosystem who provide complementary solutions. In this section, we'll look into a couple of leading SAP Solution Extensions offered for SAP Master Data Governance. This chapter will give you just an idea of various complementary solutions that work with SAP Master Data Governance but is not meant to provide detailed information.

> **Note**
>
> The complementary solutions listed in the following sections are provided by independent software vendors, and some of them may be SAP approved partners. Therefore, end-customers are recommended to do additional due diligence on the listed solutions. We encourage you to visit the *www.SAP.com* website for the latest information on these topics.

17.1 SAP Solution Extensions Partner Solutions

In the following sections you'll see some of the important solutions and how they complement the SAP Master Data Governance solution.

17.1.1   SAP Master Data Governance, Enterprise Asset Management Extension by Utopia

SAP Master Data Governance, enterprise asset management extension by Utopia (hereafter, shortened to enterprise asset management extension) has prebuilt integration to SAP. This solution is available as an add-in for SAP Master Data Governance on SAP S/4HANA and SAP Master Data Governance with SAP ERP 6.0. They follow similar release cycles of standard SAP Master Data Governance offerings. Initially, this product offering started with SAP Industry Solution for Oil & Gas, but it's now available for other industry solutions, including Discrete Manufacturing, Utilities, Defense, Telecom, and so on. The solution incorporates out-of-the-box functionality of preconfigured data structures, industry templates, workflows, and so on in the partner namespace. The enterprise asset management extension solution primarily focusses on asset management (aka plant maintenance) and service master. For some of the objects covered by the enterprise asset management extension, additional licenses and/or business functions related to the industry solutions must be activated as a prerequisite.

> **Note**
>
> Visit *www.SAP.com* and partner websites for additional information related to licensing and prerequisites for industry solutions.

The enterprise asset management extension solution is built on the framework of SAP Master Data Governance custom objects, so it shares the same look and feel of the SAP Master Data Governance standard master data domains provided directly by SAP.

The enterprise asset management extension enables the governance of the following master data objects of in plant maintenance and service master:

- Equipment master
- Functional locations
- SAP Linear Asset Management
- Maintenance, repairs, and operations (MRO) bills of materials (BOMs)
- Work centers
- Service master
- Task lists
- Maintenance plans
- Maintenance items
- Measuring points
- Object links
- Object networks
- Catalog code groups and codes
- Selected sets

Figure 17.1 shows the initial landing page of the enterprise asset management extension to process various enterprise asset management master data objects.

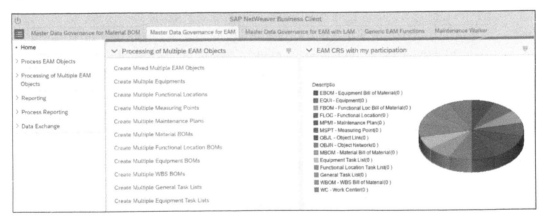

Figure 17.1 Landing Page to Process Various Enterprise Asset Management Objects

Figure 17.2 shows the landing page with options to mass-process enterprise asset management objects.

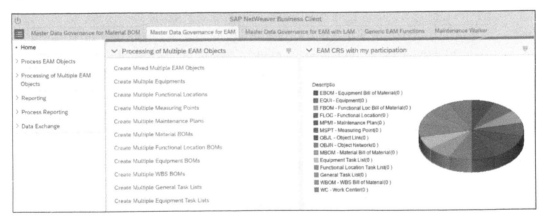

Figure 17.2 Landing Page to Process Multiple Enterprise Asset Management Objects

17.1.2   SAP Asset Information Workbench by Utopia

SAP Asset Information Workbench by Utopia is a complementary add-on solution to the enterprise asset management extension. It provides a platform for monitoring, tracking, and managing structured and unstructured asset data between multiple systems of record (SoR), for example, SAP S/4HANA, SAP ERP, engineering, product lifecycle management, and maintenance systems.

SAP Asset Information Workbench enables you to do the following:

- Integrate SAP Asset Intelligence Network and connect enterprise-wide multiple systems of record where data is stored and used.
- Synchronize asset master data across multiple SoRs.
- Quickly locate relevant records for asset master data construction.
- Accelerate acquisition, transformation, and processing of complex asset data.
- Standardize reference models of assets, work, and parts in one central location.

17.1.3   SAP Master Data Governance, Retail and Fashion Management Extension by Utopia

SAP Master Data Governance for retail and fashion management by Utopia (retail and fashion management extension) allows you to manage article master data records for the SAP Retail and Fashion Management customers. It supports a governance model through an article data lifecycle to enable master data quality. This solution is built using the custom data model framework in SAP Master Data Governance in the partner namespace and has a predefined data model AR, that is, article master in SAP Master Data Governance.

This solution is available as an add-in for SAP Master Data Governance on SAP S/4HANA and SAP Master Data Governance with SAP ERP 6.0. It's important to highlight that the activation of SAP industry solution IS-Retail is a mandatory prerequisite to enable the retail and fashion management extension with an SAP ERP system because the data models for retail article master and for material master are different. In addition, functionality related to fashion management isn't available in the SAP ERP version. With the simplification introduced with SAP S/4HANA, this prerequisite doesn't exist anymore: the material master (referred to as product master in SAP S/4HANA) and retail article master now share a common integrated data model.

As this solution is built using the SAP Master Data Governance custom data model of the standard SAP Master Data Governance framework, most of the features, such as search capabilities, duplicate checks, workflow, and so on, are available standard. Some additional features of the retail and fashion management extension solution include the following:

- Mass create/maintain various type of articles, for example, single article, generic article, variant articles, sales set, prepack, and so on.
- For integration and distribution of master data related to the retail and fashion management article master, some specific partner developed IDocs are used along with standard Electronic Data Interchange (EDI)/Application Link Enabling (ALE) IDocs.
- Integration can be enabled with the SAP Product Lifecycle Management (SAP PLM) system.

Figure 17.3 shows the landing page of the retail and fashion management extension that enables you to search and manage retail and fashion articles.

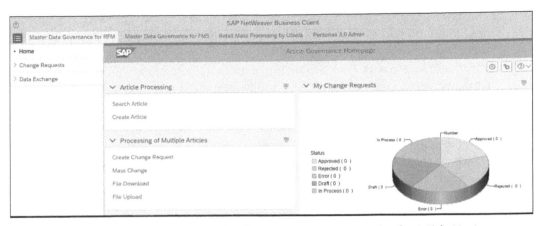

Figure 17.3 Landing Page of the Retail and Fashion Management Extension for Article Master Data Governance

17.1.4   Other Partner Add-Ons Complementing SAP Master Data Governance

Besides the previously mentioned partner solution extensions, there are many other complementary solutions for SAP Master Data Governance from different SAP partners. Many of these partner solutions provide industry-specific enhancements on top of SAP Master Data Governance or provide prepackaged specialized content that brings in added functionality. For a complete list of solution add-ons for SAP Master Data Governance, Christian Geiseler's blog from SAP Master Data Governance Product Management: *https://blogs.sap.com/2021/02/05/how-partner-add-on-solutions-enhance-saps-master-data-governance/*. You can reach out to your SAP point of contact or you can check out the SAP Store (*https://store.sap.com/dcp/en/search/master%20data%20governance*) for the latest status and updates on these add-ons.

17.2   Quick-Start for SAP Master Data Governance

In the previous chapters, we've covered all the details of SAP Master Data Governance, its various capabilities, and how to configure SAP Master Data Governance to suit your specific business requirements. The next question to answer is—what is the best way to start your implementation project?

Let's start by explaining quick-start for SAP Master Data Governance. *Quick-start for SAP Master Data Governance* is a consulting offering from SAP that delivers a preconfigured SAP Master Data Governance on SAP S/4HANA system out of the box. It's aimed at ensuring that you start your project with a best practice foundation, and it's packed with a lot of prebuilt content, including workflows, rules, and processes. Quick-start for SAP Master Data Governance includes all the standard content such as data models, SAP Fiori screens, analytics widgets, and all the other functionality that you get with SAP Master Data Governance. This ensures that, without any additional effort, you can start your project with a fully working SAP Master Data Governance system running in your landscape in a matter of days to weeks. Now let's delve deeper into this topic and see what exactly is inside this quick-start for SAP Master Data Governance box. Some SAP Master Data Governance experts even refer to it as "SAP Master Data Governance in a box" because it comes fully configured and ready out of the box.

The quick-start for SAP Master Data Governance box comes configured with all the standard SAP Master Data Governance data domains, namely, business partner (including supplier and customer), material, and finance. It covers all the SAP Master Data Governance solutions and functionalities, including central governance, consolidation, mass processing, and data quality management solutions.

Quick-start for SAP Master Data Governance is expected to delivery four key value propositions:

1. Faster time-to-value results for your SAP Master Data Governance investment
2. Reduced startup time and cost savings
3. Out-of-the-box content built with the right implementation approach
4. Support for a cleaner design and faster overall project execution

17.2.1   Benefits for Your IT Team

Customer IT teams who are implementing SAP Master Data Governance have many questions in their mind. How long does it take to install SAP Master Data Governance? What version of SAP HANA/S/4HANA should we install? Should we download and install a separate package for SAP Master Data Governance? Which switches do we have to turn on to enable SAP Master Data Governance? What notes should be applied? How do we turn on different services needed for SAP Master Data Governance?

Of course, very detailed documentation is available from SAP to answer all of these questions, but for the IT team, all of these steps can be quite overwhelming. And, of course, you don't know if you've completed all the steps correctly until somebody starts testing the system and errors pop up telling you that some services or SAP Basis settings have been left out. Plus, if you are dealing with very tight timelines to roll out SAP Master Data Governance, this could be a challenge.

Quick-start for SAP Master Data Governance enables the IT team to have a super-fast setup and installation of SAP Master Data Governance on SAP S/4HANA without all the hassles of following a guide and doing all this step by step. Quick-start for SAP Master Data Governance delivers an entire system out of the box; that is, you receive a database backup of a fully configured SAP Master Data Governance system, and you just have to bring it up in your landscape. Rest assured that it's always the latest and greatest version of SAP Master Data Governance on SAP S/4HANA with all the prerequisite notes and patches already preinstalled.

As an IT team or SAP Basis expert, the only thing you have to do is receive the database backup copy from SAP's quick-start for SAP Master Data Governance team and then install that in your landscape using the same technique that you would use to install an SAP system from a database backup. Once you've installed the system, you'll have a fully configured version of SAP Master Data Governance up and running in your landscape. You don't have to worry about all the multitude of steps that you have to do to get the system working.

In addition, if you want to leverage quick-start for SAP Master Data Governance as a foundation for all your three tiers, you just have to install the provided backup three times in your landscape for setting up the development, quality and production systems. This provides you a lot of time and effort savings because—without quick-start for SAP Master Data Governance—you would have to do all the manual steps three times to set up the entire three-tier landscape.

Now, let's see how quick-start for SAP Master Data Governance benefits the different stakeholders in a customer project.

17.2.2   Benefits for Your Business Team

For a business team in your company, one of the challenges they face is to fully understand what outcome to expect from the design and implementation exercise the IT team is doing as part of their SAP Master Data Governance project, as well as what outcomes the business users will get at the end of this exercise. How will the SAP Master Data Governance screens look and work? How easy will it be for the business team to do their day-to-day activities? Besides this, the business users are also overwhelmed with terms such as change request, business objects, actions, mass processing request, and so on, which they are expected to understand to guide the implementation team to an effective design.

Although documentation and screenshots are available, many customers say wish they had access to a system they could "touch and try" during the design phase. Usually, because installing and configuring a complete system takes some time, most implementation teams don't have a fully working SAP Master Data Governance system during their design phases. The business team is left with a set of documentation based on which they have to guide the IT/SAP Master Data Governance team in implementing a solution that meets their business need.

Quick-start for SAP Master Data Governance eases this pain by providing a fully configured SAP Master Data Governance system right at the start of the project. Therefore, during the design phase, instead of business users sitting around a table with a bunch of documentation trying to imagine how the system is going to look, the SAP Master Data Governance implementation team can actually walk the business users through existing workflows, screens, and quality dashboards to give them a firsthand feel of how an SAP Master Data Governance system looks and works. They can also get feedback from the business users on how much of the predelivered solution they would like to further customize and enhance.

When implementing the quick-start for SAP Master Data Governance approach, business users are presented with a fully configured SAP Master Data Governance system with different processes already configured, and they are asked to review this to see how well it fits their business need. A fit-gap evaluation exercise is also done to see how these predelivered processes meet the need and which gaps have to be addressed on the project.

17.2.3 Benefits for the SAP Master Data Governance Implementation Team

For the SAP Master Data Governance implementation team, one of the biggest benefits is that the SAP Master Data Governance projects are faster with lower implementation costs. Typically, installing and getting an SAP Master Data Governance system up and running will take anywhere from 8 to 12 weeks or more based on how experienced the implementation team is. Quick-start for SAP Master Data Governance provides the implementation team with the same starting point at the beginning of the project.

In addition, because the quick-start for SAP Master Data Governance system comes fully configured, the implementation team doesn't spend too much time doing mundane activities such as turning on switches and services, doing basic configuration of screens, and performing basic customization steps. Instead, they can focus their time and efforts on high-value activities and supporting a quick go-live of the SAP Master Data Governance solution.

Remember, with the traditional step-by-step manual approach, many of the basic configurations have to be done a minimum of three times in each tier of the landscape, taking up considerable effort.

The next benefit for the implementation team is that quick-start for SAP Master Data Governance comes loaded with prebuilt content, including different types of workflows, business rules and validations, data quality checks, change requests, and so on. All the content within quick-start for SAP Master Data Governance is built with an SAP recommended best practices approach. Therefore, if the delivered content isn't sufficient, the implementation team can copy and customize the delivered content, making it faster and easier to meet new requirements.

Figure 17.4 compares implementing SAP Master Data Governance following a traditional approach to a quick-start for SAP Master Data Governance implementation approach.

As an owner/sponsor of the SAP Master Data Governance project, one of the things you want to ensure is a quick time to value for the SAP Master Data Governance investment. Quick-start for SAP Master Data Governance is specifically meant to meet this requirement.

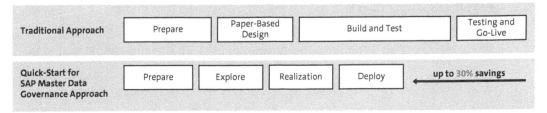

Figure 17.4 Comparison of Traditional Approach to Quick-Start for SAP Master Data Governance Approach

17.2.4   Contents Delivered as Part of Quick-Start for SAP Master Data Governance

We've been talking in detail about the benefits of quick-start for SAP Master Data Governance, but now let's go one more step to see which preconfigured contents are delivered as part of quick-start for SAP Master Data Governance. And what does "fully configured" mean when describing quick-start for SAP Master Data Governance?

From a solution perspective, quick-start for SAP Master Data Governance comes with material, business partner (including customer and supplier), and finance domains activated, configured, and working. All different master data modules, namely, central governance, consolidation, mass processing and data quality management, are also fully configured. Figure 17.5 shows all the domains and modules covered within the quick-start for SAP Master Data Governance system.

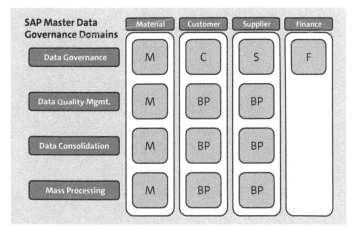

Figure 17.5 Quick-Start for SAP Master Data Governance: Scope of Solution Coverage

In the quick-start for SAP Master Data Governance solution, the following contents are delivered:

- All standard data models activated and available
- SAP HANA Search and duplicate search configured

- Lots of business rules and validations per each master data domain
- Standard and custom change request types and governance workflows
- Business configuration, including Customer-Vendor Integration (CVI) for customer/supplier domains
- SAP Fiori/Web Dynpro–based business user interfaces activated and working
- Sample key mapping
- Embedded business intelligence for change request analysis
- Business Context Viewer (BCV) for additional data insight
- Data import framework configured for IDoc XMLs
- Data distribution framework for ALE IDoc

As part of process analytics, the following content is delivered:

- SAP Fiori–based overview dashboard, including multiple analytical tiles
- SAP Fiori–based Analytical List Pages (ALPs) for monitoring the change request process and analyzing quality issues
- SAP Fiori–based analytical tiles using master data attributes

As part of Data Quality Management, the following content is delivered:

- Rule management and data quality evaluation fully configured
- Master data quality worklist
- SAP Fiori–based Data Quality Dashboard
- Process templates for data and quality evaluation
- Rule mining sample process and configurations
- Preconfigured data quality rules

As part of consolidation and mass processing, the following content is delivered:

- All SAP Fiori apps for consolidation and mass processing
- Preconfigured consolidation process, including standardization, validation, and matching steps
- Several predefined templates for mass create and mass update
- Best practice configuration for matching step configuration
- Several business rules for consolidation process

All of this content is documented, so that the implementation team is very clear on the nature of the content delivered and can adapt it as required for the project.

In addition, the package also includes some consulting support available from an SAP Master Data Governance architect to walkthrough the content for the project team and to clarify and discuss questions around best practices and architectural topics.

Many SAP Master Data Governance customers tend to implement only the central governance solution of SAP Master Data Governance suite, even though their licenses cover all the four solutions offered by SAP. Many times, the reason is that their implementation teams or partners aren't fully experienced in the other SAP Master Data Governance solutions such as mass processing and Data Quality Management. They may also not want to invest the additional effort required to explore the benefits of the other SAP Master Data Governance modules. With quick-start for SAP Master Data Governance, because all the solutions come fully configured, you can readily try out the other solutions without any extra effort to experience firsthand how they could add value to your master data processes.

All this makes the quick-start for SAP Master Data Governance approach the recommended starting point for your SAP Master Data Governance rollout.

Note

The quick-start for SAP Master Data Governance scope doesn't cover retail and fashion management extension and enterprise asset management extension.

17.2.5   Deployment Approaches

Quick-start for SAP Master Data Governance is suited for different types of deployment approaches based on your landscape architecture:

- **Quick-start template for SAP Master Data Governance approach**
  When you're deploying SAP Master Data Governance for the first time (greenfield implementation), and you've chosen a hub deployment approach for SAP Master Data Governance, then the quick-start template for SAP Master Data Governance approach is the right one to take. In this approach, an entire system copy of the template system is delivered as part of the quick-start for SAP Master Data Governance delivery. Therefore, the only thing the IT team has to do is install the provided "template" database export to get a quick-start for SAP Master Data Governance system up and running in your landscape in a matter of days/weeks.

  Because an entirely full system copy is provided in this approach, this is only suitable when you're setting up a separate SAP Master Data Governance installation as a greenfield. Nevertheless, this is the case for 90% of the customers when they roll out SAP Master Data Governance for the first time in their landscape.

- **Quick-Start Service for SAP Master Data Governance approach**
  If your SAP Master Data Governance landscape is a co-deployed landscape or you have an existing SAP Master Data Governance system already running (which means you're expanding your SAP Master Data Governance footprint, implementing one or more new domains), then it's not possible to install the quick-start for SAP Master Data Governance package as a full system copy. Therefore, the quick-

start service can be used for this purpose. It delivers a set of transport packages that brings in all the contents of the quick-start for SAP Master Data Governance offering, which can be deployed into an existing brownfield environment.

Before importing the quick-start for SAP Master Data Governance packages, the Quick Start team will do a few manual steps on the system to (1) assess the state of the system and (2) do the technical steps that can't be brought in via transport packages. After this is done, the quick-start for SAP Master Data Governance can be deployed into this brownfield environment.

These extra steps impact the deployment duration and the quick-start service takes a few days longer to complete than the template offering.

Figure 17.6 shows the comparison of steps between implementing the quick-start template for SAP Master Data Governance approach and the quick-start service for SAP Master Data Governance approach

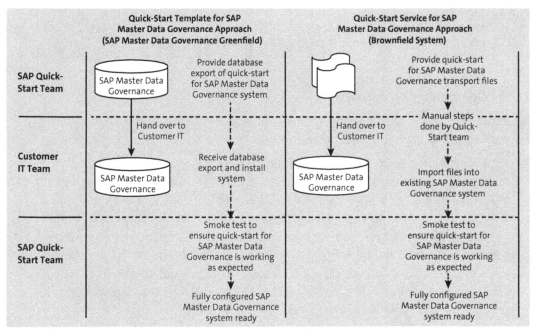

Figure 17.6 Comparison of Steps between Quick-Start for SAP Master Data Governance Deployment Approaches

Note

Irrespective of which deployment approach is chosen—either quick-start service or quick-start—the scope of the delivered content remains the same. You get all the benefits of quick-start for SAP Master Data Governance with both approaches.

17.2.6 Post-Deployment Steps

One of the advantages of the quick-start for SAP Master Data Governance offering is that not only does it deliver fantastic content as part of the quick-start delivery, but the Quick-Start for SAP Master Data Governance team is on hand to support the setup to ensure it goes hassle free. And once the setup of the system/content is done, then an SAP Master Data Governance expert from the Quick-Start team logs in to the system to perform an extensive smoke test which ensures that all the delivered content is working as expected.

Once this is done, the quick-start for SAP Master Data Governance expert will also do a walkthrough of the system for the benefit of the implementation team. There is also some time allocated within the service to discuss best practice approaches, architecture decisions, and any other question the implementation team might have for the SAP Master Data Governance expert from SAP.

> **Note**
>
> Note that the quick-start for SAP Master Data Governance approach is only available for SAP Master Data Governance on SAP S/4HANA and SAP Master Data Governance on SAP S/4HANA Cloud, private edition. It's not relevant for SAP Master Data Governance, cloud edition, nor for SAP S/4HANA Cloud for master data governance, as both of these are public cloud solutions and have a different scope within SAP Master Data Governance.
>
> In addition, note that quick-start for SAP Master Data Governance can be deployed on hyperscalers' cloud deployment environments.

17.3 Summary

In the previous sections, we saw some certified SAP Solution Extensions partner solutions that bring in additional SAP Master Data Governance domains to cover industry-specific needs. We also did a deep dive into the quick-start for SAP Master Data Governance offering, which provides a quick time-to-value result for your SAP Master Data Governance solution by accelerating your implementation.

The Authors

Bikram Dogra is a principal architect at SAP America with the Data and Technology Services (DBS) team. He has been working in the SAP Master Data Governance consulting area for more than 10 years, helping customers with master data management strategy, architecture, and implementation. He has successfully led many large SAP Master Data Governance implementation projects for Fortune 500 companies. Bikram has more than 25 years of IT experience in enterprise software implementation, architecture design, and solution consulting. He has worked in many technology areas such as Microsoft, Java/J2EE, Oracle, SAP Portal, SAP Master Data Management, SAP Master Data Governance, and middleware technologies.

Antony John Isacc is a principal architect for SAP America with a consulting focus in enterprise information management solutions. Antony has more than 14 years of SAP experience and has helped many SAP customers implement master data solutions. He has extensive technical and functional experience with master data management, business process management, user interface frameworks, and various programming languages. He is a certified architect and has a master's degree in information technology and management from Carnegie Mellon University.

Homiar Kalwachwala is a senior business development manager at SAP. He is the head of the Global Cloud Integration & Middleware services practice community at SAP and heads the data management and enterprise information management in North America. His SAP experience spans more than two decades. Homiar has contributed to SAP TechEd and ASUG as well as on SAP Community. He has won several awards at SAP and is well-respected in professional SAP data management, enterprise information management, and cloud integration communities.

Dilip Radhakrishnan has more than 15 years' experience in the enterprise software industry, designing and architecting enterprise solutions for companies globally. He has extensive experience in data management, specifically master data management, data governance, and data quality management. He has worked with a variety of SAP customers from a number of industries to implement end-to-end data management solutions. Currently Dilip is responsible for the enterprise information management portfolio in the SAP Value Prototyping team. Together with his team of experts, he works on piloting and prototyping solutions for some of the most complex EIM customer cases. Dilip was also the solution architect for SAP MDG for the retail and fashion industry before it was converted into a standard product.

Syama "Srini" Srinivasan is a principal architect in SAP North America in the enterprise information management consulting team. He has more than 25 years of experience working with SAP software. Throughout his career he has implemented SAP solutions, and defined best practices, processes, strategies, and methodologies for enterprise master data management solutions. He has worked on several complex master data governance implementation projects across industries and is currently engaged in implementing SAP MDG projects for some of the top global companies and corporations in North America. In April 2018, he co-authored the SAP PRESS E-Bite *Introducing SAP Master Data Governance (SAP MDG) on SAP S/4HANA* with Dilip Radhakrishnan.

Sandeep Chahal is a principal technology architect in the North America enterprise information management team at SAP. He is a passionate and dynamic data governance leader, creative thinker, author, visionary, and strategic professional with more than 14 years expertise in master data governance, master data management, and data migration. He has been instrumental in guiding top companies in how their data will be stored, consumed, governed, integrated, and managed by different data entities and IT systems.

Santhosh Kumar Cheekoti is principal EIM consultant at SAP America. He has more than 12 years of experience in implementing end-to-end SAP solutions. Santhosh has helped multiple Fortune 500 customers realize the full value of SAP products by providing architecture, advisory, and development services. He has been working with master data management solutions for the past five years. Santhosh also provides services like pre-sales support, bid management, and spot consulting. He has experience in providing effective solutions in high escalation scenarios. Santhosh is also certified SAP consultant and is certified in multiple technologies like SAP HANA, SAP Master Data Governance, and SAP Fiori.

Rajani Khambhampati is an expert SAP Master Data Governance architect with Nike and is helping with SAP Master Data Governance implementation across all master data domains as part of Nike's transition of retail and wholesale processes into a single SAP S/4HANA Fashion solution. In his prior role as principal technology architect at SAP America, he specialized in helping customers with all aspects of enterprise information management, including SAP Master Data Governance. He has more than 19 years of deep SAP expertise in helping organizations in their journey to achieve master data excellence. He has unique blend of expertise in the areas of preparing data governance strategies, roadmaps, data migration strategies, solution architecture, technology integration while implementing innovative master data management solutions. He has been instrumental in successfully delivering numerous large-scale globa implementations by applying thought leadership and design thinking and providing architectural guidance.

Vikas Lodha is a global technology leader with more than 25 years of experience across the full software development lifecycle, including consulting, GTM, product management, and development. At SAP, has worked on SAP Master Data Governance co-development and GTM activities, as well as on building out data management solutions for SAP HANA. Previously, he worked for Utopia, where his focus was on driving product strategy, product management, architecture, and development. This included establishing Utopia Labs for SAP support, innovation, QA, documentation, and infrastructure management. Vikas has worked as a data management advisor for global SAP customers, has been a speaker at SAP TechEd/Sapphire since 2007, and has hosted several workshops on data management and governance.

David Quirk is a senior director in the SAP EIM solution management team. He has been working in the information management field for many years, and, in his current role, his various responsibilities include formulating SAP EIM's vision and strategy and launching new products. David has been working with SAP software for more than 25 years in a variety of different roles. Prior to his current position, David worked as an implementation consultant with the SAP Master Data Governance solution. He was one of the first consultants to bring a customer live on SAP Master Data Governance and still maintains close ties to SAP Master Data Governance customers, implementations, and sales cycles.

Index

U

- Install and configure SAP Data Intelligence in the cloud or on-premise

- Govern, process, and orchestrate data workflows with tools like the Metadata Explorer and the SAP Data Intelligence Modeler

- Use machine learning, SAP Analytics Cloud, and SAP Data Warehouse Cloud to enrich business data

Dharma Teja Atluri, Devraj Bardhan, Santanu Ghosh, Snehasish Ghosh, Arindom Saha

SAP Data Intelligence

The Comprehensive Guide

Manage your data landscape with SAP Data Intelligence! Begin by understanding its architecture and capabilities and then see how to set up and install SAP Data Intelligence with step-by-step instructions. Walk through SAP Data Intelligence applications and learn how to use them for data governance, orchestration, and machine learning. Integrate with ABAP-based systems, SAP Vora, SAP Analytics Cloud, and more. Manage, secure, and operate SAP Data Intelligence with this all-in-one guide!

783 pages, pub. 10/2021
E-Book: $84.99 | **Print:** $89.95 | **Bundle:** $99.99

www.sap-press.com/5369

- Learn how to model data in SAP HANA 2.0 with SAP Web IDE

- Build calculation views and table functions, manage models, and more

- Explore advanced concepts like predictive modeling and SAP HANA spatial analysis

Anil Bavaraju

Data Modeling for SAP HANA 2.0

Find meaning in your business data. Build, manage, and secure calculation views and table functions with the SAP Web IDE for SAP HANA. See how the SAP Web IDE, SAP HANA Live, and SAP S/4HANA embedded analytics all interact to create effective data models. Explore advanced modeling concepts compatible with SAP HANA 2.0, like predictive modeling and geospatial analysis. Begin designing the perfect model today!

432 pages, pub. 07/2019

E-Book: $84.99 | **Print:** $89.95 | **Bundle:** $99.99

www.sap-press.com/4722

- Understand the technical foundation of SAP S/4HANA

- Explore the architecture of key application areas, including finance, logistics, procurement, and sales

- Learn about SAP S/4HANA Cloud's unique cloud architecture

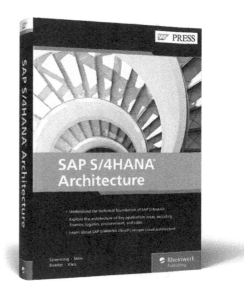

Thomas Saueressig, Tobias Stein, Jochen Boeder, Wolfram Kleis

SAP S/4HANA Architecture

Pop the hood on SAP S/4HANA with this guide to its technical and application architecture! Understand the new data and programming models that underpin SAP S/4HANA and see how they differ from SAP ERP. Learn about technology components, like embedded analytics and integration. Then walk through the architecture of individual application areas like finance and logistics to see how they work and interact. Considering SAP S/4HANA Cloud? Explore scoping, compliance, performance, and more. Get the complete blueprint to SAP S/4HANA!

520 pages, pub. 11/2020
E-Book: $74.99 | **Print:** $79.95 | **Bundle:** $89.99

www.sap-press.com/5189

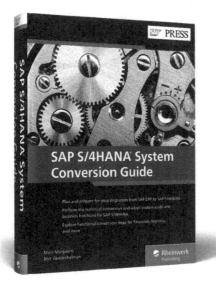

- Plan and prepare for your migration from SAP ERP to SAP S/4HANA

- Perform the technical conversion and adapt custom code and business functions for SAP S/4HANA

- Explore functional conversion steps for finance, logistics, and more

Mark Mergaerts, Bert Vanstechelman

SAP S/4HANA System Conversion Guide

If you're performing a brownfield migration from an existing SAP ERP system, this is the technical guide for you! From planning the project and preparing your system to adjusting custom code and executing the conversion, you'll get step-by-step instructions for all stages of your implementation. Troubleshooting tips and extensive coverage of the functional conversion will help you ensure that all your data makes it to where it needs to be. The time to move to SAP S/4HANA is here!

537 pages, pub. 07/2020

E-Book: $84.99 | **Print:** $89.95 | **Bundle:** $99.99

www.sap-press.com/5035

- Configure business partners in SAP
  S/4HANA for new implementations
  and system conversion projects

- Perform your customer-vendor
  integration and synchronization

- Maintain customer, vendor, and
  contact data with apps and transactions

Jawad Akhtar

Business Partners in SAP S/4HANA

The Comprehensive Guide to Customer-Vendor Integration

The distinction between "customers" and "vendors" is now a relic of the
past—jump into the future with this all-in-one guide to business partners in
SAP S/4HANA! Learn how to set up business partners from start to finish for
greenfield implementations. Or, if you're transitioning from SAP ERP to SAP
S/4HANA, walk through customer-vendor integration (CVI) with detailed
instructions. With guidance on maintaining and validating business partner
data, this is the only book on business partners you'll ever need!

353 pages, pub. 04/2022
E-Book: $84.99 | **Print:** $89.95 | **Bundle:** $99.99

www.sap-press.com/5468

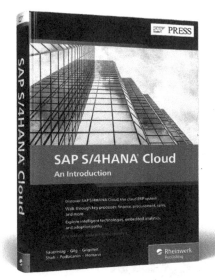

- Discover SAP S/4HANA Cloud, the cloud ERP system

- Walk through key processes: finance, procurement, sales, and more

- Explore intelligent technologies, embedded analytics, and adoption paths

Thomas Saueressig, Jan Gilg, Uwe Grigoleit, Arpan Shah, Almer Podbicanin, Marcus Homann

SAP S/4HANA Cloud

An Introduction

SAP S/4HANA Cloud has a lot to offer—see what's possible! Explore core functionality like finance, logistics, and reporting with embedded analytics. Learn how SAP S/4HANA Cloud impacts your users and how it can be extended, integrated, and adopted by your organization. Get information on the latest intelligent technologies and see how SAP S/4HANA Cloud can help unify and streamline your business. A bold new world awaits in the cloud!

538 pages, 2nd edition, pub. 05/2022
E-Book: $74.99 | **Print:** $79.95 | **Bundle:** $89.99

www.sap-press.com/5457

Interested in reading more?

Please visit our website for all new book
and e-book releases from SAP PRESS.

www.sap-press.com